sixth canadian edition

Fundamentals of Corporate Finance

STEPHEN A. ROSS
Massachusetts Institute of Technology

RANDOLPH W. WESTERFIELD
University of Southern California

BRADFORD D. JORDAN
University of Kentucky

GORDON S. ROBERTS
Schulich School of Business, York University

Toronto   Montréal   Boston   Burr Ridge, IL   Dubuque, IA   Madison, WI   New York
San Francisco   St. Louis   Bangkok   Bogotá   Caracas   Kuala Lumpur   Lisbon   London
Madrid   Mexico City   Milan   New Delhi   Santiago   Seoul   Singapore   Sydney   Taipei

Fundamentals of Corporate Finance
Sixth Canadian Edition

Statistics Canada information is used with the permission of the Minister of Industry, as Minister responsible for Statistics Canada.
Information on the availability of the wide range of data from Statistics Canada can be obtained from Statistics Canada's Regional
Offices, its World Wide Web site at http://www.statcan.ca, and its toll-free access number 1-800-263-1136.

ISBN-13: 978-0-07-095910-1
ISBN-10: 0-07-095910-2

3 4 5 6 7 8 9 10 QPD 0 9 8

Printed and bound in U.S.A.

Care has been taken to trace ownership of copyright material contained in this text; however, the publisher will welcome any information that enables them to rectify any reference or credit for subsequent editions.

Editorial Director: Joanna Cotton
Publisher: Lynn Fisher
Senior Marketing Manager: Joy Armitage Taylor
Senior Developmental Editor: Maria Chu
Editorial Associate: Stephanie Hess
Senior Production Coordinator: Paula Brown
Senior Supervising Editor: Anne Nellis
Copy Editor: Susan James
Cover Design: Liz Harasymczuk Design
Interior Design: Liz Harasymczuk Design
Cover Image Credit: © Ingram Publishing/SuperStock
Photo Credits: © CP Images for all chapters; Ch. 13 screen shot provided courtesy of *The Globe and Mail*
Composition: Brian Lehen Graphic Design Ltd.
Printer: Quebecor Printing Dubuque

Library and Archives Canada Cataloguing in Publication

    Fundamentals of corporate finance / Stephen A.
Ross ... [et al.]. -- 6th Canadian ed.
Includes bibliographical references and index.
ISBN-13: 978-0-07-095910-1
ISBN-10: 0-07-095910-2

    1. Corporations--Finance. I. Ross, Stephen A.

HG4026.F86 2007   658.15   C2006-904395-7

ABOUT THE AUTHORS

Stephen A. Ross

Sloan School of Management, Franco Modigliani Professor of Finance and Economics, Massachusetts Institute of Technology

Stephen A. Ross is the Franco Modigliani Professor of Finance and Economics at the Sloan School of Management, Massachusetts Institute of Technology. One of the most widely published authors in finance and economics, Professor Ross is recognized for his work in developing the Arbitrage Pricing Theory and his substantial contributions to the discipline through his research in signalling, agency theory, option pricing, and the theory of the term structure of interest rates, among other topics. A past president of the American Finance Association, he currently serves as an associate editor of several academic and practitioner journals. He is a trustee of CalTech and a director of the College Retirement Equity Fund (CREF) and Freddie Mac. He is also the co-chairman of Roll and Ross Asset Management Corporation.

Randolph W. Westerfield

Marshall School of Business, University of Southern California

Randolph W. Westerfield is Dean Emeritus of the University of Southern California's Marshall School of Business and is the Charles B. Thornton Professor of Finance.

He came to USC from the Wharton School, University of Pennsylvania, where he was the chairman of the finance department and a member of the finance faculty for 20 years. He is a member of several public company boards of directors, including Health Management Associates, Inc., William Lyons Homes, and the Nicholas Applegate growth fund. His areas of expertise include corporate financial policy, investment management, and stock market price behaviour.

Bradford D. Jordan

Gatton College of Business and Economics, Professor of Finance and holder of the Richard W. and Janis H. Furst Endowed Chair in Finance, University of Kentucky

Bradford D. Jordan is Professor of Finance and holder of the Richard W. and Janis H. Furst Endowed Chair in Finance at the University of Kentucky. He has a long-standing interest in both applied and theoretical issues in corporate finance and has extensive experience teaching all levels of corporate finance and financial management policy. Professor Jordan has published numerous articles on issues such as cost of capital, capital structure, and the behaviour of security prices. He is a past president of the Southern Finance Association, and he is co-author (with Charles J. Corrado) of *Fundamentals of Investments: Valuation and Management,* 3e, a leading investments text, published by McGraw-Hill/Irwin.

Gordon S. Roberts

Schulich School of Business, York University

Gordon S. Roberts is Canadian Imperial Bank of Commerce Professor of Financial Services at the Schulich School of Business, York University. His extensive teaching experience includes finance classes for undergraduate and MBA students, managers, and bankers. Professor Roberts conducts research on duration models for bond portfolio management, corporate finance, and banking. He serves on the editorial boards of several Canadian and international academic journals. Professor Roberts has been a consultant to a number of organizations, including the Office of the Superintendent of Financial Institutions, the Canada Deposit Insurance Corporation, and Canada Investment and Savings, as well as the Ontario Energy Board and the Debt Management Office of New Zealand.

BRIEF CONTENTS

CONTENTS

PREFACE

Fundamentals of Corporate Finance, Sixth Canadian Edition, provides what we believe is a modern, unified treatment of financial management in Canada that is suitable for beginning students.

Rapid and extensive changes in financial markets and instruments place new burdens on the teaching of corporate finance. On the one hand, it is much more difficult to keep materials up to date. On the other, the permanent must be distinguished from the temporary to avoid following what is merely the latest fad. Our solution is to stress the modern fundamentals of finance and to make the subject come alive with contemporary Canadian examples. As we emphasize throughout this book, we view the subject of corporate finance as the working of a small number of integrated and very powerful intuitions.

There are three basic themes in *Fundamentals of Corporate Finance*.

AN EMPHASIS ON INTUITION   We are always careful to separate and explain the principles at work on an intuitive level before launching into any specifics. The underlying ideas are discussed first in very general terms and then by way of examples that illustrate in more concrete terms how a financial manager might proceed in a given situation.

A UNIFIED VALUATION APPROACH   We treat net present value (NPV) as the basic concept underlying corporate finance. Many texts stop well short of consistently integrating this important principle. The most basic notion, that NPV represents the excess of market value over cost, tends to get lost in an overly mechanical approach to NPV that emphasizes computation at the expense of understanding. Every subject covered in *Fundamentals of Corporate Finance* is firmly rooted in valuation, and care is taken throughout the text to explain how particular decisions have valuation effects.

A MANAGERIAL FOCUS   Students won't lose sight of the fact that financial management concerns management. Throughout the text, the role of the financial manager as decision maker is emphasized, and the need for managerial input and judgement is stressed. "Black box" approaches to finance are consciously avoided.

These three themes work together to provide consistent treatment, a sound foundation, and a practical, workable understanding of how to evaluate financial decisions.

NEW TO THIS EDITION   In addition to retaining the coverage that has characterized *Fundamentals of Corporate Finance* from the beginning, the Sixth Canadian Edition features enhanced Canadian content on current issues such as corporate social responsibility, as well as both positive and negative examples of corporate governance. Key updates include income trusts (Chapters 1 and 2), where we discuss their growing importance in capital markets and recent changes in taxation, IPOs (Chapter 15), and capital market history (Chapter 12), which continues the Fifth Edition's emphasis on lower market risk premiums while introducing new material on geometric mean returns.

Learning solutions have always been a critical focus and the Sixth Canadian Edition retains features from the Fifth Edition and adds new ones: Calculator Hints and Spreadsheet Strategies walk students through time value calculations; new Mini Cases at the end of each major part of the book meet the demand for more challenging assignments.

COVERAGE

This book was designed and developed explicitly for a first course in business or corporate finance, for both finance majors and non-majors alike. In terms of background or prerequisites, the book is nearly self-contained, assuming some familiarity with basic algebra and accounting concepts, while still reviewing important accounting principles very early on. The organization of this text has been developed to give instructors the flexibility they need.

Just to get an idea of the breadth of coverage in the Sixth Canadian Edition of *Fundamentals of Corporate Finance*, the following grid presents, for each chapter, some of the most significant new features, as well as a few selected chapter highlights. Of course, in every chapter, opening vignettes, boxed features, in-chapter illustrated examples using real companies, and end-of-chapter materials have been thoroughly updated as well.

Chapters	Selected Topics of Interest	Benefits to You
PART ONE OVERVIEW OF CORPORATE FINANCE		
Chapter 1 Introduction to Corporate Finance	Goal of the firm and agency problems.	Stresses value creation as the most fundamental aspect of management and describes agency issues that can arise.
	Ethics, financial management, and executive compensation.	Brings in real-world issues concerning conflicts of interest and current controversies surrounding ethical conduct and management pay.
Chapter 2 Financial Statements, Taxes, and Cash Flow	Cash flow vs. earnings.	Clearly defines cash flow and spells out the differences between cash flow and earnings.
	Market values vs. book values.	Emphasizes the relevance of market values over book values.
PART TWO FINANCIAL STATEMENTS AND LONG-TERM FINANCIAL PLANNING		
Chapter 3 Working with Financial Statements	Using financial statement information.	Section discusses the advantages and disadvantages of using financial statements.
Chapter 4 Long-Term Financial Planning and Corporate Growth	*New material:* Explanation of alternative formulas for sustainable and internal growth rates.	Explanation of growth rate formulas clears up a common misunderstanding about these formulas and the circumstances under which alternative formulas are correct.
	Thorough coverage of sustainable growth as a planning tool.	Provides a vehicle for examining the interrelationships between operations, financing, and growth.
PART THREE VALUATION OF FUTURE CASH FLOWS		
Chapter 5 Introduction to Valuation: The Time Value of Money	First of two chapters on time value of money.	Relatively short chapter introduces just the basic ideas on time value of money to get students started on this traditionally difficult topic.
Chapter 6 Discounted Cash Flow Valuation	Second of two chapters on time value of money.	Covers more advanced time value topics with numerous examples, calculator tips, and Excel spreadsheet exhibits. Contains many real-world examples.
Chapter 7 Interest Rates and Bond Valuation	*New material:* "Clean" vs. "dirty" bond prices and accrued interest.	Clears up the pricing of bonds between coupon payment dates and also bond market quoting conventions.
	Bond ratings.	Up-to-date discussion of bond rating agencies and ratings given to debt. Includes the latest descriptions of ratings used by the DBRS.

Chapters	Selected Topics of Interest	Benefits to You
Chapter 8 Stock Valuation	Updated end-of-chapter Mini Case.	Mini Case applies material presented in chapter to a real-world situation.
	Stock market reporting.	Up-to-date discussion of stock market reporting, using Le Chateau stock as an example.

PART FOUR   CAPITAL BUDGETING

Chapters	Selected Topics of Interest	Benefits to You
Chapter 9 Net Present Value and Other Investment Criteria	First of three chapters on capital budgeting.	Relatively short chapter introduces key ideas on an intuitive level to help students with this traditionally difficult topic.
	NPV, IRR, payback, discounted payback, and accounting rate of return.	Consistent, balanced examination of advantages and disadvantages of various criteria.
Chapter 10 Making Capital Investment Decisions	Project cash flow.	Thorough coverage of project cash flows and the relevant numbers for a project analysis.
	Alternative cash flow definitions.	Emphasizes the equivalence of various formulas, thereby removing common misunderstandings.
	Special cases of DCF analysis.	Considers important applications of chapter tools.
Chapter 11 Project Analysis and Evaluation	*Mini Case:* Minor International.	This comprehensive case applies the capital budgeting concepts covered throughout Part Four.
	Sources of value.	Stresses the need to understand the economic basis for value creation in a project.
	Scenario and sensitivity "what-if" analyses.	Illustrates how to actually apply and interpret these tools in a project analysis.
	Break-even analysis.	Covers cash, accounting, and financial break-even levels.

PART FIVE   RISK AND RETURN

Chapters	Selected Topics of Interest	Benefits to You
Chapter 12 Some Lessons from Capital Market History	*New section:* Geometric vs. arithmetic returns.	Discusses calculation and interpretation of geometric returns. Clarifies common misconceptions regarding appropriate use of arithmetic vs. geometric average returns.
	Capital market history.	Extensive coverage of historical returns, volatilities, and risk premiums.
	Market efficiency.	Efficient markets hypothesis discussed along with common misconceptions.
Chapter 13 Return, Risk, and the Security Market Line	Diversification, systematic and unsystematic risk.	Illustrates basics of risk and return in a straight-forward fashion.
	Beta and the security market line.	Develops the security market line with an intuitive approach that bypasses much of the usual portfolio theory and statistics.

PART SIX   COST OF CAPITAL AND LONG-TERM FINANCIAL POLICY

Chapters	Selected Topics of Interest	Benefits to You
Chapter 14 Cost of Capital	Cost of capital estimation.	Contains a complete step-by-step illustration of cost of capital for publicly traded Loblaw Companies.
Chapter 15 Raising Capital	*New discussion:* Dutch auction IPOs.	Explains uniform price auctions using recent Google IPO as an example.
	New discussion: IPO "quiet periods."	Explains the OSC's and SEC's quiet period rules.
	New discussion: Lockup agreements.	Briefly discusses the importance of lockup agreements.
	IPOs in practice.	In-depth look at a real-world example of an IPO.
Chapter 16 Financial Leverage and Capital Structure Policy	Basics of financial leverage.	Illustrates effect of leverage on risk and return.
	Optimal capital structure.	Describes the basic trade-offs leading to an optimal capital structure.
	Financial distress and bankruptcy.	Briefly surveys the bankruptcy process.

Chapters	Selected Topics of Interest	Benefits to You
Chapter 17 Dividends and Dividend Policy	*New Mini Case:* Cost of Capital for Hubbard Computer, Inc.	New case written for this edition analyzes cost of capital estimation for a non-public firm.
	New material: Very recent survey evidence on dividend policy.	New survey results show the most important (and least important) factors considered by financial managers in setting dividend policy.
	New material: Effects of new tax laws.	Brief discussion of the implications of newer, lower dividend rates.
	Dividends and dividend policy.	Describes dividend payments and the factors favouring higher and lower payout policies.

PART SEVEN   SHORT-TERM FINANCIAL PLANNING AND MANAGEMENT

Chapters	Selected Topics of Interest	Benefits to You
Chapter 18 Short-Term Finance and Planning	Operating and cash cycles.	Stresses the importance of cash flow timing.
	Short-term financial planning.	Illustrates creation of cash budgets and potential need for financing.
Chapter 19 Cash and Liquidity Management	Float management.	Thorough coverage of float management.
	Cash collection and disbursement.	Examination of systems used by firms to handle cash inflows and outflows.
Chapter 20 Credit and Inventory Management	*New Mini Case:* Piepkorn Manufacturing Working Capital Management.	New case written for this edition evaluates working capital issues for a small firm.
	Credit management.	Analysis of credit policy and implementation.
	Inventory management.	Brief overview of important inventory concepts.

PART EIGHT   TOPICS IN CORPORATE FINANCE

Chapters	Selected Topics of Interest	Benefits to You
Chapter 21 International Corporate Finance	Foreign exchange.	Covers essentials of exchange rates and their determination.
	International capital budgeting.	Shows how to adapt basic DCF approach to handle exchange rates.
	Exchange rate and political risk.	Discusses hedging and issues surrounding sovereign risk.
Chapter 22 Leasing	*New material:* Synthetic leases.	Discusses controversial practice of custom-tailored, "off-balance-sheet" financing.
	Leases and lease valuation.	Essentials of leasing, good and bad reasons for leasing, and NPV of leasing are examined.
Chapter 23 Mergers and Acquisitions	*New material:* Alternatives to mergers and acquisitions.	Covers strategic alliances and joint ventures and why they are important alternatives.
	New material: Defensive tactics.	Expanded discussion of anti-takeover provisions.
	New section: Divestitures and restructurings.	Important actions such as equity carve-outs, spins-offs, and split-ups are examined.
	Mergers and acquisitions.	Develops essentials of M&A analysis, including financial, tax, and accounting issues.

PART NINE   DERIVATIVE SECURITIES AND CORPORATE FINANCE

Chapters	Selected Topics of Interest	Benefits to You
Chapter 24 Risk Management: An Introduction to Financial Engineering	Volatility and risk.	Illustrates need to manage risk and some of the most important types of risk.
	Hedging with forwards, options, and swaps.	Shows how many risks can be managed with financial derivatives.
Chapter 25 Options and Corporate Securities	Put-call parity and Black-Scholes.	Develops modern option valuation and factors influencing option values.
	Options and corporate finance.	Applies option valuation to a variety of corporate issues, including mergers and capital budgeting.

LEARNING SOLUTIONS

In addition to illustrating pertinent concepts and presenting up-to-date coverage, the authors of *Fundamentals of Corporate Finance* strive to present the material in a way that makes it coherent and easy to understand. To meet the varied needs of the intended audience, *Fundamentals of Corporate Finance* is rich in valuable learning tools and support.

Each feature can be categorized by the benefit to the student:

- Real Financial Decisions
- Application Tools
- Study Aids

Real Financial Decisions

We have included key features that help students connect chapter concepts to how decision makers use this material in the real world.

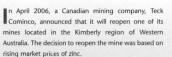

CHAPTER 11

Project Analysis and Evaluation

In April 2006, a Canadian mining company, Teck Cominco, announced that it will reopen one of its mines located in the Kimberly region of Western Australia. The decision to reopen the mine was based on rising market prices of zinc.

The case of Teck Cominco illustrates that sometimes postponing a project because of unfavourable conditions pays off. With zinc prices too low and costs too high, the strategy of closing the mine and reopening at a later date worked to the benefit of the company. Sometimes, capital budgeting decisions don't work out as well. Forecasting involves considerable risk and potential error. This chapter explores how this may happen and what companies can do to analyze (and possibly prevent) negative outcomes, as well as how companies deal with such situations when they arise.

CHAPTER-OPENING VIGNETTES These are from real-world events and introduce students to the chapter concepts. New chapter-opening vignettes can be found in many chapters. Questions about the chapter-opening vignettes are posed in the end-of-chapter material to ensure understanding of the concepts.

In Their Own Words . . . Geoff Martin on Online Billing

ELECTRONIC BILL PAYMENT and collection is finally starting to become the "killer app" that pundits have long predicted it would be, and the Government of Canada is leading the charge.

It has placed first worldwide in online services for four years running, according to a yearly study by global technology services firm Accenture. And with the leadership of the federal Government On-Line (GOL) program (gol-ged.gc.ca), which aims to provide a majority of Canadian government services securely and efficiently, our lead over the two countries tied for second place, Singapore and the United States, continues to widen.

Since it deals with virtually every Canadian citizen and business, the Canada Revenue Agency (CRA) is leading the way with the GOL program. Last year, 10 million Canadians filed their taxes online, but CRA expects to significantly expand its services before the next tax deadline, to entice even greater numbers.

With their acquisition of webdoxs from BCE Emergis in July 2004, Canada Post's online payment service, called epost,

is also poised to become a global trail-blazer in e-billing. While epost currently offers services that allow its more than 400,000 registered users in major cities such as Calgary, Winnipeg, Toronto, and Ottawa to pay their municipal taxes and other bills online, the scheduled launch of merged services between epost and webdoxs in December will connect more than one million registered customers with the services of 97 companies. In Toronto, the service will enable electronic payment for 7 of the 10 monthly bills received by an average household.

With numbers ramping upwards so sharply right across the country, it doesn't take a crystal ball to determine that e-billing is very quickly taking over in Canada. While the paperless society we've long been promised still seems like a distant fairy tale, Canadian governments and businesses seem poised to achieve one of the world's first truly cashless societies in the very near future.

This discussion is excerpted from G. Martin, "No cash please," Summit Ottawa: Oct 2004. Vol. 7, Iss. 6, p. 11. Used with permission.

IN THEIR OWN WORDS BOXES
A unique series of brief essays are written by distinguished scholars and by Canadian practitioners on key topics in the text. To name just a few, these include essays by Merton Miller on capital structure, Geoff Martin on the technology bubble, and Gérard Bérubé on corporate governance.

ENHANCED! REAL-WORLD EXAMPLES   There are many current examples integrated throughout the text, tying chapter concepts to real life through illustration and reinforcing the relevance of the material. For added reinforcement, some tie into the chapter-opening vignettes.

EXPANDED! WEB LINKS   We have added many additional website references, a key research tool directing students to websites that tie into the chapter material.

NEW! INTEGRATIVE MINI CASES   These longer problems seek to integrate a number of topics from within the chapter. The Mini Cases allow students to test and challenge their abilities to solve real-life situations for each of the key sections of the text material.

MINI CASE

Cost of Capital and Dividend Policy for Hubbard Computer, Inc.

You have recently been hired by Hubbard Computer, Inc. (HCI), in its relatively new treasury management department. HCI was founded eight years ago in Edmonton, Alberta, by Bill Hubbard and currently operates 74 stores across Canada. The company is privately owned by Bill and his family; it had sales of $97 million last year.

HCI primarily sells to customers who shop in the stores. Customers come to the store and talk with a sales representative. The sales representative assists the customer in determining the type of computer and peripherals that will meet the individual customer's computing needs. After the order is taken, the customer pays for the order immediately, and a computer is custom-made to fill the order. Delivery of the computer averages within 15 days, and it is guaranteed within 30 days.

HCI's growth to date has come from its profits. When the company had sufficient capital, it would open a new store. Other than scouting locations, relatively little formal analysis has been used in its capital budgeting process. Bill Hubbard has just read about capital budgeting techniques and has come to you for help. For starters, the company has never attempted to determine its cost of capital, and Bill would like you to perform that analysis. Since the company is privately owned, it is difficult to determine the cost of equity for the company. Bill wants you to use the pure play approach to estimating the cost of capital for HCI, and he has chosen Dell as a representative company. The following steps will enable you to calculate this estimate.

quarterly or annual report and download the form. Look on the balance sheet to find the book value of debt and the book value of equity. If you look farther down the report, you should find a section titled "Long-term Debt and Interest Rate Risk Management" that will provide a breakdown of Dell's long-term debt.

2.   To estimate the cost of equity for Dell, go to finance.yahoo.com and enter the ticker symbol DELL. Follow the links to answer the following questions: What is the most recent stock price listed for Dell? What is the market value of equity, or market capitalization? How many shares of stock does Dell have outstanding? What is the most recent annual dividend? Can you use the dividend discount model in this case? What is the beta for Dell? Now go back to *www.bankofcanada.ca* and follow the "Interest Rates" link. What is the yield on a 3-month Treasury bill? Using the historical market risk premium, what is the cost of equity for Dell using CAPM?

3.   You now need to calculate the cost of debt for Dell. Although it is much more reliable and current to use market values when calculating the cost of debt, this problem asks for the book values for simplicity. Go to *www.dell.com* and download the most recent annual report. What is the weighted average cost of debt for Dell, using the book value?

4.   You now have all the necessary information to calculate the weighted average cost of capital for Dell. Calculate the weighted average cost of capital for Dell, assuming Dell has a 37 percent marginal tax rate.

S&P PROBLEMS   At the end of each chapter there are student exercises using the **Education Version of Standard & Poor's Market Insight.** This Web-based resource, which is available with each new copy of the text, contains a wealth of current and past financial statement data plus stock price history, as well as more descriptive material from a universe of more than 1,000 firms to allow students to engage in sophisticated company and industry analysis.

S&P Problems

1.   **Calculating Required Return** A drawback of the dividend growth model is the need to estimate the growth rate of dividends. One way to estimate this growth rate is to use the sustainable growth rate. Look back at Chapter 4 and find the formula for the sustainable growth rate. Using the annual income statement and balance sheet, calculate the sustainable growth rate for MDS Inc. (MDZ). Find the most recent closing monthly stock price under the "Mthly. Adj. Prices" link. Using the growth rate you calculated, the most recent dividend per share, and the most recent stock price, calculate the required return for MDS shareholders. Does this number make sense? Why or why not?

2.   **Calculating Growth Rates** Coca-Cola (KO) is a dividend-paying company. Recently, dividends for Coca-Cola have increased at about 5.5 percent per year. Find the most recent closing monthly stock price under the "Mthly. Adj. Prices" link. Locate the most recent annual dividend for KO and calculate the dividend yield. Using your answer and the 5.5 percent dividend growth rate, what is the required return for shareholders? Suppose instead that you know that the required return is 13 percent. What price should Coca-Cola stock sell for now? What if the required return is 15 percent?

EXPANDED! INTERNET APPLICATION QUESTIONS   Many new questions, relevant to the topic discussed in each chapter, are presented for the students to explore using the Internet. From the *Fundamentals of Corporate Finance* website *www.mcgrawhill.ca/olc/ross,* students will find direct links to the websites included in these questions.

Each chapter concludes with a short, annotated list of books and articles that the interested reader may refer to for additional information.

Application Tools

Realizing that there is more than one way to solve problems in corporate finance, we include sections that will not only encourage students to learn different problem-solving methods, but will also help them learn or brush up on their financial calculator and Excel® spreadsheet skills.

CALCULATOR HINTS

We can illustrate how to calculate unknown rates using a financial calculator using these numbers. For our example, you would do the following:

Enter	8			−100	200
	N	**%i**	**PMT**	**PV**	**FV**
Solve for		9.05			

As in our previous examples, notice the minus sign on the present value.

CALCULATOR HINTS This feature introduces students to problem solving with the assistance of a financial calculator. Sample keystrokes are provided for illustrative purposes, although individual calculators will vary somewhat.

SPREADSHEET STRATEGIES

Calculating NPVs with a Spreadsheet

Spreadsheets are commonly used to calculate NPVs. Examining the use of spreadsheets in this context also allows us to issue an important warning. Let's rework Example 9.1:

	A	B	C	D	E	F	G	H
1								
2			Using a spreadsheet to calculate net present values					
3								
4	From Example 9.1, the project's cost is $10,000. The cash flows are $2,000 per year for the first							
5	two years, $4,000 per year for the next two, and $5,000 in the last year. The discount rate is							
6	10 percent; what's the NPV?							
7								
8		Year	Cash flow					
9		0	-$10,000		Discount rate =	10%		
10		1	2,000					
11		2	2,000		NPV =	$2,102.72	(wrong answer)	
12		3	4,000		NPV =	$2,312.99	(right answer)	
13		4	4,000					
14		5	5,000					
15	The formula entered in cell F11 is =NPV(F9, C9:C14). This gives the wrong answer because the NPV function							
16	calculates the sum of the present value of each number in the series, assuming that the first number occurs at							
17	the end of the first period. Therefore, in this example the year 0 value is discounted by 1 year or 10 percent							
18	(we clearly don't want this number to be discounted at all).							
19	The formula entered in cell F12 is =NPV(F9, C10:C14) + C9. This gives the right answer because the							
20	NPV function is used to calculate the present value of the cash flows for future years and then the initial cost is							
21	subtracted to calculate the answer. Notice that we added cell C9 because it is already negative.							

SPREADSHEET STRATEGIES This feature either introduces students to Excel® or helps them brush up on their Excel® spreadsheet skills, particularly as they relate to corporate finance. This feature appears in self-contained sections and shows students how to set up spreadsheets to analyze common financial problems—a vital part of every business student's education.

SPREADSHEET TEMPLATES Several questions (identified by an icon) within the end-of-chapter material can be solved using the Financial Analysis Spreadsheet Templates (FAST) available at the Ross Online Learning Centre *www.mcgrawhill.ca/olc/ross*. These Excel® templates are a valuable extension of the Spreadsheet Strategies feature.

Study Aids

We want students to get the most from this book and their course, and we realize that students have different learning styles and study needs. We therefore present a number of study features to appeal to as wide a range of students as possible.

CONCEPT BUILDING Chapter sections are intentionally kept short to promote a step-by-step, building block approach to learning. Each section is then followed by a series of short concept questions that highlight the key ideas just presented. Students use these questions to make sure they can identify and understand the most important concepts as they read.

CONCEPT QUESTIONS

1. What are the five groups of ratios? Give two or three examples of each kind.

2. Turnover ratios all have one of two figures as numerators. What are they? What do these ratios measure? How do you interpret the results?

3. Profitability ratios all have the same figure in the numerator. What is it? What do these ratios measure? How do you interpret the results?

NUMBERED EXAMPLES Separate numbered and titled examples are extensively integrated into the chapters. These examples provide detailed applications and illustrations of the text material in a step-by-step format. Each example is completely self-contained so students don't have to search for additional information. Based on our classroom testing, these examples are among the most useful learning aids because they provide both detail and explanation.

EXAMPLE 3.1: Current Events

Suppose a firm were to pay off some of its suppliers and short-term creditors. What would happen to the current ratio? Suppose a firm buys some inventory for cash. What happens in this case? What happens if a firm sells some merchandise?

The first case is a trick question. What happens is that the current ratio moves away from 1. If it is greater than 1 (the usual case), it gets bigger; but if it is less than 1, it gets smaller. To see this, suppose the firm has $4 in current assets and $2 in current liabilities for a current ratio of 2. If we use $1 in cash to reduce current liabilities, then the new current ratio is assets and $4 in current liabilities, the current ratio would fall to 1/3 from 1/2.

The second case is not quite as tricky. Nothing happens to the current ratio because cash goes down while inventory goes up—total current assets are unaffected.

In the third case, the current ratio would usually rise because inventory is normally shown at cost and the sale would normally be at something greater than cost (the difference is the markup). The increase in either cash or receivables is therefore greater than the decrease in inventory. This

---

KEY TERMS Within each chapter, key terms are highlighted in **boldface** type the first time they appear. Key terms are defined in the text, and also in a running glossary in the margins of the text for quick reminders. For reference there is a comprehensive list of key terms at the end of each chapter and a full glossary at the back of the textbook with page references for each term.

SUMMARY TABLES

These tables succinctly restate key principles, results, and equations. They appear whenever it is useful to emphasize and summarize a group of related concepts.

TABLE 4.9

Summary of internal and sustainable growth rates from Hoffman Company example

I. INTERNAL GROWTH RATE

$$\text{Internal growth rate} = \frac{\text{ROA} \times R}{1 - \text{ROA} \times R} = \frac{.132 \times 2/3}{1 - 0.132 \times 2/3} = 9.65\%$$

where

ROA = Return on assets = Net income/Total assets = 13.2%

R = Plowback (retention) ratio = $2/3$

= Addition to retained earnings/Net income

The internal growth rate is the maximum growth rate that can be achieved with no external financing of any kind.

II. SUSTAINABLE GROWTH RATE

$$\text{Sustainable growth rate} = \frac{\text{ROE} \times R}{1 - \text{ROE} \times R} = \frac{0.264 \times (2/3)}{1 - 0.264 \times (2/3)} = 21.3\%$$

where

ROE = Return on equity = Net income/Total equity = 26.4%

R = Plowback (retention) ratio = $2/3$

= Addition to retained earnings/Net income

The sustainable growth rate is the maximum growth rate that can be achieved with no external equity financing while maintaining a constant debt/equity ratio.

KEY EQUATIONS These are called out in the text and identified by equation number. An Equation Index is available at the end of the book and a Formula Sheet can be found on the Ross Online Learning Centre at *www.mcgrawhill.ca/olc/ross*.

CHAPTER SUMMARY AND CONCLUSION These paragraphs review the chapter's key points and provide closure to the chapter.

CHAPTER REVIEW PROBLEMS AND SELF-TEST Appearing after the Summary and Conclusions and Key Terms, each chapter includes Chapter Review Problems and a Self-Test section. These questions and answers allow students to test their abilities in solving key problems related to the chapter content and provide instant reinforcement.

CONCEPTS REVIEW AND CRITICAL THINKING QUESTIONS This section facilitates students' knowledge of key principles, and their intuitive understanding of chapter concepts. A number of the questions relate to the chapter-opening vignette—reinforcing students' critical-thinking skills and the learning of chapter material.

Concepts Review and Critical Thinking Questions

1. Why do you think most long-term financial planning begins with sales forecasts? Put differently, why are future sales the key input?

2. Would long-range financial planning be more important for a capital intensive company, such as a heavy equipment manufacturer, or an import-export business? Why?

3. Testaburger, Ltd., uses no external financing and maintains a positive retention ratio. When sales grow by 15 percent, the firm has a negative projected EFN. What does this tell you about the firm's internal growth rate? How about the sustainable growth rate? At this same level of sales growth, what will happen to the projected EFN if the retention ratio is increased? What if the retention ratio is decreased? What happens to the projected EFN if the firm pays out all of its earnings in the form of dividends?

4. Broslofski Co. maintains a positive retention ratio and keeps its debt-equity ratio constant every year. When sales grow by 20 percent, the firm has a negative projected EFN. What does this tell you about the firm's sustainable growth rate? Do you know, with certainty, if the internal growth rate is greater than or less than 20 percent? Why? What happens to the projected EFN if the retention ratio is increased? What if the retention ratio is decreased? What if the retention ratio is zero?

   Use the following information to answer the next six questions: A small business called The Grandmother Calendar Company began selling personalized photo calendar kits in 1992. The kits were a hit, and sales soon sharply exceeded forecasts. The rush of orders created a huge backlog, so the company leased more space and expanded capacity, but it still could not keep up with demand. Equipment failed from overuse and quality suffered. Working capital was drained to expand production, and, at the same time, payments from customers were often delayed until the product was shipped. Unable to deliver on orders, the company became so strapped for cash that employee paycheques began to bounce. Finally, out of cash, the company ceased operations entirely in January 1995.

5. Do you think the company would have suffered the same fate if its product had been less popular? Why or why not?

6. The Grandmother Calendar Company clearly had a cash flow problem. In the context of the cash flow analysis we developed in Chapter 2, what was the impact of customers not paying until orders were shipped?

7. The firm actually priced its product to be about 20 percent less than that of competitors, even though the Grandmother calendar was more detailed. In retrospect, was this a wise choice?

8. If the firm was so successful at selling, why wouldn't a bank or some other lender step in and provide it with the cash it needed to continue?

9. Which is the biggest culprit here: too many orders, too little cash, or too little production capacity?

10. What are some of the actions that a small company like The Grandmother Calendar Company can take if it finds itself in a situation in which growth in sales outstrips production capacity and available financial resources? What other options (besides expansion of capacity) are available to a company when orders exceed capacity?

QUESTIONS AND PROBLEMS We have found that many students learn better when they have plenty of opportunity to practice; therefore, we provide extensive end-of-chapter questions and problems. The end-of-chapter support greatly exceeds what is typical in an introductory textbook. The questions and problems are labelled by topic and are separated into three learning levels: Basic, Intermediate, and Challenge. Throughout the text, we have worked to supply interesting problems that illustrate real-world applications of chapter material. Answers to selected end-of-chapter material appear in Appendix B.

As described earlier in this Preface (see page xxii), students' learning and understanding of the chapter content is further supported by the following end-of-chapter materials:

- **S&P Problems**
- **Internet Application Questions**
- **Mini Cases**
- **Suggested Readings**

TECHNOLOGY SOLUTIONS

LYRYX FOR FINANCE

LYRYX LEARNING INC
Online Learning and Assessment
lyryx.com

Lyryx Assessment for Finance is a leading-edge online assessment system, designed to support both students and instructors. The assessment takes the form of a homework assignment called a Lab. The assessments are algorithmically generated and automatically graded so that students get instant grades and feedback. New Labs are randomly generated each time, providing the student with unlimited opportunities to try a type of question. After they submit a Lab for marking, students receive extensive feedback on their work, thus promoting their learning experience.

Lyryx for the student offers algorithmically generated and automatically graded assignments. Students get instant grades and instant feedback—no need to wait until the next class to find out how well they did! Grades are instantly recorded in a grade book that the student can view.

Students are motivated to do their Labs for two reasons: first because the results can be tied to assessment, and second, because they can try the Lab as many times as they wish prior to the due date, with only their best grade being recorded.

Instructors know from experience that if students do their finance homework, they will be successful in the course. Recent research regarding the use of Lyryx has shown that when Labs are tied to assessment, even if worth only a small percentage of the total grade of the course, students WILL do their homework—and MORE THAN ONCE!

Please contact your *i*Learning Sales Specialist for additional information on the Lyryx Assessment Finance system. Visit **http://lyryx.com.**

*i*STUDY

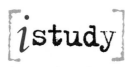

*i*Interact *i*Learn *i*Succeed

PREPARED BY KURT LOESCHER, UNIVERSITY OF SASKATCHEWAN

Available 24/7. *i*Study provides instant feedback so you can study when you want, how you want, and where you want.

This exciting and innovative online study guide provides students with a completely new way to learn. The motivating interactive exercises are not only enjoyable, but also ensure the students' active involvement in the learning process, boosting their ability to retain and apply key concepts. Each chapter of *i*Study includes chapter highlights organized by chapter sections, extensive interactive quizzes with instant feedback, and levelled problems with full solutions. Students can choose from all of these features to create their own personalized study plan—*i*Study offers the best, most convenient way to Learn, Interact, and Succeed!

To see a sample chapter, go to the Online Learning Centre at *www.mcgrawhill.ca/olc/ross*. Full access to *i*Study can be purchased at the website or by purchasing a pin code card through your campus bookstore.

Instructors: Contact your *i*Learning Sales Specialist for additional information regarding packaging access to *i*Study with the student text.

FINGAME ONLINE 5.0

BY LEROY BROOKS

In this comprehensive simulation game, students control a hypothetical company over numerous periods of operation. As student make major financial and operating decisions for their company, they will develop and enhance skills in financial management and financial accounting statement analysis. Please contact your *i*Learning Sales Specialist for additional information regarding packaging access to **FinGame** with the student text.

FINANCIAL ANALYSIS WITH AN ELECTRONIC CALCULATOR, SIXTH EDITION

BY MARK A. WHITE

This helpful guide provides you with information and procedures to master financial calculators and gain a deeper understanding of financial mathematics. Complete instructions are included for solving all major problem types on three popular models of financial calculators: Hewlett-Packard's HP-10B II, Sharp Electronics' EL-733A, and Texas Instruments' BA II Plus. Sixty hands-on problems with detailed solutions will allow you to practice the skills outlined in the book and obtain instant reinforcement. Please contact your *i*Learning Sales Specialist for additional information.

Online Learning Centre

STUDENT ONLINE LEARNING CENTRE (OLC)

Prepared by Eric Wang, Athabasca University, the OLC offers aids such as Online Quizzes, Internet Application Exercises, Annotated Web Links, Excel Templates, S&P Problems, Searchable Glossary, and *Globe and Mail* Newsfeeds. The *Fundamentals of Corporate Finance* OLC is located at ***www.mcgrawhill.ca/olc/ross.***

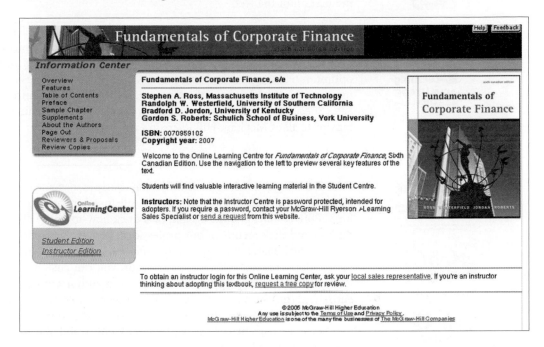

SUPPORT FOR THE INSTRUCTOR

Service takes on a whole new meaning with McGraw-Hill Ryerson and *Fundamentals of Corporate Finance*. More than just bringing you the textbook, we have consistently raised the bar in terms of innovation and educational research — both in finance and in education in general. These investments in learning and the education community have helped us to understand the needs of students and educators across the country, and allowed us to foster the growth of truly innovative, integrated learning.

INSTRUCTOR'S ONLINE LEARNING CENTRE (OLC) The OLC includes a password-protected website for Instructors; visit us at ***www.mcgrawhill.ca/olc/ross.*** The site offers downloadable supplements and PageOut, the McGraw-Hill Ryerson course website development centre.

INSTRUCTOR'S CD-ROM This CD-ROM includes the following Instructor Supplements:

Instructor's Manual Prepared by Ian Rakita, Concordia University. The IM contains two main sections. The first section contains a chapter outline with lecture tips, real-world tips, and ethics notes. The second section includes detailed solutions for all end-of-chapter problems.

Computerized Test Bank Prepared by Larry Bauer, Memorial University. This test bank contains true/false and multiple-choice questions categorized by difficulty level, type, and topic. It also includes essay and critical thinking questions. New for this edition, more than 1,000 questions have been added to the test bank.

Algorithmic Test Bank New for this edition, the Computerized Test Bank now includes a problem generator that replicates the structure of selected questions while populating them with fresh numbers. Create unique versions of every quiz, every test, or use it to provide dozens of similar but distinct problems for students to practice on.

PowerPoint® Presentation   Prepared by Anne Inglis, Ryerson University. The Microsoft® PowerPoint® Presentation slides have been enhanced to better illustrate chapter concepts.

Image Bank   All figures and tables are available in digital format in the Instructor's CD.

Excel Templates (with solutions)   Prepared by Eric Wang, Athabasca University. Excel templates are included with solutions for end-of-chapter problems indicated by an Excel icon in the margin of the text.

INTEGRATED LEARNING   Your Integrated Learning Sales Specialist is a McGraw-Hill Ryerson representative who has the experience, product knowledge, training, and support to help you assess and integrate any of our products, technology, and services into your course for optimum teaching and learning performance. Whether it's using our test bank software, helping your students improve their grades, or putting your entire course online, your *i*Learning Sales Specialist is there to help you do it. Contact your *i*Learning Sales Specialist to learn how to maximize all of McGraw-Hill Ryerson's resources!

Course Management

PAGEOUT   is the McGraw-Hill Ryerson course management system. PageOut, *www.mhhe.com/pageout*, is the easiest way to create a website for your corporate finance course. There is no need for HTML coding, graphic design, or a thick how-to book. Just fill in a series of boxes in plain English and click on one of our professional designs. In no time, your course is online!

For the integrated instructor, we offer *Fundamentals of Corporate Finance* content for complete online courses. Whatever your needs, you can customize the *Fundamentals of Corporate Finance* Online Learning Centre content and author your own online course materials. It is entirely up to you. You can offer online discussion and message boards that will complement your office hours, and reduce the lines outside your door. Content cartridges are also available for course management systems, such as **WebCT** and **Blackboard.** Ask your *i*Learning Sales Specialist for details.

iLEARNING SERVICES PROGRAM   McGraw-Hill Ryerson offers a unique *i*Service package designed for Canadian faculty. Our mission is to equip providers of higher education with superior tools and resources required for excellence in teaching. For additional information, visit *www.mcgrawhill.ca/highereducation/iservices.*

TEACHING, LEARNING & TECHNOLOGY CONFERENCE SERIES   The educational environment has changed tremendously in recent years, and McGraw-Hill Ryerson continues to be committed to helping you acquire the skills you need to succeed in this new milieu. Our innovative Teaching, Technology & Learning Conference Series brings faculty together from across Canada with 3M Teaching Excellence award winners to share teaching and learning best practices in a collaborative and stimulating environment. Preconference workshops on general topics, such as teaching large classes and technology integration, will also be offered. We will also work with you at your own institution to customize workshops that best suit the needs of your faculty.

RESEARCH REPORTS ON TECHNOLOGY AND STUDENT SUCCESS IN HIGHER EDUCATION   These landmark reports, undertaken in conjunction with academic and private sector advisory boards, are the result of research studies into the challenges professors face in helping students succeed and the opportunities that new technology presents to impact teaching and learning.

ACKNOWLEDGEMENTS

We never would have completed this book without the incredible amount of help and support we received from colleagues, editors, family members, and friends. We would like to thank, without implicating, all of you.

For starters, a great many of our colleagues read the drafts of our first and current editions. Our reviewers continued to keep us working on improving the content, organization, exposition, and Canadian content of our text. To the following reviewers, we are grateful for their many contributions to the Sixth Canadian Edition:

Mohamed Ayadi, *Brock University*

Robert Barron, *Kwantlen University College*

Ernest Biktimirov, *Brock University*

Edward Blinder, *Ryerson University*

Maria Bouchkova, *Concordia University*

Trevor Chamberlain, *McMaster University*

Kirk Collins, *University of Western Ontario*

Alex Faseruk, *Memorial University of Newfoundland*

Greg Hebb, *Dalhousie University*

Feng Liu, *McGill University*

Kurt Loescher, *University of Saskatchewan*

Basma Majerbi, *University of Victoria*

Andras Marosi, *University of Alberta*

Wilf Roesler, *University of Lethbridge*

Amir Rubin, *Simon Fraser University*

David Stangeland, *University of Manitoba*

Herman A. van den Berg, *University of Toronto*

A special thank you must be given to Helen Prankie, Academic Director, Canadian Securities Institute, for her vigilant efforts of technical proofreading and, in particular, careful checking of the solutions in the Instructor's Manual. Her keen eye and attention to detail have contributed greatly to the quality of the final product.

Also deserving of special notice is Michael Groysman, who reviewed all the chapter end problems for completeness and clarity, verifying their appropriateness and answerability.

Several of our most respected colleagues and journalists contributed essays, which are entitled "In Their Own Words" and appear in selected chapters. To these individuals we extend a special thanks:

Edward I. Altman, *New York University*

George Athanassakos, *University of Western Ontario*

Gérard Bérubé, *CA Magazine*

F. Greenslade, *National Post online*

Robert C. Higgins, *University of Washington*

Ken Hitzig, *Accord Financial Corporation*

Roger Ibbotson, *Yale School of Management*

Matthew Ingram, *The Globe and Mail*

Abolhassan Jalilvand, *Dalhousie University*

Claude Lamoureux, *Ontario Teachers' Pension Plan Board*

Richard M. Levich, *New York University*

Casey Mahood, *The Globe and Mail*

Burton Malkiel, *Princeton University*

Geoff Martin, *Summit Magazine*

Robert C. Merton, *Harvard University*
Merton H. Miller, *University of Chicago*
John Partridge, *The Globe and Mail*
Clifford W. Smith Jr., *University of Rochester*
Andrew Willis, *The Globe and Mail*

One person deserves special mention for his role in producing the Sixth Canadian Edition. Joseph Gareri, Schulich BBA student, spent the summer of 2006 capably researching updates, drafting revisions, and responding to editorial queries. His excellent input was essential to this edition.

Much credit goes to a "AAA-rated" group of people at McGraw-Hill Ryerson who worked on the Sixth Canadian Edition. Leading the team was Lynn Fisher, Publisher, who continued her role as champion of this project by arranging unparalleled support for the development of the text and support package for this edition. Maria Chu, Senior Developmental Editor, efficiently supervised the reviews and revision, cheerfully addressing the scheduling challenges arising from the sabbatical travels of the Canadian author. Production and copy-editing were handled ably by Anne Nellis, Senior Supervising Editor, and Susan James, freelance Copy Editor.

Through the development of this edition, we have taken great care to discover and eliminate errors. Our goal is to provide the best Canadian textbook available on the subject. Forward your comments to: Professor Gordon S. Roberts, Schulich School of Business, York University, 4700 Keele Street, Toronto, Ontario M3J IP3. Or, email your comments to *groberts@schulich.yorku.ca*.

Stephen A. Ross
Randolph W. Westerfield
Bradford D. Jordan
Gordon S. Roberts

PART 1

Overview of Corporate Finance

CHAPTER 1 **Introduction to Corporate Finance**

Chapter 1 describes the role of the financial manager and the goal of financial management. It also discusses some key aspects of the financial management environment.

CHAPTER 2 **Financial Statements, Taxes, and Cash Flow**

Chapter 2 describes the basic accounting statements used by the firm. The chapter focuses on the critical differences between cash flow and accounting income; it also discusses why accounting value is generally not the same as market value.

CHAPTER 1

Introduction to Corporate Finance

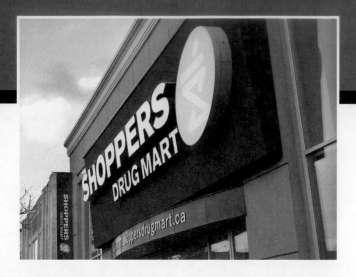

Started in 1921 as Koffler Drug Stores, Shoppers Drug Mart Corporation is now the largest pharmacy chain in Canada, running over 900 licensed stores under its own name and as Pharmaprix in Quebec. The founder, Murray Koffler, started with two family drug stores and built the chain by acquiring others. In 1983, Koffler retired and sold Shoppers, then a privately owned corporation, to Imasco. When Imasco was taken over by BAT Industries in 2000, Shoppers was sold to a group of institutional investors headed by the U.S. takeover firm Kohlberg Kravis Roberts (KKR) and including the Ontario Teachers' Pension Plan Board and CIBC Capital partners, along with Shoppers management and pharmacists who owned Shoppers stores. The next year, the firm held its initial public offering (IPO) and listed on the Toronto Stock Exchange.[1] Understanding the growth of Shoppers Drug Mart from family business to privately owned corporation to corporate giant takes us into issues involving the corporate form of organization, corporate goals, and corporate control, all of which are discussed in this chapter.

TO BEGIN OUR STUDY of modern corporate finance and financial management, we need to address two central issues: First, what is corporate finance, and what is the role of the financial manager in the corporation? Second, what is the goal of financial management? To describe the financial management environment, we look at the corporate form of organization and discuss some conflicts that can arise within the corporation. We also take a brief look at financial institutions and financial markets in Canada.

 **1.1**

CORPORATE FINANCE AND THE FINANCIAL MANAGER

In this section, we discuss where the financial manager fits in the corporation. We start by looking at what corporate finance is and what the financial manager does.

What Is Corporate Finance?

Imagine that you were to start your own business. No matter what type you started, you would have to answer the following three questions in some form or another:

1. What long-term investments should you take on? That is, what lines of business will you be in and what sorts of buildings, machinery, equipment, and research and development facilities will you need?

---

1 Our history of Shoppers Drug Mart draws on Wikipedia articles on the firm and its founder, Murray Koffler, at *http://en.wikipedia.org/wiki/Murray_Koffler*.

2. Where will you get the long-term financing to pay for your investment? Will you bring in other owners or will you borrow the money?

3. How will you manage your everyday financial activities, such as collecting from customers and paying suppliers?

These are not the only questions by any means, but they are among the most important. Corporate finance, broadly speaking, is the study of ways to answer these three questions.

Accordingly, we'll be looking at each of them in the chapters ahead. Though our discussion focuses on the role of the financial manager, these three questions are important to managers in all areas of the corporation. For example, selecting the firm's lines of business (Question 1) shapes the jobs of managers in production, marketing, and management information systems. As a result, most large corporations centralize their finance function and use it to measure performance in other areas. Most CEOs have significant financial management experience.

The Financial Manager

For current issues facing CFOs, see www.cfo.com

A striking feature of large corporations is that the owners (the shareholders) are usually not directly involved in making business decisions, particularly on a day-to-day basis. Instead, the corporation employs managers to represent the owners' interests and make decisions on their behalf. In a large corporation, the financial manager is in charge of answering the three questions we raised earlier.

It is a challenging task because changes in the firm's operations and shifts in Canadian and global financial markets mean that the best answers for each firm are changing, sometimes quite rapidly. Globalization of markets and advanced communications and computer technology, as well as increased volatility of interest rates and foreign exchange rates, have raised the stakes in financial management decisions. We discuss these major trends and how they are changing the financial manager's job after we introduce you to some of the basics of corporate financial decisions.

The financial management function is usually associated with a top officer of the firm, such as a vice president of finance or some other chief financial officer (CFO). Figure 1.1 is a simplified organization chart that highlights the finance activity in a large firm. The chief financial officer (CFO) reports to the president, who is the chief operating officer (COO) in charge of day-to-day operations. The COO reports to the chairman, who is usually chief executive officer. The CEO has overall responsibility to the board. As shown, the vice president of finance coordinates the activities of the treasurer and the controller. The controller's office handles cost and financial accounting, tax payments, and management information systems. The treasurer's office is responsible for managing the firm's cash, its financial planning, and its capital expenditures. These treasury activities are all related to the three general questions raised earlier, and the chapters ahead deal primarily with these issues. Our study thus bears mostly on activities usually associated with the treasurer's office.

Financial Management Decisions

As our discussion suggests, the financial manager must be concerned with three basic types of questions. We consider these in greater detail next.

capital budgeting
The process of planning and managing a firm's investment in long-term assets.

CAPITAL BUDGETING   The first question concerns the firm's long-term investments. The process of planning and managing a firm's long-term investments is called **capital budgeting.** In capital budgeting, the financial manager tries to identify investment opportunities that are worth more to the firm than they will cost to acquire. Loosely speaking, this means that the value of the cash flow generated by an asset exceeds the cost of that asset. The types of investment opportunities that would typically be considered depend in part on the nature of the firm's business. For example, for a retail pharmacy like Shoppers, deciding whether or not to open stores would be a major capital budgeting decision. Some decisions, such as what type of computer system to purchase, might not depend so much on a particular line of business.

Financial managers must be concerned not only with how much cash they expect to receive, but also with when they expect to receive it and how likely they are to receive it. Evaluating the size, timing, and risk of future cash flows is the essence of capital budgeting. We discuss how to do this in detail in the chapters ahead.

capital structure
The mix of debt and equity maintained by a firm.

CAPITAL STRUCTURE   The second major question for the financial manager concerns how the firm should obtain and manage the long-term financing it needs to support its long-term investments. A firm's **capital structure** (or financial structure) refers to the specific mixture of short-term debt, long-term debt, and equity the firm uses to finance its operations. The financial manager has two concerns in this area. First, how much should the firm borrow; that is, what mixture is best? The mixture chosen affects both the risk and value of the firm. Second, what are the least expensive sources of funds for the firm?

If we picture the firm as a pie, then the firm's capital structure determines how that pie is sliced. In other words, what percentage of the firm's cash flow goes to creditors and what percentage goes to shareholders? Management has a great deal of flexibility in choosing a firm's financial structure. Whether one structure is better than any other for a particular firm is the heart of the capital structure issue.

In addition to deciding on the financing mix, the financial manager has to decide exactly how and where to raise the money. The expenses associated with raising long-term financing can be considerable, so different possibilities must be carefully evaluated. Also, corporations borrow money from a variety of lenders, tapping into both Canadian and international debt markets, in a number of different—and sometimes exotic—ways. Choosing among lenders and among loan types is another of the jobs handled by the financial manager.

FIGURE 1.1

A simplified organization chart. The exact titles and organization differ from company to company.

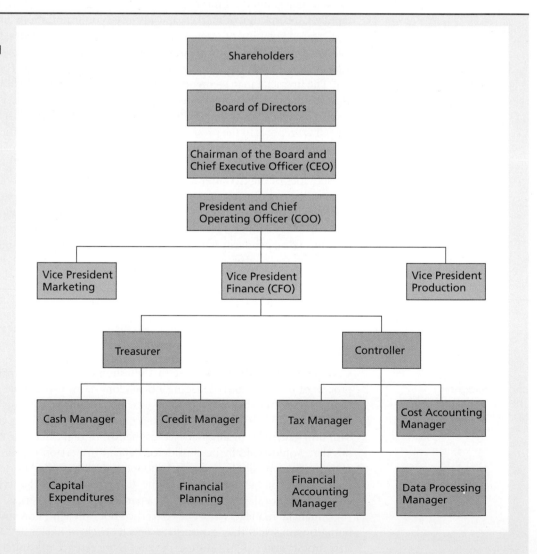

working capital management
Planning and managing the firm's current assets and liabilities.

WORKING CAPITAL MANAGEMENT The third major question concerns **working capital management.** The phrase *working capital* refers to a firm's short-term assets, such as inventory, and its short-term liabilities, such as money owed to suppliers. Managing the firm's working capital is a day-to-day activity that ensures the firm has sufficient resources to continue its operations and avoid costly interruptions. This involves a number of activities, all related to the firm's receipt and disbursement of cash.

Some of the questions about working capital that must be answered are: (1) How much cash and inventory should we keep on hand? (2) Should we sell on credit? If so, what terms should we offer, and to whom should we extend them? (3) How do we obtain any needed short-term financing? Will we purchase on credit or borrow short-term and pay cash? If we borrow short-term, how and when should we do it? This is just a small sample of the issues that arise in managing a firm's working capital.

The three areas of corporate financial management we have described—capital budgeting, capital structure, and working capital management—are very broad categories. Each includes a rich variety of topics; we have indicated only a few of the questions that arise in the different areas. The following chapters contain greater detail.

CONCEPT QUESTIONS

1. What is the capital budgeting decision?

2. Into what category of financial management does cash management fall?

3. What do you call the specific mixture of short-term debt, long-term debt, and equity that a firm chooses to use?

1.2 | FORMS OF BUSINESS ORGANIZATION

Large firms in Canada, such as CIBC and BCE, are almost all organized as corporations. We examine the three different legal forms of business organization—sole proprietorship, partnership, and corporation—to see why this is so. Each of the three forms has distinct advantages and disadvantages in the life of the business, the ability of the business to raise cash, and taxes. A key observation is that, as a firm grows, the advantages of the corporate form may come to outweigh the disadvantages.

Sole Proprietorship

sole proprietorship
A business owned by a single individual.

For more information on forms of business organization, see the "Starting a Business" section at www.canadianlawsite.com

A **sole proprietorship** is a business owned by one person. This is the simplest type of business to start and is the least regulated form of organization. Depending on where you live, you can start up a proprietorship by doing little more than getting a business licence and opening your doors. For this reason, many businesses that later become large corporations start out as sole proprietorships. There are more proprietorships than any other type of business.

As the owner of a sole proprietorship, you keep all the profits. That's the good news. The bad news is that the owner has *unlimited liability* for business debts. This means that creditors can look beyond assets to the proprietor's personal assets for payment. Similarly, there is no distinction between personal and business income, so all business income is taxed as personal income.

The life of a sole proprietorship is limited to the owner's life span, and, importantly, the amount of equity that can be raised is limited to the proprietor's personal wealth. This limitation often means that the business cannot exploit new opportunities because of insufficient capital. Ownership of a sole proprietorship may be difficult to transfer, since this requires the sale of the entire business to a new owner.

Partnership

partnership
A business formed by two or more co-owners.

A **partnership** is similar to a proprietorship, except that there are two or more owners (partners). In a *general partnership*, all the partners share in gains or losses, and all have unlimited liability for all partnership debts, not just some particular share. The way partnership gains (and losses) are divided is described in the *partnership agreement*. This agreement can be an informal oral agreement, or a lengthy, formal written document.

In a *limited partnership*, one or more *general partners* has unlimited liability and runs the business for one or more *limited partners* who do not actively participate in the business. A limited partner's liability for business debts is limited to the amount contributed to the partnership. This form of organization is common in real estate ventures, for example.

The advantages and disadvantages of a partnership are basically the same as those for a proprietorship. Partnerships based on a relatively informal agreement are easy and inexpensive to form. General partners have unlimited liability for partnership debts, and the partnership terminates when a general partner wishes to sell out or dies. All income is taxed as personal income to the partners, and the amount of equity that can be raised is limited to the partners' combined wealth. Ownership by a general partner is not easily transferred because a new partnership must be formed. A limited partner's interest can be sold without dissolving the partnership. But finding a buyer may be difficult, because there is no organized market in limited partnerships.

Based on our discussion, the primary disadvantages of sole proprietorship and partnership as forms of business organization are (1) unlimited liability for business debts on the part of the owners, (2) limited life of the business, and (3) difficulty of transferring ownership. These three disadvantages add up to a single, central problem: the ability of such businesses to grow can be seriously limited by an inability to raise cash for investment.

Corporation

corporation
A business created as a distinct legal entity owned by one or more individuals or entities.

In terms of size, the **corporation** is the most important form of business organization in Canada. A corporation is a legal entity separate and distinct from its owners; it has many of the rights, duties, and privileges of an actual person. Corporations can borrow money and own property, can sue and be sued, and can enter into contracts. A corporation can even be a general partner or a limited partner in a partnership, and a corporation can own stock in another corporation.

Not surprisingly, starting a corporation is somewhat more complicated than starting the other forms of business organization, but not greatly so for a small business. Forming a corporation involves preparing *articles of incorporation* (or a charter) and a set of *bylaws*. The articles of incorporation must contain a number of things, including the corporation's name, its intended life (which can be forever), its business purpose, and the number of shares that can be issued. This information must be supplied to regulators in the jurisdiction where the firm is incorporated. Canadian firms can be incorporated under either the federal *Canada Business Corporation Act* or provincial law.[2]

The bylaws are rules describing how the corporation regulates its own existence. For example, the bylaws describe how directors are elected. These bylaws may be a very simple statement of a few rules and procedures, or they may be quite extensive for a large corporation. The bylaws may be amended or extended from time to time by the shareholders.

In a large corporation, the shareholders and the management are usually separate groups. The shareholders elect the board of directors, which then selects the managers. Management is charged with running the corporation's affairs in the shareholders' interest. In principle, shareholders control the corporation because they elect the directors.

As a result of the separation of ownership and management, the corporate form has several advantages. Ownership (represented by shares of stock) can be readily transferred, and the life of the corporation is therefore not limited. The corporation borrows money in its own name. As a result, the shareholders in a corporation have limited liability for corporate debts. The most they can lose is what they have invested.[3]

While limited liability makes the corporate form attractive to equity investors, lenders sometimes view the limited liability feature as a disadvantage. If the borrower experiences financial

---

2 In some provinces, the legal documents of incorporation are called letters patent or a memorandum of association.

3 An important exception is negligence by a corporate director. If this can be proven, for example in a case of environmental damage, the director may be liable for more than the original investment.

distress and is unable to repay its debt, limited liability blocks lenders' access to the owners' personal assets. For this reason, chartered banks often circumvent limited liability by requiring that owners of small businesses provide personal guarantees for company debt.

www.bell.ca
www.bombardier.com

The relative ease of transferring ownership, the limited liability for business debts, and the unlimited life of the business are the reasons why the corporate form is superior when it comes to raising cash. If a corporation needs new equity, for example, it can sell new shares of stock and attract new investors. The number of owners can be huge; larger corporations have many thousands or even millions of shareholders. In a recent year, for example, BCE had more than 191,000 shareholders and Bombardier had about 11,000. In such cases, ownership can change continuously without affecting the continuity of the business.

The corporate form has a significant disadvantage. Because a corporation is a legal entity, it must pay taxes. Moreover, money paid out to shareholders in dividends is taxed again as income to those shareholders. This is *double taxation*, meaning that corporate profits are taxed twice—at the corporate level when they are earned, and again at the personal level when they are paid out.[4]

As the discussion in this section illustrates, the need of large businesses for outside investors and creditors is such that the corporate form generally is best for such firms. We focus on corporations in the chapters ahead because of the importance of the corporate form in the Canadian and world economies. Also, a few important financial management issues, such as dividend policy, are unique to corporations. However, businesses of all types and sizes need financial management, so the majority of the subjects we discuss bear on all forms of business.

A CORPORATION BY ANOTHER NAME   The corporate form of organization has many variations around the world. The exact laws and regulations differ from country to country, of course, but the essential features of public ownership and limited liability remain. These firms are often designated as joint stock companies, public limited companies, or limited liability companies, depending on the specific nature of the firm and the country of origin.

Table 1.1 gives the names of a few well-known international corporations, their country of origin, and a translation of the abbreviation that follows the company name.

In addition to international variations, there are specialized forms of corporations in Canada and the U.S. One increasingly common example is the professional corporation set up by architects, accountants, doctors, lawyers, dentists and others who are licensed by a professional governing body. A professional corporation has limited liability but each professional is still open to being sued for malpractice.

Income Trust

Starting in 2001, the income trust, a non-corporate form of business organization, has been growing in importance in Canada. As of the end of 2004, there were over 200 income trusts listed on the Toronto Stock Exchange, with a sector market capitalization of $118 billion.[5] Within this sector, the fastest growing component is business income trusts that took this form of business organization, traditionally popular in real estate and oil and gas, and applied it to businesses like telephone listing, container ports, restaurant chains and other businesses usually organized as corporations. In response to the growing importance of this sector, recent provincial legislation extended limited liability protection, previously limited to corporate shareholders, to trust unitholders. Along the same lines, at the end of 2005, the TSX began to include income trusts in its benchmark S&P / TSX composite index.

Business income trusts (also called income funds) hold the debt and equity of an underlying business and distribute the income generated to unitholders. Because income trusts are not

---

4 The dividend tax credit for individual shareholders and a corporate dividend exclusion reduce the bite of double taxation for Canadian corporations. These tax provisions are discussed in Chapter 2. Trusts and limited partnerships are designed to avoid double taxation.

5 For more on income trusts see J. Fenwick and B. Kalymon, "A Note on Income Trusts," Ivey Publishing, 2004 and Department of Finance, "Tax and Other Issues Related to Publicly Listed Flow-Through Entities (Income Trusts and Limited Partnerships)," September 8, 2005.

corporations, they are not subject to corporate income tax and their income is typically taxed only in the hands of unitholders. As a result, investors see trusts as tax-efficient and are generally willing to pay more for a company after it has converted from a corporation to a trust. This tax advantage largely disappeared on Hallowe'en 2006 when the government announced plans to tax income trusts at the same rate as corporations.

CONCEPT QUESTIONS

1. What are the three forms of business organization?

2. What are the primary advantages and disadvantages of a sole proprietorship or partnership?

3. What is the difference between a general and a limited partnership?

4. Why is the corporate form superior when it comes to raising cash?

In Their Own Words . . .   George Athanassakos on Incentives for Conversion to an Income Trust

OVER the years, BCE Inc. shareholders have not had much to smile about with regards to the company, its management and the return on their investment. As the new year dawns, can BCE make any changes to its structure to unlock shareholder value?

Yes, if that change involves converting to an income trust.

BCE is Canada's largest communications company and the owner of Bell Canada and Bell Mobility, as well as having interests in Aliant, CGI Group Inc. and Bell Globemedia, which includes Sympatico, CTV and *The Globe and Mail*.

Over the years, BCE has ventured into a number of unsuccessful acquisitions and partnerships including real estate, pipelines and international telecommunications, some of which filed for bancruptcy protection and were written off, while others were divested (usually at a loss) after shareholder pressure.

A few weeks ago, BCE said it will reduce its stake in Bell Globemedia, which it acquired for $2.3-billion in 2000, to 20 per cent from about 70 per cent.

Once again, BCE bought high and sold low. Particularly over the past five years, BCE has severely underperformed the S&P/TSX composite index and the S&P 500. And all this despite BCE generating — and being forecast to generate — significant free cash flows per share.

As free cash flows are the cash flows that remain in the company after all operating expenses, interest to service debt, taxes and capital investments have been paid, BCE has had and will continue to have surplus or excess funds even after paying dividends. Such excess funds belong to shareholders and could potentially be paid to shareholders. Since the company has not generated a satisfactory return on its equity, it may make a lot of sense for BCE to pay its shareholders all its free cash flows rather than only about half.

However, BCE has another reason to convert, and it has to do with the resolution of principal-agent problems.

As owners, shareholders hire managers to develop and manage a company's corporate strategy and capital investments. Management is supposed to act on behalf of the shareholders and in the shareholders' interest, but this relationship gives rise to conflicts of interest. While managers are supposed to act on the behalf of shareholders, they in fact often act on their own behalf in an attempt to maximize their own wealth.

One way to do this is empire building, the sometimes self-serving actions taken by management to maximize the size of a company, not market value, since size often determines managers' compensation.

Warren Buffett hit the nail on the head in 1984 when he wrote: "Many corporations that consistently show good returns, both on equity and on overall incremental capital, have, indeed, employed a large portion of their retained earnings on an economically unattractive, even disastrous basis. Their marvellous core business, however, whose earnings grow year after year, camouflage repeated failures in capital allocation elsewhere (usually involving high-priced acquisitions that have inherently mediocre economics). In such cases, shareholders would be far better off if earnings were retained only to expand the high return businesses, with the balance paid in dividends."

BCE fits this bill.

For companies such as BCE, free cash flows must be paid out to shareholders if it is to maximize its share value. However, the payout of cash reduces the resources under management's control. Moreover, witholding funds from shareholders reduces the likelihood of the company having to go to the markets to raise funds and prevents the firm's monitoring by capital markets.

An income trust, by virtue of the fact that it commits management to distributing all expected free cash flows to investors, will not only increase the payout to investors, but will also reduce the risk of management entrenchment and investor exploitation, thus leading to an even higher valuation.

Abridged from George Athanassakos, "For BCE shareholders, conversion to a trust is the logical step," *Globe and Mail* Report on Business, December 14, 2005, B13. Used with permission. George Athanassakos holds the Ben Graham Chair in Value Investing at the University of Western Ontario's Richard Ivey School of Business. BCE acted on his recommendation when it announced its plan (on hold at the time of writing) for trust conversion.

TABLE 1.1 International corporations

| Company | Country of Origin | Type of Company | |
		In Original Language	Translated
Bayerische Motorenwerke (BMW) AG	Germany	Aktiengesellschaft	Corporation
Dornier GmBH	Germany	Gesellschaft mit Beschraenkter Haftung	Limited liability company
Rolls-Royce PLC	United Kingdom	Public limited company	Public limited company
Shell UK Ltd.	United Kingdom	Limited	Corporation
Unilever NV	Netherlands	Naamloze Vennootschap	Joint stock company
Fiat SpA	Italy	Societa per Azioni	Joint stock company
Volvo AB	Sweden	Aktiebolag	Joint stock company
Peugeot SA	France	Sociedad Anonima	Joint stock company

THE GOAL OF FINANCIAL MANAGEMENT

Assuming that we restrict ourselves to for-profit businesses, the goal of financial management is to make money or add value for the owners. This goal is a little vague, of course, so we examine some different ways of formulating it to come up with a more precise definition. Such a definition is important because it leads to an objective basis for making and evaluating financial decisions.

Possible Goals

If we were to consider possible financial goals, we might come up with some ideas like the following:

Survive in business.
Avoid financial distress and bankruptcy.
Beat the competition.
Maximize sales or market share.
Minimize costs.
Maximize profits.
Maintain steady earnings growth.

These are only a few of the goals we could list. Furthermore, each of these possibilities presents problems as a goal for a financial manager.

For example, it's easy to increase market share or unit sales; all we have to do is lower our prices or relax our credit terms. Similarly, we can always cut costs simply by doing away with things such as research and development. We can avoid bankruptcy by never borrowing any money or taking any risks, and so on. It's not clear that any of these actions would be in the shareholders' best interests.

Profit maximization would probably be the most commonly cited goal, but even this is not a very precise objective. Do we mean profits this year? If so, then actions such as deferring maintenance, letting inventories run down, and other short-run cost-cutting measures tend to increase profits now, but these activities aren't necessarily desirable.

The goal of maximizing profits may refer to some sort of long-run or average profits, but it's still unclear exactly what this means. First, do we mean something like accounting net income or earnings per share? As we see in more detail in the next chapter, these accounting numbers may have little to do with what is good or bad for the firm. Second, what do we mean by the long run? What is the appropriate trade-off between current and future profits?

Although the goals we've just listed are all different, they fall into two classes. The first of these relates to profitability. The goals involving sales, market share, and cost control all relate, at least potentially, to different ways of earning or increasing profits. The second group, involving bankruptcy avoidance, stability, and safety, relate in some way to controlling risk. Unfortunately, these two types of goals are somewhat contradictory. The pursuit of profit normally involves some element of risk, so it isn't really possible to maximize both safety and profit. What we need, therefore, is a goal that encompasses both these factors.

The Goal of Financial Management

The financial manager in a corporation makes decisions for the shareholders of the firm. Given this, instead of listing possible goals for the financial manager, we really need to answer a more fundamental question: From the shareholders' point of view, what is a good financial management decision?

If we assume that shareholders buy stock because they seek to gain financially, the answer is obvious: Good decisions increase the value of the stock, and poor decisions decrease it.

Given our observation, it follows that the financial manager acts in the shareholders' best interests by making decisions that increase the value of the stock. The appropriate goal for the financial manager can thus be stated quite easily:

> The goal of financial management is to maximize the current value per share of existing stock.

The goal of maximizing the value of the stock avoids the problems associated with the different goals we listed earlier. There is no ambiguity in the criterion, and there is no short-run versus long-run issue. We explicitly mean that our goal is to maximize the current stock value. If this goal seems a little strong or one-dimensional to you, keep in mind that the shareholders in a firm are residual owners. By this we mean that they are only entitled to what is left after employees, suppliers, and creditors (and anyone else with a legitimate claim) are paid their due. If any of these groups go unpaid, the shareholders get nothing. So, if the shareholders are winning in the sense that the leftover, residual, portion is growing, it must be true that everyone else is winning also.

Because the goal of financial management is to maximize the value of the stock, we need to learn how to identify those investments and financing arrangements that favourably impact the value of the stock. This is precisely what we are studying. In fact, we could have defined corporate finance as the study of the relationship between business decisions and the value of the stock in the business.

To make the market value of the stock a valid measure of financial decisions requires an *efficient capital market*. In an efficient capital market, security prices fully reflect available information. The market sets the stock price to give the firm an accurate report card on its decisions. We return to capital market efficiency in Part Five.

A More General Goal

Given our goal of maximizing the value of the stock, an obvious question comes up: What is the appropriate goal when the firm is privately owned and has no traded stock? Corporations are certainly not the only type of business, and the stock in many corporations rarely changes hands, so it's difficult to say what the value per share is at any given time.

To complicate things further, some large Canadian companies such as Irving are privately owned. Many large firms in Canada are subsidiaries of foreign multinationals, while others are controlled by a single domestic shareholder.

Recognizing these complications, as long as we are dealing with for-profit businesses, only a slight modification is needed. The total value of the stock in a corporation is simply equal to the value of the owners' equity. Therefore, a more general way of stating our goal is to maximize the market value of the owners' equity. This market value can be measured by a business appraiser or by investment bankers if the firm eventually goes public.

With this in mind, it doesn't matter whether the business is a proprietorship, a partnership, or a corporation. For each of these, good financial decisions increase the market value of the owners' equity and poor financial decisions decrease it. In fact, although we choose to focus on corporations in the chapters ahead, the principles we develop apply to all forms of business. Many of them even apply to the not-for-profit sector.

Finally, our goal does not imply that the financial manager should take illegal or unethical actions in the hope of increasing the value of the equity in the firm. What we mean is that the financial manager best serves the owners of the business by identifying opportunities that add to the firm because they are desired and valued in the free marketplace.

In fact, truthful financial reporting is incredibly important to the long run viability of capital markets. The recent collapse of companies like Enron and Worldcom has illustrated what a dramatic impact unethical behaviour can have on public trust and confidence in our financial institutions. The ability of companies to raise capital and of our economies to function efficiently is based on this trust and confidence. If investors cannot assume that the information they receive is honest and truthful, many of the models and theories we learn through this textbook no longer apply.[6]

CONCEPT QUESTIONS

1. What is the goal of financial management?

2. What are some shortcomings of the goal of profit maximization?

3. How would you define corporate finance?

1.4 THE AGENCY PROBLEM AND CONTROL OF THE CORPORATION

We've seen that the financial manager acts in the best interest of the shareholders by taking actions that increase the value of the stock. However, we've also seen that in large corporations ownership can be spread over a huge number of shareholders. Or a large shareholder may own a whole block of shares with large minority blocks owned by pension funds. In either case, this dispersion of ownership arguably means that management effectively controls the firm. In this case, will management necessarily act in the best interests of the shareholders? Put another way, might not management pursue its own goals (or those of a small group of shareholders) at the shareholders' expense? We briefly consider some of the arguments next.

Agency Relationships

The relationship between shareholders and management is called an *agency relationship*. Such a relationship exists whenever someone (the principal) hires another (the agent) to represent his or her interests. For example, you might hire someone (an agent) to sell a car that you own. In all such relationships, there is a possibility of conflict of interest between the principal and the agent. Such conflict is called an **agency problem.**

agency problem
The possibility of conflicts of interest between the shareholders and management of a firm.

---

6 For more on ethics and financial reporting visit the website of the Canadian Centre for Ethics and Corporate Policy at *www.ethicscentre.ca.*

In hiring someone to sell your car, you agree to pay a flat fee when the car sells. The agent's incentive is to make the sale, not necessarily to get you the best price. If you paid a commission of, say, 10 percent of the sale price instead of a flat fee, this problem might not exist. This example illustrates that the way an agent is compensated is one factor that affects agency problems.

Management Goals

To see how management and shareholders' interests might differ, imagine that the firm has a new investment under consideration. The new investment favourably impacts the share value, but it is a relatively risky venture. The owners of the firm may wish to take the investment because the stock value will rise, but management may not because of the possibility that things will turn out badly and management jobs will be lost. If management does not take the investment, the shareholders may have lost a valuable opportunity. This is one example of an *agency cost*.

More generally, agency costs refer to the costs of the conflict of interests between shareholders and management. These costs can be indirect or direct. An indirect agency cost is a lost opportunity such as the one we have just described.

Direct agency costs come in two forms: The first is a corporate expenditure that benefits management but costs the shareholders. Perhaps the purchase of a luxurious and unneeded corporate jet would fall under this heading. The second direct agency cost is an expense that arises from the need to monitor management actions. Paying outside auditors to assess the accuracy of financial statement information is one example.

Some argue that if left to themselves, managers would maximize the amount of resources they have control over or, more generally, corporate power or wealth. This goal could lead to an overemphasis on corporate size or growth. For example, cases where management is accused of overpaying to buy up another company just to increase the size of the business or to demonstrate corporate power are not uncommon. Obviously, if overpayment does take place, such a purchase does not benefit the shareholders.

Our discussion indicates that management may tend to overemphasize organizational survival to protect job security. Also, management may dislike outside interference, so independence and corporate self-sufficiency may be important goals.

Do Managers Act in the Shareholders' Interests?

Whether managers do, in fact, act in the best interest of shareholders depends on two factors. First, how closely are management goals aligned with shareholder goals? This question relates to the way managers are compensated. Second, can managers be replaced if they do not pursue shareholder goals? This issue relates to control of the firm. As we discuss, there are a number of reasons to think that, even in the largest firms, management has a significant incentive to act in the interest of shareholders.

MANAGERIAL COMPENSATION Management frequently has a significant economic incentive to increase share value for two reasons: First, managerial compensation, particularly at the top, is usually tied to financial performance in general and often to the share value in particular. For example, managers are frequently given the option to buy stock at current prices. The more the stock is worth, the more valuable this option becomes.[7] The second incentive managers have relates to job prospects. Better performers within the firm get promoted. More generally, those managers who are successful in pursuing shareholder goals are in greater demand in the labour market and thus command higher salaries.

Of course, in management compensation, as with other areas of business, matters sometimes get off track. Many observers believe that top executives are overpaid. For example, Frank Stronach, the founder of auto parts manufacturer Magna International, was criticized in 2005 for his $44 million compensation for his role as non-executive chairman. Going further, creative

---

7 Employee stock options allow the manager to purchase a certain number of shares at a fixed price over a specified period of time. By providing the manager an ownership stake in the company, the options are meant to align the manager's goals and actions with the shareholders' interests. For more on employee stock options, see Chapter 25.

forms of excessive corporate compensation at U.S. companies like Worldcom, Tyco, and Adelphia led to the passage of the *Sarbanes-Oxley Act* in 2002. The act is intended to protect investors from corporate abuses. For example, one section prohibits personal loans from a company to its officers, such as the ones that were received by former Worldcom CEO Bernie Ebbers.

U.S. prosecutors have charged Conrad Black with fraud in connection with a $2.4 billion sale of hundreds of newspapers in Canada. The charges allege that Lord Black made unauthorized payments from his firm, Hollinger International, to himself and his associates. In addition to allegedly diverting over $80 million from the company, Lord Black is charged with taking a company jet on a personal vacation trip and charging his wife's $40,000 birthday party to the company.[8]

Excessive management pay and unauthorized management consumption are examples of agency costs.[9]

www.aircanada.com

CONTROL OF THE FIRM Control of the firm ultimately rests with shareholders. They elect the board of directors, who, in turn, hire and fire management. Another way that management can be replaced is by a takeover. For example, Canadian Airlines' CEO lost his job when the company was taken over by Air Canada in 1999. Poorly managed firms are more attractive as acquisitions than well-managed firms because a greater turnaround potential exists. Thus, avoiding a takeover by another firm gives management another incentive to act in the shareholders' interest.

The available theory and evidence substantiate that shareholders control the firm and that shareholder wealth maximization is the relevant goal of the corporation. Even so, at times management goals are undoubtedly pursued at the expense of the shareholders, at least temporarily. For example, management may try to avoid the discipline of a potential takeover by instituting "poison pill" provisions to make the stock unattractive. Or the firm may issue non-voting stock to thwart a takeover attempt. Canadian shareholders, particularly pension funds and other institutional investors, are becoming increasingly active in campaigning against such management actions.[10]

corporate governance
Rules for corporate organization and conduct.

Large funds like the Ontario Teachers' Pension Plan Board have set up detailed **corporate governance** and proxy voting guidelines for the companies in which they invest. Smaller funds may employ the services of firms like Institutional Shareholder Services (ISS, formerly Fairvest) to advise them on how to vote on proposed governance changes. Figure 1.2 shows an example of an ISS advisory on changes proposed by Bank of Nova Scotia in 2002.[11]

STAKEHOLDERS Our discussion thus far implies that management and shareholders are the only parties with an interest in the firm's decisions. This is an oversimplification, of course. Employees, customers, suppliers, and various levels of government all have financial interests in the firm.

stakeholder
Anyone who potentially has a claim on a firm.

Taken together, these various groups are called **stakeholders** in the firm. In general, a stakeholder is a shareholder, creditor, or other individual (or group) that potentially has a claim on the cash flows of the firm. Such groups also attempt to exert control over the firm by introducing alternate, socially oriented goals such as preserving the environment or creating employment equity. Even though stakeholder pressures may create additional costs for owners, almost all major corporations pay close attention to stakeholders because stakeholder satisfaction is consistent with shareholder wealth maximization. Table 1.2 summarizes concerns of various stakeholders.

www.jantziresearch.com

Corporate Social Responsibility and Ethical Investing

Well-managed large corporations seek to maintain a reputation as good corporate citizens with detailed policies on important social issues. Investors are becoming increasingly concerned with

---

8 BBC News, November 18, 2005.

9 Because it requires management to pay out almost all of the cash flow to unitholders, the income trust form of organization can help to control these agency costs, as explained in the earlier boxed insert.

10 We discuss takeovers and pension managers' activism in monitoring management activities in Chapter 23.

11 Updates of ISS and Teachers' governance policies are available on their websites: *www.iissproxy.com* and *www.otpp.com/website/teachers.*

FIGURE 1.2

Example of Global Proxy
Analysis

Global Proxy Analysis:

Bank Of Nova Scotia

Country: Canada

Annual Meeting: March 5, 2002

Meeting Time: 09:30

Meeting Location: The Westin Bayshore Resort & Marina 1601 Bayshore Drive, Vancouver, British Columbia

Record Date: January 15, 2002

Security ID: 0076313(SEDOL), 064149107(CUSIP)

		MEETING AGENDA		
Item	**Code**	**Proposals**	**Mgt. Rec.**	**ISS Rec.**
❑ 1	M0150	Receive Financial Statements and Statutory Reports	None	None
❑ 2	M0201	Elect Directors	For	SPLIT*
❑ 3	M0101	Ratify PricewaterhouseCoopers LLP and KPMG LLP as Auditors	For	FOR
❑ 4	S0115	Report on Bank Subsidiaries and Tax Havens	Against	AGAINST
❑ 5	S0501	Impose Restrictions on the Sale of Shares Acquired on Stock Option Exercise	Against	AGAINST
❑ 6	S0215	Require Majority of Independent Directors on Board of Publicly-Traded Companies Controlled by the Bank	Against	AGAINST

Bank Of Nova Scotia• February 13, 2002
Laura O'Neill, Analyst

Source: Fairvest Securities Corporation, used with permission.

www.scotiabank.com
www.fairvest.com

corporate social responsibility (CSR) and may turn to firms like Michael Jantzi Research Associates in Canada, or KLD in the U.S., for information. Jantzi Research provides a social responsibility rating for corporations based on over 200 indicators of responsible behaviour with respect to stakeholder issues that dovetail with those in Table 1.2: community and society, customers, corporate governance, employees, environment, and human rights. Jantzi ratings also assess controversial business activities; these include, alcohol, gaming, genetic engineering, nuclear power, pornography, tobacco, and weapons. An example Jantzi rating for Suncor Energy Inc. is shown in Figure 1.3.

Sixty companies that avoid controversial business activities and score well on Jantzi's other criteria are included in its Jantzi Social Index. Ethical investment mutual funds such as Ethical Growth and Investors Summa offer an opportunity to buy a portfolio of Canadian companies that meet criteria similar to Jantzi's. Similar funds exist in the U.S. and Europe.

You might wonder about the performance of such funds: Can investors "do well by doing good"? The results to date are mixed. A Canadian study suggests that socially responsible investing

TABLE 1.2   Inventory of typical stakeholders and issues

Company	Employees		Shareholders	Customers	Suppliers	Public Stakeholders	Competitors
Company history	General policy	Benefits	General policy	General policy	General policy	Public health, safety, and protection	General policy
Industry background	Compensation and rewards	Training and development	Shareholder communications and complaints	Customer communications	Relative power	Environmental issues	
Organization structure	Career planning	Employee assistance program	Shareholder advocacy	Product safety	Other supplier issues	Public policy involvement	
Economic performance	Health promotion	Absenteeism and turnover	Shareholder rights	Customer complaints		Community relations	
Competitive environment	Leaves of absence	Relationships with unions	Other shareholder issues	Special customer services		Social investment and donations	
Mission or purpose	Dismissal and appeal	Termination, layoff, and redundancy		Other customer issues			
Corporate codes	Retirement and termination counselling	Employment equity and discrimination					
Stakeholder and social issues	Women in management and on the board	Day care and family accommodation					
Management	Employee communication	Occupational health and safety					
	Part-time temporary, or contract employees	Other employee or human resource issues					

Source: M. B. E. Clarkson, "Analyzing Corporate Performance: A New Approach," *Canadian Investment Review*, Fall 1991, p. 70.

during the 1990s produced returns similar to those of the overall market after adjusting for risk and concludes that "investing for the soul may not hurt the bottom line." However, because ethical funds tend to invest more heavily in "clean" tech companies, it remains an open question whether this finding applies in other periods. A more recent U.S. study argues that socially responsible investing imposes a heavy penalty on return.[12] Given the mixed evidence, major Canadian institutional investors like the Ontario Teachers' Pension Plan and the Ontario Municipal Employees Retirement System pay careful attention to corporate social responsibility in selecting investments but do not eliminate companies from their portfolios based solely on environmental and other social issues.[13]

CONCEPT QUESTIONS

1. What is an agency relationship?

2. What are agency problems and how do they come about? What are agency costs?

3. What incentives do managers in large corporations have to maximize share value?

4. What role do stakeholders play in determining corporate goals?

12 P. Amundson and S.R. Foerster, "Socially Responsible Investing: Better for Your Soul or Your Bottom Line?" *Canadian Investment Review*, Winter 2001, pp. 26–34 and C. Geczy, R. F. Stambaugh and D. Levin, "Investing in Socially Responsible Mutual Funds," October 2005, available at SSRN: *http://ssrn.com/abastract=416380* .

13 For a detailed summary of arguments in favour of socially responsible investing by pension funds, see "A legal framework for the integration of environmental, social and governance issues into institutional investment," by Freshfields Bruckhaus Deringer and the UNEP Finance Initiative, October 2005, available at *http://www.unepfi.org/fineadmin/documents/freshfields_legal_resp_20051123.pdf*

FIGURE 1.3

Canadian Social
Investment Database

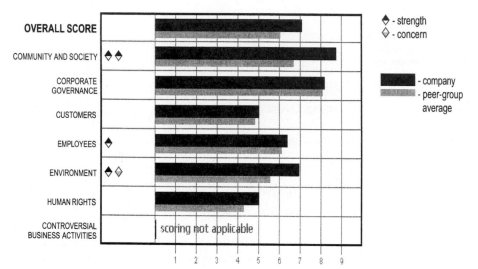

Canadian Social Investment Database

Suncor Energy Inc. (SU)   March 2005
112 - 4th Avenue S.W., P.O. Box 38, Calgary, AB T2P 2V5
www.suncor.com

Sector: Energy
Industry: Oil & Gas
Peer-Group: Integrated Oil & Gas

FY 2004 Revenue ($ millions):   8,699.0
Number of Employees: 4,261

Rating:	7.1
Rank:	1 of 5
Indexed Score:	1.17

Rating Summary

OVERALL SCORE

COMMUNITY AND SOCIETY

CORPORATE GOVERNANCE

CUSTOMERS

EMPLOYEES

ENVIRONMENT

HUMAN RIGHTS

CONTROVERSIAL BUSINESS ACTIVITIES — scoring not applicable

◆ - strength
◇ - concern

▇ - company
▒ - peer-group average

Business Description

Suncor Energy Inc. is an integrated energy company headquartered in Calgary, Alberta. Suncor's oil sands business, located near Fort McMurray, Alberta, extracts and upgrades oil sands and markets refinery feedstock and diesel fuel while operations throughout western Canada produce natural gas. Suncor operates a refining and marketing business in Ontario with retail distribution under the Sunoco brand. U.S. downstream assets include pipeline and refining operations in Colorado and Wyoming and retail sales in the Denver area under the Phillips 66 brand.

Significant Shareholders
   Widely held

Social and Environmental Profile

COMMUNITY AND SOCIETY

	Score	Rank (of 5)	Indexed Score	Peer-Group Average	Range
COMMUNITY AND SOCIETY	**8.8**	**1**	**1.31 (0.75 - 1.31)**	**6.7**	**5.1 - 8.8**
Public Reporting	10.0	1	1.04 (0.82 - 1.04)	9.6	7.9 - 10.0
Charitable Donations Program	3.8	2	1.12 (0.56 - 1.49)	3.4	1.9 - 5.0
Community Relations	9.7	1	1.43 (0.65 - 1.43)	6.8	4.4 - 9.7
Aboriginal Relations	10.0	1	1.39 (0.71 - 1.39)	7.1	5.1 - 10.0
Impact on Society	9.0	1	1.07 (0.83 - 1.07)	8.4	7.0 - 9.0

Public Reporting

In Their Own Words . . .

Clifford W. Smith Jr. on Market Incentives for Ethical Behaviour

Ethics is a topic that has been receiving increased interest in the business community. Much of this discussion has been led by philosophers and has focused on moral principles. Rather than review these issues, I want to discuss a complementary (but often ignored) set of issues from an economist's viewpoint. Markets impose potentially substantial costs on individuals and institutions that engage in unethical behaviour. These market forces thus provide important incentives that foster ethical behaviour in the business community.

At its core, economics is the study of making choices. I thus want to examine ethical behaviour simply as one choice facing an individual. Economic analysis suggests that in considering an action, you identify its expected costs and benefits. If the estimated benefits exceed the estimated costs, you take the action; if not, you don't. To focus this discussion, let's consider the following specific choice: Suppose you have a contract to deliver a product of a specified quality. Would you cheat by reducing quality to lower costs in an attempt to increase profits? Economics implies that the higher the expected costs of cheating, the more likely ethical actions will be chosen. This simple principle has several implications.

First, the higher the probability of detection, the less likely an individual is to cheat. This implication helps us understand numerous institutional arrangements for monitoring in the marketplace. For example, a company agrees to have its financial statements audited by an external public accounting firm. This periodic professional monitoring increases the probability of detection, thereby reducing any incentive to misstate the firm's financial condition.

Second, the higher the sanctions imposed if cheating is detected, the less likely an individual is to cheat. Hence, a business transaction that is expected to be repeated between the same parties faces a lower probability of cheating because the lost profits from the forgone stream of future sales provide powerful incentives for contract compliance. However, if continued corporate existence is more uncertain, so are the expected costs of forgone future sales. Therefore firms in financial difficulty are more likely to cheat than financially healthy firms. Firms thus have incentives to adopt financial policies that help credibly bond against cheating. For example, if product quality is difficult to assess prior to purchase, customers doubt a firm's claims about product quality. Where quality is more uncertain, customers are only willing to pay lower prices. Such firms thus have particularly strong incentives to adopt financial policies that imply a lower probability of insolvency. Therefore such firms should have lower leverage, enter fewer leases, and engage in more hedging.

Third, the expected costs are higher if information about cheating is rapidly and widely distributed to potential future customers. Thus information services like Consumer Reports,

which monitor and report on product quality, help deter cheating. By lowering the costs for potential customers to monitor quality, such services raise the expected costs of cheating.

Finally, the costs imposed on a firm that is caught cheating depend on the market's assessment of the ethical breach. Some actions viewed as clear transgressions by some might be viewed as justifiable behaviour by others. Ethical standards also vary across markets. For example, a payment that if disclosed in North America would be labelled a bribe might be viewed as a standard business practice in a third-world market. The costs imposed will be higher the greater the consensus that the behaviour was unethical.

Establishing and maintaining a reputation for ethical behaviour is a valuable corporate asset in the business community. This analysis suggests that a firm concerned about the ethical conduct of its employees should pay careful attention to potential conflicts among the firm's management, employees, customers, creditors, and shareholders. Consider Sears, the department store giant that was found to be charging customers for auto repairs of questionable necessity. In an effort to make the company more service oriented (in the way that competitors like Nordstrom are), Sears had initiated an across-the-board policy of commission sales. But what works in clothing and housewares does not always work the same way in the auto repair shop. A customer for a man's suit knows as much as the salesperson about the product. But many auto repair customers know little about the inner workings of their cars and thus are more likely to rely on employee recommendations in deciding on purchases. Sears's compensation policy resulted in recommendations of unnecessary repairs to customers. Sears would not have had to deal with its repair shop problems and the consequent erosion of its reputation had it anticipated that its commission sales policy would encourage auto shop employees to cheat its customers.

Clifford W. Smith Jr. is the Epstein Professor of Finance at the University of Rochester's Simon School of Business Administration. He is an advisory editor of the *Journal of Financial Economics*. His research focuses on corporate financial policy and the structure of financial institutions. Updates on his research are available on his website: *www.simon.rochester.edu/fac/smith/index.html*.

FINANCIAL MARKETS AND THE CORPORATION

We've seen that the primary advantages of the corporate form of organization are that ownership can be transferred more quickly and easily than with other forms and that money can be raised more readily. Both of these advantages are significantly enhanced by the existence of financial institutions and markets. Financial markets play an extremely important role in corporate finance.

Cash Flows to and from the Firm

The interplay between the corporation and the financial markets is illustrated in Figure 1.4. The arrows in Figure 1.4 trace the passage of cash from the financial markets to the firm and from the firm back to the financial markets.

Suppose we start with the firm selling shares of stock and borrowing money to raise cash. Cash flows to the firm from the financial market (A). The firm invests the cash in current and fixed assets (B). These assets generate some cash (C), some of which goes to pay corporate taxes (D). After taxes are paid, some of this cash flow is reinvested in the firm (E). The rest goes back to the financial markets as cash paid to creditors and shareholders (F).

Companies like Shoppers Drug Mart routinely make decisions that create such cash flows to and from the firm. For example, in 2005 the company used increased cash flow from assets to pay down a portion of the firm's debt.

A financial market, like any market, is just a way of bringing buyers and sellers together. In financial markets, it is debt and equity securities that are bought and sold. Financial markets differ in detail, however. The most important differences concern the types of securities that are traded, how trading is conducted, and who the buyers and sellers are. Some of these differences are discussed next.

FIGURE 1.4

Cash flows between the firm and the financial markets

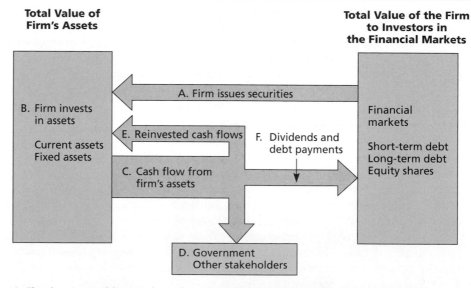

A. Firm issues securities to raise cash.
B. Firm invests in assets.
C. Firm's operations generate cash flow.
D. Cash is paid to government as taxes. Other stakeholders may receive cash.
E. Reinvested cash flows are plowed back into firm.
F. Cash is paid out to investors in the form of interest and dividends.

Money versus Capital Markets

money markets
Financial markets where short-term debt securities are bought and sold.

Financial markets can be classified as either **money markets** or **capital markets.** Short-term debt securities of many varieties are bought and sold in money markets. These short-term debt securities are often called money-market instruments and are essentially IOUs. For example, a bankers acceptance represents short-term borrowing by large corporations and is a money-market instrument. Treasury bills are an IOU of the government of Canada. Capital markets are the markets for long-term debt and shares of stock, so the Toronto Stock Exchange, for example, is a capital market.

capital markets
Financial markets where long-term debt and equity securities are bought and sold.

The money market is a dealer market. Generally, dealers buy and sell something for themselves, at their own risk. A car dealer, for example, buys and sells automobiles. In contrast, brokers and agents match buyers and sellers, but they do not actually own the commodity. A real estate agent or broker, for example, does not normally buy and sell houses.

The largest money-market dealers are chartered banks and investment dealers. Their trading facilities, like those of other market participants, are connected electronically via telephone and computer, so the money market has no actual physical location.

Primary versus Secondary Markets

Financial markets function as both primary and secondary markets for debt and equity securities. The term *primary markets* refers to the original sale of securities by governments and corporations. The *secondary markets* are where these securities are bought and sold after the original sale. Equities are, of course, issued solely by corporations. Debt securities are issued by both governments and corporations. In the following discussion, we focus only on corporate securities.

PRIMARY MARKETS   In a primary market transaction, the corporation is the seller, and the transaction raises money for the corporation. Corporations engage in two types of primary market transactions: public offerings and private placements. A public offering, as the name suggests, involves selling securities to the general public. For example, in 1999 and early 2000, investors were snapping up new issues providing equity funding to untested dot-com IPOs (initial public offerings). A private placement, on the other hand, is a negotiated sale involving a specific buyer. These topics are covered in some detail in Part 6, so we only introduce the bare essentials here.

www.rbcem.com

Most publicly offered debt and equity securities are underwritten. In Canada, underwriting is conducted by *investment dealers* specialized in marketing securities. Examples are RBC Capital Markets, Scotia Capital, BMO Capital Markets, and CIBC World Markets.

When a public offering is underwritten, an investment dealer or a group of investment dealers (called a *syndicate*) typically purchase the securities from the firm and market them to the public. The underwriters hope to profit by reselling the securities to investors at a higher price than they pay the firm.

www.osc.gov.on.ca

By law, public offerings of debt and equity must be registered with provincial authorities, of which the most important is the Ontario Securities Commission (OSC). Registration requires the firm to disclose a great deal of information before selling any securities. The accounting, legal, and underwriting costs of public offerings can be considerable.

Partly to avoid the various regulatory requirements and the expense of public offerings, debt and equity are often sold privately to large financial institutions such as life insurance companies or mutual funds. Such private placements do not have to be registered with the OSC and do not require the involvement of underwriters.

SECONDARY MARKETS   A secondary market transaction involves one owner or creditor selling to another. Therefore, the secondary markets provide the means for transferring ownership of corporate securities. There are two kinds of secondary markets: *auction markets* and *dealer markets*.

Dealer markets in stocks and long-term debt are called *over-the-counter* (OTC) markets. Trading in debt securities takes place over the counter. The expression *over-the-counter* refers to days of old when securities were literally bought and sold at counters in offices around the country.

Today, like the money market, a significant fraction of the market for stocks and all of the market for long-term debt have no central location; the many dealers are connected electronically.

TRADING IN CORPORATE SECURITIES   The equity shares of most of the large firms in Canada trade in organized auction and dealer markets. The largest stock market in Canada is the Toronto Stock Exchange (TSX). Table 1.3 shows the top ten stock markets in the world in 2004; Toronto ranked number seven based on market value. The TSX also runs the Venture Exchange for listing smaller, emerging companies. The four main industries represented on the Venture Exchange are biotechnology, information technology, mining, and oil and gas.

Auction markets differ from dealer markets in two ways: First, an auction market or exchange, unlike a dealer market, has a physical location (like Wall Street). Second, in a dealer market, most of the buying and selling is done by the dealer. The primary purpose of an auction market, on the other hand, is to match those who wish to sell with those who wish to buy. Dealers play a limited role.

In addition to the stock exchanges, there is a large OTC market for stocks. In 1971, the U.S. National Association of Securities Dealers (NASD) made available to dealers and brokers an electronic quotation system called NASDAQ (NASD Automated Quotation system, pronounced "naz-dak" and now spelled "Nasdaq"). In January 2006, Nasdaq took the next step forward when its application to be registered as a national stock exchange was accepted by the U.S. Securities and Exchange Commission. There are roughly three times as many companies on Nasdaq as there are on NYSE, but they tend to be much smaller in size and trade less actively. There are exceptions, of course. For example, tech giants Microsoft and Intel trade on Nasdaq. Nonetheless, the total value of Nasdaq stocks is considerably less than the total value of the NYSE stocks.

LISTING   Stocks that trade on an organized exchange are said to be listed on that exchange. To be listed, firms must meet certain minimum criteria concerning, for example, asset size and number of shareholders. These criteria differ for various exchanges.

The requirements for listing on the TSX Venture are not as strict as those for listing on the TSX, although the listing process is quite similar. The TSX Venture, however, has two different tiers that companies can register under. Companies can list shares on the second tier with as little as $500,000 in net tangible assets and $50,000 in pre-tax earnings. Both tiers require that there exist 300 public shareholders, holding one board lot or more; Tier 1 also requires that there be 1 million free trading shares with a market value of $1 million or more, and Tier 2 requires at least 500,000 free trading shares with a market value of $500,000 or more. These requirements make it possible for smaller companies that would not normally be able to obtain listing on the TSX to acquire equity financing.

The TSX has the most stringent requirements of the exchanges in Canada. For example, to be listed on the TSX, a company is expected to have a market value for its publicly held shares of at least $2 million and a total of at least 300 shareholders with at least 100 shares each. There are additional minimums on earnings, assets, and number of shares outstanding. Research suggests that listing on exchanges adds valuable liquidity to a company's shares.[14] In November 2002, the TSX

TABLE 1.3 Largest stock markets in the world by market capitalization in 2004	Market Value (in U.S. $ billions)	Rank in 2004
New York	12,707.6	1
Tokyo	3,557.7	2
Nasdaq	3,532.9	3
London	2,865.2	4
Euronext	2,441.3	5
Deutsche Borse	1,194.5	6
TSX Group	1,177.6	7
BmE Spain	940.7	8
Hong Kong Exchanges	861.4	9
Swiss Exchange	826.0	10

Source: World Federation of Stock Exchanges at *www.world-exchanges.org.*

---

[14] Relevant studies include S. R. Foerster and G. A. Karolyi, "The Effects of Market Segmentation and Investor Recognition on Asset Prices: Evidence from Foreign Stocks Listings in the U.S.," *Journal of Finance,* 54: 3, 1999, 981–1013 and U.R. Mittoo, "The Winners and Losers of Listings in the U.S.," *Canadian Investment Review,* Fall 1998, 13–17.

itself went public and listed its shares for the first time. With an offering of just under 19 million shares at an initial offering price of $18, the TSX easily exceeded its own listing requirements.

1.6 FINANCIAL INSTITUTIONS

Financial institutions act as *intermediaries* between investors (funds suppliers) and firms raising funds. (Federal and provincial governments and individuals also raise funds in financial markets, but our examples focus on firms.) Financial institutions justify their existence by providing a variety of services that promote the efficient allocation of funds. Canadian financial institutions include *chartered banks* and *other depository institutions—trust companies, credit unions, investment dealers, insurance companies, pension funds, and mutual funds.*

Table 1.4 ranks the top eight publicly traded financial institutions in Canada by market capitalization in 2006. They include the Big Six chartered banks and two life insurance companies. Because they are allowed to diversify by operating in all provinces, Canada's chartered banks are of a reasonable size on an international scale.

Chartered banks operate under federal regulation, accepting deposits from suppliers of funds and making commercial loans to mid-sized businesses, corporate loans to large companies, and personal loans and mortgages to individuals. Banks make the majority of their income from the *spread* between the interest paid on deposits and the higher rate earned on loans. This is *indirect finance.*

Chartered banks also provide other services that generate fees instead of spread income. For example, a large corporate customer seeking short-term debt funding can borrow *directly* from another large corporation with funds supplied through a *bankers acceptance.* This is an interest-bearing IOU stamped by a bank guaranteeing the borrower's credit. Instead of spread income, the bank receives a *stamping fee.* Bankers acceptances are an example of *direct finance.* Notice that the key difference between direct finance and indirect finance is that in direct finance funds do not pass through the bank's balance sheet in the form of a deposit and loan. Often called *securitization* because a security (the bankers acceptance) is created, direct finance is growing rapidly.

Trust companies also accept deposits and make loans. In addition, trust companies engage in fiduciary activities—managing assets for estates, registered retirement savings plans, and so on. Like trust companies, credit unions also accept deposits and make loans. Le Mouvement des caisses Desjardins is a major Quebec credit union, but does not appear in Table 1.4 because it is member-owned and not publicly traded.

Investment dealers are non-depository institutions that assist firms in issuing new securities in exchange for fee income. Investment dealers also aid investors in buying and selling securities. Chartered banks own majority stakes in five of Canada's top 15 investment dealers.

Insurance companies include property and casualty insurance and health and life insurance companies. Life insurance companies engage in indirect finance by accepting funds in a form similar to deposits and making loans. Manulife Financial and Sun Life Financial are major life insurance companies that have expanded aggressively to become rivals of the chartered banks.

Fuelled by the aging of the Canadian population and the longest bull market in history, assets in pension and mutual funds grew rapidly in the 1990s. Pension funds invest contributions from employers and employees in securities offered by financial markets. Mutual funds pool individual investments to purchase diversified portfolios of securities. There are many different types of mutual funds. Table 1.5 shows the totals of mutual fund assets by fund type. In December 2005, the two largest categories were Canadian and foreign equity.

TABLE 1.4
Largest financial institutions in Canada, by market capitalization, 2006

Rank	Company	Market Capitalization
1	Royal Bank of Canada	$59,238,910,739
2	Manulife Financial Corporation	58,330,857,790
3	Toronto-Dominion Bank	43,200,671,740
4	Bank of Nova Scotia	43,114,958,597
5	Bank of Montreal	30,992,077,055
6	Canadian Imperial Bank of Commerce	27,138,181,538
7	Sun Life Financial Inc.	26,571,300,612
8	National Bank of Canada	10,096,721,644

Source: *www.globeinvestor.com, www.tsx.com*

TABLE 1.5 Total net assets by fund type in December 2005		Net assets ($ billions)
	Balanced	123.5
	Canadian Equity	133.4
	Foreign Equity	89.4
	U.S. Equity	31.9
	Bond and Income	62.3
	Foreign Bond and Income	6.4
	Dividend and Income	69.7
	Mortgage	4.9
	Real Estate	2.2
	Canadian Money Market	44.5
	Foreign Money Market	1.9
	Total	570.0

Source: Investment Funds Institute of Canada, Monthly Statistics, December 2005, *www.ific.ca.*

We base this survey of the principal activities of financial institutions on their main activities today. Recent deregulation now allows chartered banks, trust companies, insurance companies, and investment dealers to engage in most of the activities of the others with one exception: Chartered banks are not allowed to sell life insurance through their branch networks. Although not every institution plans to become a one-stop financial supermarket, the different types of institutions are likely to continue to become more alike.

CONCEPT QUESTIONS

1. What are the principal financial institutions in Canada? What is the principal role of each?

2. What are direct and indirect finance? How do they differ?

3. How are money and capital markets different?

4. What is a dealer market? How do dealer and auction markets differ?

5. What is the largest auction market in Canada?

1.7   TRENDS IN FINANCIAL MARKETS AND FINANCIAL MANAGEMENT

Like all markets, financial markets are experiencing rapid globalization. Globalization also makes it harder for investors to shelter their portfolios from financial shocks in other countries. In the summer of 1998, the Asian financial crisis shook financial markets around the world. At the same time, interest rates, foreign exchange rates, and other macroeconomic variables have become more volatile. The toolkit of available financial management techniques has expanded rapidly in response to a need to control increased risk from volatility and to track complexities arising from dealings in many countries. Computer technology improvements are making new **financial engineering** applications practical.

financial engineering
Creation of new securities or financial processes.

When financial managers or investment dealers design new securities or financial processes, their efforts are referred to as financial engineering. Successful financial engineering reduces and controls risk and minimizes taxes. Financial engineering creates a variety of debt securities and reinforces the trend toward securitization of credit introduced earlier. A controversial example is the invention and rapid growth of trading in options, futures, and other **derivative securities.** Derivative securities are very useful in controlling risk, but they have also produced large losses when mishandled. At the time of writing, the largest financial accident with derivatives was the loss that triggered a $3.5 billion U.S. bailout of the U.S. fund Long Term Capital Management in 1998.

derivative securities
Options, futures, and other securities whose value derives from the price of another, underlying, asset.

Financial engineering also seeks to reduce financing costs of issuing securities as well as the costs of complying with rules laid down by regulatory authorities. An example is the Short Form Prospectus Distribution (SFPD) allowing firms that frequently issue new equity to bypass most of the OSC registration requirements.

www.royalbank.ca

regulatory dialectic
The pressures financial institutions and regulatory bodies exert on each other.

In addition to financial engineering, advances in technology have created e-business, bringing new challenges for the financial manager. For example, consumers ordering products on a company's website expect rapid delivery and failure to meet these expectations can damage a company's image. This means that companies doing e-business with consumers must invest in supply chain management as well as in additional inventory.

Technological advances have also created opportunities to combine different types of financial institutions to take advantage of economies of scale and scope. For example, Royal Bank, Canada's largest chartered bank, owns Royal Trust and RBC Dominion Securities. Such large institutions operate in all provinces and internationally and enjoy more lax regulations in some jurisdictions than in others. Financial institutions pressure authorities to deregulate in a push-pull process called the **regulatory dialectic.**

For example, in 1998 and again in 2002, banks planned mergers in an effort to pressure the federal government to grant approval. Although the federal governmen turned down the mergers, we believe this issue is dormant, not dead, and will reemerge in the not too distant future.

Not all trends arc driven by technology. In the aftermath of the technology bubble of the late 1990s, stakeholders and regulators have become very interested in corporate governance reform, a topic we introduced earlier in the chapter. For example, proponents of such reform argue that a stronger, independent board of directors can prevent management excesses such as ocurred at Hollinger.

These trends have made financial management a much more complex and technical activity. For this reason, many students of business find introductory finance one of their most challenging subjects. The trends we reviewed have also increased the stakes. In the face of increased global competition, the payoff for good financial management is great. The finance function is also becoming important in corporate strategic planning. The good news is that career opportunities (and compensation) in financial positions are quite attractive.

OUTLINE OF THE TEXT

Now that we've completed a quick tour of the concerns of corporate finance, we can take a closer look at the organization of this book. The text is organized into the following nine parts:

Part 1: Overview of Corporate Finance

Part 2: Financial Statements and Long-Term Financial Planning

Part 3: Valuation of Future Cash Flows

Part 4: Capital Budgeting

Part 5: Risk and Return

Part 6: Cost of Capital and Long-Term Financial Policy

Part 7: Short-Term Financial Planning and Management

Part 8: Topics in Corporate Finance

Part 9: Derivative Securities and Corporate Finance

Part 1 of the text contains some introductory material and goes on to explain the relationship between accounting and cash flow. Part 2 explores financial statements and how they are used in finance in greater depth.

Parts 3 and 4 contain our core discussion on valuation. In Part 3, we develop the basic procedures for valuing future cash flows with particular emphasis on stocks and bonds. Part 4 draws on this material and deals with capital budgeting and the effect of long-term investment decisions on the firm.

In Part 5, we develop some tools for evaluating risk. We then discuss how to evaluate the risks associated with long-term investments by the firm. The emphasis in this section is on coming up with a benchmark for making investment decisions.

Part 6 deals with the related issues of long-term financing, dividend policy, and capital structure. We discuss corporate securities in some detail and describe the procedures used to raise capital and sell securities to the public. We also introduce and describe the important concept of the cost of capital. We go on to examine dividends and dividend policy and important considerations in determining a capital structure.

The working capital question is addressed in Part 7. The subjects of short-term financial planning, cash management, and credit management are covered.

Part 8 contains the important special topic of international corporate finance. Part 9 covers risk management and derivative securities.

SUMMARY AND CONCLUSIONS

This chapter has introduced you to some of the basic ideas in corporate finance. In it, we saw that:

1. Corporate finance has three main areas of concern:
    a. What long-term investments should the firm take? This is the capital budgeting decision.
    b. Where will the firm get the long-term financing to pay for its investment? In other words, what mixture of debt and equity should we use to fund our operations? This is the capital structure decision.
    c. How should the firm manage its everyday financial activities? This is the working capital decision.

2. The goal of financial management in a for-profit business is to make decisions that increase the value of the stock or, more generally, increase the market value of the equity.

3. The corporate form of organization is superior to other forms when it comes to raising money and transferring ownership interest, but it has the disadvantage of double taxation.

4. There is the possibility of conflicts between shareholders and management in a large corporation. We called these conflicts agency problems and discussed how they might be controlled and reduced.

5. The advantages of the corporate form are enhanced by the existence of financial markets. Financial institutions function to promote the efficiency of financial markets. Financial markets function as both primary and secondary markets for corporate securities and can be organized as either dealer or auction markets. Globalization, deregulation, and financial engineering are important forces shaping financial markets and the practice of financial management.

Of the topics we've discussed thus far, the most important is the goal of financial management: maximizing the value of the stock. Throughout the text, as we analyze financial decisions, we always ask the same question: How does the decision under consideration affect the value of the shares?

Key Terms

agency problem (page 11)
capital budgeting (page 3)
capital markets (page 19)
capital structure (page 4)
corporate governance (page 13)
corporation (page 6)
derivative securities (page 22)

financial engineering (page 22)
money markets (page 19)
partnership (page 5)
regulatory dialectic (page 23)
sole proprietorship (page 5)
stakeholder (page 13)
working capital management (page 5)

Concepts Review and Critical Thinking Questions

1. **The Financial Management Decision Process** What are the three types of financial management decisions? For each type of decision, give an example of a business transaction that would be relevant.

2. **Sole Proprietorships and Partnerships** What are the three primary disadvantages to the sole proprietorship and partnership forms of business organization? What benefits are there to these types of business organization as opposed to the corporate form?

3. **Corporate Organization** What is the primary disadvantage of the corporate form of organization? Name at least two advantages of corporate organization.

4. **Corporate Finance Organizational Structure** In a large corporation, what are the two distinct groups that report to the chief financial officer? Which group is the focus of corporate finance?

5. **The Goal of Financial Management** What goal should always motivate the actions of the firm's financial manager?

6. **Corporate Agency Issues** Who owns a corporation? Describe the process whereby the owners control the firm's management. What is the main reason that an agency relationship exists in the corporate form of organization? In this context, what kind of problems can arise?

7. **Financial Markets** An initial public offering (IPO) of a company's securities is a term you've probably noticed in the financial press. Is an IPO a primary market transaction or a secondary market transaction?

8. **Financial Markets** What does it mean when we say the Toronto Stock Exchange is both an auction market and a dealer market? How are auction markets different from dealer markets? What kind of market is Nasdaq?

9. **Not-for-Profit Firm Goals** Suppose you were the financial manager of a not-for-profit business (a not-for-profit hospital, perhaps). What kinds of goals do you think would be appropriate?

10. **Firm Goals and Stock Value** Evaluate the following statement: "Managers should not focus on the current stock value because doing so will lead to an overemphasis on short-term profits at the expense of long-term profits."

11. **Firm Goals and Ethics** Can our goal of maximizing the value of the stock conflict with other goals, such as avoiding unethical or illegal behaviour? In particular, do you think subjects like customer and employee safety, the environment, and the general good of society fit in this framework, or are they essentially ignored? Try to think of some specific scenarios to illustrate your answer.

12. **Firm Goals and Multinational Firms** Would our goal of maximizing the value of the stock be different if we were thinking about financial management in a foreign country? Why or why not?

13. **Agency Issues and Corporate Control** Suppose you own shares in a company. The current price per share is $25. Another company has just announced that it wants to buy your company and will pay $35 per share to acquire all the outstanding shares. Your company's management immediately begins fighting off this hostile bid. Is management acting in the shareholders' best interests? Why or why not?

14. **Agency Issues and International Finance** Corporate ownership varies around the world. Historically, individuals have owned the majority of shares in public corporations in the United States. In Canada this is also the case, but ownership is more often concentrated in the hands of a majority shareholder. In Germany and Japan, banks, other financial institutions, and large companies own most of the shares in public corporations. How do you think these ownership differences affect the severity of agency costs in different countries?

15. **Major Institutions and Markets** What are the major types of financial institutions and financial markets in Canada?

16. **Direct versus Indirect Finance** What is the difference between direct and indirect finance? Give an example of each.

17. **Current Major Trends** What are some of the major trends in Canadian financial markets? Explain how these trends affect the practice of financial management in Canada.

S&P Problem

STANDARD & POOR'S

1. **Industry Comparison** On the Market Insight homepage, follow the "Industry" link at the top of the page to the industry page. You can use the drop down menu to select different industries. Answer the following questions for these industries: Airlines, Automobiles, Biotechnology, Computers (Software & Services), Homebuilding, Manufacturing (Diversified), Restaurants, Retail (General Merchandise), and Telecommunications (Cellular/Wireless).

   a. How many companies are in each industry?

   b. What are the total sales for each industry?

   c. Do the industries with the largest total sales have the most companies in the industry? What does this tell you about competition in the various industries?

Internet Application Questions

1. Equity markets are an important source of capital for private firms in Canada. Take a tour of the Toronto Stock Exchange at www.tsx.com. What is the TSX Composite Index? Check out Index Lists/Information under Investor Information. What does a change in the TSX Composite Index tell you?

2. Canadian banks are actively involved in financing home mortgages. Describe the role played by the Canada Mortgage and Housing Corporation in home mortgages (www.cmhc.ca/). What is the *National Housing Act*? Can an investor participate in the mortgage "pool" represented by housing loans insured by the CMHC? Click on the Investment Opportunities menu on the CMHC homepage and describe Mortgage Backed Securities offered by the CMHC.

3. The choice of business organization form depends on many factors. The following site from British Columbia outlines the pros and cons of a sole proprietorship, partnership, and corporation: www.sb.gov.bc.ca/bizstart-prop.php

   Can you suggest a few reasons why some firms that were organized as partnerships decided to incorporate (e.g., Goldman Sachs (www.goldmansachs.com) with shares traded on the NYSE (www.nyse.com))?

4. Ethical investing following socially responsible principles is gaining popularity. The Social Investment Organization website provides information about these principles and on Canadian ethical mutual funds at www.socialinvestment.ca. Michael Jantzi Research Associates offers research services to support socially responsible investing at www.jantziresearch.com. How does investing in ethical funds differ from investing in general? What has been the performance record of Canadian ethical funds?

Suggested Readings

A current survey of trends affecting chartered banks and other Canadian financial institutions is:

Saunders, A., M. Cornett and P. McGraw, *Financial Institutions Management*, Third Canadian Edition, Whitby, Ontario: McGraw-Hill Ryerson, 2006.

Another useful source is:

Freshfields Bruckhaus Deringer and the UNEP Finance Initiative, October 2005, available at http://www.unepfi.org/fineadmin/documents/freshfields_legal_resp_20051123.pdf

CHAPTER 2

Financial Statements, Taxes, and Cash Flow

In 2004, Nortel announced that it was firing its CEO, placing its CFO and controller on leave, and delaying announcement of its financial results due to problems with past overstatement of revenues. According to the newly appointed CFO, earnings for the prior year were expected to be revised downward by 50 percent. This occurred despite the fact that the past year's statements had been audited and found to express fairly the state of Nortel according to its auditors at that time.

The story of Nortel illustrates the very broad range of interpretation that can arise when applying GAAP principles, as well as the potential difficulties of relying on the accuracy of GAAP-based financial statements. These topics are discussed in this chapter.

IN THIS CHAPTER, we examine financial statements, cash flow, and taxes. Our emphasis is not on preparing financial statements. Instead, we recognize that financial statements are frequently a key source of information for financial decisions, so our goal is to briefly examine such statements and point out some of their more relevant features along with a few limitations. We pay special attention to some of the practical details of cash flow. By cash flow, we simply mean the difference between the number of dollars that come in and the number that go out. A crucial input to sound financial management, cash flow analysis is used throughout the book. For example, bankers lending to businesses are looking increasingly at borrowers' cash flows as the most reliable measures of each company's ability to repay its loans. In another example, most large companies base their capital budgets for investments in plant and equipment on analysis of cash flow. As a result, there is an excellent payoff in later chapters for knowledge of cash flow.

One very important topic is taxes because cash flows are measured after taxes. Our discussion looks at how corporate and individual taxes are computed and at how investors are taxed on different types of income. A basic understanding of the Canadian tax system is essential for success in applying the tools of financial management.

balance sheet
Financial statement showing a firm's accounting value on a particular date.

THE BALANCE SHEET

The **balance sheet** is a snapshot of the firm. It is a convenient means of organizing and summarizing what a firm owns (its *assets*), what a firm owes (its *liabilities*), and the difference between the two (the firm's *equity*) at a given time. Figure 2.1 illustrates how the balance sheet is constructed. As shown, the left-hand side lists the assets of the firm, and the right-hand side lists the liabilities and equity.

FIGURE 2.1

The balance sheet model of the firm. Left side lists total value of assets. Right side, or total value of the firm to investors, determines how the value is distributed.

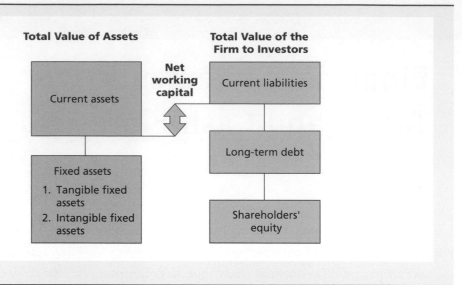

Assets: The Left-Hand Side

Assets are classified as either *current* or *fixed*. A fixed asset is one that has a relatively long life. Fixed assets can either be *tangible,* such as a truck or a computer, or *intangible,* such as a trademark or patent. Accountants refer to these assets as *capital assets.* A current asset has a life of less than one year. This means that the asset will convert to cash within 12 months. For example, inventory would normally be purchased and sold within a year and is thus classified as a current asset. Obviously, cash itself is a current asset. Accounts receivable (money owed to the firm by its customers) is also a current asset.

Liabilities and Owners' Equity: The Right-Hand Side

The firm's liabilities are the first thing listed on the right-hand side of the balance sheet. These are classified as either *current* or *long-term*. Current liabilities, like current assets, have a life of less than one year (meaning they must be paid within the year) and are listed before long-term liabilities. Accounts payable (money the firm owes to its suppliers) is one example of a current liability.

A debt that is not due in the coming year is a long-term liability. A loan that the firm will pay off in five years is one such long-term debt. Firms borrow long-term from a variety of sources. We use the terms *bond* and *bondholders* generically to refer to long-term debt and long-term creditors, respectively.

Finally, by definition, the difference between the total value of the assets (current and fixed) and the total value of the liabilities (current and long-term) is the *shareholders' equity,* also called *common equity* or *owners' equity.* This feature of the balance sheet is intended to reflect the fact that, if the firm were to sell all of its assets and use the money to pay off its debts, whatever residual value remained would belong to the shareholders. So, the balance sheet balances because the value of the left-hand side always equals the value of the right-hand side. That is, the value of the firm's assets is equal to the sum of liabilities and shareholders' equity:[1]

Assets = Liabilities + Shareholders' equity   [2.1]

This is the balance sheet identity or equation, and it always holds because shareholders' equity is defined as the difference between assets and liabilities.

---

1 The terms *owners' equity* and *shareholders' equity* are used interchangeably to refer to the equity in a corporation. The term *net worth* is also used. Variations exist in addition to these.

Net Working Capital

As shown in Figure 2.1, the difference between a firm's current assets and its current liabilities is called *net working capital*. Net working capital is positive when current assets exceed current liabilities. Based on the definitions of current assets and current liabilities, this means that the cash available over the next 12 months exceeds the cash that must be paid over that same period. For this reason, net working capital is usually positive in a healthy firm.

EXAMPLE 2.1: Building the Balance Sheet

A firm has current assets of $100, fixed assets of $500, short-term debt of $70, and long-term debt of $200. What does the balance sheet look like? What is shareholders' equity? What is net working capital?

In this case, total assets are $100 + 500 = $600 and total liabilities are $70 + 200 = $270, so shareholders' equity is the difference: $600 − 270 = $330. The balance sheet would thus look like:

Assets		Liabilities	
Current assets	$100	Current liabilities	$ 70
Fixed assets	500	Long-term debt	200
		Shareholders' equity	330
Total assets	$600	Total liabilities and shareholders' equity	$600

Net working capital is the difference between current assets and current liabilities, or $100 − 70 = $30.

Table 2.1 shows a simplified balance sheet for Canadian Enterprises Limited. The assets in the balance sheet are listed in order of the length of time it takes for them to convert to cash in the normal course of business. Similarly, the liabilities are listed in the order in which they would normally be paid.

TABLE 2.1

CANADIAN ENTERPRISES LIMITED
Balance Sheets as of December 31, 2005 and 2006
($ millions)

	2005	2006		2005	2006
Assets			*Liabilities and Owners' Equity*		
Current assets			Current liabilities		
Cash	$ 114	$ 160	Accounts payable	$ 232	$ 266
Accounts receivable	445	688	Notes payable	196	123
Inventory	553	555	Total	$ 428	$ 389
Total	$1,112	$1,403			
			Long-term debt	$ 408	$ 454
Fixed assets			Owners' equity		
Net, plant and equipment	$1,644	$1,709	Common shares	600	640
			Retained earnings	1,320	1,629
			Total	$1,920	$2,269
Total assets	$2,756	$3,112	Total liabilities and owners' equity	$2,756	$3,112

The structure of the assets for a particular firm reflects the line of business that the firm is in and also managerial decisions about how much cash and inventory to maintain and about credit policy, fixed asset acquisition, and so on.

The liabilities side of the balance sheet primarily reflects managerial decisions about capital structure and the use of short-term debt. For example, in 2006, total long-term debt for Canadian Enterprises Limited was $454 and total equity was $640 + 1,629 = $2,269, so total long-term financing was $454 + 2,269 = $2,723. Of this amount, $454/2,723 = 16.67% was long-term debt. This percentage reflects capital structure decisions made in the past by the management of Canadian Enterprises.

Three particularly important things to keep in mind when examining a balance sheet are liquidity, debt versus equity, and market value versus book value.[2]

---

2 Chapters 3 and 4 expand on financial statement analysis.

Liquidity

Liquidity refers to the speed and ease with which an asset can be converted to cash. Gold is a relatively liquid asset; a custom manufacturing facility is not. Liquidity really has two dimensions: ease of conversion versus loss of value. Any asset can be converted to cash quickly if we cut the price enough. A highly liquid asset is therefore one that can be quickly sold without significant loss of value. An illiquid asset is one that cannot be quickly converted to cash without a substantial price reduction.

Assets are normally listed on the balance sheet in order of decreasing liquidity, meaning that the most liquid assets are listed first. Current assets are relatively liquid and include cash and those assets that we expect to convert to cash over the next 12 months. Accounts receivable, for example, represents amounts not yet collected from customers on sales already made. Naturally, we hope these will convert to cash in the near future. Inventory is probably the least liquid of the current assets, at least for many businesses.

Fixed assets are, for the most part, relatively illiquid. These consist of tangible things such as buildings and equipment. Intangible assets, such as a trademark, have no physical existence but can be very valuable. Like tangible fixed assets, they won't ordinarily convert to cash and are generally considered illiquid.

Liquidity is valuable. The more liquid a business is, the less likely it is to experience financial distress (that is, difficulty in paying debts or buying needed assets). Unfortunately, liquid assets are generally less profitable to hold. For example, cash holdings are the most liquid of all investments, but they sometimes earn no return at all—they just sit there. Therefore, the trade-off is between the advantages of liquidity and forgone potential profits. We discuss this trade-off further in the rest of the book.

Debt versus Equity

To the extent that a firm borrows money, it usually gives creditors first claim to the firm's cash flow. Equity holders are only entitled to the residual value, the portion left after creditors are paid. The value of this residual portion is the shareholders' equity in the firm and is simply the asset value less the value of the firm's liabilities:

Shareholders' equity = Assets − Liabilities

This is true in an accounting sense because shareholders' equity is defined as this residual portion. More importantly, it is true in an economic sense: If the firm sells its assets and pays its debts, whatever cash is left belongs to the shareholders.

The use of debt in a firm's capital structure is called *financial leverage.* The more debt a firm has (as a percentage of assets), the greater is its degree of financial leverage. As we discuss in later chapters, debt acts like a lever in the sense that using it can greatly magnify both gains and losses. So financial leverage increases the potential reward to shareholders, but it also increases the potential for financial distress and business failure.

Market Value versus Book Value

The values shown on the balance sheet for the firm's assets are *book values* and generally are not what the assets are actually worth. Under **Generally Accepted Accounting Principles (GAAP),** audited financial statements show assets at *historical cost.* In other words, assets are carried on the books at what the firm paid for them, no matter how long ago they were purchased or how much they are worth today.

For current assets, market value and book value might be somewhat similar because current assets are bought and converted to cash over a relatively short span of time. In other circumstances, they might differ quite a bit. Moreover, for fixed assets, it would be purely a coincidence if the actual market value of an asset (what the asset could be sold for) were equal to its book value. For example, a railroad might own enormous tracts of land purchased a century or more ago. What the railroad paid for that land could be hundreds or thousands of times less than it is worth today. The balance sheet would nonetheless show the historical cost.

Financial information for most public Canadian companies can be found at www.sedar.com

Generally Accepted Accounting Principles (GAAP)
The common set of standards and procedures by which audited financial statements are prepared.

Since book values are seldom what assets are worth today, you might wonder why accountants use them. Their rationale is linked to two accounting principles: *objectivity* and *conservatism*. Book values are objective as they are a matter of record and not subject to opinion. Due to inflation, book values generally understate the market values of assets and so are conservative. When they know that asset market values are significantly *below* book values, accountants write down assets. For example, in June 2001, Nortel wrote down $12.3 billion for acquisitions that were no longer of value. Huge write-offs often go hand in hand with overstated profits in previous fiscal years, as decreases in the value of assets were not expensed properly.[3]

The balance sheet is potentially useful to many different parties. A supplier might look at the size of accounts payable relative to total purchases to see how promptly the firm pays its bills. A potential creditor would examine the liquidity and degree of financial leverage. Managers within the firm can track things like the amount of cash and the amount of inventory that the firm keeps on hand. Uses such as these are discussed in more detail in Chapter 3.

Managers and investors are frequently interested in knowing the value of the firm. This information is not on the balance sheet. The fact that balance sheet assets are listed at cost means that there is no necessary connection between the total assets shown and the value of the firm. Indeed, many of the most valuable assets that a firm might have—good management, a good reputation, talented employees—don't appear on the balance sheet at all.

Similarly, the shareholders' equity figure on the balance sheet and the true value of the stock need not be related. For financial managers, then, the accounting value of the stock is not an especially important concern; it is the market value that matters. Henceforth, whenever we speak of the value of an asset or the value of the firm, we normally mean its *market value*. So, for example, when we say the goal of the financial manager is to increase the value of the stock, we mean the market value of the stock.

EXAMPLE 2.2: Market versus Book Value

The Quebec Corporation has fixed assets with a book value of $700 and an appraised market value of about $1,000. Net working capital is $400 on the books, but approximately $600 would be realized if all the current accounts were liquidated. Quebec Corporation has $500 in long-term debt, both book value and market value. What is the book value of the equity? What is the market value?

We can construct two simplified balance sheets, one in accounting (book value) terms and one in economic (market value) terms:

QUEBEC CORPORATION
Balance Sheets
Market Value versus Book Value

	Book	Market		Book	Market
Assets			*Liabilities*		
Net working capital	$ 400	$ 600	Long-term debt	$ 500	$ 500
Net fixed assets	700	1,000	Shareholders' equity	600	1,100
	$1,100	$1,600		$1,100	$1,600

CONCEPT QUESTIONS

1. What is the balance sheet identity?

2. What is liquidity? Why is it important?

3. What do we mean by financial leverage?

4. Explain the difference between accounting value and market value. Which is more important to the financial manager? Why?

---

3 In such cases, the asset is recorded at the lesser of market or book value.

income statement
Financial statement summarizing a firm's performance over a period of time.

THE INCOME STATEMENT

The **income statement** measures performance over some period of time, usually a year. The income statement equation is

$$\text{Revenues} - \text{Expenses} = \text{Income} \qquad [2.2]$$

If you think of the balance sheet as a snapshot, then you can think of the income statement as a video recording covering the period between, before, and after pictures. Table 2.2 gives a simplified income statement for Canadian Enterprises.

The initial thing reported on an income statement would usually be revenue and expenses from the firm's principal operations. Subsequent parts include, among other things, financing expenses such as interest paid. Taxes paid are reported separately. The last item is *net income* (the so-called bottom line). Net income is often expressed on a per-share basis and called *earnings per share (EPS)*.

TABLE 2.2

CANADIAN ENTERPRISES
2006 Income Statement
($ millions)

Net sales		$1,509
Cost of goods sold		750
Depreciation		65
Earnings before interest and taxes		$ 694
Interest paid		70
Income before taxes		$ 624
Taxes		250
Net income		$ 374
Addition to retained earnings	$ 309	
Dividends	65	

As indicated, Canadian Enterprises paid cash dividends of $65. The difference between net income and cash dividends, $309, is the addition to retained earnings for the year. This amount is added to the cumulative retained earnings account on the balance sheet. If you'll look back at the two balance sheets for Canadian Enterprises, you'll see that retained earnings did go up by this amount, $1,320 + 309 = $1,629.

EXAMPLE 2.3: Calculating Earnings and Dividends per Share

Suppose that Canadian had 200 million shares outstanding at the end of 2006. Based on the preceding income statement, what was Canadian's EPS? What were the dividends per share?

From the income statement, Canadian had a net income of $374 million for the year. Since 200 million shares were out-standing, EPS was $374/200 = $1.87 per share. Similarly, dividends per share were $65/200 = $.325 per share.

When looking at an income statement, the financial manager needs to keep three things in mind: GAAP, cash versus non-cash items, and time and costs.

GAAP and the Income Statement

An income statement prepared using GAAP shows revenue when it accrues. This is not necessarily when the cash comes in. The general rule (the realization principle) is to recognize revenue when the earnings process is virtually complete and the value of an exchange of goods or services is known or can be reliably determined. In practice, this principle usually means that revenue is recognized at the time of sale, which need not be the same as the time of collection.

Costs shown on the income statement are based on the matching principle. The basic idea here is first to determine revenues as just described and then match those revenues with the costs associated with producing them. So, if we manufacture and then sell a product on credit, the revenue is realized at the time of sale. The production and other costs associated with the sale of that product would likewise be recognized at that time. Once again, the actual cash outflows may have occurred at some very different time.

As a result of the way revenues and costs are realized, the figures shown on the income statement may not be at all representative of the actual cash inflows and outflows that occurred during a particular period.

Non-Cash Items

non-cash items
Expenses charged against revenues that do not directly affect cash flow, such as depreciation.

A primary reason that accounting income differs from cash flow is that an income statement contains **non-cash items.** The most important of these is *depreciation*. Suppose a firm purchases an asset for $5,000 and pays in cash. Obviously, the firm has a $5,000 cash outflow at the time of purchase. However, instead of deducting the $5,000 as an expense, an accountant might depreciate the asset over a five-year period.

If the depreciation is straight-line and the asset is written down to zero over that period, $5,000/5 = $1,000 would be deducted each year as an expense.[4] The important thing to recognize is that this $1,000 deduction isn't cash—it's an accounting number. The actual cash outflow occurred when the asset was purchased.

The depreciation deduction is simply another application of the matching principle in accounting. The revenues associated with an asset would generally occur over some length of time. So the accountant seeks to match the expense of purchasing the asset with the benefits produced from owning it.

As we shall see, for the financial manager, the actual timing of cash inflows and outflows is critical in coming up with a reasonable estimate of market value, so we need to learn how to separate the cash flows from the non-cash accounting entries.

Time and Costs

It is often useful to think of the future as having two distinct parts: the short run and the long run. These are not precise time periods. The distinction has to do with whether costs are fixed or variable. In the long run, all business costs are variable. Given sufficient time, assets can be sold, debts can be paid, and so on.

If our time horizon is relatively short, however, some costs are effectively fixed—they must be paid no matter what (property taxes, for example). Other costs, such as wages to workers and payments to suppliers, are still variable. As a result, even in the short run, the firm can vary its output level by varying expenditures in these areas.

The distinction between fixed and variable costs is important, at times, to the financial manager, but the way costs are reported on the income statement is not a good guide as to which costs are which. The reason is that, in practice, accountants tend to classify costs as either product costs or period costs.

Product costs include such things as raw materials, direct labour expense, and manufacturing overhead. These are reported on the income statements as costs of goods sold, but they include both fixed and variable costs. Similarly, period costs are incurred during a particular time period and are reported as selling, general, and administrative expenses. Once again, some of these period costs may be fixed and others may be variable. The company president's salary, for example, is a period cost and is probably fixed, at least in the short run.

CONCEPT QUESTIONS

1. What is the income statement equation?

2. What are three things to keep in mind when looking at an income statement?

3. Why is accounting income not the same as cash flow? Give two reasons.

---

4 By straight-line, we mean that the depreciation deduction is the same every year. By written down to zero, we mean that the asset is assumed to have no value at the end of five years. Tax depreciation is discussed in more detail later in the chapter.

 **2.3**

CASH FLOW

At this point, we are ready to discuss one of the most important pieces of financial information that can be gleaned from financial statements: cash flow. There is no standard financial statement for presenting this information in the way that we wish. Therefore, we discuss how to calculate cash flow for Canadian Enterprises and point out how the result differs from standard financial statement calculations. There is a standard accounting statement called the statement of cash flows, but it is concerned with a somewhat different issue and should not be confused with what is discussed in this section. The accounting statement of cash flows is discussed in Chapter 3.

From the balance sheet identity, we know that the value of a firm's assets is equal to the value of its liabilities plus the value of its equity. Similarly, the cash flow from assets must equal the sum of the cash flow to bondholders (or creditors) plus the cash flow to shareholders (or owners):

$$\text{Cash flow from assets} = \text{Cash flow to bondholders} \qquad [2.3]$$
$$+ \text{Cash flow to shareholders}$$

This is the cash flow identity. It says that the cash flow from the firm's assets is equal to the cash flow paid to suppliers of capital to the firm. A firm generates cash through its various activities; that cash is either used to pay creditors or paid out to the owners of the firm.

Cash Flow from Assets

cash flow from assets
The total of cash flow to bondholders and cash flow to shareholders, consisting of: operating cash flow, capital spending, and additions to net working capital.

Cash flow from assets involves three components: operating cash flow, capital spending, and additions to net working capital. *Operating cash flow* refers to the cash flow that results from the firm's day-to-day activities of producing and selling. Expenses associated with the firm's financing of its assets are not included because they are not operating expenses.

As we discussed in Chapter 1, some portion of the firm's cash flow is reinvested in the firm. *Capital spending* refers to the net spending on fixed assets (purchases of fixed assets less sales of fixed assets). Finally, *additions to net working capital* is the amount spent on net working capital. It is measured as the change in net working capital over the period being examined and represents the net increase in current assets over current liabilities. The three components of cash flow are examined in more detail next.

operating cash flow
Cash generated from a firm's normal business activities.

OPERATING CASH FLOW   To calculate **operating cash flow,** we want to calculate revenues minus costs, but we don't want to include depreciation since it's not a cash outflow, and we don't want to include interest because it's a financing expense. We do want to include taxes, because taxes are, unfortunately, paid in cash.

If we look at the income statement in Table 2.2, Canadian Enterprises had earnings before interest and taxes (EBIT) of $694. This is almost what we want since it doesn't include interest paid. We need to make two adjustments: First, recall that depreciation is a non-cash expense. To get cash flow, we first add back the $65 in depreciation since it wasn't a cash deduction. The second adjustment is to subtract the $250 in taxes since these were paid in cash. The result is operating cash flow:

Canadian Enterprises thus had a 2006 operating cash flow of $509.

There is an unpleasant possibility for confusion when we speak of operating cash flow. In accounting practice, operating cash flow is often defined as net income plus depreciation. For Canadian Enterprises in Table 2.3, this would amount to $374 + 65 = $439.

The accounting definition of operating cash flow differs from ours in one important way: Interest is deducted when net income is computed. Notice that the difference between the $509 operating cash flow we calculated and this $439 is $70, the amount of interest paid for the year.

This definition of cash flow thus considers interest paid to be an operating expense. Our definition treats it properly as a financing expense. If there were no interest expense, the two definitions would be the same.

To finish our calculations of cash flow from assets for Canadian Enterprises, we need to consider how much of the $509 operating cash flow was reinvested in the firm. We consider spending on fixed assets first.

TABLE 2.3

CANADIAN ENTERPRISES 2006 Operating Cash Flow	
Earnings before interest and taxes	$694
+ Depreciation	65
– Taxes	250
Operating cash flow	$509

CAPITAL SPENDING   Net capital spending is just money spent on fixed assets less money received from the sale of fixed assets. At the end of 2005, net fixed assets were $1,644. During the year, we wrote off (depreciated) $65 worth of fixed assets on the income statement. So, if we did not purchase any new fixed assets, we would have had $1,644 – 65 = $1,579 at year's end. The 2006 balance sheet shows $1,709 in net fixed assets, so we must have spent a total of $1,709 – 1,579 = $130 on fixed assets during the year:

Ending fixed assets	$1,709
– Beginning fixed assets	1,644
+ Depreciation	65
Net investment in fixed assets	$ 130

This $130 is our net capital spending for 2006.

Could net capital spending be negative? The answer is yes. This would happen if the firm sold more assets than it purchased. The net here refers to purchases of fixed assets net of any sales.

CHANGE IN NET WORKING CAPITAL   In addition to investing in fixed assets, a firm also invests in current assets. For example, going back to the balance sheet in Table 2.1, we see that, at the end of 2006, Canadian Enterprises had current assets of $1,403. At the end of 2005, current assets were $1,112, so, during the year, Canadian Enterprises invested $1,403 – 1,112 = $291 in current assets.

As the firm changes its investment in current assets, its current liabilities usually change as well. To determine the additions to net working capital, the easiest approach is just to take the difference between the beginning and ending net working capital (NWC) figures. Net working capital at the end of 2006 was $1,403 – 389 = $1,014. Similarly, at the end of 2005, net working capital was $1,112 – 428 = $684. So, given these figures, we have:

Ending NWC	$1,014
– Beginning NWC	684
Addition to NWC	$ 330

Net working capital thus increased by $330. Put another way, Canadian Enterprises had a net investment of $330 in NWC for the year.

CONCLUSION   Given the figures we've come up with, we're ready to calculate cash flow from assets. The total cash flow from assets is given by operating cash flow less the amounts invested in fixed assets and net working capital. So, for Canadian Enterprises we have:

CANADIAN ENTERPRISES 2006 Cash Flow from Assets	
Operating cash flow	$509
– Net capital spending	130
– Additions to NWC	330
Cash flow from assets	$ 49

From the preceding cash flow identity, this $49 cash flow from assets equals the sum of the firm's cash flow to creditors and cash flow to shareholders. We consider these next.

It wouldn't be at all unusual for a growing corporation to have a negative cash flow. As we see next, the negative cash flow means that the firm raised more money by borrowing and selling shares than it paid out to creditors and shareholders that year.

free cash flow
Another name for cash flow from assets.

A NOTE ON "FREE" CASH FLOW   Cash flow from assets sometimes goes by a different name, **free cash flow.** Of course, there is no such thing as "free" cash. Instead, the name refers to cash that the firm is free to distribute to creditors and shareholders because it is not needed for working capital or fixed asset investment. We will stick with "cash flow from assets" as our label for this important concept because, in practice, there is some variation in exactly how free cash flow is computed; different users calculate it in different ways. Nonetheless, whenever you hear the phrase "free cash flow," you should understand that what is being discussed is cash flow from assets or something quite similar.

Cash Flow to Creditors and Shareholders

The cash flows to creditors and shareholders represent the net payments to creditors and owners during the year. They are calculated in a similar way. **Cash flow to creditors** is interest paid less net new borrowing; **cash flow to shareholders** is dividends less net new equity raised.

CASH FLOW TO CREDITORS   Looking at the income statement in Table 2.2, Canadian paid $70 in interest to creditors. From the balance sheets in Table 2.1, long-term debt rose by $454 − 408 = $46. So, Canadian Enterprises paid out $70 in interest, but it borrowed an additional $46. Net cash flow to creditors is thus:

CANADIAN ENTERPRISES
2006 Cash Flow to Creditors

Interest paid	$70
− Net new borrowing	46
Cash flow to creditors	$24

Cash flow to creditors is sometimes called cash flow to bondholders; we use these interchangeably.

CASH FLOW TO SHAREHOLDERS   From the income statement, we see that dividends paid to shareholders amount to $65. To calculate net new equity raised, we need to look at the common share account. This account tells us how many shares the company has sold. During the year, this account rose by $40, so $40 in net new equity was raised. Given this, we have:

CANADIAN ENTERPRISES
2006 Cash Flow to Shareholders

Dividends paid	$65
− Net new equity	40
Cash flow to shareholders	$25

The cash flow to shareholders for 2006 was thus $25.

The last thing that we need to do is to check what the cash flow identity holds to be sure that we didn't make any mistakes. Earlier we found the cash flow from assets is $49. Cash flow to creditors and shareholders is $24 + 25 = $49, so everything checks out. Table 2.4 contains a summary of the various cash flow calculations for future reference.

Two important observations can be drawn from our discussion of cash flow: First, several types of cash flow are relevant to understanding the financial situation of the firm. *Operating cash flow,* defined as earnings before interest and depreciation minus taxes, measures the cash generated from operations not counting capital spending or working capital requirements. It should usually be positive; a firm is in trouble if operating cash flow is negative for a long time because the firm is not generating enough cash to pay operating costs. *Total cash flow* of the firm includes capital spending and additions to net working capital. It will frequently be negative. When a firm is growing at a rapid rate, the spending on inventory and fixed assets can be higher than cash flow from sales.

Second, net income is not cash flow. The net income of Canadian Enterprises in 2006 was $374 million, whereas total cash flow from assets was $49 million. The two numbers are not usually the same. In determining the economic and financial condition of a firm, cash flow is more revealing.

TABLE 2.4
Cash flow summary

The cash flow identity
Cash flow from assets

= Cash flow to creditors (or bondholders)
+ Cash flow to shareholders (or owners)

Cash flow from assets
Cash flow from assets

= Operating cash flow
− Net capital spending
− Additions to net working capital (NWC)

where:
a. Operating cash flow

= Earnings before interest and taxes (EBIT)
+ Depreciation
− Taxes

b. Net capital spending

= Ending net fixed assets
− Beginning net fixed assets
+ Depreciation

c. Additions to NWC

= Ending NWC
− Beginning NWC

Cash flow to creditors (bondholders)
Cash flow to creditors = Interest paid − Net new borrowing
Cash flow to shareholders (owners)
Cash flow to shareholders = Dividends paid − Net new equity raised

EXAMPLE 2.4: Cash Flows for Dole Cola

During the year, Dole Cola, Ltd., had sales and costs of $600 and $300, respectively. Depreciation was $150 and interest paid was $30. Taxes were calculated at a straight 40 percent. Dividends were $30. All figures are in millions of dollars. What was the operating cash flow for Dole? Why is this different from net income?

The easiest thing to do here is to create an income statement. We can then fill in the numbers we need. Dole Cola's income statement follows:

DOLE COLA
2006 Income Statement ($ millions)

Net sales	$600
Cost of goods sold	300
Depreciation	150
Earnings before interest and taxes	$150
Interest paid	30
Taxable income	$120
Taxes	48
Net income	$ 72
Retained earnings	$42
Dividends	30

Net income for Dole is thus $72. We now have all the numbers we need; so referring back to the Canadian Enterprises example, we have:

DOLE COLA
2006 Operating Cash Flow ($ millions)

Earnings before interest and taxes	$150
+ Depreciation	150
− Taxes	48
Operating cash flow	$252

As this example illustrates, operating cash flow is not the same as net income, because depreciation and interest are subtracted out when net income is calculated. If you recall our earlier discussion, we don't subtract these out in computing operating cash flow because depreciation is not a cash expense and interest paid is a financing expense, not an operating expense.

Net Capital Spending

Suppose that beginning net fixed assets were $500 and ending net fixed assets were $750. What was the net capital spending for the year?

From the income statement for Dole, depreciation for the year was $150. Net fixed assets rose by $250. We thus spent $150 to cover the depreciation and an additional $250 as well, for a total of $400.

Change in NWC and Cash Flow from Assets

Suppose that Dole Cola started the year with $2,130 in current assets and $1,620 in current liabilities. The corresponding ending figures were $2,260 and $1,710. What was the addition to NWC during the year? What was cash flow from assets? How does this compare to net income?

Net working capital started out as $2,130 − 1,620 = $510 and ended up at $2,260 − 1,710 = $550. The addition to NWC was thus $550 − 510 = $40. Putting together all the information for Dole we have:

DOLE COLA
2006 Cash Flow from Assets

Operating cash flow	$252
− Net capital spending	400
− Additions to NWC	40
Cash flow from assets	−$188

Dole had a cash flow from assets of negative $188. Net income was positive at $72. Is the fact that cash flow from assets is negative a cause for alarm? Not necessarily. The cash flow here is negative primarily because of a large investment in fixed assets. If these are good investments, the resulting negative cash flow is not a worry.

CASH FLOW TO CREDITORS AND SHAREHOLDERS We saw that Dole Cola had cash flow from assets of −$188. The fact that this is negative means that Dole raised more money in the form of new debt and equity than it paid out for the year. For example, suppose we know that Dole didn't sell any new equity for the year. What was cash flow to shareholders? To bondholders?

Because it didn't raise any new equity, Dole's cash flow to shareholders is just equal to the cash dividend paid:

DOLE COLA
2006 Cash Flow to Shareholders

Dividends paid	$30
− Net new equity	0
Cash flow to shareholders	$30

Now, from the cash flow identity the total cash paid to bondholders and shareholders was −$188. Cash flow to shareholders is $30, so cash flow to bondholders must be equal to −$188 − $30 = −$218:

Cash flow to bondholders + Cash flow to shareholders = −$188
Cash flow to bondholders + $30   = −$188
Cash flow to bondholders   = −$218

From the income statement, interest paid is $30. We can determine net new borrowing as follows:

DOLE COLA
2006 Cash Flow to Bondholders

Interest paid	$ 30
− Net new borrowing	−248
Cash flow to bondholders	−$218

As indicated, since cash flow to bondholders is −$218 and interest paid is $30, Dole must have borrowed $248 during the year to help finance the fixed asset expansion.

CONCEPT QUESTIONS

1. What is the cash flow identity? Explain what it says.

2. What are the components of operating cash flow?

3. Why is interest paid not a component of operating cash flow?

TAXES

Taxes are very important because, as we just saw, cash flows are measured after taxes. In this section, we examine corporate and personal tax rates and how taxes are calculated. We apply this knowledge to see how different types of income are taxed in the hands of individuals and corporations.

The size of the tax bill is determined through tax laws and regulations in the annual budgets of the federal government (administered by Canada Revenue Agency (CRA)) and provincial governments. If the various rules of taxation seem a little bizarre or convoluted to you, keep in mind that tax law is the result of political, as well as economic, forces. According to economic theory, an ideal tax system has three features. First, it should distribute the tax burden equitably, with each taxpayer shouldering a "fair share." Second, the tax system should not change the efficient allocation of resources by markets. If this happened, such distortions would reduce economic welfare. Third, the system should be easy to administer.

The tax law is continually evolving so our discussion cannot make you a tax expert. Rather it gives you an understanding of the tax principles important for financial management along with the ability to ask the right questions when consulting a tax expert.

Individual Tax Rates

Individual tax rates in effect for federal taxes for 2006 are shown in Table 2.5. These rates apply to income from employment (wages and salary) and from unincorporated businesses. Investment income is also taxable. Interest income is taxed at the same rates as employment income, but special provisions reduce the taxes payable on dividends and capital gains. We discuss these in detail later in the chapter. Table 2.5 also provides information on provincial taxes for selected provinces. Other provinces and territories follow similar approaches, although they use different rates and brackets.

TABLE 2.5
Individual income tax rates—2006

Taxable Income	Tax Rate
Federal Taxes	
$ 0–36,378	15.0%
36,379–72,756	22.0
72,757–118,825	26.0
115,826 and over	29.0
British Columbia	
$ 0–33,755	6.05%
33,756–67,511	9.15
67,512–77,511	11.70
77,512–94,121	13.70
94,122 and over	14.70
Alberta	
All income	10.0%
Ontario	
$ 0–34,758	6.05%
34,759–69,516	9.15
69,517 and over	11.16
Quebec	
$ 0–28,710	16.0%
28,711–57,430	20.0
57,431 and over	24.0
Nova Scotia	
$ 0–29,590	8.79%
29,591–59,180	14.95
59,181–93,000	16.67
93,001 and over	17.50

Source: KPMG, *www.kpmg.ca/*

To illustrate, suppose you live in Ontario and have a taxable income over $75,000. Your tax on the next dollar is:[5]

37.16% = federal tax rate + provincial tax rate = 26% + 11.16%

Average versus Marginal Tax Rates

In making financial decisions, it is frequently important to distinguish between average and marginal tax rates. Your **average tax rate** is your tax bill divided by your taxable income; in other words, the percentage of your income that goes to pay taxes. Your **marginal tax rate** is the extra tax you would pay if you earned one more dollar. The percentage tax rates shown in Table 2.5 are all marginal rates. To put it another way, the tax rates in Table 2.5 apply to the part of income in the indicated range only, not all income.

Following the equity principle, individual taxes are designed to be progressive with higher incomes taxed at a higher rate. In contrast, with a flat rate tax, there is only one tax rate, and this rate is the same for all income levels. With such a tax, the marginal tax rate is always the same as the average tax rate. As it stands now, individual taxation in Canada is progressive but approaches a flat rate for the highest incomes. Alberta has introduced a flat tax.

Normally, the marginal tax rate is relevant for decision making. Any new cash flows are taxed at that marginal rate. Since financial decisions usually involve new cash flows or changes in existing ones, this rate tells us the marginal effect on our tax bill.

Taxes on Investment Income

When introducing the topic of taxes, we warned that tax laws are not always logical. The treatment of dividends in Canada is at least a partial exception because there are two clear goals: First, corporations pay dividends from aftertax income so tax laws shelter dividends from full tax in the hands of shareholders. This diminishes double taxation, which would violate the principle of equitable taxation. Second, tax shelters for dividends apply only to dividends paid by Canadian corporations. The result is to encourage Canadian investors to invest in Canadian firms as opposed to foreign companies.[6]

With these goals in mind, to see how dividends are taxed, we start with common shares held by individual investors. Table 2.6 shows the **dividend tax credit** calculation. The steps follow the instructions on federal tax returns. Actual dividends are grossed up by 45 percent and federal tax is calculated on the grossed up figure. A dividend tax credit of 19 percent of the grossed up dividend is subtracted from the federal tax to get the federal tax payable. The provincial tax (for Ontario in this example) is calculated and added.

As an alternative to the calculations in Table 2.6, the following equation represents the marginal tax rate on dividends in Ontario:[7]

Effective tax rate on dividends =
1.45 {[(Federal tax rate) − .19] + [(Provincial tax rate) − .0716]}

The result is that dividends are taxed far more lightly than ordinary income.

Dividend taxation became lighter under recent changes with the stated goal of making dividend-paying stocks more attractive in comparison to income trusts. The federal government announced an increase in the gross-up of the federal dividend tax credit to the levels shown in Table 2.6.

Individual Canadian investors also benefit from a tax reduction for **capital gains.** Capital gains arise when an investment increases in value above its purchase price. For capital gains, taxes

average tax rate
Total taxes paid divided by total taxable income.

marginal tax rate
Amount of tax payable on the next dollar earned.

dividend tax credit
Tax formula that reduces the effective tax rate on dividends.

capital gains
The increase in value of an investment over its purchase price.

---

5 Actual rates are somewhat higher, as we ignore surtaxes that apply in higher brackets.

6 Evidence that the dividend tax credit causes investors to favour Canadian stocks is provided in L. Booth, "The Dividend Tax Credit and Canadian Ownership Objectives," *Canadian Journal of Economics* 20 (May 1987).

7 A. H. R. Davis and G. E. Pinches, *Canadian Financial Management,* 2d ed. (New York: Harper Collins, 1991), p. 26.

TABLE 2.6

Investment income tax treatment for Ontario residents in top bracket (over $118,826) for 2006

Interest Tax Treatment

Interest	1000.00
Federal tax at 29%	290.00
Provincial tax at 11.16%	111.60
Total tax	401.60

Capital Gains Tax Treatment

Capital gains	1000.00
Taxable capital gains (50% × $1,000)	500.00
Federal tax at 29%	145.00
Provincial tax at 11.16%	55.80
Total tax	200.80

Dividend Tax Treatment

Dividends	1000.00
Gross up at 45%	450.00
Grossed up dividend	1450.00
Federal tax at 29%	420.50
Less dividend tax credit (19% × $1,450)	275.50
Federal tax payable	145.00
Provincial tax at 11.16% (11.16% × $1,450)	161.82
Less dividend tax credit (7.16% × $1,450)	103.82
Provincial tax payable	58.00
Total tax	203.00

Effective combined tax rates for Ontario residents in top bracket for 2006

Salary and interest	40.16%
Capital gains	20.08%
Dividends	20.30%

Source: KPMG, *www.kpmg.ca/*

apply at 50 percent of the applicable marginal rate. For example, individuals in the highest bracket in Table 2.6 would pay taxes on capital gains at a nominal rate of 20.08 percent = 40.16% × .50.

At the bottom of Table 2.6, we compare the effective tax rates combining federal and provincial taxes including surtaxes on salary and interest, capital gains, and dividends. The table shows that, for an Ontario resident in the top bracket, salary and interest are taxed far more heavily than investment income. It also shows that capital gains are taxed significantly less than other income.

realized capital gains
The increase in value of an investment, when converted to cash.

In practice, capital gains are lightly taxed because individuals pay taxes on **realized capital gains** only when stock is sold. Because many individuals hold shares for a long time (have unrealized capital gains), the time value of money dramatically reduces the effective tax rate on capital gains.[8] Also, investors can manage capital gain realization to offset with losses in many cases.

Corporate Taxes

Canadian corporations, like individuals, are subject to taxes levied by the federal and provincial governments. Corporate taxes are passed on to consumers through higher prices, to workers through lower wages, or to investors through lower returns.

Table 2.7 shows corporate tax rates using Ontario as an example. You can see from the table that small corporations (income less than $300,000) and, to a lesser degree, manufacturing and processing companies, receive a tax break in the form of lower rates.

Comparing the rates in Table 2.7 with the personal tax rates in Table 2.5 appears to reveal a tax advantage for small businesses and professionals that form corporations. The tax rate on corporate income of, say, $150,000 is less than the personal tax rate assessed on the income of unincorporated

---

8 D. Booth and D. J. Johnston, "The Ex-Dividend Day Behavior of Canadian Stock Prices: Tax Changes and Clientele Effects," *Journal of Finance* 39 (June 1984). Booth and Johnston find a "very low effective tax rate on capital gains" in the 1970s. They compare their results with a U.S. study that found an effective tax rate on capital gains under 7 percent.

	Federal	Ontario	Combined
Basic corporations	22.1%	14.01%	36.1%
All small corporations with a taxable income less than $300,000	13.1	5.50	18.6

TABLE 2.7
Corporate tax rates in
percentages in 2006

Source: *www.kpmg.ca/*

businesses. But this is oversimplified because dividends paid to the owners are also taxed, as we saw earlier.

Taxable Income

In Section 2.2 we discussed the income statement for Canadian Enterprises (Table 2.2); it includes both dividends and interest paid. An important difference is that interest paid is deducted from EBIT in calculating income but dividends paid are not. Because interest is a tax-deductible expense, debt financing has a tax advantage over financing with common shares. To illustrate, Table 2.2 shows that Canadian Enterprises paid $250 million in taxes on taxable income of $624 million. The firm's tax rate is $250/624 = 40%. This means that to pay another $1 in dividends, Canadian Enterprises must increase EBIT by $1.67. Of the marginal $1.67 EBIT, 40 percent, or 67 cents, goes in taxes, leaving $1 to increase dividends. In general, a taxable firm must earn 1/ (1 – Tax rate) in additional EBIT for each extra dollar of dividends. Because interest is tax deductible, Canadian Enterprises needs to earn only $1 more in EBIT to be able to pay $1 in added interest.

The tables are turned when we contrast interest and dividends earned by the firm. Interest earned is fully taxable just like any other form of ordinary income. Dividends on common shares received from other Canadian corporations qualify for a 100 percent exemption and are received tax free.[9]

Capital Gains and Carry-forward and Carry-back

When a firm disposes of an asset for more than it paid originally, the difference is a capital gain. As with individuals, firms receive favourable tax treatment on capital gains. At the time of writing, capital gains received by corporations are taxed at 50 percent of the marginal tax rate.

When calculating capital gains for tax purposes, a firm nets out all capital losses in the same year. If capital losses exceed capital gains, the net capital loss may be carried back to reduce taxable capital gains in the three prior years. Under the **carry-back** feature, a firm files a revised tax return and receives a refund of prior years' taxes. For example, suppose Canadian Enterprises experienced a net capital loss of $1 million in 2006 and net capital gains of $300,000 in 2005, $200,000 in 2004, and $150,000 in 2003. Canadian could carry back a total of $650,000 to get a refund on its taxes. The remaining $350,000 can be carried forward indefinitely to reduce future taxes on capital gains.

loss carry-forward, carry-back
Using a year's capital losses to offset capital gains in past or future years.

A similar **carry-forward** provision applies to operating losses. The carry-back period is three years and carry-forward is allowed up to seven years.

INCOME TRUST INCOME AND TAXATION

As stated in Chapter 1, business income trusts are structured so that income is taxed only once in the hands of unitholders. To achieve this, the operating entity (taxed as a corporation) pays the income trust interest, royalty or lease payments, which are usually tax deductible. Since the operating entity usually pays the income trust enough to reduce operating income to zero, the operating company pays virtually no tax. The interest, royalty or lease payments received by the trust are not taxable because it is not a corporation but a partnership. Rather, this cash flow is passed through to the unitholders, resulting in the desired level of taxation.

Table 2.8 compares income trust taxation against the tax treatment of dividends to show how the net amount received by investors is the same under current tax rates. As we explained in Chapter 1, at the end of October 2006, the federal government announced plans to tax income

---

9 The situation is more complicated for preferred stock dividends, as we discuss in Chapter 7.

TABLE 2.8
Taxation of Income Trust
Distributions vs. Dividends

	Dividends paid by large corporations	Interest and taxable distribution of income trusts
A. Income	$100	100
B. Corporate income tax[1]	32	0
C. Amount distributed to investor	68	100
D. Amount included in income	99	100
E. Personal Income tax (46%[2] of D)	46	46
F. Dividend tax credit	(32)[3]	0
G. Net personal income tax	14	46
H. Total tax paid (B + G)	46	46
I. Investor's net receipt	54	54

1 The combined average federal-provincial corporate income tax rate in 2010.
2 The average top federal-provincial personal income tax rate.
3 Assumes that the provinces and territories increase their dividend tax credits for eligible dividends to equal their general corporate income tax rates.

Source: *http://www.fin.gc.ca/budget06/bp/bpc3be.htm#dividends*

trusts as corporations. Applicable to trusts in existence in October 2006 starting in 2011 and immediately to new trusts, these plans are expected (at the time of writing) to put an end to new trust conversions.[10]

Income trust structure has worked well for trusts in stable businesses with strong cashflow generating abilities; examples are Yellow Pages Income Fund or Boston Pizza Royalty Fund. As cashflows fluctuate in riskier industries, trusts have had to reduce or suspend distributions. When this happened to Halterm — a trust based on the container port business in Halifax — in 2003, the unit price dropped by 59 percent.[11]

2.5 CAPITAL COST ALLOWANCE

capital cost allowance (CCA)
Depreciation for tax purposes, not necessarily the same as depreciation under GAAP.

Capital cost allowance (CCA) is depreciation for tax purposes in Canada. Capital cost allowance is deducted in determining income. Because the tax law reflects various political compromises, CCA is not the same as depreciation under GAAP so there is no reason calculation of a firm's income under tax rules has to be the same as under GAAP. For example, taxable corporate income may often be lower than accounting income because the company is allowed to use accelerated capital cost allowance rules in computing depreciation for tax purposes while using straight-line depreciation for GAAP reporting.[12]

CCA calculation begins by assigning every capital asset to a particular class. An asset's class establishes its maximum CCA rate for tax purposes. Intangible assets like leasehold improvements in Table 2.9 follow straight-line depreciation for CCA. For all other assets, CCA follows the declining balance method. The CCA for each year is computed by multiplying the asset's book value for tax purposes, called undepreciated capital cost (UCC), by the appropriate rate.

The CCA system is unique to Canada and differs in many respects from the ACRS depreciation method used in the United States. One key difference is that in the Canadian system, the expected salvage value (what we think the asset will be worth when we dispose of it) and the actual expected economic life (how long we expect the asset to be in service) are not explicitly considered in the calculation of capital cost allowance. Some typical CCA classes and their respective CCA rates are described in Table 2.9.

To illustrate how capital cost allowance is calculated, suppose your firm is considering buying a van costing $30,000, including any setup costs that must (by law) be capitalized. (No rational, profitable business would capitalize, for tax purposes, anything that could legally be expensed.)

---

10 ScotiaMcLeod, "Federal Government to Implement New Tax Fairness Plan," November 1, 2006.

11 R. Carrick, "Halterm Income Fund provides a cautionary tale for investors," *Globe and Mail*, Report on Business, March 27, 2003.

12 Where taxable income is less than accounting income, the difference goes into a long-term liability account on the balance sheet labelled deferred taxes.

Table 2.9 shows that vans fall in Class 10 with a 30 percent CCA rate. To calculate the CCA, we follow CRA's **half-year rule** that allows us to figure CCA on only half of the asset's installed cost in the first year it is put in use. Table 2.10 shows the CCA for our van for the first five years.

As we pointed out, in calculating CCA under current tax law, the economic life and future market value of the asset are not an issue. As a result, the UCC of an asset can differ substantially from its actual market value. With our $30,000 van, UCC after the first year is $15,000 less the first year's CCA of $4,500, or $10,500. The remaining UCC values are summarized in Table 2.10. After five years, the undepreciated capital cost of the van is $6,123.

Asset Purchases and Sales

When an asset is sold, the UCC in its asset class (or pool) is reduced by what is realized on the asset or by its original cost, whichever is less. This amount is called the adjusted cost of disposal. Suppose we wanted to sell the van in our earlier example after five years. Based on historical averages of resale prices, it will be worth, say, 25 percent of the purchase price or .25 × $30,000 = $7,500. Since the price of $7,500 is less than the original cost, the adjusted cost of disposal is $7,500 and the UCC in Class 10 is reduced by this amount.

Table 2.10 shows that the van has a UCC after five years of $6,123. The $7,500 removed from the pool is $1,377 more than the undepreciated capital cost of the van we are selling, and future CCA deductions will be reduced as the pool continues. On the other hand, if we had sold the van for, say, $4,000, the UCC in Class 10 would be reduced by $4,000 and the $2,123 excess of UCC

TABLE 2.9
Common capital cost
allowance classes

Class	Rate	Assets
1	4%	Buildings acquired after 1987
8	20	Furniture, photocopiers
10	30	Vans, trucks, tractors, and equipment
13	Straight-line	Leasehold improvements
22	50	Pollution control equipment
43	30	Manufacturing equipment

TABLE 2.10
Capital cost allowance
for a van

Year	Beginning UCC	CCA	Ending UCC
1	$15,000*	$4,500	$10,500
2	25,500†	7,650	17,850
3	17,850	5,355	12,495
4	12,495	3,748	8,747
5	8,747	2,624	6,123

*One-half of $30,000.

†Year 1 ending balance + Remaining half of $30,000.

EXAMPLE 2.5: Capital Cost Allowance Incentives in Practice

Since capital cost allowance is deducted in computing income, larger CCA rates reduce taxes and increase cash flows. As we pointed out earlier, finance ministers sometimes tinker with the CCA rates to create incentives. For example, in a federal budget a few years ago, the minister announced an increase in CCA rates from 20 to 30 percent for manufacturing and processing assets. The combined federal/provincial corporate tax rate for this sector is 36.1 percent in Ontario.

Mississauga Manufacturing was planning to acquire new processing equipment to enhance efficiency and its ability to compete with U.S. firms. The equipment had an installed cost of $1 million. How much additional tax will the new measure save Mississauga in the first year the equipment is put into use?

Under the half-year rule, UCC for the first year is 1/2 × $1 million = $500,000. The CCA deductions under the old and new rates are:

Old rate: CCA = .20 × $500,000 = $100,000
New rate: CCA = .30 × $500,000 = $150,000

Because the firm deducts CCA in figuring taxable income, taxable income will be reduced by the incremental CCA of $50,000. With $50,000 less in taxable income, Mississauga Manufacturing's combined tax bill would drop by $50,000 × .361 = $18,050.

over the sale price would remain in the pool. Then, future CCA increases as the declining balance calculations depreciate the $2,123 excess UCC to infinity.

So far we focused on CCA calculations for one asset. In practice, firms often buy and sell assets from a given class in the course of a year. In this case, we apply the **net acquisitions** rule. From the total installed cost of all acquisitions, we subtract the adjusted cost of disposal of all assets in the pool. The result is net acquisitions for the asset class. If net acquisitions are positive, we apply the half-year rule and calculate CCA as we did earlier. If net acquisitions is negative, there is no adjustment for the half-year rule.

net acquisitions
Total installed cost of capital acquisitions minus adjusted cost of any disposals within an asset pool.

WHEN AN ASSET POOL IS TERMINATED   Suppose your firm decides to contract out all transport and to sell all company vehicles. If the company owns no other Class 10 assets, the asset pool in this class is terminated. As before, the adjusted cost of disposal is the net sales proceeds or the total installed cost of all the pool assets, whichever is less. This adjusted cost of disposal is subtracted from the total UCC in the pool. So far, the steps are exactly the same as in our van example where the pool continued. What happens next is different. Unless the adjusted cost of disposal just happens to equal the UCC exactly, a positive or negative UCC balance remains and this has tax implications.

A positive UCC balance remains when the adjusted cost of disposal is less than UCC before the sale. In this case, the firm has a **terminal loss** equal to the remaining UCC. This loss is deductible from income for the year. For example, if we sell the van after two years for $10,000, the UCC of $17,850 in Table 2.10 exceeds the market value by $7,850. The terminal loss of $7,850 gives rise to a tax saving of $.40 \times \$7,850 = \$3,140$. (We assume the tax rate is 40 percent.)

terminal loss
The difference between UCC and adjusted cost of disposal when the UCC is greater.

A negative UCC balance occurs when the adjusted cost of disposal exceeds UCC, in the pool. To illustrate, return to our van example and suppose that this van is the only Class 10 asset our company owns when it sells the pool for $7,500 after five years. There is a $1,377 excess of adjusted cost of disposal ($7,500 - 6,123$) over UCC, so the final UCC credit balance is $1,377.

The company must pay tax at its ordinary tax rate on this balance. The reason that taxes must be paid is that the difference in adjusted cost of disposal and UCC is excess CCA **recaptured** when the asset is sold. We overdepreciated the asset by $7,500 - \$6,123 = \$1,377$. Because we deducted $1,377 too much in CCA, we paid $550.80 too little in taxes (at 40 percent), and we simply have to make up the difference.

recaptured depreciation
The taxable difference between adjusted cost of disposal and UCC when UCC is smaller.

EXAMPLE 2.6: CCA Calculations

Staple Supply Ltd. has just purchased a new computerized information system with an installed cost of $160,000. The computer is in Class 45 for CCA purposes. What are the yearly capital cost allowances? Based on historical experience, we think that the system will be worth only $10,000 when we get rid of it in four years. What will be the tax consequences of the sale if the company has several other computers still in use in four years? Now suppose that Staple Supply will sell all its assets and wind up the company in four years. What is the total aftertax cash flow from the sale?

In Table 2.11, at the end of Year 4, the remaining balance for the specific computer system mentioned would be $20,630.[13] The pool is reduced by $10,000, but it will continue to be depreciated. There are no tax consequences in Year 4. This is only the case when the pool is active. If this were the only computer system, we would have been closing the pool and would have been able to claim a terminal loss of $20,630 - \$10,000 = \$10,630$.

TABLE 2.11	Year	Beginning UCC	CCA	Ending UCC
CCA for computer system	1	$ 80,000*	$36,000	$44,000
	2	124,000†	55,800	68,200
	3	68,200	30,690	37,510
	4	37,510	16,880	20,630

*One-half of $160,000.
†Year 1 ending balance + Remaining half of $160,000.

---

13 In actuality, the capital cost allowance for the entire pool will be calculated at once, without specific identification of each computer system.

Notice that this is *not* a tax on a capital gain. As a general rule, a capital gain only occurs if the market price exceeds the original cost. To illustrate a capital gain, suppose that instead of buying the van, our firm purchased a classic car for $50,000. After five years, the classic car will be sold for $75,000. The sale price would exceed the purchase price, so the adjusted cost of disposal is $50,000 and UCC pool is reduced by this amount. The total negative balance left in the UCC pool is $50,000 − $6,123 = $43,877 and this is recaptured CCA. In addition, the firm has a capital gain of $75,000 − $50,000 = $25,000, the difference between the sale price and the original cost.[14]

CONCEPT QUESTIONS

1. What is the difference between capital cost allowance and GAAP depreciation?

2. Why do governments sometimes increase CCA rates?

3. Reconsider the CCA increase discussed in Example 2.5. How effective do you think it was in stimulating investment? Why?

SUMMARY AND CONCLUSIONS

This chapter has introduced you to some of the basics of financial statements, taxes, and cash flow. The Nortel example that was introduced at the start of the chapter shows just how important these issues can be for shareholders. In this chapter, we saw that:

1. The book values on an accounting balance sheet can be very different from market values. The goal of financial management is to maximize the market value of the stock, not its book value.

2. Net income as it is computed on the income statement is not cash flow. A primary reason is that depreciation, a non-cash expense, is deducted when net income is computed.

3. Marginal and average tax rates can be different; the marginal tax rate is relevant for most financial decisions.

4. There is a cash flow identity much like the balance sheet identity. It says that cash flow from assets equals cash flow to bondholders and shareholders. The calculation of cash flow from financial statements isn't difficult. Care must be taken in handling non-cash expenses, such as depreciation, and in not confusing operating costs with financial costs. Most of all, it is important not to confuse book values with market values and accounting income with cash flow.

5. Different types of Canadian investment income, dividends, interest, and capital gains are taxed differently.

6. Corporate income taxes create a tax advantage for debt financing (paying tax-deductible interest) over equity financing (paying dividends). Chapter 15 discusses this in depth.

7. Capital cost allowance (CCA) is depreciation for tax purposes in Canada. CCA calculations are important for determining cash flows.

Key Terms

---

14 This example shows that it is possible to have a recapture of CCA without closing out a pool if the UCC balance goes negative.

Chapter Review Problems and Self-Test

2.1 Cash Flow for B.C. Resources Ltd. This problem will give you some practice working with financial statements and calculating cash flow. Based on the following information for B.C. Resources Ltd., prepare an income statement for 2006 and balance sheets for 2005 and 2006. Next, following our Canadian Enterprises examples in the chapter, calculate cash flow for B.C. Resources, cash flow to bondholders, and cash flow to shareholders for 2006. Use a 40 percent tax rate throughout. You can check your answers in the next section.

	2005	2006
Sales	$4,203	$4,507
Cost of goods sold	2,422	2,633
Depreciation	785	952
Interest	180	196
Dividends	225	250
Current assets	2,205	2,429
Net fixed assets	7,344	7,650
Current liabilities	1,003	1,255
Long-term debt	3,106	2,085

Answers to Self-Test Problems

2.1 In preparing the balance sheets, remember that shareholders' equity is the residual and can be found using the equation:

Total assets = Total liabilities + Total equity

With this in mind, B.C. Resources' balance sheets are as follows:

B.C. RESOURCES LTD.
Balance Sheets as of December 31, 2005 and 2006

	2005	2006		2005	2006
Current assets	$2,205	$ 2,429	Current liabilities	$1,003	$ 1,255
Net fixed assets	7,344	7,650	Long-term debt	3,106	2,085
			Equity	5,440	6,739
Total assets	$9,549	$10,079	Total liabilities and shareholders' equity	$9,549	$10,079

The income statement is straightforward:

B.C. RESOURCES LTD.
2006 Income Statement

Sales		$4,507
Costs of goods sold		2,633
Depreciation		952
Earnings before interest and taxes		$ 922
Interest paid		196
Taxable income		$ 726
Taxes (40%)		290
Net income		436
Dividends	$250	
Addition to retained earnings	186	

Notice that we've used a flat 40 percent tax rate. Also notice that retained earnings are just net income less cash dividends. We can now pick up the figures we need to get operating cash flow:

B.C. RESOURCES LTD.
2006 Operating Cash Flow

Earnings before interest and taxes	$ 922
+ Depreciation	952
– Taxes	290
Operating cash flow	$1,584

Next, we get the capital spending for the year by looking at the change in fixed assets, remembering to account for the depreciation:

Ending net fixed assets	$7,650
– Beginning net fixed assets	7,344
+ Depreciation	952
Net capital spending	$1,258

After calculating beginning and ending NWC, we take the difference to get the addition to NWC:

Ending NWC	$1,174
– Beginning NWC	1,202
Change in NWC	–$ 28

We now combine operating cash flow, net capital spending, and the addition to net working capital to get the total cash flow from assets:

B.C. RESOURCES LTD.
2006 Cash Flow from Assets

Operating cash flow	$1,584
– Net capital spending	1,258
– Change in NWC	–28
Cash flow from assets	$ 354

To get cash flow to creditors, notice that long-term borrowing decreased by $1,021 during the year and that interest paid was $196:

B.C. RESOURCES LTD.
2006 Cash Flow to Creditors

Interest paid	$ 196
– Net new borrowing	–1,021
Cash flow to creditors	$1,217

Finally, dividends paid were $250. To get net new equity, we have to do some extra calculating. Total equity was found by balancing the balance sheets. During 2006, equity increased by $6,739 – 5,440 = $1,299. Of this increase, $186 was from additions to retained earnings, so $1,113 in new equity was raised during the year. Cash flow to shareholders was thus:

B.C. RESOURCES LTD.
2006 Cash Flow to Shareholders

Dividends paid	$ 250
– Net new equity	–1,113
Cash flow to shareholders	–$ 863

As a check, notice that cash flow from assets, $354, does equal cash flow to creditors plus cash flow to shareholders ($1,217 – 863 = $354).

Concepts Review and Critical Thinking Questions

1. What does liquidity measure? Explain the trade-off a firm faces between high liquidity and low liquidity levels.

2. Why is it that the revenue and cost figures shown on a standard income statement may not be representative of the actual cash inflows and outflows that occurred during a period?

3. In preparing a balance sheet, why do you think standard accounting practice focuses on historical cost rather than market value?

4. In comparing accounting net income and operating cash flow, what two items do you find in net income that are not in operating cash flow? Explain what each is and why it is excluded in operating cash flow.

5. Under standard accounting rules, it is possible for a company's liabilities to exceed its assets. When this occurs, the owners' equity is negative. Can this happen with market values? Why or why not?

6. Suppose a company's cash flow from assets was negative for a particular period. Is this necessarily a good sign or a bad sign?

7. Suppose a company's operating cash flow was negative for several years running. Is this necessarily a good sign or a bad sign?

8. Could a company's change in NWC be negative in a given year? Explain how this might come about. What about net capital spending?

9. Could a company's cash flow to stockholders be negative in a given year? Explain how this might come about. What about cash flow to creditors?

Questions and Problems

**Basic
(Questions
1–12)**

1. **Building a Balance Sheet**   Penguin Pucks, Inc., has current assets of $5,000, net fixed assets of $23,000, current liabilities of $4,300, and long-term debt of $13,000. What is the value of the shareholders' equity account for this firm? How much is net working capital?

Basic
(continued)

2. **Building an Income Statement**   Papa Roach Exterminators, Inc., has sales of $527,000, costs of $280,000, depreciation expense of $38,000, interest expense of $15,000, and a tax rate of 35 percent. What is the net income for this firm?

3. **Dividends and Retained Earnings**   Suppose the firm in Problem 2 paid out $48,000 in cash dividends. What is the addition to retained earnings?

4. **Per-Share Earnings and Dividends**   Suppose the firm in Problem 3 had 30,000 shares of common stock outstanding. What is the earnings per share, or EPS, figure? What is the dividends per share figure?

5. **Market Values and Book Values**   Klingon Widgets, Inc., purchased new cloaking machinery three years ago for $7 million. The machinery can be sold to the Romulans today for $3.2 million. Klingon's current balance sheet shows net fixed assets of $4,000,000, current liabilities of $2,200,000, and net working capital of $900,000. If all the current assets were liquidated today, the company would receive $2.8 million cash. What is the book value of Klingon's assets today? What is the market value?

6. **Calculating Taxes**   The Herrera Co. had $273,000 in 2005 taxable income. Using the rates from Table 2.7 in the chapter, calculate the company's 2005 income taxes.

7. **Calculating OCF**   Ranney, Inc., has sales of $13,500, costs of $5,400, depreciation expense of $1,200, and interest expense of $680. If the tax rate is 35 percent, what is the operating cash flow, or OCF?

8. **Calculating Net Capital Spending**   Gordon Driving School's 2004 balance sheet showed net fixed assets of $4.2 million, and the 2005 balance sheet showed net fixed assets of $4.7 million. The company's 2005 income statement showed a depreciation expense of $925,000. What was Gordon's net capital spending for 2005?

9. **Calculating Additions to NWC**   The 2004 balance sheet of Rock 'N' Roll Records, Inc., showed current assets of $1,600 and current liabilities of $940. The 2005 balance sheet showed current assets of $1,720 and current liabilities of $1,180. What was the company's 2005 change in net working capital, or NWC?

10. **Cash Flow to Creditors**   The 2004 balance sheet of Anna's Tennis Shop, Inc., showed long-term debt of $2.8 million, and the 2005 balance sheet showed long-term debt of $3.1 million. The 2005 income statement showed an interest expense of $340,000. What was the firm's cash flow to creditors during 2005?

11. **Cash Flow to Shareholders**   The 2004 balance sheet of Anna's Tennis Shop, Inc., showed $820,000 in the common stock account and $6.8 million in the retained earnings account. The 2005 balance sheet showed $855,000 and $7.6 million in the same two accounts, respectively. If the company paid out $600,000 in cash dividends during 2005, what was the cash flow to stockholders for the year?

12. **Calculating Total Cash Flows**   Given the information for Anna's Tennis Shop, Inc., in Problems 11 and 12, suppose you also know that the firm's net capital spending for 2005 was $760,000, and that the firm reduced its net working capital investment by $165,000. What was the firm's 2005 operating cash flow, or OCF?

Intermediate
(Questions
13–23)

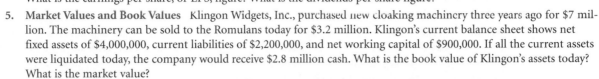

13. **Calculating Total Cash Flows**   Bedrock Gravel Corp. shows the following information on its 2005 income statement: sales = $145,000; costs = $86,000; other expenses = $4,900; depreciation expense = $7,000; interest expense = $15,000; taxes = $12,840; dividends = $8,700. In addition, you're told that the firm issued $6,450 in new equity during 2005, and redeemed $6,500 in outstanding long-term debt.

   a. What is the 2005 operating cash flow?

   b. What is the 2005 cash flow to creditors?

   c. What is the 2005 cash flow to stockholders?

   d. If net fixed assets increased by $5,000 during the year, what was the addition to NWC?

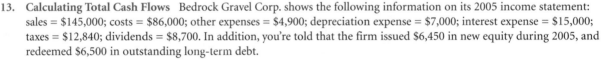

14. **Using Income Statements**   Given the following information for Papa Joe Pizza Co., calculate the depreciation expense: sales = $29,000; costs = $13,000; addition to retained earnings = $4,500; dividends paid = $900; interest expense = $1,600; tax rate = 35 percent.

15. **Preparing a Balance Sheet**   Prepare a 2005 balance sheet for Tim's Couch Corp. based on the following information: cash = $175,000; patents and copyrights = $720,000; accounts payable = $430,000; accounts receivable = $140,000; tangible net fixed assets = $2,900,000; inventory = $265,000; notes payable = $180,000; accumulated retained earnings = $1,240,000; long-term debt = $1,430,000.

16. **Residual Claims**   Clapper's Clippers, Inc., is obligated to pay its creditors $3,500 during the year.

   a. What is the market value of the shareholders' equity if assets have a market value of $4,300?

   b. What if assets equal $3,200?

17. **Marginal versus Average Tax Rates**   (Refer to Table 2.7.) Corporation Growth has $85,000 in taxable income, and Corporation Income has $8,500,000 in taxable income.

   a. What is the tax bill for each firm?

   b. Suppose both firms have identified a new project that will increase taxable income by $10,000. How much in additional taxes will each firm pay? Why is this amount the same?

Intermediate
(continued)

18. **Net Income and OCF**   During 2006, Raines Umbrella Corp. had sales of $850,000. Cost of goods sold, administrative and selling expenses, and depreciation expenses were $630,000, $120,000, and $130,000, respectively. In addition, the company had an interest expense of $85,000 and a tax rate of 35 percent. (Ignore any tax loss carry-back or carry-forward provisions.)

    a. What is Raines's net income for 2006?

    b. What is its operating cash flow?

    c. Explain your results in (a) and (b).

19. **Accounting Values versus Cash Flows**   In Problem 18, suppose Raines Umbrella Corp. paid out $30,000 in cash dividends. Is this possible? If spending on net fixed assets and net working capital was zero, and if no new stock was issued during the year, what do you know about the firm's long-term debt account?

20. **Calculating Cash Flows**   Cusic Industries had the following operating results for 2006: sales = $12,800; cost of goods sold = $10,400; depreciation expense = $1,900; interest expense = $450; dividends paid = $500. At the beginning of the year, net fixed assets were $9,100, current assets were $3,200, and current liabilities were $1,800. At the end of the year, net fixed assets were $9,700, current assets were $3,850, and current liabilities were $2,100. The tax rate for 2006 was 40 percent.

    a. What is net income for 2006?

    b. What is the operating cash flow for 2006?

    c. What is the cash flow from assets for 2006? Is this possible? Explain.

    d. If no new debt was issued during the year, what is the cash flow to creditors? What is the cash flow to stockholders? Explain and interpret the positive and negative signs of your answers in (a) through (d).

21. **Calculating Cash Flows**   Consider the following abbreviated financial statements for Parrothead Enterprises:

PARROTHEAD ENTERPRISES 2005 and 2006 Partial Balance Sheets					
Assets			**Liabilities and Owners' Equity**		
	2005	**2006**		**2005**	**2006**
Current assets	$ 650	$ 705	Current liabilities	$ 265	$ 290
Net fixed assets	2,900	3,400	Long-term debt	1,500	1,720

PARROTHEAD ENTERPRISES 2006 Income Statement	
Sales	$8,600
Costs	4,150
Depreciation	800
Interest paid	216

    a. What is owners' equity for 2005 and 2006?

    b. What is the change in net working capital for 2006?

    c. In 2006, Parrothead Enterprises purchased $1,500 in new fixed assets. How much in fixed assets did Parrothead Enterprises sell? What is the cash flow from assets for the year? (The tax rate is 35 percent.)

    d. During 2006, Parrothead Enterprises raised $300 in new long-term debt. How much long-term debt must Parrothead Enterprises have paid off during the year? What is the cash flow to creditors?

22. **Income Trust Taxation**   Quality Cars Income Trust generated $500,000 in net income before tax last year. If corporate tax is 37%, personal dividend tax is 20%, and taxes on personal income and interest are 44%, what would be the amount distributed to income trust unitholders? What amount would investors receive after taxes have been paid?

23. **Income Trust Distributions vs. Corporate Dividends**   The Payout Company is currently structured as a corporation. It is considering restructuring the company to become an income trust, but is unsure if this would benefit shareholders. Company executives have asked for your advice. They tell you that the corporate tax rate is 32%, last year's net income before tax is $450,000 and there are 10,000 outstanding shares. If the company decides to restructure into an income trust, one share will become one income trust unit. From your experience doing your own tax returns, you know that dividends are taxed at 20% and income and interest income is taxed at 46%. Is it worth it for the Payout Company to restructure into an income trust? If so, how much more would an investor gain if that investor owned 1,000 units?

Challenge
(Questions
24–36)

24. **Net Fixed Assets and Depreciation**   On the balance sheet, the net fixed assets (NFA) account is equal to the gross fixed assets (FA) account, which records the acquisition cost of fixed assets, minus the accumulated depreciation (AD) account, which records the total depreciation taken by the firm against its fixed assets. Using the fact that NFA = FA − AD, show that the expression given in the chapter for net capital spending, $NFA_{end} - NFA_{beg} + D$ (where D is the depreciation expense during the year), is equivalent to $FA_{end} - FA_{beg}$.

Challenge
(continued) Use the following information for Taco Swell, Inc., for Problems 25 and 26 (assume the tax rate is 40 percent):

	2005	2006
Sales	$4,018	$4,312
Depreciation	577	578
Cost of goods sold	1,382	1,569
Other expenses	328	274
Interest	269	309
Cash	2,107	2,155
Accounts receivable	2,789	3,142
Short-term notes payable	407	382
Long-term debt	7,056	8,232
Net fixed assets	17,669	18,091
Accounts payable	2,213	2,146
Inventory	4,959	5,096
Dividends	490	539

25. **Financial Statements** Draw up an income statement and balance sheet for this company for 2005 and 2006.

26. **Calculating Cash Flow** For 2006, calculate the cash flow from assets, cash flow to creditors, and cash flow to stock-holders.

27. **Taxes on Investment Income** Mary Song, an Alberta investor, receives $50,000 in dividends from B.C. Forest Products shares, $20,000 in interest from a deposit in a chartered bank, and a $20,000 capital gain from Central B.C. Mines shares. Use the information in Table 2.5 to calculate the aftertax cash flow from each investment. Ms. Song's federal tax rate is 29 percent.

28. **Investment Income** Assuming that Ms. Song's cash flows in Problem 27 came from equal investments of $150,000 each, find her *aftertax* rate of return on each investment.

29. **CCA** Mississauga Manufacturing Ltd. just invested in some new processing machinery to take advantage of more favourable CCA rates in a new federal budget. The machinery qualifies for 25 percent CCA rate and has an installed cost of $4,500,000. Calculate the CCA and UCC for the first five years.

30. **UCC** A piece of newly purchased industrial equipment costs $1,000,000. It is Class 8 property with a CCA rate of 20 percent. Calculate the annual depreciation allowances and end-of-year book values (UCC) for the first five years.

31. **CCA and UCC** Our new computer system cost us $600,000. We will outgrow it in three years. When we sell it, we will probably get only 20 percent of the purchase price. CCA on the computer will be calculated at a 30 percent rate (Class 10). Calculate the CCA and UCC values for five years. What will be the aftertax proceeds from the sale assuming the asset class is continued? Assume a 40 percent tax rate.

32. **CCA** Trans Canada Industries bought new manufacturing equipment (Class 8) with a CCA rate of 20 percent for $4,125,000 in 2002 and then paid $75,000 for installation it capitalized in Class 8. The firm also invested $4 million in a new brick building (Class 3) with a CCA rate of 5 percent. During 2005 Trans Canada finished the project and put it in use. Find the total CCA for Trans Canada for 2005 and 2006.

33. **UCC** Tor-Van Construction specializes in large projects in Toronto and Vancouver. In 2005, Tor-Van invested $1.3 million in new excavating equipment (Class 22). At the same time the firm sold some older equipment on the secondhand market for $145,000. When it was purchased in 2002, the older equipment cost $340,000. Calculate the UCC for the asset pool in Class 22 in each year from 2002 through 2006.

34. **Income Tax** A resident of Alberta has taxable income from employment of $170,000. This individual is considering three investments of equal risk and wishes to determine the aftertax income for each:

    a. $57,000 worth of bonds with a coupon rate of 5 percent.

    b. 250 shares of stock that will pay a dividend at the end of the year of $25 per share.

    c. 500 shares of another stock that is expected to increase in value by $15 per share during the year.

35. **Tax Loss Carry-back and Carry-forward** The Three R Company experienced an operating loss of $310,000 in 2000. Taxable income figures for recent years are given below. Show how the firm can maximize its tax refunds.

	2000	2001	2002	2003	2004	2005	2006
Taxable income ($000)	$116	$140	$168	($600)	$40	$40	$40

36. **UCC** A proposed cost-saving device has an installed cost of $99,200. It is in Class 43 (30 percent rate) for CCA purposes. It will actually function for five years, at which time it will have no value.

    a. Calculate UCC at the end of five years.

    b. What are the tax implications when the asset is sold?

MINI CASE

Consider the following financial information for the Advanced Manufacturing Corporation. You are a new financial analyst for the company, and have been asked to answer a number of questions for senior management in advance of the company's upcoming initial public offering.

a) During 2006, the company purchased a number of vehicles falling in CCA class 10 for a total cost of $725,000. All assets previous to this purchase were in class 43. What is the CCA for 2006? What is the value for net fixed assets for 2006?

b) If the company decides to sell the vehicles at the end of 2007 for $30,000, what will be the after-tax proceeds? Assume the company will have a positive net income in 2007.

c) Assuming that no dividends were paid, construct income statements and balance sheets for 2005 and 2006.

d) For 2006, calculate the cash flow from assets, cash flow to creditors, and cash flow to shareholders.

e) What is the company's tax bill for 2005? For 2006? The company is in the 35 percent tax bracket.

f) For the company's upcoming IPO, management plans to issue 250,000 shares in the company (the current owners plan to take all proceeds from the IPO). Considering the value of owner's equity, what is a fair share price?

Advanced Manufacturing Corporation
Financial Data

	2005	2006
Sales	$1,100,000	$1,200,000
Cost of goods sold	408,000	302,600
Other expenses	165,500	181,200
Interest	55,000	55,450
Cash	211,000	231,600
Accounts receivable	265,500	285,900
Short-term notes payable	55,000	57,500
Long-term debt	475,000	350,000
Net fixed assets	3,250,000	?
Accounts payable	373,500	395,750
Inventory	573,500	682,700
Depreciation	450,000	?

Internet Application Questions

1. The distinction between capital investment and current expenditure is somewhat arbitrary. Nevertheless, from the tax viewpoint, a distinction must be made to calculate depreciation and its associated tax shield. The following link at Canada Revenue Agency provides a set of pointers to distinguish whether an expenditure is considered capital in nature, or whether it is a current expense.

www.cra-arc.gc.ca/E/pub/tp/it128r/it128r-e.html

Use the guidelines in the link above to classify the following expenses as capital or current:

a. Your company buys a fleet of trucks for material delivery

b. The local barber shop buys a new chair

c. The local barber shop buys a new pair of scissors

What assumptions did you need to make to answer the above questions?

2. Capital cost allowance is not the only tax shelter available to Canadian firms. In some cases, notably cultural industries, there are both federal and provincial tax credits to offset a portion of the production costs involved in content development. The following website at Canada Revenue Agency describes the Film or Video Production Tax Credit (FTC), which is available to qualified producers.

www.cra-arc.gc.ca/tax/nonresidents/film/ftc/ftcsum-e.html

For a company with $1 million in production costs, what is the size of the federal FTC?

3. The Canadian Institute of Chartered Accountants (www.cica.ca/index.cfm) provides standards and guidance for new issues, and solicits comments for new policies. Click on What's New and pick one item from Guidance and one item from Comments. Summarize the new guidelines and critique the comments article. Note that items on this site change from time to time.

4. The home page for Air Canada can be found at www.aircanada.ca. Locate the most recent annual report, which contains a balance sheet for the company. What is the book value of equity for Air Canada? The market value of a company is the number of shares of stock outstanding times the price per share. This information can be found at finance.yahoo.com using the ticker symbol for Air Canada (AC). What is the market value of equity? Which number is more relevant for shareholders?

S&P Problems

1. **Marginal and Average Tax Rates** Download the annual income statements for Big Rock Brewery Ltd. (BEERF). Looking back at Table 2.7, what is the marginal income tax rate for Big Rock? Using the total income tax and the pre-tax income numbers calculate the tax rate for Big Rock. Is this number greater or less than the marginal rate? Why?

2. **Net Working Capital** Find the annual balance sheets for Air Canada (ACNAF) and CHC Helicopter Corp. (FLYA). Calculate the net working capital for each company. Is Air Canada's net working capital negative? If so, does this indicate potential financial difficulty for the company? What about CHC Helicopter?

3. **Per Share Earnings and Dividends** Find the annual income statements for Abitibi Consolidated Inc. (ABY), Precision Drilling Corp. (PDS), and Canwest Global Communications (CWG). What are the earnings per share (EPS Basic from operations) for each of these companies? What are the dividends per share for each company? Why do these companies pay out a different portion of income in the form of dividends?

4. **Cash Flow Identity** Download the annual balance sheets and income statements for Domtar Inc. (DTC). Using the most recent year, calculate the cash flow identity for Domtar Inc. Explain your answer.

Suggested Readings

There are many excellent textbooks on accounting and financial statements. One that we have found helpful is:

Garrison, R. H., E. Noreen, P. Brewer, G. R. Chesley, and R. G. Carroll. *Managerial Accounting,* 7th Canadian ed. Whitby, Ontario: McGraw-Hill Ryerson, 2006.

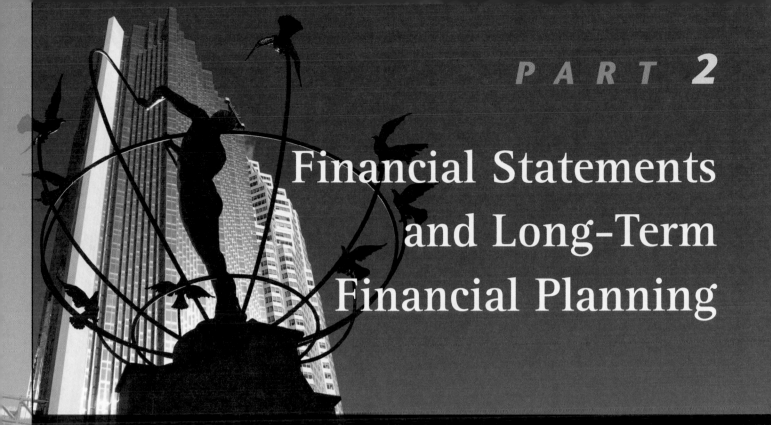

CHAPTER 3

Working with Financial Statements

On April 11, 2006, the price of common stock in software and processing provider Open Text Corporation closed at $18.51. At that price, the *Globe and Mail* reported Open Text had a price-earnings (P/E) ratio of 90.5. That is, investors were willing to pay $90.50 for every dollar in income earned by Open Text. At the same time, investors were only willing to pay $14.11 for each dollar earned by the Bank of Nova Scotia. At the other extreme was Stelco, which had recently returned to the TSX after corporate reorganization. Stelco had negative earnings, yet it was priced at $17.75 per share. Since it had negative earnings,

Stelco's P/E ratio would have been negative, so it was not reported. At that time, the typical stock in the S&P/TSX composite index was trading at a P/E of 21.39 or around 21 times earnings, as they say on Bay Street.

Price-earnings comparisons are examples of financial ratios. As we will see in this chapter, there is a wide variety of financial ratios, all designed to summarize specific aspects of a firm's financial position. In addition to discussing how to analyze financial statements and compute financial ratios, we will have quite a bit to say about who uses this information and why.

IN CHAPTER 2, we discussed some of the essential concepts of financial statements and cash flows. Part 2, this chapter and the next, continues where our earlier discussion left off. Our goal here is to expand your understanding of the uses (and abuses) of financial statement information.

Financial statement information crops up in various places in the remainder of our book. Part 2 is not essential for understanding this material, but it helps give you an overall perspective on the role of financial statement information in corporate finance.

A good working knowledge of financial statements is desirable simply because such statements, and numbers derived from those statements, are the primary means of communicating financial information both within the firm and outside the firm. In short, much of the language of corporate finance is rooted in the ideas we discuss in this chapter.

Furthermore, as we shall see, there are many different ways of using financial statement information and many different types of users. This diversity reflects the fact that financial statement information plays an important part in many types of decisions.

In the best of all worlds, the financial manager has full market value information about all the firm's assets. This rarely (if ever) happens. So the reason we rely on accounting figures for much of our financial information is that we almost always cannot obtain all (or even part) of the market information that we want. The only meaningful benchmark for evaluating business decisions is whether or not they create economic value (see Chapter 1). However, in many important situations, it is not possible to make this judgement directly because we can't see the market value effects of decisions.

We recognize that accounting numbers are often just pale reflections of economic reality, but they frequently are the best available information. For privately held corporations, not-for-profit businesses, and smaller firms, for example, very little direct market value information exists. The accountant's reporting function is crucial in these circumstances.

Clearly, one important goal of the accountant is to report financial information to the user in a form useful for decision making. Ironically, the information frequently does not come to the user in such a form. In other words, financial statements don't come with a user's guide. This chapter and the next are first steps in filling this gap.

3.1

CASH FLOW AND FINANCIAL STATEMENTS: A CLOSER LOOK

At the most fundamental level, firms do two different things: They generate cash and they spend it. Cash is generated by selling a product, an asset, or a security. Selling a security involves either borrowing or selling an equity interest (i.e., shares of stock) in the firm. Cash is spent by paying for materials and labour to produce a product and by purchasing assets. Payments to creditors and owners also require spending cash.

In Chapter 2, we saw that the cash activities of a firm could be summarized by a simple identity:

Cash flow from assets = Cash flow to creditors + Cash flow to owners

This cash flow identity summarizes the total cash result of all the transactions the firm engaged in during the year. In this section, we return to the subject of cash flows by taking a closer look at the cash events during the year that lead to these total figures.

Sources and Uses of Cash

sources of cash
A firm's activities that generate cash.

uses of cash
A firm's activities in which cash is spent.

Those activities that bring in cash are called **sources of cash.** Those activities that involve spending cash are called **uses** (or applications) **of cash.** What we need to do is to trace the changes in the firm's balance sheet to see how the firm obtained its cash and how the firm spent its cash during some time period.

To get started, consider the balance sheets for the Prufrock Corporation in Table 3.1. Notice that we have calculated the changes in each of the items on the balance sheet over the year from the end of 2005 to the end of 2006.

Looking over the balance sheets for Prufrock, we see that quite a few things changed during the year. For example, Prufrock increased its net fixed assets by $149,000 and its inventory by $29,000. Where did the money come from? To answer this and related questions, we must identify those changes that used up cash (uses) and those that brought cash in (sources). A little common sense is useful here. A firm uses cash by either buying assets or making payments. So, loosely speaking, an increase in an asset account means the firm bought some net assets, a use of cash. If an asset account went down, then, on a net basis, the firm sold some assets. This would be a net source. Similarly, if a liability account goes down, then the firm has made a net payment, a use of cash.

Given this reasoning, there is a simple, albeit mechanical, definition that you may find useful. An increase in a left-hand side (asset) account or a decrease in a right-hand side (liability or equity) account is a use of cash. Likewise, a decrease in an asset account or an increase in a liability (or equity) account is a source of cash.

Looking back at Prufrock, we see that inventory rose by $29. This is a net use since Prufrock effectively paid out $29 to increase inventories. Accounts payable rose by $32. This is a source of cash since Prufrock effectively has borrowed an additional $32 by the end of the year. Notes payable, on the other hand, went down by $35, so Prufrock effectively paid off $35 worth of short-term debt—a use of cash.

TABLE 3.1

PRUFROCK CORPORATION
Balance Sheets as of December 31, 2005 and 2006
($ thousands)

	2005	2006	Change
Assets			
Current assets			
Cash	$ 84	$ 98	+$ 14
Accounts receivable	165	188	+ 23
Inventory	393	422	+ 29
Total	$ 642	$ 708	+$ 66
Fixed assets			
Net plant and equipment	2,731	2,880	+ 149
Total assets	$3,373	$3,588	+$215
Liabilities and Owners' Equity			
Current liabilities			
Accounts payable	$ 312	$ 344	+$ 32
Notes payable	231	196	– 35
Total	$ 543	$ 540	–$ 3
Long-term debt	$ 531	$ 457	–$ 74
Owners' equity			
Common stock	500	550	+ 50
Retained earnings	1,799	2,041	+ 242
Total	$2,299	$2,591	+$292
Total liabilities			
and owners' equity	$3,373	$3,588	+$215

Based on our discussion, we can summarize the sources and uses from the balance sheet as follows:

Sources of cash:

Increase in accounts payable	$ 32
Increase in common stock	50
Increase in retained earnings	242
Total sources	$324

Uses of cash:

Increase in accounts receivable	$ 23
Increase in inventory	29
Decrease in notes payable	35
Decrease in long-term debt	74
Net fixed asset acquisitions	149
Total uses	$310
Net addition to cash	$ 14

The net addition to cash is just the difference between sources and uses, and our $14 result here agrees with the $14 change shown on the balance sheet.

This simple statement tells us much of what happened during the year, but it doesn't tell the whole story. For example, the increase in retained earnings is net income (a source of funds) less dividends (a use of funds). It would be more enlightening to have these reported separately so we could see the breakdown. Also, we have only considered net fixed asset acquisitions. Total or gross spending would be more interesting to know.

To further trace the flow of cash through the firm during the year, we need an income statement. For Prufrock, the results are shown in Table 3.2. Because we are looking at cash flow during calendar year 2006, we focus on the 2006 income statement.

Notice here that the $242 addition to retained earnings we calculated from the balance sheet is just the difference between the 2006 net income of $363 and that year's dividend of $121.

statement of cash flows
A firm's financial statement that summarizes its sources and uses of cash over a specified period.

The Statement of Cash Flows

There is some flexibility in summarizing the sources and uses of cash in the form of a financial statement. However it is presented, the result is called the **statement of cash flows.**

TABLE 3.2

PRUFROCK CORPORATION
Income Statements
($ thousands)

	2006
Sales	$2,311
Cost of goods sold	1,344
Depreciation	276
Earnings before interest and taxes	$ 691
Interest paid	141
Taxable income	$ 550
Taxes	187
Net income	$ 363

Addition to retained earnings	$242	
Dividends	121	

TABLE 3.3

PRUFROCK CORPORATION
2006 Statement of Cash Flows

Operating activities	
Net income	$ 363
Plus:	
Depreciation	276
Increase in accounts payable	32
Less:	
Increase in accounts receivable	−23
Increase in inventory	−29
Net cash from operating activity	$ 619
Investment activities:	
Fixed asset acquisitions	−$ 425
Net cash from investment activity	−$ 425
Financing activities:	
Decrease in notes payable	−$ 35
Decrease in long-term debt	−74
Dividends paid	−121
Increase in common stock	50
Net cash from financing activity	−$ 180
Net increase in cash	$ 14

We present a particular format in Table 3.3 for this statement. The basic idea is to group all the changes into one of three categories: operating activities, financing activities, and investment activities. The exact form differs in detail from one preparer to the next.

Don't be surprised if you come across different arrangements. The types of information presented may be very similar, but the exact order can differ. The key thing to remember is that we started out with $84 in cash and ended up with $98, for a net increase of $14. We're just trying to see what events led to this change.

Going back to Chapter 2, there is a slight conceptual problem here. Interest paid should really go under financing activities, but, unfortunately, that's not the way the accounting is handled. The reason, you may recall, is that interest is deducted as an expense when net income is computed. Also, notice that our net purchase of fixed assets was $149. Since we wrote off $276 worth (the depreciation), we must have actually spent a total of $149 + 276 = $425 on fixed assets.

Once we have this statement, it might seem appropriate to express the change in cash on a per-share basis, much as we did for net income. Although standard accounting practice does not report this information, it is often calculated by financial analysts. The reason is that accountants believe that cash flow (or some component of cash flow) is not an alternative to accounting income, so only earnings per share are to be reported.

Now that we have the various cash pieces in place, we can get a good idea of what happened during the year. Prufrock's major cash outlays were fixed asset acquisitions and cash dividends. The firm paid for these activities primarily with cash generated from operations.

Prufrock also retired some long-term debt and increased current assets. Finally, current liabilities were virtually unchanged, and a relatively small amount of new equity was sold. Altogether, this short sketch captures Prufrock's major sources and uses of cash for the year.

CONCEPT QUESTIONS

1. What is a source of cash? Give three examples.

2. What is a use or application of cash? Give three examples.

3.2 STANDARDIZED FINANCIAL STATEMENTS

www.bce.ca

The next thing we might want to do with Prufrock's financial statements is to compare them to those of other, similar companies. We would immediately have a problem, however. It's almost impossible to directly compare the financial statements for two companies because of differences in size. In Canada, this problem is compounded because some companies are one of a kind. BCE is an example. Further, large Canadian companies usually span two, three, or more industries, making comparisons extremely difficult.

To start making comparisons, one obvious thing we might try to do is to somehow standardize the financial statements. One very common and useful way of doing this is to work with percentages instead of total dollars. In this section, we describe two different ways of standardizing financial statements along these lines.

Common-Size Statements

common-size statement
A standardized financial statement presenting all items in percentage terms. Balance sheets are shown as a percentage of assets and income statements as a percentage of sales.

To get started, a useful way of standardizing financial statements is to express the balance sheet as a percentage of assets and to express the income statement as a percentage of sales. Such financial statements are called **common-size statements.** We consider these next.

COMMON-SIZE BALANCE SHEETS   One way, but not the only way, to construct a common-size balance sheet is to express each item as a percentage of total assets. Prufrock's 2005 and 2006 common-size balance sheets are shown in Table 3.4.

TABLE 3.4

PRUFROCK CORPORATION
Common-Size Balance Sheets
December 31, 2005 and 2006

	2005	2006	Change
Assets			
Current assets			
Cash	2.5%	2.7%	+ .2%
Accounts receivable	4.9	5.2	+ .3
Inventory	11.7	11.8	+ .1
Total	19.0	19.7	+ .7
Fixed assets			
Net plant and equipment	81.0	80.3	− .7
Total assets	100.0%	100.0%	0 %
Liabilities and Owners' Equity			
Current liabilities			
Accounts payable	9.2%	9.6%	+ .4%
Notes payable	6.8	5.5	−1.3
Total	16.1	15.1	−1.0
Long-term debt	15.7	12.7	−3.0
Owners' equity			
Common stock	14.8	15.3	+ .5
Retained earnings	53.3	56.9	+3.6
Total	68.2	72.2	+4.0
Total liabilities and owners' equity	100.0%	100.0%	0 %

Notice that some of the totals don't check exactly because of rounding errors. Also, notice that the total change has to be zero, since the beginning and ending numbers must add up to 100 percent.

In this form, financial statements are relatively easy to read and compare. For example, just looking at the two balance sheets for Prufrock, we see that current assets were 19.7 percent of total assets in 2006, up from 19 percent in 2005. Current liabilities declined from 16.1 percent to 15.1 percent of total liabilities and owners' equity over that same time. Similarly, total equity rose from 68.2 percent of total liabilities to 72.2 percent.

Overall, Prufrock's liquidity, as measured by current assets compared to current liabilities, increased over the year. Simultaneously, Prufrock's indebtedness diminished as a percentage of total assets. We might be tempted to conclude that the balance sheet has grown stronger. We say more about this later.

COMMON-SIZE INCOME STATEMENTS A useful way of standardizing income statements is to express each item as a percentage of total sales, as illustrated for Prufrock in Table 3.5.

Common-size income statements tell us what happens to each dollar in sales. For Prufrock in 2006 for example, interest expense eats up $.061 out of every sales dollar and taxes take another $.081. When all is said and done, $.157 of each dollar flows through to the bottom line (net income), and that amount is split into $.105 retained in the business and $.052 paid out in dividends.

These percentages are very useful in comparisons. For example, a very relevant figure is the cost percentage. For Prufrock, $.582 of each $1 in sales goes to pay for goods sold in 2006 as compared to $.624 in 2005. The reduction likely signals improved cost controls in 2006. To pursue this point, it would be interesting to compute the same percentage for Prufrock's main competitors to see how Prufrock's improved cost control in 2006 stacks up.

COMMON-SIZE STATEMENTS OF CASH FLOW Although we have not presented it here, it is also possible and useful to prepare a common-size statement of cash flows. Unfortunately, with the current statement of cash flows, there is no obvious denominator such as total assets or total sales. However, when the information is arranged similarly to Table 3.5, each item can be expressed as a percentage of total sources or total uses. The results can then be interpreted as the percentage of total sources of cash supplied or as the percentage of total uses of cash for a particular item.

Common-Base-Year Financial Statements: Trend Analysis

common-base-year statement
A standardized financial statement presenting all items relative to a certain base year amount.

Imagine that we were given balance sheets for the last 10 years for some company and we were trying to investigate trends in the firm's pattern of operations. Does the firm use more or less debt? Has the firm grown more or less liquid? A useful way of standardizing financial statements is to choose a base year and then express each item relative to the base amount. We call such statements **common-base-year statements.**

TABLE 3.5

PRUFROCK CORPORATION
Common-Size Income Statements

		2005		2006
Sales		100.0%		100.0%
Cost of goods sold		62.4		58.2
Depreciation		12.0		11.9
Earnings before interest and taxes		25.6		29.9
Interest paid		6.2		6.1
Taxable income		19.4		23.8
Taxes		7.8		8.1
Net income		11.6%		15.7%
Addition to retained earnings	5.8%		10.5%	
Dividends	5.8%		5.2%	

For example, Prufrock's inventory rose from $393 to $422. If we pick 2005 as our base year, then we would set inventory equal to 1 for that year. For the next year, we would calculate inventory relative to the base year as $422/$393 = 1.07. We could say that inventory grew by about 7 percent during the year. If we had multiple years, we would just divide each one by $393. The resulting series is very easy to plot, and it is then very easy to compare two or more different companies. Table 3.6 summarizes these calculations for the asset side of the balance sheet.

COMBINED COMMON-SIZE AND BASE-YEAR ANALYSIS   The trend analysis we have been discussing can be combined with the common-size analysis discussed earlier. The reason for doing this is that as total assets grow, most of the other accounts must grow as well. By first forming the common-size statements, we eliminate the effect of this overall growth.

For example, Prufrock's accounts receivable were $165, or 4.9 percent of total assets in 2005. In 2006, they had risen to $188, which is 5.2 percent of total assets. If we do our trend analysis in terms of dollars, the 2006 figure would be $188/$165 = 1.14, a 14 percent increase in receivables. However, if we work with the common-size statements, the 2006 figure would be 5.2%/4.9% = 1.06. This tells us that accounts receivable, as a percentage of total assets, grew by 6 percent. Roughly speaking, what we see is that of the 14 percent total increase, about 8 percent (14% − 6%) is attributable simply to growth in total assets. Table 3.6 summarizes this discussion for Prufrock's assets.

CONCEPT QUESTIONS

1. Why is it often necessary to standardize financial statements?

2. Name two types of standardized statements and describe how each is formed.

financial ratios
Relationships determined from a firm's financial information and used for comparison purposes.

RATIO ANALYSIS

Another way of avoiding the problem of comparing companies of different sizes is to calculate and compare **financial ratios.** Such ratios are ways of comparing and investigating the relationships between different pieces of financial information. Using ratios eliminates the size problem since the size effectively divides out. We're then left with percentages, multiples, or time periods.

There is a problem in discussing financial ratios. Since a ratio is simply one number divided by another, and since there is a substantial quantity of accounting numbers out there, there are a huge number of possible ratios we could examine. Everybody has a favourite, so we've restricted

---

TABLE 3.6

PRUFROCK CORPORATION
Summary of Standardized Balance Sheets (Asset side only)
($ thousands)

	Assets		Common Size		Common Base-Year	Combined Common-Size and Base-Year
	2005	2006	2005	2006	2006	2006
Current assets						
Cash	$ 84	$ 98	2.5%	2.7%	1.17	1.08
Accounts receivable	165	188	4.9	5.2	1.14	1.06
Inventory	393	422	11.7	11.8	1.07	1.01
Total current assets	$ 642	$ 708	19.0	19.7	1.10	1.04
Fixed assets						
Net plant and equipment	2,731	2,880	81.0	80.3	1.05	0.99
Total assets	$3,373	$3,588	100.0%	100.0%	1.06	1.00

The common-size numbers are calculated by dividing each item by total assets for that year. For example, the 2005 common-size cash amount is $84/$3,373 = 2.5%. The common-base-year numbers are calculated by dividing each 2006 item by the base-year dollar (2005) amount. The common-base cash is thus $98/$84 = 1.17, representing a 17 percent increase. The combined common-size and base-year figures are calculated by dividing each common-size amount by the base-year (2005) common-size amount. The cash figure is therefore 2.7%/2.5% = 1.08, representing an 8 percent increase in cash holdings as a percentage of total assets.

ourselves to a representative sampling. We chose the sample to be consistent with the practice of experienced financial analysts. Another way to see which ratios are used most often in practice is to look at the output of commercially available software that generates ratios.

Once you have gained experience in ratio analysis, you will find that 20 ratios do not tell you twice as much as 10. You are looking for problem areas, not an exhaustive list of ratios, so you don't have to worry about including every possible ratio.

What you do need to worry about is the fact that different people and different sources frequently don't compute these ratios in exactly the same way, and this leads to much confusion. The specific definitions we use here may or may not be the same as ones you have seen or will see elsewhere.[1] When you are using ratios as a tool for analysis, you should be careful to document how you calculate each one.

We defer much of our discussion of how ratios are used and some problems that come up with using them to the next section. For now, for each of the ratios we discuss, several questions come to mind:

1. How is it computed?
2. What is it intended to measure, and why might we be interested?
3. What might a high or low value be telling us? How might such values be misleading?
4. How could this measure be improved?

Financial ratios are traditionally grouped into the following categories:

1. Short-term solvency or liquidity ratios.
2. Long-term solvency or financial leverage ratios.
3. Asset management or turnover ratios.
4. Profitability ratios.
5. Market value ratios.

We consider each of these in turn. To illustrate ratio calculations for Prufrock, we use the ending balance sheet (2006) figures unless we explicitly say otherwise. After calculating the 2006 ratios, we illustrated the inferences you can make from ratios by making two comparisons for each ratio. The comparisons draw on numbers in Table 3.7 that summarize each ratio's 2006 value and also present corresponding values for Prufrock in 2005 and for the industry average.[2] Also notice that the various ratios are colour keyed to indicate which numbers come from the income statement (blue) and which come from the balance sheet (green). This colour key applies only to equations in this chapter.

Short-Term Solvency or Liquidity Measures

As the name suggests, short-term solvency ratios as a group are intended to provide information about a firm's liquidity, and these ratios are sometimes called liquidity measures. The primary concern is the firm's ability to pay its bills over the short run without undue stress. Consequently, these ratios focus on current assets and current liabilities.

For obvious reasons, liquidity ratios are particularly interesting to short-term creditors. Since financial managers are constantly working with banks and other short-term lenders, an understanding of these ratios is essential.

One advantage of looking at current assets and liabilities is that their book values and market values are likely to be similar. Often (but not always), these assets and liabilities just don't live long enough for the two to get seriously out of step. This is true for a going concern that has no problems in selling inventory (turning it into receivables) and then collecting the receivables, all at book values. Even in a going concern, all inventory may not be liquid, since some may be held permanently as a buffer against unforeseen delays.

---

1 For example, we compute ratios using year-end balance sheet values in the denominators, while many other sources average ending values from last year and the current year.

2 In this case the industry average figures are hypothetical. We will discuss industry average ratios in some detail later.

TABLE 3.7
Selected financial ratios
for Prufrock

Short-Term Solvency (Liquidity)	2005	2006	Industry	Rating
Current ratio	1.18	1.31	1.25	OK
Quick ratio	0.46	0.53	0.60	—
Cash ratio	0.15	0.18	0.20	OK
Net working capital	2.9%	4.7%	5.2%	OK
Interval measure (days)	182	192	202	OK
Turnover				
Inventory turnover	3.3	3.3	4.0	—
Days' sales in inventory	111	114	91	—
Receivables turnover	12.5	12.3	11.5	OK
Days' sales in receivables	29	30	32	OK
NWC turnover	20.9	13.8	14.6	—
Fixed asset turnover	0.76	0.80	0.90	OK
Total asset turnover	0.61	0.64	0.71	OK
Financial Leverage				
Total debt ratio	0.32	0.28	0.42	++
Debt/equity	0.47	0.39	0.72	++
Equity multiplier	1.47	1.39	1.72	+
Long-term debt ratio	0.16	0.15	0.16	+
Times interest earned	4.2	4.9	2.8	++
Cash coverage ratio	6.2	6.9	4.2	++
Profitability				
Profit margin	11.6%	15.7%	10.7%	++
Return on assets (ROA)	7.1%	10.1%	7.6%	+
Return on equity (ROE)	10.5%	14.0%	13.1%	+
Market Value Ratios				
Price-earnings ratio (P/E)	12.0	14.27	12.0	+
Market-to-book ratio	2.4	2.0	1.92	+

Comments: Company shows strength relative to industry in avoiding increased leverage. Profitability is above average. Company carries more inventory than the industry average, causing weakness in related ratios. Market value ratios are strong.

On the other hand, like any type of near-cash, current assets and liabilities can and do change fairly rapidly, so today's amounts may not be a reliable guide to the future. For example, when a firm experiences financial distress and undergoes a loan workout or liquidation, obsolete inventory and overdue receivables often have market values well below their book values.

CURRENT RATIO   One of the best known and most widely used ratios is the current ratio. As you might guess, the current ratio is defined as:

$$\text{Current ratio} = \text{Current assets/Current liabilities} \qquad [3.1]$$

For Prufrock, the 2006 current ratio is:

$$\text{Current ratio} = \$708/540 = 1.31$$

Because current assets and liabilities are, in principle, converted to cash over the following 12 months, the current ratio is a measure of short-term liquidity. The unit of measurement is either dollars or times. So, we could say that Prufrock has $1.31 in current assets for every $1 in current liabilities, or we could say that Prufrock has its current liabilities covered 1.31 times over. To a creditor, particularly a short-term creditor such as a supplier, the higher the current ratio, the better. To the firm, a high current ratio indicates liquidity, but it also may indicate an inefficient use of cash and other short-term assets. Absent some extraordinary circumstances, we would expect to see a current ratio of at least 1, because a current ratio of less than 1 would mean that net working capital (current assets less current liabilities) is negative. This would be unusual in a healthy firm, at least for most types of business. Some analysts use a rule of thumb that the current ratio should be at least 2.0 but this can be misleading for many industries.

Applying this to Prufrock, we see from Table 3.7 that the current ratio of 1.31 for 2006 is higher than the 1.18 recorded for 2005 and slightly above the industry average. For this reason, the analyst has recorded an OK rating for this ratio.

EXAMPLE 3.1: Current Events

Suppose a firm were to pay off some of its suppliers and short-term creditors. What would happen to the current ratio? Suppose a firm buys some inventory for cash. What happens in this case? What happens if a firm sells some merchandise?

The first case is a trick question. What happens is that the current ratio moves away from 1. If it is greater than 1 (the usual case), it gets bigger; but if it is less than 1, it gets smaller. To see this, suppose the firm has $4 in current assets and $2 in current liabilities for a current ratio of 2. If we use $1 in cash to reduce current liabilities, then the new current ratio is ($4 − $1)/($2 − $1) = 3. If we reverse this to $2 in current

assets and $4 in current liabilities, the current ratio would fall to 1/3 from 1/2.

The second case is not quite as tricky. Nothing happens to the current ratio because cash goes down while inventory goes up—total current assets are unaffected.

In the third case, the current ratio would usually rise because inventory is normally shown at cost and the sale would normally be at something greater than cost (the difference is the markup). The increase in either cash or receivables is therefore greater than the decrease in inventory. This increases current assets, and the current ratio rises.

In general, the current ratio, like any ratio, is affected by various types of transactions. For example, suppose the firm borrows long term to raise money. The short-run effect would be an increase in cash from the issue proceeds and an increase in long-term debt. Current liabilities would not be affected, so the current ratio would rise.

Finally, note that an apparently low current ratio may not be a bad sign for a company with a large reserve of untapped borrowing power.

THE QUICK (OR ACID-TEST) RATIO Inventory is often the least liquid current asset. It's also the one for which the book values are least reliable as measures of market value, since the quality of the inventory isn't considered. Some of it may be damaged, obsolete, or lost.

More to the point, relatively large inventories are often a sign of short-term trouble. The firm may have overestimated sales and overbought or overproduced as a result. In this case, the firm may have a substantial portion of its liquidity tied up in slow-moving inventory.

To further evaluate liquidity, the *quick* or *acid-test ratio* is computed just like the current ratio, except inventory is omitted:

$$\text{Quick ratio} = \frac{\text{Current assets} - \text{Inventory}}{\text{Current liabilities}} \qquad [3.2]$$

Notice that using cash to buy inventory does not affect the current ratio, but it reduces the quick ratio. Again, the idea is that inventory is relatively illiquid compared to cash.

For Prufrock, this ratio in 2006 was:

$$\text{Quick ratio} = [\$708 - 422]/\$540 = .53$$

The quick ratio here tells a somewhat different story from the current ratio, because inventory accounts for more than half of Prufrock's current assets. To exaggerate the point, if this inventory consisted of, say, unsold nuclear power plants, this is a cause for concern.

Table 3.7 provides more information. The quick ratio has improved from 2005 to 2006, but it is still less than the industry average. At a minimum, this suggests Prufrock still is carrying relatively more inventory than its competitors. We need more information to know if this is a problem.

Other Liquidity Ratios

We briefly mention three other measures of liquidity. A very short-term creditor might be interested in the *cash ratio:*

$$\text{Cash ratio} = \text{Cash/Current liabilities} \qquad [3.3]$$

You can verify that this works out to be .18 for Prufrock in 2006. According to Table 3.7, this is a slight improvement over 2005 and around the industry average. Cash adequacy does not seem to be a problem for Prufrock.

Because net working capital (NWC) is frequently viewed as the amount of short-term liquidity a firm has, we can measure the ratio of *NWC to total assets:*

$$\text{Net working capital to total assets} = \text{Net working capital/Total assets} \qquad [3.4]$$

A relatively low value might indicate relatively low levels of liquidity. For Prufrock in 2006, this ratio works out to be ($708 – 540)/$3,588 = 4.7%. As with the cash ratio, comparisons with 2005 and the industry average indicate no problems.

Finally, imagine that Prufrock is facing a strike and cash inflows are beginning to dry up. How long could the business keep running? One answer is given by the *interval measure:*

$$\text{Interval measure} = \text{Current assets/Average daily operating costs} \qquad [3.5]$$

Total costs for the year 2006, excluding depreciation and interest, were $1,344. The average daily cost was $1,344/365 = $3.68 per day. The interval measure is thus $708/$3.68 = 192 days. Based on this, Prufrock could hang on for six months or so, about in line with its competitors.[3]

Long-Term Solvency Measures

Long-term solvency ratios are intended to address the firm's long-run ability to meet its obligations or, more generally, its financial leverage. These are sometimes called *financial leverage ratios* or just *leverage ratios*. We consider three commonly used measures and some variations. These ratios all measure debt, equity, and assets at book values. As we stressed at the beginning, market values would be far better, but these are often not available.

TOTAL DEBT RATIO   The *total debt ratio* takes into account all debts of all maturities to all creditors. It can be defined in several ways, the easiest of which is:

$$\text{Total debt ratio} = [\text{Total assets} - \text{Total equity}]/\text{Total assets} \qquad [3.6]$$
$$= [\$3,588 - 2,591]/\$3,588 = .28$$

In this case, an analyst might say that Prufrock uses 28 percent debt.[4] There has been a large volume of theoretical research on how much debt is optimal, and we discuss this in Part 6. Taking a more pragmatic view here, most financial analysts would note that Prufrock's use of debt has declined slightly from 2005 and is considerably less than the industry average. To find out if this is good or bad, we would look for more information on the financial health of Prufrock's competitors. The rating and comment in Table 3.7 suggest that competitors are overleveraged and that Prufrock's more moderate use of debt is a strength.

Regardless of the interpretation, the total debt ratio shows that Prufrock has $.28 in debt for every $1 in assets in 2006. Therefore, there is $.72 in equity ($1 – $.28) for every $.28 in debt. With this in mind, we can define two useful variations on the total debt ratio, the *debt/equity ratio* and the *equity multiplier*. We illustrate each for Prufrock for 2006:

$$\text{Debt/equity ratio} = \text{Total debt/Total equity} \qquad [3.7]$$
$$= \$.28/\$.72 = .39$$

$$\text{Equity multiplier} = \text{Total assets/Total equity} \qquad [3.8]$$
$$= \$1/\$.72 = 1.39$$

The fact that the equity multiplier is 1 plus the debt/equity ratio is not a coincidence:

$$\text{Equity multiplier} = \text{Total assets/Total equity} = \$1/\$.72 = 1.39$$
$$= (\text{Total equity} + \text{Total debt})/\text{Total equity}$$
$$= 1 + \text{Debt/Equity ratio} = 1.39$$

The thing to notice here is that given any one of these three ratios, you can immediately calculate the other two, so they all say exactly the same thing. You can verify this by looking at the comparisons in Table 3.7.

---

3 Sometimes depreciation and/or interest is included in calculating average daily costs. Depreciation isn't a cash expense, so this doesn't make a lot of sense. Interest is a financing cost, so we excluded it by definition (we only looked at operating costs). We could, of course, define a different ratio that included interest expense.

4 Total equity here includes preferred stock (discussed in Chapter 14 and elsewhere), if there is any. An equivalent numerator in this ratio would be (Current liabilities + Long-term debt).

A BRIEF DIGRESSION: TOTAL CAPITALIZATION VERSUS TOTAL ASSETS

Frequently, financial analysts are more concerned with the firm's long-term debt than its short-term debt because the short-term debt is constantly changing. Also, a firm's accounts payable may be more a reflection of trade practice than debt management policy. For these reasons, the long-term debt ratio is often calculated as:

$$\text{Long-term debt ratio} = \frac{\text{Long-term debt}}{\text{Long-term debt} + \text{Total equity}} \qquad\qquad [3.9]$$

$$= \$457/[\$457 + 2,591] = \$457/\$3,048 = .15$$

The \$3,048 in total long-term debt and equity is sometimes called the firm's *total capitalization*, and the financial manager frequently focuses on this quantity rather than total assets. As you can see from Table 3.7, the long-term debt ratio follows the same trend as the other financial leverage ratios.

To complicate matters, different people (and different books) mean different things by the term *debt ratio*. Some mean total debt, and some mean long-term debt only, and, unfortunately, a substantial number are simply vague about which one they mean.

This is a source of confusion, so we choose to give two separate names to the two measures. The same problem comes up in discussing the debt/equity ratio. Financial analysts frequently calculate this ratio using only long-term debt.

TIMES INTEREST EARNED   Another common measure of long-term solvency is the times interest earned (TIE) ratio. Once again, there are several possible (and common) definitions, but we'll stick with the most traditional:

$$\text{Times interest earned ratio} = \text{EBIT/Interest} \qquad\qquad [3.10]$$

$$= \$691/\$141 = 4.9 \text{ times}$$

As the name suggests, this ratio measures how well a company has its interest obligations covered. For Prufrock, the interest bill is covered 4.9 times over in 2006. Table 3.7 shows that TIE increased slightly over 2005 and exceeds the industry average. This reinforces the signal of the other debt ratios.

CASH COVERAGE   A problem with the TIE ratio is that it is based on EBIT, which is not really a measure of cash available to pay interest. The reason is that depreciation, a non-cash expense, has been deducted out. Since interest is most definitely a cash outflow (to creditors), one way to define the cash coverage ratio is:

$$\text{Cash coverage ratio} = [\text{EBIT} + \text{Depreciation}]/\text{Interest} \qquad\qquad [3.11]$$

$$= [\$691 + 276]/\$141 = \$967/\$141 = 6.9 \text{ times}$$

The numerator here, EBIT plus depreciation, is often abbreviated EBDIT (earnings before depreciation, interest, and taxes). It is a basic measure of the firm's ability to generate cash from operations, and it is frequently used as a measure of cash flow available to meet financial obligations. If depreciation changed dramatically from one year to the next, cash coverage could give a different signal than TIE. In the case of Prufrock, the signals are reinforcing as you can see in Table 3.7.[5]

Asset Management, or Turnover, Measures

We next turn our attention to the efficiency with which Prufrock uses its assets. The measures in this section are sometimes called *asset utilization ratios*. The specific ratios we discuss can all be interpreted as measures of turnover. What they are intended to describe is how efficiently or intensively a firm uses its assets to generate sales. We first look at two important current assets, inventory and receivables.

INVENTORY TURNOVER AND DAYS' SALES IN INVENTORY   During 2006, Prufrock had a cost of goods sold of \$1,344. Inventory at the end of the year was \$422. With these numbers, *inventory turnover* can be calculated as:

---

5 Any onetime transactions, such as capital gains or losses, should be netted out of EBIT before calculating cash coverage.

$$\text{Inventory turnover} = \text{Cost of goods sold/Inventory} \qquad [3.12]$$
$$= \$1,344/\$422 = 3.2 \text{ times}$$

In a sense, the company sold or turned over the entire inventory 3.2 times.[6] As long as Prufrock is not running out of stock and thereby forgoing sales, the higher this ratio is, the more efficiently it is managing inventory.

If we turned our inventory over 3.2 times during the year, then we can immediately figure out how long it took us to turn it over on average. The result is the average *days' sales in inventory* (also known as the "inventory period"):

$$\text{Days' sales in inventory} = 365 \text{ days/Inventory turnover} \qquad [3.13]$$
$$= 365/3.2 = 114 \text{ days}$$

This tells us that, roughly speaking, inventory sits 114 days on average in 2006 before it is sold. Alternatively, assuming we used the most recent inventory and cost figures, it should take about 114 days to work off our current inventory.

Looking at Table 3.7, it would be fair to state that Prufrock has a 114 days' supply of inventory. Ninety-one days is considered normal. This means that, at current daily sales, it would take 114 days to deplete the available inventory. We could also say that we have 114 days of sales in inventory. Table 3.7 registers a negative rating for inventory because Prufrock is carrying more than the industry average. This could be a sign of poor financial management in overinvesting in inventory that will eventually be sold at a normal markup. Worse, it could be that some of Prufrock's inventory is obsolete and should be marked down. Or it could be that Prufrock is simply selling a different product mix than its competitors and nothing is wrong. What the ratio tells us is that we should investigate further.

Returning to ratio calculation, it might make more sense to use the average inventory in calculating turnover. Inventory turnover would then be $\$1,344/[(\$393 + \$422)/2] = 3.3$ times.[7] It really depends on the purpose of the calculation. If we are interested in how long it will take us to sell our current inventory, then using the ending figure (as we did initially) is probably better.

In many of the ratios we discuss next, average figures could just as well be used. Again, it really depends on whether we are worried about the past when averages are appropriate, or the future, when ending figures might be better. Also, using ending figures is very common in reporting industry averages; so, for comparison purposes, ending figures should be used. In any event, using ending figures is definitely less work, so we'll continue to use them.

RECEIVABLES TURNOVER AND DAYS IN RECEIVABLES Our inventory measures give some indications of how fast we can sell products. We now look at how fast we collect on those sales. The receivables turnover is defined in the same way as inventory turnover:

$$\text{Receivables turnover} = \text{Sales/Accounts receivable} \qquad [3.14]$$
$$= \$2,311/\$188 = 12.3 \text{ times}$$

Loosely speaking, we collected our outstanding credit accounts and reloaned the money 12.3 times during 2006.[8]

This ratio makes more sense if we convert it to days, so the *days' sales in receivables* is:

$$\text{Days' sales in receivables} = 365 \text{ days/Receivables turnover} \qquad [3.15]$$
$$= 365/12.3 = 30 \text{ days}$$

Therefore, on average, we collect on our credit sales in 30 days in 2006. For this reason, this ratio is very frequently called the *average collection period (ACP)*.

---

6 Notice that we used cost of goods sold in the top of this ratio. For some purposes, it might be more useful to use sales instead of costs. For example, if we wanted to know the amount of sales generated per dollar of inventory, then we could just replace the cost of goods sold with sales.

7 Notice we have calculated the average as (Beginning value + Ending value)/2.

8 Here we have implicitly assumed that all sales are credit sales. If they are not, then we would simply use total credit sales in these calculations, not total sales.

EXAMPLE 3.2: Payables Turnover

Here is a variation on the receivables collection period. How long, on average, does it take for Prufrock Corporation to pay its bills in 2006? To answer, we need to calculate the accounts payable turnover rate using cost of goods sold.[9] We assume that Prufrock purchases everything on credit.

The cost of goods sold is $1,344, and accounts payable are $344. The turnover is therefore $1,344/$344 = 3.9 times. So payables turned over about every 365/3.9 = 94 days. On average then, Prufrock takes 94 days to pay. As a potential creditor, we might take note of this fact.

Also, note that if we are using the most recent figures, we could also say that we have 30 days' worth of sales that are currently uncollected. Turning to Table 3.7, we see that Prufrock's average collection period is holding steady on the industry average, so no problem is indicated. You will learn more about this subject when we discuss credit policy in Chapter 20.

ASSET TURNOVER RATIOS   Moving away from specific accounts like inventory or receivables, we can consider several "big picture" ratios. For example, NWC *turnover* is:

$$\text{NWC turnover} = \text{Sales/NWC} \qquad [3.16]$$
$$= \$2,311/(\$708 - \$540) = 13.8 \text{ times}$$

Looking at Table 3.7, you can see that NWC turnover is smaller than the industry average. Is this good or bad? This ratio measures how much work we get out of our working capital. Once again, assuming that we aren't missing out on sales, a high value is preferred. Likely, sluggish inventory turnover causes the lower value for Prufrock.

Similarly, *fixed asset turnover* is:

$$\text{Fixed asset turnover} = \text{Sales/Net fixed assets} \qquad [3.17]$$
$$= \$2,311/\$2,880 = .80 \text{ times}$$

With this ratio, we see that, for every dollar in fixed assets, we generated $.80 in sales.

Our final asset management ratio, the *total asset turnover*, comes up quite a bit. We see it later in this chapter and in the next chapter. As the name suggests, the total asset turnover is:

$$\text{Total asset turnover} = \text{Sales/Total assets} \qquad [3.18]$$
$$= \$2,311/\$3,588 = .64 \text{ times}$$

In other words, for every dollar in assets, we generate $.64 in sales in 2006. Comparisons with 2005 and with the industry norm reveal no problem with fixed asset turnover. Because the total asset turnover is slower than the industry average, this points to current assets—and in this case, inventory—as the source of a possible problem.

Profitability Measures

The measures we discuss in this section are probably the best known and most widely used of all financial ratios. In one form or another, they are intended to measure how efficiently the firm uses its assets and how efficiently the firm manages its operations. The focus in this group is on the bottom line, net income.

PROFIT MARGIN   Companies pay a great deal of attention to their *profit margins*:

$$\text{Profit margin} = \text{Net income/Sales} \qquad [3.19]$$
$$= \$363/\$2,311 = 15.7\%$$

EXAMPLE 3.3: More Turnover

Suppose you find that a particular company generates $.40 in sales for every dollar in total assets. How often does this company turn over its total assets?

The total asset turnover here is .40 times per year. It takes 1/.40 = 2.5 years to turn them over completely.

---

9 This calculation could be refined by changing the denominator from cost of goods sold to purchases.

This tells us that Prufrock, in an accounting sense, generates a little less than 16 cents in profit for every dollar in sales in 2006. This is an improvement over 2005 and exceeds the industry average.

All other things being equal, a relatively high profit margin is obviously desirable. This situation corresponds to low expense ratios relative to sales. However, we hasten to add that other things are often not equal.

For example, lowering our sales price normally increases unit volume, but profit margins normally shrink. Total profit (or more importantly, operating cash flow) may go up or down; so the fact that margins are smaller isn't necessarily bad. After all, isn't it possible that, as the saying goes, "Our prices are so low that we lose money on everything we sell, but we make it up in volume!"?[10]

Two other forms of profit margin are sometimes analyzed. The simplest is gross profit margin, which considers a company's performance in making profits above the cost of goods sold (COGS). The next stage is to consider how well the company does at making money once general and administrative costs (SGA) are considered.

$$\text{Gross profit margin} = (\text{Sales} - \text{COGS})/\text{Sales}$$

$$\text{Operating profit margin} = (\text{Sales} - \text{COGS} - \text{SGA})/\text{Sales}$$

RETURN ON ASSETS *Return on assets* (ROA) is a measure of profit per dollar of assets. It can be defined several ways, but the most common is:[11]

$$\text{Return on assets} = \text{Net income}/\text{Total assets} \qquad [3.20]$$
$$= \$363/\$3,588 = 10.12\%$$

RETURN ON EQUITY *Return on equity* (ROE) is a measure of how the shareholders fared during the year. Since benefiting shareholders is our goal, ROE is, in an accounting sense, the true bottom-line measure of performance. ROE is usually measured as:[12]

$$\text{Return on equity} = \text{Net income}/\text{Total equity} \qquad [3.21]$$
$$= \$363/\$2,591 = 14\%$$

For every dollar in equity, therefore, Prufrock generated 14 cents in profit, but, again, this is only correct in accounting terms.

Because ROA and ROE are such commonly cited numbers, we stress that they are accounting rates of return. For this reason, these measures should properly be called return on *book* assets and return on *book* equity. In fact, ROE is sometimes called return on net worth. Whatever it's called, it would be inappropriate to compare the result to, for example, an interest rate observed in the financial markets. We have more to say about accounting rates of return in later chapters.

From Table 3.7, you can see that both ROA and ROE are more than the industry average. The fact that ROE exceeds ROA reflects Prufrock's use of financial leverage. We examine the relationship between these two measures in more detail next.

Market Value Measures

Our final group of measures is based, in part, on information that is not necessarily contained in financial statements—the market price per share of the stock. Obviously, these measures can only be calculated directly for publicly traded companies.

---

10 No, it's not.

11 An alternate definition abstracting from financing costs of debt and preferred shares is in R. H. Garrison, G. R. Chesley, and R. F. Carroll, *Managerial Accounting,* 5th Canadian ed. (Whitby, Ontario: McGraw-Hill Ryerson, 2001), chap. 17.

12 Alternative methods for calculating some financial ratios have also been developed. For example, the Canadian Securities Institute defines ROE as the return on common equity, which is calculated as the ratio of net income less preferred dividends to common equity.

EXAMPLE 3.4: ROE and ROA

Because ROE and ROA are usually intended to measure performance over a prior period, it makes a certain amount of sense to base them on average equity and average assets, respectively. For Prufrock, how would you calculate these for 2006?

We begin by calculating average assets and average equity:

Average assets = ($3,373 + $3,588)/2 = $3,481
Average equity = ($2,299 + $2,591)/2 = $2,445

With these averages, we can recalculate ROA and ROE as follows:

ROA = $363/$3,481 = 10.43%
ROE = $363/$2,445 = 14.85%

These are slightly higher than our previous calculations because assets grew during the year, with the result that the average is less than the ending value.

We assume that Prufrock has 33,000 shares outstanding at the end of 2006 and the stock sold for $157 per share at the end of the year. If we recall that Prufrock's net income was $363,000, its earnings per share (EPS) are:

$$EPS = \frac{Net\ Income}{Shares\ Outstanding} = \$363/33 = \$11$$

PRICE/EARNINGS RATIO The first of our market value measures, the *price/earnings (P/E) ratio* (or multiple) is defined as:

$$P/E\ ratio = Price\ per\ share/Earnings\ per\ share \qquad [\mathbf{3.22}]$$
$$= \$157/\$11 = 14.27\ times$$

In the vernacular, we would say that Prufrock shares sell for 14.27 times earnings, or we might say that Prufrock shares have or carry a P/E multiple of 14.27. In 2005, the P/E ratio was 12 times, the same as the industry average.

Because the P/E ratio measures how much investors are willing to pay per dollar of current earnings, higher P/Es are often taken to mean that the firm has significant prospects for future growth. Such expectations of higher growth likely go a long way toward explaining why Open Text had a much higher price-earnings ratio than Bank of Nova Scotia in the example we used to open the chapter. If a firm had no or almost no earnings, its P/E would probably be quite large; so, as always, care is needed in interpreting this ratio.

MARKET-TO-BOOK RATIO A second commonly quoted measure is the *market-to-book ratio*:

$$Market\text{-}to\text{-}book\ ratio = Market\ value\ per\ share/Book\ value\ per\ share \qquad [\mathbf{3.23}]$$
$$= \$157/(\$2,591/33) = \$157/\$78.5 = 2\ times$$

Notice that book value per share is total equity (not just common stock) divided by the number of shares outstanding. Table 3.7 shows that the market-to-book ratio was 2.4 in 2005.

Since book value per share is an accounting number, it reflects historical costs. In a loose sense, the market-to-book ratio therefore compares the market value of the firm's investments to their cost. A value less than 1 could mean that the firm has not been successful overall in creating value for its shareholders. Prufrock's market-to-book ratio exceeds 1 and this is a positive indication.

This completes our definitions of some common ratios. We could tell you about more of them, but these are enough for now. We'll leave it here and go on to discuss in detail some ways of using these ratios in practice. Table 3.8 summarizes the formulas for the ratios that we discussed.

CONCEPT QUESTIONS

1. What are the five groups of ratios? Give two or three examples of each kind.

2. Turnover ratios all have one of two figures as numerators. What are they? What do these ratios measure? How do you interpret the results?

3. Profitability ratios all have the same figure in the numerator. What is it? What do these ratios measure? How do you interpret the results?

TABLE 3.8
Common financial ratios

I. Short-Term Solvency or Liquidity Ratios	II. Long-Term Solvency or Financial Leverage Ratios
$\text{Current ratio} = \dfrac{\text{Current assets}}{\text{Current liabilities}}$	$\text{Total debt ratio} = \dfrac{\text{Total assets} - \text{Total equity}}{\text{Total assets}}$
$\text{Quick ratio} = \dfrac{\text{Current assets} - \text{Inventory}}{\text{Current liabilities}}$	$\text{Debt/equity ratio} = \dfrac{\text{Total debt}}{\text{Total equity}}$
$\text{Cash ratio} = \dfrac{\text{Cash}}{\text{Current liabilities}}$	$\text{Equity multiplier} = \dfrac{\text{Total assets}}{\text{Total equity}}$
$\text{Net working capital} = \dfrac{\text{Net working capital}}{\text{Total assets}}$	$\dfrac{\text{Long-term}}{\text{debt ratio}} = \dfrac{\text{Long-term debt}}{\text{Long-term debt} + \text{Total equity}}$
$\text{Interval measure} = \dfrac{\text{Current assets}}{\text{Average daily operating costs}}$	$\text{Times interest earned} = \dfrac{\text{EBIT}}{\text{Interest}}$
	$\text{Cash coverage ratio} = \dfrac{\text{EBIT} + \text{Depreciation}}{\text{Interest}}$

III. Asset Utilization Turnover Ratios	IV. Profitability Ratios
$\text{Inventory turnover} = \dfrac{\text{Cost of goods sold}}{\text{Inventory}}$	$\text{Profit margin} = \dfrac{\text{Net income}}{\text{Sales}}$
$\text{Days' sales in inventory} = \dfrac{365\ \text{days}}{\text{Inventory turnover}}$	$\text{Return on assets (ROA)} = \dfrac{\text{Net income}}{\text{Total assets}}$
$\text{Receivables turnover} = \dfrac{\text{Sales}}{\text{Accounts receivable}}$	$\text{Return on equity (ROE)} = \dfrac{\text{Net income}}{\text{Total equity}}$
$\text{Days' sales in receivables} = \dfrac{365\ \text{days}}{\text{Receivables turnover}}$	$\text{ROE} = \dfrac{\text{Net income}}{\text{Sales}} \times \dfrac{\text{Sales}}{\text{Assets}} \times \dfrac{\text{Assets}}{\text{Equity}}$
$\text{NWC turnover} = \dfrac{\text{Sales}}{\text{NWC}}$	**V. Market Value Ratios**
$\text{Fixed asset turnover} = \dfrac{\text{Sales}}{\text{Net fixed assets}}$	$\text{Price/earning ratio} = \dfrac{\text{Price per share}}{\text{Earnings per share}}$
$\text{Total asset turnover} = \dfrac{\text{Sales}}{\text{Total assets}}$	$\text{Market-to-book ratio} = \dfrac{\text{Market value per share}}{\text{Book value per share}}$

 **3.4**

THE DU PONT IDENTITY

As we mentioned in discussing ROA and ROE, the difference between these two profitability measures is a reflection of the use of debt financing or financial leverage. We illustrate the relationship between these measures in this section by investigating a famous way of decomposing ROE into its component parts.

To begin, let's recall the definition of ROE:

Return on equity = Net income/Total equity

If we were so inclined, we could multiply this ratio by Assets/Assets without changing anything:

Return on equity = Net income/Total equity × Assets/Assets
= Net income/Assets × Assets/Equity

Notice that we have expressed the return on equity as the product of two other ratios—return on assets and the equity multiplier:

ROE = ROA × Equity multiplier = ROA × (1 + Debt/Equity ratio)

Looking back at Prufrock in 2006, for example, the debt/equity ratio was .39 and ROA was 10.12 percent. Our work here implies that Prufrock's return on equity, as we previously calculated, is:

ROE = 10.12% × 1.39 = 14%

The difference between ROE and ROA can be substantial, particularly for certain businesses. For example, Royal Bank of Canada had an ROA of only 1.8% in 2005, which is actually fairly typical for a bank. However, banks tend to borrow a lot of money, and, as a result, have relatively large equity multipliers. For Royal Bank, ROE was around 18% in that year, implying an equity multiplier of 10.

We can further decompose ROE by multiplying the top and bottom by total sales:

$$\text{ROE} = \text{Net income/Sales} \times \text{Sales/Assets} \times \text{Assets/Equity} \qquad \textbf{[3.24]}$$
$$= \text{Profit margin} \times \text{Total asset turnover} \times \text{Equity multiplier}$$

Du Pont identity

Popular expression breaking ROE into three parts: profit margin, total asset turnover, and financial leverage.

What we have now done is to partition the return on assets into its two component parts, profit margin and total asset turnover. This last expression is called the **Du Pont identity,** after E. I. Du Pont de Nemours & Company, which popularized its use.

We can check this relationship for Prufrock by noting that in 2006 the profit margin was 15.7 percent and the total asset turnover was .64. ROE should thus be:

$$\text{ROE} = \text{Profit margin} \times \text{Total asset turnover} \times \text{Equity multiplier}$$
$$= 15.7\% \qquad \times \qquad .64 \qquad \times \qquad 1.39$$
$$= 14\%$$

This 14 percent ROE is exactly what we had before.

The Du Pont identity tells us that ROE is affected by three things:

1. Operating efficiency (as measured by profit margin).
2. Asset use efficiency (as measured by total asset turnover).
3. Financial leverage (as measured by the equity multiplier).

Weakness in either operating or asset use efficiency (or both) shows up in a diminished return on assets, which translates into a lower ROE.

Considering the Du Pont identity, it appears that the ROE could be leveraged up by increasing the amount of debt in the firm. It turns out that this only happens when the firm's ROA exceeds the interest rate on the debt. More importantly, the use of debt financing has a number of other effects, and, as we discuss at some length in Part VI, the amount of leverage a firm uses is governed by its capital structure policy.

The decomposition of ROE we've discussed in this section is a convenient way of systematically approaching financial statement analysis. If ROE improves, then the Du Pont identity tells you where to start looking for the reasons. To illustrate, we know from Table 3.7, that ROE for Prufrock increased from 10.4 percent in 2005 to 14 percent in 2006. The Du Pont identity can tell us why. After decomposing ROE for 2005, we can compare the parts with what we found earlier for 2006. For 2005:

$$\text{ROE} = 10.4\% = \text{Profit margin} \times \text{Total asset turnover} \times \text{Equity multiplier}$$
$$= \qquad 11.6\% \qquad \times \qquad .61 \qquad \times \qquad 1.47$$

For 2006:

$$\text{ROE} = \quad 14\% = \quad 15.7\% \qquad \times \qquad .64 \qquad \times \qquad 1.39$$

This comparison shows that the improvement in ROE for Prufrock was caused mainly by the higher profit margin.

A higher ROE is not always a sign of financial strength, however, as the example of General Motors illustrates. In 1989, GM had an ROE of 12.1 percent. By 1993, its ROE had improved to 44.1 percent, a dramatic improvement. On closer inspection, however, we find that, over the same period, GM's profit margin had declined from 3.4 to 1.8 percent, and ROA had declined from 2.4 to 1.3 percent. The decline in ROA was moderated only slightly by an increase in total asset turnover from .71 to .73 over the period.

Given this information, how is it possible for GM's ROE to have climbed so sharply? From our understanding of the Du Pont identity, it must be the case that GM's equity multiplier increased substantially. In fact, what happened was that GM's book equity value was almost wiped out overnight in 1992 by changes in the accounting treatment of pension liabilities. If a company's equity value declines sharply, its equity multiplier rises. In GM's case, the multiplier went from 4.95 in 1989 to 33.62 in 1993. In sum, the dramatic "improvement" in GM's ROE was almost entirely due to an accounting change that affected the equity multiplier and doesn't really represent an improvement in financial performance at all.

CONCEPT QUESTIONS

1. Return on assets (ROA) can be expressed as the product of two ratios. Which two?

2. Return on equity (ROE) can be expressed as the product of three ratios. Which three?

EXAMPLE 3.5: Food versus Variety Stores

Table 3.9 shows the ratios of the Du Pont identity for food and variety stores. The return on equity ratios (ROEs) for the two industries are roughly comparable. This is despite the higher profit margin achieved by variety stores. To overcome their lower profit margin, food stores turn over their assets faster and use more financial leverage. Du Pont analysis allows us to go further by asking why food stores have higher total asset turnover. The reason is higher inventory turnover—15.4 times for food stores versus 4.9 times for variety stores. Figure 3.1 shows the interaction of balance sheet and income statement items through the Du Pont analysis.

TABLE 3.9
Du Pont identity ratios for food and variety stores

Industry	Profit Margin	Total Asset Turnover	Equity Multiplier	Return on Equity
Food stores	1.0%	3.56	3.04	10.8%
Variety stores	1.8	2.60	2.58	12.1

FIGURE 3.1

The Du Pont analysis

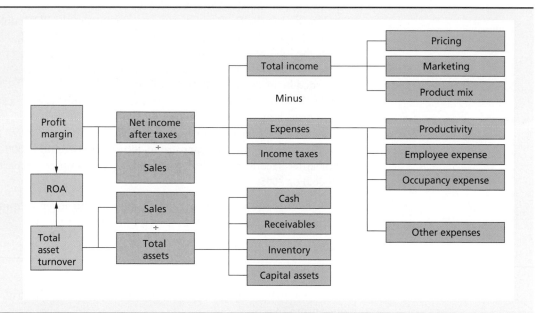

![3.5] **USING FINANCIAL STATEMENT INFORMATION**

Our last task in this chapter is to discuss in more detail some practical aspects of financial statement analysis. In particular, we look at reasons for doing financial statement analysis, how to get benchmark information, and some of the problems that come up in the process.

Why Evaluate Financial Statements?

As we have discussed, the primary reason for looking at accounting information is that we don't have, and can't reasonably expect to get, market value information. Remember that whenever we have market information, we would use it instead of accounting data. Also, when accounting and market data conflict, market data should be given precedence.

Financial statement analysis is essentially an application of management by exception. In many cases, as we illustrated with our hypothetical company, Prufrock, such analysis boils down to comparing ratios for one business with some kind of average or representative ratios. Those ratios that differ the most from the averages are tagged for further study.

INTERNAL USES   Financial information has a variety of uses within a firm. Among the most important of these is performance evaluation. For example, managers are frequently evaluated and compensated on the basis of accounting measures of performances such as profit margin and return on equity. Also, firms with multiple divisions frequently compare the performance of those divisions using financial statement information.

Another important internal use that we explore in the next chapter is planning for the future. As we see, historical financial statement information is very useful for generating projections about the future and for checking the realism of assumptions made in those projections.

EXTERNAL USES   Financial statements are useful to parties outside the firm, including short-term and long-term creditors and potential investors. For example, we would find such information quite useful in deciding whether or not to grant credit to a new customer. Chapter 20 shows how statistical models based on ratios are used in credit analysis in predicting insolvency.

If your firm borrows from a chartered bank, you can expect your loan agreement to require you to submit financial statements periodically. Most bankers use computer software to prepare common-size statements and to calculate ratios for their accounts. Standard software produces output in the format of Table 3.7. More advanced software generates a preliminary diagnosis of the account by comparing the company's ratios against benchmark parameters selected by the banker. Investment analysts also use ratio analysis software as input to their buy and sell recommendations. Credit rating agencies like Standard & Poor's, Dominion Bond Rating Service (DBRS), and Canadian Bond Rating Services rely on financial statements in assessing a firm's overall creditworthiness.

In addition to its use by investment and credit analysts, ratio analysis of competitors might be of interest to the firm. For example, Canadian Tire might be thinking of reentering the U.S. retail market. A prime concern would be the financial strength of the competition. Of course, the analyst could easily change the comparison firms if the goal were to analyze Canadian competitors. Either way, comparison firms should be in the same industries and roughly the same size.

Finally, we might be thinking of acquiring another firm. Financial statement information would be essential in identifying potential targets and deciding what to offer.

Choosing a Benchmark

Given that we want to evaluate a division or a firm based on its financial statements, a basic problem immediately comes up. How do we choose a benchmark or a standard of comparison? We describe some ways of getting started in this section.

TIME-TREND ANALYSIS   One standard we could use is history. In our Prufrock example, we looked at two years of data. More generally, suppose we find that the current ratio for a particular firm is 2.4 based on the most recent financial statement information. Looking back over the last 10 years, we might find that this ratio has declined fairly steadily.

Based on this, we might wonder if the liquidity position of the firm has deteriorated. It could be, of course, that the firm has made changes to use its current assets more efficiently, that the nature of the firm's business has changed, or that business practices have changed. If we investigate, these are all possible explanations. This is an example of what we mean by management by exception—a deteriorating time trend may not be bad, but it does merit investigation.

PEER GROUP ANALYSIS   The second means of establishing a benchmark is to identify firms that are similar in the sense that they compete in the same markets, have similar assets, and operate in similar ways. In other words, we need to identify a *peer group*. In our analysis of Prufrock, we used an industry average without worrying about where it came from. In practice, matters are not so simple because no two companies are identical. Ultimately, the choice of which companies to use as a basis for comparison involves judgement on the part of the analyst.

www.statcan.ca
www.dnb.com

For more on NAICS, see
Statistics Canada at
www.statcan.ca/english/subjects
/standard/naics/2002/naics02-
intro.htm

One common way of identifying peers is based on the North American Industry Classification System (NAICS) codes. These are five-digit codes established by the statistical agencies of Canada, Mexico, and the United States for statistical reporting purposes. Firms with the same NAICS code are frequently assumed to be similar.

Various other benchmarks are available.[13] You can turn to Statistics Canada publications and website that include typical balance sheets, income statements, and selected ratios for firms in about 180 industries. Other sources of benchmarks for Canadian companies include financial data bases available from The Financial Post Datagroup and Dun & Bradstreet Canada.[14] Several financial institutions gather their own financial ratio data bases by compiling information on their loan customers. In this way, they seek to obtain more up-to-date information than is available from services like Statistics Canada and Dun & Bradstreet.

Obtaining current information is not the only challenge facing the financial analyst. Most large Canadian corporations do business in several industries so the analyst must often compare the company against several industry averages. Also keep in mind that the industry average is not necessarily where firms would like to be. For example, agricultural analysts know that farmers are suffering with painfully low average profitability coupled with excessive debt. Despite these shortcomings, the industry average is a useful benchmark for the management by exception approach we advocate for ratio analysis.

Problems with Financial Statement Analysis

We close our chapter on financial statements by discussing some additional problems that can arise in using financial statements. In one way or another, the basic problem with financial statement analysis is that there is no underlying theory to help us identify which quantities to look at and to guide us in establishing benchmarks.

As we discuss in other chapters, there are many cases where financial theory and economic logic provide guidance to making judgements about value and risk. Very little such help exists with financial statements. This is why we can't say which ratios matter the most and what a high or low value might be.

One particularly severe problem is that many firms are conglomerates, owning more-or-less unrelated lines of business. The consolidated financial statements for such firms as Sears Canada don't really fit any neat industry category. More generally, the kind of peer group analysis we have been describing is going to work best when the firms are strictly in the same line of business, the industry is competitive, and there is only one way of operating.

www.sears.ca

Another problem that is becoming increasingly common is having major competitors and natural peer group members in an industry scattered around the globe. The automobile industry is an obvious example. The problem here is that financial statements from outside Canada and the United States do not necessarily conform to GAAP. The existence of different standards and procedures makes it very difficult to compare financial statements across national borders.

Even companies that are clearly in the same line of business may not be comparable. For example, electric utilities engaged primarily in power generation are all classified in the same group. This group is often thought to be relatively homogeneous. However, utilities generally operate as regulated monopolies, so they don't compete with each other. Many have shareholders, and many are organized as cooperatives with no shareholders. There are several different ways of generating power, ranging from hydroelectric to nuclear, so their operating activities can differ quite a bit. Finally, profitability is strongly affected by regulatory environment, so utilities in different locations can be very similar but show very different profits.

Several other general problems frequently crop up. First, different firms use different accounting procedures for inventory, for example. This makes it difficult to compare statements.

---

13 This discussion draws on L. Kryzanowski, M-C. To and R. Seguin, *Business Solvency Risk Analysis,* Institute of Canadian Bankers, 1990, chap. 3.

14 Analysts examining U.S. companies will find comparable information available from Robert Morris Associates.

Second, different firms end their fiscal years at different times. For firms in seasonal businesses (such as a retailer with a large Christmas season), this can lead to difficulties in comparing balance sheets because of fluctuations in accounts during the year. Finally, for any particular firm, unusual or transient events, such as a onetime profit from an asset sale, may affect financial performance. In comparing firms, such events can give misleading signals.

CONCEPT QUESTIONS

1. What are some uses for financial statement analysis?

2. Where do industry average ratios come from and how might they be useful?

3. Why do we say that financial statement analysis is management by exception?

4. What are some problems that can come up with financial statement analysis?

SUMMARY AND CONCLUSIONS

This chapter has discussed aspects of financial statement analysis:

1. Sources and uses of cash. We discussed how to identify the ways that businesses obtain and use cash, and we described how to trace the flow of cash through the business over the course of the year. We briefly looked at the statement of cash flows.

2. Standardized financial statements. We explained that differences in size make it difficult to compare financial statements, and we discussed how to form common-size and common-base-period statements to make comparisons easier.

3. Ratio analysis. Evaluating ratios of accounting numbers is another way of comparing financial statement information. We therefore defined and discussed a number of the most commonly reported and used financial ratios. We also developed the famous Du Pont identity as a way of analyzing financial performance.

4. Using financial statements. We described how to establish benchmarks for comparison purposes and discussed some of the types of available information. We then examined some of the problems that can arise.

After you study this chapter, we hope that you will have some perspective on the uses and abuses of financial statements. You should also find that your vocabulary of business and financial terms has grown substantially.

Key Terms

common-base-year statement (page 61)
common-size statement (page 60)
Du Pont identity (page 73)
financial ratios (page 62; Table 3.8, p. 72)

sources of cash (page 57)
statement of cash flows (page 58)
uses of cash (page 57)

Chapter Review Problems and Self-Test

3.1   Sources and Uses of Cash   Consider the following balance sheets for the Philippe Corporation. Calculate the changes in the various accounts and, where applicable, identify the change as a source or use of cash. What were the major sources and uses of cash? Did the company become more or less liquid during the year? What happened to cash during the year?

PHILIPPE CORPORATION
Balance Sheets as of December 31, 2005 and 2006
($ millions)

	2005	2006
Assets		
Current assets		
Cash	$ 210	$ 215
Accounts receivable	355	310
Inventory	507	328
Total	$1,072	$ 853
Fixed assets		
Net plant and equipment	$6,085	$6,527
Total assets	$7,157	$7,380
Liabilities and Owners' Equity		
Current liabilities		
Accounts payable	$ 207	$ 298
Notes payable	1,715	1,427
Total	$1,922	$1,725
Long-term debt	$1,987	$2,308
Owners' equity		
Common stock and paid-in surplus	$1,000	$1,000
Retained earnings	2,248	2,347
Total	$3,248	$3,347
Total liabilities and owners' equity	$7,157	$7,380

3.2   Common-Size Statements   Below is the most recent income statement for Philippe. Prepare a common-size income statement based on this information. How do you interpret the standardized net income? What percentage of sales goes to cost of goods sold?

PHILIPPE CORPORATION
2006 Income Statement
($ millions)

Sales		$4,053
Cost of goods sold		2,780
Depreciation		550
Earnings before interest and taxes		$ 723
Interest paid		502
Taxable income		$ 221
Taxes (34%)		75
Net income		$ 146
Dividends	$47	
Addition to retained earnings	99	

3.3   Financial Ratios   Based on the balance sheets and income statement in the previous two problems, calculate the following ratios for 2006:

Current ratio   _____
Quick ratio   _____
Cash ratio   _____
Inventory turnover   _____
Receivables turnover _____
Days' sales in inventory _____
Days' sales in receivables _____
Total debt ratio   _____
Long-term debt ratio _____
Times interest earned ratio _____
Cash coverage ratio _____

3.4   ROE and the Du Pont Identity   Calculate the 2006 ROE for the Philippe Corporation and then break down your answer into its component parts using the Du Pont identity.

Answers to Self-Test Problems

3.1   We've filled in the answers in the following table. Remember, increases in assets and decreases in liabilities indicate that we spent some cash. Decreases in assets and increases in liabilities are ways of getting cash.

PHILIPPE CORPORATION
Balance Sheets as of December 31, 2005 and 2006
($ millions)

	2005	2006	Change	Source or Use of Cash
Assets				
Current assets				
Cash	$ 210	$ 215	+$ 5	
Accounts receivable	355	310	− 45	Source
Inventory	507	328	− 179	Source
Total	$1,072	$ 853	−$219	
Fixed assets				
Net plant and equipment	$6,085	$6,527	+$442	Use
Total assets	$7,157	$7,380	+$223	
Liabilities and Owners' Equity				
Current liabilities				
Accounts payable	$ 207	$ 298	+$ 91	Source
Notes payable	1,715	1,427	− 288	Use
Total	$1,922	$1,725	−$197	
Long term debt	$1,987	$2,308	+$321	Source

	2005	2006	Change	Source or Use of Cash
Owners' equity				
Common stock and paid-in surplus	$1,000	$1,000	+$ 0	—
Retained earnings	2,248	2,347	+ 99	Source
Total	$3,248	$3,347	+$ 99	
Total liabilities and owners' equity	$7,157	$7,380	+$223	

Philippe used its cash primarily to purchase fixed assets and to pay off short-term debt. The major sources of cash to do this were additional long-term borrowing and, to a larger extent, reductions in current assets and additions to retained earnings.

The current ratio went from $1,072/1,922 = .56$ to $853/1,725 = .49$, so the firm's liquidity appears to have declined somewhat. Overall, however, the amount of cash on hand increased by $5.

3.2   We've calculated the common-size income statement below. Remember that we simply divide each item by total sales.

PHILIPPE CORPORATION
2006 Common-Size Income Statement

Sales		100.0%
Cost of goods sold		68.6
Depreciation		13.6
Earnings before interest and taxes		17.8
Interest paid		12.3
Taxable income		5.5
Taxes (34%)		1.9
Net income		3.6%
Dividends	1.2%	
Addition to retained earnings	2.4%	

Net income is 3.6 percent of sales. Because this is the percentage of each sales dollar that makes its way to the bottom line, the standardized net income is the firm's profit margin. Cost of goods sold is 68.6 percent of sales.

3.3   We've calculated the following ratios based on the ending figures. If you don't remember a definition, refer back to Table 3.8.

Current ratio	$853/$1,725	= .49 times
Quick ratio	$525/$1,725	= .30 times
Cash ratio	$215/$1,725	= .12 times
Inventory turnover	$2,780/$328	= 8.48 times
Receivables turnover	$4,053/$310	= 13.07 times
Days' sales in inventory	365/8.48	= 43.06 days
Days' sales in receivables	365/13.07	= 27.92 days
Total debt ratio	$4,033/$7,380	= 54.6%
Long-term debt ratio	$2,308/$5,655	= 40.8%
Times interest earned ratio	$723/$502	= 1.44 times
Cash coverage ratio	$1,273/$502	= 2.54 times

3.4   The return on equity is the ratio of net income to total equity. For Philippe, this is $146/$3,347 = 4.4%, which is not outstanding.

Given the Du Pont identity, ROE can be written as:

$$ROE = \text{Profit margin} \times \text{Total asset turnover} \times \text{Equity multiplier}$$
$$= \$146/\$4,053 \quad \times \quad \$4,053/\$7,380 \quad \times \quad \$7,380/\$3,347$$
$$= \quad 3.6\% \quad \times \quad .549 \quad \times \quad 2.20$$
$$= \quad 4.4\%$$

Notice that return on assets, ROA, is 3.6% × .549 = 1.98%.

Concepts Review and Critical Thinking Questions

1.   What effect would the following actions have on a firm's current ratio? Assume that net working capital is positive.
    a.   Inventory is purchased.
    b.   A supplier is paid.
    c.   A short-term bank loan is repaid.
    d.   A long-term debt is paid off early.
    e.   A customer pays off a credit account.
    f.   Inventory is sold at cost.
    g.   Inventory is sold for a profit.

2.   In recent years, Cheticamp Co. has greatly increased its current ratio. At the same time, the quick ratio has fallen. What has happened? Has the liquidity of the company improved?

3.   Explain what it means for a firm to have a current ratio equal to .50. Would the firm be better off if the current ratio were 1.50? What if it were 15.0? Explain your answers.

4.   Fully explain the kind of information the following financial ratios provide about a firm:
    a.   Quick ratio
    b.   Cash ratio
    c.   Interval measure
    d.   Total asset turnover
    e.   Equity multiplier
    f.   Long-term debt ratio
    g.   Times interest earned ratio
    h.   Profit margin
    i.   Return on assets
    j.   Return on equity
    k.   Price-earnings ratio

5.   What types of information do common-size financial statements reveal about the firm? What is the best use for these common-size statements? What purpose do common-base year statements have? When would you use them?

6.   Explain what peer group analysis means. As a financial manager, how could you use the results of peer group analysis to evaluate the performance of your firm?

7.   Why is the Du Pont identity a valuable tool for analyzing the performance of a firm? Discuss the types of information it reveals as compared to ROE considered by itself.

8.   Specialized ratios are sometimes used in specific industries. For example, the so-called book-to-bill ratio is closely watched for semiconductor manufacturers. A ratio of .93 indicates that for every $100 worth of chips shipped over some period, only $93 worth of new orders were received. In August 1998, the North American semiconductor equipment industry's book-to-bill ratio declined to .60, the lowest level since 1995, when analysts first began following it. Three-month average shipments in August were down 5 percent from July figures, while three-month average bookings were down 14.7 percent. What is this ratio intended to measure? Why do you think it is so closely followed?

9.   So-called "same-store sales" are a very important measure for companies as diverse as Canadian Tire and Tim Hortons. As the name suggests, examining same-store sales means comparing revenues from the same stores or restaurants at two different points in time. Why might companies focus on same-store sales rather than total sales?

10.   There are many ways of using standardized financial information beyond those discussed in this chapter. The usual goal is to put firms on an equal footing for comparison purposes. For example, for auto manufacturers, it is common to express sales, costs, and profits on a per-car basis. For each of the following industries, give an example of an actual company and discuss one or more potentially useful means of standardizing financial information:

a. Public utilities
b. Large retailers
c. Airlines

d. On-line services
e. Hospitals
f. University textbook publishers

Questions and Problems

Basic
(Questions 1–17)

1. **Calculating Liquidity Ratios**   SDJ, Inc., has net working capital of $1,320, current liabilities of $4,460, and inventory of $1,875. What is the current ratio? What is the quick ratio?

2. **Calculating Profitability Ratios**   Timber Line, Inc. has sales of $29 million, total assets of $37 million, and total debt of $13 million. If the profit margin is 9 percent, what is net income? What is ROA? What is ROE?

3. **Calculating the Average Collection Period**   Bonds Lumber Yard has a current accounts receivable balance of $421,865. Credit sales for the year just ended were $2,873,150. What is the receivables turnover? The days' sales in receivables? How long did it take on average for credit customers to pay off their accounts during the past year?

4. **Calculating Inventory Turnover**   The Sosa Cork Corporation has ending inventory of $386,500, and cost of goods sold for the year just ended was $2,532,095. What is the inventory turnover? The days' sales in inventory? How long on average did a unit of inventory sit on the shelf before it was sold?

5. **Calculating Leverage Ratios**   Kid Pet Rocks, Inc., has a total debt ratio of .44. What is its debt-equity ratio? What is its equity multiplier?

6. **Calculating Market Value Ratios**   Bellevue Corp. had additions to retained earnings for the year just ended of $310,000. The firm paid out $160,000 in cash dividends, and it has ending total equity of $6.5 million. If Bellevue currently has 180,000 shares of common stock outstanding, what are earnings per share? Dividends per share? Book value per share? If the stock currently sells for $78 per share, what is the market-to-book ratio? The price-earnings ratio?

7. **Du Pont Identity**   If Roten Rooters, Inc., has an equity multiplier of 1.75, total asset turnover of 1.30, and a profit margin of 8.5 percent, what is its ROE?

8. **Du Pont Identity**   Forester Fire Prevention Corp. has a profit margin of 9.20 percent, total asset turnover of 1.63, and ROE of 18.67 percent. What is this firm's debt-equity ratio?

9. **Sources and Uses of Cash**   Based only on the following information for Sweeney Corp., did cash go up or down? By how much? Classify each event as a source or use of cash.

Increase in inventory	$600
Increase in accounts payable	330
Decrease in notes payable	790
Increase in accounts receivable	950

10. **Calculating Average Payables Period**   For 2006, BDJ, Inc., had a cost of goods sold of $13,168. At the end of the year, the accounts payable balance was $2,965. How long on average did it take the company to pay off its suppliers during the year? What might a large value for this ratio imply?

11. **Cash Flow and Capital Spending**   For the year just ended, Dolvin Frozen Yogurt shows an increase in its net fixed assets account of $580. The company took $165 in depreciation expense for the year. How much did Dolvin spend on new fixed assets? Is this a source or use of cash?

12. **Equity Multiplier and Return on Equity**   Thomsen Fried Chicken Company has a debt-equity ratio of 1.40. Return on assets is 8.7 percent, and total equity is $520,000. What is the equity multiplier? Net income? Return on equity?

Just Dew It Corporation reports the following balance sheet information for 2004 and 2005. Use this information to work Problems 13 through 17.

JUST DEW IT CORPORATION
2005 and 2006 Balance Sheets

Assets	2005	2006	Liabilities and Owners' Equity	2005	2006
Current assets			Current liabilities		
Cash	$ 10,168	$ 10,683	Accounts payable	$ 73,185	$ 59,309
Accounts receivable	27,145	28,613	Notes payable	39,125	48,168
Inventory	59,324	64,853	Total	$112,310	$107,477
Total	$ 96,637	$104,149	Long-term debt	$ 50,000	$ 62,000
Fixed assets			Owners' equity		
Net plant and equipment	$304,165	$347,168	Common stock and		
			paid-in surplus	$ 80,000	$ 80,000
			Retained earnings	158,492	201,840
			Total	$238,492	$281,840
Total assets	$400,802	$451,317	Total liabilities and owners' equity	$400,802	$451,317

Basic
(continued)

13. **Preparing Standardized Financial Statements** Prepare the 2005 and 2006 common-size balance sheets for Just Dew It.

14. **Preparing Standardized Financial Statements** Prepare the 2006 common–base year balance sheet for Just Dew It.

15. **Preparing Standardized Financial Statements** Prepare the 2006 combined common-size, common–base year balance sheet for Just Dew It.

16. **Sources and Uses of Cash** For each account on this company's balance sheet, show the change in the account during 2006 and note whether this change was a source or use of cash. Do your numbers add up and make sense? Explain your answer for total assets as compared to your answer for total liabilities and owners' equity.

17. **Calculating Financial Ratios** Based on the balance sheets given for Just Dew It, calculate the following financial ratios for each year:

    a. Current ratio

    b. Quick ratio

    c. Cash ratio

    d. NWC to total assets ratio

    e. Debt-equity ratio and equity multiplier

    f. Total debt ratio and long-term debt ratio

Intermediate
(Questions
18–30)

18. **Using the Du Pont Identity** Y3K, Inc., has sales of $2,700, total assets of $1,185, and a debt-equity ratio of 1.00. If its return on equity is 16 percent, what is its net income?

19. **Days' Sales in Receivables** A company has net income of $173,000, a profit margin of 8.6 percent, and an accounts receivable balance of $143,200. Assuming 75 percent of sales are on credit, what is the company's days' sales in receivables?

20. **Ratios and Fixed Assets** The Le Bleu Company has a long-term debt ratio of 0.70 and a current ratio of 1.20. Current liabilities are $850, sales are $4,310, profit margin is 9.5 percent, and ROE is 21.5 percent. What is the amount of the firm's net fixed assets?

21. **Profit Margin** In response to complaints about high prices, a grocery chain runs the following advertising campaign: "If you pay your child $1 to go buy $50 worth of groceries, then your child makes twice as much on the trip as we do." You've collected the following information from the grocery chain's financial statements:

(millions)	
Sales	$770.0
Net income	7.7
Total assets	196.0
Total debt	130.0

    Evaluate the grocery chain's claim. What is the basis for the statement? Is this claim misleading? Why or why not?

22. **Return on Equity** Firm A and Firm B have debt/total asset ratios of 60% and 40% and returns on total assets of 20% and 30%, respectively. Which firm has a greater return on equity?

23. **Calculating the Cash Coverage Ratio** Titan Inc.'s net income for the most recent year was $7,850. The tax rate was 34 percent. The firm paid $2,108 in total interest expense and deducted $1,687 in depreciation expense. What was Titan's cash coverage ratio for the year?

24. **Cost of Goods Sold** Guthrie Corp. has current liabilities of $340,000, a quick ratio of 1.8, inventory turnover of 4.2, and a current ratio of 3.3. What is the cost of goods sold for the company?

25. **Ratios and Foreign Companies** Prince Albert Canning PLC had a net loss of £13,156 on sales of £147,318 (both in thousands of pounds). Does the fact that these figures are quoted in a foreign currency make any difference? Why? What was the company's profit margin? In dollars, sales were $267,661. What was the net loss in dollars?

Some recent financial statements for Smolira Golf Corp. follow. Use this information to work Problems 26 through 30.

SMOLIRA GOLF CORP.
2005 and 2006 Balance Sheets

Assets	2005	2006	Liabilities and Owners' Equity	2005	2006
Current assets			Current liabilities		
Cash	$ 815	$ 906	Accounts payable	$ 983	$ 1,292
Accounts receivable	2,405	2,510	Notes Payable	720	840
Inventory	4,608	4,906	Other	105	188
Total	$ 7,828	$ 8,322	Total	$ 1,808	$ 2,320

Intermediate (continued)	Fixed assets			Long-Term debt	$ 4,817	$ 4,960
	Net plant and equipment	$15,164	$19,167	Owners' equity		
				Common stock and paid-in surplus	$10,000	$10,000
				Retained earnings	6,367	10,209
				Total	$16,367	$20,209
	Total assets	$22,992	$27,489	Total	$22,992	$27,489

SMOLIRA GOLF CORP.
2006 Income Statement

Sales	$33,500
Cost of goods sold	18,970
Depreciation	1,980
Earnings before interest and taxes	$12,550
Interest paid	486
Taxable income	$12,064
Taxes (35%)	4,222
Net income	$ 7,842

Dividends	$4,000	
Addition to retained earnings	3,842	

26. **Calculating Financial Ratios**   Find the following financial ratios for Smolira Golf Corp. (use year-end figures rather than average values where appropriate):

   Short-term solvency ratios

   a. Current ratio   _____

   b. Quick ratio   _____

   c. Cash ratio   _____

   Asset utilization ratios

   d. Total asset turnover   _____

   e. Inventory turnover   _____

   f. Receivables turnover   _____

   Long-term solvency ratios

   g. Total debt ratio   _____

   h. Debt-equity ratio   _____

   i. Equity multiplier   _____

   j. Times interest earned ratio   _____

   k. Cash coverage ratio   _____

   Profitability ratios

   l. Profit margin   _____

   m. Return on assets   _____

   n. Return on equity   _____

27. **Du Pont Identity**   Construct the Du Pont identity for Smolira Golf Corp.

28. **Calculating the Interval Measure**   For how many days could Smolira Golf Corp. continue to operate if its cash inflows were suddenly suspended?

29. **Statement of Cash Flows**   Prepare the 2006 statement of cash flows for Smolira Golf Corp.

30. **Market Value Ratios**   Smolira Golf Corp. has 2,500 shares of common stock outstanding, and the market price for a share of stock at the end of 2006 was $67. What is the price-earnings ratio? What are the dividends per share? What is the market-to-book ratio at the end of 2006?

MINI CASE

You have just decided to start managing your own investment portfolio, and are considering the Hi-Tech Manufacturing Company as your first equity investment. The company has posted the following financial information on its website, and you want to conduct several stages of analysis in order to decide whether to invest or not.

Hi-Tech Manufacturing Company
Income Statement
(in 000s)

	2005	2006
Sales	$261,429	$313,715
Cost of goods sold	235,671	281,824
Depreciation	12,939	16,312
EBIT	$ 12,819	$ 15,579
Interest paid	4,940	6,240
Taxable income	$ 7,879	$ 9,339
Taxes (30%)	2,364	2,802
Net income	$ 5,515	$ 6,537

Hi-Tech Manufacturing Company
Balance Sheet
(in 000s)

	2005	2006
Assets		
Cash	$ 18,460	$ 7,150
Accounts receivable	38,990	42,024
Inventory	54,109	106,891
Plant and equipment	105,284	138,151
Total assets	$216,843	$294,216
Liabilities and Owners' Equity		
Accounts payable	$ 34,948	$ 35,746
Notes payable	31,993	36,415
Total current liabilities	$ 66,941	$ 72,161
Long-term debt	96,590	165,700
Total liabilities	$163,531	$237,861
Preferred shares 7%	9,750	9,750
Common shares	9,100	9,100
Retained earnings	34,462	37,505
Total liabilities and owners' equity	$216,843	$294,216

Industry Averages

Current ratio	1.75
Quick ratio	0.90
Debt/equity ratio	1.40
Total debt ratio	0.65
Times interest earned ratio	4.50
Cash coverage ratio	4.25
Inventory turnover ratio	2.90
Receivables turnover ratio	8.55
Total asset turnover ratio	1.15
Gross profit margin	15.3%
Operating profit margin	4.2%
Return on equity	9.7%

a) Calculate all ratios discussed in this chapter for 2005 and 2006.

b) Prepare common-size balance sheets for both years.

c) Prepare common-size income statements for both years.

d) Discuss the performance of the company from year-to-year from the point of view of a common shareholder, a preferred shareholder, a bondholder, and senior management.

e) Using the industry average ratios provided, what are the strengths and weaknesses of the firm? What should management set as its top three priorities for 2007?

S&P Problems

1. **Equity Multiplier** Use the balance sheets for Canadian Pacific Railway Ltd. (CP), Biovail Corp. (BVF), Barrick Gold Corp. (ABX), and Alcan Inc. (AL) to calculate the equity multiplier for each company over the most recent two years. Comment on any similarities or differences between the companies and explain how these might affect the equity multiplier.

2. **Inventory Turnover** Use the financial statements for IPSCO Inc. (IPS) and CanWest Global (CWG) to calculate the inventory turnover for each company over the past three years. Is there a difference in inventory turnover between the two companies? Is there a reason the inventory turnover differs? What does this tell you about comparing ratios across industries?

3. **SIC Codes** Find the SIC codes for Alliance Atlantis Communications (AACB) and Lions Gate Entertainment Corp. (LGF) on each company's homepage. What is the SIC code for each of these companies? What does the business description say for each company? Are these companies comparable? What does this tell you about comparing ratios for companies based on SIC codes?

4. **Calculating the Du Pont Identity** Find the annual income statements and balance sheets for BCE Inc. (BCE) and Molson Coors Brewing Company (TAP). Calculate the Du Pont identity for each company for the most recent years. Comment on the changes in each component of the Du Pont identity for each company over this period and compare the components between the two companies. Are the results what you expected? Why or why not?

5. **Ratio Analysis** Look under "Valuation" and download the "Profitability" spreadsheet for Air Canada (ACNAF), Southwest Airlines (LUV), and Continental Airlines (CAL). Find the ROA (Net ROA), ROE, PE ratio (P/E-high and P/E-low), and the market-to-book ratio (Price/Book high and Price/Book-low) for each company. Since stock prices change daily, PE and market-to-book ratios are often reported as the highest and lowest values over the year, as is done in this instance. Look at these ratios for all three companies over the past five years. Do you notice any trends in these ratios? Which company appears to be operating at a more efficient level based on these four ratios? If you were going to invest in an airline, which one (if any) of these companies would you choose, based on this information? Why?

Internet Application Questions

1. Ratio analysis is a powerful tool in determining the quality of a firm's liabilities. For example, bond rating agencies employ ratio analysis in combination with other risk assessment tools to sort companies' debt into risk categories. Higher risk debt typically carries higher yields. Go to Standard & Poor's Canada (www.standardandpoors.com) and click on Ratings Action Press Release. How do financial ratios impact ratings?

2. The Dominion Bond Rating Service (www.dbrs.com/) employs a different rating scale for short-term and long-term debt. Which ratios do you think are important for rating short-term and long-term debt? Is it possible for a firm to get a high rating for short-term debt and a lower rating for long-term debt?

3. Many Canadian companies now provide online links to their financial statements. Try the following link to Shaw Communications (www.shaw.ca/en-ca/InvestorRelations/FinancialReports/AnnualReports). How would you rate Shaw's long-term debt based on the criteria employed by DBRS?

4. Find the most recent financial statements for Loblaw at www.loblaw.com and for Stelco at www.stelco.com. Calculate the asset utilization ratio for these two companies. What does ratio measure? Is the ratio similar for both companies? Why or why not?

Suggested Readings

There are many excellent textbooks on financial statement analysis. Two that we have found helpful are:

Garrison, R. H., E. Noreen, P. Brewer, G. R. Chesley, and R. F. Carroll. *Managerial Accounting,* 7th Canadian ed. Whitby, Ontario: McGraw-Hill Ryerson, 2006, chap. 17.

White, G. I., A. C. Sondhi, and D. Fried. *The Analysis and Use of Financial Statements,* 3d ed. Wiley, 2003.

CHAPTER 4

Long-Term Financial Planning and Corporate Growth

Thirteenth Street Winery is a small producer of Old World–style wines in Jordan, Ontario. Three partners who still work at other "real jobs" founded the company as a labour of love in 1998. The winery sells its limited production from company-owned vineyards out of its winery shop, open Saturdays and Sundays only.

In contrast, Vincor International Inc. was the eighth-largest wine producer globally and TSX listed when it was bought by Constellation Brands for $1.5 billion in 2006. Started in 1989 by Donald Trigg with the purchase of a discontinued brand from Labatt's, the company grew by acquisitions in Canada with the financial backing of Gerry Schwartz and the Ontario Teachers'

Pension Plan. As the company expanded into the U.S., Australia, and New Zealand, it won numerous awards for its quality products, while Donald Trigg became Ernst & Young's 2003 Entrepreneur of the Year.

To achieve their diverse goals, both Vincor and Thirteenth Street needed proper financial planning. In the case of Vincor, rapid growth by acquisitions required financing from profits, new debt, and later new equity accessed by going public. For small companies like Thirteenth Street, keeping on mission requires planning to ensure that growth does not outrun the firm's financial resources.[1]

www.corel.com
www.gmcanada.com

A LACK OF EFFECTIVE long-range planning is a commonly cited reason for financial distress and failure. This is especially true for small businesses—a sector vital to the creation of future jobs in Canada. As we develop in this chapter, long-range planning is a means of systematically thinking about the future and anticipating possible problems before they arrive. There are no magic mirrors, of course, so the best we can hope for is a logical and organized procedure for exploring the unknown. As one member of General Motors Corporation's board was heard to say, "Planning is a process that at best helps the firm avoid stumbling into the future backwards."

Financial planning establishes guidelines for change and growth in a firm. It normally focuses on the "big picture." This means it is concerned with the major elements of a firm's financial and investment policies without examining the individual components of those policies in detail.

Our primary goals in this chapter are to discuss financial planning and to illustrate the interrelatedness of the various investment and financing decisions that a firm makes. In the chapters ahead, we examine in much more detail how these decisions are made.

---

1 Our examples of Vincor International Inc. and Thirteenth Street Winery draw on S. Ryval, "Glass half full," *The Globe and Mail,*" September 28, 2001, as well as information from *www.vincorinternational.com* and *www.13thstreetwines.com.*

We begin by describing what is usually meant by financial planning. For the most part, we talk about long-term planning. Short-term financial planning is discussed in Chapter 18. We examine what the firm can accomplish by developing a long-term financial plan. To do this, we develop a simple, but very useful, long-range planning technique: the percentage of sales approach. We describe how to apply this approach in some simple cases, and we discuss some extensions.

To develop an explicit financial plan, management must establish certain elements of the firm's financial policy. These basic policy elements of financial planning are:

1. The firm's needed investment in new assets. This arises from the investment opportunities that the firm chooses to undertake, and it is the result of the firm's capital budgeting decisions.
2. The degree of financial leverage the firm chooses to employ. This determines the amount of borrowing the firm uses to finance its investments in real assets. This is the firm's capital structure policy.
3. The amount of cash the firm thinks is necessary and appropriate to pay shareholders. This is the firm's dividend policy.
4. The amount of liquidity and working capital the firm needs on an ongoing basis. This is the firm's net working capital decision.

As we shall see, the decisions that a firm makes in these four areas directly affect its future profitability, its need for external financing, and its opportunities for growth.

A key lesson from this chapter is that the firm's investment and financing policies interact and thus cannot truly be considered in isolation from one another. The types and amounts of assets that the firm plans on purchasing must be considered along with the firm's ability to raise the necessary capital to fund those investments.

Financial planning forces the corporation to think about goals. A goal frequently espoused by corporations is growth, and almost all firms use an explicit, company-wide growth rate as a major component of their long-run financial planning. In November 2000, Molson Inc. announced it was buying a new brand of beer in Brazil for around $300 million Canadian. This was part of Molson's strategy to develop an earnings stream in emerging markets where a younger average age may produce faster sales growth. This strategy shows that growth is an important goal for most large companies.

www.molson.com

There are direct connections between the growth that a company can achieve and its financial policy. In the following sections, we show that financial planning models can help you better understand how growth is achieved. We also show how such models can be used to establish limits on possible growth. This analysis can help companies avoid the sometimes fatal mistake of growing too fast.

4.1 WHAT IS FINANCIAL PLANNING?

Financial planning formulates the way financial goals are to be achieved. A financial plan is thus a statement of what is to be done in the future. Most decisions have long lead times, which means they take a long time to implement. In an uncertain world, this requires that decisions be made far in advance of their implementation. A firm that wants to build a factory in 2005, for example, might have to begin lining up contractors and financing in 2003, or even earlier.

Growth as a Financial Management Goal

www.cott.com

Because we discuss the subject of growth in various places in this chapter, we start out with an important warning: Growth, by itself, is *not* an appropriate goal for the financial manager. In fact, as we have seen, rapid growth isn't always even good for a firm. Cott Corp., a Toronto-based bottler of private-label soft drinks, is another example of what happens when a firm grows too fast. The company aggressively marketed its soft drinks in the early 1990s, and sales exploded. However, despite its growth in sales, the company lost $29.4 million for the fiscal year ended January 27, 1996.

Cott's pains included the following: (1) aluminum prices rose; (2) the firm faced price competition; (3) costs surged as Cott built corporate infrastructure in anticipation of becoming a much bigger company; and (4) the firm botched expansion into the United Kingdom. Cott quickly grabbed a 25 percent market share by undercutting the big brands, but then had to hire an outside bottler at a cost much higher than the cost of bottling in its own plants to meet the demand. Half the cases sold in the United Kingdom in 1995 were sold below cost, bringing a loss to the company as a whole. Cott is now focusing on slower growth while keeping a line on operating costs.

As we discuss in Chapter 1, the appropriate goal is increasing the market value of the owners' equity. Of course, if a firm is successful in doing this, growth usually results. Growth may thus be a desirable consequence of good decision making, but it is not an end unto itself. We discuss growth simply because growth rates are so commonly used in the planning process. As we see, growth is a convenient means of summarizing various aspects of a firm's financial and investment policies. Also, if we think of growth as growth in the market value of the equity in the firm, then the goals of growth and increasing the market value of the equity in the firm are not all that different.

Dimensions of Financial Planning

It is often useful for planning purposes to think of the future as having a short run and a long run. The short run, in practice, is usually the coming 12 months. We focus our attention on financial planning over the long run, which is usually taken to be the coming two to five years. This is called the **planning horizon,** and it is the first dimension of the planning process that must be established.[2]

In drawing up a financial plan, all of the individual projects and investments that the firm undertakes are combined to determine the total needed investment. In effect, the smaller investment proposals of each operational unit are added up and treated as one big project. This process is called **aggregation.** This is the second dimension of the planning process.

Once the planning horizon and level of aggregation are established, a financial plan would need inputs in the form of alternative sets of assumptions about important variables. For example, suppose a company has two separate divisions: one for consumer products and one for gas turbine engines. The financial planning process might require each division to prepare three alternative business plans for the next three years.

1. A worst case. This plan would require making relatively pessimistic assumptions about the company's products and the state of the economy. This kind of disaster planning would emphasize a division's ability to withstand significant economic adversity, and it would require details concerning cost cutting, and even divestiture and liquidation. For example, the bottom was dropping out of the PC market in 2001. That left big manufacturers like Compaq, Dell, and Gateway locked in a price war, fighting for market share at a time when sales were stagnant.

2. A normal case. This plan would require making the most likely assumptions about the company and the economy.

3. A best case. Each division would be required to work out a case based on optimistic assumptions. It could involve new products and expansion and would then detail the financing needed to fund the expansion.

In this example, business activities are aggregated along divisional lines and the planning horizon is three years. This type of planning, which considers all possible events, is particularly important for cyclical businesses (businesses with sales that are strongly affected by the overall state of the economy or business cycles). For example, in 1995, Chrysler put together a forecast for the upcoming four years. According to the likeliest scenario, Chrysler would end 1999 with cash of $10.7 billion, showing a steady increase from $6.9 billion at the end of 1995. In the worst-case scenario that was reported, however, Chrysler would end 1999 with $3.3 billion in cash, having

planning horizon
The long-range time period the financial planning process focuses on, usually the next two to five years.

aggregation
Process by which smaller investment proposals of each of a firm's operational units are added up and treated as one big project.

www.daimlerchrysler.ca

---

2 The techniques we present can also be used for short-term financial planning.

reached a low of $0 in 1997. So, how did the 1999 cash picture for Chrysler actually turn out? We'll never know. Just to show you how hard it is to predict the future, Chrysler merged with Daimler Benz, maker of Mercedes automobiles, in 1998 to form DaimlerChrysler AG.

What Can Planning Accomplish?

Because the company is likely to spend a lot of time examining the different scenarios that could become the basis for the company's financial plan, it seems reasonable to ask what the planning process will accomplish.

EXAMINING INTERACTIONS   As we discuss in greater detail later, the financial plan must make explicit the linkages between investment proposals for the different operating activities of the firm and the financing choices available to the firm. In other words, if the firm is planning on expanding and undertaking new investments and projects, where will the financing be obtained to pay for this activity?

EXPLORING OPTIONS   The financial plan provides the opportunity for the firm to develop, analyze, and compare many different scenarios in a consistent way. Various investment and financing options can be explored, and their impact on the firm's shareholders can be evaluated. Questions concerning the firm's future lines of business and questions of what financing arrangements are optimal are addressed. Options such as marketing new products or closing plants might be evaluated.

www.ibm.ca

AVOIDING SURPRISES   Financial planning should identify what may happen to the firm if different events take place. In particular, it should address what actions the firm would take if things go seriously wrong or, more generally, if assumptions made today about the future are seriously in error. Thus, one of the purposes of financial planning is to avoid surprises and develop contingency plans. For example, IBM announced in September 1995 that it was delaying shipment of new mainframe computers by up to four weeks because of a shortage of a key component—the power supply. The delay in shipments was expected to reduce revenue by $250 million and cut earnings by as much as 20 cents a share, or about 8 percent in the current quarter. Apparently, IBM found itself unable to meet orders when demand accelerated. Thus, a lack of planning for sales growth can be a problem for big companies, too.

ENSURING FEASIBILITY AND INTERNAL CONSISTENCY   Beyond a specific goal of creating value, a firm normally has many specific goals. Such goals might be couched in market share, return on equity, financial leverage, and so on. At times, the linkages between different goals and different aspects of a firm's business are difficult to see. Not only does a financial plan make explicit these linkages, but it also imposes a unified structure for reconciling differing goals and objectives. In other words, financial planning is a way of checking that the goals and plans made with regard to specific areas of a firm's operations are feasible and internally consistent. Conflicting goals often exist. To generate a coherent plan, goals and objectives have to be modified therefore, and priorities have to be established.

For example, one goal a firm might have is 12 percent growth in unit sales per year. Another goal might be to reduce the firm's total debt ratio from 40 percent to 20 percent. Are these two goals compatible? Can they be accomplished simultaneously? Maybe yes, maybe no. As we discuss later, financial planning is a way of finding out just what is possible, and, by implication, what is not possible.

The fact that planning forces management to think about goals and to establish priorities is probably the most important result of the process. In fact, conventional business wisdom says that plans can't work, but planning does. The future is inherently unknown. What we can do is establish the direction that we want to travel in and take some educated guesses about what we will find along the way. If we do a good job, we won't be caught off guard when the future rolls around.

COMMUNICATION WITH INVESTORS AND LENDERS   Our discussion to this point has tried to convince you that financial planning is essential to good management. Because good management controls the riskiness of a firm, equity investors and lenders are very interested in studying a firm's financial plan. As discussed in Chapter 15, securities regulators require that firms issuing new shares or debt file a detailed financial plan as part of the *prospectus* describing the new issue. Chartered banks and other financial institutions that make loans to businesses almost always require prospective borrowers to provide a financial plan. In small businesses with limited resources for planning, pressure from lenders is often the main motivator for engaging in financial planning.

CONCEPT QUESTIONS

1. What are the two dimensions of the financial planning process?

2. Why should firms draw up financial plans?

FINANCIAL PLANNING MODELS: A FIRST LOOK

Just as companies differ in size and products, the financial planning process differs from firm to firm. In this section, we discuss some common elements in financial plans and develop a basic model to illustrate these elements.

A Financial Planning Model: The Ingredients

Most financial planning models require the user to specify some assumptions about the future. Based on those assumptions, the model generates predicted values for a large number of variables. Models can vary quite a bit in their complexity, but almost all would have the following elements:

SALES FORECAST   Almost all financial plans require an externally supplied sales forecast. In the models that follow, for example, the sales forecast is the driver, meaning that the user of the planning model supplies this value and all other values are calculated based on it. This arrangement would be common for many types of business; planning focuses on projected future sales and the assets and financing needed to support those sales.

Frequently, the sales forecast is given as a growth rate in sales rather than as an explicit sales figure. These two approaches are essentially the same because we can calculate projected sales once we know the growth rate. Perfect sales forecasts are not possible, of course, because sales depend on the uncertain future state of the economy and on industry conditions.

For example, the September 11, 2001 terrorist attacks caused many firms to scale down their sales forecasts. Some industries were hit particularly hard, such as airlines and hotels. To help firms come up with such projections, some economic consulting firms specialize in macroeconomic and industry projections. Economic and industry forecasts are also available free from the economic research departments of chartered banks.

As we discussed earlier, we are frequently interested in evaluating alternative scenarios, so it isn't necessarily crucial that the sales forecast be accurate. Our goal is to examine the interplay between investment and financing needs at different possible sales levels, not to pinpoint what we expect to happen.

PRO FORMA STATEMENTS   A financial plan has a forecasted balance sheet, an income statement, and a statement of cash flows. These are called pro forma statements, or pro formas for short. The phrase *pro forma* literally means "as a matter of form." This means that the financial statements are the forms we use to summarize the different events projected for the future. At a minimum, a financial planning model generates these statements based on projections of key items such as sales.

In the planning models we describe later, the pro formas are the output from the financial planning model. The user supplies a sales figure, and the model generates the resulting income statement and balance sheet.

ASSET REQUIREMENTS   The plan describes projected capital spending. At a minimum, the projected balance sheets contain changes in total fixed assets and net working capital. These

Spreadsheets to use for *pro forma* statements can be obtained at www.jaxworks.com

changes are effectively the firm's total capital budget. Proposed capital spending in different areas must thus be reconciled with the overall increases contained in the long-range plan.

FINANCIAL REQUIREMENTS The plan includes a section on the financial arrangements that are necessary. This part of the plan should discuss dividend policy and debt policy. Sometimes firms expect to raise cash by selling new shares of stock or by borrowing. Then, the plan has to spell out what kinds of securities have to be sold and what methods of issuance are most appropriate. These are subjects we consider in Part 6 when we discuss long-term financing, capital structure, and dividend policy.

CASH SURPLUS OR SHORTFALL After the firm has a sales forecast and an estimate of the required spending on assets, some amount of new financing is often necessary because projected total assets exceed projected total liabilities and equity. In other words, the balance sheet no longer balances.

Because new financing may be necessary to cover all the projected capital spending, a financial "plug" variable must be designated. The cash surplus or shortfall (also called the "plug") is the designated source or sources of external financing needed to deal with any shortfall (or surplus) in financing and thereby to bring the balance sheet into balance.

For example, a firm with a great number of investment opportunities and limited cash flow may have to raise new equity. Other firms with few growth opportunities and ample cash flow have a surplus and thus might pay an extra dividend. In the first case, external equity is the plug variable. In the second, the dividend is used.

ECONOMIC ASSUMPTIONS The plan has to explicitly describe the economic environment in which the firm expects to reside over the life of the plan. Among the more important economic assumptions that have to be made are the level of interest rates and the firm's tax rate, as well as sales forecasts, as discussed earlier.

A Simple Financial Planning Model

We begin our discussion of long-term planning models with a relatively simple example.[3] The Computerfield Corporation's financial statements from the most recent year are as follows:

COMPUTERFIELD CORPORATION
Financial Statements

Income Statement		Balance Sheet			
Sales	$1,000	Assets	$500	Debt	$250
Costs	800			Equity	250
Net income	$ 200	Total	$500	Total	$500

Unless otherwise stated, the financial planners at Computerfield assume that all variables are tied directly to sales and that current relationships are optimal. This means that all items grow at exactly the same rate as sales. This is obviously oversimplified; we use this assumption only to make a point.

Suppose that sales increase by 20 percent, rising from $1,000 to $1,200. Then planners would also forecast a 20 percent increase in costs, from $800 to $800 × 1.2 = $960. The pro forma income statement would thus be:

PRO FORMA
Income Statement

Sales	$1,200
Costs	960
Net income	$ 240

---

3 Computer spreadsheets are the standard way to execute this and the other examples we present. Appendix 10B gives an overview of spreadsheets and how they are used in planning with capital budgeting as the application.

The assumption that all variables would grow by 20 percent enables us to easily construct the pro forma balance sheet as well:

PRO FORMA BALANCE SHEET

Assets	$600 (+100)	Debt	$300 (+50)
		Equity	300 (+50)
Total	$600 (+100)	Total	$600 (+100)

Notice that we have simply increased every item by 20 percent. The numbers in parentheses are the dollar changes for the different items.

Now we have to reconcile these two pro formas. How, for example, can net income be equal to $240 and equity increase by only $50? The answer is that Computerfield must have paid out the difference of $240 − 50 = $190, possibly as a cash dividend. In this case, dividends are the plug variable.

Suppose Computerfield does not pay out the $190. Here, the addition to retained earnings is the full $240. Computerfield's equity thus grows to $250 (the starting amount) + 240 (net income) = $490, and debt must be retired to keep total assets equal to $600.

With $600 in total assets and $490 in equity, debt has to be $600 − 490 = $110. Since we started with $250 in debt, Computerfield has to retire $250 − 110 = $140 in debt. The resulting pro forma balance sheet would look like this:

PRO FORMA BALANCE SHEET

Assets	$600 (+100)	Debt	$110 (−140)
		Equity	490 (+240)
Total	$600 (+100)	Total	$600 (+100)

In this case, debt is the plug variable used to balance out projected total assets and liabilities.

This example shows the interaction between sales growth and financial policy. As sales increase, so do total assets. This occurs because the firm must invest in net working capital and fixed assets to support higher sales levels. Since assets are growing, total liabilities and equity, the right-hand side of the balance sheet, grow as well.

The thing to notice from our simple example is that the way the liabilities and owners' equity change depends on the firm's financing policy and its dividend policy. The growth in assets requires that the firm decide on how to finance that growth. This is strictly a managerial decision. Also, in our example the firm needed no outside funds. As this isn't usually the case, we explore a more detailed situation in the next section.

CONCEPT QUESTIONS

1. What are the basic concepts of a financial plan?

2. Why is it necessary to designate a plug in a financial planning model?

 **4.3**

THE PERCENTAGE OF SALES APPROACH

In the previous section, we described a simple planning model in which every item increased at the same rate as sales. This may be a reasonable assumption for some elements. For others, such as long-term borrowing, it probably is not, because the amount of long-term borrowing is something set by management, and it does not necessarily relate directly to the level of sales.

In this section, we describe an extended version of our simple model. The basic idea is to separate the income statement and balance sheet accounts into two groups, those that do vary directly with sales and those that do not. Given a sales forecast, we are able to calculate how much financing the firm needs to support the predicted sales level.

percentage of sales approach
Financial planning method in which accounts are projected depending on a firm's predicted sales level.

An Illustration of the Percentage of Sales Approach

The financial planning model we describe next is based on the **percentage of sales approach.** Our goal here is to develop a quick and practical way of generating pro forma statements. We defer discussion of some bells and whistles to a later section.

THE INCOME STATEMENT We start with the most recent income statement for the Rosengarten Corporation, as shown in Table 4.1. Notice that we have still simplified things by including costs, depreciation, and interest in a single cost figure. We separate these out in Appendix 4A at the end of this chapter.

Rosengarten has projected a 25 percent increase in sales for the coming year, so we are anticipating sales of $1,000 × 1.25 = $1,250. To generate a pro forma income statement, we assume that total costs continue to run at $800/$1,000 = 80% of sales. With this assumption, Rosengarten's pro forma income statement is as shown in Table 4.2. The effect here of assuming that costs are a constant percentage of sales is to assume that the profit margin is constant. To check this, notice that the profit margin was $132/$1,000 = 13.2%. In our pro forma, the profit margin is $165/$1,250 = 13.2%; so it is unchanged.

Next, we need to project the dividend payment. This amount is up to Rosengarten's management. We assume that Rosengarten has a policy of paying out a constant fraction of net income in the form of a cash dividend. From the most recent year, the **dividend payout ratio** was:

dividend payout ratio
Amount of cash paid out to shareholders divided by net income.

$$\text{Dividend payout ratio} = \text{Cash dividends/Net income} \qquad [4.1]$$
$$= \$44/\$132$$
$$= 33\frac{1}{3}\%$$

TABLE 4.1

ROSENGARTEN CORPORATION
Income Statement

Sales		$1,000
Costs		800
Taxable income		$ 200
Taxes		68
Net income		$ 132
Addition to retained earnings	$88	
Dividends	$44	

TABLE 4.2

ROSENGARTEN CORPORATION
Pro Forma Income Statement

Sales (projected)	$1,250
Costs (80% of sales)	1,000
Taxable income	$ 250
Taxes	85
Net income	$ 165

We can also calculate the ratio of the addition to retained earnings to net income as:

Retained earnings/Net income = $88/$132 = 66⅔%.

retention ratio or plowback ratio
Retained earnings divided by net income.

This ratio is called the **retention ratio** or **plowback ratio,** and it is equal to 1 minus the dividend payout ratio because everything not paid out is retained. Assuming that the payout and retention ratios are constant, the projected dividends and addition to retained earnings would be:

Projected addition to retained earnings = $165 × 2/3 = $110
Projected dividends paid to shareholders = $165 × 1/3 =   55
Net income $165

THE BALANCE SHEET To generate a pro forma balance sheet, we start with the most recent statement in Table 4.3. On our balance sheet, we assume that some of the items vary directly with sales, while others do not. For those items that do vary with sales, we express each as a percentage of sales for the year just completed. When an item does not vary directly with sales, we write "n/a" for "not applicable."

For example, on the asset side, inventory is equal to 60 percent of sales ($600/$1,000) for the year just ended. We assume that this percentage applies to the coming year, so for each $1 increase in sales, inventory rises by $.60. More generally, the ratio of total assets to sales for the year just ended is $3,000/$1,000 = 3, or 300%.

TABLE 4.3

ROSENGARTEN CORPORATION
Balance Sheet

	($)	(%)		($)	(%)
Assets			*Liabilities and Owners' Equity*		
Current assets			Current liabilities		
Cash	$ 160	16%	Accounts payable	$ 300	30%
Accounts			Notes payable	100	n/a
receivable	440	44			
Inventory	600	60	Total	$ 400	n/a
Total	$1,200	120%			
			Long-term debt	$ 800	n/a
Fixed assets			Owners' equity		
Net plant and			Common stock	$ 800	n/a
equipment	$1,800	180%	Retained earnings	1,000	n/a
			Total	$1,800	n/a
Total assets	$3,000	300%	Total liabilities and	$3,000	n/a
			owners' equity		

capital intensity ratio
A firm's total assets divided by its sales, or the amount of assets needed to generate $1 in sales.

This ratio of total assets to sales is sometimes called the **capital intensity ratio.** It tells us the assets needed to generate $1 in sales; so the higher the ratio is, the more capital intensive is the firm. Notice also that this ratio is just the reciprocal of the total asset turnover ratio we defined in the last chapter. A decrease in a firm's need for new assets as sales grow increases the sustainable growth rate.

For Rosengarten, assuming this ratio is constant, it takes $3 in total assets to generate $1 in sales (apparently Rosengarten is in a relatively capital intensive business). Therefore, if sales are to increase by $100, Rosengarten has to increase total assets by three times this amount, or $300.

On the liability side of the balance sheet, we show accounts payable varying with sales. The reason is that we expect to place more orders with our suppliers as sales volume increases, so payables should change spontaneously with sales. Notes payable, on the other hand, represent short-term debt such as bank borrowing. These would not vary unless we take specific actions to change the amount, so we mark them as n/a.

Similarly, we use n/a for long-term debt because it won't automatically change with sales. The same is true for common stock. The last item on the right-hand side, retained earnings, varies with sales, but it won't be a simple percentage of sales. Instead, we explicitly calculate the change in retained earnings based on our projected net income and dividends.

We can now construct a partial pro forma balance sheet for Rosengarten. We do this by using the percentages we calculated earlier wherever possible to calculate the projected amounts. For example, fixed assets are 180 percent of sales; so, with a new sales level of $1,250, the fixed asset amount is $1.80 \times \$1,250 = \$2,250$, an increase of $2,250 - 1,800 = \$450$ in plant and equipment. Importantly, for those items that don't vary directly with sales, we initially assume no change and simply write in the original amounts. The result is the pro forma balance sheet in Table 4.4. Notice that the change in retained earnings is equal to the $110 addition to retained earnings that we calculated earlier.

Inspecting our pro forma balance sheet, we notice that assets are projected to increase by $750. However, without additional financing, liabilities and equity only increase by $185, leaving a shortfall of $750 - 185 = \$565$. We label this amount **external financing needed** (EFN).

external financing needed (EFN)
The amount of financing required to balance both sides of the balance sheet.

A PARTICULAR SCENARIO   Our financial planning model now reminds us of one of those good news/bad news jokes. The good news is that we're projecting a 25 percent increase in sales. The bad news is that this isn't going to happen unless we can somehow raise $565 in new financing.

This is a good example of how the planning process can point out problems and potential conflicts. If, for example, Rosengarten has a goal of not borrowing any additional funds and not selling any new equity, a 25 percent increase in sales is probably not feasible.

When we take the need for $565 in new financing as a given, Rosengarten has three possible sources: short-term borrowing, long-term borrowing, and new equity. The choice of a combination among these three is up to management; we illustrate only one of the many possibilities.

Suppose that Rosengarten decides to borrow the needed funds. The firm might choose to borrow some short-term and some long-term. For example, current assets increased by $300 while current liabilities rose by only $75. Rosengarten could borrow $300 - 75 = \$225$ in short-term notes payable in

TABLE 4.4

ROSENGARTEN CORPORATION
Partial Pro Forma Balance Sheet

	Present Year	Change from Previous Year		Present Year	Change from Previous Year
Assets			*Liabilities and Owners' Equity*		
Current assets			Current liabilities		
Cash	$ 200	$ 40	Accounts payable	$ 375	$ 75
Accounts			Notes payable	100	0
receivable	550	110	Total	$ 475	$ 75
Inventory	750	150			
Total	$1,500	$300	Long-term debt	$ 800	$ 0
Fixed assets			Owners' equity		
Net plant and			Common stock	$ 800	$ 0
equipment	$2,250	$450	Retained earnings	1,110	110
			Total	$1,910	$110
Total assets	$3,750	$750	Total liabilities		
			and owners' equity	$3,185	$185
			External		
			financing needed	$ 565	

the form of a loan from a chartered bank. This would leave total net working capital unchanged. With $565 needed, the remaining $565 – 225 = $340 would have to come from long-term debt. Two examples of long-term debt discussed in Chapter 15 are a bond issue and a term loan from a chartered bank or insurance company. Table 4.5 shows the completed pro forma balance sheet for Rosengarten.

Even though we used a combination of short- and long-term debt as the plug here, we emphasize that this is just one possible strategy; it is not necessarily the best one by any means. There are many other scenarios that we could (and should) investigate. The various ratios we discussed in Chapter 3 come in very handy here. For example, with the scenario we have just examined, we would surely want to examine the current ratio and the total debt ratio to see if we were comfortable with the new projected debt levels.

Now that we have finished our balance sheet, we have all of the projected sources and uses of cash. We could finish off our pro formas by drawing up the projected statement of changes in financial position along the lines discussed in Chapter 3. We leave this as an exercise and instead investigate an important alternative scenario.

AN ALTERNATIVE SCENARIO   The assumption that assets are a fixed percentage of sales is convenient, but it may not be suitable in many cases. For example, we effectively assumed that Rosengarten was using its fixed assets at 100 percent of capacity because any increase in sales led to an increase in fixed assets. For most businesses, there would be some slack or excess capacity, and production could be increased by, perhaps, running an extra shift.

For example, in early 2004, both Ford and GM announced plans to increase production in Venezuela. The increased production was to accommodate increased sales in that country. In

TABLE 4.5

ROSENGARTEN CORPORATION
Pro Forma Balance Sheet

	Present Year	Change from Previous Year		Present Year	Change from Previous Year
Assets			*Liabilities and Owners' Equity*		
Current assets			Current liabilities		
Cash	$ 200	$ 40	Accounts payable	$ 375	$ 75
Accounts			Notes payable	325	225
receivable	550	110	Total	$ 700	$300
Inventory	750	150	Long-term debt	$1,140	$340
Total	$1,500	$300	Owners' equity		
Fixed assets			Common stock	$ 800	$0
Net plant and			Retained earnings	1,110	110
equipment	$2,250	$450	Total	$1,910	$110
Total assets	$3,750	$750	Total liabilities and	$3,750	$750
			owners' equity		

EXAMPLE 4.1: EFN and Capacity Usage

Suppose Rosengarten were operating at 90 percent capacity. What would be sales at full capacity? What is the capital intensity ratio at full capacity? What is EFN in this case?

Full capacity sales would be $1,000/.90 = $1,111. From Table 4.3, fixed assets are $1,800. At full capacity, the ratio of fixed assets to sales is thus:

Fixed assets/Full capacity sales = $1,800/$1,111 = 1.62

This tells us that we need $1.62 in fixed assets for every $1 in sales once we reach full capacity. At the projected sales level of $1,250, we need $1,250 × 1.62 = $2,025 in fixed assets. Compared to the $2,250 we originally projected, this is $225 less, so EFN is $565 − 225 = $340.

Current assets would still be $1,500, so total assets would be $1,500 + 2,025 = $3,525. The capital intensity ratio would thus be $3,525/$1,250 = 2.82, less than our original value of 3 because of the excess capacity.

Ford's case, the company planned no additional capital expenditures; in other words, the company did not plan to increase production facilities. GM's announcement of increased production came with an announcement that the company would invest in production facilities. Apparently, Ford had the capacity to expand production without significantly adding to fixed costs, while GM did not.

If we assume that Rosengarten is only operating at 70 percent of capacity, the need for external funds would be quite different. By 70 percent of capacity, we mean that the current sales level is 70 percent of the full capacity sales level:

Current sales = $1,000 = .70 × Full capacity sales
Full capacity sales = $1,000/.70 = $1,429

This tells us that sales could increase by almost 43 percent—from $1,000 to $1,429—before any new fixed assets were needed.

In our previous scenario, we assumed it would be necessary to add $450 in net fixed assets. In the current scenario, no spending on net fixed assets is needed, because sales are projected to rise to $1,250, which is substantially less than the $1,429 full capacity level.

As a result, our original estimate of $565 in external funds needed is too high. We estimated that $450 in net new fixed assets would be needed. Instead, no spending on new net fixed assets is necessary. Thus, if we are currently operating at 70 percent capacity, we only need $565 − 450 = $115 in external funds. The excess capacity thus makes a considerable difference in our projections.

These alternative scenarios illustrate that it is inappropriate to manipulate financial statement information blindly in the planning process. The output of any model is only as good as the input assumptions or, as is said in the computer field, GIGO: garbage in, garbage out. Results depend critically on the assumptions made about the relationships between sales and asset needs. We return to this point later.

CONCEPT QUESTIONS

1. What is the basic idea behind the percentage of sales approach?

2. Unless it is modified, what does the percentage of sales approach assume about fixed asset capacity usage?

 **4.4**

EXTERNAL FINANCING AND GROWTH

External financing needed and growth are obviously related. All other things being the same, the higher the rate of growth in sales or assets, the greater will be the need for external financing. In the previous section, we took a growth rate as a given, and then we determined the amount of external financing needed to support the growth. In this section, we turn things around a bit. We take the firm's financial policy as a given and then examine the relationship between that financial policy and the firm's ability to finance new investments and thereby grow.

TABLE 4.6

HOFFMAN COMPANY
Income Statement and Balance Sheet

Income Statement

Sales	$500
Costs	400
Taxable income	$100
Taxes	34
Net income	$ 66
Addition to retained earnings	$44
Dividends	$22

Balance Sheet

	$	% of Sales		$	% of Sales
Assets			*Liabilities*		
Current assets	$200	40%	Total debt	$250	n/a
Net fixed assets	300	60	Owners' equity	250	n/a
Total assets	$500	100%	Total liabilities and owners' equity	$500	n/a

This approach can be very useful because, as you have already seen, growth in sales requires financing, so it follows that growth that is too fast can cause a company to grow broke.[4] Companies that neglect to plan for financing growth can fail even when production and marketing are on track. From a positive perspective, planning growth that is financially sustainable can help an excellent company achieve its potential. This is why managers, along with their bankers and other suppliers of funds, need to look at sustainable growth.

External Financing Needed and Growth

To begin, we must establish the relationship between EFN and growth. To do this, we introduce Table 4.6, a simplified income statement and balance sheet for the Hoffman Company. Notice that we have simplified the balance sheet by combining short-term and long-term debt into a single total debt figure. Effectively, we are assuming that none of the current liabilities varies spontaneously with sales. This assumption isn't as restrictive as it sounds. If any current liabilities (such as accounts payable) vary with sales, we can assume they have been netted out in current assets.[5] Also, we continue to combine depreciation, interest, and costs on the income statement.

The following symbols are useful:

S = Previous year's sales = $500
A = Total assets = $500
D = Total debt = $250
E = Total equity = $250

In addition, based on our earlier discussions of financial ratios, we can calculate the following:

p = Profit margin = $66/$500 = 13.2%
R = Retention ratio = $44/$66 = 2/3
ROA = Return on assets = $66/$500 = 13.2%
ROE = Return on equity = $66/$250 = 26.4%
D/E = Debt/equity ratio = $250/$250 = 1.0

Suppose the Hoffman Company is forecasting next year's sales level at $600, a $100 increase. The capital intensity ratio is $500/$500 = 1, so assets need to rise by 1 × $100 = $100 (assuming

---

4 This phrase and the following discussion draws heavily on R. C. Higgins, "How Much Growth Can a Firm Afford?" *Financial Management* 6, Fall 1977, pp. 7–16.

5 This assumption makes our use of EFN here consistent with how we defined it earlier in the chapter.

full capacity usage). Notice that the percentage increase in sales is $100/$500 = 20%. The percentage increase in assets is also 20 percent: 100/$500 = 20%. As this illustrates, assuming a constant capital intensity ratio, the increase in total assets is simply $A \times g$, where g is growth rate in sales:

$$\text{Increase in total assets} = A \times g$$
$$= \$500 \times 20\%$$
$$= \$100$$

In other words, the growth rate in sales can also be interpreted as the rate of increase in the firm's total assets.

Some of the financing necessary to cover the increase in total assets comes from internally generated funds and shows up in the form of the addition to retained earnings. This amount is equal to net income multiplied by the plowback or retention ratio, R. Projected net income is equal to the profit margin, p, multiplied by projected sales, $S \times (1 + g)$. The projected addition to retained earnings for Hoffman can thus be written as:

$$\text{Addition to retained earnings} = p(S)R \times (1 + g)$$
$$= .132(\$500)(2/3) \times 1.20$$
$$= \$44 \times 1.20$$
$$= \$52.80$$

Notice that this is equal to last year's addition to retained earnings, $44, multiplied by $(1 + g)$.

Putting this information together, we need $A \times g = \$100$ in new financing. We generate $p(S)R \times (1 + g) = \$52.80$ internally, so the difference is what we need to raise. In other words, we find that EFN can be written as:

$$\text{EFN} = \text{Increase in total assets} - \text{Addition to retained earnings} \qquad [4.2]$$
$$= A(g) - p(S)R \times (1 + g)$$

For Hoffman, this works out to be

$$\text{EFN} = \$500(.20) - .132(\$500)(2/3) \times 1.20$$
$$= \$100 - \$52.80$$
$$= \$47.20$$

We can check that this is correct by filling in a pro forma income statement and balance sheet, as in Table 4.7. As we calculated, Hoffman needs to raise $47.20.

Looking at our equation for EFN, we see that EFN depends directly on g. Rearranging things to highlight this relationship, we get:

TABLE 4.7

HOFFMAN COMPANY
Pro Forma Income Statement and Balance Sheet

Income Statement

Sales	$600.0
Costs (80% of sales)	480.0
Taxable income	$120.0
Taxes	40.8
Net income	$ 79.2
Addition to retained earnings	$52.8
Dividends	$26.4

Balance Sheet

	$	% of Sales		$	% of Sales
Assets			*Liabilities*		
Current assets	$240.0	40%	Total debt	$250.0	n/a
Net fixed assets	360.0	60	Owners' equity	302.8	n/a
Total assets	$600.0	100%	Total liabilities	$552.8	n/a
			External funds needed	$ 47.2	

$$EFN = -p(S)R + [A - p(S)R] \times g \qquad [4.3]$$

Plugging in the numbers for Hoffman, the relationship between EFN and g is:

$$EFN = -.132(\$500)(2/3) + [\$500 - .132(\$500)(2/3)] \times g$$
$$= -44 + 456 \times g$$

Notice that this is the equation of a straight line with a vertical intercept of –$44 and a slope of $456.

The relationship between growth and EFN is illustrated in Figure 4.1. The y-axis intercept of our line, –$44, is equal to last year's addition to retained earnings. This makes sense because, if the growth in sales is zero, then retained earnings are $44, the same as last year. Furthermore, with no growth, no net investment in assets is needed, so we run a surplus equal to the addition to retained earnings, which is why we have a negative sign.

The slope of the line in Figure 4.1 tells us that for every .01 (1 percent) in sales growth, we need an additional $456 \times .01 = \$4.56$ in external financing to support that growth.

Internal Growth Rate

internal growth rate
The growth rate a firm can maintain with only internal financing.

Looking at Figure 4.1, there is one growth rate of obvious interest. What growth rate can we achieve with no external financing? We call this the **internal growth rate** because it is the rate the firm can maintain with only internal financing. This growth rate corresponds to the point where our line crosses the horizontal axis, that is, the point where EFN is zero. At this point, the required increase in assets is exactly equal to the addition to retained earnings, and EFN is therefore zero. Figure 4.1 shows that this rate is just under 10 percent.

We can easily calculate this rate by setting EFN equal to zero:

$$EFN = -p(S)R + [A - p(S)R] \times g \qquad [4.4]$$
$$g = pS(R)/[A - pS(R)]$$
$$= .132(\$500)(2/3)/[\$500 - .132(\$500)(2/3)]$$
$$= 44/[500 - 44]$$
$$= 44/456 = 9.65\%$$

FIGURE 4.1

External financing needed and growth in sales for the Hoffman Company

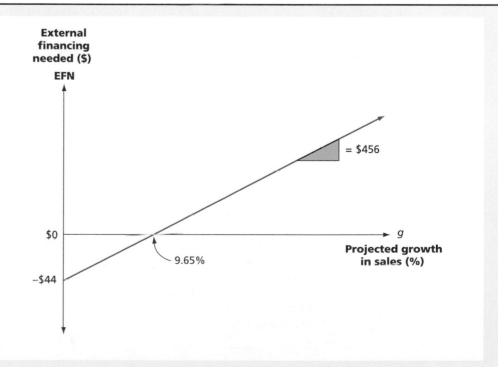

Hoffman can therefore grow at a 9.65 percent rate before any external financing is required. With a little algebra, we can restate the expression for the internal growth rate (Equation 4.4) as:[6]

$$\text{Internal growth rate} = \frac{ROA \times R}{1 - ROA \times R} \qquad [4.5]$$

For Hoffman, we can check this by recomputing the 9.65% internal growth rate

$$= \frac{.132 \times 2/3}{1 - .132 \times 2/3}$$

Financial Policy and Growth

Suppose Hoffman, for whatever reason, does not wish to sell any new equity. As we discuss in Chapter 15, one possible reason is simply that new equity sales can be very expensive. Alternatively, the current owners may not wish to bring in new owners or contribute additional equity themselves. For a small business or a start-up, the reason may be even more compelling: All sources of new equity have likely already been tapped and the only way to increase equity is through additions to retained earnings.

In addition, we assume that Hoffman wishes to maintain its current debt/equity ratio. To be more specific, Hoffman (and its lenders) regard its current debt policy as optimal. We discuss why a particular mixture of debt and equity might be better than any other in Chapters 14 and 15. For now, we say that Hoffman has a fixed **debt capacity** relative to total equity. If the debt/equity ratio declines, Hoffman has excess debt capacity and can comfortably borrow additional funds.

Assuming that Hoffman does borrow to its debt capacity, what growth rate can be achieved? The answer is the **sustainable growth rate,** the maximum growth rate a firm can achieve with no external *equity* financing while it maintains a constant debt/equity ratio. To find the sustainable growth rate, we go back to Equation 4.2 and add another term for new borrowings (up to debt capacity). One way to see where the amount of new borrowings comes from is to relate it to the addition to retained earnings. Because this addition increases equity, it reduces the debt/equity ratio. Since sustainable growth is based on a constant debt/equity ratio, we use new borrowings to top up debt. Because we are now allowing new borrowings, EFN refers to outside equity only. Because no new outside equity is available, EFN = 0.

$$\begin{aligned} \text{EFN} &= \text{Increase in total assets} - \text{Addition to retained earnings} \qquad [4.6] \\ &\quad - \text{New borrowing} \\ &= A(g) - p(S)R \times (1 + g) - pS(R) \times (1 + g)[D/E] \\ \text{EFN} &= 0 \end{aligned}$$

With some algebra we can solve for the sustainable growth rate.[7]

$$g^\star = ROE \times R/[1 - ROE \times R] \qquad [4.7]$$

This growth rate is called the firm's sustainable growth rate (SGR).

For example, for the Hoffman Company, we already know that the ROE is 26.4 percent and the retention ratio, R, is 2/3. The sustainable growth rate is thus:

$$\begin{aligned} g^\star &= (ROE \times R)/(1 - ROE \times R) \\ &= .176/.824 \\ &= 21.3\% \end{aligned}$$

This tells us that Hoffman can increase its sales and assets at a rate of 21.3 percent per year without selling any additional equity and without changing its debt ratio or payout ratio. If a growth rate in excess of this is desired or predicted, something has to give.

To better see that the SGR is 21.3 percent (and to check our answer), we can fill out the pro forma financial statements assuming that Hoffman's sales increase at exactly the SGR. We do this to verify that if Hoffman's sales do grow at 21.3 percent, all needed financing can be obtained without the need to sell new equity, and, at the same time, the debt/equity ratio can be maintained at its current level of 1.

debt capacity
The ability to borrow to increase firm value.

sustainable growth rate
The growth rate a firm can maintain given its debt capacity, ROE, and retention ratio.

---

6 To derive Equation 4.5 from (4.4) divide through by A and recognize that ROA = $p(S)/A$.

7 The derivation of the sustainable rate is shown in Appendix 4B.

To get started, sales increase from $500 to $500 × (1 + .213) = $606. Assuming, as before, that costs are proportional to sales, the income statement would be:

HOFFMAN COMPANY
Pro Forma Income Statement

Sales	$606
Costs (80% of sales)	485
Taxable income	$121
Taxes	41
Net income	$ 80

Given that the retention ratio, R, stays at 2/3, the addition to retained earnings is $80 × (2/3) = $53, and the dividend paid is $80 − 53 = $27.

We fill out the pro forma balance sheet (Table 4.8) just as we did earlier. Note that the owners' equity rises from $250 to $303 because the addition to retained earnings is $53. As illustrated, EFN is $53. If Hoffman borrows this amount, its total debt rises to $250 + 53 = $303. The debt/equity ratio therefore is $303/$303 = 1 as desired, thereby verifying our earlier calculations. At any other growth rate, something would have to change.

Pro Forma Income Statement

Sales		$1,000
Costs (80% of sales)		800
Taxable income		$ 200
Taxes		68
Net income		$ 132
Dividends (1/3)	$44	
Addition to retained earnings	88	

Pro Forma Balance Sheet

Current assets	$ 400	Total debt	$250
Fixed assets	600	Owners' equity	338
Total assets	$1,000	Total liabilities	$588
		External funds needed	$412

To maintain the debt/equity ratio at 1, Hoffman can increase debt to $338, an increase of $88. This leaves $412 − $88 = $324 to be raised by external equity. If this is not available, Hoffman could try to raise the full $412 in additional debt. This would rocket the debt/equity ratio to ($250 + $412)/$338 = 1.96, basically doubling the target amount.

TABLE 4.8

HOFFMAN COMPANY
Pro Forma Balance Sheet

	$	% of Sales		$	% of Sales
Current assets	$242	40	Total debt	$250	n/a
Net fixed assets	364	60	Owners' equity	303	n/a
Total assets	$606	100	Total liabilities	$553	n/a
			External funds needed	$ 53	

EXAMPLE 4.2: Growing Bankrupt

Suppose the management of Hoffman Company is not satisfied with a growth rate of 21 percent. Instead, the company wants to expand rapidly and double its sales to $1,000 next year. What will happen? To answer this question we go back to the starting point of our previous example.

We know that the sustainable growth rate for Hoffman is 21.3 percent, so doubling sales (100 percent growth) is not possible unless the company obtains outside equity financing or allows its debt/equity ratio to balloon beyond 1. We can prove this with simple pro forma statements.

Given that the firm's bankers and other external lenders likely had considerable say over the target D/E in the first place, it is highly unlikely that Hoffman could obtain this much additional debt. The most likely outcome is that if Hoffman insists on doubling sales, the firm would grow bankrupt.

Determinants of Growth

In the last chapter, we saw that the return on equity could be decomposed into its various components using the Du Pont identity. Because ROE appears prominently in the determination of the SGR, the important factors in determining ROE are also important determinants of growth. To see this, recall that from the Du Pont identity, ROE can be written as:

$$\text{ROE} = \text{Profit margin} \times \text{Total asset turnover} \times \text{Equity multiplier}$$

Using our current symbols for these ratios,[8]

$$\text{ROE} = p(S/A)(1 + D/E)$$

If we substitute this into our expression for g^* (SGR), we see that the sustainable growth rate can be written in greater detail as:

$$g^* = \frac{p(S/A)(1 + D/E) \times R}{1 - p(S/A)(1 + D/E) \times R} \qquad [4.8]$$

Writing the SGR out in this way makes it look a little complicated, but it does highlight the various important factors determining the ability of a firm to grow.

Examining our expression for the SGR, we see that growth depends on the following four factors:

1. Profit margin. An increase in profit margin, p, increases the firm's ability to generate funds internally and thereby increase its sustainable growth.

2. Dividend policy. A decrease in the percentage of net income paid out as dividends increases the retention ratio, R. This increases internally generated equity and thus increases sustainable growth.

3. Financial policy. An increase in the debt/equity ratio, D/E, increases the firm's financial leverage. Since this makes additional debt financing available, it increases the sustainable growth rate.

4. Total asset turnover. An increase in the firm's total asset turnover, S/A, increases the sales generated for each dollar in assets. This decreases the firm's need for new assets as sales grow and thereby increases the sustainable growth rate. Notice that increasing total asset turnover is the same thing as the decreasing capital intensity.

The sustainable growth rate is a very useful planning number. What it illustrates is the explicit relationship between the firm's four major areas of concern: its operating efficiency as measured by p, its asset use efficiency as measured by S/A, its dividend policy as measured by R, and its financial policy as measured by D/E.

Given values for all four of these, only one growth rate can be achieved. This is an important point, so it bears restating:

> If a firm does not wish to sell new equity and its profit margin, dividend policy, financial policy, and total asset turnover (or capital intensity) are all fixed, there is only one possible maximum growth rate.

As we described early in this chapter, one of the primary benefits to financial planning is to ensure internal consistency among the firm's various goals. The sustainable growth rate captures this element nicely. For this reason, sustainable growth is included in the software used by commercial lenders at several Canadian chartered banks in analyzing their accounts.

Also, we now see how to use a financial planning model to test the feasibility of a planned growth rate. If sales are to grow at a rate higher than the sustainable growth rate, the firm must

---

8 Remember that the equity multiplier is the same as 1 plus the debt/equity ratio. Appendix 4B shows the derivation in detail.

increase profit margins, increase total asset turnover, increase financial leverage, increase earnings retention, or sell new shares.

At the other extreme, suppose the firm is losing money (has a negative profit margin) or is paying out more than 100 percent of earnings in dividends so that R is negative. In each of these cases, the negative SGR signals the rate at which sales and assets must shrink. Firms can achieve negative growth by selling assets and closing divisions. The cash generated by selling assets is often used to pay down excessive debt taken on earlier to fund rapid expansion. Nortel Networks and CanWest Global Communications Corp. are examples of Canadian companies that underwent this painful negative growth in 2002. Nortel was losing money on its operations, and was selling assets to keep the remaining core businesses operating. CanWest Global, on the other hand, experienced negative growth because it paid out more in dividends than it earned. CanWest elected to sell some assets to pay down a portion of its debt.

A Note on Sustainable Growth Rate Calculations

Very commonly, the sustainable growth rate is calculated using just the numerator in our expression, ROE × R. This causes some confusion, which we can clear up here. The issue has to do with how ROE is computed. Recall that ROE is calculated as net income divided by total equity. If total equity is taken from an ending balance sheet (as we have done consistently, and is commonly done in practice), then our formula is the right one. However, if total equity is from the beginning of the period, then the simpler formula is the correct one.

In Their Own Words . . .   Robert C. Higgins on Sustainable Growth

MOST FINANCIAL OFFICERS know intuitively that it takes money to make money. Rapid sales growth requires increased assets in the form of accounts receivable, inventory, and fixed plant, which, in turn, require money to pay for assets. They also know that if their company does not have the money when needed, it can literally "grow broke." The sustainable growth equation states these intuitive truths explicitly.

Sustainable growth is often used by bankers and other external analysts to assess a company's creditworthiness. They are aided in this exercise by several sophisticated computer software packages that provide detailed analyses of the company's past financial performance, including its annual sustainable growth rate.

Bankers use this information in several ways. Quick comparison of a company's actual growth rate to its sustainable rate tells the banker what issues will be at the top of management's financial agenda. If actual growth consistently exceeds sustainable growth, management's problem will be where to get the cash to finance growth. The banker thus can anticipate interest in loan products. Conversely, if sustainable growth consistently exceeds actual, the banker had best be prepared to talk about investment products, because management's problem will be what to do with all the cash that keeps piling up in the till.

Bankers also find the sustainable growth equation useful for explaining to financially inexperienced small business owners and overly optimistic entrepreneurs that, for the long-

run viability of their business, it is necessary to keep growth and profitability in proper balance.

Finally, comparison of actual to sustainable growth rates helps a banker understand why a loan applicant needs money and for how long the need might continue. In one instance, a loan applicant requested $100,000 to pay off several insistent suppliers and promised to repay in a few months when he collected some accounts receivable that were coming due. A sustainable growth analysis revealed that the firm had been growing at four to six times its sustainable growth rate and that this pattern was likely to continue in the foreseeable future. This alerted the banker that impatient suppliers were only a symptom of the much more fundamental disease of overly rapid growth, and that a $100,000 loan would likely prove to be only the down payment on a much larger, multiyear commitment.

Robert C. Higgins is professor of finance at the University of Washington. He pioneered the use of sustainable growth as a tool for financial analysis. Updates on his research are at *www.depts.washington.edu/~finance/higgins.html.*

EXAMPLE 4.3: Sustainable Growth

The Sandar Company has a debt/equity ratio of .5, a profit margin of 3 percent, a dividend payout of 40 percent, and a capital intensity ratio of 1. What is its sustainable growth rate? If Sandar desires a 10 percent SGR and plans to achieve this goal by improving profit margins, what would you think?

The sustainable growth rate is:

$$g^* = .03(1)(1 + .5)(1 - .40)/[1 - .03(1)(1 + .5)(1 - .40)]$$
$$= 2.77\%$$

To achieve a 10 percent growth rate, the profit margin has to rise. To see this, assume that g^* is equal to 10 percent and then solve for p:

$$.10 = p(1.5)(.6)/[1 - p(1.5)(.6)]$$
$$p = .1/.99 = 10.1\%$$

For the plan to succeed, the necessary increase in profit margin is substantial, from 3 percent to about 10 percent. This may not be feasible.

In principle, you'll get exactly the same sustainable growth rate regardless of which way you calculate it (as long you match up the ROE calculation with the right formula). In reality, you may see some differences because of accounting-related complications. By the way, if you use the average of beginning and ending equity (as some advocate), yet another formula is needed. Note: all of our comments here apply to the internal growth rate as well.

One more point that is important to note is that for the sustainable growth calculations to work, all items involved in the formulas must increase at the same rate. If any items do not change at the same rate, the formulas will not work properly.

CONCEPT QUESTIONS

1. What are the determinants of growth?

2. How is a firm's sustainable growth related to its accounting return on equity (ROE)?

3. What does it mean if a firm's sustainable growth rate is negative?

 4.5

SOME CAVEATS ON FINANCIAL PLANNING MODELS

Financial planning models do not always ask the right questions. A primary reason is that they tend to rely on accounting relationships and not financial relationships. In particular, the three basic elements of firm value tend to get left out, namely, cash flow size, risk, and timing.

Because of this, financial planning models sometimes do not produce output that gives the user many meaningful clues about what strategies would lead to increases in value. Instead, they divert the user's attention to questions concerning the association of, say, the debt/equity ratio and firm growth.

The financial model we used for the Hoffman Company was simple, in fact, too simple. Our model, like many in use today, is really an accounting statement generator at heart. Such models are useful for pointing out inconsistencies and reminding us of financial needs, but they offer very little guidance concerning what to do about these problems.

In closing our discussion, we should add that financial planning is an iterative process. Plans are created, examined, and modified over and over. The final plan is a negotiated result between all the different parties to the process. In practice, long-term financial planning in some corporations relies too much on a top-down approach. Senior management has a growth target in mind and it is up to the planning staff to rework and ultimately deliver a plan to meet that target. Such plans are often made feasible (on paper or a computer screen) by unrealistically optimistic assumptions on sales growth and target debt/equity ratios. The plans collapse when lower sales make it impossible to service debt. This is what happened to Campeau's takeover of Federated Department Stores, as we discuss in Chapter 23.

As a negotiated result, the final plan implicitly contains different goals in different areas and also satisfies many constraints. For this reason, such a plan need not be a dispassionate assessment of what we think the future will bring; it may instead be a means of reconciling the planned activities of different groups and a way of setting common goals for the future.

SUMMARY AND CONCLUSIONS

Financial planning forces the firm to think about the future. We have examined a number of features of the planning process. We describe what financial planning can accomplish and the components of a financial model. We go on to develop the relationship between growth and financing needs. Two growth rates, internal and sustainable, are summarized in Table 4.9. The table recaps the key difference between the two growth rates. The internal growth rate is the maximum growth rate that can be achieved with no external financing of any kind. The sustainable growth rate is the maximum growth rate that can be achieved with no external equity financing while maintaining a constant debt/equity ratio. For Hoffman, the internal growth rate is 9.65 percent and the sustainable growth rate is 21.3 percent. The sustainable growth rate is higher because the calculation allows for debt financing up to a limit set by the target debt/equity ratio. We discuss how a financial planning model is useful in exploring that relationship.

Corporate financial planning should not become a purely mechanical activity. When it does, it probably focuses on the wrong things. In particular, plans all too often are formulated in terms of a growth target with no explicit linkage to value creation, and they frequently are overly concerned with accounting statements. Nevertheless, the alternative to financial planning is stumbling into the future backwards.

TABLE 4.9
Summary of internal and sustainable growth rates from Hoffman Company example

I.   INTERNAL GROWTH RATE

Internal growth rate $= \dfrac{\text{ROA} \times R}{1 - \text{ROA} \times R} = \dfrac{.132 \times 2/3}{1 - 0.132 \times 2/3} = 9.65\%$

where

ROA = Return on assets = Net income/Total assets = 13.2%

R = Plowback (retention) ratio = $2/3$

= Addition to retained earnings/Net income

The internal growth rate is the maximum growth rate that can be achieved with no external financing of any kind.

II.   SUSTAINABLE GROWTH RATE

Sustainable growth rate $= \dfrac{\text{ROE} \times R}{1 - \text{ROE} \times R} = \dfrac{0.264 \times (2/3)}{1 - 0.264 \times (2/3)} = 21.3\%$

where

ROE = Return on equity = Net income/Total equity = 26.4%

R = Plowback (retention) ratio = $2/3$

= Addition to retained earnings/Net income

The sustainable growth rate is the maximum growth rate that can be achieved with no external equity financing while maintaining a constant debt/equity ratio.

Key Terms

Chapter Review Problems and Self-Test

4.1   **Calculating EFN**   Based on the following information for the Skandia Mining Company, what is EFN if sales are predicted to grow by 10 percent? Use the percentage of sales approach and assume the company is operating at full capacity. The payout ratio is constant.

SKANDIA MINING COMPANY
Financial Statements

Income Statement		Balance Sheet			
		Assets		*Liabilities and Owner's Equity*	
Sales	$4,250.0				
Costs	3,876.0	Current assets	$ 900	Current liabilities	$ 500
Taxable income	$ 374.0	Net fixed assets	2,200	Long-term debt	$1,800
Taxes (34%)	127.2	Total	$3,100	Owners' equity	800
Net income	$ 246.8			Total liabilities and owners' equity	$3,100
Dividends	$ 82.4				
Addition to retained earnings	164.4				

4.2   **EFN and Capacity Use**   Based on the information in Problem 4.1, what is EFN, assuming 60 percent capacity usage for net fixed assets? Assuming 95 percent capacity?

4.3   **Sustainable Growth**   Based on the information in Problem 4.1, what growth rate can Skandia maintain if no external financing is used? What is the sustainable growth rate?

Answers to Self-Test Problems

4.1   We can calculate EFN by preparing the pro forma statements using the percentage of sales approach. Note that sales are forecasted to be $4,250 × 1.10 = $4,675.

SKANDIA MINING COMPANY
Pro Forma Financial Statements

Income Statement

Sales	$4,675.0	Forecast
Costs	4,263.6	91.2% of sales
Taxable income	$ 411.4	
Taxes (34%)	$ 139.9	
Net income	$ 271.5	
Dividends	$ 90.6	33.37% of net
Addition to retained earnings	180.9	income

Balance Sheet

Assets			*Liabilities and Owners' Equity*		
Current assets	$ 990.0	21.18%	Current liabilities	$ 550	11.76%
Net fixed assets	2,420.0	51.76%	Long-term debt	$1,800.0	n/a
Total assets	$3,410.0	72.94%	Owners' equity	980.9	n/a
			Total liabilities and owners' equity	3,330.9	n/a
			EFN	$ 79.1	n/a

4.2   Full-capacity sales are equal to current sales divided by the capacity utilization. At 60 percent of capacity:

$4,250 = .60 × Full-capacity sales
$7,083 = Full-capacity sales

With a sales level of $4,675, no net new fixed assets will be needed, so our earlier estimate is too high. We estimated an increase in fixed assets of $2,420 − 2,200 = $220. The new EFN will thus be $79.1 − 220 = −$140.9, a surplus. No external financing is needed in this case.

At 95 percent capacity, full-capacity sales are $4,474. The ratio of fixed assets to full-capacity sales is thus $2,200/4,474 = 49.17%. At a sales level of $4,675, we will thus need $4,675 × .4917 = $2,298.7 in net fixed assets, an increase of $98.7. This is $220 − 98.7 = $121.3 less than we originally predicted, so the EFN is now $79.1 − 121.3 = $42.2, a surplus. No additional financing is needed.

4.3 Skandia retains $R = 1 - .3337 = 66.63\%$ of net income. Return on assets is $\$246.8/3,100 = 7.96\%$. The internal growth rate is:

$$\frac{ROA \times R}{1 - ROA \times R} = \frac{.0796 \times .6663}{1 - .0796 \times .6663}$$
$$= 5.60\%$$

Return on equity for Skandia is $\$246.8/800 = 30.85\%$, so we can calculate the sustainable growth rate as:

$$\frac{ROE \times R}{1 - ROE \times R} = \frac{.3085 \times .6663}{1 - .3085 \times .6663}$$
$$R = 25.87\%$$

Concepts Review and Critical Thinking Questions

1. Why do you think most long-term financial planning begins with sales forecasts? Put differently, why are future sales the key input?

2. Would long-range financial planning be more important for a capital intensive company, such as a heavy equipment manufacturer, or an import-export business? Why?

3. Testaburger, Ltd., uses no external financing and maintains a positive retention ratio. When sales grow by 15 percent, the firm has a negative projected EFN. What does this tell you about the firm's internal growth rate? How about the sustainable growth rate? At this same level of sales growth, what will happen to the projected EFN if the retention ratio is increased? What if the retention ratio is decreased? What happens to the projected EFN if the firm pays out all of its earnings in the form of dividends?

4. Broslofski Co. maintains a positive retention ratio and keeps its debt-equity ratio constant every year. When sales grow by 20 percent, the firm has a negative projected EFN. What does this tell you about the firm's sustainable growth rate? Do you know, with certainty, if the internal growth rate is greater than or less than 20 percent? Why? What happens to the projected EFN if the retention ratio is increased? What if the retention ratio is decreased? What if the retention ratio is zero?

Use the following information to answer the next six questions: A small business called The Grandmother Calendar Company began selling personalized photo calendar kits in 1992. The kits were a hit, and sales soon sharply exceeded forecasts. The rush of orders created a huge backlog, so the company leased more space and expanded capacity, but it still could not keep up with demand. Equipment failed from overuse and quality suffered. Working capital was drained to expand production, and, at the same time, payments from customers were often delayed until the product was shipped. Unable to deliver on orders, the company became so strapped for cash that employee paycheques began to bounce. Finally, out of cash, the company ceased operations entirely in January 1995.

5. Do you think the company would have suffered the same fate if its product had been less popular? Why or why not?

6. The Grandmother Calendar Company clearly had a cash flow problem. In the context of the cash flow analysis we developed in Chapter 2, what was the impact of customers not paying until orders were shipped?

7. The firm actually priced its product to be about 20 percent less than that of competitors, even though the Grandmother calendar was more detailed. In retrospect, was this a wise choice?

8. If the firm was so successful at selling, why wouldn't a bank or some other lender step in and provide it with the cash it needed to continue?

9. Which is the biggest culprit here: too many orders, too little cash, or too little production capacity?

10. What are some of the actions that a small company like The Grandmother Calendar Company can take if it finds itself in a situation in which growth in sales outstrips production capacity and available financial resources? What other options (besides expansion of capacity) are available to a company when orders exceed capacity?

Questions and Problems

Basic
(Questions 1–15)

1. **Pro Forma Statements** Consider the following simplified financial statements for the Fisk Corporation (assuming no income taxes):

Income Statement		Balance Sheet			
Sales	$16,000	Assets	$8,900	Debt	$5,100
Costs	12,500			Equity	3,800
Net income	$ 3,500	Total	$8,900	Total	$8,900

Fisk has predicted a sales increase of 10 percent. It has predicted that every item on the balance sheet will increase by 10 percent as well. Create the pro forma statements and reconcile them. What is the plug variable here?

Basic
(continued)

2. Pro Forma Statements and EFN   In the previous question, assume Fisk pays out half of net income in the form of a cash dividend. Costs and assets vary with sales, but debt and equity do not. Prepare the pro forma statements and determine the external financing needed.

3. Calculating EFN   The most recent financial statements for Bradley's Bagels, Inc., are shown here (assuming no income taxes):

Income Statement			Balance Sheet			
Sales	$4,400		Assets	$13,400	Debt	$9,100
Costs	2,685				Equity	4,300
Net income	$1,715		Total	$13,400	Total	$13,400

Assets and costs are proportional to sales. Debt and equity are not. No dividends are paid. Next year's sales are projected to be $5,192. What is the external financing needed?

4. EFN   The most recent financial statements for McGillicudy, Inc., are shown here:

Income Statement			Balance Sheet			
Sales	$19,200		Assets	$93,000	Debt	$20,400
Costs	15,550				Equity	72,600
Taxable income	$3,650		Total	$93,000	Total	$93,000
Taxes (34%)	1,241					
Net income	$ 2,409					

Assets and costs are proportional to sales. Debt and equity are not. A dividend of $963.60 was paid, and McGillicudy wishes to maintain a constant payout ratio. Next year's sales are projected to be $23,040. What is the external financing needed?

5. EFN   The most recent financial statements for 2 Doors Down, Inc., are shown here:

Income Statement			Balance Sheet			
Sales	$3,600		Current Assets	$4,500	Current Liabilities	$ 920
Costs	2,900		Fixed Assets	3,900	Long-term debt	1,840
Taxable income	$ 700				Equity	$5,640
Taxes (34%)	238		Total	$8,400	Total	$8,400
Net income	$ 462					

Assets, costs, and current liabilities are proportional to sales. Long-term debt and equity are not. 2 Doors Down maintains a constant 50 percent dividend payout ratio. Like every other firm in its industry, next year's sales are projected to increase by exactly 15%. What is the external financing needed?

6. Calculating Internal Growth   The most recent financial statements for Panama Co. are shown here:

Income Statement			Balance Sheet			
Sales	$10,400		Current Assets	$11,000	Debt	$22,000
Costs	6,820		Fixed Assets	27,000	Equity	16,000
Taxable income	$ 3,580		Total	$38,000	Total	$38,000
Taxes (34%)	1,217					
Net income	$ 2,363					

Assets and costs are proportional to sales. Debt and equity are not. Panama maintains a constant 20 percent dividend payout ratio. No external equity financing is possible. What is the internal growth rate?

7. Calculating Sustainable Growth   For the company in the previous problem, what is the sustainable growth rate?

8. Sales and Growth   The most recent financial statements for Fontenot Co. are shown here:

Income Statement			Balance Sheet			
Sales	$54,000		Current Assets	$ 26,000	Long-term Debt	$ 58,000
Costs	34,800		Fixed Assets	105,000	Equity	73,000
Taxable income	$19,200		Total	$131,000	Total	$131,000
Taxes (34%)	6,528					
Net income	$12,672					

Basic
(continued)

Assets and costs are proportional to sales. The company maintains a constant 30 percent dividend payout ratio and a constant debt-equity ratio. What is the maximum increase in sales that can be sustained, assuming no new equity is issued?

9. **Calculating Retained Earnings from Pro Forma Income**   Consider the following income statement for the Armour Corporation:

ARMOUR CORPORATION
Income Statement

Sales	$29,000
Costs	11,200
Taxable income	$17,800
Taxes (34%)	6,052
Net income	$11,748

Dividends	$4,935	
Addition to retained earnings	6,813	

A 20 percent growth rate in sales is projected. Prepare a pro forma income statement assuming costs vary with sales and the dividend payout ratio is constant. What is the projected addition to retained earnings?

10. **Applying Percentage of Sales**   The balance sheet for the Armour Corporation follows. Based on this information and the income statement in the previous problem, supply the missing information using the percentage of sales approach. Assume that accounts payable vary with sales, whereas notes payable do not. Put "n/a" where needed.

ARMOUR CORPORATION
Balance Sheet

Assets	$	Percentage of Sales	Liabilities and Owners' Equity	$	Percentage of Sales
Current assets			Current liabilities		
Cash	$ 3,525	_____	Accounts payable	$ 3,000	_____
Accounts receivable	7,500	_____	Notes payable	7,500	_____
Inventory	6,000	_____	Total	$10,500	_____
Total	$17,025	_____	Long-term debt	$19,500	_____
Fixed assets			Owners' equity		
Net plant and equipment	$30,000	_____	Common stock and paid-in surplus	$15,000	_____
			Retained earnings	2,025	_____
Total assets	$47,025	_____	Total	$17,025	_____
			Total liabilities and owners' equity	$47,025	_____

11. **EFN and Sales**   From the previous two questions, prepare a pro forma balance sheet showing EFN, assuming a 15 percent increase in sales, no new external debt or equity financing, and a constant payout ratio.

12. **Internal Growth**   If Highfield Hobby Shop has a 10 percent ROA and a 20 percent payout ratio, what is its internal growth rate?

13. **Sustainable Growth**   If the Layla Corp. has a 19 percent ROE and a 25 percent payout ratio, what is its sustainable growth rate?

14. **Sustainable Growth**   Based on the following information, calculate the sustainable growth rate for Kaleb's Kickboxing:

Profit margin	= 8.9%
Capital intensity ratio	= .55
Debt-equity ratio	= .60
Net income	= $29,000
Dividends	= $15,000

What is the ROE here?

15. **Sustainable Growth**   Assuming the following ratios are constant, what is the sustainable growth rate?

Total asset turnover	= 1.40
Profit margin	= 7.6%
Equity multiplier	= 1.50
Payout ratio	= 40%

Intermediate
(Questions
16–29)

16. **Full-Capacity Sales** Thorpe Mfg., Inc., is currently operating at only 85 percent of fixed asset capacity. Current sales are $510,000. How fast can sales grow before any new fixed assets are needed?

17. **Fixed Assets and Capacity Usage** For the company in the previous problem, suppose fixed assets are $415,000 and sales are projected to grow to $680,000. How much in new fixed assets are required to support this growth in sales?

18. **Full-Capacity Sales** If a company is operating at 70 percent of fixed asset capacity and current sales are $250,000, how fast can that company grow before any new fixed assets are needed?

19. **Full-Capacity Sales** Red Brick Manufacturing sold $300,000 of red bricks in the last year. They were operating at 91 percent of fixed asset capacity. How fast can Red Brick grow before they need to purchase new fixed assets?

20. **Growth and Profit Margin** Top Hat Co. wishes to maintain a growth rate of 8 percent a year, a debt-equity ratio of .40, and a dividend payout ratio of 50 percent. The ratio of total assets to sales is constant at 1.30. What profit margin must the firm achieve?

21. **Growth and Debt-Equity Ratio** A firm wishes to maintain a growth rate of 11 percent and a dividend payout ratio of 60 percent. The ratio of total assets to sales is constant at .9, and profit margin is 9.5 percent. If the firm also wishes to maintain a constant debt-equity ratio, what must it be?

22. **Growth and Assets** A firm wishes to maintain an internal growth rate of 9 percent and a dividend payout ratio of 30 percent. The current profit margin is 8 percent and the firm uses no external financing sources. What must total asset turnover be?

23. **Sustainable Growth** Based on the following information, calculate the sustainable growth rate for Hendrix Guitars, Inc.:

Profit margin	= 6.4%
Total asset turnover	= 1.80
Total debt ratio	= .60
Payout ratio	= 60%

What is the ROA here?

24. **Sustainable Growth and Outside Financing** You've collected the following information about Bad Company, Inc.:

Sales	= $140,000
Net income	= $21,000
Dividends	= $12,000
Total debt	= $85,000
Total equity	= $49,000

What is the sustainable growth rate for Bad Company, Inc.? If it does grow at this rate, how much new borrowing will take place in the coming year, assuming a constant debt-equity ratio? What growth rate could be supported with no outside financing at all?

25. **Sustainable Growth Rate** No Return, Inc., had equity of $165,000 at the beginning of the year. At the end of the year, the company had total assets of $250,000. During the year the company sold no new equity. Net income for the year was $80,000 and dividends were $49,000. What is the sustainable growth rate for the company? What is the sustainable growth rate if you use the formula ROE × R and beginning of period equity? What is the sustainable growth rate if you use end of period equity in this formula? Is this number too high or too low? Why?

26. **Internal Growth Rates** Calculate the internal growth rate for the company in the previous problem. Now calculate the internal growth rate using ROA × R for both beginning of period and end of period total assets. What do you observe?

27. **Calculating EFN** The most recent financial statements for Moose Tours, Inc., follow. Sales for 2007 are projected to grow by 20 percent. Interest expense will remain constant; the tax rate and the dividend payout rate will also remain constant. Costs, other expenses, current assets, and accounts payable increase spontaneously with sales. If the firm is operating at full capacity and no new debt or equity is issued, what is the external financing needed to support the 20 percent growth rate in sales?

MOOSE TOURS, INC.
2006 Income Statement

Sales	$905,000
Costs	710,000
Other expenses	12,000
Earnings before interest and taxes	$183,000
Interest paid	19,700
Taxable income	$163,300
Taxes (35%)	57,155
Net income	$106,145
Dividends	$42,458
Addition to retained earnings	63,687

Intermediate
(continued)

MOOSE TOURS, INC.
Balance Sheet as of December 31, 2006

Assets		Liabilities and Owners' Equity	
Current assets		Current liabilities	
Cash	$ 25,000	Accounts payable	$ 65,000
Accounts receivable	43,000	Notes payable	9,000
Inventory	76,000	Total	$ 74,000
Total	$144,000	Long-term debt	$156,000
Fixed assets		Owners' equity	
Net plant and equipment	$364,000	Common stock and paid-in surplus	$ 21,000
		Retained earnings	257,000
		Total	$278,000
Total assets	$508,000	Total liabilities and owners' equity	$508,000

28. **Capacity Usage and Growth** In the previous problem, suppose the firm was operating at only 80 percent capacity in 2004. What is EFN now?

29. **Calculating EFN** In Problem 25, suppose the firm wishes to keep its debt-equity ratio constant. What is EFN now?

30. **EFN and Internal Growth** Redo Problem 25 using sales growth rates of 15 and 25 percent in addition to 20 percent. Illustrate graphically the relationship between EFN and the growth rate, and use this graph to determine the relationship between them. At what growth rate is the EFN equal to zero? Why is this internal growth rate different from that found by using the equation in the text?

Challenge
(Questions
30–32)

31. **EFN and Sustainable Growth** Redo Problem 27 using sales growth rates of 30 and 35 percent in addition to 20 percent. Illustrate graphically the relationship between EFN and the growth rate, and use this graph to determine the relationship between them. At what growth rate is the EFN equal to zero? Why is this sustainable growth rate different from that found by using the equation in the text?

32. **Constraints on Growth** Bulla Recording, Inc., wishes to maintain a growth rate of 14 percent per year and a debt-equity ratio of .30. Profit margin is 6.2 percent, and the ratio of total assets to sales is constant at 1.55. Is this growth rate possible? To answer, determine what the dividend payout ratio must be. How do you interpret the result?

MINI CASE

You are an analyst for a major investment bank, and your manager has asked you to develop pro forma financial information for Skyline Incorporated. You have contacted management at Skyline, who have provided you with the following financial statements for 2006:

Income Statement for the Year Ended December 31, 2006 (in 000s)

Sales	$ 10,430
Cost of goods sold	4,339
Operating expenses	2,100
Depreciation	765
EBIT	$ 3,226
Interest	315
Taxable income	$ 2,911
Taxes (at 35%)	1,019
Net income	$ 1,892

Balance Sheet as at December 31, 2006 (in 000s)

Assets	
Cash	$ 795
Accounts receivable	1,550
Inventory	963
Total current assets	$ 3,308
Fixed assets	14,743
Total assets	$ 18,051
Liabilities and Owners' Equity	
Accounts payable	$ 1,032
Short-term debt	550
Total current liabilities	$ 1,582
Long-term debt	2,527
Total liabilities	$ 4,109
Common shares	9,725
Retained earnings	4,217
Total liabilities and owners' equity	$ 18,051

MINI CASE (continued)

You also asked a number of specific questions about the company's expected performance in the next year, and were provided with the following:

- Projected sales for 2007 (in 000s)

January	$ 150	July	$1,425
February	150	August	1,275
March	150	September	1,200
April	1,275	October	450
May	2,469	November	150
June	1,950	December	150

- Whlle demand for the company's products is highly seasonal, the firm's labour availability and plant capacity mean it must undertake even production throughout the year.
- Skyline is expecting its cost of goods sold to increase with the rate of inflation, or about 0.5% each quarter through 2007.
- Accounts payable are paid two months after the material is used in production. Labour costs must be paid immediately.
- Labour is approximately 65% of the cost of goods sold.
- Depreciation for 2007 is expected to be $625,000.
- A minimum cash balance of $1,100 is required to operate the company.

- Taxes are paid each December.
- A total of $850,000 of the long-term debt will be due this June (with no more issued).
- The firm has access to a line of credit for any cash shortfalls.

a) Prepare quarterly pro forma financial statements for 2007 (discuss any necessary assumptions).

b) Your manager is concerned that with present poor economic conditions, Skyline's second quarter sales could be as much as 25 percent lower. However, an economic recovery is predicted by some and would result in sales that are 10 percent higher through the last three quarters. Adjust the pro forma statements to reflect these possibilities.

c) If there are 1,500,000 common shares in Skyline, how much is each share worth right now (at the start of 2007)? How much will they be worth at the end of 2007 if the projections in part (a) are correct?

d) Skyline's bank is considering placing a new limit of $2,500,000 on the company's line of credit. If all the company's short-term debt is on this line of credit, is there a possible cash flow concern for the company under each of the scenarios?

S&P Problems

1. **Calculating EFN** Find the income statements and balance sheets for Magna International (MGA). Assuming sales grow by 10 percent, what is the EFN for Magna next year? Assume non-operating income/expense and special items will be zero next year. Assets, costs, and current liabilities are proportional to sales. Long-term debt and equity are not. Magna will have the same tax rate next year as it does in the current year.

2. **Internal and Sustainable Growth Rates** Look up the financial statements for Potash Corporation of Saskatchewan Inc. (POT) and CanWest Global Communications (CWG). For each company, calculate the internal growth rate and sustainable growth rate over the past two years. Are the growth rates the same for each company for the two years? Why or why not?

Internet Application Questions

1. Go to www.globeinvestor.com and enter the ticker symbol "TRP-T" for TransCanada Pipelines. When you get the quote, follow the "Reports" link. What is projected earnings growth for next year? For the next five years? How do these earnings growth projections compare to the industry and to the TSX-S&P index?

2. You can find the homepage for Barrick at www.barrick.com. Go to the Annual Report. Using the growth in sales for the most recent year as the projected sales growth rate for next year, construct a pro forma income statement and balance sheet.

3. Locate the most recent annual financial statements for Canadian Tire at www.canadiantire.ca by clicking on "Investor Relations" and then on "Annual/Quarterly Reports." Using the information from the financial statements, what is the internal growth rate for Canadian Tire? What is the sustainable growth rate?

Suggested Readings

A useful textbook on financial planning is:
    Higgins, R. C. *Analysis for Financial Management.* 8th ed. McGraw-Hill Irwin, 2007.

Sustainable growth is discussed in:
    Higgins, R. C. "Sustainable Growth under Inflation." *Financial Management* 10, Autumn 1981.

For a critical discussion of sustainable growth, see:
    Rappaport, A. *Creating Shareholder Value: The New Standard for Business Performance.* New York: Free Press, 1986.

 **APPENDIX 4A**

A FINANCIAL PLANNING MODEL FOR THE HOFFMAN COMPANY

In this Appendix, we discuss how to get started with building a financial planning model in somewhat greater detail.[9] Our goal is to build a simple model for the Hoffman Company, incorporating some features commonly found in planning models. This model includes our earlier percentage of sales approach as a special case, but it is more flexible and a little more realistic. It is by no means complete, but it should give you a good idea of how to proceed.

Table 4A.1 shows the financial statements for the Hoffman Company in slightly more detail than we had before. Primarily, we have separated out depreciation and interest. We have also included some abbreviations that we use to refer to the various items on these statements.

As we have discussed, it is necessary to designate a plug. We use new borrowing as the plug in our model, and we assume Hoffman does not issue new equity. This means our model allows the debt/equity ratio to change if needed. Our model takes a sales forecast as its input and supplies the pro forma financial statements as its output.

To create our model, we take the financial statements and replace the numbers with formulas describing their relationships. In addition to the preceding symbols, we use $E0$ to stand for the beginning equity.

In Table 4A.2, the symbols a_1 through a_7 are called the *model parameters*. These describe the relationships among the variables. For example, a_7 is the relationship between sales and total assets, and it can be interpreted as the capital intensity ratio:

$$TA = a_7 \times S$$

$$a_7 = TA/S = \text{Capital intensity ratio}$$

TABLE 4A.1

HOFFMAN COMPANY
Income Statement and Balance Sheet

Income Statement

Sales	*(S)*		$500
Costs	*(C)*		235
Depreciation	*(DEP)*		120
Interest	*(INT)*		45
Taxable income	*(TI)*		100
Taxes	*(T)*		34
Net income	*(NI)*		$ 66
Addition to retained earnings	*(ARE)*	$22	
Dividends	*(DIV)*	$44	

Balance Sheet

Assets			Liabilities		
Current assets	*(CA)*	$ 400	Total debt	*(D)*	$ 450
Net fixed assets	*(FA)*	600	Owners' equity	*(E)*	550
Total assets	*(TA)*	$1,000	Total liabilities	*(L)*	$1,000

9 This Appendix draws, in part, from R. A. Brealey and S. C. Myers, *Principles of Corporate Finance*, 3d ed. (New York: McGraw-Hill Book Company, 1984), chap. 28.

TABLE 4A.2

HOFFMAN COMPANY
Long-Term Financial Planning Model

Income Statement

Sales	$S = \text{Input by user}$
Costs	$C = a_1 \times S$
Depreciation	$DEP = a_2 \times FA$
Interest	$INT = a_3 \times D$
Taxable income	$TI = S - C - DEP - INT$
Taxes	$T = a_4 \times TI$
Net income	$NI = TI - T$
Addition to retained earnings	$ARE = NI - DIV$
Dividends	$DIV = a_5 \times NI$

Balance Sheet

Assets		*Liabilities*	
Current assets	$CA = TA - FA$	Total debt	$D = TA - E$
Net fixed assets	$FA = a_6 \times TA$	Owners' equity	$E = E_0 \times ARE$
Total assets	$TA = a_7 \times S$	Total liabilities	$L = TA$

Similarly, a_3 is the relationship between total debt and interest paid, so a_3 can be interpreted as an overall interest rate. The tax rate is given by a_4, and a_5 is the dividend payout ratio.

This model uses new borrowing as the plug by first setting total liabilities and owners' equity equal to total assets. Next, the ending amount for owners' equity is calculated as the beginning amount, E_0, plus the addition to retained earnings, ARE. The difference between these amounts, $TA - E$, is the new total debt needed to balance the balance sheet.

The primary difference between this model and our earlier EFN approach is that we have separated out depreciation and interest. Notice that a_2 expresses depreciation as a fraction of beginning fixed assets. This, along with the assumption that the interest paid depends on total debt, is a more realistic approach than we used earlier. However, since interest and depreciation now do not necessarily vary directly with sales, we no longer have a constant profit margin.

Model parameters a_1 to a_7 can be based on a simple percentage of sales approach, or they can be determined by any other means that the model builder wishes. For example, they might be based on average values for the last several years, industry standards, subjective estimates, or even company targets. Alternatively, sophisticated statistical techniques can be used to estimate them.

We finish this discussion by estimating the model parameters for Hoffman using simple percentages and then generating pro forma statements for a \$600 predicted sales level. We estimate the parameters as:

$a_1 = \$235/500 = .47 = \text{Cost percentage}$
$a_2 = \$120/600 = .20 = \text{Depreciation rate}$
$a_3 = \$45/450 = .10 = \text{Interest rate}$
$a_4 = \$34/100 = .34 = \text{Tax rate}$
$a_5 = \$44/66 = 2/3 = \text{Payout ratio}$
$a_6 = \$600/1,000 = .60 = \text{Fixed assets/Total assets}$
$a_7 = \$1,000/500 = 2 = \text{Capital intensity ratio}$

With these parameters and a sales forecast of $600, our pro forma financial statements are shown in Table 4A.3.[10]

What our model is now telling us is that a sales increase of $100 requires $200 in net new assets (since the capital intensity ratio is 2). To finance this, we use $24 in internally generated funds. The balance of $200 − $24 = $176 has to be borrowed. This amount is the increase in total debt on the balance sheet: $626 − $450 = $176. If we pursue this plan, our profit margin would decline somewhat and the debt/equity ratio would rise.

Appendix Questions and Problems

Consider the following simplified financial statements from the Hoffman Company.

HOFFMAN COMPANY
Income Statement and Balance Sheet

Income Statement

Sales	$5,623
Costs	4,500
Taxable income	$ 1,123
Taxes	381
Net income	$ 742
Addition to retained earnings	$247
Dividends	$495

Balance Sheet

Assets		Liabilities	
Current assets	$3,000	Total debt	$3,375
Net fixed assets	4,500	Owners' equity	4,125
Total assets	$7,500	Total liabilities	$7,500

A.1 Prepare a financial planning model along the lines of our model for the Hoffman Company. Estimate the values for the model parameters using percentages calculated from these statements. Prepare the pro forma statements by recalculating the model by hand three or four times.

A.2 Modify the model in the previous question so that borrowing doesn't change and new equity sales are the plug.

A.3 This is a challenge question. How would you modify the model for Hoffman Company if you wanted to maintain a constant debt/equity ratio?

A.4 This is a challenge question. In our financial planning model for Hoffman, show that it is possible to solve algebraically for the amount of new borrowing. Can you interpret the resulting expression?

TABLE 4A.3

HOFFMAN COMPANY
Pro Forma Financial Statements

Income Statement

Sales	(S)	$600	= Input
Cost of sales	(C)	282	= .47 × $600
Depreciation	(DEP)	144	= .20 × $720
Interest	(INT)	63	= .10 × $626
Taxable income	(TI)	$111	= $600 − 282 − 144 − 63
Taxes	(T)	38	= .34 × $111
Net income	(NI)	$ 73	= $111 − 38

---

10 If you put this model in a standard computer spreadsheet (as we did to generate the numbers), the software may "complain" that a "circular" reference exists, because the amount of new borrowing depends on the addition to retained earnings, the addition to retained earnings depends on the interest paid, the interest paid depends on the borrowing, and so on. This isn't really a problem; we can have the spreadsheet recalculated a few times until the numbers stop changing.

There really is no circular problem with this method because there is only one unknown, the ending total debt, which we can solve for explicitly. This will usually be the case as long as there is a single plug variable. The algebra can get to be somewhat tedious, however. See the problems at the end of this Appendix for more information.

APPENDIX 4B

DERIVATION OF THE SUSTAINABLE GROWTH FORMULA

$$EFN = \text{Increase in total assets} - \text{Addition to retained earnings} \qquad [4B.1]$$
$$- \text{New borrowing}$$
$$= A(g) - p(S)R \times (1 + g) - pS(R) \times (1 + g)[D/E]$$

Since

$$EFN = 0$$
$$0 = A(g) - pS(R)(1 + g)[1 + D/E]$$
$$= -pS(R)[1 + D/E] + [A - pS(R) \times (1 + D/E)]g$$

Dividing through by A gives:

$$= -p(S/A)(R)[1 + D/E] + [1 - p(S/A)(R) \times (1 + D/E)]g$$

$$g^* = \frac{p(S/A)(R)[1 + D/E]}{1 - p(S/A)(R)[1 + D/E]}$$

In the last chapter, we saw that the return on equity could be decomposed into its various components using the Du Pont identity. Recall that from the Du Pont identity, ROE can be written as:

$$ROE = \text{Profit margin} \times \text{Total asset turnover} \times \text{Equity multiplier}$$

Using our current symbols for these ratios, ROE is:

$$ROE = p(S/A)(1 + D/E) \qquad [4B.2]$$

$$g^* = \frac{ROE \times R}{1 - ROE \times R}$$

MINI CASE

Ratios and Financial Planning at S&S Air, Inc.

Chris Guthrie was recently hired by S&S Air, Inc., to assist the company with its financial planning, and to evaluate the company's performance. Chris graduated from university five years ago with a finance degree. He has been employed in the finance department of a Fortune 500 company since then.

S&S Air was founded 10 years ago by friends Mark Sexton and Todd Story. The company has manufactured and sold light airplanes over this period, and the company's products have received high reviews for safety and reliability. The company has a niche market in that it sells primarily to individuals who own and fly their own airplanes. The company has two models, the Birdie, which sells for $53,000, and the Eagle, which sells for $78,000.

While the company manufactures aircraft, its operations are different from those of commercial aircraft companies. S&S Air builds aircraft to order. By using prefabricated parts, the company is able to complete the manufacture of an airplane in only five weeks. The company also receives a deposit on each order, as well as another partial payment before the order is complete. In contrast, a commercial airplane may take one and a half to two years to manufacture an airplane once the order is placed.

Mark and Todd have provided the following financial statements. Chris has gathered the industry ratios for the light airplane manufacturing industry.

S&S Air, Inc.
2006 Income Statement

Sales		$12,870,000
Cost of goods sold		9,070,000
Other expenses		1,538,000
Depreciation		420,000
EBIT		$ 1,842,000
Interest		231,500
Taxable income		$ 1,610,500
Taxes (40%)		644,200
Net income		$ 966,300
Dividends	$289,890	
Add. to retained earnings	676,410	

S&S Air, Inc.
2006 Balance Sheet

Assets		Liabilities & Equity	
Current assets		Current liabilities	
Cash	$ 234,000	Accounts payable	$ 497,000
Accounts receivable	421,000	Notes payable	1,006,000
Inventory	472,000	Total current liabilities	$1,503,000
Total current assets	$1,127,000		
		Long-term debt	$2,595,000
Fixed assets			
Net plant and equipment	$7,228,000	Shareholder equity	
		Common stock	$ 100,000
		Retained earnings	4,157,000
		Total equity	$4,257,000
Total assets	$8,355,000	Total liabilities & equity	$8,355,000

Light Airplane Industry Ratios

	Lower Quartile	Median	Upper Quartile
Current ratio	0.50	1.43	1.89
Quick ratio	0.21	0.38	0.62
Cash ratio	0.08	0.21	0.39
Total asset turnover	0.68	0.85	1.38
Inventory turnover	4.89	6.15	10.89
Receivables turnover	6.27	9.82	14.11
Total debt ratio	0.44	0.52	0.61
Debt-equity ratio	0.79	1.08	1.56
Equity multiplier	1.79	2.08	2.56
Times interest earned	5.18	8.06	9.83
Cash coverage ratio	5.84	8.43	10.27
Profit margin	4.05%	6.98%	9.87%
Return on assets	6.05%	10.53%	13.21%
Return on equity	9.93%	16.54%	26.15%

Questions

1. Calculate the following ratios for S&S Air: current ratio, quick ratio, cash ratio, total asset turnover, inventory turnover, receivables turnover, total debt ratio, debt-equity ratio, equity multiplier, times interest earned, cash coverage, profit margin, return on assets, and return on equity.

2. Mark and Todd agree that a ratio analysis can provide a measure of the company's performance. They have chosen Bombardier Aerospace as an aspirant company. Would you choose Bombardier Aerospace as an aspirant company? Why or why not?

3. Compare the performance of S&S Air to the industry average. For each ratio, comment on why it might be viewed as positive or negative relative to the industry. Suppose you create an inventory ratio calculated by inventory divided by current liabilities. How do you think S&S Air's ratio would compare to the industry average?

4. Calculate the internal growth rate and sustainable growth rate for S&S Air. What do these numbers mean?

5. S&S Air is planning for a growth rate of 20 percent next year. Calculate EFN assuming the company is operating at full capacity.

6. Most assets can be increased as a percentage of sales. For instance, cash can be increased by any amount. Fixed assets often must be increased in specific amounts since it is usually impossible or impractical to buy part of a new plant or machine. So, assume S&S Air cannot increase fixed assets as a percentage of sales. Instead, whenever the company needs to purchase new manufacturing equipment, it must purchase in the amount of $3,000,000. Calculate the new EFN with this assumption. What does this imply about capacity utilization for the company next year?

Valuation of Future Cash Flows

CHAPTER 5

Introduction to Valuation: The Time Value of Money

On February 5, 2000, ScotiaMcLeod, an investment dealer owned by the Bank of Nova Scotia, offered some Government of Canada stripped coupons from its inventories for sale to the public. Each coupon represented a promise to pay $100 to the holder at the maturity date on February 5, 2020, but investors would receive nothing until then. Investors paid ScotiaMcLeod $29.19 for each coupon. This means that investors paid $29.19 on February 5, 2000 for $100 to be received 20 years later. This is about the simplest type of security you will find—paying an amount today in exchange for a lump sum to be received at a future date.

Is giving up $29.19 in exchange for $100 in 20 years a good deal? On the plus side, you get back $3.43 for every $1 you put up. That probably sounds good, but, on the down side, you have to wait 20 years to get it. What you need to know is how to analyze this trade-off; this chapter give you the tools you need.

www.scotiamcleod.com

ONE OF THE BASIC problems faced by financial managers is how to determine the value today of cash flows that are expected in the future. For example, suppose your province's finance minister asked your advice on overhauling the provincial lottery with a view toward increasing revenues to help balance the budget. One attractive idea is to increase the size of the prizes while easing the strain on the treasury by spreading out the payments over time. Instead of offering $1 million paid immediately, the new lottery would pay $1 million in 10 annual payments of $100,000. How much would this save the province? The answer depends on the time value of money, the subject of this chapter.

In the most general sense, the phrase *time value of money* refers to the fact that a dollar in hand today is worth more than a dollar promised at some time in the future. On a practical level, one reason for this is that you could earn interest while you waited; so a dollar today would grow to more than a dollar later. The trade-off between money now and money later thus depends on, among other things, the rate you can earn by investing. Our goal in this chapter is to explicitly evaluate this trade-off between dollars today and dollars at some future time.

A thorough understanding of the material in this chapter is critical to understanding material in subsequent chapters, so you should study it with particular care. We will present a number of examples in this chapter. In many problems, your answer may differ from ours slightly. This can happen because of rounding and is not a cause for concern.

5.1

future value (FV)
The amount an investment is worth after one or more periods. Also compound value.

FUTURE VALUE AND COMPOUNDING

We begin by studying future value. **Future value** refers to the amount of money an investment would grow to over some length of time at some given interest rate. Put another way, future value is the cash value of an investment sometime in the future. We start out by considering the simplest case, a single period investment.

Investing for a Single Period

Suppose you were to invest $100 in a savings account that pays 10 percent interest per year. How much will you have in one year? You would have $110. This $110 is equal to your original *principal* of $100 plus $10 in interest that you earn. We say that $110 is the future value (FV) of $100 invested for one year at 10 percent, and we simply mean that $100 today is worth $110 in one year, given that 10 percent is the interest rate.

In general, if you invest for one period at an interest rate of r, your investment grows to $(1 + r)$ per dollar invested. In our example, r is 10 percent, so your investment grows to $(1 + .10)$ = 1.1 dollars per dollar invested. You invested $100 in this case, so you ended up with $100 × (1.10) = $110.

You might wonder if the single period in this example has to be a year. The answer is no. For example, if the interest rate were 2 percent per quarter, your $100 would grow to $100 × (1 + .02) = $102 by the end of the quarter. You might also wonder if 2 percent every quarter is the same as 8 percent per year. The answer is again no, and we'll explain why a little later.

Investing for More than One Period

Going back to our $100 investment, what will you have after two years, assuming the interest rate doesn't change? If you leave the entire $110 in the bank, you will earn $110 × .10 = $11 in interest during the second year, so you will have a total of $110 + 11 = $121. This $121 is the future value of $100 in two years at 10 percent. Another way of looking at it is that one year from now you are effectively investing $110 at 10 percent for a year. This is a single period problem, so you'll end up with $1.1 for every dollar invested or $110 × 1.1 = $121 total.

This $121 has four parts. The first part is the $100 original principal. The second part is the $10 in interest you earned in the first year along with another $10 (the third part) you earn in the second year, for a total of $120. The last $1 you end up with (the fourth part) is interest you earn in the second year on the interest paid in the first year: $10 × .10 = $1.

compounding
The process of accumulating interest in an investment over time to earn more interest.

This process of leaving your money and any accumulated interest in an investment for more than one period, thereby *reinvesting* the interest, is called **compounding.** Compounding the interest means earning **interest on interest,** so we call the result **compound interest.** With **simple interest,** the interest is not reinvested, so interest is earned each period only on the original principal.

interest on interest
Interest earned on the reinvestment of previous interest payments.

We now take a closer look at how we calculated the $121 future value. We multiplied $110 by 1.1 to get $121. The $110, however, was $100 also multiplied by 1.1. In other words:

compound interest
Interest earned on both the initial principal and the interest reinvested from prior periods.

$$\$121 = \$110 \times 1.1$$
$$= (\$100 \times 1.1) \times 1.1$$
$$= \$100 \times (1.1 \times 1.1)$$
$$= \$100 \times 1.1^2$$
$$= \$100 \times 1.21$$

simple interest
Interest earned only on the original principal amount invested.

As our example suggests, the future value of $1 invested for t periods at a rate of r per period is:

$$\text{Future value} = \$1 \times (1 + r)^t \qquad [5.1]$$

The expression $(1 + r)^t$ is sometimes called the *future value interest factor* (or just future value factor) for $1 invested at r percent for t periods and can be abbreviated as FVIF (r,t).

In our example, what would your $100 be worth after five years? We can first compute the relevant future value factor as:

$$(1 + r)^t = (1 + .10)^5 = 1.1^5 = 1.6105$$

Your $100 would thus grow to:

$$\$100 \times 1.6105 = \$161.05$$

EXAMPLE 5.1: Interest on Interest

Suppose you locate a two-year investment that pays 8 percent per year. If you invest $325, how much will you have at the end of the two years? How much of this is simple interest? How much is compound interest?

At the end of the first year, you would have $325 × (1 + .08) = $351. If you reinvest this entire amount and thereby compound the interest, you would have $351 × 1.08 = $379.08 at the end of the second year. The total interest you

earn is thus $379.08 – 325 = $54.08. Your $325 original principal earns $325 × .08 = $26 in interest each year, for a two-year total of $52 in simple interest. The remaining $54.08 – 52 = $2.08 results from compounding. You can check this by noting that the interest earned in the first year is $26. The interest on interest earned in the second year thus amounts to $26 × .08 = $2.08, as we calculated.

For a discussion of time value concepts (and more) see www.financeprofessor.com or www.teachmefinance.com

The growth of your $100 each year is illustrated in Table 5.1. As shown, the interest earned in each year is equal to the beginning amount multiplied by the interest rate of 10 percent.

In Table 5.1, notice that the total interest you earn is $61.05. Over the five-year span of this investment, the simple interest is $100 × .10 = $10 per year, so you accumulate $50 this way. The other $11.05 is from compounding.

Figure 5.1 illustrates the growth of the compound interest in Table 5.1. Notice how the simple interest is constant each year, but the compound interest you earn gets bigger every year. The size of the compound interest keeps increasing because more and more interest builds up and there is thus more to compound.

Future values depend critically on the assumed interest rate, particularly for long-lived investments. Figure 5.2 illustrates this relationship by plotting the growth of $1 for different rates and lengths of time. Notice that the future value of $1 after 10 years is about $6.20 at a 20 percent rate, but it is only about $2.60 at 10 percent. In this case, doubling the interest rate more than doubles the future value.

To solve future value problems, we need to come up with the relevant future value factors. There are several different ways of doing this. In our example, we could have multiplied 1.1 by itself five times. This will work just fine, but it would get to be very tedious for, say, a 30-year investment.

Fortunately, there are several easier ways to get future value factors. Most calculators have a key labelled y^x. You can usually just enter 1.1, press this key, enter 5, and press the = key to get the answer. This is an easy way to calculate future value factors because it's quick and accurate.

Alternatively, you can use a table that contains future value factors for some common interest rates and time periods. Table 5.2 contains some of these factors. Table A.1 in the Appendix at the end of the book contains a much larger set. To use the table, find the column that corresponds to 10 percent. Then look down the rows until you come to five periods. You should find the factor that we calculated, 1.6105.

Tables similar to Table 5.2 are not as common as they once were because they predate inexpensive calculators and are only available for a relatively small number of rates. Interest rates are often quoted to three or four decimal points, so the number of tables needed to deal with these accurately would be quite large. As a result, businesspeople rarely use them. We illustrate the use of a calculator in this chapter.

TABLE 5.1 Future values of $100 at 10 percent	Year	Beginning Amount	Simple Interest	Interest on Interest	Total Interest Earned	Ending Amount
	1	$100.00	10	0.00	$10.00	$110.00
	2	110.00	10	1.00	11.00	121.00
	3	121.00	10	2.10	12.10	133.10
	4	133.10	10	3.31	13.31	146.41
	5	146.41	10	4.64	14.64	161.05
			Total simple interest 50	Total interest on interest $11.05	Total interest $61.05	

FIGURE 5.1

Future value, simple interest, and compound interest

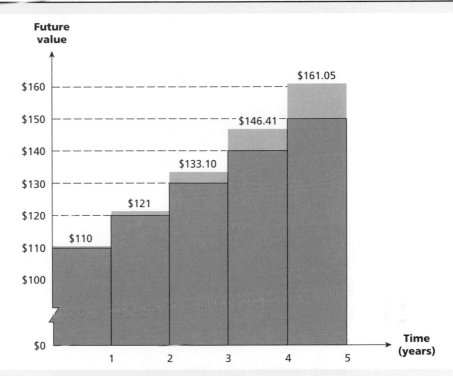

Growth of $100 original amount at 10% per year. Shaded area represents the portion of the total that results from compounding of interest.

FIGURE 5.2

Future value of $1 for different periods and rates

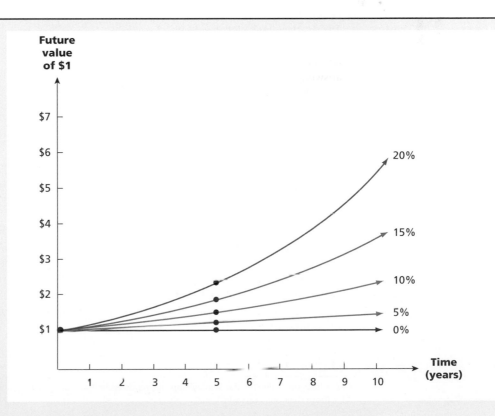

TABLE 5.2
Future value interest factors

Periods	Interest Rate			
	5%	**10%**	**15%**	**20%**
1	1.0500	1.1000	1.1500	1.2000
2	1.1025	1.2100	1.3225	1.4400
3	1.1576	1.3310	1.5209	1.7280
4	1.2155	1.4641	1.7490	2.0736
5	1.2763	1.6105	2.0114	2.4883

EXAMPLE 5.2: Compound Interest

You've located an investment that pays 12 percent. That rate sounds good to you, so you invest $400. How much will you have in three years? How much will you have in seven years? At the end of seven years, how much interest have you earned? How much of that interest results from compounding?

Based on our discussion, we can calculate the future value factor for 12 percent and three years as:

$$(1 + r)^t = 1.12^3 = 1.4049$$

Your $400 thus grows to:

$$\$400 \times 1.4049 = \$561.97$$

After seven years, you would have:

$$\$400 \times 1.12^7 = \$400 \times 2.2107 = \$884.27$$

Thus, you more than double your money over seven years.

Since you invested $400, the interest in the $884.27 future value is $884.27 – 400 = $484.27. At 12 percent, your $400 investment earns $400 × .12 = $48 in simple interest every year. Over seven years, the simple interest thus totals 7 × $48 = $336. The other $484.27 – 336 = $148.27 is from compounding.

EXAMPLE 5.3: How Much for that Cup?

To further illustrate the effect of compounding for long horizons, consider the case of the Stanley Cup. The cup, the oldest team trophy in North America, was originally purchased by the governor general of Canada, Frederick Arthur Stanley, in 1893. Lord Stanley paid $48.67 for the cup over 110 years ago. The Hockey Hall of Fame in Toronto has the cup insured for $1.5 million, although to millions of fans across Canada, it is priceless.[1] What would the sum Lord Stanley paid for the cup be worth today if he had invested it at 10 percent rather than purchasing the cup?

110 years, at 10 percent, $48.67 grows quite a bit. How much? The future value factor is approximately:

$$(1 + r)^t = (1.10)^{110} = 35,743.36$$
$$FV = \$48.67 \times 35,743.36 = \$1,739,629.30$$

Well, $1,739,629.30 is a lot of money, considerably more than $1.5 million—of course, no hockey fan would recommend that Lord Stanley should have invested the money rather than buy the cup!

This example is something of an exaggeration, of course. In 1893, it would not have been easy to locate an investment that would pay 10 percent every year without fail for the next 110 years.

These tables still serve a useful purpose. To make sure that you are doing the calculations correctly, pick a factor from the table and then calculate it yourself to see that you get the same answer. There are plenty of numbers to choose from.

The effect of compounding is not great over short time periods, but it really starts to add up as the horizon grows. To take an extreme case, suppose one of your more frugal ancestors had invested $5 for you at a 6 percent interest 200 years ago, how much would you have today? The future value factor is a substantial $(1.06)^{200} = 115,125.90$ (you won't find this one in a table), so you would have $5 × 115,125.90 = $575,629.52. Notice that the simple interest is just $5 × 0.06 = $.30 per year. After 200 years, this amounts to $60. The rest is from reinvesting. Such is the power of compound interest!

---

1 When this value for the Stanley Cup was reported in 2002, the practice of compounding interest was already more than 600 years old.

CALCULATOR HINTS

Using a Financial Calculator

Although there are the various ways of calculating future values we have described so far, many of you will decide that a financial calculator is the way to go. If you are planning on using one, you should read this extended hint; otherwise, skip it.

A financial calculator is simply an ordinary calculator with a few extra features. In particular, it knows some of the most commonly used financial formulas, so it can directly compute things like future values.

Financial calculators have the advantage that they handle a lot of the computation, but that is really all. In other words, you still have to understand the problem; the calculator just does some of the arithmetic. We therefore have two goals for this section. First, we'll discuss how to compute future values. After that, we'll show you how to avoid the most common mistakes people make when they start using financial calculators. Note that the actual keystrokes vary from calculator to calculator, so the following examples are for illustrative purposes only.

How to Calculate Future Values with a Financial Calculator   Examining a typical financial calculator, you will find five keys of particular interest. They usually look like this:

For now, we need to focus on four of these. The keys labelled **PV** and **FV** are just what you would guess, present value and future value. The key labelled **N** refers to the number of periods, which is what we have been calling t. Finally, **%i** stands for the interest rate, which we have called r.*

If we have the financial calculator set up right (see our next section), then calculating a future value is very simple. Take a look back at our question involving the future value of $100 at 10 percent for five years. We have seen that the answer is $161.05. The exact keystrokes will differ depending on what type of calculator you use, but here is basically all you do:

1. Enter −100. Press the **PV** key. (The negative sign is explained below.)
2. Enter 10. Press the **%i** key. (Notice that we entered 10, not .10; see below.)
3. Enter 5. Press the **N** key.

Now we have entered all of the relevant information. To solve for the future value, we need to ask the calculator what the FV is. Depending on your calculator, you either press the button labelled "CPT" (for compute) and then press **FV**, or else you just press **FV**. Either way, you should get 161.05. If you don't (and you probably won't if this is the first time you have used a financial calculator!), we will offer some help in our next section.

Before we explain the kinds of problems that you are likely to run into, we want to establish a standard format for showing you how to use a financial calculator. Using the example we just looked at, in the future, we will illustrate such problems like this:

---

* The reason financial calculators use N and %i is that the most common use for these calculators is determining loan payments. In this context, N is the number of payments and %i is the interest rate on the loan. But, as we will see, there are many other uses of financial calculators that don't involve loan payments and interest rates.

CALCULATOR HINTS

Enter	5	10		−100	
	N	%i	PMT	PV	FV
Solve for					161.05

If all else fails, you can read the manual that came with the calculator.

How to Get the Wrong Answer Using a Financial Calculator   There are a couple of common (and frustrating) problems that cause a lot of trouble with financial calculators. In this section, we provide some important *dos* and *don'ts*. If you just can't seem to get a problem to work out, you should refer back to this section.

There are two categories we examine, three things you need to do only once and three things you need to do every time you work a problem. The things you need to do just once deal with the following calculator settings:

1. *Make sure your calculator is set to display a large number of decimal places.* Most financial calculators only display two decimal places; this causes problems because we frequently work with numbers—like interest rates—that are very small.
2. *Make sure your calculator is set to assume only one payment per period or per year.* Most financial calculators assume monthly payments (12 per year) unless you say otherwise.
3. *Make sure your calculator is in "end" mode.* This is usually the default, but you can accidently change to "begin" mode.

If you don't know how to set these three things, see your calculator's operating manual. There are also three things you need to do every time you work a problem:

1. *Before you start, completely clear out the calculator.* This is very important. Failure to do this is the number one reason for wrong answers; you simply must get in the habit of clearing the calculator every time you start a problem. How you do this depends on the calculator, but you must do more than just clear the display. For example, on a Texas Instruments BA II Plus you must press **2nd** then **CLR TVM** for *clear time value of money.* There is a similar command on your calculator. Learn it!

    Note that turning the calculator off and back on won't do it. Most financial calculators remember everything you enter, even after you turn them off. In other words, they remember all your mistakes unless you explicitly clear them out. Also, if you are in the middle of a problem and make a mistake, *clear it out and start over.* Better to be safe than sorry.
2. *Put a negative sign on cash outflows.* Most financial calculators require you to put a negative sign on cash outflows and a positive sign on cash inflows. As a practical matter, this usually just means that you should enter the present value amount with a negative sign (because normally the present value represents the amount you give up today in exchange for cash inflows later). By the same token, when you solve for a present value, you shouldn't be surprised to see a negative sign.
3. *Enter the rate correctly.* Financial calculators assume that rates are quoted in percent, so if the rate is .08 (or 8 percent), you should enter 8, not .08.

    One way to determine if you may have made a mistake while using your financial calculator is to complete a check for reasonableness. This means that you should think about the problem logically, and consider whether your answer seems like a reasonable or even possible one. For example, if you are determining the future value of $100 invested for three years at 5 percent, an answer of $90 is clearly wrong. Future value has to be greater than the original amount invested.

    If you follow these guidelines (especially the one about clearing the calculator), you should have no problem using a financial calculator to work almost all of the problems in this and the next few chapters. We'll provide some additional examples and guidance where appropriate.

A Note on Compound Growth

If you are considering depositing money in an interest-bearing account, the interest rate on that account is just the rate at which your money grows, assuming you don't remove any of it. If that rate is 10 percent, each year you simply have 10 percent more money than you had the year before. In this case, the interest rate is just an example of a compound growth rate.

The way we calculated future values is actually quite general and lets you answer some other types of questions related to growth. For example, your company currently has 10,000 employees. You've estimated that the number of employees grows by 3 percent per year. How many employees will there be in five years? Here, we start with 10,000 people instead of dollars, and we don't think of the growth rate as an interest rate, but the calculation is exactly the same:

$$10,000 \times (1.03)^5 = 10,000 \times 1.1593 = 11,593 \text{ employees}$$

There will be about 1,593 net new hires over the coming five years.

EXAMPLE 5.4: Dividend Growth

Over the 11 years ending in 2006, the Royal Bank of Canada's dividend grew from $0.29 to $1.44, an average annual growth rate of 15.68 percent.[2] Assuming this growth continues, what will the dividend be in 2008?

Here we have a cash dividend growing because it is being increased by management, but, once again, the calculation is the same:

Future value = $1.44 × $(1.1568)^2$ = $1.44 (1.3382) = $1.93

The dividend will grow by $0.49 over that period. Dividend growth is a subject we return to in a later chapter.

CONCEPT QUESTIONS

1. What do we mean by the future value of an investment?

2. What does it mean to compound interest? How does compound interest differ from simple interest?

3. In general, what is the future value of $1 invested at r per period for t periods?

5.2 PRESENT VALUE AND DISCOUNTING

When we discuss future value, we are thinking of questions such as, What will my $2,000 investment grow to if it earns a 6.5 percent return every year for the next six years? The answer to this question is what we called the future value of $2,000 invested at 6.5 percent for six years (check that the answer is about $2,918).

Another type of question that comes up even more often in financial management is obviously related to future value. Suppose you need to have $10,000 in 10 years, and you can earn 6.5 percent on your money. How much do you have to invest today to reach your goal? You can verify that the answer is $5,327.26. How do we know this? Read on.

The Single Period Case

present value (PV)
The current value of future cash flows discounted at the appropriate discount rate.

We've seen that the future value of $1 invested for one year at 10 percent is $1.10. We now ask a slightly different question: How much do we have to invest today at 10 percent to get $1 in one year? In other words, we know the future value here is $1, but what is the **present value (PV)**?

---

2 $1.44 = $0.29 \times (1 + g)^{11}$
   $4.9655 = (1 + g)^{11}$
   $(4.9655)^{1/11} = 1 + g$
   $1.1568 = 1 + g$
   $g = 15.68\%$

The answer isn't too hard to figure out. Whatever we invest today will be 1.1 times bigger at the end of the year. Since we need $1 at the end of the year:

$$\text{Present value} \times 1.1 = \$1$$

Or:

$$\text{Present value} = \$1/1.1 = \$.909$$

discount
Calculate the present value of some future amount.

This present value is the answer to the following question: What amount, invested today, will grow to $1 in one year if the interest rate is 10 percent? Present value is thus just the reverse of future value. Instead of compounding the money forward into the future, we **discount it** back to the present.

EXAMPLE 5.5: Single Period PV

Suppose you need $400 to buy textbooks next year. You can earn 4 percent on your money. How much do you have to put up today?

We need to know the PV of $400 in one year at 4 percent. Proceeding as we just did:

$$\text{Present value} \times 1.04 = \$400$$

We can now solve for the present value:

$$\text{Present value} = \$400 \times [1/1.04] = \$384.62$$

Thus, $384.62 is the present value. Again, this just means that investing this amount for one year at 4 percent results in your having a future value of $400.

From our examples, the present value of $1 to be received in one period is generally given as:

$$PV = \$1 \times [1/(1 + r)] = \$1/(1 + r)$$

We next examine how to get the present value of an amount to be paid in two or more periods into the future.

Present Values for Multiple Periods

Suppose you needed to have $1,000 in two years. If you can earn 7 percent, how much do you have to invest to make sure that you have the $1,000 when you need it? In other words, what is the present value of $1,000 in two years if the relevant rate is 7 percent?

Based on your knowledge of future values, we know that the amount invested must grow to $1,000 over the two years. In other words, it must be the case that:

$$\begin{aligned} \$1,000 &= PV \times 1.07^2 \\ &= PV \times 1.1449 \end{aligned}$$

Given this, we can solve for the present value as:

$$\text{Present value} = \$1,000/1.1449 = \$873.44$$

Therefore, $873.44 is the amount you must invest to achieve your goal.

As you have probably recognized by now, calculating present values is quite similar to calculating future values, and the general result looks much the same. The present value of $1 to be received t periods in the future at a discount rate of r is:

EXAMPLE 5.6: Saving Up

You would like to buy a new automobile. You have about $50,000 or so, but the car costs $68,500. If you can earn 9 percent, how much do you have to invest today to buy the car in two years? Do you have enough? Assume the price will stay the same.

What we need to know is the present value of $68,500 to be paid in two years, assuming a 9 percent rate. Based on our discussion, this is:

$$PV = \$68,500/1.09^2 = \$68,500/1.1881 = \$57,655.08$$

You're still about $7,655 short, even if you're willing to wait two years.

$$PV = \$1 \times [1/(1 + r)^t] = \$1/(1 + r)^t \qquad [5.2]$$

The quantity in brackets, $1/(1 + r)^t$, goes by several different names. Since it's used to discount a future cash flow, it is often called a *discount factor*. With this name, it is not surprising that the rate used in the calculation is often called the **discount rate**. We tend to call it this in talking about present values. The discount rate is also sometimes referred to as the interest rate or rate of return. Regardless of what it is called, the discount rate is related to the risk of the cash flows. The higher the risk, the larger the discount rate and the lower the present value.

discount rate
The rate used to calculate the present value of future cash flows.

The quantity in brackets is also called the *present value interest factor* for $1 at *r* percent for *t* periods and is sometimes abbreviated as PVIF(*r*,*t*). Finally, calculating the present value of a future cash flow to determine its worth today is commonly called *discounted cash flow (DCF) valuation*.

To illustrate, suppose you needed $1,000 in three years. You can earn 15 percent on your money. How much do you have to invest today? To find out, we have to determine the present value of $1,000 in three years at 15 percent. We do this by discounting $1,000 back three periods at 15 percent. With these numbers, the discount factor is:

$$1/(1 + .15)^3 = 1/1.5209 = .6575$$

The amount you must invest is thus:

$$\$1,000 \times .6575 = \$657.50$$

We say that $657.50 is the present or discounted value of $1,000 to be received in three years at 15 percent.

There are tables for present value factors just as there are tables for future value factors, and you use them in the same way (if you use them at all). Table 5.3 contains a small set. A much larger set can be found in Table A.2 in the book's Appendix.

TABLE 5.3
Present value interest factors

Periods	Interest Rate			
	5%	**10%**	**15%**	**20%**
1	.9524	.9091	.8696	.8333
2	.9070	.8264	.7561	.6944
3	.8638	.7513	.6575	.5787
4	.8227	.6830	.5718	.4823
5	.7835	.6209	.4972	.4019

In Table 5.3, the discount factor we just calculated (.6575) can be found by looking down the column labelled 15% until you come to the third row.

CALCULATOR HINTS

You solve present value problems on a financial calculator just as you do future value problems. For the example we just examined (the present value of $1,000 to be received in three years at 15 percent), you would do the following:

Enter	3	15			1000
	N	%i	PMT	PV	FV
Solve for				−657.50	

Notice that the answer has a negative sign; as we discussed above, that's because it represents an outflow today in exchange for the $1,000 inflow later.

As the length of time until payment grows, present values decline. As Example 5.7 illustrates, present values tend to become small as the time horizon grows. If you look out far enough, they will always get close to zero. Also, for a given length of time, the higher the discount rate is, the lower is the present value. Put another way, present values and discount rates are inversely related. Increasing the discount rate decreases the PV and vice versa.

EXAMPLE 5.7: Stripped Bonds

Canadian investment dealers purchase Government of Canada bonds and resell the coupons and principal repayment separately. This process is called *bond stripping* because the coupons are stripped off. Such stripped coupons may be attractive to investors because they compound automatically with no reinvestment risk. An investor who buys a stripped coupon receives no payments before the coupon date.[3] So the price of a 25-year coupon with a face value of $10,000 is simply the present value of $10,000 in 25 years. Suppose the price of this coupon is $2,330. This discount rate, or the yield, of this bond issue is:

$$\$2,330 = \$10,000/(1 + r)^{25}$$
$$(1 + r)^{25} = 4.2918$$
$$1 + r = 1.0600$$

The discount rate, r, is found to be 6 percent. A dollar in 25 years is worth a little more than 23 cents today, assuming a 6 percent discount rate. In early 2000, the market for stripped bonds was over $140 billion with daily trading over $800 million. Zero coupon bonds are discussed in more detail in Chapter 7.

The relationship between time, discount rates, and present values is illustrated in Figure 5.3. Notice that by the time we get to 10 years, the present values are all substantially smaller than the future amounts.

CONCEPT QUESTIONS

1. What do we mean by the present value of an investment?

2. The process of discounting a future amount back to the present is the opposite of doing what?

3. What do we mean by the discounted cash flow or DCF approach?

FIGURE 5.3

Present value of $1 for different periods and rates

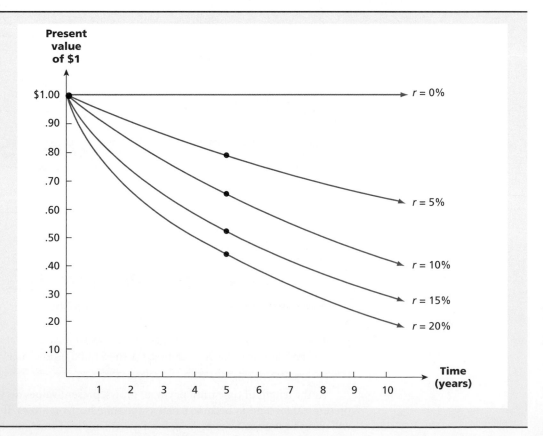

---

3 ScotiaMcLeod, "RRSP Note #5, Focus on Strip Bonds," February 21, 2000.

MORE ON PRESENT AND FUTURE VALUES

Look back at the expressions that we came up with for present and future values, and you will see a very simple relationship between the two. We explore this relationship and some related issues in this section.

Present versus Future Value

What we called the present value factor is just the reciprocal of (that is, 1 divided by) the future value factor:

Future value factor = $(1 + r)^t$
Present value factor = $1/(1 + r)^t$

In fact, the easy way to calculate a present value factor on many calculators is to first calculate the future value factor and then press the "*1/x*" key to flip it over.

If we let FV_t stand for the future value after t periods, the relationship between future value and present value can be written very simply as one of the following:

$$PV \times (1 + r)^t = FV_t$$
$$PV = FV_t/(1 + r)^t = FV_t \times [1/(1 + r)^t]$$

[5.3]

This last result we call the *basic present value equation*. We use it throughout the text. There are a number of variations that come up, but this simple equation underlies many of the most important ideas in corporate finance.[4]

EXAMPLE 5.8: Evaluating Investments

To give you an idea of how we use present and future values, consider the following simple investment. Your company proposes to buy an asset of $355,000. This investment is very safe. You will sell the asset in three years for $400,000. You know that you could invest the $335,000 elsewhere at 10 percent with very little risk. What do you think of the proposed investment?

This is not a good investment. Why not? Because you can invest the $335,000 elsewhere at 10 percent. If you do, after three years it would grow to:

$335,000 \times (1 + r)^t = $335,000 \times 1.1^3$
$= $335,000 \times 1.331$
$= $445,885$

Because the proposed investment pays out only $400,000, it is not as good as other alternatives that we have. Another way of saying the same thing is to notice that the present value of $400,000 in three years at 10 percent is:

$400,000 \times [1/(1 + r)^t] = $400,000/1.1^3 =$
$400,000/1.331 = $300,526$

This tells us that we only have to invest about $300,000 to get $400,000 in three years, not $335,000. We return to this type of analysis later.

Determining the Discount Rate

For a downloadable Windows-based financial calculator, go to www.calculator.org

Frequently, we need to determine what discount rate is implicit in an investment. We can do this by looking at the basic present value equation:

$$PV = FV_t/(1 + r)^t$$

There are only four parts to this equation: the present value (PV), the future value (FV_t), the discount rate (r), and the life of the investment (t). Given any three of these, we can always find the fourth.

To illustrate what happens with multiple periods, let's say that we are offered an investment that costs us $100 and doubles our money in eight years. To compare this to other investments, we would like to know what discount rate is implicit in these numbers. This discount rate is called the *rate of return* or sometimes just return for the investment. In this case, we have a present value

---

4 When you apply this present value equation, the process is known as discounting. If you apply the future value equation, you are compounding.

of $100, a future value of $200 (double our money), and an eight-year life. To calculate the return, we can write the basic present value equation as:

$$PV = FV_t/(1 + r)^t$$
$$\$100 = \$200/(1 + r)^8$$

It could also be written as:

$$(1 + r)^8 = 200/100 = 2$$

We now need to solve for r. There are three ways we could do it:

1. Use a financial calculator.

2. Solve the equation for $1 + r$ by taking the eighth root of both sides. Since this is the same thing as raising both sides to the power of 1/8 or .125, this is actually easy to do with the y^x key on a calculator. Just enter 2, then press y^x, enter .125, and press the = key. The eighth root should be about 1.09, which implies that r is 9 percent.

3. Use a future value table. The future value factor after eight years is equal to 2. Look across the row corresponding to eight periods in Table A.1 to see that a future value factor of 2 corresponds to the 9 percent column, again implying that the return here is 9 percent.[5]

EXAMPLE 5.9: Finding *r* for a Single Period Investment

You are considering a one-year investment. If you put up $1,250, you would get back $1,350. What rate is this investment paying?

First, in this single period case, the answer is fairly obvious. You are getting a total of $100 in addition to your $1,250. The rate of return on this investment is thus $100/1,250 = 8 percent.

More formally, from the basic present value equation, the present value (the amount you must put up today) is

$1,250. The future value (what the present value grows to) is $1,350. The time involved is one period, so we have:

$$\$1,250 = \$1,350/(1 + r)^1$$
$$(1 + r) = \$1,350/1,250 = 1.08$$
$$r = 8\%$$

In this simple case, of course, there was no need to go through this calculation, but, as we describe later, it gets a little harder when there is more than one period.

CALCULATOR HINTS

We can illustrate how to calculate unknown rates using a financial calculator using these numbers. For our example, you would do the following:

Enter	8			−100	200
	N	%i	PMT	PV	FV
Solve for		9.05			

As in our previous examples, notice the minus sign on the present value.

Not taking the time value of money into account when computing growth rates or rates of return often leads to some misleading numbers in the real world. For example, in 1997, Nissan announced plans to restore 56 vintage Datsun 240Zs and sell them to consumers. The price tag of a restored Z? About $38,000, which was at least 700 percent greater than the cost of a 240Z when it sold new 27 years earlier. As expected, many viewed the restored Zs as potential investments because they are a virtual carbon copy of the classic original.

---

5 There is a useful "back of the envelope" means of solving for r—the Rule of 72. For reasonable rates of return, the time it takes to double your money is given approximately by 72/r%. In our example, this is 72/r% = 8 years, implying that r is 9 percent as we calculated. This rule is fairly accurate for discount rates in the 5 percent to 20 percent range.

EXAMPLE 5.10: Saving for University

Many Canadian universities are increasing their tuition and fees. You estimate that you will need about $65,000 to send your child to a university in eight years. You have about $25,000 now. If you can earn 15 percent, will you make it? At what rate will you just reach your goal?

If you can earn 15 percent, the future value of your $25,000 in eight years would be:

$$FV = \$25,000 \times (1.15)^8 = \$25,000 \times 3.0590 = \$76,475.57$$

So you will make it easily. The minimum rate is the unknown r in the following:

$$FV = \$25,000 \times (1 + r)^8 = \$65,000$$
$$(1 + r)^8 = \$65,000/25,000 = 2.6000$$

Therefore, the future value factor is 2.6000. Looking at the row in Table A.1 that corresponds to eight periods, our future value factor is part way between the ones shown for 12 percent (2.4760) and 14 percent (2.8526), so you would just reach your goal if you earn slightly greater than 12 percent. To get the exact answer, we could use a financial calculator or we can solve for r:

$$(1 + r)^8 = \$65,000/25,000 = 2.6000$$
$$(1 + r) = 2.6000^{(1/8)} = 2.6000^{.125} = 1.1269$$
$$r = 12.69\%$$

EXAMPLE 5.11: Only 10,956 Days to Retirement

You would like to retire in 30 years as a millionaire. If you have $10,000 today, what rate of return do you need to earn to achieve your goal?

The future value is $1 million. The present value is $10,000, and there are 30 years until payment. We need to calculate the unknown discount rate in the following:

$$\$10,000 = \$1,000,000/(1 + r)^{30}$$
$$(1 + r)^{30} = 100$$

The future value factor is thus 100. You can verify that the implicit rate is about 16.59 percent.

If history is any guide, we can get a rough idea of how well you might expect such as investment to perform. According to the numbers quoted above, a Z that originally sold for about $5,289 twenty-seven years earlier would sell for about $38,000 in 1997. See if you don't agree that this represents a return of 7.58 percent per year, far less than the gaudy 700 percent difference in the values when the time value of money is ignored.

Our example shows it's easy to be misled when returns are quoted without considering the time value of money. However, it's not just the uninitiated who are guilty of this slight form of deception. The title of a recent feature article in a leading business magazine predicted the Dow-Jones Industrial Average would soar to a 70 percent gain over the coming five years. Do you think it meant a 70 percent return per year on your money? Think again!

Why does the Rule of 72 work? See www.moneychimp.com

Finding the Number of Periods

Suppose we were interested in purchasing an asset that costs $50,000. We currently have $25,000. If we can earn 12 percent on this $25,000, how long until we have the $50,000? The answer involves solving for the last variable in the basic present value equation, the number of periods. You already know how to get an approximate answer to this particular problem. Notice that we need to double our money. From the Rule of 72, this would take 72/12 = 6 years at 12 percent.

To come up with the exact answer, we can again manipulate the basic present value equation. The present value is $25,000, and the future value is $50,000. With a 12 percent discount rate, the basic equation takes one of the following forms:

$$\$25,000 = \$50,000/(1.12)^t$$
$$\$50,000/25,000 = (1.12)^t = 2$$

We thus have a future value factor of 2 for a 12 percent rate. We now need to solve for t. In Table A.1, if you look down the column that corresponds to 12 percent, you will see that a future value factor of 1.9738 occurs at six periods. Thus, it takes about six years, as we calculated. To get the

EXAMPLE 5.12: Waiting for Godot

You've been saving to buy the Godot Company. The total cost will be $10 million. You currently have about $2.3 million. If you can earn 5 percent on your money, how long will you have to wait? At 16 percent, how long must you wait?

At 5 percent, you'll have to wait a long time. From the basic present value equation:

$$\$2.3 = 10/(1.05)^t$$
$$1.05^t = 4.33$$
$$t = 30 \text{ years}$$

At 16 percent, things are a little better. Check for yourself that it would take about 10 years.

---

exact answer, we have to explicitly solve for t (or use a financial calculator). If you do this, the answer is 6.1163 years, so our approximation was quite close in this case.[6]

As we discussed earlier, stripped coupons are a widely-held investment. You purchase them for a fraction of their face value. For example, suppose you buy a Government of Canada stripped coupon for $50 on July 1, 2007. The coupon will mature after 12 years on July 1, 2019 and pay its face value of $100. You invest $50 and receive double your money after 12 years, what rate do you earn?

Because this investment is doubling in value in 12 years, the Rule of 72 tells you the answer right away: 72/12 = 6 percent. You can check this using the basic time value equation.

SPREADSHEET STRATEGIES

Using a Spreadsheet for Time Value of Money Calculations

More and more businesspeople from many different areas (and not just finance and accounting) rely on spreadsheets to do all the different types of calculations that come up in the real world. As a result, in this section, we will show you how to use a spreadsheet to handle the various time value of money problems we presented in this chapter. We will use Microsoft Excel™, but the commands are similar for other types of software. We assume you are already familiar with basic spreadsheet operations.

As we have seen, you can solve for any one of the following four potential unknowns: future value, present value, the discount rate, or the number of periods. With a spreadsheet, there is a separate formula for each. In Excel, these are as follows:

To Find	Enter This Formula
Future value	= FV (rate,nper,pmt,pv)
Present value	= PV (rate,nper,pmt,fv)
Discount rate	= RATE (nper,pmt,pv,fv)
Number of periods	= NPER (rate,pmt,pv,fv)

In these formulas, pv and fv are present and future value, nper is the number of periods, and rate is the discount, or interest, rate.

There are two things that are a little tricky here. First, unlike a financial calculator, the spreadsheet requires that the rate be entered as a decimal. Second, as with most financial calculators, you have to put a negative sign on either the present value or the future value to solve for the rate or the number of periods. For the same reason, if you solve for a present value, the answer will have a negative sign unless you input a negative future value. The same is true when you compute a future value.

To illustrate how you might use these formulas, we will go back to an example in the chapter. If you invest $25,000 at 12 percent per year, how long until you have $50,000? You might set up a spreadsheet like this:

Learn more about using Excel™ for time value and other calculations at www.studyfinance.com

---

6 To solve for t, we have to take the logarithm of both sides of the equation:
$$1.12^t = 2$$
$$\log 1.12^t = \log 2$$
$$t \log 1.12 = \log 2$$
We can then solve for t explicitly:
$$t = \log 2/\log 1.12$$
$$= 6.1163$$
Almost all calculators can determine a logarithm; look for a key labelled *log* or *ln*. If both are present, use either one.

SPREADSHEET STRATEGIES

	A	B	C	D	E	F	G	H
1								
2	Using a spreadsheet for time value of money calculations							
3								
4	If we invest $25,000 at 12 percent, how long until we have $50,000? We need to solve							
5	for the unknown number of periods, so we use the formula NPER(rate, pmt, pv, fv).							
6								
7	Present value (pv):	$25,000						
8	Future value (fv):	$50,000						
9	Rate (rate):	0.12						
10								
11	Periods:	6.1162554						
12								
13	The formula entered in cell b11 is = NPER(b9,0,–b7,b8); notice that pmt is zero and that pv							
14	has a negative sign on it. Also notice that rate is entered as a decimal, not a percentage.							

This example completes our introduction to basic time value concepts. Table 5.4 summarizes present and future value calculations for your reference.

TABLE 5.4

Summary of time-value calculations

I. **Symbols:**

PV = Present value, what future cash flows are worth today

FV_t = Future value, what cash flows are worth in the future

r = Interest rate, rate of return, or discount rate per period—typically, but not always, one year

t = Number of periods—typically, but not always, the number of years

C = Cash amount

II. **Future value of C invested at r percent for t periods:**

$FV_t = C \times (1 + r)^t$

The term $(1 + r)^t$ is called the *future value factor*.

III. **Present value of C to be received in t periods at r percent per period:**

$PV = C/(1 + r)^t$

The term $1/(1 + r)^t$ is called the *present value factor*.

IV. **The basic present value equation giving the relationship between present and future value is:**

$PV = FV_t/(1 + r)^t$

CONCEPT QUESTIONS

1. What is the basic present value equation?

2. In general, what is the present value of $1 to be received in t periods, assuming a discount rate of r per period?

3. What is the Rule of 72?

5.4

SUMMARY AND CONCLUSIONS

This chapter has introduced you to the basic principles of present value and discounted cash flow valuation. In it, we explained a number of things about the time value of money, including:

1. For a given rate of return, the value at some point in the future of an investment made today can be determined by calculating the future value of that investment.

2. The current worth of a future cash flow or a series of cash flows can be determined for a given rate of return by calculating the present value of the cash flow(s) involved.

3. The relationship between present value (PV) and future value (FV) for a given rate r and time t is given by the basic present value equation:

$$PV = FV_t / (1 + r)^t$$

As we have shown, it is possible to find any one of the four components (PV, FV_t, r, or t) given the other three.

The principles developed in this chapter will figure prominently in the chapters to come. The reason for this is that most investments, whether they involve real assets or financial assets, can be analyzed using the discounted cash flow (DCF) approach. As a result, the DCF approach is broadly applicable and widely used in practice. Before going on, you might want to do some of the problems that follow.

Key Terms

compound interest (page 121)
compounding (page 121)
discount (page 128)
discount rate (page 129)

future value (FV) (page 121)
interest on interest (page 121)
present value (PV) (page 127)
simple interest (page 121)

Chapter Review Problems and Self-Test

5.1   Calculating Future Values Assume you deposit $10,000 today in an account that pays 6 percent interest. How much will you have in five years?

5.2   Calculating Present Values Suppose you have just celebrated your 19th birthday. A rich uncle has set up a trust fund for you that will pay you $150,000 when you turn 30. If the relevant discount rate is 9 percent, how much is this fund worth today?

5.3   Calculating Rates of Return You've been offered an investment that will double your money in 10 years. What rate of return are you being offered? Check your answer using the Rule of 72.

5.4   Calculating the Number of Periods You've been offered an investment that will pay you 9 percent per

year. If you invest $15,000, how long until you have $30,000? How long until you have $45,000?

5.5   Compound Interest In 1867, George Edward Lee found an astrolabe (a 17th-century navigating device) originally lost by Samuel de Champlain on his property in Ontario. Lee sold the astrolabe to a stranger for $10. In 1989, the Canadian Museum of Civilization purchased the astrolabe for $250,000 from the New York Historical Society. (How it got there is a long story.) It appears that Lee had been swindled; however, suppose he had invested the $10 at 10 percent. How much would it be worth in 2007?

Answers to Self-Test Problems

5.1   We need to calculate the future value of $10,000 at 6 percent for five years. The future value factor is:

$$1.06^5 = 1.3382$$

The future value is thus $10,000 × 1.3382 = $13,382.26.

5.2   We need the present value of $150,000 to be paid in 11 years at 9 percent. The discount factor is:

$$1/1.09^{11} = 1/2.5804 = .3875$$

The present value is thus about $58,130.

5.3   Suppose you invest, say, $1,000. You will have $2,000 in 10 years with this investment. So, $1,000 is the amount you have today, or the present value, and $2,000 is the amount you will have in 10 years, or the future value. From the basic present value equation, we have:

$$\$2,000 = \$1,000 \times (1 + r)^{10}$$
$$2 = (1 + r)^{10}$$

From here, we need to solve for r, the unknown rate. As shown in the chapter, there are several different ways to do this. We will take the 10th root of 2 (by raising 2 to the power of 1/10):

$$2^{(1/10)} = 1 + r$$
$$1.0718 = 1 + r$$
$$r = 7.18\%$$

Using the Rule of 72, we have $72/t = r\%$, or $72/10 = 7.2\%$, so our answer looks good (remember that the Rule of 72 is only an approximation).

5.4   The basic equation is:

$$\$30,000 = \$15,000 \times (1 + .09)^t$$
$$2 = (1 + .09)^t$$

If we solve for t, we get that $t = 8.04$ years. Using the Rule of 72, we get $72/9 = 8$ years, so, once again, our answer looks good. To get $45,000, verify for yourself that you will have to wait 12.75 years.

5.5   At 10 percent, the $10 would have grown quite a bit over 140 years. The future value factor is:

$$(1 + r)^t = 1.1^{140} = 623,700.26$$

The future value is thus on the order of:

$$\$10 \times 623,700.26 = \$6,237,003.$$

Concepts Review and Critical Thinking Questions

1.   The basic present value equation has four parts. What are they?

2.   What is compounding? What is discounting?

3.   As you increase the length of time involved, what happens to future values? What happens to present values?

4.   What happens to a future value if you increase the rate r? What happens to a present value?

      To answer the next four questions, refer to the Government of Canada stripped coupon we discussed to open the chapter.

5.   Why would ScotiaMcLeod be willing to accept such a small amount today ($29.19) in exchange for a promise to repay over three times that amount ($100) in the future?

6.   Would you be willing to pay $500 today in exchange for $10,000 in 30 years? What would be the key con-

siderations in answering yes or no? Would your answer depend on who is making the promise to repay?

7.   Suppose that when ScotiaMcLeod offered the Government of Canada coupon for $29.19, the province of Quebec had offered an essentially identical security. Do you think it would have had a higher or lower price? Why?

8.   The Canada stripped coupon is actively bought and sold by ScotiaMcLeod and other investment dealers. If you obtained a price today, do you think the price would exceed the $29.19 original price? Why? If you looked in the year 2008, do you think the price would be higher or lower than today's price? Why?

Questions and Problems

Basic
(Questions 1–15)

1.   **Simple Interest versus Compound Interest**   Bank of Calgary pays 7 percent simple interest on its savings account balances, whereas Bank of Edmonton pays 7 percent interest compounded annually. If you made a $5,000 deposit in each bank, how much more money would you earn from your Bank of Edmonton account at the end of 10 years?

2.   **Calculating Future Values**   For each of the following, compute the future value:

Present Value	Years	Interest Rate	Future Value
$ 2,250	19	10%	
9,310	13	8	
76,355	4	22	
183,796	8	7	

3.   **Calculating Present Values**   For each of the following, compute the present value:

Present Value	Years	Interest Rate	Future Value
	6	5%	$ 15,451
	9	11	51,557
	23	16	886,073
	18	19	550,164

Basic
(continued)

4. Calculating Interest Rates Solve for the unknown interest rate in each of the following:

Present Value	Years	Interest Rate	Future Value
$ 265	2		$ 307
360	9		896
39,000	15		162,181
46,523	30		483,500

5. Calculating the Number of Periods Solve for the unknown number of years in each of the following:

Present Value	Years	Interest Rate	Future Value
$ 625		8%	$ 1,284
810		7	4,341
18,400		21	402,662
21,500		29	173,439

6. Calculating Interest Rates Assume the total cost of a university education will be $80,000 when your child enters university in 18 years. You presently have $15,000 to invest. What annual rate of interest must you earn on your investment to cover the cost of your child's university education?

7. Calculating the Number of Periods At 7 percent interest, how long does it take to double your money? To quadruple it?

8. Calculating Interest Rates In 2003, the automobile industry announced the average vehicle selling price was $28,835. Five years earlier, the average price was $21,608. What was the annual increase in vehicle selling price?

9. Calculating the Number of Periods You're trying to save to buy a new $150,000 Ferrari. You have $40,000 today that can be invested at your bank. The bank pays 5.5 percent annual interest on its accounts. How long will it be before you have enough to buy the car?

10. Calculating Present Values Imprudential, Inc., has an unfunded pension liability of $800 million that must be paid in 20 years. To assess the value of the firm's stock, financial analysts want to discount this liability back to the present. If the relevant discount rate is 9.5 percent, what is the present value of this liability?

11. Calculating Present Values You have just received notification that you have won the $1 million first prize in the provincial lottery. However, the prize will be awarded on your 100th birthday (assuming you're around to collect), 80 years from now. What is the present value of your windfall if the appropriate discount rate is 10 percent?

12. Calculating Future Values Your coin collection contains fifty 1952 silver dollars. If your grandparents purchased them for their face value when they were new, how much will your collection be worth when you retire in 2054, assuming they appreciate at a 5 percent annual rate?

13. Calculating Interest Rates and Future Values In 1895, the first U.S. Open Golf Championship was held. The winner's prize money was $150. In 2003, the winner's cheque was for $1,080,000. What was the percentage increase in the winner's cheque over this period? If the winner's prize continues to increase at the same rate, what will it be in 2040?

14. Calculating Present Values The first comic book featuring Superman was sold in 1938. In 2003, the estimated price for this comic book in good condition was about $350,000. This represented a return of 26.09 percent per year. For this to be true, what must the comic book have sold for when new?

15. Calculating Rates of Return Although appealing to more refined tastes, art as a collectible has not always performed so profitably. During 2003, Sothebys sold the Edgar Degas bronze sculpture *Petit Danseuse de Quartorze Ans* at auction for a price of $10,311,500. Unfortunately for the previous owner, he had purchased it in 1999 at a price of $12,377,500. What was his annual rate of return on this sculpture?

Intermediate
(Questions
16–20)

16. Calculating Rates of Return Referring to the Government of Canada stripped coupon we discussed at the very beginning of the chapter:

   a. Based upon the $29.19 price, what rate was the Government paying to borrow money?

   b. Suppose that, on February 5, 2001, this security's price was $35.00. If an investor had purchased it for $29.19 a year earlier and sold it on this day, what annual rate of return would she have earned?

   c. If an investor had purchased the security at market on February 5, 2001, and held it until it matured, what annual rate of return would she have earned?

17. Calculating Present Values Suppose you are still committed to owning a $150,000 Ferrari (see Question 9). If you believe your mutual fund can achieve an 11 percent annual rate of return and you want to buy the car in 10 years on the day you turn 30, how much must you invest today?

18. Calculating Future Values You have just made your first $2,000 contribution to your registered retirement saving plan (RRSP). Assuming you earn a 10 percent rate of return and make no additional contributions, what will your account be worth when you retire in 45 years? What if you wait 10 years before contributing? (Does this suggest an investment strategy?)

Intermediate (continued)

19. **Calculating Future Values** You are scheduled to receive $30,000 in two years. When you receive it, you will invest it for six more years at 6.5 percent per year. How much will you have in eight years?

20. **Calculating the Number of Periods** You expect to receive $10,000 at graduation in two years. You plan on investing it at 10 percent until you have $120,000. How long will you wait from now?

S&P Problems

1. **Calculating Future Values** Find the monthly adjusted prices for Brascan Corp. (BNN). If the stock appreciates 11 percent per year, what stock price do you expect to see in five years? In 10 years? Ignore dividends in your calculations.

2. **Calculating Interest Rates** Find the monthly adjusted prices for Domtar Inc. (DTC). What is the average annual return over the past four years?

3. **Calculating the Number of Periods** Find the monthly adjusted stock prices for Petro Canada (PCZ). You find an analyst who projects the stock price will increase 12 percent per year for the foreseeable future. Based on the most recent monthly stock price, if the projection holds true, when will the stock price reach $50? When will it reach $75?

Internet Application Questions

1. The following weblink shows the power of compound interest. The link assumes an investment of $1 made by Jesus in the year 32 B.C. Fill in the rest of the table, assuming a low interest rate (e.g., 2 percent per year). You will be amazed to find what a single dollar of investment would have grown to by 2006 A.D. www.funk.co.nz/java/jesus-investment.html

2. Go to www.dinkytown.net and follow the Net Worth Calculator link. You want to be a millionaire. You can earn 7 percent per year. Using your current age, if you have $30,000 to invest, what will your net worth be in 10 years assuming you make no other deposits (ignore inflation)?

CHAPTER 6

Discounted Cash Flow Valuation

Sports is big business and the signing of big-name athletes is often accompanied by great fanfare, but the numbers are sometimes misleading. For instance, in November 2005, the Toronto Blue Jays signed pitcher B.J. Ryan to a five-year contract paying him a total of U.S. $47 million. His contract pays him U.S. $4 million in the first year, U.S. $7 million in the second year, and U.S. $12 million each year for the final three years. After factoring in the time value of money, are the Blue Jays really spending $47 million on a pitcher?

http://toronto.bluejays.mlb.com
www.starbucks.com

IN OUR PREVIOUS CHAPTER, we covered the basics of discounted cash flow valuation. However, so far, we have only dealt with single cash flows. In reality, most investments have multiple cash flows. For example, if Starbucks or Second Cup is thinking of opening a new outlet, there will be a large cash outlay in the beginning and then cash inflows for many years. In this chapter, we begin to explore how to value such investments.

When you finish this chapter, you should have some very practical skills. For example, you will know how to calculate your own car payments or student loan payments. You will also be able to determine how long it will take to pay off a credit card if you make the minimum payment each month (a practice we do not recommend). We will show you how to compare interest rates to determine which are the highest and which are the lowest, and we will also show you how interest rates can be quoted in different, and at times deceptive, ways.

FUTURE AND PRESENT VALUES OF MULTIPLE CASH FLOWS

Thus far, we have restricted our attention to either the future value of a lump-sum present amount or the present value of some single future cash flow. In this section, we begin to study ways to value multiple cash flows. We start with future value.

Future Value with Multiple Cash Flows

Suppose you deposit $100 today in an account paying 8 percent. In one year, you will deposit another $100. How much will you have in two years? This particular problem is relatively easy. At the end of the first year, you will have $108 plus the second $100 you deposit, for a total of $208. You leave this $208 on deposit at 8 percent for another year. At the end of this second year, it is worth:

$$\$208 \times 1.08 = \$224.64$$

FIGURE 6.1

Drawing and using a time line

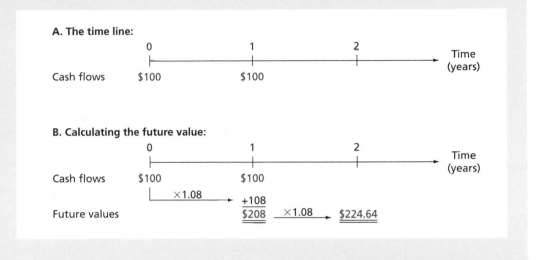

A. The time line:

B. Calculating the future value:

Figure 6.1 is a *time line* that illustrates the process of calculating the future value of these two $100 deposits. Figures such as this one are very useful for solving complicated problems. Almost any time you are having trouble with a present or future value problem, drawing a time line will help you to see what is happening.

In the first part of Figure 6.1, we show the cash flows on the time line. The most important thing is that we write them down where they actually occur. Here, the first cash flow occurs today, which we label as Time 0. We therefore put $100 at Time 0 on the time line. The second $100 cash flow occurs one year from today, so we write it down at the point labelled as Time 1. In the second part of Figure 6.1, we calculate the future values one period at a time to come up with the final $224.64.

When we calculated the future value of the two $100 deposits, we simply calculated the balance as of the beginning of each year and then rolled that amount forward to the next year. We could have done it another, quicker way. The first $100 is on deposit for two years at 8 percent, so its future value is:

$$\$100 \times 1.08^2 = \$100 \times 1.1664 = \$116.64$$

The second $100 is on deposit for one year at 8 percent, and its future value is thus:

$$\$100 \times 1.08 = \$108$$

The total future value, as we previously calculated, is equal to the sum of these two future values:

$$\$116.64 + 108 = \$224.64$$

Based on this example, there are two ways to calculate future values for multiple cash flows: (1) compound the accumulated balance forward one year at a time or (2) calculate the future

EXAMPLE 6.1: Saving Up Revisited

You think you will be able to deposit $4,000 at the end of each of the next three years in a bank account paying 8 percent interest. You currently have $7,000 in the account. How much will you have in three years? In four years?

At the end of the first year, you will have:

$$\$7,000 \times 1.08 + 4,000 = \$11,560$$

At the end of the second year, you will have:

$$\$11,560 \times 1.08 + 4,000 = \$16,484.80$$

Repeating this for the third year gives:

$$\$16,484.80 \times 1.08 + 4,000 = \$21,803.58$$

Therefore, you will have $21,803.58 in three years. If you leave this on deposit for one more year (and don't add to it), at the end of the fourth year, you'll have:

$$\$21,803.58 \times 1.08 = \$23,547.87$$

value of each cash flow first and then add them up. Both give the same answer, so you can do it either way.

To illustrate the two different ways of calculating future values, consider the future value of $2,000 invested at the end of each of the next five years. The current balance is zero, and the rate is 10 percent. We first draw a time line, as shown in Figure 6.2.

On the time line, notice that nothing happens until the end of the first year, when we make the first $2,000 investment. This first $2,000 earns interest for the next four (not five) years. Also notice that the last $2,000 is invested at the end of the fifth year, so it earns no interest at all.

Figure 6.3 illustrates the calculations involved if we compound the investment one period at a time. As illustrated, the future value is $12,210.20.

Figure 6.4 goes through the same calculations, but the second technique is used. Naturally, the answer is the same.

Present Value with Multiple Cash Flows

It will turn out that we will very often need to determine the present value of a series of future cash flows. As with future values, there are two ways we can do it. We can either discount back one period at a time, or we can just calculate the present values individually and add them up.

Suppose you need $1,000 in one year and $2,000 more in two years. If you can earn 9 percent on your money, how much do you have to put up today to exactly cover these amounts in the future? In other words, what is the present value of the two cash flows at 9 percent?

FIGURE 6.2

Time line for $2,000 per year for five years

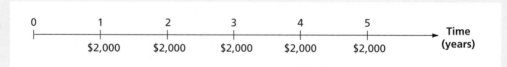

FIGURE 6.3

Future value calculated by compounding forward one period at a time

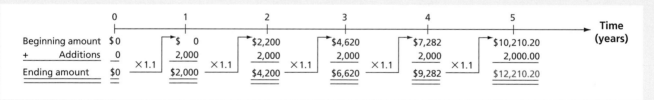

FIGURE 6.4

Future Value calculated by compounding each cash flow separately

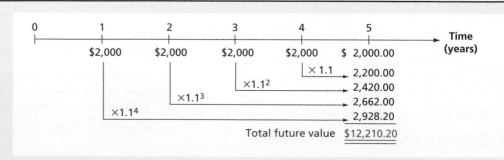

EXAMPLE 6.2: Saving Up Once Again

If you deposit $100 in one year, $200 in two years, and $300 in three years, how much will you have in three years? How much of this is interest? How much will you have in five years if you don't add additional amounts? Assume a 7 percent interest rate throughout.

We will calculate the future value of each amount in three years. Notice that the $100 earns interest for two years, and the $200 earns interest for one year. The final $300 earns no interest. The future values are thus:

$$\$100 \times 1.07^2 = \$114.49$$
$$\$200 \times 1.07 = \quad 214.00$$
$$+ \$300 \quad\quad = \quad 300.00$$
$$\text{Total future value} = \overline{\$628.49}$$

The total future value is thus $628.49. The total interest is:

$$\$628.49 - (100 + 200 + 300) = \$28.49$$

How much will you have in five years? We know that you will have $628.49 in three years. If you leave that in for two more years, it will grow to:

$$\$628.49 \times 1.07^2 = \$628.49 \times 1.1449 = \$719.56$$

Notice that we could have calculated the future value of each amount separately. Once again, be careful about the lengths of time. As we previously calculated, the first $100 earns interest for only four years, the second deposit earns three years' interest, and the last earns two years' interest:

$$\$100 \times 1.07^4 = \$100 \times 1.3108 = \$131.08$$
$$\$200 \times 1.07^3 = \$200 \times 1.2250 = \quad 245.01$$
$$\$300 \times 1.07^2 = \$300 \times 1.1449 = \quad 343.47$$
$$\text{Total future value} = \overline{\$719.56}$$

The present value of $2,000 in two years at 9 percent is:

$$\$2,000/1.09^2 = \$1,683.36$$

The present value of $1,000 in one year is:

$$\$1,000/1.09 = \$917.43$$

Therefore, the total present value is:

$$\$1,683.36 + 917.43 = \$2,600.79$$

To see why $2,600.79 is the right answer, we can check to see that after the $2,000 is paid out in two years, there is no money left. If we invest $2,600.79 for one year at 9 percent, we will have:

$$\$2,600.79 \times 1.09 = \$2,834.86$$

We take out $1,000, leaving $1,834.86. This amount earns 9 percent for another year, leaving us with:

$$\$1,834.86 \times 1.09 = \$2,000$$

This is just as we planned. As this example illustrates, the present value of a series of future cash flows is simply the amount that you would need today in order to exactly duplicate those future cash flows (for a given discount rate).

An alternative way of calculating present values for multiple future cash flows is to discount back to the present, one period at a time. To illustrate, suppose we had an investment that was going to pay $1,000 at the end of every year for the next five years. To find the present value, we could discount each $1,000 back to the present separately and then add them up. Figure 6.5 illustrates this approach for a 6 percent discount rate; as shown, the answer is $4,212.37 (ignoring a small rounding error).

Alternatively, we could discount the last cash flow back one period and add it to the next-to-the-last cash flow:

$$(\$1,000/1.06) + 1,000 = \$943.40 + 1,000 = \$1,943.40$$

We could then discount this amount back one period and add it to the Year 3 cash flow:

$$(\$1,943.40/1.06) + 1,000 = \$1,833.40 + 1,000 = \$2,833.40$$

This process could be repeated as necessary. Figure 6.6 illustrates this approach and the remaining calculations.

If we consider B.J. Ryan's five-year contract introduced at the start of the chapter, and use a 5 percent discount rate, what is the present value of his agreement? We can calculate the value as follows (assuming he is paid annually starting one year from contract signing):

$4 million/1.05   = $4 million/1.0500   = $3.8 million
$7 million/1.05^2 = $7 million/1.1025   = $6.4 million
$12 million/1.05^3 = $12 million/1.1576   = $10.4 million
$12 million/1.05^4 = $12 million/1.2155   = $9.9 million
$12 million/1.05^5 = $12 million/1.2763   = $9.4 million

Therefore, his contract is actually only worth U.S. $39.9 million at signing, not the publicized U.S. $47 million.

FIGURE 6.5

Present value calculated by discounting each cash flow separately

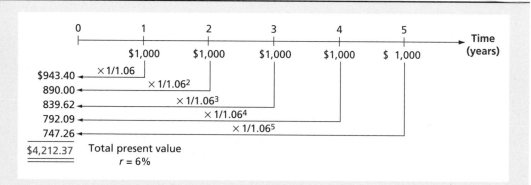

FIGURE 6.6

Present value calculated by discounting back one period at a time

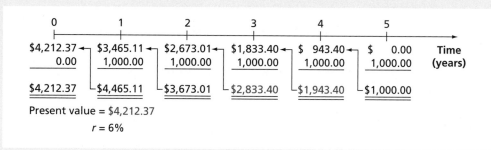

EXAMPLE 6.3: How Much Is It Worth?

You are offered an investment that will pay you $200 in one year, $400 the next year, $600 the next year, and $800 at the end of the next year. You can earn 12 percent on very similar investments. What is the most you should pay for this one?

We need to calculate the present value of these cash flows at 12 percent. Taking them one at a time gives:

$200 × 1/1.12^1 = $200/1.1200 = $ 178.57
$400 × 1/1.12^2 = $400/1.2544 = 318.88
$600 × 1/1.12^3 = $600/1.4049 = 427.07
$800 × 1/1.12^4 = $800/1.5735 = 508.41
Total present value = $1,432.93

If you can earn 12 percent on your money, then you can duplicate this investment's cash flows for $1,432.93, so this is the most you should be willing to pay.

CALCULATOR HINTS

How to Calculate Present Values with Multiple Future Cash Flows Using a Financial Calculator

To calculate the present value of multiple cash flows with a financial calculator, we will simply discount the individual cash flows one at a time using the same technique we used in our previous chapter, so this is not really new. There is a shortcut, however, that we can show you. We will use the numbers in Example 6.3 to illustrate.

To begin, of course we first remember to clear out the calculator! Next, from Example 6.3, the first cash flow is $200 to be received in one year and the discount rate is 12 percent, so we do the following:

Enter	1	12			200
	N	%i	PMT	PV	FV
Solve for				−178.57	

Now, you can write down this answer to save it, but that's inefficient. All calculators have a memory where you can store numbers. Why not just save it there? Doing so cuts way down on mistakes because you don't have to write down and/or rekey numbers, and it's much faster.

Next we value the second cash flow. We need to change N to 2 and FV to 400. As long as we haven't changed anything else, we don't have to reenter %i or clear out the calculator, so we have:

Enter	2				400
	N	%i	PMT	PV	FV
Solve for				−318.88	

You save this number by adding it to the one you saved in our first calculation, and so on for the remaining two calculations.

As we will see in a later chapter, some financial calculators will let you enter all of the future cash flows at once, but we'll discuss that subject when we get to it.

EXAMPLE 6.4: How Much Is It Worth? Part 2

You are offered an investment that will make three $5,000 payments. The first payment will occur four years from today. The second will occur in five years, and the third will follow in six years. If you can earn 11 percent, what is the most this investment is worth today? What is the future value of the cash flows?

We will answer the questions in reverse order to illustrate a point. The future value of the cash flows in six years is:

$$(\$5,000 \times 1.11^2) + (5,000 \times 1.11) + 5,000 = \$6,160.50$$
$$+ 5,550 + 5,000 = \$16,710.50$$

The present value must be:

$$\$16,710.50/1.11^6 = \$8,934.12$$

Let's check this. Taking them one at a time, the PVs of the cash flows are:

$$\$5,000 \times 1/1.11^6 = \$5,000/1.8704 = \$2,673.20$$
$$\$5,000 \times 1/1.11^5 = \$5,000/1.6851 = \ 2,967.26$$
$$\$5,000 \times 1/1.11^4 = \$5,000/1.5181 = \ 3,293.65$$
$$\text{Total present value} = \$8,934.12$$

This is as we previously calculated. The point we want to make is that we can calculate present and future values in any order and convert between them using whatever way seems most convenient. The answers will always be the same as long as we stick with the same discount rate and are careful to keep track of the right number of periods.

SPREADSHEET STRATEGIES

How to Calculate Present Values with Multiple Future Cash Flows Using a Spreadsheet

Just as we did in our previous chapter, we can set up a basic spreadsheet to calculate the present values of the individual cash flows as follows. Notice that we have simply calculated the present values one at a time and added them up:

	A	B	C	D	E
1					
2			Using a spreadsheet to value multiple future cash flows		
3					
4	What is the present value of $200 in one year, $400 the next year, $600 the next year, and				
5	$800 the last year if the discount rate is 12 percent?				
6					
7	Rate:	0.12			
8					
9	Year	Cash flows	Present values	Formula used	
10	1	$200	$178.57	=PV($B$7,A10,0,−B10)	
11	2	$400	$318.88	=PV($B$7,A11,0,−B11)	
12	3	$600	$427.07	=PV($B$7,A12,0,−B12)	
13	4	$800	$508.41	=PV($B$7,A13,0,−B13)	
14					
15		Total PV:	**$1,432.93**	=SUM(C10:C13)	
16					
17	Notice the negative signs inserted in the PV formulas. These just make the present values have				
18	positive signs. Also, the discount rate in cell b7 is entered as $B$7 (an "absolute" reference)				
19	because it is used over and over. We could have just entered ".12" instead, but our approach is more				
20	flexible.				
21					
22					

A Note on Cash Flow Timing

In working present and future value problems, cash flow timing is critically important. In almost all such calculations, it is implicitly assumed that the cash flows occur at the *end* of each period. In fact, all the formulas we have discussed, all the numbers in a standard present value or future value table, and, very importantly, all the preset (or default) settings on a financial calculator assume that cash flows occur at the end of each period. Unless you are very explicitly told otherwise, you should always assume that this is what is meant.

As a quick illustration of this point, suppose you are told that a three-year investment has a first-year cash flow of $100, a second-year cash flow of $200, and a third-year cash flow of $300. You are asked to draw a time line. Without further information, you should always assume that the time line looks like this:

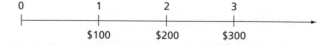

On our time line, notice how the first cash flow occurs at the end of the first period, the second at the end of the second period, and the third at the end of the third period.

CONCEPT QUESTIONS

1. Describe how to calculate the future value of a series of cash flows.

2. Describe how to calculate the present value of a series of cash flows.

3. Unless we are explicitly told otherwise, what do we always assume about the timing of cash flows in present and future value problems?

VALUING LEVEL CASH FLOWS: ANNUITIES AND PERPETUITIES

We will frequently encounter situations in which we have multiple cash flows that are all the same amount. For example, a very common type of loan repayment plan calls for the borrower to repay the loan by making a series of equal payments over some length of time. Almost all consumer loans (such as car loans and student loans) and home mortgages feature equal payments, usually made each month.

annuity
A level stream of cash flows for a fixed period of time.

More generally, a series of constant or level cash flows that occur at the end of each period for some fixed number of periods is called an ordinary **annuity**; or, more correctly, the cash flows are said to be in ordinary annuity form. Annuities appear very frequently in financial arrangements, and there are some useful shortcuts for determining their values. We consider these next.

Present Value for Annuity Cash Flows

Suppose we were examining an asset that promised to pay $500 at the end of each of the next three years. The cash flows from this asset are in the form of a three-year, $500 annuity. If we wanted to earn 10 percent on our money, how much would we offer for this annuity?

From the previous section, we know that we can discount each of these $500 payments back to the present at 10 percent to determine the total present value:

$$\text{Present value} = (\$500/1.1^1) + (500/1.1^2) + (500/1.1^3)$$
$$= (\$500/1.1) + (500/1.21) + (500/1.331)$$
$$= \$454.55 + 413.22 + 375.66$$
$$= \$1,243.43$$

This approach works just fine. However, we will often encounter situations in which the number of cash flows is quite large. For example, a typical home mortgage calls for monthly payments over 25 years, for a total of 300 payments. If we were trying to determine the present value of those payments, it would be useful to have a shortcut.

Because the cash flows of an annuity are all the same, we can come up with a very useful variation on the basic present value equation. It turns out that the present value of an annuity of C dollars per period for t periods when the rate of return or interest rate is r is given by:

$$\text{Annuity present value} = C \times \left(\frac{1 - \text{Present value factor}}{r} \right) \qquad \textbf{[6.1]}$$
$$= C \times \left\{ \frac{1 - 1/(1 + r)^t}{r} \right\}$$

The term in parentheses on the first line is sometimes called the present value interest factor for annuities and abbreviated PVIFA(r,t).

The expression for the annuity present value may look a little complicated, but it isn't difficult to use. Notice that the term in square brackets on the second line, $1/(1 + r)^t$, is the same present value factor we've been calculating. In our example from the beginning of this section, the interest rate is 10 percent and there are three years involved. The usual present value factor is thus:

$$\text{Present value factor} = 1/1.1^3 = 1/1.331 = .75131$$

To calculate the annuity present value factor, we just plug this in:

$$\text{Annuity present value factor} = (1 - \text{Present value factor})/r$$
$$= (1 - .75131)/.10$$
$$= .248685/.10 = 2.48685$$

Just as we calculated before, the present value of our $500 annuity is then:

$$\text{Annuity present value} = \$500 \times 2.48685 = \$1,243.43$$

ANNUITY TABLES   Just as there are tables for ordinary present value factors, there are tables for annuity factors as well. Table 6.1 contains a few such factors; Table A.3 in the Appendix to the book contains a larger set. To find the annuity present value factor we calculated just before Example 6.5, look for the row corresponding to three periods and then find the column for 10 percent. The number you see at that intersection should be 2.4869 (rounded to four decimal places), as we calculated. Once again, try calculating a few of these factors yourself and compare your answers to the ones in the table to make sure you know how to do it. If you are using a financial calculator, just enter $1 as the payment and calculate the present value; the result should be the annuity present value factor.

CALCULATOR HINTS

Annuity Present Values

To find annuity present values with a financial calculator, we need to use the **PMT** key (you were probably wondering what it was for). Compared to finding the present value of a single amount, there are two important differences. First, we enter the annuity cash flow using the **PMT** key, and, second, we don't enter anything for the future value, **FV**. So, for example, the problem we have been examining is a three-year, $500 annuity. If the discount rate is 10 percent, we need to do the following (after clearing out the calculator!):

Enter	3	10	500		
	N	%i	PMT	PV	FV
Solve for				−1,243.43	

As usual, we get a negative sign on the PV.

FINDING THE PAYMENT   Suppose you wish to start up a new business that specializes in the latest of health food trends, frozen yak milk. To produce and market your product, you need to borrow $100,000. Because it strikes you as unlikely that this particular fad will be long-lived, you propose to pay off the loan quickly by making five equal annual payments. If the interest rate is 18 percent, what will the payment be?

In this case, we know the present value is $100,000. The interest rate is 18 percent, and there are five years. The payments are all equal, so we need to find the relevant annuity factor and solve for the unknown cash flow:

TABLE 6.1
Annuity present value interest factors

| Periods | Interest Rate | | | |
	5%	10%	15%	20%
1	.9524	.9091	.8696	.8333
2	1.8594	1.7355	1.6257	1.5278
3	2.7232	2.4869	2.2832	2.1065
4	3.5460	3.1699	2.8550	2.5887
5	4.3295	3.7908	3.3522	2.9906

EXAMPLE 6.5: How Much Can You Afford?

After carefully going over your budget, you have determined you can afford to pay $632 per month towards a new sports car. You visit your bank's website and find that the going rate is 1 percent per month for 48 months. How much can you borrow?

To determine how much you can borrow, we need to calculate the present value of $632 per month for 48 months at 1 percent per month. The loan payments are in ordinary annuity form, so the annuity present value factor is:

Annuity PV factor = (1 − Present value factor)/r
$$= [1 − (1/1.01^{48})]/.01$$
$$= (1 − .6203)/.01 = 37.9740$$

With this factor, we can calculate the present value of the 48 payments of $632 each as:

Present value = $632 × 37.9740 = $24,000

Therefore, $24,000 is what you can afford to borrow and repay.

$$\text{Annuity present value} = \$100,000 = C \times [(1 - \text{Present value factor})/r]$$
$$= C \times \{[1 - (1/1.18^5)/.18\}$$
$$= C \times [(1 - .4371)/.18]$$
$$= C \times 3.1272$$
$$C = \$100,000/3.1272 = \$31,977$$

Therefore, you'll make five payments of just under $32,000 each.

SPREADSHEET STRATEGIES

Annuity Present Values

Using a spreadsheet to find annuity present values goes like this:

	A	B	C	D	E	F	G
1							
2	**Using a spreadsheet to find annuity present values**						
3							
4	What is the present value of $500 per year for 3 years if the discount rate is 10 percent?						
5	We need to solve for the unknown present value, so we use the formula PV(rate, nper, pmt, fv).						
6							
7	Payment amount per period:	$500					
8	Number of payments:	3					
9	Discount rate:	0.1					
10							
11	Annuity present value:	**$1,243.43**					
12							
13	The formula entered in cell b11 is =PV(b9,b8,-b7,0); notice that fv is zero and that						
14	pmt has a negative sign on it. Also notice that rate is entered as a decimal, not a percentage.						
15							
16							
17							

CALCULATOR HINTS

Annuity Payments

Finding annuity payments is easy with a financial calculator. In our example just above, the PV is $100,000, the interest rate is 18 percent, and there are five years. We find the payment as follows:

Enter	5	18		100,000	
	N	**%i**	**PMT**	**PV**	**FV**
Solve for			−31,978		

Here we get a negative sign on the payment because the payment is an outflow for us.

EXAMPLE 6.6: Finding the Number of Payments

You ran a little short on your February vacation, so you put $1,000 on your credit card. You can only afford to make the minimum payment of $20 per month. The interest rate on the credit card is 1.5 percent per month. How long will you need to pay off the $1,000?

What we have here is an annuity of $20 per month at 1.5 percent per month for some unknown length of time. The present value is $1,000 (the amount you owe today). We need to do a little algebra (or else use a financial calculator):

$$\$1,000 = \$20 \times [(1 - \text{Present value factor})/.015]$$
$$(\$1,000/20) \times .015 = 1 - \text{Present value factor}$$

$$\text{Present value factor} = .25 = 1/(1 + r)^t$$
$$1.015^t = 1/.25 = 4$$

At this point, the problem boils down to asking the question, How long does it take for your money to quadruple at 1.5 percent per month? The answer is about 93 months:

$$1.015^{93} = 3.99 \approx 4$$

It will take you about 93/12 = 7.75 years to pay off the $1,000 at this rate. If you use a financial calculator for problems like this one, you should be aware that some automatically round up to the next whole period.

SPREADSHEET STRATEGIES

Annuity Payments

Using a spreadsheet to work the same problem goes like this:

	A	B	C	D	E	F	G
1							
2		Using a spreadsheet to find annuity payments					
3							
4	What is the annuity payment if the present value is $100,000, the interest rate is 18 percent, and						
5	there are 5 periods? We need to solve for the unknown payment in an annuity, so we use the						
6	formula PMT(rate, nper, pv, fv).						
7							
8	Annuity present value:	$100,000					
9	Number of payments:	5					
10	Discount rate:	0.18					
11							
12	Annuity payment:	$31,977.78					
13							
14	The formula entered in cell b12 is =PMT(b10, b9, -b8,0); notice that fv is zero and that the payment						
15	has a negative sign because it is an outflow to us.						
16							

CALCULATOR HINTS

Finding the Number of Payments

To solve this one on a financial calculator, do the following:

Enter		1.5	−20	1,000	
	N	%i	PMT	PV	FV
Solve for	93.11				

Notice that we put a negative sign on the payment you must make, and we have solved for the number of months. You still have to divide by 12 to get our answer. Also, some financial calculators won't report a fractional value for N; they automatically (without telling you) round up to the next whole period (not to the nearest value). With a spreadsheet, use the function =NPER(rate,pmt,pv,fv); be sure to put in a zero for fv and to enter −20 as the payment.

FINDING THE RATE   The last question we might want to ask concerns the interest rate implicit in an annuity. For example, an insurance company offers to pay you $1,000 per year for 10 years if you will pay $6,710 up front. What rate is implicit in this 10-year annuity?

In this case, we know the present value ($6,710), we know the cash flows ($1,000 per year), and we know the life of the investment (10 years). What we don't know is the discount rate:

$$\$6,710 = \$1,000 \times [(1 - \text{Present value factor})/r]$$
$$\$6,710/1,000 = 6.71 = \{1 - [1/(1 + r)^{10}]\}/r$$

So, the annuity factor for 10 periods is equal to 6.71, and we need to solve this equation for the unknown value of r. Unfortunately, this is mathematically impossible to do directly. The only way to do it is to use a table or trial and error to find a value for r.

If you look across the row corresponding to 10 periods in Table A.3, you will see a factor of 6.7101 for 8 percent, so we see right away that the insurance company is offering just about 8 percent. Alternatively, we could just start trying different values until we got very close to the answer.

Using this trial-and-error approach can be a little tedious, but, fortunately, machines are good at that sort of thing.[1]

To illustrate how to find the answer by trial and error, suppose a relative of yours wants to borrow $3,000. She offers to repay you $1,000 every year for four years. What interest rate are you being offered?

The cash flows here have the form of a four-year, $1,000 annuity. The present value is $3,000. We need to find the discount rate, r. Our goal in doing so is primarily to give you a feel for the relationship between annuity values and discount rates.

We need to start somewhere, and 10 percent is probably as good a place as any to begin. At 10 percent, the annuity factor is:

Annuity present value factor $= [1 - (1/1.10^4)]/.10 = 3.1699$

The present value of the cash flows at 10 percent is thus:

Present value $= \$1,000 \times 3.1699 = \$3,169.90$

You can see that we're already in the right ballpark.

Is 10 percent too high or too low? Recall that present values and discount rates move in opposite directions: increasing the discount rate lowers the PV and vice versa. Our present value here is too high, so the discount rate is too low. If we try 12 percent:

Present value $= \$1,000 \times \{[1 - (1/1.12^4)]/.12\} = \$3,037.35$

Now we're almost there. We are still a little low on the discount rate (because the PV is a little high), so we'll try 13 percent:

Present value $= \$1,000 \times \{[1 - (1/1.13^4)]/.13\} = \$2,974.47$

This is less than $3,000, so we now know that the answer is between 12 percent and 13 percent, and it looks to be about 12.5 percent. For practice, work at it for a while longer and see if you find that the answer is about 12.59 percent.

To illustrate a situation in which finding the unknown rate can be very useful, let us consider provincial lotteries, which often offer you a choice of how to take your winnings. In a recent drawing, participants were offered the option of receiving a lump-sum payment of $400,000 or an annuity of $800,000 to be received in equal instalments over a 20-year period. (At the time, the lump-sum payment was always half the annuity option.) Which option was better?

To answer, suppose you were to compare $400,000 today to an annuity of $800,000/20 = $40,000 per year for 20 years. At what rate do these have the same value? This is the same problem we've been looking at; we need to find the unknown rate, r, for a present value of $400,000, a $40,000 payment, and a 20-year period. If you grind through the calculations (or get a little machine assistance), you should find that the unknown rate is about 7.75 percent. You should take the annuity option if that rate is attractive relative to other investments available to you.

To see why, suppose that you could find a low risk investment with a rate of return of 6 percent. Your lump sum of $400,000 would generate annual payments of only $34,874 as opposed to the $40,000 offered by the lottery. The payments are lower because they are calculated assuming a return of 6 percent while the lottery offer is based on a higher rate of 7.75 percent. This example shows why it makes sense to think of the discount rate as an opportunity cost — the return one could earn on an alternative investment of equal risk. We will have a lot more to say on this later in the text.

Future Value for Annuities

On occasion, it's also handy to know a shortcut for calculating the future value of an annuity. For example, suppose you plan to contribute $2,000 every year into a Registered Retirement Savings Plan (RRSP) paying 8 percent. If you retire in 30 years, how much will you have?

---

1 Financial calculators rely on trial and error to find the answer. That's why they sometimes appear to be "thinking" before coming up with the answer. Actually, it is possible to directly solve for r if there are fewer than five periods, but it's usually not worth the trouble.

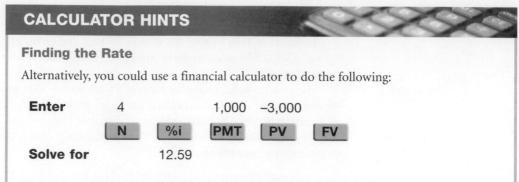

CALCULATOR HINTS

Finding the Rate

Alternatively, you could use a financial calculator to do the following:

Enter	4		1,000	–3,000	
	N	%i	PMT	PV	FV
Solve for		12.59			

Notice that we put a negative sign on the present value (why?). With a spreadsheet, use the function =RATE(nper,pmt,pv,fv); be sure to put in a zero for fv and to enter 1,000 as the payment and –3,000 as the pv.

One way to answer this particular problem is to calculate the present value of a $2,000, 30-year annuity at 8 percent to convert it to a lump sum, and then calculate the future value of that lump sum:

$$\text{Annuity present value} = \$2,000 \times (1 - 1/1.08^{30})/.08$$
$$= \$2,000 \times 11.2578$$
$$= \$22,515.57$$

The future value of this amount in 30 years is:

$$\text{Future value} = \$22,516 \times 1.08^{30} = \$22,515.57 \times 10.0627 = \$226,566.40$$

We could have done this calculation in one step:

$$\text{Annuity future value} = \text{Annuity present value} \times (1.08)^{30}$$
$$= \$2,000 \times (1 - 1/1.08^{30})/.08 \times (1.08)^{30}$$
$$= \$2,000 \times (1.08^{30} - 1)/.08$$
$$= \$2,000 \times (10.0627 - 1)/.08$$
$$= \$2,000 \times 113.2832 = \$226,566.4$$

As this example illustrates, there are future value factors for annuities as well as present value factors. In general, the future value factor for an annuity is given by:

$$\text{Annuity FV factor} = (\text{Future value factor} - 1)/r \qquad \textbf{[6.2]}$$
$$= ((1 + r)^t - 1)/r$$

For example, True North Distillers has just placed a shipment of Canadian whiskey in a bonded warehouse where it will age for the next eight years. An exporter plans to buy $1 million worth of whiskey in eight years. If the exporter annually deposits $95,000 at year-end in a bank account paying 8 percent interest, would there be enough to pay for the whiskey?

In this case, the annuity future value factor is given by:

$$\text{Annuity FV factor} = (\text{Future value factor} - 1)/r$$
$$= (1.08^8 - 1)/.08$$
$$= (1.8509 - 1)/.08$$
$$= 10.6366$$

The future value of this eight-year, $95,000 annuity is thus:

$$\text{Annuity future value} = \$95,000 \times 10.6366$$
$$= \$1,010,480$$

Thus, the exporter would make it with $10,480 to spare.

In our example, notice that the first deposit occurs in one year and the last in eight years. As we discussed earlier, the first deposit earns seven years' interest; the last deposit earns none.

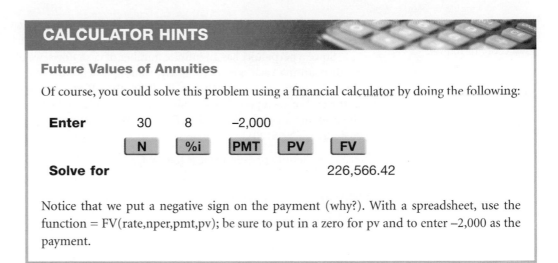

CALCULATOR HINTS

Future Values of Annuities

Of course, you could solve this problem using a financial calculator by doing the following:

Enter	30	8		−2,000	
	N	**%i**	**PMT**	**PV**	**FV**
Solve for					226,566.42

Notice that we put a negative sign on the payment (why?). With a spreadsheet, use the function = FV(rate,nper,pmt,pv); be sure to put in a zero for pv and to enter −2,000 as the payment.

A Note on Annuities Due

annuity due
An annuity for which the cash flows occur at the beginning of the period.

So far, we have only discussed ordinary annuities. These are the most important, but there is a variation that is fairly common. Remember that with an ordinary annuity, the cash flows occur at the end of each period. When you take out a loan with monthly payments, for example, the first loan payment normally occurs one month after you get the loan. However, when you lease an apartment, the first lease payment is usually due immediately. The second payment is due at the beginning of the second month, and so on. A lease is an example of an **annuity due.** An annuity due is an annuity for which the cash flows occur at the beginning of each period. Almost any type of arrangement in which we have to prepay the same amount each period is an annuity due.

There are several different ways to calculate the value of an annuity due. With a financial calculator, you simply switch it into "due" or "beginning" mode. It is very important to remember to switch it back when you are done! Another way to calculate the present value of an annuity due can be illustrated with a time line. Suppose an annuity due has five payments of $400 each, and the relevant discount rate is 10 percent. The time line looks like this:

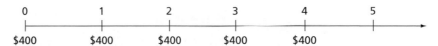

Notice how the cash flows here are the same as those for a *four*-year ordinary annuity, except that there is an extra $400 at Time 0. For practice, check to see that the value of a four-year ordinary annuity at 10 percent is $1,267.95. If we add on the extra $400, we get $1,667.95, which is the present value of this annuity due.

There is an even easier way to calculate the present or future value of an annuity due. If we assume cash flows occur at the end of each period when they really occur at the beginning, then we discount each one by one period too many. We could fix this by simply multiplying our answer by $(1 + r)$, where r is the discount rate. In fact, the relationship between the value of an annuity due and an ordinary annuity is just:

$$\text{Annuity due value} = \text{Ordinary annuity value} \times (1 + r) \qquad [6.3]$$

This works for both present and future values, so calculating the value of an annuity due involves two steps: (1) calculate the present or future value as though it were an ordinary annuity, and (2) multiply your answer by $(1 + r)$.

Perpetuities

We've seen that a series of level cash flows can be valued by treating those cash flows as an annuity. An important special case of an annuity arises when the level stream of cash flows continues

perpetuity
An annuity in which the cash flows continue forever.

consol
A type of perpetuity.

forever. Such an asset is called a **perpetuity** because the cash flows are perpetual. Some perpetuities are also called **consols**.

Since a perpetuity has an infinite number of cash flows, we obviously can't compute its value by discounting each one. Fortunately, valuing a perpetuity turns out to be the easiest possible case. Consider a perpetuity that costs $1,000 and offers a 12 percent rate of return with payments at the end of each period. The cash flow each year must be $1,000 \times .12 = $120. More generally, the present value of a perpetuity ($PV = $1,000) multiplied by the rate ($r = 12\%$) must equal the cash flow ($C = $120):

$$\text{Perpetuity present value} \times \text{Rate} = \text{Cash flow} \qquad [6.4]$$
$$PV \times r = C$$

Therefore, given a cash flow and a rate of return, we can compute the present value very easily:

$$PV \text{ for a perpetuity} = C/r = C \times (1/r)$$

For example, an investment offers a perpetual cash flow of $500 every year. The return you require on such an investment is 8 percent. What is the value of this investment? The value of this perpetuity is:

$$\text{Perpetuity } PV = C \times (1/r) = \$500/.08 = \$6,250$$

Another way of seeing why a perpetuity's value is so easy to determine is to take a look at the expression for an annuity present value factor:

$$\text{Annuity present value factor} = (1 - \text{Present value factor})/r \qquad [6.5]$$
$$= (1/r) \times (1 - \text{Present value factor})$$

As we have seen, when the number of periods involved gets very large, the present value factor gets very small. As a result, the annuity factor gets closer and closer to $1/r$. At 10 percent, for example, the annuity present value factor for 100 years is:

$$\text{Annuity present value factor} = (1/.10) \times (1 - 1/1.10^{100})$$
$$= (1/.10) \times (1 - .000073)$$
$$\approx (1/.10)$$

Table 6.2 summarizes the formulas for annuities and perpetuities.

Growing Perpetuities

growing perpetuity
A constant stream of cash flows without end that is expected to rise indefinitely.

The perpetuities we discussed so far are annuities with constant payments. In practice, it is common to find perpetuities with growing payments. For example, imagine an apartment building where cash flows to the landlord after expenses will be $100,000 next year. These cash flows are expected to rise at 5 percent per year. If we assume that this rise will continue indefinitely, the cash flow stream is termed a **growing perpetuity**. With an 11-percent discount rate, the present value of the cash flows can be represented as

---

EXAMPLE 6.7: Early Bird RRSPs

Every February, financial institutions advertise their various RRSP products. While most people contribute just before the deadline, RRSP sellers point out the advantages of contributing early—greater returns because of compounding. In our example of the future value of annuities, we found that contributing $2,000 each year at the end of the year would compound to $226,566 in 30 years at 8 percent. Suppose you made the contribution at the beginning of each year. How much more would you have after 30 years?

Annuity due future value = Payment × Annuity FV factor × (1 + r) = $2,000 × (1.08^{30} − 1)/.08 × (1.08) = $244,692

Alternatively, you could simply estimate the value as $226,566 × 1.08 = $244,691 since you are effectively earning one extra year worth of interest.[2]

You would have $244,692 − $226,566 = $18,126 more.

---

2 The answers vary slightly due to rounding.

EXAMPLE 6.8: Preferred Stock

Fixed rate preferred stock is an important example of a perpetuity.[3] When a corporation sells fixed rate preferred, the buyer is promised a fixed cash dividend every period (usually every quarter) forever. This dividend must be paid before any dividend can be paid to regular shareholders, hence the term *preferred*.

Suppose the Home Bank of Canada wants to sell preferred stock at $100 per share. A very similar issue of preferred stock already outstanding has a price of $40 per share and offers a dividend of $1 every quarter. What dividend would the Home Bank have to offer if the preferred stock is going to sell?

The issue that is already out has a present value of $40 and a cash flow of $1 every quarter forever. Since this is a perpetuity:

$$\text{Present value} = \$40 = \$1 \times (1/r)$$
$$r = 2.5\%$$

To be competitive, the new Home Bank issue would also have to offer 2.5 percent per quarter; so, if the present value is to be $100, the dividend must be such that:

$$\text{Present value} = \$100 = C \times (1/.025)$$
$$C = \$2.50 \text{ (per quarter)}$$

TABLE 6.2

Summary of annuity and perpetuity calculations

I.   Symbols:

PV = Present value, what future cash flows are worth today
FV_t = Future value, what cash flows are worth in the future
r = Interest rate, rate of return, or discount rate per period—typically, but not always, one year
t = Number of periods—typically, but not always, the number of years
C = Cash amount

II.   Future value of *C* per period for *t* periods at *r* percent per period:

$$FV_t = C \times \{[(1 + r)^t - 1]/r\}$$

A series of identical cash flows is called an annuity, and the term $[(1 + r)^t - 1]/r$ is called the *annuity future value factor*.

III.   Present value of *C* per period for *t* periods at *r* percent per period:

$$PV = C \times \{1 - [1/(1 + r)^t]\}/r$$

The term $\{1 - [1/(1 + r)^t]\}/r$ is called the *annuity present value factor*.

IV.   Present value of a perpetuity of *C* per period:

$$PV = C/r$$

A *perpetuity* has the same cash flow every year forever.

$$PV = \frac{\$100,000}{1.11} + \frac{100,000(1.05)}{(1.11)^2} + \frac{\$100,000(1.05)^2}{(1.11)^3} + \cdots$$
$$+ \frac{100,000(1.05)^{N-1}}{(1.11)^N} + \cdots$$

Algebraically, we can write the formula as

$$PV = \frac{C}{1 + r} + \frac{C \times (1 + g)}{(1 + r)^2} + \frac{C \times (1 + g)^2}{(1 + r)^3} + \cdots$$
$$+ \frac{C \times (1 + g)^{N-1}}{(1 + r)^N} + \cdots$$

where C is the cash flow to be received one period hence, g is the rate of growth per period, expressed as a percentage, and r is the interest rate.

Fortunately, the formula reduces to the following simplification:[4]

---

3 Corporations also issue floating rate preffered stock, as we discuss in Chapter 8.

4 PV is the sum of an infinite geometric series:
$$PV = a(1 + x + x^2 + \ldots)$$
where $a = C/(1 + r)$ and $x = (1 + g)/(1 + r)$ Previously we showed that the sum of an infinite geometric series is $a/(1 - x)$. Using this result and substituting for a and x, we find
$$PV = C/(r - g)$$
Note that this geometric series converges to a finite sum only when x is less than 1. This implies that the growth rate, g, must be less than the interest rate, r.

Formula for Present Value of Growing Perpetuity:

$$PV = \frac{C}{r-g}$$

[6.6]

Using this equation, the present value of the cash flows from the apartment building is

$$\frac{\$100,000}{0.11 - 0.05} = \$1,666,667$$

There are three important points concerning the growing perpetuity formula:

1. *The Numerator.* The numerator is the cash flow one period hence, not at date 0. Consider the following example:

EXAMPLE 6.9

Hoffstein Corporation is just about to pay a dividend of $3.00 per share. Investors anticipate that the annual dividend will rise by 6 percent a year forever. The applicable interest rate is 11 percent. What is the price of the stock today?

The numerator in the formula is the cash flow to be received next period. Since the growth rate is 6 percent, the dividend next year is $3.18 (or $3.00 × 1.06). The price of the stock today is

$$\$66.60 \quad = \quad \underset{\substack{\text{Imminent} \\ \text{dividend}}}{\$3.00} \quad + \quad \underset{\substack{\text{Present value} \\ \text{of all dividends} \\ \text{beginning a year} \\ \text{from now}}}{\frac{\$3.18}{0.11 - 0.06}}$$

The price of $66.60 includes both the dividend to be received immediately and the present value of all dividends beginning a year from now. The formula only makes it possible to calculate the present value of all dividends beginning a year from now. Be sure you understand this example; test questions on this subject always seem to trip up a few of our students.

2. *The Interest Rate and the Growth Rate.* The interest rate r must be greater than the growth rate g for the growing perpetuity formula to work. Consider the case in which the growth rate approaches the interest rate in magnitude. Then the denominator in the growing perpetuity formula gets infinitesimally small and the present value grows infinitely large. The present value is in fact undefined when r is less than g.

3. *The Timing Assumption.* Cash generally flows into and out of real-world firms both randomly and nearly continuously. However, our growing perpetuity formula assumes that cash flows are received and disbursed at regular and discrete points in time. In the example of the apartment, we assumed that the net cash flows only occurred once a year. In reality, rent cheques are commonly received every month. Payments for maintenance and other expenses may occur at any time within the year.

The growing perpetuity formula can be applied only by assuming a regular and discrete pattern of cash flow. Although this assumption is sensible because the formula saves so much time, the user should never forget that it is an assumption. This point will be mentioned again in the chapters ahead.

Growing Annuity

growing annuity
A finite number of growing annual cash flows.

Cash flows in business are very likely to grow over time, due either to real growth or to inflation. The growing perpetuity, which assumes an infinite number of cash flows, provides one formula to handle this growth. We now introduce a **growing annuity**, which is a *finite* number of growing cash flows. Because perpetuities of any kind are rare, a formula for a growing annuity often comes in handy. The formula is[5]

Formula for Present Value of Growing Annuity:

$$PV = \frac{C}{r-g}\left[1-\left(\frac{1+g}{1+r}\right)^t\right]$$

where, as before, C is the payment to occur at the end of the first period, r is the interest rate, g is the rate of growth per period, expressed as a percentage, and T is the number of periods for the annuity.

EXAMPLE 6.10

Gilles Lebouder, a second-year MBA student, has just been offered a job at $50,000 a year. He anticipates his salary increasing by 5 percent a year until his retirement in 40 years. Given an interest rate of 8 percent, what is the present value of his lifetime salary?

We simplify by assuming he will be paid his $50,000 salary exactly one year from now, and that his salary will continue to be paid in annual instalments. From the growing annuity formula, the calculation is

Present value
of Gilles's
lifetime salary

$= \$50,000 \times [1/(0.08 - 0.05) - 1/(0.08 - 0.05)(1.05/1.08)^{40}]$

$= \$1,126,571$

Though the growing annuity is quite useful, it is more tedious than the other simplifying formulas.

CONCEPT QUESTIONS

1. In general, what is the present value of an annuity of C dollars per period at a discount rate of r per period? The future value?

2. In general, what is the present value of a perpetuity?

3. In general, what is the present value of a growing perpetuity?

4. In general, what is the present value of a growing annuity?

6.3 COMPARING RATES: THE EFFECT OF COMPOUNDING

The last issue we need to discuss has to do with the way interest rates are quoted. This subject causes a fair amount of confusion because rates are quoted in many different ways. Sometimes

---

5 This can be proved as follows. A growing annuity can be viewed as the difference between two growing perpetuities. Consider a growing perpetuity A, where the first payment of C occurs at date 1. Next, consider growing perpetuity B, where the first payment of $C(1 + g)^T$ is made at date $T + 1$. Both perpetuities grow at rate g. The growing annuity over T periods is the difference between annuity A and annuity B. This can be represented as:

Date	0	1	2	3	...	T	$T + 1$	$T + 2$	$T + 3$
Perpetuity A		C	$C \times (1 + g)$	$C \times (1 + g)^2$	...	$C \times (1 + g)^{T-1}$	$C \times (1 + g)^T$	$C \times (1 + g)^{T+1}$	$C \times (1 + g)^{T+2}$...
Perpetuity B							$C \times (1 + g)^T$	$C \times (1 + g)^{T+1}$	$C \times (1 + g)^{T+2}$...
Annuity		C	$C \times (1 + g)$	$C \times (1 + g)^2$	...	$C \times (1 + g)^{T-1}$			

The value of perpetuity A is $\dfrac{C}{r-g}$

The value of perpetuity B is $\dfrac{C \times (1 + g)^r}{r-g} \times \dfrac{1}{(1 + r)^r}$

The difference between the two perpetuities is given by the formula for the present value of a growing annuity.

the way a rate is quoted is the result of tradition, and sometimes it's the result of legislation. Unfortunately, at times, rates are quoted in deliberately deceptive ways to mislead borrowers and investors. We will discuss these topics in this section.

Effective Annual Rates and Compounding

If a rate is quoted as 10 percent compounded semiannually, then what this means is that the investment actually pays 5 percent every six months. A natural question then arises: Is 5 percent every six months the same thing as 10 percent per year? It's easy to see that it is not. If you invest $1 at 10 percent per year, you will have $1.10 at the end of the year. If you invest at 5 percent every six months, then you'll have the future value of $1 at 5 percent for two periods, or:

$$\$1 \times 1.05^2 = \$1.1025$$

This is $.0025 more. The reason is very simple. What has occurred is that your account was credited with $1 \times .05 = 5 cents in interest after 6 months. In the following six months, you earned 5 percent on that nickel, for an extra $5 \times .05 = .25$ cents.

As our example illustrates, 10 percent compounded semiannually is actually equivalent to 10.25 percent per year. Put another way, we would be indifferent between 10 percent compounded semiannually and 10.25 percent compounded annually. Anytime we have compounding during the year, we need to be concerned about what the rate really is.

In our example, the 10 percent is called a **stated,** or **quoted interest rate.** Other names are used as well. The 10.25 percent, which is actually the rate that you will earn, is called the **effective annual rate (EAR).** To compare different investments or interest rates, we will always need to convert to effective rates. Some general procedures for doing this are discussed next.

stated interest rate
The interest rate expressed in terms of the interest payment made each period. Also, quoted interest rate.

effective annual rate (EAR)
The interest rate expressed as if it were compounded once per year.

Calculating and Comparing Effective Annual Rates

To see why it is important to work only with effective rates, suppose you've shopped around and come up with the following three rates:

Bank A: 15 percent compounded daily

Bank B: 15.5 percent compounded quarterly

Bank C: 16 percent compounded annually

Which of these is the best if you are thinking of opening a savings account? Which of these is best if they represent loan rates?

To begin, Bank C is offering 16 percent per year. Because there is no compounding during the year, this is the effective rate. Bank B is actually paying $.155/4 = .03875$ or 3.875 percent per quarter. At this rate, an investment of $1 for four quarters would grow to:

$$\$1 \times 1.03875^4 = \$1.1642$$

The EAR, therefore, is 16.42 percent. For a saver, this is much better than the 16 percent rate Bank C is offering; for a borrower, it's worse.

Bank A is compounding every day. This may seem a little extreme, but it is very common to calculate interest daily. In this case, the daily interest rate is actually:

$$.15/365 = .000411$$

This is .0411 percent per day. At this rate, an investment of $1 for 365 periods would grow to:

$$\$1 \times 1.000411^{365} = \$1.1618$$

The EAR is 16.18 percent. This is not as good as Bank B's 16.42 percent for a saver, and not as good as Bank C's 16 percent for a borrower.

This example illustrates two things. First, the highest quoted rate is not necessarily the best. Second, the compounding during the year can lead to a significant difference between the quoted rate and the effective rate. Remember that the effective rate is what you get or what you pay.

If you look at our examples, you see that we computed the EARs in three steps. We first divided the quoted rate by the number of times that the interest is compounded. We then added 1 to the result and raised it to the power of the number of times the interest is compounded. Finally, we subtracted the 1. If we let m be the number of times the interest is compounded during the year, these steps can be summarized simply as:

$$\text{EAR} = [1 + (\text{Quoted rate}/m)]^m - 1 \tag{6.7}$$

For example, suppose you are offered 12 percent compounded monthly. In this case, the interest is compounded 12 times a year; so m is 12. You can calculate the effective rate as:

$$
\begin{aligned}
\text{EAR} &= [1 + (\text{Quoted rate}/m)]^m - 1 \\
&= [1 + (.12/12)]^{12} - 1 \\
&= 1.01^{12} - 1 \\
&= 1.126825 - 1 \\
&= 12.6825\%
\end{aligned}
$$

EXAMPLE 6.11: What's the EAR?

A bank is offering 12 percent compounded quarterly. If you put $100 in an account, how much will you have at the end of one year? What's the EAR? How much will you have at the end of two years?

The bank is effectively offering 12%/4 = 3% every quarter. If you invest $100 for four periods at 3 percent per period, the future value is:

$$
\begin{aligned}
\text{Future value} &= \$100 \times 1.03^4 \\
&= \$100 \times 1.1255 \\
&= \$112.55
\end{aligned}
$$

The EAR is 12.55 percent: $100 × (1 + .1255) = $112.55.

We can determine what you would have at the end of two years in two different ways. One way is to recognize

that two years is the same as eight quarters. At 3 percent per quarter, after eight quarters, you would have:

$$\$100 \times 1.03^8 = \$100 \times 1.2668 = \$126.68$$

Alternatively, we could determine the value after two years by using an EAR of 12.55 percent; so after two years you would have:

$$\$100 \times 1.1255^2 = \$100 \times 1.2688 = \$126.68$$

Thus, the two calculations produce the same answer. This illustrates an important point. Anytime we do a present or future value calculation, the rate we use must be an actual or effective rate. In this case, the actual rate is 3 percent per quarter. The effective annual rate is 12.55 percent. It doesn't matter which one we use once we know the EAR.

EXAMPLE 6.12: Quoting a Rate

Now that you know how to convert a quoted rate to an EAR, consider going the other way. As a lender, you know you want to actually earn 18 percent on a particular loan. You want to quote a rate that features monthly compounding. What rate do you quote?

In this case, we know the EAR is 18 percent and we know this is the result of monthly compounding. Let q stand for the quoted rate. We thus have:

$$
\begin{aligned}
\text{EAR} &= [1 + (\text{Quoted rate}/m)]^m - 1 \\
.18 &= [1 + (q/12)]^{12} - 1 \\
1.18 &= [1 + (q/12)]^{12}
\end{aligned}
$$

We need to solve this equation for the quoted rate. This calculation is the same as the ones we did to find an unknown interest rate in Chapter 5:

$$
\begin{aligned}
1.18^{(1/12)} &= 1 + (q/12) \\
1.18^{.08333} &= 1 + (q/12) \\
1.0139 &= 1 + (q/12) \\
q &= .0139 \times 12 \\
&= 16.68\%
\end{aligned}
$$

Therefore, the rate you would quote is 16.68 percent, compounded monthly.

Mortgages

Mortgages are a very common example of an annuity with monthly payments. All major financial institutions have websites providing mortgage information. For example, TD Canada Trust's website has a mortgage calculator on the Tools menu. To understand mortgage calculations, keep in mind two institutional arrangements: First, although payments are monthly, regulations for Canadian financial institutions require that mortgage rates be quoted with semi-annual compounding. Second, financial institutions offer mortgages with interest rates fixed for various periods ranging from 6 months to 25 years. As the borrower, you must choose the period for which the rate is fixed. (We offer some guidance in Example 6.14.) In any case, payments on conventional mortgages are calculated to maturity (usually after 25 years).

EXAMPLE 6.13: What Are Your Payments?

A financial institution is offering a $100,000 mortgage at a quoted rate of 6 percent. To find the payments, we need to find the quoted monthly rate. To do this, we convert the quoted semiannual rate to an EAR:

$$EAR = [1 + \text{Quoted rate}/m]^m - 1$$
$$= [1 + .06/2]^2 - 1$$
$$= 1.03^2 - 1$$
$$= 6.09\%$$

Then we find the quoted monthly rate used to calculate the payments:

$$\text{Quoted rate}/m = (EAR + 1)^{1/m} - 1$$
$$\text{Quoted rate}/12 = (1.0609)^{1/12} - 1$$
$$= 1.004939 - 1$$
$$= 0.4939\%$$

Alternatively, the following formula could be applied to find the effective monthly rate (where n = number of compounding periods in a year):

$$\text{Effective rate}/m = (1 + \text{Quoted annual rate}/n)^{1/(12)} - 1$$
$$= 0.4939\%$$

The effective monthly rate is 0.4939 percent and there are $12 \times 25 = 300$ payments. To find the payment, we use the annuity present value formula:

$$\text{Annuity present value} = \$100,000$$
$$= C \times (1 - \text{Present value factor})/r$$
$$\$100,000 = C \times (1 - 1/1.004939^{300})/.004939$$
$$= C \times (1 - .22808)/.004939$$
$$= C \times 156.2907$$
$$C = \$639.83$$

Your monthly payments will be $639.83

EXAMPLE 6.14: Choosing the Mortgage Term

Earlier we pointed out that while mortgages are amortized over 300 months, the rate is fixed for a shorter period usually no longer than five years. Suppose the rate of 6 percent in Example 6.13 is fixed for five years and you are wondering whether to lock in this rate or to take a lower rate of 4 percent fixed for only one year. If you chose the one-year rate, how much lower would your payments be for the first year?

The payments at 4 percent are $525.63, a reduction of $111.40 per month. If you choose to take the shorter-

term mortgage with lower payments, you are betting that rates will not take a big jump over the next year, leaving you with a new rate after one year much higher than 6 percent. While the mortgage formula cannot make this decision for you (it depends on risk and return discussed in Chapter 12), it does give you the risk you are facing in higher monthly payments. In 1981, mortgage rates were around 20 percent!

EARs and APRs

annual percentage rate (APR)
The interest rate charged per period multiplied by the number of periods per year.

Sometimes it's not clear whether a rate is an effective annual rate. A case in point concerns what is called the **annual percentage rate** (APR) on a loan. Cost of borrowing disclosure regulations (part of the *Bank Act*) in Canada require that lenders disclose an APR on virtually all consumer loans. This rate must be displayed on a loan document in a prominent and unambiguous way.

Given that an APR must be calculated and displayed, an obvious question arises: Is an APR an effective annual rate? Put another way, if a bank quotes a car loan at 12 percent APR, is the consumer actually paying 12 percent interest? Surprisingly, the answer is no. There is some confusion over this point, which we discuss next.

The confusion over APRs arises because lenders are required by law to compute the APR in a particular way. By law, the APR is simply equal to the interest rate per period multiplied by the

EXAMPLE 6.15: What Rate Are You Paying?

Depending on the issuer, a typical credit card agreement quotes an interest rate of 18 percent APR. Monthly payments are required. What is the actual interest rate you pay on such a credit card?

Based on our discussion, an APR of 18 percent with monthly payments is really .18/12 = .015 or 1.5 percent per month. The EAR is thus:

$$\text{EAR} = [1 + (.18/12)]^{12} - 1$$
$$= 1.015^{12} - 1$$
$$= 1.1956 - 1$$
$$= 19.56\%$$

This is the rate you actually pay.

---

number of periods in a year.[6] For example, if a bank is charging 1.2 percent per month on car loans, then the APR that must be reported is $1.2\% \times 12 = 14.4\%$. So, an APR is, in fact, a quoted or stated rate in the sense we've been discussing. For example, an APR of 12 percent on a loan calling for monthly payments is really 1 percent per month. The EAR on such a loan is thus:

$$\text{EAR} = [1 + \text{APR}/12]^{12} - 1$$
$$= 1.01^{12} - 1 = 12.6825\%$$

The difference between an APR and an EAR probably won't be all that great, but it is somewhat ironic that truth-in-lending laws sometimes require lenders to be *untruthful* about the actual rate on a loan.

Taking It to the Limit: A Note on Continuous Compounding

If you made a deposit in a savings account, how often could your money be compounded during the year? If you think about it, there isn't really any upper limit. We've seen that daily compounding, for example, isn't a problem. There is no reason to stop here, however. We could compound every hour or minute or second. How high would the EAR get in this case? Table 6.3 illustrates the EARs that result as 10 percent is compounded at shorter and shorter intervals. Notice that the EARs do keep getting larger, but the differences get very small.

As the numbers in Table 6.3 seem to suggest, there is an upper limit to the EAR. If we let q stand for the quoted rate, then, as the number of times the interest is compounded gets extremely large, the EAR approaches:

$$\text{EAR} = e^q - 1 \qquad [6.8]$$

where e is the number 2.71828 (look for a key labelled "e^x" on your calculator). For example, with our 10 percent rate, the highest possible EAR is:

$$\text{EAR} = e^q - 1$$
$$= 2.71828^{.10} - 1$$
$$= 1.1051709 - 1$$
$$= 10.51709\%$$

	Compounding Period	Number of Times Compounded	Effective Annual Rate
TABLE 6.3 Compounding frequency and effective annual rates	Year	1	10.00000%
	Quarter	4	10.38129
	Month	12	10.47131
	Week	52	10.50648
	Day	365	10.51558
	Hour	8,760	10.51703
	Minute	525,600	10.51709

6 Note that we have simplified the discussion somewhat, as the *Bank Act* requires that the APR include costs such as up-front fees associated with borrowing the funds.

In this case, we say that the money is continuously, or instantaneously, compounded. What is happening is that interest is being credited the instant it is earned, so the amount of interest grows continuously.

CONCEPT QUESTIONS

1. If an interest rate is given as 12 percent compounded daily, what do we call this rate?

2. What is an APR? What is an EAR? Are they the same thing?

3. In general, what is the relationship between a stated interest rate and an effective interest rate? Which is more relevant for financial decisions?

4. What does continuous compounding mean?

LOAN TYPES AND LOAN AMORTIZATION

Whenever a lender extends a loan, some provision will be made for repayment of the principal (the original loan amount). A loan might be repaid in equal instalments, for example, or it might be repaid in a single lump sum. Because the way that the principal and interest are paid is up to the parties involved, there is actually an unlimited number of possibilities.

In this section, we describe a few forms of repayment that come up quite often, and more complicated forms can usually be built up from these. The three basic types of loans are pure discount loans, interest-only loans, and amortized loans. Working with these loans is a very straightforward application of the present value principles that we have already developed.

Pure Discount Loans

The *pure discount loan* is the simplest form of loan. With such a loan, the borrower receives money today and repays a single lump sum at some time in the future. A one-year, 10 percent pure discount loan, for example, would require the borrower to repay $1.10 in one year for every dollar borrowed today.

Because a pure discount loan is so simple, we already know how to value one. Suppose a borrower was able to repay $25,000 in five years. If we, acting as the lender, wanted a 12 percent interest rate on the loan, how much would we be willing to lend? Put another way, what value would we assign today to that $25,000 to be repaid in five years? Based on our work in Chapter 5, we know the answer is just the present value of $25,000 at 12 percent for five years:

$$\text{Present value} = \$25,000/1.12^5$$
$$= \$25,000/1.7623$$
$$= \$14,186$$

EXAMPLE 6.16: Treasury Bills

When the Government of Canada borrows money on a short-term basis (a year or less), it does so by selling what are called Treasury bills or T-bills for short. A T-bill is a promise by the government to repay a fixed amount at some time in the future, for example, 3 or 12 months.

Treasury bills are pure discount loans. If a T-bill promises to repay $10,000 in 12 months, and the market interest rate is 4 percent, how much does the bill sell for in the market?

Since the going rate is 4 percent, the T-bill sells for the present value of $10,000 to be paid in one year at 4 percent, or:

$$\text{Present value} = \$10,000/1.04 = \$9,615.38$$

In recent years, the Government of Canada has emphasized T-bills over Canada Savings Bonds when seeking short-term financing. T-bills are originally issued in denominations of $1 million. Investment dealers buy T-bills and break them up into smaller denominations, some as small as $1,000, for resale to individual investors.

Pure discount loans are very common when the loan term is short, say, a year or less. In recent years, they have become increasingly common for much longer periods.

Interest-Only Loans

A second type of loan repayment plan calls for the borrower to pay interest each period and to repay the entire principal (the original loan amount) at some point in the future. Loans with such a repayment plan are called *interest-only loans*. Notice that if there is just one period, a pure discount loan and an interest-only loan are the same thing.

For example, with a three-year, 10 percent, interest-only loan of $1,000, the borrower would pay $1,000 × .10 = $100 in interest at the end of the first and second years. At the end of the third year, the borrower would return the $1,000 along with another $100 in interest for that year. Similarly, a 50-year interest-only loan would call for the borrower to pay interest every year for the next 50 years and then repay the principal. In the extreme, the borrower pays the interest every period forever and never repays any principal. As we discussed earlier in the chapter, the result is a perpetuity.

Most bonds issued by the Government of Canada, the provinces, and corporations have the general form of an interest-only loan. Because we consider bonds in some detail in the next chapter, we defer a further discussion of them for now.

Amortized Loans

With a pure discount or interest-only loan, the principal is repaid all at once. An alternative is an *amortized loan*, with which the lender may require the borrower to repay parts of the loan amount over time. The process of providing for a loan to be paid off by making regular principal reductions is called *amortizing* the loan.

A simple way of amortizing a loan is to have the borrower pay the interest each period plus some fixed amount. This approach is common with medium-term business loans. For example, suppose a business takes out a $5,000, five-year loan at 9 percent. The loan agreement calls for the borrower to pay the interest on the loan balance each year and to reduce the loan balance each year by $1,000. Because the loan amount declines by $1,000 each year, it is fully paid in five years.

In the case we are considering, notice that the total payment will decline each year. The reason is that the loan balance goes down, resulting in a lower interest charge each year, whereas the $1,000 principal reduction is constant. For example, the interest in the first year will be $5,000 × .09 = $450. The total payment will be $1,000 + 450 = $1,450. In the second year, the loan balance is $4,000, so the interest is $4,000 × .09 = $360, and the total payment is $1,360. We can calculate the total payment in each of the remaining years by preparing a simple amortization schedule as follows:

Year	Beginning Balance	Total Payment	Interest Paid	Principal Paid	Ending Balance
1	$5,000	$1,450	$ 450	$1,000	$4,000
2	4,000	1,360	360	1,000	3,000
3	3,000	1,270	270	1,000	2,000
4	2,000	1,180	180	1,000	1,000
5	1,000	1,090	90	1,000	0
Totals		$6,350	$1,350	$5,000	

Notice that in each year, the interest paid is given by the beginning balance multiplied by the interest rate. Also notice that the beginning balance is given by the ending balance from the previous year.

Probably the most common way of amortizing a loan is to have the borrower make a single, fixed payment every period. Almost all consumer loans (such as car loans) and mortgages work this way. For example, suppose our five-year, 9 percent, $5,000 loan was amortized this way. How would the amortization schedule look?

We first need to determine the payment. From our discussion earlier in the chapter, we know that this loan's cash flows are in the form of an ordinary annuity. In this case, we can solve for the payment as follows:

$$\$5,000 = C \times \{[1 - (1/1.09^5)]/.09\}$$
$$= C \times [(1 - .6499)/.09]$$

This gives us:

$$C = \$5,000/3.8897$$
$$= \$1,285.46$$

The borrower will therefore make five equal payments of $1,285.46. Will this pay off the loan? We will check by filling in an amortization schedule.

In our previous example, we knew the principal reduction each year. We then calculated the interest owed to get the total payment. In this example, we know the total payment. We will thus calculate the interest and then subtract it from the total payment to calculate the principal portion in each payment.

In the first year, the interest is $450, as we calculated before. Because the total payment is $1,285.46, the principal paid in the first year must be:

Principal paid = $1,285.46 – 450 = $835.46

The ending loan balance is thus:

Ending balance = $5,000 – 835.46 = $4,164.54

The interest in the second year is $4,164.54 × .09 = $374.81, and the loan balance declines by $1,285.46 – 374.81 = $910.65. We can summarize all of the relevant calculations in the following schedule:

Year	Beginning Balance	Total Payment	Interest Paid	Principal Paid	Ending Balance
1	$5,000.00	$1,285.46	$ 450.00	$ 835.46	$4,164.54
2	4,164.54	1,285.46	374.81	910.65	3,253.88
3	3,253.88	1,285.46	292.85	992.61	2,261.27
4	2,261.27	1,285.46	203.51	1,081.95	1,179.32
5	1,179.32	1,285.46	106.14	1,179.32	0.00
Total		$6,427.30	$1,427.31	$5,000.00	

Because the loan balance declines to zero, the five equal payments do pay off the loan. Notice that the interest paid declines each period. This isn't surprising because the loan balance is going down. Given that the total payment is fixed, the principal paid must be rising each period.

If you compare the two loan amortizations in this section, you will see that the total interest is greater for the equal total payment case, $1,427.31 versus $1,350. The reason for this is that the loan is repaid more slowly early on, so the interest is somewhat higher. This doesn't mean that one loan is better than the other; it simply means that one is effectively paid off faster than the other. For example, the principal reduction in the first year is $835.46 in the equal total payment case as compared to $1,000 in the first case.

CALCULATOR HINTS

How to Calculate the Amortization of Loan Payments Using a Financial Calculator

The amortization of loan payments may be determined using your calculator once you have mastered the calculation of a loan payment. Once you have completed the four-step procedure to find the loan payment, you can find the amortization of any payment.

To begin, of course, we must remember to clear the calculator! Next, input the payment number (e.g., 1.0) and press AMRT. This gives you the principal returned, $835.46 in the equal payment scenario discussed in this section.

If you press AMRT again, you will be given the interest paid value. Finally, pressing AMRT a third time will give you the balance of principal after the payment number you input.

On Hewlett-Packard calculators, simply press AMRT when you are in the TVM mode and then input the number of payments to amortize by pressing the soft key corresponding to #P.

SPREADSHEET STRATEGIES

Loan Amortization Using a Spreadsheet

Loan amortization is a very common spreadsheet application. To illustrate, we will set up the problem that we have just examined, a five-year, $5,000, 9 percent loan with constant payments. Our spreadsheet looks like this:

	A	B	C	D	E	F	G	H
1								
2			Using a spreadsheet to amortize a loan					
3								
4			Loan amount:	$5,000				
5			Interest rate:	0.09				
6			Loan term:	5				
7			Loan payment:	**$1,285.46**				
8				Note: payment is calculated using PMT(rate,nper,-pv,fv)				
9			*Amortization table:*					
10								
11			Year	Beginning	Total	Interest	Principal	Ending
12				Balance	Payment	Paid	Paid	Balance
13			1	$5,000.00	$1,285.46	$450.00	$835.46	$4,164.54
14			2	4,164.54	1,285.46	374.81	910.65	3,253.88
15			3	3,253.88	1,285.46	292.85	992.61	2,261.27
16			4	2,261.27	1,285.46	203.51	1,081.95	1,179.32
17			5	1,179.32	1,285.46	106.14	1,179.32	0.00
18			Totals		6,427.31	1,427.31	5,000.00	
19								
20			*Formulas in the amortization table:*					
21								
22			Year	Beginning	Total	Interest	Principal	Ending
23				Balance	Payment	Paid	Paid	Balance
24			1	=+D4	=$D$7	=+$D$5*C13	=+D13-E13	=+C13-F13
25			2	=+G13	=$D$7	=+$D$5*C14	=+D14-E14	=+C14-F14
26			3	=+G14	=$D$7	=+$D$5*C15	=+D15-E15	=+C15-F15
27			4	=+G15	=$D$7	=+$D$5*C16	=+D16-E16	=+C16-F16
28			5	=+G16	=$D$7	=+$D$5*C17	=+D17-E17	=+C17-F17
29								
30			Note: totals in the amortization table are calculated using the SUM formula.					
31								

EXAMPLE 6.17: Partial Amortization, or the "Bullet" Loan

As we explained earlier, real estate lending usually involves mortgages with a loan period far shorter than the mortgage life. A common example might call for a five-year loan with, say, a 15-year amortization. This means the borrower makes a payment every month of a fixed amount based on a 15-year amortization. However, after 60 months, the borrower either negotiates a new five-year loan or makes a single, much larger payment called a *balloon* or *bullet* to pay off the loan. Balloon payments are common in both commercial and residential mortgages. In either case, because the monthly payments don't fully pay off the loan, the loan is said to be partially amortized.

Suppose we have a $100,000 commercial mortgage with a 12 percent rate compounded semiannually and a 20-year (240-month) amortization. Further suppose that the mortgage has a five-year balloon. What will the monthly payment be? How big will the balloon payment be?

The monthly payment can be calculated based on an ordinary annuity with a present value of $100,000. To find the monthly rate, we first have to find the EAR and then convert it to a quoted monthly rate. To do this, we convert the quoted semiannual rate to an EAR.

$$\text{EAR} = [1 + \text{Quoted rate}/m]^m - 1$$
$$= [1 + .12/2]^2 - 1$$
$$= 1.06^2 - 1$$
$$= 12.36\%$$

Then, we find the quoted monthly rate used to calculate the payments:

$$\text{Quoted rate}/m = (\text{EAR} + 1)^{1/m} - 1$$
$$\text{Quoted rate}/12 = (1.1236)^{1/12} - 1$$
$$= 1.0098 - 1 = 0.98\%$$

The quoted monthly rate is 0.98 percent and there are $12 \times 20 = 240$ payments. To find the payment amount, we use the annuity present value formula.

EXAMPLE 6.17: Partial Amortization, or the "Bullet" Loan—cont'd.

Annuity present value = $100,000
$$= C \times (1 - \text{Present value factor})/r$$
$$\$100,000 = C \times (1 - 1/1.0098^{240})/.0098$$
$$= C \times (1 - .0972)/.0098$$
$$= C \times 92.5092$$
$$C = \$1,080.97$$

Your monthly payments will be $1,080.97.

Now, there is an easy way and a hard way to determine the balloon payment. The hard way is to actually amortize the loan for 60 months to see what the balance is at that time. The easy way is to recognize that after 60 months, we have a 240 − 60 = 180-month loan. The payment is still $1,080.97 per month, and the interest rate is still .98 percent per month. The loan balance is thus the present value of the remaining payments:

Loan balance = $1,080.97 × (1 − 1/1.0098180)/.0098
$$= \$1,080.97 \times 84.6303$$
$$= \$91,482.84[17]$$

The balloon payment is a substantial $91,483. Why is it so large? To get an idea, consider the first payment on the mortgage. The interest in the first month is $100,000 × .0098 = $975.88 (rounding difference). Your payment is $1,080.97, so the loan balance declines by only $105.09. Since the loan balance declines so slowly, the cumulative pay down over five years is not great.

CONCEPT QUESTIONS

1. What is a pure discount loan? An interest-only loan?

2. What does it mean to amortize a loan?

3. What is a balloon payment? How do you determine its value?

6.5 SUMMARY AND CONCLUSIONS

This chapter rounds out your understanding of fundamental concepts related to the time value of money and discounted cash flow valuation. Several important topics were covered, including:

1. There are two ways of calculating present and future values when there are multiple cash flows. Both approaches are straightforward extensions of our earlier analysis of single cash flows.

2. A series of constant cash flows that arrive or are paid at the end of each period is called an ordinary annuity, and we described some useful shortcuts for determining the present and future values of annuities.

3. Interest rates can be quoted in a variety of ways. For financial decisions, it is important that any rates being compared be first converted to effective rates. The relationship between a quoted rate, such as an annual percentage rate (APR), and an effective annual rate (EAR) is given by:

$$\text{EAR} = [1 + (\text{Quoted rate}/m]^m - 1$$

where m is the number of times during the year the money is compounded or, equivalently, the number of payments during the year.

4. Many loans are annuities. The process of providing for a loan to be paid off gradually is called amortizing the loan, and we discussed how amortization schedules are prepared and interpreted.

The principles developed in this chapter will figure prominently in the chapters to come. The reason for this is that most investments, whether they involve real assets or financial assets, can be analyzed using the discounted cash flow (DCF) approach. As a result, the DCF approach is broadly applicable and widely used in practice. For example, the next two chapters show how to value bonds and stocks using an extension of the techniques presented in this chapter. Before going on, therefore, you might want to do some of the problems that follow.

Key Terms

annual percentage rate (APR) (page 160)
annuity (page 147)
annuity due (page 153)
consol (page 154)
effective annual rate (EAR) (page 158)

growing annuity (page 156)
growing perpetuity (page 154)
perpetuity (page 154)
stated or quoted interest rate (page 158)

Chapter Review Problems and Self-Test

6.1 **Present Values with Multiple Cash Flows** A first-round draft choice quarterback has been signed to a three-year, $25 million contract. The details provide for an immediate cash bonus of $2 million. The player is to receive $5 million in salary at the end of the first year, $8 million the next, and $10 million at the end of the last year. Assuming a 15 percent discount rate, is this package worth $25 million? How much is it worth?

6.2 **Future Value with Multiple Cash Flows** You plan to make a series of deposits in an individual retirement account. You will deposit $1,000 today, $2,000 in two years, and $2,000 in five years. If you withdraw $1,500 in three years and $1,000 in seven years, assuming no withdrawal penalties, how much will you have after eight years if the interest rate is 7 percent? What is the present value of these cash flows?

6.3 **Annuity Present Value** You are looking into an investment that will pay you $12,000 per year for the next 10 years. If you require a 15 percent return, what is the most you would pay for this investment?

6.4 **APR versus EAR** The going rate on student loans is quoted as 8 percent APR. The terms of the loans call for monthly payments. What is the effective annual rate (EAR) on such a student loan?

6.5 **It's the Principal That Matters** Suppose you borrow $10,000. You are going to repay the loan by making equal annual payments for five years. The interest rate on the loan is 14 percent per year. Prepare an amortization schedule for the loan. How much interest will you pay over the life of the loan?

6.6 **Just a Little Bit Each Month** You've recently finished your MBA at the Darnit School. Naturally, you must purchase a new BMW immediately. The car costs about $42,000. The bank quotes an interest rate of 15 percent APR for a 72-month loan with a 10 percent down payment. You plan on trading the car in for a new one in two years. What will your monthly payment be? What is the effective interest rate on the loan? What will the loan balance be when you trade the car in?

Answers to Self-Test Problems

6.1 Obviously, the package is not worth $25 million because the payments are spread out over three years. The bonus is paid today, so it's worth $2 million. The present values for the three subsequent salary payments are:

$$(\$5/1.15) + (8/1.15^2) + (10/1.15^3) = (\$5/1.15) + (8/1.32) + (10/1.52)$$
$$= \$16.9721 \text{ million}$$

The package is worth a total of $18.9721 million.

6.2 We will calculate the future values for each of the cash flows separately and then add them up. Notice that we treat the withdrawals as negative cash flows:

$1,000 × 1.07^8 =	$1,000 × 1.7182 =	$1,718.19
$2,000 × 1.07^6 =	$2,000 × 1.5007 =	3,001.46
−$1,500 × 1.07^5 =	−$1,500 × 1.4026 = −	2,103.83
$2,000 × 1.07^3 =	$2,000 × 1.2250 =	2,450.09
−$1,000 × 1.07^1 =	−$1,000 × 1.0700 = −	1,070.00
Total future value	=	$3,995.91

This value includes a small rounding error.

To calculate the present value, we could discount each cash flow back to the present or we could discount back a single year at a time. However, because we already know that the future value in eight years is $3,995.91, the easy way to get the PV is just to discount this amount back eight years:

Present value = $3,995.91/1.07^8
= $3,995.91/1.7182
= $2,325.64

We again ignore a small rounding error. For practice, you can verify that this is what you get if you discount each cash flow back separately.

6.3 The most you would be willing to pay is the present value of $12,000 per year for 10 years at a 15 percent discount rate. The cash flows here are in ordinary annuity form, so the relevant present value factor is:

$$\text{Annuity present value factor} = (1 - \text{Present value factor})/r$$
$$= [1 - (1/1.15^{10})]/.15$$
$$= (1 - .2472)/.15$$
$$= 5.0188$$

The present value of the 10 cash flows is thus:

$$\text{Present value} = \$12,000 \times 5.0188$$
$$= \$60,225$$

This is the most you would pay.

6.4 A rate of 8 percent APR with monthly payments is actually 8%/12 = .67% per month. The EAR is thus:

$$\text{EAR} = [1 + (.08/12)]^{12} - 1 = 8.30\%$$

6.5 We first need to calculate the annual payment. With a present value of $10,000, an interest rate of 14 percent, and a term of five years, the payment can be determined from:

$$\$10,000 = \text{Payment} \times \{[1 - (1/1.14^5)]/.14\}$$
$$= \text{Payment} \times 3.4331$$

Therefore, the payment is $10,000/3.4331 = $2,912.84 (actually, it's $2,912.8355; this will create some small rounding errors in the following schedule). We can now prepare the amortization schedule as follows:

Year	Beginning Balance	Total Payment	Interest Paid	Principal Paid	Ending Balance
1	$10,000.00	$ 2,912.84	$1,400.00	$ 1,512.84	$8,487.16
2	8,487.16	2,912.84	1,188.20	1,724.63	6,762.53
3	6,762.53	2,912.84	946.75	1,966.08	4,796.45
4	4,796.45	2,912.84	671.50	2,241.33	2,555.12
5	2,555.12	2,912.84	357.72	2,555.12	0.00
Totals		$14,564.17	$4,564.17	$10,000.00	

6.6 The cash flows on the car loan are in annuity form, so we only need to find the payment. The interest rate is 15%/12 = 1.25% per month, and there are 72 months. The first thing we need is the annuity factor for 72 periods at 1.25 percent per period:

$$\text{Annuity present value factor} = (1 - \text{Present value factor})/r$$
$$= [1 - (1/1.0125^{72})]/.0125$$
$$= [1 - (1/2.4459)]/.0125$$
$$= (1 - .4088)/.0125$$
$$= 47.2925$$

The present value is the amount we finance. With a 10 percent down payment, we will be borrowing 90 percent of $42,000, or $37,800.

So, to find the payment, we need to solve for C in the following:

$$\$37,800 = C \times \text{Annuity present value factor}$$
$$= C \times 47.2925$$

Rearranging things a bit, we have:

$$C = \$37,800 \times (1/47.2925)$$
$$= \$37,800 \times .02115$$
$$= \$799.47$$

Your payment is just under $800 per month.

The actual interest rate on this loan is 1.25 percent per month. Based on our work in the chapter, we can calculate the effective annual rate as:

$$\text{EAR} = (1.0125)^{12} - 1 = 16.08\%$$

The effective rate is about one point higher than the quoted rate.

To determine the loan balance in two years, we could amortize the loan to see what the balance is at that time. This would be fairly tedious to do by hand. Using the information already determined in this problem, we can instead simply calculate the present value of the remaining payments. After two years, we have made 24 payments, so there are 72 – 24 = 48 payments left. What is the present value of 48 monthly payments of $799.47 at 1.25 percent per month? The relevant annuity factor is:

$$\text{Annuity present value factor} = (1 - \text{Present value factor})/r$$
$$= [1 - (1/1.0125^{48})]/.0125$$
$$= [1 - (1/1.8154)]/.0125$$
$$= (1 - .5509)/.0125$$
$$= 35.9315$$

The present value is thus:

$$\text{Present value} = \$799.47 \times 35.9315 = \$28,726.16$$

You will owe about $28,726 on the loan in two years.

Concepts Review and Critical Thinking Questions

1. In evaluating an annuity present value, there are four pieces. What are they?

2. As you increase the length of time involved, what happens to the present value of an annuity? What happens to the future value?

3. What happens to the future value of an annuity if you increase the rate r? What happens to the present value?

4. What do you think about a lottery advertising a $500,000 prize when the lump-sum option is $250,000? Is it deceptive advertising?

5. If you were an athlete negotiating a contract, would you want a big signing bonus payable immediately and smaller payments in the future, or vice versa? How about from the team's perspective?

6. Suppose two athletes sign 10-year contracts for $80 million. In one case, we're told that the $80 million will be paid in 10 equal instalments. In the other case, we're told that the $80 million will be paid in 10 instalments, but the instalments will increase by 5 percent per year. Who got the better deal?

Questions and Problems

Basic
(Questions
1–28)

1. **Present Value and Multiple Cash Flows** Conoly Co. has identified an investment project with the following cash flows. If the discount rate is 10 percent, what is the present value of these cash flows? What is the present value at 18 percent? At 24 percent?

Year	Cash Flow
1	$1,200
2	600
3	855
4	1,480

2. **Present Value and Multiple Cash Flows** Investment X offers to pay you $4,000 per year for nine years, whereas Investment Y offers to pay you $6,000 per year for five years. Which of these cash flow streams has the higher present value if the discount rate is 5 percent? If the discount rate is 22 percent?

3. **Future Value and Multiple Cash Flows** Rasputin, Inc., has identified an investment project with the following cash flows. If the discount rate is 8 percent, what is the future value of these cash flows in Year 4? What is the future value at a discount rate of 11 percent? At 24 percent?

Year	Cash Flow
1	$ 800
2	900
3	1,000
4	1,100

4. **Calculating Annuity Present Value** An investment offers $3,600 per year for 15 years, with the first payment occurring one year from now. If the required return is 10 percent, what is the value of the investment? What would the value be if the payments occurred for 40 years? For 75 years? Forever?

5. **Calculating Annuity Cash Flows** If you put up $28,000 today in exchange for a 7.65 percent, 14-year annuity, what will the annual cash flow be?

6. **Calculating Annuity Values** Your company will generate $80,000 in annual revenue each year for the next eight years from a new information database. If the appropriate interest rate is 8.2 percent, what is the present value of the savings?

Basic
(continued)

7. **Calculating Annuity Values**   If you deposit $2,000 at the end of each of the next 20 years into an account paying 10.5 percent interest, how much money will you have in the account in 20 years? How much will you have if you make deposits for 40 years?

8. **Calculating Annuity Values**   You want to have $80,000 in your savings account 10 years from now, and you're prepared to make equal annual deposits into the account at the end of each year. If the account pays 5.8 percent interest, what amount must you deposit each year?

9. **Calculating Annuity Values**   Dinero Bank offers you a $40,000, seven-year term loan at 9 percent annual interest. What will your annual loan payment be?

10. **Calculating Perpetuity Values**   The Perpetual Life Insurance Co. is trying to sell you an investment policy that will pay you and your heirs $15,000 per year forever. If the required return on this investment is 8 percent, how much will you pay for the policy?

11. **Calculating Perpetuity Values**   In the previous problem, suppose the Perpetual Life Insurance Co. told you the policy costs $195,000. At what interest rate would this be a fair deal?

12. **Calculating EAR**   Find the EAR in each of the following cases:

Stated Rate (APR)	Number of Times Compounded	Effective Rate (EAR)
11%	Quarterly	
7	Monthly	
9	Daily	
17	Infinite	

13. **Calculating APR**   Find the APR, or stated rate, in each of the following cases:

Stated Rate (APR)	Number of Times Compounded	Effective Rate (EAR)
	Semiannually	8.1%
	Monthly	7.6
	Weekly	16.8
	Infinite	26.2

14. **Calculating EAR**   Royal Canadian Bank charges 12.2 percent compounded monthly on its business loans. First United Bank charges 12.4 percent compounded semiannually. As a potential borrower, which bank would you go to for a new loan?

15. **Calculating APR**   Copeland Credit Corp. wants to earn an effective annual return on its consumer loans of 17 percent per year. The bank uses daily compounding on its loans. What interest rate is the bank required by law to report to potential borrowers? Explain why this rate is misleading to an uninformed borrower.

16. **Calculating Future Values**   What is the future value of $800 in 20 years assuming an interest rate of 10.4 percent compounded semiannually?

17. **Calculating Future Values**   Calvani Credit Bank is offering 7.1 percent compounded daily on its savings accounts. If you deposit $6,000 today, how much will you have in the account in 5 years? In 10 years? In 20 years?

18. **Calculating Present Values**   An investment will pay you $24,000 in six years. If the appropriate discount rate is 11 percent compounded daily, what is the present value?

19. **EAR versus APR**   Big Dom's Pawn Shop charges an interest rate of 30 percent per month on loans to its customers. Like all lenders, Big Dom must report an APR to consumers. What rate should the shop report? What is the effective annual rate?

20. **Calculating Loan Payments**   You want to buy a new sports coupe for $56,850, and the finance office at the dealership has quoted you an 8.2 percent APR loan for 60 months to buy the car. What will your monthly payments be? What is the effective annual rate on this loan?

21. **Calculating Number of Periods**   One of your customers is delinquent on his accounts payable balance. You've mutually agreed to a repayment schedule of $500 per month. You will charge .9 percent per month interest on the overdue balance. If the current balance is $16,500, how long will it take for the account to be paid off?

22. **Calculating EAR**   Friendly's Quick Loans, Inc., offers you "three for four or I knock on your door." This means you get $3 today and repay $4 when you get your paycheck in one week (or else). What's the effective annual return Friendly's earns on this lending business? If you were brave enough to ask, what APR would Friendly's say you were paying?

23. **Valuing Perpetuities**   Maybepay Life Insurance Co. is selling a perpetuity contract that pays $1,150 monthly. The contract currently sells for $58,000. What is the monthly return on this investment vehicle? What is the APR? The effective annual return?

24. **Calculating Annuity Future Values**   You are to make monthly deposits of $150 into a retirement account that pays 11 percent interest compounded monthly. If your first deposit will be made one month from now, how large will your retirement account be in 20 years?

Basic
(continued)

25. **Calculating Annuity Future Values**   In the previous problem, suppose you make $1,800 annual deposits into the same retirement account. How large will your account balance be in 20 years?

26. **Calculating Annuity Present Values**   Beginning three months from now, you want to be able to withdraw $1,200 each quarter from your bank account to cover college expenses over the next four years. If the account pays 0.50 percent interest per quarter, how much do you need to have in your bank account today to meet your expense needs over the next four years?

27. **Discounted Cash Flow Analysis**   If the appropriate discount rate for the following cash flows is 13 percent compounded quarterly, what is the present value of the cash flows?

Year	Cash Flow
1	$ 900
2	750
3	0
4	1,140

28. **Discounted Cash Flow Analysis**   If the appropriate discount rate for the following cash flows is 9.75 percent per year, what is the present value of the cash flows?

Year	Cash Flow
1	$2,800
2	0
3	8,100
4	1,940

Intermediate
(Questions
29–56)

29. **Simple Interest versus Compound Interest**   First Simple Bank pays 8 percent simple interest on its investment accounts. If First Complex Bank pays interest on its accounts compounded annually, what rate should the bank set if it wants to match First Simple Bank over an investment horizon of 10 years?

30. **Calculating EAR**   You are looking at an investment that has an effective annual rate of 16 percent. What is the effective semiannual return? The effective quarterly return? The effective monthly return?

31. **Calculating Interest Expense**   You receive a credit card application from Shady Banks Savings and Loan offering an introductory rate of 1.90 percent per year, compounded monthly for the first six months, increasing thereafter to 16 percent compounded monthly. Assuming you transfer the $4,000 balance from your existing credit card and make no subsequent payments, how much interest will you owe at the end of the first year?

32. **Calculating Annuities**   You are planning to save for retirement over the next 30 years. To do this, you will invest $700 a month in a stock account and $300 a month in a bond account. The return of the stock account is expected to be 11 percent, and the bond account will pay 7 percent. When you retire, you will combine your money into an account with a 9 percent return. How much can you withdraw each month from your account assuming a 25-year withdrawal period?

33. **Calculating Future Values**   You have an investment that will pay you 1.16 percent per month. How much will you have per dollar invested in one year? In two years?

34. **Calculating Annuity Payments**   You want to be a millionaire when you retire in 40 years. How much do you have to save each month if you can earn a 10 percent annual return? How much do you have to save if you wait 10 years before you begin your deposits? 20 years?

35. **Calculating Rates of Return**   Suppose an investment offers to triple your money in 12 months (don't believe it). What rate of return per quarter are you being offered?

36. **Comparing Cash Flow Streams**   You've just joined the investment banking firm of Dewey, Cheatum, and Howe. They've offered you two different salary arrangements. You can have $80,000 per year for the next two years, or you can have $60,000 per year for the next two years, along with a $35,000 signing bonus today. The bonus is paid immediately, and the salary is paid at the end of each year. If the interest rate is 10 percent compounded monthly, which do you prefer?

37. **Calculating Present Value of Annuities**   Peter Piper wants to sell you an investment contract that pays equal $10,000 amounts at the end of each of the next 20 years. If you require a return of 0.7 percent per month on this investment, how much will you pay for the contract today?

38. **Calculating Rates of Return**   You're trying to choose between two different investments, both of which have up-front costs of $50,000. Investment G returns $85,000 in five years. Investment H returns $175,000 in 11 years. Which of these investments has the higher return?

39. **Present Value and Interest Rates**   What is the relationship between the value of an annuity and the level of interest rates? Suppose you just bought a 10-year annuity of $5,000 per year at the current interest rate of 10 percent per year. What happens to the value of your investment if interest rates suddenly drop to 5 percent? What if interest rates suddenly rise to 15 percent?

Intermediate
(continued)

40. Calculating the Number of Payments You're prepared to make monthly payments of $125, beginning at the end of this month, into an account that pays 10 percent interest compounded monthly. How many payments will you have made when your account balance reaches $20,000?

41. Calculating Annuity Present Values You want to borrow $45,000 from your local bank to buy a new sailboat. You can afford to make monthly payments of $950, but no more. Assuming monthly compounding, what is the highest rate you can afford on a 60-month APR loan?

42. Calculating Loan Payments You need a 30-year, fixed-rate mortgage to buy a new home for $200,000. Your mortgage bank will lend you the money at a 6.8 percent APR for this 360-month loan. However, you can only afford monthly payments of $1,000, so you offer to pay off any remaining loan balance at the end of the loan in the form of a single balloon payment. How large will this balloon payment have to be for you to keep your monthly payments at $1,000?

43. Present and Future Values The present value of the following cash flow stream is $5,979 when discounted at 10 percent annually. What is the value of the missing cash flow?

Year	Cash Flow
1	$1,000
2	?
3	2,000
4	2,000

44. Calculating Present Values You just won the TVM Lottery. You will receive $1 million today plus another 10 annual payments that increase by $400,000 per year. Thus, in one year you receive $1.4 million. In two years, you get $1.8 million, and so on. If the appropriate interest rate is 10 percent, what is the present value of your winnings?

45. EAR versus APR You have just purchased a new warehouse. To finance the purchase, you've arranged for a 30-year mortgage loan for 80 percent of the $1,600,000 purchase price. The monthly payment on this loan will be $10,000. What is the APR on this loan? The EAR?

46. Present Value and Break-Even Interest Consider a firm with a contract to sell an asset for $115,000 three years from now. The asset costs $72,000 to produce today. Given a relevant discount rate on this asset of 13 percent per year, will the firm make a profit on this asset? At what rate does the firm just break even?

47. Present Value and Multiple Cash Flows What is the present value of $2,000 per year, at a discount rate of 12 percent, if the first payment is received 9 years from now and the last payment is received 25 years from now?

48. Variable Interest Rates A 15-year annuity pays $1,500 per month, and payments are made at the end of each month. If the interest rate is 15 percent compounded monthly for the first seven years, and 12 percent compounded monthly thereafter, what is the present value of the annuity?

49. Comparing Cash Flow Streams You have your choice of two investment accounts. Investment A is a 15-year annuity that features end-of-month $1,000 payments and has an interest rate of 10.5 percent compounded monthly. Investment B is a 9 percent continuously compounded lump-sum investment, also good for 15 years. How much money would you need to invest in B today for it to be worth as much as Investment A 15 years from now?

50. Calculating Present Value of a Perpetuity Given an interest rate of 6.5 percent per year, what is the value at date $t = 7$ of a perpetual stream of $3,000 payments that begin at date $t = 15$?

51. Calculating EAR A local finance company quotes a 14 percent interest rate on one-year loans. So, if you borrow $20,000, the interest for the year will be $2,800. Because you must repay a total of $22,800 in one year, the finance company requires you to pay $22,800/12, or $1,900, per month over the next 12 months. Is this a 14 percent loan? What rate would legally have to be quoted? What is the effective annual rate?

52. Calculating Present Values A 5-year annuity of ten $6,000 semiannual payments will begin 9 years from now, with the first payment coming 9.5 years from now. If the discount rate is 12 percent compounded monthly, what is the value of this annuity five years from now? What is the value three years from now? What is the current value of the annuity?

53. Calculating Annuities Due As discussed in the text, an ordinary annuity assumes equal payments at the end of each period over the life of the annuity. An *annuity due* is the same thing except the payments occur at the beginning of each period instead. Thus, a three-year annual annuity due would have periodic payment cash flows occurring at Years 0, 1, and 2, whereas a three-year annual ordinary annuity would have periodic payment cash flows occurring at Years 1, 2, and 3.

a. At a 9.5 percent annual discount rate, find the present value of a six-year ordinary annuity contract of $525 payments.

b. Find the present value of the same contract if it is an annuity due.

54. Calculating Annuities Due You want to buy a new sports car from Muscle Motors for $56,000. The contract is in the form of a 48-month annuity due at an 8.15 percent APR. What will your monthly payment be?

55. Amortization with Equal Payments Prepare an amortization schedule for a five-year loan of $30,000. The interest rate is 10 percent per year, and the loan calls for equal annual payments. How much interest is paid in the third year? How much total interest is paid over the life of the loan?

56. **Amortization with Equal Principal Payments** Rework Problem 55 assuming that the loan agreement calls for a principal reduction of $6,000 every year instead of equal annual payments.

Challenge
(Questions
57–72)

57. **Calculating Annuity Values** Bilbo Baggins wants to save money to meet three objectives. First, he would like to be able to retire 30 years from now with retirement income of $25,000 per month for 20 years, with the first payment received 30 years and 1 month from now. Second, he would like to purchase a cabin in Rivendell in 10 years at an estimated cost of $350,000. Third, after he passes on at the end of the 20 years of withdrawals, he would like to leave an inheritance of $750,000 to his nephew Frodo. He can afford to save $2,100 per month for the next 10 years. If he can earn an 11 percent EAR before he retires and an 8 percent EAR after he retires, how much will he have to save each month in years 11 through 30?

58. **Calculating Annuity Values** After deciding to buy a new car, you can either lease the car or purchase it on a 3-year loan. The car you wish to buy costs $35,000. The dealer has a special leasing arrangement where you pay $1 today and $450 per month for the next three years. If you purchase the car, you will pay it off in monthly payments over the next three years at an 8% APR. You believe that you will be able to sell the car for $23,000 in three years. Should you buy or lease the car? What break-even resale price in three years would make you indifferent between buying and leasing?

59. **Calculating Annuity Values** An All-Pro defensive lineman is in contract negotiations. The team has offered the following salary structure:

Time	Salary
0	$8,000,000
1	$4,000,000
2	$4,800,000
3	$5,700,000
4	$6,400,000
5	$7,000,000
6	$7,500,000

All salaries are to be paid in a lump sum. The player has asked you as his agent to renegotiate the terms. He wants a $9 million signing bonus payable today and a contract value increase of $750,000. He also wants an equal salary paid every three months, with the first paycheque three months from now. If the interest rate is 4.5 percent compounded daily, what is the amount of his quarterly cheque? Assume 365 days in a year.

60. **Discount Interest Loans** This question illustrates what is known as *discount interest*. Imagine you are discussing a loan with a somewhat unscrupulous lender. You want to borrow $20,000 for one year. The interest rate is 12 percent. You and the lender agree that the interest on the loan will be .12 × $20,000 5 $2,400. So the lender deducts this interest amount from the loan up front and gives you $17,600. In this case, we say that the discount is $2,400. What's wrong here?

61. **Calculating Annuity Values** You are serving on a jury. A plaintiff is suing the city for injuries sustained after a freak street sweeper accident. In the trial, doctors testified that it will be five years before the plaintiff is able to return to work. The jury has already decided in favour of the plaintiff. You are the foreperson of the jury and propose that the jury give the plaintiff an award to cover the following: 1) The present value of two years' back pay. The plaintiff's annual salary for the last two years would have been $40,000 and $43,000, respectively. 2) The present value of five years' future salary. You assume the salary will be $45,000 per year. 3) $100,000 for pain and suffering. 4) $20,000 for court costs. Assume that the salary payments are equal amounts paid at the end of each month. If the interest rate you choose is a 9% EAR, what is the size of the settlement? If you were the plaintiff, would you like to see a higher or lower interest rate?

62. **EAR versus APR** There are two banks in the area that offer 30-year, $200,000 mortgages at 7.5 percent and charge a $1,500 loan application fee. However, the application fee charged by Insecurity Bank and Trust is refundable if the loan application is denied, whereas that charged by I. M. Greedy and Sons Mortgage Bank is not. The current disclosure law requires that any fees that will be refunded if the applicant is rejected be included in calculating the APR, but this is not required with nonrefundable fees (presumably because refundable fees are part of the loan rather than a fee). What are the EARs on these two loans? What are the APRs?

63. **Calculating Annuity Payments** This is a classic retirement problem. A time line will help in solving it. Your friend is celebrating her 35th birthday today and wants to start saving for her anticipated retirement at age 65. She wants to be able to withdraw $90,000 from her savings account on each birthday for 15 years following her retirement; the first withdrawal will be on her 66th birthday. Your friend intends to invest her money in the local credit union, which offers 8 percent interest per year. She wants to make equal annual payments on each birthday into the account established at the credit union for her retirement fund.

    a. If she starts making these deposits on her 36th birthday and continues to make deposits until she is 65 (the last deposit will be on her 65th birthday), what amount must she deposit annually to be able to make the desired withdrawals at retirement?

**Challlenge
(continued)**

b. Suppose your friend has just inherited a large sum of money. Rather than making equal annual payments, she has decided to make one lump-sum payment on her 35th birthday to cover her retirement needs. What amount does she have to deposit?

c. Suppose your friend's employer will contribute $1,500 to the account every year as part of the company's profit-sharing plan. In addition, your friend expects a $25,000 distribution from a family trust fund on her 55th birthday, which she will also put into the retirement account. What amount must she deposit annually now to be able to make the desired withdrawals at retirement?

64. **Calculating the Number of Periods** Your Christmas ski vacation was great, but it unfortunately ran a bit over budget. All is not lost, because you just received an offer in the mail to transfer your $10,000 balance from your current credit card, which charges an annual rate of 19.2 percent, to a new credit card charging a rate of 9.2 percent. How much faster could you pay the loan off by making your planned monthly payments of $200 with the new card? What if there was a 2 percent fee charged on any balances transferred?

65. **Future Value and Multiple Cash Flows** An insurance company is offering a new policy to its customers. Typically, the policy is bought by a parent or grandparent for a child at the child's birth. The details of the policy are as follows: The purchaser (say, the parent) makes the following six payments to the insurance company:

First birthday:	$750
Second birthday:	$750
Third birthday:	$850
Fourth birthday:	$850
Fifth birthday:	$950
Sixth birthday:	$950

After the child's sixth birthday, no more payments are made. When the child reaches age 65, he or she receives $250,000. If the relevant interest rate is 11 percent for the first six years and 7 percent for all subsequent years, is the policy worth buying?

66. **Calculating a Balloon Payment** You have just arranged for a $250,000 mortgage to finance the purchase of a large tract of land. The mortgage has an 8.5 percent APR, and it calls for monthly payments over the next 30 years. However, the loan has an eight-year balloon payment, meaning that the loan must be paid off then. How big will the balloon payment be?

 67. **Calculating Interest Rates** A financial planning service offers a college savings program. The plan calls for you to make six annual payments of $8,000 each, with the first payment occurring today, your child's 12th birthday. Beginning on your child's 18th birthday, the plan will provide $20,000 per year for four years. What return is this investment offering?

 68. **Break-Even Investment Returns** Your financial planner offers you two different investment plans. Plan X is a $10,000 annual perpetuity. Plan Y is a 10-year, $22,000 annual annuity. Both plans will make their first payment one year from today. At what discount rate would you be indifferent between these two plans?

69. **Perpetual Cash Flows** What is the value of an investment that pays $6,700 every *other* year forever, if the first payment occurs one year from today and the discount rate is 13 percent compounded daily? What is the value today if the first payment occurs four years from today?

70. **Ordinary Annuities and Annuities Due** As discussed in the text, an annuity due is identical to an ordinary annuity except that the periodic payments occur at the beginning of each period and not at the end of the period (see Question 53). Show that the relationship between the value of an ordinary annuity and the value of an otherwise equivalent annuity due is:

$$\text{Annuity due value} = \text{Ordinary annuity value} \times (1 + r)$$

Show this for both present and future values.

71. **Calculating Annuities Due** A 10-year annual annuity due with the first payment occurring at date $t = 7$ has a current value of $75,000. If the discount rate is 10 percent per year, what is the annuity payment amount?

72. **Calculating EAR** A cheque-cashing store is in the business of making personal loans to walk-up customers. The store makes only one-week loans at 10 percent interest per week.

a. What APR must the store report to its customers? What is the EAR that the customers are actually paying?

b. Now suppose the store makes one-week loans at 10 percent discount interest per week (see Question 60). What's the APR now? The EAR?

c. The cheque-cashing store also makes one-month add-on interest loans at 9 percent discount interest per week. Thus, if you borrow $100 for one month (four weeks), the interest will be ($100 × 1.09⁴) − 100 = $41.16. Because this is discount interest, your net loan proceeds today will be $58.84. You must then repay the store $100 at the end of the month. To help you out, though, the store lets you pay off this $100 in installments of $25 per week. What is the APR of this loan? What is the EAR?

MINI CASE

You have just been certified as a financial planner, and your first customer is a 65-year-old woman who is concerned about her retirement income. The woman's primary asset is her house, and she does not have sufficient money in her bank or investment accounts to pay her expenses after this year. She has brought with her some information about a reverse mortgage product available at a local bank, and wants you to advise her what her best alternative is with regards to her house. She wants the funds to last her until she is 85 years old. The following are the two alternatives:

Alternative A

Your client could sell her home for a current value of approximately $250,000. You have a friend in the real estate business who will offer her the lowest possible fee of 4.5 percent of the sale price. You have also investigated some relatively safe investments that would offer an average return of 5.5 percent. In this case, your client would need to rent accommodations, and you estimate that she would need $1,250 per month in order to maintain a comfortable lifestyle. She would require a further $400 per month for living expenses. These prices would increase with inflation, which most economists agree will be in the 1–2 percent range for the long run.

Alternative B

Your client could make use of the reverse mortgage product she has investigated. Under this situation, the company would provide her with equal monthly payments over the next 20 years. At the end of the 20 years, those payments would result in a mortgage on her home worth 75 percent of its current value. The company calculates the monthly payments based on an interest rate of 8 percent, compounded semi-annually.

a) Assuming her income from either option would be tax-free, are both alternatives viable? Which should your client prefer?

b) The federal government is considering opting for a flat-tax system, which would result in a 15 percent tax rate on all income. The reverse mortgage payment would not be considered income. Which alternative is preferred if this tax system is introduced (assume its introduction is immediate)?

c) What other considerations should you keep in mind when advising your client?

Internet Application Questions

1. Buying a house frequently involves borrowing a significant portion of the house price from a lending institution such as a bank. Often times, the bank provides repayment of the loan based on long amortization periods. The following site maintained by Royal LePage shows the effect of increasing your monthly payment on the amortization period.

   www.royallepage.ca/CMSTemplates/AsnRLP/Mortgages/SpecialOfferFS.aspx

   Note that increasing the monthly payment has a disproportionate impact on reducing the amortization period. Can you explain why this happens?

2. Alberta Treasury Branch (www.atb.com) offers a variation of GIC called a Springboard®GIC. Click on their homepage and estimate the effective annual yield on a five-year Springboard® GIC. How does this compare to the yield on a five-year standard GIC offered by CIBC? www.cibc.com

3. Toyota of Canada (www.toyota.ca) offers its own financing plans that may sometimes compare favourably to bank financing. Pick a vehicle from this website, and use Toyota's pricing calculator to estimate your monthly financing payment for this car. Assume zero down payment. How does Toyota's financing compare with the lending rates at CIBC? What is the present value of your savings if you choose to finance through Toyota?

Suggested Readings

One of the best places to learn more about the mathematics of present value is the owner's manual that comes with a financial calculator. One of the best comes with the Hewlett-Packard 12C calculator:

Hewlett-Packard HP-12C. *Owner's Handbook and Problem Solving Guide*, latest edition.
Hewlett-Packard HP-12C. *Solutions Handbook*, latest edition.

Other useful references are:

Texas Instruments. *Business Analyst/Guidebook*, latest edition.
Sharp. Business/Financial Calculator EL-731SL. *Instruction Guide and Application Manual.*

APPENDIX 6A PROOF OF ANNUITY PRESENT VALUE FORMULA

An *annuity* is a level stream of regular payments that lasts for a fixed number of periods. Not surprisingly, annuities are among the most common kinds of financial instruments. The pensions that people receive when they retire are often in the form of an annuity. Leases, mortgages, and pension plans are also annuities.

To figure out the present value of an annuity, we need to evaluate the following equation:

$$\frac{C}{1+r} + \frac{C}{(1+r)^2} + \frac{C}{(1+r)^3} + \cdots \frac{C}{(1+r)^T}$$

The present value of only receiving the coupons for T periods must be less than the present value of a consol, but how much less? To answer this, we have to look at consols a bit more closely.

Consider the following time chart:

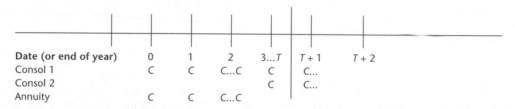

Date (or end of year)	0	1	2	3...T	T + 1	T + 2
Consol 1		C	C	C...C	C	C...
Consol 2					C	C...
Annuity		C	C	C...C		

Consol 1 is a normal consol with its first payment at date 1. The first payment of consol 2 occurs at date $T + 1$.

The present value of having cash flow of C at each of T dates is equal to the present value of consol 1 minus the present value of consol 2. The present value of consol 1 is given by

$$PV = \frac{C}{r}$$

Consol 2 is just a consol with its first payment at date $T + 1$. From the perpetuity formula, this consol will be worth C/r at date T.[7] However, we do not want the value at date T. We want the value now; in other words, the present value at date 0. We must discount C/r back by T periods. Therefore, the present value of consol 2 is

$$PV = \frac{C}{r}\left[\frac{1}{(1+r)^T}\right]$$

The present value of having cash flows for T years is the present value of a consol with its first payment at date 1 minus the present value of a consol with its first payment at date $T+1$. Thus, the present value of an annuity is the first formula minus the second formula. This can be written as

$$\frac{C}{r} - \frac{C}{r}\left[\frac{1}{(1+r)^T}\right]$$

This simplifies to the formula for the present value of an annuity:

$$PV = C\left[\frac{1}{r} - \frac{1}{r(1+r)^T}\right]$$

$$= C[1 - \{1/(1+r)^T\}]/r$$

---

7 Students frequently think that C/r is the present value at date $T + 1$ because consol's first payment is at date $T + 1$. However, the formula values the annuity as of one period before the first payment.

CHAPTER 7

Interest Rates and Bond Valuation

What do Canadian Imperial Bank of Commerce, Domtar, Loblaw, Husky Energy, and Rogers Communications all have in common? Like many other corporations, they have all borrowed money from investors by issuing bonds. Some of these companies have higher debt loads and lower bond ratings than others. Bonds issued by such riskier companies carry higher yields. In this chapter, we will learn more about bonds and what makes them risky or safe.

OUR GOAL in this chapter is to introduce you to bonds. We begin by showing how the techniques we developed in Chapters 5 and 6 can be applied to bond valuation. From there, we go on to discuss bond features and how bonds are bought and sold. One important thing we learn is that bond values depend, in large part, on interest rates. We therefore close out the chapter with an examination of interest rates and their behaviour.

7.1

www.cibc.com
www.domtar.com
www.huskyenergy.ca
www.loblaw.ca
www.rogers.com

coupons
The stated interest payments made on a bond.

face value
The principal amount of a bond that is repaid at the end of the term. Also par value.

BONDS AND BOND VALUATION

When a corporation or government wishes to borrow money from the public on a long-term basis, it usually does so by issuing or selling debt securities that are generically called bonds. In this section, we describe the various features of corporate bonds and some of the terminology associated with bonds. We then discuss the cash flows associated with a bond and how bonds can be valued using our discounted cash flow procedure.

Bond Features and Prices

A bond is normally an interest-only loan, meaning the borrower pays the interest every period, but none of the principal is repaid until the end of the loan. For example, suppose Alcan wants to borrow $1,000 for 30 years and that the interest rate on similar debt issued by similar corporations is 12 percent. Alcan thus pays .12 × $1,000 = $120 in interest every year for 30 years. At the end of 30 years, Alcan repays the $1,000. As this example suggests, a bond is a fairly simple financing arrangement. There is, however, a rich jargon associated with bonds, so we use this example to define some of the more important terms.

In our example, the $120 regular interest payments that Alcan promises to make are called the bond's **coupons.** Because the coupon is constant and paid every year, the type of bond we are describing is sometimes called a *level coupon bond.* The amount repaid at the end of the loan is called the bond's **face value** or **par value.** As in our example, this par value is usually $1,000 for corporate bonds, and a bond that sells for its par value is called a par bond. Government of Canada and provincial bonds frequently have much larger face or par values. Finally, the annual

coupon rate
The annual coupon divided by the face value of a bond.

maturity date
Specified date at which the principal amount of a bond is paid.

coupon divided by the face value is called the **coupon rate** on the bond, which is $120/1,000 = 12\%$; so the bond has a 12 percent coupon rate.

The number of years until the face value is paid is called the bond's time to **maturity**. A corporate bond would frequently have a maturity of 30 years when it is originally issued, but this varies. Once the bond has been issued, the number of years to maturity declines as time goes by.

Bond Values and Yields

As time passes, interest rates change in the marketplace. The cash flows from a bond, however, stay the same because the coupon rate and maturity date are specified when it is issued. As a result, the value of the bond fluctuates. When interest rates rise, the present value of the bond's remaining cash flows declines, and the bond is worth less. When interest rates fall, the bond is worth more.

To determine the value of a bond on a particular date, we need to know the number of periods remaining until maturity, the face value, the coupon, and the market interest rate for bonds with similar features. This interest rate required in the market on a bond is called the bond's **yield to maturity (YTM)**. This rate is sometimes called the bond's *yield* for short. Given this information, we can calculate the present value of the cash flows as an estimate of the bond's current market value.

yield to maturity (YTM)
The market interest rate that equates a bond's present value of interest payments and principal repayment with its price.

For example, suppose Royal Bank were to issue a bond with 10 years to maturity. The Royal Bank bond has an annual coupon of $56. Suppose similar bonds have a yield to maturity of 5.6 percent. Based on our previous discussion, the Royal Bank bond pays $56 per year for the next 10 years in coupon interest. In 10 years, Royal Bank pays $1,000 to the owner of the bond. The cash flows from the bond are shown in Figure 7.1. What would this bond sell for?

As illustrated in Figure 7.1, the Royal Bank bond's cash flows have an annuity component (the coupons) and a lump sum (the face value paid at maturity). We thus estimate the market value of the bond by calculating the present value of these two components separately and adding the results together. First, at the going rate of 5.6 percent, the present value of the $1,000 paid in 10 years is:

www.royalbank.com

$$\text{Present value} = \$1,000/1.056^{10} = \$1,000/1.7244 = \$579.91$$

Second, the bond offers $56 per year for 10 years, so the present value of this annuity stream is:

$$\begin{aligned}
\text{Annuity present value} &= \$56 \times (1 - 1/1.056^{10})/.056 \\
&= \$56 \times (1 - 1/1.7244)/.056 \\
&= \$56 \times 7.5016 \\
&= \$420.09
\end{aligned}$$

A good bond site to visit is www.finance.yahoo.com/bonds

We can now add the values for the two parts together to get the bond's value:

$$\text{Total bond value} = \$579.91 + 420.09 = \$1,000.00$$

This bond sells for its exact face value. This is not a coincidence. The going interest rate in the market is 5.6 percent. Considered as an interest-only loan, what interest rate does this bond have? With a $56 coupon, this bond pays exactly 5.6 percent interest only when it sells for $1,000.

FIGURE 7.1

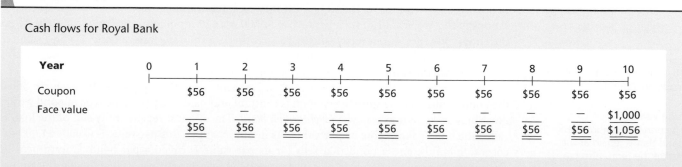

Cash flows for Royal Bank

Year	0	1	2	3	4	5	6	7	8	9	10
Coupon		$56	$56	$56	$56	$56	$56	$56	$56	$56	$56
Face value		—	—	—	—	—	—	—	—	—	$1,000
		$56	$56	$56	$56	$56	$56	$56	$56	$56	$1,056

To illustrate what happens as interest rates change, suppose a year has gone by. The Royal Bank bond now has nine years to maturity. If the interest rate in the market had risen to 7.6 percent, what would the bond be worth? To find out, we repeat the present value calculations with nine years instead of 10, and a 7.6 percent yield instead of a 5.6 percent yield. First, the present value of the $1,000 paid in nine years at 7.6 percent is:

$$\text{Present value} = \$1,000/1.076^9 = \$1,000/1.9333 = \$517.25$$

Second, the bond now offers $56 per year for nine years, so the present value of this annuity stream at 7.6 percent is:

$$\begin{aligned}\text{Annuity present value} &= \$56 \times (1 - 1/1.076^9)/.076 \\ &= \$56 \times (1 - 1/1.9333)/.076 \\ &= \$56 \times 6.3520 \\ &= \$355.71\end{aligned}$$

We can now add the values for the two parts together to get the bond's value:

$$\text{Total bond value} = \$517.25 + 355.71 = \$872.96$$

Therefore, the bond should sell for about $873. In the vernacular, we say this bond, with its 5.6 percent coupon, is priced to yield 7.6 percent at $873.

The Royal Bank bond now sells for less than its $1,000 face value. Why? The market interest rate is 7.6 percent. Considered as an interest-only loan of $1,000, this bond pays only 5.6 percent, its coupon rate. Because this bond pays less than the going rate, investors are only willing to lend something less than the $1,000 promised repayment. A bond that sells for less than face value is a *discount bond.*

The only way to get the interest rate up to 7.6 percent is for the price to be less than $1,000 so that the purchaser, in effect, has a built-in gain. For the Royal Bank bond, the price of $873 is $127 less than the face value, so an investor who purchased and kept the bond would get $56 per year and would have a $127 gain at maturity as well. This gain compensates the lender for the below-market coupon rate.

Another way to see why the bond is discounted by $127 is to note that the $56 coupon is $20 below the coupon on a newly issued par value bond, based on current market conditions. By this we mean the bond would be worth $1,000 only if it had a coupon of $76 per year. In a sense, an investor who buys and keeps the bond gives up $20 per year for nine years. At 7.6 percent, this annuity stream is worth:

$$\begin{aligned}\text{Annuity present value} &= \$20 \times (1 - 1/1.076^9)/.076 \\ &= \$20 \times 6.3520 \\ &= \$127.04\end{aligned}$$

This is just the amount of the discount.

What would the Royal Bank bond sell for if interest rates had dropped by 2 percent instead of rising by 2 percent? As you might guess, the bond would sell for more than $1,000. Such a bond is said to sell at a *premium* and is called a *premium bond.*

This case is just the opposite of a discount bond. The Royal Bank bond still has a coupon rate of 5.6 percent when the market rate is only 3.6 percent. Investors are willing to pay a premium to get this extra coupon. The relevant discount rate is 3.6 percent, and there are nine years remaining. The present value of the $1,000 face amount is:

$$\text{Present value} = \$1,000/1.036^9 = \$1,000/1.3748 = \$727.38$$

The present value of the coupon stream is:

$$\begin{aligned}\text{Annuity present value} &= \$56 \times (1 - 1/1.036^9)/.036 \\ &= \$56 \times (1 - 1/1.3748)/.036 \\ &= \$56 \times 7.5728 \\ &= \$424.08\end{aligned}$$

We can now add the values for the two parts together to get the bond's value:

$$\text{Total bond value} = \$727.38 + 424.08 = \$1,151.46$$

Total bond value is, therefore, about $151 in excess of par value. Once again, we can verify this amount by noting that the coupon is now $20 too high. The present value of $20 per year for nine years at 3.6 percent is:

$$\text{Annuity present value} = \$20 \times (1 - 1/1.036^9)/.036$$
$$= \$20 \times 7.5728$$
$$= \$151.46$$

This is just as we calculated.

Based on our examples, we can now write the general expression for the value of a bond. If a bond has (1) a face value of F paid at maturity, (2) a coupon of C paid per period, (3) t periods to maturity, and (4) a yield of r per period, its value is:

$$\text{Bond value} = C \times (1 - 1/(1 + r)^t)/r + F/(1 + r)^t \qquad [7.1]$$

$$\text{Bond value} = \begin{array}{c}\text{Present value}\\\text{of the coupons}\end{array} + \begin{array}{c}\text{Present value}\\\text{of the face amount}\end{array}$$

As we have illustrated in this section, bond prices and interest rates (or market yields) always move in opposite directions like the ends of a seesaw. Most bonds are issued at par, with the coupon rate set equal to the prevailing market yield or interest rate. This coupon rate does not change over time. The coupon yield, however, does change and reflects the return the coupon represents based on current market prices for the bond. Finally, the yield to maturity is the interest rate that equates the present value of the bond's coupons and principal repayments with the current market price (i.e., the total annual return the purchaser would receive if the bond were held to maturity).

When interest rates rise, a bond's value, like any other present value, declines. When interest rates are above the bond's coupon rate, the bond sells at a discount. Similarly, when interest rates fall, bond values rise. Interest rates below the bond's coupon rate cause the bond to sell at a premium. Even if we are considering a bond that is riskless in the sense that the borrower is certain to make all the payments, there is still risk in owning the bond. We discuss this next.

EXAMPLE 7.1: Semiannual Coupons

In practice, bonds issued in Canada usually make coupon payments twice a year. So, if an ordinary bond has a coupon rate of 8 percent, the owner gets a total of $80 per year, but this $80 comes in two payments of $40 each. Suppose we were examining such a bond. The yield to maturity is quoted at 10 percent.

Bond yields are quoted like APRs; the quoted rate is equal to the actual rate per period multiplied by the number of periods. With a 10 percent quoted yield and semiannual payments, the true yield is 5 percent per six months. The bond matures in seven years. What is the bond's price? What is the effective annual yield on this bond?

Based on our discussion, we know the bond would sell at a discount because it has a coupon rate of 4 percent every six months when the market requires 5 percent every six months. So, if our answer exceeds $1,000, we know that we made a mistake.

To get the exact price, we first calculate the present value of the bond's face value of $1,000 paid in seven years. This seven years has 14 periods of six months each. At 5 percent per period, the value is:

Present value = $1,000/1.05^{14} = $1,000/1.9799 = $505.08

The coupons can be viewed as a 14-period annuity of $40 per period. At a 5 percent discount rate, the present value of such an annuity is:

$$\text{Annuity present value} = \$40 \times (1 - 1/1.05^{14})/.05$$
$$= \$40 \times (1 - .5051)/.05$$
$$= \$40 \times 9.8980$$
$$= \$395.92$$

The total present value gives us what the bond should sell for:

Total present value = $505.08 + 395.92 = $901.00

To calculate the effective yield on this bond, note that 5 percent every six months is equivalent to:

Effective annual rate = $(1 + .05)^2 - 1$ = 10.25%

The effective yield, therefore, is 10.25 percent.

Interest Rate Risk

The risk that arises for bond owners from fluctuating interest rates (market yields) is called *interest rate risk*. How much interest risk a bond has depends on how sensitive its price is to interest rate changes. This sensitivity directly depends on two things: the time to maturity and the coupon rate. Keep the following in mind when looking at a bond:

1. All other things being equal, the longer the time to maturity, the greater the interest rate risk.
2. All other things being equal, the lower the coupon rate, the greater the interest rate risk.

We illustrate the first of these two points in Figure 7.2. As shown, we compute and plot prices under different interest rate scenarios for 10 percent coupon bonds with maturities of one year and 30 years. Notice how the slope of the line connecting the prices is much steeper for the 30-year maturity than it is for the one-year maturity.[1] This tells us that a relatively small change in interest rates could lead to a substantial change in the bond's value. In comparison, the one-year bond's price is relatively insensitive to interest rate changes.

FIGURE 7.2

Interest rate risk and time to maturity

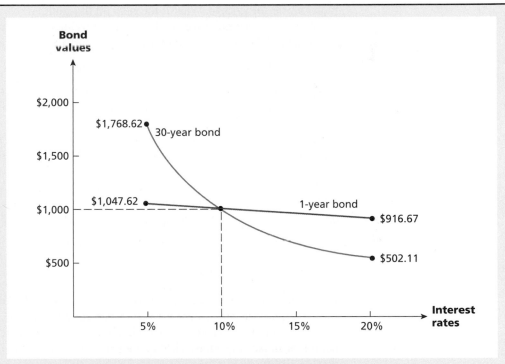

Value of a Bond with a 10% Coupon Rate for Different Interest Rates and Maturities

	Time to Maturity	
Interest Rate	1 Year	30 Years
5%	$1,047.62	$1,768.62
10%	1,000.00	1,000.00
15%	956.52	671.70
20%	916.67	502.11

---

1 We explain a more precise measure of this slope, called duration, in Appendix 7A. Our example assumes that yields of one-year and 30-year bonds are the same.

Intuitively, the reason longer-term bonds have greater interest rate sensitivity is that a large portion of a bond's value comes from the $1,000 face amount. The present value of this amount isn't greatly affected by a small change in interest rates if it is to be received in one year. If it is to be received in 30 years, however, even a small change in the interest rate can have a significant effect once it is compounded for 30 years. The present value of the face amount becomes much more volatile with a longer-term bond as a result.

The reason that bonds with lower coupons have greater interest rate risk is essentially the same. As we just discussed, the value of a bond depends on the present value of its coupons and the present value of the face amount. If two bonds with different coupon rates have the same maturity, the value of the one with the lower coupon is proportionately more dependent on the face amount to be received at maturity. As a result, all other things being equal, its value fluctuates more as interest rates change. Put another way, the bond with the higher coupon has a larger cash flow early in its life, so its value is less sensitive to changes in the discount rate.

Finding the Yield to Maturity

Frequently, we know a bond's price, coupon rate, and maturity date, but not its yield to maturity. For example, suppose we were interested in a six-year, 8 percent coupon bond. A broker quotes a price of $955.14. What is the yield on this bond?

We've seen that the price of a bond can be written as the sum of its annuity and lump-sum components. With an $80 coupon for six years and a $1,000 face value, this price is:

$$\$955.14 = \$80 \times (1 - 1/(1 + r)^6)/r + \$1,000/(1 + r)^6$$

where r is the unknown discount rate or yield to maturity. We have one equation here and one unknown, but we cannot solve it for r explicitly. The only way to find the answer exactly is to use trial and error.

This problem is essentially identical to the one we examined in the last chapter when we tried to find the unknown interest rate on an annuity. However, finding the rate (or yield) on a bond is even more complicated, because of the $1,000 face amount.

We can speed up the trial-and-error process by using what we know about bond prices and yields: The bond has an $80 coupon and is selling at a discount. We thus know that the yield is greater than 8 percent. If we compute the price at 10 percent:

$$\text{Bond value} = \$80 \times (1 - 1/1.10^6)/.10 + \$1,000/1.10^6$$
$$= \$80 \times (4.3553) + \$1,000/1.7716$$
$$= \$912.89$$

At 10 percent, the value we calculate is lower than the actual price, so 10 percent is too high. The true yield must be somewhere between 8 percent and 10 percent. At this point, it's "plug and chug" to find the answer. You would probably want to try 9 percent next. If you do, you will see that this is, in fact, the bond's yield to maturity. Our discussion of bond valuation is summarized in Table 7.1.

TABLE 7.1
Summary of bond valuation

I.	**FINDING THE VALUE OF A BOND:**

Bond value = $C \times (1 - 1/(1 + r)^t)/r + F/(1 + r)^t$
where:
C = the coupon paid each period
r = the rate per period
t = the number of periods
F = the bond's face value

II.	**FINDING THE YIELD ON A BOND:**

Given a bond value, coupon, time to maturity, and face value, it is possible to find the implicit discount rate or yield to maturity by trial and error only. To do this, try different discount rates until the calculated bond value equals the given value. Remember that increasing the rate decreases the bond value.

EXAMPLE 7.2: Bond Yields

You're looking at two bonds identical in every way except for their coupons and, of course, their prices. Both have 12 years to maturity. The first bond has a 10 percent coupon rate and sells for $935.08. The second has a 12 percent coupon rate. What do you think it would sell for?

Because the two bonds are very similar, they are priced to yield about the same rate. We begin by calculating the yield on the 10 percent coupon bond. A little trial and error reveals that the yield is actually 11 percent:

Bond value = $100 × (1 − 1/1.11^{12})/.11 + $1,000/1.11^{12}
= $100 × 6.4924 + $1,000/3.4985
= $649.24 + 285.84
= $935.08

With an 11 percent yield, the second bond sells at a premium because of its $120 coupon. Its value is:

Bond value = $120 × (1 − 1/1.11^{12})/.11 + $1,000/1.11^{12}
= $120 × 6.4924 + $1,000/3.4985
= $779.08 + 285.84
= $1,064.92

What we did in pricing the second bond is what bond traders do. Bonds trade over the counter in a secondary market made by investment dealers and banks. Suppose a bond trader at, say, BMO Nesbitt Burns receives a request for a selling price on the second bond from another trader at, say, ScotiaCapital. Suppose further that the second bond has not traded recently. The trader prices it off the first actively traded bond.

www.bmonesbittburns.com

CALCULATOR HINTS

How to Calculate Bond Prices and Yields Using a Financial Calculator

Many financial calculators have fairly sophisticated built-in bond valuation routines. However, these vary quite a lot in implementation, and not all financial calculators have them. As a result, we will illustrate a simple way to handle bond problems that will work on just about any financial calculator.

To begin, of course, we first remember to clear out the calculator! Next, for Example 7.2, we have two bonds to consider, both with 12 years to maturity. The first one sells for $935.08 and has a 10 percent coupon rate. To find its yield, we can do the following:

Enter	12		100	−935.08	1,000
	N	%i	PMT	PV	FV
Solve for		11			

Notice that here we have entered both a future value of $1,000, representing the bond's face value, and a payment of 10 percent of $1,000, or $100, per year, representing the bond's annual coupon. Also notice that we have a negative sign on the bond's price, which we have entered as the present value.

For the second bond, we now know that the relevant yield is 11 percent. It has a 12 percent coupon and 12 years to maturity, so what's the price? To answer, we just enter the relevant values and solve for the present value of the bond's cash flows:

Enter	12	11	120		1,000
	N	%i	PMT	PV	FV
Solve for		11		−1,064.92	

There is an important detail that comes up here. Suppose we have a bond with a price of $902.29, 10 years to maturity, and a coupon rate of 6 percent. As we mentioned earlier, most bonds actually make semiannual payments. Assuming that this is the case for the

CALCULATOR HINTS

bond here, what's the bond's yield? To answer, we need to enter the relevant numbers like this:

Enter	20		30	−902.29	1,000
	N	%i	PMT	PV	FV
Solve for		3.7			

Notice that we entered $30 as the payment because the bond actually makes payments of $30 every six months. Similarly, we entered 20 for N because there are actually 20 six-month periods. When we solve for the yield, we get 3.7 percent, but the tricky thing to remember is that this is the yield *per six months*, so we have to double it to get the right answer: $2 \times 3.7 = 7.4$ percent, which would be the bond's reported yield.

SPREADSHEET STRATEGIES

How to Calculate Bond Prices and Yields Using a Spreadsheet

Most spreadsheets have fairly elaborate routines available for calculating bond values and yields; many of these routines involve details that we have not discussed. However, setting up a simple spreadsheet to calculate prices or yields is straightforward, as our next two spreadsheets show:

	A	B	C	D	E	F	G	H
1								
2	Using a spreadsheet to calculate bond values							
3								
4	Suppose we have a bond with 22 years to maturity, a coupon rate of 8 percent, and a yield to							
5	maturity of 9 percent. If the bond makes semiannual payments, what is its price today?							
6								
7	Settlement date:	1/1/07						
8	Maturity date:	1/1/29						
9	Annual coupon rate:	0.08						
10	Yield to maturity:	.09						
11	Face value (% of par):	100						
12	Coupons per year:	2						
13	Bond price (% of par):	**90.49**						
14								
15	The formula entered in cell B13 is =PRICE(B7,B8,B9,B10,B11,B12); notice that face value and bond							
16	price are given as a percentage of face value.							

In our spreadsheets, notice that we had to enter two dates, a settlement date and a maturity date. The settlement date is just the date you actually pay for the bond, and the maturity date is the day the bond actually matures. In most of our problems, we don't explicitly have these dates, so we have to make them up. For example, since our bond has 22 years to maturity, we just picked 1/1/2007 (January 1, 2007) as the settlement date and 1/1/2029 (January 1, 2029) as the maturity date. Any two dates would do as long as they are exactly 22 years apart, but these are particularly easy to work with. Finally, notice that we had to enter the coupon rate and yield to maturity in annual terms and then explicitly provide the number of coupon payments per year.

SPREADSHEET STRATEGIES

	A	B	C	D	E	F	G	H
1								
2	Using a spreadsheet to calculate bond yields							
3								
4	Suppose we have a bond with 22 years to maturity, a coupon rate of 8 percent, and a price of							
5	$960.17. If the bond makes semiannual payments, what is its yield to maturity?							
6								
7	Settlement date:	1/1/07						
8	Maturity date:	1/1/29						
9	Annual coupon rate:	0.08						
10	Bond price (% of par):	96.017						
11	Face value (% of par):	100						
12	Coupons per year:	2						
13	Yield to maturity:	**0.084**						
14								
15	The formula entered in cell B13 is =YIELD(B7,B8,B9,B10,B11,B12); notice that face value and bond							
16	price are entered as a percentage of face value.							

MORE ON BOND FEATURES

In this section, we continue our discussion of corporate debt by describing in some detail the basic terms and features that make up a typical long-term corporate bond. We discuss additional issues associated with long-term debt in subsequent sections.

Securities issued by corporations may be classified roughly as *equity securities* and *debt securities*. At the crudest level, a debt represents something that must be repaid; it is the result of borrowing money. When corporations borrow, they generally promise to make regularly scheduled interest payments and to repay the original amount borrowed (that is, the principal). The person or firm making the loan is called the *creditor,* or *lender*. The corporation borrowing the money is called the *debtor,* or *borrower*.

From a financial point of view, the main differences between debt and equity are the following:

1. Debt is not an ownership interest in the firm. Creditors generally do not have voting power.
2. The corporation's payment of interest on debt is considered a cost of doing business and is fully tax deductible. Dividends paid to shareholders are *not* tax deductible.
3. Unpaid debt is a liability of the firm. If it is not paid, the creditors can legally claim the assets of the firm. This action can result in liquidation or reorganization, two of the possible consequences of bankruptcy. Thus, one of the costs of issuing debt is the possibility of financial failure. This possibility does not arise when equity is issued.

Is It Debt or Equity?

Sometimes it is not clear if a particular security is debt or equity. For example, suppose a corporation issues a perpetual bond with interest payable solely from corporate income if and only if earned. Whether or not this is really a debt is hard to say and is primarily a legal and semantic issue. Courts and taxing authorities would have the final say.

Corporations are very adept at creating exotic, hybrid securities that have many features of equity but are treated as debt. Obviously, the distinction between debt and equity is very important for tax purposes. So one reason that corporations try to create a debt security that is really equity is to obtain the tax benefits of debt and the bankruptcy benefits of equity.

As a general rule, equity represents an ownership interest, and it is a residual claim. This means that equity holders are paid after debt holders. As a result of this, the risks and benefits associated with owning debt and equity are different. To give just one example, note that the maximum reward for owning a debt security is ultimately fixed by the amount of the loan, whereas there is no upper limit to the potential reward from owning an equity interest.

Long-Term Debt: The Basics

Ultimately, all long-term debt securities are promises by the issuing firm to pay the principal when due and to make timely interest payments on the unpaid balance. Beyond this, a number of features distinguish these securities from one another. We discuss some of these features next.

The maturity of a long-term debt instrument refers to the length of time the debt remains outstanding with some unpaid balance. Debt securities can be short-term (maturities of one year or less) or long-term (maturities of more than one year).[2]

Debt securities are typically called *notes, debentures,* or *bonds.* Strictly speaking, a bond is a secured debt, but, in common usage, the word bond refers to all kinds of secured and unsecured debt. We use the term generically to refer to long-term debt.

The two major forms of long-term debt are public-issue and privately placed. We concentrate on public-issue bonds. Most of what we say about them holds true for private-issue, long-term debt as well. The main difference between public-issue and privately placed debt is that the latter is directly placed with a lender and not offered to the public. Since this is a private transaction, the specific terms are up to the parties involved.

There are many other dimensions to long-term debt, including such things as security, call features, sinking funds, ratings, and protective covenants. The following table illustrates these features for a Loblaw Companies Limited medium term note issued in January 2005. If some of these terms are unfamiliar, have no fear. We discuss them all next.

Features of Loblaw Companies—Medium Term Notes (unsecured) issue

Terms		Explanation
Amount of Issue	$300 million	The company will issue $300 million of bonds.
Issue Date	1/18/05	The bonds will be sold on January 18, 2005.
Maturity Date	1/18/36	The bonds will be paid in 31 years.
Annual Coupon	5.90	Each bondholder will receive $59.00 per bond per year.
Face Value	$1,000	The denomination of the bonds is $1,000.
Issue Price	99.859	The issue price will be 99.859% of the $1,000 face value per bond.
Yield to Maturity	5.91%	If the bond is held to maturity, bondholders will receive a stated annual rate of return equal to 5.91%.
Coupon Payment	1/18 and 7/18	Coupons of $59.00/2 = $29.50 will be paid semi-annually on these dates.
Security	Unsecured	The bonds are debentures.
Call Provision	Canada Yield Price at Canada plus 0.27%	Redeemable at the Company's option at the price calculated to provide a yield to maturity equal to Canada yield or equivalent maturity plus 0.27%.
Rating	DBRS A	The bond is of satisfactory credit quality, but is not as high as AA.

Source: www.sedar.com

Many of these features are detailed in the bond indenture, so we discuss this now.

The Indenture

The **indenture** is the written agreement between the corporation (the borrower) and its creditors. It is sometimes referred to as the deed of trust.[3] Usually, a trustee (a trust company) is appointed by the corporation to represent the bondholders. The trust company must (1) make

www.sedar.com

indenture
Written agreement between the corporation and the lender detailing the terms of the debt issue.

---

2 There is no universally agreed-upon distinction between short-term and long-term debt. In addition, people often refer to medium-term debt, which has a maturity of more than 1 year and less than 3 to 5, or even 10, years.

3 The words *loan agreement* or *loan contract* are usually used for privately placed debt and term loans.

sure the terms of the indenture are obeyed, (2) manage the sinking fund (described later), and (3) represent the bondholders in default, that is, if the company defaults on its payments to them.

The bond indenture is a legal document. It can run several hundred pages and generally makes for very tedious reading. It is an important document, however, because it generally includes the following provisions:

1. The basic terms of the bonds.
2. The amount of the bonds issued.
3. A description of property used as security if the bonds are secured.
4. The repayment arrangements.
5. The call provisions.
6. Details of the protective covenants.

We discuss these features next.

TERMS OF A BOND   Corporate bonds usually have a face value (that is, a denomination) of $1,000. This is called the *principal value*, and it is stated on the bond certificate. So, if a corporation wanted to borrow $1 million, 1,000 bonds would have to be sold. The par value (that is, initial accounting value) of a bond is almost always the same as the face value.

registered form
Registrar of company records ownership of each bond; payment is made directly to the owner of record.

Corporate bonds are usually in **registered form.** For example, the indenture might read as follows: Interest is payable semiannually on July 1 and January 1 of each year to the person in whose name the bond is registered at the close of business on June 15 or December 15, respectively.

This means the company has a registrar who records the ownership of each bond and records any changes in ownership. The company pays the interest and principal by cheque mailed directly to the address of the owner of record. A corporate bond may be registered and may have attached coupons. To obtain an interest payment, the owner must separate a coupon from the bond certificate and send it to the company registrar (the paying agent).

bearer form
Bond issued without record of the owner's name; payment is made to whoever holds the bond.

Alternatively, the bond could be in **bearer form.** This means the certificate is the basic evidence of ownership, and the corporation pays the bearer. Ownership is not otherwise recorded, and, as with a registered bond with attached coupons, the holder of the bond certificate detaches the coupons and sends them to the company to receive payment.

There are two drawbacks to bearer bonds: First, they are difficult to recover if they are lost or stolen. Second, because the company does not know who owns its bonds, it cannot notify bondholders of important events. The bearer form of ownership does have the advantage of easing transactions for investors who trade their bonds frequently.

SECURITY   Debt securities are classified according to the collateral and mortgages used to protect the bondholder.

Collateral is a general term that, strictly speaking, means securities (for example, bonds and stocks) pledged as security for payment of debt. For example, collateral trust bonds often involve a pledge of common stock held by the corporation. This pledge is usually backed by marketable securities. However, the term *collateral* often is used much more loosely to refer to any form of security.

Mortgage securities are secured by a mortgage on the real property of the borrower. The property involved may be real estate, transportation equipment, or other property. The legal document that describes a mortgage on real estate is called a mortgage trust indenture or trust deed.

Sometimes mortgages are on specific property, for example, a railroad car. This is called a chattel mortgage. More often, blanket mortgages are used. A blanket mortgage pledges all the real property owned by the company.[4]

debenture
Unsecured debt, usually with a maturity of 10 years or more.

note
Unsecured debt, usually with a maturity under 10 years.

Bonds frequently represent unsecured obligations of the company. A **debenture** is an unsecured bond, where no specific pledge of property is made. The term **note** is generally used for such instruments if the maturity of the unsecured bond is less than 10 or so years when it is originally issued. Debenture holders only have a claim on property not otherwise pledged; in other words, the property that remains after mortgages and collateral trusts are taken into account.

---

4 Real property includes land and things "affixed thereto." It does not include cash or inventories.

At the current time, most public bonds issued by industrial and finance companies are debentures. However, most utility and railroad bonds are secured by a pledge of assets.

SENIORITY   In general terms, *seniority* indicates preference in position over other lenders, and debts are sometimes labelled as "senior" or "junior" to indicate seniority. Some debt is *subordinated,* as in, for example, a subordinated debenture.

In the event of default, holders of subordinated debt must give preference to other specified creditors. Usually, this means the subordinated lenders are paid off from cash flow and asset sales only after the specified creditors have been compensated. However, debt cannot be subordinated to equity.

REPAYMENT   Bonds can be repaid at maturity, at which time the bondholder receives the stated or face value of the bonds, or they may be repaid in part or in entirety before maturity. Early repayment in some form is more typical and is often handled through a sinking fund.

sinking fund
Account managed by the bond trustee for early bond redemption.

A **sinking fund** is an account managed by the bond trustee for the purpose of repaying the bonds. The company makes annual payments to the trustee, who then uses the funds to retire a portion of the debt. The trustee does this by either buying up some of the bonds in the market or calling in a fraction of the outstanding bonds. We discuss this second option in the next section.

There are many different kinds of sinking fund arrangements. The fund may start immediately or be delayed for 10 years after the bond is issued. The provision may require the company to redeem all or only a portion of the outstanding issue before maturity. From an investor's viewpoint, a sinking fund reduces the risk that the company will be unable to repay the principal at maturity. Since it involves regular purchases, a sinking fund improves the marketability of the bonds.

call provision
Agreement giving the corporation the option to repurchase the bond at a specified price before maturity.

THE CALL PROVISION   A **call provision** allows the company to repurchase or "call" part or all of the bond issue at stated prices over a specified period. Corporate bonds are usually callable.

Generally, the call price is more than the bond's stated value (that is, the par value). The difference between the call price and the stated value is the **call premium.** The call premium may also be expressed as a percentage of the bond's face value. The amount of the call premium usually becomes smaller over time. One arrangement is to initially set the call premium equal to the annual coupon payment and then make it decline to zero the closer the call date is to maturity.

call premium
Amount by which the call price exceeds the par value of the bond.

deferred call
Call provision prohibiting the company from redeeming the bond before a certain date.

Call provisions are not usually operative during the first part of a bond's life. This makes the call provision less of a worry for bondholders in the bond's early years. For example, a company might be prohibited from calling its bonds for the first 10 years. This is a **deferred call.** During this period, the bond is said to be **call protected.**

call protected
Bond during period in which it cannot be redeemed by the issuer.

Many long-term corporate bonds outstanding in Canada have call provisions as we just described. New corporate debt features a different call provision referred to as a **Canada plus call.** This new approach is designed to replace the traditional call feature by making it unattractive for the issuer ever to call the bonds. Unlike the standard call, with the Canada call the exact amount of the call premium is not set at the time of issuance. Instead, the Canada plus call stipulates that, in the event of a call, the issuer must provide a call premium which will compensate investors for the difference in interest between the original bond and new debt issued to replace it. This compensation cancels the borrower's benefit from calling the debt and the result is that the call will not occur.

Canada plus call
Call provision which compensates bond investors for interest differential, making call unattractive for issuer.

The Canada plus call takes its name from the formula used to calculate the difference in the interest; to determine the new, lower interest rate, the formula adds a premium to the yield on Canadas. We give a numerical example of a Canada plus call in Appendix 7B, which discusses call provisions and refunding in detail.

protective covenant
Part of the indenture limiting certain transactions that can be taken during the term of the loan, usually to protect the lender's interest.

PROTECTIVE COVENANTS   A **protective covenant** is that part of the indenture or loan agreement that limits certain actions a company might otherwise wish to take during the term of the loan. Covenants are designed to reduce the agency costs faced by bondholders. By controlling company activities, they reduce the risk of the bonds.

For example, common covenants limit the dividends the firm can pay and require bondholder approval for any sale of major assets. This means that, if the firm is headed for bankruptcy, it cannot sell all the assets and pay a liquidating dividend to stockholders, leaving the bondholders with only a corporate shell. Protective covenants can be classified into two types: negative covenants and positive (or affirmative) covenants.

A *negative covenant* is a "thou shalt not." It limits or prohibits actions that the company may take. Here are some typical examples:

1. The firm must limit the amount of dividends it pays according to some formula.
2. The firm cannot pledge any assets to other lenders.
3. The firm cannot merge with another firm.
4. The firm cannot sell or lease any major assets without approval by the lender.
5. The firm cannot issue additional long-term debt.

A *positive covenant* is a "thou shalt." It specifies an action that the company agrees to take or a condition the company must abide by. Here are some examples:

1. The company must maintain its working capital at or above some specified minimum level.
2. The company must periodically furnish audited financial statements to the lender.
3. The firm must maintain any collateral or security in good condition.

This is only a partial list of covenants; a particular indenture may feature many different ones.

CONCEPT QUESTIONS

1. What are the distinguishing features of debt as compared to equity?

2. What is the indenture? What are protective covenants? Give some examples.

3. What is a sinking fund?

BOND RATINGS

www.moodys.com
www.sandp.com

Firms frequently pay to have their debt rated. The two leading bond rating firms in Canada are Standard & Poor's (S&P) and Dominion Bond Rating Service (DBRS). Moody's and Standard & Poor's (S&P) are the largest U.S. bond raters and they often rate Canadian companies that raise funds in U.S. bond markets.[5] The debt ratings are an assessment of the creditworthiness of the corporate issuer. The definitions of creditworthiness used by bond rating agencies are based on how likely the firm is to default and what protection creditors have in the event of a default.

Remember that bond ratings only concern the possibility of default. Earlier in this chapter, we discussed interest rate risk, which we defined as the risk of a change in the value of a bond from a change in interest rates. Bond ratings do not address this issue. As a result, the price of a highly rated bond can still be quite volatile.

Bond ratings are constructed from information supplied by the corporation. The rating classes and information concerning them are shown in Table 7.2. Table 7.2 shows ratings by DBRS. Standard & Poor's follows a similar system.

The highest rating a firm can have is AAA and such debt is judged to be the best quality and to have the lowest degree of risk. This rating is not awarded very often; AA ratings indicate very good quality debt and are much more common. Investment grade bonds are bonds rated at least BBB. The lowest ratings are for debt that is in default.

In the 1980s, a growing part of corporate borrowing took the form of low-grade, or junk, bonds, particularly in the United States. If they are rated at all, such low-grade bonds are rated below investment grade by the major rating agencies. Junk bonds are also called *high-yield* bonds, as they yield an interest rate 3 to 5 percentage points (300 to 500 basis points) higher than that of AAA-rated debt. Original issue junk bonds have never been a major source of funds in Canadian capital markets. Their niche has been filled in part by preferred shares and to a lesser extent, income bonds. In recent years, some Canadian corporations with large debt financing needs have issued bonds below investment grade. For example, at the time of writing, Rogers Communications Inc. (RCI) had a Standard & Poor's corporate credit rating of BB+.

www.rogers.com

---

5 They also rate bonds issued by the individual provinces.

TABLE 7.2 Descriptions of ratings used by Dominion Bond Rating Service	AAA	Long-term debt rated AAA is of the highest credit quality, with exceptionally strong protection for the timely repayment of principal and interest. Earnings are considered stable, the structure of the industry in which the entity operates is strong, and the outlook for future profitability is favourable. There are few qualifying factors present that would detract from the performance of the entity. The strength of liquidity and coverage ratios is unquestioned and the entity has established a credible track record of superior performance. Given the extremely high standard that DBRS has set for this category, few entities are able to achieve a AAA rating.
	AA	Long-term debt rated AA is of superior credit quality, and protection of interest and principal is considered high. In many cases they differ from long-term debt rated AAA only to a small degree. Given the extremely restrictive definition DBRS has for the AAA category, entities rated AA are also considered to be strong credits, typically exemplifying above-average strength in key areas of consideration and unlikely to be significantly affected by reasonably foreseeable events.
	A	Long-term debt rated "A" is of satisfactory credit quality. Protection of interest and principal is still substantial, but the degree of strength is less than that of AA-rated entities. While "A" is a respectable rating, entities in this category are considered more susceptible to adverse economic conditions and have greater cyclical tendencies than higher-rated securities.
	BBB	Long-term debt rated BBB is of adequate credit quality. Protection of interest and principal is considered acceptable, but the entity is fairly susceptible to adverse changes in financial and economic conditions, or there may be other adverse conditions present which reduce the strength of the entity and its rated securities.
	BB	Long-term debt rated BB is defined as speculative and non-investment grade, where the degree of protection afforded interest and principal is uncertain, particularly during periods of economic recession. Entities in the BB range typically have limited access to capital markets and additional liquidity support. In many cases, deficiencies in critical mass, diversification, and competitive strength are additional negative considerations.
	B	Long-term debt rated B is considered highly speculative and there is a reasonably high level of uncertainty as to the ability of the entity to pay interest and principal on a continuing basis in the future, especially in periods of economic recession or industry adversity.
	CCC CC C	Long-term debt rated in any of these categories is very highly speculative and is in danger of default of interest and principal. The degree of adverse elements present is more severe than in long-term debt rated B. Long-term debt rated below B often has features which, if not remedied, may lead to default. In practice, there is little difference between these three categories, with CC and C normally used for lower ranking debt of companies for which the senior debt is rated in the CCC to B range.
	D	A security rated D implies the issuer has either not met a scheduled payment of interest or principal or that the issuer has made it clear that it will miss such a payment in the near future. In some cases, DBRS may not assign a D rating under a bankruptcy announcement scenario, as allowances for grace periods may exist in the underlying legal documentation. Once assigned, the D rating will continue as long as the missed payment continues to be in arrears, and until such time as the rating is suspended, discontinued, or reinstated by DBRS.

Source: © 2006 Dominion Bond Rating Service Limited, *www.dbrs.com*. Used with permission.

CONCEPT QUESTIONS

1. What is a junk bond?

2. What does a bond rating say about the risk of fluctuations in a bond's value from interest rate changes?

SOME DIFFERENT TYPES OF BONDS

Thus far, we have considered "plain vanilla" bonds. In this section, we look at some more unusual types, the products of financial engineering: stripped bonds, floating-rate bonds, and others.

Financial Engineering

When financial managers or their investment bankers design new securities or financial processes, their efforts are referred to as financial engineering.[6] Successful financial engineering reduces and controls risk and minimizes taxes. It also seeks to reduce financing costs of issuing and servicing debt as well as costs of complying with rules laid down by regulatory authorities.

---

6 For more on financial engineering, see John Finnerty, "Financial Engineering in Corporate Finance: An Overview," in *The Handbook of Financial Engineering*, eds. C. W. Smith and C. W. Smithson (New York: Harper Business, 1990).

In Their Own Words . . .

Edward I. Altman on Junk Bonds

ONE OF THE most important developments in corporate finance over the last 20 years has been the reemergence of publicly owned and traded low-rated corporate debt. Originally offered to the public in the early 1900s to help finance some of our emerging growth industries, these high-yield, high-risk bonds virtually disappeared after the rash of bond defaults during the Depression. Recently, however, the junk bond market has been catapulted from being an insignificant element in the corporate fixed-income market to being one of the fastest-growing and most controversial types of financing mechanisms.

The term *junk* emanates from the dominant type of low-rated bond issues outstanding prior to 1977 when the "market" consisted almost exclusively of original-issue investment-grade bonds that fell from their lofty status to a higher–default risk, speculative-grade level. These so-called fallen angels amounted to about $8.5 billion in 1977. At the end of 1998, fallen angels comprised about 10 percent of the $450 billion publicly owned junk bond market.

Beginning in 1977, issuers began to go directly to the public to raise capital for growth purposes. Early users of junk bonds were energy-related firms, cable TV companies, airlines, and assorted other industrial companies. The emerging growth company rationale coupled with relatively high returns to early investors helped legitimize this sector.

By far the most important and controversial aspect of junk bond financing was its role in the corporate restructuring movement from 1985 to 1989. High-leverage transactions and acquisitions, such as leveraged buyouts (LBOs), which occur when a firm is taken private, and leveraged recapitalizations (debt-for-equity swaps), transformed the face of corporate America, leading to a heated debate as to the economic and social consequences of firms' being transformed with debt-equity ratios of at least 6:1.

These transactions involved increasingly large companies, and the multibillion-dollar takeover became fairly common, finally capped by the huge $25+ billion RJR Nabisco LBO in 1989. LBOs were typically financed with about 60 percent senior bank and insurance company debt, about 25–30 percent subordinated public debt (junk bonds), and 10–15 percent equity. The junk bond segment is sometimes referred to as "mezzanine" financing because it lies between the "balcony" senior debt and the "basement" equity.

These restructurings resulted in huge fees to advisors and underwriters and huge premiums to the old shareholders who were bought out, and they continued as long as the market

was willing to buy these new debt offerings at what appeared to be a favourable risk-return trade-off. The bottom fell out of the market in the last six months of 1989 due to a number of factors including a marked increase in defaults, government regulation against S&Ls' holding junk bonds, and a recession.

The default rate rose dramatically to 4 percent in 1989 and then skyrocketed in 1990 and 1991 to 10.1 percent and 10.3 percent, respectively, with about $19 billion of defaults in 1991. By the end of 1990, the pendulum of growth in new junk bond issues and returns to investors swung dramatically downward as prices plummeted and the new-issue market all but dried up. The year 1991 was a pivotal year in that, despite record defaults, bond prices and new issues rebounded strongly as the prospects for the future brightened.

In the early 1990s, the financial market was questioning the very survival of the junk bond market. The answer was a resounding "yes," as the amount of new issues soared to record annual levels of $40 billion in 1992 and almost $60 billion in 1993, and in 1997 reached an impressive $119 billion. Coupled with plummeting default rates (under 2.0 percent each year in the 1993–97 period) and attractive returns in these years, the risk-return characteristics have been extremely favourable.

The junk bond market today is a quieter one compared to that of the 1980s, but, in terms of growth and returns, it is healthier than ever before. While the low default rates in 1992–98 helped to fuel new investment funds and new issues, the market will experience its ups and downs in the future. It will continue, however, to be a major source of corporate debt financing and a legitimate asset class for investors.

Edward I. Altman is Max L. Heine Professor of Finance and vice director of the Salomon Center at the Stern School of Business of New York University. He is widely recognized as one of the world's experts on bankruptcy and credit analysis as well as on the high-yield, or junk bond, market. Updates on his research are at *www.stern.nyu.edu/~ealtman*.

Financial engineering is a response to the trends we discussed in Chapter 1, globalization, deregulation, and greater competition in financial markets.

When applied to debt securities, financial engineering creates exotic, hybrid securities that have many features of equity but are treated as debt. For example, suppose a corporation issues a perpetual bond with interest payable solely from corporate income if, and only if, earned. Whether this is really a debt or not is hard to say and is primarily a legal and semantic issue. Courts and taxing authorities would have the final say.

Obviously, the distinction between debt and equity is very important for tax purposes. So one reason that corporations try to create a debt security that is really equity is to obtain the tax benefits of debt and the bankruptcy benefits (lower agency costs) of equity.

As a general rule, equity represents an ownership interest, and it is a residual claim. This means equity holders are paid after debtholders. As a result of this, the risks and benefits associated with owning debt and equity are different. To give just one example, the maximum reward for owning a straight debt security is ultimately fixed by the amount of the loan, whereas there is no necessary upper limit to the potential reward from owning an equity interest.

Financial engineers can alter this division of claims by selling bonds with *warrants* attached giving bondholders options to buy stock in the firm. These warrants allow holders to participate in future rewards beyond the face value of the debt. We discuss other examples of financial engineering throughout this chapter.

Stripped Bonds

stripped bond/zero-coupon bond
A bond that makes no coupon payments, thus initially priced at a deep discount.

A bond that pays no coupons must be offered at a price that is much lower that its stated value. Such bonds are called **stripped bonds** or **zero-coupon bonds.**[7] Stripped bonds start life as normal coupon bonds. Investment dealers engage in bond stripping when they sell the principal and coupons separately.

Suppose the DDB Company issues a $1,000 face value five-year stripped bond. The initial price is set at $497. It is straightforward to check that, at this price, the bonds yield 15 percent to maturity. The total interest paid over the life of the bond is $1,000 − 497 = $503.

For tax purposes, the issuer of a stripped bond deducts interest every year even though no interest is actually paid. Similarly, the owner must pay taxes on interest accrued every year as well, even though no interest is actually received.[8] This second tax feature makes taxable stripped bonds less attractive to taxable investors. However, they are still a very attractive investment for tax-exempt investors with long-term dollar-denominated liabilities, such as pension funds, because the future dollar value is known with relative certainty. Stripped coupons are attractive to individual investors for tax-sheltered registered retirement savings plans (RRSPs).

Floating-Rate Bonds

The conventional bonds we have talked about in this chapter have fixed-dollar obligations because the coupon rate is set as a fixed percentage of the par value. Similarly, the principal is set equal to the par value. Under these circumstances, the coupon payment and principal are fixed.

With *floating-rate bonds (floaters)*, the coupon payments are adjustable. The adjustments are tied to the Treasury bill rate or another short-term interest rate. For example, the Royal Bank has outstanding $250 million of floating-rate notes maturing in 2083. The coupon rate is set at 0.40 percent more than the bankers acceptance rate.

Floating rate bonds were introduced to control the risk of price fluctuations as interest rates change. A bond with a coupon equal to the market yield is priced at par. In practice, the value of a floating-rate bond depends on exactly how the coupon payment adjustments are defined. In most cases, the coupon adjusts with a lag to some base rate, and so the price can deviate from par

7 A bond issued with a very low coupon rate (as opposed to a zero coupon rate) is an original issue, discount (OID) bond.

8 The way the yearly interest on a stripped bond is calculated is governed by tax law and is not necessarily the true compound interest.

within some range. For example, suppose a coupon rate adjustment is made on June 1. The adjustment might be based on the simple average of Treasury bill yields during the previous three months. In addition, the majority of floaters have the following features:

1. The holder has the right to redeem his or her note at par on the coupon payment date after some specified amount of time. This is called a put provision, and it is discussed later.

2. The coupon rate has a floor and a ceiling, meaning the coupon is subject to a minimum and a maximum.

Other Types of Bonds

Many bonds have unusual or exotic features. So-called disaster bonds provide an interesting example. In 1996, USAA, a big seller of car and home insurance based in San Antonio, Texas, announced plans to issue $500 million in "act of God" bonds. The way these work is that USAA will pay interest and principal in the usual way unless it has to cover more than $1 billion in hurricane claims from a single storm over any single one-year period. If this happens, investors stand to lose both principal and interest.

A similar issue was being planned by the proposed California Earthquake Authority, a public agency whose purpose would be to alleviate a growing home insurance availability crunch in the state. The issue, expected to be about $3.35 billion, would have a 10-year maturity, and investors would risk interest paid in the first 4 years in the event of a catastrophic earthquake.

As these examples illustrate, bond features are really only limited by the imaginations of the parties involved. Unfortunately, there are far too many variations for us to cover in detail here. We therefore close out this discussion by mentioning only a few of the more common types.

Income bonds are similar to conventional bonds, except that coupon payments depend on company income. Specifically, coupons are paid to bondholders only if the firm's income is sufficient. In Canada, income bonds are usually issued by firms in the process of reorganizing to try to overcome financial distress. The firm can skip the interest payment on an income bond without being in default. Purchasers of income bonds receive favourable tax treatment on interest received. *Real return bonds* have coupons and principal indexed to inflation to provide a stated real return. In 1993, the federal government issued a *stripped real return bond* packaging inflation protection in the form of a zero coupon bond.

A *convertible bond* can be swapped for a fixed number of shares of stock anytime before maturity at the holder's option. Convertibles are debt/equity hybrids that allow the holder to profit if the issuer's stock price rises.

A **retractable bond** or *put bond* allows the holder to force the issuer to buy the bond back at a stated price. As long as the issuer remains solvent, the put feature sets a floor price for the bond. It is, therefore, just the reverse of the call provision and is a relatively new development. We discuss convertible bonds, call provisions, and put provisions in more detail in Chapter 25.

A given bond may have many unusual features. Two of the most recent exotic bonds are CoCo bonds, which have a coupon payment, and NoNo bonds, which are zero coupon bonds. CoCo and NoNo bonds are contingent convertible, putable, callable, subordinated bonds. The contingent convertible clause is similar to the normal conversion feature, except the contingent feature must be met. For example, a contingent feature may require that the company stock trade at 110 percent of the conversion price for 20 out of the most recent 30 days. Valuing a bond of this sort can be quite complex, and the yield to maturity calculation is often meaningless. For example, in 2004, a NoNo issued by Merrill Lynch was selling at a price of $1,052.07, with a yield to maturity of negative 18.36 percent. At the same time, a NoNo issued by Countrywide Financial was selling for $1,412.50, which implied a yield to maturity of negative 28.59 percent!

retractable bond
Bond that may be sold back to the issuer at a prespecified price before maturity.

www.ml.com

CONCEPT QUESTIONS

1. Why might an income bond be attractive to a corporation with volatile cash flows? Can you think of a reason why income bonds are not more popular?

2. What do you think the effect of a put feature on a bond's coupon would be? How about a convertibility feature? Why?

BOND MARKETS

www.nyse.com

Bonds are bought and sold in enormous quantities every day. You may be surprised to learn that the trading volume in bonds on a typical day is many, many times larger than the trading volume in stocks (by trading volume, we simply mean the amount of money that changes hands). Here is a finance trivia question: What is the largest securities market in the world? Most people would guess the New York Stock Exchange. In fact, the largest securities market in the world in terms of trading volume is the U.S. Treasury market.

How Bonds Are Bought and Sold

www.tsx.com

As we mentioned all the way back in Chapter 1, most trading in bonds takes place OTC: over the counter. Recall that this means that there is no particular place where buying and selling occur. Instead, dealers around the country (and around the world) stand ready to buy and sell. The various dealers are connected electronically.

One reason the bond markets are so big is that the number of bond issues far exceeds the number of stock issues. A corporation would typically have only one common stock issue outstanding (there are exceptions to this that we discuss in our next chapter). However, a single large corporation could easily have a dozen or more note and bond issues outstanding.

Because the bond market is almost entirely OTC, it has little or no *transparency*. A financial market is transparent if it is possible to easily observe its prices and trading volume. On the Toronto Stock Exchange, for example, it is possible to see the price and quantity for every single transaction. In contrast, in the bond market, it is usually not possible to observe either. Transactions are privately negotiated between parties, and there is little or no centralized reporting of transactions.

Although the total volume of trading in bonds far exceeds that in stocks, only a very small fraction of the total bond issues that exist actually trade on a given day. This fact, combined with the lack of transparency in the bond market, means that getting up-to-date prices on individual bonds is often difficult or impossible, particularly for smaller corporate or municipal issues. Instead, a variety of sources of estimated prices exist and are very commonly used.

Bond Price Reporting

If you were to look at the *National Post* (or similar financial newspaper), you would see information on various bonds issued by the Government of Canada, the provinces and provincial crown corporations, and large corporations. Figure 7.3 reproduces excerpts from the bond quotations on May 2, 2006. If you look down the list under "Corporate," you come to an entry marked "BMO 6.685 Dec 31/11." This tells us the bond was issued by Bank of Montreal and it will mature on December 31, 2011. The 6.685 is the bond's coupon rate, so the coupon is 6.685 percent of the face value. Assuming the face value is $1000, the annual coupon on this bond is $0.06685 \times \$1000 = \$66.85$.

The column marked Bid $ gives us the last available bid price on the bond at close of business the day before. This price was supplied by RBC Dominion Securities. As with the coupon, the price is quoted as a percentage of face value; so, again assuming a face value of $1,000, this bond last sold for 108.45 percent of $1,000 or $1084.50. Quoting bond prices as percentages of face value is common practice. Because this bond is selling for about 108.45 percent of its par value, it is trading at a premium. The last column marked Yld% gives the going market yield to maturity on the BMO bond as 4.95 percent. This yield is lower than the coupon rate of 6.685 percent, which explains why the bond is selling above its par value. The market yield is below the coupon rate by 1.7350 percent, or 173.5 basis points. (In bond trader's jargon, one basis point equals 1/100 of 1 percent.) This causes the price premium to be above par.

FIGURE 7.3

Sample bond quotations

BONDS

Supplied by RBC Dominion Securities Inc. (5pm close, bid)

INDEXES

RBC Cap Index	Index level	Total ret	Price ret	MTD tot.ret
Market	497.09	-0.21	-0.23	-0.21
Short	397.35	-0.11	-0.13	-0.11
Intermed	510.88	-0.25	-0.26	-0.25
Long	669.14	-0.33	-0.35	-0.33
Govts	490.93	-0.22	-0.23	-0.22
Canadas	469.52	-0.20	-0.21	-0.20
Provs	544.02	-0.26	-0.28	-0.26
Munis	191.32	-0.25	-0.26	-0.25
Corps	537.84	-0.19	-0.21	-0.19

FEDERAL

	Coupon	Mat. date	Bid $	Yld%
Canada	3.000	Jun 01/07	98.78	4.17
Canada	7.250	Jun 01/07	103.22	4.17
Canada	4.500	Sep 01/07	100.43	4.16
Canada	2.750	Dec 01/07	97.88	4.15
Canada	12.750	Mar 01/08	114.95	4.16
Canada	10.000	Jun 01/08	111.51	4.16
Canada	6.000	Jun 01/08	103.62	4.16
Canada	3.750	Jun 01/08	99.16	4.17
Canada	4.250	Sep 01/08	100.05	4.23
Canada	11.000	Jun 01/09	119.24	4.26
Canada	5.500	Jun 01/09	103.49	4.28
Canada	4.250	Sep 01/09	99.82	4.31
Canada	10.750	Oct 01/09	120.22	4.31
Canada	5.500	Jun 01/10	104.24	4.35
Canada	9.500	Jun 01/10	119.07	4.34
Canada	4.000	Sep 01/10	98.59	4.36
Canada	9.000	Mar 01/11	119.95	4.37
Canada	6.000	Jun 01/11	107.20	4.40
Canada	8.500	Jun 01/11	118.48	4.40
Canada	3.750	Sep 01/11	96.83	4.42
Canada	5.250	Jun 01/12	104.25	4.44
Canada	5.250	Jun 01/13	104.64	4.48
Canada	10.250	Mar 15/14	137.79	4.49
Canada	5.000	Jun 01/14	103.34	4.50
Canada	11.250	Jun 01/15	149.96	4.49
Canada	4.500	Jun 01/15	99.94	4.51
Canada	4.000	Jun 01/16	95.67	4.54
Canada	9.750	Jun 01/21	155.92	4.57
Canada	9.250	Jun 01/22	153.18	4.55
Canada	8.000	Jun 01/23	140.07	4.59
Canada	9.000	Jun 01/25	155.54	4.60
Canada	8.000	Jun 01/27	145.56	4.60
Canada	5.750	Jun 01/29	116.50	4.58

	Coupon	Mat. date	Bid $	Yld%
Canada	5.000	Jun 01/37	107.99	4.52
CHT	4.750	Mar 15/07	100.41	4.26
CHT	5.100	Sep 15/07	101.10	4.26
CHT	4.400	Mar 15/08	100.19	4.29
CHT	3.700	Sep 15/08	98.61	4.32

CORPORATE

	Coupon	Mat. date	Bid $	Yld%
AGT Lt	8.800	Sep 22/25	135.51	5.74
BCE	6.750	Oct 30/07	102.94	4.68
Bell	6.550	May 01/29	103.47	6.26
BMO	6.903	Jun 30/10	107.78	4.81
BMO	6.647	Dec 31/10	107.39	4.85
BMO	4.690	Jan 31/11	99.83	4.73
BMO	6.685	Dec 31/11	108.45	4.95
BNS	3.470	Sep 02/08	97.68	4.53
BNS	4.515	Nov 19/08	99.92	4.55
BNS	3.930	Feb 18/10	97.49	4.66
BNS	7.310	Dec 31/10	110.08	4.86
CardTr2	3.869	Oct 15/10	96.81	4.67
CDP	4.200	Oct 14/08	99.48	4.43
CIBC	3.750	Sep 09/10	96.07	4.76
CIBC	4.550	Mar 28/11	98.83	4.82
Domtar	10.000	Apr 15/11	106.35	8.40
GE CAP	5.300	Jul 24/07	101.10	4.36
GE CAP	5.000	Apr 23/08	101.15	4.38
GE CAP	3.650	Jun 07/10	96.29	4.65
Genss	4.002	Mar 15/10	97.79	4.63
GldCrd	4.159	Oct 15/08	99.15	4.53
GrTAA	5.950	Dec 03/07	102.30	4.43
GrTAA	6.450	Dec 03/27	107.54	5.83
GTC Tr	6.200	Jun 01/07	101.64	4.62
Gulf C	6.450	Oct 01/07	106.75	4.39
GWLife	6.750	Aug 10/10	107.78	4.71
GWLife	5.995	Dec 31/12	105.43	5.02
GWLife	6.140	Mar 21/18	108.64	5.16
GWLife	6.740	Nov 24/31	116.09	5.55
GWLife	6.670	Mar 21/33	115.48	5.55
HSBC	7.780	Dec 31/10	111.88	4.89
HydOne	7.150	Jun 03/10	109.37	4.60
HydOne	6.400	Dec 01/11	108.14	4.72
HydOne	5.770	Nov 15/12	105.47	4.78
HydOne	7.350	Jun 03/30	125.88	5.41
HydOne	6.930	Jun 01/32	121.05	5.41
IPL	8.200	Feb 15/24	130.52	5.49
Loblaw	6.650	Nov 08/27	107.66	6.01
MLI	6.240	Feb 16/11	106.08	4.80
MLI	6.700	Jun 30/12	108.94	4.99

Source: National Post, May 2, 2006, p. FP17. Used with permission.

EXAMPLE 7.3: Bond Pricing in Action

Investment managers who specialize in bonds use bond pricing principles to try to make money for their clients by buying bonds whose prices they expect to rise. An interest rate anticipation strategy starts with a forecast for the level of interest rates. Such forecasts are extremely difficult to make consistently. In Chapter 12, we discuss in detail how difficult it is to beat the market.

Suppose a manager had predicted a significant drop in interest rates in 2006. How should such a manager have invested?

This manager would have invested heavily in bonds with the greatest price sensitivity; that is, in bonds whose prices would rise the most as rates fell. Based on the earlier discussion, you should recall that such price-sensitive bonds have longer times to maturity and low coupons.

Suppose you wanted to bet on the expectation that interest rates were going to fall significantly using the bond quotations in Figure 7.3. Suppose further that your client wanted to invest only in Government of Canada bonds. Which would you buy?

A Note on Bond Price Quotes

clean price
The price of a bond net of accrued interest; this is the price that is typically quoted.

dirty price
The price of a bond including accrued interest, also known as the *full* or *invoice price*. This is the price the buyer actually pays.

If you buy a bond between coupon payment dates, the price you pay is usually more than the price you are quoted. The reason is that standard convention in the bond market is to quote prices "net of accrued interest," meaning that accrued interest is deducted to arrive at the quoted price. This quoted price is called the **clean price**. The price you actually pay, however, includes the accrued interest. This price is the **dirty price**, also known as the "full" or "invoice" price.

An example is the easiest way to understand these issues. Suppose you buy a bond with a 12 percent annual coupon, payable semiannually. You actually pay $1,080 for this bond, so $1,080 is the dirty, or invoice, price. Further, on the day you buy it, the next coupon is due in four months, so you are between coupon dates. Notice that the next coupon will be $60.

The accrued interest on a bond is calculated by taking the fraction of the coupon period that has passed, in this case two months out of six, and multiplying this fraction by the next coupon, $60. So, the accrued interest in this example is $2/6 \times \$60 = \$20$. The bond's quoted price (i.e., its clean price) would be $1,080 − $20 = $1,060.[9]

CONCEPT QUESTIONS

1. What are the cash flows associated with a bond?

2. What is the general expression for the value of a bond?

3. Is it true that the only risk associated with owning a bond is that the issuer will not make all the payments? Explain.

4. Figure 7.3 shows two Canada bonds, both maturing on September 1, 2005. These bonds are both issued by the Government of Canada and they have identical maturities. Why do they have different yields?

 7.6

INFLATION AND INTEREST RATES

So far, we haven't considered the role of inflation in our various discussions of interest rates, yields, and returns. Because this is an important consideration, we consider the impact of inflation next.

Real versus Nominal Rates

nominal rates
Interest rates or rates of return that have not been adjusted for inflation.

real rates
Interest rates or rates of return that have been adjusted for inflation.

In examining interest rates, or any other financial market rates such as discount rates, bond yields, rates of return, and required returns, it is often necessary to distinguish between **real rates** and **nominal rates.** Nominal rates are called "nominal" because they have not been adjusted for inflation. Real rates are rates that have been adjusted for inflation.

To see the effect of inflation, suppose prices are currently rising by 5 percent per year. In other words, the rate of inflation is 5 percent. An investment is available that will be worth $115.50 in one year. It costs $100 today. Notice that with a present value of $100 and a future value in one year of $115.50, this investment has a 15.5 percent rate of return. In calculating this 15.5 percent return, we did not consider the effect of inflation, however, so this is the nominal return.

What is the impact of inflation here? To answer, suppose pizzas cost $5 apiece at the beginning of the year. With $100, we can buy 20 pizzas. Because the inflation rate is 5 percent, pizzas will cost 5 percent more, or $5.25, at the end of the year. If we take the investment, how many pizzas can we buy at the end of the year? Measured in pizzas, what is the rate of return on this investment?

Our $115.50 from the investment will buy us $115.50/5.25 = 22 pizzas. This is up from 20 pizzas, so our pizza rate of return is 10 percent. What this illustrates is that even though the

---

9 The way accrued interest is calculated actually depends on the type of bond being quoted: for example, Government of Canada or corporate. The difference has to do with exactly how the fractional period is calculated. In our example above, we implicitly treated the months as having exactly the same length (i.e., 30 days each, 360 days in a year), which is the way corporate bonds are quoted in the U.S. In Canada, the calculation assumes 365 days in a year. In contrast, Government of Canada and U.S. treasury bonds use actual day counts in quoting prices.

Current and historical Treasury yield information is available at www.bankofcanada.ca

nominal return on our investment is 15.5 percent, our buying power goes up by only 10 percent because of inflation. Put another way, we are really only 10 percent richer. In this case, we say that the real return is 10 percent.

Alternatively, we can say that with 5 percent inflation, each of the $115.50 nominal dollars we get is worth 5 percent less in real terms, so the real dollar value of our investment in a year is:

$115.50/1.05 = $110

What we have done is to *deflate* the $115.50 by 5 percent. Because we give up $100 in current buying power to get the equivalent of $110, our real return is again 10 percent. Because we have removed the effect of future inflation here, this $110 is said to be measured in current dollars.

The difference between nominal and real rates is important and bears repeating:

> The nominal rate on an investment is the percentage change in the number of dollars you have.
> The real rate on an investment is the percentage change in how much you can buy with your dollars, in other words, the percentage change in your buying power.

The Fisher Effect

Fisher effect
The relationship between nominal returns, real returns, and inflation.

Our discussion of real and nominal returns illustrates a relationship often called the **Fisher effect** (after the great economist Irving Fisher). Because investors are ultimately concerned with what they can buy with their money, they require compensation for inflation.[10] Let R stand for the nominal rate and r stand for the real rate. The Fisher effect tells us that the relationship between nominal rates, real rates, and inflation can be written as:

$$1 + R = (1 + r) \times (1 + h) \qquad [7.2]$$

where h is the inflation rate.

In the preceding example, the nominal rate was 15.50 percent and the inflation rate was 5 percent. What was the real rate? We can determine it by plugging in these numbers:

$$1 + .1550 = (1 + r) \times (1 + .05)$$
$$1 + r = 1.1550/1.05 = 1.10$$
$$r = 10\%$$

This real rate is the same as we had before. If we take another look at the Fisher effect, we can rearrange things a little as follows:

$$1 + R = (1 + r) \times (1 + h) \qquad [7.3]$$
$$R = r + h + r \times h$$

What this tells us is that the nominal rate has three components. First, there is the real rate on the investment, r. Next, there is the compensation for the decrease in the value of the money originally invested because of inflation, h. The third component represents compensation for the fact that the dollars earned on the investment are also worth less because of the inflation.

This third component is usually small, so it is often dropped. The nominal rate is then approximately equal to the real rate plus the inflation rate:

$$R \approx r + h \qquad [7.4]$$

A good example of the Fisher effect in practice comes from the history of interest rates in Canada.[11] In 1980, the average T-bill rate over the year was around 13 percent. In contrast, in

---

10 Here we are referring to the *expected* inflation rate, rather than the actual inflation rate. Buyers and sellers of investments must use their best estimate of future inflation rates at the time of a transaction. Actual rates of inflation are not known until a considerable period after the purchase or sale, when all the cash flows from the investment instrument have taken place.

11 You can find historical and international data on interest rates and inflation at
   http://www40.statcan.ca/l01/cst01/econ46.htm, www.bankofcanada.ca, and
   CIA World Factbook – *http://www.odci.gov/cia/publications/factbook/index.html*

EXAMPLE 7.4: The Fisher Effect

If investors require a 10 percent real rate of return, and the inflation rate is 8 percent, what must be the approximate nominal rate? The exact nominal rate?

First of all, the nominal rate is approximately equal to the sum of the real rate and the inflation rate: 10% + 8% = 18%. From the Fisher effect, we have:

$$1 + R = (1 + r) \times (1 + h)$$
$$= 1.10 \times 1.08$$
$$= 1.1880$$

Therefore, the nominal rate will actually be closer to 19 percent.

2005, the average rate was much lower, at 3 percent. The inflation rates for the same two years were approximately 10 percent for 1980 and under 2 percent for 2005. Lower expected inflation goes a long way toward explaining why interest rates were lower in 2005 than in 1980.

The Fisher effect also holds on an international scale. While 2005 interest rates were low in Canada compared to 1980, they were considerably higher than for the same year in Japan. In that country, the 2005 inflation rate was approximately zero, while the Bank of Japan's short-term rates were less than 0.5 percent.

It is important to note that financial rates, such as interest rates, discount rates, and rates of return, are almost always quoted in nominal terms.

CONCEPT QUESTIONS

1. What is the difference between a nominal and a real return? Which is more important to a typical investor?

2. What is the Fisher effect?

 **7.7**

DETERMINANTS OF BOND YIELDS

We are now in a position to discuss the determinants of a bond's yield. As we will see, the yield on any particular bond is a reflection of a variety of factors, some common to all bonds and some specific to the issue under consideration.

The Term Structure of Interest Rates

At any point in time, short-term and long-term interest rates will generally be different. Sometimes short-term rates are higher, sometimes lower. Through time, the difference between short- and long-term rates has ranged from essentially zero to up to several percentage points, both positive and negative.

term structure of interest rates
The relationship between nominal interest rates on default-free, pure discount securities and time to maturity; that is, the pure time value of money.

The relationship between short- and long-term interest rates is known as the **term structure of interest rates.** To be a little more precise, the term structure of interest rates tells us what *nominal* interest rates are on *default-free, pure discount* bonds of all maturities. These rates are, in essence, "pure" interest rates because they involve no risk of default and a single, lump-sum future payment. In other words, the term structure tells us the pure time value of money for different lengths of time.

When long-term rates are higher than short-term rates, we say that the term structure is upward sloping, and, when short-term rates are higher, we say it is downward sloping. The term structure can also be "humped." When this occurs, it is usually because rates increase at first, but then begin to decline as we look at longer- and longer-term rates. The most common shape of the term structure, particularly in modern times, is upward sloping, but the degree of steepness has varied quite a bit.

What determines the shape of the term structure? There are three basic components. The first two are the ones we discussed in our previous section, the real rate of interest and the rate of inflation. The real rate of interest is the compensation investors demand for forgoing the use of their money. You can think of it as the pure time value of money after adjusting for the effects of inflation.

The real rate of interest is the basic component underlying every interest rate, regardless of the time to maturity. When the real rate is high, all interest rates will tend to be higher, and vice versa. Thus, the real rate doesn't really determine the shape of the term structure; instead, it mostly influences the overall level of interest rates.

In contrast, the prospect of future inflation very strongly influences the shape of the term structure. Investors thinking about lending money for various lengths of time recognize that future inflation erodes the value of the dollars that will be returned. As a result, investors demand compensation for this loss in the form of higher nominal rates. This extra compensation is called the **inflation premium.**

inflation premium
The portion of a nominal interest rate that represents compensation for expected future inflation.

If investors believe that the rate of inflation will be higher in future, then long-term nominal interest rates will tend to be higher than short-term rates. Thus, an upward-sloping term structure may be a reflection of anticipated increases in inflation. Similarly, a downward-sloping term structure probably reflects the belief that inflation will be falling in the future.

The third, and last, component of the term structure has to do with interest rate risk. As we discussed earlier in the chapter, longer-term bonds have much greater risk of loss resulting from changes in interest rates than do shorter-term bonds. Investors recognize this risk, and they demand extra compensation in the form of higher rates for bearing it. This extra compensation is called the **interest rate risk premium.** The longer the term to maturity, the greater the interest rate risk, so the interest rate risk premium increases with maturity. However, as we discussed earlier, interest rate risk increases at a decreasing rate, so the interest rate risk premium does as well.[12]

interest rate risk premium
The compensation investors demand for bearing interest rate risk.

Putting the pieces together, we see that the term structure reflects the combined effect of the real rate of interest, the inflation premium, and the interest rate risk premium. Figure 7.4 shows how these can interact to produce an upward-sloping term structure (in the top part of Figure 7.4) or a downward-sloping term structure (in the bottom part).

In the top part of Figure 7.4, notice how the rate of inflation is expected to rise gradually. At the same time, the interest rate risk premium increases at a decreasing rate, so the combined effect is to produce a pronounced upward-sloping term structure. In the bottom part of Figure 7.4, the rate of inflation is expected to fall in the future, and the expected decline is enough to offset the interest rate risk premium and produce a downward-sloping term structure. Notice that if the rate of inflation was expected to decline by only a small amount, we could still get an upward-sloping term structure because of the interest rate risk premium.

We assumed in drawing Figure 7.4 that the real rate would remain the same. Actually, expected future real rates could be larger or smaller than the current real rate. Also, for simplicity, we used straight lines to show expected future inflation rates as rising or declining, but they do not necessarily have to look like this. They could, for example, rise and then fall, leading to a humped yield curve.

Bond Yields and the Yield Curve: Putting It All Together

Going back to Figure 7.3, recall that we saw that the yields on Government of Canada bonds of different maturities are not the same. Each day, we can plot the Canada bond prices and yields shown in Figure 7.3, relative to maturity. This plot is called the **Canada yield curve** (or just the yield curve). Figure 7.5 shows the yield curve drawn from the yields in Figure 7.3.

Canada yield curve
A plot of the yields on Government of Canada notes and bonds relative to maturity.

As you probably now suspect, the shape of the yield curve is a reflection of the term structure of interest rates. In fact, the Canada yield curve and the term structure of interest rates are almost the same thing. The only difference is that the term structure is based on pure discount bonds, whereas the yield curve is based on coupon bond yields. As a result, Canada yields depend on the three components that underlie the term structure—the real rate, expected future inflation, and the interest rate risk premium.

Canada bonds have three important features that we need to remind you of: they are default-free, they are taxable, and they are highly liquid. This is not true of bonds in general, so we need to examine what additional factors come into play when we look at bonds issued by corporations or municipalities.

---

12 In days of old, the interest rate risk premium was called a "liquidity" premium. Today, the term *liquidity premium* has an altogether different meaning, which we explore in our next section. Also, the interest rate risk premium is sometimes called a maturity risk premium. Our terminology is consistent with the modern view of the term structure.

FIGURE 7.4

The term structure of interest rates

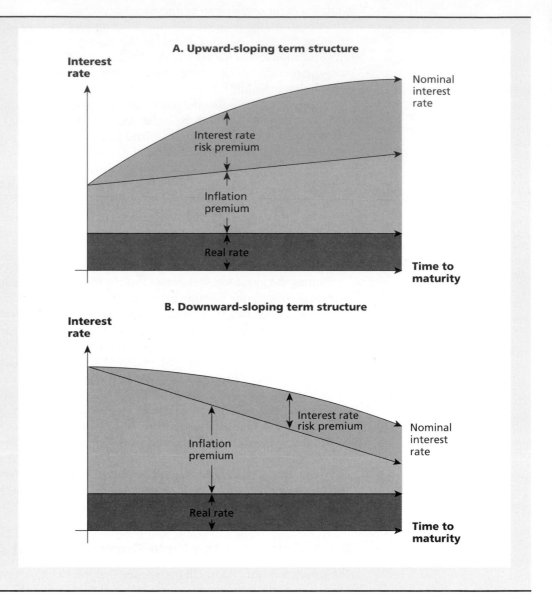

default risk premium
The portion of a nominal interest rate or bond yield that represents compensation for the possibility of default.

The first thing to consider is credit risk, that is, the possibility of default. Investors recognize that issuers other than the Government of Canada may or may not make all the promised payments on a bond, so they demand a higher yield as compensation for this risk. This extra compensation is called the **default risk premium.** Earlier in the chapter, we saw how bonds were rated based on their credit risk. What you will find if you start looking at bonds of different ratings is that lower-rated bonds have higher yields.

An important thing to recognize about a bond's yield is that it is calculated assuming that all the promised payments will be made. As a result, it is really a promised yield, and it may or may not be what you will earn. In particular, if the issuer defaults, your actual yield will be lower, probably much lower. This fact is particularly important when it comes to junk bonds. Thanks to a clever bit of marketing, such bonds are now commonly called high-yield bonds, which has a much nicer ring to it; but now you recognize that these are really high–*promised* yield bonds.

Finally, bonds have varying degrees of liquidity. As we discussed earlier, there is an enormous number of bond issues, most of which do not trade on a regular basis. As a result, if you wanted to sell quickly, you would probably not get as good a price as you could otherwise. Investors prefer liquid assets to

FIGURE 7.5

Government of Canada
yield curve

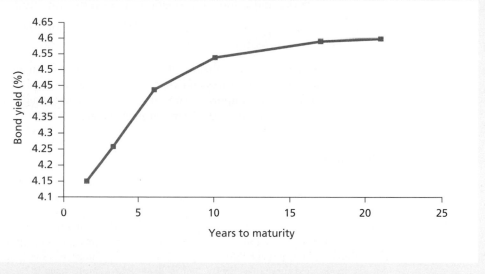

Source: *National Post,* May 2, 2006, p. FP17.

liquidity premium
The portion of a nominal
interest rate or bond
yield that represents
compensation for lack of
liquidity.

illiquid ones, so they demand a **liquidity premium** on top of all the other premiums we have discussed. As a result, all else being the same, less liquid bonds will have higher yields than more liquid bonds.

Conclusion

If we combine all of the things we have discussed regarding bond yields, we find that bond yields represent the combined effect of no fewer than six things. The first is the real rate of interest. On top of the real rate are five premiums representing compensation for (1) expected future inflation, (2) interest rate risk, (3) default risk, (4) taxability, and (5) lack of liquidity. As a result, determining the appropriate yield on a bond requires careful analysis of each of these effects.

CONCEPT QUESTIONS

1. What is the term structure of interest rates? What determines its shape?

2. What is the Canada yield curve?

3. What are the six components that make up a bond's yield?

 **7.8**

SUMMARY AND CONCLUSIONS

This chapter has explored bonds, bond yields, and interest rates. We saw that:

1. Determining bond prices and yields is an application of basic discounted cash flow principles.

2. Bond values move in the direction opposite that of interest rates, leading to potential gains or losses for bond investors.

3. Bonds have a variety of features spelled out in a document called the indenture.

4. Bonds are rated based on their default risk. Some bonds, such as Treasury bonds, have no risk of default, whereas so-called junk bonds have substantial default risk.

5. A wide variety of bonds exist, many of which contain exotic or unusual features.

6. Almost all bond trading is OTC, with little or no market transparency. As a result, bond price and volume information can be difficult to find.

7. Bond yields reflect the effect of the real rate and premiums that investors demand as compensation for inflation and interest rate risk.

In closing, we note that bonds are a vital source of financing to governments and corporations of all types. Bond prices and yields are a rich subject, and our one chapter necessarily touches on only the most important concepts and ideas. There is a great deal more we could say, but instead we will move on to stocks in our next chapter.

Key Terms

bearer form (page 187)
bond refunding (page 209)
call premium (page 188)
call protected (page 188)
call provision (page 188)
Canada plus call (page 188)
Canada yield curve (page 199)
clean price (page 196)
coupon rate (page 178)
coupons (page 177)
debenture (page 187)
default risk premium (page 200)
deferred call (page 188)
dirty price (page 196)
face value or par value (page 177)
Fisher effect (page 197)

indenture (page 186)
inflation premium (page 199)
interest rate risk premium (page 199)
liquidity premium (page 201)
maturity date (page 178)
nominal rates (page 196)
note (page 187)
protective covenant (page 188)
real rates (page 196)
registered form (page 187)
retractable bond (page 193)
sinking fund (page 188)
stripped bond/zero-coupon bond (page 192)
term structure of interest rates (page 198)
yield to maturity (YTM) (page 178)

Chapter Review Problems and Self-Test

7.1   Bond Values   A Microgates Industries bond has a 10 percent coupon rate and a $1,000 face value. Interest is paid semiannually, and the bond has 20 years to maturity. If investors require a 12 percent yield, what is the bond's value? What is the effective annual yield on the bond?

7.2   Bond Yields   A Macrohard Corp. bond carries an 8 percent coupon, paid semiannually. The par value is $1,000 and the bond matures in six years. If the bond currently sells for $911.37, what is its yield to maturity? What is the effective annual yield?

Answers to Self-Test Problems

7.1   Because the bond has a 10 percent coupon yield and investors require a 12 percent return, we know that the bond must sell at a discount. Notice that, because the bond pays interest semiannually, the coupons amount to $100/2 = $50 every six months. The required yield is 12%/2 = 6% every six months. Finally, the bond matures in 20 years, so there are a total of 40 six-month periods.

The bond's value is thus equal to the present value of $50 every six months for the next 40 six-month periods plus the present value of the $1,000 face amount:

$$\text{Bond value} = \$50 \times (1 - 1/1.06^{40})/.06 + 1,000/1.06^{40}$$
$$= \$50 \times 15.04630 + 1,000/10.2857$$
$$= \$849.54$$

Notice that we discounted the $1,000 back 40 periods at 6 percent per period, rather than 20 years at 12 percent. The reason is that the effective annual yield on the bond is $1.06^2 - 1 = 12.36\%$, not 12 percent. We thus could have used 12.36 percent per year for 20 years when we calculated the present value of the $1,000 face amount, and the answer would have been the same.

7.2   The present value of the bond's cash flows is its current price, $911.37. The coupon is $40 every six months for 12 periods. The face value is $1,000. So the bond's yield is the unknown discount rate in the following:

$$\$911.37 = \$40 \times [1 - 1/(1 + r)^{12}]/r + 1,000/(1 + r)^{12}$$

The bond sells at a discount. Because the coupon rate is 8 percent, the yield must be something in excess of that.

If we were to solve this by trial and error, we might try 12 percent (or 6 percent per six months):

$$\text{Bond value} = \$40 \times (1 - 1/1.06^{12})/.06 + 1{,}000/1.06^{12}$$
$$= \$832.32$$

This is less than the actual value, so our discount rate is too high. We now know that the yield is somewhere between 8 and 12 percent. With further trial and error (or a little machine assistance), the yield works out to be 10 percent, or 5 percent every six months.

By convention, the bond's yield to maturity would be quoted as $2 \times 5\% = 10\%$. The effective yield is thus $1.05^2 - 1 = 10.25\%$.

Concepts Review and Critical Thinking Questions

1. Is it true that a Government of Canada security is risk-free?

2. Which has greater interest rate risk, a 30-year Canada bond or a 30-year BB corporate bond?

3. With regard to bid and ask prices on a Canada bond, is it possible for the bid price to be higher? Why or why not?

4. Canada bid and ask quotes are sometimes given in terms of yields, so there would be a bid yield and an ask yield. Which do you think would be larger? Explain.

5. A company is contemplating a long-term bond issue. It is debating whether or not to include a call provision. What are the benefits to the company from including a call provision? What are the costs? How do these answers change for a put provision?

6. How does a bond issuer decide on the appropriate coupon rate to set on its bonds? Explain the difference between the coupon rate and the required return on a bond.

7. Are there any circumstances under which an investor might be more concerned about the nominal return on an investment than the real return?

8. Companies pay rating agencies such as the Dominion Bond Rating Service to rate their bonds, and the costs can be substantial. However, companies are not required to have their bonds rated in the first place; doing so is strictly voluntary. Why do you think they do it?

9. Canada bonds are not rated. Why? Often, junk bonds are not rated. Why?

10. What is the difference between the term structure of interest rates and the yield curve?

Questions and Problems

Basic
(Questions 1–14)

Unless the question states otherwise, you can assume that the face value or par value of the bond is $1,000.

1. **Interpreting Bond Yields** Is the yield to maturity on a bond the same thing as the required return? Is YTM the same thing as the coupon rate? Suppose today a 10 percent coupon bond sells at par. Two years from now, the required return on the same bond is 8 percent. What is the coupon rate on the bond now? The YTM?

2. **Interpreting Bond Yields** Suppose you buy a 7 percent coupon, 20-year bond today when it's first issued. If interest rates suddenly rise to 15 percent, what happens to the value of your bond? Why?

3. **Bond Prices** DTO, Inc., has 8 percent coupon bonds on the market that have 10 years left to maturity. The bonds make annual payments. If the YTM on these bonds is 6 percent, what is the current bond price?

4. **Bond Yields** Aragorn Co. has 9 percent coupon bonds on the market with nine years left to maturity. The bonds make annual payments. If the bond currently sells for $884.50, what is its YTM?

5. **Coupon Rates** Superstar Enterprises has bonds on the market making annual payments, with 16 years to maturity, and selling for $870. At this price, the bonds yield 6.8 percent. What must the coupon rate be on Superstar's bonds?

6. **Bond Prices** Borderline Co. issued 11-year bonds one year ago at a coupon rate of 8.2 percent. The bonds make semi-annual payments. If the YTM on these bonds is 7.4 percent, what is the current bond price?

7. **Bond Yields** Raines Umbrella Corp. issued 12-year bonds 2 years ago at a coupon rate of 8.6 percent. The bonds make semiannual payments. If these bonds currently sell for 97 percent of par value, what is the YTM?

8. **Coupon Rates** Rhiannon Corporation has bonds on the market with 14.5 years to maturity, a YTM of 7.5 percent, and a current price of $1,145. The bonds make semiannual payments. What must the coupon rate be on these bonds?

9. **Calculating Real Rates of Return** If Treasury bills are currently paying 6 percent and the inflation rate is 4.5 percent, what is the approximate real rate of interest? The exact real rate?

10. **Inflation and Nominal Returns** Suppose the real rate is 4 percent and the inflation rate is 2.5 percent. What rate would you expect to see on a Treasury bill?

Basic
(continued)

11. **Nominal and Real Returns**   An investment offers a 15 percent total return over the coming year. Alan Wingspan thinks the total real return on this investment will be only 9 percent. What does Alan believe the inflation rate will be over the next year?

12. **Nominal versus Real Returns**   Say you own an asset that had a total return last year of 13.4 percent. If the inflation rate last year was 4.5 percent, what was your real return?

13. **Bond Pricing**   This problem refers to bond quotes in Figure 7.3. Calculate the price of the Canada Sep01/09 to prove that it is 99.82 as shown. Assume that today is May 2, 2006.

14. **Bond Value**   At the time of the last referendum, Quebec provincial bonds carried a higher yield than comparable Ontario bonds because of investors' uncertainty about the political future of Quebec. Suppose you were an investment manager who thought the market was overplaying these fears. In particular, suppose you thought that yields on Quebec bonds would fall by 50 basis points. Which bonds would you buy or sell? Explain in words.

Intermediate
(Questions
15–28)

15. **Bond Price Movements**   Bond X is a premium bond making annual payments. The bond pays an 8 percent coupon, has a YTM of 6 percent, and has 13 years to maturity. Bond Y is a discount bond making annual payments. This bond pays a 6 percent coupon, has a YTM of 8 percent, and also has 13 years to maturity. If interest rates remain unchanged, what do you expect the price of these bonds to be one year from now? In three years? In eight years? In 12 years? In 13 years? What's going on here? Illustrate your answers by graphing bond prices versus time to maturity.

16. **Interest Rate Risk**   Both Bond Sam and Bond Dave have 10 percent coupons, make semiannual payments, and are priced at par value. Bond Sam has 2 years to maturity, whereas Bond Dave has 15 years to maturity. If interest rates suddenly rise by 2 percent, what is the percentage change in the price of Bond Sam? Of Bond Dave? If rates were to suddenly fall by 2 percent instead, what would the percentage change in the price of Bond Sam be then? Of Bond Dave? Illustrate your answers by graphing bond prices versus YTM. What does this problem tell you about the interest rate risk of longer-term bonds?

17. **Interest Rate Risk**   Bond J is a 5 percent coupon bond. Bond K is an 11 percent coupon bond. Both bonds have 8 years to maturity, make semiannual payments, and have a YTM of 7 percent. If interest rates suddenly rise by 2 percent, what is the percentage price change of these bonds? What if rates suddenly fall by 2 percent instead? What does this problem tell you about the interest rate risk of lower-coupon bonds?

18. **Bond Yields**   Stealers Wheel Software has 8.4 percent coupon bonds on the market with 9 years to maturity. The bonds make semiannual payments and currently sell for 104 percent of par. What is the current yield on the bonds? The YTM? The effective annual yield?

19. **Bond Yields**   Petty Co. wants to issue new 20-year bonds for some much-needed expansion projects. The company currently has 8 percent coupon bonds on the market that sell for $1,095, make semiannual payments, and mature in 20 years. What coupon rate should the company set on its new bonds if it wants them to sell at par?

20. **Accrued Interest**   You purchase a bond with a quoted price of $1,140. The bond has a coupon rate of 7.2 percent, and there are 5 months to the next semiannual coupon date. What is the clean price of the bond?

21. **Accrued Interest**   You purchase a bond with a coupon rate of 6.5 percent, and a clean price of $865. If the next semiannual coupon payment is due in three months, what is the invoice price?

22. **Finding the Bond Maturity**   Jude Corp. has 11 percent coupon bonds making annual payments with a YTM of 8.5 percent. The price of these bonds is $123.66. How many years do these bonds have left until they mature?

23. **Using Bond Quotes**   Suppose the following bond quote for IOU Corporation appear in the financial page of today's newspaper. Assume the bond has a face value of $1000 and the current date is March 21, 2006. What is the yield to maturity of the bond? What is the yield to maturity on a comparable Bank of Canada issue?

Company (Ticker)	Coupon	Maturity Date	Bid ($)	Yield (%)
IOU (IOU)	6.140	Mar 21, 2016	108.64	??

24. **Bond Prices versus Yields**

   a. What is the relationship between the price of a bond and its YTM?

   b. Explain why some bonds sell at a premium over par value while other bonds sell at a discount. What do you know about the relationship between the coupon rate and the YTM for premium bonds? What about for discount bonds? For bonds selling at par value?

   c. What is the relationship between the current yield and YTM for premium bonds? For discount bonds? For bonds selling at par value?

25. **Interest on Zeroes**   HSD Corporation needs to raise funds to finance a plant expansion, and it has decided to issue 25-year zero coupon bonds to raise the money. The required return on the bonds will be 8 percent.

   a. What will these bonds sell for at issuance?

   b. What interest deduction can HSD Corporation take on these bonds in the first year? In the last year?

   c. Repeat part (b) using the straight-line method for the interest deduction.

   d. Based on your answers in (b) and (c), which interest deduction method would HSD Corporation prefer? Why?

Intermediate **26.** **Zero Coupon Bonds** Suppose your company needs to raise $15 million and you want to issue 30-year bonds for this
(continued) purpose. Assume the required return on your bond issue will be 7 percent, and you're evaluating two issue alternatives: a 7 percent annual coupon bond and a zero coupon bond. Your company's tax rate is 35 percent.

    a. How many of the coupon bonds would you need to issue to raise the $15 million? How many of the zeroes would you need to issue?

    b. In 30 years, what will your company's repayment be if you issue the coupon bonds? What if you issue the zeroes?

    c. Based on your answers in (a) and (b), why would you ever want to issue the zeroes? To answer, calculate the firm's aftertax cash outflows for the first year under the two different scenarios.

27. **Finding the Maturity** You've just found a 10 percent coupon bond on the market that sells for par value. What is the maturity on this bond?

28. **Components of Bond Returns** Bond P is a premium bond with a 10 percent coupon. Bond D is a 6 percent coupon bond currently selling at a discount. Both bonds make annual payments, have a YTM of 8 percent, and have five years to maturity. If interest rates remain unchanged, what is the expected capital gains yield over the next year for Bond P? For Bond D? Explain your answers and the interrelationship among the YTM, coupon rate, and capital gains yield.

Challenge **29.** **Holding Period Yield** The YTM on a bond is the interest rate you earn on your investment if interest rates don't change.
(Questions If you actually sell the bond before it matures, your realized return is known as the holding period yield (HPY).
29–30)

    a. Suppose that today you buy an 8 percent annual coupon bond for $1,150. The bond has 10 years to maturity. What rate of return do you expect to earn on your investment?

    b. Two years from now, the YTM on your bond has declined by 1 percent, and you decide to sell. What price will your bond sell for? What is the HPY on your investment? Compare this yield to the YTM when you first bought the bond. Why are they different?

30. **Valuing Bonds** The Mallory Corporation has two different bonds currently outstanding. Bond M has a face value of $20,000 and matures in 20 years. The bond makes no payments for the first six years, then pays $1,200 every six months over the subsequent eight years, and finally pays $1,500 every six months over the last six years. Bond N also has a face value of $20,000 and a maturity of 20 years; it makes no coupon payments over the life of the bond. If the required return on both these bonds is 10 percent compounded semiannually, what is the current price of Bond M? Of Bond N?

MINI CASE

With current market conditions, you have decided that you want a higher weight of bonds in your investment portfolio. You have $15,000 to invest, and have narrowed down your choices to the following three options:

Option 1

A junk bond is available that sells for $93 (for each $100 in face value). The bond makes semiannual coupon payments of 6.5 percent.

Option 2

A blue-chip corporate bond is currently selling for $97 (for each $100 in face value), and pays semiannual coupons of 4 percent.

Option 3

A zero-coupon bond issued by the Province of Saskatchewan is currently available for a price of $86 (for each $100 in face value).

All bonds mature in five years, and you have decided that you will purchase only one option and hold that bond to maturity.

a) What will your annual return be from each investment option?

b) How much would you be willing to pay for each bond if you demanded a 7.5 percent annual return? A 10 percent return?

c) If market rates remain unchanged, what will the price of each bond be in 18 months? (Assume you are buying on Jan.1.)

d) If required market returns are 1 percent higher in two years and you decide to sell at that time, what is your total return? Your investment yield?

e) Which of the bonds would you pick and why?

S&P Problem

1. **Bond Rating**   Look up Biomira Inc. (BIOM), Nortel Networks Corp. (NT), Alcan Inc. (AL), and Rogers Communications (RG). For each company, follow the "Financial Highlights" link and find the bond rating. Which companies have an investment grade rating? Which companies are rated below investment grade? Are any unrated? When you find the credit rating for one of the companies, click on the "S&P Issuer Credit Rating" link. What are the three considerations listed that Standard & Poor's uses to issue a credit rating?

Internet Application Questions

1. The bond spread refers to the difference in yields between two bonds. Usually, the lower yielding bond is a risk-free bond such as a Government of Canada bond with equivalent maturity. Go to the following website and explain why bond spreads narrow as you get closer to maturity. What does the size of the spread tell you?

   www.finpipe.com/spread.htm

2. The Bank of Canada maintains a site containing historical bond yields. Pick a short-term bond and a real return bond and compare their yields. What is your expectation of inflation for the coming year? www.bankofcanada.ca/en/bond-look.htm

3. Barclays Global Investors has recently started two new exchange traded bond funds, iG5 and iG10. Explain the advantage of investing in exchange traded bond funds relative to buying the bonds outright. www.barclaysglobal.com

4. Go to the website of the Dominion Bond Rating Service at www.dbrs.com. Use Quick Search and Ticker Lookup to find Manufacturers Life Insurance Company and look up its rating. Do the same for Loblaw and Rogers Communications Inc. Which companies are investment grade? Are any junk? Now click on Rating and Methodologies. Which are the key factors in determining ratings?

Suggested Readings

The best place to look for additional information about valuing stocks and bonds is in an investments textbook. Good ones are
  Bodie, Z., A. Kane, A. Marcus, S. Perrakis, and P. Ryan. *Investments,* 5th Canadian ed. Whitby, Ontario: McGraw-Hill Ryerson, 2005.
  Sharpe, W. F., G. J. Alexander, J. V. Bailey, D. J. Fowler, and D. Domian. *Investments,* 3rd Canadian ed. Scarborough, Ont.: Prentice-Hall Canada, 1999.

For more on duration applications see Appendix 7A and the following articles:
  Fooladi, I., and G. S. Roberts. "How Effective Are Duration-Based Bond Strategies in Canada?" *Canadian Investment Review,* Spring 1989, pp. 57–61.
  Bierwag, G. O., I. J. Fooladi, and G. S. Roberts. "Risk Management with Duration: Potential and Limitations." *Canada Journal of Administrative Sciences,* 2000.

 **ON DURATION**

Our discussion of interest rate risk and applications explains how bond managers can select bonds to enhance price volatility when interest rates are falling. In this case, we recommended buying long-term, low-coupon bonds. When they apply this advice, Canadian bond managers use *duration*—a measure of a bond's effective maturity incorporating both time to maturity and coupon rate. This Appendix explains how duration is calculated and how it is used by bond managers.

Consider a portfolio consisting of two pure discount (zero coupon) bonds. The first bond matures in one year and the second after five years. As pure discount bonds, each provides a cash flow of $100 at maturity and nothing before maturity. Assuming the interest rate is 10 percent across all maturities, the bond prices are:

Value of the one-year discount bond: $\frac{\$100}{1.10} = \$90.91$

Value of the five-year discount bond: $\frac{\$100}{(1.10)^5} = \$62.09$

Which of these bonds would produce the greater percentage capital gain if rates drop to 8 percent across all maturities? From the text discussion, we know that price volatility increases with maturity and decreases with the coupon rate. Both bonds have the same coupon rate (namely zero), so the five-year bond should produce the larger percentage gain.

To prove this, we calculate the new prices and percentage changes. The one-year bond is now priced at $92.59 and has increased in price by 1.85%.[13] The five-year bond is now priced at $68.06 for a price rise of 9.61 percent. You should be able to prove that the effect works the other way. If interest rates rise to 12 percent across maturities, the five-year bond will have the greater percentage loss.

If all bonds were pure discount bonds, time to maturity would be a precise measure of price volatility. In reality, most bonds bear coupon payments. Duration provides a measure of effective maturity that incorporates the impact of differing coupon rates.

Duration

We begin by noticing that any coupon bond is actually a combination of pure discount bonds. For example, a five-year, 10 percent coupon bond, with a face value of $100, is made up of five pure discount bonds:

1. A pure discount bond paying $10 at the end of Year 1.
2. A pure discount bond paying $10 at the end of Year 2.
3. A pure discount bond paying $10 at the end of Year 3.
4. A pure discount bond paying $10 at the end of Year 4.
5. A pure discount bond paying $110 at the end of Year 5.

Because the price volatility of a pure discount bond is determined only by its maturity, we would like to determine the average maturity of the five pure discount bonds that make up a five-year coupon bond. This leads us to the concept of duration.

We calculate average maturity in three steps for the 10 percent coupon bond:

1. Calculate present value of each payment using the bond's yield to maturity. We do this as

Year	Payment	Present Value of Payment by Discounting at 10%
1	$ 10	$ 9.091
2	10	8.264
3	10	7.513
4	10	6.830
5	110	68.302
Total		$100.000

---

13 The percentage price increase is: ($92.59 − $90.91)/$90.91 = 1.85%.

2. Express the present value of each payment in relative terms. We calculate the relative value of a single payment as the ratio of the present value of the payment to the value of the bond. The value of the bond is $100. We have

Year	Payment	Present Value of Payment	Relative value = Present Value of Payment ÷ Value of Bond
1	$ 10	$ 9.091	$9.091/$100 = 0.09091
2	10	8.264	0.08264
3	10	7.513	0.07513
4	10	6.830	0.0683
5	110	68.302	0.68302
Total		$100.000	1.00000

The bulk of the relative value, 68.302 percent, occurs at Date 5 because the principal is paid back at that time.

3. Weight the maturity of each payment by its relative value. We have

$$4.1699 \text{ years} = 1 \text{ year} \times 0.09091 + 2 \text{ years} \times 0.08264 + 3 \text{ years} \times 0.07513 + 4 \text{ years} \times 0.06830 + 5 \text{ years} \times 0.68302$$

There are many ways to calculate the average maturity of a bond. We have calculated it by weighting the maturity of each payment by the payment's present value. We find that the effective maturity of the bond is 4.1699 years. *Duration* is a commonly used word for effective maturity. Thus, the bond's duration is 4.1699 years. Note that duration is expressed in units of time.[14]

Because the five-year, 10 percent coupon bond has a duration of 4.1699 years, its percentage price fluctuations should be the same as those of a zero coupon bond with a duration of 4.1699 years.[15] It turns out that a five-year, 1 percent coupon bond has a duration of 4.8742 years. Because the 1 percent coupon bond has a higher duration than the 10 percent bond, the 1 percent coupon bond should be subject to greater price fluctuations. This is exactly what we expected.

Why does the 1 percent bond have a greater duration than the 10 percent bond, even though they both have the same five-year maturity? As mentioned earlier, duration is an average of the maturity of the bond's cash flows, weighted by the present value of each cash flow. The 1 percent coupon bond receives only $1 in each of the first four years. Thus, the weights applied to Years 1 through 4 in the duration formula will be low. Conversely, the 10 percent coupon bond receives $10 in each of the first four years. The weights applied to Years 1 through 4 in the duration formula will be higher.

In general, the percentage price changes of a bond with high duration are greater than the percentage price changes for a bond with low duration. This property is useful to investment managers who seek superior performance. These managers extend portfolio duration when rates are expected to fall and reduce duration in the face of rising rates.

Because forecasting rates consistently is almost impossible, other managers hedge their returns by setting the duration of their assets equal to the duration of liabilities. In this way, market values on both sides of the balance sheet adjust in the same direction keeping the market value of net worth constant. Duration hedging is often called portfolio immunization.

Current research on Government of Canada bond returns shows that duration is a practical way of measuring bond price volatility and an effective tool for hedging interest rate risk.

Appendix Questions and Problems

A.1 Why do portfolio managers use duration instead of term to maturity as a measure of a bond's price volatility?

---

14 Also note that we discounted each payment by the interest rate of 10 percent. This was done because we wanted to calculate the duration of the bond before a change in the interest rate occurred. After a change in the rate to say 8 or 12 percent, all three of our steps would need to reflect the new interest rate. In other words, the duration of a bond is a function of the current interest rate.

15 Actually, the relationship only exactly holds true in the case of a one-time shift in the flat yield curve, where the change in the spot rate is identical for all different maturities. But duration research finds that the error is small.

A.2   Calculate the duration of a seven-year Canada bond with a 9 percent coupon and a yield of 6 percent.

A.3   You are managing a bond portfolio following a policy of interest-rate anticipation. You think that rates have bottomed and are likely to rise. The average duration of your portfolio is 3.5 years. Which bonds are more attractive for new purchases, those with a 10-year duration or three-year duration? Explain.

bond refunding
The process of replacing all or part of an issue of outstanding bonds.

CALLABLE BONDS AND BOND REFUNDING

The process of replacing all or part of an issue of outstanding bonds is called **bond refunding**.[16] As we have discussed, most corporate debt is callable. Typically, the first step in a bond refunding is to take advantage of this feature to call the entire issue of bonds at the call price.

Why would a firm want to refund a bond issue? One reason is obvious. Suppose a firm issues long-term debt with, say, a 12 percent coupon. Sometime after the issue, interest rates decline, and the firm finds that it could pay an 8 percent coupon and raise the same amount of money. Under such circumstances, the firm may wish to refund the debt. Notice that, in this case, refunding a bond issue is just a way of refinancing a higher-interest loan with a lower-interest one.

In the following discussion, we take a brief look at several issues concerning bond refunding and the call feature. First, what is the cost to the firm of a call provision? Second, what is the value of a call provision? Third, given that the firm has issued callable bonds, when should they be refunded?[17]

The Call Provision

Common sense tells us that call provisions have value. First, almost all publicly issued bonds have such a feature. Second, a call clearly works to the advantage of the issuer. If interest rates fall and bond prices go up, the issuer has an option to buy back the bond at a bargain price.

On the other hand, all other things being equal, bondholders dislike call provisions. The reason is again obvious. If interest rates do fall, the bondholder's gain is limited because of the possibility that the bond will be called away. As a result, bondholders take the call provision into account when they buy, and they require compensation in the form of a higher coupon rate.

This is an important observation. A call provision is not free. Instead, the firm pays a higher coupon than otherwise. Whether paying this higher coupon rate is a good idea or not is the subject we turn to next.

Cost of the Call Provision

To illustrate the effect of a call feature on a bond's coupon, suppose Kraus Intercable Company intends to issue some perpetual bonds with a face value of $1,000. We stick with perpetuities because doing so greatly simplifies some of the analysis without changing the general results.

The current interest rate on such bonds is 10 percent; Kraus, therefore, sets the annual coupon at $100. Suppose there is an equal chance that by the end of the year interest rates will either:

1. Fall to 6⅔ percent. If so, the bond price will increase to $100/.067 = $1,500.

2. Increase to 20 percent. If so, the bond price will fall to $100/.20 = $500.

Notice that the bond could sell for either $500 or $1,500 with equal probability, so the expected price is $1,000.

We now consider the market price of the bond assuming it is not callable, P_{NC}. This is simply equal to the expected price of the bond next year plus the coupon, all discounted at the current 10 percent interest rate:

---

16 Our discussion focuses on refunding bonds. The analysis also applies to refunding preferred stock.

17 For a more in-depth discussion of the subjects discussed in this Appendix, see John Finnerty, Andrew J. Kalotay, and Francis X. Farrell, Jr., *The Financial Manager's Guide to Evaluating Bond Refunding Opportunities*, The Institutional Investor Series in Finance and Financial Management Association Survey and Synthesis Series (Cambridge, MA: Ballinger Publishing Company, 1988). Our discussion is based in part on Alan Kraus, "An Analysis of Call Provisions and the Corporate Refunding Decision," *Midland Corporate Finance Journal*, Spring 1983.

$$P_{NC} = [\text{First-year coupon} + \text{Expected price at the end of year}]/1.10$$
$$= [\$100 + \$1,000]/1.10$$
$$= \$1,000$$

Thus, the bond sells at par.

Now suppose the Kraus Intercable Company decides to make the issue callable. To keep things as simple as possible, we assume the bonds must be called in one year or never. To call the bonds, Kraus has to pay the $1,000 face value plus a call premium of $150 for a total of $1,150. If Kraus wants the callable bond to sell for par, what coupon, C, must be offered?

To determine the coupon, we need to calculate what the possible prices are in one year. If interest rates decline, the bond will be called, and the bondholder will get $1,150. If interest rates rise, the bond will not be called, and it will thus be worth $C/.20$. So the expected price in one year is $.50 \times (C/.20) + .50 \times (\$1,150)$. If the bond sells for par, the price, P_C, is $1,000 and we have that:

$$P_C = \$1,000 = [\text{First-year coupon} + \text{Expected price at end of year}]/1.10$$
$$= [\$C + \{.50 \times (\$C/.20) + .50 \times (\$1,150)\}]/1.10$$

If we solve this for C, we find that the coupon has to be

$$C = \$525/3.5 = \$150$$

This is substantially higher than the $100 we had before and illustrates that the call provision is not free. What is the cost of the call provision here? To answer, we can calculate what the bond would sell for if it were not callable and had a coupon of $150:

$$P_{NC} = [\text{First-year coupon} + \text{Expected price at end of year}]/1.10$$
$$= [\$150 + \{.50 \times (\$150/.20) + .50 \times (\$150/.067)\}]/1.10$$
$$= \$1,500$$

What we see is that the call provision effectively costs $500 per bond in this simple case because Kraus could have raised $1,500 per bond instead of $1,000 if the bonds were not callable.

Value of the Call Provision

We have seen what Kraus has to pay to make this bond issue callable. We now need to see what the value is to Kraus from doing so. If the value is more than $500, the call provision has a positive NPV and should be included. Otherwise, Kraus should issue non-callable bonds.

If Kraus issues a callable bond and interest rates drop to 6⅔ percent in a year, then Kraus can replace the 15 percent bond with a non-callable perpetual issue that carries a coupon of 6⅔ percent. The interest saving in this case is $150 − 66.67 = $83.33 per year every year forever (since these are perpetuities). At an interest rate of 6⅔ percent, the present value of the interest savings is $83.33/.067 = $1,250.

To do the refunding, Kraus has to pay a $150 premium, so the net present value of the refunding operation in one year is $1,250 − 150 = $1,100 per bond. However, there is only a 50 percent chance that the interest rate will drop, so we expect to get $.50 \times \$1,100 = \$550$ from refunding in one year. The current value of this amount is $550/1.1 = $500. So we conclude that the value of the call feature to Kraus is $500.

It is *not* a coincidence that the cost and the value of the call provision are identical. All this says is that the NPV of the call feature is zero; the bondholders demand a coupon that exactly compensates them for the possibility of a call.

The Refunding Issue

In our preceding example, we saw that Kraus gained $1,100 per bond from the refunding operation if the interest rate fell. We now need to decide when, in general, a firm should refund an outstanding bond issue. The answer to this question can get fairly complicated, so we stick with our simplified case for the first pass and then consider a more realistic one. In particular, we continue to assume that

1. The bonds in question are perpetuities.
2. There are no taxes.

3. There are no refunding costs other than the call premium and the refunding is instantaneous. There is no overlap period when both issues are outstanding.

4. The bonds must be called now or never.[18]

When Should Firms Refund Callable Bonds?

The following notation is useful in analyzing the refunding issue:

c_o = coupon rate on the outstanding bonds
c_N = coupon rate on the new issue, equal to the current market rate
CP = call premium per bond

We assume that the face value is $1,000 per bond. If we replace the old issue, then we save $(c_o - c_N) \times 1,000$ in interest per bond every year forever.

The current interest rate is c_N, so the present value of the interest saving is $(c_o - c_N) \times \$1,000/c_N$. It costs CP to call the bond, so the NPV[19] per bond of the refunding operation can be written simply as:

$$\text{NPV} = (c_o - c_N)/c_N \times \$1,000 - CP \qquad [7B.1]$$

With our Kraus example, the bonds were originally issued with a 15 percent coupon. The going interest rate fell to $6\frac{2}{3}$ percent, and the call premium was $150. The NPV of the refunding is:

$$
\begin{aligned}
\text{NPV} &= (c_o - c_N) \times \$1,000 - CP \\
&= (.15 - .067)/.067 \times \$1,000 - \$150 \\
&= 1.25 \times \$1,000 - \$150 \\
&= \$1,100 \text{ per bond}
\end{aligned}
$$

This is as we had before (ignoring a slight rounding error): the present value of the interest savings from calling the bond is $1,250. Subtract the call premium of $150, and you have the NPV of calling the bond of $1,100 per bond.

EXAMPLE 7B.1: Who Ya Gonna Call?

Toastdusters, Inc., has an outstanding perpetuity with a 10 percent coupon rate. This issue must be called now or never. If it is called, it will be replaced with an issue that has a coupon rate of 8 percent, equal to the current interest rate. The call premium is $200 per bond. Should refunding commence? What is the NPV of a refunding?

Assuming a $1,000 face value, the interest saving would be $100 – 80 = $20 per bond, per year, forever. The present value of this saving is $20/.08 = $250 per bond. Since the call premium is $200 per bond, refunding should commence: The NPV is $50 per bond.

EXAMPLE 7B.2: Spreadsheet-Based Refunding Framework

The Nipigon Lake Mining Company has a $20 million outstanding bond issue bearing a 16 percent coupon that it issued in 1991. The bonds mature in 2015 but are callable in 2006 for a 6 percent call premium. Nipigon Lake's investment banker has assured it that up to $30 million of new nine-year bonds maturing in 2015 can be sold carrying a 6.5 percent coupon. To eliminate timing problems with the two issues, the new bonds will be sold a month before the old bonds are to be called. Nipigon Lake would have to pay the coupons on both issues during this month but can defray some of the cost by investing the issue at 4 percent, the short-term interest rate. Flotation costs for the $20 million new issue would total $1,125,000 and Nipigon Lake's marginal tax rate is 40 percent. Construct a framework to determine whether it is in Nipigon Lake's best interest to call the previous issue.

In constructing a framework to analyze a refunding operation, there are three steps: cost of refunding, interest savings, and the NPV of the refunding operation. All work described here is illustrated in Table 7B.1.

---

18 The last of these assumptions cannot be easily eliminated. The problem is that when we call a bond in, we forever destroy the option to call it in later. Conceivably, it might be better to wait and call later in hopes of even lower interest rates. This is the same issue that we discuss in Chapter 11 when we discuss options in capital budgeting, in particular, the option to wait.

19 NPV, or net present value, is the difference between an investment's market value and its cost (see Chapter 9 for more detail).

TABLE 7B.1 BOND REFUNDING WORKSHEET

	A	B	C	D	E	F	G	H	I	J	K	L	M	N
1														
2														
3														
4									**Amount**		**Amount**	**Time**	**3.9 Percent**	
5									**Beforetax**		**Aftertax**	**Period**	**PV Factor**	**PV**
6	PV Cost of Refunding													
7		Call premium									$1,200,000	0	1	$1,200,000
8		Flotation costs on new issue									1,125,000	0	1	1,125,000
9		Tax savings on new issue flotation costs									(90,000)	1-5	4.4644	(401,792)
10		Extra interest on old issue							$ 266,667		160,000	0	1	160,000
11		Interest on short-term investment							(66,667)		(40,000)	0	1	(40,000)
12		Total aftertax investment												$2,043,208
13														
14	Interest savings for the refunded issue: t = 1 – 9													
15		Interest on old bond							3,200,000		1,920,000			
16		Interest on new bond							1,300,000		780,000			
17		Net interest savings							$1,900,000		$ 1,140,000	1-9	7.4693	$8,515,036
18														
19	NPV for refunding operation													
20		NPV = PV of interest savings – PV of cost refunding												$6,471,828
21														
22														

COST OF REFUNDING   The first step in this framework consists of calculating the call premium, the flotation costs and the related tax savings, and any extra interest that must be paid or can be earned.

$$\text{Call premium} = 0.06 \times (\$20,000,000) = \$1,200,000$$

Note that a call premium is not a tax-deductible expense.

FLOTATION COSTS   Although flotation costs are a one-time expense, for tax purposes they are amortized over the life of the issue, or five years, whichever is less. For Nipigon Lake, flotation costs amount to $1,125,000. This results in an annual expense for the first five years after the issue.

$$\$1,125,000/5 = \$225,000$$

Flotation costs produce an annual tax shield of $90,000.

$$\$225,000 \times (0.4) = \$90,000$$

The tax savings on the flotation costs are a five-year annuity and would be discounted at the aftertax cost of debt ($6.5\%(1 - 0.40) = 3.9\%$). This amounts to a savings of $401,792. Therefore, the total flotation costs of issuing debt are:

Flotation costs	$1,125,000
PV of tax savings	−401,792
Total aftertax cost	$ 723,208

ADDITIONAL INTEREST   Extra interest paid on old issue:

$$\$20,000,000 \times (16\% \times 1/2) = \$266,667$$

After tax:

$$\$266,667 \times (1 - .40) = \$160,000$$

$$\$20,000,000 \times (4\% \times 1/12) = \$66,667$$

Aftertax

$$\$66,667 \times (1 - .40) = \$40,000$$

The total additional interest is:

Extra interest paid	$160,000
Extra interest earned	−40,000
Total additional interest	$120,000

These three items amount to a total aftertax investment of:

Call premium	$1,200,000
Flotation costs	723,208
Additional interest	120,000
Total investment	$2,043,208

INTEREST SAVINGS ON NEW ISSUE

Interest on old bond = $20,000,000 × 16% = $3,200,000

Interest on new bond = $20,000,000 × 6.5% = $1,300,000

Annual savings = $1,900,000

Aftertax savings = $1,900,000 × (1 − .40) = $1,140,000

PV of annual savings over nine years = $1,140,000 × 7.4693 = $8,515,036

NPV FOR THE REFUNDING OPERATION

Interest savings	$8,515,036
Investment	−2,043,208
NPV	$6,471,828

Nipigon Lake can save almost $6.5 million by proceeding with a call on its old bonds. The interest rates used in this example resemble the actual interest rates during the early 1990s. The example illustrates why firms would want to include a call provision when interest rates are very high.

CANADA PLUS CALL   In our example, the Nipigon Lake Mining bond had a traditional call feature.[20] Here we illustrate how a Canada plus call would make calling the debt unattractive. Suppose, that when the bonds were issued in 1991, Nipigon debt carried a yield 75 basis points above comparable Canadas. To set up a Canada plus call, Nipigon agrees in 1991 to compensate investors based on a yield of Canada plus 75 basis points if the bonds are ever called.

In our example, by 2006, rates on Canadas have fallen to 5.75 percent and Nipigon could issue new 9-year debt at 6.5 percent. Given this information, we can now calculate the annual interest penalty Nipigon would have to pay to call the debt:

$$16\% - [\text{Canada} + 0.75] = 16\% - [5.75 + 0.75] = 9.5\%$$

In dollars this is 9.5 percent of $20,000,000 or $1.9 million. This $1.9 million is precisely the annual savings from calling the debt with the traditional call calculated earlier. Our example shows that, with the Canada plus call, the debt will not be called.

SHOULD FIRMS ISSUE CALLABLE BONDS?

We have seen that the NPV of the call provision at the time a bond is issued is likely to be zero. This means that whether or not the issue is callable is a matter of indifference; we get exactly what we pay for, at least on average.

A company prefers to issue callable bonds only if it places a higher value on the call option than do the bondholders. We consider three reasons a company might use a call provision:

1. Superior interest rate predictions.
2. Taxes.
3. Financial flexibility for future investment opportunities.

SUPERIOR INTEREST RATE FORECASTING   The company may prefer the call provision because it assigns a higher probability to a fall in the coupon rate it must pay than the bondholders do. For example, managers may be better informed about a potential improvement in the firm's credit rating. In this way, company insiders may know more about interest rate decreases than the bondholders.

Whether or not the companies truly know more than the creditors about future interest rates is debatable, but the point is they may think they do and thus prefer to issue callable bonds.

---

20 Our discussion of the Canada plus call draws on D. J. Fowler, A. Kaplan, and W. A. Mackenzie, "A Note on Call Premiums on U.S. and Canadian Corporate Debt," York University Working Paper, April 1995.

TAXES   Call provisions may have tax advantages to both bondholders and the company. This is true if the bondholder is taxed at a lower rate than the company.

We have seen that callable bonds have higher rates than non-callable bonds. Because the coupons are a deductible interest expense to the corporation, if the corporate tax rate is higher than that of the individual holder, the corporation gains more in interest savings than the bondholders lose in extra taxes. Effectively, CRA pays for a part of the call provision in reduced tax revenues.

FUTURE INVESTMENT OPPORTUNITIES   As we have seen, bond indentures contain protective covenants that restrict a company's investment opportunities. For example, protective covenants may limit the company's ability to acquire another company or to sell certain assets (for example, a division of the company). If the covenants are sufficiently restrictive, the cost to the shareholders in lost net present value can be large.

If bonds are callable, though, by paying the call premium, the company can buy back the bonds and take advantage of a superior investment opportunity.

CONCEPT QUESTIONS

1. Why might a corporation call in a bond issue? What is this action called?

2. What is the effect on a bond's coupon rate from including a call provision? Why?

3. Why does a Canada plus call effectively make calling debt unattractive?

Appendix Review Problems and Self-Test

B.1 **Call Provisions and Bond Values**   Timberlake Industries has decided to float a perpetual bond issue. The coupon will be 8 percent (the current interest rate). In one year, there is an even chance that interest rates will be 5 percent or 20 percent. What will the market value of the bonds be if they are non-callable, if they are callable at par plus $80?

B.2 **Call Provisions and Coupon Rates**   If the Timberlake bond in Problem C.1 is callable and sells for par, what is the coupon, C? What is the cost of the call provision in this case?

Answers to Appendix Self-Test Problems

B.1 If the bond is not callable, in one year it will be worth either $80/.05 = $1,600 or $80/.2 = $400. The expected price is $1,000. The PV of the $1,000 and the first $80 coupon is $1,080/1.08 = $1,000, so the bond will sell for par.

If the bond is callable, either it will be called at $1,080 (if rates fall to 5 percent) or it will sell for $400. The expected value is ($1,080 + 400)/2 = $740. The PV is ($740 + 80)/1.08 = $759.26.

B.2 In one year, the bond either will be worth $C/.20$ or it will be called for $1,080. If the bond sells for par, then:

$$\$1,000 = [C + .5(C/.20) + .5(\$1,080)]/1.08$$
$$\$540 = [C + .5(C/.20)]$$
$$= 3.5C$$

The coupon, C, must be $540/3.5 = $154.29.

If the bond had a coupon of $154.29 and was not callable, in one year it would be worth either $154.29/.05 = $3,085.71 or $154.29/.20 = $771.43. There is an even chance of either of these, so we expect a value of $1,928.57. The bond would sell today for ($1,928.57 + 154.29)/1.08 = $1,928.57. The cost of the call provision is thus $928.57. This is quite a bit, but, as we see in a later chapter, this stems from the fact that interest rates are quite volatile in this example.

Appendix Questions and Problems

Basic
(Questions
B.1–B.8)

B.1 **NPV and Refunding** Atfan, Inc., has an outstanding callable perpetuity bond with a 9.5 percent coupon rate. This issue must be called now or never. If it is called, it will be replaced with an issue that has a coupon rate of 6.5 percent, equal to the current interest rate. The call premium is $175 per bond. Should Atfan refund its outstanding bond issue? What is the NPV of the refunding?

B.2 **Interest Rates and Refunding** In the previous problem, what would the current rate have to be for Atfan to be indifferent to refunding or not?

B.3 **Setting the Coupon Rate** Supersoft Corporation has decided to finance its expansion with a perpetual bond issue. The current interest rate is 7.5 percent. In one year, there is an equal chance that interest rates will either be 6.5 percent or 8.5 percent. If this is a callable bond issue and the call premium to be paid is $74 per bond, what does the coupon rate have to be for the bond to sell at par?

B.4 **Setting the Call Premium** In the previous problem, suppose you want to set the coupon rate on this issue at 7 percent. What would the call premium have to be for the bond to sell at par?

B.5 **Pricing Callable Bonds** In the previous problem, suppose you set the coupon rate at 7 percent and the call premium at $120. What will the issue sell for?

B.6 **Call Provision Costs** In the previous problem, what is the cost of the call provision to the firm?

B.7 **Callable Bonds** A callable bond has been issued with a face value of $1,000 and will mature in 20 years. The current interest rate is 6.5 percent, but there is a 25 percent chance that rates will be raised to 7.75 percent in two years and a 75 percent chance that it will remain the same.

  a. What is the coupon rate if the call premium is $68 per bond?

  b. How does the coupon rate change if there is a 20 percent chance that the interest rate will be 7.75 percent in two years, a 40 percent chance that it will be 7 percent in two years, and a 40 percent chance that it will remain the same?

B.8 **NPV and Refunding** Your company has an outstanding perpetual bond issue with a face value of $53 million and a coupon rate of 8.65 percent. The bonds are callable at par plus a $130 call premium per bond; in addition, any new bond issues of your firm will incur fixed costs of $9 million. The bonds must be called now or never. What would the current interest rate have to be for you to be indifferent to a refunding operation?

B.9 **NPV and Maturity** In the previous problem, suppose that the bonds in question make annual coupon payments and have 14 years to maturity, rather than being perpetual bonds. If current rates are 7.55 percent and the bonds must be called now or never, what is the NPV of the refunding operation?

Challenge
(Questions
B.10–B.11)

B.10 **NPV and Maturity** In Problem B.8, what would the current interest rate have to be for you to be indifferent to a refunding operation?

B.11 **Refunding and Taxes** In Problem B.1, suppose Atfan is in the 39 percent tax bracket. The call premium is a tax-deductible business expense, as is interest paid on the old and new bonds. What is the NPV of the refunding? Note that the appropriate discount rate will be the aftertax borrowing rate. What is the net result of including tax effects on the NPV of refunding operations? Explain.

CHAPTER 8

Stock Valuation

Telus Corp. is one of Canada's leading telecommuni- cation companies. Effective January 2006, Telus's dividend increased to $0.275 per share quarterly, or $1.10 per share annually. In contrast, Research In Motion, a leading designer, manufacturer and marketer of wireless solutions, has never paid a dividend. Even so, in May 2006, a share of Research In Motion traded on the TSX for $83, while a share of Telus Corp. was worth $48. How might investors decide on these valuations? While there are many factors that drive share prices, dividends are one of the most frequently analyzed. This chapter explores dividends, stock values, and the connection between them.

www.telus.com
www.rim.net

IN OUR PREVIOUS CHAPTER, we introduced you to bonds and bond valuation. In this chapter, we turn to the other major source of financing for corporations, common and pre- ferred stock. We first describe the cash flows associated with a share of stock and then go on to develop a very famous result, the dividend growth model. From there, we move on to examine various important features of common and preferred stock, focusing on shareholder rights. We close out the chapter with a discussion of how shares of stock are traded and how stock prices and other important information are reported in the financial press.

 **8.1**

COMMON STOCK VALUATION

A share of common stock is more difficult to value in practice than a bond for at least three rea- sons: First, not even the promised cash flows are known in advance. Second, the life of the invest- ment is essentially forever because common stock has no maturity. Third, there is no way to eas- ily observe the rate of return that the market requires. Nonetheless, there are cases under which we can come up with the present value of the future cash flows for a share of stock and thus deter- mine its value.

Common Stock Cash Flows

Imagine that you are buying a share of stock today. You plan to sell the stock in one year. You somehow know that the stock will be worth $70 at that time. You predict that the stock will also pay a $10 per share dividend at the end of the year. If you require a 25 percent return on your investment, what is the most you would pay for the stock? In other words, what is the present value of the $10 dividend along with the $70 ending value at 25 percent?

If you buy the stock today and sell it at the end of the year, you will have a total of $80 in cash. At 25 percent:

Present value = ($10 + 70)/1.25 = $64

Therefore, $64 is the value you would assign to the stock today.

More generally, let P_0 be the current price of the stock, and define P_1 to be the price in one period. If D_1 is the cash dividend paid at the end of the period, then:

$$P_0 = (D_1 + P_1)/(1 + r) \qquad\qquad [8.1]$$

where r is the required return in the market on this investment.

Notice that we really haven't said much so far. If we wanted to determine the value of a share of stock today (P_0), we would have to come up with its value in one year (P_1). This is even harder to do in the first place, so we've only made the problem more complicated.[1]

What is the price in one period, P_1? We don't know in general. Instead, suppose that we somehow knew the price in two periods, P_2. Given a predicted dividend in two periods, D_2, the stock price in one period would be:

$$P_1 = (D_2 + P_2)/(1 + r)$$

If we were to substitute this expression for P_1 into our expression for P_0, we would have:

$$P_0 = \frac{D_1 + P_1}{1 + r} = \frac{D_1 + \dfrac{D_2 + P_2}{1 + r}}{1 + r}$$

$$= \frac{D_1}{(1 + r)^1} + \frac{D_2}{(1 + r)^2} + \frac{P_2}{(1 + r)^2}$$

Now we need to get a price in two periods. We don't know this either, so we can procrastinate again and write:

$$P_2 = (D_3 + P_3)/(1 + r)$$

If we substitute this back in for P_2, we would have:

$$P_0 = \frac{D_1}{(1 + r)^1} + \frac{D_2}{(1 + r)^2} + \frac{P_2}{(1 + r)^2}$$

$$= \frac{D_1}{(1 + r)^1} + \frac{D_2}{(1 + r)^2} + \frac{\dfrac{D_3 + P_3}{1 + r}}{(1 + r)^2}$$

$$= \frac{D_1}{(1 + r)^1} + \frac{D_2}{(1 + r)^2} + \frac{D_3}{(1 + r)^3} + \frac{P_3}{(1 + r)^3}$$

Notice that we can push the problem of coming up with the stock price off into the future forever. Importantly, no matter what the stock price is, the present value is essentially zero if we push it far enough away.[2] What we would be left with is the result that the current price of the stock can be written as the present value of the dividends beginning in one period and extending out forever:

$$P_0 = \frac{D_1}{(1 + r)^1} + \frac{D_2}{(1 + r)^2} + \frac{D_3}{(1 + r)^3} + \frac{D_4}{(1 + r)^4} + \frac{D_5}{(1 + r)^5} + \dots$$

We have illustrated here that the price of the stock today is equal to the present value of all the future dividends. How many future dividends are there? In principle, there can be an infinite number. This means we still can't compute a value for the stock because we would have to forecast an infinite number of dividends and then discount them all. In the next section, we consider some special cases where we can get around this problem.

---

1 The only assumption we make about the stock price is that it is a finite number no matter how far away we push it. It can be extremely large, just not infinitely so. Since no one has ever observed an infinite stock price, this assumption is plausible.

2 One way of solving this problem is the "bigger fool" approach, which asks how much a bigger fool (than you) would pay for the stock. This approach has considerable appeal in explaining speculative bubbles that occur when prices rise to irrational levels and then fall when the bubble bursts. Our discussion focuses on more ordinary times when prices are based on rational factors.

EXAMPLE 8.1: Growth Stock

You might be wondering about shares of stock in companies that currently pay no dividends. Small, growing companies frequently plow back everything and thus pay no dividends. Many such companies are in mining, oil and gas, and high tech. For example, at the time of writing, Tim Hortons was trading at $32 per share and paid no dividends. Are such shares actually worth nothing? When we say that the value of the stock is equal to the present value of the future dividends, we don't rule out the possibility that some number of those dividends are zero. They just can't all be zero.

Imagine a hypothetical company that had a provision in its corporate charter prohibiting the paying of dividends now or ever. The corporation never borrows any money, never pays out any money to shareholders in any form whatsoever, and never sells any assets. Such a corporation couldn't really exist because the shareholders wouldn't stand for it. However, the shareholders could always vote to amend the charter if they wanted to. If it did exist, however, what would the stock be worth?

The stock is worth absolutely nothing. Such a company is a financial black hole. Money goes in, but nothing valuable ever comes out. Because nobody would ever get any return on this investment, the investment has no value. This example is a little absurd, but it illustrates that when we speak of companies that don't pay dividends, what we really mean is that they are not currently paying dividends.

www.timhortons.com

Common Stock Valuation: Some Special Cases

There are a few very useful special circumstances where we can come up with a value for the stock. What we have to do is make some simplifying assumptions about the pattern of future dividends. The three cases we consider are (1) the dividend has a zero growth rate, (2) the dividend grows at a constant rate, and (3) the dividend grows at a constant rate after some length of time. We consider each of these separately.[3]

ZERO GROWTH   The case of zero growth is one we've already seen. A share of common stock in a company with a constant dividend is much like a share of preferred stock. From Example 6.8 in Chapter 6, we know that the dividend on a share of fixed-rate preferred stock has zero growth and thus is constant through time. For a zero growth share of common stock, this implies that:

$$D_1 = D_2 = D_3 = D = \text{constant}$$

So, the value of the stock is:

$$P_0 = \frac{D}{(1+r)^1} + \frac{D}{(1+r)^2} + \frac{D}{(1+r)^3} + \frac{D}{(1+r)^4} + \frac{D}{(1+r)^5} + \dots$$

Since the dividend is always the same, the stock can be viewed as an ordinary perpetuity with a cash flow equal to D every period. The per-share value is thus given by:

$$P_0 = D/r \qquad [8.2]$$

where r is the required return.

For example, suppose the Eastcoast Energy Company has a policy of paying a $10 per share dividend every year. If this policy is to be continued indefinitely, what is the value of a share of stock if the required return is 20 percent? As it amounts to an ordinary perpetuity, the stock is worth $10/.20 = $50 per share.

CONSTANT GROWTH   Suppose we knew that the dividend for some company always grows at a steady rate. Call this growth rate g. If we let D_0 be the dividend just paid, then the next dividend, D_1 is:

$$D_1 = D_0 \times (1 + g)$$

The dividend in two periods is:

$$\begin{aligned} D_2 &= D_1 \times (1 + g) \\ &= [D_0 \times (1 + g)] \times (1 + g) \\ &= D_0 \times (1 + g)^2 \end{aligned}$$

---

3 Growth simply compares dollar dividends over time. In Chapter 12 we examine inflation and growth.

We could repeat this process to come up with the dividend at any point in the future. In general, from our discussion of compound growth in the previous chapter, we know that the dividend t periods in the future, D_t, is given by:

$$D_t = D_0 \times (1 + g)^t$$

As we showed in Chapter 6, a stock with dividends that grow a constant rate forever is an example of a growing perpetuity. This will come in handy shortly when we are ready to find the present value of this dividend stream.

The assumption of steady dividend growth might strike you as peculiar. Why would the dividend grow at a constant rate? The reason is that, for many companies—chartered banks, for example—steady growth in dividends is an explicit goal. Note also that by using a constant growth rate, we are simply trying to estimate the expected average growth rate over a long period of time. While we use this expected average value in our model, the actual growth rate does not have to be the same every year. This subject falls under the general heading of dividend policy, so we defer further discussion of it to Chapter 17.

EXAMPLE 8.2: Dividend Growth Revisited

The Bank of Manitoba has just paid a dividend of $3 per share. The dividend grows at a steady rate of 8 percent per year. Based on this information, what would the dividend be in five years?

Here we have a $3 current amount that grows at 8 percent per year for five years. The future amount is thus:

$3 \times (1.08)^5 = \$3 \times 1.4693 = \$4.41$

The dividend, therefore, increases by $1.41 over the coming five years.

See the dividend discount model in action at www.dividenddiscountmodel.com

If the dividend grows at a steady rate, we have replaced the problem of forecasting an infinite number of future dividends with the problem of coming up with a single growth rate, a considerable simplification. Taking D_0 to be the dividend just paid and g to be the constant growth rate, the value of a share of stock can be written as:

$$P_0 = \frac{D_1}{(1+r)^1} + \frac{D_2}{(1+r)^2} + \frac{D_3}{(1+r)^3} + \cdots$$

$$= \frac{D_0(1+g)^1}{(1+r)^1} + \frac{D_0(1+g)^2}{(1+r)^2} + \frac{D_0(1+g)^3}{(1+r)^3} + \cdots$$

As long as the growth rate, g, is less than the discount rate, r, the present value of this series of cash flows can be written very simply using the growing perpetuity formula from Chapter 6:

$$P_0 = \frac{D_0 \times (1+g)}{r-g} = \frac{D_1}{r-g} \qquad [8.3]$$

dividend growth model
Model that determines the current price of a stock as its dividend next period, divided by the discount rate less the dividend growth rate.

This elegant result goes by a lot of different names. We call it the **dividend growth model.**[4] By any name, it is very easy to use. To illustrate, suppose D_0 is $2.30, r is 13 percent, and g is 5 percent. The price per share is:

$$P_0 = D_0 \times (1+g)/r - g)$$
$$= \$2.30 \times (1.05)/(.13 - .05)$$
$$= \$2.415/(.08)$$
$$= \$30.19$$

We can actually use the dividend growth model to get the stock price at any point in time, not just today. In general, the price of the stock as of time t is:

$$P_t = \frac{D_t \times (1+g)}{r-g} = \frac{D_{t+1}}{r-g} \qquad [8.4]$$

In our example, suppose we were interested in the price of the stock in five years, P_5. We first need the dividend at time 5, D_5. Since the dividend just paid is $2.30 and the growth rate is 5 percent per year, D_5 is:

---

4 It is often called the Gordon Model in honour of Professor Myron Gordon, University of Toronto, its best-known developer.

$$D_5 = \$2.30 \times (1.05)^5 = \$2.30 \times 1.2763 = \$2.935$$

From the dividend growth model, the price of stock in five years is:

$$P_5 = \frac{D_5 \times (1+g)}{r-g} = \frac{\$2.935 \times (1.05)}{.13-.05} = \frac{\$3.0822}{.08} = \$38.53$$

EXAMPLE 8.3: Bank of Prince Edward Island

The next dividend for the Bank of Prince Edward Island (BPEI) will be $4.00 per share. Investors require a 16 percent return on companies such as BPEI. The bank's dividend increases by 6 percent every year. Based on the dividend growth model, what is the value of BPEI stock today? What is the value in four years?

The only tricky thing here is that the next dividend, D_1, is given as $4.00, so we won't multiply this by $(1 + g)$. With this in mind, the price per share is given by:

$$P_0 = D_1/(r-g)$$
$$= \$4.00/(.16 - .06)$$
$$= \$4.00/(.10)$$
$$= \$40.00$$

Because we already have the dividend in one year, the dividend in four years is equal to $D_1 \times (1 + g)^3 = \$4.00 \times (1.06)^3 = \$4.764$. The price in four years is therefore:

$$P_4 = [D_4 \times (1 + g)]/(r-g)$$
$$= [\$4.764 \times 1.06]/(.16 - .06)$$
$$= \$5.05/(.10)$$
$$= \$50.50$$

Notice in this example that P_4 is equal to $P_0 \times (1 + g)^4$:

$$P_4 = \$50.50 = \$40.00 \times (1.06)^4 = P_0 \times (1 + g)^4$$

To see why this is so, notice that:

$$P_4 = D_5/(r-g)$$

However, D_5 is just equal to $D_1 \times (1 + g)^4$, so we can write P_4 as:

$$P_4 = D_1 \times (1 + g)^4/(r-g)$$
$$= \{D_1/(r-g)\} \times (1 + g)^4$$
$$= P_0 \times (1 + g)^4$$

This last example illustrates that the dividend growth model has the implicit assumption that the stock price will grow at the same constant rate as the dividend. This really isn't too surprising. What it tells us is that if the cash flows on an investment grow at a constant rate through time, so does the value of that investment.

You might wonder what would happen with the dividend growth model if the growth rate, g, were greater than the discount rate, r. It looks like we would get a negative stock price because $r - g$ would be less than zero. This is not what would happen.

Instead, if the constant growth rate exceeds the discount rate, the stock price is infinitely large. Why? When the growth rate is bigger than the discount rate, the present value of the dividends keeps on getting bigger and bigger. Essentially, the same is true if the growth rate and the discount rate are equal. In both cases, the simplification that allows us to replace the infinite stream of dividends with the dividend growth model is "illegal," so the answers we get from the dividend growth model are nonsense unless the growth rate is less than the discount rate.

NON-CONSTANT GROWTH   The last case we consider is non-constant growth. The main reason to consider this is to allow for supernormal growth rates over some finite length of time. As we discussed earlier, the growth rate cannot exceed the required return indefinitely, but it certainly could do so for some number of years. To avoid the problem of having to forecast and discount an infinite number of dividends, we require that the dividends start growing at a constant rate sometime in the future.[5]

To give a simple example of non-constant growth, consider a company that is not currently paying dividends. You predict that in five years, the company will pay a dividend for the first time. The dividend will be $.50 per share. You expect this dividend to grow at 10 percent indefinitely. The required return on companies such as this one is 20 percent. What is the price of the stock today?

To see what the stock is worth today, we find out what it will be worth once dividends are paid. We can then calculate the present value of that future price to get today's price. The first dividend

---

5 This type of analysis can also be done to take into account negative growth rates, which are really just a special case of supernormal growth.

will be paid in five years, and the dividend will grow steadily from then on. Using the dividend growth model, the price in four years will be:

$$P_4 = D_5/(r - g)$$
$$= \$.50/(.20 - .10)$$
$$= \$5.00$$

If the stock will be worth $5.00 in four years, we can get the current value by discounting this back four years at 20 percent:

$$P_0 = \$5.00/(1.20)^4 = \$5.00/2.0736 = \$2.41$$

The stock is therefore worth $2.41 today.

The problem of non-constant growth is only slightly more complicated if the dividends are not zero for the first several years. For example, suppose you have come up with the following dividend forecasts for the next three years:

Year	Expected Dividend
1	$1.00
2	2.00
3	2.50

After the third year, the dividend will grow at a constant rate of 5 percent per year. The required return is 10 percent. What is the value of the stock today?

As always, the value of the stock is the present value of all the future dividends. To calculate this present value, we begin by computing the present value of the stock price three years down the road just as we did previously. We then add in the present value of the dividends paid between now and then. So, the price in three years is:

$$P_3 = D_3 \times (1 + g)/(r - g)$$
$$= \$2.50 \times (1.05)/(.10 - .05)$$
$$= \$52.50$$

We can now calculate the total value of the stock as the present value of the first three dividends plus the present value of the price at time 3, P_3:

$$P_0 = D_1/(1 + r)^1 + D_2/(1 + r)^2 + D_3/(1 + r)^3 + P_3/(1 + r)^3$$
$$= \$1.00/1.10 + \$2.00/1.10^2 + \$2.50/1.10^3 + \$52.50/1.10^3$$
$$= \$0.91 + 1.65 + 1.88 + 39.44$$
$$= \$43.88$$

Thus, the value of the stock today is $43.88.

EXAMPLE 8.4: Supernormal Growth

Genetic Engineering, Ltd., has been growing at a phenomenal rate of 30 percent per year because of its rapid expansion and explosive sales. You believe that this growth rate will last for three more years and then drop to 10 percent per year. If the growth rate remains at 10 percent indefinitely, what is the total value of the stock? Total dividends just paid were $5 million, and the required return is 20 percent.

Genetic Engineering is an example of supernormal growth. It is unlikely that 30 percent growth can be sustained for any extended time. To value the equity in this company, we calculate the total dividends over the supernormal growth period:

Year	Total Dividends (in $ millions)
1	$5.00 × (1.3) = $ 6.500
2	6.50 × (1.3) = 8.450
3	8.45 × (1.3) = 10.985

The price at time 3 can be calculated as:

$$P_3 = D_3 \times (1 + g)/(r - g)$$

where g is the long-run growth rate. So we have:

$$P_3 = \$10.985 \times (1.10)/(.20 - .10) = \$120.835$$

To determine the value today, we need the present value of this amount plus the present value of the total dividends:

$$P_0 = D_1/(1 + r)^1 + D_2/(1 + r)^2 + D_3/(1 + r)^3 + P_3/(1 + r)^3$$
$$= \$6.50/1.20 + \$8.45/1.20^2 + \$10.985/1.20^3 + \$120.835/1.20^3$$
$$= \$5.42 + 5.87 + 6.36 + 69.93$$
$$= \$87.58$$

The total value of the stock today is thus $87.58 million. If there were, for example, 20 million shares, the stock would be worth $87.58/20 = $4.38 per share.

Changing the Growth Rate

When investment analysts use the dividend valuation model, they generally consider a range of growth scenarios. The way to do this is to set up the model on a spreadsheet and vary the inputs. For example, in our original analysis of Genetic Engineering, Ltd., we chose numbers for the inputs as shown in the baseline scenario in the following table. The model calculated the price per share as $4.38. The table shows two other possible scenarios. In the best case, the supernormal growth rate is 40 percent and continues for five instead of three years. Starting in Year 6, the normal growth rate is higher at 13 percent. In the worst case, normal growth starts immediately and there is no supernormal growth spurt. The required rate of return is 20 percent in all three cases.

The table shows that the model-calculated price is very sensitive to the inputs. In the worst case, the model price drops to $2.50; in the best case, it climbs to $8.14. Of course, there are many other scenarios we could consider with our spreadsheet. For example, many investment analysts use a three-stage scenario with two supernormal and one normal growth rate. To illustrate, we could input a supernormal growth rate of 40 percent for three years, a second supernormal growth rate of 20 percent for two years, and then a normal growth rate of 10 percent indefinitely.

	Baseline	Best Case	Worst Case
Supernormal growth rate	30%	40%	n/a
Supernormal growth period	3 years	5 years	0 years
Normal growth rate	10%	13%	10%
Required rate of return	20%	20%	20%
Model calculated price	$4.38	$8.14	$2.50

The number of possible scenarios is infinite but we have done enough to show that the value of a stock depends greatly on expected growth rates and how long they last. Our examples also show that valuing stocks with the dividend growth model is far from an exact science. In fact, the model has come in for criticism based on a hindsight exercise comparing the present value of dividends against market prices for broad stock indexes. Critics raise two points. First, in the late 1990s, the level of the market, and especially tech stocks, was far higher than the present value of expected dividends. Second, market prices are far more volatile than the present value of dividends.

These criticisms suggest that, while it is a useful analytical tool, the dividend growth model is not the last word on stock valuation. We look at alternative valuation techniques later in the chapter.

Components of the Required Return

Thus far, we have taken the required return or discount rate, r, as given. We have quite a bit to say on this subject in Chapters 12 and 13. For now, we want to examine the implications of the dividend growth model for this required return. Earlier, we calculated P_0 as:

$$P_0 = D_1/(r - g)$$

If we rearrange this to solve for r, we get:

$$(r - g) = D_1/P_0$$
$$r = D_1/P_0 + g$$

[8.5]

dividend yield
A stock's cash dividend divided by its current price.

This tells us that the total return, r, has two components: The first of these, D_1/P_0, is called the **dividend yield.** Because this is calculated as the expected cash dividend divided by the current price, it is conceptually similar to the current yield on a bond.

The second part of the total return is the growth rate, g. We know that the dividend growth rate is also the rate at which the stock price grows (see Example 8.3). Thus, this growth rate can be interpreted as the **capital gains yield,** that is, the rate at which the value of the investment grows.

capital gains yield
The dividend growth rate or the rate at which the value of an investment grows.

To illustrate the components of the required return, suppose we observe a stock selling for $20 per share. The next dividend will be $1 per share. You think that the dividend will grow by 10 percent more or less indefinitely. What return does this stock offer you if this is correct?

The dividend growth model calculates total return as:

r = Dividend yield + Capital gains yield
$r = D_1/P_0 + g$

The total return works out to be:

$r = \$1/\$20 + 10\%$
$= 5\% + 10\%$
$= 15\%$

This stock, therefore, has a return of 15 percent.

We can verify this answer by calculating the price in one year, P_1, using 15 percent as the required return. Based on the dividend growth model, this price is:

$P_1 = D_1 \times (1 + g)/(r - g)$
$= \$1 \times (1.10)/(.15 - .10)$
$= \$1.1/.05$
$= \$22$

Notice that this $22 is $20 × (1.1), so the stock price has grown by 10 percent as it should. If you pay $20 for the stock today, you would get a $1 dividend at the end of the year and have a $22 − 20 = $2 gain. Your dividend yield is thus $1/$20 = 5%. Your capital gains yield is $2/$20 − 10%, so your total return would be 5% + 10% = 15%. Our discussion of stock valuation is summarized in Table 8.1.

It is important to note that dividends and dividend growth, although commonly used to estimate share value, are not the only factors that drive share prices. Factors like industry life cycle, the business cycle, supply or demand shocks (e.g., oil price spikes), liquidation value of the firm,

TABLE 8.1
Summary of stock
valuation

The General Case

In general, the price today of a share of stock, P_0, is the present value of all of its future dividends, $D_1, D_2, D_3 \ldots$

$$P_0 = \frac{D_1}{(1 + r)^1} + \frac{D_2}{(1 + r)^2} + \frac{D_3}{(1 + r)^3} + \cdots$$

where r is the required return.

Constant Growth Case

If the dividend grows at a steady rate, g, the price can be written as:

$$P_0 = \frac{D_1}{(r - g)}$$

This result is called the *dividend growth model*.

Supernormal Growth

If the dividend grows steadily after t periods, the price can be written as:

$$P_0 = \frac{D_1}{(1 + r)^1} + \frac{D_2}{(1 + r)^2} + \cdots + \frac{D_t}{(1 + r)^t} + \frac{P_t}{(1 + r)^t}$$

where

$$P_t = \frac{D_t \times (1 + g)}{(r - g)}$$

The Required Return

The required return, r, can be written as the sum of two things:

$$R = D_1/P_0 + g$$

where D_1/P_0 is the dividend yield and g is the *capital gains yield* (which is the same thing as the growth rate in the dividends for the steady growth case).

replacement cost of the firm's assets, and investor psychology are examples of other potentially important price drivers.[6]

common stock
Equity without priority for dividends or in bankruptcy.

COMMON STOCK FEATURES

The term **common stock** means different things to different people, but it is usually applied to stock that has no special preference either in dividends or in bankruptcy.

Shareholders' Rights

The conceptual structure of the corporation assumes that shareholders elect directors who, in turn, hire management to carry out their directives. Shareholders, therefore, control the corporation through their right to elect the directors. Generally, only shareholders have this right.

Directors are elected each year at an annual meeting. Despite the exceptions we discuss later, the general idea is "one share, one vote" (not one shareholder, one vote). Corporate democracy is thus very different from our political democracy. With corporate democracy, the "golden rule" prevails absolutely.[7] Large institutional investors, like the Caisse de depot and Ontario Teachers' Pension Plan Board, take an active interest in exercising their votes to influence the corporate governance practices of the companies in their portfolios. For example, they are concerned that the elections for directors allow large investors to have an independent voice on the board.[8]

Directors are elected at an annual shareholders' meeting by a vote of the holders of a majority of shares present and entitled to vote. However, the exact mechanism for electing directors differs across companies. The two most important methods are cumulative voting and straight voting; we discuss these in Appendix 8A.

Recent concern over company performance, including issues like managerial compensation and option packages, has renewed focus on shareholder activism. While shareholders often vote for the recommendations of management and/or the board of directors, concerned shareholders could also enter into a proxy contest. A proxy contest is essentially a fight for shareholder votes between parties attempting to control the corporation. For example, in April 2006, a dissident group of directors at Vancouver-based AnorMed Inc. were successful in taking over the board of directors. The dissident shareholder group initiated the takeover because they were concerned that the previous board of directors was not providing adequate guidance to management and was therefore failing to create shareholder value.

OTHER RIGHTS The value of a share of common stock in a corporation is directly related to the general rights of shareholders. In addition to the right to vote for directors, shareholders usually have the following rights:

1. The right to share proportionally in dividends paid.
2. The right to share proportionally in assets remaining after liabilities have been paid in a liquidation.
3. The right to vote on stockholder matters of great importance, such as a merger, usually done at the annual meeting or a special meeting.

In addition, stockholders sometimes have the right to share proportionally in any new stock sold. This is called the *preemptive right*. Essentially, a preemptive right means that a company wishing to sell stock must first offer it to the existing stockholders before offering it to the general public. The purpose is to give a stockholder the opportunity to protect his or her proportionate ownership in the corporation.

---

6 A readable article on behavioural finance is: Robert J. Shiller, 2003. "From Efficient Markets Theory to Behavioral Finance," *Journal of Economic Perspectives,* American Economic Association, vol. 17(1), pages 83–104, Winter.

7 The golden rule: Whosoever has the gold makes the rules.

8 A good shareholder resource is the Canadian Coalition for Good Governance (*www.ccgg.ca*). You can find current examples of governance policies at *www.lacaisse.com* and *www.otpp.com*.

Dividends

dividends
Return on capital of corporation paid by company to shareholders in either cash or stock.

A distinctive feature of corporations is that they have shares of stock on which they are authorized by their bylaws to pay dividends to their shareholders. **Dividends** paid to shareholders represent a return on the capital directly or indirectly contributed to the corporation by the shareholders. The payment of dividends is at the discretion of the board of directors.

Some important characteristics of dividends include the following:

1. Unless a dividend is declared by the board of directors of a corporation, it is not a liability of the corporation. A corporation cannot default on an undeclared dividend. As a consequence, corporations cannot become bankrupt because of nonpayment of dividends. The amount of the dividend and even whether it is paid are decisions based on the business judgement of the board of directors.

2. The payment of dividends by the corporation is not a business expense. Dividends are not deductible for corporate tax purposes. In short, dividends are paid out of aftertax profits of the corporation.

3. Dividends received by individual shareholders are partially sheltered by a dividend tax credit discussed in detail in Chapter 2. Corporations that own stock in other corporations are permitted to exclude 100 percent of the dividend amounts they receive from taxable Canadian corporations. The purpose of this provision is to avoid the double taxation of dividends.

Classes of Stock

www.canadiantire.com

Some firms have more than one class of common stock.[9] Often, the classes are created with unequal voting rights. Canadian Tire Corporation, for example, has two classes of common stock both publicly traded. The voting common stock was distributed as follows in 1990: 61 percent to three offspring of the company founder and the rest divided among Canadian Tire dealers, pension funds, and the general public. The non-voting, Canadian Tire A stock was more widely held.

There are many other Canadian corporations with restricted (non-voting) stock. Such stock made up around 15 percent of the market values of TSX listed shares at the end of 1989. Non-voting shares must receive dividends no lower than dividends on voting shares. Some companies pay a higher dividend on the non-voting shares. In 1990, Canadian Tire paid $.40 per share on both classes of stock.

A primary reason for creating dual classes of stock has to do with control of the firm. If such stock exists, management of a firm can raise equity capital by issuing non-voting or limited-voting stock while maintaining control.

Because it is only necessary to own 51 percent of the voting stock to control a company, non-voting shareholders could be left out in the cold in the event of a takeover bid for the company. To protect the non-voting shareholders, most companies have a "coattail" provision giving non-voting shareholders either the right to vote or to convert their shares into voting shares that can be tendered to the takeover bid. In the Canadian Tire case, all Class A shareholders become entitled to vote and the coattail provision is triggered if a bid is made for "all or substantially all" of the voting shares.

The effectiveness of the coattail provision was tested in 1986 when the Canadian Tire Dealers Association offered to buy 49 percent of the voting shares from the founding Billes family. In the absence of protection, the non-voting shareholders stood to lose substantially. The dealers bid at a large premium for the voting shares that were trading at $40 before the bid. The non-voting shares were priced at $14. Further, since the dealers were the principal buyers of Canadian Tire products, control of the company would have allowed them to adjust prices to benefit themselves over the non-voting shareholders.

The key question was whether the bid triggered the coattail. The dealers and the Billes family argued that the offer was for 49 percent of the stock not for "all or substantially all" of the voting

---

9 This section draws heavily on Elizabeth Maynes, Chris Robinson, and Alan White, "How Much Is a Share Vote Worth?" *Canadian Investment Review*, Spring 1990, pp. 49–56.

shares. In the end, the Ontario Securities Commission ruled that the offer was unfair to the holders of the A shares and its view was upheld in two court appeals.

As a result, investors believe that coattails have protective value but remain skeptical that they afford complete protection. In December 2002, Canadian Tire voting stock traded at a substantial premium over non-voting stock.

CONCEPT QUESTIONS

1. What is a company's book value?

2. What rights do shareholders have?

3. Why do some companies have two classes of stock?

preferred stock
Stock with dividend priority over common stock, normally with a fixed dividend rate, often without voting rights.

www.bankofmontreal.com

PREFERRED STOCK FEATURES

Preferred stock differs from common stock because it has preference over common stock in the payment of dividends and in the distribution of corporation assets in the event of liquidation. Preference means the holders of the preferred shares must receive a dividend (in the case of an ongoing firm) before holders of common shares are entitled to anything. If the firm is liquidated, preferred shareholders rank behind all creditors but ahead of common stockholders.

Preferred stock is a form of equity from a legal, tax, and regulatory standpoint. In the last decade, chartered banks were important issuers of preferred stock as they moved to meet higher capital requirements. Importantly, however, holders of preferred stock generally have no voting privileges.

Stated Value

Preferred shares have a stated liquidating value. The cash dividend is described in dollars per share or as a percentage of the stated value. For example, Bank of Montreal's "$2.25" translates easily into a dividend yield of 9 percent of $25 stated value.

Cumulative and Non-Cumulative Dividends

A preferred dividend is not like interest on a bond. The board of directors may decide not to pay the dividends on preferred shares, and their decision may have nothing to do with the current net income of the corporation.

Dividends payable on preferred stock are either cumulative or non-cumulative; most are cumulative. If preferred dividends are cumulative and are not paid in a particular year, they are carried forward as an *arrearage*. Usually both the cumulated (past) preferred dividends plus the current preferred dividends must be paid before the common shareholders can receive anything.

Unpaid preferred dividends are not debts of the firm. Directors elected by the common shareholders can defer preferred dividends indefinitely. However, in such cases:

1. Common shareholders must also forgo dividends.
2. Holders of preferred shares are often granted voting and other rights if preferred dividends have not been paid for some time.

Because preferred shareholders receive no interest on the cumulated dividends, some have argued that firms have an incentive to delay paying preferred dividends.

Is Preferred Stock Really Debt?

A good case can be made that preferred stock is really debt in disguise, a kind of equity bond. Preferred shareholders receive a stated dividend only, and, if the corporation is liquidated, preferred shareholders get a stated value. Often, preferreds carry credit ratings much like bonds.

Furthermore, preferred stock is sometimes convertible into common stock. Preferred stocks are often callable by the issuer and the holder often has the right to sell the preferred stock back to the issuer at a set price.

In addition, in recent years, many new issues of preferred stock have had obligatory sinking funds. Such a sinking fund effectively creates a final maturity since the entire issue is ultimately retired. For example, if a sinking fund required that 2 percent of the original issue be retired each year, the issue would be completely retired in 50 years.

On top of all of this, preferred stocks with adjustable dividends have been offered in recent years. For example, a CARP is a cumulative, adjustable rate, preferred stock. There are various types of floating-rate preferreds, some of which are quite innovative in the way the dividend is determined. For example, Royal Bank of Canada used to have First Preferred Shares Series C where dividends were set at 2/3 of the bank's average Canadian prime rate with a floor dividend of 6.67 percent per year.

For all these reasons, preferred stock seems to be a lot like debt. In comparison to debt, the yields on preferred stock can appear very low. For example, the Royal Bank has another preferred stock with a $1.18 stated dividend. In May 2006, the market price of the $1.18 Royal Bank preferred was $25.37. This is a $1.18/$25.37 = 4.65% yield, less than the yield on Royal Bank long-term debt (about 5% at that time). Also at that time, long-term Government of Canada bonds were yielding around 4.5 percent.

Despite the apparently low yields, corporate investors have an incentive to hold the preferred stock issued by other corporations rather than holding their debt because 100 percent of the dividends they receive are exempt from income taxes. While individual investors do receive a dividend tax credit for preferred dividends, it is much smaller than the corporate tax break and most preferred stock in Canada is purchased by corporate investors. Corporate investors pay a premium for preferred stock because of the tax exclusion on dividends; as a consequence, the yields are low.

Preferred Stock and Taxes

Turning to the issuers' point of view, a tax loophole encourages corporations that are lightly taxed or not taxable due to losses or tax shelters to issue preferred stock. Such low-tax companies can make little use of the tax deduction on interest. However, they can issue preferred stock and enjoy lower financing costs because preferred dividends are significantly lower than interest payments.

In 1987, the federal government attempted to close this tax loophole by introducing a tax of 40 percent of the preferred dividends to be paid by the issuer of preferred stock. The tax is refunded (through a deduction) to taxable issuers only. The effect of this (and associated) tax change was to narrow but not close the loophole.

Table 8.2 shows how Zero Tax Ltd., a corporation not paying any income taxes, can issue preferred shares attractive to Full Tax Ltd., a second corporation taxable at a combined federal and provincial rate of 45 percent. The example assumes that Zero Tax is seeking $1,000 in financing through either debt or preferred stock and that Zero Tax can issue either debt with a 10 percent coupon or preferred stock with a 6.7 percent dividend.[10]

Table 8.2 shows that with preferred stock financing, Zero Tax pays out 6.7% × $1,000 = $67.00 in dividends and 40% × $67.00 = $26.80 in tax on the dividends for a total aftertax outlay of $93.80. This represents an aftertax cost of $93.80/$1,000 = 9.38%. Debt financing is more expensive with an outlay of $100 and an aftertax yield of 10 percent. So Zero Tax is better off issuing preferred stock.

From the point of view of the purchaser, Full Tax Ltd., the preferred dividend is received tax free for an aftertax yield of 6.7 percent. If it bought debt issued by Zero Tax instead, Full Tax would pay income tax of $45 for a net aftertax receipt of $55 or 5.5 percent. So again, preferred stock is better than debt.

---

10 We set the preferred dividend at around two thirds of the debt yield to reflect market practice as exemplified by the Royal Bank issue discussed earlier. Further discussion of preferred stock and taxes is in I. Fooladi, P. A. McGraw, and G. S. Roberts, "Preferred Share Rules Freeze Out the Individual Investor," *CA Magazine*, April 11, 1988, pp. 38–41.

TABLE 8.2
Tax loophole on
preferred stock

	Preferred	Debt
Issuer: Zero Tax Ltd.		
Preferred dividend/interest paid	$67.00	$100.00
Dividend tax at 40%	26.80	0.00
Tax deduction on interest	0.00	0.00
Total financing cost	$93.80	$100.00
Aftertax cost	9.38%	10.00%
Purchaser: Full Tax Ltd.		
Beforetax income	$67.00	$100.00
Tax	0.00	45.00
Aftertax income	$67.00	$ 55.00
Aftertax yield	6.70%	5.50%

Of course, if we change the example to make the issuer fully taxable, the aftertax cost of debt drops to 5.5 percent making debt financing more attractive. This reinforces our point that the tax motivation for issuing preferred stock is limited to lightly taxed companies.

Beyond Taxes

For fully taxed firms, the fact that dividends are not an allowable deduction from taxable corporate income is the most serious obstacle to issuing preferred stock, but there are a couple of reasons beyond taxes why preferred stock is issued.

First, firms issuing preferred stock can avoid the threat of bankruptcy that might otherwise exist if debt were relied on. Unpaid preferred dividends are not debts of a corporation, and preferred shareholders cannot force a corporation into bankruptcy because of unpaid dividends.

A second reason for issuing preferred stock concerns control of the firm. Since preferred shareholders often cannot vote, preferred stock may be a means of raising equity without surrendering control.

On the demand side, most preferred stock is owned by corporations. Corporate income from preferred stock dividends enjoys a tax exemption, which can substantially reduce the tax disadvantage of preferred stock. Some of the new types of adjustable-rate preferred stocks are highly suited for corporations needing short-term investments for temporarily idle cash.

> ### CONCEPT QUESTIONS
>
> **1.** What is preferred stock?
>
> **2.** Why is it arguably more like debt than equity?
>
> **3.** Why is it attractive for firms that are not paying taxes to issue preferred stock?
>
> **4.** What are two reasons unrelated to taxes why preferred stock is issued?

8.4   STOCK MARKET REPORTING

www.lechateau.ca

If you look through the pages of the *National Post,* in another financial newspaper, or at www.globeinvestor.com, you find information on a large number of stocks in several different markets.[11] Figure 8.1 reproduces a small section of the stock page for the Toronto Stock Exchange (TSX) for May 4, 2006. In Figure 8.1, locate the line for Le Chateau Inc. The first two numbers, 59.40 and 29.10, are the high and low prices for the last 52 weeks.

The 1.00 is the annual dividend rate. Since Le Chateau Inc., like most companies, pays dividends quarterly, this dividend is actually the last quarterly dividend multiplied by four. So the last cash dividend paid was $1.00/4 = $.25. The column marked Yield % gives the dividend yield

---

11 To look up detailed stock information on line, any one of the following Web pages can provide excellent data: *http://finance.canada.com, http://www.globeinvestor.com, http://ca.finance.yahoo.com,* or *http://ca.moneycentral.msn.com.*

FIGURE 8.1

Sample stock market quotation from the *National Post*

Figures supplied by Thomson Financial.

Securities must trade a minimum of 1,000 shares to be listed.

52W high	52W low	Stock Ticker	Div	Yield %	P/E	Vol 00s	High	Low	Close	Net chg
		A B								
1.15	0.37	ACD Sys ....ASA	-	-	-	702	0.39	0.37	0.38	-
43.00	30.25	ACE Aviatn B. ACE	p2.37	7.4	12.1	2129	32.08	31.07	31.92	+0.89
43.03	30.25	ACE Aviatn RV..	p2.37	7.4	12.2	7213	32.15	31.05	32.10	+0.95
0.28	0.135	ADB Sys ...ADY	-	-	-	2196	0.205	0.19	0.20	-
2.05	0.42	ADF SV....DRX	-	-	26.3	135	1.05	1.00	1.05	-0.09
2.20	0.96	ADS MV....AAL	0.05	3.0	16.4	80	1.66	1.64	1.64	+0.03
8.79	4.85	AEterna.....AEZ	-	-	39.5	1690	8.08	7.80	7.87	-0.10
25.77	16.01	AGFMgmtB NV▲AGF	0.72	3.0	28.0	616	24.75	23.76	24.10	-0.35
28.28	25.71	AIC Divrs pf . ADC	1.50	5.8	-	27	26.00	26.00	26.00	+0.24
15.25	12.50	AIC Glbl.......ASC	1.20	7.5	7.5	47	16.15	16.10	16.10	+0.09
≤ 26.35	14.75	AKITA A NV. AKT	0.24	1.0	13.5	25	23.00	22.50	22.90	+0.14
12.47	6.85	AMVESCAP. AVZ	p0.19	1.6	44.7	283	12.28	12.02	12.08	-0.04
1.00	0.455	ART Advd ... ARA	-	-	-	75	0.82	0.78	0.82	+0.09
s 44.08	31.20	ATCO 1 NV◆ .ACO	0.82	2.4	12.3	5805	35.10	34.41	34.75	+0.25
21.18	12.40	ATI Tech ...ATY	-	-	-	19169	18.59	17.70	18.46	+0.56
18.45	11.95	ATS Auto.. ATA	-	-	90.2	1877	18.06	17.87	18.04	-0.01
0.97	0.46	AZCAR.. .AZZ	-	-	11.4	110	0.83	0.80	0.80	-
39.99	18.25	AastraTch.. AAH	-	-	21.0	363	33.02	33.01	33.11	-0.39
49.35	33.08	AberDia.. ABZ	u1.00	2.6	27.2	1812	42.86	41.58	42.25	-0.50
9.75	7.87	AberdnAP ..FAP	0.72	9.0	35.1	1045	8.00	7.93	7.98	+0.01
6.33	3.48	AbitibiCons... A	0.10	2.3	-	28548	4.60	4.35	4.37	-0.18
n 4.00	2.75	AbsltSftwr.. ABT	-	-	-	711	3.85	3.75	3.83	-0.02

52W high	52W low	Stock Ticker	Div	Yield %	P/E	Vol 00s	High	Low	Close	Net chg
8.40	6.65	AccordFn ...ACD	0.18	2.3	11.4	800	8.10	7.85	7.90	+0.05
10.35	7.01	AccreteEng... GZ	-	-	36.1	32	8.35	8.21	8.30	-
4.10	2.22	Adaltis.....ADS	-	-	-	304	3.00	2.98	3.00	+0.01
3.78	1.13	AdastraMin.. AAA	-	-	-	886	3.70	3.56	3.56	-0.10
n 31.00	19.65	Addax Pete.. AXC	-	-	-	1693	30.00	29.30	29.30	-0.36
33.00	23.50	Addenda.. ADV	1.20	4.5	19.3	176	27.00	26.50	26.50	-0.50
0.29	0.11	Adeptron... ATQ	-	-	-	358	0.20	0.18	0.20	+0.02
c 2.70	0.80	Adherex .. AHX	-	-	-	112	1.05	1.01	1.01	-0.05
0.25	0.05	Advantex... ADX	-	-	-	1160	0.145	0.13	0.14	+0.01
7.04	5.25	AeconGrp ... ARE	-	-	-	64	5.93	5.90	5.93	+0.03
n 2.60	0.82	AfrcnCppr... ACU	-	-	-	369	1.79	1.64	1.71	+0.08
4.80	1.30	AfriOre ....AFO	-	-	-	490	4.80	4.70	4.71	-0.04
42.41	13.63	AgnicoEag .. AEM	u0.03	0.1	88.2	13019	42.28	39.73	41.06	-0.79
↑ 20.95	1.18	AgncEaglwt*.	-	-	-	130	20.95	19.00	19.75	-0.25
9.25	6.40	Agricore LV◆ .AU	0.12	1.4	42.0	110	8.43	8.30	8.39	+0.04
32.66	22.39	Agrium ...AGU	u0.11	0.4	11.9	2551	29.10	28.15	28.30	-0.20
43.82	26.55	CdnWstBk ..CWB	0.48	1.1	22.5	201	43.29	42.75	43.29	+0.54
1.63	0.38	Cdn Zinc ....CZN	-	-	-	5348	1.31	1.22	1.25	-0.05
11.66	6.02	Canam A SV▲CAM	0.16	1.5	10.7	1210	10.70	10.20	10.39	-0.20
0.95	0.31	CanarcRes .. CCM	-	-	-	1302	0.91	0.83	0.89	-
27.00	25.51	CanCap5.4 .. CAC	1.35	5.3	-	20	25.51	25.51	25.51	-
0.42	0.15	CancorMns.. KCR	-	-	-	125	0.34	0.34	0.34	-
n 1.48	0.39	Candax En... CAX	-	-	-	12237	1.31	1.23	1.27	-0.04
1.11	0.31	Candente ... DNT	-	-	-	794	1.02	0.97	0.97	-0.03
16.12	11.26	Canfor ....CFP	-	-	33.5	8950	14.09	13.65	14.06	-0.06
10.63	7.25	Cangene ... CNJ	-	-	-	132	9.75	9.75	9.75	+0.05
15.75	8.80	CanWest NV◆ CGS	-	-	-	20	9.58	9.56	9.56	-0.02
15.78	8.80	CanWest SV◆....	-	-	-	1756	9.66	9.55	9.60	-0.03
↑n14.50	13.00	Canam Enrg .. FRC	-	-	-	4705	14.50	14.00	14.15	+0.15
15.95	14.25	CapQneqdv .CGO	1.05	7.0	-	30	14.92	14.92	14.92	+0.04
x 2.68	0.67	Capstone .. CS	-	-	-	8683	2.07	1.85	1.95	-0.60
16.39	6.47	Cardiome... COM	-	-	-	215	11.65	11.40	11.62	-0.07
12.27	10.50	CaribUtilA*.. CUP	u0.66	5.6	14.0	23	11.80	11.75	11.80	-

52W high	52W low	Stock Ticker	Div	Yield %	P/E	Vol 00s	High	Low	Close	Net chg
n 4.19	2.80	Carmanah .. CMH	-	-	-	310	3.61	3.50	3.61	-
0.65	0.33	cars4U......CFU	0.04	6.3	63.0	95	0.63	0.63	0.63	+0.03
12.60	7.35	Cascades....CAS	0.16	1.5	-	3769	11.55	10.86	10.99	-0.49
3.68	1.33	Caspian En .. CEK	-	-	-	593	2.98	2.92	2.94	-0.06
3.51	2.40	CatalystPpr.. CTL	-	-	-	5144	3.04	2.77	2.93	-0.12
18.06	10.18	CelesticaSV◆. CLS	-	-	-	2716	12.75	12.40	12.61	+0.08
14.80	8.91	CelticExp... CLT	-	-	21.2	123	14.03	13.65	14.00	+0.15
47.90	16.81	CenterraGld .. CG	-	-	60.3	670	46.75	44.75	44.75	-0.73
11.30	6.05	CentFundA NV◆CEF	u0.01	0.1	4.8	2786	11.04	10.50	10.64	+0.22
15.25	9.66	CentrnEng... CUX	-	-	-	11780	11.57	10.85	11.00	-0.55
4.25	1.12	Centuryll.... CH	-	-	12.8	48	4.24	4.10	4.10	+0.10
n 23.50	13.25	CermicPro... CEP	-	-	22.1	18	23.06	23.00	23.00	-
8.75	3.97	Certicom ... CIC	-	-	-	392	7.01	6.77	6.79	-0.13
1.35	0.225	CervusFinl... CFG	-	-	-	1816	0.33	0.25	0.33	+0.06
n 8.38	5.57	ChamaeloEx. CXN	-	-	-	763	6.70	6.65	6.70	+0.05
0.65	0.27	ChariotRs .. CHD	-	-	-	38472	0.56	0.51	0.53	-
0.31	0.05	ChariotRs wt ..	-	-	-	6021	0.26	0.235	0.26	-
↓ 11.90	3.45	Chartwell... CWH	-	-	21.6	468	3.49	3.45	3.45	-0.04
59.40	29.10	LeChateauSV◆CTU	1.00	1.8	14.4	118	57.25	56.80	56.91	-0.19
1.43	0.89	Chemokine... CTI	-	-	-	1924	1.05	1.00	1.05	-
0.29	0.14	ChromosMl... CHR	-	-	-	95	0.24	0.24	0.24	-
4.70	2.36	Chrchill A ... CUQ	-	-	19.2	228	4.60	4.50	4.60	-
3.77	2.00	Cinch Enrg. CNH	-	-	28.5	585	2.37	2.20	2.28	-0.14
30.30	22.05	Cinram.... CRW	0.12	0.4	18.3	867	29.50	29.11	29.25	-0.25
5.40	1.00	CipherPhrm . DND	-	-	-	1810	4.95	4.85	4.95	-
11.49	9.14	Clairvest... CVG	0.10	0.9	40.8	17	11.01	11.01	11.01	-0.09
s 12.25	7.00	Clarke.....CKI	0.15	1.4	8.4	17	11.40	11.01	11.01	+0.01
1.69	0.82	ClaudeRes ... CRJ	-	-	-	1741	1.62	1.52	1.57	-0.03
n 10.52	9.92	ClaymorETFs CRQ	-	-	-	177	10.38	10.22	10.22	-0.07
6.03	3.68	Clear Enrg... CEN	-	-	79.2	461	4.75	4.62	4.75	+0.03
n 1.17	0.50	ClineMng ... CMK	-	-	-	913	0.60	0.57	0.57	-0.03
27.05	25.70	Co-opApt....CCS	f1.37	5.3	-	10	26.10	26.10	26.10	-

Source: Reprinted with permission of the *National Post*, May 4, 2006, p. FP14.

based on the current dividend and the closing price. For Le Chateau Inc., this is $1/56.91 = 0.018% or 1.8% as shown.

The High, Low, and Close figures are the high, low, and closing prices during the day. The Net Chg of –0.19 tells us the closing price of $56.91 per share is $0.19 lower than the closing price the day before.

The remaining column, marked Vol 00s, tells us how many shares traded during the day (in hundreds). For example, the 118 for Le Chateau Inc. tells us that 11,800 shares changed hands. If the average price during the day was $57.00 or so, the dollar volume of transactions was on the order of $57.00 × 11,800 = $672,600 worth of Le Chateau stock.

Growth Opportunities

We previously spoke of the growth rate of dividends. We now want to address the related concept of growth opportunities. Imagine a company with a level stream of earnings per share in perpetuity. The company pays all these earnings out to shareholders as dividends. Hence,

$$EPS = Div$$

here EPS is *earnings per share* and Div is dividends per share. A company of this type is frequently called a *cash cow*.

From the perpetuity formula of the previous chapter, the value of a share of stock is:

Value of a share of stock when firm acts as a cash cow: $\dfrac{EPS}{r} = \dfrac{Div}{r}$

where r is the discount rate on the firm's stock.

The preceding policy of paying out all earnings as dividends may not be the optimal one. Many firms have growth opportunities, that is, opportunities to invest in profitable projects. Because these projects can represent a significant fraction of the firm's value, it would be foolish to forgo them to pay out all earnings as dividends.

Although management frequently thinks of a set of growth opportunities, let's focus on only one opportunity; that is, the opportunity to invest in a single project. Suppose the firm retains the entire dividend at Date 1 to invest in a particular capital budgeting project. The net present value per share of the project as of Date 0 is NPVGO, which stands for the *net present value (per share) of the growth opportunity*.

What is the price of a share of stock at Date 0 if the firm decides to take on the project at Date 1? Because the per-share value of the project is added to the original stock price, the stock price must now be:

Stock price after firm commits to new project: $\dfrac{EPS}{r} + NPVGO$

This equation indicates that the price of a share of stock can be viewed as the sum of two different items: The first term (EPS/r) is the value of the firm if it rested on its laurels, that is, if it simply distributed all earnings to the shareholders. The second term is the additional value if the firm retains earnings to fund new projects.

Application: The Price Earnings Ratio

Even though our stock valuation formulas focused on dividends, not earnings, financial analysts often rely on price earnings ratios (P/Es). You can see in Figure 8.1 that financial newspapers report P/Es.

We showed in the previous section that

Price per share $= \dfrac{EPS}{r} + NPVGO$

Dividing by EPS yields

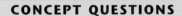

$\dfrac{\text{Price per share}}{EPS} = \dfrac{1}{r} + \dfrac{NPVGO}{EPS}$

The left-hand side is the formula for the price-earnings ratio. The equation shows that the P/E ratio is related to the net present value of growth opportunities. As an example, consider two firms each having just reported earnings per share of $1. However, one firm has many valuable growth opportunities while the other firm has no growth opportunities at all. The firm with growth opportunities should sell at a higher price because an investor is buying both current income of $1 and growth opportunities. Suppose the firm with growth opportunities sells for $16 and the other firm sells for $8. The $1 earnings per share appears in the denominator of the P/E ratio for both firms. Thus, the P/E ratio is 16 for the firm with growth opportunities, but only 8 for the firm without the opportunities.

Because P/E ratios are based on earnings and not cash flows, investors should follow up with cash flow analysis using the dividend valuation model. Using a spreadsheet to look at different growth scenarios lets investors quantify projected growth in cash flows.

As you can see in the boxed insert, in May 2000, Internet stocks like Yahoo! and Research in Motion were trading at P/Es over 1000! Clearly the P/E analysis we present could never explain these prices in terms of growth opportunities. As covered in the boxed insert, some analysts who recommended buying these stocks developed a new measure called the PEG ratio to justify their recommendation. Although it is not based on any theory, the PEG ratio became popular among proponents of Internet stocks. On the other side, many analysts believed that the market had lost touch with reality. To these analysts, Internet stock prices were the result of speculative fever. Subsequent events support the second group of analysts.

www.yahoo.com
www.rim.net

CONCEPT QUESTIONS

1. What are the relevant cash flows for valuing a share of common stock?

2. Does the value of a share of stock depend on how long you expect to keep it?

3. How does expected dividend growth impact on the stock price in the dividend valuation model? Is this consistent with the NPVGO approach?

8.5

SUMMARY AND CONCLUSIONS

This chapter has covered the basics of stocks and stock valuation. The key points include:

1. The cash flows from owning a share of stock come in the form of future dividends. We saw that in certain special cases it is possible to calculate the present value of all the future dividends and thus come up with a value for the stock.

In Their Own Words . . .   Matthew Ingram on the New Tally for Tech Stocks

AT THE annual meeting of his holding company, Berkshire Hathaway, last May, legendary value investor and billionaire Warren Buffett told his audience that if he were a business professor, he would ask his students to pick an Internet company and try to determine how much it was worth. "And anybody who turned in an answer would fail," he quipped.

Mr. Buffett is just one of the many traditional value-oriented investors who have given up trying to explain why technology shares have been trading the way they have. Who can blame them? Some of these tiny companies were worth billions of dollars not long ago, and now they are worth a fraction of that — and yet some feel they are still overvalued.

It's easy enough for Mr. Buffett to avoid investing in tech stocks, since he's made billions by buying insurance companies, shoe stocks and shares in Coca-Cola. But plenty of people believe they have to be invested in technology stocks, despite the recent turmoil, and they are trying to figure out how to separate the winners from the losers.

Looking at a stock's price compared to its earnings is one way of doing so, but it's only a broad measure — like using binoculars instead of a magnifying glass. It doesn't really tell you whether a stock that was $250 and is now $75 is cheap or not.

Instead of just relying on one such measure, analysts say investors should try to use as many tools as possible. That includes old standbys such as the price-earnings ratio, newer ones such as the PEG (price-earnings-growth) ratio, price-to-cash-flow multiples, and various measures of how a company is spending its money — including its "customer-acquisition" costs, or its sales per customer or per registered user.

The investor's task is made even more difficult by the fact that, during the tech stock runup last year, even some industry analysts apparently gave up trying to figure out what stocks were worth.

Last fall, for example, analysts expected Research In Motion Ltd. to reach $150 (Canadian) in a year. The stock hit that level in just a few months, and peaked at $220, giving it a market value of $15-billion.

"Valuing tech stocks became a very difficult process in the past 18 months or so," says one analyst, who didn't want to be named. "As casino-style investing took over . . . valuation became nearly irrelevant."

Despite the recent pullback in some share prices, arriving at a value for a high-flying tech stock hasn't gotten any easier. For example, Research In Motion has fallen by 70 per cent from its peak, but it is still trading at 250 times its earnings per share. Yahoo! Inc. (540 times earnings), eBay Inc. (1,600 times) and Nortel Networks Corp. (105 times) are also still at lofty levels. Of course, those multiples are based on last year's earnings, and most analysts look at next year's — but even that doesn't reduce the multiple very much.

Broadly speaking, there are two kinds of tech stocks: those that have earnings, and those that don't. If they do, you have to decide how much you're willing to pay for those earnings. But arriving at a value for a company like Amazon.com Inc. — which lost $720-million last year — is a lot more difficult, to the point where some professional money managers advise ordinary investors not to buy these kinds of stocks at all.

One way to try and value such a company is to look at its revenue per share, and compare that to similar companies. Analysts say this should always be used in combination with other measures, such as how much the company spends per customer and its revenue per user — as well as its gross profit margin, since having sales isn't worth much if a company is losing money with each sale. Many retailing stocks, on-line or not, are valued this way because such companies live or die on their customer base.

One point analysts make is that for most tech stocks, the current level of earnings isn't what is really important: growth is. For that reason, an increasingly popular valuation method combines the price-earnings multiple with a company's earnings growth rate, to get something called the PEG ratio, for price-earnings-growth.

RATING THE HIGH-FLYERS

For an investor interested in growth, using PEG ratios to evaluate high-tech stocks shows that Yahoo is about as valuable as Coca-Cola, and Microsoft is probably a bargain.

Stock	Highest intraday price ($U.S.)	P/E ratio	PEG ratio*	Tuesday close ($U.S.)	P/E ratio	PEG ratio*
Microsoft	$120	72	4	$68	41	2.5
Yahoo	250	1,136	19	123	569	9.0
America Online	95	232	11	58	145	7.0
Research in Motion	175	1,029	20	46	265	4.5
IBM	139	33	3	111	26	2.6
Coca-Cola	70	76	15	46	48	9.6

*Price/earnings ratio divided by growth.

The Globe and Mail

PEG, EXPLAINED

A company's price-earnings-growth (PEG) ratio compares its price-to-earnings multiple — its share price divided by its earnings per share — to its earnings growth rate. The PEG ratio is calculated by dividing the P/E ratio by the percentage growth rate in earnings. A company with a P/E ratio of 100 and an earnings growth rate of 25 has a PEG ratio of 4. The PEG ratio makes it easier to compare stocks that trade at dramatically different levels.

If a stock is trading at 40 times earnings, and earnings are expected to grow at 40 per cent a year, that stock has a PEG ratio of 1 to 1. A stock trading at 20 times earnings may look a lot cheaper than one at 50 times earnings — but if the first company is only growing at 10 per cent a year, and the second is growing at 50 per cent, the first has a PEG of 2 to 1 and the second 1 to 1. If you want growth, the second is the better buy.

Duncan Stewart, a portfolio manager with Tera Capital in Toronto, says such a method is useful when a single sector, technology, takes on more importance in the overall economy. "There are parts of the economy that aren't growing at all, and then there are parts with companies like JDS Uniphase, that are growing at 150 per cent a year," he says. "You can't value them the same way."

For example, he says, Coca-Cola Co. is trading at about 50 times its earnings, and yet most analysts don't see it growing much more than 5 per cent a year. That means the stock has a PEG ratio of 10 to 1, higher than a tech company such as Yahoo! or even Microsoft Corp. By contrast, Nortel is expected to increase its earnings by 30 to 40 per cent a year, giving it a PEG ratio of between 2.5 and 3.3 and allowing some analysts to justify its 100 times price-earnings multiple.

At the moment, the average price-earnings multiple for the technology sector is about 40 times — but many analysts expect the sector to produce earnings growth of about 20 per cent a year, which makes for a 2 to 1 ratio. The average price-earnings multiple on the Standard & Poor's 500 index is about 28, but the average forecast growth rate is only 7 per cent, for a ratio of 4 to 1. Which one is more expensive?

Coming up with a company's PEG ratio is far from an exact science, mind you. For one thing, analysts often use projected earnings in their calculations, which leaves plenty of room for error. It also used to be assumed that a company's price-earnings multiple should be the same as its growth rate — but some analysts say firms growing at high rates deserve premiums of up to three or four times their growth rate.

None of these valuation methods is a one-size-fits-all tool, and that's why investors should use as many as possible to try and separate the wheat from the chaff. It's harder than buying a stock knowing it will double without you lifting a finger, but those days appear to be gone.

Matthew Ingram writes for *The Globe and Mail.* His comments are reproduced with permission from the May 4, 2000 edition.

2. As the owner of shares of common stock in a corporation, you have various rights, including the right to vote to elect corporate directors. Voting in corporate elections can be either cumulative or straight. Most voting is actually done by proxy, and a proxy battle breaks out when competing sides try to gain enough votes to have their candidates for the board elected.

3. In addition to common stock, some corporations have issued preferred stock. The name stems from the fact that preferred stockholders must be paid first, before common stockholders can receive anything. Preferred stock has a fixed dividend.

This chapter completes Part 3 of our book. By now, you should have a good grasp of what we mean by present value. You should also be familiar with how to calculate present values, loan payments, and so on. In Part 4, we cover capital budgeting decisions. As you will see, the techniques you learned in Chapters 5–8 form the basis for our approach to evaluating business investment decisions.

Key Terms

Chapter Review Problems and Self-Test

8.1 **Dividend Growth and Stock Valuation** The Brigapenski Co. has just paid a cash dividend of $2 per share. Investors require a 16 percent return from investments such as this. If the dividend is expected to grow at a steady 8 percent per year, what is the current value of the stock? What will the stock be worth in five years?

8.2 **More Dividend Growth and Stock Valuation** In Self-Test Problem 8.1, what would the stock sell for today if the dividend was expected to grow at 20 percent per year for the next three years and then settle down to 8 percent per year, indefinitely?

Answers to Self-Test Problems

8.1 The last dividend, D_0, was $2. The dividend is expected to grow steadily at 8 percent. The required return is 16 percent. Based on the dividend growth model, we can say that the current price is:

$$P_0 = D_1/(r - g) = D_0 \times (1 + g)/(r - g)$$
$$= \$2 \times 1.08/(.16 - .08)$$
$$= \$2.16/.08$$
$$= \$27$$

We could calculate the price in five years by calculating the dividend in five years and then using the growth model again. Alternatively, we could recognize that the stock price will increase by 8 percent per year and calculate the future price directly. We'll do both. First, the dividend in five years will be:

$$D_5 = D_0 \times (1 + g)^5$$
$$= \$2 \times 1.4693$$
$$= 2.9387$$

The price in five years would therefore be:

$$P_5 = D_5 \times (1 + g)/(r - g)$$
$$= \$2.9387 \times 1.08/.08$$
$$= \$3.1738/.08$$
$$= \$39.67$$

Once we understand the dividend model, however, it's easier to notice that:

$$P_5 = P_0 \times (1 + g)^5$$
$$= \$27 \times (1.08)^5$$
$$= \$27 \times 1.4693$$
$$= \$39.67$$

Notice that both approaches yield the same price in five years.

8.2 In this scenario, we have supernormal growth for the next three years. We'll need to calculate the dividends during the rapid-growth period and the stock price in three years. The dividends are:

$$D_1 = \$2.00 \times 1.20 = \$2.400$$
$$D_2 = \$2.40 \times 1.20 = \$2.880$$
$$D_3 = \$2.88 \times 1.20 = \$3.456$$

After three years, the growth rate falls to 8 percent indefinitely. The price at that time, P_3, is thus:

$$P_3 = D_3 \times (1 + g)/(r - g)$$
$$= \$3.456 \times 1.08/(.16 - .08)$$
$$= \$3.7325/.08$$
$$= \$46.656$$

To complete the calculation of the stock's present value, we have to determine the present value of the three dividends and the future price:

$$P_0 = \frac{D_1}{(1 + r)^1} + \frac{D_2}{(1 + r)^2} + \frac{D_3}{(1 + r)^3} + \frac{P_3}{(1 + r)^3}$$

$$= \frac{\$2.40}{1.16} + \frac{2.88}{1.16^2} + \frac{3.456}{1.16^3} + \frac{46.656}{1.16^3}$$

$$= \$2.07 + 2.14 + 2.21 + 29.89$$

$$= \$36.31$$

Concepts Review and Critical Thinking Questions

1. Why does the value of a share of stock depend on dividends?

2. A substantial percentage of the companies listed on the TSX and the Nasdaq don't pay dividends, but investors are nonetheless willing to buy shares in them. How is this possible given your answer to the previous question?

3. Referring to the previous question, under what circumstances might a company choose not to pay dividends?

4. Under what two assumptions can we use the dividend growth formula presented in the chapter to determine the value of a share of stock? Comment on the reasonableness of these assumptions.

5. Suppose a company has a preferred stock issue and a common stock issue. Both have just paid a $2 dividend. Which do you think will have a higher price, a share of the preferred or a share of the common?

6. Based on the dividend growth model, what are the two components of the total return on a share of stock? Which do you think is typically larger?

7. In the context of the dividend growth model, is it true that the growth rate in dividends and the growth rate in the price of the stock are identical?

8. When it comes to voting in elections, what are the differences between political democracy and corporate democracy?

9. Is it unfair or unethical for corporations to create classes of stock with unequal voting rights?

10. Some companies, such as Canadian Tire, have created classes of stock with no voting rights at all. Why would investors buy such stock?

Questions and Problems

Basic
(Questions 1–8)

1. **Stock Values**   The Jackson–Timberlake Wardrobe Co., just paid a dividend of $1.40 per share on its stock. The dividends are expected to grow at a constant rate of 6 percent per year, indefinitely. If investors require a 12 percent return on The Jackson–Timberlake Wardrobe Co., stock, what is the current price? What will the price be in three years? In 15 years?

2. **Stock Values**   The next dividend payment by MUG, Inc., will be $3.10 per share. The dividends are anticipated to maintain a 5 percent growth rate, forever. If MUG stock currently sells for $48.00 per share, what is the required return?

3. **Stock Values**   For the company in the previous problem, what is the dividend yield? What is the expected capital gains yield?

4. **Stock Values**   Warren Corporation will pay a $3.60 per share dividend next year. The company pledges to increase its dividend by 4.5 percent per year, indefinitely. If you require a 13 percent return on your investment, how much will you pay for the company's stock today?

5. **Stock Valuation**   Joe Elvis Co. is expected to maintain a constant 6 percent growth rate in its dividends, indefinitely. If the company has a dividend yield of 3.9 percent, what is the required return on the company's stock?

6. **Stock Valuation**   Suppose you know that a company's stock currently sells for $70 per share and the required return on the stock is 12 percent. You also know that the total return on the stock is evenly divided between a capital gains yield and a dividend yield. If it's the company's policy to always maintain a constant growth rate in its dividends, what is the current dividend per share?

7. **Stock Valuation**   Rocket Man Corp. pays a constant $12 dividend on its stock. The company will maintain this dividend for the next eight years and will then cease paying dividends forever. If the required return on this stock is 10 percent, what is the current share price?

8. **Valuing Preferred Stock**   Ayden, Inc., has an issue of preferred stock outstanding that pays an $8.25 dividend every year, in perpetuity. If this issue currently sells for $113 per share, what is the required return?

Intermediate
(Questions 9–18)

9. **Stock Valuation**   Smashed Pumpkin Farms (SPF) just paid a dividend of $3.00 on its stock. The growth rate in dividends is expected to be a constant 5 percent per year, indefinitely. Investors require a 16 percent return on the stock for the first three years, a 14 percent return for the next three years, and then an 11 percent return, thereafter. What is the current share price for SPF stock?

10. **Nonconstant Growth**   Metallica Bearings, Inc., is a young start-up company. No dividends will be paid on the stock over the next nine years, because the firm needs to plow back its earnings to fuel growth. The company will pay an $8 per share dividend in 10 years and will increase the dividend by 6 percent per year, thereafter. If the required return on this stock is 13 percent, what is the current share price?

11. **Nonconstant Dividends**   Corn, Inc., has an odd dividend policy. The company has just paid a dividend of $9 per share and has announced that it will increase the dividend by $3 per share for each of the next four years, and then never pay another dividend. If you require an 11 percent return on the company's stock, how much will you pay for a share today?

12. **Nonconstant Dividends**   South Side Corporation is expected to pay the following dividends over the next four years: $8, $6, $3, and $2. Afterwards, the company pledges to maintain a constant 5 percent growth rate in dividends, forever. If the required return on the stock is 13 percent, what is the current share price?

Intermediate (continued)

13. **Supernormal Growth** Rizzi Co. is growing quickly. Dividends are expected to grow at a 25 percent rate for the next three years, with the growth rate falling off to a constant 7 percent thereafter. If the required return is 13 percent and the company just paid a $2.80 dividend, what is the current share price?

14. **Supernormal Growth** Janicek Corp. is experiencing rapid growth. Dividends are expected to grow at 30 percent per year during the next three years, 18 percent over the following year, and then 8 percent per year, indefinitely. The required return on this stock is 14 percent, and the stock currently sells for $70.00 per share. What is the projected dividend for the coming year?

15. **Negative Growth** Antiques R Us is a mature manufacturing firm. The company just paid a $10 dividend, but management expects to reduce the payout by 8 percent per year, indefinitely. If you require an 11 percent return on this stock, what will you pay for a share today?

16. **Finding the Dividend** Hollin Corporation stock currently sells for $50 per share. The market requires a 14 percent return on the firm's stock. If the company maintains a constant 8 percent growth rate in dividends, what was the most recent dividend per share paid on the stock?

17. **Valuing Preferred Stock** Mark Bank just issued some new preferred stock. The issue will pay a $9 annual dividend in perpetuity, beginning six years from now. If the market requires a 7 percent return on this investment, how much does a share of preferred stock cost today?

18. **Using Stock Quotes** You have found the following stock quote for RJW Enterprises, Inc., in the financial pages of today's newspaper. What was the closing price for this stock that appeared in *yesterday's* paper? If the company currently has 25 million shares of stock outstanding, what was net income for the most recent four quarters?

YTD % CHG	52 WEEK		STOCK	TICKER	DIV	YLD %	PE	VOL 100s	CLOSE	NET CHG
	HI	LO								
22.4	70.80	39.93	RJW	RJW	.15	.2	14	35215	??	2.20

Challenge (Questions 19–25)

19. **Capital Gains versus Income** Consider four different stocks, all of which have a required return of 15 percent and a most recent dividend of $4.50 per share. Stocks W, X, and Y are expected to maintain constant growth rates in dividends for the foreseeable future of 10 percent, 0 percent, and –5 percent per year, respectively. Stock Z is a growth stock that will increase its dividend by 20 percent for the next two years and then maintain a constant 12 percent growth rate, thereafter. What is the dividend yield for each of these four stocks? What is the expected capital gains yield? Discuss the relationship among the various returns that you find for each of these stocks.

20. **Stock Valuation** Most corporations pay quarterly dividends on their common stock rather than annual dividends. Barring any unusual circumstances during the year, the board raises, lowers, or maintains the current dividend once a year and then pays this dividend out in equal quarterly installments to its shareholders.

    a. Suppose a company currently pays a $3.00 annual dividend on its common stock in a single annual installment, and management plans on raising this dividend by 6 percent per year, indefinitely. If the required return on this stock is 14 percent, what is the current share price?

    b. Now suppose that the company in (a) actually pays its annual dividend in equal quarterly installments; thus, this company has just paid a $.75 dividend per share, as it has for the previous three quarters. What is your value for the current share price now? (Hint: Find the equivalent annual end-of-year dividend for each year.) Comment on whether or not you think that this model of stock valuation is appropriate.

21. **Nonconstant Growth** Storico Co. just paid a dividend of $3.50 per share. The company will increase its dividend by 20 percent next year and will then reduce its dividend growth rate by 5 percentage points per year until it reaches the industry average of 5 percent dividend growth, after which the company will keep a constant growth rate, forever. If the required return on Storico stock is 13 percent, what will a share of stock sell for today?

22. **Nonconstant Growth** This one's a little harder. Suppose the current share price for the firm in the previous problem is $98.65 and all the dividend information remains the same. What required return must investors be demanding on Storico stock? (Hint: Set up the valuation formula with all the relevant cash flows, and use trial and error to find the unknown rate of return.)

23. **Nonconstant Growth** HRM manufactures state of the art sound systems targeted at the young professional market. Analysts following HRM Corporation predict that the company's earnings and dividends will continue to grow at 18 percent for the next period. After that, growth will level off at 4 percent for the indefinite future. Last year's dividend was $1.50 per share and analysts figure that the required return on this stock should be 18 percent.

    a. What is the value of an HRM share assuming that growth at the rate of 18 percent will continue for seven years?

    b. What is the value of an HRM share assuming that growth will drop immediately to the long-run rate of 6 percent?

    c. Suppose that HRM is currently trading at $47 per share. How many years of growth at 18 percent is the market predicting? How could you use your answer to decide whether to buy HRM shares?

24. Futrell Fixtures expects net cash flows of $53,000 by the end of this year. Net cash flows will grow 2.5 percent if the firm makes no new investments. Mike Futrell, the president of the firm, has the opportunity to add a line of kitchen

Challenge (continued)

and bathroom cabinets to the business. The immediate outlay for this opportunity is $125,000, and the net cash flows from the line will begin one year from now. The cabinet business will generate $31,500 in additional net cash flows. These net cash flows will also grow at 2.5 percent. The firm's discount rate is 12 percent, and 200,000 shares of Futrell stock are outstanding.

a. What is the price per share of Futrell stock without the cabinet line?

b. What is the value of the growth opportunities that the cabinet line offers?

c. Once Futrell adds the cabinet line, what is the price of Futrell stock?

25. **Price-Earnings Ratio**   Consider Pacific Energy Company and Ottawa Valley Bluechips, Inc., both of which reported recent earnings of $1,000,000 and both have 650,000 shares of common stocks outstanding. Assume both firms have the same appropriate discount rate of return of 15 percent a year.

a. Pacific Energy Company has a new project that will generate net cash flows of $125,000 each year in perpetuity. Calculate the P/E ratio of the company.

b. Ottawa Valley Bluechips has a new project that will increase earnings by $200,000 in the coming year. The increased earnings will grow at 9 percent a year in perpetuity. Calculate the P/E ratio of the firm.

MINI CASE

As an investment advisor, you have been asked to pick one of the following three stock options for your latest client. The client will be investing $25,000 in whichever option you pick. Your client plans to hold the investment over the long run, so is not particularly concerned with "quick money."

Option	Market Price	Current Dividend	Expected Firm Growth
Common shares	$25.00	$0.90	5.5%
Preferred shares	$15.00	$1.35	4%
Risky Venture	$ 3.70	—	40% for the first 4 years, 25% for the next 5 years, and 9% thereafter

You have also learned that a majority of stock analysts expect that the risky venture will begin paying a dividend of $0.30 in five years. The market demands a 9.5 percent return on most equity investments, but demands a 15 percent return for risky shares.

a) What should you be willing to pay for each investment given the available information?

b) Over a 15-year period, what is your expected annual return from each option?

c) If inflation is expected to be 2.5 percent annually, what price should you be willing to pay for the shares?

d) If there is a 20 percent chance that each firm will grow at a rate 1.5 times the expected rate and a 30 percent chance that each will grow at only 2/3 the expected rate, how would this change your valuation of each option?

e) Which option would you recommend to your client? Why?

S&P Problems

1. **Calculating Required Return**   A drawback of the dividend growth model is the need to estimate the growth rate of dividends. One way to estimate this growth rate is to use the sustainable growth rate. Look back at Chapter 4 and find the formula for the sustainable growth rate. Using the annual income statement and balance sheet, calculate the sustainable growth rate for MDS Inc. (MDZ). Find the most recent closing monthly stock price under the "Mthly. Adj. Prices" link. Using the growth rate you calculated, the most recent dividend per share, and the most recent stock price, calculate the required return for MDS shareholders. Does this number make sense? Why or why not?

2. **Calculating Growth Rates**   Coca-Cola (KO) is a dividend-paying company. Recently, dividends for Coca-Cola have increased at about 5.5 percent per year. Find the most recent closing monthly stock price under the "Mthly. Adj. Prices" link. Locate the most recent annual dividend for KO and calculate the dividend yield. Using your answer and the 5.5 percent dividend growth rate, what is the required return for shareholders? Suppose instead that you know that the required return is 13 percent. What price should Coca-Cola stock sell for now? What if the required return is 15 percent?

Internet Application Questions

1. What are the latest corporate governance policies of institutional investors? Go to www.lacaisse.com and www.otpp.com to see. How do these large Canadian institutions seek to ensure the practice of corporate governance?

2. Stock valuation is difficult because dividends are difficult to forecast. Go to Petro-Canada's website (www.petro-canada.ca) and click on Investors. Use the information provided and the dividend growth model to estimate the implied growth for Petro-Canada's dividends. Is this reasonable? Can you form a similar conclusion by looking at Petro-Canada's P/E ratio?

3. Barclays Global Investors (www.barclaysglobal.com) has an exchange traded equity fund, i60 (www.ishares.ca/product_info/fund_ overview.do?ticker=XIU). The i60 trades on the Toronto Stock Exchange (www.tsx.com) and invests in 60 firms that comprise the S&P/TSX 60 Index. Explain the advantage of investing in exchange traded funds relative to buying the stocks outright, and relative to buying index funds from banks.

4. Explore the wealth of online materials about stocks by going to www.globeinvestor.com. Generate the latest report on BCE Inc. by clicking on reports and entering the ticker symbol, BCE-T. You can get the current stock price by clicking on quotes.

Suggested Readings

Two current Canadian investment texts expanding our discussion of stock valuation are:
Bodie, Z., A. Kane, A. Marcus, S. Perrakis, and P. Ryan. *Investments,* 5th Canadian ed. Whitby, Ontario: McGraw-Hill Ryerson, 2005.
Sharpe, W.F., G.J. Alexander, J.V. Bailey, D.J. Fowler, and D. Domian. *Investments,* 3rd Canadian ed. Scarborough, Ontario: Prentice-Hall Canada, 1999.

Further insight into using the dividend growth model in Canada is in:
Ackert, L. and J. Schnabel. "The Dividend Discount Model: A Victim of the Tumultuous Eighties?" *Canadian Investment Review* 6, no. 3, Fall 1993, pp. 7–10.

CORPORATE VOTING

To illustrate the two different voting procedures, imagine that a corporation has two shareholders: Smith with 20 shares and Jones with 80 shares. Both want to be directors. Jones, however, does not want Smith to be a director. We assume that four directors are to be elected.

cumulative voting
Procedure where a shareholder may cast all votes for one member of the board of directors.

CUMULATIVE VOTING   The effect of **cumulative voting** is to permit minority participation.[12] If cumulative voting is permitted, the total number of votes that each shareholder may cast is determined first. This is usually calculated as the number of shares (owned or controlled) multiplied by the number of directors to be elected.

With cumulative voting, the directors are elected all at once. In our example, this means that the top four vote getters will be the new directors. A shareholder can distribute votes however he or she wishes.

Will Smith get a seat on the board? If we ignore the possibility of a five-way tie, the answer is yes. Smith casts $20 \times 4 = 80$ votes, and Jones casts $80 \times 4 = 320$ votes. If Smith gives all his votes to himself, he is assured of a directorship. The reason is that Jones can't divide 320 votes among four candidates in such a way as to give all of them more than 80 votes, so Smith would finish fourth at worst.

In general, if there are N directors up for election, $1/(N + 1)$ percent of the stock (plus one share) would guarantee you a seat. In our current example, this is $1/(4 + 1) = 20\%$. So the more seats that are up for election at one time, the easier (and cheaper) it is to win one.

straight voting
Procedure where a shareholder may cast all votes for each member of the board of directors.

STRAIGHT VOTING   With **straight voting,** the directors are elected one at a time. Each time, Smith can cast 20 votes and Jones can cast 80. As a consequence, Jones elects all the candidates. The only way to guarantee a seat is to own 50 percent plus one share. This also guarantees that you would win every seat, so it's really all or nothing.

proxy
Grant of authority by shareholder allowing for another individual to vote his or her shares.

PROXY VOTING   A **proxy** is the grant of authority by a shareholder to someone else to vote his or her shares. For convenience, much of the voting in large public corporations is actually done by proxy.

---

12 By minority participation, we mean participation by shareholders with relatively small amounts of stock.

EXAMPLE 8A.1: Buying the Election

Stock in JRJ Corporation sells for $20 per share and features cumulative voting. There are 10,000 shares outstanding. If three directors are up for election, how much does it cost to ensure yourself a seat on the board?

The question here is how many shares of stock it will take to get a seat. The answer is 2,501, so the cost is 2,501 × $20 = $50,020. Why 2,501? Because there is no way the remaining 7,499 votes can be divided among three people to give all of them more than 2,501 votes. For example, suppose two people receive 2,502 votes and the first two seats. A third person can receive at most 10,000 − 2,502 − 2,502 − 2,501 = 2,495, so the third seat is yours.

As we've illustrated, straight voting can "freeze out" minority shareholders; that is the rationale for cumulative voting. But devices have been worked out to minimize its impact.

One such device is to stagger the voting for the board of directors. With staggered elections, only a fraction of the directorships are up for election at a particular time. Thus, if only two directors are up for election at any one time, it takes 1/(2 + 1) = 33.33% of the stock to guarantee a seat. Overall, staggering has two basic effects:

1. Staggering makes it more difficult for a minority to elect a director when there is cumulative voting because there are fewer to be elected at one time.
2. Staggering makes takeover attempts less likely to be successful because it is more difficult to vote in a majority of new directors.

We should note that staggering may serve a beneficial purpose. It provides "institutional memory," that is, continuity on the board of directors. This may be important for corporations with significant long-range plans and projects.

As we have seen, with straight voting, each share of stock has one vote. The owner of 10,000 shares has 10,000 votes. Many companies have hundreds of thousands or even millions of shareholders. Shareholders can come to the annual meeting and vote in person, or they can transfer their right to vote to another party.

Obviously, management always tries to get as many proxies transferred to it as possible. However, if the shareholders are not satisfied with management, an outside group of shareholders can try to obtain votes via proxy. They can vote by proxy to replace management by adding enough directors. Or they can vote to oppose certain specific measures proposed by management. For example, proxyholders can vote against granting generous stock options to management. This activity is called a proxy battle and we come back to it in more detail in Chapter 23.

Appendix Review Problem and Self-Test

A.1 **Cumulative versus Straight Voting** The Krishnamurti Corporation has 500,000 shares outstanding. There are four directors up for election. How many shares would you need to own to guarantee that you will win a seat if straight voting is used? If cumulative voting is used? Ignore possible ties.

Answer to Appendix Self-Test Problem

A.1 If there is straight voting, you need to own half the shares, or 250,000. In this case, you could also elect the other three directors. With cumulative voting, you need $1/(N + 1)$ percent of the shares, where N is the number of directors up for election. With four directors, this is 20 percent, or 100,000 shares.

Appendix Question and Problem

A.1 **Voting for Directors** The shareholders of Vycom, Inc., need to elect six new directors to the board. There are 1 million shares of common stock outstanding. How many shares do you need to own to guarantee yourself a seat on the board if:

  a. The company uses cumulative voting procedures?

  b. The company uses straight voting procedures?

Capital Budgeting

CHAPTER 9

Net Present Value and Other Investment Criteria

Zenon Environmental Inc. is a world leader in ultra-filtration technology for use in water treatment systems. In March 2006, General Electric announced an agreement to acquire the Oakville, Ontario–based company for $760 million. The acquisition is aimed at growing revenues in GE's Water & Process Technologies Platform at 30 percent per year for the next few years. GE's investment illustrates how advanced ultrafiltration technology is becoming increasingly important in water and wastewater treatment systems.

General Electric's purchase is an example of a capital budgeting decision. Investing $760 million in advanced ultrafiltration technology is a major undertaking that requires serious evaluation of the potential risks and rewards. In this chapter, we will discuss the basic tools in making such decisions.

www.zenon.ca

IN CHAPTER 1, we identified the three key areas of concern to the financial manager. The first of these was deciding which fixed assets to buy. We called this the capital budgeting decision. In this chapter, we begin to deal with the issues that arise in answering this question.

The process of allocating or budgeting capital is usually more involved than just deciding whether to buy a particular fixed asset. We frequently face broader issues such as whether to launch a new product or enter a new market. Decisions such as these determine the nature of a firm's operations and products for years to come, primarily because fixed asset investments are generally long-lived and not easily reversed once they are made.

The most fundamental decision that a business must make concerns its product line. What services will we offer or what will we sell? In what markets will we compete? What new products will we introduce? The answer to any of these questions requires that the firm commit its scarce and valuable capital to certain types of assets. As a result, all these strategic issues fall under the general heading of capital budgeting. The process of capital budgeting could thus be given a more descriptive (not to mention impressive) name: strategic asset allocation.

For the reasons we have discussed, the capital budgeting question is probably the most important issue in corporate finance. How a firm chooses to finance its operations (the capital structure question) and how a firm manages its short-term operating activities (the working capital question) are certainly issues of concern; however, fixed assets define the business of the firm. Airlines, for example, are airlines because they operate airplanes, regardless of how they finance them.

Any firm possesses a huge number of possible investments. Each of these possible investments is an option available to the firm. Some of these options are valuable and some are not. The essence of successful financial management, of course, is learning to identify which are which. With this in mind, our goal in this chapter is to introduce you to the techniques used to analyze potential business ventures to decide which are worth undertaking.

We present and compare a number of different procedures used in practice. Our primary goal is to acquaint you with the advantages and disadvantages of the various approaches. As we shall see, the most important concept in this area is the idea of net present value. We consider this next.

NET PRESENT VALUE

In Chapter 1, we argued that the goal of financial management is to create value for the shareholders. The financial manager must thus examine a potential investment in light of its likely effect on the price of the firm's shares. In this section, we describe a widely used procedure for doing this, the net present value approach.

The Basic Idea

An investment is worth undertaking if it creates value for its owners. In the most general sense, we create value by identifying an investment that is worth more in the marketplace than it costs us to acquire. How can something be worth more than it costs? It's a case of the whole being worth more than the cost of the parts.

For example, suppose you buy a run-down house for $65,000 and spend another $25,000 on painters, plumbers, and so on to get it fixed. Your total investment is $90,000. When the work is completed, you place the house back on the market and find that it's worth $100,000. The market value ($100,000) exceeds the cost ($90,000) by $10,000. What you have done here is to act as a manager and bring together some fixed assets (a house), some labour (plumbers, carpenters, and others), and some materials (carpeting, paint, and so on). The net result is that you have created $10,000 in value by employing business skills like human resources (hiring labour), project management, and marketing. Put another way, this $10,000 is the *value added* by management.

With our house example, it turned out after the fact that $10,000 in value was created. Things thus worked out very nicely. The real challenge, of course, was to somehow identify ahead of time whether or not investing the necessary $90,000 was a good idea. This is what capital budgeting is all about, namely, trying to determine whether a proposed investment or project will be worth more than it costs once it is in place.

For reasons that will be obvious in a moment, the difference between an investment's market value and its cost is called the **net present value (NPV)** of the investment. In other words, net present value is a measure of how much value is created or added today by undertaking an investment. Given our goal of creating value for the shareholders, the capital budgeting process can be viewed as a search for investments with positive net present values.

With our run-down house, you can probably imagine how we would make the capital budgeting decision. We would first look at what comparable, fixed-up properties were selling for in the market. We would then get estimates of the cost of buying a particular property and bringing it up to market. At this point, we have an estimated total cost and an estimated market value. If the difference is positive, this investment is worth undertaking because it has a positive estimated net present value. There is risk, of course, because there is no guarantee that our estimates will turn out to be correct.

As our example illustrates, investment decisions are greatly simplified when there is a market for assets similar to the investment we are considering. Capital budgeting becomes much more difficult when we cannot observe the market price for at least roughly comparable investments. We are then faced with the problem of estimating the value of an investment using only indirect market information. Unfortunately, this is precisely the situation the financial manager usually encounters. We examine this issue next.

Estimating Net Present Value

Imagine that we are thinking of starting a business to produce and sell a new product, say, organic fertilizer. We can estimate the start-up costs with reasonable accuracy because we know what we need to buy to begin production. Would this be a good investment? Based on our discussion, you know that the answer depends on whether the value of the new business exceeds the cost of starting it. In other words, does this investment have a positive NPV?

This problem is much more difficult than our fixer-upper house example because entire fertilizer companies are not routinely bought and sold in the marketplace, so it is essentially impossible to observe the market value of a similar investment. As a result, we must somehow estimate this value by other means.

Based on our work in Chapters 5 and 6, you may be able to guess how we estimate the value of our fertilizer business. We begin by trying to estimate the future cash flows that we expect the

net present value (NPV)
The difference between an investment's market value and its cost.

discounted cash flow (DCF) valuation
The process of valuing an investment by discounting its future cash flows.

new business to produce. We then apply our basic discounted cash flow procedure to estimate the present value of those cash flows. Once we have this number, we estimate NPV as the difference between the present value of the future cash flows and the cost of the investment. As we mentioned in Chapter 6, this procedure is often called **discounted cash flow (DCF) valuation.**

To see how we might estimate NPV, suppose we believe that the cash revenues from our fertilizer business will be $20,000 per year, assuming everything goes as expected. Cash costs (including taxes) will be $14,000 per year. We will wind down the business in eight years. The plant, property, and equipment will be worth $2,000 as salvage at that time. The project costs $30,000 to launch. We use a 15 percent discount rate on new projects such as this one. Is this a good investment? If there are 1,000 shares of stock outstanding, what will be the effect on the price per share from taking it?

From a purely mechanical perspective, we need to calculate the present value of the future cash flows at 15 percent. The net cash flow inflow will be $20,000 cash income less $14,000 in costs per year for eight years. These cash flows are illustrated in Figure 9.1. As Figure 9.1 suggests, we effectively have an eight-year annuity of $20,000 − 14,000 = $6,000 per year along with a single lump-sum inflow of $2,000 in eight years. Calculating the present value of the future cash flows thus comes down to the same type of problem we considered in Chapter 6. The total present value is:

$$\text{Present value} = \$6,000 \times (1 - 1/1.15^8)/.15 + 2,000/1.15^8$$
$$= \$6,000 \times 4.4873 + 2,000/3.0590$$
$$= \$26,924 + 654$$
$$= \$27,578$$

When we compare this to the $30,000 estimated cost, the NPV is:

$$\text{NPV} = -\$30,000 + 27,578 = -\$2,422$$

Therefore, this is not a good investment. Based on our estimates, taking it would decrease the total value of the stock by $2,422. With 1,000 shares outstanding, our best estimate of the impact of taking this project is a loss of value of $2,422/1,000 = $2.422 per share.

Our fertilizer example illustrates how NPV estimates can help determine whether or not an investment is desirable. From our example, notice that, if the NPV is negative, the effect on share value would be unfavourable. If the NPV is positive, the effect would be favourable. As a consequence, all we need to know about a particular proposal for the purpose of making an accept/reject decision is whether the NPV is positive or negative.

Given that the goal of financial management is to increase share value, our discussion in this section leads us to the *net present value rule*:

> An investment should be accepted if the net present value is positive and rejected if it is negative.

FIGURE 9.1

Project cash flows ($ 000s)

Time (years)	0	1	2	3	4	5	6	7	8
Initial cost	−$30								
Inflows		$20	$20	$20	$20	$20	$20	$20	$20
Outflows		− 14	− 14	− 14	− 14	− 14	− 14	− 14	− 14
Net inflow		$ 6	$ 6	$ 6	$ 6	$ 6	$ 6	$ 6	$ 6
Salvage									2
Net cash flow	−$30	$ 6	$ 6	$ 6	$ 6	$ 6	$ 6	$ 6	$ 8

In the unlikely event that the net present value turned out to be zero, we would be indifferent to taking the investment or not taking it.

Two comments about our example are in order: First, it is not the rather mechanical process of discounting the cash flows that is important. Once we have the cash flows and the appropriate discount rate, the required calculations are fairly straightforward. The task of coming up with the cash flows and the discount rate in the first place is much more challenging. We have much more to say about this in the next several chapters. For the remainder of this chapter, we take it as given that we have estimates of the cash revenues and costs and, where needed, an appropriate discount rate.

The second thing to keep in mind about our example is that the −$2,422 NPV is an estimate. Like any estimate, it can be high or low. The only way to find out the true NPV would be to place the investment up for sale and see what we could get for it. We generally won't be doing this, so it is important that our estimates be reliable. Once again, we have more to say about this later. For the rest of this chapter, we assume the estimates are accurate.

As we have seen in this section, estimating NPV is one way of assessing the merits of a proposed investment. It is certainly not the only way that profitability is assessed, and we now turn to some alternatives. As we shall see, when compared to NPV, each of the ways of assessing profitability that we examine is flawed in some key way; so NPV is the preferred approach in principle, if not always in practice.

EXAMPLE 9.1: Using the NPV Rule

Suppose we are asked to decide whether or not a new consumer product should be launched. Based on projected sales and costs, we expect that the cash flows over the five-year life of the project will be $2,000 in the first two years, $4,000 in the next two, and $5,000 in the last year. It will cost about $10,000 to begin production. We use a 10 percent discount rate to evaluate new products. What should we do here?

Given the cash flows and discount rate, we can calculate the total value of the product by discounting the cash flows back to the present:

$$\text{Present value} = \$2,000/1.1 + 2,000/1.1^2 + 4,000/1.1^3 +$$
$$4,000/1.1^4 + 5,000/1.1^5$$
$$= \$1,818 + 1,653 + 3,005 + 2,732 + 3,105$$
$$= \$12,313$$

The present value of the expected cash flows is $12,313, but the cost of getting those cash flows is only $10,000, so the NPV is $12,313 − 10,000 = $2,313. This is positive; so, based on the net present value rule, we should take on the project.

SPREADSHEET STRATEGIES

Calculating NPVs with a Spreadsheet

Spreadsheets are commonly used to calculate NPVs. Examining the use of spreadsheets in this context also allows us to issue an important warning. Let's rework Example 9.1:

	A	B	C	D	E	F	G	H
1								
2			Using a spreadsheet to calculate net present values					
3								
4	From Example 9.1, the project's cost is $10,000. The cash flows are $2,000 per year for the first							
5	two years, $4,000 per year for the next two, and $5,000 in the last year. The discount rate is							
6	10 percent; what's the NPV?							
7								
8		Year	Cash flow					
9		0	-$10,000		Discount rate =		10%	
10		1	2,000					
11		2	2,000		NPV =	$2,102.72	(*wrong* answer)	
12		3	4,000		NPV =	$2,312.99	(*right* answer)	
13		4	4,000					
14		5	5,000					
15	The formula entered in cell F11 is =NPV(F9, C9:C14). This gives the wrong answer because the NPV function							
16	calculates the sum of the present value of each number in the series, assuming that the first number occurs at							
17	the end of the first period. Therefore, in this example the year 0 value is discounted by 1 year or 10 percent							
18	(we clearly don't want this number to be discounted at all).							
19	The formula entered in cell F12 is =NPV(F9, C10:C14) + C9. This gives the right answer because the							
20	NPV function is used to calculate the present value of the cash flows for future years and then the initial cost is							
21	subtracted to calculate the answer. Notice that we added cell C9 because it is already negative.							

SPREADSHEET STRATEGIES

In our spreadsheet example just above, notice that we have provided two answers. By comparing the answers to that found in Example 9.1, we see that the first answer is wrong even though we used the spreadsheet's NPV formula. What happened is that the "NPV" function in our spreadsheet is actually a PV function; unfortunately, one of the original spreadsheet programs many years ago got the definition wrong, and subsequent spreadsheets have copied it! Our second answer shows how to use the formula properly.

The example here illustrates the danger of blindly using calculators or computers without understanding what is going on; we shudder to think of how many capital budgeting decisions in the real world are based on incorrect use of this particular function. We will see another example of something that can go wrong with a spreadsheet later in the chapter.

CALCULATOR HINTS

Finding NPV

You can solve this problem using a financial calculator by doing the following:

CFo = -$10,000
C01 = $2,000
F01 = 2
C02 = $4,000
F02 = 2   I = 10%
C03 = $5,000
F03 = 1   NPV = CPT

CF   NPV

The answer to the problem is: $2,312.99

NOTE: To toggle between the different cash flow and NPV options, use the ↑↓ arrows found on the calculator.

CONCEPT QUESTIONS

1. What is the net present value rule?

2. If we say that an investment has an NPV of $1,000, what exactly do we mean?

9.2 | THE PAYBACK RULE

It is very common in practice to talk of the payback on a proposed investment. Loosely, the payback is the length of time it takes to recover our initial investment. Because this idea is widely understood and used, we examine and critique it in some detail.

Defining the Rule

We can illustrate how to calculate a payback with an example. Figure 9.2 shows the cash flows from a proposed investment. How many years do we have to wait until the accumulated cash flows from this investment equal or exceed the cost of the investment? As Figure 9.2 indicates, the initial investment is $50,000. After the first year, the firm has recovered $30,000, leaving $20,000.

payback period
The amount of time required for an investment to generate cash flows to recover its initial cost.

The cash flow in the second year is exactly $20,000, so this investment pays for itself in exactly two years. Put another way, the **payback period** is two years. If we require a payback of, say, three years or less, then this investment is acceptable. This illustrates the *payback period rule*:

> Based on the payback rule, an investment is acceptable if its calculated payback is less than some prespecified number of years.

In our example, the payback works out to be exactly two years. This won't usually happen, of course. When the numbers don't work out exactly, it is customary to work with fractional years. For example, suppose the initial investment is $60,000, and the cash flows are $20,000 in the first year and $90,000 in the second. The cash flows over the first two years are $110,000, so the project obviously pays back sometime in the second year. After the first year, the project has paid back $20,000, leaving $40,000 to be recovered. To figure out the fractional year, note that this $40,000 is $40,000/$90,000 = 4/9 of the second year's cash flow. Assuming that the $90,000 cash flow is paid uniformly throughout the year, the payback would thus be $1^4/9$ years.

FIGURE 9.2

Net project cash flows

Year	0	1	2	3	4
	−$50,000	$30,000	$20,000	$10,000	$5,000

Analyzing the Payback Period Rule

When compared to the NPV rule, the payback period rule has some rather severe shortcomings. Perhaps the biggest problem with the payback period rule is coming up with the right cutoff period because we don't really have an objective basis for choosing a particular number. Put another way, there is no economic rationale for looking at payback in the first place, so we have no guide as to how to pick the cutoff. As a result, we end up using a number that is arbitrarily chosen.

Another critical disadvantage is that the payback period is calculated by simply adding the future cash flows. There is no discounting involved, so the time value of money is ignored. Finally, a payback rule does not consider risk differences. The payback rule would be calculated the same way for both very risky and very safe projects.

Suppose we have somehow decided on an appropriate payback period, say two years or less. As we have seen, the payback period rule ignores the time value of money for the first two years. More seriously, cash flows after the second year are ignored. To see this, consider the two investments, Long and Short, in Table 9.1. Both projects cost $250. Based on our discussion, the payback on Long is 2 + $50/100 = 2.5 years, and the payback on Short is 1 + $150/200 = 1.75 years. With a cutoff of two years, Short is acceptable and Long is not.

Is the payback period rule giving us the right decisions? Maybe not. Suppose again that we require a 15 percent return on this type of investment. We can calculate the NPV for these two investments as:

$$NPV(Short) = -\$250 + 100/1.15 + 200/1.15^2 = -\$11.81$$
$$NPV(Long) = -\$250 + 100 \times (1 - 1/1.15^4)/.15 - \$35.50$$

Now we have a problem. The NPV of the shorter-term investment is actually negative, meaning that taking it diminishes the value of the shareholders' equity. The opposite is true for the longer-term investment—it increases share value.

Our example illustrates two primary shortcomings of the payback period rule. First, by ignoring time value, we may be led to take investments (like Short) that actually are worth less than they cost. Second, by ignoring cash flows beyond the cutoff, we may be led to reject profitable long-term investments (like Long). More generally, using a payback period rule tends to bias us toward shorter-term investments.

TABLE 9.1
Investment projected
cash flows

Year	Long	Short
1	$100	$100
2	100	200
3	100	0
4	100	0

Redeeming Qualities

Despite its shortcomings, the payback period rule is often used by small businesses whose managers lack financial skills. It is also used by large and sophisticated companies when making relatively small decisions. There are several reasons for this. The primary reason is that many decisions simply do not warrant detailed analysis because the cost of the analysis would exceed the possible loss from a mistake. As a practical matter, an investment that pays back rapidly and has benefits extending beyond the cutoff period probably has a positive NPV.

Small investment decisions are made by the hundreds every day in large organizations. Moreover, they are made at all levels. As a result, it would not be uncommon for a corporation to require, for example, a two-year payback on all investments of less than $10,000. Investments larger than this are subjected to greater scrutiny. The requirement of a two-year payback is not perfect for reasons we have seen, but it does exercise some control over expenditures and thus limits possible losses.

In addition to its simplicity, the payback rule has several other features to recommend it. First, because it is biased toward short-term projects, it is biased toward liquidity. In other words, a payback rule favours investments that free up cash for other uses more quickly. This could be very important for a small business; it would be less so for a large corporation. Second, the cash flows that are expected to occur later in a project's life are probably more uncertain. Arguably, a payback period rule adjusts for the extra riskiness of later cash flows, but it does so in a rather draconian fashion—by ignoring them altogether.

We should note here that some of the apparent simplicity of the payback rule is an illusion. We still must come up with the cash flows first, and, as we discussed previously, this is not easy to do. Thus, it would probably be more accurate to say that the concept of a payback period is both intuitive and easy to understand.

Summary of the Rule

To summarize, the payback period is a kind of "break-even" measure. Because time value is ignored, you can think of the payback period as the length of time it takes to break even in an accounting sense, but not in an economic sense. The biggest drawback to the payback period rule is that it doesn't ask the right question. The relevant issue is the impact an investment will have on the value of our stock, not how long it takes to recover the initial investment.

Nevertheless, because it is so simple, companies often use it as a screen for dealing with the myriad of minor investment decisions they have to make. There is certainly nothing wrong with this practice. As with any simple rule of thumb, there will be some errors in using it, but it would not have survived all this time if it weren't useful. Now that you understand the rule, you can be on the alert for those circumstances under which it might lead to problems. To help you remember, the following table lists the pros and cons of the payback period rule.

Advantages and Disadvantages of the Payback Period Rule	
Advantages	**Disadvantages**
1. Easy to understand.	1. Ignores the time value of money.
2. Adjusts for uncertainty of later cash flows.	2. Requires an arbitrary cutoff point.
3. Biased towards liquidity.	3. Ignores cash flows beyond the cutoff date.
	4. Biased against long-term projects, such as research and development, and new projects.

The Discounted Payback Rule

discounted payback period
The length of time required for an investment's discounted cash flows to equal its initial cost.

We saw that one of the shortcomings of the payback period rule was that it ignored time value. There is a variation of the payback period, the **discounted payback period,** that fixes this particular problem. The discounted payback period is the length of time until the sum of the discounted cash flows equals the initial investment. The *discounted payback rule* is:

> An investment is acceptable if its discounted payback is less than some prescribed number of years.

To see how we might calculate the discounted payback period, suppose we require a 12.5 percent return on new investments. We have an investment that costs $300 and has cash flows of $100 per year for five years. To get the discounted payback, we have to discount each cash flow at 12.5 percent and then start adding them. We do this in Table 9.2. We have both the discounted and the undiscounted cash flows in Table 9.2. Looking at the accumulated cash flows, the regular payback is exactly three years (look for the arrow in Year 3). The discounted cash flows total $300 only after four years, so the discounted payback is four years as shown.[1]

How do we interpret the discounted payback? Recall that the ordinary payback is the time it takes to break even in an accounting sense. Since it includes the time value of money, the discounted payback is the time it takes to break even in an economic or financial sense. Loosely speaking, in our example, we get our money back along with the interest we could have earned elsewhere in four years.

Based on our example, the discounted payback would seem to have much to recommend it. You may be surprised to find out that it is rarely used. Why? Probably because it really isn't any simpler than NPV. To calculate a discounted payback, you have to discount cash flows, add them up, and compare them to the cost, just as you do with NPV. So, unlike an ordinary payback, the discounted payback is not especially simple to calculate.

A discounted payback period rule still has a couple of significant drawbacks. The biggest one is that the cutoff still has to be arbitrarily set and cash flows beyond that point are ignored.[2] As a result, a project with a positive NPV may not be acceptable because the cutoff is too short. Also, just because one project has a shorter discounted payback than another does not mean it has a larger NPV.

TABLE 9.2
Ordinary and discounted payback

Year	Cash Flow		Accumulated Cash Flow	
	Undiscounted	**Discounted**	**Undiscounted**	**Discounted**
1	$100	$89	$100	$ 89
2	100	79	200	168
3	100	70	⇒300	238
4	100	62	400	⇒300
5	100	55	500	355

All things considered, the discounted payback is a compromise between a regular payback and NPV that lacks the simplicity of the first and the conceptual rigour of the second. Nonetheless, if we need to assess the time it takes to recover the investment required by a project, the discounted payback is better than the ordinary payback because it considers time value. In other words, the discounted payback recognizes that we could have invested the money elsewhere and earned a return on it. The ordinary payback does not take this into account.

The advantages and disadvantages of the discounted payback are summarized in the following table:

---

1 In this case, the discounted payback is an even number of years. This won't ordinarily happen, of course. However, calculating a fractional year for the discounted payback period is more involved than for the ordinary payback, and it is not commonly done.

2 If the cutoff were forever, then the discounted payback rule would be the same as the NPV rule. It would also be the same as the profitability index rule considered in a later section.

Discounted Payback Period Rule	
Advantages	**Disadvantages**
1. Includes time value of money.	1. May reject positive NPV investments.
2. Easy to understand.	2. Requires an arbitrary cutoff point.
3. Does not accept negative estimated NPV investments.	3. Ignores cash flows beyond the cutoff date.
4. Biased toward liquidity.	4. Biased against long-term projects, such as research and development, and new projects.

CONCEPT QUESTIONS

1. What is the payback period? The payback period rule?

2. Why do we say that the payback period is, in a sense, an accounting break-even?

average accounting return (AAR)
An investment's average net income divided by its average book value.

THE AVERAGE ACCOUNTING RETURN

Another attractive, but flawed, approach to making capital budgeting decisions is the **average accounting return (AAR)**. There are many different definitions of the AAR. However, in one form or another, the AAR is always defined as:

$$\frac{\text{Some measure of average accounting profit}}{\text{Some measure of average accounting value}}$$

The specific definition we use is:

$$\frac{\text{Average net income}}{\text{Average book value}}$$

To see how we might calculate this number, suppose we are deciding whether to open a store in a new shopping mall. The required investment in improvements is $500,000. The store would have a five-year life because everything reverts to the mall owners after that time. The required investment would be 100 percent depreciated (straight-line) over five years, so the depreciation would be $500,000/5 = $100,000 per year. The tax rate for this small business is 25 percent.[3] Table 9.3 contains the projected revenues and expenses. Based on these figures, net income in each year is also shown.

To calculate the average book value for this investment, we note that we started out with a book value of $500,000 (the initial cost) and ended up at $0. The average book value during the life of the investment is thus ($500,000 + 0)/2 = $250,000. As long as we use straight-line depreciation, the average investment is always 1⁄2 of the initial investment.[4]

Looking at Table 9.3, net income is $100,000 in the first year, $150,000 in the second year, $50,000 in the third year, $0 in Year 4, and –$50,000 in Year 5. The average net income, then, is:

$$[\$100,000 + 150,000 + 50,000 + 0 + (-\$50,000)]/5 = \$50,000$$

The average accounting return is:

$$\text{AAR} = \text{Average net income/Average book value} = \$50,000/\$250,000$$
$$= 20\%$$

If the firm has a target AAR less than 20 percent, this investment is acceptable; otherwise it is not. The *average accounting return rule* is thus:

---

3 These depreciation and tax rates are chosen for simplicity. Chapter 10 discusses depreciation and taxes.

4 We could, of course, calculate the average of the six book values directly. In thousands, we would have ($500 + 400 + 300 + 200 + 100 + 0)/6 = $250.

TABLE 9.3   Projected yearly revenue and costs for average accounting return

	Year 1	Year 2	Year 3	Year 4	Year 5
Revenue	$433,333	$450,000	$266,667	$200,000	$133,333
Expenses	200,000	150,000	100,000	100,000	100,000
Earnings before depreciation	$233,333	$300,000	$166,667	$100,000	$ 33,333
Depreciation	100,000	100,000	100,000	100,000	100,000
Earnings before taxes	$133,333	$200,000	$ 66,667	$ 0	–$ 66,667
Taxes	33,333	50,000	16,667	0	–16,667
(Tc = 0.25)					
Net income	$100,000	$150,000	$ 50,000	$ 0	–$ 50,000

$$\text{Average net income} = \frac{(\$100{,}000 + 150{,}000 + 50{,}000 + 0 - 50{,}000)}{5} = \$50{,}000$$

$$\text{Average investment} = \frac{\$500{,}000 + 0}{2} = \$250{,}000$$

> Based on the average accounting return rule, a project is acceptable if its average accounting return exceeds a target average accounting return.

As we see in the next section, this rule has a number of problems.

Analyzing the Average Accounting Return Method

You recognize the first drawback to the AAR immediately. Above all else, the AAR is not a rate of return in any meaningful economic sense. Instead, it is the ratio of two accounting numbers, and it is not comparable to the returns offered, for example, in financial markets.[5]

One of the reasons the AAR is not a true rate of return is that it ignores time value. When we average figures that occur at different times, we are treating the near future and the more distant future the same way. There was no discounting involved when we computed the average net income, for example.

The second problem with the AAR is similar to the problem we had with the payback period rule concerning the lack of an objective cutoff period. Since a calculated AAR is really not comparable to a market return, the target AAR must somehow be specified. There is no generally agreed-on way to do this. One way of doing it is to calculate the AAR for the firm as a whole and use this for a benchmark, but there are lots of other ways as well.

The third, and perhaps worst, flaw in the AAR is that it doesn't even look at the right things. Instead of cash flow and market value, it uses net income and book value. These are both poor substitutes because the value of the firm is the present value of future cash flows. As a result, an AAR doesn't tell us what the effect on share price will be from taking an investment, so it does not tell us what we really want to know.

Does the AAR have any redeeming features? About the only one is that it almost always can be computed. The reason is that accounting information is almost always available, both for the project under consideration and for the firm as a whole. We hasten to add that once the accounting information is available, we can always convert it to cash flows, so even this is not a particularly important fact. The AAR is summarized in the following table:

Average Accounting Return Rule

Advantages	Disadvantages
1. Easy to calculate.	1. Not a true rate of return; time value of money is ignored.
2. Needed information is usually available.	2. Uses an arbitrary benchmark cutoff rate.
	3. Based on accounting (book) values, not cash flows and market values.

---

5 The AAR is closely related to the return on assets (ROA) discussed in Chapter 3. In practice, the AAR is sometimes computed by first calculating the ROA for each year and then averaging the results. This produces a number that is similar, but not identical, to the one we computed.

internal rate of return (IRR)
The discount rate that makes the NPV of an investment zero.

CONCEPT QUESTIONS

1. What is an accounting rate of return (AAR)?

2. What are the weaknesses of the AAR rule?

THE INTERNAL RATE OF RETURN

We now come to the most important alternative to NPV, the **internal rate of return,** universally known as the IRR. As we see, the IRR is closely related to NPV. With the IRR, we try to find a single rate of return that summarizes the merits of a project. Furthermore, we want this rate to be an internal rate in the sense that it depends only on the cash flows of a particular investment, not on rates offered elsewhere.

To illustrate the idea behind the IRR, consider a project that costs $100 today and pays $110 in one year. Suppose you were asked, "What is the return on this investment?" What would you say? It seems both natural and obvious to say that the return is 10 percent because, for every dollar we put in, we get $1.10 back. In fact, as we see in a moment, 10 percent is the internal rate of return or IRR on this investment.

Is this project with its 10 percent IRR a good investment? Once again, it would seem apparent that this is a good investment only if our required return is less than 10 percent. This intuition is also correct and illustrates the *IRR rule:*

> Based on the IRR rule, an investment is acceptable if the IRR exceeds the required return. It should be rejected otherwise.

If you understand the IRR rule, you should see that we used the IRR (without defining it) when we calculated the yield to maturity of a bond in Chapter 7. In fact, the yield to maturity is the bond's IRR.[6] More generally, many returns for different types of assets are calculated the same way.

Imagine that we wanted to calculate the NPV for our simple investment. At a discount rate of r, the NPV is:

$$\text{NPV} = -\$100 + 110/(1 + r)$$

Suppose we didn't know the discount rate. This presents a problem, but we could still ask how high the discount rate would have to be before this project was unacceptable. We know that we are indifferent to taking or not taking this investment when its NPV is just equal to zero. In other words, this investment is economically a break-even proposition when the NPV is zero because value is neither created nor destroyed. To find the break-even discount rate, we set NPV equal to zero and solve for r:

$$\text{NPV} = 0 = -\$100 + 110/(1 + r)$$
$$\$100 = \$110/(1 + r)$$
$$1 + r = \$110/100 = 1.10$$
$$r = 10\%$$

This 10 percent is what we already have called the return on this investment. What we have now illustrated is that the internal rate of return on an investment (or just return for short) is the discount rate that makes the NPV equal to zero. This is an important observation, so it bears repeating:

> The IRR on an investment is the return that results in a zero NPV when it is used as the discount rate.

6 Strictly speaking, this is true for bonds with annual coupons. Typically, bonds carry semiannual coupons so yield to maturity is the six-month IRR expressed as a stated rate per year. Further, the yield to maturity is based on cash flows promised by the bond issuer as opposed to cash flows expected by a firm.

FIGURE 9.3

Project cash flows

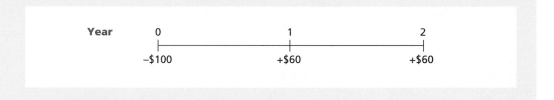

The fact that the IRR is simply the discount rate that makes the NPV equal to zero is important because it tells us how to calculate the returns on more complicated investments. As we have seen, finding the IRR turns out to be relatively easy for a single period investment. However, suppose you were now looking at an investment with the cash flows shown in Figure 9.3. As illustrated, this investment costs $100 and has a cash flow of $60 per year for two years, so it's only slightly more complicated than our single period example. If you were asked for the return on this investment, what would you say? There doesn't seem to be any obvious answer (at least to us). Based on what we now know, we can set the NPV equal to zero and solve for the discount rate:

$$NPV = 0 = -\$100 + 60/(1 + IRR) + 60/(1 + IRR)^2$$

Unfortunately, the only way to find the IRR in general is by trial and error, either by hand or by calculator. This is precisely the same problem that came up in Chapter 5 when we found the unknown rate for an annuity and in Chapter 7 when we found the yield to maturity on a bond. In fact, we now see that, in both of those cases, we were finding an IRR.

In this particular case, the cash flows form a two-period, $60 annuity. To find the unknown rate, we can try various different rates until we get the answer. If we were to start with a 0 percent rate, the NPV would obviously be $120 – 100 = $20. At a 10 percent discount rate, we would have:

$$NPV = -\$100 + 60/1.1 + 60/(1.1)^2 = \$4.13$$

Now, we're getting close. We can summarize these and some other possibilities as shown in Table 9.4. From our calculations, the NPV appears to be zero between 10 and 15 percent, so the IRR is somewhere in that range. With a little more effort, we can find that the IRR is about 13.1 percent.[7] So, if our required return is less than 13.1 percent, we would take this investment. If our required return exceeds 13.1 percent, we would reject it.

By now, you have probably noticed that the IRR rule and the NPV rule appear to be quite similar. In fact, the IRR is sometimes simply called the discounted cash flow or DCF return. The easiest way to illustrate the relationship between NPV and IRR is to plot the numbers we calculated in Table 9.4. On the vertical or y-axis we put the different NPVs. We put discount rates on the horizontal or x-axis. If we had a very large number of points, the resulting picture would be a smooth curve called a **net present value profile**. Figure 9.4 illustrates the NPV profile for this project. Beginning with a 0 percent discount rate, we have $20 plotted directly on the y-axis. As the discount rate increases, the NPV declines smoothly. Where does the curve cut through the x-axis? This occurs where the NPV is just equal to zero, so it happens right at the IRR of 13.1 percent.

net present value profile
A graphical representation of the relationship between an investment's NPVs and various discount rates.

In our example, the NPV rule and the IRR rule lead to identical accept/reject decisions. We accept an investment using the IRR rule if the required return is less than 13.1 percent. As

TABLE 9.4
NPV at different discount rates

Discount Rate	NPV
0%	$20.00
5	11.56
10	4.13
15	–2.46
20	–8.33

7 With a lot more effort (or a calculator or personal computer), we can find that the IRR is approximately (to 15 decimal points) 13.0662386291808 percent, not that anybody would ever want this many decimal points.

FIGURE 9.4

An NPV profile

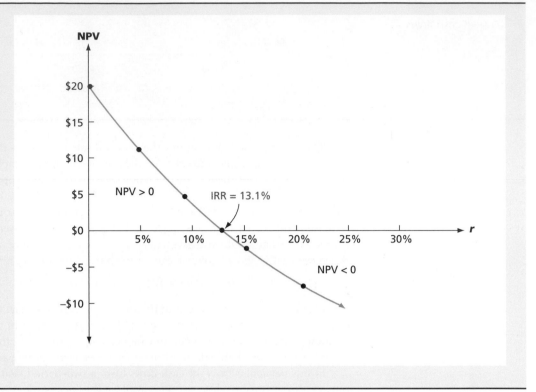

EXAMPLE 9.2: Calculating the IRR

A project has a total up-front cost of $435.44. The cash flows are $100 in the first year, $200 in the second year, and $300 in the third year. What's the IRR? If we require an 18 percent return, should we take this investment?

We'll describe the NPV profile and find the IRR by calculating some NPVs at different discount rates. You should check our answers for practice. Beginning with 0 percent, we have:

Discount Rate	NPV
0%	$164.56
5	100.36
10	46.15
15	0.00
20	−39.61

The NPV is zero at 15 percent, so 15 percent is the IRR. If we require an 18 percent return, we should not take the investment. The reason is that the NPV is negative at 18 percent (check that it is −$24.47). The IRR rule tells us the same thing in this case. We shouldn't take this investment because its 15 percent return is less than our required 18 percent return.

Figure 9.4 illustrates, however, the NPV is positive at any discount rate less than 13.1 percent, so we would accept the investment using the NPV rule as well. The two rules are equivalent in this case.

At this point, you may be wondering whether the IRR and the NPV rules always lead to identical decisions. The answer is yes as long as two very important conditions are met: First, the project's cash flows must be conventional, meaning that the first cash flow (the initial investment) is negative and all the rest are positive. Second, the project must be independent, meaning the decision to accept or reject this project does not affect the decision to accept or reject any other. The first of these conditions is typically met, but the second often is not. In any case, when one or both of these conditions is not met, problems can arise. We discuss some of these next.

Problems with the IRR

Problems with the IRR come about when the cash flows are not conventional or when we are trying to compare two or more investments to see which is best. In the first case, surprisingly, the simple question—What's the return?—can become very difficult to answer. In the second case, the IRR can be a misleading guide.

SPREADSHEET STRATEGIES

Calculating IRRs with a Spreadsheet

Because IRRs are so tedious to calculate by hand, financial calculators and, especially, spreadsheets are generally used. The procedures used by various financial calculators are too different for us to illustrate here, so we will focus on using a spreadsheet. As the following example illustrates, using a spreadsheet is very easy.

	A	B	C	D	E	F	G	H
1								
2			Using a spreadsheet to calculate internal rates of return					
3								
4	Suppose we have a four-year project that costs $500. The cash flows over the four-year life will be							
5	$100, $200, $300, and $400. What is the IRR?							
6								
7		Year	Cash flow					
8		0	-$500					
9		1	100		IRR =	27.3%		
10		2	200					
11		3	300					
12		4	400					
13								
14								
15	The formula entered in cell F9 is =IRR(C8:C12). Notice that the Year 0 cash flow has a negative							
16	sign representing the initial cost of the project.							
17								

CALCULATOR HINTS

Finding IRR

You can solve this problem using a financial calculator by doing the following:

CFo = -$5000
C01 = $100
F01 = 1
C02 = $200
F02 = 1
C03 = $300
F03 = 1
C04 = $400   IRR = **CPT**
F04 = 1

CF   **IRR**

The answer to the problem is: 27.2732%

NOTE: To toggle between the different cash flow options, use the **↑↓** arrows found on the calculator.

NON-CONVENTIONAL CASH FLOWS   Suppose we have an oil sands project that requires a $60 investment. Our cash flow in the first year will be $155. In the second year, the mine is depleted, but we have to spend $100 to restore the terrain. As Figure 9.5 illustrates, both the first and third cash flows are negative.

To find the IRR on this project, we can calculate the NPV at various rates:

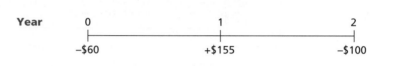

Discount Rate	NPV
0%	–$ 5.00
10	–1.74
20	–0.28
30	0.06
40	–0.31

The NPV appears to be behaving in a very peculiar fashion here. As the discount rate increases from 0 percent to 30 percent, the NPV starts out negative and becomes positive. This seems backward because the NPV is rising as the discount rate rises. It then starts getting smaller and becomes negative again. What's the IRR? To find out, we draw the NPV profile in Figure 9.6.

In Figure 9.6, notice that the NPV is zero when the discount rate is 25 percent, so this is the IRR. Or is it? The NPV is also zero at 33⅓ percent. Which of these is correct? The answer is both or neither; more precisely, there is no unambiguously correct answer. This is the **multiple rates of return** problem. Many financial computer packages (including the best seller for personal computers) aren't aware of this problem and just report the first IRR that is found. Others report only the smallest positive IRR, even though this answer is no better than any other.

multiple rates of return
One potential problem in using the IRR method if more than one discount rate makes the NPV of an investment zero.

FIGURE 9.5

Project cash flows

Year	0	1	2
	–$60	+$155	–$100

FIGURE 9.6

NPV and the multiple IRR problem

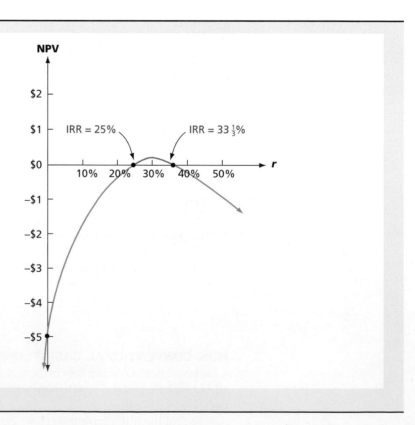

In our current example, the IRR rule breaks down completely. Suppose our required return were 10 percent. Should we take this investment? Both IRRs are greater than 10 percent, so, by the IRR rule, maybe we should. However, as Figure 9.6 shows, the NPV is negative at any discount rate less than 25 percent, so this is not a good investment. When should we take it? Looking at Figure 9.6 one last time, the NPV is positive only if our required return is between 25 and $33\frac{1}{3}$ percent.

www.opgdirect.com
www.oeb.gov.on.ca

Non-conventional cash flows occur when a project has an outlay (negative cash flow) at the end (or in some intermediate period in the life of a project) as well as the beginning. Earlier, we gave the example of a strip mine with its major environmental cleanup costs at the end of the project life. Another common example faces utilities like Ontario Hydro that invested in nuclear power plants. Heightened safety and environmental concerns are forcing utilities to begin planning to decommission nuclear plants. To make matters worse, utilities regulators, like the Ontario Energy Board, are deregulating electricity markets so that Ontario Hydro cannot pass on the decommissioning costs to consumers. This creates a major expense for Ontario Hydro on plant closedown and gives the project a non-conventional cash flow pattern.

The moral of the story is that when the cash flows aren't conventional, strange things can start to happen to the IRR. This is not anything to get upset about, however, because the NPV rule, as always, works just fine. This illustrates that, oddly enough, the obvious question—What's the rate of return?—may not always have a good answer.

mutually exclusive investment decisions
One potential problem in using the IRR method if the acceptance of one project excludes that of another.

MUTUALLY EXCLUSIVE INVESTMENTS   Even if there is a single IRR, another problem can arise concerning mutually exclusive investment decisions. If two investments, X and Y, are mutually exclusive, then taking one of them means we cannot take the other. For example, if we own one corner lot, we can build a gas station or an apartment building, but not both. These are mutually exclusive alternatives.

Thus far, we have asked whether or not a given investment is worth undertaking. A related question, however, comes up very often: Given two or more mutually exclusive investments, which one is the best? The answer is simple enough: The best one is the one with the largest NPV. Can we also say that the best one has the highest return? As we show, the answer is no.

To illustrate the problem with the IRR rule and mutually exclusive investments, consider the cash flows from the following two mutually exclusive investments:

EXAMPLE 9.3: What's the IRR?

You are looking at an investment that requires you to invest $51 today. You'll get $100 in one year, but you must pay out $50 in two years. What is the IRR on this investment?

You're on the alert now to the non-conventional cash flow problem, so you probably wouldn't be surprised to see more than one IRR. However, if you start looking for an IRR by trial and error, it will take you a long time. The reason is that there is no IRR. The NPV is negative at every discount rate, so we shouldn't take this investment under any circumstances. What's the return of this investment? Your guess is as good as ours.

EXAMPLE 9.4: "I Think, Therefore I Know How Many IRRs There Can Be."

We've seen that it's possible to get more than one IRR. If you wanted to make sure that you had found all of the possible IRRs, how could you tell? The answer comes from the great mathematician, philosopher, and financial analyst Descartes (of "I think; therefore I am" fame). Descartes's rule of signs says that the maximum number of IRRs is equal to the number of times that the cash flows change sign from positive to negative and/or negative to positive.[8]

In our example with the 25 and $33\frac{1}{3}$ percent IRRs, could there be yet another IRR? The cash flows flip from negative to positive, then back to negative, for a total of two sign changes. As a result, the maximum number of IRRs is two, and, from Descartes's rule, we don't need to look for any more. Note that the actual number of IRRs can be less than the maximum (see Example 9.3).

---

8 To be more precise, the number of IRRs that are bigger than −100 percent is generally equal to the number of sign changes, or it differs from the number of sign changes by an even number. Thus, for example, if there are five sign changes, there are either five, three, or one IRRs. If there are two sign changes, there are either two IRRs or no IRRs.

Year	Investment A	Investment B
0	–$100	–$100
1	50	20
2	40	40
3	40	50
4	30	60
IRR	24%	21%

Since these investments are mutually exclusive, we can take only one of them. Simple intuition suggests that Investment A is better because of its higher return. Unfortunately, simple intuition is not always correct.

To see why investment A is not necessarily the better of the two investments, we've calculated the NPV of these investments for different required returns:

Discount Rate	NPV(A)	NPV(B)
0%	$60.00	$70.00
5	43.13	47.88
10	29.06	29.79
15	17.18	14.82
20	7.06	2.31
25	–1.63	–8.22

The IRR for A (24 percent) is larger than the IRR for B (21 percent). However, if you compare the NPVs, you'll see that which investment has the higher NPV depends on our required return. B has greater total cash flow, but it pays back more slowly than A. As a result, it has a higher NPV at lower discount rates.

In our example, the NPV and IRR rankings conflict for some discount rates. If our required return is 10 percent, for instance, B has the higher NPV and is thus the better of the two even though A has the higher return. If our required return is 15 percent, there is no ranking conflict: A is better.

The conflict between the IRR and NPV for mutually exclusive investments can be illustrated as we have done in Figure 9.7 by plotting their NPV profiles. In Figure 9.7, notice that the NPV profiles cross at about 11 percent. Notice also that at any discount rate less than 11 percent, the NPV for B is higher. In this range, taking B benefits us more than taking A, even though A's IRR is higher. At any rate greater than 11 percent, project A has the greater NPV.

What this example illustrates is that whenever we have mutually exclusive projects, we shouldn't rank them based on their returns. More generally, anytime we are comparing investments to determine which is best, IRRs can be misleading. Instead, we need to look at the relative NPVs to avoid the possibility of choosing incorrectly. Remember, we're ultimately interested in creating value for the shareholders, so the option with the higher NPV is preferred, regardless of the relative returns.

If this seems counterintuitive, think of it this way. Suppose you have two investments. One has a 10 percent return and makes you $100 richer immediately. The other has a 20 percent return and makes you $50 richer immediately. Which one do you like better? We would rather have $100 than $50, regardless of the returns, so we like the first one better.

A final, important consideration in choosing between investment options is the actual amount of funds to be invested. In our example above, the options involve different amounts of money ($70,000 versus $60,000). In this case, we must consider whether we have sufficient funds to undertake a particular option, and if we choose the smaller investment, what to do with the excess funds. Some important tools to handle this situation, like the profitability index and capital rationing, will be discussed further in this section of the text.

Redeeming Qualities of the IRR

Despite its flaws, the IRR is very popular in practice, more so than even the NPV. It probably survives because it fills a need that the NPV does not. In analyzing investments, people in general and financial analysts in particular seem to prefer talking about rates of return rather than dollar values.

FIGURE 9.7

NPV and the IRR ranking
problem

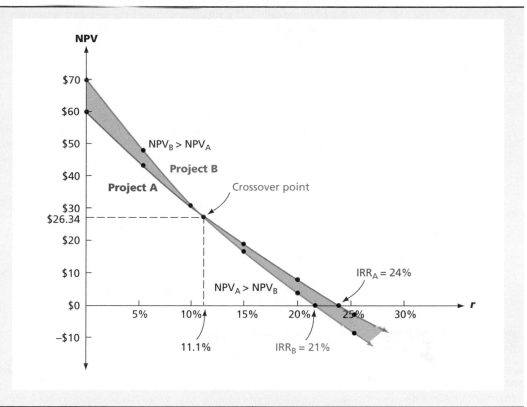

EXAMPLE 9.5: Calculating the Crossover Rate

In Figure 9.7, the NPV profiles cross at about 11 percent. How can we determine just what this crossover point is? The crossover rate, by definition, is the discount rate that makes the NPVs of two projects equal. To illustrate, suppose we have the following two mutually exclusive investments:

Year	Investment A	Investment B
0	–$400	–$500
1	250	320
2	280	340

What's the crossover rate?

To find the crossover, consider moving out of Investment A and into Investment B. If you make the move, you'll have to invest an extra $100 = ($500 – 400). For this $100 investment, you'll get an extra $70 = ($320 – 250) in the first year and an extra $60 = ($340 – 280) in the second year. Is this a good move? In other words, is it worth investing the extra $100?

Based on our discussion, the NPV of the switch, NPV(B – A) is:

$$NPV(B – A) = –\$100 + \$70/(1 + r) + \$60/(1 + r)^2$$

We can calculate the return on this investment by setting the NPV equal to zero and solving for the IRR;

$$NPV(B – A) = 0 = –\$100 + \$70/(1 + r) + \$60/(1 + r)^2$$

If you go through this calculation, you will find the IRR is exactly 20 percent. What this tells us is that at a 20 percent discount rate, we are indifferent between the two investments because the NPV of the difference in their cash flows is zero. As a consequence, the two investments have the same value, so this 20 percent is the crossover rate. Check that the NPV at 20 percent is $2.78 for both.

In general, you can find the crossover rate by taking the difference in the cash flows and calculating the IRR using the differences. It doesn't make any difference which one you subtract from which. To see this, find the IRR for (A – B); you'll see it's the same number. Also, for practice, you might want to find the exact crossover in Figure 9.7. (Hint: It's 11.0704 percent.)

In a similar vein, the IRR also appears to provide a simple way of communicating information about a proposal. One manager might say to another: "Remodelling the clerical wing has a 20 percent return." This may somehow be simpler than saying: "At a 10 percent discount rate, the net present value is $4,000."

Finally, under certain circumstances, the IRR may have a practical advantage over NPV. We can't estimate the NPV unless we know the appropriate discount rate, but we can still estimate the IRR. Suppose we only had a rough estimate of the required return on an investment, but we found, for example, that it had a 40 percent return. We would probably be inclined to take it since it is very unlikely that the required return is that high. The advantages and disadvantages of the IRR follow:

Internal Rate of Return Rule

Advantages	Disadvantages
1. Closely related to NPV, generally leading to identical decisions.	1. May result in multiple answers or no answer with non-conventional cash flows.
2. Easy to understand and communicate.	2. May lead to incorrect decisions in comparisons of mutually exclusive investments.

CONCEPT QUESTIONS

1. Under what circumstances will the IRR and NPV rules lead to the same accept/reject decisions? When might they conflict?

2. Is it generally true that an advantage of the IRR rule over the NPV rule is that we don't need to know the required return to use the IRR rule?

9.5

profitability index (PI)
The present value of an investment's future cash flows divided by its initial cost. Also benefit/cost ratio.

benefit/cost ratio
The profitability index of an investment project.

THE PROFITABILITY INDEX

Another method used to evaluate projects is called the **profitability index (PI)** or **benefit/cost ratio.** This index is defined as the present value of the future cash flows divided by the initial investment. So, if a project costs $200 and the present value of its future cash flows is $220, the profitability index value would be $220/200 = 1.10. Notice that the NPV for this investment is $20, so it is a desirable investment.

More generally, if a project has a positive NPV, the present value of the future cash flows must be bigger than the initial investment. The profitability index would thus be bigger than 1.00 for a positive NPV investment and less than 1.00 for a negative NPV investment.

How do we interpret the profitability index? In our example, the PI was 1.10. This tells us that, per dollar invested, $1.10 in value or $.10 in NPV results. The profitability index thus measures "bang for the buck," that is, the value created per dollar invested. For this reason, it is often proposed as a measure of performance for government or other not-for-profit investments. They can use the index by attempting to quantify both tangible and intangible costs and benefits of a particular program. For example, the cost of a tree planting program might be simply the value of the trees and the labour to plant them. The benefits might be improvement to the environment and public enjoyment (the dollar value of which would have to be estimated). Also, when capital is scarce, it may make sense to allocate it to those projects with the highest PIs. We return to this issue in a later chapter.

The PI is obviously very similar to the NPV. However, consider an investment that costs $5 and has a $10 present value and an investment that costs $100 with a $150 present value. The first of these investments has an NPV of $5 and a PI of 2. The second has an NPV of $50 and a PI of 1.50. If these were mutually exclusive investments, the second one is preferred even though it has a lower PI. This ranking problem is very similar to the IRR ranking problem we saw in the previous section. In all, there seems to be little reason to rely on the PI instead of the NPV. Our discussion of the PI is summarized in the following table:

Profitability Index Rule

Advantages	Disadvantages
1. Closely related to NPV, generally leading to identical decisions.	1. May lead to incorrect decisions in comparisons of mutually exclusive investments.
2. Easy to understand and communicate.	
3. May be useful when available investment funds are limited.	

> **CONCEPT QUESTIONS**
>
> **1.** What does the profitability index measure?
>
> **2.** How would you state the profitability index rule?

9.6 THE PRACTICE OF CAPITAL BUDGETING

So far, this chapter has asked the question: Which capital budgeting methods should companies be using? An equally important question is: Which methods are companies using? Table 9.5 goes a long way toward answering this question. As can be seen from the table, approximately three-quarters of large Canadian and U.S. companies use the IRR and NPV methods. An exclusively Canadian study reached a similar conclusion.[9] This is not surprising, given the theoretical advantages of these approaches.

Over half of these companies use the payback method, a rather surprising result given the conceptual problems with this approach. And while discounted payback represents a theoretical improvement over regular payback, the usage here is far less. Perhaps companies are attracted to the user-friendly nature of payback.

You might expect the capital budgeting methods of large firms to be more sophisticated than the methods of small firms. After all, large firms have the financial resources to hire more sophisticated employees. Table 9.6 provides some support for this idea. Here, firms indicate frequency of use of the various capital budgeting methods on a scale of 0 (never) to 4 (always). Both the IRR and NPV methods are used more frequently, and payback less frequently, in large firms than in small firms. Conversely, large and small firms employ the last three approaches about equally.

The use of quantitative techniques in capital budgeting varies with the industry. As you would imagine, firms that are better able to estimate cash flows precisely are more likely to use NPV. For example, estimation of cash flow in certain aspects of the oil business is quite feasible. Because of this, energy-related firms were among the first to use NPV analysis. Conversly, the flows in the motion picture business are very hard to project. The grosses of great hits like *Spiderman, Pirates of the Caribbean, Shrek 2* and *Lord of the Rings* were far, far greater than anyone imagined. The big failures like *Waterworld* were unexpected as well. Consequently, NPV analysis is frowned upon in the movie business.

In Chapter 11 we discuss what types of capital budgeting techniques firms with less predictable cash flows can use.

TABLE 9.5 Percent of CFOs who always or almost always use a given technique	
Internal rate of return (IRR)	75.6%
Net present value (NPV)	74.9
Payback method	56.7
Discounted payback	29.5
Accounting rate of return	30.3
Profitability index	11.9

Source: Figure 2 from John R. Graham and Campbell R. Harvey, "The Theory and Practice of Corporate Finance: Evidence from the Field," *Journal of Financial Economics* 60 (2001). Based on a survey of 392 CFOs.

TABLE 9.6 Frequency of use of various capital budgeting methods		
Internal rate of return (IRR)	3.41	2.87
Net present value (NPV)	3.42	2.83
Payback method	2.25	2.72
Discounted payback	1.55	1.58
Accounting rate of return	1.25	1.41
Profitability index	0.75	0.78

Firms indicate frequency of use on a scale from 0 (never) to 4 (always). Number in table are averages across respondents.

Source: Table 2 from J. R. Graham and C. R. Harvey, "The Theory and Practice of Corporate Finance: Evidence From the Field," *Journal of Financial Economics* 60 (May 2001).

---

9 V. M. Jog and A. Srivastava, "Capital Budgeting Practices in Corporate Canada," *Financial Practice and Education* 5 (Fall/Winter 1995), pp. 37–43.

Table 9.7 provides a summary of investment criteria for capital budgeting. The table discusses the benefits and flaws of each approach.

TABLE 9.7
Summary of investment criteria

I.   DISCOUNTED CASH FLOW CRITERIA

A.   NET PRESENT VALUE (NPV). The NPV of an investment is the difference between its market value and its cost. The NPV rule is to take a project if its NPV is positive. NPV is frequently estimated by calculating the present value of the future cash flows (to estimate market value) and then subtracting the cost. NPV has no serious flaws; it is the preferred decision criterion.

B.   INTERNAL RATE OF RETURN (IRR). The IRR is the discount rate that makes the estimated NPV of investment equal to zero; it is sometimes called the discounted cash flow (DCF) return. The IRR rule is to take a project when its IRR exceeds the required return. IRR is closely related to NPV, and it leads to exactly the same decisions as NPV for conventional, independent projects. When project cash flows are not conventional, there may be no IRR or there may be more than one. More seriously, the IRR cannot be used to rank mutually exclusive projects; the project with the highest IRR is not necessarily the preferred investment.

C.   PROFITABILITY INDEX. The profitability index, also called the benefit/cost ratio, is the ratio of present value to cost. The profitability index rule is to take an investment if the index exceeds one. The profitability index measures the present value of an investment per dollar invested. It is quite similar to NPV, but, like IRR, it cannot be used to rank mutually exclusive projects. However, it is sometimes used to rank projects when a firm has more positive NPV investments than it can currently finance.

II.   PAYBACK CRITERIA

A.   PAYBACK PERIOD. The payback period is the length of time until the sum of an investment's cash flows equals its cost. The payback period rule is to take a project if its payback is less than some cutoff. The payback period is a flawed criterion primarily because it ignores risk, the time value of money, and cash flows beyond the cutoff point.

B.   DISCOUNTED PAYBACK PERIOD. The discounted payback period is the length of time until the sum of an investment's discounted cash flows equals its cost. The discounted payback period rule is to take an investment if the discounted payback is less than some cutoff. The discounted payback rule is flawed primarily because it ignores cash flows after the cutoff.

III.   ACCOUNTING CRITERIA

A.   AVERAGE ACCOUNTING RETURN (AAR). The AAR is a measure of accounting profit relative to book value. It is not related to the IRR, but it is similar to the accounting return on assets (ROA) measure in Chapter 3. The AAR rule is to take an investment if its AAR exceeds a benchmark AAR. The AAR is seriously flawed for a variety of reasons, and it has little to recommend it.

CONCEPT QUESTIONS

1. What are the most commonly used capital budgeting procedures?

2. Since NPV is conceptually the best procedure for capital budgeting, why do you think that multiple measures are used in practice?

9.7

SUMMARY AND CONCLUSIONS

This chapter has covered the different criteria used to evaluate proposed investments. The six criteria, in the order we discussed them, are:

1. Net present value (NPV)
2. Payback period
3. Discounted payback period
4. Average accounting return (AAR)
5. Internal rate of return (IRR)
6. Profitability index (PI)

We illustrated how to calculate each of these and discussed the interpretation of the results. We also described the advantages and disadvantages of each of them. Ultimately, a good capital budgeting criterion must tell us two things. First, is a particular project a good investment? Second, if we have more than one good project, but we can only take one of them, which one should we take? The main point of this chapter is that only the NPV criterion can always provide the correct answer to both questions.

For this reason, NPV is one of the two or three most important concepts in finance, and we will refer to it many times in the chapters ahead. When we do, keep two things in mind: (1) NPV is always just the difference between the market value of an asset or project and its cost, and (2) the financial manager acts in the shareholders' best interests by identifying and taking positive NPV projects.

Finally, we noted that NPVs can't normally be observed in the market; instead, they must be estimated. Because there is always the possibility of a poor estimate, financial managers use multiple criteria for examining projects. These other criteria provide additional information about whether a project truly has a positive NPV.

Key Terms

average accounting return (AAR) (page 248)
benefit/cost ratio (page 258)
discounted cash flow (DCF) valuation (page 242)
discounted payback period (page 247)
internal rate of return (IRR) (page 250)
multiple rates of return (page 254)

mutually exclusive investment decisions (page 255)
net present value (NPV) (page 241)
net present value profile (page 251)
payback period (page 245)
profitability index (PI) (page 258)

Chapter Review Problems and Self-Test

9.1   **Investment Criteria**   This problem will give you some practice calculating NPVs and paybacks. A proposed overseas expansion has the following cash flows

Year	Cash Flow
0	–$200
1	50
2	60
3	70
4	200

Calculate the payback, the discounted payback, and the NPV at a required return of 10 percent.

9.2   **Mutually Exclusive Investments**   Consider the following two mutually exclusive investments. Calculate the IRR for each and the crossover rate. Under what circumstances will the IRR and NPV criteria rank the two projects differently?

Year	Investment A	Investment B
0	–$75	–$75
1	20	60
2	40	50
3	70	15

9.3   **Average Accounting Return**   You are looking at a three-year project with a projected net income of $2,000 in Year 1, $4,000 in Year 2, and $6,000 in Year 3. The cost is $12,000, which will be depreciated straight-line to zero over the three-year life of the project. What is the average accounting return (AAR)?

Answers to Self-Test Problems

9.1   In the following table, we have listed the cash flow, cumulative cash flow, discounted cash flow (at 10 percent), and cumulative discounted cash flow for the proposed project.

	Cash Flow		Accumulated Cash Flow	
Year	Undiscounted	Discounted	Undiscounted	Discounted
1	$ 50	$ 45.45	$ 50	$ 45.45
2	60	49.59	110	95.04
3	70	52.59	180	147.63
4	200	136.60	380	284.23

Recall that the initial investment was $200. When we compare this to accumulated undiscounted cash flows, we see that payback occurs between Years 3 and 4. The cash flows for the first three years are $180 total, so, going into the fourth year, we are short by $20. The total cash flow in Year 4 is $200, so the payback is $3 + ($20/200) = 3.10$ years.

Looking at the accumulated discounted cash flows, we see that the discounted payback occurs between Years 3 and 4. The sum of the discounted cash flows is $284.23, so the NPV is $84.23. Notice that this is the present value of the cash flows that occur after the discounted payback.

9.2   To calculate the IRR, we might try some guesses, as in the following table:

Discount Rate	NPV(A)	NPV(B)
0%	$55.00	$50.00
10	28.83	32.14
20	9.95	18.40
30	–4.09	7.57
40	–14.80	–1.17

Several things are immediately apparent from our guesses. First, the IRR on A must be between 20 percent and 30 percent (why?). With some more effort, we find that it's 26.79 percent. For B, the IRR must be a little less than 40 percent (again, why?); it works out to be 38.54 percent. Also, notice that at rates between 0 percent and 10 percent, the NPVs are very close, indicating that the crossover is in that vicinity.

To find the crossover exactly, we can compute the IRR on the difference in the cash flows. If we take the cash flows from A minus the cash flows from B, the resulting cash flows are:

Year	A – B
0	$ 0
1	–40
2	–10
3	55

These cash flows look a little odd, but the sign only changes once, so we can find an IRR. With some trial and error, you'll see that the NPV is zero at a discount rate of 5.42 percent, so this is the crossover rate.

The IRR for B is higher. However, as we've seen, A has the larger NPV for any discount rate less than 5.42 percent, so the NPV and IRR rankings will conflict in that range. Remember, if there's a conflict, we will go with the higher NPV. Our decision rule is thus very simple: take A if the required return is less than 5.42 percent, take B if the required return is between 5.42 percent and 38.54 percent (the IRR on B), and take neither if the required return is more than 38.54 percent.

9.3   Here we need to calculate the ratio of average net income to average book value to get the AAR. Average net income is:

Average net income = ($2,000 + 4,000 + 6,000)/3 = $4,000

Average book value is:

Average book value = $12,000/2 = $6,000

So the average accounting return is:

AAR = $4,000/$6,000 = 66.67%

This is an impressive return. Remember, however, that it isn't really a rate of return like an interest rate or an IRR, so the size doesn't tell us a lot. In particular, our money is probably not going to grow at a rate of 66.67 percent per year, sorry to say.

Concepts Review and Critical Thinking Questions

1.   If a project with conventional cash flows has a payback period less than the project's life, can you definitively state the algebraic sign of the NPV? Why or why not? If you know that the discounted payback period is less than the project's life, what can you say about the NPV? Explain.

2. Suppose a project has conventional cash flows and a positive NPV. What do you know about its payback? Its discounted payback? Its profitability index? Its IRR? Explain.

3. Concerning payback:
   a. Describe how the payback period is calculated and describe the information this measure provides about a sequence of cash flows. What is the payback criterion decision rule?
   b. What are the problems associated with using the payback period as a means of evaluating cash flows?
   c. What are the advantages of using the payback period to evaluate cash flows? Are there any circumstances under which using payback might be appropriate? Explain.

4. Concerning discounted payback:
   a. Describe how the discounted payback period is calculated and describe the information this measure provides about a sequence of cash flows. What is the discounted payback criterion decision rule?
   b. What are the problems associated with using the discounted payback period as a means of evaluating cash flows?
   c. What conceptual advantage does the discounted payback method have over the regular payback method? Can the discounted payback ever be longer than the regular payback? Explain.

5. Concerning AAR:
   a. Describe how the average accounting return is usually calculated and describe the information this measure provides about a sequence of cash flows. What is the AAR criterion decision rule?
   b. What are the problems associated with using the AAR as a means of evaluating a project's cash flows? What underlying feature of AAR is most troubling to you from a financial perspective? Does the AAR have any redeeming qualities?

6. Concerning NPV:
   a. Describe how NPV is calculated and describe the information this measure provides about a sequence of cash flows. What is the NPV criterion decision rule?
   b. Why is NPV considered to be a superior method of evaluating the cash flows from a project? Suppose the NPV for a project's cash flows is computed to be $2,500. What does this number represent with respect to the firm's shareholders?

7. Concerning IRR:
   a. Describe how the IRR is calculated and describe the information this measure provides about a sequence of cash flows. What is the IRR criterion decision rule?
   b. What is the relationship between IRR and NPV? Are there any situations in which you might prefer one method over the other? Explain.
   c. Despite its shortcomings in some situations, why do most financial managers use IRR along with NPV when evaluating projects? Can you think of a situation in which IRR might be a more appropriate measure to use than NPV? Explain.

8. Concerning the profitability index:
   a. Describe how the profitability index is calculated and describe the information this measure provides about a sequence of cash flows. What is the profitability index decision rule?
   b. What is the relationship between the profitability index and NPV? Are there any situations in which you might prefer one method over the other? Explain.

9. A project has perpetual cash flows of C per period, a cost of I, and a required return of R. What is the relationship between the project's payback and its IRR? What implications does your answer have for long-lived projects with relatively constant cash flows?

10. In 1996, Fuji Film, the Japanese manufacturer of photo film and related products, broke ground on a film plant in South Carolina. Fuji apparently thought that it would be better able to compete and create value with a U.S.-based facility. Other companies, such as BMW and Mercedes-Benz, have reached similar conclusions and taken similar actions. What are some of the reasons that foreign manufacturers of products as diverse as photo film and luxury automobiles might arrive at this same conclusion?

11. What are some of the difficulties that might come up in actual applications of the various criteria we discussed in this chapter? Which one would be the easiest to implement in actual applications? The most difficult?

12. Are the capital budgeting criteria we discussed applicable to not-for-profit corporations? How should such entities make capital budgeting decisions? What about different levels of government, i.e., federal, provincial, and municipal? Should they evaluate spending proposals using these techniques?

Questions and Problems

Basic (Questions 1–18)

1. **Calculating Payback** What is the payback period for the following set of cash flows?

Year	Cash Flow
0	–$4,800
1	1,200
2	2,500
3	3,400
4	1,700

Basic
(continued)

2. **Calculating Payback** An investment project provides cash inflows of $840 per year for eight years. What is the project payback period if the initial cost is $3,000? What if the initial cost is $5,000? What if it is $7,000?

3. **Calculating Payback** Old Country, Inc., imposes a payback cutoff of three years for its international investment projects. If the company has the following two projects available, should they accept either of them?

Year	Cash Flow (A)	Cash Flow (B)
0	–$50,000	–$ 70,000
1	30,000	9,000
2	18,000	25,000
3	10,000	35,000
4	5,000	425,000

4. **Calculating Discounted Payback** An investment project has annual cash inflows of $7,000, $7,500, $8,000, and $8,500, and a discount rate of 14 percent. What is the discounted payback period for these cash flows if the initial cost is $8,000? What if the initial cost is $13,000? What if it is $18,000?

5. **Calculating Discounted Payback** An investment project costs $10,000 and has annual cash flows of $2,100 for six years. What is the discounted payback period if the discount rate is zero percent? What if the discount rate is 5 percent? If it is 15 percent?

6. **Calculating AAR** You're trying to determine whether or not to expand your business by building a new manufacturing plant. The plant has an installation cost of $15 million, which will be depreciated straight-line to zero over its four-year life. If the plant has projected net income of $1,416,000, $1,868,000, $1,562,000, and $985,000 over these four years, what is the project's average accounting return (AAR)?

7. **Calculating IRR**   A firm evaluates all of its projects by applying the IRR rule. If the required return is 18 percent, should the firm accept the following project?

Year	Cash Flow
0	–$30,000
1	20,000
2	14,000
3	11,000

8. **Calculating NPV** For the cash flows in the previous problem, suppose the firm uses the NPV decision rule. At a required return of 11 percent, should the firm accept this project? What if the required return was 30 percent?

9. **Calculating NPV and IRR** A project that provides annual cash flows of $14,000 for nine years costs $70,000 today. Is this a good project if the required return is 8 percent? What if it's 16 percent? At what required return would you be indifferent between accepting the project and rejecting it?

10. **Calculating IRR** What is the IRR of the following set of cash flows?

Year	Cash Flow
0	–$8,000
1	3,200
2	4,000
3	6,100

11. **Calculating NPV** For the cash flows in the previous problem, what is the NPV at a discount rate of zero percent? What if the discount rate is 10 percent? If it is 20 percent? If it is 30 percent?

12. **NPV versus IRR** Bumble's Bees, Inc., has identified the following two mutually exclusive projects:

Year	Cash Flow (A)	Cash Flow (B)
0	–$34,000	–$34,000
1	16,500	5,000
2	14,000	10,000
3	10,000	18,000
4	6,000	19,000

a. What is the IRR for each of these projects? If you apply the IRR decision rule, which project should the company accept? Is this decision necessarily correct?

b. If the required return is 11 percent, what is the NPV for each of these projects? Which project will you choose if you apply the NPV decision rule?

c. Over what range of discount rates would you choose Project A? Project B? At what discount rate would you be indifferent between these two projects? Explain.

Basic **13.** **NPV versus IRR** Consider the following two mutually exclusive projects:
(continued)

Year	Cash Flow (X)	Cash Flow (Y)
0	−$5,000	−$5,000
1	2,700	2,300
2	1,700	1,800
3	2,300	2,700

Sketch the NPV profiles for X and Y over a range of discount rates from zero to 25 percent. What is the crossover rate for these two projects?

14. **Problems with IRR** Cutler Petroleum, Inc., is trying to evaluate a generation project with the following cash flows:

Year	Cash Flow
0	−$28,000,000
1	53,000,000
2	− 8,000,000

a. If the company requires a 10 percent return on its investments, should it accept this project? Why?

b. Compute the IRR for this project. How many IRRs are there? If you apply the IRR decision rule, should you accept the project or not? What's going on here?

15. **Calculating Profitability Index** What is the profitability index for the following set of cash flows if the relevant discount rate is 10 percent? What if the discount rate is 15 percent? If it is 22 percent?

Year	Cash Flow
0	−$7,000
1	3,200
2	3,900
3	2,600

16. **Problems with Profitability Index** The Robb Computer Corporation is trying to choose between the following two mutually exclusive design projects:

Year	Cash Flow (I)	Cash Flow (II)
0	−$30,000	−$5,000
1	15,000	2,800
2	15,000	2,800
3	15,000	2,800

a. If the required return is 10 percent and Robb Computer applies the profitability index decision rule, which project should the firm accept?

b. If the company applies the NPV decision rule, which project should it take?

c. Explain why your answers in (*a*) and (*b*) are different.

17. **Comparing Investment Criteria** Consider the following two mutually exclusive projects:

Year	Cash Flow (A)	Cash Flow (B)
0	−$210,000	−$21,000
1	15,000	11,000
2	30,000	9,000
3	30,000	11,000
4	370,000	9,000

Whichever project you choose, if any, you require a 15 percent return on your investment.

a. If you apply the payback criterion, which investment will you choose? Why?

b. If you apply the discounted payback criterion, which investment will you choose? Why?

c. If you apply the NPV criterion, which investment will you choose? Why?

d. If you apply the IRR criterion, which investment will you choose? Why?

e. If you apply the profitability index criterion, which investment will you choose? Why?

f. Based on your answers in (*a*) through (*e*), which project will you finally choose? Why?

18. **NPV and Discount Rates** An investment has an installed cost of $568,240. The cash flows over the four-year life of the investment are projected to be $289,348, $196,374, $114,865, and $93,169. If the discount rate is zero, what is the

NPV? If the discount rate is infinite, what is the NPV? At what discount rate is the NPV just equal to zero? Sketch the NPV profile for this investment based on these three points.

Intermediate (Questions 19–20)

19. NPV and the Profitability Index   If we define the NPV index as the ratio of NPV to cost, what is the relationship between this index and the profitability index?

20. Cash Flow Intuition   A project has an initial cost of I, has a required return of R, and pays C annually for N years.

   a. Find C in terms of I and N such that the project has a payback period just equal to its life.

   b. Find C in terms of I, N, and R such that this is a profitable project according to the NPV decision rule.

   c. Find C in terms of I, N, and R such that the project has a benefit-cost ratio of 2.

Challenge (Questions 21–24)

21. Payback and NPV   An investment under consideration has a payback of seven years and a cost of $483,000. If the required return is 12 percent, what is the worst-case NPV? The best-case NPV? Explain. Assume the cash flows are conventional.

22. Multiple IRRs   This problem is useful for testing the ability of financial calculators and computer software. Consider the following cash flows. How many different IRRs are there (hint: search between 20 percent and 70 percent)? When should we take this project?

Year	Cash Flow
0	–$ 504
1	2,862
2	–$6,070
3	5,700
4	–$2,000

23. NPV Valuation   The Yurdone Corporation wants to set up a private cemetery business. According to the CFO, Barry M. Deep, business is "looking up." As a result, the cemetery project will provide a net cash inflow of $50,000 for the firm during the first year, and the cash flows are projected to grow at a rate of 6 percent per year forever. The project requires an initial investment of $780,000.

   a. If Yurdone requires a 13 percent return on such undertakings, should the cemetery business be started?

   b. The company is somewhat unsure about the assumption of a 6 percent growth rate in its cash flows. At what constant growth rate would the company just break even if it still required a 13 percent return on investment?

24. Project Choice and NPV Intuition   Atlantic Megaprojects has a contract to build a tunnel connecting two Atlantic provinces. The contract calls for the firm to complete the tunnel in three years with an annual cash outlay of $350 million at the end of years 1 and 2. At the end of the third year, governments will pay Atlantic Megaprojects $860 million. If it wishes, the firm can exercise an option to build the tunnel in just two years by subcontracting part of the work to a government-sponsored entity designed to create employment in the region. Under this option, Atlantic Megaprojects will make a cash payment of $728 million at the end of the first year and will receive $860 million after the second year.

   a. Suppose Atlantic Megaprojects has a cost of capital of 13 percent. Should the firm subcontract the work?

   b. Now suppose Atlantic Megaprojects can estimate its cost of capital only up to a range. Over what range of discount rates is subcontracting attractive?

MINI CASE

Ted Black, chief financial officer of Consumers Cable Ltd. (CCL), is looking at two capital projects designed to correct the company's current restricted ability to service expanding customer demand. Project Refit revolves around upgrading transmission technology to allow an increased number of programs to be supplied over CCL's existing cable network. Because the network is aging, future cost increases will produce a declining stream of cash flows over the project's four-year life. In contrast, Project Hightech would upgrade the cable network to expand capacity beyond immediately projected needs. Project Hightech has cash flows that increase over time as increased demand catches up with supply capabilities. Like Project Refit, Project Hightech has a four-year life as Black expects that a new generation of technology will come in after four years.

The following estimates include all elements of cash flows in millions.

Year	Project Hightech	Project Refit
0	($80)	($80)
1	11	56
2	53	48
3	65.5	27
4	84	9.5

Ted Black's staff conducted risk analysis of the two projects and found that both are similar in risk to what the firm is currently doing. Consequently, both have an assigned cost of capital (discount rate) of 11 percent.

MINI CASE (continued)

As Ted Black's executive assistant, you are assigned the task of completing the capital budgeting analysis and drafting a memo to the board to go forward over Black's signature. In preparing the memo, be sure to address the following questions.

a) State the rationale for capital budgeting and how it links to the goal of the financial manager—maximizing the value of the shareholders' wealth.

b) Are these projects independent or mutually exclusive and how does this affect your analysis?

c) Calculate the payback period for each project. Which project is better according to this method? Relate the advantages and disadvantages of the payback method in this case.

d) Use the NPV method to analyze the projects. Which project(s) should the firm undertake according to this method?

e) Use the IRR method to analyze the projects. Which project(s) should the firm undertake according to this method?

f) Do the NPV and IRR methods give the same recommendations in this case? Use NPV profiles to see whether the two methods ever disagree over these two projects. How would you resolve such a disagreement if it occurred?

g) What is your recommendation to the board? Justify your position.

Internet Application Questions

1. Net Present Value analysis assumes market efficiency. In fact, we can back out whether a particular investment had positive NPV by observing the market reaction to its announcement. For example, go to the homepage of Coca-Cola (www.coke.com/) and click on Press Center. These are typically made over the wire to news agencies, and are also reported on the company's website. On November 21, 2000, Coca-Cola announced that it would no longer pursue its bid for the Quaker Oats company. Go to the Coca-Cola Investor Relations site (http://www2.coca-cola.com/investors/index.html) and get the company's stock price chart surrounding this date. Assuming that all of the price movement was due to the announcement, discuss whether the Quaker Oats bid was a positive NPV investment for Coca-Cola.

2. NPV analysis assumes that managers' objective is to maximize shareholders' value. Directors on the boards of Canadian firms are required to look after the best interests of the corporation. Traditionally, this has meant the best interests of shareholders. The law firm of Osler, Hoskin and Harcourt maintains a public website providing detailed descriptions of the duties and responsibilities of Canadian directors (follow the Publications link to the reference guides at www.osler.com). What are some of the difficulties in broadening the definition of corporate stakeholders? Do you think shareholders' interests alone should be considered by directors? Why or why not?

3. The Ontario Teachers' Pension Plan has the responsibility to manage the retirement investments of teachers in the Province of Ontario. The plan presents its views and policies on corporate governance under the Governance link at the site www.otpp.com. From the shareholders' perspective, what role should social responsibility and ethical considerations play in a firm's investment analysis? Can these non-financial factors actually enhance shareholder value in the long term? How should companies take this into account in NPV decisions?

4. Here's a concept most finance classes tiptoe around: a captive capital provider. Can a conglomerate successfully grow around its own capital-providing corporation? Or will internal capital ruin all NPV calculations? For GE Corp (www.ge.com), the answer is a big affirmative in favour of GE Capital (www.gecapital.com).

    Do you think this is a successful strategy to imitate by other conglomerates? Do you see parallels with the Main Bank system of financing within Japanese keiretsu firms?

5. You have a project that has an initial cash outflow of –$20,000 and cash inflows of $6,000, $5,000, $4,000 and $3,000, respectively, for the next four years. Go to www.datadynamica.com, and follow the "On-line IRR NPV Calculator" link. Enter the cash flows. If the required return is 12 percent, what is the NPV of the project? The IRR?

Suggested Readings

For a discussion of the capital budgeting techniques used by large firms in Canada, see:

Jog, V.M. and A.K. Srivastava. "Corporate Financial Decision Making in Canada." *Canadian Journal of Administrative Sciences* 11, June 1994, pp. 156–76.

Graham, J. R., and C.R. Harvey. "The Theory and Practice of Corporate Finance: Evidence From the Field," *Journal of Financial Economics* 60 (May 2001).

CHAPTER 10

Making Capital Investment Decisions

In late 2001, Air Canada began operations of Tango, its first discount airline, flying to 18 cities in North America. Tango grew out of the increasing demand for "no-frills air travel"[1] by Canadian travellers. Air Canada's decision was primarily a reaction to the outstanding success of other low-fare air carriers such as American-based JetBlue and Canada's WestJet. These airlines were boasting considerable profits, indicating that it was no longer viable for Air Canada to ignore this lucrative market.

Some analysts questioned Air Canada's decision to launch Tango. At a time when the company was facing many financial problems, entering a new market, where an already established airline ruled, was seen as dangerous. Looking back on the decision shows that the critics may have been right. A number of problems, including a high cost structure, significant debt load, and world events like the war in Iraq and the SARS health crisis forced the company into bankruptcy protection in April 2003. In October of 2003, Air Canada decided to stop Tango service entirely and sell discount fares on its other aircraft. The Tango project was immediately billed a failure by analysts. This example shows that companies like Air Canada must make capital investment decisions very carefully. As you will see in this chapter, many factors must be taken into account.

www.aircanada.com

SO FAR, we've covered various parts of the capital budgeting decision. Our task in this chapter is to start bringing these pieces together. In particular, we show you how to "spread the numbers" for a proposed investment or project and, based on those numbers, make an initial assessment about whether or not the project should be undertaken.

In the discussion that follows, we focus on setting up a discounted cash flow analysis. From the last chapter, we know that the projected future cash flows are the key element in such an evaluation. Accordingly, we emphasize working with financial and accounting information to come up with these figures.

In evaluating a proposed investment, we pay special attention to deciding what information is relevant to the decision at hand and what information is not. As we shall see, it is easy to overlook important pieces of the capital budgeting puzzle.

We wait until the next chapter to describe in detail how to evaluate the results of our discounted cash flow analysis. Also, where needed, we assume that we know the relevant required return or discount rate reflecting the risk of the project. We continue to defer discussion of this subject to Part 5.

---

1 *www.aircanada.com*

PROJECT CASH FLOWS: A FIRST LOOK

The effect of undertaking a project is to change the firm's overall cash flows today and in the future. To evaluate a proposed investment, we must consider these changes in the firm's cash flows and then decide whether they add value to the firm. The most important step, therefore, is to decide which cash flows are relevant and which are not.

Relevant Cash Flows

incremental cash flows
The difference between a firm's future cash flows with a project and without the project.

What is a relevant cash flow for a project? The general principle is simple enough: A relevant cash flow for a project is a change in the firm's overall future cash flow that comes about as a direct consequence of the decision to take that project. Because the relevant cash flows are defined in terms of changes in or increments to the firm's existing cash flow, they are called the **incremental cash flows** associated with the project.

The concept of incremental cash flow is central to our analysis, so we state a general definition and refer back to it as needed:

> The incremental cash flows for project evaluation consist of any and all changes in the firm's future cash flows that are a direct consequence of taking the project.

This definition of incremental cash flows has an obvious and important corollary: Any cash flow that exists regardless of whether or not a project is undertaken is not relevant.

The Stand-Alone Principle

stand-alone principle
Evaluation of a project based on the project's incremental cash flows.

In practice, it would be very cumbersome to actually calculate the future total cash flows to the firm with and without a project, especially for a large firm. Fortunately, it is not really necessary to do so. Once we identify the effect of undertaking the proposed project on the firm's cash flows, we need focus only on the resulting project's incremental cash flows. This is called the **stand-alone principle.**

What the stand-alone principle says is that, once we have determined the incremental cash flows from undertaking a project, we can view that project as a kind of minifirm with its own future revenues and costs, its own assets, and, of course, its own cash flows. We are then primarily interested in comparing the cash flows from this minifirm to the cost of acquiring it. An important consequence of this approach is that we evaluate the proposed project purely on its own merits, in isolation from any other activities or projects.

CONCEPT QUESTIONS

1. What are the relevant incremental cash flows for project evaluation?

2. What is the stand-alone principle?

INCREMENTAL CASH FLOWS

We are concerned here only with those cash flows that are incremental to a project. Looking back at our general definition, it seems easy enough to decide whether a cash flow is incremental or not. Even so, there are a few situations when mistakes are easy to make. In this section, we describe some of these common pitfalls and how to avoid them.

Sunk Costs

sunk cost
A cost that has already been incurred and cannot be removed and therefore should not be considered in an investment decision.

A **sunk cost,** by definition, is a cost we have already paid or have already incurred the liability to pay. Such a cost cannot be changed by the decision today to accept or reject a project. Put another way, the firm has to pay this cost no matter what. Based on our general definition of cash flow, such a cost is clearly not relevant to the decision at hand. So, we are always careful to exclude sunk costs from our analysis.

That a sunk cost is not relevant seems obvious given our discussion. Nonetheless, it's easy to fall prey to the sunk cost fallacy. For example, suppose True North Distillery Ltd. hires a financial consultant to help evaluate whether or not a line of maple sugar liqueur should be launched. When the consultant turns in the report, True North objects to the analysis because the consultant did not include the hefty consulting fee as a cost to the liqueur project.

Who is correct? By now, we know that the consulting fee is a sunk cost, because the consulting fee must be paid whether or not the liqueur line is launched (this is an attractive feature of the consulting business).

A more subtle example of a cost that can sometimes be sunk is overhead. To illustrate, suppose True North Distillery is now considering building a new warehouse to age the maple sugar liqueur. Should a portion of overhead costs be allocated to the proposed warehouse project? If the overhead costs are truly sunk and independent of the project, the answer is no. An example of such an overhead cost is the cost of maintaining a corporate jet for senior executives. But if the new warehouse requires additional reporting, supervision, or legal input, these overheads should be part of the project analysis.

Opportunity Costs

When we think of costs, we normally think of out-of-pocket costs, namely, those that require us to actually spend some amount of cash. An **opportunity cost** is slightly different; it requires us to give up a benefit. A common situation arises where another division of a firm already owns some of the assets that a proposed project will be using. For example, we might be thinking of converting an old rustic water-powered mill that we bought years ago for $100,000 into upscale condominiums.

If we undertake this project, there will be no direct cash outflow associated with buying the old mill since we already own it. For purposes of evaluating the condo project, should we then treat the mill as free? The answer is no. The mill is a valuable resource used by the project. If we didn't use it here, we could do something else with it. Like what? The obvious answer is that, at a minimum, we could sell it. Using the mill for the condo complex thus has an opportunity cost: We give up the valuable opportunity to do something else with it.

There is another issue here. Once we agree that the use of the mill has an opportunity cost, how much should the condo project be charged? Given that we paid $100,000, it might seem we should charge this amount to the condo project. Is this correct? The answer is no, and the reason is based on our discussion concerning sunk costs.

The fact that we paid $100,000 some years ago is irrelevant. It's sunk. At a minimum, the opportunity cost that we charge the project is what it would sell for today (net of any selling costs) because this is the amount that we give up by using it instead of selling it.[2]

Side Effects

Remember that the incremental cash flows for a project include all the resulting changes in the *firm's* future cash flows. It would not be unusual for a project to have side, or spillover, effects, both good and bad. For example, as we discussed at the beginning of the chapter, Air Canada had to recognize the possibility that sales from Tango would come at the expense of sales from its main fleet. The negative impact on cash flows is called **erosion,** and the same general problem anticipated by Air Canada could occur for any multiline consumer product producer or seller.[3] In this case, the cash flows from the new line should be adjusted downwards to reflect lost profits on other lines.

---

2 Economists sometimes use the acronym TANSTAAFL, which is short for there ain't no such thing as a free lunch, to describe the fact that only very rarely is something truly free. Further, if the asset in question is unique, the opportunity cost might be higher because there might be other valuable projects we could undertake that would use it. However, if the asset in question is of a type that is routinely bought and sold (a used car, perhaps), the opportunity cost is always the going price in the market because that is the cost of buying another one.

3 More colourfully, erosion is sometimes called *piracy* or *cannibalism.*

www.disneyworld.com
www.hp.com

In accounting for erosion, it is important to recognize that any sales lost as a result of launching a new product might be lost anyway because of future competition. Erosion is only relevant when the sales would not otherwise be lost.

Side effects show up in a lot of different ways. For example, one of Walt Disney's concerns when it built Euro Disney was that the new park would drain visitors from the Florida park, a popular vacation destination for Europeans.

There are beneficial side effects, of course. For example, you might think that Hewlett-Packard would have been concerned when the price of a printer that sold for $500 to $600 in 1994 declined to below $100 by 2003, but they weren't. What HP realized was that the big money is in the consumables that printer owners buy to keep their printers going, such as ink-jet cartridges, laser toner cartridges, and special paper. The profit margins for these products are astounding, reaching as high as 70 percent.

Net Working Capital

Normally, a project requires that the firm invest in net working capital in addition to long-term assets. For example, a project generally needs some amount of cash on hand to pay any expenses that arise. In addition, a project needs an initial investment in inventories and accounts receivable (to cover credit sales). Some of this financing would be in the form of amounts owed to suppliers (accounts payable), but the firm has to supply the balance. This balance represents the investment in net working capital.

It's easy to overlook an important feature of net working capital in capital budgeting. As a project winds down, inventories are sold, receivables are collected, bills are paid, and cash balances can be drawn down. These activities free up the net working capital originally invested. So, the firm's investment in project net working capital closely resembles a loan. The firm supplies working capital at the beginning and recovers it toward the end.

Financing Costs

In analyzing a proposed investment, we do not include interest paid or any other financing costs such as dividends or principal repaid, because we are interested in the cash flow generated by the assets from the project. As we mentioned in Chapter 2, interest paid, for example, is a component of cash flow to creditors, not cash flow from assets.

More generally, our goal in project evaluation is to compare the cash flow from a project to the cost of acquiring that project to estimate NPV. The particular mixture of debt and equity that a firm actually chooses to use in financing a project is a managerial variable and primarily determines how project cash flow is divided between owners and creditors. This is not to say that financing costs are unimportant. They are just something to be analyzed separately, and are included as a component of the discount rate. We cover this in later chapters.

Inflation

Because capital investment projects generally have long lives, price inflation or deflation is likely to occur during the project's life. It is possible that the impact of inflation will cancel out—changes in the price level will impact all cash flows equally—and that the required rate of return will also shift exactly with inflation. But this is unlikely, so we need to add a brief discussion of how to handle inflation.

As we explained in more detail in Chapter 7, investors form expectations of future inflation. These are included in the discount rate as investors wish to protect themselves against inflation. Rates including inflation premiums are called nominal rates. In Brazil, for example, where the inflation rate is very high, discount rates are much higher than in Canada.

Given that nominal rates include an adjustment for expected inflation, cash flow estimates must also be adjusted for inflation.[4] Ignoring inflation in estimating the cash inflows would lead

---

4 In Chapter 7, we explained how to calculate real discount rates. The term, *real,* in finance and economics means adjusted for inflation, that is, net of the inflation premium. A less common alternative approach uses real discount rates to discount real cash flows.

to a bias against accepting capital budgeting projects. As we go through detailed examples of capital budgeting, we comment on making these inflation adjustments. Appendix 10A discusses inflation effects further.

Government Intervention

In Canada, various levels of government commonly offer incentives to promote certain types of capital investment. These include grants, investment tax credits, more favourable rates for **capital cost allowance,** and subsidized loans. Since these change a project's cash flows, they must be factored into capital budgeting analysis.

Other Issues

There are other things to watch for. First, we are interested only in measuring cash flow. Moreover, we arc interested in measuring it when it actually occurs, not when it arises in an accounting sense. Second, we are always interested in aftertax cash flow since tax payments are definitely a cash outflow. In fact, whenever we write incremental cash flows, we mean aftertax incremental cash flows. Remember, however, that aftertax cash flow and accounting profit or net income are different things.

> **capital cost allowance (CCA)**
> Depreciation method under Canadian tax law allowing for the accelerated write-off of property under various classifications.

CONCEPT QUESTIONS

1. What is a sunk cost? An opportunity cost?

2. Explain what erosion is and why it is relevant.

3. Explain why interest paid is not a relevant cash flow for project valuation.

4. Explain how consideration of inflation comes into capital budgeting.

10.3 | PRO FORMA FINANCIAL STATEMENTS AND PROJECT CASH FLOWS

When we begin evaluating a proposed investment, we need a set of pro forma or projected financial statements. Given these, we can develop the projected cash flows from the project. Once we have the cash flows, we can estimate the value of the project using the techniques we described in the previous chapter.

In calculating the cash flows, we make several simplifying assumptions to avoid bogging down in technical details at the outset. We use straight-line depreciation as opposed to capital cost allowance. We also assume that a full year's depreciation can be taken in the first year. In addition, we construct the example so the project's market value equals its book cost when it is scrapped. Later, we address the real-life complexities of capital cost allowance and salvage values introduced in Chapter 2.

Getting Started: Pro Forma Financial Statements

> **pro forma financial statements**
> Financial statements projecting future years' operations.

Pro forma financial statements are a convenient and easily understood means of summarizing much of the relevant information for a project. To prepare these statements, we need estimates of quantities such as unit sales, the selling price per unit, the variable cost per unit, and total fixed costs. We also need to know the total investment required, including any investment in net working capital.

To illustrate, suppose we think we can sell 50,000 cans of shark attractant per year at a price of $4.30 per can. It costs us about $2.50 per can to make the attractant, and a new product such as this one typically has only a three-year life (perhaps because the customer base dwindles rapidly). We require a 20 percent return on new products.

Fixed operating costs for the project, including such things as rent on the production facility, would run $12,000 per year.[5] Further, we need to invest $90,000 in manufacturing equipment. For simplicity, we assume this $90,000 will be 100 percent depreciated over the three-year life of the project in equal annual amounts.[6] Furthermore, the cost of removing the equipment roughly equals its actual value in three years, so it would be essentially worthless on a market value basis as well. Finally, the project requires a $20,000 investment in net working capital. This amount remains constant over the life of the project.

In Table 10.1, we organize these initial projections by first preparing the pro forma income statements.

Once again, notice that we have not deducted any interest expense. This is always so. As we described earlier, interest paid is a financing expense, not a component of operating cash flow.

We can also prepare a series of abbreviated balance sheets that show the capital requirements for the project as we've done in Table 10.2. Here we have net working capital of $20,000 in each year. Fixed assets are $90,000 at the start of the project's life (Year 0), and they decline by the $30,000 in depreciation each year, ending at zero. Notice that the total investment given here for future years is the total book or accounting value, not market value.

At this point, we need to start converting this accounting information into cash flows. We consider how to do this next.

Project Cash Flows

To develop the cash flows from a project, we need to recall (from Chapter 2) that cash flow from assets has three components: operating cash flow, capital spending, and additions to net working capital. To evaluate a project or minifirm, we need to arrive at estimates for each of these.

Once we have estimates of the components of cash flow, we can calculate cash flow for our minifirm just as we did in Chapter 2 for an entire firm:

Project cash flow = Project operating cash flow
 – Project additions to net working capital
 – Project capital spending

We consider these components next.

PROJECT OPERATING CASH FLOW   To determine the operating cash flow associated with a project, recall the definition of operating cash flow:

TABLE 10.1
Projected income statement, shark attractant project

Sales (50,000 units at $4.30/unit)	$215,000
Variable costs ($2.50/unit)	125,000
	$ 90,000
Fixed costs	$ 12,000
Depreciation ($90,000/3)	30,000
EBIT	$ 48,000
Taxes (40%)	19,200
Net income	$ 28,800

Operating cash flow = Earnings before interest and taxes (EBIT)
 + Depreciation
 – Taxes

---

5 By fixed cost, we literally mean a cash outflow that occurs regardless of the level of sales. This should not be confused with some sort of accounting period charge.

6 We also assume that a full year's depreciation can be taken in the first year. Together with the use of straight-line depreciation, this unrealistic assumption smooths the exposition. We bring in real-life complications of capital cost allowance and taxes (introduced in Chapter 2) later in the chapter.

TABLE 10.2
Projected capital requirements, shark attractant project

	Year			
	0	1	2	3
Net working capital	$ 20,000	$20,000	$20,000	$20,000
Net fixed assets	90,000	60,000	30,000	0
Total investment	$110,000	$80,000	$50,000	$20,000

As before, taxes in our equation are taxes assuming that there is no interest expense. To illustrate the calculation of operating cash flow, we use the projected information from the shark attractant project. For ease of reference, Table 10.3 contains the income statement.

Given the income statement in Table 10.3, calculating the operating cash flow is very straightforward. As we see in Table 10.4, projected operating cash flow for the shark attractant project is $58,800.

PROJECT NET WORKING CAPITAL AND CAPITAL SPENDING We next need to take care of the fixed asset and net working capital requirements. Based on our preceding balance sheets, the firm must spend $90,000 up front for fixed assets and invest an additional $20,000 in net working capital. The immediate outflow is thus $110,000. At the end of the project's life, the fixed assets are worthless, but the firm recovers the $20,000 tied up in working capital.[7] This leads to a $20,000 inflow in the last year.

TABLE 10.3
Projected income statement, shark attractant project

Sales	$215,000
Variable costs	125,000
Fixed costs	12,000
Depreciation	30,000
EBIT	$ 48,000
Taxes (40%)	19,200
Net income	$ 28,800

TABLE 10.4
Projected operating cash flow, shark attractant project

EBIT	$ 48,000
Depreciation	30,000
Taxes	−19,200
Operating cash flow	$ 58,800

TABLE 10.5
Projected total cash flows, shark attractant project

	Year			
	0	1	2	3
Operating cash flow	0	$58,800	$58,800	$58,800
Additions to NWC	−$ 20,000	0	0	20,000
Capital spending	−90,000	0	0	0
Total cash flow	−$110,000	$58,800	$58,800	$78,800
DCF	−$110,000	$49,000	$40,833	$45,602
NPV	$ 25,435			

On a purely mechanical level, notice that whenever we have an investment in net working capital, that investment has to be recovered; in other words, the same number needs to appear with the opposite sign.

Project Total Cash Flow and Value

Given the information we've accumulated, we can finish the preliminary cash flow analysis as illustrated in Table 10.5.

Now that we have cash flow projections, we are ready to apply the various criteria we discussed in the last chapter. The NPV at the 20 percent required return is:

---

7 In reality, the firm would probably recover something less than 100 percent of this amount because of bad debts, inventory loss, and so on. If we wanted to, we could just assume that, for example, only 90 percent was recovered and proceed from there.

$$NPV = -\$110,000 + \$58,800/1.2 + \$58,800/1.2^2 + 78,800/1.2^3$$
$$= \$25,435$$

So, based on these projections, the project creates more than $25,000 in value and should be accepted. Also, the return on this investment obviously exceeds 20 percent (since the NPV is positive at 20 percent). After some trial and error, we find that the IRR works out to be about 34 percent.

In addition, if required, we could go ahead and calculate the payback and the average accounting return (AAR). Inspection of the cash flows shows that the payback on this project is just a little under two years (check that it's about 1.85 years).[8]

From the last chapter, the AAR is average net income divided by average book value. The net income each year is $28,800. The average (in thousands) of the four book values (from Table 10.2) for total investment is ($110 + 80 + 50 + 20)/4 = $65, so the AAR is $28,800/65,000 = 44.31 percent.[9] We've already seen that the return on this investment (the IRR) is about 34 percent. The fact that the AAR is larger illustrates again why the AAR cannot be meaningfully interpreted as the return on a project.

CONCEPT QUESTIONS

1. What is the definition of project operating cash flow? How does this differ from net income?

2. In the shark attractant project, why did we add back the firm's net working capital investment in the final year?

MORE ON PROJECT CASH FLOW

In this section, we take a closer look at some aspects of project cash flow. In particular, we discuss project net working capital in more detail. We then examine current tax laws regarding depreciation. Finally, we work through a more involved example of the capital investment decision.

A Closer Look at Net Working Capital

In calculating operating cash flow, we did not explicitly consider the fact that some of our sales might be on credit. Also, we may not have actually paid some of the costs shown. In either case, the cash flow has not yet occurred. We show here that these possibilities are not a problem as long as we don't forget to include additions to net working capital in our analysis. This discussion thus emphasizes the importance and the effect of doing so.

Suppose that during a particular year of a project we have the following simplified income statement:

Sales	$500
Costs	310
Net income	$190

Depreciation and taxes are zero. No fixed assets are purchased during the year. Also, to illustrate a point, we assume the only components of net working capital are accounts receivable and payable. The beginning and ending amounts for these accounts are:

	Beginning of Year	End of Year	Change
Accounts receivable	$880	$910	+$ 30
Accounts payable	550	605	+55
Net working capital	$330	$305	−$ 25

---

8 We're guilty of a minor inconsistency here. When we calculated the NPV and the IRR, we assumed all the cash flows occurred at end of year. When we calculated the payback, we assumed the cash flow occurred uniformly through the year.

9 Notice that the average total book value is not the initial total of $110,000 divided by 2. The reason is that the $20,000 in working capital doesn't depreciate. Notice that the average book value could be calculated as (beginning book value + ending book value)/2 = ($110,000 + 20,000)/2 = $65,000.

Based on this information, what is total cash flow for the year? We can begin by mechanically applying what we have been discussing to come up with the answer. Operating cash flow in this particular case is the same as EBIT since there are no taxes or depreciation; thus, it equals $190. Also, notice that net working capital actually *declined* by $25, so the addition to net working capital is negative. This just means that $25 was freed up during the year. There was no capital spending, so the total cash flow for the year is:

$$
\begin{aligned}
\text{Total cash flow} &= \text{Operating cash flow} - \text{Additions to NWC} \\
&\quad - \text{Capital spending} \\
&= \$190 - (-\$25) - \$0 \\
&= \$215
\end{aligned}
$$

Now, we know that this $215 total cash flow has to be "dollars in" less "dollars out" for the year. We could, therefore, ask a different question: What were cash revenues for the year? Also, what were cash costs?

To determine cash revenues, we need to look more closely at net working capital. During the year, we had sales of $500. However, accounts receivable rose by $30 over the same time period. What does this mean? The $30 increase tells us that sales exceeded collections by $30. In other words, we haven't yet received the cash from $30 of the $500 in sales. As a result, our cash inflow is $500 − 30 = $470. In general, cash income is sales minus the increase in accounts receivable.

Cash outflows can be similarly determined. We show costs of $310 on the income statement, but accounts payable increased by $55 during the year. This means we have not yet paid $55 of the $310, so cash costs for the period are just $310 − 55 = $255. In other words, in this case, cash costs equal costs less the increase in accounts payable.[10]

Putting this information together, cash inflows less cash outflows is $470 − 255 = $215, just as we had before. Notice that:

$$
\begin{aligned}
\text{Cash flow} &= \text{Cash inflow} - \text{Cash outflow} \\
&= (\$500 - 30) - (\$310 - 55) \\
&= (\$500 - \$310) - (30 - 55) \\
&= \text{Operating cash flow} - \text{Change in NWC} \\
&= \$190 - (-25) \\
&= \$215
\end{aligned}
$$

More generally, this example illustrates that including net working capital changes in our calculations has the effect of adjusting for the discrepancy between accounting sales and costs and actual cash receipts and payments.

EXAMPLE 10.1: Cash Collections and Costs

For the year just completed, Combat Wombat Telestat Ltd. (CWT) reports sales of $998 and costs of $734. You have collected the following beginning and ending balance sheet information:

	Beginning	Ending
Accounts receivable	$100	$110
Inventory	100	80
Accounts payable	100	70
Net working capital	$100	$120

Based on these figures, what are cash inflows? Cash outflows? What happened to each? What is net cash flow?

Sales were $998, but receivables rose by $10. So cash collections were $10 less than sales, or $988. Costs were $734, but inventories fell by $20. This means we didn't replace $20 worth of inventory, so cash costs are actually overstated by this amount. Also, payables fell by $30. This means that, on a net basis, we actually paid our suppliers $30 more than the value of what we received from them, resulting in a $30 understatement of cash costs. Adjusting for these events, cash costs are $734 − 20 + 30 = $744. Net cash flow is $988 − 744 = $244.

Finally, notice that net working capital increased by $20 overall. We can check our answer by noting that the original accounting sales less costs of $998 − 734 is $264. In addition, CWT spent $20 on net working capital, so the net result is a cash flow of $264 − 20 = $244, as we calculated.

---

10 If there were other accounts, we might have to make some further adjustments. For example, a net increase in inventory would be a cash outflow.

Depreciation and Capital Cost Allowance

As we note elsewhere, accounting depreciation is a noncash deduction. As a result, depreciation has cash flow consequences only because it influences the tax bill. The way that depreciation is computed for tax purposes is thus the relevant method for capital investment decisions. Chapter 2 introduced the capital cost allowance (CCA) system—Canada Revenue Agency's version of depreciation. We use CCA in the example that follows.

An Example: The Majestic Mulch and Compost Company (MMCC)

At this point, we want to go through a somewhat more involved capital budgeting analysis. Keep in mind as you read that the basic approach here is exactly the same as that in the earlier shark attractant example. We have only added more real-world detail (and a lot more numbers).

MMCC is investigating the feasibility of a new line of power mulching tools aimed at the growing number of home composters. Based on exploratory conversations with buyers for large garden shops, we project unit sales as follows:

Year	Unit Sales
1	3,000
2	5,000
3	6,000
4	6,500
5	6,000
6	5,000
7	4,000
8	3,000

The new power mulcher would be priced to sell at $120 per unit to start. When the competition catches up after three years, however, we anticipate that the price would drop to $110.[11]

The power mulcher project requires $20,000 in net working capital at the start. Subsequently, total net working capital at the end of each year would be about 15 percent of sales for that year. The variable cost per unit is $60, and total fixed costs are $25,000 per year.

It costs about $800,000 to buy the equipment necessary to begin production. This investment is primarily in industrial equipment and thus falls in Class 8 with a CCA rate of 20 percent.[12] The equipment will actually be worth about $150,000 in eight years. The relevant tax rate is 40 percent, and the required return is 15 percent. Based on this information, should MMCC proceed?

OPERATING CASH FLOWS   There is a lot of information here that we need to organize. The first thing we can do is calculate projected sales. Sales in the first year are projected at 3,000 units at $120 apiece, or $360,000 total. The remaining figures are shown in Table 10.6.

Next, we compute the CCA on the $800,000 investment in Table 10.7. Notice how, under the half-year rule (Chapter 2), UCC is only $400,000 in Year 1.

With this information, we can prepare the pro forma income statements, as shown in Table 10.8.

From here, computing the operating cash flows is straightforward. The results are illustrated in the first part of Table 10.9.

ADDITIONS TO NWC   Now that we have the operating cash flows, we need to determine the additions to NWC. By assumption, net working capital requirements change as sales change. In each year, we generally either add to or recover some of our project net working capital. Recalling that NWC starts at $20,000 and then rises to 15 percent of sales, we can calculate the amount of NWC for each year as illustrated in Table 10.10.

11 To be consistent, these prices include an inflation estimate.

12 Chapter 2 explains CCA classes.

TABLE 10.6
Projected revenues, power mulcher project

Year	Unit Price	Unit Sales	Revenues
1	$120	3,000	$360,000
2	120	5,000	600,000
3	120	6,000	720,000
4	110	6,500	715,000
5	110	6,000	660,000
6	110	5,000	550,000
7	110	4,000	440,000
8	110	3,000	330,000

TABLE 10.7
Annual CCA, power mulcher project (Class 8, 20% rate)

Year	Beginning UCC	CCA	Ending UCC
1	$400,000	$ 80,000	$320,000
2	720,000	144,000	576,000
3	576,000	115,200	460,800
4	460,800	92,160	368,640
5	368,640	73,728	294,912
6	294,912	58,982	235,930
7	235,930	47,186	188,744
8	188,744	37,749	150,995

TABLE 10.8 Projected income statements, power mulcher project

	Year							
	1	2	3	4	5	6	7	8
Unit price	$ 120	$ 120	$ 120	$ 110	$ 110	$ 110	$ 110	$ 110
Unit sales	3,000	5,000	6,000	6,500	6,000	5,000	4,000	3,000
Revenues	$360,000	$600,000	$720,000	$715,000	$660,000	$550,000	$440,000	$330,000
Variable costs	180,000	300,000	360,000	390,000	360,000	300,000	240,000	180,000
Fixed costs	25,000	25,000	25,000	25,000	25,000	25,000	25,000	25,000
CCA	80,000	144,000	115,200	92,160	73,728	58,982	47,186	37,749
EBIT	75,000	131,000	219,800	207,840	201,272	166,018	127,814	87,251
Taxes	30,000	52,400	87,920	83,136	80,509	66,407	51,126	34,901
Net income	$ 45,000	$ 78,600	$131,880	$124,704	$120,763	$ 99,611	$ 76,688	$ 52,350

TABLE 10.9 Projected cash flows, power mulcher project

	Year								
	0	1	2	3	4	5	6	7	8
I. Operating Cash Flow									
EBIT		$ 75,000	$131,000	$219,800	$207,840	$201,272	$166,018	$127,814	$ 87,251
CCA		80,000	144,000	115,200	92,160	73,728	58,982	47,186	37,749
Taxes		30,000	52,400	87,920	83,136	80,509	66,407	51,126	34,901
Operating cash flow		$125,000	$222,600	$247,080	$216,864	$194,491	$158,593	$123,874	$ 90,099
II. Net Working Capital									
Initial NWC									
NWC increases	$ 20,000	$ 34,000	$ 36,000	$ 18,000	-$ 750	-$ 8,250	-$16,500	-$16,500	-$ 16,500
NWC recovery									-$ 49,500
Additions to NWC	$ 20,000	$ 34,000	$ 36,000	$ 18,000	-$ 750	-$ 8,250	-$16,500	-$16,500	-$ 66,000
III. Capital Spending									
Initial outlay	$800,000								
Aftertax salvage									-$150,000
Capital spending	$800,000								-$150,000

As illustrated in Table 10.10, during the first year, net working capital grows from $20,000 to .15 × 360,000 = $54,000. The increase in net working capital for the year is thus $54,000 – 20,000 = $34,000. The remaining figures are calculated the same way.

TABLE 10.10

Additions to net working capital, power mulcher project

Year	Revenues	Net Working Capital	Increase
0		$ 20,000	
1	$360,000	54,000	$ 34,000
2	600,000	90,000	36,000
3	720,000	108,000	18,000
4	715,000	107,250	–750
5	660,000	99,000	–8,250
6	550,000	82,500	–16,500
7	440,000	66,000	–16,500
8	330,000	49,500	–16,500

Remember that an increase in net working capital is a cash outflow and a decrease in net working capital is a cash inflow. This means that a negative sign in this table represents net working capital returning to the firm. Thus, for example, $16,500 in NWC flows back to the firm in Year 6. Over the project's life, net working capital builds to a peak of $108,000 and declines from there as sales begin to drop.

We show the result for additions to net working capital in the second part of Table 10.9. Notice that at the end of the project's life there is $49,500 in net working capital still to be recovered. Therefore, in the last year, the project returns $16,500 of NWC during the year and then returns the remaining $49,500 for a total of $66,000 (the addition to NWC is –$66,000).

Finally, we have to account for the long-term capital invested in the project. In this case, we invest $800,000 at Time 0. By assumption, this equipment would be worth $150,000 at the end of the project. It will have an undepreciated capital cost of $150,995 at that time as shown in Table 10.7. As we discussed in Chapter 2, this $995 shortfall of market value below UCC creates a tax refund ($995 × 40 percent tax rate = $398) only if MMCC has no continuing Class 8 assets. However, we assume the company would continue in this line of manufacturing so there is no tax refund. Making this assumption is standard practice unless we have specific information about plans to close an asset class. Given our assumption, the difference of $995 stays in the asset pool, creating future tax shields.[13] The investment and salvage are shown in the third part of Table 10.9.

TOTAL CASH FLOW AND VALUE   We now have all the cash flow pieces, and we put them together in Table 10.11. In addition to the total project cash flows, we have calculated the cumulative cash flows and the discounted cash flows. At this point, it's essentially "plug and chug" to calculate the net present value, internal rate of return, and payback.

If we sum the discounted flows and the initial investment, the net present value (at 15 percent) works out to be $4,604. This is positive, so, based on these preliminary projections, the power mulcher project is acceptable. The internal or DCF rate of return is slightly greater than 15 percent since the NPV is positive. It works out to be 15.15, again indicating that the project is acceptable.[14]

Looking at the cumulative cash flows, we see that the project has almost paid back after four years since the cumulative cash flow is almost zero at that time. As indicated, the fractional year works out to be 95,706/202,741 = .47, so the payback is 4.47 years. We can't say whether or not this is good since we don't have a benchmark for MMCC. This is the usual problem with payback periods.

CONCLUSION   This completes our preliminary DCF analysis. Where do we go from here? If we have a great deal of confidence in our projections, there is no further analysis to be done. We should begin production and marketing immediately. It is unlikely that this would be the case. For one thing, NPV is not that far above zero and IRR is only marginally more than the 15 percent required rate of return. Remember that the result of our analysis is an estimate of NPV, and we usually have less than complete confidence in our projections. This means we have more work to do. In particular, we almost surely want to evaluate the quality of our estimates.

---

13 We show the detailed calculations in Section 10.6.

14 Appendix 10B shows how to analyze Majestic Mulch using a spreadsheet.

TABLE 10.11 Projected total cash flow, power mulcher project

	Year								
	0	1	2	3	4	5	6	7	8
Operating cash flow		$125,000	$222,600	$247,080	$216,864	$194,491	$158,593	$123,874	$ 90,099
Additions to NWC	–$ 20,000	–34,000	–36,000	–18,000	750	8,250	16,500	16,500	66,000
Capital spending	–800,000	0	0	0	0	0	0	0	150,000
Total project cash flow	–$ 820,000	$ 91,000	$186,600	$229,080	$217,614	$202,741	$175,093	$140,374	$306,099
Cumulative cash flow	–$ 820,000	–$729,000	–$542,400	–$313,320	–$ 95,706	$107,035	$282,128	$422,503	$728,602
Discounted cash flow @ 15%	–$ 820,000	$ 79,130	$141,096	$150,624	$124,422	$100,798	$ 75,698	$ 52,772	$100,064
NPV	$ 4,604								
IRR	15.15%								
PB	4.47								

We take up this subject in the next chapter. For now, we look at alternative definitions of operating cash flow, and we illustrate some different cases that arise in capital budgeting.

CONCEPT QUESTIONS

1. Why is it important to consider additions to net working capital in developing cash flows? What is the effect of doing so?

2. How is depreciation calculated for fixed assets under current tax law? What effect do expected salvage value and estimated economic life have on the calculated capital cost allowance?

 **10.5**

ALTERNATIVE DEFINITIONS OF OPERATING CASH FLOW

The analysis we have been through in the previous section is quite general and can be adapted to almost any capital investment problem. In the next section, we illustrate some particularly useful variations. Before we do so, we need to discuss the fact that different definitions of project operating cash flow are commonly used, both in practice and in finance texts.

As we see, the different definitions of operating cash flow all measure the same thing. If they are used correctly, they all produce the same answer, and one is not necessarily any better or more useful than another. Unfortunately, the fact that alternative definitions are used sometimes leads to confusion. For this reason, we examine several of these variations next to see how they are related.

In the following discussion, keep in mind that when we speak of cash flow, we literally mean dollars in less dollars out. This is all that we are concerned with. Different definitions of operating cash flow simply amount to different ways of manipulating basic information about sales, costs, depreciation, and taxes to get at cash flow.

To begin, it will be helpful to define the following:

$$OCF = \text{Project operating cash flow}$$
$$S = \text{Sales}$$
$$C = \text{Operating costs}$$
$$D = \text{Depreciation for tax purposes, i.e., CCA}^{15}$$
$$T_c = \text{Corporate tax rate}$$

For a particular project and year under consideration, suppose we have the following estimates:

$$S = \$1,500$$
$$C = \$700$$
$$D = \$600$$
$$T_c = 40\%$$

---

15 In this discussion, we use the terms *depreciation* and *CCA* interchangeably.

With these definitions, notice that EBIT is:

$$EBIT = S - C - D$$
$$= \$1,500 - 700 - 600$$
$$= \$200$$

Once again, we assume no interest is paid, so the tax bill is:

$$Taxes = EBIT \times T_c = (S - C - D) \times T_c$$
$$= \$200 \times .40 = \$80$$

When we put all of this together, project operating cash flow (OCF) is:

$$OCF = EBIT + D - Taxes \qquad \text{[10.1]}$$
$$= (S - C - D) + D - (S - C - D) \times T_c$$
$$= \$200 + 600 - 80 = \$720$$

If we take a closer look at this definition of OCF, we see that there are other definitions that could be used. We consider these next.

The Bottom-Up Approach

Since we are ignoring any financing expenses such as interest in our calculations of project OCF, we can write project net income as:

$$Project\ net\ income = EBIT - Taxes$$
$$= (S - C - D) - (S - C - D) \times T_c$$
$$= (S - C - D) \times (1 - T_c)$$
$$= (\$1,500 - 700 - 600) \times (1 - .40)$$
$$= \$200 \times .60$$
$$= \$120$$

With this in mind, we can develop a slightly different and very common approach to the cash flow question by restating Equation (10.1) as follows:

$$OCF = (S - C - D) + D - (S - C - D) \times T_c \qquad \text{[10.2]}$$
$$= (S - C - D) \times (1 - T_c) + D$$
$$= Project\ net\ income + Depreciation$$
$$= \$120 + 600$$
$$= \$720$$

This is the bottom-up approach. Here we start with the accountant's bottom line (net income) and add back any non-cash deductions such as depreciation. It is important to remember that this definition of operating cash flow as net income plus depreciation is only equivalent to our definition, and thus correct, when there is no interest expense subtracted in the calculation of net income.

For the shark attractant project, net income was $28,800 and depreciation was $30,000, so the bottom-up calculation is:

$$OCF = \$28,800 + 30,000 = \$58,800$$

This again is the correct answer.

The Top-Down Approach

A closely related, and perhaps more obvious, manipulation of our definition is to cancel the depreciation expense where possible:

$$OCF = (S - C - D) + D - (S - C - D) \times T_c \qquad \text{[10.3]}$$
$$= (S - C) - (S - C - D) \times T_c$$
$$= Sales - Costs - Taxes$$
$$= \$1,500 - 700 - 80 = \$720$$

This is the top-down approach. Here we start at the top of the income statement with sales and work our way down to net cash flow by subtracting costs, taxes, and other expenses. Along the way, we simply leave out any strictly non-cash items such as depreciation.

For the shark attractant project, the top-down cash flow can be readily calculated. With sales of $215,000, total costs (fixed plus variable) of $137,000, and a tax bill of $19,200, the OCF is:

$$OCF = \$215,000 - 137,000 - 19,200 = \$58,800$$

This is just as we had before.

The Tax Shield Approach

The final variation on our basic definition of OCF is the tax shield approach. This approach will be very useful for some problems we consider in the next section. The tax shield definition of OCF is:

$$\begin{aligned} OCF &= (S - C - D) + D - (S - C - D) \times T_c \\ &= (S - C) \times (1 - T_c) + D \times T_c \end{aligned}$$

[10.4]

With our numbers, this works out to be:

$$\begin{aligned} &= (S - C) \times (1 - T_c) + D \times T_c \\ &= \$800 \times .60 + \$600 \times .40 \\ &= \$480 + 240 \\ &= \$720 \end{aligned}$$

This is just as we had before.

This approach views OCF as having two components: The first part, $(S - C) \times (1 - T_c)$, is what the project's cash flow would be if there were no depreciation expense. In this case, this would-have-been cash flow is $480.

depreciation (CCA) tax shield
Tax saving that results from the CCA deduction, calculated as depreciation multiplied by the corporate tax rate.

The second part of OCF in this expression, $D \times T_c$, is called the **depreciation (CCA) tax shield.** We know that depreciation is a non-cash expense. The only cash flow effect from deducting depreciation is to reduce our taxes, a benefit to us. At the current 40 percent corporate tax rate, every dollar in CCA expense saves us 40 cents in taxes. So, in our example, the $600 in depreciation saves us $600 \times .40 = $240 in taxes.

For the shark attractant project we considered earlier in the chapter, the CCA tax shield would be $30,000 \times .40 = $12,000. The aftertax value for sales less costs would be ($240,000 − 162,000) \times (1 − .40) = $46,800. Adding these together yields the right answer:

$$OCF = \$46,800 + 12,000 = \$58,800$$

This verifies this approach.

Conclusion

Table 10.12 summarizes the four approaches to computing OCF. Now that we've seen that all these definitions are the same, you're probably wondering why everybody doesn't just agree on one of them. One reason, as we see in the next section, is that different definitions are useful in different circumstances. The best one to use is whichever happens to be the most convenient for the problem at hand.

TABLE 10.12
Alternative definitions of operating cash flow

Approach	Formula
Basic	OCF = EBIT + Depreciation − Taxes
Bottom-up	OCF = Net income + Depreciation
Top-down	OCF = Sales − Costs − Taxes
Tax shield	OCF = (Sales − Costs) $(1 − T_c)$ + Depreciation $\times T_c$

 **10.6**

APPLYING THE TAX SHIELD APPROACH TO THE MAJESTIC MULCH AND COMPOST COMPANY PROJECT

If you look back over our analysis of MMCC, you'll see that most of the number crunching involved finding CCA, EBIT, and net income figures. The tax shield approach has the potential to save us considerable time.[16] To realize on that potential, we do the calculations in a different order from Table 10.11. Instead of adding the cash flow components down the columns for each year and finding the present value of the total cash flows, we find the present values of each source of cash flows and add the present values.

The first source of cash flow is $(S - C)(1 - T_c)$ as shown for each year on the first line of Table 10.13. The figure for the first year, $93,000, is the first part of the OCF equation.

$$OCF = (S - C)(1 - T_c) + DT_c$$
$$= (360,000 - 180,000 - 25,000)(1 - .40) + 80,000(.40)$$
$$= 93,000 + 32,000 = \$125,000$$

Calculating the present value of the $93,000 for the first year and adding the present values of the other $(S - C)(1 - T_c)$ figures in Table 10.13 gives a total present value for this source of $645,099 as seen in the lower part of Table 10.13.

The second term is the tax shield on CCA for the first year. Table 10.14 reproduces the first year's tax shield of $32,000 along with the corresponding tax shields for each year. The total present value of the CCA tax shield is shown as $159,649.

The additions to net working capital and capital expenditure are essentially the same as in Table 10.11. Their present values are shown in the lower part of Table 10.13. The NPV is the sum of the present value of the four sources of cash flow. The answer, $4,604 is identical to what we found earlier in Table 10.11.

TABLE 10.13 Tax shield solution, power mulcher project

					Year				
	0	1	2	3	4	5	6	7	8
$(S - C)(1 - T_c)$		$93,000	$165,000	$201,000	$180,000	$165,000	$135,000	$105,000	$ 75,000
Additions to NWC	–$ 20,000	–34,000	–36,000	–18,000	750	8,250	16,500	16,500	66,000
Capital spending	–800,000								150,000
Totals									
PV of $(S - C)(1 - T_c)$		$645,099							
PV of additions to NWC		–49,179							
PV of capital spending		–750,965							
PV of CCA tax shield		159,649							
NPV		$ 4,604							

TABLE 10.14
PV of tax shield on CCA

	Tax Shield		
Year	CCA	.40 × CCA	PV at 15%
1	$ 80,000	$32,000	$ 27,826
2	144,000	57,600	43,554
3	115,200	46,080	30,298
4	92,160	36,864	21,077
5	73,728	29,491	14,662
6	58,982	23,593	10,200
7	47,186	18,874	7,096
8	37,749	15,100	4,936
	PV of tax shield on CCA		$159,649

---

16 This is particularly true if we set it up using a spreadsheet. See Appendix 10B.

Present Value of the Tax Shield on CCA

Further time savings are possible by using a formula that replaces the detailed calculation of yearly CCA. The formula is based on the idea that tax shields from CCA continue in perpetuity as long as there are assets remaining in the CCA class.[17] This idea is important because it gives us insight into when we can apply the formula in solving a problem in practice. The formula applies when the CCA asset class (or pool) will remain open when the project is completed. As we explained earlier, it is standard practice to assume that the asset class remains open unless we have specific information to the contrary. If, however, in a special case, we find that the pool will be closed out at the end of the project's life, we should not use this formula. The pool will only close if there are no remaining assets in the class. If this happens, the annual CCA values should be calculated to determine the UCC at the end of the project. If there is a terminal loss (i.e., the salvage value is less than this UCC), then there is a further tax shield when the asset is sold. If there is a gain (i.e., the salvage value is greater than this UCC), then there will be a recapture of a portion of the tax savings.[18] To calculate the present value of the tax shield on CCA, we find the present value of an infinite stream of tax shields abstracting from two practical implications—the half-year rule for CCA and disposal of the asset. We then adjust the formula.

Our derivation uses the following terms:

I = Total capital investment in the asset which is added to the pool
d = CCA rate for the asset class
T_c = Company's marginal tax rate
k = Discount rate
S = Salvage or disposal value of the asset in year n
S_n = Asset life in years

We can use the dividend valuation formula from Chapter 8 to derive the present value of the CCA tax shield. Recall that when dividends grow at a constant rate, g, the stock price is

$$P_0 = \frac{D_1}{k-g}$$

To apply this to the tax shield problem, we recognize that the formula can be generalized for any growing perpetuity where for example, Payment 3 = (Payment 2) × (1 + g)

$$PV = \frac{1st\ payment}{(Discount\ rate) - (Growth\ rate)}$$

Since we are temporarily ignoring the half-year rule, the growth rate in CCA payments is equal to $(-d)$. For example, in Table 10.14:

CCA 3 = CCA2 (1 + (−d))
CCA 3 = 144,000 (1 + (−.20))
CCA 3 = 144,000 (.8) = 115,200

Given the growth rate as $(-d)$, we need the 1st payment to complete the formula. This is the first year's tax shield IdT_c. We can now complete the formula:

$$PV(CCA\ tax\ shield) = \frac{1st\ payment}{(Discount\ rate) - (Growth\ rate)}$$

$$= \frac{IdT_c}{k-(-d)}$$

$$= \frac{IdT_c}{k+d}$$

The next step is to extend the formula to adjust for CCRA's half-year rule. This rule implies that a firm adds one-half of the incremental capital cost of a new project in Year 1 and the other half

17 Strictly speaking, the UCC for a class remains positive as long as there are physical assets in the class and the proceeds from disposal of assets is less than total UCC for the class.

18 Alternatively, the formula could be applied and the end-of-project effects calculated and discounted appropriately.

in Year 2. The result is that we now calculate the present value of the tax shield in two parts: The present value of the stream starting the first year is simply one-half of the original value:

$$\text{PV of 1st half} = 1/2\,\frac{IdT_c}{k+d}$$

The PV of the second half (deferred one year) is the same quantity (bracketed term) discounted back to time zero. The total present value of the tax shield on CCA under the half-year rule is the sum of the two present values.

$$\text{PV tax shield on CCA} = \frac{1/2\ IdTc}{k+d} + \left[\frac{1/2\ IdTc}{k+d}\right]/(1+k)$$

With a little algebra we can simplify the formula:

$$\text{PV} = \frac{1/2\ IdTc}{k+d}\,[1+1/(1+k)] = \frac{1/2\ IdTc}{k+d}\left[\frac{1+k+1}{1+k}\right]$$

$$\text{PV} = \frac{IdT_c}{k+d}\left[\frac{1+.5k}{1+k}\right]$$

The final adjustment for salvage-value begins with the present value in the salvage year, n of future tax shields beginning in Year $n+1$:

$$\frac{S_n dT_c}{d+k}$$

We discount this figure back to today and subtract it to get the complete formula:[19]

$$\text{PV tax shield on CCA} = \frac{[IdT_c]}{d+k}\times\frac{[1+.5k]}{1+k} - \frac{S_n dT_c}{d+k}\times\frac{1}{(1+k)^n}$$

Using the first part of the formula, the present value of the tax shield on MMCC's project is $170,932 assuming the tax shield goes on in perpetuity:

$$= \frac{800,000(.20)(.40)}{.20+.15}\times\frac{1+.5\times(.15)}{1+.15}$$

$$= 182,857 \times 1.08/1.15 = \$170,932.$$

The adjustment for the salvage value is

$$\frac{-150,000(.20)(.40)}{.20+.15}\times\frac{1}{(1+.15)^8}$$

$$= -34,286 \times 1/(1.15)^8 = -\$11,208$$

The present value of the tax shield on CCA is the sum of the two present values:

$$\text{Present value of tax shield from CCA} = \$170,932 - \$11,208$$
$$= \$159,724$$

Salvage Value versus UCC

There is a slight difference between this calculation for the present value of the tax shield on CCA and what we got in Table 10.14 by adding the tax shields over the project life. The difference arises whenever the salvage value of the asset differs from its UCC. The formula solution is more accurate as it takes into account the future CCA on this difference. In this case, the asset was sold for $150,000 and had UCC of $150,995. The $995 left in the pool after eight years creates an infinite stream of CCA. At Time 8, this stream has a present value of [$995(.20)(.40)]/[.20 + .15] = $227.43. At Time 0, the present value of this stream at 15 percent is about $75. To get the precise estimate of the present value of the CCA tax shield, we need to add this to the approximation in Table 10.14: $159,649 + $75 = $159,724.

EXAMPLE 10.2: The Ogopogo Paddler

Harvey Bligh, of Kelowna, British Columbia, is contemplating purchasing a paddle-wheel boat that he will use to give tours of Okanagan Lake in search of the elusive Ogopogo. Bligh has estimated cash flows from the tours and discounted them back over the eight-year expected life of the boat at his 20 percent required rate of return. The summary of his calculations follows:

Investment	–$250,000.00
Working capital	–50,000.00
PV of salvage	11,628.40
PV of NWC recovery	11,628.40
PV of aftertax operating income	251,548.33
PV of CCATS	?
NPV	?

He is struggling with the CCA tax shield calculation and is about to dump the project as it appears to be unprofitable. Is the project as unprofitable as Bligh believes?

The salvage value of the boat is $50,000, the combined federal and provincial corporate tax rate in British Columbia is 43 percent, and the CCA rate is 15 percent on boats.

$$PV \text{ tax shield on CCA} = \frac{[IdT_c]}{d + k} \times \frac{[1 + .5k]}{1 + k} - \frac{S_n dT_c}{d + k} \times \frac{1}{(1 + k)^n}$$

$$\text{1st term} = [(\$250,000 \times .15 \times .43)/(.15 + .20)]$$
$$\times [(1 + .50 \times .20)/(1 + .20)]$$
$$= \$42,232.14$$
$$\text{2nd term} = [(\$50,000 \times .15 \times .43)/(.15 + .20)]$$
$$\times 1/(1 + .20)^8$$
$$= \$2,142.95$$
$$PV \text{ of CCATS} = \$42,232.14 - 2,142.95$$
$$= \$40,089.19$$

The NPV of the investment is $14,894.32. Bligh should pursue this venture.

CONCEPT QUESTIONS

1. What is meant by the term depreciation (CCA) tax shield?
2. What are the top-down and bottom-up definitions of operating cash flow?

 **10.7**

SOME SPECIAL CASES OF DISCOUNTED CASH FLOW ANALYSIS

To finish our chapter, we look at four common cases involving discounted cash flow analysis. The first case involves investments that are primarily aimed at improving efficiency and thereby cutting costs. The second case demonstrates analysis of a replacement decision. The third case arises in choosing between equipment with different economic lives. The fourth and final case we consider comes up when a firm is involved in submitting competitive bids.

There are many other special cases that we should consider, but these four are particularly important because problems similar to these are so common. Also, they illustrate some very diverse applications of cash flow analysis and DCF valuation.

Evaluating Cost-Cutting Proposals

One decision we frequently face is whether to upgrade existing facilities to make them more cost-effective. The issue is whether the cost savings are large enough to justify the necessary capital expenditure.

For example, suppose we are considering automating some part of an existing production process presently performed manually in one of our plants. The necessary equipment costs $80,000 to buy and install. It will save $35,000 per year (pretax) by reducing labour and material costs. The equipment has a five-year life and is in Class 8 with a CCA rate of 20 percent. Due to rapid obsolescence, it will actually be worth nothing in five years. Should we do it? The tax rate is 40 percent, and the discount rate is 10 percent.

As always, the initial step in making this decision is to identify the relevant incremental cash flows. We keep track of these in the following table. First, determining the relevant capital spending is easy enough. The initial cost is $80,000 and the salvage value after five years is zero. Second, there are no working capital consequences here, so we don't need to worry about additions to net working capital.

Operating cash flows are the third component. Buying the new equipment affects our operating cash flows in two ways. First, we save $35,000 pretax every year. In other words, the firm's operating income increases by $35,000, so this is the relevant incremental project operating income. After taxes, this represents an annual cash flow of $21,000 as shown in the following table:

			Year			
	0	**1**	**2**	**3**	**4**	**5**
Investment	–$ 80,000					
NWC	0					
Subtotal	–80,000					
Op. income		$35,000	$35,000	$35,000	$35,000	$35,000
Taxes		14,000	14,000	14,000	14,000	14,000
Subtotal		21,000	21,000	21,000	21,000	21,000
Salvage						0
Total	–$ 80,000	$21,000	$21,000	$21,000	$21,000	$21,000

Present value of the tax shield on the CCA:

$$PV = \frac{80,000(.20)(.40)}{.20 + .10} \times \frac{1 + .5(.10)}{1 + .10}$$
$$= \$20,364$$

Present value of the aftertax operating savings:

$$PV = \$21,000 \times (1 - (1/1.10^5))/.10$$
$$= \$21,000 \times 3.7908$$
$$= \$79,607$$

NPV	
Investment	–$80,000
Operating cash flows	79,607
PV of salvage	0
CCATS	20,364
NPV	$19,971

Second, we have a tax shield on the incremental CCA created by the new equipment. This equipment has zero salvage so the formula is simplified as shown. CCA goes on forever and the present value of the tax shield is the sum of an infinite series. The present value is $20,364.

We can now finish our analysis by finding the present value of the $21,000 aftertax operating savings and adding the present values. At 10 percent, it's straightforward to verify that the NPV here is $19,971, so we should go ahead and automate.

Replacing an Asset

Instead of cutting costs by automating a manual production process, companies often need to decide whether it is worthwhile to enhance quality control by replacing existing equipment with newer models or more advanced technology. Suppose the promising numbers we calculated for the automation proposal encourage you to look into buying three more sets of equipment to replace older technology on your company's other production lines. Three new sets of equipment cost $200,000 to buy and install. (Your projected cost is less than the earlier $80,000 per machine because you receive a quantity discount from the manufacturer.)

This time, the analysis is more complex because you are going to replace existing equipment. You bought it four years ago for $150,000 and expect it to last for six more years. Due to rapid technological advances, the existing equipment is only worth $50,000 if you sell it today. The

EXAMPLE 10.3: To Buy or Not to Buy

We are considering the purchase of a $200,000 computer-based inventory management system. It is in Class 10 with a CCA rate of 30 percent. The computer has a four-year life. It will be worth $30,000 at that time. The system would save us $60,000 pretax in inventory-related costs. The relevant tax rate is 43.5 percent. Because the new setup is more efficient than our existing one, we would be able to carry less total inventory and thus free $45,000 in net working capital. What is the NPV at 16 percent? What is the DCF return (the IRR) on this investment?

We begin by calculating the operating cash flow. The aftertax cost savings are $60,000 \times (1 - .435) = $33,900$. The present value of the tax shield on the CCA is found using the formula we first used in the Majestic Mulch and Compost Company problem.

$$PV = \frac{200,000(.30)(.435)}{.30 + .16} \times \frac{1 + .5(.16)}{1 + .16}$$

$$- \frac{30,000(.30)(.435)}{.30 + .16} \times \frac{1}{(1 + .16)^4}$$

$$= \$48,126$$

The capital spending involves $200,000 up front to buy the system. The salvage is $30,000. Finally, and this is the somewhat tricky part, the initial investment in net working capital is a $45,000 inflow because the system frees working capital. Furthermore, we have to put this back in at the end of the project's life. What this really means is simple: While the system is in operation, we have $45,000 to use elsewhere.

To finish our analysis, we can compute the total cash flows:

	Year				
	0	1	2	3	4
Investment	−$200,000				
NWC	45,000				
Subtotal	−155,000				
Operating income		$60,000	$60,000	$60,000	$ 60,000
Taxes		26,100	26,100	26,100	26,100
Aftertax operating income		33,900	33,900	33,900	33,900
NWC returned					−45,000

NPV	
Investment	−$200,000
NWC recovered now	45,000
Operating income	94,858
PV of salvage	16,569
PV of NWC returned	−24,853
CCATS	48,126
NPV	−$ 20,300

At 16 percent, the NPV is −$20,300, so the investment is not attractive. After some trial and error, we find that the NPV is zero when the discount rate is 8.28 percent, so the IRR on this investment is about 8.3 percent.[20]

more efficient newer technology would save you $75,000 per year in production costs over its projected six-year life.[21] These savings could be realized through reduced wastage and downtime on the shop floor.

If you retain the current equipment for the rest of its working life, you can expect to realize $10,000 in scrap value after six years. The new equipment, on the other hand, is saleable in the second-hand market and is expected to have a salvage value of $30,000 after six years.

With regard to working capital, the new equipment requires a greater stock of specialized spare parts but offers an offsetting reduction in wastage of work in process. On balance, no change in net working capital is predicted.

You determine that both the existing and new equipment are Class 8 assets with a CCA rate of 20 percent. Your firm requires a return of 15 percent on replacement investments and faces a tax rate of 44 percent. Should you recommend purchase of the new technology?

---

20 This IRR is tricky to compute without a spreadsheet because the asset is sold for $30,000, which is less than its undepreciated capital cost (after four years) of $48,000. Capital cost allowance on the difference remains in the pool and goes on to infinity. For this reason, we need to solve for the CCATS by trial and error.

21 For simplicity, we assume that both the old and new equipment have six-year remaining lives. Later, we discuss how to analyze cases in which lives differ.

There is a lot of information here and we organize it in Table 10.15. The first cash flow is the capital outlay—and the difference between the cost of the new and the sale realization on the old equipment. To address CCA, we draw on the discussion in Chapter 2. There will still be undepreciated capital cost in the Class 8 pool because the amount we are adding to the pool (purchase price of new equipment) is greater than the amount we are subtracting (salvage on old equipment). Because we are not creating a negative balance of undepreciated capital cost (recapturing CCA) or selling all the pool's assets, there are no tax adjustments to the net outlay. The incremental salvage in six years is treated in the same way.[22]

The fact that we are making a net addition to the asset pool in Class 8 simplifies calculation of the tax shield on CCA. In this common case, Canada Customs and Revenue Agency's half-year rule applies to the net addition to the asset class. So, we simply substitute the incremental outlay for C in the present value of tax shield formula. Finally, we substitute the incremental salvage for S and crank the formula.[23]

$$PV = \frac{150,000(.20)(.44)}{.20 + .15} \times \frac{1 + .5(.15)}{1 + .15}$$
$$- \frac{20,000(.20)(.44)}{.20 + .15} \times \frac{1}{(1 + .15)^6}$$
$$= \$33,081$$

Additions to net working capital are not relevant here. Aftertax operating savings are calculated in the same way as in our prior examples. Table 10.15 shows that the replacement proposal has a substantial positive NPV and seems attractive.

Evaluating Equipment with Different Lives

Our previous examples assumed, a bit unrealistically, that competing systems had the same life. The next problem we consider involves choosing among different possible systems, equipment, or procedures with different lives. For example, an automobile fleet manager needs to know whether it is

TABLE 10.15
Replacement of existing asset ($ 000s)

		Year					
	0	**1**	**2**	**3**	**4**	**5**	**6**
Investment	–$ 200						
Salvage on old	50						
NWC additions	0						
Subtotal	–150						
Op. savings		$75	$75	$75	$75	$75	$ 75
Taxes		33	33	33	33	33	33
Subtotal		42	42	42	42	42	42
Salvage forgone							–10
Salvage							30

NPV

Investment	–$200,000
Salvage recovered now	50,000
Operating cash flows	158,948
PV of salvage forgone	–4,323
PV of salvage recovered	12,970
CCATS	33,081
NPV	$ 50,676

22 Here we are making an implicit assumption that at the end of six years the deduction of salvage will not exhaust the Class 8 pool. If this were not the case, the excess, recaptured depreciation would be taxable at the firm's tax rate of 44 percent.

23 The present value of tax shield formula does not adjust the salvage for the half-year rule. This means we are assuming that, while the asset class will continue beyond Year 6, no new assets will be added in that year. We make this and the other tax assumptions to illustrate common situations without bogging down in the fine points of taxes.

EXAMPLE 10.4: Replacement

Theatreplex Oleum is considering replacing a projector system in one of its cinemas. The new projector has super-holographic sound and is able to project laser-sharp images. These features would increase the attendance at the theatre; and the new projector could cut repair costs dramatically. The new projector costs $250,000 and has a useful life of 15 years, at which time it could be sold for $20,000. The projector currently being used was purchased for $150,000 five years ago and can be sold now for $50,000. In 15 years the old projector would be scrapped for $5,000. The new projector would increase operating income by $50,000 annually; it belongs to Class 9 for CCA calculations with a rate of 25 percent. Theatreplex requires a 15 percent return on replacement assets and the corporate tax rate is 43.5 percent. Should Theatreplex replace the projector?

We begin calculating the profitability of such an investment by finding the present value of the increased operating income:

$$\text{Aftertax flow} = \$50,000 \times (1 - .435)$$
$$= \$28,250$$
$$PV = \$28,250 \times (1 - 1/(1.15)^{15})/.15$$
$$= \$28,250 \times 5.84737$$
$$= \$165,188$$

The next step is to calculate the present value of the net salvage value of the new projector:

$$PV = (\$20,000 - 5,000) \times 1/(1.15)^{15}$$
$$= \$1,843$$

The last step is to calculate the present value tax shield on the CCA:

$$PV = \frac{200,000(.25)(.435)}{.25 + .15} \times \frac{1 + .5(.15)}{1 + .15}$$
$$- \frac{15,000(.25)(.435)}{.25 + .15} \times \frac{1}{(1 + .15)^{15}}$$
$$= 54,375 \times 1.075/1.15 - 4,078 \times 1/(1.15)^{15}$$
$$= \$50,829 - \$501$$
$$= \$50,328$$

The NPV is found by adding these present values to the original investment:

Net investment	−$200,000
Increased operating income	165,188
Net salvage	1,843
CCATS	50,328
NPV	$ 17,359

The investment surpasses the required return on investments for Theatreplex Oleum and should be pursued.

better to replace cars every year or to keep cars until they are five years old. As always, our goal is to maximize net present value. To do this, we place the projects on a common horizon for comparison.

The approach we consider here is only necessary when two special circumstances exist: First, the possibilities under evaluation have different economic lives. Second, and just as important, we need whatever we buy more or less indefinitely. As a result, when it wears out, we buy another one.

We can illustrate this problem with a simple example that holds the benefits constant across different alternatives. This way we can focus on finding the least-cost alternative.[24] Imagine that we are in the business of manufacturing stamped metal subassemblies. Whenever a stamping mechanism wears out, we have to replace it with a new one to stay in business. We are considering which of two stamping mechanisms to buy.

Machine A costs $100 to buy and $10 per year to operate. It wears out and must be replaced every two years. Machine B costs $140 to buy and $8 per year to operate. It lasts for three years and must then be replaced. Ignoring taxes, which one should we go with if we use a 10 percent discount rate?

In comparing the two machines, we notice that the first is cheaper to buy, but it costs more to operate and it wears out more quickly. How can we evaluate these trade-offs? We can start by computing the present value of the costs for each:

Machine A: $PV = -\$100 + -\$10/1.1 + -10/1.1^2 = -\$117.36$
Machine B: $PV = -\$140 + -\$8/1.1 + -\$8/1.1^2 + -\$8/1.1^3 = -\$159.89$

Notice that all the numbers here are costs, so they all have negative signs. If we stopped here, it might appear that A is the more attractive since the PV of the costs is less. However, all we have really discovered so far is that A effectively provides two years' worth of stamping service for $117.36, while B effectively provides three years' worth for $159.89. These are not directly comparable because of the difference in service periods.

---

24 Alternatively, in another case, the costs could be constant and the benefits differ. Then we would maximize the equivalent annual benefit.

We need to somehow work out a cost per year for these two alternatives. To do this, we ask the question: What amount, paid each year over the life of the machine, has the same PV of costs? This amount is called the **equivalent annual cost (EAC)**.

equivalent annual cost (EAC)
The present value of a project's costs calculated on an annual basis.

Calculating the EAC involves finding an unknown payment amount. For example, for Machine A, we need to find a two-year ordinary annuity with a PV of −$117.36 at 10 percent. Going back to Chapter 4, the two-year annuity factor is:

$$\text{Annuity factor} = [1 - 1/1.10^2]/.10 = 1.7355$$

For Machine A, then, we have:

$$\text{PV of costs} = -\$117.36 = \text{EAC} \times 1.7355$$
$$\text{EAC} = -\$117.36/1.7355$$
$$= -\$67.62$$

For Machine B, the life is three years, so we first need the three-year annuity factor:

$$\text{Annuity factor} = [1 - 1/1.10^3]/.10 = 2.4869$$

We calculate the EAC for B just as we did for A:

EXAMPLE 10.5: Equivalent Annual Costs

This extended example illustrates what happens to the EAC when we consider taxes. You are evaluating two different pollution control options. A filtration system costs $1.1 million to install and $60,000 pretax annually to operate. It would have to be replaced every five years. A precipitation system costs $1.9 million to install, but only $10,000 per year to operate. The precipitation equipment has an effective operating life of eight years. The company rents its factory and both systems are considered leasehold improvements so straight-line capital cost allowance is used throughout, and neither system has any salvage value. Which method should we select if we use a 12 percent discount rate? The tax rate is 40 percent.

We need to consider the EACs for the two approaches because they have different service lives, and they will be replaced as they wear out. The relevant information is summarized in Table 10.16.

Notice that the operating cash flow is actually positive in both cases because of the large CCA tax shields.[25] This can occur whenever the operating cost is small relative to the purchase price.

To decide which system to purchase, we compute the EACs for both using the appropriate annuity factors:

TABLE 10.16 Equivalent annual cost

	Filtration System	Precipitation System
Aftertax operating cost	−$ 36,000	−$ 6,000
Annual CCATS	88,000	95,000
Operating cash flow	$ 52,000	$ 89,000
Economic life	5 years	8 years
Annuity factor (12%)	3.6048	4.9676
Present value of operating cash flow	$ 187,450	$ 442,116
Capital spending	−1,100,000	−1,900,000
Total PV of costs	−$ 912,550	−$ 1,457,884

Filtration system: −$912,550 = EAC × 3.6048
EAC = −$253,149 per year
Precipitation system: −$1,457,884 = EAC × 4.9676
EAC = −$293,479 per year

The filtration system is the cheaper of the two, so we select it. The longer life and smaller operating cost of the precipitation system are not sufficient to offset its higher initial cost.

---

25 We ignore the half-year rule for simplicity here. Also note that it is possible to rework Example 10.5 (and reach the same answer) treating the EAC as equivalent annual cash flows. In this case, the inflows have minus signs and the EAC is positive.

$$\text{PV of costs} = \$159.89 = \text{EAC} \times 2.4869$$
$$\text{EAC} = -\$159.89/2.4869$$
$$= -\$64.29$$

Based on this analysis, we should purchase B because it effectively costs $64.29 per year versus $67.62 for A. In other words, all things considered, B is cheaper. Its longer life and lower operating cost are more than enough to offset the higher initial purchase price.

Setting the Bid Price

Early on, we used discounted cash flow to evaluate a proposed new product. A somewhat different (and very common) scenario arises when we must submit a competitive bid to win a job. Under such circumstances, the winner is whoever submits the lowest bid.

There is an old saw concerning this process: the low bidder is whoever makes the biggest mistake. This is called the winner's curse. In other words, if you win, there is a good chance that you underbid. In this section, we look at how to set the bid price to avoid the winner's curse. The procedure we describe is useful anytime we have to set a price on a product or service.

To illustrate how to set a bid price, imagine that we are in the business of buying stripped-down truck platforms and then modifying them to customer specifications for resale. A local distributor has requested bids for five specially modified trucks each year for the next four years, for a total of 20 trucks.

We need to decide what price per truck to bid. The goal of our analysis is to determine the lowest price we can profitably charge. This maximizes our chances of being awarded the contract while guarding against the winner's curse.

Suppose we can buy the truck platforms for $10,000 each. The facilities we need can be leased for $24,000 per year. The labour and material cost to do the modification works out to be about $4,000 per truck. Total cost per year would thus be

$$\$24,000 + 5 \times (\$10,000 + 4,000) = \$94,000.$$

We need to invest $60,000 in new equipment. This equipment falls in Class 8 with a CCA rate of 20 percent. It would be worth about $5,000 at the end of the four years. We also need to invest $40,000 in raw materials inventory and other working capital items. The relevant tax rate is 43.5 percent. What price per truck should we bid if we require a 20 percent return on our investment?

We start by looking at the capital spending and net working capital investment. We have to spend $60,000 today for new equipment. The aftertax salvage value is simply $5,000 assuming as usual that at the end of four years, other assets remain in Class 8. Furthermore, we have to invest $40,000 today in working capital. We get this back in four years.

We can't determine the aftertax operating income just yet because we don't know the sales price. The present value of the tax shield on CCA works out to be $11,438. The calculations are in Table 10.17 along with the other data. With this in mind, here is the key observation: The lowest possible price we can profitably charge results in a zero NPV at 20 percent. The reason is, at that price we earn exactly the required 20 percent on our investment.

TABLE 10.17
Setting the bid price

	Cash Flow	Year	PV at 20%
Capital spending	-$ 60,000	0	-$60,000
Salvage	5,000	4	2,411
Additions to NWC	-40,000	0	-40,000
	40,000	4	19,290
Aftertax operating income	(S − 94,000)(1 − .435)	1-4	?
Tax shield on CCA			$ 11,438
NPV			$ 0

$$\text{PV} = \frac{60,000(.20)(.435)}{.20 + .20} \times \frac{1 + .5(.20)}{1 + .20}$$

$$- \frac{5,000(.20)(.435)}{.20 + .20} \times \frac{1}{(1 + .20)^4}$$

$$= \$11,438$$

Given this observation, we first need to determine what the aftertax operating income must be for the NPV to be equal to zero. To do this, we calculate the present values of the salvage and return of net working capital in Table 10.17 and set up the NPV equation.

$$\text{NPV} = 0 = -\$60,000 + 2,411 - 40,000 + 19,290 + \text{PV}$$
$$\text{(annual aftertax incremental operating income)} + 11,438$$
$$\text{PV (annual aftertax incremental operating income)} = \$66,861$$

Since this represents the present value of an annuity, we can find the annual "payments,"

$$\text{PV (annuity)} = \$66,861 = P\,[1 - 1/1.20^4]/.20$$
$$P = \$25,828$$

The annual incremental aftertax operating income is $25,828. Using a little algebra we can solve for the necessary sales proceeds, S.

$$\$25,828 = (S - 94,000)(1 - .435)$$
$$\$45,713 = S - 94,000$$
$$S = \$139,713.$$

Since the contract is for five trucks, this represents $27,943 per truck. If we round this up a bit, it looks like we need to bid about $28,000 per truck. At this price, were we to get the contract, our return would be a bit more than 20 percent.

> **CONCEPT QUESTIONS**
>
> **1.** Under which circumstances do we have to worry about unequal economic lives? How do you interpret the EAC?
>
> **2.** In setting a bid price, we used a zero NPV as our benchmark. Explain why this is appropriate.

10.8   SUMMARY AND CONCLUSIONS

This chapter describes how to put together a discounted cash flow analysis. In it, we covered:

1. The identification of relevant project cash flows. We discussed project cash flows and described how to handle some issues that often come up, including sunk costs, opportunity costs, financing costs, net working capital, and erosion.

2. Preparing and using pro forma or projected financial statements. We showed how such financial statement information is useful in coming up with projected cash flows, and we also looked at some alternative definitions of operating cash flow.

3. The role of net working capital and depreciation in project cash flows. We saw that including the additions to net working capital was important because it adjusted for the discrepancy between accounting revenues and costs and cash revenues and costs. We also went over the calculation of capital cost allowance under current tax law.

4. Some special cases in using discounted cash flow analysis. Here we looked at four special issues: cost-cutting investments, replacement decisions, the unequal lives problem, and how to set a bid price.

The discounted cash flow analysis we've covered here is a standard tool in the business world. It is a very powerful tool, so care should be taken in its use. The most important thing is to get the cash flows identified in a way that makes economic sense. This chapter gives you a good start on learning to do this.

Key Terms

capital cost allowance (CCA) (page 272)
depreciation (CCA) tax shield (page 282)
equivalent annual cost (EAC) (page 291)
erosion (page 270)
incremental cash flows (page 269)

opportunity cost (page 270)
pro forma financial statements (page 272)
stand-alone principle (page 269)
sunk cost (page 269)

Chapter Review Problems and Self-Test

These problems give you some practice with discounted cash flow analysis. The answers follow.

10.1   Capital Budgeting for Project X Based on the following information for Project X, should we undertake the venture? To answer, first prepare a pro forma income statement for each year. Second, calculate the operating cash flow. Finish the problem by determining total cash flow and then calculating NPV assuming a 20 percent required return. Use a 40 percent tax rate throughout. For help, look back at our shark attractant and power mulcher examples.

Project X is a new type of audiophile-grade stereo amplifier. We think we can sell 500 units per year at a price of $10,000 each. Variable costs per amplifier run about $5,000 per unit, and the product should have a four-year life. We require a 20 percent return on new products such as this one.

Fixed costs for the project run $610,000 per year. Further, we need to invest $1,100,000 in manufacturing equipment. This equipment belongs to class 8 for CCA purposes. In four years, the equipment can be sold for its UCC value. We would have to invest $900,000 in

working capital at the start. After that, net working capital requirements would be 30 percent of sales.

10.2   Calculating Operating Cash Flow Mater Pasta, Ltd., has projected a sales volume of $1,432 for the second year of a proposed expansion project. Costs normally run 70 percent of sales, or about $1,002 in this case. The capital cost allowance will be $80, and the tax rate is 40 percent. What is the operating cash flow? Calculate your answer using the top-down, bottom-up, and tax shield approaches described in the chapter.

10.3   Spending Money to Save Money For help on this one, refer back to the computerized inventory management system in Example 10.3. Here, we're contemplating a new, mechanized welding system to replace our current manual system. It costs $600,000 to get the new system. The cost will be depreciated at a 30 percent CCA rate. Its expected life is four years. The system would actually be worth $100,000 at the end of four years.

We think the new system could save us $180,000 per year pretax in labour costs. The tax rate is 44 percent. What is the NPV of buying the new system? The required return is 15 percent.

Answers to Self-Test Problems

10.1   To develop the pro forma income statements, we need to calculate the depreciation for each of the four years. The relevant CCA percentages, allowances, and UCC values for the first four years are:

Year	CCA rate	Eligible UCC	Allowance	Ending UCC
1	20.0%	$550,000	$110,000	$990,000
2	20.0	990,000	198,000	792,000
3	20.0	792,000	158,400	633,600
4	20.0	633,600	126,720	506,880

The projected income statements, therefore, are as follows:

	Year			
	1	2	3	4
Sales	$5,000,000	$5,000,000	$5,000,000	$5,000,000
Variable costs	2,500,000	2,500,000	2,500,000	2,500,000
Fixed costs	610,000	610,000	610,000	610,000
CCA deduction	110,000	198,000	158,400	126,720
EBIT	$1,780,000	$1,692,000	$1,731,600	$1,763,280
Taxes (40%)	712,000	676,800	692,640	705,312
Net income	$1,068,000	$1,015,200	$1,038,960	$1,057,968

Based on this information, the operating cash flows are:

	Year			
	1	**2**	**3**	**4**
EBIT	$1,780,000	$1,692,000	$1,731,600	$1,763,280
CCA deduction	110,000	198,000	158,400	126,720
Taxes	–712,000	–676,800	–692,640	–705,312
Operating cash flow	$1,178,000	$1,213,200	$1,197,360	$1,184,688

We now have to worry about the non-operating cash flows. Net working capital starts at $900,000 and then rises to 30 percent of sales, or $1,500,000. This is a $600,000 addition to net working capital.

Finally, we have to invest $1,100,000 to get started. In four years, the market and book value of this investment would be identical, $506,880. Under our usual going-concern assumption, other Class 8 assets remain in the pool. There are no tax adjustments needed to the salvage value.

When we combine all this information, the projected cash flows for Project X are:

	Year				
	0	**1**	**2**	**3**	**4**
Operating cash flow		$1,178,000	$1,213,200	$1,197,360	$1,184,688
Additions to NWC	–$ 900,000	–600,000			1,500,000
Capital spending	–1,100,000				506,880
Total cash flow	–$ 2,000,000	$ 578,000	$1,213,200	$1,197,360	$3,191,568

With these cash flows, the NPV at 20 percent is:

$$NPV = -\$2,000,000 + 578,000/1.2 + 1,213,200/1.2^2$$
$$+ 1,197,360/1.2^3 + 3,191,568/1.2^4$$
$$= \$1,556,227$$

So this project appears quite profitable.

10.2 We begin by calculating the project's EBIT, its tax bill, and its net income.

$$EBIT = \$1,432 - 1,002 - 80 = \$350$$
$$Taxes = \$350 \times .40 = \$140$$
$$Net\ income = \$350 - 140 = \$210$$

With these numbers, operating cash flow is:

$$OCF = EBIT + D - Taxes$$
$$= \$350 + 80 - 140$$
$$= \$290$$

Using the other OCF definitions, we have:

$$Tax\ shield\ OCF = (S - C) \times (1 - .40) + D \times .40$$
$$= (\$1,432 - \$1,002) \times .60 + 80 \times .40$$
$$= \$290$$
$$Bottom\text{-}up\ OCF = Net\ income + D$$
$$= \$210 + 80$$
$$= \$290$$
$$Top\text{-}down\ OCF = S - C - Taxes$$
$$= \$1,432 - 1,002 - 140$$
$$= \$290$$

As expected, all of these definitions produce exactly the same answer.

10.3 The $180,000 pretax saving gives an aftertax amount of:

$$(1 - .44) \times \$180,000 = \$100,800$$

The present value of this four-year annuity amounts to:

$$PV = \$100,800 \times (1 - \frac{1}{1.15^4})/.15$$

$$= \$100,800 \times 2.8550$$

$$= \$287,782$$

The present value of the tax shield on the CCA is:

$$PV = \frac{600,000(.30)(.44)}{.15 + .30} \times \frac{(1 + .5(.15))}{1 + .15}$$

$$- \frac{100,000(.30)(.44)}{.15 + .30} \times \frac{1}{(1.15)^4}$$

$$= 164,522 - 16,771$$

$$= \$147,750$$

The only flow left undiscounted is the salvage value of the equipment. The present value of this flow is:

$$PV = \$100,000 \times 1/1.15^4$$

$$= \$100,000 \times .5718$$

$$= \$57,175$$

There are no working capital consequences, so the NPV is found by adding these three flows and the initial investment.

Investment	−$600,000
PV of labour savings	287,782
PV of salvage	57,175
CCATS	147,750
NPV	−$107,293

You can verify that the NPV is −$107,293, and the return on the new welding system is only about 5.4 percent. The project does not appear to be profitable.

Concepts Review and Critical Thinking Questions

1. In the context of capital budgeting, what is an opportunity cost?

2. In our capital budgeting examples, we assumed that a firm would recover all of the working capital it invested in a project. Is this a reasonable assumption? When might it not be valid?

3. When is EAC analysis appropriate for comparing two or more projects? Why is this method used? Are there any implicit assumptions required by this method that you find troubling? Explain.

4. "When evaluating projects, we're only concerned with the relevant incremental aftertax cash flows. Therefore, because depreciation is a noncash expense, we should ignore its effects when evaluating projects." Critically evaluate this statement.

5. A major textbook publisher has an existing finance textbook. The publisher is debating whether or not to produce an "essentialized" version, meaning a shorter (and lower-priced) book. What are some of the considerations that should come into play?

To answer the next two questions, refer back to the case of Tango we discussed to open the chapter.

6. In evaluating the decision to start Tango, under what circumstances might Air Canada have concluded that erosion was irrelevant?

7. In evaluating Tango, what do you think Air Canada needs to assume regarding the profit margins that exist in this market? Is it likely they will be maintained when Air Canada and others enter this market?

Questions and Problems

Basic
(Questions 1–34)

1. **Relevant Cash Flows** Parker & Stone, Inc., is looking at setting up a new manufacturing plant in South Park to produce garden tools. The company bought some land six years ago for $5 million in anticipation of using it as a warehouse and distribution site, but the company has since decided to rent these facilities from a competitor instead. If the land were sold today, the company would net $5.4 million. The company wants to build its new manufacturing plant on this land; the plant will cost $10.4 million to build, and the site requires $650,000 worth of grading before it is suitable for construction. What is the proper cash flow amount to use as the initial investment in fixed assets when evaluating this project? Why?

2. **Relevant Cash Flows** Winnebagel Corp. currently sells 30,000 motor homes per year at $45,000 each, and 12,000 luxury motor coaches per year at $85,000 each. The company wants to introduce a new portable camper to fill out its product line; it hopes to sell 21,000 of these campers per year at $12,000 each. An independent consultant has determined that if Winnebagel introduces the new campers, it should boost the sales of its existing motor homes by 5,000

**Basic
(continued)**

units per year, and reduce the sales of its motor coaches by 1,300 units per year. What is the amount to use as the annual sales figure when evaluating this project? Why?

3. **Calculating Projected Net Income** A proposed new investment has projected sales of $650,000. Variable costs are 60 percent of sales, and fixed costs are $158,000; depreciation is $75,000. Prepare a pro forma income statement assuming a tax rate of 35 percent. What is the projected net income?

4. **Calculating OCF** Consider the following income statement:

Sales	$912,400
Costs	593,600
Depreciation	135,000
EBIT	?
Taxes (34%)	?
Net income	?

Fill in the missing numbers and then calculate the OCF. What is the CCA tax shield?

5. **OCF from Several Approaches** A proposed new project has projected sales of $85,000, costs of $43,000, and CCA of $3,000. The tax rate is 40 percent. Calculate operating cash flow using the four different approaches described in the chapter and verify that the answer is the same in each case.

6. **Calculating Net Income** A proposed new investment has projected sales in Year 5 of $900,000. Variable costs are 52 percent of sales and fixed costs are $190,000. CCA for the year will be $112,000. Prepare a projected income statement, assuming a 39 percent tax rate.

7. **Calculating Depreciation** A new electronic process monitor costs $850,000. This cost could be depreciated at 30 percent per year (Class 10). The monitor would actually be worthless in five years. The new monitor would save $490,000 per year before taxes and operating costs. If we require a 12 percent return, what is the NPV of the purchase? Assume a tax rate of 40 percent.

8. **NPV and NWC Requirements** In the previous question, suppose the new monitor also requires us to increase net working capital by $37,500 when we buy it. Further suppose that the monitor could actually be worth $100,000 in five years. What is the new NPV?

9. **NPV and CCA** In the previous question, suppose the monitor was assigned a 25 percent CCA rate. All the other facts are the same. Will the NPV be larger or smaller? Why? Calculate the new NPV to verify your answer.

10. **Identifying Relevant Costs** Rick Bardles and Ed James are considering building a new bottling plant to meet expected future demand for their new line of tropical coolers. They are considering putting it on a plot of land they have owned for three years. They are analyzing the idea and comparing it to some others. Bardles says, "Ed, when we do this analysis, we should put in an amount for the cost of the land equal to what we paid for it. After all, it did cost us a pretty penny." James retorts, "No, I don't care how much it cost—we have already paid for it. It is what they call a sunk cost. The cost of the land shouldn't be considered." What would you say to Bardles and James?

 11. **Calculating Salvage Value**[26] Consider an asset that costs $400,000 and can be depreciated at 20 percent per year (Class 8) over its 10-year life. The asset is to be used in a six-year project; at the end of the project, the asset can be sold for $100,000. If the relevant tax rate is 40 percent, what is the aftertax cash flow from the sale of the asset? You can assume that there will be no assets left in the class in six years.

12. **Identifying Cash Flows** Last year, Little Brutus Pizza Corporation reported sales of $67,000 and costs of $28,500. The following information was also reported for the same period:

	Beginning	Ending
Accounts receivable	$41,250	$37,000
Inventory	51,639	54,244
Accounts payable	66,380	72,570

Based on this information, what was Little Brutus' change in net working capital for last year? What was the net cash flow?

13. **Calculating Project OCF** Tectonic Plating Inc. is considering a new three-year expansion project that requires an initial fixed asset investment of $1.76 million. The fixed asset falls into Class 10 for tax purposes (CCA rate of 30 percent per year), and at the end of the three years can be sold for a salvage value equal to its UCC. The project is estimated to generate $2,027,000 in annual sales, with costs of $595,000. If the tax rate is 38 percent, what is the OCF for each year of this project?

14. **Calculating Project NPV** In the previous problem, supposed the required return on the project is 20 percent. What is the project's NPV?

---

26 Recall that terminal losses and recapture in CCA calculations were covered in Chapter 2.

Basic
(continued)

15. **Calculating Project Cash Flow from Assets**   In the previous problem, suppose the project requires an initial investment in net working capital of $300,000 and the fixed asset will have a market value of $215,000 at the end of the project. What is the project's Year 0 net cash flow? Year 1? Year 2? Year 3? What is the new NPV?

16. **NPV Applications**   We believe we can sell 60,000 home security devices per year at $140 a piece. They cost $100 to manufacture (variable cost). Fixed production costs run $205,000 per year. The necessary equipment costs $625,000 to buy and would be depreciated at a 25 percent CCA rate. The equipment would have a zero salvage value after the five-year life of the project. We need to invest $160,000 in net working capital up front; no additional net working capital investment is necessary. The discount rate is 17 percent, and the tax rate is 38 percent. What do you think of the proposal?

17. **Identifying Cash Flows**   Suppose a company has $8,000 in sales during a quarter. Over the quarter, accounts receivable increased by $4,500. What were cash collections?

18. **Stand-Alone Principle**   Suppose a financial manager is quoted as saying: "Our firm uses the stand-alone principle. Since we treat projects like minifirm in our evaluation process, we include financing costs, because financing costs are relevant at the firm level." Critically evaluate this statement.

19. **Relevant Cash Flows**   Perfect Plexiglass, Inc., is looking to set up a new manufacturing plant to produce surfboards. The company bought some land seven years ago for $7.5 million in anticipation of using it as a warehouse and distribution site, but the company decided to rent the facilities from a competitor instead. The land was appraised last week for $985,000. The company wants to build its new manufacturing plant on this land; the plant will cost $19 million to build, and the site requires $425,000 in grading before it will be suitable for construction. What is the proper cash flow amount to use as the initial investment in fixed assets when evaluating this project? Why?

20. **Relevant Cash Flows**   Stevinator Motorworks Corp. currently sells 18,000 compact cars per year at $12,500 each, and 36,700 luxury sedans at $42,600 each. The company wants to introduce a new mid-sized sedan to fill out its product line; it hopes to sell 24,500 of the cars per year at $31,500 each. An independent consultant has determined that if Stevinator introduces the new cars, it should boost the sales of its existing compacts by 9,000 units per year, while reducing the unit sales of its luxury sedans by 7,500 units per year. What is the annual cash flow amount to use as the sales figure when evaluating this project? Why?

21. **Project Evaluation**   Bendog's Franks is looking at a new system with an installed cost of $450,000. This equipment is depreciated at a rate of 20 percent per year (Class 8) over the project's six-year life, at the end of which the sausage system can be sold for $100,000. The sausage system will save the firm $105,000 per year in pre-tax operating costs, and the system requires an initial investment in net working capital of $23,500. If the tax rate is 37 percent and the discount rate is 12.5 percent, what is the NPV of this project?

22. **Project Evaluation**   Your firm is contemplating the purchase of a new $1.1 million computer-based order entry system. The PVCCATS is $240,000, and the machine will be worth $260,000 at the end of the five-year life of the system. You will save $364,000 before taxes per year in order processing costs and you will be able to reduce working capital by $104,000 (this is a one-time reduction). If the tax rate is 35 percent, what is the IRR for this project?

23. **Project Evaluation**   In the previous problem, suppose your required return on the project is 16 percent, your pre-tax cost savings are only $350,000 per year, and the machine can be depreciated at 30 percent (Class 10). Will you accept the project? What if the pre-tax savings are only $275,000 per year? At what level of pre-tax cost savings would you be indifferent between accepting the project and not accepting it?

24. **Calculating a Bid Price**   We have been requested by a large retailer to submit a bid for a new point-of-sale credit checking system. The system would be installed, by us, in 50 stores per year for three years. We would need to purchase $725,000 worth of specialized equipment. This will be depreciated at a 20 percent CCA rate. We will sell it in three years, at which time it will be worth about half of what we paid for it. Labour and material cost to install the system is about $75,000 per site. Finally, we need to invest $175,000 in working capital items. The relevant tax rate is 38 percent. What price per system should we bid if we require a 20 percent return on our investment? Try to avoid the winner's curse.

25. **Alternative OCF Definitions**   Next year, Billy Adams Corporation estimates that they will have $150,000 in sales, $80,000 in operating costs, and their corporate tax rate will be 32 percent. Undepreciated capital costs (UCC) will be $250,000 and the CCA rate will be 20 percent.

    a. What is estimated EBIT for next year?

    b. Using the bottom-up approach, what is the operating cash flow?

    c. Using the tax shield method, what is the operating cash flow?

26. **Alternating OCF Definitions**   The Logging Company is considering a new logging project in British Columbia, requiring new equipment with a cost of $200,000. For the upcoming year, they estimate that the project will produce sales of $400,000 and $305,000 in operating costs. The CCA rate will be 25 percent and their net profits will be taxed at a corporate rate of 36 percent. Use the top-down approach and the tax shield approach to calculate the operating cash flow for the first year of the project for The Logging Company.

Basic
(continued)

27. **EAC** Olivaw is a leading manufacturer of positronic brains, a key component in robots. The company is considering two alternative production methods. The costs and lives associated with each are:

Year	Method 1	Method 2
0	$5,800	$8,300
1	350	580
2	350	580
3	350	580
4		580

Assuming that Olivaw will not replace the equipment when it wears out, which should it buy? If Olivaw is going to replace the equipment, which should it buy (r = 12%)? Ignore depreciation and taxes in answering.

28. **Calculating Cash Flows and EAC** In the previous question, suppose all the costs are before taxes and the tax rate is 37 percent. Both types of equipment would be depreciated at a CCA rate of 25 percent (Class 9), and would have no value after the project. What are the EACs in this case? Which is the preferred method?

29. **Calculating EAC** A five-year project has an initial fixed asset investment of $210,000, an initial NWC investment of $20,000, and an annual OCF of –$32,000. The fixed asset is fully depreciated over the life of the project and has no salvage value. If the required return is 15 percent, what is this project's equivalent annual cost, or EAC?

30. **Calculating EAC** You are evaluating two different silicon wafer milling machines. The Techron I costs $210,000, has a three-year life, and has pretax operating costs of $34,000 per year. The Techron II costs $320,000, has a five-year life, and has pretax operating costs of $23,000 per year. Both milling machines are in Class 8 (CCA rate of 20 percent per year). Assume a salvage value of $20,000. If your tax rate is 35 percent and your discount rate is 14 percent, compute the EAC for both machines. Which do you prefer? Why?

31. **Calculating EAC** You are considering two different methods for constructing a new warehouse site. The first method would use prefabricated building segments, would have an initial cost of $4.8 million, would have annual maintenance costs of $100,000, and would last for 25 years. The second alternative would employ a new carbon-fibre panel technology, would have an initial cost of $6 million, would have maintenance costs of $525,000 every 10 years, and is expected to last for 40 years. Both buildings would be in CCA Class 1 (at a rate of 4 percent) and it is expected that each would have a salvage value equivalent to 25 percent of its construction cost at the end of its useful life. The discount rate the firm uses in evaluating projects is 15 percent. The tax rate is 38 percent. What is the annual cost for each option, and which would you pick?

32. **Calculating EAC** A seven-year project has an initial investment of $350,000 and an annual operating cost of $16,000 in the first year. The operating costs are expected to increase at the rate of inflation, which is projected at 3 percent for the life of the project. The investment is in Class 7 for CCA purposes, and will therefore be depreciated at 15 percent annually. The salvage value at the end of the project will be $105,000. The firm's discount rate is 11.5 percent, and the company falls in the 35 percent tax bracket. What is the EAC for the investment?

33. **Calculating a Bid Price** Alton Enterprises needs someone to supply it with 175,000 cartons of machine screws per year to support its manufacturing needs over the next five years, and you've decided to bid on the contract. It will cost you $570,000 to install the equipment necessary to start production. The equipment will be depreciated at 30 percent (Class 10), and you estimate that it can be salvaged for $77,000 at the end of the five-year contract. Your fixed production costs will be $182,000 per year, and your variable production costs should be $6.25 per carton. You also need an initial net working capital of $75,000. If your tax rate is 37 percent and you require a 20 percent return on your investment, what bid price should you submit?

34. **Cost-cutting Proposals** Doohan's Machine Shop is considering a four-year project to improve its production efficiency. Buying a new machine press for $450,000 is estimated to result in $150,000 in annual pretax cost savings. The press falls into Class 8 for CCA purposes (CCA rate of 20 percent per year), and it will have a salvage value at the end of the project of $75,000. The press also requires an initial investment in spare parts inventory of $22,000, along with an additional $2,000 in inventory for each succeeding year of the project. If the shop's tax rate is 36 percent and its discount rate is 18 percent, should Doohan's buy and install the machine press?

Intermediate
(Questions
35–45)

35. **Cash Flows and NPV** We project unit sales for a new household-use laser-guided cockroach search and destroy system as follows:

Year	Unit Sales
1	82,000
2	115,000
3	144,300
4	150,500
5	51,275

The new system will be priced to sell at $179 each.

The cockroach eradicator project will require $975,000 in net working capital to start, and total net working capital will rise to 37 percent of the change in sales. The variable cost per unit is $137, and total fixed costs are $47,700 per year. The equipment necessary to begin production will cost a total of $11.3 million. This equipment is mostly industrial machinery and thus qualifies for CCA at a rate of 20 percent. In five years, this equipment will actually be worth about 25 percent of its cost.

The relevant tax rate is 37 percent, and the required return is 20 percent. Based on these preliminary estimates, what is the NPV of the project?

36. **Replacement Decisions**   An officer for a large construction company is feeling nervous. The anxiety is caused by a new excavator just released onto the market. The new excavator makes the one purchased by the company a year ago obsolete. As a result, the market value for the company's excavator has dropped significantly, from $400,000 a year ago to $35,000 now. In 10 years, it would be worth only $5,000. The new excavator costs only $700,000 and would increase operating revenues by $65,000 annually. The new equipment has a 10-year life and expected salvage value of $115,000. What should the officer do? The tax rate is 39 percent, the CCA rate, 25 percent for both excavators, and the required rate of return for the company is 14 percent.

37. **Replacement Decisions**   A university student painter is considering the purchase of a new air compressor and paint gun to replace an old paint sprayer. (Both items belong to Class 9 and have a 25 percent CCA rate.) These two new items cost $8,000 and have a useful life of four years, at which time they can be sold for $1,100. The old paint sprayer can be sold now for $300 and could be scrapped for $150 in four years. The entrepreneurial student believes that operating revenues will increase annually by $8,000. Should the purchase be made? The tax rate is 22 percent and the required rate of return is 17 percent.

38. **Different Lives**   The Briar Patch Golf and Country Club in Calgary is evaluating two different irrigation system options. An underground automatic irrigation system will cost $9.5 million to install and $62,000 pretax annually to operate. It will not have to be replaced for 20 years. An aboveground system will cost $5 million to install, but $165,000 per year to operate. The aboveground equipment has an effective operating life of nine years. The country club leases its land from the city and both systems are considered leasehold improvements; as a result, straight-line capital cost allowance is used throughout, and neither system has any salvage value. Which method should we select if we use a 10.5 percent discount rate? The tax rate is 37 percent.

39. **Comparing Mutually Exclusive Projects**   Victoria Enterprises, Inc., is evaluating alternative uses for a three-story manufacturing and warehousing building that it has purchased for $745,000. The company could continue to rent the building to the present occupants for $45,000 per year. These tenants have indicated an interest in staying in the building for at least another 15 years. Alternatively, the company could make leasehold improvements to modify the existing structure to use for its own manufacturing and warehousing needs. Victoria's production engineer feels the building could be adapted to handle one of two new product lines. The cost and revenue data for the two product alternatives follow.

	Product A	Product B
Initial cash outlay for building modifications	$ 99,000	$180,850
Initial cash outlay for equipment	372,000	428,000
Annual pretax cash revenues (generated for 15 years)	301,900	375,000
Annual pretax cash expenditures (generated for 15 years)	169,500	210,500

The building will be used for only 15 years for either product A or product B. After 15 years, the building will be too small for efficient production of either product line. At that time, Victoria plans to rent the building to firms similar to the current occupants. To rent the building again, Victoria will need to restore the building to its present layout. The estimated cash cost of restoring the building if product A has been undertaken is $14,750; if product B has been produced, the cash cost will be $112,550. These cash costs can be deducted for tax purposes in the year the expenditures occur.

Victoria will depreciate the original building shell (purchased for $745,000) at a CCA rate of 5 percent, regardless of which alternative it chooses. The building modifications fall into CCA Class 13 and are depreciated using the straight-line method over a 15-year life. Equipment purchases for either product are in Class 8 and have a CCA rate of 20 percent. The firm's tax rate is 39 percent, and its required rate of return on such investments is 15 percent.

For simplicity, assume all cash flows for a given year occur at the end of the year. The initial outlays for modifications and equipment will occur at $t = 0$, and the restoration outlays will occur at the end of year 15. Also, Victoria has other profitable ongoing operations that are sufficient to cover any losses.

Which use of the building would you recommend to management?

40. **Valuation of the Firm**   The Regina Wheat Company (RWC) has wheat fields that currently produce annual profits of $800,000. These fields are expected to produce average annual profits of $700,000 in real terms forever. RWC has no depreciable assets, so the annual cash flow is also $700,000. RWC is an all-equity firm with 275,000 shares outstanding. The appropriate discount rate for its stock is 17 percent. RWC has an investment opportunity with a

Intermediate
(continued)

gross present value of $1,800,000. The investment requires a $1,100,000 outlay now. RWC has no other investment opportunities. Assume all cash flows are received at the end of each year. What is the price per share of RWC?

41. **Comparing Mutually Exclusive Projects** Hagar Industrial Systems Company (HISC) is trying to decide between two different conveyor belt systems. System A costs $430,000, has a four-year life, and requires $120,000 in pre-tax annual operating costs. System B costs $540,000, has a six-year life, and requires $80,000 in pre-tax annual operating costs. Both systems are to be depreciated at 30 percent per year (Class 10) and will have no salvage value. Whichever project is chosen, it will *not* be replaced when it wears out. If the tax rate is 34 percent and the discount rate is 20 percent, which project should the firm choose?

42. **Comparing Mutually Exclusive Projects** Suppose in the previous problem that HISC always needs a conveyor belt system; when one wears out, it must be replaced. Which project should the firm choose now?

43. **Calculating a Bid Price** Consider a project to supply 80 million postage stamps per year to Canada Post for the next five years. You have an idle parcel of land available that cost $1,000,000 five years ago; if you sold the land today, it would net you $1,200,000, after-tax. You will need to install $3.1 million in new manufacturing plant and equipment to actually produce the stamps; this plant and equipment will be depreciated straight-line to zero over the project's five-year life. The equipment can be sold for $600,000 at the end of the project. You will also need $600,000 in initial net working capital for the project, and an additional investment of $50,000 every year thereafter. Your production costs are 0.75 cents per stamp, and you have fixed costs of $800,000 per year. If your tax rate is 34 percent and your required return on this project is 15 percent, what bid price should you submit on the contract?

44. **Replacement with Unequal Lives** BIG Industries needs computers. Management has narrowed the choices to the SAL 5000 and the DET 1000. It would need 12 SALs. Each SAL costs $12,000 and requires $1,750 of maintenance each year. At the end of the computer's six-year life, BIG expects to be able to sell each one for $1,200. On the other hand, BIG could buy 10 DETs. DETs cost $14,000 each and each machine requires $1,400 maintenance every year. They last for 4 years and have no resale value. Whichever model BIG chooses, it will buy that model forever. Ignore tax effects, and assume that maintenance costs occur at year-end. Which model should BIG buy if the cost of capital is 15 percent?

45. **Replacement with Unequal Lives** Station CJXT is considering the replacement of its old, fully depreciated sound mixer. Two new models are available. Mixer X has a cost of $550,000, a five-year expected life, and after-tax cash flow savings of $195,000 per year. Mixer Y has a cost of $950,000, a 10-year life, and after-tax cash flow of $247,000 per year. No new technological developments are expected. The cost of capital is 14.5 percent. Should CJXT replace the old mixer with X or Y?

Challenge
(Questions
46–53)

46. **Abandonment Decisions** For some projects, it may be advantageous to terminate the project early. For example, if a project is losing money, you might be able to reduce your losses by scrapping out the assets and terminating the project, rather than continuing to lose money all the way through to the project's completion. Consider the following project of Hand Clapper, Inc. The company is considering a four-year project to manufacture clap-command garage door openers. This project requires an initial investment of $5 million with a CCA of 40 percent over the project's life. An initial investment in net working capital of $1 million is required to support spare parts inventory; this cost is fully recoverable whenever the project ends. The company believes it can generate $4 million in pretax revenues with $1.5 million in total pretax operating costs. The tax rate is 36 percent and the discount rate is 13 percent. The market value of the equipment over the life of the project is as follows:

Year	Market Value (millions)
1	$4.00
2	3.34
3	1.50
4	0.00

   a. Assuming Hand Clapper operates this project for four years, what is the NPV?

   b. Now compute the project NPV assuming the project is abandoned after only one year, after two years, and after three years. What economic life for this project maximizes its value to the firm? What does this problem tell you about not considering abandonment possibilities when evaluating projects?

47. **Capital Budgeting Renovations** Suppose we are thinking about renovating a leased office. The renovations would cost $240,000. The renovations will be depreciated straight-line to zero over the five-year remainder of the lease.

   The new office would save us $30,000 per year in heating and cooling costs. Also, absenteeism should be reduced and the new image should increase revenues. These last two items would result in increased operating revenues of $25,000 annually. The tax rate is 38 percent, and the discount rate is 13 percent. Strictly from a financial perspective, should the renovations take place?

48. **Calculating Required Savings** A proposed cost-saving device has an installed cost of $190,000. It is in Class 8 (CCA rate = 20%) for CCA purposes. It will actually function for five years, at which time it will have no value. There are no working capital consequences from the investment, and the tax rate is 37 percent.

Challenge
(continued)

    a. What must the pretax cost savings be for us to favour the investment? We require a 14 percent return. Hint: This one is a variation on the problem of setting a bid price.

    b. Suppose the device will be worth $28,500 in salvage (before taxes). How does this change your answer?

49. **Cash Flows and Capital Budgeting Choices** Klaatu Company has recently completed a $1.2 million, two-year marketing study. Based on the results, Klaatu has estimated that 16,900 of its new RUR-class robots could be sold annually over the next eight years at a price of $23,900 each. Variable costs per robot are $20,000 and fixed costs total $28.4 million.

    Start-up costs include $85.5 million to build production facilities, $4.5 million in land, and $16.3 million in net working capital. The $85.5 million facility is made up of a building valued at $10 million that will belong to CCA Class 3 and $75.5 million of manufacturing equipment (belonging to CCA Class 8). Class 3 has a CCA rate of 5 percent, while Class 8 has a rate of 20 percent. At the end of the project's life, the facilities (including the land) will be sold for an estimated $20.9 million; assume the building's value will be $7.7 million. The value of the land is not expected to change.

    Finally, start-up would also entail fully deductible expenses of $3.3 million at Year 0. Klaatu is an ongoing, profitable business and pays taxes at a 37 percent rate. Klaatu uses a 16 percent discount rate on projects such as this one. Should Klaatu produce the RUR-class robots?

50. **Project Evaluation** Pavarotti-in-You (PIY), Inc., projects unit sales for a new opera tenor emulation implant as follows:

Year	Unit Sales
1	95,000
2	105,000
3	105,000
4	112,000
5	62,500

Production of the implants will require $600,000 in net working capital to start and additional net working capital investments each year equal to 35 percent of the projected sales increase for the following year. (Because sales are expected to fall in Year 5, there is no NWC cash flow occurring for Year 4.) Total fixed costs are $160,000 per year, variable production costs are $240 per unit, and the units are priced at $360 each. The equipment needed to begin production has an installed cost of $16.7 million. Because the implants are intended for professional singers, this equipment is considered industrial machinery and thus falls into Class 8 for tax purposes (20 percent). In five years, this equipment can be sold for about 25 percent of its acquisition cost. PIY is in the 40 percent marginal tax bracket and has a required return on all its projects of 22 percent. Based on these preliminary project estimates, what is the NPV of the project? What is the IRR?

51. **Calculating Required Savings** A proposed cost-saving device has an installed cost of $600,000. The device will be used in a five-year project, but is classified as manufacturing and processing equipment for tax purposes. The required initial net working capital investment is $20,000, the marginal tax rate is 37 percent, and the project discount rate is 12.5 percent. The device has an estimated Year 5 salvage value of $90,000. What level of pretax cost savings do we require for this project to be profitable?

52. **Replacement Decisions** Suppose we are thinking about replacing an old computer with a new one. The old one cost us $350,000; the new one will cost $625,000. The new machine will be in CCA Class 10 (30 percent). It will probably be worth about $100,000 after five years.

    The old computer is being depreciated at a rate of $62,500 per year. It will be completely written off in three years. If we don't replace it now, we will have to replace it in two years. We can sell it now for $150,000; in two years, it will probably be worth half that. The new machine will save us $100,000 per year in maintenance costs. The tax rate is 36 percent and the discount rate is 11 percent.

    a. Suppose we only consider whether or not we should replace the old computer now without worrying about what's going to happen in two years. What are the relevant cash flows? Should we replace it or not? Hint: Consider the net change in the firm's aftertax cash flows if we do the replacement.

    b. Suppose we recognize that if we don't replace the computer now, we will be replacing it in two years. Should we replace now or should we wait? Hint: What we effectively have here is a decision either to "invest" in the old computer (by not selling it) or to invest in the new one. Notice that the two investments have unequal lives.

53. **Financial Break-Even Analysis** To solve the bid price problem presented in the text, we set the project NPV equal to zero and found the required price using the definition of OCF. Thus the bid price represents a financial break-even level for the project. This type of analysis can be extended to many other types of problems.

    a. In Problem 33, assume that the price per carton is $10 and find the project NPV. What does your answer tell you about your bid price? What do you know about the number of cartons you can sell and still break even? How about your level of costs?

Challenge
(continued)

    b. Solve Problem 33 again with the price still at $10 but find the quantity of cartons per year that you can supply and still break even.

    c. Repeat (b) with a price of $10 and a quantity of 175,000 cartons per year, and find the highest level of fixed costs you could afford and still break even.

MINI CASE

As a financial analyst at Minor International (MI) you have been asked to evaluate two capital investment alternatives submitted by the production department of the firm. Before beginning your analysis, you note that company policy has set the cost of capital at 16 percent for all proposed projects. As a small business, MI pays corporate taxes at the rate of 35 percent.

The proposed capital project calls for developing new computer software to facilitate partial automation of production in MI's plant. Alternative A has initial software development costs projected at $175,000, while Alternative B would cost $290,000. Software development costs would be capitalized and qualify for a capital cost allowance (CCA) rate of 30 percent. In addition, IT would hire a software consultant under either alternative to assist in making the decision whether to invest in the project for a fee of $15,000 and this cost would be expensed when it is incurred.

To recover its costs, MI's IT department would charge the production department for the use of computer time at the rate of $310 per hour and estimates that it would take 100 hours of computer time per year to run the new software under either alternative. MI owns all its computers and does not currently operate them at capacity. The information technology (IT) plan calls for this excess capacity to continue in the future. For security reasons, it is company policy not to rent excess computing capacity to outside users.

If the new partial automation of production is put in place, expected savings in production cost (before tax) are projected as follows:

Year	Alternative A	Alternative B
1	$70,000	$100,000
2	70,000	105,000
3	60,000	90,000
4	30,000	50,000
5	20,000	30,000

As the capital budgeting analyst, you are required to answer the following in your memo to the production department:

a) Calculate the net present value of each of the alternatives. Which would you recommend?

b) The CFO suspects that there is a high risk that new technology will render the production equipment and this automation software obsolete after only three years. Which alternative would you now recommend? (Cost savings for years 1 to 3 would remain the same.)

c) MI could use excess resources in its Engineering department to develop a way to eliminate this step of the manufacturing process by the end of year 3. The salvage value of the equipment (including any CCA and tax impact) would be $30,000 at the end of year 3, $20,000 at the end of year 4, and zero after five years. Should Engineering develop the solution and remove the equipment before the five years are up? Which alternative? When?

Internet Application Questions

1. From time to time, governments at various levels provide tax incentives to promote capital investments in key industries. The Province of Ontario (www.gov.on.ca) introduced in 2000 the Mining Investment Incentives program in the form of bonus tax credits (on top of normal deductions). Information on this program is found in the following release:

    http://www.mndm.gov.on.ca/mndm/pub/newrel/NRPrint.asp?NRNUM=254&NRYear=2000&NRLAN=EN&NRID=1022

    Explain how this incentive will affect new exploration activity. Is it possible that such tax incentives alter the NPV of a project?

2. Syncrude Canada Limited (www.syncrude.com) is a consortium of several oil companies. In August 2000, Syncrude announced the opening of Aurora, a new oil sands project, at a total capital cost of $8 billion spread over 10 years. Aurora is expected to increase production from approximately 80 million barrels of oil to 170 million barrels per year. Assuming a 10-year horizon and a cost of capital of 10 percent, do you think Aurora is a positive NPV project? Oil price at the time was $30 per barrel, and cost of extraction was $10 per barrel. Ignore taxes. Information on the Aurora project is provided on Syncrude's homepage.

3. In addition to NPV and IRR, Economic Value Added (EVA®) analysis (www.sternstewart.com/cvaabout/whatis.php) has emerged as a popular tool for capital budgeting and valuation. EVA was developed and is patented by Stern Stewart & Co (www.sternstewart.com). Explain the mechanics of EVA and show its equivalence to NPV. Provide at least two reasons why EVA and NPV may differ in implementation.

4. Toyota Canada expected the capital expansion of its Cambridge, Ontario facility to total $680 million (CDN). The plant began production of 60,000 Lexus RX300 (which have since been renamed RX330 and RX350) luxury SUVs annually in September 2003. Information on the expansion can be found in the press releases section of Toyota's site (www.toyota.co.jp) or at the Government of Canada's Strategis business information site (http://strategis.ic.gc.ca/epic/internet/inauto-auto.nsf/en/am01519e.html). Assuming profit of $5000 on the Lexus, a 15-year production horizon, and a 15 percent discount rate, do you think Toyota made a good investment decision? What other factors need to be considered? Why?

Suggested Readings

For more on the capital budgeting decision, see:

Garrison, R., E. Noreen, G.R. Chesley, and R. Carroll. *Managerial Accounting*, 5th Canadian ed. Whitby, Ontario: McGraw-Hill Ryerson, 2001.

Graham, John R. and Campbell R. Harvey. "The Theory and Practice of Corporate Finance: Evidence From the Field." *Journal of Financial Economics* 60, May/June 2001, pp. 187–243.

MORE ON INFLATION AND CAPITAL BUDGETING

This text states that interest rates can be expressed in either nominal or real terms. For example, suppose the nominal interest rate is 12 percent and inflation is expected to be 8 percent next year. Then the real interest rate is approximately

Real rate = Nominal rate – Expected inflation rate
= 12% – 8% = 4%.

Similarly, cash flows can be expressed in either nominal or real terms. Given these choices, how should one express interest rates and cash flows when performing capital budgeting?

Financial practitioners correctly stress the need to maintain consistency between cash flows and discount rates. That is, nominal cash flows must be discounted at the nominal rate. Real cash flows must be discounted at the real rate. The NPV is the same when cash flows are expressed in real quantities. The NPV is always the same under the two different approaches.

Because both approaches always yield the same result, which one should be used? Students will be happy to learn the following rule: Use the approach that is simpler. In the Shields Electric case, nominal quantities produce a simpler calculation. That is because the problem gave us nominal cash flows to begin with.

However, firms often forecast unit sales per year. They can easily convert these forecasts to real quantities by multiplying expected unit sales each year by the product price at Date 0. (This assumes the price of

EXAMPLE 10A.1: Real or Nominal?

Shields Electric forecasts the following nominal cash flows on a particular project:

	Date		
	0	1	2
Cash flow	–$1,000	$600	$650

The nominal interest rate is 14 percent, and the inflation rate is forecast to be 5 percent. What is the value of the project?

<u>Using Nominal Quantities</u>   The NPV can be calculated as:

$$\$26.47 = -\$1,000 + \frac{\$600}{1.14} + \frac{\$650}{(1.14)^2}$$

The project should be accepted.

Using Real Quantities   The real cash flows are:

	Date		
	0	1	2
Cash flow	–$1,000	$571.43	$589.57
		$\frac{\$600}{1.05}$	$\frac{\$650}{(1.05)^2}$

The real interest rate is approximately 9 percent (14 percent – 5 percent); precisely it is 8.57143 percent.[27] The NPV can be calculated as

$$\$26.47 = -\$1,000 + \frac{\$571.32}{1.0857143} + \frac{\$589.57}{(1.0857143)^2}$$

---

27 The exact calculation is 8.57143% = (1.14/1.05) – 1. It is explained in Chapter 12.

the product rises at exactly the rate of inflation.) Once a real discount rate is selected, NPV can easily be calculated from real quantities. Conversely, nominal quantities complicate the example, because the extra step of converting all real cash flows to nominal cash flows must be taken.

CONCEPT QUESTIONS

1. What is the difference between the nominal and the real interest rate?

2. What is the difference between nominal and real cash flows?

Appendix Question and Problem

A.1 Repeat Question 27, assuming that all cash flows and discount rates provided are nominal rates, and that the inflation rate is 3 percent. What are the real cash flows and the real rate of return? What is the new EAC for the production methods if inflation is taken into account?

CAPITAL BUDGETING WITH SPREADSHEETS

Spreadsheets are almost essential for constructing a capital budgeting framework or for using pro forma financial statements. Table 10B.2 is an example of a capital budgeting framework, using the data from the Majestic Mulch and Compost Company. The framework is completely integrated, changing one of the input variables at the top reformulates the whole problem. This is useful for sensitivity calculations as it would be tedious to recalculate each column in the framework by hand.

The highlighted cells exhibit the more complicated procedures in the framework. The first, E16, is the CCA calculation. The IF statement is used to decide what year it is, to take into consideration the half-year effect. The second, G32, uses another IF statement; this one is needed to assess whether there is a deficiency or excess of working capital. The last cell, S49, simply discounts the future cash flows back to Year 0 dollars.

A well-designed capital budgeting framework allows most inputs to be easily changed, simplifying sensitivity calculations. We now turn our attention to a simple sensitivity calculation, to explain the usefulness of spreadsheets.

Table 10B.1 shows two sensitivity tables: One varies the initial investment and the other varies the discount rate. Notice in the first that if the initial investment runs over budget by as little as $25,000, it makes the whole project unprofitable. The second sensitivity analysis demonstrates that the project is even more sensitive to discount rate fluctuations.

Spreadsheets are invaluable in problems such as these; they decrease the number of silly errors and make all values easier to check. They also allow for what-if analyses such as these.

Recall that many problems in each chapter are labelled, with an icon, as Spreadsheet Problems. For some good practice at capital budgeting on a spreadsheet, we suggest that you consider completing Problem 48 in particular.

TABLE 10B.1
Sensitivity analysis

Initial Investment	NPV	Discount Rate	NPV
Base case	$ 4,604	15.0%	$ 4,604
$750,000	44,626	10.0	177,240
775,000	24,615	12.5	84,796
800,000	4,604	15.0	4,604
825,000	–15,407	17.5	–65,319
850,000	–35,418	20.0	–126,589

TABLE 10B.2 Capital budgeting framework

The Majestic Mulch and Compost Company

Input variables:

Tax rate	40.0%	Discount rate	15.0%
CCA rate	20.0%	NWC as a % of sale	15.0%
Initial investment	$800,000		

Income statements

Year	0	1	2	3	4	5	6	7	8
Unit price		$ 120	$ 120	$ 120	$ 110	$ 110	$ 110	$ 110	$ 110
Unit sales		3,000	5,000	6,000	6,500	6,000	5,000	4,000	3,000
Revenues		$360,000	$600,000	$720,000	$715,000	$660,000	$550,000	$440,000	$330,000
Variable costs		180,000	300,000	360,000	390,000	360,000	300,000	240,000	180,000
Fixed costs		25,000	25,000	25,000	25,000	25,000	25,000	25,000	25,000
CCA		80,000	144,000	115,200	92,160	73,728	58,982	47,186	37,749
EBIT		$ 75,000	$131,000	$219,800	$207,840	$201,272	$166,018	$127,814	$ 87,251
Taxes		30,000	52,400	87,920	83,136	80,509	66,407	51,126	34,901
Net income		$ 45,000	$ 78,600	$131,880	$124,704	$120,763	$ 99,611	$ 76,688	$ 52,351

Projected cash flows

Year	0	1	2	3	4	5	6	7	8
Operating cash flows									
EBIT		$ 75,000	$131,000	$219,800	$207,840	$201,272	$166,018	$127,814	$ 87,251
CCA		80,000	144,000	115,200	92,160	73,728	58,982	47,186	37,749
Taxes		30,000	52,400	87,920	83,136	80,509	66,407	51,126	34,901
Op. cash flow		$125,000	$222,600	$247,080	$216,864	$194,491	$158,593	$123,874	$ 90,099
Net working capital									
Initial NWC	$20,000								
NWC increases		$ 34,000	36,000	$ 18,000	–$ 750	–$ 8,250	–$ 16,500	–$ 16,500	–$ 16,500
NWC recovery									–$ 49,500
Add'ns to NWC	$20,000	$ 34,000	$ 36,000	$ 18,000	–$ 750	–$ 8,250	–$ 16,500	–$ 16,500	–$ 66,000

continued

TABLE 10B.2 concluded

#	A	B	C	D	E	F	G	H	I	J	K	L	M	N	O	P	Q	R	S
36	Capital spending																		
37	Initial inv.		$800,000																-$150,000
38	Aftertax salvage																		
39	Net cap. spending		$800,000																-$150,000
40																			
41			0		1		2		3		4		5		6		7		8
42	Total project cash flow																		
43			-$820,000		$ 91,000		$186,600		$229,080		$217,614		$202,741		$175,093		$140,374		$306,099
44																			
45	Cumulative cash flow																		
46			-$820,000		-$729,000		-$542,400		-$313,320		-$ 95,706		$107,035		$282,128		$422,503		$728,602
47																			
48	Discounted cash flow (@15%)																		
49			-$820,000		$ 79,130		$141,096		$150,624		$124,422		$100,798		$ 75,698		$ 52,772		$100,064
50																			
51	NPV		$ 4,604																
52																			
53	IRR		15.15%		Cash flows														
54					-$820,000														
55					91,000														
56					186,600														
57					229,080														
58					217,614														
59					202,741														
60					175,093														
61					140,374														
62					306,099														

Cell formulas

E16: =IF(E10=1,$C$6/2*$C$5,($C$6–SUM(D16:$E$16))*$C$5)

G32: =IF(SUM(F32..$E$32)+$C$31<G13*$G$5,G13*$G$5–(SUM(F32:$E$32)
+ $C$31),G13*$G$5–(@SUM(F32:$E$32)+$C$31))

S49= S43/((1+$C$4)^S41)

CHAPTER 11

Project Analysis and Evaluation

In April 2006, a Canadian mining company, Teck Cominco, announced that it will reopen one of its mines located in the Kimberly region of Western Australia. The decision to reopen the mine was based on rising market prices of zinc.

The case of Teck Cominco illustrates that sometimes postponing a project because of unfavourable conditions pays off. With zinc prices too low and costs too high, the strategy of closing the mine and reopening at a later date worked to the benefit of the company. Sometimes, capital budgeting decisions don't work out as well. Forecasting involves considerable risk and potential error. This chapter explores how this may happen and what companies can do to analyze (and possibly prevent) negative outcomes, as well as how companies deal with such situations when they arise.

IN OUR PREVIOUS CHAPTER, we discussed how to identify and organize the relevant cash flows for capital investment decisions. Our primary interest there was in coming up with a preliminary estimate of the net present value for a proposed project. In this chapter, we focus on assessing the reliability of such an estimate and avoiding forecasting risk, the possibility that errors in projected cash flow may lead to incorrect decisions.

We begin by discussing the need for an evaluation of cash flow and NPV estimates. We go on to develop some tools that are useful for doing so. We also examine complications and concerns that can arise in project evaluation.

11.1   EVALUATING NPV ESTIMATES

As we discussed in Chapter 9, an investment has a positive net present value if its market value exceeds its cost. Such an investment is desirable because it creates value for its owner. The primary problem in identifying such opportunities is that most of the time we can't actually observe the relevant market value. Instead, we estimate it. Having done so, it is only natural to wonder whether our estimates are at least close to the true values or whether we have fallen prey to forecasting risk. We consider this question next.

The Basic Problem

Suppose we are working on a preliminary DCF analysis along the lines we described in the previous chapter. We carefully identify the relevant cash flows, avoiding such things as sunk costs, and we remember to consider working capital requirements. We add back any depreciation; we account for possible erosion; and we pay attention to opportunity costs. Finally, we double-check our calculations, and, when all is said and done, the bottom line is that the estimated NPV is positive.

Now what? Do we stop here and move on to the next proposal? Probably not. The fact that the estimated NPV is positive is definitely a good sign, but, more than anything, this tells us we need to take a closer look.

If you think about it, there are two circumstances under which a discounted cash flow analysis could lead us to conclude that a project has a positive NPV. The first possibility is that the project really does have a positive NPV. That's the good news. The bad news is the second possibility: A project may appear to have a positive NPV because our estimate is inaccurate.

Notice that we could also err in the opposite way. If we conclude that a project has a negative NPV when the true NPV is positive, we lose a valuable opportunity.

Projected versus Actual Cash Flows

There is a somewhat subtle point we need to make here. When we say something like: "The projected cash flow in Year 4 is $700," what exactly do we mean? Does this mean we think the cash flow will actually be $700? Not really. It could happen, of course, but we would be surprised to see it turn out exactly that way. The reason is that the $700 projection is based only on what we know today. Almost anything could happen between now and then to change that cash flow.

Loosely speaking, we really mean that, if we took all the possible cash flows that could occur in four years and averaged them, the result would be $700. In other words, $700 is the expected cash flow. So, we don't really expect a projected cash flow to be exactly right in any one case. What we do expect is that, if we evaluate a large number of projects, our projections are right on the average.

Forecasting Risk

The key inputs into a DCF analysis are expected future cash flows. If these projections are seriously in error, we have a classic GIGO (garbage-in, garbage-out) system. In this case, no matter how carefully we arrange the numbers and manipulate them, the resulting answer can still be grossly misleading. This is the danger in using a relatively sophisticated technique like DCF. It is sometimes easy to get caught up in number crunching and forget the underlying nuts-and-bolts economic reality.

forecasting risk
The possibility that errors in projected cash flows lead to incorrect decisions.

As stated above, the possibility that we can make a bad decision because of errors in the projected cash flows is called **forecasting risk** (or estimation risk). Because of forecasting risk, there is the danger that we think a project has a positive NPV when it really does not. How is this possible? It happens if we are overly optimistic about the future and, as a result, our projected cash flows don't realistically reflect the possible future cash flows.

So far, we have not explicitly considered what to do about the possibility of errors in our forecasts, so one of our goals in this chapter is to develop some tools that are useful in identifying areas where potential errors exist and where they might be especially damaging. In one form or another, we try to assess the economic reasonableness of our estimates. We also consider how much damage can be done by errors in those estimates.

Sources of Value

www.rubbermaid.com

The first line of defence against forecasting risk is simply to ask: What is it about this investment that leads to a positive NPV? We should be able to point to something specific as the source of value. For example, if the proposal under consideration involved a new product, we might ask questions such as: Are we certain that our new product is significantly better than that of the competition? Can we truly manufacture at lower cost, or distribute more effectively, or identify undeveloped market niches, or gain control of a market?

These are just a few of the potential sources of value. There are many others. For example, in 2004, Google announced a new, free e-mail service, g.mail. Why? Free e-mail service is widely available from big hitters like Microsoft and Yahoo! and, obviously, it's free! The answer is that Google's mail service will be integrated with its acclaimed search engine, thereby giving it an edge. Also, offering e-mail will let Google expand its lucrative keyword-based advertising delivery. So, Google's source of value is leveraging its proprietary Web search and ad delivery technologies.

A key factor to keep in mind is the degree of competition in the market. It is a basic principle of economics that positive NPV investments are rare in a highly competitive environment. Therefore, proposals that appear to show significant value in the face of stiff competition are particularly troublesome, and the likely reaction of the competition to any innovations must be closely examined.

Similarly, beware of forecasts that simply extrapolate past trends without taking into account changes in technology or human behaviour. Forecasts similar to the following fall prey to the forecaster's trap:

> In 1860, several forecasters were secured from the financial community by the city of New York to forecast the future level of pollution caused by the use of chewing tobacco and horses . . . In 1850, the spit level in the gutter and manure level in the middle of the road had both averaged half an inch (approximately 1 cm). By 1860, each had doubled to a level of one inch. Using this historical growth rate, the forecasters projected levels of two inches by 1870, four inches by 1880 and 1,024 inches (22.5 metres) by 1960![1]

To avoid the forecaster's trap, the point to remember is that positive NPV investments are probably not all that common, and the number of positive NPV projects is almost certainly limited for any given firm. If we can't articulate some sound economic basis for thinking ahead of time that we have found something special, the conclusion that our project has a positive NPV should be viewed with some suspicion.

CONCEPT QUESTIONS

1. What is forecasting risk? Why is it a concern for the financial manager?

2. What are some potential sources of value in a new project?

SCENARIO AND OTHER WHAT-IF ANALYSES

Our basic approach to evaluating cash flow and NPV estimates involves asking what-if questions. Accordingly, we discuss some organized ways of going about a what-if analysis. Our goal in doing so is to assess the degree of forecasting risk and to identify those components most critical to the success or failure of an investment.

Getting Started

We are investigating a new project. Naturally, we begin by estimating NPV based on our projected cash flows. We call this the *base case*. Now, however, we recognize the possibility of error in those cash flow projections. After completing the base case, we wish to investigate the impact of different assumptions about the future on our estimates.

One way to organize this investigation is to put an upper and lower bound on the various components of the project. For example, suppose we forecast sales at 100 units per year. We know this estimate may be high or low, but we are relatively certain that it is not off by more than 10 units in either direction. We would thus pick a lower bound of 90 and an upper bound of 110. We go on to assign such bounds to any other cash flow components that we are unsure about.

When we pick these upper and lower bounds, we are not ruling out the possibility that the actual values could be outside this range. What we are saying, again loosely speaking, is that it is unlikely that the true average (as opposed to our estimated average) of the possible values is outside this range.

An example is useful to illustrate the idea here. The project under consideration costs $200,000, has a five-year life, and no salvage value. Depreciation is straight-line to keep our

---

1 This apocryphal example comes from L. Kryzanowski, T. Minh-Chau, and R. Seguin, *Business Solvency Risk Analysis* (Montreal: Institute of Canadian Bankers, 1990), chap. 5, p. 10.

example simpler.[2] The required return is 12 percent, and the tax rate is 34 percent. In addition, we have compiled the following information:

	Base Case	Lower Bound	Upper Bound
Unit sales	6,000	5,500	6,500
Price per unit	$ 80	$ 75	$ 85
Variable costs per unit	60	58	62
Fixed costs per year	50,000	45,000	55,000

With this information, we can calculate the base case NPV by first calculating net income:

Sales	$480,000
Variable costs	360,000
Fixed costs	50,000
Depreciation	40,000
EBIT	$ 30,000
Taxes (34%)	10,200
Net income	$ 19,800

Cash flow is thus $30,000 + 40,000 − 10,200 = $59,800 per year. At 12 percent, the five-year annuity factor is 3.6048, so the base case NPV is:

$$\text{Base case NPV} = -\$200,000 + (59,800 \times 3.6048)$$
$$= \$15,567$$

Thus, the project looks good so far.

What we are going to do next is recalculate NPV varying some key inputs such as unit sales, price per unit, variable costs per unit, and fixed costs. With the base case calculations completed, you can see why we assumed straight-line depreciation. It allows us to focus on key variables without the complications of calculating net income separately for each year or using the PVC-CATS formula. Of course, for full accuracy you should employ the CCA rules.

Scenario Analysis

scenario analysis
The determination of what happens to NPV estimates when we ask what-if questions.

The basic form of what-if analysis is called **scenario analysis.** What we do is investigate the changes in our NPV estimates that result from asking questions such as: What if unit sales realistically should be projected at 5,500 units instead of 6,000?

Once we start looking at alternative scenarios, we might find that most of the plausible ones result in positive NPVs. This gives us some confidence in proceeding with the project. If a substantial percentage of the scenarios looks bad, the degree of forecasting risk is high and further investigation is in order.

There are a number of possible scenarios we could consider. A good place to start is the worst-case scenario. This tells us the minimum NPV of the project. If this were positive, we would be in good shape. While we are at it, we also determine the other extreme, the best case. This puts an upper bound on our NPV.

To get the worst case, we assign the least favourable value to each item. This means low values for items such as units sold and price per unit and high values for costs. We do the reverse for the best case. For our project, these values would be:

	Worst Case	Best Case
Unit sales	5,500	6,500
Price per unit	$ 75	$ 85
Variable costs per unit	62	58
Fixed costs	55,000	45,000

2 We discuss how to change this later.

With this information, we can calculate the net income and cash flows under each scenario (check these for yourself):

Scenario	Net Income	Cash Flow	Net Present Value	IRR
Base case	$ 19,800	$59,800	$ 15,567	15.1%
Worst case*	−15,510	24,490	−111,719	−14.4
Best case	59,730	99,730	159,504	40.9

*We assume a tax credit is created in our worst-case scenario.

What we learn is that under the worst scenario, the cash flow is still positive at $24,490. That's good news. The bad news is that the return is −14.4 percent in this case, and the NPV is −$111,719. Since the project costs $200,000, we stand to lose a little more than half of the original investment under the worst possible scenario. The best case offers an attractive 41 percent return.

The terms *best case* and *worst case* are very commonly used, and we will stick with them, but we should note they are somewhat misleading. The absolutely best thing that could happen would be something absurdly unlikely, such as launching a new diet soda and subsequently learning that our (patented) formulation also just happens to cure the common cold. Similarly, the true worst case would involve some incredibly remote possibility of total disaster. We're not claiming that these things don't happen; once in a while they do. Some products, such as personal computers, succeed beyond the wildest of expectations, and some, such as asbestos, turn out to be absolute catastrophes. Instead, our point is that in assessing the reasonableness of an NPV estimate, we need to stick to cases that are reasonably likely to occur.

Instead of *best* and *worst*, then, it is probably more accurate to use the words *optimistic* and *pessimistic*. In broad terms, if we were thinking about a reasonable range for, say, unit sales, then what we call the best case would correspond to something near the upper end of that range. The worst case would simply correspond to the lower end.

As we have mentioned, we could examine an unlimited number of different scenarios. At a minimum, we might want to investigate two intermediate cases by going halfway between the base amounts and the extreme amounts. This would give us five scenarios in all, including the base case.

Beyond this point, it is hard to know when to stop. As we generate more and more possibilities, we run the risk of paralysis by analysis. The difficulty is that no matter how many scenarios we run on our spreadsheet, all we can learn are possibilities, some good and some bad. Beyond that, we don't get any guidance as to what to do. Scenario analysis is thus useful in telling us what can happen and in helping us gauge the potential for disaster, but it does not tell us whether to take the project.

Unfortunately, in practice, even the worst case scenarios may not be low enough. Two recent examples show what we mean. The Eurotunnel, or Chunnel, may be one of the new Seven Wonders of the World. The tunnel under the English Channel connects England to France and covers 24 miles. It took 8,000 workers eight years to remove 9.8 million cubic yards of rock. When the tunnel was finally built, it cost $17.9 billion, or slightly more than twice the original estimate of $8.8 billion. And things only got worse. Forecasts called for 16.8 million passengers in the first year, but only 4 million actually used it. Revenue estimates for 2003 were $2.88 billion, but actual revenue was only about one-third of that. The major problems faced by the Eurotunnel were the increased competition from ferry services, which dropped their prices, and the rise of low-cost airlines.

Sensitivity Analysis

sensitivity analysis
Investigation of what happens to NPV when only one variable is changed.

Sensitivity analysis is a variation on scenario analysis that is useful in pinpointing the areas where forecasting risk is especially severe. The basic idea with a sensitivity analysis is to freeze all the variables except one and see how sensitive our estimate of NPV is to changes in that one variable. The logic is exactly the same as for *ceteris paribus* analysis in economics.

If our NPV estimate turns out to be very sensitive to relatively small changes in the projected value of some component of project cash flow, the forecasting risk associated with that variable is high. To put it another way, NPV depends critically on the assumptions we made about this variable.

Sensitivity analysis is a very commonly used tool. For example, in 1998, Cumberland Resources announced that it had completed a preliminary study of plans to spend $94 million building a gold-mining operation in the then Northwest Territories. Cumberland reported that the project would have a life of 10 years, a payback of 2.7 years, and an IRR of 18.9 percent assuming a gold price of $325 per ounce. However, Cumberland further estimated that, at a price of $300 per ounce, the IRR would fall to 15.1 percent, and, at $275 per ounce, it would be only 11.1 percent. Thus, Cumberland focused on the sensitivity of the project's IRR to the price of gold. As of May 2006, Cumberland has been very fortunate with gold prices well above the best-case scenario. Since May 2003, gold prices have soared from $379 per ounce to 25-year highs of $700 (USD) per ounce in May 2006.

To illustrate how sensitivity analysis works, we go back to our base case for every item except unit sales. We can then calculate cash flow and NPV using the largest and smallest unit sales figures. This is very easy to do on a spreadsheet program.

Scenario	Unit Sales	Cash Flow	Net Present Value	IRR
Base case	6,000	$59,800	$15,567	15.1%
Worst case	5,500	53,200	–8,226	10.3
Best case	6,500	66,400	39,357	19.7

By way of comparison, we now freeze everything except fixed costs and repeat the analysis:

Scenario	Fixed Costs	Cash Flow	Net Present Value	IRR
Base case	$50,000	$59,800	$15,567	15.1%
Worst case	55,000	56,500	3,670	12.7
Best case	45,000	63,100	27,461	17.4

What we see here is that, given our ranges, the estimated NPV of this project is more sensitive to projected unit sales than it is to projected fixed costs. In fact, under the worst case for fixed costs, the NPV is still positive.

The results of our sensitivity analysis for unit sales can be illustrated graphically as in Figure 11.1. Here we place NPV on the vertical axis and unit sales on the horizontal axis. When we plot the combinations of unit sales versus NPV, we see that all possible combinations fall on a straight line. The steeper the resulting line is, the greater the sensitivity of the estimated NPV to the projected value of the variable being investigated.

As we have illustrated, sensitivity analysis is useful in pinpointing those variables that deserve the most attention. If we find that our estimated NPV is especially sensitive to a variable that is difficult to forecast (such as unit sales), the degree of forecasting risk is high. We might decide that further market research would be a good idea in this case.

Because sensitivity analysis is a form of scenario analysis, it suffers from the same drawbacks. Sensitivity analysis is useful for pointing out where forecasting errors could do the most damage, but it does not tell us what to do about possible errors.

Simulation Analysis

Scenario analysis and sensitivity analysis are widely used in part because they are easily executed on spreadsheets. With scenario analysis, we let all the different variables change, but we let them take on only a small number of values. With sensitivity analysis, we let only one variable change, but we let it take on a large number of values. If we combine the two approaches, the result is a crude form of **simulation analysis.**

simulation analysis
A combination of scenario and sensitivity analyses.

Simulation analysis is potentially useful to measure risk in a complex system of variables. The technique is sometimes called *Monte Carlo simulation* and has been used successfully to test gambling strategies.

For example, researchers believed that casino gamblers could shift the odds in their favour in blackjack by varying their bets during the game. In blackjack, you play against the dealer and

FIGURE 11.1

Sensitivity analysis for
unit sales

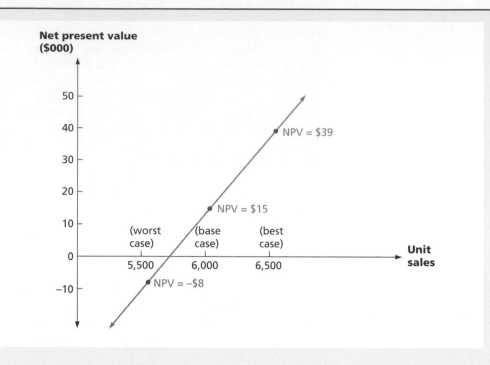

win if the dealer "goes bust" drawing cards that add to more than 21. The dealer must always take another card if his or her cards add to 16 or less. The probability of the dealer going bust increases as there are more face cards (worth 10) in the deck. To make the strategy work, players count all the cards as they are played and increase their bets when a high number of 10s remain in the deck.

Clearly, it would have been very expensive to test this strategy in a casino using real money. Researchers developed a computer simulation of blackjack and measured hypothetical winnings. They found that the strategy worked but required a substantial stake because it often took considerable time for the winnings to occur.[3]

As our blackjack example illustrates, simulation analysis allows all variables to vary at the same time. If we want to do this, we have to consider a very large number of scenarios, and computer assistance is almost certainly needed. In the simplest case, we start with unit sales and assume that any value in our 5,500 to 6,500 range is equally likely. We start by randomly picking one value (or by instructing a computer to do so).[4] We then randomly pick a price, a variable cost, and so on.

Once we have values for all the relevant components, we calculate an NPV. Since we won't know the project's risk until the simulation is finished, we avoid prejudging risk by discounting the cash flows at a riskless rate.[5] We repeat this sequence as much as we desire, probably several thousand times. The result is a large number of NPV estimates that we summarize by calculating the average value and some measure of how spread out the different possibilities are. For example, it would be of some interest to know what percentage of the possible scenarios result in negative estimated NPVs.

Because simulation is an extended form of scenario analysis, it has the same problems. Once we have the results, there is no simple decision rule that tells us what to do. Also, we have

---

3 To learn more about simulation, blackjack, and what happened when the strategy was implemented in Las Vegas, read *Beat the Dealer* by Edward O. Thorp (New York: Random House, 1962).

4 Two popular software packages for simulation analysis are Crystal Ball (*www.decionneering.com/crystal_ball/index.html*) and @Risk (*www.palisade.com/risk/default.asp*).

5 The rate on Government of Canada Treasury bills is a common example of a riskless rate.

described a relatively simple form of simulation. To really do it right, we would have to consider the interrelationships between the different cash flow components. Furthermore, we assumed that the possible values were equally likely to occur. It is probably more realistic to assume that values near the base case are more likely than extreme values, but coming up with the probabilities is difficult, to say the least.

For these reasons, the use of simulation is somewhat limited in practice. A recent survey found that about 40 percent of large corporations use sensitivity and scenario analyses as compared to around 20 percent using simulation. However, recent advances in computer software and hardware (and user sophistication) lead us to believe that simulation may become more common in the future, particularly for large-scale projects.

11.3 BREAK-EVEN ANALYSIS

It frequently turns out that the crucial variable for a project is sales volume. If we are thinking of a new product or entering a new market, for example, the hardest thing to forecast accurately is how much we can sell. For this reason, in order to control forecasting risk, sales volume is usually analyzed more closely than other variables.

Break-even analysis is a popular and commonly used tool for analyzing the relationships between sales volume and profitability. There are a variety of different break-even measures, and we have already seen several types. All break-even measures have a similar goal. Loosely speaking, we are always asking: How bad do sales have to get before we actually begin to lose money? Implicitly, we are also asking: Is it likely that things will get that bad? To get started on this subject, we discuss fixed and variable costs.

Fixed and Variable Costs

In discussing break-even, the difference between fixed and variable costs becomes very important. As a result, we need to be a little more explicit about the difference than we have been so far.

variable costs
Costs that change when the quantity of output changes.

VARIABLE COSTS By definition, **variable costs** change as the quantity of output changes, and they are zero when production is zero. For example, direct labour costs and raw material costs are usually considered variable. This makes sense because, if we shut down operations tomorrow, there will be no future costs for labour or raw materials.

We assume that variable costs are a constant amount per unit of output. This simply means that total variable cost is equal to the cost per unit multiplied by the number of units. In other words, the relationship between total variable cost (VC), cost per unit of output (v), and total quantity of output (Q) can be written simply as:

Variable cost = Total quantity of output × Cost per unit of output
$$VC = Q \times v$$

For example, suppose that v is $2 per unit. If Q is 1,000 units, what will VC be?

$$
\begin{aligned}
VC &= Q \times v \\
&= \$1,000 \times \$2 \\
&= \$2,000
\end{aligned}
$$

Similarly, if Q is 5,000 units, then VC is $5,000 \times \$2 = \$10,000$. Figure 11.2 illustrates the relationship between output level and variable costs in this case. In Figure 11.2, notice that increasing output by one unit results in variable costs rising by $2, so the "rise over the run" (the slope of the line) is given by $2/1 = \$2$.

fixed costs
Costs that do not change when the quantity of output changes during a particular time period.

FIXED COSTS By definition, **fixed costs** do not change during a specified time period. So, unlike variable costs, they do not depend on the amount of goods or services produced during a period (at least within some range of production). For example, the lease payment on a production facility and the company president's salary are fixed costs, at least over some period.

Naturally, fixed costs are not fixed forever. They are fixed only during some particular time, say a quarter or a year. Beyond that time, leases can be terminated and executives retired. More

FIGURE 11.2

Output level and variable costs

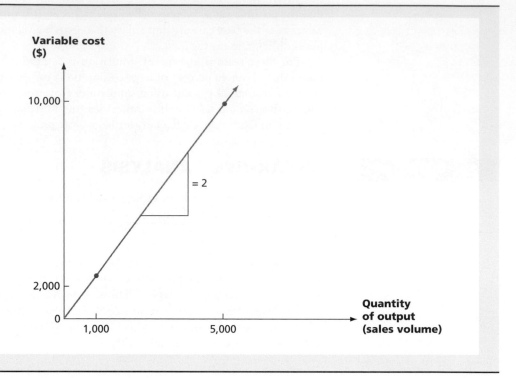

to the point, any fixed cost can be modified or eliminated given enough time; so, in the long run, all costs are variable.

Notice that during the time that a cost is fixed, that cost is effectively a sunk cost because we are going to have to pay it no matter what.

TOTAL COSTS   Total costs (TC) for a given level of output are the sum of variable costs (VC) and fixed costs (FC):

$$TC = VC + FC$$
$$TC = v \times Q + FC$$

So, for example, if we have a variable cost of $3 per unit and fixed costs of $8,000 per year, our total cost is:

$$TC = \$3 \times Q + \$8,000$$

If we produce 6,000 units, our total production cost would be $3 × 6,000 + $8,000 = $26,000. At other production levels, we have:

Quantity Produced	Total Variable Cost	Fixed Costs	Total Cost
0	$ 0	$8,000	$ 8,000
1,000	3,000	8,000	11,000
5,000	15,000	8,000	23,000
10,000	30,000	8,000	38,000

marginal or incremental cost
The change in costs that occurs when there is a small change in output.

By plotting these points in Figure 11.3, we see that the relationship between quantity produced and total cost is given by a straight line. In Figure 11.3, notice that total costs are equal to fixed costs when sales are zero. Beyond that point, every one-unit increase in production leads to a $3 increase in total costs, so the slope of the line is 3. In other words, the **marginal** or **incremental cost** of producing one more unit is $3.

Output level and total costs

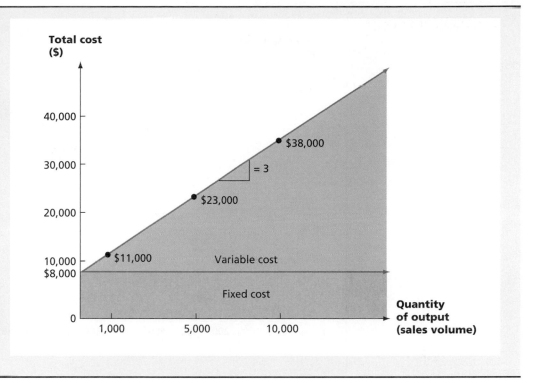

Accounting Break-Even

accounting break-even
The sales level that results in zero project net income.

The most widely used measure of break-even is **accounting break-even.** The accounting break-even point is simply the sales level that results in a zero project net income.

To determine a project's accounting break-even, we start with some common sense. Suppose we retail one-terabyte CDs for $5 a piece. We can buy CDs from a wholesale supplier for $3 a piece. We have accounting expenses of $600 in fixed costs and $300 in depreciation. How many CDs do we have to sell to break even, that is, for net income to be zero?

For every CD we sell, we pick up $5 − 3 = $2 toward covering our other expenses. We have to cover a total of $600 + 300 = $900 in accounting expenses, so we obviously need to sell $900/$2 = 450 CDs. We can check this by noting that, at a sales level of 450 units, our revenues are $5 × 450 = $2,250 and our variable costs are $3 × 450 = $1,350. The income statement is thus:

Sales	$2,250
Variable costs	1,350
Fixed costs	600
Depreciation	300
EBIT	$ 0
Taxes	$ 0
Net income	$ 0

Remember, since we are discussing a proposed new project, we do not consider any interest expense in calculating net income or cash flow from the project. Also, notice that we include depreciation in calculating expenses here, even though depreciation is not a cash outflow. That is why we call it accounting break-even. Finally, notice that when net income is zero, so are pretax income and, of course, taxes. In accounting terms, our revenues are equal to our costs, so there is no profit to tax.

Figure 11.4 is another way to see what is happening. This figure looks like Figure 11.3 except that we add a line for revenues. As indicated, total revenues are zero when output is zero. Beyond that, each unit sold brings in another $5, so the slope of the revenue line is 5.

FIGURE 11.4

Accounting break-even

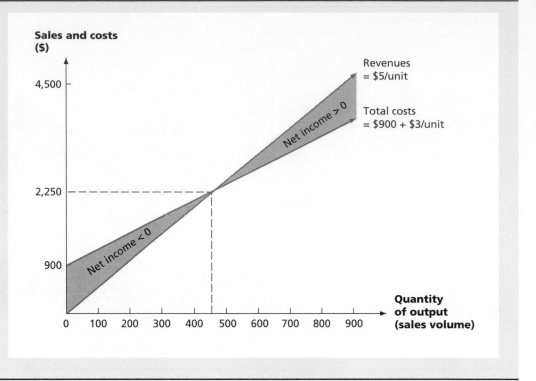

From our preceding discussion, we break even when revenues are equal to total costs. The line for revenues and the line for total cost cross right where output is 450 units. As illustrated, at any level below 450, our accounting profit is negative and, at any level above 450, we have a positive net income.

Accounting Break-Even: A Closer Look

In our numerical example, notice that the break-even level is equal to the sum of fixed costs and depreciation divided by price per unit less variable costs per unit. This is always true. To see why, we recall the following set of abbreviations for the different variables:

$$P = \text{Selling price per unit}$$
$$v = \text{Variable cost per unit}$$
$$Q = \text{Total units sold}$$
$$FC = \text{Fixed costs}$$
$$D = \text{Depreciation}$$
$$t = \text{Tax rate}$$
$$VC = \text{Variable cost in dollars}$$

Project net income is given by:

$$\text{Net income} = (\text{Sales} - \text{Variable costs} - \text{Fixed costs} - \text{Depreciation}) \times (1 - t)$$
$$= (S - VC - FC - D) \times (1 - t)$$

From here, it is not difficult to calculate the break-even point. If we set this net income equal to zero, we get:

$$\text{Net income} = 0 = (S - VC - FC - D) \times (1 - t)$$

Divide both sides by $(1 - t)$ to get:

$$S - VC - FC - D = 0$$

As we have seen, this says, when net income is zero, so is pretax income. If we recall that $S = P \times Q$ and $VC = v \times Q$, we can rearrange this to solve for the break-even level:

$$S - VC = FC + D$$
$$P \times Q - v \times Q = FC + D$$
$$(P - v) \times Q = FC + D \qquad \qquad [11.1]$$
$$Q = (FC + D)/(P - v)$$

This is the same result we described earlier.

Uses for the Accounting Break-Even

Why would anyone be interested in knowing the accounting break-even point? To illustrate how it can be useful, suppose we are a small specialty ice cream manufacturer in Vancouver with a strictly local distribution. We are thinking about expanding into new markets. Based on the estimated cash flow, we find that the expansion has a positive NPV.

Going back to our discussion of forecasting risk, it is likely that what makes or breaks our expansion is sales volume. The reason is that, in this case at least, we probably have a fairly good idea of what we can charge for the ice cream. Further, we know relevant production and distribution costs with a fair degree of accuracy because we are already in the business. What we do not know with any real precision is how much ice cream we can sell.

Given the costs and selling price, however, we can immediately calculate the break-even point. Once we have done so, we might find that we need to get 30 percent of the market just to break even. If we think that this is unlikely to occur because, for example, we only have 10 percent of our current market, we know that our forecast is questionable and there is a real possibility that the true NPV is negative.

On the other hand, we might find that we already have firm commitments from buyers for about the break-even amount, so we are almost certain that we can sell more. Because the forecasting risk is much lower, we have greater confidence in our estimates. If we need outside financing for our expansion, this break-even analysis would be useful in presenting our proposal to our banker.

COMPLICATIONS IN APPLYING BREAK-EVEN ANALYSIS   Our discussion ignored several complications you may encounter in applying this useful tool. To begin, it is only in the short run that revenues and variable costs fall along straight lines. For large increases in sales, price may decrease with volume discounts while variable costs increase as production runs up against capacity limits. If you have sufficient data, you can redraw cost and revenue as curves. Otherwise, remember that the analysis is most accurate in the short run.

Further, while our examples classified costs as fixed or variable, in practice some costs are semivariable (i.e., partly fixed and partly variable). A common example is telephone expense, which breaks down into a fixed charge plus a variable cost depending on the volume of calls. In applying break-even analysis, you have to make judgements on the breakdown.

CONCEPT QUESTIONS

1. How are fixed costs similar to sunk costs?

2. What is net income at the accounting break-even point? What about taxes?

3. Why might a financial manager be interested in the accounting break-even point?

11.4   OPERATING CASH FLOW, SALES VOLUME, AND BREAK-EVEN

Accounting break-even is one tool that is useful for project analysis. Ultimately, however, we are more interested in cash flow than accounting income. So, for example, if sales volume is the critical variable in avoiding forecasting risk, we need to know more about the relationship between sales volume and cash flow than just the accounting break-even.

Our goal in this section is to illustrate the relationship between operating cash flow and sales volume. We also discuss some other break-even measures. To simplify matters somewhat, we ignore the effect of taxes.[6] We start by looking at the relationship between accounting break-even and cash flow.

Accounting Break-Even and Cash Flow

Now that we know how to find the accounting break-even, it is natural to wonder what happens with cash flow. To illustrate, suppose that Victoria Sailboats Limited is considering whether to launch its new Mona-class sailboat. The selling price would be $40,000 per boat. The variable costs would be about half that, or $20,000 per boat, and fixed costs will be $500,000 per year.

THE BASE CASE The total investment needed to undertake the project is $3.5 million for leasehold improvements to the company's factory. This amount will be depreciated straight-line to zero over the five-year life of the equipment. The salvage value is zero, and there are no working capital consequences. Victoria has a 20 percent required return on new projects.

Based on market surveys and historical experience, Victoria projects total sales for the five years at 425 boats, or about 85 boats per year. Should this project be launched?

To begin (ignoring taxes), the operating cash flow at 85 boats per year is:

$$
\begin{aligned}
\text{Operating cash flow} &= \text{EBIT} + \text{Depreciation} - \text{Taxes} \\
&= (S - VC - FC - D) + D - 0 \\
&= 85 \times (\$40,000 - 20,000) - \$500,000 \\
&= \$1,200,000 \text{ per year}
\end{aligned}
$$

At 20 percent, the five-year annuity factor is 2.9906, so the NPV is:

$$
\begin{aligned}
\text{NPV} &= -\$3,500,000 + 1,200,000 \times 2.9906 \\
&= -\$3,500,000 + 3,588,720 \\
&= \$88,720
\end{aligned}
$$

In the absence of additional information, the project should be launched.

CALCULATING THE ACCOUNTING BREAK-EVEN LEVEL To begin looking a little more closely at this project, you might ask a series of questions. For example, how many new boats does Victoria need to sell for the project to break even on an accounting basis? If Victoria does break even, what would be the annual cash flow from the project? What would be the return on the investment?

Before fixed costs and depreciation are considered, Victoria generates $40,000 − 20,000 = $20,000 per boat (this is revenue less variable cost). Depreciation is $3,500,000/5 = $700,000 per year. Fixed costs and depreciation together total $1.2 million, so Victoria needs to sell $(FC + D)/(P − v) = $1.2 million/$20,000 = 60 boats per year to break even on an accounting basis. This is 25 boats less than projected sales; so, assuming that Victoria is confident that its projection is accurate to within, say, 15 boats, it appears unlikely that the new investment will fail to at least break even on an accounting basis.

To calculate Victoria's cash flow, we note that if 60 boats are sold, net income is exactly zero. Recalling from our previous chapter that operating cash flow for a project can be written as net income plus depreciation (the bottom-up definition), the operating cash flow is obviously equal to the depreciation, or $700,000 in this case. The internal rate of return would be exactly zero (why?).

The bad news is that a project that just breaks even on an accounting basis has a negative NPV and a zero return. For our sailboat project, the fact that we would almost surely break even on an accounting basis is partially comforting since our downside risk (our potential loss) is limited, but we still don't know if the project is truly profitable. More work is needed.

---

6 This is a minor simplification because the firm pays no taxes when it just breaks even in the accounting sense. We also use straight-line depreciation, realistic in this case for leasehold improvements, for simplicity.

SALES VOLUME AND OPERATING CASH FLOW   At this point, we can general-ize our example and introduce some other break-even measures. As we just discussed, we know that, ignoring taxes, a project's operating cash flow (OCF) can be written simply as EBIT plus depreciation:[7]

$$OCF = [(P - v) \times Q - FC - D] + D \qquad\qquad [11.2]$$
$$= (P - v) \times Q - FC$$

For the Victoria Sailboats project, the general relationship between operating cash flow and sales volume is thus:

$$OCF = (P - v) \times Q - FC$$
$$= (\$40,000 - 20,000) \times Q - \$500,000$$
$$= -\$500,000 + \$20,000 \times Q$$

What this tells us is that the relationship between operating cash flow and sales volume is given by a straight line with a slope of \$20,000 and a *y*-intercept of –\$500,000. If we calculate some different values, we get:

Quantity Sold	Operating Cash Flow
0	–\$ 500,000
15	–200,000
30	100,000
50	500,000
75	1,000,000

These points are plotted in Figure 11.5. In Figure 11.5, we have indicated three different break-even points. We already covered the accounting break-even. We discuss the other two next.

FIGURE 11.5

Operating cash flow and sales volume

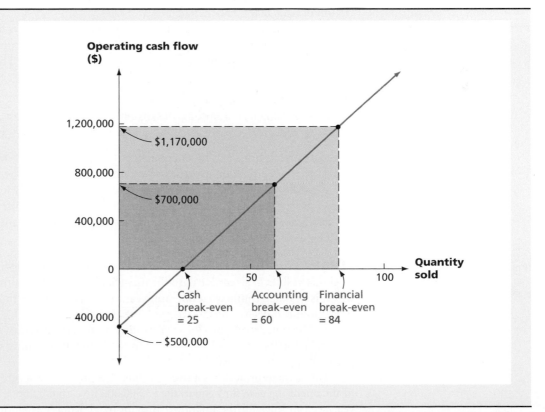

7 With no taxes, depreciation drops out of cash flow because there is no tax shield.

Cash Flow and Financial Break-Even Points

We know that the relationship between operating cash flow and sales volume (ignoring taxes) is:

$$OCF = (P - v) \times Q - FC$$

If we rearrange this and solve it for Q, we get:

$$Q = (FC + OCF)/(P - v) \qquad [11.3]$$

This tells us what sales volume (Q) is necessary to achieve any given OCF, so this result is more general than the accounting break-even. We use it to find the various break-even points in Figure 11.5.

CASH BREAK-EVEN   We have seen that our sailboat project that breaks even on an accounting basis has a net income of zero, but it still has a positive cash flow. At some sales level below the accounting break-even, the operating cash flow actually goes negative. This is a particularly unpleasant occurrence. If it happens, we actually have to supply additional cash to the project just to keep it afloat.

To calculate the **cash break-even** (the point where operating cash flow is equal to zero), we put in a zero for OCF:

$$
\begin{aligned}
Q &= (FC + 0)/(P - v) \\
&= \$500{,}000/\$20{,}000 \\
&= 25
\end{aligned}
$$

> **cash break-even**
> The sales level where operating cash flow is equal to zero.

Victoria must therefore sell 25 boats to cover the $500,000 in fixed costs. As we show in Figure 11.5, this point occurs right where the operating cash flow line crosses the horizontal axis.

In this example, cash break-even is lower than accounting break-even. Equation 11.3 shows why; when we calculated accounting break-even we substituted depreciation of $700,000 for OCF. The formula for cash break-even sets OCF equal to zero. Figure 11.5 shows that accounting break-even is 60 boats and cash break-even, 25 boats. Accounting break-even is 35 boats higher. Since Victoria generates a $20,000 contribution per boat, the difference exactly covers the depreciation of $700,000 = 35 × $20,000.

This analysis also shows that cash break-even does not always have to be lower than accounting break-even. To see why, suppose Victoria had to make a cash outlay in Year 1 of $1 million for working capital. Accounting break-even remains at 60 boats. The new cash break-even is 75 boats:

$$
\begin{aligned}
Q &= (FC + OCF)/(P - v) \\
&= (\$500{,}000 + 1{,}000{,}000)/(\$20{,}000) \\
&= 75
\end{aligned}
$$

In general, retail firms and other companies that experience substantial needs for working capital relative to depreciation expenses have cash break-evens greater than accounting break-evens.

Regardless of whether the cash break-even point is more or less than the accounting break-even, a project that just breaks even on a cash flow basis can cover its own fixed operating costs, but that is all. It never pays back anything, so the original investment is a complete loss (the IRR is −100 percent).

FINANCIAL BREAK-EVEN   The last case we consider is **financial break-even,** the sales level that results in a zero NPV. To the financial manager, this is the most interesting case. What we do is first determine what operating cash flow has to be for the NPV to be zero. We then use this amount to determine the sales volume.

> **financial break-even**
> The sales level that results in a zero NPV.

To illustrate, recall that Victoria requires a 20 percent return on its $3,500,000 investment. How many sailboats does Victoria have to sell to break even once we account for the 20 percent per year opportunity cost?

The sailboat project has a five-year life. The project has a zero NPV when the present value of the operating cash flow equals the $3,500,000 investment. Since the cash flow is the same each year, we can solve for the unknown amount by viewing it as an ordinary annuity. The five-year annuity factor at 20 percent is 2.9906, and the OCF can be determined as follows:

$$\$3,500,000 = OCF \times 2.9906$$
$$OCF = \$3,500,000/2.9906$$
$$= \$1,170,000$$

Victoria thus needs an operating cash flow of $1,170,000 each year to break even. We can now plug this OCF into the equation for sales volume:

$$Q = (\$500,000 + \$1,170,000)/\$20,000$$
$$= 83.5$$

So Victoria needs to sell about 84 boats per year. This is not good news.

As indicated in Figure 11.5, the financial break-even is substantially higher than the accounting break-even point. This is often the case. Moreover, what we have discovered is that the sailboat project has a substantial degree of forecasting risk. We project sales of 85 boats per year, but it takes 84 just to earn our required return.

CONCLUSION Overall, it seems unlikely that the Victoria Sailboats project would fail to break even on an accounting basis. However, there appears to be a very good chance that the true NPV is negative. This illustrates the danger in just looking at the accounting break-even.

Victoria can learn this lesson from the U.S. government. In the early 1970s, the U.S. Congress voted a guarantee for Lockheed Corporation, the airplane manufacturer, based on analysis that showed the L1011-TriStar would break even on an accounting basis. It subsequently turned out that the financial break-even point was much higher.

What should Victoria Sailboats do? Is the new project all wet? The decision at this point is essentially a managerial issue—a judgement call. The crucial questions are:

1. How much confidence do we have in our projections? Do we think that forecasting risk is too high?
2. How important is the project to the future of the company?
3. How badly will the company be hurt if sales do turn out low?

What options are available to the company?

We consider questions such as these in a later section. For future reference, our discussion of different break-even measures is summarized in Table 11.1.

www.lockheedmartin.com

CONCEPT QUESTIONS

1. If a project breaks even on an accounting basis, what is its operating cash flow?

2. If a project breaks even on a cash basis, what is its operating cash flow?

3. If a project breaks even on a financial basis, what do you know about its discounted payback?

11.5 OPERATING LEVERAGE

We have discussed how to calculate and interpret various measures of break-even for a proposed project. What we have not explicitly discussed is what determines these points and how they might be changed. We now turn to this subject.

The Basic Idea

operating leverage
The degree to which a firm or project relies on fixed costs.

Operating leverage is the degree to which a project or firm is committed to fixed production costs. A firm with low operating leverage has low fixed costs (as a proportion of total costs) compared to a firm with high operating leverage. Generally, projects with a relatively heavy investment in plant and equipment have a relatively high degree of operating leverage. Such projects are said to be capital intensive.

TABLE 11.1
Summary of break-even
measures

The general expression. Ignoring taxes, the relation between operating cash flow (OCF) and quantity of output or sales volume (Q) is

$$Q = \frac{FC + OCF}{P - v}$$

where
FC = Total fixed costs
P = Price per unit
v = Variable cost per unit

As shown next, this relation can be used to determine the accounting, cash, and financial break-even points.

The accounting break-even point. Accounting break-even occurs when net income is zero. Operating cash flow (OCF) is equal to depreciation when net income is zero, so the accounting break-even point is:

$$Q = \frac{FC + D}{P - v}$$

A project that always just breaks even on an accounting basis has a payback exactly equal to its life, a negative NPV, and an IRR of zero.

The cash break-even point. Cash break-even occurs when operating cash flow (OCF) is zero; the cash break-even point is thus:

$$Q = \frac{FC}{P - v}$$

A project that always just breaks even on a cash basis never pays back, its NPV is negative and equal to the initial outlay, and the IRR is –100%.

The financial break-even point. Financial break-even occurs when the NPV of the project is zero. The financial break-even point is thus:

$$Q = \frac{FC + OCF^*}{P - v}$$

where OCF* is the level of OCF that results in a zero NPV. A project that breaks even on a financial basis has a discounted payback equal to its life, a zero NPV, and an IRR just equal to the required return.

Any time we are thinking about a new venture, there are normally alternative ways of producing and delivering the product. For example, Victoria Sailboats can purchase the necessary equipment and build all the components for its sailboats in-house. Alternatively, some of the work could be farmed out to other firms. The first option involves a greater investment in plant and equipment, greater fixed costs and depreciation, and, as a result, a higher degree of operating leverage.

Implications of Operating Leverage

Regardless of how it is measured, operating leverage has important implications for project evaluation. Fixed costs act like a lever in the sense that a small percentage change in operating revenue can be magnified into a large percentage change in operating cash flow and NPV. This explains why we call it operating leverage.

The higher the degree of operating leverage, the greater is the potential danger from forecasting risk. The reason is that relatively small errors in forecasting sales volume can get magnified or "levered up" into large errors in cash flow projections.

From a managerial perspective, one way of coping with highly uncertain projects is to keep the degree of operating leverage as low as possible.[8] This generally has the effect of keeping the break-even point (however measured) at its minimum level. We illustrate this point after discussing how to measure operating leverage.

degree of operating leverage
The percentage change in operating cash flow relative to the percentage change in quantity sold.

Measuring Operating Leverage

One way of measuring operating leverage is to ask: If the quantity sold rises by 5 percent, what will be the percentage change in operating cash flow? In other words, the **degree of operating leverage** (DOL) is defined such that

---

8 Another response is to keep the amount of debt low. We cover financial leverage in Chapter 16.

Percentage change in OCF = DOL × Percentage change in Q

Based on the relationship between OCF and Q, DOL can be written as:[9]

DOL = 1 + FC/OCF

The ratio FC/OCF simply measures fixed costs as a percentage of total operating cash flow. Notice that zero fixed costs would result in a DOL of 1, implying that changes in quantity sold would show up one for one in operating cash flow. In other words, no magnification or leverage effect would exist.

To illustrate this measure of operating leverage, we go back to the Victoria Sailboats project. Fixed costs were $500 and $(P - v)$ was $20, so OCF was:

OCF = –$500 + 20 × Q

Suppose Q is currently 50 boats. At this level of output, OCF is –$500 + 1,000 = $500.

If Q rises by 1 unit to 51, then the percentage change in Q is (51 – 50)/50 = .02, or 2%. OCF rises to $520, a change of $(P - v) = $20. The percentage change in OCF is ($520 – 500)/500 = .04, or 4%. So a 2 percent increase in the number of boats sold leads to a 4 percent increase in operating cash flow. The degree of operating leverage must be exactly 2.00. We can check this by noting that:

DOL = 1 + FC/OCF
= 1 + $500/$500
= 2

This verifies our previous calculations.

Our formulation of DOL depends on the current output level, Q. However, it can handle changes from the current level of any size, not just one unit. For example, suppose Q rises from 50 to 75, a 50 percent increase. With DOL equal to 2, operating cash flow should increase by 100 percent, or exactly double. Does it? The answer is yes, because, at a Q of 75, OCF is:

–$500 + $20 × 75 = $1,000

Notice that operating leverage declines as output (Q) rises. For example, at an output level of 75, we have:

DOL = 1 + $500/1,000
= 1.50

The reason DOL declines is that fixed costs, considered as a percentage of operating cash flow, get smaller and smaller, so the leverage effect diminishes.[10]

What do you think DOL works out to at the cash break-even point, an output level of 25 boats? At the cash break-even point, OCF is zero. Since you cannot divide by zero, DOL is undefined.

Operating Leverage and Break-Even

We illustrate why operating leverage is an important consideration by examining the Victoria Sailboats project under an alternative scenario. At a Q of 85 boats, the degree of operating leverage for the sailboat project under the original scenario is:

---

9 To see this, note that, if Q goes up by 1 unit, OCF goes up by $(P - v)$. The percentage change in Q is $1/Q$, and the percentage change in OCF is $(P - v)$/OCF. Given this, we have:
Percentage change in OCF = DOL × Percentage change in Q
$(P - v)$/OCF = DOL × $1/Q$
DOL = $(P - v)$ × Q/OCF
Also, based on our definition of OCF:
OCF + FC = $(P - v)$ × Q
Thus, DOL can be written as:
DOL = (OCF + FC)/OCF
= 1 + FC/OCF

10 Students who have studied economics will recognize DOL as an elasticity. Recall that elasticities vary with quantity along demand and supply curves. For the same reason, DOL varies with unit sales, Q.

EXAMPLE 11.1: Operating Leverage

The Huskies Corporation currently sells gourmet dog food for $1.20 per can. The variable cost is 80 cents per can, and the packaging and marketing operation has fixed costs of $360,000 per year. Depreciation is $60,000 per year. What is the accounting break-even? Ignoring taxes, what will be the increase in operating cash flow if the quantity sold rises to 10 percent more than the break-even point?

The accounting break-even is $420,000/.40 = 1,050,000 cans. As we know, the operating cash flow is equal to the $60,000 depreciation at this level of production, so the degree of operating leverage is:

$$DOL = 1 + FC/OCF$$
$$= 1 + \$360,000/\$60,000$$
$$= 7$$

Given this, a 10 percent increase in the number of cans of dog food sold increases operating cash flow by a substantial 70 percent.

To check this answer, we note that if sales rise by 10 percent, the quantity sold rises to $1,050,000 \times 1.1 = 1,155,000$. Ignoring taxes, the operating cash flow is $1,155,000 \times .40 - \$360,000 = \$102,000$. Compared to the $60,000 cash flow we had, this is exactly 70 percent more: $102,000/60,000 = 1.70$.

$$DOL = 1 + FC/OCF$$
$$= 1 + \$500/1,200$$
$$= 1.42$$

Also, recall that the NPV at a sales level of 85 boats was $88,720, and that the accounting break-even was 60 boats.

An option available to Victoria is to subcontract production of the boat hull assemblies. If it does, the necessary investment falls to $3.2 million, and the fixed operating costs fall to $180,000. However, variable costs rise to $25,000 per boat since subcontracting is more expensive than doing it in-house. Ignoring taxes, evaluate this option.

For practice, see if you don't agree with the following:

NPV at 20% (85 units) = $74,720
Accounting break-even = 55 boats
Degree of operating leverage = 1.16

What has happened? This option results in slightly lower estimated net present value, and the accounting break-even point falls to 55 boats from 60 boats.

Given that this alternative has the lower NPV, is there any reason to consider it further? Maybe there is. The degree of operating leverage is substantially lower in the second case. If we are worried about the possibility of an overly optimistic projection, we might prefer to subcontract.

There is another reason we might consider the second arrangement. If sales turned out better than expected, we always have the option of starting to produce in-house later. As a practical matter, it is much easier to increase operating leverage (by purchasing equipment) than to decrease it (by selling equipment).[11] As we discuss later, one of the drawbacks to discounted cash flow is that it is difficult to explicitly include options of this sort, even though they may be quite important.

CONCEPT QUESTIONS

1. What is operating leverage?

2. How is operating leverage measured?

3. What are the implications of operating leverage for the financial manager?

---

11 In the extreme case, if firms were able to readjust the ratio of variable and fixed costs continually, there would be no increased risk associated with greater operating leverage.

MANAGERIAL OPTIONS

managerial options
Opportunities that managers can exploit if certain things happen in the future.

www.disneylandparis.com

In our capital budgeting analysis thus far, we have more or less ignored the possibility of future managerial actions. Implicitly, we assumed that once a project is launched, its basic features cannot be changed. For this reason, we say that our analysis is static (as opposed to dynamic).

In reality, depending on what actually happens in the future, there are always ways to modify a project. We call these opportunities **managerial (or real) options.** As we will see, in many cases managerial options can improve project cash flows, making the best case better while placing a floor under the worst case. As a result, ignoring such options would lead to forecasting risk in underestimating NPV. There are a great number of these options. The way a product is priced, manufactured, advertised, and produced can all be changed, and these are just a few of the possibilities.[12]

For example, in April 1992, Euro Disney (ED), the $3.9 billion, 5,000-acre theme park located east of Paris, opened for business. The owners, including Walt Disney Co. with a 49 percent share, thought Europeans would go goofy over the park and envisioned enormous profits. Instead, by the end of its first fiscal year, the park was actually losing about $2.5 million per day.

Originally, ED's owners thought that the park would draw 11 million visitors annually, far more than the 7 to 8 million visitors it would take to break even. In this they were correct; the park actually drew about one million per month.

Unfortunately, however, ED opened in the middle of a European recession. ED quickly realized that whereas it had expected customers to stay more than four days, they were staying only two on average. Part of the problem was that the park's hotels were overpriced. In addition, ED suffered from dramatic seasonal swings in attendance. The number of visitors per day during peak times could be 10 times larger than that during slack times. The need to lay off employees in quiet times did not square well with France's inflexible labour schedules. ED responded by cutting hotel room rates and offering lower admission prices in off-season times.

ED had also miscalculated by initially banning alcohol in the park, in a country where wine is customary with meals. This policy was reversed. Also, ED had been told that Europeans don't eat breakfast, so it had built smaller-than-usual cafés, only to find that customers showed up in large numbers. The owners found that they were trying to serve 2,500 breakfasts in 350-seat restaurants.

Many other changes were considered and implemented, but despite averaging 12 million visitors a year and having 160 million total visitors since opening, Euro Disney still posted a loss of €101 million in the first half of 2006. It would appear that, as of 2006, Euro Disney has not yet been able to bounce back from the variety of problems the corporation has faced. As this example suggests, the possibility of future actions is important. We discuss some of the most common types of managerial actions in the next few sections.

CONTINGENCY PLANNING   The various what-if procedures, particularly the break-even measures, in this chapter have another use. We can also view them as primitive ways of exploring the dynamics of a project and investigating managerial options. What we think about are some of the possible futures that could come about and what actions we might take if they do.

contingency planning
Taking into account the managerial options that are implicit in a project.

For example, we might find that a project fails to break even when sales drop below 10,000 units. This is a fact that is interesting to know, but the more important thing is to go on and ask: What actions are we going to take if this actually occurs? This is called **contingency planning,** and it amounts to an investigation of some of the managerial options implicit in a project.

There is no limit to the number of possible futures or contingencies that we could investigate. However, there are some broad classes, and we consider these next.

THE OPTION TO EXPAND   One particularly important option that we have not explicitly addressed is the option to expand. If we truly find a positive NPV project, there is an obvious consideration. Can we expand the project or repeat it to get an even larger NPV? Our static analysis implicitly assumes that the scale of the project is fixed.

---

12 We introduce managerial options here and return to the topic in more depth in Chapter 25.

For example, if the sales demand for a particular product were to greatly exceed expectations, we might investigate increasing production. If this is not feasible for some reason, we could always increase cash flow by raising the price. Either way, the potential cash flow is higher than we have indicated because we have implicitly assumed that no expansion or price increase is possible. Overall, because we ignore the option to expand in our analysis, we underestimate NPV (all other things being equal).

www.ml.com
www.cibcwoodgundy.com

THE OPTION TO ABANDON   At the other extreme, the option to scale back or even abandon a project is also quite valuable. For example, if a project does not break even on a cash flow basis, it can't even cover its own expenses. We would be better off if we just abandoned it. Our DCF analysis implicitly assumes that we would keep operating even in this case.

Sometimes the best thing to do is to reverse direction. For example, Merrill Lynch Canada has done this three times. First, it built up a retail brokerage operation in the 1980s and sold it to CIBC Wood Gundy in 1990. Later, in 1998, Merrill Lynch made headlines by paying $1.26 billion for Midland Walwyn, the last independently owned retail brokerage firm in Canada. The reason? Merrill Lynch wanted to continue its globalization drive and get back into the business it had earlier abandoned. However, in November 2001, Merrill Lynch Canada once again sold its retail brokerage and mutual fund and securities services businesses to CIBC Wood Gundy. This sale was part of an effort to cut back expenses on its international operations.

In reality, if sales demand were significantly below expectations, we might be able to sell some capacity or put it to another use. Maybe the product or service could be redesigned or otherwise improved. Regardless of the specifics, we once again underestimate NPV if we assume the project must last for some fixed number of years, no matter what happens in the future.

THE OPTION TO WAIT   Implicitly, we have treated proposed investments as if they were go or no-go decisions. Actually, there is a third possibility. The project can be postponed, perhaps in hope of more favourable conditions. We call this the option to wait.

For example, suppose an investment costs $120 and has a perpetual cash flow of $10 per year. If the discount rate is 10 percent, the NPV is $10/.10 − 120 = −$20, so the project should not be undertaken now. However, this does not mean we should forget about the project forever, because in the next period, the appropriate discount rate could be different. If it fell to, say, 5 percent, the NPV would be $10/.05 − 120 = $80, and we would take it.

More generally, as long as there is some possible future scenario under which a project has a positive NPV, the option to wait is valuable. Related to the option to wait is the option to suspend operations. For example, in May 2004, General Motors announced a voluntary temporary shutdown of its Oklahoma City sport utility vehicle plant to reduce inventories of unsold SUVs. Such actions are common in the auto industry; plants are temporarily idled when inventories become too large.

THE TAX OPTION   Investment decisions may trigger favourable or unfavourable tax treatment of existing assets. This can occur because, as you recall from Chapter 2, capital cost allowance calculations are usually based on assets in a pooled class. Tax liabilities for recaptured CCA and tax shelters from terminal losses occur only when an asset class is liquidated either by selling all the assets or writing the undepreciated capital cost below zero. As a result, management has a potentially valuable tax option.

For example, suppose your firm is planning to replace all its company delivery vans at the end of the year. Because of unfavourable conditions in the used vehicle market, prices are depressed and you expect to realize a loss. Since you are replacing the vehicles, as opposed to closing out the class, no immediate tax shelter results from the loss. If your company is profitable and the potential tax shelter sizable, you could exercise your tax option by closing out Class 12. To do this, you could lease the new vehicles or set up a separate firm to purchase the vehicles.

OPTIONS IN CAPITAL BUDGETING: AN EXAMPLE   Suppose we are examining a new project. To keep things relatively simple, we expect to sell 100 units per year at $1 net cash flow apiece into perpetuity. We thus expect the cash flow to be $100 per year.

In one year, we will know more about the project. In particular, we will have a better idea of whether it is successful or not. If it looks like a long-run success, the expected sales could be revised upward to 150 units per year. If it does not, the expected sales could be revised downward to 50 units per year.

Success and failure are equally likely. Notice that with an even chance of selling 50 or 150 units, the expected sales are still 100 units as we originally projected.

The cost is $550, and the discount rate is 20 percent. The project can be dismantled and sold in one year for $400, if we decide to abandon it. Should we take it?

A standard DCF analysis is not difficult. The expected cash flow is $100 per year forever and the discount rate is 20 percent. The PV of the cash flows is $100/.20 = $500, so the NPV is $500 − 550 = −$50. We shouldn't take it.

This analysis is static, however. In one year, we can sell out for $400. How can we account for this? What we have to do is to decide what we are going to do one year from now. In this simple case, there are only two contingencies that we need to evaluate, an upward revision and a downward revision, so the extra work is not great.

In one year, if the expected cash flows are revised to $50, the PV of the cash flows is revised downward to $50/.20 = $250. We get $400 by abandoning the project, so that is what we will do (the NPV of keeping the project in one year is $250 − 400 = −$150).

If the demand is revised upward, the PV of the future cash flows at Year 1 is $150/.20 = $750. This exceeds the $400 abandonment value, so we would keep the project.

We now have a project that costs $550 today. In one year, we expect a cash flow of $100 from the project. In addition, this project would either be worth $400 (if we abandon it because it is a failure) or $750 (if we keep it because it succeeds). These outcomes are equally likely, so we expect it to be worth ($400 + 750)/2, or $575.

Summing up, in one year, we expect to have $100 in cash plus a project worth $575, or $675 total. At a 20 percent discount rate, this $675 is worth $562.50 today, so the NPV is $562.50 − 550 = $12.50. We should take it.

The NPV of our project has increased by $62.50. Where did this come from? Our original analysis implicitly assumed we would keep the project even if it was a failure. At Year 1, however, we saw that we were $150 better off ($400 versus $250) if we abandoned. There was a 50 percent chance of this happening, so the expected gain from abandoning is $75. The PV of the amount is the value of the option to abandon, $75/1.20 = $62.50.

www.google.com/corporate

strategic options
Options for future, related business products or strategies.

STRATEGIC OPTIONS   Companies sometimes undertake new projects just to explore possibilities and evaluate potential future business strategies. This is a little like testing the water by sticking a toe in before diving. When Google decided to buy YouTube for US$1.65 billion in 2006, strategic considerations likely dominated immediate cash flow analysis.

Such projects are difficult to analyze using conventional DCF because most of the benefits come in the form of **strategic options,** that is, options for future, related business moves. Projects that create such options may be very valuable, but that value is difficult to measure. Research and development, for example, is an important and valuable activity for many firms precisely because it creates options for new products and procedures.

To give another example, a large manufacturer might decide to open a retail outlet as a pilot study. The primary goal is to gain some market insight. Because of the high start-up costs, this one operation won't break even. However, based on the sales experience from the pilot, we can then evaluate whether or not to open more outlets, to change the product mix, to enter new markets, and so on. The information gained and the resulting options for actions are all valuable, but coming up with a reliable dollar figure is probably not feasible.

CONCLUSION   We have seen that incorporating options into capital budgeting analysis is not easy. What can we do about them in practice? The answer is that we can only keep them in the back of our minds as we work with the projected cash flows. We tend to underestimate NPV by ignoring options. The damage might be small for a highly structured, very specific proposal, but it might be great for an exploratory one such as a gold mine. The value of a gold mine depends on management's ability to shut it down if the price of gold falls below a certain point, and the ability to reopen it subsequently if conditions are right.[13]

---

13 M. J. Brennan and E. S. Schwartz, "A New Approach to Evaluating Natural Resource Investments," *Midland Corporate Financial Journal* 3 (Spring 1985).

CAPITAL RATIONING

Our final topic in this chapter is capital rationing. While not strictly related to forecasting risk, the theme of this chapter, capital rationing also represents a complication in capital budgeting, so we discuss it here. **Capital rationing** is said to exist when we have profitable (positive NPV) investments available but we can't get the needed funds to undertake them. For example, as division managers for a large corporation, we might identify $5 million in excellent projects, but find that, for whatever reason, we can spend only $2 million. Now what? Unfortunately, for reasons we discuss next there may be no truly satisfactory answer.

capital rationing
The situation that exists if a firm has positive NPV projects but cannot find the necessary financing.

SOFT RATIONING   The situation we have just described is **soft rationing.** This occurs when, for example, different units in a business are allocated some fixed amount of money each year for capital spending. Such an allocation is primarily a means of controlling and keeping track of overall spending. The important thing about soft rationing is that the corporation as a whole isn't short of capital; more can be raised on ordinary terms if management so desires.

soft rationing
The situation that occurs when units in a business are allocated a certain amount of financing for capital budgeting.

If we face soft rationing, the first thing to do is try to get a larger allocation. Failing that, then one common suggestion is to generate as large a net present value as possible within the existing budget. This amounts to choosing those projects with the largest benefit/cost ratio (profitability index).

Strictly speaking, this is the correct thing to do only if the soft rationing is a one-time event; that is, it won't exist next year. If the soft rationing is a chronic problem, something is amiss. The reason goes all the way back to Chapter 1. Ongoing soft rationing means we are constantly by-passing positive NPV investments. This contradicts our goal of the firm. When we are not trying to maximize value, the question of which projects to take becomes ambiguous because we no longer have an objective goal in the first place.

hard rationing
The situation that occurs when a business cannot raise financing for a project under any circumstances.

HARD RATIONING   With **hard rationing,** a business cannot raise capital for a project under any circumstances. For large, healthy corporations, this situation probably does not occur very often. This is fortunate because with hard rationing our DCF analysis breaks down, and the best course of action is ambiguous.

The reason that DCF analysis breaks down has to do with the required return. Suppose we say our required return is 20 percent. Implicitly, we are saying we will take a project with a return that exceeds this. However, if we face hard rationing, we are not going to take a new project no matter what the return on that project is, so the whole concept of a required return is ambiguous. About the only interpretation we can give this situation is that the required return is so large that no project has a positive NPV in the first place.

Hard rationing can occur when a company experiences financial distress, meaning that bankruptcy is a possibility. Also, a firm may not be able to raise capital without violating a pre-existing contractual agreement. We discuss these situations in greater detail in a later chapter.

CONCEPT QUESTIONS

1. Why do we say that our standard discounted cash flow analysis is static?

2. What are managerial options in capital budgeting? Give some examples.

3. What is capital rationing? What types are there? What problem does it create for discounted cash flow analysis?

SUMMARY AND CONCLUSIONS

In this chapter, we looked at some ways of evaluating the results of a discounted cash flow analysis. We also touched on some problems that can come up in practice. We saw that:

1. Net present value estimates depend on projected future cash flows. If there are errors in those projections, our estimated NPVs can be misleading. We called this forecasting risk.

2. Scenario and sensitivity analyses are useful tools for identifying which variables are critical to a project and where forecasting problems can do the most damage.

3. Break-even analysis in its various forms is a particularly common type of scenario analysis that is useful for identifying critical levels of sales.

4. Operating leverage is a key determinant of break-even levels. It reflects the degree to which a project or a firm is committed to fixed costs. The degree of operating leverage tells us the sensitivity of operating cash flow to changes in sales volume.

5. Projects usually have future managerial options associated with them. These options may be very important, but standard discounted cash flow analysis tends to ignore them.

6. Capital rationing occurs when apparently profitable projects cannot be funded. Standard discounted cash flow analysis is troublesome in this case because NPV is not necessarily the appropriate criterion anymore.

The most important thing to carry away from reading this chapter is that estimated NPVs or returns should not be taken at face value. They depend critically on projected cash flows. If there is room for significant disagreement about those projected cash flows, the results from the analysis have to be taken with a grain of salt.

Despite the problems we have discussed, discounted cash flow is still the way of attacking problems, because it forces us to ask the right questions. What we learn in this chapter is that knowing the questions to ask does not guarantee that we get all the answers.

Key Terms

accounting break-even (page 317)
capital rationing (page 330)
cash break-even (page 322)
contingency planning (page 327)
degree of operating leverage (page 324)
financial break-even (page 322)
fixed costs (page 315)
forecasting risk (page 309)
hard rationing (page 330)

managerial options (page 327)
marginal or incremental cost (page 316)
operating leverage (page 323)
scenario analysis (page 311)
sensitivity analysis (page 312)
simulation analysis (page 313)
soft rationing (page 330)
strategic options (page 329)
variable costs (page 315)

Chapter Review Problems and Self-Test

Use the following base-case information to work the self-test problems.

A project under consideration costs $750,000, has a five-year life, and has no salvage value. Depreciation is straight-line to zero. The required return is 17 percent, and the tax rate is 34 percent. Sales are projected at 500 units per year. Price per unit is $2,500, variable cost per unit is $1,500, and fixed costs are $200,000 per year.

11.1 Scenario Analysis Suppose you think that the unit sales, price, variable cost, and fixed cost projections given here are accurate to within 5 percent. What are the upper and lower bounds for these projections? What is the base case NPV? What are the best- and worst-case scenario NPVs?

11.2 Break-Even Analysis Given the base-case projections in the previous problem, what are the cash, accounting, and financial break-even sales levels for this project? Ignore taxes in answering.

Answers to Self-Test Problems

11.1 We can summarize the relevant information as follows:

	Base Case	Lower Bound	Upper Bound
Unit sales	500	475	525
Price per unit	$ 2,500	$ 2,375	$ 2,625
Variable cost per unit	$ 1,500	$ 1,425	$ 1,575
Fixed cost per year	$200,000	$190,000	$210,000

Depreciation is $150,000 per year; knowing this, we can calculate the cash flows under each scenario. Remember that we assign high costs and low prices and volume for the worst-case and just the opposite for the best-case scenario.

Scenario	Unit Sales	Unit Price	Unit Variable Cost	Fixed Costs	Cash Flow
Base case	500	$2,500	$1,500	$200,000	$249,000
Best case	525	2,625	1,425	190,000	341,400
Worst case	475	2,375	1,575	210,000	163,200

At 17 percent, the five-year annuity factor is 3.19935, so the NPVs are:

$$\text{Base-case NPV} = -\$750,000 + 3.19935 \times \$249,000$$
$$= \$46,638$$
$$\text{Best-case NPV} = -\$750,000 + 3.19935 \times \$341,400$$
$$= \$342,258$$
$$\text{Worst-case NPV} = -\$750,000 + 3.19935 \times \$163,200$$
$$= -\$227,866$$

11.2 In this case, we have $200,000 in cash fixed costs to cover. Each unit contributes $2,500 − 1,500 = $1,000 towards covering fixed costs. The cash break-even is thus $200,000/$1,000 = 200 units. We have another $150,000 in depreciation, so the accounting break-even is ($200,000 + 150,000)/$1,000 = 350 units.

To get the financial break-even, we need to find the OCF such that the project has a zero NPV. As we have seen, the five-year annuity factor is 3.19935 and the project costs $750,000, so the OCF must be such that:

$$\$750,000 = \text{OCF} \times 3.19935$$

So, for the project to break even on a financial basis, the project's cash flow must be $750,000/3.19935, or $234,423 per year. If we add this to the $200,000 in cash fixed costs, we get a total of $434,423 that we have to cover. At $1,000 per unit, we need to sell $434,423/$1,000 = 435 units.

Concepts Review and Critical Thinking Questions

1. What is forecasting risk? In general, would the degree of forecasting risk be greater for a new product or a cost-cutting proposal? Why?

2. What is the essential difference between sensitivity analysis and scenario analysis?

3. If you were to include the effect of taxes in break-even analysis, what do you think would happen to the cash, accounting, and financial break-even points?

4. A co-worker claims that looking at all this marginal this and incremental that is just a bunch of nonsense, and states, "Listen, if our average revenue doesn't exceed our average cost, then we will have a negative cash flow, and we will go broke!" How do you respond?

5. What is the option to abandon? Explain why we underestimate NPV if we ignore this option.

6. In our previous chapter, we discussed Air Canada's launch of Tango. Suppose Tango ticket sales had gone extremely well and Air Canada was forced to expand capacity to meet demand. Air Canada's action in this case would be an example of exploiting what kind of option?

7. At one time at least, many Japanese companies had a "no layoff" policy (for that matter, so did IBM). What are the implications of such a policy for the degree of operating leverage a company faces?

8. Airlines offer an example of an industry in which the degree of operating leverage is fairly high. Why?

9. Natural resource extraction facilities (e.g., oil wells or gold mines) provide a good example of the value of the option to suspend operations. Why?

10. In looking at Euro Disney, and its "Mickey Mouse" financial performance early on, note that the subsequent actions taken amount to a product reformulation. Is this a marketing issue, a finance issue, or both? What does Euro Disney's experience suggest about the importance of coordination between marketing and finance?

Questions and Problems

Basic
(Questions 1–15)

1. **Calculating Costs and Break-Even** Bob's Bikes Inc. (BBI) manufactures biotech sunglasses. The variable materials cost is $1.43 per unit and the variable labour cost is $2.44 per unit.

    a. What is the variable cost per unit?

    b. Suppose BBI incurs fixed costs of $650,000 during a year in which total production is 320,000 units. What are the total costs for the year?

    c. If the selling price is $10.00 per unit, does BBI break even on a cash basis? If depreciation is $190,000 per year, what is the accounting break-even point?

2. **Computing Average Cost** Everest Everwear Corporation can manufacture mountain climbing shoes for $16.15 per pair in variable raw material costs and $18.50 per pair in variable labour expense. The shoes sell for $105 per pair. Last year, production was 150,000 pairs. Fixed costs were $800,000. What were total production costs? What is the marginal cost per pair? What is the average cost? If the company is considering a one-time order for an extra 10,000 pairs, what is the minimum acceptable total revenue from the order? Explain.

3. **Scenario Analysis** Bellevue Transmissions, Inc., has the following estimates for its new gear assembly project: price = $1,900 per unit; variable costs = $170 per unit; fixed costs = $6 million; quantity = 105,000 units. Suppose the company believes all of its estimates are accurate only to within ±15 percent. What values should the company use for the four variables given here when it performs its best-case scenario analysis? What about the worst-case scenario?

4. **Sensitivity Analysis** For the company in the previous problem, suppose management is most concerned about the impact of its price estimate on the project's profitability. How could you address this concern for Bellevue Transmissions? Describe how you would calculate your answer. What values would you use for the other forecast variables?

5. **Sensitivity Analysis and Break-Even** We are evaluating a project that costs $896,000, has a eight-year life, and has no salvage value. Assume that depreciation is straight line to zero over the life of the project. Sales are projected at 100,000 units per year. Price per unit is $38, variable cost per unit is $25, and fixed costs are $900,000 per year. The tax rate is 35 percent, and we require a 15 percent return on this project.

    a. Calculate the accounting break-even point. What is the degree of operating leverage at the accounting break-even point?

    b. Calculate the base-case cash flow and NPV. What is the sensitivity of NPV to changes in the sales figure? Explain what your answer tells you about a 500-unit decrease in projected sales.

    c. What is the sensitivity of OCF to changes in the variable cost figure? Explain what your answer tells you about a $1 decrease in estimated variable costs.

6. **Scenario Analysis** In the previous problem, suppose the projections given for price, quantity, variable costs, and fixed costs are all accurate to within ±10 percent. Calculate the best-case and worst-case NPV figures.

7. **Calculating Break-Even** In each of the following cases, calculate the accounting break-even and the cash break-even points. Ignore any tax effects in calculating the cash break-even.

Unit Price	Unit Variable Cost	Fixed Costs	Depreciation
$3,000	$2,275	$15,000,000	$6,500,000
39	27	73,000	140,000
8	3	1,200	840

8. **Calculating Break-Even** In each of the following cases, find the unknown variable.

Accounting Break-Even	Unit Price	Unit Variable Cost	Fixed Costs	Depreciation
130,200	$ 41	$30	$ 820,000	?
135,000	?	56	3,200,000	$1,150,000
5,478	105	?	160,000	105,000

9. **Calculating Break-Even** A project has the following estimated data: price = $70 per unit; variable costs = $37 per unit; fixed costs = $6,000; required return = 15 percent; initial investment = $12,000; life = four years. Ignoring the effect of taxes, what is the accounting break-even quantity? The cash break-even quantity? The financial break-even quantity? What is the degree of operating leverage at the financial break-even level of output?

10. **Using Break-Even Analysis** Consider a project with the following data: accounting break-even quantity = 19,000 units; cash break-even quantity = 13,000 units; life = five years; fixed costs = $120,000; variable costs = $23 per unit; required return = 16 percent. Ignoring the effect of taxes, find the financial break-even quantity.

Basic
(continued)

11. **Calculating Operating Leverage** At an output level of 40,000 units, you calculate that the degree of operating leverage is 2.5. If output rises to 47,000 units, what will the percentage change in operating cash flow be? Will the new level of operating leverage be higher or lower? Explain.

12. **Leverage** In the previous problem, suppose fixed costs are $150,000. What is the operating cash flow at 35,000 units? The degree of operating leverage?

13. **Operating Cash Flow and Leverage** A proposed project has fixed costs of $45,000 per year. The operating cash flow at 8,000 units is $71,000. Ignoring the effect of taxes, what is the degree of operating leverage? If units sold rises from 8,000 to 8,500, what will be the increase in operating cash flow? What is the new degree of operating leverage?

14. **Cash Flow and Leverage** At an output level of 10,000 units, you have calculated that the degree of operating leverage is 2.75. The operating cash flow is $16,000 in this case. Ignoring the effect of taxes, what are fixed costs? What will the operating cash flow be if output rises to 11,000 units? If output falls to 9,000 units?

15. **Leverage** In the previous problem, what will be the new degree of operating leverage in each case?

Intermediate
(Questions
16–25)

16. **Break-Even Intuition** Consider a project with a required return of R% that costs I and will last for N years. The project uses straight-line depreciation to zero over the N-year life; there is no salvage value or net working capital requirements.

   a. At the accounting break-even level of output, what is the IRR of this project? The payback period? The NPV?

   b. At the cash break-even level of output, what is the IRR of this project? The payback period? The NPV?

   c. At the financial break-even level of output, what is the IRR of this project? The payback period? The NPV?

17. **Sensitivity Analysis** Consider a four-year project with the following information: initial fixed asset investment = $420,000; straight-line depreciation to zero over the four-year life; zero salvage value; price = $28; variable costs = $19; fixed costs = $190,000; quantity sold = 110,000 units; tax rate = 34 percent. How sensitive is OCF to changes in quantity sold?

18. **Operating Leverage** In the previous problem, what is the degree of operating leverage at the given level of output? What is the degree of operating leverage at the accounting break-even level of output?

19. **Project Analysis** You are considering a new product launch. The project will cost $720,000, have a four-year life, and have no salvage value; depreciation is straight-line to zero. Sales are projected at 190 units per year; price per unit will be $21,000, variable cost per unit will be $15,000, and fixed costs will be $225,000 per year. The required return on the project is 15 percent, and the relevant tax rate is 35 percent.

   a. Based on your experience, you think the unit sales, variable cost, and fixed cost projections given here are probably accurate to within ±10 percent. What are the upper and lower bounds for these projections? What is the base-case NPV? What are the best-case and worst-case scenarios?

   b. Evaluate the sensitivity of your base-case NPV to changes in fixed costs.

   c. What is the cash break-even level of output for this project (ignoring taxes)?

   d. What is the accounting break-even level of output for this project? What is the degree of operating leverage at the accounting break-even point? How do you interpret this number?

20. **Abandonment Value** We are examining a new project. We expect to sell 6,250 units per year at $145 net cash flow apiece (including CCA) for the next 11 years. In other words, the annual operating cash flow is projected to be $145 × 6,250 = $906,250. The relevant discount rate is 17 percent, and the initial investment required is $3,900,000.

   a. What is the base-case NPV?

   b. After the first year, the project can be dismantled and sold for $2,700,000. If expected sales are revised based on the first year's performance, when would it make sense to abandon the investment? In other words, at what level of expected sales would it make sense to abandon the project?

   c. Explain how the $2,700,000 abandonment value can be viewed as the opportunity cost of keeping the project one year.

21. **Abandonment** In the previous problem, suppose you think it is likely that expected sales will be revised upwards to 7,700 units if the first year is a success and revised downwards to 3,500 units if the first year is not a success.

   a. If success and failure are equally likely, what is the NPV of the project? Consider the possibility of abandonment in answering.

   b. What is the value of the option to abandon?

22. **Abandonment and Expansion** In the previous problem, supposed the scale of the project can be doubled in one year in the sense that twice as many units can be produced and sold. Naturally, expansion would only be desirable if the project is a success. This implies that if the project is a success, projected sales after expansion will be 15,400. Again, assuming that success and failure are equally likely, what is the NPV of the project? Note that abandonment is still an option if the project is a failure. What is the value of the option to expand?

23. **Project Analysis** McGilla Golf has decided to sell a new line of golf clubs. The clubs will sell for $700 per set and have a variable cost of $320 per set. The company has spent $150,000 for a marketing study that determined the company will sell 55,000 sets per year for seven years. The marketing study also determined that the company will lose sales of

Intermediate
(continued)

13,000 sets of its high-priced clubs. The high-priced clubs sell at $1,100 and have variable costs of $600. The company will also increase sales of its cheap clubs by 10,000 sets. The cheap clubs sell for $400 and have variable costs of $180 per set. The fixed costs each year will be $7,500,000. The company has also spent $1,000,000 on research and development for the new clubs. The plant and equipment required will cost $18,200,000 and will be depreciated on a straight-line basis. The new clubs will also require an increase in net working capital of $950,000 that will be returned at the end of the project. The tax rate is 40 percent, and the cost of capital is 14 percent. Calculate the payback period, the NPV, and the IRR.

24. **Scenario Analysis**   In the previous problem, you feel that the values are accurate to within only ±10 percent. What are the best-case and worst-case NPVs? (Hint: The price and variable costs for the two existing sets of clubs are known with certainty; only the sales gained or lost are uncertain.)

25. **Sensitivity Analysis**   McGilla Golf would like to know the sensitivity of NPV to changes in the price of the new clubs and the quantity of new clubs sold. What is the sensitivity of the NPV to each of these variables?

Challenge
(Questions
26–31)

26. **Break-Even and Taxes**   This problem concerns the effect of taxes on the various break-even measures.

   a. Show that, when we consider taxes, the general relationship between operating cash flow, OCF, and sales volume, Q, can be written as:

   $$Q = \frac{FC + \frac{OCF - T \times D}{1 - T}}{P - v}$$

   b. Use the expression in part (a) to find the cash, accounting, and financial break-even points for the Victoria sailboat example in the chapter. Assume a 38 percent tax rate.

   c. In part (b), the accounting break-even should be the same as before. Why? Verify this algebraically.

27. **Operating Leverage and Taxes**   Show that if we consider the effect of taxes, the degree of operating leverage can be written as:

   $$DOL = 1 + [FC \times (1 - T) - T \times D]/OCF$$

   Notice that this reduces to our previous result if $T = 0$. Can you interpret this in words?

28. **Scenario Analysis**   Consider a project to supply Oshawa with 40,000 tonnes of machine screws annually for five years for automobile production. The sales price will be $280 per tonne. You will need an initial $1,750,000 investment in threading equipment to get the project started; the project will last for five years. The accounting department estimates that annual fixed costs will be $350,000 and that variable costs should be $225 per tonne; the CCA rate for threading equipment is 20 percent. It also estimates a salvage value of $550,000 after dismantling costs. The marketing department estimates you will need an initial net working capital investment of $475,000. You require a 14 percent return and face a marginal tax rate of 39 percent on this project.

   a. What is the estimated OCF for this project? The NPV? Should you pursue this project?

   b. Suppose you believe that the accounting department's initial cost and salvage value projections are accurate only to within +/- 15 percent; the marketing department's price estimate is accurate only within +/- 10 percent; and the engineering department's net working capital estimate is accurate only to within +/- 5 percent. What is your worst-case scenario for this project? Best-case scenario? Do you still want to pursue the project?

29. **Sensitivity Analysis**   In Problem 28, suppose you're confident about your own projections, but you're a little unsure about Oshawa's actual machine screw requirement. What is the sensitivity of the project OCF to changes in the quantity supplied? What about the sensitivity of NPV to changes in quantity supplied? Given the sensitivity number you calculated, is there some minimum level of output below which you wouldn't want to operate? Why?

30. **Break-Even Analysis**   Use the results of Problem 26 to find the accounting, cash, and financial break-even quantities for the company in Problem 28.

31. **Operating Leverage**   Use the results of Problem 27 to find the degree of operating leverage for the company in Problem 28 at the base-case output level of 40,000 units. How does this number compare to the sensitivity figure you found in Problem 29? Verify that either approach will give you the same OCF figure at any new quantity level.

MINI CASE

As a financial analyst at Minor International (MI) you have been asked to revisit your analysis of the two capital investment alternatives submitted by the production department of the firm. (Detailed discussion of these alternatives is in the Mini Case at the end of Chapter 10.) The CFO is concerned that the analysis to date has not really addressed the risk in this project. Your task is to employ scenario and sensitivity analysis to explore how your original recommendation might change when subjected to a number of "what-ifs."

In your discussions with the CFO, the CIO and the head of the production department, you have pinpointed two key inputs to the capital budgeting decision: initial software development costs and expected savings in production costs (before tax). By properly designing the contract for software development, you are confident that initial software costs for each alternative can be kept in a range of plus or minus 18 percent of the original estimates. Savings in production costs are less certain because the software will involve new technology that has not been implemented before. An appropriate range for these costs is plus or minus 45 percent of the original estimates.

As the capital budgeting analyst, you are required to answer the following in your memo to the CFO:

a)   Conduct sensitivity analysis to determine which of the two inputs has a greater input on the choice between the two projects.

b)   Conduct scenario analysis to assess the risks of each alternative in turn. What are your conclusions?

c)   Explain what your sensitivity and scenario analyses tell you about your original recommendations.

*We recommend using a spreadsheet in analyzing this Mini Case.

Internet Application Questions

1. The following website allows you to download a cash flow sensitivity analysis spreadsheet: www.toolkit.cch.com/tools/cfsens_m.asp. You are faced with two technologies, one with a higher cash flow but greater risk, and the second with a lower cash flow and less risk. How would you use the cash flow sensitivity spreadsheet to pick the right technology? What factors would you consider in the analysis?

2. The Motley Fool site (www.fool.com) provides a discussion of operating leverage (www.fool.com/portfolios/rulemaker/2000/rulemaker000814.htm) in the context of new economy firms characterized by very large developmental costs and virtually zero variable costs. Do you think this model will work for old economy industries? What assumptions do you need to make in answering such questions?

3. Sometimes investments are associated with catastrophic risk. It is important for managers to control this risk within reasonable limits. Value at Risk provides an easily understood and measured statistic to quantify this risk. The following site provides discussions of Value at Risk: VaR Measure (www.valueatrisk.com)

   Under what conditions will VaR and standard deviation provide identical information?

Suggested Readings

For a more in-depth (and highly readable) discussion of break-even analysis and operating leverage, see:
   Viscione, J. A. *Financial Analysis: Tools and Concepts.* New York: National Association of Credit Management, 1984, chap. 4.

A discussion of break-even applications in Canada is in:
   Kilpatrick, I. "Customized Control." *CA Magazine,* Toronto, October 1995.

The following articles are classics on the subject of risk analysis in investment decisions:
   Hertz, D. B. "Risk Analysis in Capital Investment." *Harvard Business Review* 42 (January–February 1964).
   _____. "Investment Policies that Pay Off." *Harvard Business Review* 46 (January–February 1968).

A trade book on competitive strategy and advantage is:
   Porter, M. E. *Competitive Advantage: Creating and Sustaining Superior Performance.* New York: The Free Press, 1985.

Risk and Return

CHAPTER 12

Some Lessons from Capital Market History

The S&P/TSX Composite was up over 31 percent in 1999 on the strength of high tech stocks like Nortel Networks. Although it was basically flat (down around 1.5 percent) in 1998, the two prior years both saw strong returns—over 14 percent in 1997 and around 28 percent in 1996. From January 2000 to the end of 2002, however, the TSX was down almost 18 percent as tech stocks collapsed. The S&P/TSX Composite rebounded, posting annual returns of 26.7% in 2003, 14.5% in 2004, and 23.3% in 2005.

Based on this historical experience, what return should you expect if you invest in Canadian common stocks? In this chapter we study five decades of capital market history to find out.

www.nortel.com

THUS FAR, we haven't had much to say about what determines the required return on an investment. In one sense, the answer is very simple: The required return depends on the risk of the investment. The greater the risk is, the greater is the required return.

Having said this, we are left with a somewhat more difficult problem. How can we measure the amount of risk present in an investment? Put another way, what does it mean to say that one investment is riskier than another? Obviously, we need to define what we mean by risk if we are going to answer these questions. This is our task in the next two chapters.

From the last several chapters, we know that one of the responsibilities of the financial manager is to assess the value of proposed real asset investments. In doing this, it is important to know what financial investments have to offer. Going further, we saw in Chapter 2 that the cash flow of a firm equals the cash flow to creditors and shareholders. So the returns and risks of financial investments provide information on the real investments firms undertake.

Our goal in this chapter is to provide a perspective on what capital market history can tell us about risk and return. The most important thing to get out of this chapter is a feel for the numbers. What is a high return? What is a low one? More generally, what returns should we expect from financial assets and what are the risks from such investments? This perspective is essential for understanding how to analyze and value risky investment projects.

We start our discussion on risk and return by describing the historical experience of investors in Canadian financial markets. In 1931, for example, the stock market lost about 33 percent of its value. Just two years later, the stock market gained 51 percent. In more recent memory, the U.S. market lost about 23 percent of its value in 2002. What lessons, if any, can financial managers learn from such shifts in the stock market? We explore the last half-century of market history to find out.

Not everyone agrees on the value of studying history. On the one hand, there is philosopher George Santayana's famous comment, "Those who cannot remember the past are condemned to repeat it." On the other hand, there is industrialist Henry Ford's equally famous comment, "History is more or less bunk." Nonetheless, based on recent events, perhaps everyone would agree with Mark Twain when he observed, "October. This is one of the peculiarly dangerous months to speculate in stocks in. The others are July, January, September, April, November, May, March, June, December, August, and February."

Two central lessons emerge from our study of market history: First, there is a reward for bearing risk. Second, the greater the risk, the greater the potential reward. To understand these facts about market returns, we devote much of this chapter to reporting the statistics and numbers that make up modern capital market history in Canada. Canadians also invest in the United States so we include some discussion of U.S. markets. In the next chapter, these facts provide the foundation for our study of how financial markets put a price on risk.

RETURNS

We wish to discuss historical returns on different types of financial assets. We do this after briefly discussing how to calculate the return from investing.

Dollar Returns

If you buy an asset of any sort, your gain (or loss) from that investment is called the return on your investment. This return usually has two components: First, you may receive some cash directly while you own the investment. This is called the income component of your return. Second, the value of the asset you purchase often changes. In this case, you have a capital gain or capital loss on your investment.[1]

To illustrate, suppose Canadian Atlantic Enterprises has several thousand shares of stock outstanding. You purchased some of these shares at the beginning of the year. It is now year-end, and you want to find out how well you have done on your investment.

Over the year, a company may pay cash dividends to its shareholders. As a shareholder in Canadian Atlantic Enterprises, you are a part owner of the company. If the company is profitable, it may choose to distribute some of its profits to shareholders (we discuss the details of dividend policy in Chapter 17). So, as the owner of some stock, you receive some cash. This cash is the income component from owning the stock.

In addition to the dividend, the other part of your return is the capital gain or capital loss on the stock. This part arises from changes in the value of your investment. For example, consider the cash flows illustrated in Figure 12.1. The stock is selling for $37 per share. If you buy 100 shares, you have a total outlay of $3,700. Suppose that, over the year, the stock paid a dividend of $1.85 per share. By the end of the year, then, you would have received income of:

$$\text{Dividend} = \$1.85 \times 100 = \$185$$

Also, the value of the stock rises to $40.33 per share by the end of the year. Your 100 shares are worth $4,033, so you have a capital gain of:

$$\text{Capital gain} = (\$40.33 - \$37) \times 100 = \$333$$

On the other hand, if the price had dropped to, say, $34.78, you would have a capital loss of:

$$\text{Capital loss} = (\$34.78 - \$37) \times 100 = -\$222$$

Notice that a capital loss is the same thing as a negative capital gain.

---

[1] The aftertax dollar returns would be reduced by taxes levied differently for dividends and capital gains, as we discussed in Chapter 2.

FIGURE 12.1

Dollar returns

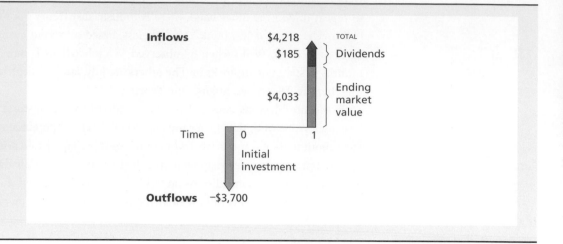

The total dollar return on your investment is the sum of the dividend and the capital gain:

$$\text{Total dollar return} = \text{Dividend income} + \text{Capital gain (or loss)} \qquad [12.1]$$

In our first example, the total dollar return is thus given by:

$$\text{Total dollar return} = \$185 + 333 = \$518$$

If you sold the stock at the end of the year, the total amount of cash you would have would be your initial investment plus the total return. In the preceding example, then:

$$\begin{aligned}\text{Total cash if stock is sold} &= \text{Initial investment} + \text{Total return} \qquad [12.2]\\ &= \$3{,}700 + 518\\ &= \$4{,}218\end{aligned}$$

As a check, notice that this is the same as the proceeds from the sale of the stock plus the dividends:

$$\begin{aligned}\text{Proceeds from stock sale} + \text{Dividends} &= \$40.33 \times 100 + \$185\\ &= \$4{,}033 + 185\\ &= \$4{,}218\end{aligned}$$

Suppose you hold on to your Canadian Atlantic stock and don't sell it at the end of the year. Should you still consider the capital gain as part of your return? Isn't this only a paper gain and not really a cash flow if you don't sell it?

The answer to the first question is a strong yes, and the answer to the second is an equally strong no. The capital gain is every bit as much a part of your return as the dividend, and you should certainly count it as part of your return. That you actually decided to keep the stock and not sell (you don't realize the gain) is irrelevant because you could have converted it to cash if you wanted to. Whether you choose to do so or not is up to you.

After all, if you insisted on converting your gain to cash, you could always sell the stock at year-end and immediately reinvest by buying the stock back. There is no net difference between doing this and just not selling (assuming there are no tax consequences from selling the stock). Again, the point is that whether you actually cash out or reinvest by not selling doesn't affect the return you earn.

Percentage Returns

It is usually more convenient to summarize information about returns in percentage terms, rather than dollar terms, because that way your return doesn't depend on how much you actually invest. The question we want to answer is: How much do we get for each dollar we invest?

To answer this question, let P_t be the price of the stock at the beginning of the year and let D_t be the dividend paid on the stock during the year. Consider the cash flows in Figure 12.2.

These are the same as those in Figure 12.1, except we have now expressed everything on a per-share basis.

In our example, the price at the beginning of the year was $37 per share and the dividend paid during the year on each share was $1.85. As we discussed in Chapter 8, expressing the dividend as a percentage of the beginning stock price results in the dividend yield:

$$\text{Dividend yield} = D_t/P_t$$
$$= \$1.85/\$37 = .05 = 5\%$$

This says that, for each dollar we invest, we get 5 cents in dividends.

The other component of our percentage return is the capital gains yield. This is calculated as the change in the price during the year (the capital gain) divided by the beginning price:

$$\text{Capital gains yield} = (P_{t+1} - P_t)/P_t$$
$$= (\$40.33 - 37)/\$37$$
$$= \$3.33/\$37$$
$$= 9\%$$

So, per dollar invested, you get 9 cents in capital gains.

Putting it together, per dollar invested, we get 5 cents in dividends and 9 cents in capital gains, a total of 14 cents. Our percentage return is 14 cents on the dollar, or 14 percent.

To check this, notice that you invested $3,700 and ended with $4,218. By what percentage did your $3,700 increase? As we saw, you picked up $4,218 − 3,700 = $518. This is a $518/$3,700 = 14% increase.

FIGURE 12.2

Percentage, dollar, and per-share returns

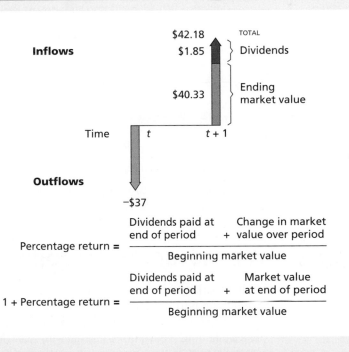

EXAMPLE 12.1: Calculating Returns

Suppose you buy some stock for $25 per share. At the end of the year, the price is $35 per share. During the year, you got a $2 dividend per share. This is the situation illustrated in Figure 12.3. What is the dividend yield? The capital gains yield? The percentage return? If your total investment was $1,000, how much do you have at the end of the year?

Your $2 dividend per share works out to a dividend yield of:

$$\text{Dividend yield} = D_t/P_t$$
$$= \$2/\$25 = .08 = 8\%$$

EXAMPLE 12.1: Calculating Returns—cont'd.

The per-share capital gain is $10, so the capital gains yield is:

$$
\begin{aligned}
\text{Capital gains yield} &= (P_{t+1} - P_t)/P_t \\
&= (\$35 - 25)/\$25 \\
&= \$10/\$25 \\
&= 40\%
\end{aligned}
$$

The total percentage return is thus 48 percent.

If you had invested $1,000, you would have $1,480 at the end of the year, a 48 percent increase. To check this, note that your $1,000 would have bought you $1,000/25 = 40 shares. Your 40 shares would then have paid you a total of 40 × $2 = $80 in cash dividends. Your $10 per-share gain would give you a total capital gain of $10 × 40 = $400. Add these together, and you get the $480.

FIGURE 12.3

Cash flow—an investment example

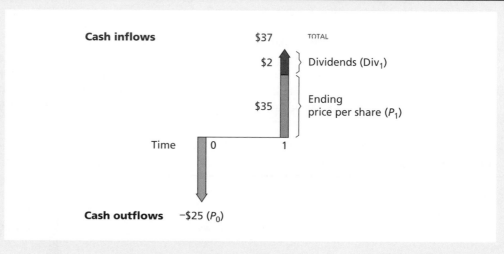

CONCEPT QUESTIONS

1. What are the two parts of total return?

2. Why are unrealized capital gains or losses included in the calculation of returns?

3. What is the difference between a dollar return and a percentage return? Why are percentage returns more convenient?

www.merceric.com

12.2 THE HISTORICAL RECORD

Capital market history is of great interest to investment consultants who advise institutional investors on portfolio strategy. The data set we use is in Table 12.1. It was assembled by Mercer Investment Consulting, drawing on two major studies. Roger Ibbotson and Rex Sinquefield conducted a famous set of studies dealing with rates of return in U.S. financial markets. James Hatch and Robert White examined Canadian returns.[2] Our data present year-to-year historical rates of return on five important types of financial investments. The returns can be interpreted as what you would have earned if you held portfolios of the following:

---

2 The two classic studies are R. G. Ibbotson and R. A. Sinquefield, *Stocks, Bonds, Bills, and Inflation* (Charlottesville, Va.: Financial Analysts Research Foundation, 1982), and J. Hatch and R. White, *Canadian Stocks, Bonds, Bills, and Inflation: 1950–1983* (Charlottesville, Va.: Financial Analysts Research Foundation, 1985). Additional sources used by Mercer Investment Consulting are Nesbitt Burns for small capitalization for small stocks, Scotia Capital Markets for Canada Treasury bills and long bonds, and Statistics Canada CANSIM for rates of exchange and inflation.

www.bmonesbittburns.com

www.statcan.ca

1. Canadian common stocks. The common stock portfolio is based on a sample of the largest companies (in total market value of outstanding stock) in Canada.[3]

2. U.S. common stocks. The U.S. common stock portfolio consists of 500 of the largest U.S. companies. The full historical series is given in U.S. dollars. A separate series presents U.S. stock returns in Canadian dollars adjusting for shifts in exchange rates.

3. Small stocks. The small stock portfolio is composed of the small capitalization Canadian stocks as compiled by BMO Nesbitt Burns.

4. Long bonds. The long bond portfolio has high-quality, long-term corporate, provincial, and Government of Canada bonds.

5. Canada Treasury bills. The T-bill portfolio has Treasury bills with a three-month maturity.

These returns are not adjusted for inflation or taxes; thus, they are nominal, pretax returns.

In addition to the year-to-year returns on these financial instruments, the year-to-year percentage change in the Statistics Canada Consumer Price Index (CPI) is also computed. This is a commonly used measure of inflation, so we can calculate real returns using this as the inflation rate.

The five asset classes included in Table 12.1 cover a broad range of investments popular with Canadian individuals and financial institutions. We include U.S. stocks since Canadian investors often invest abroad—particularly in the United States.[4]

A First Look

Before looking closely at the different portfolio returns, we take a look at the "big picture." Figure 12.4 shows what happened to $1 invested in three of these different portfolios at the beginning of 1957. We work with a sample period of 1957–2005 for two reasons: the years immediately after the Second World War do not reflect trends today and the TSE 300 (predecessor of the TSX) was introduced in 1956, making 1957 the first really comparable year. This decision is somewhat controversial and we return to it later as we draw lessons from our data. The growth in value for each of the different portfolios over the 49-year period ending in 2005 is given separately. Notice that, to get everything on a single graph, some modification in scaling is used. As is commonly done with financial series, the vertical axis is on a logarithmic scale such that equal distances measure equal percentage changes (as opposed to equal dollar changes) in value.

Looking at Figure 12.4, we see that the common stock investments did the best overall. Every dollar invested in Canadian stocks grew to $96.61 over the 49 years.

At the other end, the T-bill portfolio grew to only $22.53. Long bonds did better with an ending value of $52.56. These values are less impressive when we consider inflation over this period. As illustrated, the price level climbed such that $7.36 is needed just to replace the original $1.

Given the historical record as discussed so far, why would any investor hold any asset class other than common stocks? A close look at Figure 12.4 provides an answer. The T-bill portfolio and the long-term bond portfolio grew more slowly than did the stock portfolio, but they also grew much more steadily. The common stocks ended up on top, but as you can see, they grew erratically at times. For example, comparing Canadian stocks with T-bills, the stocks had a smaller return in 19 years during this period.

A Closer Look

To illustrate the variability of the different investments, we look at a few selected years in Table 12.1. For example, looking at long-term bonds, we see the largest historical return (45.82 percent) occurred in 1982. This was a good year for bonds. The largest single-year return in the table is a very healthy 52.62 percent for the S&P 500 in 1954. In the same year, T-bills returned only 1.62 percent. In contrast, the largest Treasury bill return was 19.11 percent (in 1981).

---

3 From 1956 on, the S&P/TSX Composite is used. For earlier years, Mercer Investment Consulting used a sample provided by the TSX.

4 Chapter 21 discusses exchange rate risk and other risks of foreign investments.

TABLE 12.1 Annual market index returns: 1948–2005

Year	Statistics Canada inflation	Canadian stocks S&P/TSX Composite	Scotia Capital Markets 91-day T-bill	Scotia Capital Markets long bonds	U.S. stocks S&P 500 (Cdn.$)	Nesbitt Burns small stocks
1948	8.88	12.25	0.40	−0.08	5.50	
1949	1.09	23.85	0.45	5.18	22.15	
1950	5.91	51.69	0.51	1.74	39.18	
1951	10.66	25.44	0.71	−7.89	15.00	
1952	−1.38	0.01	0.95	5.01	13.68	
1953	0.00	2.56	1.54	5.00	−0.99	
1954	0.00	39.37	1.62	12.23	52.62	
1955	0.47	27.68	1.22	0.13	35.51	
1956	3.24	12.68	2.63	−8.87	2.35	
1957	1.79	−20.58	3.76	7.94	−8.51	
1958	2.64	31.25	2.27	1.92	40.49	
1959	1.29	4.59	4.39	−5.07	10.54	
1960	1.27	1.78	3.66	12.19	5.15	
1961	0.42	32.75	2.86	9.16	32.85	
1962	1.67	−7.09	3.81	5.03	−5.77	
1963	1.64	15.60	3.58	4.58	23.19	
1964	2.02	25.43	3.73	6.16	15.75	
1965	3.16	6.67	3.79	0.05	12.58	
1966	3.45	−7.07	4.89	−1.05	−9.33	
1967	4.07	18.09	4.38	−0.48	23.61	
1968	3.91	22.45	6.22	2.14	10.26	
1969	4.79	−0.81	6.83	−2.86	−8.50	
1970	1.31	−3.57	6.89	16.39	−1.96	−11.69
1971	5.16	8.01	3.86	14.84	13.28	15.83
1972	4.91	27.37	3.43	8.11	18.12	44.72
1973	9.36	0.27	4.78	1.97	−14.58	−7.82
1974	12.30	−25.93	7.68	−4.53	−26.87	−26.89
1975	9.52	18.48	7.05	8.02	40.72	41.00
1976	5.87	11.02	9.10	23.64	22.97	22.77
1977	9.45	10.71	7.64	9.04	0.65	39.93
1978	8.44	29.72	7.90	4.10	15.50	44.41
1979	9.69	44.77	11.01	−2.83	16.52	46.04
1980	11.20	30.13	12.23	2.18	35.51	42.86
1981	12.20	−10.25	19.11	−2.09	−5.57	−15.10
1982	9.23	5.54	15.27	45.82	25.84	4.55
1983	4.51	35.49	9.39	9.61	24.07	44.30
1984	3.77	−2.39	11.21	16.90	12.87	−2.33
1985	4.38	25.07	9.70	26.68	39.82	38.98
1986	4.19	8.95	9.34	17.21	16.96	12.33
1987	4.12	5.88	8.20	1.77	−0.96	−5.47
1988	3.96	11.08	8.94	11.30	7.21	5.46
1989	5.17	21.37	11.95	15.17	27.74	10.66
1990	5.00	−14.80	13.28	4.32	−3.06	−27.32
1991	3.78	12.02	9.90	25.30	30.05	18.51
1992	2.14	−1.43	6.65	11.57	18.42	13.01
1993	1.70	32.55	5.63	22.09	14.40	52.26
1994	0.23	−0.18	4.76	−7.39	7.48	−9.21
1995	1.75	14.53	7.39	26.34	33.68	13.88
1996	2.17	28.35	5.02	14.18	23.62	28.66
1997	0.73	14.98	3.20	18.46	39.18	6.97
1998	1.02	−1.58	4.74	12.85	37.71	−17.90
1999	2.58	31.59	4.66	−5.98	14.14	20.29
2000	3.23	7.41	5.49	12.97	−5.67	−4.29
2001	0.60	−12.60	4.70	8.10	−6.50	0.70
2002	4.30	−12.40	2.50	8.70	−22.70	−0.90
2003	1.60	26.70	2.90	6.70	5.30	42.70
2004	2.40	14.50	2.30	7.20	3.30	14.10
2005	2.00	23.29	2.58	5.86	3.80	13.70

Source: Mercer Investment Consulting, Bloomberg Financial Services, Fortress Small Cap Equity Fund, BMO, and Scotia Capital.

FIGURE 12.4

Returns to a $1
investment, 1957–2005

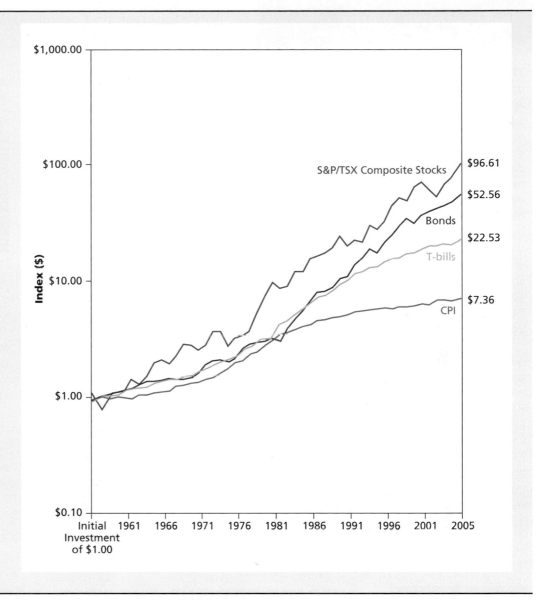

CONCEPT QUESTIONS

1. With 20-20 hindsight, what was the best investment for the period 1981–82?

2. Why doesn't everyone just buy common stocks as investments?

3. What was the smallest return observed over the 48 years for each of these investments? When did it occur?

4. How many times did large Canadian stocks (common stocks) return more than 30 percent? How many times did they return less than 20 percent?

5. What was the longest winning streak (years without a negative return) for large Canadian stocks? For long-term bonds?

6. How often did the T-bill portfolio have a negative return?

7. How have Canadian stocks compared with U.S. stocks over the last 10 years?

In Their Own Words . . .   Roger Ibbotson on Capital Market History

THE financial markets are perhaps the most carefully documented human phenomena in history. Every day, approximately 2,000 NYSE stocks are traded, and at least 5,000 more are traded on other exchanges and in over-the-counter markets. Bonds, commodities, futures, and options also provide a wealth of data. These data daily fill a dozen pages of *The Wall Street Journal* (and numerous other newspapers), and these pages are only summaries of the day's transactions. A record actually exists of every transaction, providing not only a real-time data base, but a historical record extending back, in many cases, more than a century.

The global market adds another dimension to this wealth of data. The Japanese stock market trades a billion shares on active days, and the London exchange reports trades on over 10,000 domestic and foreign issues a day. [The Toronto Stock Exchange ranks seventh in the world by market capitalization, as seen in Chapter 1.]

The data generated by these transactions are quantifiable, quickly analyzed and disseminated, and made easily accessible by computer. Because of this, finance has increasingly come to resemble one of the exact sciences. The use of financial market data ranges from the simple, such as using the S&P 500 to measure the performance of a portfolio, to the incredibly complex. For example, only a generation ago, the bond market was the staidest province on Wall Street. Today, it attracts swarms of traders seeking to exploit arbitrage opportunities—small temporary mispricings—using real-time data and supercomputers to analyze them.

Financial market data are the foundation for the extensive empirical understanding we now have of the financial markets. The following is a list of some of the principal findings of such research: Risky securities, such as stocks, have higher average returns than riskless securities such as Treasury bills. Stocks of small companies have higher average returns than those of larger companies. Long-term bonds have higher average yields and returns than short-term bonds. The cost of capital for a company, project, or division can be predicted using data from the markets. Because phenomena in the financial markets are so well measured, finance is the most readily quantifiable branch of economics. Researchers are able to do more extensive empirical research than in any other economic field, and the research can be quickly translated into action in the marketplace.

Roger Ibbotson is Professor in the Practice of Management at the Yale School of Management. He is the founder and president of Ibbotson Associates, a major supplier of financial data bases to the financial services industry. An outstanding scholar, he is best known for his original estimates of the historical rates of return realized by investors in different markets and for his research on new issues.

12.3   AVERAGE RETURNS: THE FIRST LESSON

As you've probably begun to notice, the history of capital market returns is too complicated to be of much use in its undigested form. We need to begin summarizing all these numbers. Accordingly, we discuss how to consider the detailed data. We start by calculating average returns.

Calculating Average Returns

The obvious way to calculate the average returns from 1957–2005 on the different investments in Table 12.1 is simply to add up the yearly returns and divide by 49. The result is the historical average of the individual values. Statisticians call this the arithmetic average or arithmetic mean return. It has the advantage of being easy to calculate and interpret, so we use it here to measure expected return.

For example, if you add the returns for the Canadian common stocks for the 49 years, you get about 537.7. The average annual return is thus 537.7/49 = 10.97%. You interpret this 10.97 percent just like any other average. If you picked a year at random from the 49-year history and you had to guess what the return in that year was, the best guess is 10.97 percent.

Average Returns: The Historical Record

Table 12.2 shows the average returns computed from Table 12.1. As shown, in a typical year, the small stocks increased in value by 14.1 percent. Notice also how much larger the stock returns are than the bond returns.

These averages are, of course, nominal since we haven't worried about inflation. Notice that the average inflation rate was 4.21 percent per year over this 49-year span. The nominal return on Canada Treasury bills was 6.62 percent per year. The average real return on Treasury bills was thus approximately 2.41 percent per year; so the real return on T-bills has been quite low historically.

At the other extreme, Canadian common stocks had an average real return of about 11% − 4% = 7%, which is relatively large. If you remember the Rule of 72 (Chapter 5), then a quick "back of the envelope" calculation tells us that 7 percent real growth doubles your buying power about every 10 years.

Risk Premiums

Now that we have computed some average returns, it seems logical to see how they compare with each other. Based on our discussion so far, one such comparison involves government-issued securities. These are free of much of the variability we see in, for example, the stock market.

The Government of Canada borrows money by issuing debt securities in different forms. The ones we focus on are Treasury bills. These have the shortest time to maturity of the different government securities. Because the government can always raise taxes to pay its bills, this debt is virtually free of any default risk over its short life. Thus, we call the rate on such debt the risk-free return, and we use it as a kind of benchmark.

A particularly interesting comparison involves the virtually risk-free return on T-bills and the very risky return on common stocks. The difference between these two returns can be interpreted as a measure of the excess return on the average risky asset (assuming that the stock of a large Canadian corporation has about average risk compared to all risky assets).

risk premium
The excess return required from an investment in a risky asset over a risk-free investment.

We call this the excess return because it is the additional return we earn by moving from a relatively risk-free investment to a risky one. Because it can be interpreted as a reward for bearing risk, we call it a **risk premium.**

From Table 12.2, we can calculate the risk premiums for the different investments. We report only the nominal risk premium in Table 12.3 because there is only a slight difference between the historical nominal and real risk premiums. The risk premium on T-bills is shown as zero in the table because we have assumed that they are riskless.

The First Lesson

Looking at Table 12.3, we see that the average risk premium earned by a typical Canadian common stock is around 4 percent: 10.97 − 6.62 = 4.35. This is a significant reward. The fact that it exists historically is an important observation, and it is the basis for our first lesson: Risky assets, on average, earn a risk premium. Put another way, there is a reward for bearing risk.

Why is this so? Why, for example, is the risk premium for common stocks larger than the risk premium for long bonds? More generally, what determines the relative sizes of the risk premiums for the different assets? The answers to these questions are at the heart of modern finance, and

TABLE 12.2
Average annual returns, 1957–2005

Investment	Arithmetic Average Return (%)
Canadian common stocks	10.97
U.S. common stocks (Cdn. $)	12.31
Long bonds	8.88
Small stocks	14.16
Inflation	4.21
Treasury bills	6.62

Average return on small stocks is based on data from 1970 to 2005.

TABLE 12.3
Average annual returns and risk premiums, 1957–2005

Investment	Arithmetic Average Return (%)	Risk Premium (%)
Canadian common stocks	10.97	4.35
U.S. common stocks (Cdn. $)	12.31	5.69
Long bonds	8.88	2.25
Small stocks	14.16	7.53
Inflation	4.21	−2.42
Treasury bills	6.62	0.00

Average return on small stocks is based on data from 1970 to 2005.

the next chapter is devoted to them. For now, part of the answer can be found by looking at the historical variability of the returns on these different investments. So, to get started, we now turn our attention to measuring variability in returns.

CONCEPT QUESTIONS

1. What do we mean by excess return and risk premium?

2. What was the nominal risk premium on long bonds? The real risk premium?

3. What is the first lesson from capital market history?

THE VARIABILITY OF RETURNS: THE SECOND LESSON

We have already seen that the year-to-year returns on common stocks tend to be more volatile than the returns on, say, long-term bonds. Next we discuss measuring this variability so we can begin examining the subject of risk.

Frequency Distributions and Variability

To get started, we can draw a frequency distribution for the common Canadian stock returns similar to the one in Figure 12.5. What we have done here is to count the number of times the annual return on the common stock portfolio falls within each 5 percent range. For example, in Figure 12.5, the height of 1 in the range −25 percent to −30 percent means that 1 of the 49 annual returns was in that range.

Now we need to measure the spread in returns. We know, for example, that the return on Canadian common stocks in a typical year was 10.97 percent. We now want to know how far the actual return deviates from this average in a typical year. In other words, we need a measure of how volatile the return is. The **variance** and its square root, the **standard deviation,** are the most commonly used measures of volatility. We describe how to calculate them next.

variance
The average squared deviation between the actual return and the average return.

standard deviation
The positive square root of the variance.

The Historical Variance and Standard Deviation

The variance essentially measures the average squared difference between the actual returns and the average return. The bigger this number is, the more the actual returns tend to differ from the average return. Also, the larger the variance or standard deviation is, the more spread out the returns are.

The way we calculate the variance and standard deviation depends on the situation. In this chapter, we are looking at historical returns; so the procedure we describe here is the correct one for calculating the historical variance and standard deviation. If we were examining projected future returns, the procedure would be different. We describe this procedure in the next chapter.

To illustrate how we calculate the historical variance, suppose a particular investment had returns of 10 percent, 12 percent, 3 percent, and −9 percent over the last four years. The average return is $(.10 + .12 + .03 − .09)/4 = 4\%$. Notice that the return is never actually equal to 4 percent. Instead, the first return deviates from the average by $.10 − .04 = .06$, the second return deviates from the average by .12 − .04 = .08, and so on. To compute the variance, we square each of these deviations, add them up, and divide the result by the number of returns less one, or three in this case. This information is summarized in the following table:

	(1) Actual Returns	(2) Average Return	(3) Deviation (1) − (2)	(4) Squared Deviation
	.10	.04	.06	.0036
	.12	.04	.08	.0064
	.03	.04	−.01	.0001
	−.09	.04	−.13	.0169
Totals	.16		.00	.0270

In the first column, we write down the four actual returns. In the third column, we calculate the difference between the actual returns and the average by subtracting out 4 percent. Finally, in the fourth column, we square the numbers in column 3 to get the squared deviations from the average.

The variance can now be calculated by dividing .0270, the sum of the squared deviations, by the number of returns less one. Let Var(R) or σ^2 (read this as sigma squared) stand for the variance of the return:

$$\text{Var}(R) = \sigma^2 = .027/(4-1) = .009$$

The standard deviation is the square root of the variance. So, if SD(R) or σ stands for the standard deviation of return:

$$\text{SD}(R) = \sigma = \sqrt{0.009} = .09487$$

The square root of the variance is used because the variance is measured in squared percentages and, thus, is hard to interpret. The standard deviation is an ordinary percentage, so the answer here could be written as 9.487 percent.

FIGURE 12.5

Frequency distribution of returns on Canadian common stocks

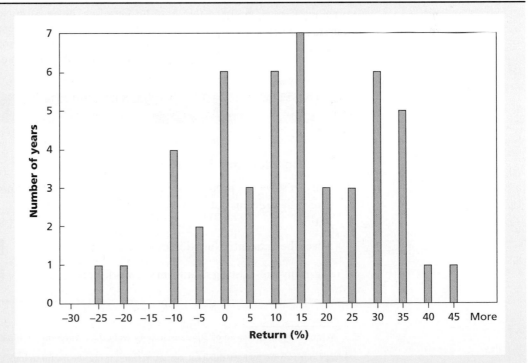

In the preceding table, notice that the sum of the deviations is equal to zero. This is always the case, and it provides a good way to check your work. In general, if we have T historical returns, where T is some number, we can write the historical variance as:

$$Var(R) = (1/(T-1)) \, [(R_1 - \overline{R})^2 + \ldots + (R_T - \overline{R})^2] \qquad [12.3]$$

This formula tells us to do just what we did above: Take each of the T individual returns $(R_1, R_2, \ldots)$ and subtract the average return, $\overline{R}$; square the result, and add them up; finally, divide this total by the number of returns less one $(T-1)$.[5] The standard deviation is always the square root of Var(R).

Each of the above calculations can also be completed using an Excel spreadsheet. Once your data are entered, you can use the following functions:

$$\text{Average} = \text{AVERAGE( )}$$
$$\text{Variance} = \text{VAR( )}$$
$$\text{Standard Deviation} = \text{STDEV( )}$$

EXAMPLE 12.2: Calculating the Variance and Standard Deviation

Suppose Northern Radio Comm and the Canadian Empire Bank have experienced the following returns in the last four years:

Year	Northern Radio Comm Returns	Canadian Empire Bank Returns
2001	−.20	.05
2002	.50	.09
2003	.30	−.12
2004	.10	.20

What are the average returns? The variances? The standard deviations? Which investment was more volatile?

To calculate the average returns, we add the returns and divide by four. The results are:

Northern Radio Comm average return = $\overline{R}$ = .70/4 = .175
Canadian Empire Bank average return = $\overline{R}$ = .22/4 = .055

To calculate the variance for Northern Radio Comm, we can summarize the relevant calculations as follows:

Year	(1) Actual Returns	(2) Average Returns	(3) Deviation (1) − (2)	(4) Squared Deviation
2001	−.20	.175	−.375	.140625
2002	.50	.175	.325	.105625
2003	.30	.175	.125	.015625
2004	.10	.175	−.075	.005625
Totals	.70		.000	.267500

Since there are four years of returns, we calculate the variances by dividing .2675 by (4 − 1) = 3:

	Northern Radio Comm	Canadian Empire Bank
Variance (σ^2)	.2675/3 = .0892	.0529/3 = .0176
Standard deviation (σ)	$\sqrt{.0892}$ = .2987	0176 = .1327

For practice, check that you get the same answer as we do for Canadian Empire Bank. Notice that the standard deviation for Northern Radio Comm, 29.87 percent, is a little more than twice Canadian Empire's 13.27 percent; Northern Radio Comm is thus the more volatile investment.[6]

CALCULATOR HINTS

(Using Texas Instruments BA II Plus Financial Calculator)

Finding Standard Deviation (s) and Mean (x)

You can solve this problem using a financial calculator by doing the following:
Clear any previous data:

Action	Keystrokes
Select the data entry function of the calculator	**2nd** [DATA]
Clear any pre-existing data from the worksheet	**2nd** [CLR WORK]

---

5 We divide by $T-1$ instead of T because our 49 years' data represent a sample, not the full population.

6 Since our two stocks have different average returns, it may be useful to look at their risks in comparison to the average returns. The coefficient of variation shows this. It equals (Standard deviation)/(Average return).

CALCULATOR HINTS

Enter the data into the calculator:

Keystrokes			Calculator Display	
−0.20 ENTER ↓			X01 =	−0.20
		↓	Y01 =	1.00
0.50 ENTER ↓			X02 =	0.50
		↓	Y02 =	1.00
0.30 ENTER ↓			X03 =	0.30
		↓	Y03 =	1.00
0.10 ENTER ↓			X04 =	0.10
		↓	Y04 =	1.00

Before calculating the statistics:

Action	Keystroke		Calculator Display
Select the statistics calculation function of the calculator	2nd	[STAT]	Will display any pre-existing date from prior use
Clear any pre-existing data from the worksheet	2nd	[CLR WORK]	LIN
Set the calculator to 1-variable calculation mode	2nd	[SET]	
	Repeatedly tap the [SET] key to toggle the different options.		1-V

To view statistics of data set:

Action	Keystroke	Calculator Display	
To view mean (x), toggle down	↓	x =	0.1750
To view sample standard deviation (s), toggle downward	↓	Sx =	0.2986

The Historical Record

Table 12.4 summarizes much of our discussion of capital market history so far. It displays average returns and standard deviations of annual returns. We used spreadsheet software to calculate these standard deviations. For example, in Excel it is STDEV. In Table 12.4, notice, for example, that the standard deviation for the Canadian common stock portfolio (16.17 percent per year) is about four times as large as the T-bill portfolio's standard deviation (3.66 percent per year). We return to these figures momentarily.

Normal Distribution

normal distribution
A symmetric, bell-shaped frequency distribution that can be defined by its mean and standard deviation.

For many different random events in nature, a particular frequency distribution, the **normal distribution** (or bell curve), is useful for describing the probability of ending up in a given range. For example, the idea behind grading on a curve comes from the fact that exam scores often resemble a bell curve.

Figure 12.6 illustrates a normal distribution and its distinctive bell shape. As you can see, this distribution has a much cleaner appearance than the actual return distributions illustrated in

Figure 12.5. Even so, like the normal distribution, the actual distributions do appear to be at least roughly mound-shaped and symmetrical. When this is true, the normal distribution is often a very good approximation.[7]

Also, keep in mind that the distributions in Figure 12.5 are based on only 49 yearly observations while Figure 12.6 is, in principle, based on an infinite number. So, if we had been able to observe returns for, say, 1,000 years, we might have filled in a lot of the irregularities and ended up with a much smoother picture. For our purposes, it is enough to observe that the returns are at least roughly normally distributed.

The usefulness of the normal distribution stems from the fact that it is completely described by the average and standard deviation. If you have these two numbers, there is nothing else to know. For example, with a normal distribution, the probability that we end up within one standard deviation of the average is about two-thirds. The probability that we end up within two standard deviations is about 95 percent. Finally, the probability of being more than three standard deviations away from the average is less than 1 percent. These ranges and the probabilities are illustrated in Figure 12.6.

To see why this is useful, recall from Table 12.4 that the standard deviation of returns on Canadian common stocks is 16.17 percent. The average return is 10.97 percent. So, assuming that the frequency distribution is at least approximately normal, the probability that the return in a given year is in the range −5.20 percent to 27.14 percent (10.97 percent plus or minus one standard deviation, 16.17 percent) is about two-thirds. This range is illustrated in Figure 12.6. In other words, there is about one chance in three that the return is outside the range. This literally tells you that, if you buy stocks in larger companies, you should expect to be outside this range in one year out of every three. This reinforces our earlier observations about stock market volatility. However, there is only a 5 percent chance (approximately) that we would end up outside the range −21.37 percent to 43.31 percent (10.97 percent plus or minus $2 \times 16.17\%$). These points are also illustrated in Figure 12.6.

TABLE 12.4

Historical returns and standard deviations, 1957–2005

Investment	Arithmetic Average Return (%)	Standard Deviation (%)
Canadian common stocks	10.97	16.17
U.S. common stocks (Cdn. $)	12.31	16.99
Long bonds	8.88	10.15
Small stocks	14.16	22.58
Inflation	4.21	3.22
Treasury bills	6.62	3.66

Average return and standard deviation on small stocks is based on data from 1970 to 2005.

FIGURE 12.6

The normal distribution. Illustrated returns are based on the historical return and standard deviation for a portfolio of large common stocks.

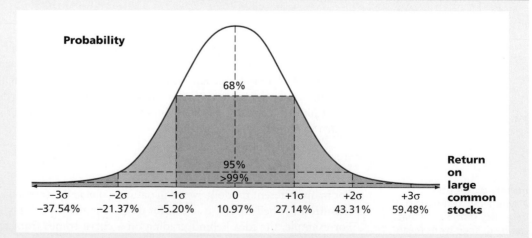

---

7 It is debatable whether such a smooth picture would necessarily always be a normal distribution. But we assume it would be normal to make the statistical discussion as simple as possible.

Value at Risk

We can take this one step further to create a measure of risk that is widely used. Suppose you are a risk management executive at a bank that has $100 million invested in stocks. You want to know how much you can lose in any one year. We just showed that based on historical data you would be outside the range of –21.37 percent to 43.31 percent only 5 percent of the time. Because we based this on a normal distribution, you know that the distribution is symmetric. In other words, the 5 percent chance of being outside the range breaks down into a 2.5 percent probability of a return above 43.31 percent and an equal 2.5 percent chance of a return below –21.37 percent. You want to find out how much you can lose, so you can safely ignore the chance of a return above 43.31 percent. Instead you focus on the 2.5 percent probability of a loss of more than 21.37 percent of the portfolio.

value at risk (VaR)
Statistical measure of maximum loss used by banks and other financial institutions to manage risk exposures.

What you have discovered is that 97.5 percent of the time, your loss will not exceed this level. On a portfolio of $100 million, this means that your maximum loss estimate is $100 million × (–21.37%) = –$21.37 million. This number is called **value at risk** or **VaR.** You can find examples of VaR in the annual report of Bank of Montreal and all other Canadian banks. Since VaR is a measure of possible loss, financial institutions use it in determining adequate capital levels.

The Second Lesson

Our observations concerning the year-to-year variability in returns are the basis for our second lesson from capital market history. On average, bearing risk is handsomely rewarded, but in a given year, there is a significant chance of a dramatic change in value. Thus, our second lesson is: The greater the potential reward, the greater is the risk.

Small stocks in Table 12.4 illustrate the second lesson over again, as this investment has both the highest return and the largest standard deviation of any Canadian investment.

Using Capital Market History

Based on the discussion in this section, you should begin to have an idea of the risks and rewards from investing. For example, suppose Canada Treasury bills are paying about 5 percent. Suppose further we have an investment that we think has about the same risk as a portfolio of large-firm Canadian common stocks. At a minimum, what return would this investment have to offer to catch our interest?

From Table 12.3, the risk premium on Canadian common stocks has been 4.35 percent historically, so a reasonable estimate of our required return would be this premium plus the T-bill rate, 5.0% + 4.35% = 9.35%. This may strike you as low, as during the 1990s, as well as in the years immediately after World War II, double-digit returns on Canadian and U.S. stocks were common, as Table 12.1 shows. Currently most financial executives and professional investment managers expect lower returns and smaller risk premiums in the future.[8]

We agree with their expectation and this relates to our earlier discussion of which data to use to calculate the market risk premium. In Table 12.1 we display returns data back to 1948 but only go back to 1957 when we calculate risk premiums in Table 12.3. This drops off the high returns experienced in many of the post-war years. If we recalculate the returns and risk premiums in Table 12.3 going all the way back to 1948, we arrive at a market risk premium of 6.94 percent. We think this is too high looking to the future but we have to recognize that this is a controversial point over which experts disagree.

We discuss the relationship between risk and required return in more detail in the next chapter.

---

8 A survey of academic views on the market risk premium is in I. Welch, "Views of Financial Economists on the Equity Risk Premium and Other Issues," *Journal of Business* 73 (October 2000), pp. 501–537. Mercer Investment Consulting surveys professional investment managers in its annual *Fearless Forecast* available in the Knowledge Center at *http://merceric.com.*

EXAMPLE 12.3: Investing in Growth Stocks

The phrase *growth stock* is frequently a euphemism for *small-company stock*. Are such investments suitable for elderly, conservative investors? Before answering, you should consider the historical volatility. For example, from the historical record, what is the approximate probability that you could actually lose 10 percent or more of your money in a single year if you buy a portfolio of such companies?

Looking back at Table 12.4, the average return on small stocks is 14.16 percent and the standard deviation is 22.58 percent. Assuming the returns are approximately normal, there is about a one-third probability that you could experience a return outside the range –8.42 percent to 36.74 percent (14.16 plus or minus 22.58 percent).

Because the normal distribution is symmetric, the odds of being above or below this range are equal. There is thus a one-sixth chance (half of one-third) that you could lose more than 8.42 percent. So you should expect this to happen once in every six years, on average. Such investments can thus be very volatile, and they are not well suited for those who cannot afford the risk.[9]

CONCEPT QUESTIONS

1. In words, how do we calculate a variance? A standard deviation?

2. With a normal distribution, what is the probability of ending up more than one standard deviation below the average?

3. Assuming that long-term bonds have an approximately normal distribution, what is the approximate probability of earning 17 percent or more in a given year? With T-bills, what is this probability?

4. What is the first lesson from capital market history? The second?

 **12.5**

MORE ON AVERAGE RETURNS

Thus far in this chapter, we have looked closely at simple average returns. But there is another way of computing an average return. The fact that average returns are calculated two different ways leads to some confusion, so our goal in this section is to explain the two approaches and also the circumstances under which each is appropriate.

Arithmetic versus Geometric Averages

Let's start with a simple example. Suppose you buy a particular stock for $200. Unfortunately, the first year you own it, it falls to $100. The second year you own it, it rises back to $200, leaving you where you started (no dividends were paid).

What was your average return on this investment? Common sense seems to say that your average return must be exactly zero since you started with $200 and ended with $200. But if we calculate the returns year-by-year, we see that you lost 50 percent the first year (you lost half of your money). The second year, you made 100 percent (you doubled your money). Your average return over the two years was thus (–50% + 100%)/2 = 25%!

So which is correct, 0 percent or 25 percent? The answer is that both are correct: They just answer different questions. The 0 percent is called the **geometric average return**. The 25 percent is called the **arithmetic average return**. The geometric average return answers the question *"What was your average compound return per year over a particular period?"* The arithmetic average return answers the question *"What was your return in an average year over a particular period?"*

Notice that, in previous sections, the average returns we calculated were all arithmetic averages, so we already know how to calculate them. What we need to do now is (1) learn how to calculate geometric averages and (2) learn the circumstances under which one average is more meaningful than the other.

geometric average return
The average compound return earned per year over a multiyear period.

arithmetic average return
The return earned in an average year over a multiyear period.

---

9 Some researchers argue that elderly investors should hold equities to protect against outliving their assets:
M. A. Milevsky, K. Ho, and C. Robinson, "Asset Allocation via the Conditional First Exit Time or How to Avoid Outliving Your Money," *Review of Quantitative Finance and Accounting* 9 (July 1997), pp. 53–70.

Calculating Geometric Average Returns

First, to illustrate how we calculate a geometric average return, suppose a particular investment had annual returns of 10 percent, 12 percent, 3 percent, and –9 percent over the last four years. The geometric average return over this four-year period is calculated as $(1.10 \times 1.12 \times 1.03 \times .91)^{1/4} - 1 = 3.66\%$. In contrast, the average arithmetic return we have been calculating is $(.10 + .12 + .03 - .09)/4 = 4.0\%$.

In general, if we have T years of returns, the geometric average return over these T years is calculated using this formula:

$$\text{Geometric average return} = [(1 + R_1) \times (1 + R_2) \times \cdots \times (1 + R_T)]^{1/T} - 1 \qquad [\textbf{12.4}]$$

This formula tells us that four steps are required:

1. Take each of the T annual returns $R_1, R_2, \ldots, R_T$ and add a one to each (after converting them to decimals!).

2. Multiply all the numbers from step 1 together.

3. Take the result from step 2 and raise it to the power of $1/T$.

4. Finally, subtract one from the result of step 3. The result is the geometric average return.

EXAMPLE 12.4: Calculating the Geometric Average Return

Calculate the geometric average return for S&P 500 large-cap stocks for the first five years in Table 12.1, 1948–1952.

First, convert percentages to decimal returns, add one, and then calculate their product:

S&P 500 Returns	Product
5.50	1.055
22.15	×1.2215
39.18	×1.3918
15.00	×1.15
13.68	×1.1368
	2.3448

Notice that the number 2.3448 is what our investment is worth after five years if we started with a one dollar investment. The geometric average return is then calculated as

Geometric average return = $2.3448^{1/5} - 1 = 0.1858$, or 18.58%

Thus the geometric average return is about 18.58 percent in this example. Here is a tip: If you are using a financial calculator, you can put $1 in as the present value, $2.3448 as the future value, and 5 as the number of periods. Then, solve for the unknown rate. You should get the same answer we did.

One thing you may have noticed in our examples thus far is that the geometric average returns seem to be smaller. It turns out that this will always be true (as long as the returns are not all identical, in which case the two "averages" would be the same).

As shown in Table 12.5, the geometric averages are all smaller, but the magnitude of the difference varies quite a bit. The reason is that the difference is greater for more volatile investments. In fact, there is useful approximation. Assuming all the numbers are expressed in decimals (as opposed to percentages), the geometric average return is approximately equal to the arithmetic average return minus half the variance. For example, looking at the Canadian stocks, the arithmetic average is .1097% and the standard deviation is .1617, implying that the variance is .0261. The approximate geometric average is thus $.1097 - .0251/2 = .0966$, which is quite close to the actual value.

TABLE 12.5 Geometric versus Arithmetic Average Returns, 1957–2005	Average Return		
Investment	Arithmetic (%)	Geometric (%)	Standard Deviation (%)
Canadian common stocks	10.97	9.78	16.17
U.S. common stocks (Cdn. $)	12.31	11.00	16.99
Long bonds	8.88	8.42	10.15
Small stocks	14.16	11.53	22.58
Inflation	4.21	4.16	3.22
Treasury bills	6.62	6.56	3.66

Average return and standard deviation on small stocks is based on data from 1970 to 2005.

EXAMPLE 12.5: More Geometric Averages

Take a look back at Figure 12.4. There, we showed the value of a $1 investment after 49 years. Use the value for the S&P/TSX Composite stocks to check the geometric average in Table 12.5.

In Figure 12.4, the S&P/TSX Composite stocks grew to $96.61 over 49 years. The geometric average return is thus:

Geometric average return = $96.61^{1/49} - 1 = 0.978$ or 9.78%

This 9.78% is the value shown in Table 12.5. For practice, check some of the other numbers in Table 12.5 the same way.

Arithmetic Average Return or Geometric Average Return?

When we look at historical returns, the difference between the geometric and arithmetic average returns isn't too hard to understand. To put it slightly differently, the geometric average tells you what you actually earned per year on average, compounded annually. The arithmetic average tells you what you earned in a typical year. You should use whichever one answers the question you want answered.

A somewhat trickier question concerns which average return to use when forecasting future wealth levels, and there's a lot of confusion on this point among analysts and financial planners. First, let's get one thing straight: If you *know* the true arithmetic average return, then this is what you should use in your forecast. So, for example, if you know the arithmetic return is 10 percent, then your best guess of the value of a $1,000 investment in 10 years is the future value of $1,000 at 10 percent for 10 years, or $2,593.74.

The problem we face, however, is that we usually only have *estimates* of the arithmetic and geometric returns, and estimates have errors. In this case, the arithmetic average return is probably too high for longer periods and the geometric average is probably too low for shorter periods. So, you should regard long-run projected wealth levels calculated using arithmetic averages as optimistic. Short-run projected wealth levels calculated using geometric averages are probably pessimistic.

As a practical matter, if you are using averages calculated over a long period of time (such as the 49 years we use) to forecast, then you should just split the difference between the arithmetic and geometric average returns. What this means is calculating the geometric mean market risk premium from Table 12.5: 9.78% − 6.56% = 3.22%. Our revised estimate of the market risk premium then becomes the average of this number and the arithmetic mean risk premium on Canadian common stocks of 4.35 percent from Table 12.3: (3.22% + 4.35%) /2 = 3.79%.[10]

This concludes our discussion of geometric versus arithmetic averages. One last note: In the future, when we say "average return," we mean arithmetic unless we explicitly say otherwise.

CONCEPT QUESTIONS

1. If you wanted to forecast what the stock market is going to do over the next year, should you use an arithmetic or geometric average?

2. If you wanted to forecast what the stock market is going to do over the next century, should you use an arithmetic or geometric average?

 12.6

CAPITAL MARKET EFFICIENCY

Capital market history suggests that the market values of stocks and bonds can fluctuate widely from year to year. Why does this occur? At least part of the answer is that prices change because new information arrives, and investors reassess asset values based on that information.

The behaviour of market prices has been extensively studied. A question that has received particular attention is whether prices adjust quickly and correctly when new information arrives.

10 Our approach here is adapted from M.E. Blume, "Unbiased Estimators of Long-Run Expected Rates of Return," *Journal of the American Statistical Association* 69:347 (September 1974), pp. 634–638.

efficient capital market
Market in which security prices reflect available information.

A market is said to be efficient if this is the case. To be more precise, in an **efficient capital market,** current market prices fully reflect available information. By this we simply mean that, based on available information, there is no reason to believe the current price is too low or too high.

The concept of market efficiency is a rich one, and much has been written about it. A full discussion of the subject goes beyond the scope of our study of corporate finance. However, because the concept figures so prominently in studies of market history, we briefly describe the key points here.

Price Behaviour in an Efficient Market

To illustrate how prices behave in an efficient market, suppose the F-Stop Camera Corporation (FCC) has, through years of secret research and development, developed a camera that doubles the speed of available autofocusing systems. FCC's capital budgeting analysis suggests that launching the new camera is a highly profitable move; in other words, the NPV appears to be positive and substantial. The key assumption thus far is that FCC has not released any information about the new system, so the fact of its existence is only inside information.

Now consider a share of stock in FCC. In an efficient market, its price reflects what is known about FCC's current operations and profitability, and it reflects market opinion about FCC's potential for future growth and profits. The value of the new autofocusing system is not reflected, however, because the market is unaware of its existence.

If the market agrees with FCC's assessment of the value of the new project, FCC's stock price rises when the decision to launch is made public. For example, assume the announcement is made in a press release on Wednesday morning. In an efficient market, the price of shares in FCC adjusts quickly to this new information. Investors should not be able to buy the stock on Wednesday afternoon and make a profit on Thursday. This would imply that it took the stock market a full day to realize the implication of the FCC press release. If the market is efficient, on Wednesday afternoon the price of FCC shares already reflects the information contained in that morning's press release.

Figure 12.7 presents three possible stock price adjustments for FCC. In Figure 12.7, Day 0 represents the announcement day. As illustrated, before the announcement, FCC's stock sells for $140 per share. The NPV per share of the new system is, say, $40, so the new price would be $180 once the value of the new project is fully reflected.

The solid line in Figure 12.7 represents the path taken by the stock price in an efficient market. In this case, the price adjusts immediately to the new information and no further changes in the price of the stock occur. The broken line in Figure 12.7 depicts a delayed reaction. Here it takes the market eight days or so to fully absorb the information. Finally, the dotted line illustrates an overreaction and subsequent adjustments to the correct price.

The broken line and the dotted line in Figure 12.7 illustrate paths that the stock price might take in an inefficient market. If, for example, stock prices don't adjust immediately to new information (the broken line), buying stock immediately following the release of new information and then selling it several days later would be a positive NPV activity because the price is too low for several days after the announcement.

The Efficient Markets Hypothesis

efficient markets hypothesis (EMH)
The hypothesis is that actual capital markets, such as the TSX, are efficient.

The **efficient markets hypothesis (EMH)** asserts that well-organized capital markets such as the TSX and the NYSE are efficient markets, at least as a practical matter. In other words, an advocate of the EMH might argue that while inefficiencies may exist, they are relatively small and not common.

When a market is efficient, there is a very important implication for market participants: All investments in an efficient market are zero NPV investments. The reason is not complicated. If prices are neither too low nor too high, the difference between the market value of an investment and its cost is zero; hence, the NPV is zero. As a result, in an efficient market, investors get exactly what they pay for when they buy securities, and firms receive exactly what their stocks and bonds are worth when they sell them.

What makes a market efficient is competition among investors. Many individuals spend their lives trying to find mispriced stocks. For any given stock, they study what has happened in the

FIGURE 12.7

Reaction of stock price to new information in efficient and inefficient markets

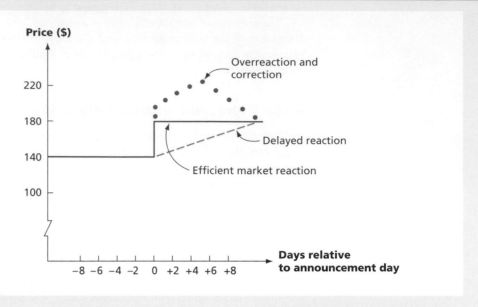

Efficient market reaction: The price instantaneously adjusts to and fully reflects new information; there is no tendency for subsequent increases and decreases.
Delayed reaction: The price partially adjusts to the new information; 10 days elapse before the price completely reflects the new information.
Overreaction: The price overadjusts to the new information; it "overshoots" the new price and subsequently corrects.

past to the stock price and its dividends. They learn, to the extent possible, what a company's earnings have been, how much it owes to creditors, what taxes it pays, what businesses it is in, what new investments are planned, how sensitive it is to changes in the economy, and so on.

Not only is there a great deal to know about any particular company, but there is also a powerful incentive for knowing it; namely, the profit motive. If you know more about some company than other investors in the marketplace, you can profit from that knowledge by investing in the company's stock if you have good news and selling it if you have bad news.

The logical consequence of all this information being gathered and analyzed is that mispriced stocks will become fewer and fewer. In other words, because of competition among investors, the market is becoming increasingly efficient. A kind of equilibrium comes into being where there is just enough mispricing around for those who are best at identifying it to make a living at it. For most other investors, the activity of information gathering and analysis does not pay. We can use Microsoft to illustrate the competition for information. A survey found that there are 60 analysts on Wall Street, Bay Street, and around the world assigned to following this stock. As a result, the chances are very low that one analyst will discover some information or insight into the company that is unknown to the other 59.

No idea in finance has attracted as much attention as that of efficient markets, and not all the attention has been flattering. Rather than rehash the arguments here, we are content to observe that some markets are more efficient than others. For example, financial markets on the whole are probably much more efficient than real asset markets.

Efficiency does imply that the price a firm obtains when it sells a share of its stock is a fair price in the sense that it reflects the value of that stock given the information available about it. Shareholders do not have to worry that they are paying too much for a stock with a low dividend or some other sort of characteristic because the market has already incorporated that characteristic into the price. We sometimes say that the information has been "priced out."

The concept of efficient markets can be explained further by replying to a frequent objection. It is sometimes argued that the market cannot be efficient because stock prices fluctuate from day to day. If the prices are right, the argument goes, then why do they change so much and so often? From our prior discussion, these price movements are in no way inconsistent with

www.microsoft.com/canada

In Their Own Words . . .

Air Canada, WestJet get "good news" from demise

WestJet can resurrect old business model; Air Canada says it'll add flights if needed

AIR CANADA AND WESTJET AIRLINES LTD. will be big winners from the demise of small but aggresive deep-discount airline **Jetsgo Corp.**, which comes at a time of continued major turbulence for global aviation, industry analysts say.

Jetsgo's forced landing is "very good news" for the other carriers, said Joe d'Cruz, who heads the aerospace management program at the University of Toronto's Rotman School of Management. "It means WestJet can heave a huge sigh of relief. It can go back to its old business model, which was very successful, and that will take pressure off Air Canada."

"What happened today is very unfortunate for the employees and travellers who have been stranded, but this will stabilize the industry," said analyst Ben Cherniavsky of Raymond James Ltd. in Vancouver.

Investors placed their bets firmly on that outcome yesterday.

Shares of Calgary-based WestJet, Canada's second-largest carrier, skyrocketed to as high as $16.90 on the Toronto Stock Exchange, up more than 51 per cent from Thursday's finish, as investors considered the prospect of it regaining a large chunk of Jetsgo's estimated 10-percent share of the domestic market and of a return to more rational pricing. The shares closed at $15.60, up $4.43.

Meanwhile the stock of **ACE Aviation Holdings Inc.**, the Montreal-based parent of Air Canada, the nation's largest airline, which emerged last fall from 18 months of protection under the Companies' Creditors Arrangement Act (CCAA), closed at $37, a new high, up $4.81 or nearly 15 percent.

Montreal-based Jetsgo announced just after midnight Thursday that it was grounding its 25-plane fleet and seeking CCAA protection. The 2 1/2-year-old airline, which had expanded at breakneck speed to a total of 19 routes in Canada and 10 in the United States, is credited with helping force down ticket prices across the domestic industry.

The company's crash comes as air carriers around the world are still trying to cope with five years of turmoil that has led to an orgy of liquidation and consolidation, whipped up by vicious fare wars and soaring fuel costs and worsened by such events as the Sept. 11, 2001, terrorist attacks.

WestJet chief executive officer Clive Beddoe responded to Jetsgo's demise yesterday by delaying plans to retire 18 older aircraft later this year as the Calgary airline takes delivery of 15 new ones it has ordered.

The loss of a competitor, he said, "opens up the opportunity for us to expand our service to more cities, with more flights."

Mr. Beddoe added: "I've maintained for a long time that Canada is only large enough to sustain two significant carriers."

He also said he expects to raise fares by about 10 per cent. "The reality is you can't fly around with $55 oil, burning fuel at the pace we do, and not have higher prices."

One person close to Air Canada said it expects WestJet to gain most from the Jetsgo development.

Still, Air Canada vice-president Ben Smith said the company will add flights on a number of routes "where we see demand increase for Air Canada service as a direct result of the withdrawal of Jetsgo."

Analyst Jacques Kavafian at Research Capital Corp. said Jetsgo's disappearance will allow Air Canada and WestJet to raise prices to more profitable levels. "They don't have to gouge consumers," he said. "They just have to go up a little bit, enough that consumers are reliably transported. You can have cheap fares if you want, but if you're stranded, that doesn't help you."

As well, he does not expect a new competitor to replace Jetsgo. "WestJet and Air Canada are almost everywhere ... so I don't think there'll be another carrier coming out and starting up in a big way."

Jetsgo's pain: Their gain

ACE Aviation Holdings
Market capitalization: $3.3-billion
Street view: Analysts were quick to boost target prices and earnings estimates on shares in Air Canada's parent. Fadi Chamoun of UBS Investment Research dramatically raised his earnings forecast for this year to $3.30 a share from $2.26. He also tacked on $10 to his 12-month share target price to $45 from $35.

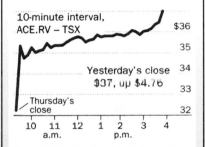

WestJet Airlines
Market capitalization: $2-billion
Street view: WestJet is seen by analysts as the airline with the most to gain from Jetsgo's demise. "WestJet is in a good position to capture much of Jetsgo's business because it has sufficient capacity," said Jacques Kavafian, an analyst at Research Capital.

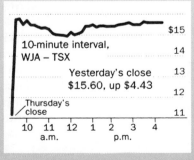

Source: Bloomberg financial services

Source: *The Globe and Mail*, March 12, 2005, p. B5. By John Partridge. Used with permission.

efficiency. Investors are bombarded with information every day. The fact that prices fluctuate is, at least in part, a reflection of that information flow. In fact, the absence of price movements in a world that changes as rapidly as ours would suggest inefficiency.[11]

Market Efficiency—Forms and Evidence

It is common to distinguish between three forms of market efficiency. Depending on the degree of efficiency, we say that markets are either weak form efficient, semistrong form efficient, or strong form efficient. The difference between these forms relates to what information is reflected in prices.

We start with the extreme case. If the market is strong form efficient, then all information of every kind is reflected in stock prices. In such a market, there is no such thing as inside information. Thus, in our previous FCC example, we apparently were assuming the market was not strong form efficient.

Casual observation, particularly in recent years, suggests that inside information exists and it can be valuable to possess. Whether it is lawful or ethical to use that information is another issue. In any event, we conclude that private information about a particular stock may exist that is not currently reflected in the price of the stock. For example, prior knowledge of a takeover attempt could be very valuable.[12]

The second form of efficiency, semistrong efficiency, is the most controversial. In a market that is semistrong form efficient, all public information is reflected in the stock price. The reason this form is controversial is that it implies that a security analyst who tries to identify mispriced stocks using, for example, financial statement information is wasting time because that information is already reflected in the current price.

Studies of semistrong form efficiency include event studies that measure whether prices adjust rapidly to new information following the efficient markets pattern in Figure 12.7. Announcements of mergers, dividends, earnings, capital expenditures, and new issues of securities are a few examples. Although there are exceptions, event study tests for major exchanges including the TSX, NYSE, and Nasdaq generally support the view that these markets are semistrong efficient with respect to the arrival of new information. In fact, the tests suggest these markets are gifted with a certain amount of foresight. By this, we mean that news tends to leak out and be reflected in stock prices even before the official release of the information.

Referring back to Figure 12.7, what this means is that for stocks listed on major exchanges, the stock price reaction to new information is typically the one shown for an efficient market. In some cases, the price follows the pattern shown for overreaction and correction. For example, a recent study found that stocks recommended in *The Financial Post* "Hot Stock" column experienced price increases followed by declines.[13] Our conclusion here is that the market is mainly efficient but that there are some exceptions.

If the market is efficient in the semistrong form, no matter what publicly available information mutual fund managers rely on to pick stocks, their average returns should be the same as those of the average investor in the market as a whole. Researchers have tested mutual fund performance against a market index and found that, on average, fund managers have no special ability to beat the market.[14] This supports semistrong form efficiency. An important practical result

www.nationalpost.com/
financialpost

www.tdwaterhouse.ca

---

11 For a current Canadian study showing the impact of some of this daily information flow related to business relocation announcements, see, H. Bhabra, U. Lel, and D. Tirtiroglu, "Stock Market's Reaction to Business Relocations: Canadian Evidence," *Canadian Journal of Administrative Sciences,* December 2002, Vol. 19, Number 4, pp. 346–358.

12 The film, *Wall Street,* Twentieth Century Fox, 1987, realistically illustrates how valuable the information can be. The trading activities of company insiders in Canada can now be tracked on the System for Electronic Disclosure by Insiders at *www.sedi.ca.*

13 For more details see V. Mehrotra, W.W. Yu, and C. Zhang, "Market Reactions to *The Financial Post's* 'Hot Stock' Column," *Canadian Journal of Administrative Sciences* 16, June 1999, pp. 118-131.

14 A Canadian study is G. Athanassakos, P. Carayannopoulos, and M. Racine, "Mutual Fund Performance: The Canadian Experience Between 1985 and 1996," *Canadian Journal of Financial Planning of the CAFP,* June 2000, Vol. 1, Issue 2, pp. 5–9.

In Their Own Words . . .   A Case of Insider Trading in Canada

MICHAEL DEGROOTE AND AN ASSOCIATE settled one of the largest insider trading cases [in April 1993]. Mr DeGroote, who built Laidlaw over 30 years from a small trucking company into a waste management and transportation giant, resigned as an officer and director of the company in December 1990. He had sold control of Laidlaw to Canadian Pacific Ltd. two years earlier for $500 million.

Rather than a smooth transition, the first few months after Mr. DeGroote left Laidlaw have become a recurring nightmare for the company and many of those associated with it.

Laidlaw had been a favourite growth stock for investors in the 1980s, but its earnings fell apart in early 1991, shocking shareholders who believed the waste management sector was recession-proof.

[In] April [1993], Ontario securities regulators alleged that Seakist Overseas Ltd., which was based in the Channel Islands and directed by Mr. Henri Herbots, sold Laidlaw stock short using Mr. DeGroote's money and inside knowledge as a former Laidlaw officer and director that the company was doing much worse than the investing public knew.

Investors sell stock short when they expect its price to fall. When investors take short positions to "sell" stock they don't own at its current price and then "buy" it back in the future. If the price falls, investors can make a profit.

Mr. DeGroote lent Seakist $27 million (Canadian), at an annual interest rate of 20 percent, to run the short-selling effort, but he maintained he did not have or use inside information about Laidlaw in making the loan on an arm's-length basis.

Seakist opened an account with Midland Walwyn Capital Inc. on January 31, 1991, and, through former Midland broker, Keith Walker, sold short three million Laidlaw shares for about $61 million by March 13, when Laidlaw warned about its poor earnings. The stock fell 18.6 percent in the next trading session and by March 21, Seakist had covered its short positions for $44.5 million, making a $16.5 million profit on the deal.

Mr. Herbots said he devised the short-selling plan based solely on publicly available information.

The two sides agreed to disagree on many of the facts in the settlement, with Mr. DeGroote, Mr. Herbots, and Seakist losing their trading privileges in Ontario for five years, paying $5 million to the provincial treasury and $18 million to compensate investors adversely affected by the short selling. Midland and Mr. Walker paid their total commissions from Seakist's short selling—$304,286—to the provincial treasury.

Source: Abridged from Casey Mahood, "DeGroote Faces U.S. Suit," *The Globe and Mail's* "Report on Business," September 28, 1993, p. B1. Used with permission.

---

of such studies is the growth of index funds that follows a passive investment strategy of investing in the market index. For example, TD Waterhouse Canadian Index Fund invests in the S&P/TSX Composite and its performance tracks that of the index. The fund has lower expenses than an actively managed fund because it does not employ analysts to pick stocks. Investors who believe in market efficiency prefer index investing because market efficiency means that the analysts will not beat the market consistently.

The third form of efficiency, weak form efficiency, suggests that, at a minimum, the current price of a stock reflects its own past prices. In other words, studying past prices in an attempt to identify mispriced securities is futile if the market is weak form efficient. Research supporting weak form efficiency suggests that successive price changes are generally consistent with a random walk where deviations from expected return are random. Tests on both the TSX and NYSE support weak form efficiency, although the results are more conclusive for the NYSE. This form of efficiency might seem rather mild; however, it implies that searching for patterns in historical prices that identify mispriced stocks does not work in general. An exception to this statement occurred in the hot high tech market of the late 1990s. Some investors were able to achieve superior returns following momentum strategies based on the idea that stocks that went up yesterday are likely also to go up today. Day trading became very popular in this "momentum market."[15]

Although the bulk of the evidence supports the view that major markets such as the TSX, NYSE, and Nasdaq are reasonably efficient, we would not be fair if we did not note the existence of selected contrary results often termed anomalies. The most striking anomaly is the seasonality

www.tsx.com
www.nyse.com
www.nasdaq.com

---

15 A Canadian study on momentum is M. Inglis and S. Cleary, "Momentum in Canadian Stock Returns," *Canadian Journal of Administrative Sciences*, September 1998, pp. 279–291.

of stock prices. For instance, the January effect is the well-documented tendency for firms with small capitalizations to have abnormally high returns in the first five days of that month in both the United States and Canada.[16] While the effect is small relative to commissions on stock purchases and sales, investors who have decided to buy small capitalization stocks can exploit the anomaly by buying in December rather than in January.

In addition, the stock market crash of October 19, 1987, is extremely puzzling. The NYSE dropped by more than 20 percent and the TSE by more than 11 percent on a Monday following a weekend during which little surprising news was released. A drop of this magnitude for no apparent reason is not consistent with market efficiency. One theory sees the crash as evidence consistent with the bubble theory of speculative markets. That is, security prices sometimes move wildly above their true values. Eventually, prices fall back to their original level, causing great losses for investors. The tulip craze of the 17th century in Holland and the South Sea Bubble in England the following century are perhaps the two best-known bubbles. From the vantage point of 2003, it is clear that stocks of Internet startups experienced a speculative bubble in 1999.[17]

In summary, what does research on capital market history say about market efficiency? At risk of going out on a limb, the evidence does seem to tell us three things: First, prices do appear to respond very rapidly to new information, and the response is at least not grossly different from what we would expect in an efficient market. Second, the future of market prices, particularly in the short run, is very difficult to predict based on publicly available information. Third, if mispriced stocks do exist, there is no obvious means of identifying them. Put another way, simpleminded schemes based on public information will probably not be successful.[18]

EXAMPLE 12.6: The EMH and the Accounting Veil

The accounting profession provides firms with a significant amount of leeway in their reporting practices. Firms and their accountants have frequently been accused of misusing this leeway in hopes of boosting earning and stock prices.

However, accounting choice should not affect stock price if two conditions hold. First, enough information must be provided in the annual report so financial analysts can recast earnings under their own choice of accounting methods. Second, the market must be efficient in the semistrong form. In other words, the market must appropriate-

ly use all this accounting information to "lift the accounting veil" in determining the market price.

One example in which this occurred involved the Northland Bank. Before its failure in 1985, the bank used questionable accounting to cover up its exposure to bad energy loans in western Canada. According to the Estey Commission, which investigated the bank failure, "The financial statements became gold fillings covering cavities in the assets and in the earnings of the bank." Yet, research on stock prices prior to the collapse has shown that stock market investors were aware the bank was highly risky.[19]

CONCEPT QUESTIONS

1. What is an efficient market?

2. What are the forms of market efficiency?

3. What evidence exists that major stock markets are efficient?

4. Explain anomalies in the efficient market hypothesis.

---

16 The effect is international and has been documented in most stock exchanges around the world occurring immediately after the close of the tax year. See V. Jog, "Stock Pricing Anomalies Revisited," *Canadian Investment Review,* Winter 1998, pp. 28–33 and S. Elfakhani, L.J. Lockwood, and R.S. Zaher, "Small Firm and Value Effects in the Canadian Stock Market," *Journal of Financial Research* 21, Fall 1998, pp. 277–291.

17 See Matthew Bishop, "Bubble Trouble," *The Economist,* May 18, 2002 for an interesting discussion of the response to the Internet speculative bubble. This article is available online at *www.cfo.com/Article?article=7240.*

18 The suggested readings for this chapter give references to the large body of U.S. and Canadian research on efficient markets.

19 R. Giammarino, E. Schwartz, and J. Zechner, "Market Valuation of Bank Assets and Deposit Insurance in Canada," *Canadian Journal of Economics* 22 (February 1989), pp. 109–26.

In Their Own Words . . .   A Random Talk with Burton Malkiel

HOW WILL THE TECHNOLOGY BUBBLE BE REMEMBERED?

Historians will record the Internet bubble of the late 1990s as one of the greatest bubbles of all time. Valuations became truly unbelievable. During the Nifty Fifty craze, the well-known growth stocks may have sold at 60-, 70- or even 80-times earnings. During the Internet bubble, stocks would sell at 60-, 70- or 80-times sales. Priceline.com, one of the Internet companies that sold discounted airline tickets, was valued at one time with a market capitalization that was larger than the combined market capitalizations of Delta Airlines, American Airlines and United Airlines. At its low, Priceline sold for about a dollar a share. You even had enormous multi-billion dollar capitalizations from companies that had essentially no sales at all. They were just selling on a promise.

People confused the correct idea that the Internet was real, that it was going to mean some profound changes in the way we live and shop and get information, to saying that the ordinary rules of valuation didn't apply. Whatever business you are in, an asset can only be worth the present value of the cash flows that are going to be generated in the future.

Look at reports that were issued by Wall Street firms. You find statements such as "the old metrics are different this time." That has certainly proved to be wrong. Most of these Internet stocks today are selling at a tiny fraction of their high market valuations. It is not clear that any of them have a business model that is going to allow them to make money. In one sense, Amazon.com is a very successful company. But they have yet to show that they are able to make any money.

To be sure, the same thing happened in our past history. There were many people who laid railroad tracks during the railroad-ization of North America. There was overbuilding and most of them collapsed. We had hundreds of automobile manufacturers at one time.

But what didn't happen in the past were the market valuations assigned to these companies. Why did firms like Morgan Stanley and Merrill Lynch put out buy recommendations on all of these stocks when they were at or near their peaks? The real problem is that their well-known analysts were paid a lot of money, not necessarily to make correct judgments about whether stocks were good buys or not, but rather based on their success in bringing investment banking clients into the firm. Who knows whether they knew better or not? But there was a clear conflict of interest.

Here's another thing—the CNBC effect. You had people talking about these extraordinary gains, and [producers] didn't want a fuddy duddy value manager being interviewed on CNBC. [They] wanted the person who said Amazon.com has a price target of $500 a share. Those were the people who got on those shows. That fed the public enthusiasm. There were some people who got it right. They were generally the value managers who actually underperformed the market as a whole very badly during that period.

HOW DID INSTITUTIONAL INVESTORS COMPARE TO RETAIL INVESTORS?

The retail investors probably did a bit worse. Some of the institutional investors were sucked up in the enthusiasm and probably did overweight some of these stocks. But I think the real damage occurred with individual investors. It really worries me how sensitive the public money flows are to recent performance.

Having said that, everyone is ranked each quarter in the institutional business versus everyone else. The institutions—not quite to the extent that the public is—are not immune at all. Presumably the savvy institutions should be precisely the ones who lean against the wind. But if you look at the cash balances of mutual fund managers and institutional money managers, you find almost invariably their lowest cash balances are just at the peak of the market. They're almost perfect contrarian indicators.

I can remember arguments that I had with institutional investors in 1999, when I'd talk about the Pricelines of the world. People would say "You don't understand the value of the first mover. What a brilliant idea Priceline has. Don't worry that they're losing money now." Very clearly, there is soul searching to be done by the institutions.

Burton Malkiel is the Chemical Bank Chairman's Professor of Economics at Princeton University and author of *A Random Walk Down Wall Street*. His comments are excerpted (with permission) from *Canadian Investment Review*, Summer 2001.

12.7   SUMMARY AND CONCLUSIONS

This chapter explores the subject of capital market history. Such history is useful because it tells us what to expect in the way of returns from risky assets. We summed up our study of market history with two key lessons:

1. Risky assets, on average, earn a risk premium. There is a reward for bearing risk.

2. The greater the risk from a risky investment, the greater is the required reward.

These lessons have significant implications for financial managers. We consider these implications in the chapters ahead.

We also discussed the concept of market efficiency. In an efficient market, prices adjust quickly and correctly to new information. Consequently, asset prices in efficient markets are rarely too high or too low. How efficient capital markets (such as the TSX and NYSE) are is a matter of debate, but, at a minimum, they are probably much more efficient than most real asset markets.

Key Terms

arithmetic average return (page 354)
efficient capital market (page 357)
efficient markets hypothesis (EMH) (page 357)
geometric average return (page 354)
normal distribution (page 351)

risk premium (page 347)
standard deviation (page 348)
value at risk (VaR) (page 353)
variance (page 348)

Chapter Review Problems and Self-Test

12.1   Recent Return History Use Table 12.1 to calculate the average return over the five years 1998–2002 for Canadian common stocks, small stocks, and Treasury bills.

12.2   More Recent Return History Calculate the standard deviations using information from Problem 12.1. Which of the investments was the most volatile over this period?

Answers to Self-Test Problems

12.1   We calculate the averages as follows:

Year	TSX	Small	T-bills
1998	−0.01580	−0.1790	0.04740
1999	0.31590	0.2029	0.04660
2000	0.07410	−0.0429	0.05490
2001	−0.12600	0.0070	0.04700
2002	−0.12400	−0.0090	0.02500
Average	0.02484	−0.0042	0.04418

12.2   We first need to calculate the deviations from the average returns. Using the averages from Problem 12.1, we get:

Year	TSX	Small	T-bills
1998	−0.04064	−0.1748	0.00322
1999	0.29106	0.2071	0.00242
2000	0.04926	−0.0387	0.01072
2001	−0.15084	0.0112	0.00282
2002	−0.14884	−0.0048	−0.01918

We square the deviations and calculate the variances and standard deviations:

Year	TSX	Small	T-bills
1998	0.001652	0.030555	0.00001037
1999	0.084716	0.042890	0.00000586
2000	0.002427	0.001498	0.00011492
2001	0.022753	0.000125	0.00000795
2002	0.022153	0.000023	0.00036787
Variance	0.033425	0.018773	0.00012674
Standard deviation	0.182825	0.137014	0.01125797

To calculate the variances, we added the squared deviations and divided by four, the number of returns less one. Notice that the small stocks had substantially greater volatility with a smaller average return. Once again, such investments are risky, particularly over short periods.

Concepts Review and Critical Thinking Questions

1. Given that Nortel was up by more than 300 percent in the 12 months ending in July 2000, why didn't all investors hold Nortel?

2. Given that Hayes was down by 98 percent for 1998, why did some investors hold the stock? Why didn't they sell out before the price declined so sharply?

3. We have seen that, over long periods of time, stock investments have tended to substantially outperform bond investments. However, it is not at all uncommon to observe investors with long horizons holding entirely bonds. Are such investors irrational?

4. Explain why a characteristic of an efficient market is that investments in that market have zero NPVs.

5. A stock market analyst is able to identify mispriced stocks by comparing the average price for the last 10 days to the average price for the last 60 days. If this is true, what do you know about the market?

6. If a market is semistrong form efficient, is it also weak form efficient? Explain.

7. What are the implications of the efficient markets hypothesis for investors who buy and sell stocks in an attempt to "beat the market"?

8. Critically evaluate the following statement: Playing the stock market is like gambling. Such speculative investing has no social value, other than the pleasure people get from this form of gambling.

9. There are several celebrated investors and stock pickers frequently mentioned in the financial press who have recorded huge returns on their investments over the past two decades. Is the success of these particular investors an invalidation of the EMH? Explain.

10. For each of the following scenarios, discuss whether profit opportunities exist from trading in the stock of the firm under the conditions that (1) the market is not weak form efficient, (2) the market is weak form but not semistrong form efficient, (3) the market is semistrong form but not strong form efficient, and (4) the market is strong form efficient.

a. The stock price has risen steadily each day for the past 30 days.

b. The financial statements for a company were released three days ago, and you believe you've uncovered some anomalies in the company's inventory and cost control reporting techniques that are causing the firm's true liquidity strength to be understated.

c. You observe that the senior management of a company has been buying a lot of the company's stock on the open market over the past week.

Questions and Problems

**Basic
(Questions
1–14)**

1. **Calculating Returns** Suppose a stock had an initial price of $64 per share, paid a dividend of $1.75 per share during the year, and had an ending share price of $72. Compute the percentage total return.

2. **Calculating Yields** In Problem 1, what was the dividend yield? The capital gains yield?

3. **Return Calculations** Rework Problems 1 and 2 assuming the ending share price is $55.

4. **Calculating Arithmetic Returns** What is the arithmetic return for the S&P/TSX Composite Index from 1996 to 2005? The Scotia Capital Markets long bonds? You can find the data to solve this problem in Table 12.1.

5. **Calculating Geometric Returns** For the same time period as Problem 4, calculate the geometric return for the S&P/TSX Composite Index and the Scotia Capital Markets long bonds. What is the difference between the two averages?

6. **Calculating Returns** Suppose you bought a 9 percent coupon bond one year ago for $1,050. The bond sells for $1,080 today.

a. Assuming a $1,000 face value, what was your total dollar return on this investment over the past year?

**Basic
(continued)**

b. What was your total nominal rate of return on this investment over the past year?

c. If the inflation rate last year was 4 percent, what was your total real rate of return on this investment?

7. **Nominal versus Real Returns** What was the average annual return on Canadian stock from 1957 through 2005:

a. In nominal terms?

b. In real terms?

8. **Bond Returns** What is the historical real return on Scotia Capital Markets long bonds?

9. **Calculating Returns and Variability** Using the following returns, calculate the arithmetic average returns, the variances, and the standard deviations for X and Y.

	Returns	
Year	X	Y
1	14%	29%
2	20	– 7
3	– 9	–12
4	3	56
5	17	8

10. **Risk Premiums** Refer to Table 12.1 in the text and look at the period from 1970 through 1975.

a. Calculate the arithmetic average returns for large-company stocks and T-bills over this time period.

b. Calculate the standard deviation of the returns for large-company stocks and T-bills over this time period.

c. Calculate the observed risk premium in each year for the large-company stocks versus the T-bills. What was the average risk premium over this period? What was the standard deviation of the risk premium over this period?

d. Is it possible for the risk premium to be negative before an investment is undertaken? Can the risk premium be negative after the fact? Explain.

11. **Calculating Returns and Variability** You've observed the following returns on Crash-n-Burn Computer's stock over the past five years: 9 percent, –12 percent, 16 percent, 38 percent, and 11 percent.

a. What was the arithmetic average return on Crash-n-Burn's stock over this five-year period?

b. What was the variance of Crash-n-Burn's returns over this period? The standard deviation?

12. **Calculating Real Returns and Risk Premiums** For Problem 11, suppose the average inflation rate over this period was 3.5 percent and the average T-bill rate over the period was 4.2 percent.

a. What was the average real return on Crash-n-Burn's stock?

b. What was the average nominal risk premium on Crash-n-Burn's stock?

13. **Calculating Real Rates** Given the information in Problem 12, what was the average real risk-free rate over this time period? What was the average real risk premium?

14. **Effects of Inflation** Look at Table 12.1 in the text. When were T-bill rates at their highest over the period from 1957 through 2005? Why do you think they were so high during this period? What relationship underlies your answer?

**Intermediate
(Questions
15–21)**

15. **Calculating Investment Returns** You bought one of Great White Shark Repellant Co.'s 8 percent coupon bonds one year ago for $980. These bonds make annual payments and mature six years from now. Suppose you decide to sell your bonds today, when the required return on the bonds is 9 percent. If the inflation rate was 4.2 percent over the past year, what was your total real return on investment?

16. **Calculating Returns and Variability** You find a certain stock that had returns of 8 percent, –13 percent, –7 percent, and 29 percent for four of the last five years. If the average return of the stock over this period was 11 percent, what was the stock's return for the missing year? What is the standard deviation of the stock's return?

17. **Arithmetic and Geometric Returns** A stock has had returns of 29 percent, 14 percent, 23 percent, –8 percent, 9 percent, and –14 percent over the last six years. What are the arithmetic and geometric returns for the stock?

18. **Arithmetic and Geometric Returns** A stock has had the following year-end prices and dividends:

Year	Price	Dividend
1	$43.12	—
2	49.07	$0.55
3	51.19	0.60
4	47.24	0.63
5	56.09	0.72
6	67.21	0.81

What are the arithmetic and geometric returns for the stock?

Intermediate (continued)

19. **Using Return Distributions** Suppose the returns on long-term government bonds are normally distributed. Based on the historical record, what is the approximate probability that your return on these bonds will be less than −3.6 percent in a given year? What range of returns would you expect to see 95 percent of the time? What range would you expect to see 99 percent of the time?

20. **Using Return Distributions** Assuming that the returns from holding small-company stocks are normally distributed, what is the approximate probability that your money will double in value in a single year? What about triple in value?

21. **Distributions** In Problem 20, what is the probability that the return is less than −100 percent (think)? What are the implications for the distribution of returns?

Challenge (Questions 22–23)

22. **Using Probability Distributions** Suppose the returns on Canadian stocks are normally distributed. Based on the historical record, use the cumulative normal probability table (rounded to the nearest table value) in the appendix of the text to determine the probability that in any given year you will lose money by investing in common stock.

23. **Using Probability Distributions** Suppose the returns on Scotia Capital Markets long bonds and T-bills are normally distributed. Based on the historical record, use the cumulative normal probability table (rounded to the nearest table value) in the appendix of the text to answer the following questions:

    a. What is the probability that in any given year, the return on long bonds will be greater than 10 percent? Less than 0 percent?

    b. What is the probability that in any given year, the return on T-bills will be greater than 10 percent? Less than 0 percent?

    c. In 1979, the return on long bonds was −2.83 percent. How likely is it that this low of a return will recur at some point in the future? T-bills had a return of 11.01 percent in this same year. How likely is it that this high of a return on T-bills will recur at some point in the future?

S&P Problems

1. **Calculating Yields** Download the historical stock prices for Suncor Energy Inc. (SU) under the "Mthly. Adj. Prices" link. Find the closing stock price for the beginning and end of the prior two years. Now use the annual financial statements to find the dividend for each of these years. What was the capital gains yield and dividend yield for Suncor stock for each of these years? Now calculate the capital gains yield and dividend for Nexen Inc. (NXY). How do the returns for these two companies compare?

2. **Calculating Average Returns** Download the Monthly Adjusted Prices for ATI Technologies Inc. (ATYT). What is the return on the stock over the past 12 months? Now use the 1 Month Total Return and calculate the average monthly return. Is this one-twelfth of the annual return you calculated? Why or why not? What is the monthly standard deviation of ATI's stock over the past year?

Internet Application Questions

1. Russell Fuller and Richard Thaler operate an asset management company that capitalizes on market inefficiencies caused by investors' misprocessing of information. Explain the strategies for their

   a. Small/Mid-Cap Growth Fund

   b. Small-Cap Value Fund

   The website for the Fuller and Thaler Asset Management company is provided below:

   www.fullerthaler.com/

2. While evidence favouring the Efficient Market Hypothesis (EMH) is generally favourable for stock markets in the U.S. and Canada, there are several documented cases of persistent anomalies that defy the EMH. Pick two anomalies from the site listed below, and discuss whether investment strategies based on them can be profitably exploited in the future.

   www.investorhome.com/anomaly.htm

3. Valuing Internet stocks rattles even the best of professional analysts. The following sites provide pointers to understanding valuation of Internet stocks.

   a. stocks.miningco.com/money/stocks/library/weekly/aa040300a.htm

   b. FOOL ON THE HILL: An Investment Opinion at www.fool.com/EveningNews/1998/EveningNews981120.htm

   Pick an Internet stock such as Yahoo! at www.yahoo.com. Based on the comments in the sites above, do you think the Internet stock you have chosen is over- or under-valued?

4. You want to find the current market risk premium. Go to www.bmo.com/economic/index.html, follow the link to "The Monthly." What is the shortest maturity interest rate shown? What is the interest rate for this maturity? Using the Canadian common stock return in Table 12.3, what is the current market risk premium? What assumption are you making when calculating the risk premium?

Suggested Readings

Two good reviews of research on efficient markets in Canada are:

Z. Bodie, A. Kane, A. Marcus, S. Perrakis, and P. J. Ryan. *Investments.* 5th Canadian ed. Whitby, Ontario: McGraw-Hill Ryerson, 2005.

W. F. Sharpe, G. J. Alexander, J. V. Bailey, D. J. Fowler, and D. Domian. *Investments.* 3rd Canadian ed. Scarborough, Ontario: Prentice-Hall, 2000.

A useful source of highly readable current Canadian capital markets research is the *Canadian Investment Review.*

A readable article on behavioural finance and bubbles is:

Robert J. Shiller, "From Efficient Markets Theory to Behavioral Finance," *Journal of Economic Perspectives*, American Economic Association, vol. 17(1), pages 83–104, Winter 2003.

A readable article on forecasting returns is:

Eric, Jacquier. "Optimal Estimation of the Risk Premium for the Long Run and Asset Allocation: A Case of Compounded Estimation Risk." *Journal of Financial Econometrics* 3.1 (2005): 37–55.

CHAPTER 13

Return, Risk, and the Security Market Line

The Globe and Mail's website provides detailed statistics on mutual funds available to Canadian investors. For Bank of Montreal, Money Market Fund and TD Canadian Equity, and hundreds of others, the website shows past returns for periods from one month to 10 years and compares them against those of comparable funds and a relevant market index. The website also gives quantitative risk measures like standard deviation and beta.

The inclusion of such statistics on a popular website aimed at individual investors shows that they are of practical interest. It raises the question—how can investors use this information to rate securities such as mutual funds and equities? This chapter introduces the theory and practice of asset pricing and illustrates how to answer this question.

www.globefund.com

IN OUR LAST CHAPTER, we learned some important lessons from capital market history. Most importantly, there is a reward, on average, for bearing risk. We called this reward a *risk premium.* The second lesson is that this risk premium is larger for riskier investments. The principle that higher returns can be earned only by taking greater risks appeals to our moral sense that we cannot have something for nothing. This chapter explores the economic and managerial implications of this basic idea.

Thus far, we have concentrated mainly on the return behaviour of a few large portfolios. We need to expand our consideration to include individual assets and mutual funds. Accordingly, the purpose of this chapter is to provide the background necessary for learning how the risk premium is determined for such assets.

When we examine the risks associated with individual assets, we find two types of risk: systematic and unsystematic. This distinction is crucial because, as we see, systematic risks affect almost all assets in the economy, at least to some degree, while a particular unsystematic risk affects at most a small number of assets. We then develop the principle of diversification, which shows that highly diversified portfolios tend to have almost no unsystematic risk.

The principle of diversification has an important implication: To a diversified investor, only systematic risk matters. It follows that in deciding whether to buy a particular individual asset, a diversified investor is concerned only with that asset's systematic risk. This is a key observation, and it allows us to say a great deal about the risks and returns on individual assets. In particular, it is the basis for a famous relationship between risk and return called the security market line, or SML. To develop the SML, we introduce the equally famous beta coefficient, one of the centrepieces of modern finance. Beta and the SML are key concepts because they supply us with at least part of the answer to the question of how to determine the required return on an investment.

13.1   EXPECTED RETURNS AND VARIANCES

In our previous chapter, we discussed how to calculate average returns and variances using historical data. We now begin to discuss how to analyze returns and variances when the information we have concerns future possible returns and their possibilities.

Expected Return

We start with a straightforward case. Consider a single period of time, say, a year. We have two stocks, L and U, with the following characteristics: Stock L is expected to have a return of 25 percent in the coming year. Stock U is expected to have a return of 20 percent for the same period.[1]

In a situation like this, if all investors agreed on the expected returns, why would anyone want to hold Stock U? After all, why invest in one stock when the expectation is that another will do better? Clearly, the answer must depend on the risk of the two investments. The return on Stock L, although it is expected to be 25 percent, could actually be higher or lower.

For example, suppose the economy booms. In this case, we think Stock L would have a 70 percent return. If the economy enters a recession, we think the return would be −20 percent. Thus, we say there are two *states of the economy,* meaning that these are the only two possible situations. This setup is oversimplified, of course, but it allows us to illustrate some key ideas without a lot of computation.

Suppose we think a boom and a recession are equally likely to happen, a 50-50 chance of each. Table 13.1 illustrates the basic information we have described and some additional information about Stock U. Notice that Stock U earns 30 percent if there is a recession and 10 percent if there is a boom.

Obviously, if you buy one of these stocks, say Stock U, what you earn in any particular year depends on what the economy does during that year. However, suppose the probabilities stay the same through time. If you hold U for a number of years, you'll earn 30 percent about half the time and 10 percent the other half. In this case, we say that your **expected return** on Stock U, $E(R_U)$, is 20 percent:

$$E(R_U) = .50 \times 30\% + .50 \times 10\% = 20\%$$

In other words, you should expect to earn 20 percent from this stock, on average.

For Stock L, the probabilities are the same, but the possible returns are different. Here we lose 20 percent half the time, and we gain 70 percent the other half. The expected return on L, $E(R_L)$, is thus 25 percent:

$$E(R_L) = .50 \times -20\% + .50 \times 70\% = 25\%$$

expected return
Return on a risky asset expected in the future.

TABLE 13.1
States of the economy and stock returns

State of the Economy	Probability of State of the Economy	Security Returns if State Occurs	
		L	U
Recession	0.5	−20%	30%
Boom	0.5	70	10
	1.0		

Table 13.2 illustrates these calculations.

---

1 This is a good point to clarify the difference between expected return and required return. While the expected return reflects how investors think the stock will actually perform over a future period, the required return is the amount that investors must receive to compensate them for the risk they are accepting on any given investment.

In our previous chapter, we defined the risk premium as the difference between the return on a risky investment and a risk-free investment, and we calculated the historical risk premiums on some different investments. Using our projected returns, we can calculate the *projected or expected risk premium* as the difference between the expected return on a risky investment and the certain return on a risk-free investment.

For example, suppose risk-free investments are currently offering 8 percent. We say the risk-free rate (which we label as R_f) is 8 percent. Given this, what is the projected risk premium on Stock U? On Stock L? Since the expected return on Stock U, $E(R_U)$, is 20 percent, the projected risk premium is:

$$\text{Risk premium} = \text{Expected return} - \text{Risk-free rate} \qquad [13.1]$$
$$= E(R_U) - R_f$$
$$= 20\% - 8\%$$
$$= 12\%$$

Similarly, the risk premium on Stock L is 25% − 8% = 17%.

In general, the expected return on a security or other asset is simply equal to the sum of the possible returns multiplied by their probabilities. So, if we have 100 possible returns, we would multiply each one by its probability and add the results. The result would be the expected return. The risk premium would be the difference between this expected return and the risk-free rate.

A useful generalized equation for expected return is:

$$E(R) = \sum_j O_j \times P_j \qquad [13.2]$$

where

O_j = value of the jth outcome

P_j = associated probability of occurrence

$\sum_j$ = the sum over all j

Calculating the Variance

To calculate the variances of the returns on our two stocks, we determine the squared deviations from the expected return. We then multiply each possible squared deviation by its probability. We

TABLE 13.2
Calculation of expected return

		Stock L		Stock U	
(1) State of Economy	(2) Probability of State of Economy	(3) Rate of Return if State Occurs	(4) Product (2) × (3)	(5) Rate of Return if State Occurs	(6) Product (2) × (5)
Recession	0.5	−.20	−.10	.30	.15
Boom	0.5	.70	.35	.10	.05
	1.0		$E(R_L) = 25\%$		$E(R_U) = 20\%$

EXAMPLE 13.1: Unequal Probabilities

Look back at Tables 13.1 and 13.2. Suppose you thought that a boom would only occur 20 percent of the time instead of 50 percent. What are the expected returns on Stocks U and L in this case? If the risk-free rate is 10 percent, what are the risk premiums?

The first thing to notice is that a recession must occur 80 percent of the time (1 − .20 = .80) because there are only two possibilities. With this in mind, Stock U has a 30 percent return in 80 percent of the years and a 10 percent return in 20 percent of the years. To calculate the expected return, we again just multiply the possibilities by the probabilities and add up the results:

$$E(R_U) = .80 \times 30\% + .20 \times 10\% = 26\%$$

Table 13.3 summarizes the calculations for both stocks. Notice that the expected return on L is −2 percent.

The risk premium for Stock U is 26% − 10% = 16% in this case. The risk premium for Stock L is negative: −2% − 10% = −12%. This is a little odd, but, for reasons we discuss later, it is not impossible.

TABLE 13.3

Expected return calculation

(1) State of Economy	(2) Probability of State of Economy	Stock L (3) Rate of Return if State Occurs	(4) Product (2) × (3)	Stock U (5) Rate of Return if State Occurs	(6) Product (2) × (5)
Recession	.80	−.20	−.16	.30	.24
Boom	.20	.70	.14	.10	.02
	1.0		E(R_L) = −2%		E(R_U) = 26%

add these, and the result is the variance. The standard deviation, as always, is the square root of the variance. It is important to note that later on in the chapter another alternative to calculating variance will be introduced, using the correlation coefficient.

Generalized equations for variance and standard deviation are

$$\sigma^2 = \sum_j [O_j - E(R)]^2 \times P_j \qquad\qquad [13.3]$$
$$\sigma = \sqrt{\sigma^2}$$

To illustrate, Stock U has an expected return of E(R_U) = 20%. In a given year, it could actually return either 30 percent or 10 percent. The possible deviations are thus 30% − 20% = 10% or 10% − 20% = −10%. In this case, the variance is:

Variance = σ^2 = .50 × (10%)^2 + .50 × (−10%)^2 = .01

The standard deviation is the square root of this: = .10 = 10%

Standard deviation = σ = $\sqrt{.01}$ = .10 = 10%

Table 13.4 summarizes these calculations for both stocks. Notice that Stock L has a much larger variance.

TABLE 13.4

Calculation of variance

(1) State of Economy	(2) Probability of State of Economy	(3) Return Deviation from Expected Return	(4) Squared Return Deviation from Expected Return	(5) Product (2) × (4)
Stock L				
Recession	0.5	−.20 − .25 = −.45	(−.45)^2 = .2025	.10125
Boom	0.5	.70 − .25 = .45	(.45)^2 = .2025	.10125
				σ^2_L = .2025
Stock U				
Recession	0.5	.30 − .20 = .10	(.10)^2 = .01	.005
Boom	0.5	.10 − .20 = −.10	(−.10)^2 = .01	.005
				σ^2_U = .010

When we put the expected return and variability information for our two stocks together, we have:

	Stock L	Stock U
Expected return, E(R)	25%	20%
Variance, σ^2	.2025	.0100
Standard deviation, σ	45%	10%

Stock L has a higher expected return, but U has less risk. You could get a 70 percent return on your investment in L, but you could also lose 20 percent. Notice that an investment in U always pays at least 10 percent.

Which of these two stocks should you buy? We can't really say; it depends on your personal preferences. We can be reasonably sure that some investors would prefer L to U and some would prefer U to L.

You've probably noticed that the way we calculated expected returns and variances here is somewhat different from the way we did it in the last chapter. The reason is that, in Chapter 12, we were examining actual historical returns, so we estimated the average return and the variance

EXAMPLE 13.2: More Unequal Probabilities

Going back to Example 13.1, what are the variances on the two stocks once we have unequal probabilities? The standard deviations?

We can summarize the needed calculations as follows:

(1) State of Economy	(2) Probability of State of Economy	(3) Return Deviation from Expected Return	(4) Squared Return Deviation from Expected Return	(5) Product (2) × (4)
Stock L				
Recession	.80	$-.20 - (-.02) = -.18$	.0324	.02592
Boom	.20	$.70 - (-.02) = .72$	.5184	.10368
				$\sigma^2_L = .12960$
Stock U				
Recession	.80	$.30 - .26 = .04$	.0016	.00128
Boom	.20	$.10 - .26 = -.16$	.0256	.00512
				$\sigma^2_U = .00640$

Based on these calculations, the standard deviation for L is $\sigma_L = \sqrt{.1296} = 36$ percent. The standard deviation for U is much smaller, $\sigma_U = \sqrt{.0064} = .08$ or 8 percent.

based on some actual events. Here, we have projected future returns and their associated probabilities, so this is the information with which we must work.

CONCEPT QUESTIONS

1. How do we calculate the expected return on a security?

2. In words, how do we calculate the variance of the expected return?

 **13.2**

portfolio
Group of assets such as stocks and bonds held by an investor.

portfolio weights
Percentage of a portfolio's total value in a particular asset.

PORTFOLIOS

Thus far in this chapter, we have concentrated on individual assets considered separately. However, most investors actually hold a **portfolio** of assets. All we mean by this is that investors tend to own more than just a single stock, bond, or other asset. Given that this is so, portfolio return and portfolio risk are of obvious relevance. Accordingly, we now discuss portfolio expected returns and variances.

Portfolio Weights

There are many equivalent ways of describing a portfolio. The most convenient approach is to list the percentages of the total portfolio's value that are invested in each portfolio asset. We call these percentages the **portfolio weights.**

For example, if we have $50 in one asset and $150 in another, our total portfolio is worth $200. The percentage of our portfolio in the first asset is $50/$200 = .25. The percentage of our portfolio in the second asset is $150/$200, or .75. Our portfolio weights are thus .25 and .75. Notice that the weights have to add up to 1.00 since all of our money is invested somewhere.[2]

Portfolio Expected Returns

Let's go back to Stocks L and U. You put half your money in each. The portfolio weights are obviously .50 and .50. What is the pattern of returns on this portfolio? The expected return?

---

2 Some of it could be in cash, of course, but we would just consider the cash to be one of the portfolio assets.

To answer these questions, suppose the economy actually enters a recession. In this case, half your money (the half in L) loses 20 percent. The other half (the half in U) gains 30 percent. Your portfolio return, R_p, in a recession is thus:

$$R_p = .50 \times (-20\%) + .50 \times 30\% = 5\%$$

Table 13.5 summarizes the remaining calculations. Notice that when a boom occurs, your portfolio would return 40 percent:

$$R_p = .50 \times 70\% + .50 \times 10\% = 40\%$$

As indicated in Table 13.5, the expected return on your portfolio, $E(R_p)$, is 22.5 percent.

We can save ourselves some work by calculating the expected return more directly. Given these portfolio weights, we could have reasoned that we expect half of our money to earn 25 percent (the half in L) and half of our money to earn 20 percent (the half in U). Our portfolio expected return is thus:

$$\begin{aligned} E(R_p) &= .50 \times E(R_L) + .50 \times E(R_U) \\ &= .50 \times 25\% + .50 \times 20\% \\ &= 22.5\% \end{aligned}$$

TABLE 13.5

Expected return on an equally weighted portfolio of Stock L and Stock U

(1) State of Economy	(2) Probability of State of Economy	(3) Portfolio Return if State Occurs	(4) Product (2) × (3)
Recession	.50	1/2 × (−20%) + 1/2 × (30%) = 5%	2.5%
Boom	.50	1/2 × (70%) + 1/2 × (10%) = 40%	20.0
			$E(R_p)$ = 22.5%

This is the same portfolio expected return we had before.

This method of calculating the expected return on a portfolio works no matter how many assets are in the portfolio. Suppose we had n assets in our portfolio, where n is any number. If we let x_i stand for the percentage of our money in asset i, the expected return is:

$$E(R_p) = x_1 \times E(R_1) + x_2 \times E(R_2) + \ldots + x_n \times E(R_n) \qquad \text{[13.4]}$$

This says that the expected return on a portfolio is a straightforward combination of the expected returns on the assets in that portfolio. This seems somewhat obvious, but, as we examine next, the obvious approach is not always the right one.

EXAMPLE 13.3: Portfolio Expected Returns

Suppose we have the following projections on three stocks:

State of Economy	Probability of State	Returns		
		Stock A	Stock B	Stock C
Boom	.40	10%	15%	20%
Bust	.60	8%	4%	0%

What would be the expected return on a portfolio with equal amounts invested in each of the three stocks? What would the expected return be if half the portfolio were in A, with the remainder equally divided between B and C?

From our earlier discussions, the expected returns on the individual stocks are (check these for practice):

$E(R_A) = 8.8\%$
$E(R_B) = 8.4\%$
$E(R_C) = 8.0\%$

If a portfolio has equal investments in each asset, the portfolio weights are all the same. Such a portfolio is said to be equally weighted. Since there are three stocks, the weights are all equal to 1/3. The portfolio expected return is thus:

$E(R_p) = (1/3) \times 8.8\% + (1/3) \times 8.4\% + (1/3) \times 8.0\% = 8.4\%$

In the second case, check that the portfolio expected return is 8.5 percent.

Portfolio Variance

From our previous discussion, the expected return on a portfolio that contains equal investment in Stocks U and L is 22.5 percent. What is the standard deviation of return on this portfolio? Simple intuition might suggest that half the money has a standard deviation of 45 percent and the other half has a standard deviation of 10 percent, so the portfolio's standard deviation might be calculated as:

$$\sigma_p = .50 \times 45\% + .50 \times 10\% = 27.5\%$$

Unfortunately, this approach is incorrect.

Let's see what the standard deviation really is. Table 13.6 summarizes the relevant calculations. As we see, the portfolio's variance is about .031, and its standard deviation is less than we thought—it's only 17.5 percent. What is illustrated here is that the variance on a portfolio is not generally a simple combination of the variances of the assets in the portfolio.

We can illustrate this point a little more dramatically by considering a slightly different set of portfolio weights. Suppose we put 2/11 (about 18 percent) in L and the other 9/11 (about 82 percent) in U. If a recession occurs, this portfolio would have a return of:

$$R_p = \left(\frac{2}{11}\right) \times (-20\%) + \left(\frac{9}{11}\right) \times (30\%) = 20.91\%$$

If a boom occurs, this portfolio would have a return of:

$$R_p = \left(\frac{2}{11}\right) \times (70\%) + \left(\frac{9}{11}\right) \times (10\%) = 20.91\%$$

Notice that the return is the same no matter what happens. No further calculations are needed: This portfolio has a zero variance. Apparently, combining assets into portfolios can substantially alter the risks faced by the investor. This is a crucial observation, and we explore its implications in the next section.

EXAMPLE 13.4: Portfolio Variance and Standard Deviation

In Example 13.3, what are the standard deviations on the two portfolios? To answer, we first have to calculate the portfolio returns in the two states. We will work with the second portfolio, which has 50 percent in Stock A and 25 percent in each of Stocks B and C. The relevant calculations can be summarized as follows:

State of Economy	Probability of State	Returns			
		Stock A	Stock B	Stock C	Portfolio
Boom	.40	10%	15%	20%	13.75%
Bust	.60	8%	4%	0%	5.00%

The portfolio return when the economy booms is calculated as:

$$.50 \times 10\% + .25 \times 15\% + .25 \times 20\% = 13.75\%$$

The return when the economy goes bust is calculated the same way. The expected return on the portfolio is 8.5 percent. The variance is thus:

$$\sigma^2 = .40 \times (.1375 - .085)^2 + .60 \times (.05 - .085)^2$$
$$= .0018375$$

The standard deviation is thus about 4.3 percent. For our equally weighted portfolio, check to see that the standard deviation is about 5.4 percent.

TABLE 13.6

Variance on an equally weighted portfolio of Stock L and Stock U

(1) State of Economy	(2) Probability of State of Economy	(3) Portfolio Return if State Occurs	(4) Squared Deviation from Expected Return	(5) Product (2) × (4)
Recession	.50	5%	$(.05 - .225)^2 = .030625$	.0153125
Boom	.50	40%	$(.40 - .225)^2 = .030625$	.0153125
				$\sigma^2_p = .030625$

$$\sigma_p = \sqrt{.030625} = 17.5\%$$

Portfolio Standard Deviation and Diversification

How diversification reduces portfolio risk as measured by the portfolio standard deviation is worth exploring in some detail.[3] The key concept is *correlation,* which provides a reading on the extent to which the returns on two assets move together. If correlation is positive, we say that Assets A and B are positively correlated; if it is negative, we say they are negatively correlated; and if it is zero, the two assets are uncorrelated.

Figure 13.1 shows these three benchmark cases for two assets, A and B. The graphs on the left side plot the separate returns on the two securities through time. Each point on the graphs on the right side represents the returns for both A and B over a particular time interval. The figure shows examples of different values for the correlation coefficient, CORR (R_a, R_b), that range from −1.0 to 1.0.

To show how the graphs are constructed, we need to look at points 1 and 2 (on the upper left graph) and relate them to point 3 (on the upper right graph). Point 1 is a return on Company B and point 2 is a return on Company A. They both occur over the same time period, say, for example, the month of June. Both returns are above average. Point 3 represents the returns on both stocks in June. Other dots in the upper right graph represent the returns on both stocks in other months.

Because the returns on Security B have bigger swings than the returns on Security A, the slope of the line in the upper right graph is greater than one. Perfect positive correlation does not imply that the slope is one. Rather, it implies that all points lie exactly on the line. Less-than-perfect positive correlation implies a positive slope, but the points do not lie exactly on the line. An example of less-than-perfect positive correlation is provided in the left side of Figure 13.2. As before, each point in the graph represents the returns on both securities in the same month. In a graph like this, the closer the points lie to the line, the closer the correlation is to one. In other words, a high correlation between the two returns implies that the graph has a tight fit.[4]

Less-than-perfect negative correlation implies a negative slope, but the points do not lie exactly on the line, as shown on the right side of Figure 13.2.

EXAMPLE 13.5: Correlation between Stocks U and L

What is the correlation between Stocks U and L from our earlier example if we assume the two states of the economy are equally probable? Table 13.2 shows the returns on each stock in recession and boom states.

	Stock L	Stock U
Recession	−.20	.30
Boom	.70	.10

Figure 13.3 plots the line exactly the same way as we plotted the graphs on the right sides of Figures 13.1 and 13.2. You can see from the figure that the line has a negative slope and all the points lie exactly on the line. (Since we only have two outcomes for each stock, the points must plot exactly on a straight line.) You can conclude that the correlation between Stocks U and L is equal to −1.0.

Our discussion of correlation provides us with a key building block of a formula for portfolio standard variance and its square root, portfolio standard deviation.

$$\sigma^2_P = x^2_L\sigma^2_L + x^2_U\sigma^2_U + 2x_L \times {}_U\text{CORR}_{L,U}\sigma_L\sigma_U \qquad [13.5]$$

$$\sigma_P = \sqrt{\sigma^2_P}$$

Recall that x_L and x_U are, respectively, the portfolio weights for Stocks U and L. $\text{CORR}_{L,U}$ is the correlation of the two stocks.

We can use the formula to check our previous calculation of portfolio standard deviation for a portfolio invested 50 percent in each stock.

$$= (.5)^2 \times (.45)^2 + (.5)^2 \times (.10)^2 + (2) \times (.5) \times (.5) \times (-1.0) \times (.45) \times (.10)$$
$$= .030625$$
$$= \sqrt{.030625} = 17.5\%$$

These are the same results we got in Table 13.6.

---

3 The ideas in this section were first developed systematically in an article written in 1952 by Harry Markowitz, "Portfolio Selection," *Journal of Finance* 7 (March 1952), pp. 77–91. His work laid the foundation for the development of the capital asset pricing model, principally by William F. Sharpe, "Capital Asset Prices: A Theory of Market Equilibrium under Conditions of Risk," *Journal of Finance* 19 (1964), pp. 425–42. These pioneers of modern portfolio theory were awarded the Nobel Prize in Economics in 1991.

4 If we measure the correlation by regression analysis, the *correlation coefficient* is the square root of R squared, the regression coefficient of determination. For a perfect fit, R squared is one and the correlation coefficient is also one.

FIGURE 13.1

Examples of different correlation coefficients

The graphs on the left-hand side of the figure plot the separate returns on the two securities through time. Each point on the graphs on the right-hand side represents the returns for both A and B over a particular time period.

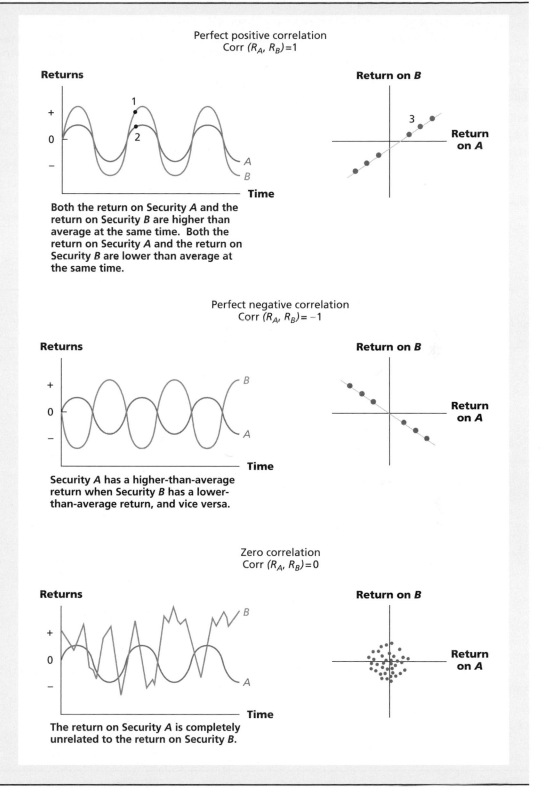

Perfect positive correlation
Corr $(R_A, R_B) = 1$

Both the return on Security A and the return on Security B are higher than average at the same time. Both the return on Security A and the return on Security B are lower than average at the same time.

Perfect negative correlation
Corr $(R_A, R_B) = -1$

Security A has a higher-than-average return when Security B has a lower-than-average return, and vice versa.

Zero correlation
Corr $(R_A, R_B) = 0$

The return on Security A is completely unrelated to the return on Security B.

The Efficient Set

Suppose U and L actually have a correlation of about +0.70. The opportunity set is graphed in Figure 13.4. In this figure, we have marked the minimum variance portfolio, MV. No risk-averse

FIGURE 13.2

Graphs of possible relationships between two stocks

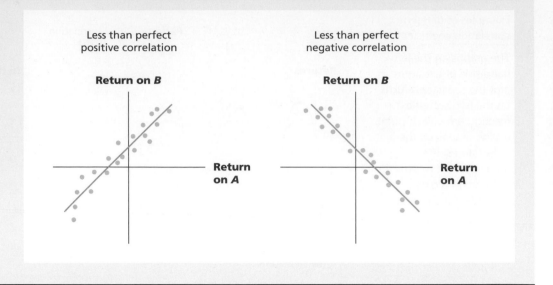

FIGURE 13.3

Correlation between Stocks U and L

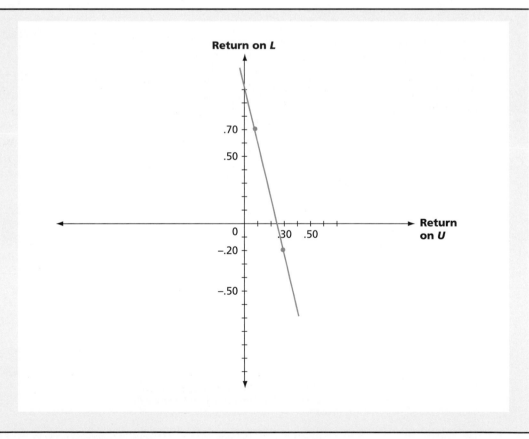

investor would hold any portfolio with expected return below MV. For example, no such investor would invest 100 percent in Stock U because such a portfolio has lower expected return and higher standard deviation than the minimum variance portfolio. We say that portfolios such as U are dominated by the minimum variance portfolio. (Since standard deviation is the square root of variance, the minimum variance portfolios also have minimum standard deviations as shown in

Figures 13.4 and 13.5.) Though the entire curve from U to L is called the *feasible set*, investors only consider the curve from MV to L. This part of the curve is called the *efficient set*.

EXAMPLE 13.6: The Zero-Variance Portfolio

Can you find a portfolio of Stocks U and L with zero variance? Earlier, we showed that investing 2/11 (about 18) percent of the portfolio in L and the other 9/11 (about 82 percent) in U gives the same expected portfolio return in either recession or boom. As a result, the portfolio variance and standard deviation should both be zero. We can check this with the formula for portfolio variance.

$$\sigma^2_p = \left(\frac{2}{11}\right)^2 \times (.45)^2 + \left(\frac{9}{11}\right)^2 \times (.10)^2 + 2 \times \left(\frac{2}{11}\right) \times \left(\frac{9}{11}\right) \times$$

$$(-1.0) \times (.45) \times (.10)$$

$$= .006694 + .006694 - .013388$$

$$= 0$$

You can see that the portfolio variance (and standard deviation) are zero because the weights were chosen to make the negative third term exactly offset the first two positive terms. This third term is called the *covariance term* because the product of the correlation times the two security standard deviations is the covariance of U and L.[5]

To explore how the portfolio standard deviation depends on correlation, Table 13.7 recalculates the portfolio standard deviation, changing the correlation between U and L, yet keeping the portfolio weights and all the other input data unchanged. When the correlation is perfectly negative, $CORR_{U,L} = -1.0$, the portfolio standard deviation is 0 as we just calculated. If the two stocks were uncorrelated ($CORR_{L,U} = 0$), the portfolio standard deviation becomes 11.5708 percent. And, with perfect positive correlation ($CORR_{L,U} = +1.0$) the portfolio standard deviation is 16.3636 percent.

When the returns on the two assets are perfectly correlated, the portfolio standard deviation is simply the weighted average of the individual standard deviations. In this special case:

$$16.3636 = \left(\frac{2}{11}\right) \times 45\% + \left(\frac{9}{11}\right) \times 10\%$$

With perfect correlation, all possible portfolios lie on a straight line between U and L in expected return/standard deviation space as shown in Figure 13.4. In this polar case, there is no benefit from diversification. But, as soon as correlation is less than perfectly positive, $CORR_{L,U} = +1.0$, diversification reduces risk.

As long as CORR is less than +1.0, the standard deviation of a portfolio of two securities is less than the weighted average of the standard deviations of the individual securities.

Figure 13.4 shows this important result by graphing all possible portfolios of U and L for the three cases for $CORR_{L,U}$, given in Table 13.7. The portfolios marked 1, 2, and 3 in Figure 13.4 all have an expected return of 20.91 percent as calculated in Table 13.7. Their standard deviations also come from Table 13.7. The other points on the respective lines or curves are derived by varying the portfolio weights for each value of $CORR_{L,U}$. Each line or curve represents all the possible portfolios of U and L for a given correlation. Each is called an *opportunity set* or *feasible set*. The lowest opportunity set representing $CORR_{L,U} = 1.0$ always has the largest standard deviation for any return level. Once again, this shows how diversification reduces risk as long as correlation is less than perfectly positive.

TABLE 13.7
Portfolio standard deviation and correlation

Stock L	$x_L = \frac{2}{11}$	$\sigma_L = 45\%$	$E(R_L) = 25\%$
Stock U	$x_U = \frac{9}{11}$	$\sigma_U = 10\%$	$E(R_U) = 20\%$

$E(R_P) = \left(\frac{2}{11}\right) \times 25\% + \frac{9}{11} \times 20\% = 20.91\%$

$CORR_{L,U}$ Portfolio	Standard Deviation of Portfolio s_P
1. −1.0	0.0000%
2. 0.0	11.5708%
3. +1.0	16.3636%

CONCEPT QUESTIONS

1. What is a portfolio weight?

2. How do we calculate the expected return on a portfolio?

3. Is there a simple relationship between the standard deviation on a portfolio and the standard deviation of the assets in the portfolio?

---

5 As the number of stocks in the portfolio increases beyond the two in our example, the number of covariance terms increases geometrically. In general, for a portfolio of N securities, the number of covariance terms is $(N^2 - N)/2$. For example, a 10-stock portfolio has 45 covariance terms.

FIGURE 13.4

Opportunity sets composed of holdings in Stock L and Stock U

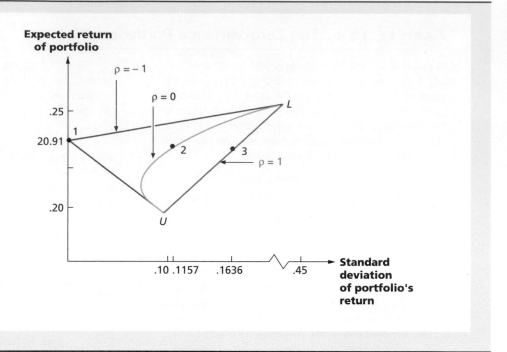

FIGURE 13.5

Efficient frontier

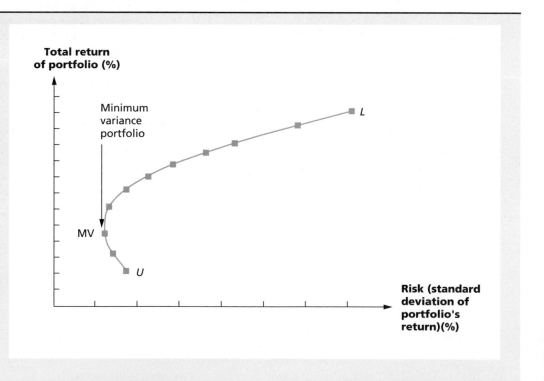

EXAMPLE 13.7: Benefits of Foreign Investment

Research on diversification extends our discussion of historical average returns and risks in Chapter 12 to include foreign investment portfolios. It turns out that the feasible set looks like Figure 13.5 where points like U and L represent portfolios instead of individual stocks. Portfolio U represents 100 percent investment in Canadian equities and Portfolio L represents 100 percent in foreign equities. The domestic stock portfolio is less risky than the foreign portfolio. Does this mean Canadian portfolio managers should invest entirely in Canada?

The answer is no because the minimum variance portfolio with approximately 20 percent foreign content dominates portfolio U, the 100 percent domestic portfolio. Going from 0 percent to around 20 percent foreign content actually reduces portfolio standard deviation due to the diversification effect. Increasing the foreign content beyond around 20 percent increases portfolio risk but also raises expected return. Recognizing this point led pension managers to lobby successfully in 2000 for an increase in allowable foreign content to 25 percent immediately and to 30 percent over time.[6]

ANNOUNCEMENTS, SURPRISES, AND EXPECTED RETURNS

Now that we know how to construct portfolios and evaluate their returns, we begin to describe more carefully the risks and returns associated with individual securities. Thus far, we have measured volatility by looking at the differences between the actual returns on an asset or portfolio, R, and the expected return, $E(R)$. We now look at why those deviations exist.

Expected and Unexpected Returns

To begin, for concreteness, we consider the return on the stock of TransCanada Industries. What will determine this stock's return in, say, the coming year? The return on any stock traded in a financial market is composed of two parts: First, the normal or expected return from the stock is the part of the return that shareholders in the market predict or expect. This return depends on the information shareholders have that bears on the stock, and it is based on the market's understanding today of the important factors that influence the stock in the coming year.

The second part of the return on the stock is the uncertain or risky part. This is the portion that comes from unexpected information that is revealed within the year. A list of all possible sources of such information is endless, but here are a few examples:

News about TransCanada's research.

Government figures released on gross national product (GNP).

The imminent bankruptcy of an important competitor.

The news that TransCanada's sales figures are higher than expected.

A sudden, unexpected drop in interest rates.

Based on this discussion, one way to write the return on TransCanada's stock in the coming year would be:

$$\text{Total return} = \text{Expected return} + \text{Unexpected return} \qquad [13.6]$$
$$R = E(R) + U$$

where R stands for the actual total return in the year, $E(R)$ stands for the expected part of the return, and U stands for the unexpected part of the return. What this says is that the actual return, R, differs from the expected return, $E(R)$, because of surprises that occur during the day.

---

6 These data come from Harry S. Marmer, "International Investing: A New Canadian Perspective," *Perspectives on Institutional Investment Management*. Toronto: Rogers Publishing, 2002, pp. 92–97, and *Canadian Investment Review*, Winter 1998, pp. 49–51.

Announcements and News

We need to be careful when we talk about the effect of news items on the return. For example, suppose that TransCanada Industries' business is such that the company prospers when GNP grows at a relatively high rate and suffers when GNP is relatively stagnant. In deciding what return to expect this year from owning stock in TransCanada, shareholders either implicitly or explicitly must think about what the GNP is likely to be for the year.

When the government actually announces GNP figures for the year, what will happen to the value of TransCanada Industries stock? Obviously, the answer depends on what figure is released. More to the point, however, the impact depends on how much of that figure is new information.

At the beginning of the year, market participants have some idea or forecast of what the yearly GNP will be. To the extent that shareholders had predicted the GNP, that prediction is already factored into the expected part of the return on the stock, $E(R)$. On the other hand, if the announced GNP is a surprise, the effect is part of U, the unanticipated portion of the return. As an example, suppose shareholders in the market had forecast that the GNP increase this year would be 0.5 percent. If the actual announcement this year is exactly 0.5 percent, the same as the forecast, the shareholders didn't really learn anything, and the announcement isn't news. There would be no impact on the stock price as a result. This is like receiving confirmation of something that you suspected all along; it doesn't reveal anything new.

www.bmo.com

To give a more concrete example, on April 25, 2005, Petro-Canada announced that its first quarter profit had risen 70 percent based on robust energy prices. This seems like very good news, but the stock price increased by only 0.51% on the announcement. Why? Because market participants had already expected that the oil company would achieve these improved results. This meant the stock price had already risen, based on the expectation of improved results. If the announcement had, in fact, not met expectations, the stock price could actually have dropped.

A common way of saying that an announcement isn't news is to say that the market has already "discounted" the announcement. The use of the word *discount* here is different from the use of the term in computing present values, but the spirit is the same. When we discount a dollar in the future, we say it is worth less to us because of the time value of money. When we discount an announcement or a news item, we mean it has less of an impact on the market because the market already knew much of it.

For example, going back to TransCanada Industries, suppose the government announced that the actual GNP increase during the year was 1.5 percent. Now shareholders have learned something, namely, that the increase is 1 percentage point higher than they had forecast. This difference between the actual result and the forecast, 1 percentage point in this example, is sometimes called the *innovation* or the *surprise*.

An announcement, then, can be broken into two parts, the anticipated or expected part and the surprise or innovation:

$$\text{Announcement} = \text{Expected part} + \text{Surprise} \qquad [13.7]$$

The expected part of any announcement is the part of the information that the market uses to form the expectation $E(R)$, of the return on the stock. The surprise is the news that influences the unanticipated return on the stock, U.

Our discussion of market efficiency in the previous chapter bears on this discussion. We are assuming that relevant information that is known today is already reflected in the expected return. This is identical to saying that the current price reflects relevant publicly available information. We are thus implicitly assuming that markets are at least reasonably efficient in the semi-strong form sense.

Henceforth, when we speak of news, we mean the surprise part of an announcement and not the portion that the market has expected and, therefore, already discounted.

CONCEPT QUESTIONS

1. What are the two basic parts of a return?

2. Under what conditions does an announcement have no effect on common stock prices?

 **13.4**

RISK: SYSTEMATIC AND UNSYSTEMATIC

The unanticipated part of the return, that portion resulting from surprises, is the true risk of any investment. After all, if we always receive exactly what we expect, the investment is perfectly predictable and, by definition, risk-free. In other words, the risk of owning an asset comes from surprises—unanticipated events.

There are important differences, though, among various sources of risk. Look back at our previous list of news stories. Some of these stories are directed specifically at TransCanada Industries, and some are more general. Which of the news items are of specific importance to TransCanada Industries?

Announcements about interest rates or GNP are clearly important for nearly all companies, whereas the news about TransCanada Industries' president, its research, or its sales are of specific interest to TransCanada Industries. We distinguish between these two types of events however because, as we shall see, they have very different implications.

Systematic and Unsystematic Risk

systematic risk
A risk that influences a large number of assets. Also called market risk.

The first surprise, the one that affects a large number of assets, we label **systematic risk.** A systematic risk is one that influences a large number of assets, each to a greater or lesser extent. Because systematic risks are market-wide effects, they are sometimes called *market risks.*

The second type of surprise we call **unsystematic risk.** An unsystematic risk is one that affects a single asset or a small group of assets. Because these risks are unique to individual companies or assets, they are sometimes called *unique* or *asset-specific risks.* We use these terms interchangeably.

unsystematic risk
A risk that affects at most a small number of assets. Also called unique or asset-specific risks.

As we have seen, uncertainties about general economic conditions, such as GNP, interest rates, or inflation, are examples of systematic risks. These conditions affect nearly all companies to some degree. An unanticipated increase or surprise in inflation, for example, affects wages and the costs of the supplies that companies buy; it affects the value of the assets that companies own; and it affects the prices at which companies sell their products. Forces such as these, to which all companies are susceptible, are the essence of systematic risk.

In contrast, the announcement of an oil strike by a company primarily affects that company and, perhaps, a few others (such as primary competitors and suppliers). It is unlikely to have much of an effect on the world oil market, however, or on the affairs of companies not in the oil business.

Systematic and Unsystematic Components of Return

The distinction between a systematic risk and an unsystematic risk is never really as exact as we make it out to be. Even the most narrow and peculiar bits of news about a company ripple through the economy. This is true because every enterprise, no matter how tiny, is a part of the economy. It's like the tale of a kingdom that was lost because one horse lost a shoe. This is mostly hairsplitting, however. Some risks are clearly much more general than others. We'll see some evidence on this point in just a moment.

The distinction between the types of risk allows us to break down the surprise portion, U, of the return on TransCanada Industries stock into two parts. As before, we break the actual return down into its expected and surprise components:

$$R = E(R) + U$$

We now recognize that the total surprise for TransCanada Industries, U, has a systematic and an unsystematic component, so:

$$R = E(R) + \text{Systematic portion} + \text{Unsystematic portion} \qquad [13.8]$$

Because it is traditional, we use the Greek letter epsilon, ϵ, to stand for the unsystematic portion. Since systematic risks are often called market risks, we use the letter m to stand for the systematic part of the surprise. With these symbols, we can rewrite the total return:

$$R = E(R) + U$$
$$= E(R) + m + \epsilon$$

The important thing about the way we have broken down the total surprise, U, is that the unsystematic portion, ϵ, is more or less unique to TransCanada Industries. For this reason, it is unrelated to the unsystematic portion of return on most other assets. To see why this is important, we need to return to the subject of portfolio risk.

CONCEPT QUESTIONS

1. What are the two basic types of risk?

2. What is the distinction between the two types of risk?

13.5   DIVERSIFICATION AND PORTFOLIO RISK

We've seen earlier that portfolio risks can, in principle, be quite different from the risks of the assets that make up the portfolio. We now look more closely at the riskiness of an individual asset versus the risk of a portfolio of many different assets. We once again examine some market history to get an idea of what happens with actual investments in capital markets.

The Effect of Diversification: Another Lesson from Market History

In our previous chapter, we saw that the standard deviation of the annual return on a portfolio of several hundred large common stocks has historically been about 16 percent per year for the Toronto Stock Exchange and 17 percent per year for the New York Stock Exchange (see Table 12.4, for example). Does this mean the standard deviation of the annual return on a typical stock is about 16 or 17 percent? As you might suspect by now, the answer is no. This is an extremely important observation.

To examine the relationship between portfolio size and portfolio risk, Table 13.8 illustrates typical average annual standard deviations for equally weighted portfolios that contain different numbers of randomly selected NYSE securities.[7]

www.nyse.com
www.tsx.com

TABLE 13.8
Standard deviations of annual portfolio returns

(1) Number of Stocks in Portfolio	(2) Average Standard Deviation of Annual Portfolio Returns	(3) Ratio of Portfolio Standard Deviation to Standard Deviation of a Single Stock
1	49.24%	1.00
2	37.36	0.76
4	29.69	0.60
6	26.64	0.54
8	24.98	0.51
10	23.93	0.49
20	21.68	0.44
30	20.87	0.42
40	20.46	0.42
50	20.20	0.41
100	19.69	0.40
200	19.42	0.39
300	19.34	0.39
400	19.29	0.39
500	19.27	0.39
1,000	19.21	0.39

---

7 These figures are from Table 1 in Meir Statman, "How Many Stocks Make a Diversified Portfolio?" *Journal of Financial and Quantitative Analysis* 22 (September 1987), pp. 353–64. They were derived from E. J. Elton and M. J. Gruber, "Risk Reduction and Portfolio Size: An Analytic Solution," *Journal of Business* 50 (October 1977), pp. 415–37.

In Column 2 of Table 13.8, we see that the standard deviation for a "portfolio" of one security is about 49 percent. What this means is that, if you randomly selected a single NYSE stock and put all your money into it, your standard deviation of return would typically have been a substantial 49 percent per year. If you were to randomly select two stocks and invest half your money in each, your standard deviation would have been about 37 percent on average, and so on.

The important thing to notice in Table 13.8 is that the standard deviation declines as the number of securities is increased. By the time we have 30 randomly chosen stocks, the portfolio's standard deviation has declined by about 60 percent, from 49 to about 20 percent. With 500 securities, the standard deviation is 19.27 percent, similar to the 21 percent we saw in our previous chapter for the large common stock portfolio. The small difference exists because the portfolio securities and time periods examined are not identical.

The Principle of Diversification

Figure 13.6 illustrates the point we've been discussing. What we have plotted is the standard deviation of return versus the number of stocks in the portfolio. Notice in Figure 13.6 that the benefit in risk reduction from adding securities drops as we add more and more. By the time we have 10 securities, the portfolio standard deviation has dropped from 49.2 to 23.9 percent, most of the effect is already realized, and by the time we get to 30 or so, there is very little remaining benefit. The data in Table 13.8 and Figure 13.6 are from the NYSE but a Canadian study documented the same effect. However, the Canadian researchers found that Canadian investors need to hold a larger number of stocks to achieve diversification. This is likely due to Canadian stocks being more concentrated in a few industries than in the U.S.[8]

FIGURE 13.6

Portfolio diversification

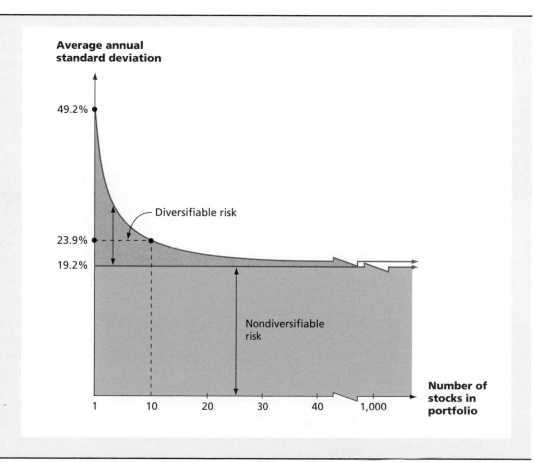

---

8 For more on the Canadian study, see S. Cleary and D. Copp, "Diversification with Canadian stocks: How much is enough?" *Canadian Investment Review* 12, Fall 1999, pp. 21–25.

principle of diversification
Principle stating that spreading an investment across a number of assets eliminates some, but not all, of the risk.

Figure 13.6 illustrates two key points: First, the **principle of diversification** (discussed earlier) tells us that spreading an investment across many assets eliminates some of the risk. The shaded area in Figure 13.6, labelled diversifiable risk, is the part that can be eliminated by diversification.

The second point is equally important. A minimum level of risk cannot be eliminated simply by diversifying. This minimum level is labelled nondiversifiable risk in Figure 13.6. Taken together, these two points are another important lesson from capital market history: Diversification reduces risk, but only up to a point. Put another way, some risk is diversifiable and some is not.

Diversification and Unsystematic Risk

From our discussion of portfolio risk, we know that some of the risk associated with individual assets can be diversified away and some cannot. We are left with an obvious question: Why is this so? It turns out that the answer hinges on the distinction we made earlier between systematic and unsystematic risk.

By definition, an unsystematic risk is one that is particular to a single asset or, at most, a small group. For example, if the asset under consideration is stock in a single company, the discovery of positive NPV projects such as successful new products and innovative cost savings tend to increase the value of the stock. Unanticipated lawsuits, industrial accidents, strikes, and similar events tend to decrease future cash flows and thereby reduce share values.

Here is the important observation: If we only held a single stock, the value of our investment would fluctuate because of company-specific events. If we held a large portfolio, on the other hand, some of the stocks in the portfolio would go up in value because of positive company-specific events and some would go down in value because of negative events. The net effect on the overall value of the portfolio is relatively small, however, as these effects tend to cancel each other out.

Now we see why some of the variability associated with individual assets is eliminated by diversification. By combining assets into portfolios, the unique or unsystematic events—both positive and negative—tend to wash out once we have more than just a few assets.

This important point bears repeating: *Unsystematic risk is essentially eliminated by diversification, so a relatively large portfolio has almost no unsystematic risk.* In fact, the terms *diversifiable risk* and *unsystematic risk* are often used interchangeably.

Diversification and Systematic Risk

We've seen that unsystematic risk can be eliminated by diversifying. What about systematic risk? Can it also be eliminated by diversification? The answer is no because, by definition, a systematic risk affects almost all assets to some degree. As a result, no matter how many assets we put into a portfolio, the systematic risk doesn't go away. Thus, for obvious reasons, the terms *systematic risk* and *nondiversifiable risk* are used interchangeably.

Because we have introduced so many different terms, it is useful to summarize our discussion before moving on. What we have seen is that the total risk of an investment, as measured by the standard deviation of its return, can be written as:

$$\text{Total risk} = \text{Systematic risk} + \text{Unsystematic risk} \qquad [13.9]$$

Systematic risk is also called nondiversifiable risk or market risk. Unsystematic risk is also called diversifiable risk, unique risk, or asset-specific risk. For a well-diversified portfolio, the unsystematic risk is negligible. For such a portfolio, essentially all of the risk is systematic.

Risk and the Sensible Investor

Having gone to all this trouble to show that unsystematic risk disappears in a well-diversified portfolio, how do we know that investors even want such portfolios? Suppose they like risk and don't want it to disappear?

We must admit that, theoretically at least, this is possible, but we argue that it does not describe what we think of as the typical investor. Our typical investor is *risk averse*. Risk-averse behaviour can be defined in many ways, but we prefer the following example: A fair gamble is one with zero expected return; a risk-averse investor would prefer to avoid fair gambles.

Why do investors choose well-diversified portfolios? Our answer is that they are risk averse, and risk-averse people avoid unnecessary risk, such as the unsystematic risk on a stock. If you do not think this is much of an answer to why investors choose well-diversified portfolios and avoid unsystematic risk, consider whether you would take on such a risk. For example, suppose you had worked all summer and had saved $5,000, which you intended to use for your university expenses. Now, suppose someone came up to you and offered to flip a coin for the money: heads, you would double your money, and tails, you would lose it all.

Would you take such a bet? Perhaps you would, but most people would not. Leaving aside any moral question that might surround gambling and recognizing that some people would take such a bet, it's our view that the average investor would not.

To induce the typical risk-averse investor to take a fair gamble, you must sweeten the pot. For example, you might need to raise the odds of winning from 50-50 to 70-30 or higher. The risk-averse investor can be induced to take fair gambles only if they are sweetened so that they become unfair to the investor's advantage.

www.sap.com
www.microsoft.com
www.ebay.com

EXAMPLE 13.8: Risk of Canadian Mutual Funds

Table 13.9 shows the returns and standard deviations for two Canadian mutual funds over the three-year period ending December 31, 2005. The table also shows comparable statistics for the S&P/TSX Composite. As you would expect, the TSX portfolio is the most widely diversified of the three portfolios and has the lowest unsystematic risk. For this reason, it has the lowest portfolio standard deviation. The next lowest standard deviation is the TD Canadian Equity fund, which invests in equities across different Canadian industries.

The TD Precious Metals fund focuses on one sector of the economy. For example, its top three holdings at the end of December 2005 were Goldcorp Inc., Barrick Gold Corp., and Glamis Gold Ltd. The narrower focus of this fund makes it less diversified, with higher standard deviations.

What does this example tell us about how good these funds were as investments? To answer this question, we have to investigate asset pricing, our next topic.

TABLE 13.9

Average returns and standard deviations for two Canadian mutual funds and the S&P/TSX Composite, 2003–2005

Fund	Annual Return	Standard Deviation
S&P/TSX Composite	21.39%	6.29%
TD Canadian Equity	7.16%	11.88%
TD Precious Metals	12.08%	25.38%

www.tdcanadatrust.com

CONCEPT QUESTIONS

1. What happens to the standard deviation of return for a portfolio if we increase the number of securities in the portfolio?

2. What is the principle of diversification?

3. Why is some risk diversifiable? Why is some risk not diversifiable?

4. Why can't systematic risk be diversified away?

5. Explain the concept of risk aversion.

SYSTEMATIC RISK AND BETA

The question that we now begin to address is: What determines the size of the risk premium on a risky asset? Put another way, why do some assets have a larger risk premium than other assets? The answer to these questions, as we discuss next, is also based on the distinction between systematic and unsystematic risk.

The Systematic Risk Principle

Thus far, we've seen that the total risk associated with an asset can be decomposed into two components: systematic and unsystematic risk. We have also seen that unsystematic risk can be essentially eliminated by diversification. The systematic risk present in an asset, on the other hand, cannot be eliminated by diversification.

systematic risk principle
Principle stating that the expected return on a risky asset depends only on that asset's systematic risk.

Based on our study of capital market history, we know that there is a reward, on average, for bearing risk. However, we now need to be more precise about what we mean by risk. The **systematic risk principle** states that the reward for bearing risk depends only on the systematic risk of an investment. The underlying rationale for this principle is straightforward: Because unsystematic risk can be eliminated at virtually no cost (by diversifying), there is no reward for bearing it. Put another way, the market does not reward risks that are born unnecessarily.

The systematic risk principle has a remarkable and very important implication: *The expected return on an asset depends only on that asset's systematic risk.* There is an obvious corollary to this principle: No matter how much total risk an asset has, only the systematic portion is relevant in determining the expected return (and the risk premium) on that asset.

Measuring Systematic Risk

Since systematic risk is the crucial determinant of an asset's expected return, we need some way of measuring the level of systematic risk for different investments. The specific measure that we use is called the **beta coefficient,** for which we will use the Greek symbol β. A beta coefficient, or beta for short, tells us how much systematic risk a particular asset has relative to an average asset. By definition, an average asset has a beta of 1.0 relative to itself. An asset with a beta of .50, therefore, has half as much systematic risk as an average asset; an asset with a beta of 2.0 has twice as much. These different levels of beta are illustrated in Figure 13.7. You can see that high beta assets display greater volatility over time.

beta coefficient
Amount of systematic risk present in a particular risky asset relative to an average risky asset.

Table 13.10 contains the estimated beta coefficients for the stocks of some well-known companies ranging from 0.56 to 3.28.

FIGURE 13.7

Volatility: High and low betas

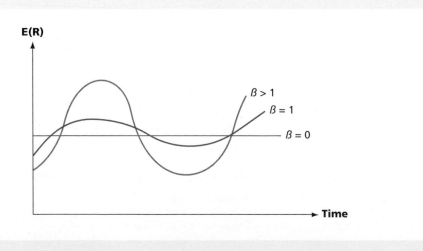

	Beta coefficient
TABLE 13.10	
Beta coefficients for selected companies	
Bank of Nova Scotia	0.56
Investors Group	0.84
Meridian Gold	0.89
Talisman Energy	0.99
Suncor Energy	1.01
Rogers Communications	1.43
Teck Cominco	1.94
Nortel Networks	3.28

Source: Financial Post Advisor, 2006.

EXAMPLE 13.9: Total Risk versus Beta

Consider the following information on two securities. Which has greater total risk? Which has greater systematic risk? Greater unsystematic risk? Which asset has a higher risk premium?

	Standard Deviation	Beta
Security A	40%	.50
Security B	20	1.50

From our discussion in this section, Security A has greater total risk, but it has substantially less systematic risk. Since total risk is the sum of systematic and unsystematic risk, Security A must have greater unsystematic risk. Finally, from the systematic risk principle, Security B has a higher risk premium and a greater expected return, despite the fact that it has less total risk.

Remember that the expected return, and thus the risk premium, on an asset depends only on its systematic risk. Because assets with larger betas have greater systematic risks, they have greater expected returns. Thus, in Table 13.10, an investor who buys stock in Bank of Nova Scotia with a beta of 0.56, should expect to earn less, on average, than an investor who buys stock in Rogers Communications, with a beta of 1.43.

Portfolio Betas

www.scotiabank.ca

Earlier, we saw that the riskiness of a portfolio does not have any simple relationship to the risks of the assets in the portfolio. A portfolio beta, however, can be calculated just like a portfolio expected return. For example, looking at Table 13.10, suppose you put half of your money in Bank of Nova Scotia and half in Nortel Networks. What would the beta of this combination be? Since Bank of Nova Scotia (BNS) has a beta of 0.56 and Nortel has a beta of 3.28, the portfolio's beta, β_P, would be:

$$\beta_P = .50 \times \beta_{BNS} + .50 \times \beta_{Nortel}$$
$$= .50 \times 0.56 + .50 \times 3.28$$
$$= 1.92$$

EXAMPLE 13.10: Portfolio Betas

Suppose we had the following investments:

Security	Amount Invested	Expected Return	Beta
Stock A	$1,000	8%	.80
Stock B	2,000	12	.95
Stock C	3,000	15	1.10
Stock D	4,000	18	1.40

What is the expected return on this portfolio? What is the beta of this portfolio? Does this portfolio have more or less systematic risk than an average asset?

To answer, we first have to calculate the portfolio weights. Notice that the total amount invested is $10,000. Of this, $1,000/$10,000 − 10% is invested in Stock A. Similarly, 20 percent is invested in Stock B, 30 percent is

invested in Stock C, and 40 percent is invested in Stock D. The expected return, $E(R_P)$, is thus:

$$E(R_P) = .10 \times E(R_A) + .20 \times E(R_B) + .30 \times E(R_C) + .40 \times E(R_D)$$
$$= .10 \times 8\% + .20 \times 12\% + .30 \times 15\% + .40 \times 18\%$$
$$= 14.9\%$$

Similarly, the portfolio beta, β_P, is:

$$\beta_P = .10 \times \beta_A + .20 \times \beta_B + .30 \times \beta_C + .40 \times \beta_D$$
$$= .10 \times .80 + .20 \times .95 + .30 \times 1.10 + .40 \times 1.40$$
$$= 1.16$$

This portfolio thus has an expected return of 14.9 percent and a beta of 1.16. Since the beta is larger than 1.0, this portfolio has greater systematic risk than an average asset.

In general, if we had a large number of assets in a portfolio, we would multiply each asset's beta by its portfolio weight and then add the results to get the portfolio's beta.

CONCEPT QUESTIONS

1. What is the systematic risk principle?

2. What does a beta coefficient measure?

3. How do you calculate a portfolio beta?

4. Does the expected return on a risky asset depend on that asset's total risk? Explain.

 **13.7**

THE SECURITY MARKET LINE

We're now in a position to see how risk is rewarded in the marketplace. To begin, suppose Asset A has an expected return of $E(R_A) = 20\%$ and a beta of $\beta_A = 1.6$. Furthermore, the risk-free rate is $R_f = 8\%$. Notice that a risk-free asset, by definition, has no systematic risk (or unsystematic risk), so a risk-free asset has a beta of 0.

Beta and the Risk Premium

Consider a portfolio made up of Asset A and a risk-free asset. We can calculate some different possible portfolio expected returns and betas by varying the percentages invested in these two assets. For example, if 25 percent of the portfolio is invested in Asset A, the expected return is:

$$E(R_p) = .25 \times E(R_A) + (1 - .25) \times R_f$$
$$= .25 \times 20\% + .75 \times 8\%$$
$$= 11.0\%$$

Similarly, the beta on the portfolio, β_p, would be:

$$\beta_P = .25 \times \beta_A + (1 - .25) \times 0$$
$$= .25 \times 1.6$$
$$= .40$$

Notice that, since the weights have to add up to 1, the percentage invested in the risk-free asset is equal to 1 minus the percentage invested in Asset A.

One thing that you might wonder about is whether it is possible for the percentage invested in Asset A to exceed 100 percent. The answer is yes. This can happen if the investor borrows at the risk-free rate. For example, suppose an investor has $100 and borrows an additional $50 at 8 percent, the risk-free rate. The total investment in Asset A would be $150, or 150 percent of the investor's wealth. The expected return in this case would be:

$$E(R_p) = 1.50 \times E(R_A) + (1 - 1.50) \times R_f$$
$$= 1.50 \times 20\% - .50 \times 8\%$$
$$= 26\%$$

The beta on the portfolio would be:

$$\beta_P = 1.50 \times \beta_A + (1 - 1.50) \times 0$$
$$= 1.50 \times 1.6$$
$$= 2.4$$

We can calculate some other possibilities as follows:

Percentage of Portfolio in Asset A	Portfolio Expected Return	Portfolio Beta
0%	8%	0.0
25	11	0.4
50	14	0.8
75	17	1.2
100	20	1.6
125	23	2.0
150	26	2.4

In Figure 13.8A, these portfolio expected returns are plotted against the portfolio betas. Notice that all the combinations fall on a straight line.

THE REWARD-TO-RISK RATIO   What is the slope of the straight line in Figure 13.8A? As always, the slope of a straight line is equal to the "rise over the run." As we move out of the risk-free asset into Asset A, the beta increases from zero to 1.6 (a "run" of 1.6). At the same time, the expected return goes from 8 to 20 percent, a "rise" of 12 percent. The slope of the line is thus 12%/1.6 = 7.50%.

Notice that the slope of our line is just the risk premium on Asset A, $E(R_A) - R_f$, divided by Asset A's beta, β_A:

$$\text{Slope} = \frac{[E(R_A) - R_f]}{\beta_A}$$

$$= \frac{[20\% - 8\%]}{1.6} = 7.50\%$$

What this tells us is that Asset A offers a reward-to-risk ratio of 7.50 percent.[9] In other words, Asset A has a risk premium of 7.50 percent per unit of systematic risk.

THE BASIC ARGUMENT   Now suppose we consider a second asset, Asset B. This asset has a beta of 1.2 and an expected return of 16 percent. Which investment is better, Asset A or Asset B? You might think that, once again, we really cannot say. Some investors might prefer A; some investors might prefer B. Actually, however, we can say: A is better because, as we demonstrate, B offers inadequate compensation for its level of systematic risk, at least relative to A.

FIGURE 13.8A

Portfolio expected returns and betas for Asset A

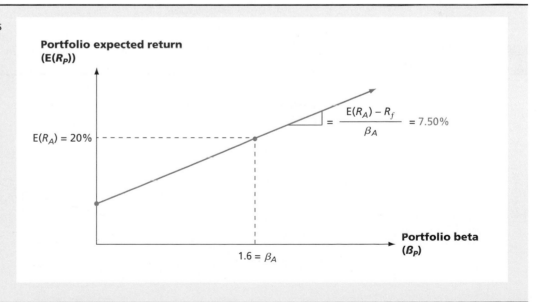

9 This ratio is sometimes called the Treynor index, after one of its originators.

To begin, we calculate different combinations of expected returns and betas for portfolios of Asset B and a risk-free asset just as we did for Asset A. For example, if we put 25 percent in Asset B and the remaining 75 percent in the risk-free asset, the portfolio's expected return would be:

$$
\begin{aligned}
E(R_P) &= .25 \times E(R_B) + (1 - .25) \times R_f \\
&= .25 \times 16\% + .75 \times 8\% \\
&= 10\%
\end{aligned}
$$

Similarly, the beta on the portfolio, β_P, would be:

$$
\begin{aligned}
\beta_P &= .25 \times \beta_B + (1 - .25) \times 0 \\
&= .25 \times 1.2 \\
&= .30
\end{aligned}
$$

Some other possibilities are as follows:

Percentage of Portfolio in Asset B	Portfolio Expected Return	Portfolio Beta
0%	8%	0.0
25	10	0.3
50	12	0.6
75	14	0.9
100	16	1.2
125	18	1.5
150	20	1.8

When we plot these combinations of portfolio expected returns and portfolios betas in Figure 13.8B, we get a straight line just as we did for Asset A.

The key thing to notice is that when we compare the results for Assets A and B, as in Figure 13.8C, the line describing the combinations of expected returns and betas for Asset A is higher than the one for Asset B. This tells us that for any given level of systematic risk (as measured by β), some combination of Asset A and the risk-free asset always offers a larger return. This is why we were able to state that Asset A is a better investment than Asset B.

Another way of seeing that A offers a superior return for its level of risk is to note that the slope of our line for Asset B is:

$$
\begin{aligned}
\text{Slope} &= \left[\frac{E(R_B) - R_f}{\beta_B}\right] \\
&= \frac{[16\% - 8\%]}{1.2} = 6.67\%
\end{aligned}
$$

FIGURE 13.8B

Portfolio expected returns and betas for Asset B

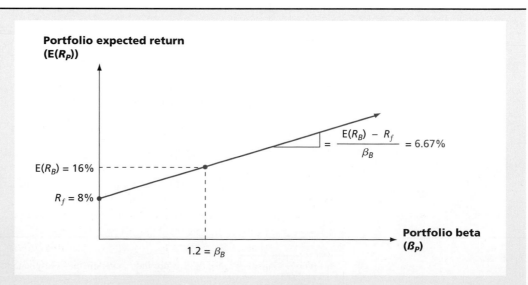

FIGURE 13.8C

Portfolio expected returns and betas for both assets

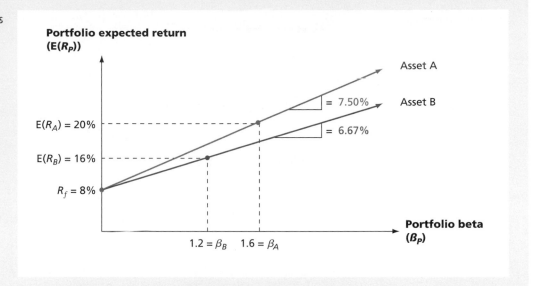

Thus, Asset B has a reward-to-risk ratio of 6.67 percent, which is less than the 7.5 percent offered by Asset A.

THE FUNDAMENTAL RESULT   The situation we have described for Assets A and B cannot persist in a well-organized, active market, because investors would be attracted to Asset A and away from Asset B. As a result, Asset A's price would rise and Asset B's price would fall. Since prices and returns move in opposite directions, the result is that A's expected return would decline and B's would rise.

This buying and selling would continue until the two assets plotted on exactly the same line, which means they offer the same reward for bearing risk. In other words, in an active, competitive market, we must have:

$$\frac{E(R_A) - R_f}{\beta_A} = \frac{E(R_B) - R_f}{\beta_B}$$

This is the fundamental relationship between risk and return.

Our basic argument can be extended to more than just two assets. In fact, no matter how many assets we had, we would always reach the same conclusion:

> The reward-to-risk ratio must be the same for all the assets in the market.

This result is really not so surprising. What it says, for example, is that, if one asset has twice as much systematic risk as another asset, its risk premium is simply twice as large.

Since all the assets in the market must have the same reward-to-risk ratio, they all must plot on the same line. This argument is illustrated in Figure 13.9. As shown, Assets A and B plot directly on the line and thus have the same reward-to-risk ratio. If an asset plotted above the line, such as C in Figure 13.9, its price would rise, and its expected return would fall until it plotted exactly on the line. Similarly, if an asset plotted below the line, such as D in Figure 13.9, its expected return would rise until it too plotted directly on the line.

The arguments we have presented apply to active, competitive, well-functioning markets. The financial markets, such as the TSX, NYSE, and Nasdaq, best meet these criteria. Other markets, such as real asset markets, may or may not. For this reason, these concepts are most useful in examining financial markets. We thus focus on such markets here. However, as we discuss in a later section, the information about risk and return gleaned from financial markets is crucial in evaluating the investments that a corporation makes in real assets.

www.nasdaq.com

FIGURE 13.9

Expected returns and systematic risk

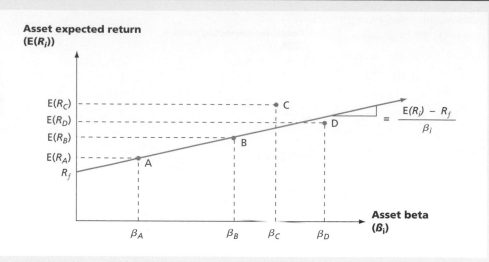

The fundamental relationship between beta and expected return is that all assets must have the same reward-to-risk ratio $[E(R_i) - R_f]/\beta_i$. This means they would all plot on the same straight line. Assets A and B are examples of this behaviour. Asset C's expected return is too high; Asset D's is too low.

EXAMPLE 13.11: Beta and Stock Valuation

An asset is said to be overvalued if its price is too high given its expected return and risk. Suppose you observe the following situation:

Security	Beta	Expected Return
SWMS Company	1.3	14%
Insec Company	.8	10

The risk-free rate is currently 6 percent. Is one of the two preceding securities overvalued relative to the other?

To answer, we compute the reward-to-risk ratio for both. For SWMS, this ratio is (14% – 6%)/1.3 = 6.15%. For Insec, this ratio is 5 percent. What we conclude is that Insec offers an insufficient expected return for its level of risk, at least relative to SWMS. Since its expected return is too low, its price is too high. To see why this is true, recall that the

dividend valuation model presented in Chapter 8 treats price as the present value of future dividends.

$$P_0 = \frac{D_1}{(r - g)}$$

Projecting the dividend stream gives us D_1 and g. If the required rate of return is too low, the stock price will be too high. For example, suppose D_1 = $2.00 and g = 7 percent. If the expected rate of return on the stock is wrongly underestimated at 10 percent, the stock price estimate is $66.67. This price is too high if the true expected rate of return is 14 percent. At this higher rate of return, the stock price should fall to $28.57. In other words, Insec is overvalued relative to SWMS, and we would expect to see its price fall relative to SWMS's. Notice that we could also say that SWMS is undervalued relative to Insec.

TABLE 13.11

Average returns and betas for selected Canadian mutual funds, the S&P/TSX Composite, and Canadian 3-month Treasury bills, 10 years ending April 30, 2006

Fund	Annual Return	Beta
S&P/TSX Composite	10.88%	1
3-month Treasury bills	3.60%	0
Altamira Equity	5.42%	0.93
Saxon Stock	13.41%	0.86

Source: *www.globefund.com, www.bankofcanada.ca.*

Calculating Beta

The beta of a security measures the responsiveness of that security's return to the return on the market as a whole. To calculate beta, we draw a line relating the expected return on the security to different returns on the market. This line, called the *characteristic line* of the security, has a slope equal to the stock's beta.

EXAMPLE 13.12: Mutual Fund Performance

Table 13.11 gives the inputs needed to compute the reward-to-risk ratios for the TSX and two mutual funds. Starting with the TSX, the reward-to-risk ratio was:

(Average return − Riskless rate)/Beta

(10.88 − 3.60)/1.00 = 7.28%

You can verify that the reward-to-risk ratio for Altamira Equity is 1.96 percent and the ratio for Saxon

Stock was 11.41 percent. Saxon Stock beat the market by earning a higher reward-to-risk ratio than the TSX, while Altamira Equity underperformed over this period.

Unfortunately, in an efficient market, past performance can guide expectations of future returns, but these expectations may not be realized in actual returns. So we would not expect that Saxon Stock would beat the market consistently over time.

Consider Figure 13.10, which displays returns for both a hypothetical company and the market as a whole.[10] Each point represents a pair of returns over a particular month. The vertical dimension measures the return on the stock over the month and the horizontal dimension that of the S&P/TSX Composite. (The S&P/TSX Composite is considered a reasonable proxy for the general market.)

Figure 13.10 also shows the line of *best fit* superimposed on these points. In practical applications, this line is calculated from regression analysis. As one can see from the graph, the slope is 1.28. Because the average beta is 1, this indicates the stock's beta of 1.28 is higher than that for the average stock.

The goal of a financial analyst is to determine the beta that a stock will have in the future, because this is when the proceeds of an investment are received. Of course, past data must be used in regression analysis. Thus, it is incorrect to think of 1.28 as the beta of our example company. Rather it is our estimate of the firm's beta from past data.

The bottom of Figure 13.10 indicates that the company's R^2 over the time period is 0.584. What does this mean? R^2 measures how close the points in the figure are to the characteristic line. The highest value for R^2 is 1, a situation that would occur if all points lay exactly on the characteristic line. This would be the case where the security's return is determined only by the market's return without the security having any independent variation. The R^2 is likely to approach one for a large portfolio of securities. For example, many widely diversified mutual funds have R^2s of 0.80 or more. The lowest possible R^2 is zero, a situation occurring when two variables are entirely unrelated to each other. Those companies whose returns are pretty much independent of returns on the stock market would have R^2s near zero.

The risk of any security can be broken down into unsystematic and systematic risk. Whereas beta measures the amount of systematic risk, R^2 measures the *proportion* of total risk that is systematic. Thus, a low R^2 indicates that most of the risk of a firm is unsystematic.[11]

The mechanics for calculating betas are quite simple. People in business frequently estimate beta by using commercially available computer programs. Certain handheld calculators are also able to perform the calculation. In addition, a large number of services sell or even give away estimates of beta for different firms. For example, Table 13.10 presents a set of betas calculated by *The Financial Post* in May 2006.

In calculating betas, analysts make a number of assumptions consistent with Canadian research on the capital asset pricing model.[12] First, they generally choose monthly data, as do

www.nationalpost.com/
financialpost

---

10 As we mentioned in Chapter 12, the return on a security includes both the dividend and the capital gain (or loss).

11 Standard computer packages generally provide confidence intervals (error ranges) for beta estimates. One has greater confidence in beta estimates where the confidence interval is small. While stocks with high R^2s generally have small confidence intervals, it is the size of the confidence interval, not the R^2 itself, that is relevant here. Because expected return is related to systematic risk, the R^2 of a firm is of no concern to us once we know the firm's beta. This often surprises students trained in statistics, because R^2 is an important concept for many other purposes.

12 See Z. Bodie, A. Kane, A. J. Marcus, S. Perrakis and P. J. Ryan, *Investments*, 5th Canadian ed. (Whitby, Ontario: McGraw-Hill Ryerson, 2005).

FIGURE 13.10

Graphic representation of beta

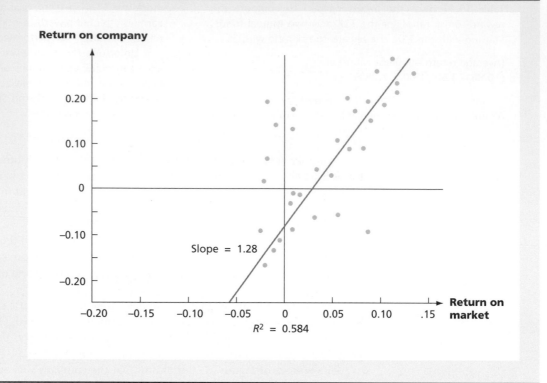

Return on company

Slope = 1.28

$R^2 = 0.584$

Return on market

many financial economists. On the one hand, statistical problems frequently arise when time intervals shorter than a month are used. On the other hand, important information is lost when longer intervals are employed. Thus, the choice of monthly data can be viewed as a compromise.

Second, analysts typically use just under five years of data, the result of another compromise. Due to changes in production mix, production techniques, management style, and/or financial leverage, a firm's nature adjusts over time. A long time period for calculating beta implies many out-of-date observations. Conversely, a short time period leads to statistical imprecision, because few monthly observations are used.

CONCEPT QUESTIONS

1. What is the statistical procedure employed for calculating beta?

2. Why do financial analysts use monthly data when calculating beta?

3. What is R^2?

The Security Market Line

The line that results when we plot expected returns and beta coefficients is obviously of some importance, so it's time we gave it a name. This line, which we use to describe the relationship between systematic risk and expected return in financial markets, is usually called the **security market line (SML).** After NPV, the SML is arguably the most important concept in modern finance.

security market line (SML)
Positively sloped straight line displaying the relationship between expected return and beta.

MARKET PORTFOLIOS   It will be very useful to know the equation of the SML. There are many different ways that we could write it, but one way is particularly common. Suppose we were to consider a portfolio made up of all of the assets in the market. Such a portfolio is called a *market portfolio*, and we write the expected return on this market portfolio as $E(R_M)$.

Since all the assets in the market must plot on the SML, so must a market portfolio made of those assets. To determine where it plots on the SML, we need to know the beta of the market portfolio, β_M. Because this portfolio is representative of all the assets in the market, it must have average systematic risk. In other words, it has a beta of one. We could therefore write the slope of the SML as:

$$\text{SML slope} = \frac{[E(R_M) - R_f]}{\beta_M} = \frac{[E(R_M) - R_f]}{1} = E(R_M) - R_f$$

market risk premium
Slope of the SML, the difference between the expected return on a market portfolio and the risk-free rate.

The term $E(R_M) - R_f$ is often called the **market risk premium** since it is the risk premium on a market portfolio.

THE CAPITAL ASSET PRICING MODEL   To finish up, if we let $E(R_i)$ and β_i stand for the expected return and beta, respectively, on any asset in the market, we know it must plot on the SML. As a result, we know that its reward-to-risk ratio is the same as the overall market's:

$$\frac{[E(R_i) - R_f]}{\beta_i} = E(R_M) - R_f$$

capital asset pricing model (CAPM)
Equation of the SML showing the relationship between expected return and beta.

If we rearrange this, we can write the equation for the SML as:

$$E(R_i) = R_f + [E(R_M) - R_f] \times \beta_i \qquad\qquad [13.10]$$

This result is identical to the famous **Capital Asset Pricing Model (CAPM).**[13]

What the CAPM shows is that the expected return for a particular asset depends on three things:

FIGURE 13.11

The security market line (SML)

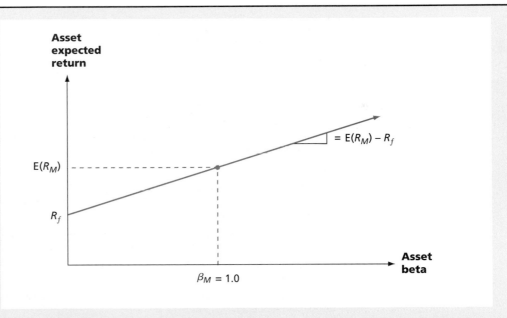

The slope of the security market line is equal to the market risk premium; i.e., the reward for bearing an average amount of systematic risk. The equation describing the SML can be written:

$E(R_i) = R_f + \beta_i \times [E(R_M) - R_f]$

which is the capital asset pricing model (CAPM).

---

13 Our discussion leading up to the CAPM is actually much more closely related to a more recently developed theory, known as the arbitrage pricing theory (APT). The theory underlying the CAPM is a great deal more complex than we have indicated here, and the CAPM has a number of other implications that go beyond the scope of this discussion. As we present here, the CAPM and the APT have essentially identical implications, so we don't distinguish between them. Appendix 13A presents another way to develop the CAPM.

1. *The pure time value of money.* As measured by the risk-free rate, R_f, this is the reward for merely waiting for your money, without taking any risk.
2. *The reward for bearing systematic risk.* As measured by the market risk premium $[E(R_M) - R_f]$, this component is the reward the market offers for bearing an average amount of systematic risk in addition to waiting.
3. *The amount of systematic risk.* As measured by β_i, this is the amount of systematic risk present in a particular asset, relative to an average asset.

By the way, the CAPM works for portfolios of assets just as it does for individual assets. In an earlier section, we saw how to calculate a portfolio's β. To find the expected return on a portfolio, we simply use this β in the CAPM equation.

Figure 13.11 summarizes our discussion of the SML and the CAPM. As before, we plot the expected return against beta. Now we recognize that, based on the CAPM, the slope of the SML is equal to the market risk premium $[E(R_M) - R_f]$. This concludes our presentation of concepts related to the risk-return trade-off. For future reference, Table 13.12 summarizes the various concepts in the order we discussed them in.

EXAMPLE 13.13: Risk and Return

Suppose the risk-free rate is 4 percent, the market risk premium is 8.6 percent, and a particular stock has a beta of 1.3. Based on the CAPM, what is the expected return on this stock? What would the expected return be if the beta were to double?

With a beta of 1.3, the risk premium for the stock would be $1.3 \times 8.6\%$, or 11.18 percent. The risk-free rate is 4 percent, so the expected return is 15.18 percent. If the beta doubles to 2.6, the risk premium would double to 22.36 percent, so the expected return would be 26.36 percent.

TABLE 13.12
Summary of risk and return

Total risk. The *total risk* of an investment is measured by the variance or, more commonly, the standard deviation of its return.

Total return. The *total return* on an investment has two components: the expected return and the unexpected return. The unexpected return comes about because of unanticipated events. The risk from investing stems from the possibility of unanticipated events.

Systematic and unsystematic risks. Systematic risks (also called market risks) are unanticipated events that affect almost all assets to some degree because they are economywide. Unsystematic risks are unanticipated events that affect single assets or small groups of assets. Unsystematic risks are also called *unique* or *asset-specific risks.*

The effect of diversification. Some, but not all, of the risk associated with a risky investment can be eliminated by diversification. The reason is that unsystematic risks, which are unique to individual assets, tend to wash out in a large portfolio; systematic risks, which affect all of the assets in a portfolio to some extent, do not.

The systematic risk principle and beta. Because unsystematic risk can be freely eliminated by diversification, the *systematic risk principle* states that the reward for bearing risk depends only on the level of systematic risk. The level of systematic risk in a particular asset, relative to average, is given by the beta of that asset.

The reward-to-risk ratio and the security market line. The reward-to-risk ratio for asset i is the ratio of its risk premium $E(R_i) - R_f$ to its beta, β_i:

$$\frac{E(R_i) - R_f}{\beta i}$$

In a well-functioning market, this ratio is the same for every asset. As a result, when asset expected returns are plotted against asset betas, all assets plot on the same straight line, called the *security market line* (SML).

The capital asset pricing model. From the SML, the expected return on asset i can be written:

$$E(R_i) = R_f + [E(R_M) - R_f] \times \beta_i$$

This is the *capital asset pricing model* (CAPM). The expected return on a risky asset thus has three components: The first is the pure time value of money (R_f), the second is the market risk premium $[E(R_M) - R_f]$, and the third is the beta for that asset, β_i.

CONCEPT QUESTIONS

1. What is the fundamental relationship between risk and return in well-functioning markets?

2. What is the security market line? Why must all assets plot directly on it in a well-functioning market?

3. What is the capital asset pricing model (CAPM)? What does it tell us about the required return on a risky investment?

arbitrage pricing theory (APT)

An equilibrium asset pricing theory that is derived from a factor model by using diversification and arbitrage. It shows that the expected return on any risky asset is a linear combination of various factors.

ARBITRAGE PRICING THEORY

The CAPM and the **arbitrage pricing theory** (APT) are alternative models of risk and return. One advantage of the APT is that it can handle multiple factors that the CAPM ignores. Although the bulk of our presentation in this chapter focused on the one-factor model, a multifactor model is probably more reflective of reality.[14]

The APT assumes that stock returns are generated according to factor models. For example, we have described a stock's return as

Total return = Expected return + Unexpected return
$$R = E(R) + U$$

In APT, the unexpected return is related to several market factors. Suppose there are three such factors: unanticipated changes in inflation, GNP, and interest rates. The total return can be expanded as

$$R = E(R) + \beta_I F_I + \beta_{GNP} F_{GNP} + \beta_r F_r + \epsilon \qquad [13.11]$$

The three factors F_I, F_{GNP}, and F_r represent systematic risk because these factors affect many securities. The term ϵ is considered unsystematic risk because it is unique to each individual security.

Under this multifactor APT, we can generalize from three to K factors to express the relationship between risk and return as:

$$E(R) = R_F + E[(R_1) - R_F]\beta_1 + E[(R_2) - R_F]\beta_2 \qquad [13.12]$$
$$+ E[(R_3) - R_F]\beta_3 + \dots E[(R_K) - R_F]\beta_K$$

In this equation, β_1 stands for the security's beta with respect to the first factor, β_2 stands for the security's beta with respect to the second factor, and so on. For example, if the first factor is inflation, β_1 is the security's inflation beta. The term $E(R_1)$ is the expected return on a security (or portfolio) whose beta with respect to the first factor is one and whose beta with respect to all other factors is zero. Because the market compensates for risk, $E((R_1) - R_F)$ is positive in the normal case.[15] (An analogous interpretation can be given to $E(R_2)$, $E(R_3)$, and so on.)

The equation states that the security's expected return is related to its factor betas. The argument is that each factor represents risk that cannot be diversified away. The higher a security's beta with regard to a particular factor, the higher the risk that security bears. In a rational world, the expected return on the security should compensate for this risk. The preceding equation states that the expected return is a summation of the risk-free rate plus the compensation for each type of risk the security bears.

As an example, consider a Canadian study where the factors were

1. The rate of growth in industrial production (INDUS).

---

14 A well-known extension of the CAPM employs three factors to explain returns: a market factor, firm size and the market-to-book-value ratio: E.F. Fama and K.R. French, "Common Risk Factors in the Returns on Stocks and Bonds," *Journal of Financial Economics* 33 (1) (February 1993).

15 Actually $(R_i - R_F)$ could be negative in the case where factor i is perceived as a hedge of some sort.

2. The changes in the slope of the term structure of interest rates (the difference between the yield on long-term and short-term Canada bonds) (TERMS).

3. The default risk premium for bonds (measured as the difference between the yield on long-term Canada bonds and the yield on the ScotiaMcLeod corporate bond index) (RISKPREM).

4. The inflation (measured as the growth of the consumer price index) (INFL).

5. The value-weighted return on the market portfolio (S&P/TSX Composite) (MKRET).[16]

Using the period 1970–84, the empirical results of the study indicated that expected monthly returns on a sample of 100 TSX stocks could be described as a function of the risk premiums associated with these five factors.

Because many factors appear on the right side of the APT equation, the APT formulation explained expected returns in this Canadian sample more accurately than did the CAPM. However, as we mentioned earlier, one cannot easily determine which are the appropriate factors. The factors in this study were included for reasons of both common sense and convenience. They were not derived from theory and the choice of factors varies from study to study. A more recent Canadian study, for example, includes changes in a U.S. stock index and in exchange rates as factors.[17]

CONCEPT QUESTIONS

1. What is the main advantage of the APT over the CAPM?

SUMMARY AND CONCLUSIONS

This chapter covered the essentials of risk. Along the way, we introduced a number of definitions and concepts. The most important of these is the security market line, or SML. The SML is important because it tells us the reward offered in financial markets for bearing risk. Once we know this, we have a benchmark against which to compare the returns expected from real asset investments and to determine if they are desirable.

Because we covered quite a bit of ground, it's useful to summarize the basic economic logic underlying the SML as follows:

1. Based on capital market history, there is a reward for bearing risk. This reward is the risk premium on an asset.

2. The total risk associated with an asset has two parts: systematic risk and unsystematic risk. Unsystematic risk can be freely eliminated by diversification (this is the principle of diversification), so only systematic risk is rewarded. As a result, the risk premium on an asset is determined by its systematic risk. This is the systematic risk principle.

3. An asset's systematic risk, relative to average, can be measured by its beta coefficient, β_i. The risk premium on an asset is then given by its beta coefficient multiplied by the market risk premium $[E(R_M) - R_f] \times \beta_i$.

4. The expected return on an asset, $E(R_i)$, is equal to the risk-free rate, R_f, plus the risk premium:

$$E(R_i) = R_f + [E(R_M) - R_f] \times \beta_i$$

---

16 E. Otuteye, "How Economic Forces Explain Canadian Stock Returns," *Canadian Investment Review*, Spring 1991, pp. 93–99.

17 L. Kryzanowski, S. Lalancette, and M.C. To, "Performance Attribution using an APT with Prespecified Macro-factors and Time-Varying Risk Premia and Betas," *Journal of Financial and Quantitative Analysis* 32 (June 1997), pp. 205–224. A further Canadian study is: B.F. Smith, "A Study of the Arbitrage Pricing Theory Using Daily Returns of Canadian Stocks," in M.J. Robinson and B.F. Smith, eds., *Canadian Capital Markets*, London, Ont., Ivey Business School, 1993.

This is the equation of the SML, and it is often called the capital asset pricing model (CAPM).

This chapter completes our discussion of risk and return and concludes Part 5 of our book. Now that we have a better understanding of what determines a firm's cost of capital for an investment, the next several chapters examine more closely how firms raise the long-term capital needed for investment.

Key Terms

arbitrage pricing theory (APT) (page 399)
beta coefficient (page 388)
capital asset pricing model (CAPM) (page 397)
expected return (page 370)
market risk premium (page 397)
portfolio (page 373)

portfolio weights (page 373)
principle of diversification (page 386)
security market line (SML) (page 396)
systematic risk (page 383)
systematic risk principle (page 388)
unsystematic risk (page 383)

Chapter Review Problems and Self-Test

13.1   Expected Return and Standard Deviation This problem gives you some practice calculating measures of prospective portfolio performance. There are two assets and three states of the economy:

State of Economy	Probability of State of Economy	Rate of Return if State Occurs	
		Stock A	Stock B
Recession	.20	−.15	.20
Normal	.50	.20	.30
Boom	.30	.60	.40

What are the expected returns and standard deviations for these two stocks?

13.2   Portfolio Risk and Return Using the information in the previous problem, suppose you have $20,000 total. If you put $15,000 in Stock A and the remainder in

Stock B, what will be the expected return and standard deviation on your portfolio?

13.3   Risk and Return Suppose you observe the following situation:

Security	Beta	Expected Return
Cooley, Inc.	1.8	22.00%
Moyer Company	1.6	20.44

If the risk-free rate is 7 percent, are these securities correctly priced? What would the risk-free rate have to be if they are correctly priced?

13.4   CAPM Suppose the risk-free rate is 8 percent. The expected return on the market is 16 percent. If a particular stock has a beta of .7, what is its expected return based on the CAPM? If another stock has an expected return of 24 percent, what must its beta be?

Answers to Self-Test Problems

13.1   The expected returns are just the possible returns multiplied by the associated probabilities:

$$E(R_A) = (.20 \times -.15) + (.50 \times .20) + (.30 \times .60) = 25\%$$
$$E(R_B) = (.20 \times .20) + (.50 \times .30) + (.30 \times .40) = 31\%$$

The variances are given by the sums of the squared deviations from the expected returns multiplied by their probabilities:

$$\begin{aligned}
\sigma^2_A &= .20 \times (-.15 - .25)^2 + .50 \times (.20 - .25)^2 + .30 \times (.60 - .25)^2 \\
&= (.20 \times -.40^2) + (.50 \times -.05^2) + (.30 \times .35^2) \\
&= (.20 \times .16) + (.50 \times .0025) + (.30 \times .1225) \\
&= .0700
\end{aligned}$$

$$\begin{aligned}
\sigma^2_B &= .20 \times (.20 - .31)^2 + .50 \times (.30 - .31)^2 + .30 \times (.40 - .31)^2 \\
&= (.20 \times -.11^2) + (.50 \times -.01^2) + (.30 \times .09^2) \\
&= (.20 \times .0121) + (.50 \times .0001) + (.30 \times .0081) \\
&= .0049
\end{aligned}$$

The standard deviations are thus:

$$\sigma_A = \sqrt{.0700} = 26.46\%$$
$$\sigma_B = \sqrt{.0049} = 7\%$$

13.2   The portfolio weights are $15,000/20,000 = .75$ and $5,000/20,000 = .25$. The expected return is thus:

$$E(R_p) = .75 \times E(R_A) + .25 \times E(R_B)$$
$$= (.75 \times 25\%) + (.25 \times 31\%)$$
$$= 26.5\%$$

Alternatively, we could calculate the portfolio's return in each of the states:

State of Economy	Probability of State of Economy	Portfolio Return if State Occurs
Recession	.20	$(.75 \times -.15) + (.25 \times .20) = -.0625$
Normal	.50	$(.75 \times .20) + (.25 \times .30) = .2250$
Boom	.30	$(.75 \times .60) + (.25 \times .40) = .5500$

The portfolio's expected return is:

$$E(R_p) = (.20 \times -.0625) + (.50 \times .2250) + (.30 \times .5500) = 26.5\%$$

This is the same as we had before.

The portfolio's variance is:

$$\sigma^2_p = .20 \times (-.0625 - .265)^2 + .50 \times (.225 - .265)^2$$
$$+ .30 \times (.55 - .265)^2$$
$$= .0466$$

So the standard deviation is $\sqrt{.0466} = 21.59\%$.

13.3   If we compute the reward-to-risk ratios, we get $(22\% - 7\%)/1.8 = 8.33\%$ for Cooley versus 8.4% for Moyer. Relative to that of Cooley, Moyer's expected return is too high, so its price is too low.

If they are correctly priced, they must offer the same reward-to-risk ratio. The risk-free rate would have to be such that:

$$(22\% - R_f)/1.8 = (20.44\% - R_f)/1.6$$

With a little algebra, we find that the risk-free rate must be 8 percent:

$$22\% - R_f = (20.44\% - R_f)(1.8/1.6)$$
$$22\% - 20.44\% \times 1.125 = R_f - R_f \times 1.125$$
$$R_f = 8\%$$

13.4   Because the expected return on the market is 16 percent, the market risk premium is $16\% - 8\% = 8\%$ (the risk-free rate is 8 percent). The first stock has a beta of .7, so its expected return is $8\% + .7 \times 8\% = 13.6\%$.

For the second stock, notice that the risk premium is $24\% - 8\% = 16\%$. Because this is twice as large as the market risk premium, the beta must be exactly equal to 2. We can verify this using the CAPM:

$$E(R_i) = R_f + [E(R_M) - R_f] \times \beta_i$$
$$24\% = 8\% + (16\% - 8\%) \times \beta_i$$
$$\beta_i = 16\%/8\%$$
$$= 2.0$$

Concepts Review and Critical Thinking Questions

1. In broad terms, why is some risk diversifiable? Why are some risks nondiversifiable? Does it follow that an investor can control the level of unsystematic risk in a portfolio, but not the level of systematic risk?

2. Suppose the government announces that, based on a just-completed survey, the growth rate in the economy is likely to be 2 percent in the coming year, as compared to 5 percent for the year just completed. Will security prices increase, decrease, or stay the same following this announcement? Does it make any difference whether or not the 2 percent figure was anticipated by the market? Explain.

3. Classify the following events as mostly systematic or mostly unsystematic. Is the distinction clear in every case?
   a. Short-term interest rates increase unexpectedly.
   b. The interest rate a company pays on its short-term debt borrowing is increased by its bank.
   c. Oil prices unexpectedly decline.
   d. An oil tanker ruptures, creating a large oil spill.
   e. A manufacturer loses a multimillion-dollar product liability suit.
   f. A Supreme Court of Canada decision substantially broadens producer liability for injuries suffered by product users.

4. Indicate whether the following events might cause stocks in general to change price, and whether they might cause Big Widget Corp.'s stock to change price.
    u. The government announces that inflation unexpectedly jumped by 2 percent last month.
    b. Big Widget's quarterly earnings report, just issued, generally fell in line with analysts' expectations.
    c. The government reports that economic growth last year was at 3 percent, which generally agreed with most economists' forecasts.
    d. The directors of Big Widget die in a plane crash.
    e. The Government of Canada approves changes to the tax code that will increase the top marginal corporate tax rate. The legislation had been debated for the previous six months.

5. If a portfolio has a positive investment in every asset, can the expected return on the portfolio be greater than that on every asset in the portfolio? Can it be less than that on every asset in the portfolio? If you answer yes to one or both of these questions, give an example to support your answer.

6. True or false: The most important characteristic in determining the expected return of a well-diversified portfolio is the variances of the individual assets in the portfolio. Explain.

7. If a portfolio has a positive investment in every asset, can the standard deviation on the portfolio be less than that on every asset in the portfolio? What about the portfolio beta?

8. Is it possible that a risky asset could have a beta of zero? Explain. Based on the CAPM, what is the expected return on such an asset? Is it possible that a risky asset could have a negative beta? What does the CAPM predict about the expected return on such an asset? Can you give an explanation for your answer?

9. In recent years, it has been common for companies to experience significant stock price changes in reaction to announcements of massive layoffs. Critics charge that such events encourage companies to fire long-time employees and that Bay Street is cheering them on. Do you agree or disagree?

10. As indicated by a number of examples in this chapter, earnings announcements by companies are closely followed by, and frequently result in, share price revisions. Two issues should come to mind. First, earnings announcements concern past periods. If the market values stocks based on expectations of the future, why are numbers summarizing past performance relevant? Second, these announcements concern accounting earnings. Going back to Chapter 2, such earnings may have little to do with cash flow, so, again, why are they relevant?

Questions and Problems

Basic
(Questions 1–22)

1. **Determining Portfolio Weights**   What are the portfolio weights for a portfolio that has 70 shares of Stock A that sell for $40 per share and 110 shares of Stock B that sell for $22 per share?

2. **Portfolio Expected Return**   You own a portfolio that has $1,200 invested in Stock A and $1,900 invested in Stock B. If the expected returns on these stocks are 11 percent and 16 percent, respectively, what is the expected return on the portfolio?

3. **Portfolio Expected Return**   You own a portfolio that is 50 percent invested in Stock X, 30 percent in Stock Y, and 20 percent in Stock Z. The expected returns on these three stocks are 11 percent, 17 percent, and 14 percent, respectively. What is the expected return on the portfolio?

4. **Portfolio Expected Return**   You have $10,000 to invest in a stock portfolio. Your choices are Stock X with an expected return of 14 percent and Stock Y with an expected return of 9 percent. If your goal is to create a portfolio with an expected return of 12.2 percent, how much money will you invest in Stock X? In Stock Y?

5. **Calculating Expected Return**   Based on the following information, calculate the expected return.

State of Economy	Probability of State of Economy	Rate of Return if State Occurs
Recession	.30	−.08
Boom	.70	.28

6. **Calculating Expected Return**   Based on the following information, calculate the expected return.

State of Economy	Probability of State of Economy	Rate of Return if State Occurs
Recession	.20	−.05
Normal	.50	.12
Boom	.30	.25

7. **Calculating Returns and Standard Deviations**   Based on the following information, calculate the expected return and standard deviation for the two stocks.

State of Economy	Probability of State of Economy	Rate of Return if State Occurs	
		Stock A	Stock B
Recession	.10	.06	−.20
Normal	.60	.07	.13
Boom	.30	.11	.33

Basic **8.** **Calculating Expected Returns**   A portfolio is invested 20 percent in Stock G, 70 percent in Stock J, and 10 percent in
(continued)   Stock K. The expected returns on these stocks are 8 percent, 15 percent, and 24 percent, respectively. What is the portfolio's expected return? How do you interpret your answer?

9. **Returns and Standard Deviations**   Consider the following information:

State of Economy	Probability of State of Economy	Rate of Return if State Occurs		
		Stock A	Stock B	Stock C
Boom	.70	.07	.15	.33
Bust	.30	.13	.03	−.06

a. What is the expected return on an equally weighted portfolio of these three stocks?

b. What is the variance of a portfolio invested 20 percent each in A and B, and 60 percent in C?

10. **Returns and Standard Deviations**   Consider the following information:

State of Economy	Probability of State of Economy	Rate of Return if State Occurs		
		Stock A	Stock B	Stock C
Boom	.30	.30	.45	.33
Good	.40	.12	.10	.15
Poor	.25	.01	−.15	−.05
Bust	.05	−.06	−.30	−.09

a. Your portfolio is invested 30 percent each in A and C, and 40 percent in B. What is the expected return of the portfolio?

b. What is the variance of this portfolio? The standard deviation?

11. **Standard Deviations**   You own a portfolio of two stocks (X and Y), with 43 percent of the portfolio invested in
Stock X. You have observed over many years that the variance of your portfolio value is 0.0212, and that the correlation
between Stock X and Stock Y is 0.85. If the standard deviation of Stock X is 0.18, what is the standard deviation of
Stock Y?

12. **Variance and Standard Deviations**   You have $6,000 invested in Stock A and $15,000 invested in Stock B. The return
for Stock A has a variance of 0.03225, while the return for Stock B has a variance of 0.02112. You have also determined
that the correlation coefficient between the two stocks is 0.60. What is the variance and the standard deviation for the
portfolio? How would this change if the correlation was 0.5? 1.0?

 13. **Calculating Portfolio Betas**   You own a stock portfolio invested 25 percent in Stock Q, 20 percent in Stock R,
15 percent in Stock S, and 40 percent in Stock T. The betas for these four stocks are .6, 1.70, 1.15, and 1.34, respectively.
What is the portfolio beta?

14. **Calculating Portfolio Betas**   You own a portfolio equally invested in a risk-free asset and two stocks. If one of the
stocks has a beta of 1.9 and the total portfolio is equally as risky as the market, what must the beta be for the other
stock in your portfolio?

15. **Using CAPM**   A stock has a beta of 1.3, the expected return on the market is 14 percent, and the risk-free rate is
5 percent. What must the expected return on this stock be?

16. **Using CAPM**   A stock has an expected return of 14 percent, the risk-free rate is 4 percent, and the market risk premium is 6 percent. What must the beta of this stock be?

17. **Using CAPM**   A stock has an expected return of 11 percent, its beta is .85, and the risk-free rate is 5.5 percent.
What must the expected return on the market be?

18. **Using CAPM**   A stock has an expected return of 17 percent, a beta of 1.9, and the expected return on the market is
11 percent. What must the risk-free rate be?

 19. **Using CAPM**   A stock has a beta of 1.2 and an expected return of 16 percent. A risk-free asset currently earns 5 percent.

a. What is the expected return on a portfolio that is equally invested in the two assets?

b. If a portfolio of the two assets has a beta of .75, what are the portfolio weights?

c. If a portfolio of the two assets has an expected return of 8 percent, what is its beta?

d. If a portfolio of the two assets has a beta of 2.40, what are the portfolio weights? How do you interpret the weights
for the two assets in this case? Explain.

20. **Using the SML**   Asset W has an expected return of 16 percent and a beta of 1.3. If the risk-free rate is 5 percent, complete the following table for portfolios of Asset W and a risk-free asset. Illustrate the relationship between portfolio

**Basic
(continued)**

expected return and portfolio beta by plotting the expected returns against the betas. What is the slope of the line that results?

Percentage of Portfolio in Asset W	Portfolio Expected Return	Portfolio Beta
0%		
25		
50		
75		
100		
125		
150		

21. **Reward-to-Risk Ratios**   Stock Y has a beta of 1.50 and an expected return of 17 percent. Stock Z has a beta of .80 and an expected return of 10.5 percent. If the risk-free rate is 5.5 percent and the market risk premium is 7.5 percent, are these stocks correctly priced?

22. **Reward-to-Risk Ratios**   In the previous problem, what would the risk-free rate have to be for the two stocks to be correctly priced?

Intermediate 23. **Portfolio Returns**   Using information from the previous chapter on capital market history, determine the return on a
(Questions   portfolio that is equally invested in large-company stocks and long-term government bonds. What is the return on a
23–29)   portfolio that is equally invested in small-company stocks and Treasury bills?

24. **CAPM**   Using the CAPM, show that the ratio of the risk premiums on two assets is equal to the ratio of their betas.

25. **Portfolio Returns and Deviations**   Consider the following information on three stocks:

State of Economy	Probability of State of Economy	Rate of Return if State Occurs		
		Stock A	Stock B	Stock C
Boom	.4	.20	.35	.60
Normal	.4	.15	.12	.05
Bust	.2	.01	−.25	−.50

a. If your portfolio is invested 40 percent each in A and B and 20 percent in C, what is the portfolio expected return? The variance? The standard deviation?

b. If the expected T-bill rate is 3.80 percent, what is the expected risk premium on the portfolio?

c. If the expected inflation rate is 3.50 percent, what are the approximate and exact expected real returns on the portfolio? What are the approximate and exact expected real risk premiums on the portfolio?

26. **Analyzing a Portfolio**   You want to create a portfolio equally as risky as the market, and you have $1,000,000 to invest. Given this information, fill in the rest of the following table:

Asset	Investment	Beta
Stock A	$200,000	.80
Stock B	$250,000	1.30
Stock C		1.50
Risk-free asset		

27. **Analyzing a Portfolio**   You have $100,000 to invest in a portfolio containing Stock X, Stock Y, and a risk-free asset. You must invest all of your money. Your goal is to create a portfolio that has an expected return of 13.5 percent and that has only 70 percent of the risk of the overall market. If X has an expected return of 31 percent and a beta of 1.8, Y has an expected return of 20 percent and a beta of 1.3, and the risk-free rate is 7 percent, how much money will you invest in Stock X? How do you interpret your answer?

28. **Systematic versus Unsystematic Risk**   Consider the following information on Stocks I and II:

State of Economy	Probability of State of Economy	Rate of Return if State Occurs	
		Stock I	Stock II
Recession	.15	.09	−.30
Normal	.70	.42	.12
Irrational exuberance	.15	.26	.44

The market risk premium is 10 percent, and the risk-free rate is 4 percent. Which stock has the most systematic risk? Which one has the most unsystematic risk? Which stock is "riskier"? Explain.

Intermediate
(continued)

29. SML Suppose you observe the following situation:

Security	Beta	Expected Return
Pete Corp.	1.3	.23
Repete Co.	.6	.13

Assume these securities are correctly priced. Based on the CAPM, what is the expected return on the market? What is the risk-free rate?

S&P Problem

1. **Using CAPM** You can find estimates of beta for each company under the "Mthly. Val. Data" link. Locate the beta for Nortel Networks Corp. (NT) and Imperial Oil Ltd. (IMO). How has the beta for each of these companies changed over the period reported? Using the historical risk-free rate and market risk premium found in the chapter, calculate the expected return for each company based on the most recent beta. Is the expected return for each company what you would expect? Why or why not?

Internet Application Questions

1. You have decided to invest in an equally weighted portfolio consisting of Petro-Canada, Royal Bank of Canada, Canadian Tire, and WestJet Airlines and need to find the beta of your portfolio. Go to finance.yahoo.com and follow the "Global Symbol Lookup" link to find the ticker symbols for each of these companies. Next, go back to finance.yahoo.com, enter one of the ticker symbols and get a stock quote. Follow the "Profile" link to find the beta for this company. You will then need to find the beta for each of the companies. What is the beta for your portfolio?

2. Go to moneycentral.msn.com or FP Advisor and search for Reitmans Canada. Follow the "Profile" link to get the beta for the company. Go to www.bankofcanada.ca, follow the "Interest Rates" link, and find the current interest rate for three-month Treasury bills. Using this information, calculate the expected return on the market using the reward-to-risk ratio. What would be the expected stock price one year from now?

3. Recall that the site www.globefund.com contains considerable information on Canadian mutual funds. Visit the site and update the calculations in Example 13.12 to reflect the most recent three-year period.

4. You want to find the expected return for Bank of Montreal using the CAPM. First you need the market risk premium. Go to www.bmo.com, follow the "BMO Economics" link and find "The Daily" under regular publications. Find the current interest rate for three-month Treasury bills. Use the average Canadian common stock return in Table 12.3 to calculate the market risk premium. If the beta for Bank of Montreal is 1.01, what is the expected return using CAPM?[18] What assumptions have you made to arrive at this number? As you may recall from Chapter 8, stock growth is often assumed to be equal to earnings growth. Compare your answer above with an EPS growth estimate from www.globeinvestor.com. What does this tell you about analyst estimates?

5. You have decided to invest in an equally weighted portfolio consisting of Rogers Communications, Bank of Montreal, and Inco and need to find the beta of your portfolio. Go to finance.yahoo.com and follow the "Symbol Lookup" link to find the ticker symbols for each of these companies. Next, go back to finance.yahoo.com, enter one of the ticker symbols and get a stock quote. Follow the "Profile" link to find the beta for this company. You will then need to find the beta for each of the companies. What is the beta for your portfolio? (Note that this beta will compare the stock to the NYSE.)

6. Go to finance.yahoo.com and enter the ticker symbol FS for Four Seasons Hotels. Follow the "Profile" link to get the beta for the company. Next, follow the "Research" link to find the estimated price in 12 months according to market analysts. Using the current share price and the mean target price, compute the expected return for this stock. Don't forget to include the expected dividend payments over the next year. Now go to www.cnnfn.com and find the current interest rate for three-month Treasury bills. Using this information, calculate the expected return on the market using the reward-to-risk ratio. Does this number make sense? Why or why not? (Note that the beta value you locate will compare Four Seasons to the NYSE volatility. You should analyze this question from a U.S. perspective.)

Suggested Readings

For greater detail on the subject of risk and return see Chapters 8, 9, and 10 of:
  Ross, S.A., R. W. Westerfield, J. J. Jaffe, and G. S. Roberts. *Corporate Finance,* 4th Canadian ed. Whitby, Ontario: McGraw-Hill Ryerson, 2005.

---

18 Note that if you have access to investment research services like those offered by TD Waterhouse or ScotiaMcLeod you could update the beta value by accessing their stock research section.

Two intuitive discussions of APT are:

Bower, D. H., R. S. Bower, and D. Logue. "A Primer on Arbitrage Pricing Theory." *Midland Corporate Finance Journal,* Fall 1984.

Roll, R., and S. Ross. "The Arbitrage Pricing Theory Approach to Strategic Portfolio Planning." *Financial Analysts Journal,* May–June 1984.

Discussions of Canadian tests of APT are found in:

Bodie, Z., A. Kane, A. J. Marcus, S. Perrakis, and P. J. Ryan, *Investments,* 5th Canadian ed. Whitby, Ontario: McGraw-Hill Ryerson, 2005.

Otuteye, E. "How Economic Forces Explain Canadian Stock Returns." *Canadian Investment Review,* Spring 1991.

Sharpe, W.F., G.J. Alexander, J.V. Bailey, D.J. Fowler, and D. Domian, *Investments,* 3rd Canadian ed. Scarborough, Ontario: Prentice-Hall Canada, 2000.

DERIVATION OF THE CAPITAL ASSET PRICING MODEL

Up to this point, we have assumed that all assets on the efficient frontier are risky. Alternatively, an investor could easily combine a risky investment with an investment in a riskless or risk-free security, such as a Canada Treasury bill. Using the equation for portfolio variance (Equation 13A.1) we can find the variance of a portfolio with one risky and one risk-free asset:

$$\sigma^2_P = x^2_L\sigma^2_L + x^2_U\sigma^2_U + 2x_Lx_U\text{CORR}_{L,U}\sigma_L\sigma_U \qquad [13A.1]$$

However, by definition, the risk-free asset (say, L in this example) has no variability so the equation for portfolio standard deviation reduces to:

$$\sigma^2_P = x^2_U\sigma^2_U$$

$$\sigma_P = \sqrt{\sigma^2_P} = x_U\sigma_U$$

The relationship between risk and return for one risky and one riskless asset is represented on a straight line between the risk-free rate and a pure investment in the risky asset as shown in Figure 13A.1. The line extends to the right of the point representing the risky asset when we assume the investor can borrow at the risk-free rate to take a leveraged position of more than 100 percent in the risky asset.

FIGURE 13A.1

Relationship between expected return and standard deviation for an investment in a combination of risky securities and the riskless asset

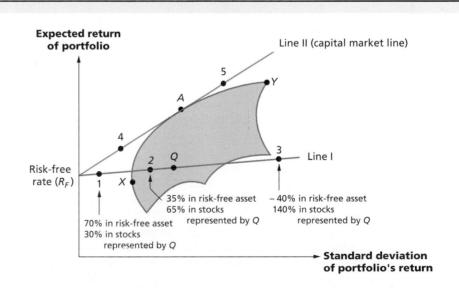

Portfolio Q is composed of
30 percent BCE
45 percent Bank of Montreal
25 percent Northern Telecom

To form an optimal portfolio, an investor is likely to combine an investment in the riskless asset with a portfolio of risky assets. Figure 13A.1 illustrates our discussion by showing a risk-free asset and four risky assets: A, X, Q, and Y. If there is no riskless asset, the efficient set is the curve from X to Y. With a risk-free asset, it is possible to form portfolios like 1, 2, and 3 combining Q with the risk-free asset. Portfolios 4 and 5 combine the riskless asset with A.

The graph illustrates an important point. With riskless borrowing and lending, the portfolio of risky assets held by any investor would always be point A. Regardless of the investor's tolerance for risk, he or she would never choose any other point on the efficient set of risky assets. Rather, an investor with a high aversion to risk would combine the securities of A with riskless assets. The investor would borrow the riskless asset to invest more funds in A had he or she low aversion to risk. In other words, all investors would choose portfolios along Line II, called the *capital market line*.

To move from our description of a single investor to market equilibrium, financial economists imagine a world where all investors possess the same estimates of expected returns, variance, and correlations. This assumption is called *homogeneous expectations*.

If all investors have homogeneous expectations, Figure 13A.1 becomes the same for all individuals. All investors sketch out the same efficient set of risky assets because they are working with the same inputs. This efficient set of risky assets is represented by the curve XAY. Because the same risk-free rate applies to everyone, all investors view point A as the portfolio of risky assets to be held. In a world with homogeneous expectations, all investors would hold the portfolio of risky assets represented by point A.

If all investors choose the same portfolio of risky assets, A, then A must be the market portfolio. This is because, in our simplified world of homogeneous expectations, no asset would be demanded (and priced) if it were not in portfolio A. Since all assets have some demand and non-zero price, A has to be the market portfolio including all assets.

The variance of the market portfolio can be represented as:

$$\sigma^2_P \sum_{i=1}^{N} \sum_{j=1}^{N} x_j \sigma_{ij} \qquad [13A.2]$$

where we define σ_{ij} as the covariance of i with j if $i \neq j$ and σ_{ij} is the variance or σ^2_i if $i = j$.

$$\sigma_{ij} = \text{CORR}_{ij} \, \sigma_i \sigma_j$$

Using a little elementary calculus, we can represent a security's systematic risk (the contribution of security i to the risk of the market portfolio) by taking the partial derivative of the portfolio risk with respect to a change in the weight of the security. This measures the change in the portfolio variance when the weight of the security is increased slightly. For security 2,

$$\frac{\delta \sigma^2_P}{\delta x_2} = 2 \sum_{j=1}^{N} x_j \sigma_{i2} = 2[x_1 \text{COV}(R_1, R_2) + x_2 \sigma^2_2 + x_3 \text{COV}(R_3, R_2) \qquad [13A.3]$$
$$+ \dots + x_N \text{COV}(R_N, R_2)]$$

The term within brackets in (13A.3) is $\text{COV}(R_2, R_M)$. This shows that systematic risk is proportional to a security's covariance with the market portfolio.

The final step is to standardize systematic risk by dividing by the variance of the market portfolio. The result is β_2 as presented in the text.

$$\beta_2 = \frac{\text{COV}(R_2, R_M)}{\sigma^2(R_M)} \qquad [13A.4]$$

If you consult any basic statistics text, you will see that this formula is identical to the β_2 obtained from a regression of R_2 on R_M.

We can now redraw Figure 13A.1 in expected return-β space, as shown in Figure 13A.2. The vertical axis remains the same, but on the horizontal axis we replace total risk (σ) with systematic risk as measured by β. We plot the two points on the capital market line from Figure 13A.1: R_F with $\beta = 0$ and M (the market portfolio represented by A) with a $\beta = 1$. To see that $\beta_M = 1$, substitute portfolio M for i in Equation 13A.4.

$$\beta_M = \frac{COV(R_M, R_M)}{\sigma^2(R_M)}$$

$$= \frac{CORR_{M,M}\sigma_M\sigma_M}{\sigma^2(R_M)}$$

$$= \frac{1.0 \times \sigma 2_M}{\sigma^2(R_M)}$$

$$\beta_M = 1.0$$

The result is the security market line shown in Figure 13A.2. We can use the slope-intercept method to find that the intercept of the SML is R_F and the slope is $(R_M - R_F)$. The equation for the SML is:

$$E(R) = R_F + \beta(R_M - R_F)$$

And this completes the derivation of the capital asset pricing model.

FIGURE 13A.2

Relationship between expected return on an individual security and beta of the security

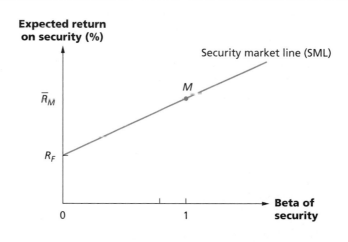

$\underline{R}_F$ is the risk-free rate.
$\overline{R}_M$ is the expected return on the market portfolio.

PART 6

Cost of Capital and Long-Term Financial Policy

CHAPTER 14

Cost of Capital

ALCAN

Alcan Inc. is a multinational leader in aluminum, rolled aluminum products, and specialty packaging with annual revenue of more than U.S. $20 billion in 2005. Alcan's key business objective is maximizing shareholder value. As such, Alcan Inc. has become one of a growing number of Canadian companies who measure performance based on the amount by which their return on capital for the year exceeds the cost of capital. This measure is used to increase shareholder value, to prioritize investment and operational decisions, and as part of each business unit's annual compensation formula. In this chapter, we learn how to compute a firm's cost of capital and find out what it means to the firm and its investors.

www.alcan.com

SUPPOSE YOU HAVE just become the president of a large company and the first decision you face is whether to go ahead with a plan to renovate the company's warehouse distribution system. The plan will cost the company $50 million, and it is expected to save $12 million per year after taxes over the next six years.

This is a familiar problem in capital budgeting. To address it, you would determine the relevant cash flows, discount them, and, if the net present value is positive, take on the project; if the NPV is negative, you would scrap it. So far so good, but what should you use as the discount rate?

From our discussion of risk and return, you know that the correct discount rate depends on the riskiness of the warehouse distribution system. In particular, the new project would have a positive NPV only if its return exceeds what the financial markets offer on investments of similar risks. We called this minimum required return the cost of capital associated with the project.

Thus, to make the right decision as president, you must examine the returns that investors expect to earn on the securities represented in the pool of funds that would finance the project. You then use this information to arrive at an estimate of the project's cost of capital. Our primary purpose in this chapter is to describe how to do this. There are a variety of approaches to this task, and a number of conceptual and practical issues arise.

One of the most important concepts we develop is the weighted average cost of capital (WACC). This is the cost of capital for the firm as a whole, and it can be interpreted as the required return on the overall firm. In discussing the WACC, we recognize the fact that a firm normally raises capital in a variety of forms and that these different forms of capital may have different costs associated with them.

We also recognize in this chapter that taxes are an important consideration in determining the required return on an investment, because we are always interested in valuing the aftertax cash flows from a project. We therefore discuss how to incorporate taxes explicitly into our estimates of the cost of capital.

THE COST OF CAPITAL: SOME PRELIMINARIES

In Chapter 13, we developed the security market line (SML) and used it to explore the relationship between the expected return on a security and its systematic risk. We concentrated on how the risky returns from buying securities looked from the viewpoint of, for example, a shareholder in the firm. This helped us understand more about the alternatives available to an investor in the capital markets.

In this chapter, we turn things around and look more closely at the other side of the problem, which is how these returns and securities look from the viewpoint of the companies that issue them. Note that the return an investor in a security receives is the cost of that security to the company that issued it.

Required Return versus Cost of Capital

When we say that the required return on an investment is, say, 10 percent, we usually mean the investment has a positive NPV only if its return exceeds 10 percent. Another way of interpreting the required return is to observe that the firm must earn 10 percent on the investment just to compensate its investors for the use of the capital needed to finance the project. This is why we could also say that 10 percent is the cost of capital associated with the investment.

To illustrate the point further, imagine that we were evaluating a risk-free project. In this case, how to determine the required return is obvious: We look at the capital markets and observe the current rate offered by risk-free investments, and we use this rate to discount the project's cash flows. Thus, the cost of capital for a risk-free investment is the risk-free rate.

If this project were risky, then, assuming that all the other information is unchanged, the required return is obviously higher. In other words, the cost of capital for this project, if it is risky, is greater than the risk-free rate, and the appropriate discount rate would exceed the risk-free rate.

We henceforth use the terms *required return, appropriate discount rate,* and *cost of capital* more or less interchangeably because, as the discussion in this section suggests, they all mean essentially the same thing. The key fact to grasp is that the cost of capital associated with an investment depends on the risk of that investment. This is one of the most important lessons in corporate finance, so it bears repeating: *The cost of capital depends primarily on the use of the funds, not the source.*

It is a common error to forget this crucial point and fall into the trap of thinking that the cost of capital for an investment depends primarily on how and where the capital is raised.

Financial Policy and Cost of Capital

We know that the particular mixture of debt and equity that a firm chooses to employ—its capital structure—is a managerial variable. In this chapter, we take the firm's financial policy as given. In particular, we assume the firm has a fixed debt/equity ratio that it maintains. This *D/E* ratio reflects the firm's target capital structure. How a firm might choose that ratio is the subject of Chapter 16.

From our discussion, we know that a firm's overall cost of capital reflects the required return on the firm's assets as a whole. Given that a firm uses both debt and equity capital, this overall cost of capital is a mixture of the returns needed to compensate its creditors and its shareholders. In other words, a firm's cost of capital reflects both its cost of debt capital and its cost of equity capital. We discuss these costs separately in the following sections

14.2

cost of equity
The return that equity investors require on their investment in the firm.

THE COST OF EQUITY

We begin with the most difficult question on the subject of cost of capital: What is the firm's over-all **cost of equity**? The reason this is a difficult question is that there is no way of directly observing the return that the firm's equity investors require on their investment. Instead, we must somehow estimate it. This section discusses two approaches to determining the cost of equity: the dividend growth model approach and the security market line (SML) approach.

The Dividend Growth Model Approach

The easiest way to estimate the cost of equity capital is to use the dividend growth model that we developed in Chapter 8. Recall that, under the assumption that the firm's dividend will grow at a constant rate, g, the price per share of the stock, P_0, can be written as:

$$P_0 = \frac{D_0 \times (1 + g)}{[R_E - g]} = \frac{D_1}{[R_E - g]}$$

where D_0 is the dividend just paid, and D_1 is the next period's projected dividend. Notice that we have used the symbol R_E (the E stands for equity) for the required return on the stock.

As we discussed in Chapter 8, we can arrange this to solve for R_E as follows:

$$R_E = (D_1/P_0) + g \tag{14.1}$$

Since R_E is the return that the shareholders require on the stock, it can be interpreted as the firm's cost of equity capital.

IMPLEMENTING THE APPROACH   To estimate R_E using the dividend growth model approach, we obviously need three pieces of information: P_0, D_0, and g.[1] Of these, for a publicly traded, dividend-paying company, the first two can be observed directly, so they are easily obtainable. Only the third component, the expected growth rate in dividends, must be estimated.

For example, suppose Provincial Telephone Company, a large public utility, paid a dividend of $4 per share last year. The stock currently sells for $60 per share. You estimate the dividend will grow steadily at 6 percent per year into the indefinite future. What is the cost of equity capital for Provincial Telephone? Using the dividend growth model, the expected dividend for the coming year, D_1, is:

$$
\begin{aligned}
D_1 &= D_0 \times (1 + g) \\
&= \$4 \times (1.06) \\
&= \$4.24
\end{aligned}
$$

Given this, the cost of equity, R_E, is:

$$
\begin{aligned}
R_E &= D_1/P_0 + g \\
&= \$4.24/\$60 + .06 \\
&= 13.07\%
\end{aligned}
$$

The cost of equity is thus 13.07 percent.

ESTIMATING g   To use the dividend growth model, we must come up with an estimate for g, the growth rate. There are essentially two ways of doing this: (1) use historical growth rates, or (2) use analysts' forecasts of future growth rates. Analysts' forecasts are available from the

---

1 Notice that if we have D_0 and g, we can simply calculate D_1 by multiplying D_0 by $(1 + g)$.

research departments of investment dealers. Naturally, different sources have different estimates, so one approach might be to obtain multiple estimates and then average them.

Alternatively, we might observe dividends for the previous, say, five years, and calculate the compound growth rate. For example, suppose we observe the following for the James Bay Company:

Individual firm growth estimates can be found at www.globeinvestor.ca in the Estimate Snapshot section.

Year	Dividend
2000	$1.10
2001	1.20
2002	1.35
2003	1.40
2004	1.55

The compound growth rate, g, is the rate at which $1.10 grew to $1.55 during four periods of growth.

$$\$1.10 (1 + g)^4 = \$1.55$$
$$\$1.10/(\$1.55) = 0.7097 = 1/(1 + g)^4$$
$$g = 8.95\%$$

If historical growth has been volatile, the compound growth rate would be sensitive to our choice of beginning and ending years. In this case, it is better to calculate the year-to-year growth rates and average them.

Year	Dividend	Dollar Change	Percentage Change
2000	$1.10	—	—
2001	1.20	$.10	9.09%
2002	1.35	.15	12.50
2003	1.40	.05	3.70
2004	1.55	.15	10.71

Notice that we calculated the change in the dividend on a year-to-year basis and then expressed the change as a percentage. Thus, in 2001 for example, the dividend rose from $1.10 to $1.20, an increase of $.10. This represents a $.10/1.10 = 9.09% increase.

If we average the four growth rates, the result is (9.09 + 12.50 + 3.70 + 10.71)/ 4 = 9%, so we could use this as an estimate for the expected growth rate, g. In this case, averaging annual growth rates gives about the same answer as the compound growth rate. Other more sophisticated statistical techniques could be used, but they all amount to using past dividend growth to predict future dividend growth.[2]

AN ALTERNATIVE APPROACH   Another way to find g starts with earnings retention. Consider a business whose earnings next year are expected to be the same as earnings this year unless a net investment is made. The net investment will be positive only if some earnings are not paid out as dividends, that is, only if some earnings are retained. This leads to the following equation:

$$\text{Earnings next year} = \text{Earnings this year} + \text{Retained earnings this year} \times \text{Return on retained earnings}$$

The increase in earnings is a function of both the retained earnings and the return on retained earnings.

We now divide both sides of the equation by earnings this year yielding

$$\frac{\text{Earnings next year}}{\text{Earnings this year}} = \frac{\text{Earnings this year}}{\text{Earnings this year}} + \frac{\text{Retained earnings this year}}{\text{Earnings this year}} \times \text{Return on retained earnings}$$

---

2 Statistical techniques for calculating g include linear regression, geometric averaging, and exponential smoothing.

retention ratio
Retained earnings divided by
net income.

The left side of the last equation is simply one plus the growth rate in earnings, which we write as $1 + g$.[3] The ratio of retained earnings to earnings is called the **retention ratio.** Thus we can write:

$$1 + g = 1 + \text{Retention ratio} \times \text{Return on retained earnings}$$

It is difficult for a financial analyst to determine the return to be expected on currently retained earnings, because the details on forthcoming projects are not generally public information. However, it is frequently assumed that the projects selected in the current year have the same risk and therefore the same anticipated return as projects in other years. Here, we can estimate the anticipated return on current retained earnings by the historical **return on equity** or **ROE.** After all, ROE is simply the return on the firm's entire equity, which is the return on the cumulation of all the firm's past projects.

return on equity (ROE)
Net income after interest and
taxes divided by average
common shareholders'
equity.

We now have a simple way to estimate growth:

$$g = \text{Retention ratio} \times \text{ROE}$$

ADVANTAGES AND DISADVANTAGES OF THE APPROACH Whichever way we estimate g, the primary advantage of the dividend growth model approach is its simplicity. It is both easy to understand and easy to use. There are a number of associated practical problems and disadvantages.

First and foremost, the dividend growth model is most applicable to companies that pay dividends. For companies that do not pay dividends, we can use the model and estimate g from earnings/growth. This is equivalent to assuming that one day dividends will be paid. Either way, the key underlying assumption is that the dividend grows at a constant rate. As our previous example illustrates, this will never be exactly the case. More generally, the model is really only applicable to cases where reasonably steady growth is likely to occur.

A second problem is that the estimated cost of equity is very sensitive to the estimated growth rate. An upward revision of g by just 1 percentage point, for example, increases the estimated cost of equity by at least a full percentage point. Since D_1 would probably be revised upwards as well, the increase would actually be somewhat larger than that.

Finally, this approach really does not explicitly consider risk. Unlike the SML approach (which we consider next), there is no direct adjustment for the riskiness of the investment. For example, there is no allowance for the degree of certainty or uncertainty surrounding the estimated growth rate in dividends. As a result, it is difficult to say whether or not the estimated return is commensurate with the level of risk.[4]

The SML Approach

In Chapter 13, we discussed the security market line (SML). Our primary conclusion was that the required or expected return on a risky investment depends on three things:

1. The risk-free rate, R_f.
2. The market risk premium, $E(R_M) - R_f$.
3. The systematic risk of the asset relative to average, which we called its beta coefficient, β.

Using the SML, the expected return on the company's equity, $E(R_E)$, can be written as:

$$E(R_E) = R_F + \beta_E \times [E(R_M) - R_F]$$

where β_E is the estimated beta for the equity. For the SML approach to be consistent with the dividend growth model, we drop the expectation sign, E, and henceforth write the required return from the SML, R_E, as:

$$R_E = R_f + \beta_E \times [R_M - R_f] \qquad \text{[14.2]}$$

---

3 Previously g referred to growth in dividends. However, the growth in earnings is equal to the growth rate in dividends in this context, because we assume the ratio of dividends to earnings is held constant.

4 There is an implicit adjustment for risk because the current stock price is used. All other things being equal, the higher the risk, the lower the stock price. Further, the lower the stock price, the greater the cost of equity, again assuming all the other information is the same.

IMPLEMENTING THE APPROACH   To use the SML approach, we need a risk-free rate, R_f, an estimate of the market risk premium, $R_M - R_f$, and an estimate of the relevant beta, β_E. In Chapter 12 (Table 12.3), we saw that one estimate of the market risk premium (based on large capitalization Canadian common stocks) is around 4.35 percent. Three-month Canada Treasury bills are paying about 4.2 percent as this is written, so we use this as our risk-free rate. Beta coefficients for publicly traded companies are widely available. Chapter 13 showed how to calculate betas from historical returns.

T-bill rates can be found at www.bmo.com

To illustrate, in Chapter 13 we saw that Investors Group had an estimated beta of 0.84 (Table 13.10). We could thus estimate Investors Group's cost of equity as:

$$R_{ntl} = R_f + \beta \times [R_M - R_f]$$
$$= 4.2\% + 0.84 \times (4.35\%)$$
$$= 7.854\%$$

Thus, using the SML approach, Investors Group's cost of equity is about 7.854 percent.

ADVANTAGES AND DISADVANTAGES OF THE APPROACH   The SML approach has two primary advantages: First, it explicitly adjusts for risk. Second, it is applicable to companies other than those with steady dividend growth. Thus, it may be useful in a wider variety of circumstances.

There are drawbacks, of course. The SML approach requires that two things be estimated, the market risk premium and the beta coefficient. To the extent that our estimates are poor, the resulting cost of equity is inaccurate. For example, our estimate of the market risk premium, 3.4 percent, is based on about 50 years of returns on a particular portfolio of stocks. Using different time periods or different stocks could result in very different estimates.

Finally, as with the dividend growth model, we essentially rely on the past to predict the future when we use the SML approach. Economic conditions can change very quickly, so, as always, the past may not be a good guide to the future. In the best of all worlds, the two approaches (dividend growth model and SML) are both applicable and both result in similar answers. If this happens, we might have some confidence in our estimates. We might also wish to compare the results to those for other, similar companies as a reality check.

The Cost of Equity in Rate Hearings

Suppose that Provincial Hydro, a regulated utility, has just applied for increases in the rates charged some of its customers. One test that regulators apply is called the "fair rate of return" rule. This means that they determine the fair rate of return on capital for the company and allow an increase in rates only if the company can show that revenues are insufficient to achieve this fair rate. For example, suppose a company had capital in the form of equity of $100 and net

---

EXAMPLE 14.1: The Cost of Equity

At the time of writing, stock in Bank of Nova Scotia was trading on the TSX at $42.80. Bank of Nova Scotia had a 120-month beta of 0.71. The market risk premium historically has been around 4.35 percent and the risk-free rate in 2006 was 3.97 percent. Bank of Nova Scotia's last dividend was $1.44 and some analysts expected that the dividends would grow at 8 percent indefinitely. What is Bank of Nova Scotia's cost of equity?

$$R_E = R_f + \beta_E \times [R_M - R_f]$$
$$= 3.97\% + 0.71 \times 4.35$$
$$= 7.06\%$$

This suggests that 7.06% percent is Bank of Nova Scotia's cost of equity. We next use the dividend growth model. The projected dividend is $D_0 \times (1+g) = \$1.44 \times (1.08) = \$1.56$, so the expected return using this approach is:

$$RE = D_1/P_0 + g$$
$$= \$1.56/\$42.80 + 0.08$$
$$= 11.7\%$$

Our two estimates differ significantly, so we will use the one in which we have the greater confidence. If the inputs are fairly reliable for the SML, it is preferred over the growth model, which may not apply in all companies. One key reason for this preference is that the SML considers risk (as measured by beta), while the growth model does not. We should also note that in our example the 8 percent indefinite growth rate seems quite high, so the dividend growth model may be overestimating the cost of equity. In this case, this gives us a cost of equity for Bank of Nova Scotia of 7.06 percent. If the two estimates had been reasonably close, we might have chosen to average them to find the cost of equity.

income of $8 providing a return of 8 percent. If the fair rate of return were 9 percent, the company would be allowed a rate increase sufficient to generate one additional dollar of net income.

Regulatory authorities determine the fair rate of return after hearing presentations by the company and by consumer groups. Since a higher fair rate of return helps make the case for rate increases, it is no surprise to find that consultants engaged by the company argue for a higher fair rate and consultants representing consumer groups argue for a lower fair rate. Because the fair rate of return depends on capital market conditions, consultants use the dividend growth approach and the SML approach, along with other techniques.

Suppose that Provincial Hydro has presented the regulators with a cost of equity of 11 percent. You are a consultant for a consumer group. What flaws would you look for?

If you think that the cost of equity is too high, you should challenge the assumed growth rate in dividends. Also, the market risk premium used in the SML may be too high.[5] If you are clever at working with these models and can remain unruffled when testifying, you may have career potential as a financial expert witness.

CONCEPT QUESTIONS

1. What do we mean when we say that a corporation's cost of equity capital is 16 percent?

2. What are two approaches to estimating the cost of equity capital?

THE COSTS OF DEBT AND PREFERRED STOCK

In addition to ordinary equity, firms use debt and, to a lesser extent, preferred stock to finance their investments. As we discuss next, determining the costs of capital associated with these sources of financing is much easier than determining the cost of equity.

The Cost of Debt

cost of debt
The return that lenders require on the firm's debt.

The **cost of debt** is the return that the firm's long-term creditors demand on new borrowing. In principle, we could determine the beta for the firm's debt and then use the SML to estimate the required return on debt just as we estimate the required return on equity. This isn't really necessary, however.

Unlike a firm's cost of equity, its cost of debt can normally be observed either directly or indirectly, because the cost of debt is simply the interest rate the firm must pay on new borrowing, and we can observe interest rates in the financial markets. For example, if the firm already has bonds outstanding, then the yield to maturity on those bonds is the market-required rate on the firm's debt.

Alternatively, if we knew that the firm's bonds were rated, say, A, we can simply find out what the interest rate on newly issued A-rated bonds is. Either way, there is no need to actually estimate a beta for the debt since we can directly observe the rate we want to know.

There is one thing to be careful about, though. The coupon rate on the firm's outstanding debt is irrelevant here. That just tells us roughly what the firm's cost of debt was back when the bonds were issued, not what the cost of debt is today.[6] This is why we have to look at the yield on

---

EXAMPLE 14.2: The Cost of Debt

At the time of writing, Union Gas had a bond outstanding with approximately 19.2 years to maturity (38.4 semi-annual coupons) and a coupon rate of 8.65 percent. The bond was currently selling for $136.03. What is Union Gas's cost of debt?

To answer this question, we need to solve the bond pricing formula for R, the yield to maturity:

$$\$136.03 = \sum_{t=1}^{38.4} \$4.325/(1 + \tfrac{R}{2})^t + 100/(1 + \tfrac{R}{2})^{38.4}$$

Using a spreadsheet or a financial calculator, we find that R is 5.57 percent. Union Gas's cost of debt is thus 5.57 percent.

---

5 If you were the consultant for the company, you should counter that, at the time of writing, long-term bonds issued by Canadian utilities were yielding around 6.5 percent. Since equity is riskier than bonds, the cost of equity should be higher than 6.5 percent.

6 The firm's cost of debt based on its historic borrowing is sometimes called the *embedded debt cost.*

the debt in today's marketplace. For consistency with our other notation, we use the symbol R_D for the cost of debt.

The Cost of Preferred Stock

Determining the cost of fixed rate preferred stock is quite straightforward. As we discussed in Chapters 7 and 8, this type of preferred stock has a fixed dividend paid every period forever, so a share of preferred stock is essentially a perpetuity. The cost of preferred stock, R_P, is thus:

$$R_P = D/P_0 \qquad\qquad [14.3]$$

www.telus.com
www.tsx.com

where D is the fixed dividend and P_0 is the current price per share of the preferred stock. Notice that the cost of preferred stock is simply equal to the dividend yield on the preferred stock. Alternatively, preferred stocks are rated in much the same way as bonds, so the cost of preferred stock can be estimated by observing the required returns on other, similarly rated shares of preferred stock.

EXAMPLE 14.3: Great-West Life Assurance's Cost of Preferred Stock

On May 18, 2006, Great-West Life Assurance's preferred stock (GWL.PR.L-T) traded on the TSX with a dividend of $1.30 annually and a price of $26.00. What is Great-West Life Assurance's cost of preferred stock?

The cost of preferred stock is:

$$
\begin{aligned}
R_P &= D/P_0 \\
&= \$1.30/\$26 \\
&= 5\%
\end{aligned}
$$

So Great-West Life Assurance's cost of preferred stock is 5%.

CONCEPT QUESTIONS

1. How can the cost of debt be calculated?

2. How can the cost of preferred stock be calculated?

3. Why is the coupon rate a bad estimate of a firm's cost of debt?

14.4

THE WEIGHTED AVERAGE COST OF CAPITAL

Now that we have the costs associated with the main sources of capital that the firm employs, we need to worry about the specific mix. As we mentioned earlier, we take this mix (the firm's capital structure) as given for now.

One of the implications of using WACC for a project is that we are assuming that money is raised in the optimal proportions. For instance, if the optimal weight for debt is 25 percent, raising $100 million means that $25 million will come from new debt and $75 million from common and preferred shares. Practically speaking, the firm would not raise these sums simultaneously by issuing both debt and equity. Instead, the firm may issue just debt, or just equity, which, at that point, has the effect of upsetting the optimal debt ratio. Issuing just one type of security and temporarily upsetting the optimal weights presents no problem as long as a subsequent issue takes the firm back to the optimal ratio for which it is striving. The point is that the firm's capital structure weights may fluctuate within some range in the short term, but the target weights should always be used in computing WACC.

In Chapter 3, we mentioned that financial analysts frequently focus on a firm's total capitalization, which is the sum of its long-term debt and equity. This is particularly true in determining the cost of capital; short-term liabilities are often ignored in the process. Some short-term liabilities such as accounts payable and accrued wages rise automatically with sales increases and have already been incorporated into cash flow estimates. We ignore them in calculating the cost of capital to avoid the error of double counting. Other current liabilities, short-term bank borrowing for example, are excluded because they support seasonal needs and are not part of the permanent capital structure.[7]

---

[7] If a firm used short-term bank loans as part of its permanent financing, we would include their cost as part of the cost of debt.

The Capital Structure Weights

We use the symbol E (for equity) to stand for the market value of the firm's equity. We calculate this by taking the number of shares outstanding and multiplying it by the price per share. Similarly, we use the symbol D (for debt) to stand for the market value of the firm's debt. For long-term debt, we calculate this by multiplying the market price of a single bond by the number of bonds outstanding.

For multiple bond issues (as there normally would be), we repeat this calculation for each and then add the results. If there is debt that is not publicly traded (because it was privately placed with a life insurance company, for example), we must observe the yields on similar, publicly traded debt and estimate the market value of the privately held debt using this yield as the discount rate.

Finally, we use the symbol V (for value) to stand for the combined market value of the debt and equity:

$$V = E + D \qquad\qquad [14.4]$$

If we divide both sides by V, we can calculate the percentages of the total capital represented by the debt and equity:

$$100\% = E/V + D/V \qquad\qquad [14.5]$$

These percentages can be interpreted just like portfolio weights, and they are often called the capital structure weights.

For example, if the total market value of a company's stock were calculated as $200 million and the total market value of the company's debt were calculated as $50 million, the combined value would be $250 million. Of this total, $E/V = \$200/250 = 80\%$, so 80 percent of the firm's financing is equity and the remaining 20 percent is debt.

We emphasize here that the correct way to proceed is to use the market values of the debt and equity. The reason is that, as we discussed in Chapters 1 and 2, market values measure management's success in achieving its goal: maximizing shareholder wealth. Under certain circumstances, such as a privately owned company, it may not be possible to get reliable estimates of these quantities. Even for publicly traded firms, market value weights present some difficulties. If there is a major shift in stock or bond prices, market value weights may fluctuate significantly so that the **weighted average cost of capital (WACC)** is quite another number by the time a weekend is over. In fact, because practitioners encounter some of these difficulties in computing WACC using market value weights, book values are usually the best alternative when market values are not readily available.

weighted average cost of capital (WACC)
The weighted average of the costs of debt and equity.

Taxes and the Weighted Average Cost of Capital

There is one final issue associated with the WACC. We called the preceding result the unadjusted WACC because we haven't considered taxes. Recall that we are always concerned with aftertax cash flows. If we are determining the discount rate appropriate to those cash flows, the discount rate also needs to be expressed on an aftertax basis.

As we discussed previously in various places in this book (and as we discuss later), the interest paid by a corporation is deductible for tax purposes. Payments to shareholders, such as dividends, are not. What this means, effectively, is that the government pays some of the interest provided the firm expects to have positive taxable income. Thus, in determining an aftertax discount rate, we need to distinguish between the pretax and the aftertax cost of debt.

To illustrate, suppose a firm borrows $1 million at 9 percent interest. The corporate tax rate is 40 percent. What is the aftertax interest rate on this loan? The total interest bill would be $90,000 per year. This amount is tax deductible, however, so the $90,000 interest reduces our tax bill by $.40 \times \$90,000 = \$36,000$. The aftertax interest bill is thus $90,000 - 36,000 = \$54,000$. The aftertax interest rate is $54,000/\$1 million = 5.4\%$.

Notice that, in general, the aftertax interest rate is simply equal to the pretax rate multiplied by one minus the tax rate. For example, using the preceding numbers, we find that the aftertax interest rate is $9\% \times (1 - .40) = 5.4\%$.

If we use the symbol T_C to stand for the corporate tax rate, the aftertax rate that we use in our WACC calculation can be written as $R_D \times (1 - T_C)$. Thus, once we consider the effect of taxes, the WACC is:

$$\text{WACC} = (E/V) \times R_E + (P/V) \times R_P + (D/V) \times R_D \times (1 - T_C) \qquad [14.6]$$

From now on, when we speak of the WACC, this is the number we have in mind.

This WACC has a very straightforward interpretation. It is the overall return that the firm must earn on its existing assets to maintain the value of its stock. It is also the required return on any investments by the firm that have essentially the same risks as existing operations. So, if we were evaluating the cash flows from a proposed expansion of our existing operations, this is the discount rate we would use.

EXAMPLE 14.4: Calculating the WACC

The B. B. Lean Company has 1.4 million shares of stock outstanding. The stock currently sells for $20 per share. The firm's debt is publicly traded and was recently quoted at 93 percent of face value. It has a total face value of $5 million, and it is currently priced to yield 11 percent. The risk-free rate is 8 percent, and the market risk premium is 3.4 percent. You've estimated that Lean has a beta of .74. If the corporate tax rate is 40 percent, what is the WACC of Lean Co.?

We can first determine the cost of equity and the cost of debt. From the SML, the cost of equity is 8% + .74 × 3.4% = 10.52%. The total value of the equity is 1.4 million × $20 = $28 million. The pretax cost of debt is the current yield to maturity on the outstanding debt, 11 percent. The debt sells for 93 percent of its face value, so its current

market value is .93 × $5 million = $4.65 million. The total market value of the equity and debt together is $28 + 4.65 = $32.65 million.

From here, we can calculate the WACC easily enough. The percentage of equity used by Lean to finance its operations is $28/$32.65 = 85.76%. Because the weights have to add up to 1, the percentage of debt is 1 − .8576 = 14.24%. The WACC is thus:

$$\begin{aligned}\text{WACC} &= (E/V) \times R_E + (D/V) \times R_D \times (1 - T_C) \\ &= .8576 \times 10.52\% + .1424 \times 11\% \times (1 - .40) \\ &= 9.96\%\end{aligned}$$

B. B. Lean thus has an overall weighted average cost of capital of 9.96 percent.

Solving the Warehouse Problem and Similar Capital Budgeting Problems

Now we can use the WACC to solve the warehouse problem that we posed at the beginning of the chapter. However, before we rush to discount the cash flows at the WACC to estimate NPV, we need to make sure we are doing the right thing.

Going back to first principles, we must find an alternative in the financial markets that is comparable to the warehouse renovation. To be comparable, an alternative must be of the same risk as the warehouse project. Projects that have the same risk are said to be in the same risk class.

The WACC for a firm reflects the risk and the target capital structure of the firm's existing assets as a whole. As a result, strictly speaking, the firm's WACC is the appropriate discount rate only if the proposed investment is a replica of the firm's existing operating activities.

In broader terms, whether or not we can use the firm's WACC to value the warehouse project depends on whether the warehouse project is in the same risk class as the firm. We assume that this project is an integral part of the overall business of the firm. In such cases, it is natural to think that the cost savings are as risky as the general cash flows of the firm, and the project is thus in the same risk class as the overall firm. More generally, projects like the warehouse renovation that are intimately related to the firm's existing operations are often viewed as being in the same risk class as the overall firm.

We can now see what the president should do. Suppose the firm has a target debt/equity ratio of 1/3. In this case, E/V is .75 and D/V is .25. The cost of debt is 10 percent, and the cost of equity is 20 percent. Assuming a 40 percent tax rate, the WACC is:

$$\begin{aligned}\text{WACC} &= (E/V) \times R_E + (D/V) \times (R_D \times (1 - T_C)) \\ &= .75 \times 20\% + .25 \times 10\% \times (1 - .40) \\ &= 16.5\%\end{aligned}$$

EXAMPLE 14.5: Using the WACC

A firm is considering a project that will result in initial cash savings of $5 million at the end of the first year. These savings will grow at the rate of 5 percent per year. The firm has a debt/equity ratio of 0.5, a cost of equity of 29.2 percent, and a cost of debt of 10 percent. The cost-saving proposal is closely related to the firm's core business, so it is viewed as having the same risks as the overall firm. Should the firm take on the project?

Assuming a 40 percent tax rate, the firm should take on this project if it costs less than $30.36 million. To see this, first note that the PV is:

PV = $5 million/[WACC − 0.05]

This is an example of a growing perpetuity as discussed in Chapter 8. The WACC is:

$$\text{WACC} = (E/V) \times R_E + (D/V) \times R_D \times (1 - T_C)$$
$$= 2/3 \times 29.2\% + 1/3 \times 10\% \times (1 - .40)$$
$$= 21.47\%$$

The PV is thus:

PV = $5 million/[.2147 − .05] = $30.36 million

The NPV is positive only if the cost is less than $30.36 million.

Recall that the warehouse project had a cost of $50 million and expected aftertax cash flows (the cost savings) of $12 million per year for six years. The NPV is thus:

$$\text{NPV} = -\$50 + \$12/(1 + \text{WACC})^1 + \ldots + \$12/(1 + \text{WACC})^6$$

Since the cash flows are in the form of an ordinary annuity, we can calculate this NPV using 16.5 percent (the WACC) as the discount rate as follows:

$$\text{NPV} = -\$50 + \$12 \times [1 - (1/(1 + 0.165)^6)]/0.165$$
$$= -\$50 + \$12 \times 3.6365$$
$$= -\$6.36$$

Should the firm take on the warehouse renovation? The project has a negative NPV using the firm's WACC. This means the financial markets offer superior projects in the same risk class (namely, the firm itself). The answer is clear: The project should be rejected.

For future reference, Table 14.1 summarizes our discussion of the WACC.

TABLE 14.1

Summary of capital cost calculations

THE COST OF EQUITY, R_E

❏   Dividend growth model approach (from Chapter 8):
$R_E = D_1/P_0 + g$,
where D_1 is the expected dividend in one period, g is the dividend growth rate, and P_0 is the current stock price.

❏   SML approach (from Chapter 13):
$R_E = R_f + (R_M - R_f) \times \beta_E$,
where R_f is the risk-free rate, R_M is the expected return on the overall market, and β_E is the systematic risk of the equity.

THE COST OF DEBT, R_D

❏   For a firm with publicly held debt, the cost of debt can be measured as the yield to maturity on the outstanding debt. The coupon rate is irrelevant. Yield to maturity is covered in Chapter 7.

❏   If the firm has no publicly traded debt, the cost of debt can be measured as the yield to maturity on similarly rated bonds (bond ratings are discussed in Chapter 7).

THE WEIGHTED AVERAGE COST OF CAPITAL, WACC

❏   The firm's WACC is the overall required return on the firm as a whole. It is the appropriate discount rate to use for cash flows similar in risk to the overall firm.

o   The WACC is calculated as
$\text{WACC} = E/V \times R_E + D/V \times R_D \times (1 - T_C)$,
where T_C is the corporate tax rate, E is the market value of the firm's equity, D is the market value of the firm's debt, and $V = E + D$. Note that E/V is the percentage of the firm's financing (in market value terms) that is equity, and D/V is the percentage that is debt.

CONCEPT QUESTIONS

1. How is the WACC calculated?

2. Why do we multiply the cost of debt by $(1 - T_C)$ when we compute the WACC?

3. Under what conditions is it correct to use the WACC to determine NPV?

---

www.sternstewart.com

economic value added (EVA)
Performance measure based on WACC.

www.leons.ca
www.sceptre.ca

Performance Evaluation: Another Use of the WACC

Looking back to the Alcan Inc. example we used to open the chapter, we see another use of the WACC—for performance evaluation. Probably the best-known approach in this area is the **economic value added (EVA)** (also called economic value contribution (EVC)) method developed by Stern Stewart and Co. Companies such as Cogeco, Domtar, and Grand & Toy are among the Canadian firms that have been using EVA as a means of evaluating corporate performance. In Canada, a CICA survey showed that 45 percent of public companies and 27 percent of private firms are using some type of EVA analysis.[8]

Although the details differ, the basic idea behind EVA and similar strategies is straightforward. Suppose we have $100 million in capital (debt and equity) tied up in our firm and our overall WACC is 12 percent. If we multiply these together, we get $12 million. Referring back to Chapter 2, if our cash flow from assets is less than this, we are, on an overall basis, destroying value. If cash flow from assets exceeds $12 million, we are creating value.

In addition to evaluating the performance of employees and management, EVA is used in the search for undervalued stocks. The Corporate Renaissance Group of Ottawa calculates its version of EVA and then compares it with share price performance. When it finds that EVA is high and share performance poor, the prediction is for share price turnaround.

In 2003, the Corporate Renaissance Group identified Leon's Furniture Limited, Cognos Inc., and Sceptre Investment Counsel Ltd. as the top consistent value creators based on EVA. In comparison, Canlan Ice Sports Corp., Napier Environmental Technologies, and Asia Pacific Resources were identified as the most consistent value destroyers based on EVA performance. The top seven consistent value creators and consistent value destroyers for 1995–2002 are shown in Table 14.2.

Despite being listed as a consistent value creator in the past, Biovail's stock price has dropped from a high of approximately $90 per share in October of 2002 to $30 per share in May of 2006. The exact opposite of Biovail would be F N X Mining Co. Inc. The company's stock price rose to a high of $16 per share in February 2006 from a low of almost $6 per share in June 2003. These are two examples that show that it is not always possible to predict a future share price turnaround by using past EVA calculations.

In practice, strategies such as these suffer to a certain extent from problems with implementation. For example, it appears that the Corporate Renaissance Group makes extensive use of

---

TABLE 14.2
Consistent value creators and value destroyers based on EVA

Consistent Value Creators 1995–2002 Company	Consistent Value Destroyers 1995–2002 Company
Leon's Furniture	Canlan Ice Sports Corp.
Cognos Inc.	Napier Environmental Technologies
Sceptre Investment Counsel Ltd.	Asia Pacific Resources Ltd.
Pason Systems Inc.	Ballard Power Systems Inc.
Dupont Canada Inc.	F N X Mining Co. Inc.
Metro Inc.	Sterlite Gold Ltd.
Biovail Corporation	Aldeavision Inc.

Source: From V. Jog, "Value and Wealth Creation in Canada," *Canadian Investment Review,* Winter 2003, pp. 45–50.

---

8 Our discussion of EVA applications in Canada draws on S. Northfield, "A New Way to Measure Wealth," *The Globe and Mail,* June 13, 1998, B22; V. Jog, "Value and Wealth Creation in Canada," *Canadian Investment Review,* Winter 2003, pp. 45–50; and John M. Griffith, "The True Value of EVA," *Journal of Applied Finance,* Fall/Winter 2004, Vol. 14, No. 2, pp. 25–29. Appendix 14B discusses EVA in more detail.

book values for debt and equity in computing cost of capital. Evidence is mixed on the track record of EVA in identifying undervalued securities. Even so, by focusing on value creation, WACC-based evaluation procedures force employees and management to pay attention to the real bottom line: increasing share prices.

DIVISIONAL AND PROJECT COSTS OF CAPITAL

As we have seen, using the WACC as the discount rate for future cash flows is only appropriate when the proposed investment is similar to the firm's existing activities. This is not as restrictive as it sounds. If we were in the pizza business, for example, and we were thinking of opening a new location, the WACC is the discount rate to use. The same is true of a retailer thinking of opening a new store, a manufacturer thinking of expanding production, or a consumer products company thinking of expanding its markets.

Nonetheless, despite the usefulness of the WACC as a benchmark, there are clearly situations where the cash flows under consideration have risks distinctly different from those of the overall firm. We consider how to cope with this problem next.

The SML and the WACC

When we are evaluating investments with risks substantially different from the overall firm, the use of the WACC can potentially lead to poor decisions. Figure 14.1 illustrates why.

In Figure 14.1, we have plotted an SML corresponding to a risk-free rate of 7 percent and a market risk premium of 8 percent. To keep things simple, we consider an all-equity company with a beta of 1. As we have indicated, the WACC and the cost of equity are exactly equal to 15 percent for this company, since there is no debt.

Suppose our firm uses its WACC to evaluate all investments. This means any investment with a return of greater than 15 percent is accepted and any investment with a return of less than 15 percent is rejected. We know from our study of risk and return, however, that a desirable

FIGURE 14.1

The security market line (SML) and the weighted average cost of capital (WACC)

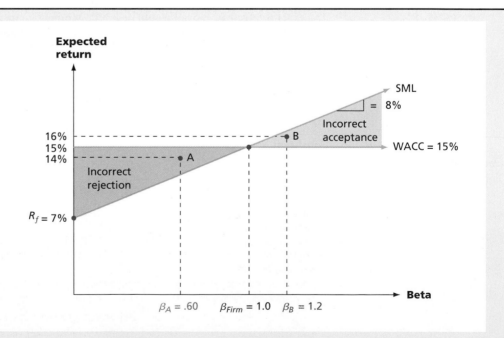

If a firm uses its WACC to make accept/reject decisions for all types of projects, it will have a tendency toward incorrectly accepting risky projects and incorrectly rejecting less risky projects.

investment is one that plots above the SML. As Figure 14.1 illustrates, using the WACC for all types of projects can result in the firm incorrectly accepting relatively risky projects and incorrectly rejecting relatively safe ones.

For example, consider point A. This project has a beta of .6 compared to the firm's beta of 1.0. It has an expected return of 14 percent. Is this a desirable investment? The answer is yes, because its required return is only:

$$\text{Required return} = R_f + \beta \times (R_M - R_f)$$
$$= 7\% + .60 \times 8\%$$
$$= 11.8\%$$

However, if we use the WACC as a cutoff, this project would be rejected because its return is less than 15 percent. This example illustrates that a firm using its WACC as a cutoff tends to reject profitable projects with risks less than those of the overall firm.

At the other extreme, consider point B. This project offers a 16 percent return, which exceeds the firm's cost of capital. This is not a good investment, however, because its return is inadequate, given its level of systematic risk. Nonetheless, if we use the WACC to evaluate it, it appears to be attractive. So the second error that arises if we use the WACC as a cutoff is that we tend to make unprofitable investments with risks greater than the overall firm. As a consequence, through time, a firm that uses its WACC to evaluate all projects has a tendency to both accept unprofitable investments and become increasingly risky.

Divisional Cost of Capital

The same type of problem with the WACC can arise in a corporation with more than one line of business. Imagine, for example, a corporation that has two divisions, a regulated telephone company and a high-tech communications company. The first of these (the telephone company) has relatively low risk; the second has relatively high risk. Companies like this spanning several industries are very common in Canada.

In this case, the firm's overall cost of capital is really a mixture of two different costs of capital, one for each division. If the two divisions were competing for resources, and the firm used a single WACC as a cutoff, which division would tend to be awarded greater funds for investment?

The answer is that the riskier division would tend to have greater returns (ignoring the greater risk), so it would tend to be the winner. The less glamorous operation might have great profit potential that ends up being ignored. Large corporations in Canada and the United States are aware of this problem and many work to develop separate divisional costs of capital.

The Pure Play Approach

We've seen that using the firm's WACC inappropriately can lead to problems. How can we come up with the appropriate discount rates in such circumstances? Because we cannot observe the returns on these investments, there generally is no direct way of coming up with a beta, for example. Instead, what we must do is examine other investments outside the firm that are in the same risk class as the one we are considering and use the market-required returns on these investments as the discount rate. In other words, we determine what the cost of capital is for such investments by locating some similar investments in the marketplace.

For example, going back to our telephone division, suppose we wanted to come up with a discount rate to use for that division. What we can do is to identify several other phone companies that have publicly traded securities. We might find that a typical phone company stock has a beta of .40, AA-rated debt, and a capital structure that is about 50 percent debt and 50 percent equity. Using this information, we could develop a WACC for a typical phone company and use this as our discount rate.

Alternatively, if we are thinking of entering a new line of business, we would try to develop the appropriate cost of capital by looking at the market-required returns on companies already in that business. In the language of Bay Street, a company that focusses only on a single line of business is called a pure play. For example, if you wanted to bet on the price of crude oil by purchasing common stocks, you would try to identify companies that dealt exclusively with this

pure play approach
Use of a WACC that is unique to a particular project.

product because they would be the most affected by changes in the price of crude oil. Such companies would be called pure plays on the price of crude oil.

What we try to do here is to find companies that focus as exclusively as possible on the type of project in which we are interested. Our approach, therefore, is called the **pure play approach** to estimating the required return on an investment.

The pure play approach is also useful in finding the fair rate of return for utility companies. Going back to our earlier example, we use the pure play approach if Provincial Hydro is not a public company. Because a number of electric utilities in Canada are crown corporations, consultants for the two sides use Canadian telephone companies and U.S. public utilities for comparison.

In Chapter 3, we discussed the subject of identifying similar companies for comparison purposes. The same problems that we described there come up here. The most obvious one is that we may not be able to find any suitable companies. In this case, how to determine a discount rate objectively becomes a very difficult question. Alternatively, a comparable company may be found but the comparison complicated by a different capital structure. In this case, we have to adjust the beta for the effect of leverage. Appendix 14A on adjusted present value (APV) explains how to do this.[9] The important thing is to be aware of the issue so we at least reduce the possibility of the kinds of mistakes that can arise when the WACC is used as a cutoff on all investments.

The Subjective Approach

Because of the difficulties that exist in objectively establishing discount rates for individual projects, firms often adopt an approach that involves making subjective adjustments to the overall WACC. To illustrate, suppose a firm has an overall WACC of 14 percent. It places all proposed projects into four categories as follows:

Category	Examples	Adjustment Factor	Discount Rate
High risk	New products	+6%	20%
Moderate risk	Cost savings, expansion of existing lines	+0	14
Low risk	Replacement of existing equipment	−4	10
Mandatory	Pollution control equipment	n.a.*	n.a.

*n.a. = Not applicable

The effect of this crude partitioning is to assume that all projects either fall into one of three risk classes or else they are mandatory. In this last case, the cost of capital is irrelevant since the project must be taken. Examples are safety and pollution control projects. With the subjective approach, the firm's WACC may change through time as economic conditions change. As this happens, the discount rates for the different types of projects also change.

Within each risk class, some projects presumably have more risk than others, and the danger of incorrect decisions still exists. Figure 14.2 illustrates this point. Comparing Figures 14.1 and 14.2, we see that similar problems exist, but the magnitude of the potential error is less with the subjective approach. For example, the project labelled A would be accepted if the WACC were used, but it is rejected once it is classified as a high-risk investment. What this illustrates is that some risk adjustment, even if it is subjective, is probably better than no risk adjustment.

It would be better, in principle, to determine the required return objectively for each project separately. However, as a practical matter, it may not be possible to go much beyond subjective adjustments because either the necessary information is unavailable or else the cost and effort required are simply not worthwhile.

CONCEPT QUESTIONS

1. What are the likely consequences if a firm uses its WACC to evaluate all proposed investments?

2. What is the pure play approach to determining the appropriate discount rate? When might it be used?

---

9 Another approach is to develop an accounting beta using a formula that makes beta a function of the firm's financial ratios.

FIGURE 14.2

The security market line (SML) and the subjective approach

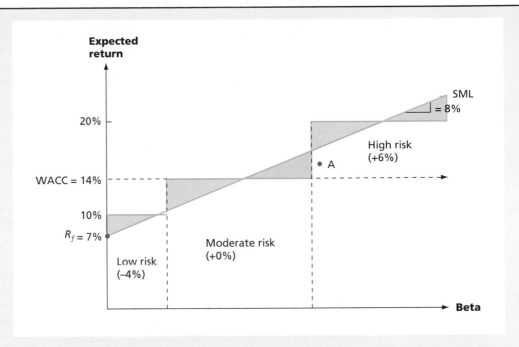

With the subjective approach, the firm places projects into one of several risk classes. The discount rate used to value the project is then determined by adding (for high risk) or subtracting (for low risk) an adjustment factor to or from the firm's WACC.

 **14.6**

FLOTATION COSTS AND THE WEIGHTED AVERAGE COST OF CAPITAL

So far, we have not included issue or flotation costs in our discussion of the weighted average cost of capital. If a company accepts a new project, it may be required to issue or float new bonds and stocks. This means the firm incurs some costs that we call flotation costs. The nature and magnitude of flotation costs are discussed in some detail in Chapter 15.

Sometimes it is suggested that the firm's WACC should be adjusted upward to reflect flotation costs. This is really not the best approach because, once again, the required return on an investment depends on the risk of the investment, not the source of the funds. This is not to say that flotation costs should be ignored. Because these costs arise as a consequence of the decision to undertake a project, they are relevant cash flows. We therefore briefly discuss how to include them in a project analysis.

The Basic Approach

We start with a simple case. The Spatt Company, an all-equity firm, has a cost of equity of 20 percent. Since this firm is 100 percent equity, its WACC and its cost of equity are the same. Spatt is contemplating a large-scale $100 million expansion of its existing operations. The expansion would be funded by selling new stock.

Based on conversations with its investment dealer, Spatt believes its flotation costs would run 10 percent of the amount issued. This means that Spatt's proceeds from the equity sale would be only 90 percent of the amount sold. When flotation costs are considered, what is the cost of the expansion?

As we discuss in Chapter 15, Spatt needs to sell enough equity to raise $100 million after covering the flotation costs. In other words:

$100 million = (1 − .10) × Amount raised
Amount raised = $100/.90 = $111.11 million

Spatt's flotation costs are thus $11.11 million, and the true cost of the expansion is $111.11 million once we include flotation costs.

Things are only slightly more complicated if the firm uses both debt and equity. For example, suppose Spatt's target capital structure is 60 percent equity, 40 percent debt. The flotation costs associated with equity are still 10 percent, but the flotation costs for debt are less, say 5 percent.

Earlier, when we had different capital costs for debt and equity, we calculated a weighted average cost of capital using the target capital structure weights. Here, we do much the same thing. We can calculate a weighted average flotation cost, f_A, by multiplying the equity flotation cost, f_E, by the percentage of equity (E/V) and the debt flotation cost, f_D, by the percentage of debt (D/V) and then adding the two together:

$$f_A = (E/V) \times f_E + (D/V) \times f_D \qquad [14.7]$$
$$= 60\% \times .10 + 40\% \times .05$$
$$= 8\%$$

The weighted average flotation cost is thus 8 percent. What this tells us is that for every dollar in outside financing needed for new projects, the firm must actually raise $1/(1 - .08) = 1.087. In our previous example, the project cost is $100 million when we ignore flotation costs. If we include them, the true cost is $100/(1 - f_A) = $100/.92 = 108.7 million.

In taking issue costs into account, the firm must be careful not to use the wrong weights. The firm should use the target weights, even if it can finance the entire cost of the project with either debt or equity. The fact that a firm can finance a specific project with debt or equity is not directly relevant. If a firm has a target debt/equity ratio of 1, for example, but chooses to finance a particular project with all debt, it has to raise additional equity later to maintain its target debt/equity ratio. To take this into account, the firm should always use the target weights in calculating the flotation cost.[10]

EXAMPLE 14.6: Calculating the Weighted Average Flotation Cost

The Weinstein Corporation has a target capital structure that is 80 percent equity, 20 percent debt. The flotation costs for equity issues are 20 percent of the amount raised; the flotation costs for debt issues are 6 percent. If Weinstein needs $65 million for a new manufacturing facility, what is the true cost once flotation costs are considered?

We first calculate the weighted average flotation cost, f_A:

$$f_A = (E/V) \times f_E + (D/V) \times f_D$$
$$= 80\% \times .20 + 20\% \times .06$$
$$= 17.2\%$$

The weighted average flotation cost is thus 17.2 percent. The project cost is $65 million when we ignore flotation costs. If we include them, the true cost is $65/(1 - f_A) = $65/.828 = 78.5 million, again illustrating that flotation costs can be a considerable expense.

Flotation Costs and NPV

To illustrate how flotation costs can be included in an NPV analysis, suppose the Tripleday Printing Company is currently at its target debt/equity ratio of 100 percent. It is considering building a new $500,000 printing plant. This new plant is expected to generate aftertax cash flows of $73,150 per year forever. There are two financing options:

1. A $500,000 new issue of common stock. The issuance costs of the new common stock would be about 10 percent of the amount raised. The required return on the company's new equity is 20 percent.

2. A $500,000 issue of 30-year bonds. The issuance costs of the new debt would be 2 percent of the proceeds. The company can raise new debt at 10 percent. The company faces a 40 percent combined federal/provincial tax rate.

What is the NPV of the new printing plant?

To begin, since printing is the company's main line of business, we use the company's weighted average cost of capital to value the new printing plant:

---

10 Since flotation costs may be amortized for tax purposes, there is a tax adjustment as explained in Appendix 14A.

In Their Own Words . . .
Samuel Weaver on Cost of Capital and Hurdle Rates at Hershey Foods Corporation

AT HERSHEY, we re-evaluate our cost of capital annually or as market conditions warrant. The calculation of the cost of capital essentially involves three different issues, each with a few alternatives:

- *Capital structure weighting*
  Historical book value
  Target capital structure
  Market-based weights

- *Cost of debt*
  Historical interest rates
  Market-based interest rates

- *Cost of equity*
  Dividend growth model
  Capital asset pricing model, or CAPM

At Hershey, we calculate our cost of capital officially based upon the projected "target" capital structure at the end of our three-year intermediate planning horizon. This allows management to see the immediate impact of strategic decisions related to the planned composition of Hershey's capital pool. The cost of debt is calculated as the anticipated weighted average aftertax cost of debt in that final plan year based upon the coupon rates attached to that debt. The cost of equity is computed via the dividend growth model.

We recently conducted a survey of the 11 food processing companies that we consider our industry group competitors. The result of this survey indicated that the cost of capital for most of these companies was in the 10 to 12 percent range. Furthermore, without exception, all 11 of these companies employed the CAPM when calculating their cost of equity. Our experience has been that the dividend growth model works better for Hershey. We do pay dividends, and we do experience steady, stable growth in our dividends. This

growth is also projected within our strategic plan. Consequently, the dividend growth model is technically applicable and appealing to management since it reflects their best estimate of the future long-term growth rate.

In addition to the calculation already described, the other possible combinations and permutations are calculated as barometers. Unofficially, the cost of capital is calculated using market weights, current marginal interest rates, and the CAPM cost of equity. For the most part, and due to rounding the cost of capital to the nearest whole percentage point, these alternative calculations yield approximately the same results.

From the cost of capital, individual project hurdle rates are developed using a subjectively determined risk premium based on the characteristics of the project. Projects are grouped into separate project categories, such as cost savings, capacity expansion, product line extension, and new products. For example, in general, a new product is more risky than a cost savings project. Consequently, each project category's hurdle rate reflects the level of risk and commensurate required return as perceived by senior management.

Samuel Weaver, Ph.D., was formerly director, financial planning and analysis, for Hershey Chocolate North America. He is a certified management accountant. His position combined the theoretical with the pragmatic and involved the analysis of many different facets of finance in addition to capital expenditure analysis.

$$\begin{aligned}
\text{WACC} &= (E/V) \times R_E + (D/V) \times R_D \text{ v} (1 - T_C) \\
&= .50 \times 20\% + .50 \times 10\% \times (1 - .40) \\
&= 13.0\%
\end{aligned}$$

Since the cash flows are $73,150 per year forever, the PV of the cash flows at 13.0 percent per year is:

$$\text{PV} = \$73,150/.13 = \$562,692$$

If we ignore flotation costs, the NPV is:

$$\text{NPV} = \$562,692 - 500,000 = \$62,692$$

The project generates an NPV greater than zero, so it should be accepted.

What about financing arrangements and issue costs? From the information just given, we know that the flotation costs are 2 percent for debt and 10 percent for equity. Since Tripleday uses equal amounts of debt and equity, the weighted average flotation cost, f_A, is:

$$f_A = (E/V) \times f_E + (D/V) \times f_D$$
$$= .50 \times 10\% + .50 \times 2\%$$
$$= 6\%$$

Remember that the fact that Tripleday can finance the project with all debt or equity is irrelevant. Because Tripleday needs $500,000 to fund the new plant, the true cost, once we include flotation costs, is $500,000/(1 − f_A) = \$500,000/.94 = \$531,915$. Since the PV of the cash flows is $562,692, the plant has an NPV of $562,692 − 531,915 = \$30,777$, so it is still a good investment. However, its return is lower than we initially might have thought.[11]

CONCEPT QUESTIONS

1. What are flotation costs?

2. How are flotation costs included in an NPV analysis?

CALCULATING WACC FOR LOBLAW

We illustrate the practical application of the weighted average cost of capital by calculating it for a prominent Canadian company. Loblaw is a large food distribution company with operations across Canada. The company operates grocery stores under various banners. Loblaw's revenue for the year ending December 2005 was about $27.8 billion, with a net profit of $746 million.

As we pointed out, WACC calculations depend on market values as observed on a particular date. In this application, market values for Loblaw were observed on May 19, 2006.[12] Other information comes from annual statements at Loblaw's year-end on December 31, 2005.

Estimating Financing Proportions

Table 14.3 shows an abbreviated balance sheet for Loblaw. Recall from our earlier discussion that when calculating the cost of capital, it is common to ignore short-term financing, such as payables and accruals. We also ignore short-term debt unless it is a permanent source of financing. As both current assets and current liabilities are ignored for our purposes, increases (or decreases) in current liabilities are netted against changes in current assets. Leases are included in long-term debt for the purposes of this analysis.

Ideally, we should calculate the market value of all sources of financing and determine the relative weights of each source. Sometimes, difficulties arise in finding the market value of non-traded bonds. This would require us to use book values for debt. This is not a problem for Loblaw as the company does not have any non-traded bonds. It is much more important to use the market value for calculation of equity weights than for debt, as the market value of common equity differs markedly from the book value.

TABLE 14.3
Book value balance sheet on December 31, 2005 ($ millions)

Assets		Liabilities and Equity	
Current	$3,701	Current	$ 3,162
		Deferred taxes and other	519
Long-term	10,060	Long-term debt	4,194
		Equity	
		Common equity	5,886
Total	$13,761	Total	$13,761

Obtained from *www.loblaw.ca*. Used with permission.

---

11 Our example abstracts from the tax deductibility of some parts of flotation costs.

12 Obtained from *www.globeinvestor.com* and *www.loblaw.ca*. Used with permission.

Market Value Weights for Loblaw

To find the market value weights of debt and common stock we find the total market value of each. The market values are calculated as the number of shares times the share price. The figures for Loblaw, as of December 31, 2005, were 274,054,814 common shares outstanding. Multiplying each by its price gives:

Security	Book Value ($ millions)	Market Price	Market Value ($ millions)
Interest-bearing debt	$4,194	—	$4,653*
Common equity	5,886	$54.75	15,005

Proportions	Dollars	Market Value Weights
Debt	$4,653	23.67%
Common stock	15,005	76.33%
	$19,658	100.00%

*We calculate market value of interest-bearing debt below.

As you can see from the market value weights, Loblaw uses common equity and debt for all of its financing needs so there is no preferred stock in its capital structure.

Cost of Debt

Loblaw has 21 relatively long-term bond issues that account for virtually all of its long-term debt. To calculate the cost of debt, we combine these twenty-one issues and compute a weighted average. We use Bloomberg Financial Services to find quotes on the bonds. We should note here that finding the yield to maturity for all of a company's outstanding bond issues on a single day is unusual. If you remember our previous discussion on bonds, the bond market is not as liquid as the stock market, and on many days individual bond issues may not trade. To find the book value of the bonds, we also used Bloomberg Financial Services. The basic information is as follows:

Coupon Rate	Maturity Date	Book Value (Face value, in millions)	Price (% of par)	Yield to Maturity
6.000%	2-Jun-08	$390	103.16	4.345%
5.750%	22-Jan-09	125	103.16	4.472%
7.100%	11-May-10	300	108.78	4.633%
6.500%	19-Jan-11	350	107.54	4.665%
5.400%	20-Nov-13	200	103.25	4.872%
6.000%	3-Mar-14	100	106.72	4.940%
5.100%	1-Jun-16	8	100.47	5.039%
7.100%	1-Jun-16	300	115.26	5.117%
6.650%	8-Nov-27	100	109.99	5.823%
6.450%	9-Feb-28	200	107.49	5.833%
6.500%	22-Jan-29	175	107.59	5.885%
11.400%	23-May-31	200	175.68	5.667%
6.850%	1-Mar-32	200	112.70	5.881%
6.540%	17-Feb-33	200	109.06	5.861%
8.750%	23-Nov-33	200	141.42	5.725%
6.050%	9-Jun-34	200	102.35	5.877%
6.150%	29-Jan-35	200	103.97	5.861%
5.900%	18-Jan-36	300	100.57	5.859%
6.450%	1-Mar-39	200	108.10	5.887%
7.000%	7-Jun-40	150	116.42	5.874%
5.860%	18-Jun-43	55	100.72	5.812%

To calculate the total average cost of debt, we take the percentage of the total debt represented by each issue and multiply by the yield on the issue. We then add to get the overall weighted average debt cost. We use both book values and market values here for comparison. The results of the calculations are as follows:

Coupon Rate	Book Value (Face value, in millions)	Percentage of Total	Market Value (in millions)	Percentage of Total	Yield to Maturity	Book Values	Market Values
6.000%	$390	9.39%	$402.32	8.65%	4.345%	0.408%	0.376%
5.750%	125	3.01%	128.95	2.77%	4.472%	0.135%	0.124%
7.100%	300	7.22%	326.33	7.01%	4.633%	0.335%	0.325%
6.500%	350	8.43%	376.39	8.09%	4.665%	0.393%	0.377%
5.400%	200	4.82%	206.51	4.44%	4.872%	0.235%	0.216%
6.000%	100	2.41%	106.72	2.29%	4.940%	0.119%	0.113%
5.100%	8	0.19%	8.04	0.17%	5.039%	0.010%	0.009%
7.100%	300	7.22%	345.79	7.43%	5.117%	0.370%	0.380%
6.650%	100	2.41%	109.99	2.36%	5.823%	0.140%	0.138%
6.450%	200	4.82%	214.98	4.62%	5.833%	0.281%	0.270%
6.500%	175	4.21%	188.29	4.05%	5.885%	0.248%	0.238%
11.400%	200	4.82%	351.36	7.55%	5.667%	0.273%	0.428%
6.850%	200	4.82%	225.40	4.84%	5.881%	0.283%	0.285%
6.540%	200	4.82%	218.12	4.69%	5.861%	0.282%	0.275%
8.750%	200	4.82%	282.83	6.08%	5.725%	0.276%	0.348%
6.050%	200	4.82%	204.70	4.40%	5.877%	0.283%	0.259%
6.150%	200	4.82%	207.94	4.47%	5.861%	0.282%	0.262%
5.900%	300	7.22%	301.71	6.48%	5.859%	0.423%	0.380%
6.450%	200	4.82%	216.19	4.65%	5.887%	0.284%	0.274%
7.000%	150	3.61%	174.64	3.75%	5.874%	0.212%	0.220%
5.860%	55	1.32%	55.40	1.19%	5.812%	0.077%	0.069%
Total	$4,153	100.00%	$4,653	100.00%		5.348%	5.365%

As these calculations show, Loblaw's cost of debt is 5.348% on a book value basis and 5.365% on a market value basis. They are very similar. Thus, for Loblaw, whether market values are used or book values are used makes only a small difference. The reason is simply that the market values and book values are similar to total values. This will often be the case and explains why companies frequently use book values for debt in WACC calculations.

The last step that needs to be done is to convert the before-tax cost of debt to an after-tax cost. To do this, we use the average tax rate for Loblaw during 2005: 34.8 percent.

$$RD(1 - T_C) = \text{Cost of Debt (Market Value)} \times (1 - T_C) = 5.365\% \, (1 - 0.348) = 3.50\%$$

Cost of Common Stock

To determine the cost of common stock for Loblaw, we use both the dividend valuation model and CAPM. The two methods will be used and compared to come up with an appropriate value.

To calculate the cost of equity using the dividend valuation model, we need a growth rate for Loblaw. A geometric regression would be the most accurate; however, a geometric average is simpler and nearly as accurate. We use the EPS figures to determine the growth rate for Loblaw.

Year	EPS
2005	$2.72
2004	3.53
2003	3.07
2002	2.64
2001	2.04
2000	1.71
1999	1.37
1998	1.06
1997	0.88
1996	0.72

Source: FP Advisor.

Dividend Valuation Model Growth Rate

$$(1 + g)^{10} = (\$2.72/0.72)$$
$$1 + g = (3.78)^{1/10} - 1$$
$$g = 14.22\%$$

The geometric growth rate over the period 1996–2005 was 14.22 percent.[13] This rather high growth rate is likely a supernormal one in the language of Chapter 8. Since the formula calls for normal growth rate continuing indefinitely, we adjust the calculated growth rate downward by 50 percent to get:[14]

$$50\% \times 14.22 = 7.11\%$$
$$\text{Dividend valuation model} = D_1/P_P + g$$

To get next year's dividend, D_1, we adjust the current dividend of $0.84 for projected growth:

$$D_1 = D_0 (1 + g) = \$0.84(1.0711) = \$0.8997$$
$$P_0 = \$54.75$$
$$R_E = D_1/P_0 + g$$
$$= \$0.8997/\$54.75 + 0.0711$$
$$= 8.75\%$$

CAPM

$$\beta = 0.19$$
$$\text{Market risk premium} = 4.35\%[15]$$
$$\text{Risk-free rate} = 4.6\%$$
$$R_E = R_f + \beta(\text{Market risk premium})[16]$$
$$= 4.6\% + 0.19(4.35\%)$$
$$= 5.43\%$$
$$\text{Cost of common stock} = (2/3 \times 8.75\% + 1/3 \times 5.43\%)$$
$$= 7.64\%$$

Notice that the estimates for the cost of equity are quite different. Remember that each method of estimating the cost of equity relies on different assumptions, so different estimates of the cost of equity should not surprise us. If the estimates are different, there are two simple solutions: First, we could ignore one of the estimates. We would look at each estimate to see if one of them seemed too high or too low to be reasonable. In this case, the CAPM estimate seems rather low. Second, we could take some kind of average of the two estimates. In this case we attach a $2/3$ weight to the 8.75 percent from the dividend valuation model and $1/3$ to the CAPM number to obtain:

$$2/3 \times 8.75\% + 1/3 \times 5.43\% = 7.64\%$$

Since this seems like a reasonable number, we will use it in calculating the cost of equity in this example.

Loblaw's WACC

To find the weighted average cost of capital, we weight the cost of each source by the weights:

$$\text{WACC} = (E/V) R_E + (P/V) R_P + (D/V) R_D (1 - T_C)$$
$$= 0.7633(7.64\%) + 0 + 0.2367 (3.5\%)$$
$$= 6.66\%$$

Our analysis shows that in May 2006 Loblaw's weighted average cost of capital was just over 6.6 percent.

---

13 Strictly speaking, the two growth rates will diverge unless the payment ratio is constant.

14 We could justify the 50 percent adjustment by looking at analysts' forecasts for Loblaw's future EPS growth, such as that made available in Scotia Capital's May 5, 2006 Daily Edge company comment.

15 We use the 60-month beta calculated by FP Advisor and the arithmetic mean market risk premium from Chapter 12 for the period 1957–2005. A further refinement would compute the market risk premium as the average of the arithmetic and geometric mean values.

16 We consider Loblaw a going concern, so we use the risk-free rate on a long-term government bond. In this case, the bond used matures in 2027 and has an approximate yield to maturity of 4.6%.

14.8   SUMMARY AND CONCLUSIONS

This chapter discussed cost of capital. The most important concept is the weighted average cost of capital (WACC) that we interpreted as the required rate of return on the overall firm. It is also the discount rate appropriate for cash flows that are similar in risk to the overall firm. We described how the WACC can be calculated as the weighted average of different sources of financing. We also illustrated how it can be used in certain types of analyses.

In addition, we pointed out situations in which it is inappropriate to use the WACC as the discount rate. To handle such cases, we described some alternative approaches to developing discount rates such as the pure play approach. We also discussed how the flotation costs associated with raising new capital can be included in an NPV analysis.

Key Terms

adjusted present value (APV) (page 439)
cost of debt (page 418)
cost of equity (page 414)
economic value added (EVA) (page 423)

pure play approach (page 426)
retention ratio (page 416)
return on equity (ROE) (page 416)
weighted average cost of capital (WACC) (page 420)

Chapter Review Problems and Self-Test

14.1   Calculating the Cost of Equity   Suppose that stock in Boone Corporation has a beta of .90. The market risk premium is 7 percent, and the risk-free rate is 8 percent. Boone's last dividend was $1.80 per share, and the dividend is expected to grow at 7 percent indefinitely. The stock currently sells for $25. What is Boone's cost of equity capital?

14.2   Calculating the WACC   In addition to the information in the previous problem, suppose Boone has a target debt/equity ratio of 50 percent. Its cost of debt is

8 percent, before taxes. If the tax rate is 40 percent, what is the WACC?

14.3   Flotation Costs   Suppose that in the previous question Boone is seeking $40 million for a new project. The necessary funds have to be raised externally.

Boone's flotation costs for selling debt and equity are 3 percent and 12 percent, respectively. If flotation costs are considered, what is the true cost of the new project?

Answers to Self-Test Problems

14.1   We start with the SML approach. Based on the information given, the expected return on Boone's common stock is:

$$R_E = R_f + \beta_E \times [R_M - R_f]$$
$$= 8\% + .9 \times 7\%$$
$$= 14.3\%$$

We now use the dividend growth model. The projected dividend is $D_0 \times (1 + g) = \$1.80 \times (1.07) = \$1.926$, so the expected return using this approach is:

$$r = D_1/P_0 + g$$
$$= \$1.926/25 + .07$$
$$= 14.704\%$$

Since these two estimates, 14.3 percent and 14.7 percent, are fairly close, we average them. Boone's cost of equity is approximately 14.5 percent.

14.2   Since the target debt/equity ratio is .50, Boone uses $.50 in debt for every $1.00 in equity. In other words, Boone's target capital structure is 1/3 debt and 2/3 equity. The WACC is thus:

$$WACC = (E/V) \times R_E + (D/V) \times R_D \times (1 - T_C)$$
$$= 2/3 \times 14.5\% + 1/3 \times 8\% \times (1 - .40)$$
$$= 11.267\%$$

14.3   Since Boone uses both debt and equity to finance its operations, we first need the weighted average flotation cost. As in the previous problem, the percentage of equity financing is 2/3, so the weighted average cost is:

$$f_A = (E/V) \times f_E + (D/V) \times f_D$$
$$= 2/3 \times 12\% + 1/3 \times 3\%$$
$$= 9\%$$

If Boone needs $40 million after flotation costs, the true cost of the project is $40/(1 - f_A) = \$40/.91 = \$43.96$ million.

Concepts Review and Critical Thinking Questions

1. On the most basic level, if a firm's WACC is 12 percent, what does this mean?

2. In calculating the WACC, if you had to use book values for either debt or equity, which would you choose? Why?

3. If you can borrow all the money you need for a project at 6 percent, doesn't it follow that 6 percent is your cost of capital for the project?

4. Why do we use an aftertax figure for cost of debt but not for cost of equity?

5. What are the advantages of using the DCF model for determining the cost of equity capital? What are the disadvantages? What specific piece of information do you need to find the cost of equity using this model? What are some of the ways in which you could get this estimate?

6. What are the advantages of using the SML approach to finding the cost of equity capital? What are the disadvantages? What are the specific pieces of information needed to use this method? Are all of these variables observable, or do they need to be estimated? What are some of the ways you could get these estimates?

7. How do you determine the appropriate cost of debt for a company? Does it make a difference if the company's debt is privately placed as opposed to being publicly traded? How would you estimate the cost of debt for a firm whose only debt issues are privately held by institutional investors?

8. Suppose Tom O'Bedlam, president of Bedlam Products, Inc., has hired you to determine the firm's cost of debt and cost of equity capital.

    a. The stock currently sells for $50 per share, and the dividend per share will probably be about $5. Tom argues, "It will cost us $5 per share to use the stockholders' money this year, so the cost of equity is equal to 10 percent ($5/50)." What's wrong with this conclusion?

    b. Based on the most recent financial statements, Bedlam Products' total liabilities are $8 million. Total interest expense for the coming year will be

about $1 million. Tom therefore reasons, "We owe $8 million, and we will pay $1 million interest. Therefore, our cost of debt is obviously $1 million/8 million = 12.5%." What's wrong with this conclusion?

    c. Based on his own analysis, Tom is recommending that the company increase its use of equity financing, because "debt costs 12.5 percent, but equity only costs 10 percent; thus equity is cheaper." Ignoring all the other issues, what do you think about the conclusion that the cost of equity is less than the cost of debt?

9. Both Dow Chemical Company, a large natural gas user, and Superior Oil, a major natural gas producer, are thinking of investing in natural gas wells near Edmonton. Both are all-equity-financed companies. Dow and Superior are looking at identical projects. They've analyzed their respective investments, which would involve a negative cash flow now and positive expected cash flows in the future. These cash flows would be the same for both firms. No debt would be used to finance the projects. Both companies estimate that their project would have a net present value of $1 million at an 18 percent discount rate and a −$1.1 million NPV at a 22 percent discount rate. Dow has a beta of 1.25, whereas Superior has a beta of .75. The expected risk premium on the market is 8 percent, and risk-free bonds are yielding 12 percent. Should either company proceed? Should both? Explain.

10. Under what circumstances would it be appropriate for a firm to use different costs of capital for its different operating divisions? If the overall firm WACC were used as the hurdle rate for all divisions, would the riskier divisions or the more conservative divisions tend to get most of the investment projects? Why? If you were to try to estimate the appropriate cost of capital for different divisions, what problems might you encounter? What are two techniques you could use to develop a rough estimate for each division's cost of capital?

Questions and Problems

Basic
(Questions 1–19)

1. **Calculating Cost of Equity**   The Say Hey! Co. just issued a dividend of $2.45 per share on its common stock. The company is expected to maintain a constant 6 percent growth rate in its dividends indefinitely. If the stock sells for $45 a share, what is the company's cost of equity?

2. **Calculating Cost of Equity**   The Tubby Ball Corporation's common stock has a beta of 1.3. If the risk-free rate is 4.5 percent and the expected return on the market is 12 percent, what is Tubby Ball's cost of equity capital?

Basic
(continued)

3. **Calculating Cost of Equity** Stock in Parrothead Industries has a beta of 1.15. The market risk premium is 8 percent, and T-bills are currently yielding 4 percent. Parrothead's most recent dividend was $1.80 per share, and dividends are expected to grow at a 5 percent annual rate indefinitely. If the stock sells for $34 per share, what is your best estimate of Parrothead's cost of equity?

4. **Estimating the DCF Growth Rate** Suppose Massey Ltd. just issued a dividend of $1.22 per share on its common stock. The company paid dividends of $.78, $.91, $.93, and $1.00 per share in the last four years. If the stock currently sells for $45, what is your best estimate of the company's cost of equity capital using the arithmetic average growth rate in dividends? What if you use the geometric average growth rate?

5. **Calculating Cost of Preferred Stock** Holdup Bank has an issue of preferred stock with a $6 stated dividend that just sold for $92 per share. What is the bank's cost of preferred stock?

6. **Calculating Cost of Debt** Advance, Inc., is trying to determine its cost of debt. The firm has a debt issue outstanding with 12 years to maturity that is quoted at 105 percent of face value. The issue makes semiannual payments and has an embedded cost of 8 percent annually. What is Advance's pretax cost of debt? If the tax rate is 35 percent, what is the aftertax cost of debt?

7. **Calculating Cost of Debt** Jiminy's Cricket Farm issued a 30-year, 10 percent semiannual bond 7 years ago. The bond currently sells for 108 percent of its face value. The company's tax rate is 35 percent.

   a. What is the pretax cost of debt?

   b. What is the aftertax cost of debt?

   c. Which is more relevant, the pretax or the aftertax cost of debt? Why?

8. **Calculating Cost of Debt** For the firm in Problem 7, suppose the book value of the debt issue is $20 million. In addition, the company has a second debt issue on the market, a zero coupon bond with seven years left to maturity; the book value of this issue is $80 million and the bonds sell for 58 percent of par. What is the company's total book value of debt? The total market value? What is your best estimate of the aftertax cost of debt now?

9. **Calculating WACC** Mullineaux Corporation has a target capital structure of 50 percent common stock, 5 percent preferred stock, and 45 percent debt. Its cost of equity is 16 percent, the cost of preferred stock is 7.5 percent, and the cost of debt is 9 percent. The relevant tax rate is 35 percent.

   a. What is Mullineaux's WACC?

   b. The company president has approached you about Mullineaux's capital structure. He wants to know why the company doesn't use more preferred stock financing, since it costs less than debt. What would you tell the president?

10. **Taxes and WACC** Miller Manufacturing has a target debt-equity ratio of .60. Its cost of equity is 18 percent and its cost of debt is 10 percent. If the tax rate is 35 percent, what is Miller's WACC?

11. **Finding the Target Capital Structure** Captain's Llamas has a weighted average cost of capital of 11.5 percent. The company's cost of equity is 16 percent and its cost of debt is 8.5 percent. The tax rate is 35 percent. What is Captain's target debt-equity ratio?

12. **Book Value versus Market Value** Filer Manufacturing has 9.5 million shares of common stock outstanding. The current share price is $53, and the book value per share is $5. Filer Manufacturing also has two bond issues outstanding. The first bond issue has a face value of $75 million, an 8 percent coupon, and sells for 93 percent of par. The second issue has a face value of $60 million, a 7.5 percent coupon, and sells for 96.5 percent of par. The first issue matures in 10 years, the second in 6 years.

   a. What are Filer's capital structure weights on a book value basis?

   b. What are Filer's capital structure weights on a market value basis?

   c. Which are more relevant, the book or market value weights? Why?

13. **Calculating the WACC** In Problem 12, suppose the most recent dividend was $4.10 and the dividend growth rate is 6 percent. Assume that the overall cost of debt is the weighted average of that implied by the two outstanding debt issues. Both bonds make semiannual payments. The tax rate is 35 percent. What is the company's WACC?

14. **WACC** Jungle, Inc., has a target debt-equity ratio of .80. Its WACC is 10.5 percent, and the tax rate is 35 percent.

   a. If Jungle's cost of equity is 15 percent, what is its pretax cost of debt?

   b. If instead you know that the aftertax cost of debt is 6.4 percent, what is the cost of equity?

15. **Finding the WACC** Given the following information for Huntington Power Co., find the WACC. Assume the company's tax rate is 35 percent.

Debt:	4,000 7 percent coupon bonds outstanding, $1,000 par value, 20 years to maturity, selling for 103 percent of par; the bonds make semiannual payments.
Common stock:	90,000 shares outstanding, selling for $57 per share; the beta is 1.10.
Preferred stock:	13,000 shares of 6 percent preferred stock outstanding, currently selling for $104 per share.
Market:	8 percent market risk premium and 6 percent risk-free rate.

Basic
(continued)

16. **Finding the WACC** Titan Mining Corporation has 9 million shares of common stock outstanding, .5 million shares of 7 percent preferred stock outstanding, and 120,000 8.5 percent semiannual bonds outstanding, par value $1,000 each. The common stock currently sells for $34 per share and has a beta of 1.20, the preferred stock currently sells for $83 per share, and the bonds have 15 years to maturity and sell for 93 percent of par. The market risk premium is 10 percent, T-bills are yielding 5 percent, and Titan Mining's tax rate is 35 percent.

    a. What is the firm's market value capital structure?

    b. If Titan Mining is evaluating a new investment project that has the same risk as the firm's typical project, what rate should the firm use to discount the project's cash flows?

17. **SML and WACC** An all-equity firm is considering the following projects:

Project	Beta	Expected Return
W	.60	11%
X	.90	13
Y	1.20	14
Z	1.70	16

The T-bill rate is 5 percent, and the expected return on the market is 12 percent.

    a. Which projects have a higher expected return than the firm's 12 percent cost of capital?

    b. Which projects should be accepted?

    c. Which projects would be incorrectly accepted or rejected if the firm's overall cost of capital were used as a hurdle rate?

18. **Calculating Flotation Costs** Suppose your company needs $15 million to build a new assembly line. Your target debt-equity ratio is .90. The flotation cost for new equity is 10 percent, but the flotation cost for debt is only 4 percent. Your boss has decided to fund the project by borrowing money, because the flotation costs are lower and the needed funds are relatively small.

    a. What do you think about the rationale behind borrowing the entire amount?

    b. What is your company's weighted average flotation cost?

    c. What is the true cost of building the new assembly line after taking flotation costs into account? Does it matter in this case that the entire amount is being raised from debt?

19. **Calculating Flotation Costs** Southern Alliance Company needs to raise $25 million to start a new project and will raise the money by selling new bonds. The company has a target capital structure of 60 percent common stock, 10 percent preferred stock, and 30 percent debt. Flotation costs for issuing new common stock are 11 percent, for new preferred stock, 7 percent, and for new debt, 4 percent. What is the true initial cost figure Southern should use when evaluating its project?

Intermediate
(Questions
20–21)

20. **WACC and NPV** Och, Inc., is considering a project that will result in initial aftertax cash savings of $3.5 million at the end of the first year, and these savings will grow at a rate of 5 percent per year indefinitely. The firm has a target debt-equity ratio of .65, a cost of equity of 15 percent, and an aftertax cost of debt of 5.5 percent. The cost-saving proposal is somewhat riskier than the usual project the firm undertakes; management uses the subjective approach and applies an adjustment factor of +2 percent to the cost of capital for such risky projects. Under what circumstances should Och take on the project?

21. **Flotation Costs** Knight, Inc., recently issued new securities to finance a new TV show. The project cost $2.1 million and the company paid $128,000 in flotation costs. In addition, the equity issued had a flotation cost of 8 percent of the amount raised, whereas the debt issued had a flotation cost of 3 percent of the amount raised. If Knight issued new securities in the same proportion as its target capital structure, what is the company's target debt-equity ratio?

Challenge
(Question
22)

22. **Flotation Costs and NPV** Photochronograph Corporation (PC) manufactures time series photographic equipment. It is currently at its target debt-equity ratio of 1.3. It's considering building a new $45 million manufacturing facility. This new plant is expected to generate aftertax cash flows of $5.7 million in perpetuity. There are three financing options:

    1. A new issue of common stock. The flotation costs of the new common stock would be 8 percent of the amount raised. The required return on the company's new equity is 17 percent.

    2. A new issue of 20-year bonds. The flotation costs of the new bonds would be 4 percent of the proceeds. If the company issues these new bonds at an annual coupon rate of 9 percent, they will sell at par.

    3. Increased use of accounts payable financing. Because this financing is part of the company's ongoing daily business, it has no flotation costs and the company assigns it a cost that is the same as the overall firm WACC. Management has a target ratio of accounts payable to long-term debt of .20. (Assume there is no difference between the pretax and aftertax accounts payable cost.)

    What is the NPV of the new plant? Assume that PC has a 35 percent tax rate.

MINI CASE

This is a comprehensive project evaluation problem bringing together much of what you have learned in this and previous chapters. Suppose you have been hired as a financial consultant to Defense Electronics, Inc. (DEI), a large, publicly traded firm that is the market share leader in radar detection systems (RDSs). The company is looking at setting up a manufacturing plant overseas to produce a new line of RDSs. This will be a five-year project. The company bought some land three years ago for $7 million in anticipation of using it as a toxic dump site for waste chemicals, but it built a piping system to safely discard the chemicals instead. The land was appraised last week for $9.6 million. The company wants to build its new manufacturing plant on this land; the plant will cost $15 million to build. The following market data on DEI's securities are current:

Debt:	15,000 7 percent coupon bonds outstanding, 15 years to maturity, selling for 92 percent of par; the bonds have a $1,000 par value each and make semiannual payments.
Common stock:	300,000 shares outstanding, selling for $75 per share; the beta is 1.3.
Preferred stock:	20,000 shares of 5 percent preferred stock outstanding, selling for $72 per share.
Market:	8 percent expected market risk premium; 5 percent risk-free rate.

DEI uses G. M. Wharton as its lead underwriter. Wharton charges DEI spreads of 9 percent on new common stock issues, 7 percent on new preferred stock issues, and 4 percent on new debt issues. Wharton has included all direct and indirect issuance costs (along with its profit) in setting these spreads. Wharton has recommended to DEI that it raise the funds needed to build the plant by issuing new shares of common stock. DEI's tax rate is 35 percent. The project requires $900,000 in initial net working capital investment to get operational.

a) Calculate the project's initial Time 0 cash flow, taking into account all side effects.

b) The new RDS project is somewhat riskier than a typical project for DEI, primarily because the plant is being located overseas. Management has told you to use an adjustment factor of +2 percent to account for this increased riskiness. Calculate the appropriate discount rate to use when evaluating DEI's project.

c) The manufacturing plant has an eight-year tax life, and as a Class 43 asset, has an assigned CCA rate of 30 percent. At the end of the project (i.e., the end of Year 5), the plant can be scrapped for $5 million. The company will incur $400,000 in annual fixed costs. The plan is to manufacture 12,000 RDSs per year and sell them at $10,000 per machine; the variable production costs are $9,000 per RDS. What are the operating cash flows, OCF, from this project?

d) DEI's controller is primarily interested in the impact of DEI's investments on the bottom line of reported accounting statements. What will you tell her is the accounting break-even quantity of RDSs sold for this project?

e) Finally, DEI's president wants you to throw all your calculations, assumptions, and everything else into the report for the chief financial officer; all he wants to know is what the RDS project's internal rate of return, IRR, and net present value, NPV, are. What will you report?

Internet Application Questions

The following problems are interrelated and involve the steps necessary to calculate the WACC for Nortel Networks.

1. Most publicly traded companies in the United States are required to submit quarterly (10Q) and annual (10K) reports to the SEC detailing the financial operations of the company over the past quarter or year, respectively. These corporate filings are available on the SEC website at www.sec.gov. In Canada, companies make filings with the local regulatory body such as the Ontario Securities Commission, and the filings can be found at www.sedar.com. Go to the SEC website and search for the most recent filings made by Nortel Networks. Locate the book value of debt, the book value of equity, and information breaking down the company's long-term debt.

2. You wish to calculate the cost of equity for Nortel. Go to finance.yahoo.com and enter the ticker symbol "NT.TO" to locate information on the firm's stock, listed on the TSX. Locate the most recent price for Nortel, the market capitalization, the number of shares outstanding, the beta, and the most recent annual dividend. Can you use the dividend discount model in this case? Go to www.bankofcanada.ca and follow the "Interest Rates" link to locate the yield on the 3-month Treasury bills. Assuming a 4 percent market risk premium, what is the cost of equity for Nortel using CAPM?

3. You now need to calculate the cost of debt for Nortel. Go to www.bondsonline.com and search for yield to maturity data for some of Nortel's bonds. What is the weighted average cost of debt for Nortel using the book value weights and the market value weights? Does it make a difference if you use book value weights or market value weights?

4. Now you can calculate the weighted average cost of capital for Nortel, using book value weights and market value weights, assuming Nortel has a 35 percent marginal tax rate. Which number is more relevant?

Suggested Readings

The following article contains an excellent discussion of some of the subtleties of using the WACC for project evaluation:
  Miles, J., and R. Ezzel. "The Weighted Average Cost of Capital, Perfect Capital Markets and Project Life: A Clarification." *Journal of Financial and Quantitative Analysis* 15 (September 1980).

Canadian examples of economic value added analysis are in:
  Jog, V. "Value and Wealth Creation in Canada." *Canadian Investment Review,* Winter 2003, pp. 45–50.

adjusted present value (APV)
Base case net present value of a project's operating cash flows plus present value of any financing benefits.

ADJUSTED PRESENT VALUE

Adjusted present value (APV) is an alternative to WACC in analyzing capital budgeting proposals. Under APV, we first analyze a project under all-equity financing and then add the additional effects of debt. This can be written as

Adjusted present value = All-equity value + Additional effects of debt

We illustrate the APV methodology with a simple example.[17] Suppose BDE is considering a $10 million project that will last five years. Projected operating cash flows are $3 million annually. The risk-free rate is 10 percent and the cost of equity is 20 percent. This is often called the cost of unlevered equity because we assume initially that the firm has no debt.

All-Equity Value

Assuming that the project is financed with all equity, its value is

$$-\$10,000,000 + \$3,000,000 \times [1 - 1/(1.20)5]/.20 = -\$1,028,164$$

An all-equity firm would clearly reject this project because the NPV is negative. And equity flotation costs (not considered yet) would only make the NPV more negative. However, debt financing may add enough value to the project to justify acceptance. We consider the effects of debt next.

Additional Effects of Debt

BDE can obtain a five-year, balloon payment loan for $7.5 million after flotation costs. The interest rate is the risk-free cost of debt of 10 percent. The flotation costs are 1 percent of the amount raised. The amount of the loan is determined using the firm's target capital structure. In this case, debt represents 75 percent of firm value so the loan for the $10 million project is $7.5 million. If the firm borrowed only $5 million, the difference of $2.5 million would remain as unused debt capacity for another project. This unused debt capacity would be a benefit of the current project. For this reason, we would still use $7.5 million in calculating the additional effects of debt for the current project.[18] We look at three ways in which debt financing alters the NPV of the project.

Flotation Costs

The formula introduced in the chapter gives us the flotation costs.

$$\$7,500,000 = (1 - .01) \times \text{Amount raised}$$
$$\text{Amount raised} = \$7,500,000/.99 = \$7,575,758$$

So flotation costs are $75,758 and in the text we added these to the initial outlay reducing NPV.

---

17 To make it easier to illustrate what is new in APV, we simplify the project details by assuming the operating cash flows are an annuity. Most Canadian projects generate variable cash flows due to the CCA rules. This is handled within APV by finding the the present value of each source of cash flow separately exactly, as presented in Chapter 10.

18 We base this explanation on teaching materials kindly provided by Alan Marshall.

The APV method refines the estimate of flotation costs by recognizing that they generate a tax shield. Flotation costs are paid immediately but are deducted from taxes by amortizing over the life of the loan. In this example, the annual tax deduction for flotation costs is $75,758/5 years = $15,152. At a tax rate of 40 percent, the annual tax shield is $15,152 \times .40 = $6,061.

To find the net flotation costs of the loan, add the present value of the tax shield to the flotation costs.

$$\text{Net flotation costs} = -\$75,758 + \$6,061 \times [1 - 1/(1.10)^5]/.10$$
$$= -\$75,758 + \$22,976 = -\$52,782$$

The net present value of the project after debt flotation costs but before the benefits of debt is

$$-\$1,028,164 - \$52,782 = -\$1,080,946$$

Tax Subsidy

The loan of $7.5 million is received at Date 0. Annual interest is $750,000 ($7,500,000 \times .10). The interest cost after tax is $450,000 ($750,000 \times (1 - .40)). The loan has a balloon payment of the full $7.5 million at the end of five years. The loan gives rise to three sets of cash flows—the loan received, the annual interest cost after taxes, and the repayment of principal. The net present value of the loan is simply the sum of three present values.

$$
\begin{array}{lll}
\text{NPV (Loan)} = + \text{Amount} & - \begin{array}{l}\text{Present value}\\\text{of after tax}\end{array} & - \begin{array}{l}\text{Present value}\\\text{of loan}\end{array} \\
\qquad\qquad\quad \text{borrowed} & \quad\text{interest payments} & \quad\text{repayments}
\end{array}
$$

$$= + \$7,500,000 - \$450,000 \times [1 - 1/(1.10)^5]/.10$$
$$\quad - \$7,500,000/(1.10)^5$$
$$= + \$7,500,000 - \$1,705,854$$
$$\quad - \$4,656,910$$
$$= \$1,137,236$$

The NPV of the loan is positive, reflecting the interest tax shield.[19]

The adjusted present value of the project with this financing is:

$$\text{APV} = \text{All-equity value} - \text{Flotation costs of debt} + \text{NPV (Loan)}$$
$$\$56,290 = -\$1,028,164 - \$52,782 + \$1,137,236$$

Though we previously saw that an all-equity firm would reject the project, a firm would accept the project if a $7.5 million loan could be obtained.

Because this loan discussed was at the market rate of 10 percent, we have considered only two of the three additional effects of debt (flotation costs and tax subsidy) so far. We now examine another loan where the third effect arises.

Non–Market Rate Financing

In Canada a number of companies are fortunate enough to obtain subsidized financing from a governmental authority. Suppose the project of BDE is deemed socially beneficial and a federal governmental agency grants the firm a $7.5 million loan at 8 percent interest. In addition, the agency absorbs all flotation costs. Clearly, the company would choose this loan over the one we previously calculated. At 8 percent interest, the annual interest payments are $7,500,000 \times .08 = $600,000. The aftertax payments are $360,000 = $600,000 \times (1 - .40). Using the equation we developed,

---

19 The NPV (Loan) must be zero in a no-tax world, because interest provides no tax shield there. To check this intuition, we calculate

$$0 = +\$7,500,000 - \$750,000 [1 - 1/(1.10)^5]/.10 - \$7,500,000/(1.10)^5$$

$$
\begin{aligned}
\text{NPV (Loan)} = \; & + \text{Amount} && - \begin{array}{c}\text{Present value}\\ \text{of after tax}\end{array} && - \begin{array}{c}\text{Present value}\\ \text{of loan}\end{array}\\
& \;\;\text{borrowed} && \;\;\text{interest payments} && \;\;\text{repayments}
\end{aligned}
$$

$$
\begin{aligned}
&= + \$7{,}500{,}000 - \$360{,}000 \times [1 - 1/(1.10)^5]/.10\\
&\quad - \$7{,}500{,}000/(1.10)^5\\
&= + \$7{,}500{,}000 - \$1{,}364{,}683\\
&\quad - \$4{,}656{,}910\\
&= \$1{,}478{,}407
\end{aligned}
$$

Notice that we still discount the cash flows at 10 percent when the firm is borrowing at 8 percent. This is done because 10 percent is the fair, marketwide rate. That is, 10 percent is the rate at which one could borrow without benefit of subsidization. The net present value of the subsidized loan is larger than the net present value of the earlier loan because the firm is now borrowing at the below-market rate of 8 percent. Note that the NPV (Loan) calculation captures both the tax effect and the non-market rate effect.

The net present value of the project with subsidized debt financing is:

$$
\begin{aligned}
\text{APV} &= \text{All-equity value} - \text{Flotation costs of debt} + \text{NPV (Loan)}\\
\$450{,}243 &= -\$1{,}028{,}164 \qquad\quad\; - 0 \qquad\qquad\qquad\quad + \$1{,}478{,}407
\end{aligned}
$$

Subsidized financing has enhanced the NPV substantially. The result is that the government debt subsidy program will likely achieve its result—encouraging the firm to invest in the kind of project the government agency wishes to encourage.

This example illustrates the adjusted (APV) approach. The approach begins with the present value of a project for the all-equity firm. Next, the effects of debt are added in. The approach has much to recommend it. It is intuitively appealing because individual components are calculated separately and added together in a simple way. And, if the debt from the project can be specified precisely, the present value of the debt can be calculated precisely.

APV and Beta

The APV approach discounts cash flows from a scale-enhancing project at the cost of unlevered equity, which is also the cost of capital for the all-equity firm. Because in this chapter we are considering firms that have debt, this unlevered equity does not exist. One must somehow use the beta of the levered equity (which really exists) to calculate the beta for the hypothetical unlevered firm. Then the SML line can be employed to determine the cost of equity capital for the unlevered firm.

We now show how to compute the unlevered firm's beta from the levered equity's beta. To begin, we treat the case of no corporate taxes to explain the intuition behind our results. However, corporate taxes must be included to achieve real-world applicability. We therefore consider taxes in the second case.

No Taxes

In the previous two chapters, we defined the value of the firm to be equal to the value of the firm's debt plus the value of its equity. For a levered firm, this can be represented as $V_L = B + S$. Imagine an individual who owns all the firm's debt and all its equity. In other words, this individual owns the entire firm. What is the beta of his or her portfolio of the firm's debt and equity?

As with any portfolio, the beta of this portfolio is a weighted average of the betas of the individual items in the portfolio. Hence, we have

$$
\beta_{Portfolio} = \beta_{Levered\ firm} = \frac{\text{Debt}}{\text{Debt} + \text{Equity}} \times \beta_{Debt} \qquad\qquad \text{[14A.1]}
$$
$$
+ \frac{\text{Equity}}{\text{Debt} + \text{Equity}} \times \beta_{Equity}
$$

where β_{Equity} is the beta of the equity of the *levered* firm. Notice that the beta of debt is multiplied by Debt/(Debt + Equity), the percentage of debt in the capital structure. Similarly, the beta of equity is multiplied by the percentage of equity in the capital structure. Because the portfolio is the levered firm, the beta of the portfolio is equal to the beta of the levered firm.

The previous equation relates the betas of the financial instruments (debt and equity) to the beta of the levered firm. We need an extra step, however, because we want to relate the betas of the financial instruments to the beta of the firm had it been *unlevered*. Only in this way can we apply APV, because APV begins by discounting the project's cash flows for an all-equity firm.

Ignoring taxes, the cash flows to both the debtholders and the equityholders of a levered firm are equal to the cash flows to the equityholders of an otherwise identical unlevered firm. Because the cash flows are identical for the two firms, the betas of the two firms must be equal as well.

Because the beta of the unlevered firm is equal to Equation 14A.1, we have

$$\beta_{Unlevered\ firm} = \frac{Debt}{Debt + Equity} \times \beta_{Debt} + \frac{Equity}{Debt + Equity} \times \beta_{Equity}$$

The beta of debt is very low in practice. If we make the common assumption that the beta of debt is zero, we have the no-tax case:

$$\beta_{Unlevered\ firm} = \frac{Equity}{Debt + Equity} \times \beta_{Equity} \qquad\qquad [14A.2]$$

Because Equity/(Debt + Equity) must be below 1 for a levered firm, it follows that $\beta_{Unlevered\ firm} < \beta_{Equity}$. In words, the beta of the unlevered firm must be less than the beta of the equity in an otherwise identical levered firm. This is consistent with our work on capital structure. We showed there that leverage increases the risk of equity. Because beta is a measure of risk, it is sensible that leverage increases the beta of equity.

Real-world corporations pay taxes, whereas the above results are for no taxes. Thus, although the previous discussion presents the intuition behind an important relationship, it does not help apply the APV method in practice. We examine the tax case next.

Corporate Taxes

It can be shown that the relationship between the beta of the unlevered firm and the beta of the levered equity in the corporate-tax case is:[20]

$$\beta_{Unlevered\ firm} = \frac{Equity}{Equity + (1 - T_C) \times Debt} \times \beta_{Equity} \qquad\qquad [14A.3]$$

Equation 14A.3 holds when (1) the corporation is taxed at the rate of T_C and (2) the debt has a zero beta.

Because Equity/(Equity + $(1 - T_C) \times$ Debt) must be less than 1 for a levered firm, it follows that $\beta_{Unlevered\ firm} < \beta_{Equity}$. The corporate-tax case of (14A.3) is quite similar to the no-tax case of (14A.2), because the beta of levered equity must be greater than the beta of the unlevered firm in either case. The intuition that leverage increases the risk of equity applies in both cases.

---

20 This result holds if the beta of debt equals zero. To see this, note that

$$V_U + T_C B = V_L = B + S \qquad\qquad (a)$$

where

V_U = value of unlevered firm B = value of debt in a levered firm
V_L = value of levered firm S = value of equity in a levered firm

As we stated in the text, the beta of the levered firm is a weighted average of the debt beta and the equity beta:

$$\frac{B}{B+S} \times \beta_B + \frac{S}{B+S} \times \beta_S$$

where β_B and β_S are the betas of the debt and the equity of the levered firm, respectively. Because $V_L = B + S$, we have

$$\frac{B}{V_L} \times \beta_B + \frac{S}{V_L} \times \beta_S \qquad\qquad (b)$$

The beta of the leveraged firm can also be expressed as a weighted average of the beta of the unlevered firm and the beta of the tax shield:

$$\frac{V_U}{V_U + T_C B} \times \beta_U + \frac{T_C B}{V_U + T_C B} \times \beta_B$$

where β_U is the beta of the unlevered firm. This follows from Equation (a). Because $V_L = V_U + T_C B$, we have

$$\frac{V_U}{V_L} \times \beta_U + \frac{T_C B}{V_L} \times \beta_B \qquad\qquad (c)$$

We can equate (b) and (c) because both represent the beta of a levered firm. Equation (a) tells us that $V_U = S + (1 - T_C) \times B$. Under the assumption that $\beta_B = 0$, equating (b) and (c) and using Equation (a) yields Equation 14A.3.

However, notice that the two equations are not equal. It can be shown that leverage increases the equity beta less rapidly under corporate taxes. This occurs because, under taxes, leverage creates a riskless tax shield, thereby lowering the risk of the entire firm.

EXAMPLE 14A.1: Applying APV

Trans Canada Industries is considering a scale-enhancing project. The market value of the firm's debt is $100 million, and the market value of the firm's equity is $200 million. The debt is considered riskless. The corporate tax rate is 34 percent. Regression analysis indicates that the beta of the firm's equity is 2. The risk-free rate is 10 percent, and the expected market premium is 8.5 percent. What is the project's discount rate in the hypothetical case that Trans Canada is all equity?

We can answer this question in two steps.

1. *Determining beta of hypothetical all-equity firm.* Using Equation 14A.3, we have:

Unlevered beta: [$200 million/$200 million + (1 − 0.34) × $100 million] × 2 = 1.50

2. *Determining discount rate.* We calculate the discount rate from the SML as:

Discount rate: $R_S = R_f + \beta \times [E(R_M) - R_f]$
$$22.75\% = 10\% + 1.50 \times 8.5\%$$

Thus, the APV method says that the project's NPV should be calculated by discounting the cash flows at the all equity rate of 22.75 percent. As we discussed earlier in this chapter, the tax shield should then be added to the NPV of the cash flows, yielding APV.

The Project Is Not Scale-Enhancing

This example assumed that the project is scale-enhancing, doing what the firm does already on a larger scale. So, we began with the beta of the firm's equity. If the project is not scale-enhancing, one could begin with the equity betas of firms in the industry of the project. For each firm, the hypothetical beta of the unlevered equity could be calculated by Equation 14A.3. The SML could then be used to determine the project's discount rate from the average of these betas.

Comparison of WACC and APV

In Chapter 14 we provided two approaches to capital budgeting for firms that use debt financing. Both WACC and APV attempt the same task: to value projects when debt financing is allowed. However, as we have shown, the approaches are markedly different in technique. Because of this, it is worthwhile to compare the two approaches.[21]

WACC is an older approach that has been used extensively in business. APV is a newer approach that, while attracting a large following in academic circles, is used less commonly in business. Over the years, we have met with many executives in firms using both approaches. They have frequently pointed out to us that the cost of equity, the cost of debt, and the proportions of debt and equity can easily be calculated for a firm as a whole.

Some projects are scale-enhancing with the same risk as the whole firm. An example is a fast-food chain adding more company-owned outlets. In this case, it is straightforward to calculate the project's NPV with WACC. However, both the proportions and the costs of debt and equity are different for the project than for the firm as a whole if the project is not scale-enhancing. WACC is more difficult to use in that case.

As a result, firms may switch between approaches using WACC for scale-enhancing projects and APV for special situations. For example, an acquisition of a firm in a completely different industry is clearly not scale-enhancing. So when Campeau Corporation, originally a real estate firm, acquired Federated Department Stores, APV analysis would have been appropriate because Federated was in a different industry. Also, the acquisition was through a leveraged buyout involving a large (with hindsight, too large) amount of debt and the APV approach values the NPV of the loan.

---

21 In some circumstances faced by multinational firms, APV breaks down. See L. Booth, "Capital Budgeting Frameworks for the Multinational Corporation," *Journal of International Business Studies*, Fall 1982, pp. 113–23.

> **CONCEPT QUESTIONS**
>
> 1. What are the steps in using adjusted present value (APV) to value a project?
>
> 2. Compare APV with WACC. In what situations is each best applied?

Appendix Questions and Problems

A.1 **APV Problem**   A mining company has discovered a small silver deposit neighbouring its existing mine site. It has been estimated that there is a 10-year supply of silver in the deposit that would return $13.5 million annually to the firm. The estimated cost of developing the site is $63.6 million and could be financed by the issuance of shares. The firm has experienced significant growth, and this is reflected in a cost of equity of 21.6 percent. After analyzing the returns to the project, the firm's chief financial officer (CFO) recommends to the board not to continue with it as it is not profitable to the firm. However, in speaking with an investment dealer the following week, the CFO is told that it would be possible to float bonds for up to $42 million carrying a coupon of 12 percent. The flotation costs for debt and equity are both 1.2 percent and the marginal tax rate for the firm is 40 percent. Is it profitable for the firm to continue with the project now?

A.2 **APV Problem**   What would be the marginal benefit to the mining company if it could obtain a government loan for $42 million at 8.4 percent that has a balloon payment for the full amount at the end of 10 years? Assume there are no flotation costs for this loan.

ECONOMIC VALUE ADDED AND THE MEASUREMENT OF FINANCIAL PERFORMANCE

Chapter 13 shows how to calculate the appropriate discount rate for capital budgeting and other valuation problems. We now consider the measurement of financial performance. We introduce the concept of economic value added, which uses the same discount rate developed for capital budgeting. We begin with a simple example.

Calculating Economic Value Added

Many years ago, Henry Bodenheimer started Bodie's Blimps, one of the largest high-speed blimp manufacturers. Because growth was so rapid, Henry put most of his effort into capital budgeting. His approach to capital budgeting parallelled that of Chapter 13. He forecasted cash flows for various projects and discounted them at the cost of capital appropriate to the beta of the blimp business. However, these projects have grown rapidly, in some cases becoming whole divisions. He now needs to evaluate the performance of these divisions in order to reward his division managers. How does he perform the appropriate analysis?

Henry is aware that capital budgeting and performance measurement are essentially mirror images of each other. Capital budgeting is forward-looking by nature because one must estimate future cash flows to value a project. By contrast, performance measurement is backward-looking. As Henry stated to a group of his executives, "Capital budgeting is like looking through the windshield while driving a car. You need to know what lies further down the road to calculate a net present value. Performance measurement is like looking into the rearview mirror. You find out where you have been."

Henry first measured the performance of his various divisions by return on assets (ROA), an approach, which we treated in the appendix to Chapter 3. For example, if a division had earnings after tax of $1,000 and had assets of $10,000, the ROA would be[22]

$$\frac{\$1,000}{\$10,000} = 10\%.$$

He calculated the ROA ratio for each of his divisions, paying a bonus to each of his division managers based on the size of that division's ROA. However, while ROA was generally effective in motivating his managers, there were a number of situations where it appeared that ROA was counterproductive.

---

[22] Earnings after tax is EBIT $(1 - T_c)$ where EBIT is earnings before interest and taxes and T_c is the tax rate. Stern Stewart and other EVA users refer to EBIT $(1 - T_c)$ as net operating profit after tax.

For example, Henry always believed that Sharon Smith, head of the supersonic division, was his best manager. The ROA of Smith's division was generally in the high double digits, but the best estimate of the weighted average cost of capital for the division was only 20 percent. Furthermore, the division had been growing rapidly. However, as soon as Henry paid bonuses based on ROA, the division stopped growing. At that time, Smith's division had after-tax earnings of $2,000,000 on an asset base of $2,000,000, for an ROA of 100 percent ($2 million/$2 million).

Henry found out why the growth stopped when he suggested a project to Smith that would earn $1,000,000 per year on an investment of $2,000,000. This was clearly an attractive project with an ROA of 50 percent ($1 million/$2 million). He thought that Smith would jump at the chance to place his project into her division, because the ROA of the project was much higher than the cost of capital of 20 percent. However, Smith did everything she could to kill the project. And, as Henry later figured out, Smith was rational to do so. Smith must have realized that if the project were accepted, the division's ROA would become

$$\frac{\$2,000,000 + \$1,000,000}{\$2,000,000 + \$2,000,000} = 75\%$$

Thus, the ROA of Smith's division would fall from 100 percent to 75 percent if the project were accepted, with Smith's bonus falling in tandem.

Henry was later exposed to the economic-value-added (EVA) approach,[23] which seems to solve this particular problem. The formula for EVA is

[ROA – Weighted average cost of capital] × Total capital

Without the new project, the EVA of Smith's division would be:

[100% – 20%] × $2,000,000 = $1,600,000

This is an annual number. That is, the division would bring in $1.6 million above and beyond the cost of capital to the firm each year.

With the new project included, the EVA jumps to

[75% – 20%] × $4,000,000 = $2,200,000

If Sharon Smith knew that her bonus was based on EVA, she would now have an incentive to accept, not reject, the project. Although ROA appears in the EVA formula, EVA differs substantially from ROA. The big difference is that ROA is a percentage number and EVA is a dollar value. In the preceding example, EVA increased when the new project was added even though the ROA actually decreased. In this situation, EVA correctly incorporates the fact that a high return on a large division may be better than a very high return on a smaller division.

Further understanding of EVA can be achieved by rewriting the EVA formula. Because ROA × total capital is equal to earnings after tax, we can write the EVA formula as:

Earnings after tax – Weighted average cost of capital × Total capital

Thus, EVA can simply be viewed as earnings after capital costs. Although accountants subtract many costs (including depreciation) to get the earnings number shown in financial reports, they do not subtract out capital costs. One can see the logic of accountants, because the cost of capital is very subjective. By contrast, costs such as COGS (cost of goods sold), SGA (sales, general and administration), and even depreciation can be measured more objectively.[24] However, even if the cost of capital is difficult to estimate, it is hard to justify ignoring it completely. After all, this textbook argues that the cost of capital is a necessary input to capital budgeting. Shouldn't it also be a necessary input to performance measurement?

This example argues that EVA can increase investment for those firms that are currently underinvesting. However, there are many firms in the reverse situation; the managers are so focused on increasing earnings that they take on projects for which the profits do not justify the capital outlays. These managers either

---

23 Stern Stewart & Company have a copyright on the terms *economic value added* and *EVA*. Details on the Stern Stewart & Company EVA can be found in J. M. Stern, G. B. Stewart, and D. A. Chew, "The EVA Financial Management System," *Journal of Applied Corporate Finance* (Summer 1999).

24 Some EVA users add back depreciation and other non-cash items. A Canadian example is: B.A. Schofield, "Evaluating Stocks," *Canadian Investment Review* (Spring 2000).

are unaware of capital costs or, knowing these costs, choose to ignore them. Because the cost of capital is right in the middle of the EVA formula, managers will not easily ignore these costs when evaluated on an EVA system.

One other advantage of EVA is that the number is either positive or it is negative. Plenty of divisions have negative EVAs for a number of years. Because these divisions are destroying more value than they are creating, a strong point can be made for liquidating these divisions. Although managers are generally emotionally opposed to this type of action, EVA analysis makes liquidation harder to ignore.

EXAMPLE 14B.1

Assume the following figures for the International Trade Corporation

$$EBIT = \$2.5 \text{ billion}$$
$$T_c = 0.4$$
$$r_{WACC} = 11\%$$

$$
\begin{aligned}
\text{Total capital contributed} &= \text{Total debt} + \text{Equity} \\
&= \$10 \text{ billion} + \$10 \text{ billion} \\
&= \$20 \text{ billion}
\end{aligned}
$$

Now we can calculate International Trade's EVA:

$$
\begin{aligned}
\text{EVA} &= \text{EBIT} (1 - T_c) - r_{WACC} \times \text{Total capital} \\
&= (\$2.5 \text{ billion} \times 0.6) - (0.11 \times \$20 \text{ billion}) \\
&= \$1.5 \text{ billion} - \$2.2 \text{ billion} \\
&= -\$700 \text{ million}
\end{aligned}
$$

In this example, International Trade Corporation has a negative EVA—it is destroying shareholder value.

Some Caveats on EVA

The preceding discussion puts EVA in a very positive light. However, one can certainly find much to criticize with EVA as well. We now focus on two well-known problems with EVA. First, the preceding example uses EVA for performance measurement, where we believe it properly belongs. To us, EVA seems a clear improvement over ROA and other financial ratios. However, EVA has little to offer for capital budgeting because EVA focuses only on current earnings. By contrast, net-present-value analysis uses projections of all future cash flows, where the cash flows will generally differ from year to year. Although supporters may argue that EVA correctly incorporates the weighted average cost of capital, one must remember that the discount rate in NPV analysis is the same weighted average cost of capital. That is, both approaches take the cost of equity capital based on beta and combine it with the cost of debt to get an estimate of this weighted average.

A second problem with EVA is that it may increase the shortsightedness of managers. Under EVA, a manager will be well rewarded today if earnings are high today. Future losses may not harm the manager, because there is a good chance that she will be promoted or have left the firm by then. Thus, the manager has an incentive to run a division with more regard for short-term than long-term value. By raising prices or cutting quality, the manager may increase current profits (and, therefore, current EVA). However, to the extent that customer satisfaction is reduced, future profits (and therefore future EVA) are likely to fall. However, one should not be too harsh with EVA here, because the same problem occurs with ROA. A manager who raises prices or cuts quality will increase current ROA at the expense of future ROA. The problem, then, is not EVA per se but with the use of accounting numbers in general. Because shareholders want the discounted present value of all cash flows to be maximized, managers with bonuses based on some function of current profits or current cash flows are likely to behave in a shortsighted way.

Despite these shortcomings EVA or something similar is used widely by corporations in Canada and the U.S. Table 14B.1 lists some examples.

TABLE 14B.1
Selected economic value
added users

United States	Canada
Bausch & Lomb	Alcan Aluminum
Briggs and Stratton Crop.	Cogeco, Inc.
Coca-Cola Company	Domtar, Inc.
Dun & Bradstreet Corp.	Grand & Toy
Eli Lilly & Co.	Long Manufacturing
JC Penney	Robin Hood Multifoods
Monsanto	
Rubbermaid Inc.	
Print	
Toys R Us	
U.S. Postal Service	
Whirlpool	

Source: Adapted from *sternstewart.com*.

CONCEPT QUESTIONS

1. Why is capital budgeting important to a firm?

2. What is the major difference between EVA and ROA?

3. What are the advantages of using EVA?

4. What are the well-known problems of EVA?

Appendix Questions and Problems

B.1 As a new financial analyst at ABC Co., your manager has decided to give you two projects to evaluate for the company. Prior to undertaking either of these projects, the company has an ROA of 37 percent on total assets of $12 million. Project A would involve an investment of $5.5 million, and would derive after-tax earnings of $1.3 million. Project B would involve an investment of $3 million, but would only produce after-tax earnings of $450,000. The cost of capital for the firm is 17.5 percent. You have been asked to undertake an EVA analysis to determine which of these projects should be selected (if any).

B.2 You are the manager of a department that recently launched a new product line for High Flyer Incorporated. High Flyer invested $3.8 million of equity and $2.2 million of debt in the project, and the project has earned the company earnings before taxes of $1.25 million in 2006. The firm's capital structure has a market value of $110 million for debt and $185 million of equity. The cost of debt is 6.8 percent, and the cost of equity is currently 11.3 percent. If the firm pays taxes at a rate of 36 percent, what is the EVA of the project your department launched?

Suggested Readings

More on economic value added can be found in:

Grant, James L. *Foundations of Economic Value Added,* 2d edition. Hoboken, NJ: Wiley, 2003.

Leahy, Tad. "Capitalizing on Economic Value Added," *Business Finance,* July 2000 (available online at *www.businessfinancemag.com*).

Stern, J.M., G.B. Stewart, and D.A. Chew, "The EVA Financial Management System," *Journal of Applied Corporate Finance,* Summer 1999, and at *www.sternstewart.com*.

Useful Canadian articles on EVA are:

Armitage, H.M., and V. Jog. "Economic Value Creation—What Every Management Accountant Should Know," *CMA Magazine,* October 1996.

Jog, V. "Value Creation and Credibility of Financial Reporting in Canada." *Canadian Investment Review,* Fall 2002, pp. 12–20.

Jog, V. "Value and Wealth Creation in Canada." *Canadian Investment Review,* Winter 2003, pp. 45–50.

Keys, D., M. Azamhuzjaev, and J. Mackey. "EVA, to Boldly Go," *CMA Magazine,* September 1999.

Schofield, B.A. "Evaluating Stocks," *Canadian Investment Review,* Spring 2000.

CHAPTER 15

Raising Capital

On August 19, 2004, in an eagerly awaited initial public offering (IPO), the Internet search engine company Google went public. Initially, the company expected to sell about 26 million shares of stock at a price of $108 to $135 U.S. per share through an unusual (for an IPO) "Dutch auction" process. Just before the company went public, it reduced the price to $85 U.S. per share and also reduced the number of shares to 19.6 million. Even with these reductions, the company's value when it first sold shares to investors was $23 billion U.S. By the end of the first day of trading, the stock price had jumped 18 percent to just over $100 U.S., which meant that the company missed out on almost $300 million U.S. by pricing the stock too low. The underpricing Google experienced is not unusual. For example, in March 2006, Canadian corporate icon Tim Hortons announced the pricing of its initial public offering of 29 million shares of common stock, at a price of $27. Tim Hortons stock price closed at $33.10 – 22.6 percent higher than the IPO price. In this chapter, we will examine the process by which companies such as Google and Tim Hortons sell stock to the public, the costs of doing so, and the role of investment banks in the process.

www.celestica.com
www.versus.com

ALL FIRMS MUST, at varying times, obtain capital. To do so, a firm must either borrow the money (debt financing), sell a portion of the firm (equity financing), or both. How a firm raises capital depends a great deal on the size of the firm, its life cycle stage, and its growth prospects.

In this chapter, we examine some of the ways in which firms actually raise capital. We begin by looking at companies in the early stages of their lives and the importance of venture capital for such firms. We then look at the process of going public and the role of investment banks. Along the way, we discuss many of the issues associated with selling securities to the public and their implications for all types of firms. We close the chapter with a discussion of sources of debt capital.

15.1

THE FINANCING LIFE CYCLE OF A FIRM: EARLY-STAGE FINANCING AND VENTURE CAPITAL

One day, you and a friend have a great idea for a new computer software product that helps users communicate using the Internet. Filled with entrepreneurial zeal, you christen the product InterComm and set about bringing it to market.

Working nights and weekends, you are able to create a prototype of your product. It doesn't actually work, but at least you can show it around to illustrate your idea. To develop the product, you need to hire programmers, buy computers, rent office space, and so on. Unfortunately, because you are both university students, your combined assets are not sufficient to fund a pizza party, much less a start-up company. You need what is often referred to as OPM—other people's money.

Your first thought might be to approach a bank for a loan. You would probably discover, however, that banks are generally not interested in making loans to start-up companies with no assets (other than an idea) run by fledgling entrepreneurs with no track record. Instead, your search for capital would very likely lead you to use your own wealth (mortgaging the home) as well as borrowing from relatives and wealthy friends. If more capital needs to be raised, the next step would lead you to the venture capital market.

Venture Capital

venture capital
Financing for new, often high-risk ventures.

www.netscape.com

The term **venture capital** does not have a precise meaning, but it generally refers to financing for new, often high-risk, ventures. For example, before it went public, Netscape Communications was venture capital financed. Individual venture capitalists invest their own money; so-called "angels" are usually individual investors, but they tend to specialize in smaller deals.[1] Venture capital firms specialize in pooling funds from various sources and investing them. The underlying sources of funds for such firms include individuals, pension funds, insurance companies, large corporations, and even university endowment funds. The broad term *private equity* is often used to label the rapidly growing area of equity financing for nonpublic companies.[2]

Venture capitalists and venture capital firms recognize that many or even most new ventures will not fly, but the occasional one will. The potential profits are enormous in such cases. To limit their risk, venture capitalists generally provide financing in stages. At each stage, enough money is invested to reach the next milestone or planning stage. For example, the *first-stage financing* might be enough to get a prototype built and a manufacturing plan completed. Based on the results, the *second-stage financing* might be a major investment needed to begin manufacturing, marketing, and distribution. There might be many such stages, each of which represents a key step in the process of growing the company.

Venture capital firms often specialize in different stages. Some specialize in very early "seed money," or ground floor, financing. In contrast, financing in the later stages might come from venture capitalists specializing in so-called mezzanine level financing, where *mezzanine level* refers to the level just above the ground floor.

The fact that financing is available in stages and is contingent on specified goals being met is a powerful motivating force for the firm's founders. Often, the founders receive relatively little in the way of salary and have substantial portions of their personal assets tied up in the business. At each stage of financing, the value of the founder's stake grows and the probability of success rises.

In addition to providing financing, venture capitalists often actively participate in running the firm, providing the benefit of experience with previous start-ups as well as general business expertise. This is especially true when the firm's founders have little or no hands-on experience in running a company.

Some Venture Capital Realities

Although there is a large venture capital market, the truth is that access to venture capital is really very limited. Venture capital companies receive huge numbers of unsolicited proposals, the vast majority of which end up in the circular file unread. Venture capitalists rely heavily on informal networks of lawyers, accountants, bankers, and other venture capitalists to help identify potential investments. As a result, personal contacts are important in gaining access to the venture capital market; it is very much an "introduction" market.

---

1 For discussion of this topic in Canada see A. Riding, "Roundtable on Angel Investment in Canada," *Canadian Investment Review*, Fall 2000; and Joseph Lo, "Note on Venture Capital," Richard Ivey School of Business, 9B04N005, 2004.

2 So-called vulture capitalists specialize in high-risk investments in established, but financially distressed, firms.

Another simple fact about venture capital is that it is incredibly expensive, a fact that is inevitable given the high risk involved in such firms. In a typical deal, the venture capitalist will demand (and get) 40 percent or more of the equity in the company. The venture capitalist will frequently hold voting preferred stock, giving them various priorities in the event that the company is sold or liquidated. The venture capitalist will typically demand (and get) several seats on the company's board of directors and may even appoint one or more members of senior management.

Choosing a Venture Capitalist

Some start-up companies, particularly those headed by experienced, previously successful entrepreneurs, will be in such demand that they will have the luxury of looking beyond the money in choosing a venture capitalist. There are some key considerations in such a case, some of which can be summarized as follows:

1. Financial strength is important. The venture capitalist needs to have the resources and financial reserves for additional financing stages should they become necessary. This does not mean that bigger is necessarily better, however, because of our next consideration.

2. Style is important. Some venture capitalists will wish to be very much involved in day-to-day operations and decision making, whereas others will be content with monthly reports. Which are better depends on the firm and also on the venture capitalists' business skills. In addition, a large venture capital firm may be less flexible and more bureaucratic than a smaller "boutique" firm.

3. References are important. Has the venture capitalist been successful with similar firms? Of equal importance, how has the venture capitalist dealt with situations that didn't work out?

4. Contacts are important. A venture capitalist may be able to help the business in ways other than helping with financing and management by providing introductions to potentially important customers, suppliers, and other industry contacts. Venture capitalist firms frequently specialize in a few particular industries, and such specialization could prove quite valuable.

5. Exit strategy is important. Venture capitalists are generally not long-term investors. How and under what circumstances the venture capitalist will "cash out" of the business should be carefully evaluated.

Conclusion

If a start-up succeeds, the big payoff frequently comes when the company is sold to another company or goes public. The IPO process has created many "dot-com" millionaires. Either way, investment bankers are often involved in the process. We discuss the process of selling securities to the public in the next several sections, paying particular attention to the process of going public.

CONCEPT QUESTIONS

1. What is venture capital?

2. Why is venture capital often provided in stages?

THE PUBLIC ISSUE

public issue
Creation and sale of securities on public markets.

As the term implies, a **public issue** refers to the creation and sale of securities, which are intended to be traded on the public markets. A firm issuing securities must satisfy a number of requirements set out by provincial regulations and statutes and enforced by provincial securities commissions. Regulation of the securities market in Canada is carried out by provincial commissions and through provincial securities acts. However, only five of the provinces have commissions, due

www.sec.gov
www.osc.gov.on.ca

in large part to an absence of exchanges in some provinces. This is in contrast to the United States, where regulation is handled by a federal body, the Securities and Exchange Commission (SEC). The goal of the regulators is to promote the efficient flow of information about securities and the smooth functioning of securities markets.

All companies listed on the Toronto Stock Exchange come under the jurisdiction of the Ontario Securities Commission (OSC). The *Securities Act* sets forth the provincial regulations for all new securities issues involving the province of Ontario and the Toronto Stock Exchange. The OSC administers the act. Other provinces have similar legislation and regulating bodies; however, the OSC is the most noteworthy because of the scope of the TSX.[3] The Canadian Securities Administration (CSA) coordinates across provinces. One of the most recent efforts by the CSA has been to streamline Canadian securities regulations by establishing guidelines for uniform securities laws to be applied in Canada's 13 securities jurisdictions. In general terms, OSC rules seek to ensure that investors receive all material information on new issues in the form of a registration statement and prospectus.

The OSC's responsibilities for efficient information flow go beyond new issues. It continues to regulate the trading of securities after they have been issued to ensure adequate disclosure of information. For example, in July 2000, the OSC disciplined investment manager, RT Capital, for practices leading to inflated closing prices for stocks and portfolios under its management.

Another role of the OSC is gathering and publishing *insider reports* filed by major shareholders, officers, and directors of TSX-listed firms. To ensure efficient functioning of markets, the OSC oversees the training and supervision that investment dealers provide for their personnel. It also works with the Investment Dealers' Association to monitor investment dealers' capital positions. Increasing market volatility and the popularity of bought deals where the dealer assumes all the price risk make capital adequacy important.

THE BASIC PROCEDURE FOR A NEW ISSUE

There is a series of steps involved in issuing securities to the public. In general terms, the basic procedure is as follows:

1. Management's first step in issuing any securities to the public is to obtain approval from the board of directors. In some cases, the number of authorized shares of common stock must be increased. This requires a vote of the shareholders.

2. The firm must prepare and distribute copies of a preliminary **prospectus** to the OSC and to potential investors. The preliminary prospectus contains some of the financial information that will be contained in the final prospectus; it does not contain the price at which the security will be offered. The preliminary prospectus is sometimes called a **red herring,** in part because bold red letters are printed on the cover warning that the OSC has neither approved nor disapproved of the securities. The OSC studies the preliminary prospectus and notifies the company of any changes required. This process is usually completed within about two weeks.

3. Once the revised, final prospectus meets with the OSC's approval, a price is determined, and a full-fledged selling effort gets under way. A final prospectus must accompany the delivery of securities or confirmation of sale, whichever comes first. You can find current examples of Canadian prospectuses at the website of the System for Electronic Documents and Retrieval (SEDAR).

Tombstone advertisements are placed during and after the waiting period. The tombstone contains the name of the company whose securities are involved. It provides some information about the issue, and it lists the investment dealers (the underwriters) who are involved with selling the issue. We discuss the role of the investment dealers in selling securities more fully later.

prospectus
Legal document describing details of the issuing corporation and the proposed offering to potential investors.

red herring
Preliminary prospectus distributed to prospective investors in a new issue of securities.

www.sedar.com

---

3 The TSX is Canada's largest exchange and its dollar trading ranked 7th in the world behind the NYSE (number 1) and Tokyo (number 2) in 2002. Chapter 8 discusses equity markets in more detail.

The investment dealers are divided into groups called *brackets* on the tombstone and prospectus, and the names of the dealers are listed alphabetically within each bracket. The brackets are a kind of pecking order. In general, the higher the bracket, the greater the underwriter's prestige.

While an underwriter's prestige is important for a **seasoned new issue** by a well-known company already traded on the TSX, it is even more critical for the first public equity issue referred to as an **initial public offering (IPO),** or an unseasoned new issue. An IPO occurs when a company decides to go public. Researchers have found that IPOs with prestigious underwriters perform better. This is likely because investors believe that prestigious underwriters, jealous of their reputations, shun questionable IPOs.[4]

Securities Registration

The SEC employs a shelf registration system designed to reduce repetitive filing requirements for large companies. The OSC's SFPD (short form prospectus distribution) system has a similar goal. The five provinces with securities commissions all have compatible legislation allowing certain securities issuers prompt access to capital markets without preparing a full preliminary and final prospectus before a distribution.

The SFPD system, accessible only by large companies, lets issuers file annual and interim financial statements regardless of whether they issue securities in a given year. To use the SFPD system, issuers must have not only reported for 36 months but also complied with the continuous disclosure requirements. Because the OSC has an extensive file of information on these companies, only a short prospectus is required when securities are issued.

In the early 1990s, securities regulators in Canada and the SEC in the United States introduced a Multi-Jurisdictional Disclosure System (MJDS). Under MJDS, large issuers in the two countries are allowed to issue securities in both countries under disclosure documents satisfactory to regulators in the home country. In its day, this was an important simplification of filing requirements for certain large Canadian companies. While MJDS is based on a model of companies issuing securities simultaneously at home and in foreign markets, many Canadian companies are cross-listed on the NYSE or Nasdaq. Cross-listing refers to the practice of listing a firm's shares for trading on other exchanges, usually in foreign countries. For Canadian firms, cross-listing opens up the alternative of issuing in larger U.S. stock markets. Possible advantages of U.S. listing include greater liquidity, lower trading costs, greater visibility, and greater investor protection under more stringent U.S. securities laws such as *Sarbanes-Oxley* on corporate governance. U.S. listing also brings possible disadvantages in the form of higher accounting and compliance costs. On balance, it remains undecided whether U.S. listing adds shareholder value.

Alternative Issue Methods

For equity sales, there are two kinds of public issues: a **general cash offer** and a **rights offer** (or *rights offering*). With a cash offer, securities are offered to the general public. With a rights offer, securities are initially offered only to existing owners. Rights offers are fairly common in other countries, but they are relatively rare in Canada (and the United States), particularly in recent years. We therefore focus primarily on cash offers in this chapter.

The first public equity issue that is made by a company is referred to as an initial public offering, IPO, or an *unseasoned new issue*. This issue occurs when a company decides to go public. Obviously, all initial public offerings are cash offers. If the firm's existing shareholders wanted to buy the shares, the firm wouldn't have to sell them publicly in the first place.

A **seasoned equity offering (SEO)** is a new issue for a company with securities that have been previously issued. A seasoned equity offering of common stock can be made by using a cash offer or a rights offer.

These methods of issuing new securities are shown in Table 15.1. They are discussed in Sections 15.4 through 15.8.

seasoned new issue
A new issue of securities by a firm that has already issued securities in the past.

initial public offering (IPO)
A company's first equity issue made available to the public. Also an unseasoned new issue.

www.nasdaq.com
www.tsx.com

general cash offer
An issue of securities offered for sale to the general public on a cash basis.

rights offer
A public issue of securities in which securities are first offered to existing shareholders. Also called a rights offering.

seasoned equity offering (SEO)
A new equity issue of securities by a company that has previously issued securities to the public.

4 Richard Carter and Steven Manaster, "Initial Public Offerings and Underwriter Reputation," *Journal of Finance* 1990, 45(4), 1045–1067.

	Method	Type	Definition
TABLE 15.1 The Methods of Issuing New Securities	Public Traditional negotiated cash offer	Firm commitment cash offer	Company negotiates an agreement with an investment banker to underwrite and distribute the new shares. A specified number of shares are bought by underwriters and sold at a higher price.
		Best efforts cash offer	Company has investment bankers sell as many of the new shares as possible at the agreed-upon price. There is no guarantee concerning how much cash will be raised.
		Dutch auction cash offer	Company has investment bankers auction shares to determine the highest offer price obtainable for a given number of shares to be sold.
	Privileged subscription	Direct rights offer	Company offers the new stock directly to its existing shareholders.
		Standby rights offer	Like the direct rights offer, this contains a privileged subscription arrangement with existing shareholders. The net proceeds are guaranteed by the underwriters.
	Nontraditional cash offer	Shelf cash offer	Qualifying companies can authorize all shares they expect to sell over a two-year period and sell them when needed.
		Competitive firm cash offer	Company can elect to award the underwriting contract through a public auction instead of negotiation.
	Private	Direct placement	Securities are sold directly to the purchaser, who, at least until recently, generally could not resell securities for 4 months.

www.ipohome.com
www.hoovers.com

CONCEPT QUESTIONS

1. What are the basic procedures in selling a new issue?

2. What is a preliminary prospectus?

3. What is the POP system and what advantages does it offer?

4. What is the difference between a rights offer and a cash offer?

5. Why is an initial public offering necessarily a cash offer?

15.4

www.rbcds.com

syndicate
A group of underwriters formed to reduce the risk and help to sell an issue.

spread
Compensation to the underwriter, determined by the difference between the underwriter's buying price and offering price.

THE CASH OFFER

If the public issue of securities is a cash offer, underwriters are usually involved. Underwriters perform the following services for corporate issuers:

> Formulating the method used to issue the securities.

> Pricing the new securities.

> Selling the new securities.

Typically, the underwriter buys the securities for less than the offering price and accepts the risk of not being able to sell them. Because underwriting involves risk, underwriters combine to form an underwriting group called a **syndicate** or a *banking group* to share the risk and help to sell the issue.

In a syndicate, one or more managers arrange or co-manage the offering. This manager is designated as the lead manager and typically has the responsibility for packaging and executing the deal. The other underwriters in the syndicate serve primarily to distribute the issue.

The difference between the underwriter's buying and the offering price is called the **spread** or *discount*. It is the basic compensation received by the underwriter.

In Canada, firms often establish long-term relationships with their underwriters. With the growth in popularity of **bought deals,** competition among underwriters has increased. At the same time, mergers among investment dealers have reduced the number of underwriters. For example, RBC Dominion Securities grew through merger with six other investment dealers and a major capital injection by the Royal Bank.

Types of Underwriting

Two basic types of underwriting are possible in a cash offer: regular underwriting and a bought deal.

With **regular underwriting** the banking group of underwriters buys the securities from the issuing firm and resells them to the public for the purchase price plus an underwriting spread. Regular underwriting includes a market out clause that gives the banking group the option to decline the issue if the price drops dramatically. In this case, the deal is usually withdrawn. The issue might be repriced and/or reoffered at a later date. **Firm commitment underwriting** is like regular underwriting without the market out clause.

A close counterpart to regular underwriting is called **best efforts underwriting.** The underwriter is legally bound to use its best efforts to sell the securities at the agreed-on offering price. Beyond this, the underwriter does not guarantee any particular amount of money to the issuer. This form of underwriting is more common with initial public offerings (IPOs), and with smaller, less well-known companies.

Bought Deal

In a bought deal, the issuer sells the entire issue to one investment dealer or to a group that attempts to resell it. As in firm commitment underwriting, the investment dealer assumes all the price risk. The dealer usually markets the prospective issue to a few large, institutional investors. Issuers in bought deals are large, well-known firms qualifying for the use of SPDF to speed up OSC filings. For these reasons, bought deals are usually executed swiftly. Bought deals are the most popular form of underwriting in Canada today.

Dutch Auction Underwriting

With **Dutch auction underwriting**, the underwriter does not set a fixed price for the shares to be sold. Instead, the underwriter conducts an auction in which investors bid for shares. The offer price is determined based on the submitted bids. A Dutch auction is also known by the more descriptive name *uniform price auction*. This approach to selling securities to the public is relatively new in the IPO market and has not been widely used there, but it is very common in the bond markets. For example, it is the sole procedure used by the U.S. Treasury to sell enormous quantities of notes, bonds, and bills to the public.

Dutch auction underwriting was much in the news in 2004 because, as we mentioned to open the chapter, Web search company Google elected to use this approach. The best way to understand a Dutch or uniform price auction is to consider a simple example. Suppose the Rial Company wants to sell 400 shares to the public. The company receives five bids as follows:

Bidder	Quantity	Price
A	100 shares	$16
B	100 shares	14
C	200 shares	12
D	200 shares	12
E	200 shares	10

Thus, bidder A is willing buy 100 shares at $16 each, bidder B is willing to buy 100 shares at $14, and so on. The Rial Company examines the bids to determine the highest price that will result in all 400 shares being sold. So, for example, at $14, A and B would buy only 200 shares, so that price is too high. Working our way down, all 400 shares won't be sold until we hit a price of $12, so $12 will be the offer price in the IPO. Bidders A through D will receive shares; bidder E will not.

There are two additional important points to observe in our example: First, all the winning bidders will pay $12, even bidders A and B, who actually bid a higher price. The fact that all

---

bought deal
One underwriter buys securities from an issuing firm and sells them directly to a small number of investors.

regular underwriting
The purchase of securities from the issuing company by an investment banker for resale to the public.

firm commitment underwriting
Underwriter buys the entire issue, assuming full financial responsibility for any unsold shares.

best efforts underwriting
Underwriter sells as much of the issue as possible, but can return any unsold shares to the issuer without financial responsibility.

Dutch auction underwriting
The type of underwriting in which the offer price is set based on competitive bidding by investors. Also known as a *uniform price auction.*

www.wrhambrecht.com

successful bidders pay the same price is the reason for the name "uniform price auction." The idea in such an auction is to encourage bidders to bid aggressively by providing some protection against bidding a price that is too high.

Second, notice that at the $12 offer price, there are actually bids for 600 shares, which exceeds the 400 shares Rial wants to sell. Thus, there has to be some sort of allocation. How this is done varies a bit, but, in the IPO market, the approach has been to simply compute the ratio of shares offered to shares bid at the offer price or better, which, in our example, is 400/600 = 0.67, and allocate bidders that percentage of their bids. In other words, bidders A through D would each receive 67 percent of the shares they bid for at a price of $12 per share.

The Selling Period

While the issue is being sold to the public, the underwriting group agrees not to sell securities for less than the offering price until the syndicate dissolves. The principal underwriter is permitted to buy shares if the market price falls below the offering price. The purpose would be to support the market and stabilize the price from temporary downward pressure. If this issue remains unsold after a time (for example, 30 days), members can leave the group and sell their shares at whatever price the market allows.

The Overallotment Option

Many underwriting contracts contain an overallotment option or *Green Shoe provision* that gives the members of the underwriting group the option to purchase additional shares at the offering price less fees and commissions.[5] The stated reason for the overallotment option is to cover excess demand and oversubscriptions. The option has a short maturity, around 30 days, and is limited to about 15 percent of the original number of shares issued.

The overallotment option is a benefit to the underwriting syndicate and a cost to the issuer. If the market price of the new issue rises immediately, the overallotment option allows the underwriters to buy additional shares from the issuer and immediately resell them to the public.

Lockup Agreements

lockup agreement
The part of the underwriting contract that specifies how long insiders must wait after an IPO before they can sell stock.

Although they are not required by law, almost all underwriting contracts contain so-called **lockup agreements**. Such agreements specify how long insiders must wait after an IPO before they can sell some or all of their stock. Lockup periods have become fairly standardized in recent years at 180 days. Thus, following an IPO, insiders can't cash out until six months have gone by, which ensures that they maintain a significant economic interest in the company going public.

Lockup periods are also important because it is not unusual for the number of locked-up shares to exceed the number of shares held by the public, sometimes by a substantial multiple. On the day the lockup period expires, there is the possibility that a large number of shares will hit the market on the same day and thereby depress values. The evidence suggests that, on average, venture capital–backed companies are particularly likely to experience a loss in value on the lockup expiration day.

The Quiet Period

For 40 calendar days following an IPO, both the OSC and the SEC require that a firm and its managing underwriters observe a "quiet period." This means that all communications with the public must be limited to ordinary announcements and other purely factual matters. The OSC's logic is that all relevant information should be contained in the prospectus. An important result of this requirement is that the underwriter's analysts are prohibited from making recommendations to investors. As soon as the quiet period ends, however, the managing underwriters typically publish research reports, usually accompanied by a favourable "buy" recommendation.

---

5 The term *Green Shoe provision* sounds quite exotic, but the origin is relatively mundane. It comes from the Green Shoe Company, which once granted such an option.

In 2004, Google experienced notable quiet period-related problems. Just before the IPO, an interview with Google co-founders Sergy Brin and Larry Page appeared in *Playboy*. The interview almost caused a postponement of the IPO, but Google was able to amend its prospectus in time.

The Investment Dealers

Investment dealers are at the heart of new security issues. They provide advice, market the securities (after investigating the market's receptiveness to the issue), and provide a guarantee of the amount an issue will raise (with a bought deal).

Table 15.2 lists the top IPO underwriters in 2004, ranked by total estimated underwriting commissions. The table shows that CIBC World Markets was the leading IPO underwriter.

The Offering Price and Underpricing

Determining the correct offering price is the most difficult thing an underwriter must do. The issuing firm faces a potential cost if the offering price is set too high or too low. If the issue is priced at less than the true market price, the issuer's existing shareholders experience an opportunity loss when they sell their shares for less than they are worth. If the issue is priced too high, it may be unsuccessful and have to be withdrawn. Of course, this is the underwriter's problem under a bought deal.

Underpricing is fairly common. It obviously helps new shareholders earn a higher return on the shares they buy as in our Tim Hortons example at the beginning of this chapter. However, the existing shareholders of the issuing firm are not helped by underpricing. To them it is an indirect cost of issuing new securities. In the case of an IPO, underpricing reduces the proceeds received by the original owners.

IPOS AND UNDERPRICING

Determining the correct offering price is the most difficult thing an underwriter must do for an initial public offering. The issuing firm faces a potential cost if the offering price is set too high or too low. If the issue is priced too high, it may be unsuccessful and have to be withdrawn. If the issue is priced below the true market value, the issuer's existing shareholders will experience an opportunity loss when they sell their shares for less than they are worth.

Underpricing is fairly common. It obviously helps new shareholders earn a higher return on the shares they buy. However, the existing shareholders of the issuing firm are not helped by underpricing. To them, it is an indirect cost of issuing new securities. For example, on May 25, 2006, Mastercard Inc., the second largest credit card brand in the world next to Visa, went public on the Nasdaq, selling 61.52 million shares at a price of US $39, thereby raising $2.4 billion. At the end of the first day of trading, the stock sold for US $46.00, up about 18 percent for the day. Based on these numbers, Mastercard's shares were apparently underpriced by US $7 each, which means that the company missed out on an additional US $430.6 million. On a much smaller scale, Lakeport Brewing Income Fund began trading on the TSX at $10 per unit on June 21, 2005. The unit price jumped approximately 9% within the first two days of trading. The initial

TABLE 15.2 **Top IPO underwriters, 2004** **Ranked by estimated total** **underwriting commissions**	1. CIBC World Markets 2. BMO Nesbitt Burns 3. RBC Dominion Securities 4. TD Securities 5. National Bank Financial 6. Scotia Capital 7. Canaccord 8. HSBC 9. Raymond James 10. First Associates 11. Desjardins

Source: Investment Executive, April 2005, p. 6. Used with permission.

public offering was for 5,195,746 units, thus the money "left on the table" was $4.7 million. A classic example of money "left on the table" is that of eToys, whose 8.2-million-share 1999 IPO was underpriced by $57 per share, or almost half a billion dollars in all! eToys could have used the money; it was bankrupt within two years.

IPO Underpricing: The 1999–2000 Experience

Figure 15.1 shows that 1999 and 2000 were extraordinary years in the IPO market. Almost 900 companies went public, and the average first-day return across the two years was about 65 percent. During this time, 194 IPOs doubled, or more than doubled, in value on the first day. In contrast, only 39 percent did so in the preceding 24 years combined. One company, VA Linux, shot up 698 percent!

The dollar amount raised in 2000, $66 billion, was a record, followed closely by 1999 at $65 billion. The underpricing was so severe in 1999 that companies left another $36 billion on the table, which was substantially more than 1990–1998 combined, and, in 2000, the amount was at least $27 billion. In other words, over the two-year period, companies missed out on $63 billion because of underpricing.

October 19, 1999, was one of the more memorable days during this time. The World Wrestling Federation (WWF) (now known as World Wrestling Entertainment, or WWE) and Martha Stewart Omnimedia both went public, so it was Martha Stewart versus "Stone Cold" Steve Austin in a Wall Street version of MTV's *Celebrity Deathmatch*. When the closing bell rang, it was a clear smack-down as Martha Stewart gained 98 percent on the first day compared to 48 percent for the WWF.

Evidence on Underpricing

Figure 15.1 provides a more general illustration of the underpricing phenomenon. What is shown is the month-by-month history of underpricing for SEC-registered IPOs.[6] The period

FIGURE 15.1

Average initial returns by month for SEC-registered Initial Public Offerings: 1960–2003

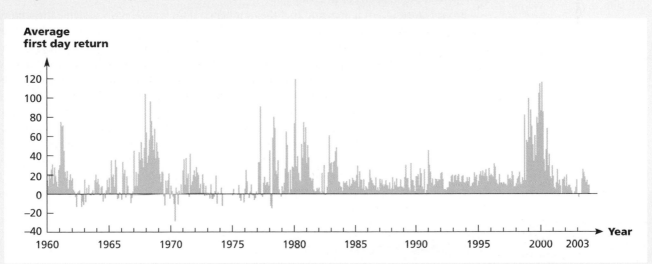

Source: Roger G. Ibbotson, Jody L. Sindelar, and Jay R. Ritter, "The Market's Problems with the Pricing of Initial Public Offerings," *Journal of Applied Corporate Finance* 7 (Spring 1994), as updated by the authors.

6 The discussion in this section draws on Roger G. Ibbotson, Jody L. Sindelar, and Jay R. Ritter, "The Market's Problems with the Pricing of Initial Public Offerings," *Journal of Applied Corporate Finance* 7 (Spring 1994).

FIGURE 15.2

Number of offerings by month for SEC-registered Initial Public Offerings: 1960–2003

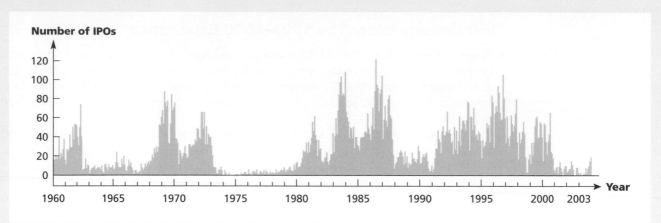

Source: Roger G. Ibbotson, Jody L. Sindelar, and Jay R. Ritter, "The Market's Problems with the Pricing of Initial Public Offerings," *Journal of Applied Corporate Finance* 7 (Spring 1994), as updated by the authors.

covered is 1960 through 2003. Figure 15.2 presents the number of offerings in each month for the same period.

Figure 15.1 shows that underpricing can be quite dramatic, exceeding 100 percent in some months. In such months, the average IPO more than doubled in value, sometimes in a matter of hours. Also, the degree of underpricing varies through time, and periods of severe underpricing ("hot issue" markets) are followed by periods of little underpricing ("cold issue" markets). For example, in the 1960s, the average U.S. IPO was underpriced by 21.2 percent. In the 1970s, the average underpricing was much smaller (9.0 percent), and the amount of underpricing was actually very small or even negative for much of that time. Underpricing in the 1980s ran about 6.8 percent. For 1990–99, U.S. IPOs were underpriced by 20.9 percent on average, and they were underpriced by 39.5 percent in 2000–03.

From Figure 15.2, it is apparent that the number of IPOs is also highly variable through time. Further, there are pronounced cycles in both the degree of underpricing and the number of IPOs. Comparing Figures 15.1 and 15.2, we see that increases in the number of new offerings tend to follow periods of significant underpricing by roughly six months. This probably occurs because companies decide to go public when they perceive that the market is highly receptive to new issues.

Table 15.3 contains a year-by-year summary of underpricing for the years 1975–2003. As indicated, a grand total of 7,253 companies were included in this analysis. The degree of underpricing averaged 17.6 percent overall for the 29 years examined. Securities were overpriced on average in only 1 of the 29 years; in 1975, the average decrease in value was −1.5 percent. At the other extreme, in 1999, the 490 issues were underpriced, on average, by a remarkable 69.1 percent. Since the tech boom at the turn of the century, IPO volumes have stayed relatively high, mainly due to the popularity of income trust IPOs, but underpricing has declined because income trusts represent more mature, more easily valued businesses.

Why Does Underpricing Exist?

Based on the evidence we've examined, an obvious question is, Why does underpricing continue to exist? As we discuss, there are various explanations, but, to date, there is a lack of complete agreement among researchers as to which is correct.

We present some pieces of the underpricing puzzle by stressing two important caveats to our preceding discussion. First, the average figures we have examined tend to obscure the fact that much of the apparent underpricing is attributable to the smaller, more highly speculative issues.

TABLE 15.3

Number of Offerings, Average First-Day Return, and Gross Proceeds of Initial Public Offerings: 1975–2003

Year	Number of Offerings*	Average First-Day Return, %†	Gross Proceeds, $ Millions‡
1975	12	–1.5	262
1976	26	1.9	214
1977	15	3.6	127
1978	20	11.2	209
1979	39	8.5	312
1980	75	13.9	934
1981	197	6.2	2,366
1982	82	10.6	1,064
1983	522	9.0	11,323
1984	222	2.6	2,841
1985	216	6.2	5,492
1986	485	5.9	16,349
1987	344	5.6	13,069
1988	129	5.4	4,181
1989	120	7.9	5,402
1990	113	10.4	4,480
1991	288	11.7	15,771
1992	397	10.0	22,204
1993	507	12.7	29,257
1994	416	9.7	18,300
1995	465	21.0	28,872
1996	666	16.5	42,479
1997	484	13.9	33,218
1998	319	20.0	35,112
1999	490	69.1	65,460
2000	385	55.4	65,677
2001	81	13.7	34,368
2002	71	8.5	22,220
2003	67	12.3	10,114
1975–79	112	5.7	1,124
1980–89	2,392	6.8	63,021
1990–99	4,145	20.9	295,153
2000–03	604	39.5	132,379
1975–2003	**7,253**	**17.6**	**491,677**

*The number of offerings excludes IPOs with an offer price of less than $5.00, ADRs, best efforts, units, and Regulation A offers (small issues, raising less than $1.5 million during the 1980s), real estate investment trusts (REITs), partnerships, and closed-end funds. Banks and S&Ls and non-CRSP-listed IPOs are included.

†First-day returns are computed as the percentage return from the offering price to the first closing market price.

‡Gross proceeds data are from Securities Data Co., and exclude overallotment options but include the international tranche, if any. No adjustments for inflation have been made.

SOURCE: Professor Jay R. Ritter, University of Florida.

This point is illustrated in Table 15.4, which shows the extent of under pricing for 6,086 firms over the period from 1980 through 2003. Here, the firms are grouped based on their total sales in the 12 months prior to the IPO.

As illustrated in Table 15.4, the underpricing tends to be higher for firms with little to no sales in the previous year. These firms tend to be young firms, and such young firms can be very risky investments. Arguably, they must be significantly underpriced, on average, just to attract investors, and this is one explanation for the underpricing phenomenon.

The second caveat is that relatively few IPO buyers will actually get the initial high average returns observed in IPOs, and many will actually lose money. Although it is true that, on average, IPOs have positive initial returns, a significant fraction of them have price drops. Furthermore, when the price is too low, the issue is often "oversubscribed." This means investors will not be able to buy all the shares they want, and the underwriters will allocate the shares among investors.

In Their Own Words . . .   Jay Ritter on IPO Underpricing around the World

THE UNITED STATES is not the only country in which initial public offerings (IPOs) of common stock are underpriced. The phenomenon exists in every country with a stock market, although the extent of underpricing varies from country to country.

In general, countries with developed capital markets have more moderate underpricing than in emerging markets. During the Internet bubble of 1999–2000, however, underpricing in the developed capital markets increased dramatically. In the United States, for example, the average first-day return during 1999–2000 was 65 percent. At the same time that underpricing in the developed capital markets

increased, the underpricing of IPOs sold to residents of China moderated. The Chinese average has come down to a mere 257 percent, which is lower than it had been in the early and mid-1990s. After the bursting of the Internet bubble in mid-2000, the level of underpricing in the United States, Germany, and other developed capital markets has returned to more traditional levels.

The table below gives a summary of the average first-day returns on IPOs in a number of countries around the world, with the figures collected from a number of studies by various authors.

Country	Sample Size	Time Period	Avg. Initial Return	Country	Sample Size	Time Period	Avg. Initial Return
Australia	381	1976–1995	12.1%	Mexico	37	1987–1990	33.0%
Austria	83	1984–2002	6.3	Netherlands	143	1982–1999	10.2
Belgium	86	1984–1999	14.6	New Zealand	201	1979–1999	23.0
Brazil	62	1979–1990	78.5	Nigeria	63	1989–1993	19.1
Canada	500	1971–1999	6.3	Norway	68	1984–1996	12.5
Chile	55	1982–1997	8.8	Philippines	104	1987–1997	22.7
China	432	1990–2000	256.9	Poland	140	1991–1998	27.4
Denmark	117	1984–1998	5.4	Portugal	21	1992–1998	10.6
Finland	99	1984–1997	10.1	Singapore	441	1973–2001	29.6
France	571	1983–2000	11.6	South Africa	118	1980–1991	32.7
Germany	407	1978–1999	27.7	Spain	99	1986–1998	10.7
Greece	338	1987–2002	49.0	Sweden	332	1980–1998	30.5
Hong Kong	857	1980–2001	17.3	Switzerland	120	1983–2000	34.9
India	98	1992–1993	35.3	Taiwan	293	1986–1998	31.1
Indonesia	237	1989–2001	19.7	Thailand	292	1987–1997	46.7
Israel	285	1990–1994	12.1	Turkey	163	1990–1996	13.1
Italy	181	1985–2001	21.7	United Kingdom	3,122	1959–2001	17.4
Japan	1,689	1970–2001	28.4	United States	14,978	1960–2003	18.3
Korea	477	1980–1996	74.3				
Malaysia	401	1980–1998	104.1				

Jay R. Ritter is Cordell Professor of Finance at the University of Florida. An outstanding scholar, he is well known for his insightful analyses of new issues and going public.

The average investor will find it difficult to get shares in a "successful" offering (one in which the price increases) because there will not be enough shares to go around. On the other hand, an investor blindly submitting orders for IPOs tends to get more shares in issues that go down in price.

To illustrate, consider this tale of two investors. Smith knows very accurately what the Bonanza Corporation is worth when its shares are offered. She is confident that the shares are underpriced. Jones knows only that prices usually rise one month after an IPO. Armed with this information, Jones decides to buy 1,000 shares of every IPO. Does he actually earn an abnormally high return on the initial offering?

The answer is no, and at least one reason is Smith. Knowing about the Bonanza Corporation, Smith invests all her money in its IPO. When the issue is oversubscribed, the underwriters have to somehow allocate the shares between Smith and Jones. The net result is that when an issue is underpriced, Jones doesn't get to buy as much of it as he wanted.

TABLE 15.4   Average first-day returns, categorized by sales, for IPOs: 1980–2003*

Annual Sales of Issuing Firms	1980–89		1990–98		1999–2000		2001–2003	
	Number of Firms	First-Day Average Return	Number of Firms	First-Day Average Return	Number of Firms	First-Day Average Return	Number of Firms	First-Day Average Return
$0 ≤ Sales < $10m	389	10.2%	642	16.9%	17	69.5%	28	7.2%
$10m ≤ Sales < $20m	247	8.8	358	18.2	128	81.0	11	14.3
$20m ≤ Sales < $50m	484	7.9	753	8.8	140	77.9	22	14.5
$50m ≤ Sales < $100m	334	6.5	562	13.1	83	62.5	26	14.4
$100m ≤ Sales < $200m	229	4.8	432	11.9	50	30.9	26	12.6
$200m ≤ Sales	264	3.6	603	8.9	82	25.0	96	11.2
All	1,947	7.3	3,350	14.8	800	65.1	209	11.7

*Sales, measured in millions, are for the last twelve months prior to going public. All sales have been converted into dollars of 2003 purchasing power, using the Consumer Price Index. There are 6,306 IPOs, after excluding IPOs with an offer price of less than $5.00 per share, units, REITs, ADRs, closed-end funds, banks and S&Ls, firms not listed on CRSP within six months of the offer date, and 85 firms with missing sales. The average first-day return is 18.7 percent.

SOURCE: Professor Jay R. Ritter, University of Florida.

Smith also knows that the Blue Sky Corporation IPO is overpriced. In this case, she avoids its IPO altogether, and Jones ends up with a full 1,000 shares. To summarize this tale, Jones gets fewer shares when more knowledgeable investors swarm to buy an underpriced issue and gets all he wants when the smart money avoids the issue.

This is an example of a "winner's curse," and it is thought to be another reason why IPOs have such a large average return. When the average investor "wins" and gets the entire allocation, it may be because those who knew better avoided the issue. The only way underwriters can counteract the winner's curse and attract the average investor is to underprice new issues (on average) so that the average investor still makes a profit.

Another reason for underpricing is that the underpricing is a kind of insurance for the investment banks. Conceivably, an investment bank could be sued successfully by angry customers if it consistently overpriced securities. Underpricing guarantees that, at least on average, customers will come out ahead.

A final reason for underpricing is that before the offer price is established, investment banks talk to big institutional investors to gauge the level of interest in the stock and to gather opinions about a suitable price. Underpricing is a way that the bank can reward these investors for truthfully revealing what they think the stock is worth and the number of shares they would like to buy.

CONCEPT QUESTIONS

1. Why is underpricing a cost to the issuing firm?

2. Suppose a stockbroker calls you up out of the blue and offers to sell you "all the shares you want" of a new issue. Do you think the issue will be more or less underpriced than average?

15.6

NEW EQUITY SALES AND THE VALUE OF THE FIRM

It seems reasonable to believe that new long-term financing is arranged by firms after positive net present value projects are put together. As a consequence, when the announcement of external financing is made, the firm's market value should go up. Interestingly, this is not what happens. Stock prices tend to decline following the announcement of a new equity issue, and they tend to rise following a debt announcement. A number of researchers have studied this issue. Plausible reasons for this strange result include:

1. *Managerial information.* If management has superior information about the market value of the firm, it may know when the firm is overvalued. If it does, it attempts to issue new

shares of stock when the market value exceeds the correct value. This benefits existing shareholders. However, the potential new shareholders are not stupid, and they anticipate this superior information and discount it in lower market prices at the new issue date.

2. *Debt usage.* Issuing new equity may reveal that the company has too much debt or too little liquidity. One version of this argument is that the equity issue is a bad signal to the market. After all, if the new projects are favourable ones, why should the firm let new shareholders in on them? As you read earlier, in IPOs it is regarded as a positive signal when the original owners keep larger amounts of stock for themselves. Taking this argument to the limit, the firm could just issue debt and let the existing shareholders have all the gain.

3. *Issue costs.* As we discuss next, there are substantial costs associated with selling securities.

CONCEPT QUESTIONS

1. What are some possible reasons that the price of stock drops on the announcement of a new equity issue?

2. Explain why we might expect a firm with a positive NPV investment to finance it with debt instead of equity.

 **15.7**

THE COST OF ISSUING SECURITIES

Issuing securities to the public isn't free, and the costs of different methods are important determinants of which method is used. These costs associated with *floating* a new issue are generically called *flotation* costs. In this section, we take a closer look at the flotation costs associated with equity sales to the public.

The costs of selling stock fall into six categories: (1) the spread, (2) other direct expenses, (3) indirect expenses, (4) abnormal returns (discussed earlier), (5) underpricing, and (6) the overallotment option. We look at these costs first for United States and then for Canadian equity sales.

The Costs of Issuing Securities

Spread	The spread consists of direct fees paid by the issuer to the underwriting syndicate—the difference between the price the issuer receives and the offer price.
Other direct expenses	These are direct costs, incurred by the issuer, that are not part of the compensation to underwriters. These costs include filing fees, legal fees, and taxes—all reported on the prospectus.
Indirect expenses	These costs are not reported on the prospectus and include the costs of management time spent working on the new issue.
Abnormal returns	In a seasoned issue of stock, the price drops on average by 3 percent on the announcement of the issue.
Underpricing	For initial public offerings, losses arise from selling the stock below the correct value.
Overallotment (Green Shoe) option	The Green Shoe option gives the underwriters the right to buy additional shares at the offer price to cover overallotments.

Table 15.5 reports direct costs as a percentage of the gross amount raised for IPOs, SEOs, straight (ordinary) bonds, and convertible bonds sold by U.S. companies over the 13-year period from 1990 through 2003. These are direct costs only. Not included are indirect expenses, the cost of the overallotment option, underpricing (for IPOs), and abnormal returns (for SEOs).

As Table 15.5 shows, the direct costs alone can be very large, particularly for smaller issues (less than $10 million). On a smaller IPO, for example, the total direct costs amount to 15.36 percent of the amount raised. This means that if a company sells $10 million in stock, it will only net about $8.5 million; the other $1.5 million goes to cover the underwriter spread and other direct

TABLE 15.5 Direct costs as a percentage of gross proceeds for equity (IPOs and SEOs) and straight and convertible bonds offered by U.S. operating companies: 1990–2003

| | Equity | | | | | | | | Bonds | | | | | | | |
| | IPOs | | | | SEOs | | | | Convertible Bonds | | | | Straight Bonds | | | |
Proceeds ($ in millions)	Number of Issues	Gross Spread	Other Direct Expense	Total Direct Cost	Number of Issues	Gross Spread	Other Direct Expense	Total Direct Cost	Number of Issues	Gross Spread	Other Direct Expense	Total Direct Cost	Number of Issues	Gross Spread	Other Direct Expense	Total Direct Cost
2–9.99	624	9.15%	6.21%	15.36%	267	7.56%	5.32%	12.88%	8	5.73%	2.78%	8.51%	70	1.39%	2.35%	3.74%
10–19.99	704	7.33	4.30	11.63	519	6.32	2.49	8.81	20	5.26	2.90	8.16	104	1.33	1.59	2.92
20–39.99	1336	6.99	2.82	9.81	904	5.73	1.51	7.24	27	4.74	1.72	6.46	159	1.22	0.90	2.12
40–59.99	771	6.96	2.25	9.21	677	5.28	0.92	6.20	33	3.29	1.01	4.30	152	0.72	0.63	1.35
60–79.99	403	6.88	1.77	8.65	489	5.07	0.74	5.81	61	2.70	0.61	3.31	113	1.52	0.76	2.28
80–99.99	245	6.79	1.55	8.34	292	4.95	0.61	5.56	17	2.16	0.56	2.72	159	1.39	0.56	1.95
100–199.99	438	6.48	1.19	7.67	657	4.57	0.43	5.00	100	2.56	0.39	2.95	677	1.60	0.52	2.12
200–499.99	197	5.91	0.81	6.72	275	3.99	0.27	4.26	53	2.34	0.22	2.56	333	1.43	0.37	1.80
500 and up	72	4.66	0.49	5.15	83	3.48	0.16	3.64	17	2.05	0.11	2.16	118	0.62	0.20	0.82
Total	4,790	7.17	3.22	10.39	4,163	5.37	1.35	6.72	336	2.99	0.81	3.80	1,885	1.36	0.61	1.97

Source: Inmoo Lee, Scott Lochhead, Jay Ritter, and Quanshui Zhao, "The Costs of Raising Capital," *Journal of Financial Research* 19 (Spring 1996), updated by the authors.

expenses. Typical underwriter spreads on an IPO range from about 5 percent up to 10 percent or so, but, for well over half of the IPOs in Table 15.5, the spread is exactly 7 percent, so this is, by far, the most common spread.

Overall, four clear patterns emerge from Table 15.5. First of all, with the possible exception of straight debt offerings (about which we will have more to say later), there are substantial economies of scale. The underwriter spreads are smaller on larger issues, and the other direct costs fall sharply as a percentage of the amount raised, a reflection of the mostly fixed nature of such costs. Second, the costs associated with selling debt are substantially less than the costs of selling equity. Third, IPOs have higher expenses than SEOs, but the difference is not as great as might originally be guessed. Finally, straight bonds are cheaper to float than convertible bonds.

Table 15.5 tells only part of the story. For IPOs, the effective costs can be much greater because of the indirect costs. Table 15.6 reports both the direct costs of going public and the degree of underpricing, based on IPOs that occurred on the Toronto Stock Exchange between 1984 and 1997. These figures understate the total cost because the study did not consider indirect expenses or the overallotment option.

The total costs of going public over these years averaged 18 percent. This is somewhat higher than the U.S. figures for smaller IPOs. Once again we see that the costs of issuing securities can be considerable.

Overall, three conclusions emerge from our discussion of underwriting:

1. Substantial economies of size are evident. Larger firms can raise equity more easily.

2. The cost associated with underpricing can be substantial and can exceed the direct costs.

3. The issue costs are higher for an initial public offering than for a seasoned offering.

TABLE 15.6
Costs of going public in Canada: 1984–97

Fees	6.00%
Underpricing (first day trading return)	12.00
Total	18.00%

Sources: Fees are from L. Kryzanowski and I. Rakita, "Is the U.S. 7% Solution Equivalent to the Canadian 6% Solution?" *Canadian Investment Review,* Fall 1999, pp. 27–34. Underpricing is from V. Jog and L. Wang, "Aftermarket Volatility and Underpricing of Canadian initial public offerings, *Canadian Journal of Administrative Sciences,* September 2002, pp. 231–249.

CONCEPT QUESTIONS

1. What are the different costs associated with security offerings?

2. What lessons do we learn from studying issue costs?

IPOs in Practice: The Case of Hydrogenics Corporation

www.hydrogenics.com

In October 2000, Hydrogenics Corporation began trading on the Toronto Stock Exchange. Hydrogenics Corporation designs, develops, and manufactures fuel cell automated test stations. Hydrogenics sold 7 million shares at $18.22 each, generating $118 million after flotation costs.[7] At the time of issue, the hype surrounding alternative energy sources such as fuel cell research and production was very high, due to rising oil prices and the search for sustainable alternate sources of energy.

The shares issued in this IPO were common voting shares, but the 7 million issued would only be a small portion of the 35 million shares outstanding after the offering. The proceeds of the issue were used for research and product development, capital expenditures, potential acquisitions and investments, and general corporate purposes. A syndicate of underwriters was used in the offering: Salomon Smith Barney, CIBC World Markets, and BMO Nesbitt Burns. The underwriters had an overallotment option in place. Stating all figures in U.S. dollars, it read:

> We expect to receive approximately $76.5 million in net proceeds from the sale of 7,000,000 common shares being offered by us in this offering, based on an

---

7 Hydrogenics was also listed on Nasdaq, where the offer price was $12 at the prevailing exchange rate.

initial public offering price of $12.00 per common share. We expect that the net proceeds will be approximately $88.2 million if the underwriters' overallotment option is exercised in full.

Immediate underpricing was not evident. The stock rose from $18.22 to $18.65 on the first day of trading and then declined to a low of $6.40 within the month after the issue. The stock did eventually climb back to around $12 from October 2001 to March of 2002.

On February 3, 2004, Hydrogenics issued another 11,000,000 shares at $7.63. The stock price by the end of February was $8.55. The return to investors after the issue was ($8.55 – $7.63)/$7.63 = 12%. So in the second offering, or tranche, underpricing was significant but in line with the average underpricing reported in Table 15.6. The longer-term performance of Hydrogenics has not been favourable. By May 2006 the price declined to around $4 and the stock has never been able to rebound and trade at its initial public offering price of $18.22.

15.8 RIGHTS

When new shares of common stock are sold to the general public, the proportional ownership of existing shareholders is likely reduced. However, if a preemptive right is contained in the firm's articles of incorporation, the firm must first offer any new issue of common stock to existing shareholders. If the articles of incorporation do not include a preemptive right, the firm has a choice of offering the issue of common stock directly to existing shareholders or to the public. In some industries, regulatory authorities set rules concerning rights. For example, before the *Bank Act of 1980*, chartered banks were required to raise equity exclusively through rights offerings.

An issue of common stock offered to existing shareholders is called a *rights offering*. In a rights offering, each shareholder is issued one right for every share owned. The rights give the shareholder an option to buy a specified number of new shares from the firm at a specified price within a specified time, after which time the rights are said to expire.

The terms of the rights offering are evidenced by certificates known as rights. Such rights are often traded on securities exchanges or over the counter.

The Mechanics of a Rights Offering

To illustrate the various considerations a financial manager has in a rights offering, we examine the situation faced by the National Power Company, whose abbreviated initial financial statements are given in Table 15.7.

As indicated in Table 15.7, National Power earns $2 million after taxes and has 1 million shares outstanding. Earnings per share are thus $2, and the stock sells for $20, or 10 times earnings (that is, the price-earnings ratio is 10). To fund a planned expansion, the company intends to raise $5 million of new equity funds by a rights offering.

To execute a rights offering, the financial management of National Power has to answer the following questions:

1. What should the price per share be for the new stock?
2. How many shares will have to be sold?
3. How many shares will each shareholder be allowed to buy?

Also, management would probably want to ask:

4. What is the likely effect of the rights offering on the per share value of the existing stock?

It turns out that the answers to these questions are highly interrelated. We get to them in a moment.

The early stages of a rights offering are the same as for the general cash offer. The difference between a rights offering and a general cash offer lies in how the shares are sold. As we discussed earlier, in a cash offer, shares are sold to retail and institutional investors through investment dealers. With a rights offer, National Power's existing shareholders are informed that they own one right for each share of stock they own. National Power then specifies how many rights a shareholder needs to buy one additional share at a specified price.

To take advantage of the rights offering, shareholders have to exercise the rights by filling out a subscription form and sending it, along with payment, to the firm's subscription agent. Shareholders of National Power actually have several choices: (1) exercise and subscribe to the entitled shares, (2) sell the rights, or (3) do nothing and let the rights expire. This third action is inadvisable, as long as the rights have value.

Number of Rights Needed to Purchase a Share

National Power wants to raise $5 million in new equity. Suppose the subscription price is set at $10 per share. How National Power arrived at that price is something we discuss later, but notice that the subscription price is substantially less than the current $20 per share market price.

At $10 per share, National Power will have to issue 500,000 new shares. This can be determined by dividing the total amount of funds to be raised by the subscription price:

$$\text{Number of new shares} = \text{Funds to be raised/Subscription price} \qquad [15.1]$$
$$= \$5,000,000/\$10 = 500,000 \text{ shares}$$

Because stockholders always get one right for each share of stock they own, 1 million rights would be issued by National Power. To determine how many rights are needed to buy one new share of stock, we can divide the number of existing outstanding shares of stock by the number of new shares:

$$\text{Number of rights needed to buy a share of stock} = \text{Old shares/New shares} \qquad [15.2]$$
$$= 1,000,000/500,000 = 2 \text{ rights}$$

Thus, a shareholder needs to give up two rights plus $10 to receive a share of new stock. If all the shareholders do this, National Power could raise the required $5 million.

It should be clear that the subscription price, the number of new shares, and the number of rights needed to buy a new share of stock are interrelated. For example, National Power can lower the subscription price. If so, more new shares will have to be issued to raise $5 million in new equity. Several alternatives are worked out here:

Subscription Price	New Shares	Rights Needed to Buy a Share of Stock
$20	250,000	4
10	500,000	2
5	1,000,000	1

The Value of a Right

Rights clearly have value. In the case of National Power, the right to buy a share of stock worth $20 for $10 is definitely worth something. In fact, if you think about it, a right is essentially a call option. A call option gives the holder of the option the ability to buy a particular asset, in this case a stock, at a fixed price for a particular period of time. The most important difference

TABLE 15.7

National Power Company financial statements before rights offering

Balance Sheet

Assets		Shareholders' Equity	
		Common stock	$ 5,000,000
		Retained earnings	10,000,000
Total	$15,000,000	Total	$15,000,000

Income Statement

Earnings before taxes	$ 3,333,333
Taxes (40%)	1,333,333
Net income	2,000,000
Earnings per share	2
Shares outstanding	1,000,000
Market price per share	20
Total market value	$20,000,000

TABLE 15.8
The value of rights:
the individual shareholder

	Initial Position	
Number of shares		2
Share price		$20
Value of holding		$40
	Terms of Offer	
Subscription price		$10
Number of rights issued		2
Number of rights for a new share		2
	After Offer	
Number of shares		3
Value of holdings		$50
Share price		$16.67
Value of a right		
Old price – New price		$20 – 16.67 = $3.33

between a right and an ordinary call option is that rights are issued by the firm, so they closely resemble warrants. In general, the valuation of options, rights, and warrants can be fairly complex, so we defer discussion of this to a later chapter. However, we can discuss the value of a right just prior to expiration in order to illustrate some important points.

Suppose a shareholder of National Power owns two shares of stock just before the rights offering. This situation is depicted in Table 15.8. Initially, the price of National Power is $20 per share, so the shareholder's total holding is worth $2 \times \$20 = \$40$. The National Power rights offer gives shareholders with two rights the opportunity to purchase one additional share for $10. The additional share does not carry a right.

The shareholder who has two shares receives two rights. The holding of the shareholder who exercises these rights and buys the new share would increase to three shares. The total investment would be $40 + 10 = $50 (the $40 initial value plus the $10 paid to the company).

The shareholder now holds three shares, all of which are identical because the new share does not have a right and the rights attached to the old shares have been exercised. Since the total cost of buying these three shares is $40 + 10 = $50, the price per share must end up at $50/3 = $16.67 (rounded to two decimal places).

Table 15.9 summarizes what happens to National Power's stock price. If all shareholders exercise their rights, the number of shares increases to 1 million + .5 million = 1.5 million. The value of the firm increases to $20 million + 5 million = $25 million. The value of each share thus drops to $25 million/1.5 million = $16.67 after the rights offering.

The difference between the old share price of $20 and the new share price of $16.67 reflects the fact that the old shares carried rights to subscribe to the new issue. The difference must be equal to the value of one right, that is, $20 – 16.67 = $3.33.

Although holding no shares of outstanding National Power stock, an investor who wants to subscribe to the new issue can do so by buying some rights. Suppose an outside investor buys two rights. This costs $3.33 \times 2 = $6.67 (to account for previous rounding). If the investor exercises the rights at a subscription price of $10, the total cost would be $10 + 6.67 = $16.67. In return

TABLE 15.9
National Power Company
rights offering

	Initial Position	
Number of shares		1 million
Share price		$20
Value of firm		$20 million
	Terms of Offer	
Subscription price		$10
Number of rights issued		1 million
Number of rights for a share		2
	After Offer	
Number of shares		1.5 million
Share price		$16.67
Value of firm		$25 million
Value of one right		$20 – 16.67 = $3.33

for this expenditure, the investor receives a share of the new stock, which, as we have seen, is worth $16.67.

Theoretical Value of a Right

We can summarize the discussion with an equation for the theoretical value of a right during the rights-on period:

$$R_o = (M_o - S)/(N + 1) \qquad\qquad [15.3]$$

where

M_o = common share price during the rights-on period
S = subscription price
N = number of rights required to buy one new share

We can illustrate the use of Equation 15.3 by checking our answer for the value of one right in Example 15.1.

$$R_o = (\$20 - 8)/(1.6 + 1) = \$4.62$$

This is the same answer we got below.

EXAMPLE 15.1: Exercising Your Rights: Part I

In the National Power example, suppose the subscription price was set at $8. How many shares have to be sold? How many rights would you need to buy a new share? What is the value of a right? What will the price per share be after the rights offer?

To raise $5 million, $5 million/$8 = 625,000 shares need to be sold. There are 1 million shares outstanding, so it will take 1 million/625,000 = 8/5 = 1.6 rights to buy a new share of stock (you can buy five new shares for every eight you own). After the rights offer, there will be 1.625 million shares, worth $25 million all together, so the per share value is $25/1.625 = $15.38 each. The value of a right is the $20 original price less the $15.38 ending price, or $4.62.

Ex Rights

National Power's rights have substantial value. In addition, the rights offering would have a large impact on the market price of National Power's stock price. It would drop by $3.33 on the day when the shares trade **ex rights.**

The standard procedure for issuing rights involves the firm's setting a **holder-of-record date.** Following stock exchange rules, the stock typically goes ex-rights two trading days before the holder-of-record date. If the stock is sold before the ex-rights date—rights-on, with rights, or cum rights—the new owner receives the rights. After the ex-rights date, an investor who purchases the shares will not receive the rights. This is depicted for National Power in Figure 15.3

As illustrated, on September 30, National Power announced the terms of the rights offering, stating that the rights would be mailed on, say, November 1 to stockholders of record as of October 15. Since October 13 is the ex-rights date, only those shareholders who own the stock on or before October 12 receive the rights.

ex rights
Period when stock is selling without a recently declared right, normally beginning four business days before the holder-of-record date.

holder-of-record date
The date on which existing shareholders on company records are designated as the recipients of stock rights. Also the date of record.

EXAMPLE 15.2: Exercising Your Rights: Part II

The Lagrange Point Company has proposed a rights offering. The stock currently sells for $40 per share. Under the terms of the offer, stockholders are allowed to buy one new share for every five that they own at a price of $25 per share. What is the value of a right? What is the ex-rights price?

You can buy five rights on shares for 5 × $40 = $200 and then exercise the rights for another $25. Your total investment is $225, and you end up with six ex-rights shares. The ex-rights price per share is $225/6 = $37.50 per share. The rights are thus worth $40 − 37.50 = $2.50 apiece.

Using Equation 15.3 we have:

$$R_o = (\$40 - 25)/(5 + 1) = \$2.50$$

FIGURE 15.3

Ex-rights stock prices: the effect of rights on stock prices

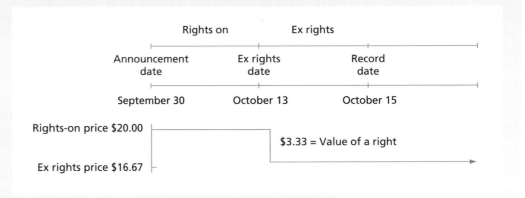

In a rights offering, there is a date of record, which is the last day that a shareholder can establish legal ownership. However, stocks are sold ex rights two business days before the record date. Before the ex rights day, the stock sells rights on, which means the purchaser receives the rights.

Value of Rights after Ex-Rights Date

When the stock goes ex rights, we saw that its price drops by the value of one right. Until the rights expire, holders can buy one share at the subscription price by exercising N rights. In equation form:[8]

$$M_e = M_o - R_o \qquad\qquad\qquad [15.4]$$
$$R_e = (M_e - S)/N \qquad\qquad [15.5]$$

where M_e = common share price during the ex-rights period and M_o = rights-on common share price. Checking the formula using Example 15.2 gives

$$M_e = \$40 - 2.50 = \$37.50$$
$$R_e = (\$37.50 - 25)/5 = \$2.50$$

The Underwriting Arrangements

standby underwriting
Agreement where the underwriter agrees to purchase the unsubscribed portion of the issue.

Rights offerings are typically arranged using **standby underwriting.** In standby underwriting, the issuer makes a rights offering, and the underwriter makes a firm commitment to "take up" (that is, purchase) the unsubscribed portion of the issue. The underwriter usually gets a **standby fee** and additional amounts based on the securities taken up.

Standby underwriting protects the firm against undersubscription. This can occur if investors throw away rights or if bad news causes the market price of the stock to fall to less than the subscription price.

standby fee
Amount paid to underwriter participating in standby underwriting agreement.

In practice, a small percentage (less than 10 percent) of shareholders fail to exercise valuable rights. This can probably be attributed to ignorance or vacations. Furthermore, shareholders are usually given an **oversubscription privilege** enabling them to purchase unsubscribed shares at the subscription price. The oversubscription privilege makes it unlikely that the corporate issuer would have to turn to its underwriter for help.

oversubscription privilege
Allows shareholders to purchase unsubscribed shares in a rights offering at the subscription price.

Effects on Shareholders

Shareholders can exercise their rights or sell them. In either case, the shareholder does not win or lose by the rights offering. The hypothetical holder of two shares of National Power has a port-

---

8 During the ex-rights period, a right represents a short-lived option to buy the stock. Equation 15.5 gives the minimum value of this option. The market value of rights is generally higher, as explained in our discussion of options in Chapter 25.

folio worth $40. If the shareholder exercises the rights, he or she ends up with three shares worth a total of $50. In other words, by spending $10, the investor's holding increases in value by $10, which means the shareholder is neither better nor worse off.

On the other hand, if the shareholder sells the two rights for $3.33 each, he or she would obtain $3.33 × 2 = $6.67 and end up with two shares worth $16.67 and the cash from selling the right:

$$\begin{aligned} \text{Shares held} = 2 \times \$16.67 &= \underline{\$33.33} \\ \text{Rights sold} = 2 \times \$3.33 &= \$\ 6.67 \\ \text{Total} = &\quad\ \$40.00 \end{aligned}$$

The new $33.33 market value plus $6.67 in cash is exactly the same as the original holding of $40. Thus, shareholders cannot lose or gain from exercising or selling rights.

It is obvious that after the rights offering, the new market price of the firm's stock would be lower than it was before the rights offering. As we have seen, however, shareholders have suffered no loss because of the rights offering. Thus, the stock price decline is very much like a stock split, a device that is described in Chapter 17. The lower the subscription price, the greater is the price decline of a rights offering. It is important to emphasize that because shareholders receive rights equal in value to the price drop, the rights offering does not hurt shareholders.

There is one last issue. How do we set the subscription price in a rights offering? If you think about it, in theory, the subscription price really does not matter. It has to be less than the market price of the stock for the rights to have value, but, beyond this, the price is arbitrary. In principle, it could be as low as we cared to make it as long as it is not zero.

In practice, however, the subscription price is typically 20 to 25 percent less than the prevailing stock price. Once we recognize market inefficiencies and frictions, a subscription price too close to the share price may result in undersubscription due simply to market imperfections.

Cost of Rights Offerings

Until the early 1980s, rights offerings were the most popular method of raising new equity in Canada for seasoned issuers. (Obviously, you cannot use rights offerings for IPOs.) The reason was lower flotation costs from the simpler underwriting arrangements. In the last decade, with the advent and popularity of POP, bought deals replaced rights offers as the prevalent form of equity issue.

CONCEPT QUESTIONS

1. How does a rights offering work?

2. What are the questions that financial management must answer in a rights offering?

3. How is the value of a right determined?

4. When does a rights offering affect the value of a company's shares?

5. Does a rights offer cause a share price decrease? How are existing shareholders affected by a rights offer?

EXAMPLE 15.3: Right on or Rights-On?

In Example 15.2, suppose you could buy the rights for only $0.25 instead of the $2.50 we calculated. What could you do?

You can get rich quick, because you have found a money machine. Here's the recipe: Buy five rights for $1.25. Exercise them and pay $25 to get a new share. Your total investment to get one ex rights share is 5 × $0.25 + $25 = $26.25. Sell the share for $37.50 and pocket the $11.25 difference. Repeat as desired.

A variation on this theme actually occurred in the course of a rights offering by a major Canadian chartered bank in the mid-1980s. The bank's employee stock ownership plan had promoted share ownership by tellers and clerical staff who were unfamiliar with the workings of rights offerings. When they received notification of the rights offering, many employees did not bother to respond until they were personally solicited by other, more sophisticated employees who bought the rights for a fraction of their value. We do not endorse the ethics behind such transactions. But the incident does show why it pays for everyone who owns shares to understand the workings of rights offers.

dilution
Loss in existing shareholders' value, in terms of either ownership, market value, book value, or EPS.

DILUTION

A subject that comes up quite a bit in discussions involving the selling of securities is **dilution**. Dilution refers to a loss in existing shareholders' value. There are several kinds:

1. Dilution of percentage ownership.
2. Dilution of market value.
3. Dilution of book value and earnings per share.

The difference between these three types can be a little confusing and there are some common misconceptions about dilution, so we discuss it in this section.

Dilution of Proportionate Ownership

The first type of dilution can arise whenever a firm sells shares to the general public. For example, Joe Smith owns 5,000 shares of Merit Shoe Company. Merit Shoe currently has 50,000 shares of stock outstanding; each share gets one vote. Smith thus controls 10 percent (5,000/50,000) of the votes and gets 10 percent of the dividends.

If Merit Shoe issues 50,000 new shares of common stock to the public via a general cash offer, Smith's ownership in Merit Shoe may be diluted. If Smith does not participate in the new issue, his ownership drops to 5 percent (5,000/100,000). Notice that the value of Smith's shares is unaffected; he just owns a smaller percentage of the firm.

Because a rights offering would ensure Joe Smith an opportunity to maintain his proportionate 10 percent share, dilution of the ownership of existing shareholders can be avoided by using a rights offering.

Dilution of Value: Book versus Market Values

We now examine dilution of value by looking at some accounting numbers. We do this to illustrate a fallacy concerning dilution; we do not mean to suggest that accounting dilution is more important than market value dilution. As we illustrate, quite the reverse is true.

Suppose Provincial Telephone Company (PTC) wants to build a new switching facility to meet future anticipated demands. PTC currently has 1 million shares outstanding and no debt. Each share is selling for $5, and the company has a $5 million market value. PTC's book value is $10 million total, or $10 per share.

PTC has experienced a variety of difficulties in the past, including cost overruns, regulatory delays, and below normal profits. These difficulties are reflected in the fact that PTC's market-to-book ratio is $5/$10 = .50 (successful firms rarely have market prices less than book values).

Net income for PTC is currently $1 million. With 1 million shares, earnings per share (EPS) are $1, and the return on equity (ROE) is $1/$10 = 10%.[9] PTC thus sells for five times earnings (the price/earnings ratio is five). PTC has 200 shareholders, each of whom hold 5,000 shares each. The new plant will cost $2 million, so PTC has to issue 400,000 new shares ($5 × 400,000 = $2,000,000). There will thus be 1.4 million shares outstanding after the issue.

The ROE on the new plant is expected to be the same as for the company as a whole. In other words, net income is expected to go up by .10 × $2 million = $200,000. Total net income will thus be $1.2 million. The following things would occur:

1. With 1.4 million shares outstanding, EPS would be $1.2/1.4 = $.857 per share, down from $1.
2. The proportionate ownership of each old shareholder drops to 5,000/1.4 million = .36 percent from .50 percent.
3. If the stock continues to sell for five times earnings, the value would drop to 5 × .857 = $4.29, a loss of $.71 per share.
4. The total book value is the old $10 million plus the new $2 million for a total of $12 million. Book value per share falls to $12 million/1.4 million = $8.57 per share.

---

9 Return on equity (ROE) is equal to earnings per share divided by book value per share or, equivalently, net income divided by common equity. We discuss this and other financial ratios in some detail in Chapter 3.

TABLE 15.10

New issues and dilution: the case of Provincial Telephone Company

	(1) Initial	After (2) Dilution	After (3) No Dilution
Number of shares	1,000,000	1,400,000	1,400,000
Book value (B)	$10,000,000	$12,000,000	$12,000,000
Book value per share	$10	$8.57	$8.57
Market value	$5,000,000	$6,000,000	$8,000,000
Market price (P)	$5	$4.29	$5.71
Net income	$1,000,000	$1,200,000	$1,600,000
Return on equity (ROE)	0.10	0.10	0.13
Earnings per share (EPS)	$1	$0.86	$1.14
EPS/P	0.20	0.20	0.20
P/EPS	5	5	5
P/B	0.5	0.5	0.67
PROJECT			
Cost $2,000,000		NPV = –$1,000,000	NPV = $1,000,000

If we take this example at face value, dilution of proportionate ownership, accounting dilution, and market value dilution all occur. PTC's stockholders appear to suffer significant losses.

A MISCONCEPTION   Our example appears to show that selling stock when the market-to-book ratio is less than 1 is detrimental to the stockholders. Some managers claim that this dilution occurs because EPS goes down whenever shares are issued where the market value is less than the book value.

When the market-to-book ratio is less than 1, increasing the number of shares does cause EPS to go down. Such a decline in EPS is accounting dilution, and accounting dilution always occurs under these circumstances.

Is it furthermore true that market value dilution will also necessarily occur? The answer is no. There is nothing incorrect about our example, but why the market value has decreased is not obvious. We discuss this next.

THE CORRECT ARGUMENTS   In this example, the market price falls from $5 per share to $4.29. This is true dilution, but why does it occur? The answer has to do with the new project. PTC is going to spend $2 million on the new switching facility. However, as shown in Table 15.10, the total market value of the company is going to rise from $5 million to $6 million, an increase of only $1 million. This simply means that the NPV of the new project is – $1 million. With 1.4 million shares, the loss per share is $1/1.4 = .71, as we calculated before.

So, true dilution takes place for the shareholders of PTC because the NPV of the project is negative and the market knows it, not because the market-to-book ratio is less than 1. This negative NPV causes the market price to drop, and the accounting dilution has nothing to do with it.

Suppose that the new project had a positive NPV of $1 million. The total market value would rise by $2 + 1 = $3 million. As shown in Table 15.10 (third column), the price per share rises to $5.71. Notice that accounting dilution still occurs because the book value per share still falls, but there is no economic consequence to that fact. The market value of the stock rises.

The $.71 increase in share value comes about because of the $1 million NPV, which amounts to an increase in value of about $.71 per share. Also, as shown, if the ratio of price to EPS remains at 5, EPS must rise to $5.71/5 = $1.14. Total earnings (net income) rises to $1.14 per share × 1.4 million shares = $1.6 million. Finally, ROE would rise to $1.6 million/$12 million = 13.33%.

CONCEPT QUESTIONS

1. What are the different kinds of dilution?

2. Is dilution important?

15.10

ISSUING LONG-TERM DEBT

The general procedures followed in a public issue of bonds are the same as those for stocks. The issue must be registered with the OSC and any other relevant provincial securities commissions, there must be a prospectus, and so on. The registration statement for a public issue of bonds, however, is different from the one for common stock. For bonds, the registration statement must indicate an indenture.

Another important difference is that debt is more likely to be issued privately. There are two basic forms of direct private long-term financing: term loans and private placement.

Term loans are direct business loans. These loans have maturities of between one and five years. Most term loans are repayable during the life of the loan. The lenders include chartered banks, insurance companies, trust companies, and other lenders that specialize in corporate finance. The interest rate on a term loan may be either a fixed or floating rate.

Syndicated loans are loans made by a group (or syndicate) of banks and other institutional investors. They are used because large banks such as Citigroup and Royal Bank of Canada typically have a larger demand for loans than they can supply, and small regional banks frequently have more funds on hand than they can profitably lend to existing customers. As a result, a very large bank may arrange a loan with a firm or country and then sell portions of it to a syndicate of other banks. With a syndicated loan, each bank has a separate loan agreement with the borrowers.

A syndicated loan may be publicly traded. It may be a line of credit and be "undrawn" or it may be drawn and be used by a firm. Syndicated loans are always rated investment grade. However, a *leveraged* syndicated loan is rated speculative grade (i.e., it is "junk"). Every week, the *Wall Street Journal* reports on a number of syndicated loan deals, credit costs, and yields. In addition, syndicated loan prices are reported for a group of publicly traded loans. Research finds slightly higher default rates for syndicated loans when compared to corporate bonds.[10]

While there is no market for the public trading of syndicated loans, commercial and investment banks in the U.S. have created loan trading desks and a secondary loan market for syndicated loans. Further, the Loan Syndications and Trading Association was formed to help develop regulations and practices for this market. There is currently no similar market in Canada.[11]

Private placements are very similar to term loans except that the maturity is longer. Unlike term loans, privately placed debt usually employs an investment dealer. The dealer facilitates the process but does not underwrite the issue. A private placement does not require a full prospectus. Instead, the firm and its investment dealer only need to draw up an offering memorandum briefly describing the issuer and the issue. Most privately placed debt is sold to exempt purchasers. These are large insurance companies, pension funds, and other institutions, which, as sophisticated market participants, do not require the protection provided by studying a full prospectus.

The important differences between direct private long-term financing—term loans and private debt placements—and public issues of debt are:

1. Registration costs are lower for direct financing. A term loan avoids the cost of OSC registration. Private debt placements require an offering memorandum, but this is cheaper than preparing a full prospectus.

2. Direct placement is likely to have more restrictive covenants.

3. It is easier to renegotiate a term loan or a private placement in the event of a default. It is harder to renegotiate a public issue because hundreds of holders are usually involved.

term loans
Direct business loans of, typically, one to five years.

syndicated loans
Loans made by a group of banks or other institutions.

private placements
Loans, usually long term in nature, provided directly by a limited number of investors.

---

10 Edward I. Altman and Heather J. Suggitt, "Default Rates in the Syndicated Bank Loan Market: A Longitudinal Analysis," *Journal of Banking and Finance*, vol. 24, 2000.

11 This discussion of the secondary syndicated loan market is largely based upon the following Bank of Canada paper available at *www.bankofcanada.ca*: Jim Armstrong, "The Syndicated Loan Market: Developments in the North American Context," Bank of Canada Working Paper 2003-15.

4. Life insurance companies and pension funds dominate the private-placement segment of the bond market. Chartered banks are significant participants in the term loan market.

5. The costs of distributing bonds are lower in the private market because fewer buyers are involved and the issue is not underwritten.

The interest rates on term loans and private placements are usually higher than those on an equivalent public issue. This reflects the trade-off between a higher interest rate and more flexible arrangements in the event of financial distress, as well as the lower costs associated with private placements.

An additional, and very important, consideration is that the flotation costs associated with selling debt are much less than the costs associated with selling equity.

CONCEPT QUESTIONS

1. What is the difference between private and public bond issues?

2. A private placement is likely to have a higher interest rate than a public issue. Why?

SUMMARY AND CONCLUSIONS

This chapter looks at how corporate securities are issued. The following are the main points:

1. The costs of issuing securities can be quite large. They are much lower (as a percentage) for larger issues.

2. The bought deal type of underwriting is far more prevalent for large issues than regular underwriting. This is probably connected to the savings available through Prompt Offering Prospectuses and concentrated selling efforts.

3. The direct and indirect costs of going public can be substantial. However, once a firm is public it can raise additional capital with much greater ease.

4. Rights offerings are cheaper than general cash offers. Even so, most new equity issues in the United States are underwritten general cash offers. In Canada, the bought deal is cheaper and dominates the new issue market.

Key Terms

best efforts underwriting (page 454)
bought deal (page 454)
dilution (page 471)
Dutch auction underwriting (454)
ex rights (page 468)
firm commitment underwriting (page 454)
general cash offer (452)
holder-of-record date (page 468)
initial public offering (IPO) (page 452)
lockup agreement (page 455)
oversubscription privilege (page 469)
private placements (page 473)
prospectus (page 451)

public issue (page 450)
red herring (page 451)
regular underwriting (page 454)
rights offer (page 452)
seasoned equity offering (SEO) (page 452)
seasoned new issue (page 452)
spread (page 453)
standby fee (page 469)
standby underwriting (page 469)
syndicate (page 453)
syndicated loans (page 473)
term loans (page 473)
venture capital (page 449)

Chapter Review Problems and Self-Test

15.1   Flotation Costs   The L5 Corporation is considering an equity issue to finance a new space station. A total of $10 million in new equity is needed. If the direct costs are estimated at 6 percent of the amount raised, how large does the issue need to be? What is the dollar amount of the flotation cost?

15.2 **Rights Offerings** The Hadron Corporation currently has 4 million shares outstanding. The stock sells for $50 per share. To raise $30 million for a new particle accelerator, the firm is considering a rights offering at $20 per share. What is the value of a right in this case? The ex-rights price?

Answers to Self-Test Problems

15.1 The firm needs to net $10 million after paying the 6 percent flotation costs. So the amount raised is given by:

Amount raised × (1 − .06) = $10 million
Amount raised = $10/.94 = $10.638 million

The total flotation cost is thus $638,000.

15.2 To raise $30 million at $20 per share, $30 million/$20 = 1.5 million shares will have to be sold. Before the offering, the firm is worth 4 million × $50 = $200 million. The issue raised $30 million and there will be 5.5 million shares outstanding. The value of an ex-rights share will therefore be $230/5.5 = $41.82. The value of a right is thus $50 − 41.82 = $8.18.

Concepts Review and Critical Thinking Questions

1. In the aggregate, debt offerings are much more common than equity offerings and typically much larger as well. Why?

2. Why are the costs of selling equity so much larger than the costs of selling debt?

3. Why do noninvestment-grade bonds have much higher direct costs than investment-grade issues?

4. Why is underpricing not a great concern with bond offerings?

   Use the following information in answering the next three questions: Netscape Communications, maker of Internet and World Wide Web software, went public in August of 1995. Assisted by the investment bank of Morgan Stanley, Netscape sold five million shares at $28 each, thereby raising a total of $140 million. At the end of the first day of trading, the stock sold for $58.25 per share, down from a high of $71 reached earlier in the day in frenzied trading. Based on the end-of-day numbers, Netscape's shares were apparently underpriced by about $30 each, meaning that the company missed out on an additional $150 million.

5. The Netscape IPO was severely underpriced. This occurred even though the offering price of $28 had already been doubled from a planned $14 just weeks earlier. Should Netscape be upset with Morgan Stanley over the remaining underpricing?

6. In the previous question, would it affect your thinking to know that, at the time of the IPO, Netscape was only 16 months old, had only $16.6 million in revenues for the first half of the year, had never earned a profit, and was giving away its primary product over the Internet for free?

7. In the previous two questions, would it affect your thinking to know that, of 38 million shares total in Netscape, only 5 million were actually offered to the public? The remaining 33 million were retained by various founders of the company. For example, 24-year-old Marc Andreessen held a million shares, so he picked up $58.3 million for his 16-month effort (and that didn't include options he held to buy more shares).

8. Ren-Stimpy International is planning to raise fresh equity capital by selling a large new issue of common stock. Ren-Stimpy is currently a publicly traded corporation, and it is trying to choose between an underwritten cash offer and a rights offering (not underwritten) to current shareholders. Ren-Stimpy management is interested in minimizing the selling costs and has asked you for advice on the choice of issue methods. What is your recommendation and why?

9. In 1999, a certain assistant professor of finance bought 12 initial public offerings of common stock. He held each of these for approximately one month and then sold. The investment rule he followed was to submit a purchase order for every initial public offering of Internet companies. There were 22 of these offerings, and he submitted a purchase order for approximately $1,000 in stock for each of the companies. With 10 of these, no shares were allocated to this assistant professor. With 5 of the 12 offerings that were purchased, fewer than the requested number of shares were allocated.

   The year 1999 was very good for Internet company owners: on average, for the 22 companies that went public, the stocks were selling for 80 percent above the offering price a month after the initial offering date. The assistant professor looked at his performance record and found that the $8,400 invested in the 12 companies had grown to $10,000, representing a return of only about 20 percent (commissions were negligible). Did he have bad luck, or should he have expected to do worse than the average initial public offering investor? Explain.

Questions and Problems

Basic
(Questions
1–8)

1. **Rights Offerings** Again, Inc., is proposing a rights offering. Presently there are 350,000 shares outstanding at $85 each. There will be 70,000 new shares offered at $70 each.

   a. What is the new market value of the company?

   b. How many rights are associated with one of the new shares?

Basic
(continued)

c. What is the ex-rights price?

d. What is the value of a right?

e. Why might a company have a rights offering rather than a general cash offer?

2. **Rights Offerings**   The Clifford Corporation has announced a rights offer to raise $50 million for a new journal, the *Journal of Financial Excess*. This journal will review potential articles after the author pays a nonrefundable reviewing fee of $5,000 per page. The stock currently sells for $40 per share, and there are 5.2 million shares outstanding.

   a. What is the maximum possible subscription price? What is the minimum?

   b. If the subscription price is set at $35 per share, how many shares must be sold? How many rights will it take to buy one share?

   c. What is the ex-rights price? What is the value of a right?

   d. Show how a shareholder with 1,000 shares before the offering and no desire (or money) to buy additional shares is not harmed by the rights offer.

3. **Rights**   Stone Shoe Co. has concluded that additional equity financing will be needed to expand operations and that the needed funds will be best obtained through a rights offering. It has correctly determined that as a result of the rights offering, the share price will fall from $80 to $74.50 ($80 is the rights-on price; $74.50 is the ex-rights price, also known as the *when-issued* price). The company is seeking $15 million in additional funds with a per-share subscription price equal to $40. How many shares are there currently, before the offering? (Assume that the increment to the market value of the equity equals the gross proceeds from the offering.)

4. **IPO Underpricing**   The Woods Co. and the Weir Co. have both announced IPOs at $40 per share. One of these is undervalued by $11, and the other is overvalued by $6, but you have no way of knowing which is which. You plan on buying 1,000 shares of each issue. If an issue is underpriced, it will be rationed, and only half your order will be filled. If you *could* get 1,000 shares in Woods and 1,000 shares in Weir, what would your profit be? What profit do you actually expect? What principle have you illustrated?

5. **Calculating Flotation Costs**   The St. Anger Corporation needs to raise $25 million to finance its expansion into new markets. The company will sell new shares of equity via a general cash offering to raise the needed funds. If the offer price is $35 per share and the company's underwriters charge an 8 percent spread, how many shares need to be sold?

6. **Calculating Flotation Costs**   In the previous problem, if the SEC filing fee and associated administrative expenses of the offering are $900,000, how many shares need to be sold?

7. **Calculating Flotation Costs**   The Green Hills Co. has just gone public. Under a firm commitment agreement, Green Hills received $19.75 for each of the 5 million shares sold. The initial offering price was $21 per share, and the stock rose to $26 per share in the first few minutes of trading. Green Hills paid $800,000 in direct legal and other costs, and $250,000 in indirect costs. What was the flotation cost as a percentage of funds raised?

8. **Price Dilution**   Raggio, Inc., has 100,000 shares of stock outstanding. Each share is worth $90, so the company's market value of equity is $9,000,000. Suppose the firm issues 20,000 new shares at the following prices: $90, $85, and $70. What will the effect be of each of these alternative offering prices on the existing price per share?

Intermediate
(Questions
9–15)

9. **Dilution**   Teardrop Inc., wishes to expand its facilities. The company currently has 10 million shares outstanding and no debt. The stock sells for $50 per share, but the book value per share is $40. Net income for Teardrop is currently $15 million. The new facility will cost $35 million, and it will increase net income by $500,000.

   a. Assuming a constant price-earnings ratio, what will the effect be of issuing new equity to finance the investment? To answer, calculate the new book value per share, the new total earnings, the new EPS, the new stock price, and the new market-to-book ratio. What is going on here?

   b. What would the new net income for Teardrop have to be for the stock price to remain unchanged?

10. **Dilution**   The Metallica Heavy Metal Mining (MHMM) Corporation wants to diversify its operations. Some recent financial information for the company is shown here:

Stock price	$ 98
Number of shares	14,000
Total assets	$6,000,000
Total liabilities	$2,400,000
Net income	$ 630,000

MHMM is considering an investment that has the same PE ratio as the firm. The cost of the investment is $1,100,000, and it will be financed with a new equity issue. The return on the investment will equal MHMM's current ROE. What will happen to the book value per share, the market value per share, and the EPS? What is the NPV of this investment? Does dilution take place?

11. **Dilution**   In the previous problem, what would the ROE on the investment have to be if we wanted the price after the offering to be $98 per share (assume the PE ratio still remains constant)? What is the NPV of this investment? Does any dilution take place?

Intermediate
(continued) 12. **Rights** Hoobastink Mfg. is considering a rights offer. The company has determined that the ex-rights price would be $52. The current price is $55 per share, and there are 5 million shares outstanding. The rights offer would raise a total of $60 million. What is the subscription price?

13. **Underwriting** Performance Enhancement Corporation (PEC), a pharmaceutical company specializing in athletic "supplements," would like to issue an IPO. The underwriter, SEC Securities, has given PEC the option of choosing between a firm commitment, and regular underwriting. Under the firm commitment, SEC would buy all 15,000 shares of PEC for $50 a share. If PEC chooses to go with regular underwriting, SEC's fee will be $2 a share.

    a. How much money would be raised for PEC in a firm commitment if the stock sells for $65 a share on the open market? $45 a share? What would the profit or loss be for SEC under both conditions?

    b. How much money would be raised for PEC in regular underwriting if the stock sells for $65 a share? $45 a share? What would the profit or loss be for SEC under both conditions?

    c. Repeat a) and b) with the assumption that only 80% of the issue is sold. How does this effect the profit/loss for PEC and SEC?

14. **Selling Rights** Wuttke Corp. wants to raise $3.65 million via a rights offering. The company currently has 490,000 shares of common stock outstanding that sell for $30 per share. Its underwriter has set a subscription price of $22 per share and will charge Wuttke a 6 percent spread. If you currently own 6,000 shares of stock in the company and decide not to participate in the rights offering, how much money can you get by selling your rights?

15. **Valuing a Right** Mitsi Inventory Systems, Inc., has announced a rights offer. The company has announced that it will take four rights to buy a new share in the offering at a subscription price of $40. At the close of business the day before the ex-rights day, the company's stock sells for $80 per share. The next morning, you notice that the stock sells for $72 per share and the rights sell for $6 each. Are the stock and/or the rights correctly priced on the ex-rights day? Describe a transaction in which you could use these prices to create an immediate profit.

MINI CASE

The following material represents the cover page and summary of the prospectus for the initial public offering of the Pest Investigation Control Corporation (PICC), which is going public tomorrow with a firm commitment initial public offering managed by the investment banking firm of Erlanger and Ritter. Answer the following questions:

a) Assume that you know nothing about PICC other than the information contained in the prospectus. Based on your knowledge of finance, what is your prediction for the price of PICC tomorrow? Provide a short explanation of why you think this will occur.

b) Assume that you have several thousand dollars to invest. When you get home from class tonight, you find that your stockbroker, whom you have not talked to for weeks, has called. She has left a message that PICC is going public tomorrow and that she can get you several hundred shares at the offering price if you call her back first thing in the morning. Discuss the merits of this opportunity.

Prospectus   PICC

PEST INVESTIGATION CONTROL CORPORATION

Of the shares being offered hereby, all 300,000 are being sold by the Pest Investigation Control Corporation, Inc. ("the Company"). Before the offering there has been no public market for the shares of PICC, and no guarantee can be given that any such market will develop.

These securities have not been approved or disapproved by the OSC, nor has the commission passed upon the accuracy or adequacy of this prospectus. Any representation to the contrary is a criminal offence.

	Price to Public	Underwriting Discount	Proceeds to Company*
Per share	$10.00	$1.00	$9.00
Total	$3,000,000	$300,000	$2,700,000

*Before deducting expenses estimated at $27,000 and payable by the Company.

This is an initial public offering. The common shares are being offered, subject to prior sale, when, as, and if delivered to and accepted by the Underwriters and subject to approval of certain legal matters by their Counsel and by Counsel for the Company. The Underwriters reserve the right to withdraw, cancel, or modify such offer and to reject offers in whole or in part.

Erlanger and Ritter, Investment Bankers
May 3, 2006

Prospectus Summary

The Company	The Pest Investigation Control Corporation (PICC) breeds and markets toads and tree frogs as ecologically safe insect-control mechanisms.
The Offering	300,000 shares of common stock, no par value.
Listing	The Company will seek listing on the TSX.
Shares Outstanding	As of December 31, 2005, 400,000 shares of common stock were outstanding. After the offering, 700,000 shares of common stock will be outstanding.

MINI CASE (continued)

Use of Proceeds	To finance expansion of inventory and receivables and general working capital, and to pay for country club memberships for certain finance professors.

As of December 31, 2003

	Actual	As Adjusted for This Offering
Working capital	$10.00	$2,200
Total assets	$550	$2,856
Stockholders' equity	460	2,712

Selected Financial Information
(amounts in thousands except per share data)

	Fiscal Year Ended December 31		
	2003	2004	2005
Revenues	$65.00	$130.00	$260.00
Net earnings	4.50	17.00	30.00
Earnings per share	0.011	0.043	0.075

Internet Application Questions

1. What is the Investment Dealers' Association of Canada (www.ida.ca)? Describe its mandate, with particular attention on how the IDA protects the investors' funds (www.cipf.ca) from insolvent member dealers.

2. What comprises the Canadian regulatory landscape (www.ida.ca/Investors/SeRegulation_en.asp) for securities trading? Also go to the website for the newest stock exchange in Canada, the TSX Venture Exchange. Describe the role played by the capital pool program (142.201.0.1/en/pdf/CPCBrochure.pdf) at the Venture Exchange. As a bonus reference, bookmark the following site that contains a neat translation of financial jargon into simple English.

    142.201.0.1/en/aboutUs/education/mandate/resources/resourcesGlossary.html

3. What is the most recent Canadian IPO? Go to ipo.investcom.com and search under the "Date of Filing" link. What is the company? What exchange trades the stock? What was the IPO price? Is the company currently trading? If so, find the current price and calculate the return since inception.

4. What were the biggest first day returns in the latest quarter for IPOs in the U.S. markets? Go to www.hoovers.com, follow the "IPO Central" link, then the "IPO Scorecard" link.

5. You want to look at the most recent initial public offering filings on SEDAR. Go to ipo.investcom.com and locate the most recent company making a filing (note the name and ticker symbol of the company). Then go to www.sedar.com and search for the company. What is the name of the document files with SEDAR for the IPO? What does this company do? What purpose does the company propose for the funds raised by the IPO?

6. Go to ipo.investcom.com and locate the largest Canadian offering listed. What is the name of the company? What industry is it in? What is the final offering price per share? How much does the company expect to raise in the offering? Who is the lead underwriter(s)?

Suggested Readings

For further reading on underwriting in Canada and the role of the OSC see:
   Ontario Securities Commission Annual Reports and other information at *www.osc.gov.on.ca.*
Two studies of IPO costs in Canada are:
   Kryzanowski. L., and I. Rakita, "Is the U.S. 7% Solution Equivalent to the Canadian 6% Solution?" *Canadian Investment Review,* Fall 1999, pp. 27–34.
   L. Wang. "Aftermarket Volatility and Underpricing of Canadian Initial Public Offerings." *Canadian Journal of Administrative Sciences*, September 2002, pp. 231–249.

Some interesting papers on IPOs in Canada can also be found on the Web at *www.cirano.qc.ca:*
   Suret, Jean-Marc, and Maher Kooli. "How Cost-Effective are Canadian IPO Markets?" October 2002.
   Kooli, Maher, Jean-Francois L'Her, and Jean-Marc Suret. "Do IPOs Underperform in the Long-Run? New Evidence From the Canadian Stock Market," April 2003.

CHAPTER 16

Financial Leverage and Capital Structure Policy

omputing the weighted average cost of capital for Loblaw took up most of Chapter 14. Our calculations took the capital structure weights as observed. While this was fine for our purpose of introducing WACC, we must now recognize that the choice of capital structure is an important decision. The question of how much debt a firm should have relative to equity, known as its capital structure, has many implications for a firm and is far from being a settled issue in either theory or practice. In this chapter, we discuss the basic ideas underlying capital structures and how firms choose them.

THUS FAR, we have taken the firm's capital structure as given. Debt/equity ratios don't just drop on firms from the sky, of course, so now it's time to wonder where they do come from. Going back to Chapter 1, we call decisions about a firm's debt/equity ratio capital structure decisions.[1]

For the most part, a firm can choose any capital structure it wants. If management so desired, a firm could issue some bonds and use the proceeds to buy back some stock, thereby increasing the debt/equity ratio. Alternatively, it can issue stock and use the money to pay off some debt, thereby reducing the debt/equity ratio. These activities that alter the firm's existing capital structure are called capital *restructurings*. In general, such restructurings occur whenever the firm substitutes one capital structure for another while leaving the firm's assets unchanged.

Since the assets of a firm are not directly affected by a capital restructuring, we can examine the firm's capital structure decision separately from its other activities. This means a firm can consider capital restructuring decisions in isolation from its investment decisions. In this chapter then, we ignore investment decisions and focus on the long-term financing, or capital structure, question. We consider only long-term financing because, as we explained in Chapter 14, short-term sources of financing are excluded in calculating capital structure weights.

What we see in this chapter is that capital structure decisions can have important implications for the value of the firm and its cost of capital. We also find that important elements of the capital structure decision are easy to identify, but precise measures of these elements are generally not obtainable. As a result, we are able to give only an incomplete answer to the question of what the best capital structure might be for a particular firm at a particular time.

---

1 It is conventional to refer to decisions regarding debt and equity as capital structure decisions. However, the term *financial structure* would be more accurate, and we use the terms interchangeably.

 16.1

THE CAPITAL STRUCTURE QUESTION

How should a firm choose its debt/equity ratio? Here, as always, we assume that the guiding principle is to choose the action that maximizes the value of a share of stock. As we discuss next, however, when it comes to capital structure decisions, this is essentially the same thing as maximizing the value of the firm, and, for convenience, we frame our discussion in terms of firm value.

Firm Value and Stock Value: An Example

The following example illustrates that the capital structure that maximizes the value of the firm is the one that financial managers should choose for the shareholders, so there is no conflict in our goals. To begin, suppose the market value of the J. J. Sprint Company is $1,000. The company currently has no debt, and J. J. Sprint's 100 shares sell for $10 each. Further suppose that J. J. Sprint restructures itself by borrowing $500 and then paying out the proceeds to shareholders as an extra dividend of $500/100 = $5 per share.

This restructuring changes the capital structure of the firm with no direct effect on the firm's assets. The immediate effect is to increase debt and decrease equity. However, what would be the final impact of the restructuring? Table 16.1 illustrates three possible outcomes in addition to the original no-debt case. Notice that in scenario II the value of the firm is unchanged at $1,000. In scenario I, firm value rises by $250; it falls by $250 in scenario III. We haven't yet said what might lead to these changes. For now, we just take them as possible outcomes to illustrate a point.

Since our goal is to benefit the shareholders, we next examine, in Table 16.2, the net payoffs to the shareholders in these scenarios. For now we ignore the impact of taxes on dividends, capital gains and losses. We see that, if the value of the firm stays the same, then shareholders experience a capital loss that exactly offsets the extra dividend. This is outcome II. In outcome I, the value of the firm increases to $1,250 and the shareholders come out ahead by $250. In other words, the restructuring has an NPV of $250 in this scenario. The NPV in scenario III is –$250.

The key observation to make here is that the change in the value of the firm is the same as the net effect on the shareholders. Financial managers can therefore try to find the capital structure that maximizes the value of the firm. Put another way, the NPV rule applies to capital structure decisions, and the change in the value of the overall firm is the NPV of a restructuring. Thus, J. J. Sprint should borrow $500 if it expects outcome I. The crucial question in determining a firm's capital structure is, of course, which scenario is likely to occur.

Capital Structure and the Cost of Capital

In Chapter 14, we discussed the concept of the firm's weighted average cost of capital (WACC). Recall that the WACC tells us that the firm's overall cost of capital is a weighted average of the costs of the various components of the firm's capital structure. When we described the WACC, we took the firm's capital structure as given. Thus, one important issue that we want to explore

TABLE 16.1

Possible firm values: No debt versus debt plus dividend

| | No Debt | Debt plus Dividend | | |
		I	II	III
Debt	$ 0	$ 500	$ 500	$500
Equity	1,000	750	500	250
Firm value	$1,000	$1,250	$1,000	$750

TABLE 16.2

Possible payoffs to shareholders: Debt plus dividend

| | Debt plus Dividend | | |
	I	II	III
Equity value reduction	–$250	–$500	–$750
Dividends	500	500	500
Net effect	+$250	$ 0	–$250

in this chapter is what happens to the cost of capital when we vary the amount of debt financing or the debt/equity ratio.[2]

A primary reason for studying the WACC is that the value of the firm is maximized when the WACC is minimized. To see this, recall that the WACC is the discount rate that is appropriate for the firm's overall cash flows. Because values and discount rates move in opposite directions, minimizing the WACC maximizes the value of the firm's cash flows.

Thus, we want to choose the firm's capital structure so that the WACC is minimized. For this reason, we say that one capital structure is better than another if it results in a lower weighted average cost of capital. Further, we say that a particular debt/equity ratio represents the *optimal capital structure* if it results in the lowest possible WACC. This is sometimes called the firm's target capital structure as well.

CONCEPT QUESTIONS

1. Why should financial managers choose the capital structure that maximizes the value of the firm?

2. What is the relationship between the WACC and the value of the firm?

3. What is an optimal capital structure?

THE EFFECT OF FINANCIAL LEVERAGE

The previous section describes why the capital structure that produces the highest firm value (or the lowest cost of capital) is the one most beneficial to shareholders. In this section, we examine the impact of financial leverage on the payoffs to stockholders. As you may recall, financial leverage refers to the extent to which a firm relies on debt. The more debt financing a firm uses in its capital structure, the more financial leverage it employs.

As we describe, financial leverage can dramatically alter the payoffs to shareholders in the firm. Remarkably, however, financial leverage may not affect the overall cost of capital. If this is true, then a firm's capital structure is irrelevant because changes in capital structure won't affect the value of the firm. We return to this issue a little later.

The Basics of Financial Leverage

We start by illustrating how financial leverage works. For now, we ignore the impact of taxes. Also, for ease of presentation, we describe the impact of leverage in its effects on earnings per share (EPS) and return on equity (ROE). These are, of course, accounting numbers, and, as such, are not our primary concern. Using cash flows instead of these accounting numbers would lead to precisely the same conclusions, but a little more work would be needed. We discuss the impact on market values in a subsequent section.

FINANCIAL LEVERAGE, EPS, AND ROE: AN EXAMPLE The Trans Can Corporation currently has no debt in its capital structure. The CFO, Kim Morris, is considering a restructuring that would involve issuing debt and using the proceeds to buy back some of the outstanding equity. Table 16.3 presents both the current and proposed capital structures. As shown, the firm's assets have a value of $8 million, and there are 400,000 shares outstanding. Because Trans Can is an all-equity firm, the price per share is $20.

The proposed debt issue would raise $4 million; the bonds would be issued at par with a coupon rate of 10 percent for a required return on debt of 10 percent. Since the stock sells for $20 per share, the $4 million in new debt would be used to purchase $4 million/$20 = 200,000 shares, leaving 200,000. After the restructuring, Trans Can would have a capital structure that was 50 percent debt, so the debt/equity ratio would be 1. Notice that, for now, we assume the stock price remains at $20.

---

2 Note that when we looked at WACC, we considered the cost of debt to be related to bond issues. This cost could also be a bank debt financing rate if the firm predominantly uses that form of debt.

To investigate the impact of the proposed restructuring, Morris has prepared Table 16.4, that compares the firm's current capital structure to the proposed capital structure under three scenarios. The scenarios reflect different assumptions about the firm's EBIT. Under the expected scenario, the EBIT is $1 million. In the recession scenario, EBIT falls to $500,000. In the expansion scenario, it rises to $1.5 million.

To illustrate some of the calculations in Table 16.4, consider the expansion case. EBIT is $1.5 million. With no debt (the current capital structure) and no taxes, net income is also $1.5 million. In this case, there are 400,000 shares worth $8 million total. EPS is therefore $1.5 million/400,000 = $3.75 per share. Also, since accounting return on equity (ROE) is net income divided by total equity, ROE is $1.5 million/$8 million = 18.75%.[3]

With $4 million in debt (the proposed capital structure), things are somewhat different. Since the interest rate is 10 percent, the interest bill is $400,000. With EBIT of $1.5 million, interest of $400,000, and no taxes, net income is $1.1 million. Now there are only 200,000 shares worth $4 million total. EPS is therefore $1.1 million/200,000 = $5.50 per share versus the $3.75 per share that we calculated earlier. Furthermore, ROE is $1.1 million/$4 million = 27.5 percent. This is well above the 18.75 percent we calculated for the current capital structure. So our example in Table 16.4 shows how increased debt can magnify ROE when profitability is good.

Greater use of debt also magnifies ROE in the other direction. To see this, look at the recession case in Table 16.4. Under the current capital structure, EPS falls to $1.25 in a recession bringing ROE down to 6.25 percent. With more debt under the proposed capital structure, EPS is only $.50 and ROE drops to 2.50 percent. In brief, Table 16.4 shows that using more debt makes EPS and ROE more risky.

DEGREE OF FINANCIAL LEVERAGE   As our example shows, financial leverage measures how much earnings per share (and ROE) respond to changes in EBIT. It is the financial counterpart to operating leverage that we discussed in Chapter 11. We can generalize our discussion of financial leverage by introducing a formula for the degree of financial leverage:

$$\text{Degree of financial leverage} = \frac{\text{Percentage change in EPS}}{\text{Percentage change in EBIT}} \qquad [16.1]$$

TABLE 16.3
Current and proposed capital structures for the Trans Can Corporation

	Current	Proposed
Assets	$8,000,000	$8,000,000
Debt	0	4,000,000
Equity	8,000,000	4,000,000
Debt/equity ratio	0	1
Share price	$ 20	$ 20
Shares outstanding	400,000	200,000
Interest rate	10%	10%

TABLE 16.4
Capital structure scenarios for the Trans Can Corporation

	Recession	Expected	Expansion
Current Capital Structure: No Debt			
EBIT	$500,000	$1,000,000	$1,500,000
Interest	0	0	0
Net income	$500,000	$1,000,000	$1,500,000
ROE	6.25%	12.50%	18.75%
EPS	$ 1.25	$ 2.50	$ 3.75
Proposed Capital Structure: Debt = $4 million			
EBIT	$500,000	$1,000,000	$1,500,000
Interest	400,000	400,000	400,000
Net income	$100,000	$ 600,000	$1,100,000
ROE	2.50%	15.00%	27.50%
EPS	$ .50	$ 3.00	$ 5.50

---

3 ROE is discussed in some detail in Chapter 3.

Like the degree of operating leverage, DFL varies for different ranges of EPS and EBIT. To illustrate the formula, we calculate DFL for Trans Can for an EBIT of $1 million. There are two calculations, one for the current and one for the proposed capital structure. Starting with the current capital structure:

$$DFL = \frac{(\$3.75 - 2.50)/2.50}{(\$1,500,000 - 1,000,000)/1,000,000}$$

$$= \frac{.50}{.50}$$

$$DFL = 1.0$$

So for the existing capital structure, the degree of financial leverage is 1.0. For the proposed capital structure:

$$DFL = \frac{(\$5.50 - 3.00)/3.00}{(\$1,500,000 - 1,000,000)/1,000,000}$$

$$DFL = \frac{.83}{.50}$$

$$DFL = 1.67$$

The proposed capital structure includes debt and this increases the degree of financial leverage. Calculating DFL adds precision to our earlier observation that increasing financial leverage magnifies the gains and losses to shareholders. We can now say that EPS increases or decreases by a factor of 1.67 times the percentage increase or decrease in EBIT.

Many analysts use a convenient alternative formula for DFL:

$$DFL = \frac{EBIT}{EBIT - Interest} \qquad [16.2]$$

We recalculate DFL for the proposed capital structure at EBIT of $1 million to show that the new formula gives the same answer.

$$DFL = \frac{\$1,000,000}{\$1,000,000 - 400,000}$$

$$DFL = \frac{\$1,000,000}{\$600,000}$$

$$DFL = 1.67$$

EPS VERSUS EBIT   The impact of leverage is evident when the effect of the restructuring on EPS and ROE is examined. In particular, the variability in both EPS and ROE is much larger under the proposed capital structure. This illustrates how financial leverage acts to magnify gains and losses to shareholders.

In Figure 16.1, we take a closer look at the effect of the proposed restructuring. This figure plots earnings per share (EPS) against earnings before interest and taxes (EBIT) for the current and proposed capital structures. The first line, labelled "No debt," represents the case of no leverage. This line begins at the origin, indicating that EPS would be zero if EBIT were zero. From there, every $400,000 increase in EBIT increases EPS by $1 (because there are 400,000 shares outstanding).

The second line represents the proposed capital structure. Here, EPS is negative if EBIT is zero. This follows because $400,000 of interest must be paid regardless of the firm's profits. Since there are 200,000 shares in this case, the EPS is –$2 per share as shown. Similarly, if EBIT were $400,000, EPS would be exactly zero.

The important thing to notice in Figure 16.1 is that the slope of the line in this second case is steeper. In fact, for every $400,000 increase in EBIT, EPS rises by $2, so the line is twice as steep. This tells us that EPS is twice as sensitive to changes in EBIT because of the financial leverage employed.

Another observation to make in Figure 16.1 is that the lines intersect. At that point, EPS is exactly the same for both capital structures. To find this point, note that EPS is equal to EBIT/400,000 in the no-debt case. In the with-debt case, EPS is (EBIT – $400,000)/200,000. If we set these equal to each other, EBIT is:

$$EBIT/400,000 = (EBIT - 400,000)/200,000$$
$$EBIT = 2 \times (EBIT - \$400,000)$$
$$EBIT = \$800,000$$

EXAMPLE 16.1: Indifference EBIT

The MPD Corporation has decided in favour of a capital restructuring. Currently, MPD uses no debt financing. Following the restructuring, however, debt would be $1 million. The interest rate on the debt would be 9 percent. MPD currently has 200,000 shares outstanding, and the price per share is $20. If the restructuring is expected to increase EPS, what is the minimum level for EBIT that MPD's management must be expecting? Ignore taxes in answering.[4]

To answer, we calculate EBIT at the indifferent point. At any EBIT above this, the increased financial leverage increases EPS, so this tells us the minimum level for EBIT. Under the old capital structure, EPS is simply EBIT/200,000. Under the new capital structure, the interest expense is

$1 million × .09 = $90,000. Furthermore, with the $1 million proceeds, MPD could repurchase $1 million/$20 = 50,000 shares of stock, leaving 150,000 outstanding. EPS is thus (EBIT − $90,000)/150,000.

Now that we know how to calculate EPS under both scenarios, we set them equal to each other and solve for the indifference point EBIT:

$$EBIT/200,000 = (EBIT − \$90,000)/150,000$$
$$EBIT = (4/3) × (EBIT − \$90,000)$$
$$EBIT = \$360,000$$

Check that, in either case, EPS is $1.80 when EBIT is $360,000. Management at MPD is apparently of the opinion that EPS will exceed $1.80.

FIGURE 16.1

Financial leverage, EPS, and EBIT for the Trans Can Corporation

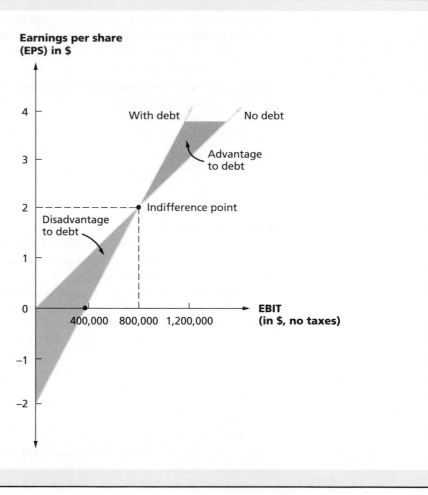

When EBIT is $800,000, EPS is $2 per share under either capital structure. This is labelled as the indifference point in Figure 16.1. If EBIT is above this level, leverage is beneficial; if it is below this point, it is not.

---

4 Note that at the breakeven point, taxes are irrelevant.

There is another, more intuitive way of seeing why the indifferent point is $800,000. Notice that, if the firm has no debt and its EBIT is $800,000, its net income is also $800,000. In this case, the ROE is 10 percent. This is precisely the same as the interest rate on the debt, so the firm earns a return that is just sufficient to pay the interest.

Corporate Borrowing and Homemade Leverage

Based on Tables 16.3 and 16.4 and Figure 16.1, Morris draws the following conclusions:

1. The effect of financial leverage depends on Trans Can's EBIT. When EBIT is expected to increase, leverage is beneficial.
2. Under the expected scenario, leverage increases the returns to shareholders, both as measured by ROE and EPS.
3. Shareholders are exposed to more risk under the proposed capital structure since the EPS and ROE are more sensitive to changes in EBIT in this case.
4. Because of the impact that financial leverage has on both the expected return to shareholders and the riskiness of the stock, capital structure is an important consideration.

The first three of these conclusions are clearly correct. Does the last conclusion necessarily follow? Surprisingly, the answer is not necessarily—at least in a world of perfect capital markets where individual investors can borrow at the same rate as corporations. As we discuss next, the reason is that shareholders can adjust the amount of financial leverage by borrowing and lending on their own. This use of personal borrowing to alter the degree of financial leverage is called **homemade leverage.**

homemade leverage
The use of personal borrowing to change the overall amount of financial leverage to which the individual is exposed.

We now assume perfect markets and illustrate that it actually makes no difference whether or not Trans Can adopts the proposed capital structure, because any shareholder who prefers the proposed capital structure can simply create it using homemade leverage. To begin, the first part of Table 16.5 shows what would happen to an investor who buys $2,000 worth of Trans Can stock if the proposed capital structure were adopted. This investor purchases 100 shares of stock. From Table 16.4, EPS will either be $.50, $3.00, or $5.50, so the total earnings for 100 shares is either $50, $300, or $550 under the proposed capital structure.

Now, suppose that Trans Can does not adopt the proposed capital structure. In this case, EPS is $1.25, $2.50, or $3.75. The second part of Table 16.5 demonstrates how a shareholder who preferred the payoffs under the proposed structure can create them using personal borrowing. To do this, the shareholder borrows $2,000 at 10 percent on his or her own. Our investor uses this amount, along with the original $2,000, to buy 200 shares of stock. As shown, the net payoffs are exactly the same as those for the proposed capital structure.

How did we know to borrow $2,000 to create the right payoffs? We are trying to replicate Trans Can's proposed capital structure at the personal level. The proposed capital structure results in a debt/equity ratio of 1. To replicate it at the personal level, the shareholder must borrow enough to create this same debt/equity ratio. Since the shareholder has $2,000 in equity invested, borrowing another $2,000 creates a personal debt/equity ratio of 1.

This example demonstrates that investors can always increase financial leverage themselves to create a different pattern of payoffs. It thus makes no difference whether or not Trans Can chooses the proposed capital structure.

TABLE 16.5
Proposed capital structure versus original capital structure with homemade leverage

	Recession	Expected	Expansion
Proposed Capital Structure			
EPS	$ .50	$ 3.00	$ 5.50
Earnings for 100 shares	50.00	300.00	550.00
Net cost = 100 shares at $20 = $2,000			
Original Capital Structure and Homemade Leverage			
EPS	$ 1.25	$ 2.50	$ 3.75
Earnings for 200 shares	250.00	500.00	750.00
Less: Interest on $2,000 at 10%	200.00	200.00	200.00
Net earnings	$ 50.00	$300.00	$550.00
Net cost = 200 shares at $20/share – Amount borrowed = $4,000 – 2,000 = $2,000			

EXAMPLE 16.2: Unlevering the Stock

In our Trans Can example, suppose management adopts the proposed capital structure. Further suppose that an investor who owned 100 shares preferred the original capital structure. Show how this investor could "unlever" the stock to re-create the original payoffs.

	Recession	Expected	Expansion
EPS (proposed structure)	$ .50	$ 3.00	$ 5.50
Earnings for 50 shares	25.00	150.00	275.00
Plus: Interest on $1,000	100.00	100.00	100.00
Total payoff	$125.00	$250.00	$375.00

To create leverage, investors borrow on their own. To undo leverage, investors must lend money. For Trans Can, the corporation borrowed an amount equal to half its value. The investor can unlever the stock by simply lending money in the same proportion. In this case, the investor sells 50 shares for $1,000 total and then lends out the $1,000 at 10 percent. The payoffs are calculated in the accompanying table. These are precisely the payoffs the investor would have experienced under the original capital structure.

CONCEPT QUESTIONS

1. What is the impact of financial leverage on shareholders?

2. What is homemade leverage?

3. Why is Trans Can's capital structure irrelevant?

16.3   CAPITAL STRUCTURE AND THE COST OF EQUITY CAPITAL

We have seen that there is nothing special about corporate borrowing because investors can borrow or lend on their own. As a result, whichever capital structure Trans Can chooses, the stock price is the same. Trans Can's capital structure is thus irrelevant, at least in the simple world we examined.

Our Trans Can example is based on a famous argument advanced by two Nobel laureates, Franco Modigliani and Merton Miller, whom we henceforth call M&M. What we illustrated for the Trans Can Company is a special case of **M&M Proposition I**. M&M Proposition I states that it is completely irrelevant how a firm chooses to arrange its finances.

M&M Proposition I
The value of the firm is independent of its capital structure.

M&M Proposition I: The Pie Model

One way to illustrate M&M Proposition I is to imagine two firms that are identical on the left side of the balance sheet. Their assets and operations are exactly the same. Each firm earns $EBIT every year indefinitely. No EBIT growth is projected. The right sides are different because the two firms finance their operations differently. We can view the capital structure question as a pie model. Why we chose this name is apparent in Figure 16.2. Figure 16.2 gives two possible ways of cutting up this pie between the equity slice, E, and the debt slice, D: 40–60 percent and 60–40 percent. However, the size of the pie in Figure 16.2 is the same for both firms because the value of the assets is the same. This is precisely what M&M Proposition I states: The size of the pie does not depend on how it is sliced.

Proposition I is expressed in the following formula:

$$V_u = EBIT/R_E^u = V_L = E_L + D_L$$ [16.3]

where

$$V_u = \text{Value of the unlevered firm}$$
$$V_L = \text{Value of the levered firm}$$
$$EBIT = \text{Perpetual operating income}$$
$$R_E^u = \text{Equity required return for the unlevered firm}$$
$$E_L = \text{Market value of equity}$$
$$D_L = \text{Market value of debt}$$

The Cost of Equity and Financial Leverage: M&M Proposition II

Although changing the capital structure of the firm may not change the firm's total value, it does cause important changes in the firm's debt and equity. We now examine what happens to a firm financed with debt and equity when the debt/equity ratio is changed. To simplify our analysis, we continue to ignore taxes.

M&M PROPOSITION II   In Chapter 14, we saw that if we ignore taxes the weighted average cost of capital, WACC, is:

$$WACC = (E/V) \times R_E + (D/V) \times R_D$$

where $V = E + D$. We also saw that one way of interpreting the WACC is that it is the required return on the firm's overall assets. To remind us of this, we use the symbol R_A to stand for the WACC and write:

$$R_A = (E/V) \times R_E + (D/V) \times R_D$$

If we rearrange this to solve for the cost of equity capital, we see that:

$$R_E = R_A + (R_A - R_D) \times (D/E) \qquad \text{[16.4]}$$

M&M Proposition II
A firm's cost of equity capital is a positive linear function of its capital structure.

This is the famous **M&M Proposition II,** which tells us that the cost of equity depends on three things: the required rate of return on the firm's assets, R_A; the firm's cost of debt, R_D; and the firm's debt/equity ratio, D/E.

Figure 16.3 summarizes our discussion thus far by plotting the cost of equity capital, R_E, against the debt/equity ratio. As shown, M&M Proposition II indicates that the cost of equity, R_E, is given by a straight line with a slope of $(R_A - R_D)$. The y-intercept corresponds to a firm with a debt/equity ratio of zero, so $R_A = R_E$ in that case. Figure 16.3 shows that, as the firm raises its debt/equity ratio, the increase in leverage raises the risk of the equity and, therefore, the required return or cost of equity (R_E).

Notice in Figure 16.3 that the WACC doesn't depend on the debt/equity ratio; it's the same no matter what the debt/equity ratio is. This is another way of stating M&M Proposition I: The firm's overall cost of capital is unaffected by its capital structure. As illustrated, the fact that the cost of debt is lower than the cost of equity is exactly offset by the increase in the cost of equity from borrowing. In other words, the change in the capital structure weights (E/V and D/V) is exactly offset by the change in the cost of equity (R_E), so the WACC stays the same.

Business and Financial Risk

In our previous chapter, we discussed the use of the security market line (SML) to estimate the cost of equity capital. If we now combine the SML and M&M Proposition II, we can develop a particularly valuable insight into the cost of equity. Using the SML, we can write the required return on the firm's assets as:

FIGURE 16.2

Two pie models of capital structure

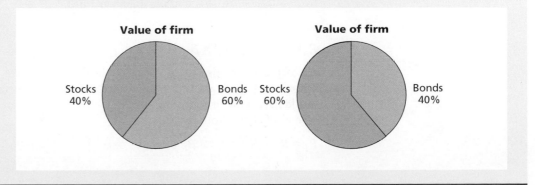

Value of firm

Stocks 40%   Bonds 60%

Value of firm

Stocks 60%   Bonds 40%

In Their Own Words . . .

Merton H. Miller on Capital Structure— M&M 30 Years Later

HOW DIFFICULT it is to summarize briefly the contribution of these papers was brought home to me very clearly after Franco Modigliani was awarded the Nobel Prize in Economics, in part—but, of course, only in part—for the work in finance. The television camera crews from our local stations in Chicago immediately descended upon me. "We understand," they said, "that you worked with Modigliani some years back in developing these M&M theorems, and we wonder if you could explain them briefly to our television viewers." "How briefly?" I asked. "Oh, take 10 seconds," was the reply.

Ten seconds to explain the work of a lifetime! Ten seconds to describe two carefully reasoned articles, each running to more than 30 printed pages and each with 60 or so long footnotes! When they saw the look of dismay on my face, they said: "You don't have to go into details. Just give us the main points in simple, commonsense terms."

The main point of the cost-of-capital article was, in principle at least, simple enough to make. It said that in an economist's ideal world, the total market value of all the securities issued by a firm would be governed by the earning power and risk of its underlying real assets and would be independent of how the mix of securities issued to finance it was divided between debt instruments and equity capital. Some corporate treasurers might well think that they could enhance total value by increasing the proportion of debt instruments because yields on debt instruments, given their lower risk, are, by and large, substantially below those on equity capital. But, under the ideal conditions assumed, the added risk to the shareholders from issuing more debt will raise required yields on the equity by just enough to offset the seeming gain from use of low cost debt.

Such a summary would not only have been too long, but it relied on shorthand terms and concepts that are rich in connotations to economists, but hardly so to the general public. I thought, instead, of an analogy that we ourselves had invoked in the original paper. "Think of the firm," I said, "as a gigantic tub of whole milk. The farmer can sell the whole milk as is. Or he can separate out the cream and sell it at a considerably higher price

than the whole milk would bring. (Selling cream is the analog of a firm selling low-yield and hence high-priced debt securities.) But, of course, what the farmer would have left would be skim milk, with low butter-fat content and that would sell for much less than whole milk. Skim milk corresponds to the levered equity. The M&M proposition says that if there were no costs of separation (and, of course, no government dairy support programs), the cream plus the skim milk would bring the same price as the whole milk."

The television people conferred among themselves for a while. They informed me that it was still too long, too complicated, and too academic. "Have you anything simpler?" they asked. I thought for another way that the M&M proposition is presented which stresses the role of securities as devices for "partitioning" a firm's payoffs among the group of its capital suppliers. "Think of the firm," I said, "as a gigantic pizza, divided into quarters. If now, you cut each quarter in half into eighths, the M&M proposition says that you will have more pieces, but not more pizza."

Once again widespread conversation. This time, they shut the lights off. They folded up their equipment. They thanked me for my cooperation. They said they would get back to me. But I knew that I had somehow lost my chance to start a new career as a packager of economic wisdom for TV viewers in convenient 10-second sound bites. Some have the talent for it; and some just don't.

The late Merton H. Miller was Robert R. McCormick Distinguished Service Professor at the University of Chicago Graduate School of Business. He was famous for his path-breaking work with Franco Modigliani on corporate capital structure, cost of capital, and dividend policy. He received the Nobel Prize in Economics for his contributions shortly after this essay was prepared.

$$R_A = R_f + (R_M - R_f) \times \beta_A$$

The beta coefficient in this case, β_A, is called the firm's asset beta, and it is a measure of the systematic risk of the firm's assets. It is also called the unlevered beta because it is the beta that the stock would have if the firm had no debt.

The cost of equity from the SML is:

$$R_E = R_f + (R_M - R_f) \times \beta_E$$

FIGURE 16.3

The cost of equity and
the WACC; M&M
Propositions I and II with
no taxes

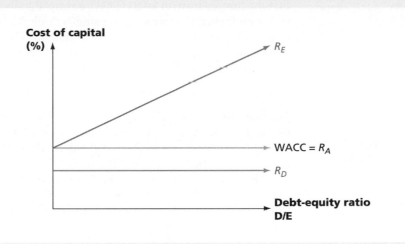

$$R_E = R_A + (R_A - R_D) \times (D/E) \text{ by Proposition II}$$
$$\text{WACC} = \left(\frac{E}{V}\right) R_E + \left(\frac{D}{V}\right) R_D$$
$$V = D + E$$

EXAMPLE 16.3: The Cost of Equity Capital

The Ricardo Corporation has a weighted average cost of capital (unadjusted) of 12 percent. It can borrow at 8 percent. Assuming that Ricardo has a target capital structure of 80 percent equity and 20 percent debt, what is its cost of equity? What is the cost of equity if the target capital structure is 50 percent equity (D/E of 1.0)? Calculate the unadjusted WACC using your answers to verify that it is the same.

According to M&M Proposition II, the cost of equity, R_E, is:

$$R_E = R_A + (R_A - R_D) \times (D/E)$$

In the first case, the debt/equity ratio is .2/.8 = .25, so the cost of the equity is:

$$R_E = 12\% + (12\% - 8\%) \times (.25)$$
$$= 13\%$$

In the second case, check that the debt/equity ratio is 1.0, so the cost of equity is 16 percent.

We can now calculate the unadjusted WACC assuming that the percentage of equity financing is 80 percent and the cost of equity is 13 percent:

$$\text{WACC} = (E/V) \times R_E + (D/V) \times R_D$$
$$= .80 \times 13\% + .20 \times 8\%$$
$$= 12\%$$

In the second case, the percentage of equity financing is 50 percent and the cost of equity is 16 percent. The WACC is:

$$\text{WACC} = (E/V) \times R_E + (D/V) \times R_D$$
$$= .50 \times 16\% \times .50 \times 8\%$$
$$= 12\%$$

As we calculated, the WACC is 12 percent in both cases.

When this is combined with M&M Proposition II, it is straightforward to show the relationship between the equity beta, β_E, and the asset beta, β_A, is:[5]

$$\beta_E = \beta_A \times (1 + D/E) \qquad\qquad [16.5]$$

---

5 To see this, assume the firm's debt has a beta of zero. This means that $R_D = R_f$. If we substitute for R_A and R_D in M&M Proposition II, we see that:

$$R_E = R_A + (R_A - R_D) \times (D/E)$$
$$= [R_f + \beta_A \times (R_M - R_f)] + ([R_f + \beta_A \times (R_M - R_f)] - R_f) \times (D/E)$$
$$= R_f + (R_M - R_f) \times \beta_A \times (1 + D/E)$$

Thus, the equity beta, β_E, equals the asset beta, β_A, multiplied by the equity multiplier, $(1 + D/E)$.

The term $(1 + D/E)$ here is the same as the equity multiplier described in Chapter 3, except here it is measured in market values instead of book values. In fact, from the Du Pont identity, we saw that the firm's return on assets (ROA) was equal to its return on equity (ROE) multiplied by the equity multiplier. Here we see a very similar result: The risk premium on the firm's equity is equal to the risk premium on the firm's assets multiplied by the equity multiplier.

We are now in a position to examine directly the impact of financial leverage on the firm's cost of equity. Rewriting things a bit, we see the equity beta has two components:

$$\beta_E = \beta_A + \beta_A \times (D/E)$$

The first component, β_A, is a measure of the riskiness of the firm's assets. Since this is determined primarily by the nature of the firm's operations, we say it measures the **business risk** of the equity. The second component, $\beta_A \times (D/E)$, depends on the firm's financial policy. We therefore say it measures the **financial risk** of the equity.

The total systematic risk of the firm's equity thus has two parts: business risk and financial risk. As we have illustrated, the firm's cost of equity rises when it increases its use of financial leverage because the financial risk of the stock increases. Shareholders require compensation in the form of a larger risk premium, thereby increasing the firm's cost of equity capital.

business risk
The equity risk that comes from the nature of the firm's operating activities.

financial risk
The equity risk that comes from the financial policy (i.e., capital structure) of the firm.

CONCEPT QUESTIONS

1. What does M&M Proposition I state?

2. What are the two determinants of a firm's cost of equity?

M&M PROPOSITIONS I AND II WITH CORPORATE TAXES

Debt has two distinguishing features that we have not taken into proper account: First, as we have mentioned in a number of places, interest paid on debt is tax deductible. This is good for the firm, and it may be an added benefit to debt financing. Second, failure to meet debt obligations can result in bankruptcy. This is not good for the firm, and it may be an added cost of debt financing. Since we haven't explicitly considered either of these two features of debt, we may get a different answer about capital structure once we do. Accordingly, we consider taxes in this section and bankruptcy in the next one.

We can start by considering what happens to M&M Propositions I and II when we look at the effect of corporate taxes. To do this, we examine two firms, Firm U (unlevered) and Firm L (levered). These two firms are identical on the left side of the balance sheet, so their assets and operations are the same.

We assume EBIT is expected to be $1,000 every year forever for both firms. The difference between them is that Firm L has issued $1,000 worth of perpetual bonds on which it pays 8 percent interest every year. The interest bill is thus $.08 \times \$1,000 = \$80$ every year forever. Also, we assume the corporate tax rate is 30 percent.

For our two firms, U and L, we can now calculate the following:

	Firm U	Firm L
EBIT	$1,000	$1,000
Interest	0	80
Taxable income	$1,000	$ 920
Taxes (30%)	300	276
Net income	$ 700	$ 644

The Interest Tax Shield

To simplify things, we assume depreciation is equal to zero. We also assume capital spending is zero and there are no additions to NWC. In this case, the cash flow from assets is simply equal to EBIT − Taxes. For firms U and L we thus have:

Cash Flow from Assets	Firm U	Firm L
EBIT	$1,000	$1,000
– Taxes	300	276
Total	$ 700	$ 724

We immediately see that capital structure is now having some effect because the cash flows from U and L are not the same even though the two firms have identical assets.

To see what's going on, we can compute the cash flow to stockholders and bondholders.

Cash Flow	Firm U	Firm L
To stockholders	$700	$644
To bondholders	0	80
Total	$700	$724

What we are seeing is that the total cash flow to L is $24 more. This occurs because L's tax bill (which is a cash outflow) is $24 less. The fact that interest is deductible for tax purposes has generated a tax saving equal to the interest payment ($80) multiplied by the corporate tax rate (30 percent): $80 × .30 = $24. We call this tax saving the **interest tax shield.**

Taxes and M&M Proposition I

Since the debt is perpetual, the same $24 shield would be generated every year forever. The after-tax cash flow to L would thus be the same $700 that U earns plus the $24 tax shield. Since L's cash flow is always $24 greater, Firm L is worth more than Firm U by the value of this perpetuity.

Because the tax shield is generated by paying interest, it has the same risk as the debt, and 8 percent (the cost of debt) is therefore the appropriate discount rate. The value of the tax shield is thus:

$$PV = \$24/.08 = .30 \times 1{,}000 \times .08/.08 = .30(1{,}000) = \$300$$

As our example illustrates, the value of the tax shield can be written as:

$$\text{Value of the interest tax shield} = (T_C \times R_D \times D)/R_D \qquad [16.6]$$
$$= T_C \times D$$

We have now come up with another famous result, M&M Proposition I with corporate taxes. We have seen that the value of Firm L, V_L, exceeds the value of Firm U, V_U, by the present value of the interest tax shield, $T_C \times D$. M&M Proposition I with taxes therefore states that:

$$V_L = V_U + T_C \times D \qquad [16.7]$$

The effect of borrowing is illustrated in Figure 16.4. We have plotted the value of the levered firm, V_L, against the amount of debt, D. M&M Proposition I with corporate taxes implies that the relationship is given by a straight line with a slope of T_C and a y-intercept of V_U.

In Figure 16.4, we have also drawn a horizontal line representing V_U. As indicated, the distance between the two lines is $T_C \times D$, the present value of the tax shield.

Suppose the cost of capital for Firm U is 10 percent. We call this the **unlevered cost of capital,** (R_U). We can think of R_U as the cost of the capital the firm would have if it had no debt. Firm U's cash flow is $700 every year forever, and since U has no debt, the appropriate discount rate is $R_U = 10\%$. The value of the unlevered firm, V_U, is simply:

$$V_U = EBIT \times (1 - T_C)/R_U$$
$$= 700/.10$$
$$= \$7{,}000$$

The value of the levered firm, V_L, is:

$$V_L = V_U + T_C \times D$$
$$= \$7{,}000 + .30 \times \$1{,}000$$
$$= \$7{,}300$$

FIGURE 16.4

M&M Proposition I with taxes

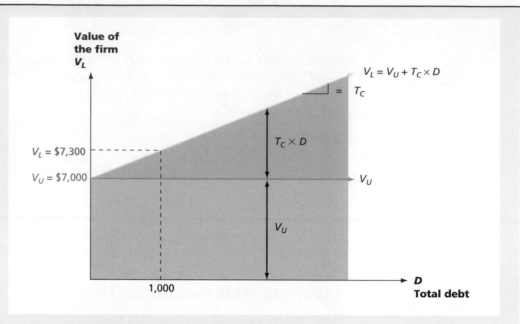

The value of the firm increases as total debt increases because of the interest tax shield. This is the basis of M&M Proposition I with taxes.

As Figure 16.4 indicates, the value of the firm goes up by $.30 for every $1 in debt. In other words, the NPV per dollar in debt is $.30. It is difficult to imagine why any corporation would not borrow to the absolute maximum under these circumstances.

The result of our analysis in this section is that, once we include taxes, capital structure definitely matters. However, we immediately reach the illogical conclusion that the optimal capital structure is 100 percent debt.

Taxes, the WACC, and Proposition II

The conclusion that the best capital structure is 100 percent debt also can be seen by examining the weighted average cost of capital. From our previous chapter, we know that, once we consider the effect of taxes, the WACC is:

$$\text{WACC} = (E/V) \times R_E + (D/V) \times R_D \times (1 - T_C)$$

To calculate this WACC, we need to know the cost of equity. M&M Proposition II with corporate taxes states that the cost of equity is:

$$R_E = R_U + (R_U - R_D) \times (D/E) \times (1 - T_C)$$ [16.8]

To illustrate, we saw a moment ago that Firm L is worth $7,300 total. Since the debt is worth $1,000, the equity must be worth $7,300 - 1,000 = $6,300. For Firm L, the cost of equity is thus:

$$R_E = .10 + (.10 - .08) \times (\$1,000/\$6,300) \times (1 - .30)$$
$$= 10.22\%$$

The weighted average cost of capital is:

$$\text{WACC} = \$6,300/\$7,300 \times 10.22\% + \$1,000/\$7,300 \times 8\% \times (1 - .30)$$
$$= 9.6\%$$

Without debt, the WACC is 10 percent; with debt, it is 9.6 percent. Therefore, the firm is better off with debt.

This is a comprehensive example that illustrates most of the points we have discussed thus far.

Figure 16.5 summarizes our discussion concerning the relationship between the cost of equity, the aftertax cost of debt, and the weighted average cost of capital. For reference, we have included R_U, the unlevered cost of capital. In Figure 16.5, we have the debt/equity ratio on the horizontal axis. Notice how the WACC declines as the debt/equity ratio grows. This illustrates again that the more debt the firm uses, the lower is its WACC. Table 16.6 summarizes the key results for future reference.

EXAMPLE 16.4: The Cost of Equity and the Value of the Firm

You are given the following information for the Format Company:

$$\text{EBIT} = \$166.67$$
$$T_C = .40$$
$$D = \$500$$
$$R_U = .20$$

The cost of debt capital is 10 percent. What is the value of Format's equity? What is the cost of equity capital for Format? What is the WACC?

This one's easier than it looks. Remember that all the cash flows are perpetuities. The value of the firm if it had no debt, V_U, is:

$$V_U = \text{EBIT} \times (1 - T_C)/R_U$$
$$= 100/.20$$
$$= \$500$$

From M&M Proposition I with taxes, we know that the value of the firm with debt is:

$$V_L = V_U + T_C \times D$$
$$= \$500 + .40 \times \$500$$
$$= \$700$$

Since the firm is worth $700 total and the debt is worth $500, the equity is worth $200.

$$E = V_L - D$$
$$= \$700 - 500$$
$$= \$200$$

Thus, from M&M Proposition II with taxes, the cost of equity is:

$$R_E = R_U + (R_U - R_D) \times (D/E) \times (1 - T_C)$$
$$= .20 + (.20 - .10) \times (\$500/200) \times (1 - .40)$$
$$= 35\%$$

Finally, the WACC is:

$$\text{WACC} = (\$200/700) \times 35\% + (\$500/700) \times 10\% \times$$
$$(1 - .40)$$
$$= 14.29\%$$

Notice that this is substantially lower than the cost of capital for the firm with no debt ($R_U = 20\%$), so debt financing is highly advantageous.

FIGURE 16.5

The cost of equity and the WACC; M&M Propositions I and II with taxes

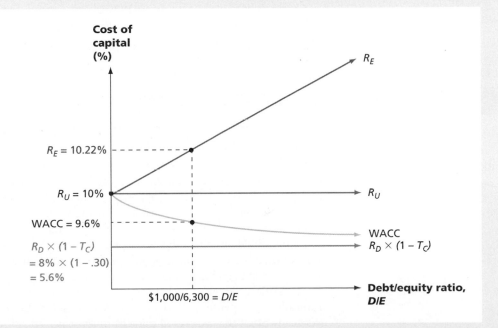

$R_E = R_U + (R_U - R_D) \times (D/E) \times (1 - T_C)$ by Proposition II with taxes

$\text{WACC} = \left(\frac{E}{V}\right) \times R_E + \left(\frac{D}{V}\right) \times R_D \times (1 - T_C)$

TABLE 16.6
Modigliani and Miller
summary

The no tax case

❏ Proposition I: The value of the firm leveraged (V_L) is equal to the value of the firm unleveraged (V_U):

$$V_L = V_U$$

Implications of Proposition I:

1. A firm's capital structure is irrelevant.
2. A firm's weighted average cost of capital (WACC) is the same no matter what mixture of debt and equity is used to finance the firm.

❏ Proposition II: The cost of equity, R_E, is

$$R_E = R_A + (R_A - R_D) \times D/E,$$

where R_A is the WACC, R_D is the cost of debt, and D/E is the debt/equity ratio.

Implications of Proposition II:

1. The cost of equity rises as the firm increases its use of debt financing.
2. The risk of the equity depends on two things, the riskiness of the firm's operations (business risk) and the degree of financial leverage (*financial risk*).

With taxes

❏ Proposition I with taxes: The value of the firm leveraged (V_L) is equal to the value of the firm unleveraged (V_U) plus the present value of the interest tax shield:

$$V_L = V_U + T_C \times D$$

where T_C is the corporate tax rate and D is the amount of debt.

Implications of Proposition I:

1. Debt financing is highly advantageous, and, in the extreme, a firm's optimal capital structure is 100 percent debt.
2. A firm's weighted average cost of capital (WACC) decreases as the firm relies on debt financing.

❏ Proposition II with taxes: The cost of equity, R_E, is

$$R_E = R_U + (R_U - R_D) \times (D/E) \times (1 - T_C),$$

where R_U is the unleveraged cost of capital, that is, the cost of capital for the firm if it had no debt. Unlike Proposition I, the general implications of Proposition II are the same whether there are taxes or not.

CONCEPT QUESTIONS

1. What is the relationship between the value of an unlevered firm and the value of a levered firm once we consider the effect of corporate taxes?

2. If we only consider the effect of taxes, what is the optimum capital structure?

 **16.5**

BANKRUPTCY COSTS

One limit to the amount of debt a firm might use comes in the form of *bankruptcy costs*. Bankruptcy costs are a form of the agency costs of debt introduced in Chapter 1. As the debt/equity ratio rises, so too does the probability that the firm could be unable to pay its bondholders what was promised to them. When this happens, ownership of the firm's assets is ultimately transferred from the shareholders to the bondholders.

In principle, a firm is bankrupt when the value of its assets equals the value of the debt. When this occurs, the value of equity is zero and the shareholders turn over control of the firm to the bondholders. When this takes place, the bondholders hold assets whose value is exactly equal to what is owed on the debt. In a perfect world, there are no costs associated with this transfer of ownership, and the bondholders don't lose anything.

This idealized view of bankruptcy is not, of course, what happens in the real world. Ironically, it is expensive to go bankrupt. As we discuss, the costs associated with bankruptcy may eventually offset the tax-related gains from leverage.

Direct Bankruptcy Costs

When the value of a firm's assets equals the value of its debt, the firm is economically bankrupt in the sense that the equity has no value. However, the formal means of turning over the assets to the bondholders is a legal process, not an economic one. There are legal and administrative costs to bankruptcy, and it has been remarked that bankruptcies are to lawyers what blood is to sharks.

Because of the expenses associated with bankruptcy, bondholders won't get all that they are owed. Some fraction of the firm's assets disappear in the legal process of going bankrupt. These are the legal and administrative expenses associated with the bankruptcy proceeding. We call these costs **direct bankruptcy costs.**

direct bankruptcy costs
The costs that are directly associated with bankruptcy, such as legal and administrative expenses.

These direct bankruptcy costs are a disincentive to debt financing. When a firm goes bankrupt, suddenly, a piece of the firm disappears. This amounts to a bankruptcy tax. So a firm faces a trade-off: Borrowing saves a firm money on its corporate taxes, but the more a firm borrows, the more likely it is that the firm becomes bankrupt and has to pay the bankruptcy tax.

Indirect Bankruptcy Costs

Because it is expensive to go bankrupt, a firm spends resources to avoid doing so. When a firm is having significant problems in meeting its debt obligations, we say it is experiencing financial distress. Some financially distressed firms ultimately file for bankruptcy, but most do not because they are able to recover or otherwise survive.

The costs of avoiding a bankruptcy filing by a financially distressed firm are one example of **indirect bankruptcy costs.** We use the term **financial distress costs** to refer generically to the direct and indirect costs associated with going bankrupt and/or avoiding a bankruptcy filing.

indirect bankruptcy costs
The difficulties of running a business that is experiencing financial distress.

financial distress costs
The direct and indirect costs associated with going bankrupt or experiencing financial distress.

The problems that come up in financial distress are particularly severe, and the financial distress costs are thus larger, when the shareholders and the bondholders are different groups. Until the firm is legally bankrupt, the shareholders control it. They, of course, take actions in their own economic interests. Since the shareholders can be wiped out in a legal bankruptcy, they have a very strong incentive to avoid a bankruptcy filing.

The bondholders, on the other hand, are primarily concerned with protecting the value of the firm's assets and try to take control away from shareholders. They have a strong incentive to seek bankruptcy to protect their interests and keep shareholders from further dissipating the assets of the firm. The net effect of all this fighting is that a long, drawn-out, and potentially quite expensive, legal battle gets started.

www.cdic.ca

Long before the wheels of justice begin to turn, the assets of the firm lose value because management is busy trying to avoid bankruptcy instead of running the business. Further, as they get desperate, managers may adopt go-for-broke strategies that increase the risk of the firm. A good example of this occurred in the failure of two banks in Western Canada in 1985. Because they were allowed to stay in business although they were economically insolvent, the banks had nothing to lose by taking great risks. Solvent banks had to pay increased deposit insurance premiums to shore up the resources of the Canada Deposit Insurance Corporation.

When firms are on the brink of bankruptcy, normal operations are disrupted, and sales are lost. Valuable employees leave, potentially fruitful programs are dropped to preserve cash, and otherwise profitable investments are not taken.

These are all indirect bankruptcy costs, or costs of financial distress. Whether or not the firm ultimately goes bankrupt, the net effect is a loss of value because the firm chose to use too much debt in its capital structure. This possibility of loss limits the amount of debt a firm chooses to use.

Agency Costs of Equity

Bankruptcy costs are agency costs of debt that increase with the amount of debt a firm uses. Agency costs of equity can result from shirking by owner-managers and work in the opposite direction. The idea is that when a firm run by an owner-entrepreneur issues debt, the entrepreneur has an incentive to work harder because he or she retains the claim to all the payoffs beyond the fixed interest on the debt. If the firm issues equity instead, the owner-entrepreneur's stake is diluted. In this case, the entrepreneur has more incentive to work shorter hours and to consume more perquisites (a big office, a company car, more expense account meals) than if the firm issues debt. Adelphia and Hollinger are two famous examples of publicly traded companies where owner-entrepreneurs allegedly used company funds to finance all sorts of perquisites.

Agency costs of equity are likely to be more significant for smaller firms where the dilution of ownership by issuing equity is significant. Underpricing of new equity issues, especially IPOs, discussed in Chapter 15, is the market's response to the agency costs of equity. In effect, underpricing passes most of these agency costs back to owner-entrepreneurs. The final effect is that firms may use more debt than otherwise.

In the 1980s, it was argued that *leveraged buyouts (LBOs)* significantly reduced the agency costs of equity. In an LBO, a purchaser (usually a team of existing management) buys out the shareholders at a price above the current market. In other words, the company goes private since the stock is placed in the hands of only a few people. Because the managers now own a substantial chunk of the business, they are likely to work harder than when they were simply employees. The track record of LBOs is at best mixed, and we discuss them in detail in Chapter 23.

> ### CONCEPT QUESTIONS
>
> **1.** What are direct bankruptcy costs?
>
> **2.** What are indirect bankruptcy costs?
>
> **3.** What are the agency costs of equity?

16.6 OPTIMAL CAPITAL STRUCTURE

Our previous two sections have established the basis for an optimal capital structure. A firm borrows because the interest tax shield is valuable. At relatively low debt levels, the probability of bankruptcy and financial distress is low, and the benefit from debt outweighs the cost. At very high debt levels, the possibility of financial distress is a chronic, ongoing problem for the firm, so the benefit from debt financing may be more than offset by the financial distress costs. Based on our discussion, it would appear that an optimal capital structure exists somewhere between these extremes.

The Static Theory of Capital Structure

static theory of capital structure
Theory that a firm borrows up to the point where the tax benefit from an extra dollar in debt is exactly equal to the cost that comes from the increased probability of financial distress.

The theory of capital structure that we have outlined is called the **static theory of capital structure.** It says that firms borrow up to the point where the tax benefit from an extra dollar in debt is exactly equal to the cost that comes from the increased probability of financial distress. We call this the static theory because it assumes the firm's assets and operations are fixed and it only considers possible changes in the debt/equity ratio.

The static theory is illustrated in Figure 16.6, which plots the value of the firm, V_L, against the amount of debt, D. In Figure 16.6, we have drawn lines corresponding to three different stories. The first is M&M Proposition I with no taxes. This is the horizontal line extending from V_U, and it indicates that the value of the firm is unaffected by its capital structure. The second case, M&M Proposition I with corporate taxes, is given by the upward-sloping straight line. These two cases are exactly the same as the ones we previously illustrated in Figure 16.4.

The third case in Figure 16.6 illustrates our current discussion: The value of the firm rises to a maximum and then declines beyond that point. This is the picture that we get from our static theory. The maximum value of the firm, V_L^*, is reached at D^*, so this is the optimal amount of borrowing. Put another way, the firm's optimal capital structure is composed of D^*/V_L^* in debt and $(1 - D^*/V_L^*)$ in equity.

The final thing to notice in Figure 16.6 is that the difference between the value of the firm in our static theory and the M&M value of the firm with taxes is the loss in value from the

FIGURE 16.6

The static theory of
capital structure. The
optimal capital structure
and the value of the firm.

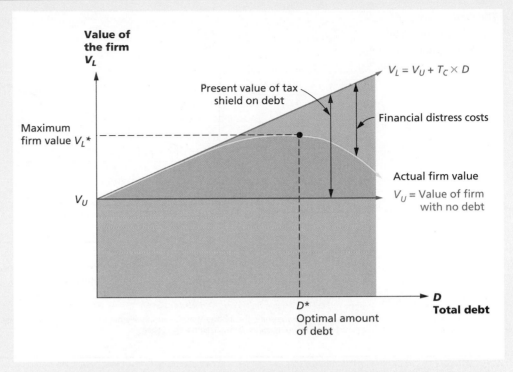

According to the static theory, the gain from the tax shield on debt is offset by financial distress costs. An optimal capital structure exists that just balances the additional gain from leverage against the added financial distress cost.

possibility of financial distress. Also, the difference between the static theory value of the firm and the M&M value with taxes is the gain from leverage, net of distress costs.[6]

Optimal Capital Structure and the Cost of Capital

As we discussed earlier, the capital structure that maximizes the value of the firm is also the one that minimizes the cost of capital. Figure 16.7 illustrates the static theory of capital structure in the weighted average cost of capital and the costs of debt and equity. Notice in Figure 16.7 that we have plotted the various capital costs against the debt/equity ratio, D/E.

Figure 16.7 is much the same as Figure 16.5 except that we have added a new line for the WACC. This line, which corresponds to the static theory, declines at first. This occurs because the aftertax cost of debt is cheaper than equity, at least initially, so the overall cost of capital declines.

At some point, the cost of debt begins to rise and the fact that debt is cheaper than equity is more than offset by the financial distress costs. At this point, further increases in debt actually increase the WACC. As illustrated, the minimum WACC occurs at the point D^*/E^*, just as we described earlier.

Optimal Capital Structure: A Recap

With the help of Figure 16.8, we can recap (no pun intended) our discussion of capital structure and cost of capital. As we have noted, there are essentially three cases. We will use the simplest of

6 Another way of arriving at Figure 16.6 is to introduce personal taxes on interest and equity disbursements. Interest is taxed more heavily than dividends and capital gains in Canada. This creates a tax disadvantage to leverage that partially offsets the corporate tax advantage to debt. This argument is developed in Appendix 16A.

FIGURE 16.7

The static theory of capital structure. The optimal capital structure and the cost of capital.

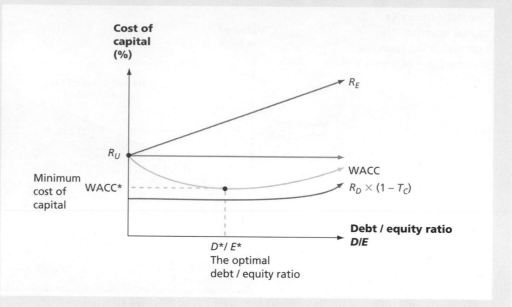

According to the static theory, the WACC falls initially because of the tax advantage to debt. Beyond the point $D*/E*$, it begins to rise because of financial distress costs.

the three cases as a starting point and then build up to the static theory of capital structure. Along the way, we will pay particular attention to the connection between capital structure, firm value, and cost of capital.

Figure 16.8 illustrates the original Modigliani and Miller (M&M) no-tax, no-bankruptcy argument in Case I. This is the most basic case. In the top part, we have plotted the value of the firm, V_L, against total debt, D. When there are no taxes, bankruptcy costs, or other real-world imperfections, we know that the total value of the firm is not affected by its debt policy, so V_L is simply constant. The bottom part of Figure 16.8 tells the same story in terms of the cost of capital. Here, the weighted average cost of capital, WACC, is plotted against the debt to equity ratio, D/E. As with total firm value, the overall cost of capital is not affected by debt policy in this basic case, so the WACC is constant.

Next, we consider what happens to the original M&M arguments once taxes are introduced. As Case II illustrates, we now see that the firm's value critically depends on its debt policy. The more the firm borrows, the more it is worth. From our earlier discussion, we know this happens because interest payments are tax deductible, and the gain in firm value is just equal to the present value of the interest tax shield.

In the bottom part of Figure 16.8, notice how the WACC declines as the firm uses more and more debt financing. As the firm increases its financial leverage, the cost of equity does increase, but this increase is more than offset by the tax break associated with debt financing. As a result, the firm's overall cost of capital declines.

To finish our story, we include the impact of bankruptcy of financial distress costs to get Case III. As shown in the top part of Figure 16.8, the value of the firm will not be as large as we previously indicated. The reason is that the firm's value is reduced by the present value of the potential future bankruptcy costs. These costs grow as the firm borrows more and more, and they eventually overwhelm the tax advantage of debt financing. The optimal capital structure occurs at $D*$, the point at which the tax saving from an additional dollar in debt financing is exactly balanced by the increased bankruptcy costs associated with the additional borrowing. This is the essence of the static theory of capital structure.

The bottom part of Figure 16.8 presents the optimal capital structure in terms of the cost of capital. Corresponding to $D*$, the optimal debt level, is the optimal debt to equity ratio, $D*/E*$. At this level of debt financing, the lowest possible weighted average cost of capital, WACC*, occurs.

FIGURE 16.8

The capital structure
question

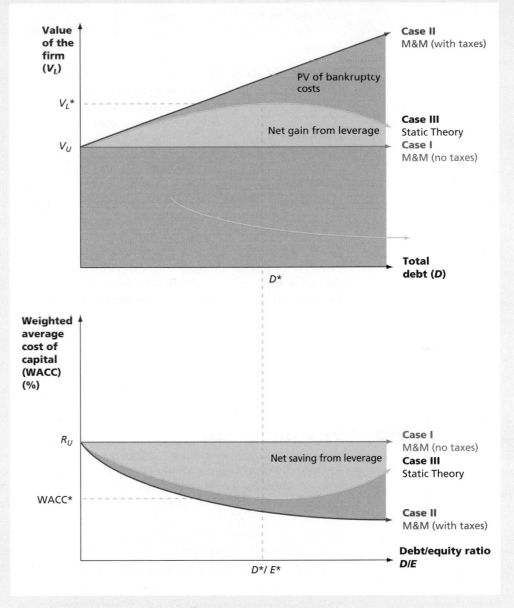

Case I

With no taxes or bankruptcy costs, the value of the firm and its weighted average cost
of capital are not affected by capital structure.

Case II

With corporate taxes and no bankruptcy costs, the value of the firm increases and the
weighted average cost of capital decreases as the amount of debt goes up.

Case III

With corporate taxes and bankruptcy costs, the value of the firm V_L^* reaches a
maximum at D^*, the optimal amount of borrowing. At the same time, the weighted
average cost of capital, WACC*, is minimized at D^*/E^*.

Capital Structure: Some Managerial Recommendations

The static model that we described is not capable of identifying a precise optimal capital structure, but it does point out two of the more relevant factors: taxes and financial distress. We can
draw some limited conclusions concerning these.

TAXES   First, the tax benefit from leverage is obviously important only to firms that are in a tax-paying position. Firms with substantial accumulated losses get little value from the tax shield. Furthermore, firms that have substantial tax shields from other sources, such as depreciation, get less benefit from leverage.

Also, not all firms have the same tax rate. The higher the tax rate, the greater the incentive to borrow.

FINANCIAL DISTRESS   Firms with a greater risk of experiencing financial distress borrow less than firms with a lower risk of financial distress. For example, all other things being equal, the greater the volatility in EBIT, the less a firm should borrow.

In addition, financial distress is more costly for some firms than others. The costs of financial distress depend primarily on the firm's assets. In particular, financial distress costs are determined by how easily ownership of those assets can be transferred.

For example, a firm with mostly tangible assets that can be sold without great loss in value has an incentive to borrow more. If a firm has a large investment in land, buildings, and other tangible assets, it has less financial distress than a firm with a large investment in research and development. Research and development typically has less resale value than land; thus, most of its value disappears in financial distress.

Air Canada provides an excellent example of the effects financial distress can have on a company. The firm faced considerable unexpected volatility in its earnings with the terrorist attacks, the war in Iraq, and the SARS health crisis. As a result, it appears to have relied too heavily on borrowing and was forced to enter into bankruptcy protection in 2003.

CONCEPT QUESTIONS

1. Describe the trade-off that defines the static theory of capital structure.

2. What are the important factors in making capital structure decisions?

16.7   THE PIE AGAIN

Although it is comforting to know that the firm might have an optimal capital structure when we take account of such real-world matters as taxes and financial distress costs, it is disquieting to see the elegant, original M&M intuition (that is, the no-tax version) fall apart in the face of them.

Critics of the M&M theory often say it fails to hold as soon as we add in real-world issues and that the M&M theory is really just that, a theory that doesn't have much to say about the real world that we live in. In fact, they would argue that it is the M&M theory that is irrelevant, not capital structure. As we discuss next, however, taking that view blinds critics to the real value of the M&M theory.

The Extended Pie Model

To illustrate the value of the original M&M intuition, we briefly consider an expanded version of the pie model that we introduced earlier. In the extended pie model, taxes just represent another claim on the cash flows of the firm. Since taxes are reduced as leverage is increased, the value of the government's claim *(G)* on the firm's cash flows decreases with leverage.

Bankruptcy costs are also a claim on the cash flows. They come into play as the firm comes close to bankruptcy and has to alter its behaviour to attempt to stave off the event itself, and they become large when bankruptcy actually occurs. Thus, the value of the cash flows to this claim (B) rises with the debt/equity ratio.

The extended pie theory simply holds that all of these claims can be paid from only one source, the cash flows (CF) of the firm. Algebraically, we must have:

$$CF = \text{Payments to shareholders} + \text{Payments to bondholders}$$
$$+ \text{Payments to the government}$$
$$+ \text{Payments to bankruptcy courts and lawyers}$$
$$+ \text{Payments to any and all other claimants to the cash flow of the firm}$$

The extended pie model is illustrated in Figure 16.9. Notice that we have added a few slices for the other groups. Notice also the relative size of the slices as the firm's use of debt financing is increased.

With this list, we have not even begun to exhaust the potential claims to the firm's cash flows. To give an unusual example, everyone reading this book has an economic claim to the cash flows of General Motors Corporation (GM). After all, if you are injured in an accident, you might sue GM, and, win or lose, GM expends some of its cash flow in dealing with the matter. For GM, or any other company, there should thus be a slice of the pie representing the potential lawsuits.

This is the essence of the M&M intuition and theory: The value of the firm depends on the total cash flow of the firm. The firm's capital structure just cuts that cash flow up into slices without altering the total. What we recognize now is that the stockholders and the bondholders may not be the only ones who can claim a slice.

Marketed Claims versus Non-Marketed Claims

With our extended pie model, there is an important distinction between claims such as those of shareholders and bondholders, on the one hand, and those of the government and potential litigants in lawsuits on the other. The first set of claims are *marketed claims,* and the second set are *non-marketed claims.* A key difference is that the marketed claims can be bought and sold in financial markets and the non-marketed claims cannot be.

When we speak of the value of the firm, we are generally referring just to the value of the marketed claims, V_M, and not the value of the non-marketed claims, V_N. If we write V_T for the total value of all the claims against a corporation's cash flows, then:

$$V_T = E + D + G + B + \ldots$$
$$= V_M + V_N$$

The essence of our extended pie model is that this total value, V_T, of all the claims to the firm's cash flows is unaltered by capital structure. However, the value of the marketed claims, V_M, may be affected by changes in the capital structure.

By the pie theory, any increase in V_M must imply an identical decrease in V_N. The optimal capital structure is thus the one that maximizes the value of the marketed claims, or, equivalently, minimizes the value of non-marketed claims such as taxes and bankruptcy costs.

FIGURE 16.9

The extended pie model

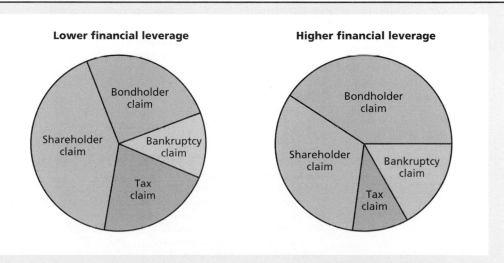

In the extended pie model, the value of all the claims against the firm's cash flows is not affected by capital structure, but the relative value of claims changes as the amount of debt financing is increased.

16.8   OBSERVED CAPITAL STRUCTURES

No two firms have identical capital structures. Nonetheless, we see some regular elements when we start looking at actual capital structures. We discuss a few of these next.

A pattern is apparent when we compare capital structures across industries. Table 16.7 shows Canadian debt/equity ratios for selected industries measured at book values. You can see rather large differences in the use of debt among industries. Real estate developers and operators, for example, carry about eight times as much debt as manufacturers of electronic equipment and computer services. This is consistent with our discussion of the costs of financial distress. Real estate developers have large tangible assets while electronic equipment and computer services firms carry significant intangible assets in the form of research and development.

Further, because different industries have different operating characteristics, for example, EBIT volatility and asset types, there does appear to be some connection between these characteristics and capital structure. Our story involving tax savings and financial distress costs is undoubtedly part of the reason, but, to date, there is no fully satisfactory theory that explains these regularities.

In practice, firms (and lenders) also look at the industry's debt/equity ratio as a guide. If the industry is sound, the industry average provides a useful benchmark. Of course, if the entire industry is in distress, the average leverage is likely too high. For example, in 1998, the average debt/equity ratio of 4.938 for real estate developers and operators was probably too high.

The leverage ratios in Table 16.7 are considerably higher than they were in the 1960s. Most of the increase in Canada came in the 1970s and early 1980s—periods of low interest rates and economic growth particularly in Western Canada. Significant corporate tax rates encouraged corporations to use debt financing. Table 16.7 shows that the construction industry had one of the highest uses of leverage in 2005 and this industry accounts for a major portion of the

TABLE 16.7

Book value debt/equity ratios for selected industries in Canada, 2005

Industry	Ratio
All industries	**0.916**
Non-financial	**0.989**
Agriculture, forestry, fishing and hunting	1.296
Oil and gas extraction and support activities	0.967
Mining (except oil and gas)	0.454
Utilities	0.905
Construction	2.006
Manufacturing	0.618
Wholesale trade	0.855
Retail trade	1.072
Transportation and warehousing	1.454
Information and cultural industries	1.238
Real estate and rental and leasing	2.061
Professional, scientific and technical services	0.846
Administrative and support, waste management and remediation services	1.427
Educational, healthcare and social assistance services	0.930
Arts, entertainment and recreation	2.393
Accommodation and food services	3.592
Repair, maintenance and personal services	0.838
Insurance carriers and related activities	0.177

Source: "Book value debt/equity ratios for selected industries in Canada 2005," adapted from the Statistics Canada publication "Quarterly financial statistics for enterprises," Catalogue 61-008, Fourth Quarter, 2005, vol. 16, no. 4, April 2006.

leverage increase for Canadian companies over the last 40 years. In the U.S., the increase in leverage was similar but occurred in the leveraged buyout period of the 1980s.[7]

CONCEPT QUESTIONS

1. Do Canadian corporations rely heavily on debt financing? What about U.S. corporations?

2. What regularities do we observe in capital structures?

LONG-TERM FINANCING UNDER FINANCIAL DISTRESS AND BANKRUPTCY

One of the consequences of using debt is the possibility of financial distress, which can be defined in several ways:

1. *Business failure.* Although this term usually refers to a situation where a business has terminated with a loss to creditors, even an all-equity firm can fail.[8]
2. *Legal bankruptcy.* Firms bring petitions to a federal court for bankruptcy. **Bankruptcy** is a legal proceeding for liquidating or reorganizing a business.
3. *Technical insolvency.* Technical insolvency occurs when a firm defaults on a current legal obligation; for example, it does not pay a bill. Technical insolvency is a short-term condition that may be reversed to avoid bankruptcy.
4. *Accounting insolvency.* Firms with negative net worth are insolvent on the books. This happens when the total book liabilities exceed the book value of the total assets.

For future reference, we define bankruptcy as the transfer of some or all of the firm's assets to creditors. We now very briefly discuss what happens in financial distress and some of the relevant issues associated with bankruptcy.[9]

Liquidation and Reorganization

Firms that cannot or choose not to make contractually required payments to creditors have two basic options: liquidation or reorganization. Both of these options are covered under the *Bankruptcy and Insolvency Act (1992)*. **Liquidation** means termination of the firm as a going concern, and it involves selling the assets of the firm. The proceeds, net of selling costs, are distributed to creditors in order of established priority. **Reorganization** is the option of keeping the firm a going concern; it often involves issuing new securities to replace old securities. Liquidation or reorganization is the result of a bankruptcy proceeding. Which occurs depends on whether the firm is worth more dead or alive.

Before the early 1990s, most legal bankruptcies in Canada ended with liquidation. More recently, more frequent cases of financial distress along with new bankruptcy laws are encouraging restructuring and reorganizations. For example, in 2003, Air Canada's cash flow was not enough to cover its operating expenses, including interest and principal payments on its $13 billion in debt. The company had experienced several unusual business circumstances including the terrorist attacks in 2001 and the SARS health crisis in Asia and Canada, and was said to be using up to $5 million a day in cash. The company decided to seek court protection to allow it to restructure its assets and avoid formal bankruptcy liquidation.

BANKRUPTCY LIQUIDATION Liquidation occurs when the court directs sale of all assets of the firm. The following sequence of events is typical:

bankruptcy
A legal proceeding for liquidating or reorganizing a business. Also, the transfer of some or all of a firm's assets to its creditors.

liquidation
Termination of the firm as a going concern.

reorganization
Financial restructuring of a failing firm to attempt to continue operations as a going concern.

---

7 Our discussion of trends in leverage draws on M. Zyblock, "Corporate Financial Leverage: A Canada–U.S. Comparison, 1961–1996," *Statistics Canada,* Paper no. 111, December 1997 and P.M. Shum, "Taxes and Corporate Debt Policy in Canada: An Empirical Investigation," *Canadian Journal of Economics* 29, August 1996.

8 Dun & Bradstreet Canada Ltd. compiles failure statistics in "The Canadian Business Failure Record."

9 Our discussion of bankruptcy procedures is based on the 1992 *Bankruptcy and Insolvency Act.*

www.dnb.com

1. A petition is filed in a federal court. Corporations may file a voluntary petition, or involuntary petitions may be filed against the corporation by creditors.

2. A trustee-in-bankruptcy is elected by the creditors to take over the assets of the debtor corporation. The trustee attempts to liquidate the assets.

3. When the assets are liquidated, after the payment of the bankruptcy administration costs, the proceeds are distributed among the creditors.

4. If any assets remain, after expenses and payments to creditors, they are distributed to the shareholders.

The distribution of the proceeds of the liquidation occurs according to the following priority. The higher a claim is on the list, the more likely it is to be paid. In many of these categories, we omit various limitations and qualifications for the sake of brevity.

1. Administrative expenses associated with the bankruptcy.

2. Other expenses arising after the filing of an involuntary bankruptcy petition but before the appointment of a trustee.

3. Wages, salaries, and commissions.

4. Contributions to employee benefit plans.

5. Consumer claims.

6. Government tax claims.

7. Unsecured creditors.

8. Preferred stockholders.

9. Common stockholders.

Two qualifications to this list are in order: The first concerns secured creditors. Such creditors are entitled to the proceeds from the sale of the security and are outside this ordering. However, if the secured property is liquidated and provides cash insufficient to cover the amount owed, the secured creditors join with unsecured creditors in dividing the remaining liquidated value. In contrast, if the secured property is liquidated for proceeds greater than the secured claim, the net proceeds are used to pay unsecured creditors and others.

The second qualification is that, in reality, courts have a great deal of freedom in deciding what actually happens and who actually gets what in the event of bankruptcy; as a result, the priority just set out is not always followed.

The 1988 restructuring of Dome Petroleum is an example. Declining oil prices in 1986 found Dome already in difficulties after a series of earlier debt rescheduling. Dome's board believed that if the company went into bankruptcy, secured creditors could force disposal of assets at fire sale prices producing losses for unsecured creditors and shareholders. One estimate obtained at the time projected that unsecured creditors would receive at best 15 cents per dollar of debt under liquidation. As a result, the board sought and received court and regulatory approval for sale of the company as a going concern to Amoco Canada. Unsecured creditors eventually received 45 cents on the dollar.

BANKRUPTCY REORGANIZATION   The general objective of corporate reorganization is to plan to restructure the corporation with some provision for repayment of creditors. A typical sequence of events follows:

1. A voluntary petition can be filed by the corporation, or an involuntary petition can be filed by creditors.

2. A federal judge either approves or denies the petition. If the petition is approved, a time for filing proofs of claims is set. A stay of proceedings of 30 days is effected against all creditors.

3. In most cases, the corporation (the "debtor in possession") continues to run the business.

4. The corporation is required to submit a reorganization plan.

5. Creditors and shareholders are divided into classes. A class of creditors accepts the plan if a majority of the class (in dollars or in number) agrees to the plan. The secured creditors must vote before the unsecured creditors.

6. After acceptance by creditors, the plan is confirmed by the court.

7. Payments in cash, property, and securities are made to creditors and shareholders. The plan may provide for the issuance of new securities.

The corporation may wish to allow the old shareholders to retain some participation in the firm. Needless to say, this may involve some protest by the holders of unsecured debt.

So-called prepackaged bankruptcies are a relatively new phenomenon. What happens is that the corporation secures the necessary approval of a bankruptcy plan by a majority of its creditors first, and then it files for bankruptcy. As a result, the company enters bankruptcy and re-emerges almost immediately. In some cases, the bankruptcy procedure is needed to invoke the "cram down" power of the bankruptcy court. Under certain circumstances, a class of creditors can be forced to accept a bankruptcy plan even if they vote not to approve it, hence the remarkably descriptive phrase *cram down*.

Returning to our Air Canada example, the company underwent a major restructuring effort in June 2003. Air Canada sought court protection to reorganize, and reached agreements with all of its employee unions to workplace rule changes, job cuts, and wage reductions that would reduce operating expenses by approximately $1.1 billion per year. Creditors approved Air Canada's restructuring plan in August 2004. The plan called for creditors to receive a very small percentage of every dollar they were owed, but their approval of the plan opened up the option of picking up a 45.8 per cent interest in the parent company of Air Canada.

Air Canada has enjoyed many successes since. The company recorded a $118 million net profit in the first quarter of 2006, compared to a $77 million net loss in the first quarter of 2005. As well, the stock price was trading at approximately $33 a share in May 2006, compared to $1 a share in June 2003.

Agreements to Avoid Bankruptcy

A firm can default on an obligation and still avoid bankruptcy. Because the legal process of bankruptcy can be lengthy and expensive, it is often in everyone's best interest to devise a "work out" that avoids a bankruptcy filing. Much of the time creditors can work with the management of a company that has defaulted on a loan contract. Voluntary arrangements to restructure the company's debt can be and often are made. This may involve *extension,* which postpones the date of payment, or *composition,* which involves a reduced payment.

CONCEPT QUESTIONS

1. What is a bankruptcy?

2. What is the difference between liquidation and reorganization?

SUMMARY AND CONCLUSIONS

The ideal mixture of debt and equity for a firm—its optimal capital structure—is the one that maximizes the value of the firm and minimizes the overall cost of capital. If we ignore taxes, financial distress costs, and any other imperfections, we find that there is no ideal mixture. Under these circumstances, the firm's capital structure is simply irrelevant, as we see in M&M Proposition I and II.

If we consider the effect of corporate taxes, we find that capital structure matters a great deal. This conclusion is based on the fact that interest is tax deductible and thus generates a valuable tax shield. Unfortunately, we also find that the optimal capital structure is 100 percent debt, which is not something we observe for healthy firms.

We next introduced costs associated with bankruptcy, or, more generally, financial distress. These costs reduce the attractiveness of debt financing. We concluded that an optimal capital structure exists when the net tax saving from an additional dollar in interest just equals the increase in expected financial distress costs. This is the essence of the static theory of capital structure.

When we examine actual capital structures, we find two regularities: First, firms in Canada typically do not use great amounts of debt, but they pay substantial taxes. This suggests there is a limit to the use of debt financing to generate tax shields. Second, firms in similar industries tend to have similar capital structures, suggesting that the nature of their assets and operations is an important determinant of capital structure.

Key Terms

bankruptcy (page 503)
business risk (page 490)
direct bankruptcy costs (page 495)
financial distress costs (page 495)
financial risk (page 490)
homemade leverage (page 485)
indirect bankruptcy costs (page 495)

interest tax shield (page 491)
liquidation (page 503)
M&M Proposition I (page 486)
M&M Proposition II (page 487)
reorganization (page 503)
static theory of capital structure (page 496)
unlevered cost of capital (page 491)

Chapter Review Problems and Self-Test

16.1   EBIT and EPS   Suppose the GNR Corporation has decided in favour of a capital restructuring that involves increasing its existing $5 million in debt to $25 million. The interest rate on the debt is 12 percent and is not expected to change. The firm currently has 1 million shares outstanding, and the price per share is $40. If the restructuring is expected to increase the ROE, what is the minimum level for EBIT that GNR's management must be expecting? Ignore taxes in your answer.

16.2   M&M Proposition II (no taxes)   The Pro Bono Corporation has a WACC of 20 percent. Its cost of debt is 12 percent. If Pro Bono's debt/equity ratio is 2, what is its cost of equity capital? If Pro Bono's equity beta is 1.5, what is its asset beta? Ignore taxes in your answer.

16.3   M&M Proposition I (with corporate taxes)   The Deathstar Telecom Company (motto: "Reach out and clutch someone") expects an EBIT of $4,000 every year forever. Deathstar can borrow at 10 percent.

Suppose that Deathstar currently has no debt and its cost of equity is 14 percent. If the corporate tax rate is 30 percent, what is the value of the firm? What will the value be if Deathstar borrows $6,000 and uses the proceeds to buy up stock?

Answers to Self-Test Problems

16.1   To answer, we can calculate the break-even EBIT. At any EBIT more than this, the increased financial leverage increases EPS. Under the old capital structure, the interest bill is $5 million × .12 = $600,000. There are 1 million shares of stock, so, ignoring taxes, EPS is (EBIT − $600,000)/1 million.

Under the new capital structure, the interest expense is $25 million × .12 = $3 million. Furthermore, the debt rises by $20 million. This amount is sufficient to repurchase $20 million/$40 = 500,000 shares of stock, leaving 500,000 outstanding. EPS is thus (EBIT − $3 million)/500,000.

Now that we know how to calculate EPS under both scenarios, we set them equal to each other and solve for the break-even EBIT;

$$(EBIT − \$600,000)/1 \text{ million} = (EBIT − \$3 \text{ million})/500,000$$
$$(EBIT − \$600,000) = 2 × (EBIT − \$3 \text{ million})$$
$$EBIT = \$5,400,000$$

Check that, in either case, EPS is $4.80 when EBIT is $5.4 million.

16.2   According to M&M Proposition II (no taxes), the cost of equity is:

$$R_E = R_A + (R_A − R_D) × (D/E)$$
$$= 20\% + (20\% − 12\%) × 2$$
$$= 36\%$$

Also, we know that the equity beta is equal to the asset beta multiplied by the equity multiplier:

$$\beta_E = \beta_A × (1 + D/E)$$

In this case, D/E is 2 and β_E is 1.5, so the asset beta is 1.5/3 = .50.

16.3   With no debt, Deathstar's WACC is 14 percent. This is also the unlevered cost of capital. The aftertax cash flow is $4,000 × (1 − .30) = $2,800, so the value is just $V_U = $2,800/.14 = $20,000.

After the debt issue, Deathstar is worth the original $20,000 plus the present value of the tax shield. According to M&M Proposition I with taxes, the present value of the tax shield is $T_c \times D$, or .30 × $6,000 = $1,800, so the firm is worth $20,000 + 1,800 = $21,800.

Concepts Review and Critical Thinking Questions

1. Explain what is meant by business and financial risk. Suppose Firm A has greater business risk than Firm B. Is it true that Firm A also has a higher cost of equity capital? Explain.

2. How would you answer in the following debate?

   Q: Isn't it true that the riskiness of a firm's equity will rise if the firm increases its use of debt financing?

   A: Yes, that's the essence of M&M Proposition II.

   Q: And isn't it true that, as a firm increases its use of borrowing, the likelihood of default increases, thereby increasing the risk of the firm's debt?

   A: Yes.

   Q: In other words, increased borrowing increases the risk of the equity and the debt?

   A: That's right.

   Q: Well, given that the firm uses only debt and equity financing, and given that the risks of both are increased by increased borrowing, does it not follow that increasing debt increases the overall risk of the firm and therefore decreases the value of the firm?

   A: ??

3. Is there an easily identifiable debt-equity ratio that will maximize the value of a firm? Why or why not?

4. Refer to the observed capital structures given in Table 16.7 of the text. What do you notice about the types of industries with respect to their average debt-equity ratios? Are certain types of industries more likely to be highly leveraged than others? What are some possible reasons for this observed segmentation? Do the oper-ating results and tax history of the firms play a role? How about their future earnings prospects? Explain.

5. Why is the use of debt financing referred to as financial "leverage"?

6. What is homemade leverage?

7. As mentioned in the text, some firms have filed for bankruptcy because of actual or likely litigation-related losses. Is this a proper use of the bankruptcy process?

8. Firms sometimes use the threat of a bankruptcy filing to force creditors to renegotiate terms. Critics argue that in such cases, the firm is using bankruptcy laws "as a sword rather than a shield." Is this an ethical tactic?

9. In the context of the extended pie model, what is the basic goal of financial management with regard to capital structure?

10. What basic options does a firm have if it cannot (or chooses not to) make a contractually required payment such as interest? Describe them.

11. Absolute Priority Rule   In the event of corporate liquidation proceedings, rank the following claimants of the firm from highest to lowest in order of their priority for being paid:

   a. Preferred shareholders.
   b. Canada Customs and Revenue Agency.
   c. Unsecured debtholders.
   d. The company pension plan.
   e. Common shareholders.
   f. Employee wages.
   g. The law firm representing the company in the bankruptcy proceedings.

Questions and Problems

Basic (Questions 1–15)

1. **EBIT and Leverage**   Money, Inc., has no debt outstanding and a total market value of $150,000. Earnings before interest and taxes, EBIT, are projected to be $14,000 if economic conditions are normal. If there is strong expansion in the economy, then EBIT will be 30 percent higher. If there is a recession, then EBIT will be 60 percent lower. Money is considering a $60,000 debt issue with a 5 percent interest rate. The proceeds will be used to repurchase shares of stock. There are currently 2,500 shares outstanding. Ignore taxes for this problem.

   a. Calculate earnings per share, EPS, under each of the three economic scenarios before any debt is issued. Also, calculate the percentage changes in EPS when the economy expands or enters a recession.

   b. Repeat part (a) assuming that Money goes through with recapitalization. What do you observe?

2. **EBIT, Taxes, and Leverage**   Repeat parts (a) and (b) in Problem 1 assuming Money has a tax rate of 35 percent.

3. **ROE and Leverage**   Suppose the company in Problem 1 has a market-to-book ratio of 1.0.

   a. Calculate return on equity, ROE, under each of the three economic scenarios before any debt is issued. Also, calculate the percentage changes in ROE for economic expansion and recession, assuming no taxes.

   b. Repeat part (a) assuming the firm goes through with the proposed recapitalization.

   c. Repeat parts (a) and (b) of this problem assuming the firm has a tax rate of 35 percent.

Basic
(continued)

4. **Break-Even EBIT** ZZ Pop Corporation is comparing two different capital structures, an all-equity plan (Plan I) and a levered plan (Plan II). Under Plan I, ZZ Pop would have 150,000 shares of stock outstanding. Under Plan II, there would be 60,000 shares of stock outstanding and $1.5 million in debt outstanding. The interest rate on the debt is 10 percent and there are no taxes.

   a. If EBIT is $200,000, which plan will result in the higher EPS?

   b. If EBIT is $700,000, which plan will result in the higher EPS?

   c. What is the break-even EBIT?

5. **M&M and Stock Value** In Problem 4, use M&M Proposition I to find the price per share of equity under each of the two proposed plans. What is the value of the firm?

6. **Break-Even EBIT and Leverage** Kolby Corp. is comparing two different capital structures. Plan I would result in 1,100 shares of stock and $16,500 in debt. Plan II would result in 900 shares of stock and $27,500 in debt. The interest rate on the debt is 10 percent.

   a. Ignoring taxes, compare both of these plans to an all-equity plan assuming that EBIT will be $10,000. The all-equity plan would result in 1,400 shares of stock outstanding. Which of the three plans has the highest EPS? The lowest?

   b. In part (*a*), what are the break-even levels of EBIT for each plan as compared to that for an all-equity plan? Is one higher than the other? Why?

   c. Ignoring taxes, when will EPS be identical for Plans I and II?

   d. Repeat parts (*a*), (*b*), and (*c*) assuming that the corporate tax rate is 40 percent. Are the break-even levels of EBIT different from before? Why or why not?

7. **Leverage and Stock Value** Ignoring taxes in Problem 6, what is the price per share of equity under Plan I? Plan II? What principle is illustrated by your answers?

8. **Homemade Leverage** Star, Inc., a prominent consumer products firm, is debating whether or not to convert its all-equity capital structure to one that is 40 percent debt. Currently, there are 2,000 shares outstanding and the price per share is $70. EBIT is expected to remain at $16,000 per year forever. The interest rate on new debt is 8 percent, and there are no taxes.

   a. Ms. Knowles, a shareholder of the firm, owns 100 shares of stock. What is her cash flow under the current capital structure, assuming the firm has a dividend payout rate of 100 percent?

   b. What will Ms. Knowles's cash flow be under the proposed capital structure of the firm? Assume that she keeps all 100 of her shares.

   c. Suppose Star does convert, but Ms. Knowles prefers the current all-equity capital structure. Show how she could unlever her shares of stock to recreate the original capital structure.

   d. Using your answer to part (*c*), explain why Star's choice of capital structure is irrelevant.

9. **Homemade Leverage and WACC** ABC Co. and XYZ Co. are identical firms in all respects except for their capital structure. ABC is all-equity financed with $600,000 in stock. XYZ uses both stock and perpetual debt; its stock is worth $300,000 and the interest rate on its debt is 10 percent. Both firms expect EBIT to be $73,000. Ignore taxes.

   a. Rico owns $30,000 worth of XYZ's stock. What rate of return is she expecting?

   b. Show how Rico could generate exactly the same cash flows and rate of return by investing in ABC and using homemade leverage.

   c. What is the cost of equity for ABC? What is it for XYZ?

   d. What is the WACC for ABC? For XYZ? What principle have you illustrated?

10. **M&M** Nina Corp. uses no debt. The weighted average cost of capital is 13 percent. If the current market value of the equity is $35 million and there are no taxes, what is EBIT?

11. **M&M and Taxes** In the previous question, suppose the corporate tax rate is 35 percent. What is EBIT in this case? What is the WACC? Explain.

12. **Calculating WACC** Moon Beam Industries has a debt-equity ratio of 1.5. Its WACC is 12 percent, and its cost of debt is 12 percent. The corporate tax rate is 35 percent.

   a. What is Moon Beam's cost of equity capital?

   b. What is Moon Beam's unlevered cost of equity capital?

   c. What would the cost of equity be if the debt-equity ratio were 2? What if it were 1.0? What if it were zero?

13. **Calculating WACC** Shadow Corp. has no debt but can borrow at 8 percent. The firm's WACC is currently 12 percent, and the tax rate is 35 percent.

   a. What is Shadow's cost of equity?

   b. If the firm converts to 25 percent debt, what will its cost of equity be?

   c. If the firm converts to 50 percent debt, what will its cost of equity be?

   d. What is Shadow's WACC in part (*b*)? In part (*c*)?

Basic
(continued)

14. M&M and Taxes   Bruce & Co. expects its EBIT to be $95,000 every year forever. The firm can borrow at 11 percent. Bruce currently has no debt, and its cost of equity is 22 percent. If the tax rate is 35 percent, what is the value of the firm? What will the value be if Bruce borrows $60,000 and uses the proceeds to repurchase shares?

15. M&M and Taxes   In Problem 14, what is the cost of equity after recapitalization? What is the WACC? What are the implications for the firm's capital structure decision?

Intermediate
(Questions
16–17)

16. M&M   Tool Manufacturing has an expected EBIT of $35,000 in perpetuity and a tax rate of 35 percent. The firm has $70,000 in outstanding debt at an interest rate of 9 percent, and its unlevered cost of capital is 14 percent. What is the value of the firm according to M&M Proposition I with taxes? Should Tool change its debt-equity ratio if the goal is to maximize the value of the firm? Explain.

17. Firm Value   Old School Corporation expects an EBIT of $9,000 every year forever. Old School currently has no debt, and its cost of equity is 17 percent. The firm can borrow at 10 percent. If the corporate tax rate is 35 percent, what is the value of the firm? What will the value be if Old School converts to 50 percent debt? To 100 percent debt?

Challenge
(Questions
18–23)

18. M&M   A firm with a capital investment of $2 million is financed solely through common shares and generates a steady stream of operating cash flows of $500,000 per year. The corporate tax rate is 38 percent, and the appropriate equity required return for the unlevered firm (R_U) is 22 percent. The firm considers raising $825,000 through debt at an interest rate of 12 percent, using the proceeds to retire outstanding equity by repurchasing shares.

   a. For both the unlevered and levered firm:

   i.   What are the total cash flows to security holders?

   ii. What is the total value of the firm?

   iii. What is the value of shareholders' equity?

   b. Should the firm take on the debt?

   c. Would your answer change if the interest rate on debt increased to 15 percent?

19. M&M   A firm financed solely by equity is considering issuing debt and using the proceeds to repurchase some of the outstanding shares at the current market price of $34.61. There are currently 195,000 shares outstanding. EBIT is expected to remain at $1.1 million, with all earnings paid out as dividends. The firm can issue debt at a rate of 8.5 percent, and the firm's tax rate is 36 percent. Three alternative amounts of debt are being considered:

Amount of debt	0	$500,000	$1,000,000
Required return on equity	13%	13.41%	13.88%

   a. What is the optimum amount of debt?

   b. Show that, at the optimum capital structure, the firm minimizes the WACC and maximizes both the total firm value and the price of the outstanding shares.

20. Business and Financial Risk   Assume a firm's debt is risk-free, so that the cost of debt equals the risk-free rate, R_f. Define β_A as the firm's *asset* beta, that is, the systematic risk of the firm's assets. Define β_E to be the beta of the firm's equity. Use the capital asset pricing model, CAPM, along with M&M Proposition II to show that $\beta_E = \beta_A \times (1 + D/E)$, where D/E is the debt-equity ratio. Assume the tax rate is zero.

21. Shareholder Risk   Suppose a firm's business operations are such that they mirror movements in the economy as a whole very closely, that is, the firm's asset beta is 1.0. Use the result of Problem 20 to find the equity beta for this firm for debt-equity ratios of 0, 1, 5, and 20. What does this tell you about the relationship between capital structure and shareholder risk? How is the shareholders' required return on equity affected? Explain.

22. Bankruptcy   A petition for the reorganization of the Dew Drop Inn Company has been filed under the Insolvency Act. The trustees estimate the firm's liquidation value, after considering costs, is $68 million. Alternatively, the trustees, using the analysis of the PH Consulting firm, predict that the reorganized business will generate $12 million annual cash flows in perpetuity. The discount rate is 16.8 percent. Should Dew Drop be liquidated or reorganized? Why?

23. Bankruptcy   The Lead Zeppelin Corporation (LZC) has filed for bankruptcy. All of LZC's assets would fetch $22 million on the open market today if put up for sale. The other alternative would be to reorganize the business. If this occurs, the company would generate $2.5 million cash flows in perpetuity. Since there are no competitors making lead zeppelins, there is no company that can offer a comparable discount rate. Analysts estimate that the discount rate can be between 8 percent and 16 percent. If the company's discount rate is 8 percent, should the company be liquidated or reorganized? Is the answer the same for a 16 percent discount rate? What other factors may play a role in deciding whether to liquidate the company or reorganize it?

The management of Canada Textile Corporation (CTC) has decided to relocate the firm to Quebec after four more years of operating its factory in Cotton City, Saskatchewan. Because of transportation costs and a nonexistent secondary market for used textile machines, all of CTC's machines will be worthless after four years.

Mr. Rayon, plant engineer, recommends that a Spool Pfitzer machine be purchased. His analysis of the only two available models shows that:

	Heavy-Duty Model	Lightweight Model
Annual savings in costs	$380	$335
Economic life	4 years	2 years
Price of machine	$1,150	$580

CTC's accountant, Mr. Wool, must decide on two actions.

a) Purchase the Heavy-Duty Spool Pfitzer now, or

b) Purchase the Lightweight Spool Pfitzer now and replace it after two years with a second Lightweight Spool Pfitzer.

The manufacturer of the Spool Pfitzers is willing to guarantee that the prices he charges to CTC won't change during the next four years. The annual cost savings are known with certainty because of CTC's backlog of orders to supply the Canadian Army and because of CTC's long-term contracts with its workers and suppliers. Spool Pfitzer machines have a CCA rate of 30 percent (Class 43), and the company's tax rate will be 37 percent.

Mr. Wool obtained the following information for his analysis of various investment and financial proposals:

Asset	Expected Value	Variance	Covariance with Market Return
Risk-free asset	0.11		
Market portfolio	0.18	0.03	
CTC common stock			0.051

As a matter of company policy, CTC has never borrowed in the past; it is 100 percent equity financed. The market value of CTC common stock is $10 million.

a) What is the cost of capital for CTC?

b) Which of the two Spool Pfitzers should CTC purchase? If Spool Pfitzers are a bad investment, show why.

c) Assuming that the Heavy-Duty Spool Pfitzer will be purchased, what is the minimum annual savings in costs necessary for it to be an acceptable investment?

d) Mr. Wool has long believed that CTC's capital structure is not optimal; however, he was afraid to suggest changing the company's traditional all-equity financing policy. He believes in the Miller-Modigliani analysis and thinks that by selling $2.3 million of 10 percent perpetual bonds (no maturity) at par ("par" = "face" or "principal" amount) and using the proceeds to repurchase CTC stock, the total value of the firm would increase.

If Mr. Wool is correct and if his financial plan is adopted, what would be the new:

i) Total value of the firm?

ii) Total value of CTC stock?

iii) Weighted average cost of capital for CTC?

e) Ms. Nylon, the company's chief financial officer, says that Mr. Wool is mistaken. Because CTC is a high-risk firm in a declining industry, it would have to pay a 20 percent interest rate on its bonds, and the "increase in the value of the firm would be much less." Mr. Rayon says that a 20 percent interest rate "would mean that the value of the firm would increase more than Mr. Wool expects because of a larger tax shield." Mr. Orlon, chairman of the board of CTC, says that Wool, Nylon, and Rayon are all wrong and that the total value of the firm would remain at $10 million "because bond investors are risk-averse too!" Discuss the arguments given by Wool, Rayon, Nylon, and Orlon.

f) Suppose that, because of the new debt, there are new costs associated with possible financial distress. These costs can be expressed as 2 percent of the new firm value. Does this new information change the analysis?

g) Mr. Buck, loan officer at the Royal Canadian Imperial Bank (RCIB), received an application for a 20-year $2 million loan from CTC. RCIB is one of the few banks in Canada that make long-term loans. Although CTC is a well-known and respected local firm, Mr. Buck is worried about whether he should approve the loan. Does he have any reason to examine this loan application more carefully than (for example) one from Quebec Electric Utility Company? What (if any) are the risks of making the loan to CTC?

S&P Problem

1. Visit the "Student Centre" at the Online Learning Centre for this textbook (www.mcgrawhill.ca/college/ross). By using the passcode that came with your textbook, access the information in the S&P Market Insight tool. Find the annual balance sheets for Corel Corp. (CORL) and Imperial Oil Ltd. (IMO). For each company, calculate the long-term debt-to-equity ratio for the two most recent years. Why would these companies use such different capital structures?

Internet Application Questions

1. Capital structure choice in textbooks usually revolves around debt versus equity. In reality, there are several shades of gray in between. For example, subordinated debt can often be a useful source of capital for many firms. The following site lists the benefits of including subordinated debt in a firm's capital structure. What types of firms would find this financing attractive? Go to http://www.bctechnology.com/frameset_cc.html, click on the FINANCING button on the left of the screen, and then find the Subordinated Debt article.

2. Highly leveraged transactions called LBOs attempt to gain control of a firm through the use of borrowed funds, and their perpetrators hope to profit from de-leveraging the acquired assets in the future and doing a reverse LBO. Onex Corp. (www.onex.com) is an example of a Canadian company that specializes in doing LBO deals. Click on their website and explain the principles that underlie Onex's operating philosophy.

3. Go to yahoo.marketguide.com and enter the ticker symbols for JDS Uniphase (JDSU), Suncor Energy (SU), and BCE Inc. (BCE). Follow the "Ratio" link for each one and look under "Financial Condition" ratios. What are the long-term debt-to-equity and total debt-to-equity ratios for each of the companies? How do these values compare to the industry, sector, and S&P 500 for each company? Can you think of possible explanations for the differences among the three companies in terms of their financial structures?

4. A useful site for information on bankruptcy and reorganizations is found at www.abiworld.org. For the latest news, follow the "Bankruptcy Headlines" link on the site. How many companies filed for bankruptcy on this day? What conditions or issues caused these filings?

Suggested Readings

The classic articles on capital structure are:

Modigliani, F., and M. H. Miller. "The Cost of Capital, Corporate Finance, and the Theory of Investment." *American Economic Review* 48 (June 1958).

_____. "Corporation Income Taxes and the Cost of Capital: A Correction." *American Economic Review* 53 (June 1963).

Some research on capital structure is summarized in:

Smith, C. "Raising Capital: Theory and Evidence." *Midland Corporate Finance Journal,* Spring 1986.

The text of Stewart Myers's 1984 presidential address to the American Finance Association is in the following article. It summarizes the academic insights on capital structure until the early 1980s and points out directions for future research:

Myers, S. "The Capital Structure Puzzle." *Midland Corporate Finance Journal,* Fall 1985.

CAPITAL STRUCTURE AND PERSONAL TAXES

Up to this point, we considered corporate taxes only. Unfortunately, Canada Customs and Revenue Agency does not let us off that easily. As we saw in Chapter 2, income to individuals is taxed at different rates. For individuals in the top brackets, some kinds of personal income can be taxed more heavily than corporate income.

Earlier, we showed that the value of a levered firm equals the value of an identical unlevered firm, V_U plus the present value of the interest tax shield $T_C \times D$.

$$V_L = V_U + T_C \times D$$

This approach considered only corporate taxes. In a classic paper, Miller derived another expression for the value of the levered firm taking into account personal taxes.[10] In Equation 16A.1, T_b is the personal tax rate on ordinary income, such as interest and T_S is the personal tax rate on equity distributions—dividends and capital gains.[11]

$$V_L = V_U + \left[1 - \frac{(1 - T_C) \times (1 - T_S)}{(1 - T_b)} \right] \times B \qquad\qquad \textbf{[16A.1]}$$

Value of the Firm with Personal and Corporate Taxes

If the personal tax rates on interest (T_b) and on equity distributions (T_S) happen to be the same, then our new, more complex expression (Equation 16A.1) simplifies to Equation 16.7, which is the result when there are no personal taxes. It follows that introducing personal taxes does not affect our valuation formula as long as equity distributions are taxed identically to interest at the personal level.

However, the gain from leverage is reduced when equity distributions are taxed more lightly than interest, that is when T_S is less than T_b. Here, more taxes are paid at the personal level for a levered firm than for an unlevered firm. In fact, imagine that $(1 - T_C) \times (1 - T_S) = 1 - T_b$. Formula 16A.1 tells us there is no gain from leverage at all! In other words, the value of the levered firm is equal to the value of the unlevered firm. The reason there is no gain from leverage is that the lower corporate taxes for a levered firm are exactly offset by higher personal taxes. These results are presented in Figure 16A.1.

---

10 M. H. Miller, "Debt and Taxes," *Journal of Finance* 32 (May 1977), pp. 261–75.

11 Stockholders receive

$$(\text{EBIT} - r_B B) \times (1 - T_C) \times (1 - T_S)$$

Bondholders receive

$$r_B B \times (1 - T_b)$$

Thus, the total cash flow to all stakeholders is

$$(\text{EBIT} - r_B B) \times (1 - T_C) \times (1 - T_S) + r_B B \times (1 - T_b)$$

which can be rewritten as

$$\text{EBIT} \times (1 - T_C) \times (1 - T_S) + r_B B \times (1 - T_b) \times \left[1 - \frac{(1 - T_C) \times (1 - T_S)}{1 - T_b} \right] \qquad (a)$$

The first term in Equation (a) is the cash flow from an unlevered firm after all taxes. The value of this stream must be V_U, the value of an unlevered firm. An individual buying a bond for B receives $r_B B \times (1 - T_b)$ after all taxes. Thus, the value of the second term in (a) must be

$$B \times \left[1 - \frac{(1 - T_C) \times (1 - T_S)}{1 - T_b} \right]$$

Therefore, the value of the stream in (a), which is the value of the levered firm, must be

$$V_U + \left[1 - \frac{(1 - T_C) \times (1 - T_S)}{1 - T_b} \right] \times B$$

EXAMPLE 16A.1: Financial Leverage with Personal Taxes

Acme Industries anticipates a perpetual pretax earning stream of $100,000 and faces a 36 percent corporate tax rate. Investors discount the earnings stream after corporate taxes at 15 percent. The personal tax rate on equity distributions is 20 percent and the personal tax rate on interest is 40 percent. Acme currently has an all-equity capital structure but is considering borrowing $120,000 at 10 percent.

The value of the all-equity firm is:[12]

$$V_U = \frac{\$100,000 \times (1 - .36)}{0.15} = \$426,667$$

The value of the levered firm is

$$V_L = \$426,667 + \left[\frac{1 - (1 - .36) \times (1 - .20)}{(1 - .40)} \right] \times \$120,000$$

$$= \$444,267$$

The advantage to leverage here is $444,267 − $426,667 = $17,600. This is much smaller than the $43,200 = .36 × $120,000 = $T_C \times B$, which would have been the gain in a world with no personal taxes.

Acme had previously considered the choice years earlier when T_B = 60 percent, T_C = 45 percent and T_S = 18 percent. Here

$$V_L = \$366,667 + \left[\frac{1 - (1 - .45) \times (1 - .18)}{(1 - .60)} \right] \times \$120,000$$

$$= \$351,367$$

In this case, the value of the levered firm, V_L, is $351,367 which is less than the value of the unlevered firm, V_U = $366,667. Hence, Acme was wise not to increase leverage years ago. Leverage causes a loss of value because the personal tax rate on interest is much higher than the personal tax rate on equity distributions. In other words, the reduction in corporate taxes from leverage is more than offset by the increase in taxes from leverage at the personal level.

Figure 16A.1 summarizes the different cases we considered. Which one is the most applicable to Canada? While the numbers are different for different firms in different provinces, Chapter 2 showed that interest income is taxed at the full marginal rate, around 40 percent for the top bracket. Equity distributions take the form of either dividends or capital gains and both are taxed more lightly than interest. As we showed in Chapter 2, dividend income is sheltered by the dividend tax credit.

While the exact numbers depend on the type of portfolio chosen, our first scenario for Acme is a reasonable tax scenario for Canadian investors and companies. In Canada, personal taxes reduce, but do not eliminate, the advantage to corporate leverage.

This result is still unrealistic. It suggests that firms should add debt, moving out on the second line from the top in Figure 16A.1, until 100 percent leverage is reached. Firms do not do this. One reason is that interest on debt is not the firm's only tax shield. Investment tax credits, capital cost allowance, and depletion allowances give rise to tax shields regardless of the firm's decision on leverage. Because these other tax shields exist, increased leverage brings with it a risk that income will not be high enough to utilize the debt tax shield fully. The result is that firms use a limited amount of debt.[13]

Of course, as we argued in the chapter, the costs of bankruptcy and financial distress are another reason healthy firms do not use 100 percent debt financing.

CONCEPT QUESTIONS

1. How does considering personal taxes on interest and equity distributions change the M&M conclusions on optimal debt?

2. Explain in words the logic behind Miller's theory of capital structure.

3. How does this theory apply in Canada?

---

12 Alternatively, we could have said that investors discount the earnings stream after both corporate and personal taxes at 12% = 15% (1 − .20):

$$V_U = \frac{\$100,000 \times (1 - .36) \times (1 - .20)}{.12} = \$426,667$$

13 This argument was first advanced by H. DeAngelo and R. Masulis, "Optimal Capital Structure under Corporate and Personal Taxation," *Journal of Financial Economics*, March 1980, pp. 3–30. and is further discussed by Alfred H.R. Davis, "The Corporate Use of Debt Substitutes in Canada: A Test of Competing Versions of the Substitution Hypothesis," *Canadian Journal of Administrative Sciences*, March 1994, vol. 11, issue 1, p. 105.

FIGURE 16A.1

Gains from financial leverage with both corporate and personal taxes

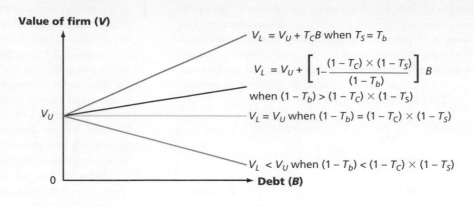

$V_L = V_U + T_C B$ when $T_S = T_b$

$V_L = V_U + \left[1 - \dfrac{(1 - T_C) \times (1 - T_S)}{(1 - T_b)} \right] B$
when $(1 - T_b) > (1 - T_C) \times (1 - T_S)$

$V_L = V_U$ when $(1 - T_b) = (1 - T_C) \times (1 - T_S)$

$V_L < V_U$ when $(1 - T_b) < (1 - T_C) \times (1 - T_S)$

T_C is the corporate tax rate.
T_b is the personal tax rate on interest.
T_S is the personal tax rate on dividends and other equity distributions.
Both personal taxes and corporate taxes are included. Bankruptcy costs and agency costs are ignored.
The effect of debt on firm value depends on T_S, T_C, and T_b.

Appendix Questions and Problems

A.1   Miller's model introduces personal taxes into the theory of capital structure. With both personal and corporate taxes, we got the same indifference result as with no taxes. Explain why.

A.2   This question is a follow-up to Question A.1 on Miller's model. In comparing this approach to M&M with corporate taxes, you can see that in one case both models imply that firms should use 100 percent debt financing. Explain how this conclusion occurs in each case. Why does it not occur in practice?

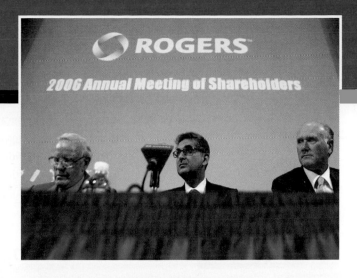

CHAPTER 17

Dividends and Dividend Policy

In 2006, some Canadian firms like Bank of Montreal prided themselves on paying sizable dividends for over 175 years. Other well-known companies paid low dividends (Talisman Energy) or no dividends at all (Research in Motion). In 2000, Rogers Communications Inc., announced that it would begin paying a regular divi-dend to shareholders at $0.05 per share for the first time in company history. By 2006, Rogers Communications Inc. had increased its dividend payout to $0.15 per share. Explaining dividends and dividend policy is the subject of this chapter.

www.rim.net

DIVIDEND POLICY is an important subject in corporate finance, and dividends are a major cash outlay for many corporations. At first glance, it may seem obvious that a firm would always want to give as much as possible back to its shareholders by paying dividends. It might seem equally obvious, however, that a firm can always invest the money for its shareholder instead of paying it out. The heart of the dividend policy question is just this: Should the firm pay out money to its shareholders, or should the firm take that money and invest it for its shareholders?

It may seem surprising, but much research and economic logic suggest that dividend policy doesn't matter. In fact, it turns out that the dividend policy issue is much like the capital structure question. The important elements are not difficult to identify, but the interactions between those elements are complex and no easy answer exists.

Dividend policy is controversial. Many implausible reasons are given for why dividend policy might be important, and many of the claims made about dividend policy are economically illogical. Even so, in the real world of corporate finance, determining the most appropriate dividend policy is considered an important issue. It could be that financial managers who worry about dividend policy are wasting time, but it could be true that we are missing something important in our discussions.

In part, all discussions of dividends are plagued by the "two-handed lawyer" problem. Former U.S. President Harry S. Truman, while discussing the legal implications of a possible presidential decision, asked his staff to set up a meeting with a lawyer. Supposedly, Truman said, "But I don't want one of those two-handed lawyers." When asked what a two-handed lawyer was, he replied, "You know, a lawyer who says, 'On the one hand I recommend you do so and so because of the following reasons, but on the other hand I recommend that you don't do it because of these other reasons.'"

Unfortunately, any sensible treatment of dividend policy appears to be written by a two-handed lawyer (or, in fairness, several two-handed financial economists). On the one hand, there are many good reasons for corporations to pay high dividends; on the other hand, there are also many good reasons to pay low dividends or no dividends.

We cover three broad topics that relate to dividends and dividend policy in this chapter. First, we describe the various kinds of dividends and how dividends are paid. Second, we consider an idealized case in which dividend policy doesn't matter. We then discuss the limitations of this case and present some practical arguments for both high- and low-dividend payouts. Finally, we conclude the chapter by looking at some strategies that corporations might employ to implement a dividend policy.

17.1 CASH DIVIDENDS AND DIVIDEND PAYMENT

dividend
Payment made out of a firm's earnings to its owners, either in the form of cash or stock.

distribution
Payment made by a firm to its owners from sources other than current or accumulated earnings.

The term **dividend** usually refers to cash paid out of earnings. If a payment is made from sources other than current or accumulated retained earnings, the term **distribution** rather than dividend is sometimes used. However, it is acceptable to refer to a distribution from earnings as a dividend and a distribution from capital as a liquidating dividend. More generally, any direct payment by the corporation to the shareholders may be considered a dividend or a part of dividend policy. Figure 17.1 shows how the dividend decision is part of distributing the firm's cash flow over different uses.

Dividends come in several different forms. The basic types of cash dividends are:

1. Regular cash dividends.
2. Extra dividends.
3. Liquidating dividends.

Later in the chapter, we discuss dividends that are paid in stock instead of cash, and we also consider an alternative to cash dividends, stock repurchase.

Cash Dividends

regular cash dividend
Cash payment made by a firm to its owners in the normal course of business, usually made four times a year.

The most common type of dividend is a cash dividend. Commonly, public companies pay **regular cash dividends** four times a year. As the name suggests, these are cash payments made directly to shareholders, and they are made in the regular course of business. In other words, management sees nothing unusual about the dividend and no reason it won't be continued.

FIGURE 17.1

Distribution of corporate cash flow

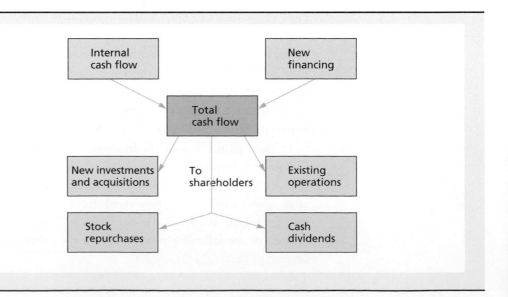

Sometimes firms pay a regular cash dividend and an extra cash dividend. By calling part of the payment extra, management is indicating it may or may not be repeated in the future.

Finally, a *liquidating dividend* usually means that some or all of the business has been liquidated, that is, sold off. Debt covenants, discussed in Chapter 7, offer the firm's creditors protection against liquidating dividends that could violate their prior claim against assets and cash flows.

However it is labelled, a cash dividend payment reduces corporate cash and retained earnings, except in the case of a liquidating dividend (where capital may be reduced).

Standard Method of Cash Dividend Payment

The decision to pay a dividend rests in the hands of the board of directors of the corporation. When a dividend has been declared, it becomes a debt of the firm and cannot be rescinded easily. Sometime after it has been declared, a dividend is distributed to all shareholders as of some specific date.

Commonly, the amount of the cash dividend is expressed in dollars per share (*dividends per share*). As we have seen in other chapters, it is also expressed as a percentage of the market price (the *dividend yield*) or as a percentage of earnings per share (the *dividend payout*).

Dividend Payment: A Chronology

The mechanics of a dividend payment can be illustrated by the example in Figure 17.2 and the following description:

declaration date
Date on which the board of directors passes a resolution to pay a dividend.

1. **Declaration date.** On January 15, the board of directors passes a resolution to pay a dividend of $1 per share on February 16 to all holders of record as of January 30.

ex-dividend date
Date two business days before the date of record, establishing those individuals entitled to a dividend.

2. **Ex-dividend date.** To make sure that dividend cheques go to the right people, brokerage firms and stock exchanges establish an ex-dividend date. This date is two business days before the date of record (discussed next). If you buy the stock before this date, then you are entitled to the dividend. If you buy on this date or after, then the previous owner gets it.

   The ex-dividend date convention removes any ambiguity about who is entitled to the dividend. Since the dividend is valuable, the stock price is affected when it goes "ex." We examine this effect later.

   In Figure 17.2, Wednesday, January 28, is the ex-dividend date. Before this date, the stock is said to trade "with dividend" or "cum dividend." Afterwards the stock trades "ex dividend."

date of record
Date on which holders of record are designated to receive a dividend.

3. **Date of record.** Based on its records, the corporation prepares a list on January 30 of all individuals believed to be shareholders as of this date. These are the *holders of record* and January 30 is the *date of record*. The word believed is important here. If you buy the stock

---

FIGURE 17.2

Procedure for dividend payment

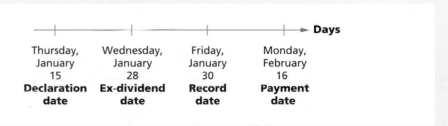

1. *Declaration date:* The board of directors declares a payment of dividends.
2. *Ex-dividend date:* A share of stock goes ex dividend on the date the seller is entitled to keep the dividend; under TSX rules, shares are traded ex dividend on and after the second business day before the record date.
3. *Record date:* The declared dividends are distributable to shareholders of record on a specific date.
4. *Payment date:* The dividend cheque date.

just before this date, the corporation's records may not reflect that fact because of mailing or other delays. Without some modification, some of the dividend cheques would get mailed to the wrong people. This is the reason for the ex-dividend day convention.

date of payment
Date on the dividend cheques.

4. **Date of payment.** The dividend cheques are mailed on February 16.

More on the Ex-Dividend Date

The ex-dividend date is important and is a common source of confusion. We examine what happens to the stock when it goes ex, meaning that the ex-dividend date arrives. To illustrate, suppose we have a stock that sells for $10 per share. The board of directors declares a dividend of $1 per share, and the record date is Thursday, June 14. Based on our previous discussion, we know that the ex date will be two business (not calendar) days earlier on Tuesday, June 12.

If you buy the stock on Monday, June 11, right as the market closes, you'll get the $1 dividend because the stock is trading cum dividend. If you wait and buy it right as the market opens on Tuesday, you won't get the $1 dividend. What will happen to the value of the stock overnight?

If you think about it, the stock is obviously worth about $1 less on Tuesday morning, so its price will drop by this amount between close of business on Monday and the Tuesday opening. In general, we expect the value of a share of stock to go down by about the dividend amount when the stock goes ex dividend. The key word here is *about.* Since dividends are taxed, the actual price drop might be closer to some measure of the aftertax value of the dividend. Determining this value is complicated because of the different tax rates and tax rules that apply for different buyers. The series of events described here is illustrated in Figure 17.3.

The amount of the price drop is a matter for empirical investigation. Researchers have argued that, due to personal taxes, the stock price should drop by less than the dividend.[1] For example, consider the case with no capital gains taxes. On the day before a stock goes ex dividend, shareholders must decide either to buy the stock immediately and pay tax on the forthcoming dividend, or to buy the stock tomorrow, thereby missing the dividend. If all investors are in a 30 percent bracket for dividends and the quarterly dividend is $1, the stock price should fall by $.70 on the ex-dividend date. If the stock price falls by this amount on the ex-dividend date, then purchasers receive the same return from either strategy.

FIGURE 17.3

Price behaviour around ex-dividend date for a $1 cash dividend

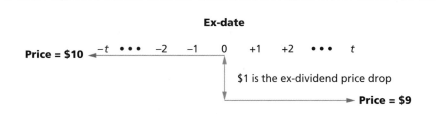

The stock price will fall by the amount of the dividend on the ex date (time 0). If the dividend is $1 per share, the price will be equal to $10 − $1 = $9 on the ex date:

Before ex date (−1) dividend = 0   Price = $10
Ex-date (0) dividend = $1   Price = $9

1 The original argument was advanced and tested for the United States by E. Elton and M. Gruber, "Marginal Stockholder Tax Rates and the Clientele Effect," *Review of Economics and Statistics* 52 (February 1970). Canadian evidence (discussed briefly later in this chapter) is from J. Lakonishok and T. Vermaelen, "Tax Reform and Ex-Dividend Day Behavior," *Journal of Finance* 38 (September 1983) pp. 1157–80, and L. D. Booth and D. J. Johnston, "The Ex-Dividend Day Behavior of Canadian Stock Prices: Tax Changes and Clientele Effects," *Journal of Finance* 39 (June 1984), pp. 457–76.

EXAMPLE 17.1: "Ex" Marks the Day

The board of directors of Divided Airlines has declared a dividend of $2.50 per share payable on Tuesday, May 30, to shareholders of record as of Tuesday, May 9. Cal Icon buys 100 shares of Divided on Tuesday, May 2, for $150 per share. What is the ex date? Describe the events that will occur with regard to the cash dividend and the stock price.

The ex date is two business days before the date of record, Tuesday, May 9, so the stock will go ex on Friday,

May 5. Cal buys the stock on Tuesday, May 2, so Cal has purchased the stock cum dividend. In other words, Cal gets $2.50 × 100 = $250 in dividends. The cheque is mailed on Tuesday, May 30. When the stock does go ex on Friday, its value drops overnight by about $2.50 per share (or maybe a little less due to personal taxes).

CONCEPT QUESTIONS

1. What are the different types of cash dividends?

2. What are the mechanics of the cash dividend payment?

3. How should the price of a stock change when it goes ex dividend?

DOES DIVIDEND POLICY MATTER?

To decide whether or not dividend policy matters, we first have to define what we mean by dividend policy. All other things being the same, of course dividends matter. Dividends are paid in cash, and cash is something that everybody likes. The question we are discussing here is whether the firm should pay out cash now or invest the cash and pay it out later. Dividend policy, therefore, is the time pattern of dividend payout. In particular, should the firm pay out a large percentage of its earnings now or a small (or even zero) percentage? This is the dividend policy question.

An Illustration of the Irrelevance of Dividend Policy

A powerful argument can be made that dividend policy does not matter. We illustrate this by considering the simple case of Wharton Corporation. Wharton is an all-equity firm that has existed for 10 years. The current financial managers plan to dissolve the firm in two years. The total cash flows that the firm will generate, including the proceeds from liquidation, are $10,000 in each of the next two years.

CURRENT POLICY: DIVIDENDS SET EQUAL TO CASH FLOW   At the present time, dividends at each date are set equal to the cash flow of $10,000. There are 100 shares outstanding, so the dividend per share will be $100. In Chapter 8, we stated that the value of the stock is equal to the present value of the future dividends. Assuming a 10 percent required return, the value of a share of stock today, P_0, is:

$$P_0 = D_1/(1 + R)^1 + D_2/(1 + R)^2$$
$$= \$100/1.10 + \$100/1.21 = \$173.55$$

The firm as a whole is thus worth 100 × $173.55 = $17,355.

Several members of the board of Wharton have expressed dissatisfaction with the current dividend policy and have asked you to analyze an alternative policy.

ALTERNATIVE POLICY: INITIAL DIVIDEND IS GREATER THAN CASH FLOW
Another policy is for the firm to pay a dividend of $110 per share on the first date, which is, of course, a total dividend of $11,000. Because the cash flow is only $10,000, an extra $1,000 must somehow be raised. One way to do it is to issue $1,000 of bonds or stock at Date 1. Assume that stock is issued. The new shareholders desire enough cash flow at Date 2 so that they earn the required 10 percent return on their Date 1 investment.[2]

---

2 The same results would occur after an issue of bonds, though the arguments would be less easily presented.

What is the value of the firm with this new dividend policy? The new shareholders invest $1,000. They require a 10 percent return, so they demand $1,000 \times 1.10 = $1,100 of the Date 2 cash flow, leaving only $8,900 to the old stockholders. The dividends to the old shareholders would be:

	Date 1	Date 2
Aggregate dividends to old stockholders	$11,000	$8,900
Dividends per share	110	89

The present value of the dividends per share is therefore:

$$P_0 = \$110/1.10 + \$89/1.10^2 = \$173.55$$

This is the same present value as we had before.

The value of the stock is not affected by this switch in dividend policy even though we had to sell some new stock just to finance the dividend. In fact, no matter what pattern of dividend payout the firm chooses, the value of the stock is always the same in this example. In other words, for the Wharton Corporation, dividend policy makes no difference. The reason is simple: Any increase in a dividend at some point in time is exactly offset by a decrease somewhere else, so the net effect, once we account for time value, is zero.

HOMEMADE DIVIDENDS   There is an alternative and perhaps more intuitively appealing explanation about why dividend policy doesn't matter in our example. Suppose individual investor X prefers dividends per share of $100 at both Dates 1 and 2. Would he or she be disappointed when informed that the firm's management is adopting the alternative dividend policy (dividends of $110 and $89 in the two dates, respectively)? Not necessarily, because the investor could easily reinvest the $10 of unneeded funds received on Date 1 by buying more Wharton stock. At 10 percent, this investment grows to $11 at Date 2. Thus, the investor would receive the desired net cash flow of $110 − 10 = $100 at Date 1 and $89 + 11 = $100 at Date 2.

Conversely, imagine Investor Z, preferring $110 of cash flow at Date 1 and $89 of cash flow at Date 2, finds that management pays dividends of $100 at both Dates 1 and 2. This investor can simply sell $10 worth of stock to boost his or her total cash at Date 1 to $110. Because this investment returns 10 percent, Investor Z gives up $11 at Date 2 ($10 × 1.1), leaving him with $100 − 11 = $89.

Our two investors are able to transform the corporation's dividend policy into a different policy by buying or selling on their own. The result is that investors are able to create **homemade dividends.** This means dissatisfied shareholders can alter the firm's dividend policy to suit themselves. As a result, there is no particular advantage to any one dividend policy that the firm might choose.

Many corporations actually assist their stockholders in creating homemade dividend policies by offering *automatic dividend reinvestment plans* (ADPs or DRIPs). As the name suggests, with such a plan, shareholders have the option of automatically reinvesting some or all of their cash dividends in shares of stock.

Under a new issue dividend reinvestment plan, investors buy new stock issued by the firm. They may receive a small discount on the stock, usually under 5 percent, or be able to buy without a broker's commission. This makes dividend reinvestment very attractive to investors who do not need cash flow from dividends. Since the discount or lower commission compares favourably with issue costs for new stock discussed in Chapter 15, dividend reinvestment plans are popular with large companies like BCE that periodically seek new common stock.[3]

Investment dealers also use financial engineering to create homemade dividends (or homemade capital gains). Called **stripped common shares,** these vehicles entitle holders to receive either all the dividends from one or a group of well-known companies or an instalment receipt that packages any capital gain in the form of a call option. The option gives the investor the right to buy the underlying shares at a fixed price and so it is valuable if the shares appreciate beyond that price.

homemade dividends
Idea that individual investors can undo corporate dividend policy by reinvesting dividends or selling shares of stock.

www.bell.ca

stripped common shares
Common stock on which dividends and capital gains are repackaged and sold separately.

---

3 Reinvested dividends are still taxable.

A TEST   Our discussion to this point can be summarized by considering the following true/false test questions:

1. True or false: Dividends are irrelevant.
2. True or false: Dividend policy is irrelevant.

The first statement is surely false, and the reason follows from common sense. Clearly, investors prefer higher dividends to lower dividends at any single date if the dividend level is held constant at every other date. To be more precise regarding the first question, if the dividend per share at a given date is raised while the dividend per share at each other date is held constant, the stock price rises. The reason is that the present value of the future dividends must go up if this occurs. This action can be accomplished by management decisions that improve productivity, increase tax savings, strengthen product marketing, or otherwise improve cash flow.

The second statement is true, at least in the simple case we have been examining. Dividend policy by itself cannot raise the dividend at one date while keeping it the same at all other dates. Rather, dividend policy merely establishes the trade-off between dividends at one date and dividends at another date. Once we allow for time value, the present value of the dividend stream is unchanged. Thus, in this simple world, dividend policy does not matter, because managers choosing either to raise or to lower the current dividend do not affect the current value of their firm. However, we have ignored several real-world factors that might lead us to change our minds; we pursue some of these in subsequent sections.

CONCEPT QUESTIONS

1. How can an investor create a homemade dividend?

2. Are dividends irrelevant?

REAL-WORLD FACTORS FAVOURING A LOW PAYOUT

The example we used to illustrate the irrelevance of dividend policy ignored taxes and flotation costs. In other words, we assumed perfect capital markets in which these and other imperfections did not exist. In this section, we see that these factors might lead us to prefer a low-dividend payout.

Taxes

The logic we used to establish that dividend policy does not affect firm value ignored the real-world complication of taxes. In Canada, both dividends and capital gains are taxed at effective rates less than the marginal tax rates.

For dividends, we showed in Chapter 2 that individual investors face a lower tax rate due to the dividend tax credit. Capital gains in the hands of individuals are taxed at 50 percent of the marginal tax rate. Since taxation only occurs when capital gains are realized, capital gains are very lightly taxed in Canada. On balance, capital gains are subject to lower taxes than dividends.

A firm that adopts a low-dividend payout reinvests the money instead of paying it out. This reinvestment increases the value of the firm and of the equity. All other things being equal, the net effect is that the capital gains portion of the return is higher in the future. So, the fact that capital gains are taxed favourably may lead us to prefer this approach.

This tax disadvantage of dividends doesn't necessarily lead to a policy of paying no dividends. Suppose a firm has some excess cash after selecting all positive NPV projects. The firm might consider the following alternatives to a dividend:

1. *Select additional capital budgeting projects.* Because the firm has taken all the available positive NPV projects already, it must invest its excess cash in negative NPV projects. This is clearly a policy at variance with the principles of corporate finance and represents an example of the agency costs of equity introduced in Chapter 1. Still, research suggests that

some companies are guilty of doing this.[4] It is frequently argued that managers who adopt negative NPV projects are ripe for takeover, leveraged buyouts, and proxy fights.

2. *Repurchase shares.* A firm may rid itself of excess cash by repurchasing shares of stock. In both the United States and Canada, investors can treat profits on repurchased stock in public companies as capital gains and pay lower taxes than they would if the cash were distributed as a dividend.

3. *Acquire other companies.* To avoid the payment of dividends, a firm might use excess cash to acquire another company. This strategy has the advantage of acquiring profitable assets. However, a firm often incurs heavy costs when it embarks on an acquisition program. In addition, acquisitions are invariably made above the market price. Premiums of 20 to 80 percent are not uncommon. Because of this, a number of researchers have argued that mergers are not generally profitable to the acquiring company, even when firms are merged for a valid business purpose.[5] Therefore, a company making an acquisition merely to avoid a dividend is unlikely to succeed.

4. *Purchase financial assets.* The strategy of purchasing financial assets in lieu of a dividend payment can be illustrated with the following example.

Suppose the Regional Electric Company has $1,000 of extra cash. It can retain the cash and invest it in Treasury bills yielding 8 percent, or it can pay the cash to shareholders as a dividend. Shareholders can also invest in Treasury bills with the same yield. Suppose, realistically, that the tax rate is 44 percent on ordinary income like interest on Treasury bills for both the company and individual investors and the individual tax rate on dividends is 30 percent. What is the amount of cash that investors have after five years under each policy?

If dividends are paid now, shareholders will receive $1,000 before taxes, or $1,000 \times (1 - .30) = $700 after taxes. This is the amount they invest. If the rate on T-bills is 8 percent, before taxes, then the aftertax return is $8\% \times (1 - .44) = 4.48\%$ per year. Thus, in five years, the shareholders have:

$$\$700 \times (1 + 0.0448)^5 = \$871.49$$

If Regional Electric Company retains the cash, invests in Treasury bills, and pays out the proceeds five years from now, then $1,000 will be invested today. However, since the corporate tax rate is 44 percent, the aftertax return from the T-bills will be $8\% \times (1 - .44) = 4.48\%$ per year. In five years, the investment will be worth:

$$\$1,000 \times (1 + 0.0448)^5 = \$1,244.99$$

If this amount is then paid out as a dividend, after taxes the stockholders receive:

$$\$1,244.99 \times (1 - .30) = \$871.49$$

In this case, dividends are the same after taxes whether the firm pays them now or later after investing in Treasury bills. The reason is that the firm invests exactly as profitably as the shareholders do on an aftertax basis.

This example shows that for a firm with extra cash, the dividend payout decision depends on personal and corporate tax rates. All other things the same, when personal tax rates are higher than corporate tax rates, a firm has an incentive to reduce dividend payouts. This would have occurred if we changed our example to have the firm invest in preferred stock instead of T-bills. (Recall from Chapter 8 that corporations enjoy a 100 percent exclusion of dividends from taxable income.) However, if personal tax rates on dividends are lower than corporate tax rates (for investors in lower tax brackets or tax-exempt investors), a firm has an incentive to pay out any excess cash in dividends.

These examples show that dividend policy is not always irrelevant when we consider personal and corporate taxes. To continue the discussion, we go back to the different tax treatment of dividends and capital gains.

---

4 M. C. Jensen, "Agency Costs of Free Cash Flows, Corporate Finance and Takeovers," *American Economic Review,* May 1986, pp. 323–29.

5 The original hypothesis comes from R. Roll, "The Hubris Hypothesis of Corporate Takeovers," *Journal of Business* (1986). Chapter 23 presents some Canadian examples.

EXPECTED RETURN, DIVIDENDS, AND PERSONAL TAXES We illustrate the effect of personal taxes by considering a situation where dividends are taxed and capital gains are not taxed—a scenario that is not unrealistic for many Canadian individual investors. We show that a firm that provides more return in the form of dividends has a lower value (or a higher pretax required return) than one whose return is in the form of untaxed capital gains.

Suppose every shareholder is in the top tax bracket (tax rate on dividends of 30 percent) and is considering the stocks of Firm G and Firm D. Firm G pays no dividend, and Firm D pays a dividend. The current price of the stock of Firm G is $100, and next year's price is expected to be $120. The shareholder in Firm G thus expects a $20 capital gain. With no dividend, the return is $20/$100 = 20%. If capital gains are not taxed, the pretax and aftertax returns must be the same.[6]

Suppose the stock of Firm D is expected to pay a $20 dividend next year. If the stocks of Firm G and Firm D are equally risky, the market prices must be set so that their aftertax expected returns are equal. The aftertax return on Firm D thus has to be 20 percent.

What will be the price of stock in Firm D? The aftertax dividend is $20 × (1 − .30) = $14, so our investor has a total of $114 after taxes. At a 20 percent required rate of return (after taxes), the present value of this aftertax amount is:

Present value = $114/1.20 = $95.00

The market price of the stock in Firm D thus must be $95.00.

Some Evidence on Dividends and Taxes in Canada

Is our example showing higher pretax returns for stocks that pay dividends realistic for Canadian capital markets? Since tax laws change from budget to budget, we have to exercise caution in interpreting research results. Before 1972, capital gains were untaxed in Canada (as in our simplified example). Research suggests stocks that paid dividends had higher pretax returns prior to 1972. From 1972 to 1977, the same study detected no difference in pretax returns.[7]

In 1985, the lifetime exemption on capital gains was introduced. Recent research found that investors anticipated this tax break for capital gains and bid up the prices of stocks with low dividend yields. Firms responded by lowering their dividend payouts. This all ended in 1994 when the federal budget ended the capital gains exemption.[8] In 2000, the federal budget lowered the taxable portion of capital gains from 75 to 50 percent. In November 2005, the government of Canada initiated changes with the goal of making dividend-paying stocks more attractive by increasing the gross-up and the dividend tax credit. We suspect that from the viewpoint of individual investors, higher dividends require larger pretax returns.

Another way of measuring the effective tax rates on dividends and capital gains in Canada is to look at ex-dividend day price drops. We showed earlier that, ignoring taxes, a stock price should drop by the amount of the dividend when it goes ex dividend. This is because the price drop offsets what investors lose by waiting to buy the stock until it goes ex dividend. If dividends are taxed and capital gains are tax free, the price drop should be lower, equal to the aftertax value of the dividend. However, if gains are taxed too, the price drop needs to be adjusted for the gains tax. An investor who waits for the stock to go ex dividend buys at a lower price and hence has a larger capital gain when the stock is sold later.

---

6 Under current tax law, if the shareholder in Firm G does not sell the shares for a gain, it will be an unrealized capital gain, which is not taxed.

7 I. G. Morgan, "Dividends and Stock Price Behaviour in Canada," *Journal of Business Administration* 12 (Fall 1989).

8 B. Amoako-adu, M. Rashid, and M. Stebbins, "Capital Gains Tax and Equity Values: Empirical Test of Stock Price Reaction to the Introduction and Reduction of Capital Gains Tax Exemption, *Journal of Banking and Finance* 16 (1992), pp. 275–87; F. Adjaoud and D. Zeghal, "Taxation and Dividend Policy in Canada: New Evidence," *FINECO* (2nd Semester) 1993, pp. 141–54.

All this allowed researchers to infer tax rates from ex-dividend day behaviour. One study concludes that marginal investors who set prices are taxed more heavily on dividends than on capital gains.[9] This supports our argument: Individual investors likely look for higher pretax returns on dividend paying stocks.

Flotation Costs

In our example illustrating that dividend policy doesn't matter, we saw that the firm could sell some new stock if necessary to pay a dividend. As we mentioned in Chapter 15, selling new stock can be very expensive. If we include flotation costs in our argument, then we find that the value of the stock decreases if we sell new stock.

More generally, imagine two firms that are identical in every way except that one pays out a greater percentage of its cash flow in the form of dividends. Since the other firm plows back more, its equity grows faster. If these two firms are to remain identical, the one with the higher payout has to sell some stock periodically to catch up. Since this is expensive, a firm might be inclined to have a low payout.

Dividend Restrictions

In some cases, a corporation may face restrictions on its ability to pay dividends. For example, as we discussed in Chapter 7, a common feature of a bond indenture is a covenant prohibiting dividend payments above some level.

CONCEPT QUESTIONS

1. What are the tax benefits of low dividends?

2. Why do flotation costs favour a low payout?

 **17.4**

REAL-WORLD FACTORS FAVOURING A HIGH PAYOUT

In this section, we consider reasons a firm might pay its shareholders higher dividends even if it means the firm must issue more shares of stock to finance the dividend payments.

In a classic textbook, Benjamin Graham, David Dodd, and Sidney Cottle have argued that firms should generally have high-dividend payouts because:

1. "The discounted value of near dividends is higher than the present worth of distant dividends."

2. Between "two companies with the same general earning power and same general position in an industry, the one paying the larger dividend will almost always sell at a higher price."[10]

Two factors favouring a high-dividend payout have been mentioned frequently by proponents of this view: the desire for current income and the resolution of uncertainty.

Desire for Current Income

It has been argued that many individuals desire current income. The classic example is the group of retired people and others living on fixed incomes, the proverbial "widows and orphans." It is

---

9 L. Booth and D. Johnston, "Ex-Dividend Day Behavior." Their research also showed that interlisted stocks, traded on exchanges in both the United States and Canada, tended to be priced by U.S. investors and not be affected by Canadian tax changes. J. Lakonishok and T. Vermaelen, "Tax Reforms and Ex-Dividend Day Behavior," *Journal of Finance*, September 1983, pp. 1157–58, gives a competing explanation in terms of tax arbitrage by short-term traders

10 G. Graham, D. Dodd, and S. Cottle, *Security Analysis* (New York: McGraw-Hill, 1962).

argued that this group is willing to pay a premium to get a higher dividend yield. If this is true, it lends support to the second claim by Graham, Dodd, and Cottle.

It is easy to see, however, that this argument is not relevant in our simple case. An individual preferring high current cash flow but holding low-dividend securities could easily sell shares to provide the necessary funds. Similarly, an individual desiring a low current cash flow but holding high-dividend securities can just reinvest the dividend. This is just our homemade dividend argument again. Thus, in a world of no transaction costs, a high current dividend policy would be of no value to the shareholder.

The current income argument may have relevance in the real world. Here the sale of low-dividend stocks would involve brokerage fees and other transaction costs. Such a sale might also trigger capital gains taxes. These direct cash expenses could be avoided by an investment in high-dividend securities. In addition, the expenditure of the stockholder's own time when selling securities and the natural (but not necessarily rational) fear of consuming out of principal might further lead many investors to buy high-dividend securities.

Even so, to put this argument in perspective, remember that financial intermediaries such as mutual funds can (and do) perform these repackaging transactions for individuals at very low cost. Such intermediaries could buy low-dividend stocks, and, by a controlled policy of realizing gains, they could pay their investors at a higher rate.

Uncertainty Resolution

We have just pointed out that investors with substantial current consumption needs prefer high current dividends. In another classic treatment, Professor Myron Gordon has argued that a high-dividend policy also benefits stockholders because it resolves uncertainty.[11]

According to Gordon, investors price a security by forecasting and discounting future dividends. Gordon then argues that forecasts of dividends to be received in the distant future have greater uncertainty than do forecasts of near-term dividends. Because investors dislike uncertainty, the stock price should be low for those companies that pay small dividends now in order to remit higher dividends later.

Gordon's argument is essentially a "bird-in-hand" story. A $1 dividend in a shareholder's pocket is somehow worth more than that same $1 in a bank account held by the corporation. By now, you should see the problem with this argument. A shareholder can create a bird in hand very easily just by selling some stock.

Tax and Legal Benefits from High Dividends

Earlier, we saw that dividends were taxed more heavily than capital gains for individual investors. This fact is a powerful argument for a low payout. However, a number of other investors do not receive unfavourable tax treatment from holding high-dividend yield, rather than low-dividend yield, securities.

CORPORATE INVESTORS A significant tax break on dividends occurs when a corporation owns stock in another corporation. A corporate shareholder receiving either common or preferred dividends is granted a 100 percent dividend exclusion.[12] Since the 100 percent exclusion does not apply to capital gains, this group is taxed unfavourably on capital gains.

As a result of the dividend exclusion, high-dividend, low capital gains stocks may be more appropriate for corporations to hold. As we discuss elsewhere, this is why corporations hold a substantial percentage of the outstanding preferred stock in the economy. This tax advantage of dividends also leads some corporations to hold high-yielding stocks instead of long-term bonds because there is no similar tax exclusion of interest payments to corporate bondholders.

---

11 M. Gordon, *The Investment, Financing and Valuation of the Corporation* (Homewood, IL: Richard D. Irwin, 1961).

12 For preferred stock, we assume the issuer has elected to pay the refundable withholding tax on preferred dividends.

TAX-EXEMPT INVESTORS   We have pointed out both the tax advantages and disadvantages of a low-dividend payout. Of course, this discussion is irrelevant to those in zero tax brackets. This group includes some of the largest investors in the economy, such as pension funds, endowment funds, and trust funds.

There are some legal reasons for large institutions to favour high-dividend yields: First, institutions such as pension funds and trust funds are often set up to manage money for the benefit of others. The managers of such institutions have a *fiduciary responsibility* to invest the money prudently. It has been considered imprudent in courts of law to buy stock in companies with no established dividend record.

Second, institutions such as university endowment funds and trust funds are frequently prohibited from spending any of the principal. Such institutions might, therefore, prefer high-dividend yield stocks so they have some ability to spend. Like widows and orphans, this group thus prefers current income. Unlike widows and orphans, in terms of the amount of stock owned, this group is very large and its market share is expanding rapidly.

Conclusion

Overall, individual investors (for whatever reason) may have a desire for current income and may thus be willing to pay the dividend tax. In addition, some very large investors such as corporations and tax-free institutions may have a very strong preference for high-dividend payouts.

CONCEPT QUESTIONS

1. Why might some individual investors favour a high dividend payout?
2. Why might some nonindividual investors prefer a high dividend payout?

17.5   A RESOLUTION OF REAL-WORLD FACTORS?

In the previous sections, we presented some factors that favour a low-dividend policy and others that favour high dividends. In this section, we discuss two important concepts related to dividends and dividend policy: the information content of dividends and the clientele effect. The first topic illustrates both the importance of dividends in general and the importance of distinguishing between dividends and dividend policy. The second topic suggests that, despite the many real-world considerations we have discussed, the dividend payout ratio may not be as important as we originally imagined.

Information Content of Dividends

To begin, we quickly review some of our earlier discussion. Previously, we examined three different positions on dividends:

1. Based on the homemade dividend argument, dividend policy is irrelevant.
2. Because of tax effects for individual investors and new issues costs, a low-dividend policy is the best.
3. Because of the desire for current income and related factors, a high-dividend policy is the best.

If you wanted to decide which of these positions is the right one, an obvious way to get started would be to look at what happens to stock prices when companies announce dividend changes. You would find with some consistency that stock prices rise when the current dividend is unexpectedly increased, and they generally fall when the dividend is unexpectedly decreased. What does this imply about any of the three positions just stated?

At first glance, the behaviour we describe seems consistent with the third position and inconsistent with the other two. In fact, many writers have argued this. If stock prices rise on dividend increases and fall on dividend decreases, isn't the market saying it approves of higher dividends?

Other authors have pointed out that this observation doesn't really tell us much about dividend policy. Everyone agrees that dividends are important, all other things being equal. Companies only cut dividends with great reluctance. Thus, a dividend cut is often a signal that the firm is in trouble.

More to the point, a dividend cut is usually not a voluntary, planned change in dividend policy. Instead, it usually signals that management does not think the current dividend policy can be maintained. As a result, expectations of future dividends should generally be revised downward. The present value of expected future dividends falls and so does the stock price.

In this case, the stock price declines following a dividend cut because future dividends are generally lower, not because the firm changes the percentage of its earnings it will pay out in the form of dividends.

Dividend Signalling in Practice

www.conedison.com

To give a particularly dramatic example, consider what happened to Consolidated Edison, the largest investor-owned U.S. electric utility, in the second quarter of 1974. Faced with poor operating results and problems associated with the OPEC oil embargo, Con Ed announced after the market closed that it was omitting its regular quarterly dividend of 45 cents per share. This was somewhat surprising given Con Ed's size, prominence in the industry, and long dividend history. Also, Con Ed's earnings at that time were sufficient to pay the dividend, at least by some analysts' estimates.

The next morning was not pleasant. Sell orders were so heavy that a market could not be established for several hours. When trading finally got started, the stock opened at about $12 per share, down from $18 the day before. In other words, Con Ed, a very large company, lost about one-third of its market value overnight. As this case illustrates, shareholders can react very negatively to unanticipated cuts in dividends.

In a similar vein, an unexpected increase in the dividend signals good news. Management raises the dividend only when future earnings, cash flow, and general prospects are expected to rise enough so that the dividend does not have to be cut later. A dividend increase is management's signal to the market that the firm is expected to do well. The stock reacts favourably because expectations of future dividends are revised upward, not because the firm has increased its payout. Since the firm has to come up with cash to pay dividends, this kind of signal is more convincing than calling a press conference to announce good earnings prospects.

www.bankofmontreal.com

Management behaviour is consistent with the notion of dividend signalling. In 1989, for example, the Bank of Montreal's earnings per share dropped from $4.89 the previous year to $.04 due to increased loan loss provisions for LDC debt. Yet the annual dividend was increased slightly from $2.00 to $2.12 per share. The payout ratio skyrocketed to 5,300 percent ($2.12/$.04). Management signalled the market that earnings would recover in 1990, which they did.

In both these cases, the stock price reacts to the dividend change. The reaction can be attributed to changes in the amount of future dividends, not necessarily a change in dividend payout policy. This signal is called the **information content effect** of the dividend. The fact that dividend changes convey information about the firm to the market makes it difficult to interpret the effect of dividend policy of the firm.

information content effect
The market's reaction to a change in corporate dividend payout.

The Clientele Effect

www.suncor.com

clientele effect
Stocks attract particular groups based on dividend yield and the resulting tax effects.

In our earlier discussion, we saw that some groups (wealthy individuals, for example) have an incentive to pursue low-payout (or zero-payout) stocks. Other groups (corporations, for example) have an incentive to pursue high-payout stocks. Companies with high payouts thus attract one group and low-payout companies attract another.

Table 17.1 shows the dividends paid by the 25 largest Canadian companies in terms of market capitalization. In May 2006, all of these companies paid dividends, although mining stocks such as Barrick Gold and oil and gas stocks like Talisman Energy paid low dividends. Banks and utilities paid relatively high dividends.

Groups of investors attracted to different payouts are called *clienteles*, and what we have described is a **clientele effect.** The clientele effect argument states that different groups of investors desire different levels of dividends. When a firm chooses a particular dividend policy, the only effect is to attract a particular clientele. If a firm changes its dividend policy, it just attracts a different clientele.

What we are left with is a simple supply and demand argument. Suppose that 40 percent of all investors prefer high dividends, but only 20 percent of the firms pay high dividends. Here the high-dividend firms are in short supply; thus, their stock prices rise. Consequently, low-dividend firms would find it advantageous to switch policies until 40 percent of all firms have high payouts. At this point, the *dividend market* is in equilibrium. Further changes in dividend policy are pointless because all of the clienteles are satisfied. The dividend policy for any individual firm is now irrelevant.

To see if you understand the clientele effect, consider the following statement: "In spite of the theoretical argument that dividend policy is irrelevant or that firms should not pay dividends, many investors like high dividends. Because of this fact, a firm can boost its share price by having a higher dividend payout ratio." True or false?

The answer is false if clienteles exist. As long as enough high-dividend firms satisfy the dividend-loving investors, a firm won't be able to boost its share price by paying high dividends.

CONCEPT QUESTIONS

1. How does the market react to unexpected dividend changes? What does this tell us about dividends? About dividend policy?

2. What is a dividend clientele? All things considered, would you expect a risky firm with significant but highly uncertain growth prospects to have a low- or high-dividend payout?

TABLE 17.1   Largest TSX companies by market capitalization and dividends for May 30, 2006

Symbol	Company	Market Capitalization	Dividend per share
TSX: RY	Royal Bank of Canada	$59,238,910,739	1.44
TSX: MFC	Manulife Financial Corporation	58,330,857,790	0.70
TSX: ECA	EnCana Corporation	46,462,276,922	0.44
TSX: TD	Toronto-Dominion Bank	43,200,671,740	1.76
TSX: BNS	Bank of Nova Scotia	43,114,958,597	1.56
TSX: SU	Suncor Energy Inc.	41,582,670,041	0.32
TSX: IMO	Imperial Oil Ltd.	41,508,199,639	0.32
TSX: CNQ	Canadian Natural Resources Ltd.	32,861,448,398	0.30
TSX: BMO	Bank of Montreal	30,992,077,055	2.48
TSX: ABX	Barrick Gold Corp.	29,439,900,547	0.24 u
TSX: TOC	Thomson Corporation	28,599,442,552	0.97 u
TSX: HSE	Husky Energy Inc.	27,444,252,612	1.00
TSX: CM	Canadian Imperial Bank of Commerce	27,138,181,538	2.72
TSX: SLF	Sun Life Financial Inc.	26,571,300,612	1.10
TSX: CNR	Canadian National Railway Company	26,448,507,286	0.65
TSX: PCA	Petro-Canada Inc.	26,023,591,955	0.40
TSX: BCE	BCE Inc.	23,991,893,375	1.32
TSX: TLM	Talisman Energy Inc.	23,054,065,387	0.15
TSX: AL	Alcan Inc.	21,251,973,933	0.66 u
TSX: FAL.LV	FalconBridge Ltd.	20,834,295,838	0.48
TSX: BAM.LV.A	Brookfield Asset Management Inc.	17,624,352,166	0.71
TSX: NXY	Nexen Inc.	16,506,772,641	0.20
TSX: CCO	Cameco Corporation	16,272,422,911	0.16
TSX: TRP	TransCanada Corporation	15,892,356,221	1.28
TSX: L	Loblaw Companies Ltd.	14,733,186,801	0.84

u = dividends are paid in U.S. dollars

Source: www.tsx.com, www.globeinvestor.com

www.scotiabank.com

17.6

ESTABLISHING A DIVIDEND POLICY

How do firms actually determine the level of dividends that they pay at a particular time? As we have seen, there are good reasons for firms to pay high dividends and there are good reasons to pay low dividends.

We know some things about how dividends are paid in practice. Firms don't like to cut dividends. We saw this with Bank of Montreal earlier. As Table 17.2 shows, two chartered banks, Bank of Montreal and Bank of Nova Scotia, have been paying dividends for over 170 years.

In the next section, we discuss a particular dividend policy strategy. In doing so, we emphasize the real-world features of dividend policy. We also analyze an alternative to cash dividends, a stock repurchase.

Residual Dividend Approach

Earlier, we noted that firms with higher dividend payouts have to sell stock more often. As we have seen, such sales are not very common and they can be very expensive. Consistent with this, we assume that the firm wishes to minimize the need to sell new equity. We also assume that the firm wishes to maintain its current capital structure.[13]

If a firm wishes to avoid new equity sales, then it has to rely on internally generated equity to finance new, positive NPV projects.[14] Dividends can only be paid out of what is left over. This leftover is called the *residual,* and such a dividend policy would be called a **residual dividend approach.**

With a residual dividend policy, the firm's objective is to meet its investment needs and maintain its desired debt/equity ratio before paying dividends. To illustrate, imagine that a firm has $1,000 in earnings and a debt/equity ratio of .50. Notice that, since the debt/equity ratio is .50, the firm has 50 cents in debt for every $1.50 in value. The firm's capital structure is thus 1/3 debt and 2/3 equity.

The first step in implementing a residual dividend policy is to determine the amount of funds that can be generated without selling new equity. If the firm reinvests the entire $1,000 and pays no dividend, equity increases by $1,000. To keep the debt/equity ratio at .50, the firm must borrow an additional $500. The total amount of funds that can be generated without selling new equity is thus $1,000 + 500 = $1,500.

The second step is to decide whether or not a dividend will be paid. To do this, we compare the total amount that can be generated without selling new equity ($1,500 in this case) with planned capital spending. If funds needed exceed funds available, no dividend is paid. In addition, the firm will have to sell new equity to raise the needed finance or else (more likely) postpone some planned capital spending.

If funds needed are less than funds generated, a dividend will be paid. The amount of the dividend is the residual, that is, that portion of the earnings not needed to finance new projects. For example, suppose we have $900 in planned capital spending. To maintain the firm's capital structure, this $900 must be financed 2/3 equity and 1/3 debt. So, the firm actually borrows

residual dividend approach
Policy where a firm pays dividends only after meeting its investment needs while maintaining a desired debt-to-equity ratio.

TABLE 17.2
Paying dividends

Stock	Year Dividend Payments Began
Bank of Montreal	1829
Bank of Nova Scotia	1833
Royal Bank	1870

---

13 As in our discussion of the cost of capital in Chapter 14, the capital structure should be measured using market value weights.

14 Our discussion of sustainable growth in Chapter 4 is relevant here. We assumed there that a firm has a fixed capital structure, profit margin, and capital intensity. If the firm raises no new equity and wishes to grow at some target rate, there is only one payout ratio consistent with these assumptions.

TABLE 17.3
Dividend policy under the residual approach

Row	(1) Aftertax Earnings	(2) New Investment	(3) Additional Debt	(4) Retained Earnings	(5) Additional Stock	(6) Dividends
1	$1,000	$3,000	$1,000	$1,000	$1,000	$ 0
2	1,000	2,000	667	1,000	333	0
3	1,000	1,500	500	1,000	0	0
4	1,000	1,000	333	667	0	333
5	1,000	500	167	333	0	667
6	1,000	0	0	0	0	1,000

FIGURE 17.4

Relationship between dividends and investment in residual dividend policy

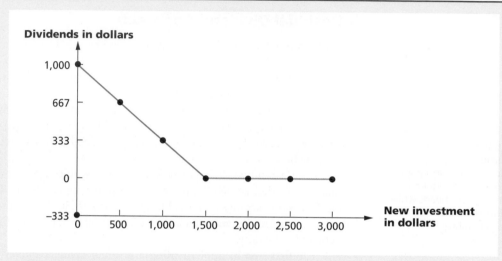

This figure illustrates that a firm with many investment opportunities will pay small amounts of dividends and a firm with few investment opportunities will pay relatively large amounts of dividends.

$1/3 \times \$900 = \$300$. The firm spends $2/3 \times \$900 = \$600$ of the $1,000 in equity available. There is a $\$1,000 - 600 = \$400$ residual, so the dividend is $400.

In sum, the firm has aftertax earnings of $1,000. Dividends paid are $400. Retained earnings are $600, and new borrowing totals $300. The firm's debt/equity ratio is unchanged at .50.

The relationship between physical investment and dividend payout is presented for six different levels of investment in Table 17.3 and illustrated in Figure 17.4. The first three rows of the table can be discussed together, because in each case no dividends are paid.

In row 1, for example, note that new investment is $3,000. Additional debt of $1,000 and equity of $2,000 must be raised to keep the debt/equity ratio constant. Since this latter figure is greater than the $1,000 of earnings, all earnings are retained. Additional stock to be raised is also $1,000. In this example, since new stock is issued, dividends are not simultaneously paid out.

In rows 2 and 3, investment drops. Additional debt needed goes down as well since it is equal to 1/3 of investment. Because the amount of new equity needed is still greater than or equal to $1,000, all earnings are retained and no dividends are paid.

We finally find a situation in row 4 where a dividend is paid. Here, total investment is $1,000. To keep our debt/equity ratio constant, 1/3 of this investment, or $333, is financed by debt. The remaining 2/3 or $667, comes from internal funds, implying that the residual is $1,000 − 667 = $333. The dividend is equal to this $333 residual.

In this case, note that no additional stock is issued. Since the needed investment is even lower in rows 5 and 6, new debt is reduced further, retained earnings drop, and dividends increase. Again, no additional stock is issued.

Given our discussion, we expect those firms with many investment opportunities to pay a small percentage of their earnings as dividends and other firms with fewer opportunities to pay a high percentage of their earnings as dividends. Young, fast-growing firms commonly employ a

www.canadiantire.ca

low payout ratio, whereas older, slower-growing firms in more mature industries use a higher ratio. This pattern is consistent with firms' practice in the U.S. and Canada.[15]

We see this pattern somewhat in Table 17.4 where the Bank of Montreal is a slower-growing firm with a high payout; Canadian Tire is a faster-growing firm with a pattern of low payouts. Canadian Tire had a steady payout in most of the years, but the payout exceeded 300 percent on one occasion in 1994. This illustrates that firms will sometimes accept a significantly different payout ratio in order to avoid or soften dividend cuts. In the case of Canadian Tire, the change was driven by a substantial drop in EPS in 1994 (a change that reversed the following year).

Dividend Stability

The key point of the residual dividend approach is that dividends are paid only after all profitable investment opportunities are exhausted. Of course, a strict residual approach might lead to a very unstable dividend policy. If investment opportunities in one period are quite high, dividends would be low or zero. Conversely, dividends might be high in the next period if investment opportunities are considered less promising.

Consider the case of Big Department Stores, Inc., a retailer whose annual earnings are forecasted to be equal from year to year but whose quarterly earnings change throughout the year. They are low in each year's first quarter because of the post-Christmas business slump. Although earnings increase only slightly in the second and third quarters, they advance greatly in the fourth quarter as a result of the Christmas season. A graph of this firm's earnings is presented in Figure 17.5.

The firm can choose between at least two types of dividend policies. First, each quarter's dividend can be a fixed fraction of that quarter's earnings. Here, dividends vary throughout the year.

TABLE 17.4
The stability of dividends

	EPS	DPS	Payout
Bank of Montreal			
1993	$1.30	$0.56	43%
1994	1.51	0.60	40
1995	1.73	0.66	38
1996	2.10	0.74	35
1997	2.35	0.82	35
1998	2.36	0.88	37
1999	2.38	0.94	39
2000	3.30	1.00	30
2001	2.72	1.12	41
2002	2.73	1.20	44
2003	3.51	1.34	38
2004	4.53	1.59	35
2005	4.74	1.85	39
Canadian Tire			
1993	$0.90	$0.40	44%
1994	0.12	0.40	333
1995	1.39	0.40	29
1996	1.54	0.40	26
1997	1.84	0.40	22
1998	2.09	0.40	19
1999	2.09	0.40	19
2000	1.89	0.40	21
2001	2.25	0.40	18
2002	2.56	0.40	16
2003	3.06	0.40	13
2004	3.60	0.475	13
2005	4.04	0.56	14

Source: Financial Post Advisor.

---

15 Current research shows that in many other countries where shareholders have weaker legal rights, dividends are not linked to firm growth. Rather, they are seen as a way of prying wealth loose from the hands of controlling shareholders: R. LaPorta, F. Lopez-de-Silanes, A. Schleifer, and R.W. Vishny, "Agency Problems and Dividend Policies Around the World," *Journal of Finance* 2000.

This is a cyclical dividend policy. Second, each quarter's dividend can be a fixed fraction of yearly earnings, implying that all dividend payments would be equal. This is a stable dividend policy. These two types of dividend policies are displayed in Figure 17.6.

Corporate executives generally agree that a stable policy is in the interest of the firm and its stockholders. Dividend stability complements investor objectives of information content, income, and reduction in uncertainty. Institutional investors often follow "prudence" tests that restrict investment in firms that do not pay regular dividends. For all these reasons a stable dividend policy is common. For example, looking back at Table 17.4, the dividends paid by these large Canadian firms are much less volatile through time than their earnings.

FIGURE 17.5

Earnings for Big
Department Stores, Inc.

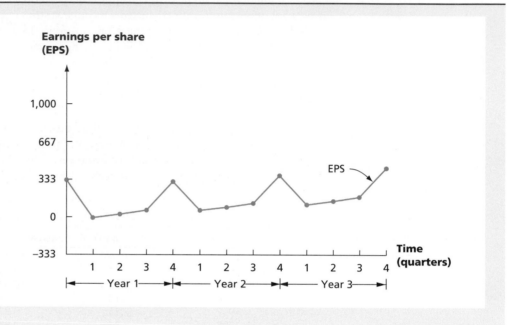

FIGURE 17.6

Alternative dividend
policies for Big
Department Stores, Inc.

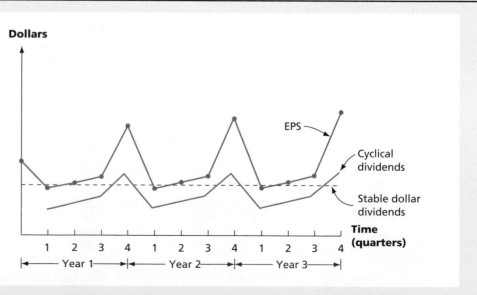

Cyclical dividend policy: Dividends are a constant proportion of earnings at each pay date. Stable dividend policy: Dividends are a constant porportion of earnings over an earnings cycle.

A Compromise Dividend Policy

In practice, many firms appear to follow what amounts to a compromise dividend policy. Such a policy is based on five main goals:

1. Avoid cutting back on positive NPV projects to pay a dividend.
2. Avoid dividend cuts.
3. Avoid the need to sell equity.
4. Maintain a target debt/equity ratio.
5. Maintain a target dividend payout ratio.

These goals are ranked more or less in order of their importance. In our strict residual approach, we assumed that the firm maintained a fixed debt/equity ratio. Under the compromise approach, that debt/equity ratio is viewed as a long-range goal. It is allowed to vary in the short run if necessary to avoid a dividend cut or the need to sell new equity.

target payout ratio
A firm's long-term desired dividend-to-earnings ratio.

In addition to a strong reluctance to cut dividends, financial managers tend to think of dividend payments in terms of a proportion of income, and they also tend to think investors are entitled to a "fair" share of corporate income. This share is the long-run **target payout ratio**, and it is the fraction of the earnings that the firm expects to pay as dividends under ordinary circumstances. Again, this is viewed as a long-range goal, so it might vary in the short run if needed. As a result, in the long run, earnings growth is followed by dividend increases, but only with a lag.

One can minimize the problems of dividend instability by creating two types of dividends: regular and extra. For companies using this approach, the regular dividend would likely be a relatively small fraction of permanent earnings, so that it could be sustained easily. Extra dividends would be granted when an increase in earnings was expected to be temporary.

Since investors look on an extra dividend as a bonus, there is relatively little disappointment when an extra dividend is not repeated.

Some Survey Evidence on Dividends

A recent study surveyed a large number of U.S. financial executives regarding dividend policy. One of the questions asked was "Do these statements describe factors that affect your company's dividend decisions?" Table 17.5 shows some of the results.

As shown in Table 17.5, financial managers are very disinclined to cut dividends. Moreover, they are very conscious of their previous dividends and desire to maintain a relatively steady dividend. In contrast, the cost of external capital and the desire to attract "prudent man" investors (such as pension funds with fiduciary duties to ultimate beneficaries) are less important.

Table 17.6 is drawn from the same survey, but here the responses are to the question, "How important are the following factors to your company's dividend decision?" Not surprisingly given the responses in Table 17.5 and our earlier discussion, the highest priority is maintaining a consistent

TABLE 17.5

Survey responses on dividend decisions*

Policy Statements	Percent Who Agree or Strongly Agree
1. We try to avoid reducing dividends per share.	93.8%
2. We try to maintain a smooth dividend from year to year.	89.6
3. We consider the level of dividends per share that we have paid in recent quarters.	88.2
4. We are reluctant to make dividend changes that might have to be reversed in the future.	77.9
5. We consider the change or growth in dividends per share.	66.7
6. We consider the cost of raising external capital to be smaller than the cost of cutting dividends.	42.8
7. We pay dividends to attract investors subject to "prudent man" investment restrictions.	41.7

*Survey respondents were asked the question, "Do these statements describe factors that affect your company's dividend decisions?"

Source: Adapted from Table 4 of A. Brav, J.R. Graham, C.R. Harvey, and R. Michaely, "Payout Policy in the 21st Century," *Journal of Financial Economics*, Vol. 77, Iss. 3, September 2005.

TABLE 17.6
Survey responses on
dividend decisions*

Policy Statements	Percent Who Think This Is Important or Very Important
1. Maintaining consistency with our historic dividend policy.	84.1%
2. Stability of future earnings.	71.9
3. A sustainable change in earnings.	67.1
4. Attracting institutional investors to purchase our stock.	52.5
5. The availability of good investment opportunities for our firm to pursue.	47.6
6. Attracting retail investors to purchase our stock.	44.5
7. Personal taxes our stockholders pay when receiving dividends.	21.1
8. Flotation costs to issuing new equity.	9.3

*Survey respondents were asked the question, "How important are the following factors to your company's dividend decision?"
Source: Adapted from Table 5 of A. Brav, J.R. Graham, C.R. Harvey, and R. Michaely, "Payout Policy in the 21st Century," *Journal of Financial Economics*, Vol. 77, Iss. 3, September 2005.

dividend policy. The next several items are also consistent with our previous analysis. Financial managers are very concerned about earnings stability and future earnings levels in making dividend decisions, and they consider the availability of good investment opportunities. Survey respondents also believed that attracting both institutional and individual (retail) investors was relatively important.

In contrast to our discussion in the earlier part of this chapter on taxes and flotation costs, the U.S. financial managers in this survey did not think that personal taxes paid on dividends by shareholders are very important. And even fewer think that equity flotation costs are relevant. In contrast to our discussion in the earlier part of this chapter on taxes and flotation costs, the U.S. managers in this survey did not think that the latter were relevant. They also did not consider that personal taxes paid on dividends by shareholders were very important. Since Canada has a different taxation system, it is likely that personal taxes are more important to financial managers here.

CONCEPT QUESTIONS

1. What is a residual dividend policy?

2. What is the chief drawback to a strict residual policy? What do many firms do in practice?

17.7

STOCK REPURCHASE: AN ALTERNATIVE TO CASH DIVIDENDS

When a firm wants to pay cash to its shareholders, it normally pays a cash dividend. Another way is to **repurchase** its own stock. Stock repurchasing has been a major financial activity, and it appears that it will continue to be one.

repurchase
Another method used to pay out a firm's earnings to its owners, which provides more preferable tax treatment than dividends.

Cash Dividends versus Repurchase

Imagine an all-equity company with excess cash of $300,000. The firm pays no dividends, and its net income for the year just ended is $49,000. The market value balance sheet at the end of the year is represented below.

Market Value Balance Sheet
(before paying out excess cash)

Excess cash	$ 300,000	$ 0	Debt
Other assets	700,000	1,000,000	Equity
Total	$1,000,000	$1,000,000	

There are 100,000 shares outstanding. The total market value of the equity is $1 million, so the stock sells for $10 per share. Earnings per share (EPS) were $49,000/100,000 = $.49, and the price/earnings ratio (P/E) is $10/$.49 = 20.4.

One option the company is considering is a $300,000/100,000 = $3 per share extra cash dividend. Alternatively, the company is thinking of using the money to repurchase $300,000/$10 = 30,000 shares of stock.

If commissions, taxes, and other imperfections are ignored in our example, the shareholders shouldn't care which option is chosen. Does this seem surprising? It shouldn't, really. What is happening here is that the firm is paying out $300,000 in cash. The new balance sheet is represented below.

**Market Value Balance Sheet
(before paying out excess cash)**

Excess cash	$ 0		$ 0	Debt
Other assets	700,000		700,000	Equity
Total	$700,000		$700,000	

If the cash is paid out as a dividend, there are still 100,000 shares outstanding, so each is worth $7.

The fact that the per-share value fell from $10 to $7 isn't a cause for concern. Consider a shareholder who owns 100 shares. At $10 per share before the dividend, the total value is $1,000.

After the $3 dividend, this same shareholder has 100 shares worth $7 each, for a total of $700, plus 100 × $3 = $300 in cash, for a combined total of $1,000. This just illustrates what we saw earlier: A cash dividend doesn't affect a shareholder's wealth if there are no imperfections. In this case, the stock price simply fell by $3 when the stock went ex dividend.

Also, since total earnings and the number of shares outstanding haven't changed, EPS is still 49 cents. The price/earnings ratio (P/E), however, falls to $7/.49 = 14.3. Why we are looking at accounting earnings and P/E ratios will be apparent just below.

Alternatively, if the company repurchases 30,000 shares, there will be 70,000 left outstanding. The balance sheet looks the same.

**Market Value Balance Sheet
(before paying out excess cash)**

Excess cash	$ 0		$ 0	Debt
Other assets	700,000		700,000	Equity
Total	$700,000		$700,000	

The company is worth $700,000 again, so each remaining share is worth $700,000/70,000 = $10 each. Our shareholder with 100 shares is obviously unaffected. For example, if the shareholder were so inclined, he or she could sell 30 shares and end up with $300 in cash and $700 in stock, just as if the firm pays the cash dividend. This is another example of a homemade dividend.

In this second case, EPS goes up since total earnings are the same while the number of shares goes down. The new EPS will be $49,000/70,000 = $.70 per share. However, the important thing to notice is that the P/E ratio is $10/$.70 = 14.3, just as it was following the dividend.

This example illustrates the important point that, if there are no imperfections, a cash dividend and a share repurchase are essentially the same thing. This is just another illustration of dividend policy irrelevance when there are no taxes or other imperfections.

Real-World Considerations in a Repurchase

In the real world, there are some accounting differences between a share repurchase and a cash dividend, but the most important difference is in the tax treatment. A repurchase has a significant tax advantage over a cash dividend. A dividend is taxed, and a shareholder has no choice about whether or not to receive the dividend. In a repurchase, a shareholder pays taxes only if (1) the shareholder actually chooses to sell, and (2) the shareholder has a taxable capital gain on the sale.

Normally, at any time, about one-third of TSX listed companies have announced their intentions to repurchase stock through the exchange. This means they plan to buy up to 5 percent of their stock for their treasury. Because of the favourable tax treatment of capital gains, a repurchase is a very sensible alternative to an extra dividend.

Share repurchases can be used to achieve other corporate goals such as altering the firm's capital structure or as a takeover defence. Many firms repurchase shares because management believes the stock is undervalued. This reason for repurchasing is controversial because it contradicts the efficient market hypothesis. However, there is considerable evidence that firms repurchasing shares do experience an increase in shareholder return.[16]

Share Repurchase and EPS

You may read in the popular financial press that a share repurchase is beneficial because earnings per share increase. As we have seen, this will happen. The reason is simply that a share repurchase reduces the number of outstanding shares, but it has no effect on total earnings. As a result, EPS rises.

However, the financial press may place undue emphasis on EPS figures in a repurchase agreement. In our example above, we saw that the value of the stock wasn't affected by the EPS change. In fact, the price/earnings ratio was exactly the same when we compared a cash dividend to a repurchase.

Since the increase in earnings per share is exactly tracked by the increase in the price per share, there is no net effect. Put another way, the increase in EPS is just an accounting adjustment that reflects (correctly) the change in the number of shares outstanding.

In the real world, to the extent that repurchases benefit the firm, we would argue that they do so primarily because of the tax considerations we discussed above.

CONCEPT QUESTIONS

1. Why might a stock repurchase make more sense than an extra cash dividend?

2. Why don't all firms use stock repurchases instead of cash dividends?

stock dividend
Payment made by a firm to its owners in the form of stock, diluting the value of each share outstanding.

stock split
An increase in a firm's shares outstanding without any change in owner's equity.

STOCK DIVIDENDS AND STOCK SPLITS

Another type of dividend is paid out in shares of stock. This type of dividend is called a **stock dividend.** A stock dividend is not a true dividend because it is not paid in cash. The effect of a stock dividend is to increase the number of shares that each owner holds. Since there are more shares outstanding, each is simply worth less.

A stock dividend is commonly expressed as a percentage; for example, a 20 percent stock dividend means that a shareholder receives one new share for every five currently owned (a 20 percent increase). Since every shareholder owns 20 percent more stock, the total number of shares outstanding rises by 20 percent. As we see in a moment, the result would be that each share of stock is worth about 20 percent less.

A **stock split** is essentially the same thing as a stock dividend, except that a split is expressed as a ratio instead of a percentage. When a split is declared, each share is split to create additional shares. For example, Nortel Networks' stock split two-for-one in 2000 and each old share was split into two new shares.

Some Details on Stock Splits and Stock Dividends

Stock splits and stock dividends have essentially the same impacts on the corporation: They increase the number of shares outstanding and reduce the value per share. Also, both options will have a similar impact on future cash dividends. When stocks split, the cash dividend per share is reduced accordingly. The accounting treatment is not the same, however. Under TSX rules, the maximum stock dividend is 25 percent, anything larger is considered a stock split. Further, stock dividends are taxable, but stock splits are not.

---

16 This evidence is in: D. Ikenberry, J. Lakonishok, and T. Vermaelen, "Stock Repurchases in Canada: Performance and Strategic Trading," *Journal of Finance,* October 2000. For a contradictory view, see K. Li and W. McNally, "Information Signalling or Agency Conflicts: What Explains Canadian Open Market Share Repurchases?" *Working Paper,* Wilfrid Laurier University, March 2000.

EXAMPLE OF A STOCK DIVIDEND   The Peterson Company, a consulting firm specializing in difficult accounting problems, has 10,000 shares of stock, each selling at $66. The total market value of the equity is $66 × 10,000 = $660,000. With a 10 percent stock dividend, each stockholder receives one additional share for each 10 presently owned, and the total number of shares outstanding after the dividend is 11,000.

Before the stock dividend, the equity portion of Peterson's balance sheet might look like this:

Common stock (10,000 shares outstanding)	$210,000
Retained earnings	290,000
Total owners' equity	$500,000

The amount of the stock dividend is transferred from retained earnings to common stock. Since 1,000 new shares are issued, the common stock account is increased by $66,000 (1,000 shares at $66 each). Total owners' equity is unaffected by the stock dividend because no cash has come in or out, so retained earnings is reduced by the entire $66,000. The net effect of these machinations is that Peterson's equity accounts now look like this:

Common stock (11,000 shares outstanding)	$276,000
Retained earnings	224,000
Total owners' equity	$500,000

EXAMPLE OF A STOCK SPLIT   A stock split is conceptually similar to a stock dividend, but it is commonly expressed as a ratio. For example, in a three-for-two split, each shareholder receives one additional share of stock for each two held originally, so a three-for-two split amounts to a 50 percent stock dividend. Again, no cash is paid out, and the percentage of the entire firm that each shareholder owns is unaffected.

The accounting treatment of a stock split is a little different (and simpler) from that of a stock dividend. Suppose Peterson decides to declare a two-for-one stock split. The number of shares outstanding doubles to 20,000. The owner's equity after the split is the same as before the split except the new number of shares is noted.

Common stock (20,000 shares outstanding)	$210,000
Retained earnings	290,000
Total owners' equity	$500,000

Value of Stock Splits and Stock Dividends

The laws of logic tell us that stock splits and stock dividends can (1) leave the value of the firm unaffected, (2) increase its value, or (3) decrease its value. Unfortunately, the issues are complex enough that one cannot easily determine which of the three relationships holds.

THE BENCHMARK CASE   A strong case can be made that stock dividends and splits do not change either the wealth of any shareholder or the wealth of the firm as a whole. In our prior example, the equity was worth a total of $660,000. With the stock dividend, the number of shares increased to 11,000, so it seems that each would be worth $660,000/11,000 = $60.

For example, a shareholder who had 100 shares worth $66 each before the dividend would have 110 shares worth $60 each afterwards. The total value of the stock is $6,600 either way; so the stock dividend doesn't really have any economic affect.

With the stock split, there were 20,000 shares outstanding, so each should be worth $660,000/20,000 = $33. In other words, the number of shares doubles and the price halves. From these calculations, it appears that stock dividends and splits are just paper transactions.

Although these results are relatively obvious, there are reasons that are often given to suggest that there may be some benefits to these actions. The typical financial manager is aware of many real-world complexities, and, for that reason, the stock split or stock dividend decision is not treated lightly in practice.

trading range
Price range between highest and lowest prices at which a stock is traded.

TRADING RANGE   Proponents of stock dividends and stock splits frequently argue that a security has a proper **trading range.** When the security is priced above this level, many investors do not have the funds to buy the common trading unit called a *round lot (usually 100 shares).*

Although this argument is a popular one, its validity is questionable for a number of reasons. Mutual funds, pension funds, and other institutions have steadily increased their trading activity since World War II and now handle a sizeable percentage of total trading volume (over half of the trading volume on both the TSX and NYSE). Because these institutions buy and sell in huge amounts, the individual share price is of little concern. Furthermore, we sometimes observe share prices that are quite large without appearing to cause problems.

Finally, there is evidence that stock splits may actually decrease the liquidity of the company's shares. Following a two-for-one split, the number of shares traded should more than double if liquidity is increased by the split. This doesn't appear to happen, and the reverse is sometimes observed.

Regardless of the impact on liquidity, firms do split their stock. Some managers believe that keeping the share price within a range attractive to individual investors helps promote Canadian ownership.

Reverse Splits

reverse split
Procedure where a firm's number of shares outstanding is reduced.

A less frequently encountered financial maneuver is the **reverse split.** In a one-for-three reverse split, each investor exchanges three old shares for one new share. As mentioned previously with reference to stock splits and stock dividends, a case can be made that a reverse split changes nothing substantial about the company.

Given real-world imperfections, three related reasons are cited for reverse splits. First, transaction costs to shareholders may be less after the reverse split. Second, the liquidity and marketability of a company's stock might be improved when its price is raised to the popular trading range. Third, stocks selling below a certain level are not considered respectable, meaning that investors underestimate these firms' earnings, cash flow, growth, and stability. Some financial analysts argue that a reverse split can achieve instant respectability. As with stock splits, none of these reasons is particularly compelling, especially the third one.

There are two other reasons for reverse splits. First, stock exchanges have minimum price per share requirements. A reverse split may bring the stock price up to such a minimum. Second, companies sometimes perform reverse splits and, at the same time, buy out any shareholders who end up with less than a certain number of shares. This second tactic can be abusive if used to force out minority shareholders.

In the aftermath of the tech bubble, a number of technology firms made the decision to undertake reverse splits. For example, Nortel Networks sought shareholder approval in early 2003 for a reverse split between one-for-five and one-for-10 shares, and Call-Net Enterprises conducted a one-for-20 consolidation of shares at about the same time. Nortel management cited three reasons for undertaking a reverse split—to return the company's share price to a level similar to that of other widely owned companies, to meet the investing guidelines for some institutional investors and investment funds, and to reduce trading costs for shareholders.

CONCEPT QUESTIONS

1. What is the effect of a stock split on shareholder wealth?

2. How does the accounting treatment of a stock split differ from that used with a small stock dividend?

17.9 SUMMARY AND CONCLUSIONS

In this chapter, we discussed the types of dividends and how they are paid. We then defined dividend policy and examined whether or not dividend policy matters. Finally, we illustrated how a firm might establish a dividend policy and described an important alternative to cash dividends, a share repurchase.

In covering these subjects, we saw that:

1. Dividend policy is irrelevant when there are no taxes or other imperfections because shareholders can effectively undo the firm's dividend strategy. A shareholder who receives a dividend greater than desired can reinvest the excess. Conversely, the shareholder who receives a dividend that is smaller than desired can sell extra shares of stock.

2. Individual shareholder income taxes and new issue flotation costs are real-world considerations that favour a low-dividend payout. With taxes and new issue costs, the firm should pay out dividends only after all positive NPV projects have been fully financed.

3. There are groups in the economy that may favour a high payout. These include many large institutions such as pension plans. Recognizing that some groups prefer a high payout and some prefer a low payout, the clientele effect supports the idea that dividend policy responds to the needs of shareholders. For example, if 40 percent of the shareholders prefer low dividends and 60 percent of the shareholders prefer high dividends, approximately 40 percent of companies will have a low-dividend payout, while 60 percent will have a high payout. This sharply reduces the impact of any individual firm's dividend policy on its market price.

4. A firm wishing to pursue a strict residual dividend payout will have an unstable dividend. Dividend stability is usually viewed as highly desirable. We therefore discussed a compromise strategy that provides for a stable dividend and appears to be quite similar to the dividend policies many firms follow in practice.

5. A stock repurchase acts much like a cash dividend, but can have a significant tax advantage. Stock repurchases are therefore a very useful part of over-all dividend policy.

To close our discussion of dividends, we emphasize one last time the difference between dividends and dividend policy. Dividends are important, because the value of a share of stock is ultimately determined by the dividends that are paid. What is less clear is whether or not the time pattern of dividends (more now versus more later) matters. This is the dividend policy question, and it is not easy to give a definitive answer to it.

Key Terms

clientele effect (page 527)
date of payment (page 518)
date of record (page 517)
declaration date (page 517)
distribution (page 516)
dividend (page 516)
ex-dividend date (page 517)
homemade dividends (page 520)
information content effect (page 527)

regular cash dividend (page 516)
repurchase (page 534)
residual dividend approach (page 529)
reverse split (page 538)
stock dividend (page 536)
stock split (page 536)
stripped common shares (page 520)
target payout ratio (page 533)
trading range (page 537)

Chapter Review Problems and Self-Test

17.1 Residual Dividend Policy The Rapscallion Corporation practices a strict residual dividend policy and maintains a capital structure of 40 percent debt, 60 percent equity. Earnings for the year are $2,500. What is the maximum amount of capital spending possible without new equity? Suppose that planned investment outlays for the coming year are $3,000. Will Rapscallion be paying a dividend? If so, how much?

17.2 Repurchase versus Cash Dividend Trantor Corporation is deciding whether to pay out $300 in excess cash in the form of an extra dividend or a share repurchase. Current earnings are $1.50 per share and the stock sells for $15. The market value balance sheet before paying out the $300 is as follows:

Market Value Balance Sheet (before paying out excess cash)			
Excess cash	$ 300	$ 400	Debt
Other assets	1,600	1,500	Equity
Total	$1,900	$1,900	

Evaluate the two alternatives for the effect on the price per share of the stock, the EPS, and the P/E ratio.

Answers to Self-Test Problems

17.1   Rapscallion has a debt/equity ratio of .40/.60 = 2/3. If the entire $2,500 in earnings were reinvested, $2,500 × 2/3 = $1,667 in new borrowing would be needed to keep the debt/equity unchanged. Total new financing possible without external equity is thus $2,500 + 1,667 = $4,167.

   If planned outlays are $3,000, this amount can be financed 60 percent with equity. The needed equity is thus $3,000 × .60 = $1,800. This is less than the $2,500 in earnings, so a dividend of $2,500 − 1,800 = $700 would be paid.

17.2   The market value of the equity is $1,500. The price per share is $15, so there are 100 shares outstanding. The cash dividend would amount to $300/100 = $3 per share. When the stock goes ex dividend, the price drops by $3 per share to $12. Put another way, the total assets decrease by $300, so the equity value goes down by this amount to $1,200. With 100 shares, this is $12 per share. After the dividend, EPS is the same, $1.50, but the P/E ratio is $12/1.50 = 8 times.

   With a repurchase, $300/15 = 20 shares would be bought up, leaving 80. The equity again is worth $1,200 total. With 80 shares, this is $1,200/80 = $15 per share, so the price doesn't change. Total earnings for Trantor must be $1.5 × 100 = $150. After the repurchase, EPS is higher at $150/80 = $1.875. The P/E ratio, however, is still $15/1.875 = 8 times.

Concepts Review and Critical Thinking Questions

1.   How is it possible that dividends are so important, but, at the same time, dividend policy could be irrelevant?

2.   What is the impact of a stock repurchase on a company's debt ratio? Does this suggest another use for excess cash?

3.   What is the chief drawback to a strict residual dividend policy? Why is this a problem? How does a compromise policy work? How does it differ from a strict residual policy?

4.   On Tuesday, December 8, Hometown Power Co.'s board of directors declares a dividend of 75 cents per share payable on Wednesday, January 17, to shareholders of record as of Wednesday, January 3. When is the ex-dividend date? If a shareholder buys stock before that date, who gets the dividends on those shares, the buyer or the seller?

5.   Some corporations, like one British company that offers its large shareholders free crematorium use, pay dividends in kind (that is, offer their services to shareholders at below-market cost). Should mutual funds invest in stocks that pay these dividends in kind? (The fundholders do not receive these services.)

6.   If increases in dividends tend to be followed by (immediate) increases in share prices, how can it be said that dividend policy is irrelevant?

7.   Last month, East Coast Power Company, which had been having trouble with cost overruns on a nuclear power plant that it had been building, announced that it was "temporarily suspending payments due to the cash flow crunch associated with its investment program." The company's stock price dropped from $28.50 to $25 when this announcement was made. How would you interpret this change in the stock price (that is, what would you say caused it)?

8.   The DRK Corporation has recently developed a dividend reinvestment plan, or DRIP. The plan allows investors to reinvest cash dividends automatically in DRK in exchange for new shares of stock. Over time, investors in DRK will be able to build their holdings by reinvesting dividends to purchase additional shares of the company.

   Over 1,000 companies offer dividend reinvestment plans. Most companies with DRIPs charge no brokerage or service fees. In fact, the shares of DRK will be purchased at a 10 percent discount from the market price.

   A consultant for DRK estimates that about 75 percent of DRK's shareholders will take part in this plan. This is somewhat higher than the average.

   Evaluate DRK's dividend reinvestment plan. Will it increase shareholder wealth? Discuss the advantages and disadvantages involved here.

9.   For initial public offerings of common stock, 1993 was a very big year, with over $43 billion raised by the process. Relatively few of the firms involved paid cash dividends. Why do you think that most chose not to pay cash dividends?

10.   York University pays no taxes on its capital gains or on its dividend income and interest income. Would it be irrational to find low-dividend, high-growth stocks in its portfolio? Would it be irrational to find preferred shares in its portfolio? Explain.

Questions and Problems

Basic
(Questions 1–13)

1.   **Dividends and Taxes**   Lee Ann, Inc., has declared a $6.00 per share dividend. Suppose capital gains are not taxed, but dividends are taxed at 15 percent. Lee Ann sells for $80 per share, and the stock is about to go ex dividend. What do you think the ex-dividend price will be?

2.   **Stock Dividends**   The owners' equity accounts for Hexagon International are shown here:

Common stock ($1 par value)	$ 10,000
Capital surplus	180,000
Retained earnings	586,500
Total owners' equity	$776,500

Basic
(continued)

a. If Hexagon stock currently sells for $25 per share and a 10 percent stock dividend is declared, how many new shares will be distributed? Show how the equity accounts would change.

b. If Hexagon declared a 25 percent stock dividend, how would the accounts change?

3. **Stock Splits** For the company in Problem 2, show how the equity accounts will change if:

a. Hexagon declares a four-for-one stock split. How many shares are outstanding now? What is the new par value per share?

b. Hexagon declares a one-for-five reverse stock split. How many shares are outstanding now? What is the new par value per share?

4. **Stock Splits and Stock Dividends** Rooster Rocks Corporation (RRC) currently has 150,000 shares of stock outstanding that sell for $65 per share. Assuming no market imperfections or tax effects exist, what will the share price be after:

a. RRC has a five-for-three stock split?

b. RRC has a 15 percent stock dividend?

c. RRC has a 42.5 percent stock dividend?

d. RRC has a four-for-seven reverse stock split?

e. Determine the new number of shares outstanding in parts (a) through (d).

5. **Regular Dividends** The balance sheet for Cherry Pie Corp. is shown here in market value terms. There are 5,000 shares of stock outstanding.

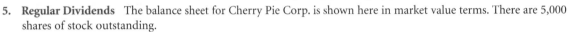

Market Value Balance Sheet			
Cash	$ 20,000	Debt	$175,000
Fixed assets	155,000		
Total	$175,000	Total	$175,000

The company has declared a dividend of $1.50 per share. The stock goes ex dividend tomorrow. Ignoring any tax effects, what is the stock selling for today? What will it sell for tomorrow? What will the balance sheet look like after the dividends are paid?

6. **Share Repurchase** In the previous problem, suppose Cherry Pie has announced it is going to repurchase $4,025 worth of stock. What effect will this transaction have on the equity of the firm? How many shares will be outstanding? What will the price per share be after the repurchase? Ignoring tax effects, show how the share repurchase is effectively the same as a cash dividend.

7. **Stock Dividends** The market value balance sheet for Outbox Manufacturing is shown here. Outbox has declared a 25 percent stock dividend. The stock goes ex dividend tomorrow (the chronology for a stock dividend is similar to that for a cash dividend). There are 15,000 shares of stock outstanding. What will the ex dividend price be?

Market Value Balance Sheet			
Cash	$190,000	Debt	$160,000
Fixed assets	330,000	Equity	360,000
Total	$520,000	Total	$520,000

8. **Stock Dividends** The company with the common equity accounts shown here has declared a 12 percent stock dividend at a time when the market value of its stock is $20 per share. What effects on the equity accounts will the distribution of the stock dividend have?

Common stock ($1 par value)	$ 350,000
Retained earnings	4,650,000
Total owners' equity	$5,000,000

9. **Stock Splits** In the previous problem, suppose the company instead decides on a five-for-one stock split. The firm's 70-cent per share cash dividend on the new (post-split) shares represents an increase of 10 percent over last year's dividend on the pre-split stock. What effect does this have on the equity accounts? What was last year's dividend per share?

10. **Residual Dividend Policy** Soprano, Inc., a litter recycling company, uses a residual dividend policy. A debt-equity ratio of .80 is considered optimal. Earnings for the period just ended were $1,200, and a dividend of $480 was declared. How much in new debt was borrowed? What were total capital outlays?

11. **Residual Dividend Policy** Worthington Corporation has declared an annual dividend of $0.80 per share. For the year just ended, earnings were $7 per share.

a. What is Worthington's payout ratio?

Basic
(continued)

b. Suppose Worthington has seven million shares outstanding. Borrowing for the coming year is planned at $18 million. What are planned investment outlays assuming a residual dividend policy? What target capital structure is implicit in these calculations?

12. **Residual Dividend Policy** Red Zeppelin Corporation follows a strict residual dividend policy. Its debt-equity ratio is 3.

   a. If earnings for the year are $180,000, what is the maximum amount of capital spending possible with no new equity?

   b. If planned investment outlays for the coming year are $760,000, will Red Zeppelin pay a dividend? If so, how much?

   c. Does Red Zeppelin maintain a constant dividend payout? Why or why not?

13. **Residual Dividend Policy** Preti Rock (PR), Inc., predicts that earnings in the coming year will be $56 million. There are 12 million shares, and PR maintains a debt-equity ratio of 2.

   a. Calculate the maximum investment funds available without issuing new equity and the increase in borrowing that goes along with it.

   b. Suppose the firm uses a residual dividend policy. Planned capital expenditures total $72 million. Based on this information, what will the dividend per share be?

   c. In part (b), how much borrowing will take place? What is the addition to retained earnings?

   d. Suppose PR plans no capital outlays for the coming year. What will the dividend be under a residual policy? What will new borrowing be?

Intermediate
(Questions
14–16)

14. **Homemade Dividends** You own 1,000 shares of stock in Avondale Corporation. You will receive a 70-cent per share dividend in one year. In two years, Avondale will pay a liquidating dividend of $40 per share. The required return on Avondale stock is 15 percent. What is the current share price of your stock (ignoring taxes)? If you would rather have equal dividends in each of the next two years, show how you can accomplish this by creating homemade dividends. Hint: Dividends will be in the form of an annuity.

15. **Homemade Dividends** In the previous problem, suppose you want only $200 total in dividends the first year. What will your homemade dividend be in two years?

16. **Stock Repurchase** Flychucker Corporation is evaluating an extra dividend versus a share repurchase. In either case, $5,000 would be spent. Current earnings are $0.95 per share, and the stock currently sells for $40 per share. There are 200 shares outstanding. Ignore taxes and other imperfections in answering the first two questions.

   a. Evaluate the two alternatives in terms of the effect on the price per share of the stock and shareholder wealth.

   b. What will be the effect on Flychucker's EPS and PE ratio under the two different scenarios?

   c. In the real world, which of these actions would you recommend? Why?

Challenge
(Questions
17–19)

17. **Expected Return, Dividends, and Taxes** The Gecko Company and the Gordon Company are two firms whose business risk is the same but that have different dividend policies. Gecko pays no dividend, whereas Gordon has an expected dividend yield of 6 percent. Suppose the capital gains tax rate is zero, whereas the income tax rate is 35 percent. Gecko has an expected earnings growth rate of 15 percent annually, and its stock price is expected to grow at this same rate. If the aftertax expected returns on the two stocks are equal (because they are in the same risk class), what is the pretax required return on Gordon's stock?

18. **Dividends and Taxes** As discussed in the text, in the absence of market imperfections and tax effects, we would expect the share price to decline by the amount of the dividend payment when the stock goes ex dividend. Once we consider the role of taxes, however, this is not necessarily true. One model has been proposed that incorporates tax effects into determining the ex-dividend price:[17]

   $$(P_0 - P_X)/D = (1 - T_P)/(1 - T_G)$$

   where P0 is the price just before the stock goes ex, PX is the ex-dividend share price, D is the amount of the dividend per share, TP is the relevant marginal personal tax rate on dividends, and TG is the effective marginal tax rate on capital gains.

   a. If $T_P = T_G = 0$, how much will the share price fall when the stock goes ex?

   b. If $T_P = 30$ percent and $T_G = 0$, how much will the share price fall?

   c. If $T_P = 25$ percent and $T_G = 20$ percent, how much will the share price fall?

   d. Suppose the only owners of stock are corporations. Corporations get 100% percent exemption from taxation on the dividend income they receive, but they do not get such an exemption on capital gains. If the corporation's income and capital gains tax rates are both 35 percent, what does this model predict the ex-dividend share price will be?

   e. What does this problem tell you about real-world tax considerations and the dividend policy of the firm?

---

17 Elton and M. Gruber, "Marginal Stockholder Tax Rates and the Clientele Effect," *Review of Economics and Statistics* 52 (February 1970).

Challenge **19.** **Residual Dividends** BelTech Corporation is debating between one of two projects. The chosen project would maxi-
(continued) mize the dividends paid out to shareholders. The company currently has a debt-to-equity ratio of 0.40 and retained
earnings of $400,000. The chart below shows the details of each project.

	Project 1	Project 2
Project Costs	$100,000	$150,000
IRR	9%	10.5%
Years	2	2

Calculate the residual dividends for both projects. Which project maximizes the residual dividends for the shareholders?

MINI CASE

Cost of Capital and Dividend Policy for Hubbard Computer, Inc.

You have recently been hired by Hubbard Computer, Inc. (HCI), in its relatively new treasury management department. HCI was founded eight years ago in Edmonton, Alberta, by Bill Hubbard and currently operates 74 stores across Canada. The company is privately owned by Bill and his family; it had sales of $97 million last year.

HCI primarily sells to customers who shop in the stores. Customers come to the store and talk with a sales representative. The sales representative assists the customer in determining the type of computer and peripherals that will meet the individual customer's computing needs. After the order is taken, the customer pays for the order immediately, and a computer is custom-made to fill the order. Delivery of the computer averages within 15 days, and it is guaranteed within 30 days.

HCI's growth to date has come from its profits. When the company had sufficient capital, it would open a new store. Other than scouting locations, relatively little formal analysis has been used in its capital budgeting process. Bill Hubbard has just read about capital budgeting techniques and has come to you for help. For starters, the company has never attempted to determine its cost of capital, and Bill would like you to perform that analysis. Since the company is privately owned, it is difficult to determine the cost of equity for the company. Bill wants you to use the pure play approach to estimating the cost of capital for HCI, and he has chosen Dell as a representative company. The following steps will enable you to calculate this estimate.

1. Most publicly traded corporations are required to submit quarterly and annual reports detailing the financial operations of the company over the past quarter or year. Canadian corporate filings are available at *www.sedar.com*. Since Dell Computer is an American company, the company's corporate filings can be found on the SEC website, at *www.sec.gov*. Follow the "Search for Company Filings" link, the "Companies & Other Files" link, enter "Dell Computer," and search for SEC filings made by Dell.

Find the most recent quarterly or annual report and download the form. Look on the balance sheet to find the book value of debt and the book value of equity. If you look farther down the report, you should find a section titled "Long-term Debt and Interest Rate Risk Management" that will provide a breakdown of Dell's long-term debt.

2. To estimate the cost of equity for Dell, go to finance.yahoo.com and enter the ticker symbol DELL. Follow the links to answer the following questions: What is the most recent stock price listed for Dell? What is the market value of equity, or market capitalization? How many shares of stock does Dell have outstanding? What is the most recent annual dividend? Can you use the dividend discount model in this case? What is the beta for Dell? Now go back to *www.bankofcanada.ca* and follow the "Interest Rates" link. What is the yield on a 3-month Treasury bill? Using the historical market risk premium, what is the cost of equity for Dell using CAPM?

3. You now need to calculate the cost of debt for Dell. Although it is much more reliable and current to use market values when calculating the cost of debt, this problem asks for the book values for simplicity. Go to *www.dell.com* and download the most recent annual report. What is the weighted average cost of debt for Dell, using the book value?

4. You now have all the necessary information to calculate the weighted average cost of capital for Dell. Calculate the weighted average cost of capital for Dell, assuming Dell has a 37 percent marginal tax rate.

5. You used Dell as a pure play company to estimate the cost of capital for HCI. Are there any potential problems with this approach in this situation?

6. If Bill Hubbard decides to finance an expansion by taking on $50 million in debt, how would this change in capital structure affect the cost of capital?

7. If Bill Hubbard decides that he no longer wants to grow the company using profits and would like to pay out any profits as dividend, how would this change in dividend policy affect the cost of capital?

S&P Problem

1. **Dividend Payouts** Use the annual financial statements for Enbridge Inc. (ENB), Celestica Inc. (CLS), and the Nortel Networks Corp. (NT) to find the dividend payout ratio for each company for the last three years. Why would these companies pay out a different percentage of income as dividends? Is there anything unusual about the dividends paid by Nortel? How is this possible?

Internet Application Questions

1. Buying back a company's own shares is an alternative way of distributing corporate assets. Share buybacks involve both capital structure and dividend policy. In fact, share repurchases have overtaken dividends as the most popular means of cash payouts by corporations in the U.S. The following link explains the advantages of share repurchases, and also cautions against cases where repurchases have not or will not work.

   www.fool.com/EveningNews/FOTH/1998/foth981019.htm

   Discuss the following questions after reading the link above.

   a. Show that share repurchases and dividend payments are equivalent, in the sense that they do not affect relative corporate value.

   b. The link above argues that Circus Circus (NYSE: CIR) and Trump (NYSE: DJT) should have avoided buying back their shares. Do you agree with the admonition that highly leveraged firms should not use share buybacks? What are you assuming about dividend policy when you answer this question?

   c. The link also contends that share buybacks enhance shareholder value when done properly and cites three companies as virtuous examples: Coke (NYSE: KO), Intel (Nasdaq: INTC), and Chrysler (NYSE: C). Keeping in mind that the article was written in October 1998, what lessons do you draw from the successful repurchase strategies of these firms?

2. Dividend reinvestment plans (DRIPs) permit shareholders to automatically reinvest cash dividends in the company. To find out more about DRIPs go to www.fool.com, follow the "Fool's School" link and then the "DRIP Investing" link. What are the advantages that Motley Fool lists for DRIPs? What are the different types of DRIPs? What is a Direct Purchase Plan? How does a Direct Purchase Plan differ from a DRIP?

3. Information on recently announced dividends and stock splits for the U.S. markets can be found at www.earnings.com. How many companies went "ex" today? What is the largest declared dividend? Are there any reverse splits listed? What is the largest split in terms of the number of shares?

4. How many times has Royal Bank of Canada stock split? Go to the Web page www.rbc.com and visit the "Investor Relations" section. You will find share information, including dates of stock splits. Were there any splits accomplished in unique ways? When did the splits occur?

Suggested Readings

Our dividend irrelevance argument is based on a classic article:
   Miller, M. H., and F. Modigliani. "Dividend Policy, Growth and the Valuation of Shares." *Journal of Business* 34, (October 1961).

Higgins describes the residual dividend approach in:
   Higgins, R. C. "The Corporate Dividend-Saving Decision." *Journal of Financial and Quantitative Analysis* 7, (March 1972).

The following examine taxes and dividends in Canada:
   Adjaoud, F., and D. Zeghal. "Taxation and Dividend Policy in Canada: New Evidence." *FINECO* (2nd Semester) 1993, pp. 141–54.
   Amoako-Adu, B., M. Rashid, and M. Stebbins. "Capital Gains Tax and Equity Values: Empirical Test of Stock Price Reaction to the Introduction and Reduction of Capital Gains Tax Exemption." *Journal of Banking and Finance* 16 (1992), pp. 275–87.
   Booth, L. D., and D. J. Johnston. "The Ex-Dividend Day Behavior of Canadian Stock Prices: Tax Changes and Clientele Effects." *Journal of Finance* 39 (June 1984).

A relevant article on share repurchases in Canada is:
   Ikenberry, D., J. Lakonishok, and T. Vermaelen. "Stock Repurchases in Canada: Performance and Strategic Trading." *Journal of Finance*, October 2000.

CHAPTER 18

Short-Term Finance and Planning

In 2005, Home Depot continued expansion of its business, opening 20 new stores in Canada and 10 new stores in Mexico, while overall sales increased by 11.5 percent. During the same year, cash and short-term investments decreased by $1.4 billion. On the other hand, short-term debt increased by $900 million, which is a sizeable portion of the $3.9 billion that Home Depot invested back into the company to help finance expansion, rapid growth, and rising inventory levels.

In May 2005, Home Depot announced that it would be upgrading its current logistics platform and inventory and supply chain management systems to compete more effectively with other big players encroaching on its territory.

As this chapter will illustrate, choosing the best financing policies to effectively manage growth and inventory levels is an important element of short-term financial management, and companies like Home Depot pay close attention to these decisions.

www.homedepot.ca
Interested in a career in short-term finance? Visit the Treasury Management Association of Canada at
www.tmac.ca

TO THIS POINT, we have described many of the decisions of long-term finance, for example, capital budgeting, dividend policy, and financial structure. In this chapter, we begin to discuss short-term finance. Short-term finance is primarily concerned with the analysis of decisions that affect current assets and current liabilities.

Financial managers spend major blocks of time daily on short-term financial management. What types of questions fall under the general heading of short-term finance? To name just a very few:

1. What is a reasonable level of cash to keep on hand (in a bank) to pay bills?
2. How much should the firm borrow short-term?
3. How much credit should be extended to customers?
4. How much inventory should the firm carry?

Answering these questions is central to the financial manager's job. Short-term financial management is often an important part of entry-level jobs for new finance graduates.[1]

Frequently, the term *net working capital* is associated with short-term financial decision making. As we describe in Chapter 2 and elsewhere, net working capital is the difference between current assets and current liabilities. Often, short-term financial management is called *working capital management.* These terms mean the same thing.

---

1 N. C. Hill and W. L. Sartoris, *Short-Term Financial Management* (New York: Macmillan, 1988), p. 3.

There is no universally accepted definition of short-term finance. The most important difference between short-term and long-term finance is the timing of cash flows. Short-term financial decisions typically involve cash inflows and outflows that occur within a year or less. For example, short-term financial decisions are involved when a firm orders raw materials, pays in cash, and anticipates selling finished goods in one year for cash. In contrast, long-term financial decisions are involved when a firm purchases a special machine that reduces operating costs over, say, the next five years.

This chapter introduces the basic elements of short-term financial decisions. We begin by discussing the short-term operating activities of the firm. We then identify some alternative short-term financial policies. Finally, we outline the basic elements in a short-term financial plan and describe short-term financing instruments.

18.1 TRACING CASH AND NET WORKING CAPITAL

In this section, we examine the components of cash and net working capital as they change from one year to the next. We have already discussed various aspects of this subject in Chapters 2, 3, and 4. We briefly review some of that discussion as it relates to short-term financing decisions. Our goal is to describe the short-term operating activities of the firm and their impact on cash and working capital.

To begin, recall that *current assets* are cash and other assets expected to convert to cash within the year. Current assets are presented in the balance sheet in order of their accounting liquidity—the ease with which they can be converted to cash and the time it takes to do so. Four of the most important items found in the current asset section of a balance sheet are cash, marketable securities (or cash equivalents), accounts receivable, and inventories.

Analogous to their investment in current assets, firms use several kinds of short-term debt, called *current liabilities*. Current liabilities are obligations expected to require cash payment within one year (or within the operating period if it is different from one year). The three major items found as current liabilities are accounts payable; expenses payable, including accrued wages and taxes; and notes payable.

Because we want to focus on changes in cash, we start by defining cash in terms of the other elements of the balance sheet. This lets us isolate the cash account and explore the impact on cash from the firm's operating and financing decisions. The basic balance sheet identity can be written as:

$$\text{Net working capital} + \text{Fixed assets} = \text{Long-term debt} + \text{Equity} \qquad \text{[18.1]}$$

Net working capital is cash plus other current assets less current liabilities; that is,

$$\text{Net working capital} = (\text{Cash} + \text{Other current assets}) \qquad \text{[18.2]}$$
$$- \text{Current liabilities}$$

If we substitute this for net working capital in the basic balance sheet identity and rearrange things a bit, cash is:

$$\text{Cash} = \text{Long-term debt} + \text{Equity} + \text{Current liabilities} \qquad \text{[18.3]}$$
$$- \text{Current assets (other than cash)} - \text{Fixed assets}$$

This tells us in general terms that some activities naturally increase cash and some activities decrease it. We can list these along with an example of each as follows:

Activities that Increase Cash

> Increasing long-term debt (borrowing long-term).
> Increasing equity (selling some stock).
> Increasing current liabilities (getting a 90-day loan).
> Decreasing current assets other than cash (selling some inventory for cash).
> Decreasing fixed assets (selling some property).

Activities that Decrease Cash

> Decreasing long-term debt (paying off a long-term debt).
>
> Decreasing equity (repurchasing some stock).
>
> Decreasing current liabilities (paying off a 90-day loan).
>
> Increasing current assets other than cash (buying some inventory for cash).
>
> Increasing fixed assets (buying some property).

Notice that our two lists are exact opposites. For example, floating a long-term bond issue increases cash (at least until the money is spent). Paying off a long-term bond issue decreases cash.

As we discussed in Chapter 3, those activities that increase cash are sources of cash. Those activities that decrease cash are uses of cash. Looking back at our list, sources of cash always involve increasing a liability (or equity) account or decreasing an asset account. This makes sense because increasing a liability means we have raised money by borrowing it or by selling an ownership interest in the firm. A decrease in an asset means we have sold or otherwise liquidated an asset. In either case, there is a cash inflow.

Uses of cash are just the reverse. A use of cash involves decreasing a liability by paying it off, perhaps, or an increase in assets from purchasing something. Both of these activities require that the firm spend some cash.

EXAMPLE 18.1: Sources and Uses

Here is a quick check of your understanding of sources and uses: If accounts payable goes up by $100, is this a source or use? If accounts receivable goes up by $100, is this a source or use?

Accounts payable are what we owe our suppliers. This is a short-term debt. If it rises by $100, we have effectively borrowed the money, so this is a source of cash. Receivables is what our customers owe to us, so an increase of $100 means that we loaned the money; this is a use of cash.

CONCEPT QUESTIONS

1. What is the difference between net working capital and cash?

2. Will net working capital always increase when cash increases?

3. List five potential uses of cash.

4. List five potential sources of cash.

 **18.2**

THE OPERATING CYCLE AND THE CASH CYCLE

The primary concern in short-term finance is the firm's short-run operating and financing activities. For a typical manufacturing firm, these short-run activities might consist of the following sequence of events and decisions:

Events	Decisions
1. Buying raw materials	1. How much inventory to order?
2. Paying cash	2. Borrow or draw down cash balance?
3. Manufacturing the product	3. What choice of production technology?
4. Selling the product	4. Should credit be extended to a particular customer?
5. Collecting cash	5. How to collect?

These activities create patterns of cash inflows and cash outflows. These cash flows are both unsynchronized and uncertain. They are unsynchronized because, for example, the payment of cash for raw materials does not happen at the same time as the receipt of cash from selling the product. They are uncertain because future sales and costs cannot be predicted precisely.

Small businesses in particular must pay attention to the timing of inflows and outflows. For example, Earthly Elements, a maker of dried floral gifts and accessories, was formed in March 1993. The owners of the firm rejoiced when they received a $10,000 order from a national home shopping service in November 1993. The order represented 20 percent of total orders for the year and was expected to give a big boost to the young company. Unfortunately, it cost Earthly Elements 25 percent more than expected to fill the order. Then, its customer was slow to pay. By the end of February 1994, the payment was 30 days late, and the company was running out of cash. By the time the payment was received in April, the firm had already closed its doors in March, a victim of the cash cycle.

Defining the Operating and Cash Cycles

We can start with a simple case. One day, call it Day 0, you purchase $1,000 worth of inventory on credit. You pay the bill 30 days later, and, after 30 more days, someone buys the $1,000 in inventory for $1,400. Your buyer does not actually pay for another 45 days. We can summarize these events chronologically as follows:

Day	Activity	Cash effect
0	Acquire inventory	none
30	Pay for inventory	–$1,000
60	Sell inventory on credit	none
105	Collect on sale	+$1,400

THE OPERATING CYCLE   There are several things to notice in our example: First, the entire cycle, from the time we acquire some inventory to the time we collect the cash, takes 105 days. This is called the **operating cycle.**

As we illustrate, the operating cycle is the length of time it takes to acquire inventory, sell it, and collect for it. This cycle has two distinct components. The first part is the time it takes to acquire and sell the inventory. This 60-day span (in our example) is called the **inventory period.** The second part is the time it takes to collect on the sale, 45 days in our example. This is called the **accounts receivable period.**

Based on our definitions, the operating cycle is obviously just the sum of the inventory and receivables periods:

$$\text{Operating cycle} = \text{Inventory period} + \text{Accounts receivable period} \qquad \text{[18.4]}$$
$$105 \text{ days} = 60 \text{ days} + 45 \text{ days}$$

What the operating cycle describes is how a product moves through the current asset accounts. It begins life as inventory, it is converted to a receivable when it is sold, and it is finally converted to cash when we collect from the sale. Notice that, at each step, the asset is moving closer to cash.

THE CASH CYCLE   The second thing to notice is that the cash flows and other events that occur are not synchronized. For example, we didn't actually pay for the inventory until 30 days after we acquired it. This 30-day period is called the **accounts payable period.** Next, we spend cash on Day 30, but we don't collect until Day 105. Somehow or the other, we have to arrange to finance the $1,000 for $105 - 30 = 75$ days. This period is called the **cash cycle.**

The cash cycle, therefore, is the number of days that pass until we collect the cash from a sale, measured from when we actually pay for the inventory. Notice that, based on our definitions, the cash cycle is the difference between the operating cycle and the accounts payable period:

$$\text{Cash cycle} = \text{Operating cycle} - \text{Accounts payable period} \qquad \text{[18.5]}$$
$$75 \text{ days} = 105 \text{ days} - 30 \text{ days}$$

Figure 18.1 depicts the short-term operating activities and cash flows for a typical manufacturing firm by looking at the cash flow time line. As shown, the **cash flow time line** is made up of the operating cycle and the cash cycle. In Figure 18.1, the need for short-term financial management is suggested by the gap between the cash inflows and cash outflows. This is related to the length of the operating cycle and accounts payable period.

operating cycle
The time period between the acquisition of inventory and when cash is collected from receivables.

inventory period
The time it takes to acquire and sell inventory.

accounts receivable period
The time between sale of inventory and collection of the receivable.

accounts payable period
The time between receipt of inventory and payment for it.

cash cycle
The time between cash disbursement and cash collection.

cash flow time line
Graphical representation of the operating cycle and the cash cycle.

The gap between short-term inflows and outflows can be filled either by borrowing or by holding a liquidity reserve in the form of cash or marketable securities. Alternatively, the gap can be shortened by changing the inventory, receivable, and payable periods. These are all managerial options that we discuss in this and subsequent chapters.

THE OPERATING CYCLE AND THE FIRM'S ORGANIZATION CHART   Before we look at detailed examples of operating and cash cycles, realism dictates a look at the people involved in implementing a firm's policies. This is important because short-term financial management in a large corporation involves non-financial managers as well and there is potential for conflict as each manager looks at only part of the picture.[2] As you can see in Table 18.1,

---

FIGURE 18.1

Cash flow time line and the short-term operating activities of a typical manufacturing firm

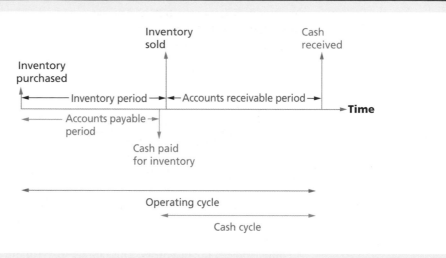

The operating cycle is the time period from inventory purchase until the receipt of cash. (Sometimes the operating cycle includes the time from placement of the order until arrival of the stock.) The cash cycle is the time period from when cash is paid out to when cash is received.

TABLE 18.1
Managers who deal with short-term financial problems

Title	Short-Term Financial Management Duties	Assets/Liabilities Influenced
Cash manager	Collection, concentration, disbursement; short-term investment; short-term borrowing; banking relations	Cash, marketable securities, short-term loans
Credit manager	Monitoring and control of accounts receivable; credit policy decisions	Accounts receivable
Marketing manager	Credit policy decisions	Accounts receivable
Purchasing manager	Decisions on purchase, suppliers; may negotiate payment terms	Inventory, accounts payable
Production manager	Setting of production schedules and materials requirements	Inventory, accounts payable
Payables manager	Decisions on payment policies and on whether to take discounts	Accounts payable
Controller	Accounting information on cash flows; reconciliation of accounts payable; application of payments to accounts receivable	Accounts receivable, accounts payable

Source: Ned C. Hill and William L. Sartoris, *Short-Term Financial Management*, 2d ed. (New York: Macmillan Publishing Company, 1992), p. 15.

---

2 This discussion draws on N.C. Hill and W.L. Sartoris, *Short-Term Financial Management* (New York: Macmillan, 1988), chap. 1.

selling on credit involves the credit manager, the marketing manager, and the controller. Of these three, only two are responsible to the vice president of finance, as the marketing function has its own vice president in most large corporations. If the marketing function is trying to land a new account, it may seek more liberal credit terms as an inducement. Since this may increase the firm's investment in receivables or its exposure to the bad debt risk, conflict may result. To resolve such conflict, the firm must look beyond personalities to the ultimate impact on shareholder wealth.

Calculating the Operating and Cash Cycles

In our example, the lengths of time that made up the different periods were obvious. When all we have is financial statement information, however, we have to do a little more work. We illustrate these calculations next.

To begin, we need to determine various things like how long it takes, on average, to sell inventory and how long it takes, on average, to collect. We start by gathering some balance sheet information such as the following (in $ thousands):

Item	Beginning	Ending	Average
Inventory	$2,000	$3,000	$2,500
Accounts receivable	1,600	2,000	1,800
Accounts payable	750	1,000	875

Also, from the most recent income statement, we might have the following figures (in $ thousands):

Net sales	$11,500
Cost of goods sold	8,200

We now need to calculate some financial ratios. We discussed these in some detail in Chapter 3; here we just define them and use them as needed.

THE OPERATING CYCLE   First, we need the inventory period. We spent $8.2 million on inventory (our cost of goods sold). Our average inventory was $2.5 million. We thus turned our inventory over 8.2/2.5 times during the year:[3]

$$\text{Inventory turnover} = \text{Cost of goods sold/Average inventory}$$
$$= \$8.2 \text{ million}/\$2.5 \text{ million} = 3.28 \text{ times}$$

Loosely speaking, this tells us that we bought and sold off our inventory 3.28 times during the year. This means that, on average, we held our inventory for:

$$\text{Inventory period} = 365 \text{ days/Inventory turnover}$$
$$= 365/3.28 = 111.3 \text{ days}$$

So the inventory period is about 111 days. On average, in other words, inventory sat for about 111 days before it was sold.

Similarly, receivables averaged $1.8 million, and sales were $11.5 million. Assuming that all sales were credit sales, the receivables turnover is:[4]

$$\text{Receivables turnover} = \text{Credit sales/Average accounts receivable}$$
$$= \$11.5 \text{ million}/\$1.8 \text{ million} = 6.4 \text{ times}$$

If we turn over our receivables 6.4 times, then the receivables period is:

$$\text{Receivables period} = 365 \text{ days/Receivables turnover}$$
$$= 365/6.4 = 57 \text{ days}$$

---

3 Notice that we have used the cost of goods sold in calculating inventory turnover. Sales is sometimes used instead. Also, rather than average inventory, ending inventory is often used. See Chapter 3 for some examples.

4 If less than 100 percent of our sales are credit sales, we would just need a little more information, namely, credit sales for the year. See Chapter 3 for more discussion of this measure.

The receivables period is also called the *days' sales in receivables* or the *average collection period*. Whatever it is called, it tells us that our customers took an average of 57 days to pay.

The operating cycle is the sum of the inventory and receivables periods:

$$\text{Operating cycle} = \text{Inventory period} + \text{Accounts receivables period}$$
$$= 111 \text{ days} + 57 \text{ days} = 168 \text{ days}$$

This tells us that, on average, 168 days elapse between the time we acquire inventory, sell it, and collect for the sale.

THE CASH CYCLE   We now need the payables period. From the information just given, average payables were $875,000, and cost of goods sold was again $8.2 million. Our payables turnover is thus:

$$\text{Payables turnover} = \text{Cost of goods sold/Average payables}$$
$$= \$8.2 \text{ million}/\$.875 \text{ million} = 9.4 \text{ times}$$

The payables period is:

$$\text{Payables period} = 365 \text{ days/Payables turnover}$$
$$= 365/9.4 = 39 \text{ days}$$

Thus, we took an average of 39 days to pay our bills.

Finally, the cash cycle is the difference between the operating cycle and the payables period:

$$\text{Cash cycle} = \text{Operating cycle} - \text{Accounts payables period}$$
$$= 168 \text{ days} - 39 \text{ days} = 129 \text{ days}$$

So, on average, there is a 129-day delay from the time we pay for merchandise and the time we collect on the sales.

Interpreting the Cash Cycle

Our examples show how the cash cycle depends on the inventory, receivables, and payables periods. Taken one at a time, the cash cycle increases as the inventory and receivables periods get longer. It decreases if the company is able to stall payment of payables, lengthening the payables period. Suppose a firm could purchase inventory, sell its product, collect receivables (perhaps selling for cash) and then pay suppliers all on the same day. This firm would have a cash cycle of zero days.

Some firms may meet this description but it is hard to think of many examples (gas retailing or dry cleaners might meet the description). Most firms have a positive cash cycle. Such firms require some additional financing for inventories and receivables. The longer the cash cycle, the

---

EXAMPLE 18.2: The Operating and Cash Cycles

You have collected the following information for the Slowpay Company.

Item	Beginning	Ending
Inventory	$5,000	$7,000
Accounts receivable	1,600	2,400
Accounts payable	2,700	4,800

Sales for the year just ended were $50,000, and cost of goods sold was $30,000. How long does it take Slowpay to collect on its receivables? How long does merchandise stay around before it is sold? How long does Slowpay take to pay its bills? We can first calculate the three turnover ratios:

Inventory turnover = $30,000/$6,000 = 5 times
Receivables turnover = $50,000/$2,000 = 25 times

Payables turnover = $30,000/$3,750 = 8 times

We use these to get the various periods:

Inventory period = 365/5 = 73 days
Receivables period = 365/25 = 14.6 days
Payables period = 365/8 = 45.6 days

All told, Slowpay collects on a sale in 14.6 days, inventory sits around for 73 days, and bills get paid after about 46 days. The operating cycle here is the sum of the inventory and receivables: 73 + 14.6 = 87.6 days. The cash cycle is the difference between the operating cycle and the payables period: 87.6 − 45.6 = 42 days.

more financing is required, other things being equal. You could also think of this concept in terms of liquidity. All firms need liquidity to operate. That means that a firm must create liquidity quickly (as in the case of a company with a short cash cycle), or it must invest in working capital on its balance sheet. Since bankers are conservative and dislike surprises, they monitor the firm's cash cycle. A lengthening cycle may indicate obsolete, unsalable inventory or problems in collecting receivables. Unless these problems are detected and solved, the firm may require emergency financing or face insolvency.

Our calculations of the cash cycle used financial ratios introduced in Chapter 3. We can use some other ratio relationships from Chapter 3 to see how the cash cycle relates to profitability and sustainable growth. A good place to start is with the Du Pont equation for profitability as measured by return on assets (ROA):

$$\text{ROA} = \text{Profit margin} \times \text{Total asset turnover}$$
$$\text{Total asset turnover} = \text{Sales/Total assets}$$

Go back to the case of the firm with a lengthening cash cycle. Increased inventories and receivables that caused the cash cycle problem also reduce total asset turnover. The result is lower profitability. In other words, with more assets tied up over a longer cash cycle, the firm is less efficient and therefore less profitable. And, as if its troubles were not enough already, this firm suffers a drop in its sustainable growth rate.

Chapter 4 (in the discussion of Equation 4.5) showed that total asset turnover is directly linked to sustainable growth. Reducing total asset turnover lowers sustainable growth. This makes sense because our troubled firm must divert its financial resources into financing excess inventory and receivables.[5]

CONCEPT QUESTIONS

1. What does it mean to say that a firm has an inventory turnover ratio of 4?

2. Describe the operating cycle and cash cycle. What are the differences?

3. Explain the connection between a firm's accounting-based profitability and its cash cycle.

SOME ASPECTS OF SHORT-TERM FINANCIAL POLICY

The short-term financial policy that a firm adopts is reflected in at least two ways:

1. *The size of the firm's investment in current assets.* This is usually measured relative to the firm's level of total operating revenues. A *flexible* or accommodative short-term financial policy would maintain a relatively high ratio of current assets to sales. A *restrictive* short-term financial policy would entail a low ratio of current assets to sales.[6]

2. *The financing of current assets.* This is measured as the proportion of short-term debt (that is, current liabilities) and long-term debt used to finance current assets. A restrictive short-term financial policy means a high proportion of short-term debt relative to long-term financing, and a flexible policy means less short-term debt and more long-term debt.

If we take these two areas together, a firm with a flexible policy would have relatively large investment in current assets. It would finance this investment with relatively less in short-term debt. The net effect of a flexible policy is thus a relatively high level of net working capital. Put another way, with a flexible policy, the firm maintains a larger overall level of liquidity.

At the beginning of this chapter, we introduced the example of Canadian Tire and its efforts to reduce inventory levels. We can now see that Canadian Tire's working capital policy in relation

---

5 Further discussion of the cash cycle is in L. Kryzanowski, *Business Solvency Risk Analysis* (Montreal: Institute of Canadian Bankers, 1990), chap. 10.

6 Some people use the term *conservative* in place of flexible and the term *aggressive* in place of restrictive.

to inventory management is moving from a more flexible to a more restrictive approach. More generally, a survey of Canadian firms revealed that a flexible working capital policy is more popular.[7]

The Size of the Firm's Investment in Current Assets

Flexible short-term financial policies with regard to current assets include such actions as:

1. Keeping large balances of cash and marketable securities.
2. Making large investments in inventory.
3. Granting liberal credit terms, which result in a high level of accounts receivable.

Restrictive short-term financial policies would just be the opposite of these:

1. Keeping low cash balances and little investment in marketable securities.
2. Making small investments in inventory.
3. Allowing little or no credit sales, thereby minimizing accounts receivable.

Determining the optimal investment level in short-term assets requires an identification of the different costs of alternative short-term financing policies. The objective is to trade off the cost of a restrictive policy against the cost of a flexible one to arrive at the best compromise.

Current asset holdings are highest with a flexible short-term financial policy and lowest with a restrictive policy. So flexible short-term financial policies are costly in that they require a greater investment in cash and marketable securities, inventory, and accounts receivable. However, we expect future cash inflows to be higher with a flexible policy. For example, sales are stimulated by the use of a credit policy that provides liberal financing to customers. A large amount of finished inventory on hand ("on the shelf") provides a quick delivery service to customers and may increase sales. Similarly, a large inventory of raw materials may result in fewer production stoppages because of inventory shortages.[8]

A more restrictive short-term financial policy probably reduces future sales levels below those that would be achieved under flexible policies. It is also possible that higher prices can be charged to customers under flexible working capital policies. Customers may be willing to pay higher prices for the quick delivery service and more liberal credit terms implicit in flexible policies.

carrying costs
Costs that rise with increases in the level of investment in current assets.

Managing current assets can be thought of as involving a trade-off between costs that rise and costs that fall with the level of investment. Costs that rise with increases in the level of investment in current assets are called **carrying costs.** The larger the investment a firm makes in its current assets, the higher its carrying costs are. Costs that fall with increases in the level of investment in current assets are called **shortage costs.**

shortage costs
Costs that fall with increases in the level of investment in current assets.

In a general sense, carrying costs are the opportunity costs associated with current assets. The rate of return on current assets is very low when compared to other assets. For example, the rate of return on Treasury bills is usually considerably less than the rate of return firms would like to achieve overall. (Treasury bills are an important component of cash and marketable securities.)

Shortage costs are incurred when the investment in current assets is low. If a firm runs out of cash, it is forced to sell marketable securities. Of course, if a firm runs out of cash and marketable securities to sell, it may have to borrow, sell assets at fire-sale prices, or default on an obligation. This situation is called a cash out. A firm loses customers if it runs out of inventory (a stock out) or if it cannot extend credit to customers.

More generally, there are two kinds of shortage costs:

1. *Trading or order costs.* Order costs are the costs of placing an order for more cash (brokerage costs, for example) or more inventory (production set-up costs, for example).
2. *Costs related to lack of safety reserves.* These are costs of lost sales, lost customer goodwill, and disruption of production schedules.

---

7 For more on this survey, see N.T. Khoury, K.V. Smith, and P.I. MacKay, "Comparing Working Capital Practices in Canada, the United States and Australia," *Canadian Journal of Administrative Sciences* 16, March 1999, pp. 53–57.

8 Many industries are reducing inventory through new technology. We discuss this approach, called just-in-time inventory (or production), in Chapter 20.

The top part of Figure 18.2 illustrates the basic trade-off between carrying costs and shortage costs. On the vertical axis, we have costs measured in dollars and, on the horizontal axis, we have the amount of current assets. Carrying costs start at zero when current assets are zero and then climb steadily as current assets grow. Shortage costs start very high and then decline as we add current assets. The total cost of holding current assets is the sum of the two. Notice how the combined costs reach a minimum at CA*. This is the optimum level of current assets.

Current asset holdings are highest under a flexible policy. This is one in which the carrying costs are perceived to be low relative to shortage costs. This is Case A in Figure 18.2. In comparison, under restrictive current asset policies, carrying costs are perceived to be high relative to shortage costs. This is Case B in Figure 18.2.

Alternative Financing Policies for Current Assets

In previous sections, we looked at the basic determinants of the level of investment in current assets, and we thus focused on the asset side of the balance sheet. Now we turn to the financing side of the question. Here we are concerned with the relative amounts of short-term and long-term debt, assuming the investment in current assets is constant.

AN IDEAL CASE We start with the simplest possible case: an ideal economy. In such an economy, short-term assets can always be financed with short-term debt, and long-term assets can be financed with long-term debt and equity. In this economy, net working capital is always zero.

Consider a simplified case for a grain elevator operator. Grain elevator operators buy crops after harvest, store them, and sell them during the year. They have high inventories of grain after the harvest and end up with low inventories just before the next harvest.

Bank loans with maturities of less than one year are used to finance the purchase of grain and the storage costs. These loans are paid off from the proceeds of the sale of grain.

The situation is shown in Figure 18.3. Long-term assets are assumed to grow over time, whereas current assets increase at the end of the harvest and then decline during the year. Short-term assets end up at zero just before the next harvest. Current (short-term) assets are financed by short-term debt, and long-term assets are financed with long-term debt and equity. Net working capital—current assets minus current liabilities—is always zero. Figure 18.3 displays a sawtooth pattern that we see again when we get to our discussion on cash management in the next chapter. For now, we need to discuss some alternative policies for financing current assets under less idealized conditions.

DIFFERENT POLICIES IN FINANCING CURRENT ASSETS In the real world, it is not likely that current assets would ever drop to zero. For example, a long-term rising level of sales results in some permanent investment in current assets. Moreover, the firm's investments in long-term assets may show a great deal of variation.

A growing firm can be thought of as having a total asset requirement consisting of the current assets and long-term assets needed to run the business efficiently. The total asset requirement may exhibit change over time for many reasons, including (1) a general growth trend, (2) seasonal variation around the trend, and (3) unpredictable day-to-day and month-to-month fluctuations. This situation is depicted in Figure 18.4. (We have not tried to show the unpredictable day-to-day and month-to-month variations in the total asset requirement.)

The peaks and valleys in Figure 18.4 represent the firm's total asset needs through time. For example, for a lawn and garden supply firm, the peaks might represent inventory buildups prior to the spring selling season. The valleys would come about because of lower off-season inventories. There are two strategies such a firm might consider to meet its cyclical needs. First, the firm could keep a relatively large pool of marketable securities. As the need for inventory and other current assets began to rise, the firm would sell off marketable securities and use the cash to purchase whatever was needed. Once the inventory was sold and inventory holdings began to decline, the firm would reinvest in marketable securities. This approach is the flexible policy illustrated in Figure 18.5 as Policy F. Notice that the firm essentially uses a pool of marketable securities as a buffer against changing current asset needs.

FIGURE 18.2

Carrying costs and
shortage costs

Short-term financial policy: the optimal investment in current assets.

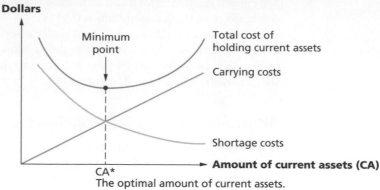

Carrying costs increase with the level of investment in current assets. They include the costs of maintaining economic value and opportunity costs. Shortage costs decrease with increases in the level of investment in current assets. They include trading costs and the costs related to being short of the current asset (for example, being short of cash). The firm's policy can be characterized as flexible or restrictive.

A. Flexible policy

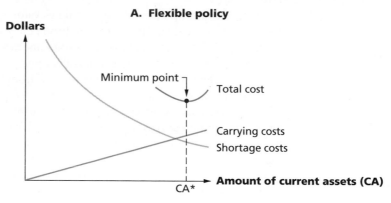

A flexible policy is most appropriate when carrying costs are low relative to shortage costs.

B. Restrictive policy

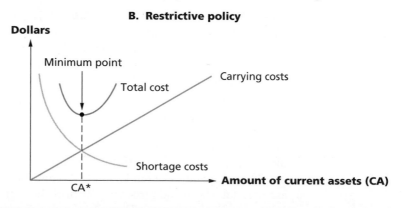

A restrictive policy is most appropriate when carrying costs are high relative to shortage costs.

At the other extreme, the firm could keep relatively little in marketable securities. As the need for inventory and other assets began to rise, the firm would simply borrow the needed cash on a short-term basis. The firm would repay the loans as the need for assets cycled back down. This approach is the restrictive policy illustrated in Figure 18.5 as Policy R.

In comparing the two strategies illustrated in Figure 18.5, notice that the chief difference is the way in which the seasonal variation in asset needs is financed. In the flexible case, the firm finances

FIGURE 18.3

Financing policy for an ideal economy

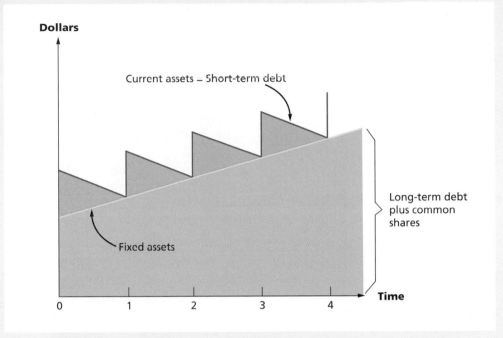

In an ideal world, net working capital is always zero because short-term assets are financed by short-term debt.

FIGURE 18.4

The total asset requirement over time

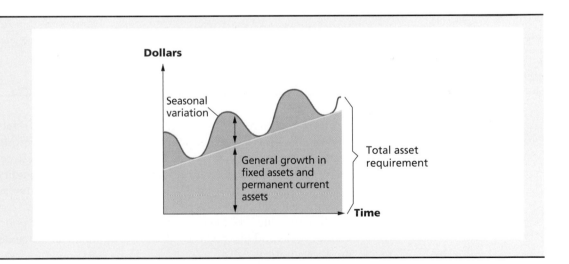

internally, using its own cash and marketable securities. In the restrictive case, the firm finances the variation externally, borrowing the needed funds on a short-term basis. As we discussed previously, all else being the same, a firm with a flexible policy will have a greater investment in net working capital.

Which Financing Policy is Best?

What is the most appropriate amount of short-term borrowing? There is no definitive answer. Several considerations must be included in a proper analysis:

1. *Cash reserves.* The flexible financial policy implies surplus cash and little short-term borrowing. This policy reduces the probability that a firm would experience financial distress.

FIGURE 18.5

Alternative asset
financing policies

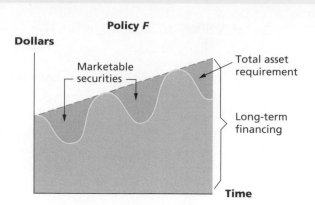

Policy *F* always implies a short-term cash surplus and a large investment in cash and marketable securities.

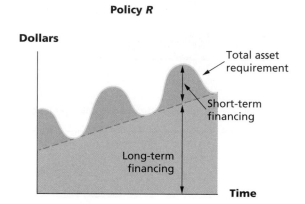

Policy *R* uses long-term financing for permanent asset requirements only and short-term borrowing for seasonal variations.

Firms may not have to worry as much about meeting recurring, short-run obligations. However, this higher level of liquidity comes at a price. Investments in cash and marketable securities generally produce lower returns than investments in real assets. For example, suppose the firm invests any temporary excess liquidity in Treasury bills. The price of a Treasury bill is simply the present value of its future cash flow. It follows that, since present value and the cost of a Treasury bill are equal, Treasury bills are always zero net present value investments. If the firm followed another policy, the funds tied up in Treasury bills and other zero NPV short-term financial instruments could be invested to produce a positive NPV.

2. *Maturity hedging.* Most firms attempt to match the maturities of assets and liabilities. They finance inventories with short-term bank loans and fixed assets with long-term financing. Firms tend to avoid financing long-lived assets with short-term borrowing. This type of maturity mismatching is inherently more risky for two reasons: First, the cost of the financing is more uncertain because short-term interest rates are more volatile than longer rates. For example, in 1981, many short-term borrowers faced financial distress when short-term rates exceeded 20 percent.

Second, maturity mismatching necessitates frequent refinancing and this produces rollover risk, the risk that renewed short-term financing may not be available. A recent example is the financial distress faced in 1992 by Olympia & York (O&Y), a real estate development firm privately owned by the Reichmann family of Toronto. O&Y's main assets were office towers, including First Canadian Place in Toronto and Canary Wharf outside London, England. Financing for these long-term assets was short-term bank loans and commercial paper. In early 1992, investor fears about real estate prospects prevented O&Y from rolling over its commercial paper. To avoid default, the company turned to its bankers to negotiate emergency longer-term financing and, when that failed, had to file for bankruptcy protection.

3. *Relative interest rates.* Short-term interest rates are usually lower than long-term rates. This implies that it is, on the average, more costly to rely on long-term borrowing as compared to short-term borrowing. This is really a statement about the yield curve we introduced in Appendix 7B. What we are saying is that the yield curve is normally upward sloping.

Policies F and R, which are shown in Figure 18.5, are, of course, extreme cases. With F, the firm never does any short-term borrowing; with R, the firm never has a cash reserve (an investment in marketable securities). Figure 18.6 illustrates these two policies along with a compromise, Policy C.

With this compromise approach, the firm borrows short-term to cover peak financing needs, but it maintains a cash reserve in the form of marketable securities during slow periods. As current assets build up, the firm draws down this reserve before doing any short-term borrowing. This allows for some run-up in current assets before the firm has to resort to short-term borrowing.

Current Assets and Liabilities in Practice

www.candiantire.ca

Table 18.2 shows that current assets made up just over 45 percent of all assets for Canadian Tire in 2005. Short-term financial management deals with a significant portion of the balance sheet for this large firm. For small firms, especially in the retailing and service sectors, current assets make up an even larger portion of total assets.

FIGURE 18.6

A compromise financing policy

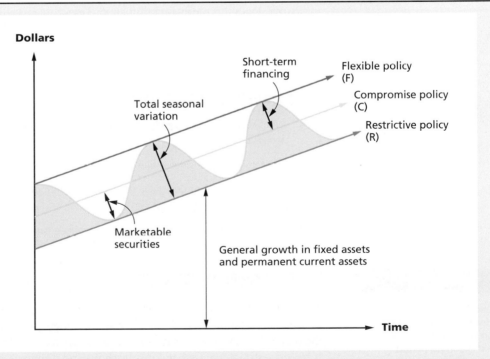

With a compromise policy, the firm keeps a reserve of liquidity, which it uses to initially finance seasonal variations in current asset needs. Short-term borrowing is used when the reserve is exhausted.

TABLE 18.2		2005	2004
Current assets and current liabilities as percentages of total assets for Canadian Tire 2004–2005	**Current assets:**		
	Cash and cash equivalents	14.07%	15.30%
	Accounts receivable	10.96%	7.07%
	Loans receivable	12.24%	11.03%
	Inventories	11.37%	11.84%
	Prepaid expenses and deposits	0.71%	0.46%
	Future income taxes	0.73%	0.47%
	Total current assets	50.08%	46.44%
	Current liabilities:		
	Accounts payable and other	49.15%	53.40%
	Income taxes payable	2.26%	1.64%
	Current portion of long-term debt	6.50%	0.21%
	Total current liabilities	57.91%	55.25%

Source: Drawn from Canadian Tire's *Annual Report*, 2005.

Over time, advances in technology are changing the way Canadian firms manage current assets. With new techniques such as just-in-time inventory and business-to-business e-business sales (B2B), firms are moving away from flexible policies and toward a more restrictive approach to current assets.

Current liabilities are also declining as a percentage of total assets. Firms are practising maturity hedging as they match lower current liabilities with decreased current assets. The previously discussed Canadian Tire example indicates that maturity hedging is occurring. Table 18.2 shows that Canadian Tire is attempting to match the maturities of assets and liabilities, as current assets as a percentage of total assets moved closer to the current liabilities as a percentage of total assets from 2004 to 2005. In addition to these differences over time, there are differences between industries in policies on current assets and liabilities.

The cash cycle is longer in some industries; various products and industry practices require different levels of inventory and receivables. This is why we saw in Chapter 3 that industry average ratios are not the same. Levels of current assets and liabilities differ across industries.[9] For example, the aircraft industry carries more than twice the amount of inventory of the other industries. Does this mean aircraft manufacturers are less efficient? Most likely, the higher inventory consists of airplanes under construction. Because building planes takes more time than most printing processes, it makes sense that aircraft manufacturers carry higher inventories than printing and publishing firms.

CONCEPT QUESTIONS

1. What keeps the real world from being an ideal one where net working capital could always be zero?

2. What considerations determine the optimal size of the firm's investment in current assets?

3. What considerations determine the optimal compromise between flexible and restrictive net working capital policies?

4. How are industry differences reflected in working capital policies?

18.4

cash budget
A forecast of cash receipts and disbursements for the next planning period.

THE CASH BUDGET

The **cash budget** is a primary tool in short-run financial planning. It allows the financial manager to identify short-term financial needs and opportunities. Importantly, the cash budget helps the manager explore the need for short-term borrowing. The idea of the cash budget is simple: It records estimates of cash receipts (cash in) and disbursements (cash out). The result is an estimate of the cash surplus or deficit.

---

9 See N.G. Hill and W.L. Sartoris, *Short-Term Financial Management* (New York: Macmillan, 1988) chap. 1.

Sales and Cash Collections

We start with an example for the Fun Toys Corporation for which we prepare a quarterly cash budget. We could just as well use a monthly, weekly, or even daily basis. We choose quarters for convenience and also because a quarter is a common short-term business planning period.

All of Fun Toys' cash inflows come from the sale of toys. Cash budgeting for Fun Toys must therefore start with a sales forecast for the next year, by quarters:

	Q1	Q2	Q3	Q4
Sales (in $ millions)	$200	$300	$250	$400

Note that these are predicted sales, so there is forecasting risk here because actual sales could be more or less. Also, Fun Toys started the year with accounts receivable equal to $120.

Fun Toys has a 45-day receivables or average collection period. This means that half of the sales in a given quarter are collected the following quarter. This happens because sales made during the first 45 days of a quarter are collected in that quarter. Sales made in the second 45 days are collected in the next quarter. Note that we are assuming that each quarter has 90 days, so the 45-day collection period is the same as a half-quarter collection period.

Based on the sales forecasts, we now need to estimate Fun Toys' projected cash collections. First, any receivables that we have at the beginning of a quarter would be collected within 45 days, so all of them are collected sometime during the quarter. Second, as we discussed, any sales made in the first half of the quarter are collected, so total cash collections are:

$$\text{Cash collections} = \text{Beginning accounts receivable} + 1/2 \times \text{Sales} \qquad [18.6]$$

For example, in the first quarter, cash collections would be the beginning receivables of $120 plus half of sales, $1/2 \times \$200 = \$100$, for a total of $220.

Since beginning receivables are all collected along with half of sales, ending receivables for a particular quarter would be the other half of sales. First-quarter sales are projected at $200, so ending receivables are $100. This would be the beginning receivables in the second quarter. Cash collections in the second quarter are thus $100 plus half of the projected $300 in sales, or $250 total.

Continuing this process, we can summarize Fun Toys' projected cash collections as shown in Table 18.3. In this table, collections are shown as the only source of cash. Of course, this need not be the case. Other sources of cash could include asset sales, investment income, and receipts from planned long-term financing.

Cash Outflows

Next, we consider the cash disbursements or payments. These come in four basic categories:

1. *Payments of accounts payable.* These are payments for goods or services rendered from suppliers, such as raw materials. Generally, these payments are made sometime after purchases.
2. *Wages, taxes, and other expenses.* This category includes all other regular costs of doing business that require actual expenditures. Depreciation, for example, is often thought of as a regular cost of business, but it requires no cash outflow, and is not included.
3. *Capital expenditures.* These are payments of cash for long-lived assets.

TABLE 18.3
Cash collections for Fun Toys (in $ millions)

	Q1	Q2	Q3	Q4
Beginning receivables	$120	$100	$150	$125
Sales	200	300	250	400
Cash collections	220	250	275	325
Ending receivables	100	150	125	200

Notes.   Collections = Beginning receivables + ½ × Sales
Ending receivables = Beginning receivables + Sales − Collections
= ½ × Sales

4. *Long-term financing expenses.* This category, for example, includes interest payments on long-term outstanding debt and dividend payments to shareholders.

Fun Toys' purchases from suppliers (in dollars) in a quarter are equal to 60 percent of next quarter's predicted sales. Fun Toys' payments to suppliers are equal to the previous quarter's purchases, so the accounts payable period is 90 days. For example, in the quarter just ended, Fun Toys ordered .60 × $200 = $120 in supplies. This would actually be paid in the first quarter (Q1) of the coming year.

Wages, taxes, and other expenses are routinely 20 percent of sales; interest and dividends are currently $20 per quarter. In addition, Fun Toys plans a major plant expansion (a capital expenditure) of $100 in the second quarter. If we put all this information together, the cash outflows are as shown in Table 18.4.

The Cash Balance

The predicted net cash inflow is the difference between cash collections and cash disbursements. The net cash inflow for Fun Toys is shown in Table 18.5. What we see immediately is that there is a cash surplus in the first and third quarters and a cash deficit in the second and fourth.

We assume that Fun Toys starts the year with a $20 cash balance. Furthermore, Fun Toys maintains a $10 minimum cash balance to guard against unforeseen contingencies and forecasting errors. So we start the first quarter with $20 in cash. This increases by $40 during the quarter, and the ending balance is $60. Of this, $10 is reserved as a minimum, so we subtract it out and find that the first-quarter surplus is $60 – 10 = $50.

Fun Toys starts the second quarter with $60 in cash (the ending balance from the previous quarter). There is a net cash inflow of –$110, so the ending balance is $60 – 110 = –$50. We need another $10 as a buffer, so the total deficit is –$60. These calculations and those for the last two quarters are summarized in Table 18.6.

Beginning in the second quarter, Fun Toys has a cash shortfall of $60. This occurs because of the seasonal pattern of sales (higher toward the end of the second quarter), the delay in collections, and the planned capital expenditure.

The cash situation at Fun Toys is projected to improve to a $5 deficit in the third quarter, but, by year's end, Fun Toys still has a $20 deficit. Without some sort of financing, this deficit would carry over into the next year. We explore financing sources in the next section.

TABLE 18.4 Cash disbursements for Fun Toys (in $ millions)	**Q1**	**Q2**	**Q3**	**Q4**
Payment of accounts (60% of sales)	$120	$180	$150	$240
Wages, taxes, other expenses	40	60	50	80
Capital expenditures	0	100	0	0
Long-term financing expenses (interest and dividends)	20	20	20	20
Total	$180	$360	$220	$340

TABLE 18.5 Net cash inflow for Fun Toys (in $ millions)	**Q1**	**Q2**	**Q3**	**Q4**
Total cash collections	$220	$250	$275	$325
Total cash disbursements	180	360	220	340
Net cash inflow	$ 40	–$110	$ 55	–$ 15

TABLE 18.6 Cash balance for Fun Toys (in $ millions)	**Q1**	**Q2**	**Q3**	**Q4**
Beginning cash balance	$ 20	$ 60	–$ 50	$ 5
Net cash inflow	40	–110	55	–15
Ending cash balance	$ 60	–$ 50	$ 5	–$ 10
Minimum cash balance	–10	–10	–10	–10
Cumulative surplus (deficit)	$ 50	–$ 60	–$ 5	–$ 20

For now, we can make the following general comments on Fun Toys' cash needs:

1. Fun Toys' large outflow in the second quarter is not necessarily a sign of trouble. It results from delayed collections on sales and a planned capital expenditure (presumably a worthwhile one).

2. The figures in our example are based on a forecast. Sales could be much worse (or better) than the forecast.

CONCEPT QUESTIONS

1. How would you do a sensitivity analysis (discussed in Chapter 11) for Fun Toys' net cash balance?

2. What could you learn from such an analysis?

A SHORT-TERM FINANCIAL PLAN

To illustrate a completed short-term financial plan, we assume Fun Toys arranges to borrow any needed funds on a short-term basis. The interest rate is 20 percent APR, and it is compounded on a quarterly basis. From Chapter 6, we know that the rate is 20%/4 = 5% per quarter. We assume that Fun Toys starts the year with no short-term debt.

From Table 18.6, Fun Toys has a second-quarter deficit of $60 million. We have to borrow this amount. Net cash inflow in the following quarter is $55 million. We now have to pay $60 × .05 = $3 million in interest out of that, leaving $52 million to reduce the borrowing.

We still owe $60 – 52 = $8 million at the end of the third quarter. Interest in the last quarter is thus $8 × .05 = $.4 million. In addition, net inflows in the last quarter are –$15 million, so we have to borrow $15.4 million, bringing our total borrowing up to $15.4 + 8 = $23.4 million. Table 18.7 extends Table 18.6 to include these calculations.

Notice that the ending short-term debt is just equal to the cumulative deficit for the entire year, $20, plus the interest paid during the year, $3 + .4 = $3.4, for a total of $23.4.

Our plan is very simple. For example, we ignored the fact that the interest paid on the short-term debt is tax deductible. We also ignored the fact that the cash surplus in the first quarter would earn some interest (which would be taxable). We could add on a number of refinements. Even so, our plan highlights the fact that in about 90 days, Fun Toys would need to borrow $60 million or so on a short-term basis. It's time to start lining up the source of the funds.

Our plan also illustrates that financing the firm's short-term needs costs more than $3 million in interest (before taxes) for the year. This is a starting point for Fun Toys to begin evaluating alternatives to reduce this expense. For example, can the $100 million planned expenditure be postponed or spread out? At 5 percent per quarter, short-term credit is expensive.

Also, if Fun Toys' sales are expected to keep growing, the $20 million plus deficit would probably also keep growing, and the need for additional financing is permanent. Fun Toys may wish to think about raising money on a long-term basis to cover this need.

TABLE 18.7
Short-term financial plan for Fun Toys (in $ millions)

	Q1	Q2	Q3	Q4
Beginning cash balance	$ 20	$ 60	$ 10	$ 10.0
Net cash inflow	40	–110	55	–15.0
New short-term borrowing	—	60	—	15.4
Interest on short-term borrowing	—	—	3	.4
Short-term borrowing repaid	—	—	–52	—
Ending cash balance	$ 60	$ 10	$ 10	$ 10.0
Minimum cash balance	–10	–10	–10	–10.0
Cumulative surplus (deficit)	$ 50	$ 0	$ 0	$ 0.0
Beginning short-term borrowing	0	0	60	8.0
Change in short-term debt	0	60	–52	15.4
Ending short-term debt	$ 0	$ 60	$ 8	$ 23.4

As our example for Fun Toys illustrates, cash budgeting is a planning exercise because it forces the financial manager to think about future cash flows. This is important because, as we showed in Chapter 4, firms, can "grow bankrupt" if there is no planning. This is why bankers, venture capitalists, and other financing sources stress the importance of management and planning.

Short-Term Planning and Risk

After it is revised, the short-term financial plan in Table 18.7 represents Fun Toys' best guess for the future. Large firms go beyond the best guess to ask what-if questions using scenario analysis, sensitivity analysis, and simulation. We introduced these techniques in Chapter 11's discussion of project analysis. They are tools for assessing the degree of forecasting risk and identifying those components most critical to the success or failure of a financial plan.

Recall that scenario analysis involves varying the base case plan to create several others—a best case, worst case, and so on. Each produces different financing needs to give the financial manager a first look at risk.

Sensitivity analysis is a variation on scenario analysis that is useful in pinpointing the areas where forecasting risk is especially severe. The basic idea of sensitivity analysis is to freeze all the variables except one and then see how sensitive our estimate of financing needs is to changes in that one variable. If our projected financing turns out to be very sensitive to, say, sales, then we know that extra effort in refining the sales forecast would pay off.

Since the original financial plan was almost surely developed on a computer spreadsheet, scenario and sensitivity analysis are quite straightforward and widely used.

Simulation analysis combines the features of scenario and sensitivity analysis varying all the variables over a range of outcomes simultaneously. The result of simulation analysis is a probability distribution of financing needs.

Air Canada uses simulation analysis in forecasting its cash needs. The simulation is useful in capturing the variability of cash flow components in the airline industry in Canada. Bad weather, for example, causes delays and cancelled flights, with unpredictable dislocation payments to travellers and crew overtime. This and other risks are reflected in a probability distribution of cash needs, giving the treasurer better information for planning borrowing needs.

www.aircanada.ca

18.6 SHORT-TERM BORROWING

Fun Toys has a short-term financing problem. It cannot meet the forecasted cash outflows in the second quarter from internal sources. How it finances that shortfall depends on its financial policy. With a very flexible policy, Fun Toys might seek up to $60 million in long-term debt financing.

In addition, much of the cash deficit comes from the large capital expenditure. Arguably, this is a candidate for long-term financing. Examples discussed in Chapter 15 include issuing shares or bonds or taking a term loan from a chartered bank or other financial institution. If it chose equity financing through an initial public offering (IPO), Fun Toys would be following the example of Chapters Online. As the firm's Internet division, Chapters Online sells books, CD ROMs, DVDs and videos through its website. In September 1999, Chapters Online went public, raising equity at an offering price of $13.50 per share. A little under a year later, in August 2000, analysts calculated Chapters Online's "burn rate," the rate at which the firm was using cash, to determine its cash position. Given that the stock price had fallen from the offering price of $13.50 to $2.80 per share, a further equity offering seemed unlikely and the discussion of the firm's financial health focused on the availability of short-term borrowing.

Here we concentrate on two short-term borrowing alternatives: (1) unsecured borrowing and (2) secured borrowing.

Operating Loans

operating loan
Loan negotiated with banks for day-to-day operations.

The most common way to finance a temporary cash deficit is to arrange a short-term **operating loan** from a chartered bank. This is an agreement under which a firm is authorized to borrow up to a specified amount for a given period, usually one year (much like a credit card).[10] Operating loans can be either unsecured or secured by collateral. Large corporations with excellent credit ratings usually structure the facility as an unsecured line of credit. Because unsecured credit lines are backed only by projections of future cash flows, bankers offer this cash flow lending only to those with top-drawer credit.

Short-term lines of credit are classified as either *committed* or *noncommitted*. The latter is an informal arrangement. Committed lines of credit are more formal legal arrangements and usually involve a commitment fee paid by the firm to the bank (usually the fee is 0.25 percent of the total committed funds per year). A firm that pays a commitment fee for a committed line of credit is essentially buying insurance to guarantee that the bank can't back out of the agreement (absent some material change in the borrower's status).

COMPENSATING THE BANK   The interest rate on an operating loan is usually set equal to the bank's prime lending rate plus an additional percentage, and the rate usually floats. For example, suppose that the prime rate is 9 percent when the loan is initiated and the loan is at prime plus 1.5 percent. The original rate charged the borrower is 10.5 percent. If after, say, 125 days, prime increases to 9.5 percent, the company's borrowing rate goes up to 11 percent and interest charges are adjusted accordingly.

The premium charged over prime reflects the banker's assessment of the borrower's risk. Table 18.8 lists factors bankers use in assessing risk in loans to small business. Notice that risks related to management appear most often because poor management is considered the major risk with small business. There is a trend among bankers to look more closely at industry and economic risk factors. A similar set of risk factors applies to loans to large corporations.

Banks are in the business of lending mainly to low-risk borrowers. For this reason, bankers generally prefer to decline risky business loans that would require an interest rate more than prime plus 3 percent. Many of the loan requests that banks turn down are from small business, especially start-ups. Around 60 percent of these turn-downs find financing elsewhere. Alternative sources include venture capital financing discussed in Chapter 15 and federal and provincial government programs to assist small business.

In addition to charging interest, banks also levy fees for account activity and loan management. Small businesses may also pay application fees to cover the costs of processing loan applications.

	Factor	Percent of Mentions
TABLE 18.8		(1,539 cases)
Factors mentioned in the credit files	1. **Economic environment** Opportunities and risks	6.1%
	2. **Industry environment** Competitive conditions, prospects, and risks	40.4
	3. **Client's marketing activities** Strategies, strengths, and weaknesses	30.8
	4. **Firm's operations management** Strengths and weaknesses	59.5
	5. **Client's financial resources, skills, and performance**	44.9
	Financial management expertise	84.8
	Historical or future profitability	41.6
	Future cash flows	20.5
	Future financing needs (beyond the current year)	
	6. **Management capabilities and character**	79.6
	Strengths and weaknesses	95.1
	Length of ownership of the firm	57.1
	Past management experience relevant to the business	
	7. **Collateral security and the firm's net worth position**	97.7
	8. **Borrower's past relationship with bank**	65.3

Source: Larry Wynant and James Hatch, *Banks and Small Business Borrowers* (London: University of Western Ontario, 1991), p. 136.

---

10 Descriptions of bank loans draw on L. Wynant and J. Hatch, *Banks and Small Business Borrowers* (London: University of Western Ontario, 1991).

Fees are becoming increasingly important in bank compensation.[11] Fees and other details of any short-term business lending arrangements are highly negotiable. Banks generally work with firms to design a package of fees and interest.

Letters of Credit

letter of credit
A written statement by a bank that money will be paid, provided conditions specified in the letter are met.

A **letter of credit** is a common arrangement in international finance. With a letter of credit, the bank issuing the letter promises to make a loan if certain conditions are met. Typically, the letter guarantees payment on a shipment of goods provided that the goods arrive as promised. A letter of credit can be revocable (subject to cancellation) or irrevocable (not subject to cancellation if the specified conditions are met).

Secured Loans

Banks and other financial institutions often require security for an operating loan just as they do for a long-term loan. Table 18.8 shows that collateral security is a factor in virtually every small-business loan. Security for short-term loans usually consists of accounts receivable, inventories, or both because these are the assets most likely to retain value if the borrower goes bankrupt. Security is intended to reduce the lender's risk by providing a second "line of defence" behind the borrower's projected cash flows. To achieve this intention, the ideal collateral is Treasury bills or another asset whose value is independent of the borrower's business. We say this because, under the NPV principle, business assets derive their value from cash flow. When business is bad and cash flow low (or negative), the collateral value is greatly reduced. Several Canadian banks found this out in the early 1990s when they wrote off billions in real estate loans, and again in 2002 when the deteriorating financial health of several large telecom companies including Worldcom, Teleglobe, and Global Crossing resulted in significant loan write-downs.

covenants
A promise by the firm, included in the debt contract, to perform certain acts. A restrictive covenant imposes constraints on the firm to protect the interests of the debtholder.

In addition, banks routinely limit risk through loan conditions called **covenants.** Table 18.9 lists common covenants in Canadian small-business loans. You can see that bankers expect to have a detailed knowledge of their clients' businesses.

accounts receivable financing
A secured short-term loan that involves either the assignment or factoring of receivables.

Accounts receivable financing from chartered banks typically involves assigning receivables to the lender under a general assignment of book debts. Under assignment, the bank or other lender has the receivables as security, but the borrower is still responsible if a receivable can't be collected. The lending agreement establishes a margin usually 75 percent of current (under 90 days) receivables. As the firm makes sales, it submits its invoices to the bank and can borrow up to 75 percent of their value.

Inventory margins are set similarly to accounts receivable. Since inventory is often less liquid than receivables (bringing a lower percentage of book value in liquidations), inventory lending margins are lower, typically 50 percent.

Many small and medium-sized businesses secure their operating loans with both receivables and inventory. In this case, the lending limit fluctuates with both accounts according to the lending margins.

Factoring

In addition to bank borrowing, accounts receivable financing is also possible through factoring. A factor is an independent company that acts as "an outside credit department" for the client. It checks the credit of new customers, authorizes credit, handles collections and bookkeeping. As the accounts are collected, the factor pays the client the face amount of the invoice less a 1 or 2 percent discount.[12] If any accounts are late, the factor still pays the selling firm on an average

---

11 U.S. banks sometimes require that the firm keep some account of money on deposit. This is called a compensating balance. A *compensating balance* is some of the firm's money kept by the bank in low-interest or non-interest-bearing accounts. By leaving these funds with the bank and receiving no interest, the firm further increases the effective interest rate earned by the bank on the line of credit, thereby compensating the bank.

12 Our discussion of factoring draws on D. Reidy, "Factoring Smooths Banking Relationships," *Profit*, November 1991; and S. Horvitch, "Busy Days for Factoring Firms," *The Financial Post*, February 15, 1991.

	Percent of Cases*
Condition	(1,382 cases)
Postponement of shareholder claims	39.8%
Life insurance on key principals	39.4
Fire insurance on company premises	35.7
Accounts receivable and inventory reporting	27.8
Limits on withdrawals and dividends	11.9
Limits on capital expenditures	10.5
Maintenance of minimum working capital levels	2.9
Restrictions on further debt	2.5
Restrictions on disposal of company assets	1.7
Maintenance of minimum cash balances	0.9
Other conditions	6.2

TABLE 18.9
Loan conditions for approved bank credits in the credit file sample

*Adds up to more than 100 percent because of multiple responses.
Source: Larry Wynant and James Hatch, *Banks and Small Business Borrowers* (London: University of Western Ontario, 1991), p. 173.

EXAMPLE 18.3: Secured Borrowing for Fun Toys

Based on the cash budget we drew up earlier, the financial manager of Fun Toys has decided to seek a bank operating loan to cover the projected deficit of $60 million. The Royal Canadian National Bank has offered Fun Toys an operating loan at prime plus 1 percent to be secured by inventories. The lending officer has set a 75 percent margin on current receivables and 50 percent on inventory. Fun Toys has assured you that all its receivables are current and that two-thirds of payables were for inventory purchases. Can Fun Toys provide sufficient security for a $60 million operating loan?

Tables 18.3 and 18.4 show receivables and payables for Fun Toys for the next three quarters. Since the bank lends only against existing receivables and inventory, we use the Q1 beginning figures of $120 million for receivables and the same figure for payables. The full amount of the inventory is eligible for margining but only two-thirds of payables ($80) are inventory. We can calculate the amount that Fun Toys can secure as follows:

	Amount	×	Margin	=	Security
Receivables	$120		.75		$ 90
Inventory	80		.50		40
Total eligible security					$130

So Fun Toys could borrow up to $130 million under the margin formula and have no trouble securing a loan of $60 million.

maturity date determined in advance. The legal arrangement is that the factor purchases the accounts receivable from the firm. Thus, factoring provides insurance against bad debts because any defaults on bad accounts are the factor's problem.

Factoring in Canada is conducted by independent firms whose main customers are small businesses. Factoring is popular with manufacturers of retail goods, especially in the apparel business. The attraction of factoring to small businesses is that it allows outside professionals to handle the headaches of credit. To avoid magnifying those headaches, factors must offer cost savings and avoid alienating their clients' customers in the collection process.

maturity factoring
Short-term financing in which the factor purchases all of a firm's receivables and forwards the proceeds to the seller as soon as they are collected.

What we have described so far is **maturity factoring** and does not involve a formal financing arrangement. What factoring does is remove receivables from the balance sheet and so, indirectly, it reduces the need for financing. It may also reduce the costs associated with granting credit. Because factors do business with many firms, they may be able to achieve scale economies, reduce risks through diversification, and carry more clout in collection.

Firms financing their receivables through a chartered bank may also use the services of a factor to improve the receivables' collateral value. In this case, the factor buys the receivables and assigns them to the bank. This is called *maturity factoring with assignment of equity*. Or the factor provides an advance on the receivables and charges interest at prime plus 2.5 to 3 percent. In advance factoring, the factor provides financing as well as other services.

Securitized Receivables—A Financial Innovation

Financial engineers have come up with a new approach to receivables financing. When a large corporation such as Sears Canada, Ltd., securitized receivables, it sold them to Sears Canada Receivables Trust (SCRT), a wholly owned subsidiary. SCRT issued debentures and commercial paper backed by a diversified portfolio of receivables. Because receivables are liquid, SCRT debt is less risky than lending to Sears Canada and the company hopes to benefit through interest

www.sears.ca

EXAMPLE 18.4: Cost of Factoring

For the year just ended, LuLu's Fashions had $500,000 in credit sales monthly with an average maturity of receivables of 45 days. LuLu's uses a factor to obtain funds 15 days after the sale. This means the factor is advancing funds for 45 – 15 = 30 days. The factor charges 10.5 percent interest (APR), 2.5 percent over the current prime rate of 8 percent. In addition, the factor charges a 1.5 percent fee for processing the receivables and assuming all credit risk. If LuLu's ran its own credit department, it would cost $2,000 per month in variable expenses and this is saved with factoring. What is the effective interest cost of factoring?

The costs are:

		Per Month
Interest = .105 × 30/365 × $500,000	=	$ 4,315
Factor's fee = .015 × $500,000	=	7,500
Variables expenses saved	=	–2,000
Total cost		$ 9,815

$9,815/$500,000 = 1.96 percent per month.

The effective annual rate (EAR) is $(1.0196)^{12} - 1 = 26.23$ percent.

Note that the factor takes on the risk of default by a buyer, thus providing insurance as well as immediate cash. More generally, the factor essentially takes over the firm's credit operations. This can result in a significant saving. The interest rate we calculated is therefore overstated, particularly if default is a significant possibility.

savings. According to the Dominion Bond Rating Service, the total market for asset-backed securities has grown from $84.5 billion at the end of 2001 to $130.2 billion at the end of 2005. This represents a growth rate of 11.41%, which indicates clearly that asset-backed securities are increasing in importance.

Inventory Loans

inventory loan
A secured short-term loan to purchase inventory.

Inventory loans, or operating loans to finance inventory, feature assignment of inventory to the lender who then advances funds according to a predetermined margin as we discussed earlier. The specific legal arrangements depend on the type of inventory. The most sweeping form is the general security agreement that registers security over all a firm's assets. Inventory as a whole can be assigned under Section 178 of the *Bank Act,* or *Bill 97* in Quebec. If the inventory consists of equipment or large, movable assets, the appropriate legal form is a chattel mortgage (commercial pledge of equipment in Quebec).

trust receipt
An instrument acknowledging that the borrower holds certain goods in trust for the lender.

The legal form of the security arrangement can be tailored to the type of inventory. For example, with large, expensive items in inventory, the security agreement is often based on **trust receipts** listing the individual items by serial numbers. Trust receipts are used to support *floor plan financing* for automobile dealers and sellers of household appliances and other equipment. The advantage of floor plan financing is that it gives the lender a systematic way to monitor the inventory as it moves through the cash cycle. As the vehicles are sold, the dealer reports the sale to the lender and repays the financing.

Warehouse financing is a similar system in which the inventory that serves as security is identified and monitored. In this case, the inventory is segregated in a designated field or public warehouse run by a third party. The warehouse issues a *warehouse receipt* providing legal evidence of the existence of the security. Because the goods are segregated, warehouse financing is not suitable for work-in-progress inventory. On the other hand, this form of financing is ideally suited for inventories that improve with age such as whiskey or wine.

Trade Credit

When a firm purchases supplies on credit, the increase in accounts payable is a source of funds and automatic financing. As compared with bank financing, trade credit has the advantage of arising automatically from the firm's business. It does not require a formal financing agreement with covenants that may restrict the borrower's business activities. Suppliers offer credit to remain competitive; in many industries, the terms of credit include a cash discount for paying

In Their Own Words . . .   Ken Hitzig on Keeping Business Liquid through Factoring

THROUGH SUBSIDIARIES in Canada and the United States, Accord Financial Corp. provides factoring services to small and medium-sized companies. Accord's customers are engaged in temporary staff placement, computer services, textiles, apparel, medical services, food distribution, sporting goods, leisure products, transportation, footwear, floor coverings, home furnishings, and industrial products.

Accord is engaged in the factoring business on both a recourse and non-recourse basis. Non-recourse factoring is a service provided to companies desiring to outsource their customer accounts receivable departments, including the risk of customer default. Almost all the work involving credit checking, recordkeeping, collections, and credit losses is effectively off-loaded on Accord for a predetermined fee. Financing is available, but few of Accord's clients avail themselves of this facility, preferring instead to fund their business through banks.

Accord's non-recourse service appeals to medium-sized companies (annual sales of $1–$10 million) which view the virtual elimination of customer credit risk as the single, most important benefit. Most of these clients are privately owned and the owners are very aware of preserving capital and avoiding unnecessary risk. The failure of a large customer could cause the bank to reduce or cancel the operating line of credit and jeopardize the owner's life savings. Non-recourse factoring with Accord solves the problem. As one client described it: "Accord's credit is best described in three words—Ship and Sleep."

Recourse factoring is similar to non-recourse but the customer credit risk remains with the client company. Accord purchases the invoices from the client for cash; however, in the event of customer default, Accord has the right to resell the account back to the client. Recourse factoring is attractive to small and medium-sized companies needing liquidity but unable to borrow from banks on the strength of their financial statements. These companies are usually thinly capitalized, going through a turnaround phase, growing rapidly or a combination of some or all of these traits. They usually have better-than-average quality customers, and by factoring their sales, they effectively exchange paper for cash.

Ken Hitzig is a Commerce graduate of McGill University and a Chartered Accountant. After an 18-year career at Aetna Factors Corp. Ltd., he left to start Accord Business Credit Inc. in 1978. Along with Montcap Financial Corp. in Canada and J.T.A. Factors, Inc. in South Carolina, Accord is now a subsidiary of Accord Financial Corp., a publicly-held company listed on the Toronto Stock Exchange. Mr. Hitzig is Chief Executive Officer of Accord Financial Corp.

within a certain period. For example, suppose a supplier offers terms of 2/10, net 30.[13] If your firm makes a $1,000 purchase, you have a choice of paying after 10 days, taking the cash discount, or paying the full $1,000 after 30 days. Or you could stretch your payables by paying the $1,000 after, say, 45 days. The longer you wait, the longer the supplier is providing you with trade credit financing.

In making your decision, you should ask whether the cash discount provides a significant incentive for early payment. The answer is yes because the implicit interest rate is extremely high.

To see why the discount is important, we calculate the cost to the buyer of not paying early. To do this, we find the interest rate that the buyer is effectively paying for the trade credit. Suppose the order is for $1,000. The buyer can pay $980 in 10 days or wait another 20 days and pay $1,000. (For the moment, we ignore the possibility of stretching.) It's obvious that the buyer is effectively borrowing $980 for 20 days and that the buyer pays $20 in interest on the loan. What's the interest rate?

This interest is ordinary discount interest, which we discussed in Chapter 5. With $20 in interest on $980 borrowed, the rate is $20/$980 = 2.0408%. This is relatively low, but remember that this is the rate per 20-day period. There are 365/20 = 18.25 such periods in a year, so the buyer is paying an effective annual rate (EAR) of:

---

13 Chapter 20 provides a full discussion of credit terms from the seller's viewpoint.

$$EAR = (1.020408)^{18.25} - 1 = 44.6\%$$

From the buyer's point of view, this is an expensive source of financing.

Now suppose the buyer decides to stretch its payables and pay in 45 days. What is the EAR now? The interest is still $20 on $980 borrowed so the rate is still 2.0408%. What stretching changes is the length of the loan period. Since we are paying on Day 45, the loan period is now $45 - 10 = 35$ days. There are $365/35 = 10.43$ such periods in a year. The new EAR is:

$$EAR = (1.020408)^{10.43} - 1 = 23.5\%$$

So you can see that stretching reduces the EAR somewhat but this does not make it a recommended practice. Companies that habitually pay their suppliers late risk supplier ill will. This may impact unfavourably on delivery schedules and, in the extreme case, suppliers may cut off the firm or ship only terms of C.O.D. (cash on delivery). Late payment may also harm the firm's credit rating.

EXAMPLE 18.5: What's the Rate?

Ordinary tiles are often sold 3/30, net 60. What effective annual rate does a buyer pay by not taking the discount? What would the APR be if one were quoted?

Here we have 3 percent discount interest on $60 - 30 = 30$ days' credit. The rate per 30 days is $.03/.97 = 3.093\%$. There are $365/30 = 12.17$ such periods in a year, so the effective annual rate is:

$$EAR = (1.03093)^{12.17} - 1 = 44.9\%$$

The APR, as always, would be calculated by multiplying the rate per period by the number of periods:

$$APR = .03093 \times 12.17 = 37.6\%$$

An interest rate calculated like this APR is often quoted as the cost of the trade credit, and, as this example illustrates, the true cost can be seriously understated.

Money Market Financing

Large firms with excellent credit ratings can obtain financing directly from money markets. Two of the most important money market instruments for short-term financing are commercial paper and bankers acceptances.

www.dbrs.com
www.standardandpoors.com

Commercial paper consists of short-term notes issued by large and highly rated firms. Firms issuing commercial paper in Canada generally have borrowing needs over $20 million. Rating agencies, the Dominion Bond Rating Service and Standard & Poor's (S&P) discussed in Chapter 7, rate commercial paper similarly to bonds. Typically, these notes are of short maturity, ranging from 30 to 90 days with some maturities up to 365 days. Commercial paper is offered in denominations of $100,000 and up. Because the firm issues paper directly and because it usually backs the issue with a special bank line of credit, the interest rate the firm obtains is less than the rate a bank would charge for a direct loan, usually by around 1 percent. Another advantage is that commercial paper offers the issuer flexibility in tailoring the maturity and size of the borrowing.

Bankers acceptances are a variant on commercial paper. When a bank accepts paper, it charges a stamping fee in return for a guarantee of the paper's principal and interest. Stamping fees vary from .20 percent to .75 percent. Bankers acceptances are more widely used than commercial paper in Canada because Canadian chartered banks enjoy stronger credit ratings than all but the largest corporations.[14] The main buyers of bankers acceptances and commercial paper are institutions, including mutual funds, insurance companies, and banks.

A disadvantage of borrowing through bankers acceptances or commercial paper is the risk that the market might temporarily dry up when it comes time to roll over the paper. Extendible commercial paper is an innovation designed to address the risk of market disruption. In the event that the issuer cannot obtain new financing through normal channels, the extension feature makes it possible to keep maturing paper in force beyond its stated maturity.

---

14 The reverse situation prevails in the United States, with commercial paper being more common.

CONCEPT QUESTIONS

1. What are the two basic forms of short-term financing?

2. Describe two types of secured operating loans.

3. Describe factoring and the services it provides.

4. How does trade credit work? Should firms stretch their accounts payable?

5. Describe commercial paper and bankers acceptances. How do they differ?

18.7   SUMMARY AND CONCLUSIONS

1. This chapter introduces the management of short-term finance. Short-term finance involves short-lived assets and liabilities. We trace and examine the short-term sources and uses of cash as they appear on the firm's financial statements. We see how current assets and current liabilities arise in the short-term operating activities and the cash cycle of the firm. This chapter shows why managing the cash cycle is critical to small businesses.

2. Managing short-term cash flows involves the minimizing of costs. The two major costs are carrying costs, the return forgone by keeping too much invested in short-term assets such as cash, and shortage costs, the cost of running out of short-term assets. The objective of managing short-term finance and doing short-term financial planning is to find the optimal trade-off between these two costs.

3. In an ideal economy, the firm could perfectly predict its short-term uses and sources of cash, and net working capital could be kept at zero. In the real world we live in, cash and net working capital provide a buffer that lets the firm meet its ongoing obligations. The financial manager seeks the optimal level of each of the current assets.

4. The financial manager can use the cash budget to identify short-term financial needs. The cash budget tells the manager what borrowing is required or what lending will be possible in the short run. The firm has available to it a number of possible ways of acquiring funds to meet short-term shortfalls, including unsecured and secured loans.

Key Terms

accounts payable period (page 549)
accounts receivable financing (page 566)
accounts receivable period (page 549)
carrying costs (page 554)
cash budget (page 560)
cash cycle (page 549)
cash flow time line (page 549)
covenants (page 566)

inventory loan (page 568)
inventory period (page 549)
letter of credit (page 566)
maturity factoring (page 567)
operating cycle (page 549)
operating loan (page 564)
shortage costs (page 554)
trust receipt (page 568)

Chapter Review Problems and Self-Test

18.1   The Operating and Cash Cycles   Consider the following financial statement information for the Glory Road Company:

Item	Beginning		Ending
Inventory	$1,543		$1,669
Accounts receivable	4,418		3,952
Accounts payable	2,551		2,673
Net sales		$11,500	
Cost of goods sold		8,200	

Calculate the operating and cash cycles.

18.2 **Cash Balance for Masson Corporation** The Masson Corporation has a 60-day average collection period and wishes to maintain a $5 million minimum cash balance. Based on this and the following information, complete the cash budget. What conclusions do you draw?

MASSON CORPORATION
Cash Budget
(in $ millions)

	Q1	Q2	Q3	Q4
Beginning receivables	$120			
Sales	90	120	150	120
Cash collections				
Ending receivables				
Total cash collections				
Total cash disbursements	80	160	180	160
Net cash inflow				
Beginning cash balance	$ 5			
Net cash inflow				
Ending cash balance				
Minimum cash balance				
Cumulative surplus (deficit)				

Answers to Self-Test Problems

18.1 **We first need the turnover ratios.** Note that we have used the average values for all balance sheet items and that we have based the inventory and payables turnover measures on cost of goods sold.

$$\text{Inventory turnover} = \$8,200/[(1,543 + 1,669)/2] = 5.11 \text{ times}$$
$$\text{Receivables turnover} = \$11,500/[(4,418 + 3,952)/2] = 2.75 \text{ times}$$
$$\text{Payables turnover} = \$8,200/[(2,551 + 2,673)/2] = 3.14 \text{ times}$$

We can now calculate the various periods:

$$\text{Inventory period} = 365 \text{ days}/5.11 \text{ times} = 71.43 \text{ days}$$
$$\text{Receivables period} = 365 \text{ days}/2.75 \text{ times} = 132.73 \text{ days}$$
$$\text{Payables period} = 365 \text{ days}/3.14 \text{ times} = 116.24 \text{ days}$$

So the time it takes to acquire inventory and sell it is about 71 days. Collection takes another 133 days, and the operating cycle is thus 71 + 133 = 204 days. The cash cycle is thus 204 days less the payables period, 204 − 116 = 88 days.

18.2 Since Masson has a 60-day collection period, only those sales made in the first 30 days of the quarter are collected in the same quarter. Total cash collections in the first quarter thus equal 30/90 = 1/3 of sales plus beginning receivables, or $120 + 1/3 × $90 = $150. Ending receivables for the first quarter (and the second quarter beginning receivables) are the other 2/3 of sales, or 2/3 × $90 = $60. The remaining calculations are straightforward, and the completed budget follows:

MASSON CORPORATION
Cash Budget
(in $ millions)

	Q1	Q2	Q3	Q4
Beginning receivables	$120	$ 60	$ 80	$100
Sales	90	120	150	120
Cash collection	150	100	130	140
Ending receivables	$ 60	$ 80	$100	$ 80
Total cash collections	$150	$100	$130	$140
Total cash disbursements	80	160	180	160
Net cash inflow	$ 70	–$ 60	–$ 50	–$ 20
Beginning cash balance	$5	$ 75	$ 15	–$ 35
Net cash inflow	70	–60	–50	–20
Ending cash balance	$ 75	$ 15	–$ 35	–$ 55
Minimum cash balance	–$ 5	–$ 5	–$ 5	–$ 5
Cumulative surplus (deficit)	$ 70	$ 10	–$ 40	–$ 60

The primary conclusion from this schedule is that beginning in the third quarter, Masson's cash surplus becomes a cash deficit. By the end of the year, Masson needs to arrange for $60 million in cash beyond what is available.

Concepts Review and Critical Thinking Questions

1. What are some of the characteristics of a firm with a long operating cycle?

2. What are some of the characteristics of a firm with a long cash cycle?

3. For the year just ended, you have gathered the following information on the Holly Corporation:

   a. A $200 dividend was paid.

   b. Accounts payable increased by $500.

   c. Fixed asset purchases were $900.

   d. Inventories increased by $625.

   e. Long-term debt decreased by $1,200.

   Label each as a source or use of cash and describe its effect on the firm's cash balance.

   Use the following information to answer Questions 4–7: In August 2000, Chapters Inc. announced that it

was returning unsold books to suppliers to pay overdue bills and pare down its inventory. Larry Stevenson, Chapters' CEO, stated his firm would no longer "effectively finance the book industry" by purchasing large quantities of books in the spring and holding them for sales in the Christmas season.[15]

4. What impact did this change in inventory policy have on Chapters' operating cycle? Its cash cycle?

5. What was the impact on Chapters' suppliers from the announcement?

6. Why don't all large retailers follow the same policy as Chapters?

7. What was the benefit to Chapters from this policy change?

Questions and Problems

Basic
(Questions 1–11)

1. **Changes in the Cash Account**   Indicate the impact of the following corporate actions on cash, using the letter *I* for an increase, *D* for a decrease, or *N* when no change occurs.

   a. A dividend is paid with funds received from a sale of debt.

   b. Real estate is purchased and paid for with short-term debt.

   c. Inventory is bought on credit.

   d. A short-term bank loan is repaid.

   e. Next year's taxes are prepaid.

   f. Preferred stock is redeemed.

   g. Sales are made on credit.

   h. Interest on long-term debt is paid.

   i. Payments for previous sales are collected.

   j. The accounts payable balance is reduced.

   k. A dividend is paid.

   l. Production supplies are purchased and paid for with a short-term note.

   m. Utility bills are paid.

   n. Cash is paid for raw materials purchased for inventory.

   o. Marketable securities are sold.

2. **Cash Equation**   Kaleb's Korndog Corp. has a book net worth of $9,300. Long-term debt is $1,900. Net working capital, other than cash, is $2,450. Fixed assets are $2,300. How much cash does the company have? If current liabilities are $1,250, what are current assets?

3. **Changes in the Operating Cycle**   Indicate the effect that the following will have on the operating cycle. Use the letter *I* to indicate an increase, the letter *D* for a decrease, and the letter *N* for no change.

   a. Average receivables goes up.

   b. Credit repayment times for customers are increased.

   c. Inventory turnover goes from 3 times to 6 times.

   d. Payables turnover goes from 6 times to 11 times.

   e. Receivables turnover goes from 7 times to 9 times.

   f. Payments to suppliers are accelerated.

4. **Changes in Cycles**   Indicate the impact of the following on the cash and operating cycles, respectively. Use the letter *I* to indicate an increase, the letter *D* for a decrease, and the letter *N* for no change.

   a. The terms of cash discounts offered to customers are made less favourable.

   b. The cash discounts offered by suppliers are decreased; thus, payments are made earlier.

---

15 Our description of Chapters' policies is drawn from M. Strauss, "Chapters admits to aggressive returns," *The Globe and Mail, Report on Business,* August 2000, pp. B1 and B4.

Basic
(continued)

c. An increased number of customers begin to pay in cash instead of with credit.

d. Fewer raw materials than usual are purchased.

e. A greater percentage of raw material purchases are paid for with credit.

f. More finished goods are produced for inventory instead of for order.

5. **Calculating Cash Collections**   The Kolby Coffee Company has projected the following quarterly sales amounts for the coming year:

	Q1	Q2	Q3	Q4
Sales	$800	$760	$940	$870

a. Accounts receivable at the beginning of the year are $300. Kolby has a 45-day collection period. Calculate cash collections in each of the four quarters by completing the following:

	Q1	Q2	Q3	Q4
Beginning receivables				
Sales				
Cash collections				
Ending receivables				

b. Rework (*a*) assuming a collection period of 60 days.

c. Rework (*a*) assuming a collection period of 30 days.

6. **Calculating Cycles**   Consider the following financial statement information for the Bulldog Icers Corporation:

Item	Beginning	Ending
Inventory	$8,413	$10,158
Accounts receivable	5,108	5,439
Accounts payable	6,927	7,625
Net sales	$67,312	
Cost of goods sold	52,827	

Calculate the operating and cash cycles. How do you interpret your answer?

7. **Factoring Receivables**   Your firm has an average collection period of 34 days. Current practice is to factor all receivables immediately at a 2 percent discount. What is the effective cost of borrowing in this case? Assume that default is extremely unlikely.

8. **Calculating Payments**   Iron Man Products has projected the following sales for the coming year:

	Q1	Q2	Q3	Q4
Sales	$540	$630	$710	$785

Sales in the year following this one are projected to be 15 percent greater in each quarter.

a. Calculate payments to suppliers assuming that Iron Man places orders during each quarter equal to 30 percent of projected sales for the next quarter. Assume that Iron Man pays immediately. What is the payables period in this case?

	Q1	Q2	Q3	Q4
Payment of accounts	$	$	$	$

b. Rework (*a*) assuming a 90-day payables period.

	Q1	Q2	Q3	Q4
Payment of accounts	$	$	$	$

c. Rework (*a*) assuming a 60-day payables period.

	Q1	Q2	Q3	Q4
Payment of accounts	$	$	$	$

9. **Calculating Payments**   The Thunder Dan Corporation's purchases from suppliers in a quarter are equal to 75 percent of the next quarter's forecasted sales. The payables period is 60 days. Wages, taxes, and other expenses are 20 percent of sales, and interest and dividends are $60 per quarter. No capital expenditures are planned. Projected quarterly sales are:

	Q1	Q2	Q3	Q4
Sales	$750	$920	$890	$790

Basic
(continued)

Sales for the first quarter of the following year are projected at $970. Calculate Thunder's cash outlays by completing the following:

	Q1	Q2	Q3	Q4
Payments of accounts				
Wages, taxes, other expenses				
Long-term financing expenses				
(interest and dividends)				
Total				

10. **Calculating Cash Collections**   The following is the sales budget for Duck-n-Run, Inc., for the first quarter of 2004:

	January	February	March
Sales budget	$150,000	$173,000	194,000

Credit sales are collected as follows:

   65 percent in the month of the sale

   20 percent in the month after the sale

   15 percent in the second month after the sale

The accounts receivable balance at the end of the previous quarter was $57,000 ($41,000 of which was uncollected December sales).

a.   Compute the sales for November.

b.   Compute the sales for December.

c.   Compute the cash collections from sales for each month from January through March.

11. **Calculating the Cash Budget**   Here are some important figures from the budget of Nashville Nougats, Inc., for the second quarter of 2004:

	April	May	June
Credit sales	$380,000	$396,000	$438,000
Credit purchases	147,000	175,500	200,500
Cash disbursements			
Wages, taxes, and expenses	39,750	48,210	50,300
Interest	11,400	11,400	11,400
Equipment purchases	83,000	91,000	0

The company predicts that 5 percent of its credit sales will never be collected, 35 percent of its sales will be collected in the month of the sale, and the remaining 60 percent will be collected in the following month. Credit purchases will be paid in the month following the purchase.

   In March 2004, credit sales were $210,000, and credit purchases were $156,000. Using this information, complete the following cash budget:

	April	May	June
Beginning cash balance	$280,000		
Cash receipts			
Cash collections from credit sales			
Total cash available			
Cash disbursements			
Purchases			
Wages, taxes, and expenses			
Interest			
Equipment purchases			
Total cash disbursements			
Ending cash balance			

Intermediate
(Questions
12–17)

12. **Costs of Borrowing**   You've worked out a line of credit arrangement that allows you to borrow up to $60 million at any time. The interest rate is .61 percent per month. In addition, 4 percent of the amount that you borrow must be deposited in a non-interest-bearing account. Assume that your bank uses compound interest on its line of credit loans.

a.   What is the effective annual interest rate on this lending arrangement?

b.   Suppose you need $15 million today and you repay it in six months. How much interest will you pay?

Intermediate
(continued)

13. **Costs of Borrowing** A bank offers your firm a revolving credit arrangement for up to $100 million at an interest rate of 2.20 percent per quarter. The bank also requires you to maintain a compensating balance of 5 percent against the *unused* portion of the credit line, to be deposited in a non-interest-bearing account. Assume you have a short-term investment account at the bank that pays 1.40 percent per quarter, and assume that the bank uses compound interest on its revolving credit loans.

    a. What is your effective annual interest rate (an opportunity cost) on the revolving credit arrangement if your firm does not use it during the year?

    b. What is your effective annual interest rate on the lending arrangement if you borrow $60 million immediately and repay it in one year?

    c. What is your effective annual interest rate if you borrow $100 million immediately and repay it in one year?

14. **Costs of Borrowing** You've gone to the bank and asked for a line of credit. The banker allows you to borrow up to $10 million at any time but 2 percent of the amount borrowed has to be deposited in a non-interest-bearing account. You agree with the banker on these terms. You disagree on the interest rate. You want an interest rate of 0.55 percent per month and the banker refuses to negotiate below 0.62 percent per month. Assume that your bank uses compound interest on its line of credit loans.

    a. What is the bank's effective annual interest rate? What will be the effective annual interest rate if you manage to win the negotiation?

    b. Suppose you need $10 million today and repay it entirely in 13 months. How much interest will you save if you obtain the interest rate you want? How much total interest will you be paying?

15. **Calculating the Cash Budget** Timberwolf, Inc. has estimated sales (in millions) for the next four quarters as:

	Q1	Q2	Q3	Q4
Sales	$2	$2.5	$2	$1.5

Sales for the first quarter next year are $2.5 million. Accounts receivable at the beginning of the year were $750,000. Timberwolf has a 30-day collection period.

Timberwolf's purchases from suppliers in a quarter are equal to 37 percent of the next quarter's forecasted sales, and suppliers are normally paid in 24 days. Wages, taxes and other expenses run about 25 percent of sales. Interest and dividends are $120,000 per quarter.

Timberwolf is not planning any major cash outlays in the future. The company started the year with an $8 million cash balance and would like to maintain a minimum balance of no less than $750,000. Complete a cash budget for Timberwolf by filling in the following:

Timberwolf, Inc.
Cash Budget
(in millions)

	Q1	Q2	Q3	Q4
Beginning cash balance	$8			
Net cash inflow				
Ending cash balance				
Minimum cash balance	$0.75			
Cumulative surplus (deficit)				

16. **Calculating the Cash Budget** Wildcat, Inc., has estimated sales (in millions) for the next four quarters as:

	Q1	Q2	Q3	Q4
Sales	$230	$195	$270	$290

Sales for the first quarter of the year after this one are projected at $250 million. Accounts receivable at the beginning of the year were $79 million. Wildcat has a 45-day collection period.

Wildcat's purchases from suppliers in a quarter are equal to 45 percent of the next quarter's forecasted sales, and suppliers are normally paid in 36 days. Wages, taxes, and other expenses run about 30 percent of sales. Interest and dividends are $15 million per quarter.

Wildcat plans a major capital outlay in the second quarter of $90 million. Finally, the company started the year with a $73 million cash balance and wishes to maintain a $30 million minimum balance.

    a. Complete a cash budget for Wildcat by filling in the following:

Intermediate
(continued)

WILDCAT, Inc.
Cash Budget
(in millions)

	Q1	Q2	Q3	Q4
Beginning cash balance	$73			
Net cash inflow				
Ending cash balance				
Minimum cash balance	30			
Cumulative surplus (deficit)				

b. Assume that Wildcat can borrow any needed funds on a short-term basis at a rate of 3 percent per quarter, and can invest any excess funds in short-term marketable securities at a rate of 2 percent per quarter. Prepare a short-term financial plan by filling in the following schedule. What is the net cash cost (total interest paid minus total investment income earned) for the year?

WILDCAT, INC.
Short-Term Financial Plan
(in millions)

	Q1	Q2	Q3	Q4
Beginning cash balance	$73			
Net cash inflow				
New short-term investments				
Income from short-term investments				
Short-term investments sold				
New short-term borrowing				
Interest on short-term borrowing				
Short-term borrowing repaid				
Ending cash balance				
Minimum cash balance	30			
Cumulative surplus (deficit)				
Beginning short-term investments				
Ending short-term investments				
Beginning short-term debt				
Ending short-term debt				

17. **Cash Management Policy** Rework Problem 16 assuming:

   a. Wildcat maintains a minimum cash balance of $45 million.

   b. Wildcat maintains a minimum cash balance of $15 million.

   Based on your answers in (*a*) and (*b*), do you think the firm can boost its profit by changing its cash management policy? Are there other factors that must be considered as well? Explain.

Challenge
(Questions 18–19) 18. **Costs of Borrowing** In exchange for a $500 million fixed commitment line of credit, your firm has agreed to do the following:

   1. Pay 1.3 percent per quarter on any funds actually borrowed.

   2. Maintain a 4 percent compensating balance on any funds actually borrowed.

   3. Pay an up-front commitment fee of .105 percent of the amount of the line.

   Based on this information, answer the following:

   a. Ignoring the commitment fee, what is the effective annual interest rate on this line of credit?

   b. Suppose your firm immediately uses $210 million of the line and pays it off in one year. What is the effective annual interest rate on this $210 million loan?

19. **Costs of Borrowing** Stream Bank offers your firm an 8 percent *discount* interest loan for up to $8 million, and in addition requires you to maintain a 6 percent compensating balance against the amount borrowed. What is the effective annual interest rate on this lending arrangement?

S&P Problems

1. Visit the "Student Centre" at the Online Learning Centre for this textbook (www.mcgrawhill.ca/college/ross). Using the pass code that came with your textbook, access the information in the S&P Market Insight tool. Find the most recent financial statements for Alcan Inc. and Biomira Inc. Calculate the cash and operating cycles for each company for the most recent year. Are the numbers similar for the companies? Why or why not?

2.   Download the most recent quarterly financial statements for Celestica from the above website. Calculate the operating and cash cycle for Celestica over each of the last four quarters. Comment on any changes in the operating or cash cycle over this period.

Internet Application Questions

1. For many medium-sized firms, commercial paper and other direct means of short-term capital are difficult to obtain due to lack of name recognition, lack of sufficient scale, and the costs of rating the paper. Bank of Montreal is one of many Canadian institutions that arranges a "backdoor" entry into the commercial paper market for these firms through Asset Backed Commercial Paper. The idea is to pool current assets of many medium-sized firms, and securitize them by issuing high quality paper against this pool. The following link from Bank of Montreal provides numbers on the ABS market in Canada, and describes the main products. List three reasons to account for the success of the ABS market in Canada.

    www.bmo.com/products/investment/securitization

2. Short-term financing is structured in many different ways. The following site from British Columbia describes different types of short-term credit.

    www.smallbusinessbc.ca

    What type of loan will suit the following companies' short-term financing needs?

    a. Small garment store with seasonal sales.

    b. Mid-sized pulp producer with level sales.

3. In many cases, a straight bank loan may not be the best source of funds. The following link describes a few of the alternative debt sources available to small businesses today.

    www.smallbusinessbc.ca

    Pick any three financing alternatives from the link above, and give an example of a business that would find the particular type of financing attractive.

Suggested Readings

Gallinger, G. W., and P. B. Healey. *Liquidity Analysis and Management,* 2d ed. Reading, MA: Addison-Wesley Publishing, 1991.

Kahlberg, J. G., and K. Parkinson. *Current Asset Management: Cash, Credit and Inventory.* New York: John Wiley & Sons, 1984.

Vander Weide, J., and S. F. Maier. *Managing Corporate Liquidity: An Introduction to Working Capital Management.* New York: John Wiley & Sons, 1985.

CHAPTER 19

Cash and Liquidity Management

Most often, when news breaks about a firm's cash position, it's because the firm is running low on cash. This happened to Air Canada in 2003, when it entered bankruptcy protection and had only $492 million in cash (falling considerably short of its obligations to creditors).[1] Around the same time, some firms had sizeable cash reserves. In 2004, Microsoft made the news regarding its cash position, but not because it was running low on cash. Cash reserves were at $76.6 billion until the company issued a special dividend of $3 a share, paying out a total of $30 billion to investors. Why would firms such as these hold so much cash? We examine cash management in this chapter to explore this question and some related issues.

THIS CHAPTER IS ABOUT how firms manage cash. Cash management is not as complex and conceptually challenging as capital budgeting and asset pricing. Still this is a very important activity and financial managers in many companies, especially in the retail and services industries, spend a significant portion of their time on cash management.

The basic objective in cash management is to keep the investment in cash as low as possible while still keeping the firm operating efficiently and effectively. The goal usually reduces to the dictum, "Collect early and pay late." Accordingly, we discuss ways of accelerating collections and managing disbursements. Our examples feature large firms and how they use computer-based cash management services offered by banks.

In addition, firms must invest temporarily idle cash in short-term marketable securities. As we discuss in various places, these securities can be bought and sold in the financial markets. As a group, they have very little default risk, and most are highly marketable. There are different types of marketable securities and we discuss a few of the most important ones.

 **19.1**

REASONS FOR HOLDING CASH

John Maynard Keynes, in his great work, *The General Theory of Employment, Interest, and Money*, identified three reasons liquidity is important: the precautionary motive, the speculative motive, and the transaction motive. We discuss these next.

---

1 See Eric Reguly, "Gamble may pay off for Air Canada pilots," *The Globe and Mail*, May 31, 2003.

Speculative and Precautionary Motives

speculative motive
The need to hold cash to take advantage of additional investment opportunities, such as bargain purchases.

The **speculative motive** is the need to hold cash to be able to take advantage of, for example, bargain purchases that might arise, attractive interest rates, and (in the case of international firms) favourable exchange rate fluctuations.

For most firms, reserve borrowing ability and marketable securities can be used to satisfy speculative motives. Thus, for a modern firm, there might be a speculative motive for liquidity, but not necessarily for cash per se. Think of it this way: If you have a credit card with a very large credit limit, you can probably take advantage of any unusual bargains that come along without carrying any cash.

precautionary motive
The need to hold cash as a safety margin to act as a financial reserve.

This is also true, to a lesser extent, for precautionary motives. The **precautionary motive** is the need for a safety supply to act as a financial reserve. Once again, there probably is a precautionary motive for liquidity. However, given that the value of money market instruments is relatively certain and that instruments such as T-bills are extremely liquid, there is no real need to literally hold substantial amounts of cash for precautionary purposes.

www.daimlerchrysler.com
www.ford.ca

Take the examples of DaimlerChrysler and Ford: both companies had argued during the late 1990s that they needed huge cash reserves to weather a downturn in the economy if one came. The automotive industry experiences large capital expenditures to engineer new models and update plant and equipment. Thus, the motive for these companies at the time was largely precautionary. The economic slowdown in 2001–2002 resulted in increased competition and larger sales incentives for these companies, and appeared to prove their arguments to be good ones. However, the cost of such reserves is high. If Ford could earn a 10 percent greater return by investing the money it has in reserves, the company would earn an additional $329,000 per day.

The Transaction Motive

transaction motive
The need to hold cash to satisfy normal disbursement and collection activities associated with a firm's ongoing operations.

Cash is needed to satisfy the **transaction motive,** the need to have cash on hand to pay bills. Transaction-related needs come from the normal disbursement and collection activities of the firm. The disbursement of cash includes the payment of wages and salaries, trade debts, taxes, and dividends.

Cash is collected from sales, the selling of assets, and new financing. The cash inflows (collections) and outflows (disbursements) are not perfectly synchronized, and some level of cash holdings is necessary to serve as a buffer. Perfect liquidity is the characteristic of cash that allows it to satisfy the transaction motive.

As electronic funds transfers and other high-speed, paperless payment mechanisms continue to develop, even the transaction demand for cash may all but disappear. Even if it does, however, there is still a demand for liquidity and a need to manage it efficiently.

Costs of Holding Cash

When a firm holds cash in excess of some necessary minimum, it incurs an opportunity cost. The opportunity cost of excess cash (held in currency or bank deposits) is the interest income that could be earned in the next best use, such as investment in marketable securities.

Given the opportunity cost of holding cash, why would a firm hold any cash? The answer is that a cash balance must be maintained to provide the liquidity necessary for transaction needs—paying bills. If the firm maintains too small a cash balance, it may run out of cash. When this happens, the firm may have to raise cash on a short-term basis. This could involve, for example, selling marketable securities or borrowing.

Activities such as selling marketable securities and borrowing involve various costs. As we've discussed, holding cash has an opportunity cost. To determine the target cash balance, the firm must weigh the benefits of holding cash against these costs. We discuss this subject in more detail in the next section.

Cash Management versus Liquidity Management

Before we move on, we should note that it is important to distinguish between true cash management and a more general subject, liquidity management. The distinction is a source of confusion because the word *cash* is used in practice in two different ways. First of all, it has its literal meaning, actual cash on hand. However, financial managers frequently use the word to describe a firm's holdings of cash along with its marketable securities, and marketable securities are sometimes called cash equivalents or near-cash. In the case of Ford's cash position, for example, what was actually being described was Ford's total cash and cash equivalents.

The distinction between liquidity management and cash management is straightforward. Liquidity management concerns the optimal quantity of liquid assets a firm should have on hand, and it is one particular aspect of the current asset management policies we discussed in our previous chapter. Cash management is much more closely related to optimizing mechanisms for collecting and disbursing cash, and it is this subject that we primarily focus on in this chapter.

CONCEPT QUESTIONS

1. What is the transaction motive, and how does it lead firms to hold cash?

2. What is the cost to the firm of holding excess cash?

19.2

target cash balance
A firm's desired cash level as determined by the trade-off between carrying costs and shortage costs.

adjustment costs
The costs associated with holding too little cash. Also shortage costs.

DETERMINING THE TARGET CASH BALANCE

Based on our general discussion of current assets in the previous chapter, the **target cash balance** involves a trade-off between the opportunity costs of holding too much cash (the carrying costs) and the costs of holding too little (the shortage costs, also called **adjustment costs**). The nature of these costs depends on the firm's working capital policy.

If the firm has a flexible working capital policy, it probably maintains a marketable securities portfolio. As we showed earlier, large Canadian corporations carry portfolios of marketable securities. In this case, the adjustment or shortage costs are the trading costs associated with buying and selling securities. In addition to these costs, firms holding large amounts of cash may be too flexible. This can occur if management prefers the comfort of sitting on a large cash balance instead of investing in projects with positive net present values. If this happens, shareholders face an unwanted agency cost. In Chapter 23, we discuss how takeover bids can discipline such managers.[2]

If the firm has a restrictive working capital policy, it probably borrows short-term to meet cash shortages. The costs are the interest and other expenses associated with arranging a loan. The restrictive case is more realistic for small- and medium-sized companies.

In the following discussion, we assume the firm has a flexible policy. Its cash management consists of moving money in and out of marketable securities. This is a very traditional approach to the subject, and it is a nice way of illustrating the costs and benefits of holding cash. Keep in mind, however, that the distinction between cash and money market investments is becoming increasingly blurred as electronic technology allows easy and fast transfers.

The Basic Idea

Figure 19.1 presents the cash management problem for our flexible firm. If a firm tries to keep its cash holdings too low, it finds itself running out of cash more often than is desirable, and thus selling marketable securities (and perhaps later buying marketable securities to replace those sold) more frequently than it would if the cash balance were higher. Thus, trading costs are high when the size of the cash balance is low. These fall as the cash balance becomes larger.

In contrast, the opportunity costs of holding cash are very low if the firm holds very little cash. These costs increase as the cash holdings rise because the firm is giving up more and more in interest that could have been earned.

At point C^* in Figure 19.1, the sum of the costs is given by the total cost curve. As shown, the minimum total cost occurs where the two individual cost curves cross. At this point, the

---

2 This argument was originated in M.C. Jensen, "Agency Costs of Free Cash Flow, Corporate Finance and Takeovers," *American Economic Review*, May 1986.

opportunity costs and the trading costs are equal. This is the target cash balance, and it is the point the firm should try to find.

Figure 19.1 is essentially the same as one in the previous chapter. However, if we use real data on holding and opportunity costs, we can come up with a precise dollar optimum investment in cash. Appendix 19A covers two models that do this in varying degrees of complexity. Here, we focus only on their implications. All other things being equal:

1. The greater the interest rate, the lower is the target cash balance.
2. The greater the trading cost, the higher is the target balance.

These are both fairly obvious from looking at Figure 19.1, but they bring out an important point on the evolution of computerized cash management techniques. In the early 1980s, high interest rates (the prime rate was over 22 percent) caused the cost of idle cash to skyrocket. In response, large corporations and banks invested in applying computer and communications technologies to cash management. The result was lower trading costs. With systems in place, banks are now able to offer cash management services to smaller customers.

Going beyond the simple framework of Figure 19.1, the more advanced models also show that the target cash balance should be higher for firms facing greater uncertainty in forecasting their cash needs. This makes sense because such firms need a larger cash balance as a cushion against unexpected outflows. We cover cash management under uncertainty later in the chapter.

Other Factors Influencing the Target Cash Balance

Before moving on, we briefly discuss two additional considerations that affect the target cash balance.

First, in our discussion of cash management, we assume cash is invested in marketable securities such as Treasury bills. The firm obtains cash by selling these securities. Another alternative is to borrow cash. Borrowing introduces additional considerations to cash management:

1. Borrowing is likely to be more expensive than selling marketable securities because the interest rate is likely to be higher. For example, Figure 19.7 in a later section shows that the prime rate considerably exceeds all money market rates.

FIGURE 19.1

Costs of holding cash

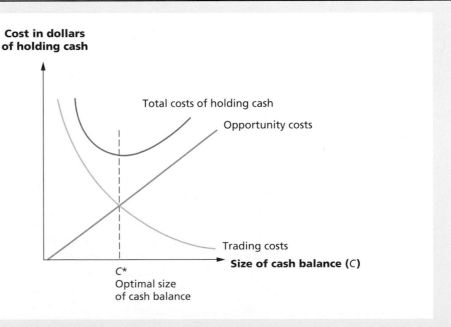

Trading costs are increased when the firm must sell securities to establish a cash balance. Opportunity costs are increased when there is a cash balance because there is no return to cash.

2. The need to borrow depends on management's desire to hold low cash balances. A firm is more likely to have to borrow to cover an unexpected cash outflow the greater its cash flow variability and the lower its investment in marketable securities.

Second, for large firms, the trading costs of buying and selling securities are very small when compared to the opportunity costs of holding cash. For example, suppose a firm has $1 million in cash that won't be needed for 24 hours. Should the firm invest the money or leave it sitting?

Suppose the firm can invest the money overnight at the call money rate. To do this, the treasurer arranges through a chartered bank to lend funds for 24 hours to an investment dealer. According to Figure 19.7 in Section 19.4, this is an annualized rate of 4.25 percent per year. The daily rate is about 1.2 basis points (.012 percent or .00012).[3]

The daily return earned on $1 million is thus $0.00012 \times \$1$ million = $120. In most cases, the order cost would be much less than this. Following up on our earlier point about technology and cash management, large corporations buy and sell securities daily so they are unlikely to leave substantial amounts of cash idle.

CONCEPT QUESTIONS

1. What is a target cash balance?

2. How do changes in interest rates affect the target cash balance? Changes in trading costs?

UNDERSTANDING FLOAT

As you no doubt know, the amount of money you have according to your chequebook can be very different from the amount of money that your bank thinks you have. The reason is that some of the cheques you have written haven't yet been presented to the bank for payment. The same thing is true for a business. The cash balance that a firm shows on its books is called the firm's *book* or *ledger balance*. The balance shown in its bank account is called its *available* or *collected balance*. The difference between the available balance and the ledger balance is called the **float**, and it represents the net effect of cheques in the process of clearing (moving through the banking system).

float
The difference between book cash and bank cash, representing the net effect of cheques in the process of clearing.

Disbursement Float

Cheques written by a firm generate disbursement float, causing a decrease in its book balance but no change in its available balance. For example, suppose General Mechanics, Inc. (GMI), currently has $100,000 on deposit with its bank. On June 8, it buys some raw materials and puts a cheque in the mail for $100,000. The company's book balance is immediately reduced by $100,000 as a result.

GMI's bank, however, does not find out about this cheque until it is presented to GMI's bank for payment on, say, June 14. Until the cheque is presented, the firm's available balance is greater than its book balance by $100,000. In other words, before June 8, GMI has a zero float:

Float = Firm's available balance – Firm's book balance
        − $100,000   − $100,000   = $0

GMI's position from June 8 to June 14 is:

Disbursement float = Firm's available balance – Firm's book balance
               = $100,000   − $0
               = $100,000

---

3 A basis point is 1 percent of 1 percent. Also, the annual interest rate is calculated as $(1 + R)^{365} = 1.0425$, implying a daily rate of .012 percent.

During this period while the cheque is clearing (moving through the mail and the banking system), GMI has a balance with the bank of $100,000. It can obtain the benefit of this cash while the cheque is clearing. For example, the available balance could be temporarily invested in marketable securities and thus earn more interest. We return to this subject a little later.

Collection Float and Net Float

Cheques received by the firm create collection float. Collection float increases book balances but does not immediately change available balances. For example, suppose GMI receives a cheque from a customer for $100,000 on October 8. Assume, as before, that the company has $100,000 deposited at its bank and a zero float. It processes the cheque through the bookkeeping department and increases its book balance by $100,000 to $200,000. However, the additional cash is not available to GMI until the cheque is deposited in the firm's bank. This occurs on, say, October 9, the next day. In the meantime, the cash position at GMI reflects a collection float of $100,000. We can summarize these events. Before October 8, GMI's position is:

$$\begin{aligned}\text{Float} &= \text{Firm's available balance} - \text{Firm's book balance}\\ &= \$100,000 \qquad\qquad\quad - \$100,000\\ &= \$0\end{aligned}$$

GMI's position from October 8 to October 9 is:

$$\begin{aligned}\text{Collection float} &= \text{Firm's available balance} - \text{Firm's book balance}\\ &= \$100,000 \qquad\qquad\quad - \$200,000\\ &= -\$100,000\end{aligned}$$

In general, a firm's payment (disbursement) activities generate disbursement float, and its collection activities generate collection float. The net effect, that is, the sum of the total collection and disbursement floats, is the net float. The net float at a point in time is simply the overall difference between the firm's available balance and its book balance.

If the net float is positive, the firm's disbursement float exceeds its collection float and its available balance exceeds its book balance. In other words, the bank thinks the firm has more cash than it really does. This, of course, is desirable. If the available balance is less than the book balance, the firm has a net collection float. This is undesirable because we actually have more cash than the bank thinks we do, but we can't use it.

A firm should be concerned with its net float and available balance more than its book balance. Knowing that a cheque will not clear for several days, a financial manager can keep a lower cash balance at the bank than might be true otherwise. This can generate a great deal of money.

For example, take the case of ExxonMobil. The average daily sales of ExxonMobil are about U.S. $650 million. If ExxonMobil's collections could be speeded up by a single day, then ExxonMobil could free up $650 million for investing. At a relatively modest 0.015 percent daily rate, the interest earned would be on the order of $97,500 per day. This could represent the annual salary of a senior financial manager.

www.exxon.com

EXAMPLE 19.1: Staying Afloat

Suppose you have $5,000 on deposit. You write and mail a cheque for $1,000. You receive a cheque for $2,000 and put it in your wallet to deposit the next time you use a bank machine. What are your disbursement, collection, and net floats?

After you write the $1,000 cheque, you show a balance of $4,000 on your books, but the bank shows $5,000 while the cheque is moving through the mail. This is a disbursement float of $1,000.

After you receive the $2,000 cheque, you show a balance of $6,000. Your available balance doesn't rise until you deposit

the cheque. This is a collection float of –$2,000. Your net float is the sum of the collection and disbursement floats, or –$1,000.

Overall, you show $6,000 on your books, but the bank only shows $5,000 cash. The discrepancy between your available balance and your book balance is the net float (–$1,000), and it is bad for you. If you write another cheque for $5,500, it might bounce even though, net, it shouldn't. This is the reason the financial manager has to be more concerned with available balances than book balances.

Float Management

Float management involves controlling the collection and disbursement of cash. The objective in cash collection is to speed up collections and reduce the lag between the time customers pay their bills and the time the cheques are collected. The objective in cash disbursement is to control payments and minimize the firm's costs associated with making payments.

Float can be broken down into three parts: mail float, processing float, and availability float:

1. *Mail float* is the part of the collection and disbursement process where cheques are trapped in the postal system.
2. *Processing float* is the time it takes the receiver of a cheque to process the payment and deposit it in a bank.
3. *Availability float* refers to the time required to clear a cheque through the banking system. In the Canadian banking system, availability float does not exceed one day for creditworthy firms and is often zero, so this is the least important part.

Speeding collections involves reducing one or more of these float components. Slowing disbursements involves increasing one of them. Later, we describe some procedures for managing float times; before that, we need to discuss how float is measured.

MEASURING FLOAT The size of the float depends on both the dollars and time delay involved. For example, suppose you receive a cheque for $500 from another province each month. It takes five days in the mail to reach you (the mail float) and one day for you to get over to the bank (the processing float). The bank gives you immediate availability (so there is no availability float). The total delay is $5 + 1 = 6$ days.

What is your average daily float? There are two equivalent ways of calculating the answer: First, you have a $500 float for six days, so we say the total float is $6 \times \$500 = \$3,000$. Assuming 30 days in the month, the average daily float is $\$3,000/30 = \$100$.

Second, your float is $500 for 6 days out of the month and zero the other 24 days (again assuming 30 days in a month). Your average daily float is thus:

$$
\begin{aligned}
\text{Average daily float} &= (6 \times \$500 + 24 \times 0)/30 \\
&= 6/30 \times \$500 + 24/30 \times 0 \\
&= \$3,000/30 \\
&= \$100
\end{aligned}
$$

This means that, on an average day, there is $100 that is not available to spend. In other words, on average, your book balance is $100 greater than your available balance, a $100 average collection float.

Things are only a little more complicated when there are multiple receipts. Suppose Concepts, Ltd., receives two items each month as follows:

	Amount	Days Delay	Total Float
Item 1:	$5,000,000	× 9	= $45,000,000
Item 2:	3,000,000	× 5	= 15,000,000
Total	$8,000,000		$60,000,000

The average daily float is equal to:

$$
\begin{aligned}
\text{Average daily float} &= \text{Total float/Total days} \\
&= \$60,000,000/30 = \$2,000,000
\end{aligned}
$$

So, on an average day, $2 million is uncollected and not available.

Another way to see this is to calculate the average daily receipts and multiply by the weighted average delay. Average daily receipts are:

$$
\begin{aligned}
\text{Average daily receipts} &= \text{Total receipts/Total days} \\
&= \$8,000,000/30 = \$266,666.67
\end{aligned}
$$

Of the $8 million total receipts, $5 million, or 5/8 of the total, is delayed for nine days. The other 3/8 is delayed for five days. The weighted average delay is thus:

$$\text{Weighted average delay} = (5/8) \times 9 \text{ days} + (3/8) \times 5 \text{ days}$$
$$= 5.625 + 1.875 = 7.50 \text{ days}$$

The average daily float is thus:

$$\text{Average daily float} = \text{Average daily receipts} \times \text{Weighted average delay} \qquad \textbf{[19.1]}$$
$$= \$266{,}666.67 \times 7.50 \text{ days} = \$2{,}000{,}000$$

This is just as we had before.

See www.cfoasia.com for an
international view on cash
management.

COST OF THE FLOAT The basic cost to the firm of collection float is simply the opportunity cost from not being able to use the cash. At a minimum, the firm could earn interest on the cash if it were available for investing.

Suppose the Lambo Corporation has average daily receipts of $1,000 and a weighted average delay of three days. The average daily float is thus $3 \times \$1,000 = \$3,000$. This means that, on a typical day, there is $3,000 that is not earning interest. Suppose Lambo could eliminate the float entirely. What would be the benefit? If it costs $2,000 to eliminate the float, what is the NPV of doing it?

After the float is eliminated, daily receipts are still $1,000. We collect the same day since the float is eliminated, so daily collections are also still $1,000. The only change occurs the first day. On that day, we catch up and collect $1,000 from the sale made three days ago. Because the float is gone, we also collect on the sales made two days ago, one day ago, and today, for an additional $3,000. Total collections today are thus $4,000 instead of $1,000.

What we see is that Lambo generates an extra $3,000 today by eliminating the float. On every subsequent day, Lambo receives $1,000 in cash just as it did before the float was eliminated. If you recall our definition of relevant cash flow, the only change in the firm's cash flow from eliminating the float is this extra $3,000 that comes in immediately. No other cash flows are affected, so Lambo is $3,000 richer.

In other words, the PV of eliminating the float is simply equal to the total float. Lambo could pay this amount out as a dividend, invest it in interest-bearing assets, or do anything else with it. If it costs $2,000 to eliminate the float, the NPV is $3,000 − 2,000 = $1,000, so Lambo should do it.

ELECTRONIC DATA INTERCHANGE: THE END OF FLOAT? *Electronic data interchange* (EDI) is a general term that refers to the growing practice of direct, electronic information exchange between all types of businesses. One important use of EDI, often called financial EDI, or FEDI, is to electronically transfer financial information and funds between parties, thereby eliminating paper invoices, paper cheques, mailing, and handling. For example, it is now possible to arrange to have your chequing account directly debited each month to pay many types of bills, and corporations now routinely directly deposit paycheques into employee accounts. More generally, EDI allows a seller to send a bill electronically to a buyer, thereby avoiding the mail. The seller can then authorize payment, which also occurs electronically. Its bank then transfers the funds to the seller's account at a different bank. Major banks have implemented a financial EDI system for personal banking. Canadian banks have added personal banking services for clients using their Web-based systems whereby clients can pay bills online and can also receive their bills electronically instead of by mail. The net effect is that the length of time required to initiate and complete a business or personal transaction is shortened considerably, and much of what we normally think of as float is sharply reduced or eliminated. As the use of FEDI increases (which it will), float management will evolve to focus much more on issues surrounding computerized information exchange and funds transfers.

EXAMPLE 19.2: Reducing the Float

Instead of eliminating the float, suppose Lambo can reduce it to one day. What is the maximum Lambo should be willing to pay for this?

If Lambo can reduce the float from three days to one day, the amount of the float will fall from $3,000 to $1,000. We see immediately that the PV of doing this is just equal to the $2,000 float reduction. Lambo should thus be willing to pay up to $2,000.

At the time of writing, the popularity of extranet portals is growing over EDI, especially in the electronics and high-tech industries.[4] Original equipment manufacturers (OEMs) are putting pressure on manufacturing suppliers to abandon EDI for Web-based business-to-business (B2B) extranets. One example of a B2B platform is RosettaNet, a non-profit consortium of 40 of the largest high-tech companies, including Motorola, IBM, and Sony. Two of the drawbacks that firms face switching away from EDI (and FEDI) are that it is very expensive and complex for many companies to set up and that they would be losing efficiency in the switch because the extranets require more manual work than EDI. Because of security concerns and lack of standardization, don't look for e-commerce and extranets to completely eliminate the need for EDI any time soon. In fact, it appears these complementary systems will most likely be used in tandem.

CONCEPT QUESTIONS

1. Which would a firm be most interested in reducing, collection or disbursement float? Why?

2. How is daily average float calculated?

3. What is the benefit from reducing or eliminating float?

Accelerating Collections

Based on our discussion, we can depict the basic parts of the cash collection process in Figure 19.2. The total time in this process is made up of mailing time, cheque-processing time, and the bank's cheque-clearing time. The amount of time that cash spends in each part of the cash collection process depends on where the firm's customers are located and how efficient the firm is at collecting cash.

Coordinating the firm's efforts in all areas in Figure 19.2 is its cash flow information system. Tracking payments through the system and providing the cash manager with up-to-date daily cash balances and investment rates are its key tasks. Chartered banks offer cash information systems that all but put the bank on the manager's desk. Linking the manager's computer with the bank's system gives the manager access to account balances and transactions and information on money market rates. The system also allows the manager to transfer funds and make money market investments.

The cash management system has security features to prevent unauthorized use. Different passwords allow access to each level of authority. For example, you could give your receivables clerk access to deposit activity files but not to payroll. Some systems use **smart cards** for security. A smart card looks like a credit card but contains a computer chip that can be programmed to grant access to certain files only. The card must be inserted into an access device attached to a personal computer and provides another safeguard in addition to a password.

We next discuss several techniques used to accelerate collections and reduce collection time: systems to expedite mailing and cheque processing and concentration banking.

smart card
Much like an automated teller machine card; one use is within corporations to control access to information by employees.

Over-the-Counter Collections

In an over-the-counter system, customers pay in person at field offices or stores. Most large retailers, utilities, and many other firms receive some payments this way. Because the payments are made at a company location, there is no mail delay. The manager of the field location is responsible for ensuring that cheques and cash collected are deposited promptly and for reporting daily deposit amounts to the head office.

When payments are received by mail, a company may instruct customers to mail cheques to a collection point address on its invoices. By distributing the collection points locally throughout

---

4 Extranet portals are private networks that use Internet protocol and public telecommunication systems to securely share information with certain stakeholders, while EDI implies direct computer-to-computer transactions into vendors' databases and ordering systems. Levinson, Meridith. "How to Keep the Web from Becoming a Trap; Smart companies are taking their transition from EDI to the Internet slowly, to keep IT costs down and let suppliers and customers investments in technology catch up," *CIO*, Framingham: May 1, 2006. Vol. 19, Iss. 14, p. 1.

FIGURE 19.2

Float time line

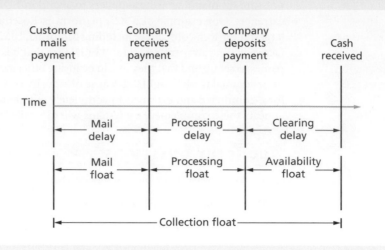

its market area, the company avoids the delays occurring when all payments are mailed to its head office. If the collection points are field offices, the next steps are the same as for over-the-counter collections. A popular alternative, lockboxes, contracts out the collection points to a bank.

lockboxes
Special post office boxes set up to intercept and speed up accounts receivable payments.

LOCKBOXES   **Lockboxes** are special post office boxes set up to intercept accounts receivable payments. Figure 19.3 illustrates a lockbox system. The collection process is started by business and retail customers mailing their cheques to a post office box instead of sending them to the firm. The lockbox is maintained at a local bank branch. Large corporations may maintain a number of lockboxes, one in each significant market area. The location depends on a trade-off between bank fees and savings on mailing time.

In the typical lockbox system, the local bank branch collects the lockbox cheques from the post office daily. The bank deposits the cheques directly to the firm's account. Details of the operation are recorded in some computer-usable form and sent to the firm.

A lockbox system reduces mailing time because cheques are received at a nearby post office instead of at corporate headquarters. Lockboxes also reduce the processing time because the corporation doesn't have to open the envelopes and deposit cheques for collection. In all, a bank lockbox should enable a firm to get its receipts processed, deposited, and cleared faster than if it were to receive cheques at its headquarters and deliver them itself to the bank for deposit and clearing.

ELECTRONIC COLLECTION SYSTEMS   Over-the-counter and lockbox systems are standard ways to reduce mail and processing float time. They are used by almost all large Canadian firms that can benefit from them. Newer approaches focus on reducing float virtually to zero by replacing cheques with electronic funds transfer. Examples used in Canada include preauthorized payments, point-of-sale transfers, and electronic trade payables. We discuss the first two here and the third later when we look at disbursement systems.

Preauthorized payments are paperless transfers of contractual or instalment payments from the customer's account directly to the firm's. Common applications are mortgage payments and installment payments for insurance, rent, cable TV, telephone, and so on. This system eliminates all invoice paperwork and the deposit and reconciliation of cheques. There is no mail or processing float.

debit card
An automated teller machine card used at the point of purchase to avoid the use of cash. As this is not a credit card, money must be available in the user's bank account.

Point-of-sale systems use **debit cards** to transfer funds directly from a customer's bank account to a retailer's. A debit card works like a bank machine (ATM) card with a personal identification card (PIN) for security. Unlike a credit card, the funds are transferred immediately. Point-of-sale systems are common in Canada.

The next generation of cards for point-of-sale applications is the smart card mentioned earlier in its role of security for corporate cash management systems. Smart cards differ from debit

FIGURE 19.3

Overview of lockbox processing

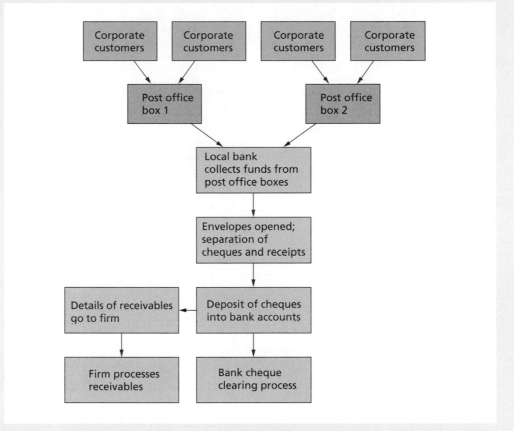

The flow starts when a corporate customer mails remittances to a post office box number instead of to the corporation. Several times a day the bank collects the lockbox receipts from the post office. The cheques are then put into the company bank accounts.

cards in that they contain a chip that can hold a cash balance. Consumers can download small amounts of money (usually under $300) directly on the card and then spend it at point-of-sale terminals. The advantage of smart cards is that, with the balance programmed on the card's chip, there is no need for the merchant to have technology that goes online to the customer's bank. Several Canadian banks test marketed smart card technology in several Canadian communities in the late 1990s, and are currently sponsoring the Dexit smart card in Toronto, but there has not yet been any commitment to a broad application of smart card payment.

CASH CONCENTRATION   Using lockboxes or other collection systems helps firms collect cheques from customers and get them deposited rapidly. But the job is not finished yet since these systems give the firm cash at a number of widely dispersed branches. Until it is concentrated in a central account, the cash is of little use to the firm for paying bills, reducing loans, or investing.

With a concentration banking system, sales receipts are processed at field sales offices and banks providing lockbox services and deposited locally. Surplus funds are transferred from the various local branches to a single, central concentration account. This process is illustrated in Figure 19.4, where concentration banks are combined with over-the-counter collection and lockboxes in a total cash management system.

Large firms in Canada may manage collections through one chartered bank across the country. Chartered banks offer a concentrator account that automatically electronically transfers deposits at any branch in Canada to the firm's concentration account. These funds receive **same day value.** This means the firm has immediate use of the funds even though it takes 24 hours for

same day value
Bank makes proceeds of cheques deposited available the same day before cheques clear.

FIGURE 19.4

Lockboxes and concentration banks in a cash management system

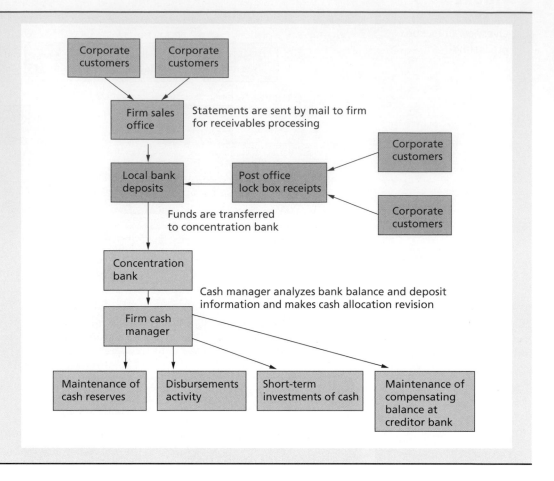

a cheque to clear in Canada.[5] If the concentration involves branches of more than one bank, electronic transfers take place between banks.

Once the funds are in the concentration account, the bank can make automatic transfers to pay down the firm's credit line or, if there is a surplus, to an investment account. Transfers are made in units of minimum size agreed in advance. A common practice is in units of $5,000. Mid-sized firms lacking in money market expertise may invest in bank accounts at competitive interest rates. The largest firms have the capability to purchase money market instruments electronically.

Controlling Disbursements

Accelerating collections is one method of cash management; slowing disbursements is another. This can be a sensitive area and some practices exist that we do not recommend. For example, some small firms that are short of working capital make disbursements on the "squeaky wheel" principle." Payables invoices are processed before their due dates and cheques printed. When the cheques are ready, the firm's controller puts them all in a desk drawer. As suppliers call and ask for their money, the cheques come out of the drawer and go into the mail! We do not recommend the desk drawer method because it is bad for supplier relations and borders on being unethical.

CONTROLLING DISBURSEMENTS IN PRACTICE   As we have seen, float in terms of slowing down payments comes from mail delivery, cheque-processing time, and collection of funds. In the United States, disbursement float can be increased by writing a cheque on a geographically distant bank. For example, a New York supplier might be paid with cheques drawn on a Los Angeles bank. This increases the time required for the cheques to clear through the

---

5 Since the bank is providing availability in advance of receiving funds, same day availability creates collection float for the bank. An interest charge on this float is usually included in the bank's fees.

banking system. Mailing cheques from remote post offices is another way firms slow disbursement. Because there are significant ethical (and legal) issues associated with deliberately delaying disbursements in these and similar ways, such strategies appear to be disappearing. In Canada, banks provide same day availability so the temptation is easy to resist.

For these reasons, the goal is to control rather than simply delay disbursements. A treasurer should try to pay payables on the last day appropriate for net terms or a discount.[6] The traditional way is to write a cheque and mail it timed to arrive on the due date. With the cash management system we described earlier, the payment can be programmed today for electronic transfer on the future due date. This eliminates paper along with guesswork about mail times.

The electronic payment is likely to come from a disbursement account, kept separate from the concentration account to ease accounting and control. Firms keep separate accounts for payroll, vendor disbursements, customer refunds, and so on. This makes it easy for the bank to provide each cost or profit centre with its own statement.

zero-balance account
A chequing account in which a zero balance is maintained by transfers of funds from a master account in an amount only large enough to cover cheques presented.

Firms use **zero-balance accounts** to avoid carrying extra balances in each disbursement account. With a zero-balance account, the firm, in cooperation with its bank, transfers in just enough funds to cover cheques presented that day. Figure 19.5 illustrates how such a system might work. In this case, the firm maintains two disbursement accounts, one for suppliers and one for payroll. As shown, when the firm does not use zero-balance accounts, each of these accounts must have a safety stock of cash to meet unanticipated demands. A firm that uses zero-balance accounts can keep one safety stock in a master account and transfer in the funds to the two subsidiary accounts as needed. The key is that the total amount of cash held as a buffer is smaller under the zero-balance arrangement, thereby freeing cash to be used elsewhere.

CONCEPT QUESTIONS

1. What are collection and disbursement floats?

2. What are lockboxes? Concentration banking? Zero-balance accounts?

3. How do computer and communications technologies aid in cash management by large corporations?

FIGURE 19.5

Zero-balance accounts

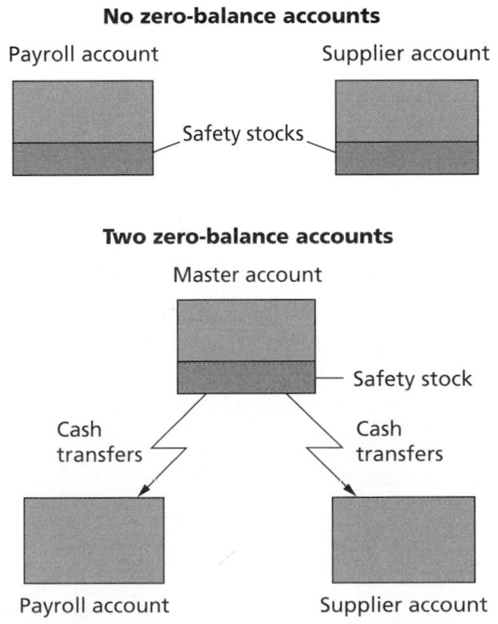

No zero-balance accounts

Payroll account   Supplier account

Safety stocks

Two zero-balance accounts

Master account

Safety stock

Cash transfers   Cash transfers

Payroll account   Supplier account

---

6 We discuss credit terms in depth in Chapter 20.

19.4

INVESTING IDLE CASH

If a firm has a temporary cash surplus, it can invest in short-term securities. As we have mentioned at various times, the market for short-term financial assets is called the money market. The maturity of short-term financial assets that trade in the money market is one year or less.

Most large firms manage their own short-term financial assets through transactions with banks and investment dealers. Some firms use money market funds that invest in short-term financial assets for a management fee. The management fee is compensation for the professional expertise and diversification provided by the fund manager.

Money market funds are becoming increasingly popular in Canada. Also, Canadian chartered banks offer arrangements in which the bank takes all excess available funds at the close of each business day and invests them for the firm.

Temporary Cash Surpluses

Firms have temporary cash surpluses for various reasons. Two of the most important are the financing of seasonal or cyclical activities and the financing of planned or possible expenditures.

www.tru.com

SEASONAL OR CYCLICAL ACTIVITIES   Some firms have a predictable cash flow pattern. They have surplus cash flows during part of the year and deficit cash flows the rest of the year. For example, Toys "R" Us, a retail toy firm, has a seasonal cash flow pattern influenced by Christmas.

A firm such as Toys "R" Us may buy marketable securities when surplus cash flows occur and sell marketable securities when deficits occur. Of course, bank loans are another short-term financing device. The use of bank loans and marketable securities to meet temporary financing needs is illustrated in Figure 19.6. In this case, the firm is following a compromise working capital policy in the sense we discussed in the previous chapter.

PLANNED OR POSSIBLE EXPENDITURES   Firms frequently accumulate temporary investments in marketable securities to provide the cash for a plant construction program,

FIGURE 19.6

Seasonal cash demands

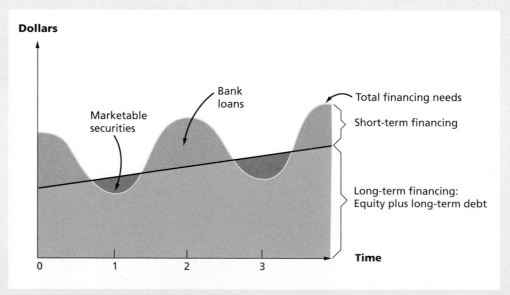

Time 1: A surplus cash flow exists. Seasonal demand for assets is low. The surplus cash flow is invested in short-term marketable securities.

Time 2: A deficit cash flow exists. Seasonal demand for assets is high. The financial deficit is financed by selling marketable securities and by bank borrowing.

dividend payment, and other large expenditures. Thus, firms may issue bonds and stocks before the cash is needed, investing the proceeds in short-term marketable securities, and then selling the securities to finance the expenditures. Also, firms may face the possibility of having to make a large cash outlay. An obvious example would be the possibility of losing a large lawsuit. Firms may build up cash surpluses against such a contingency.

Characteristics of Short-Term Securities

Given that a firm has some temporarily idle cash, there are a variety of short-term securities available for investing. The most important characteristics of these short-term marketable securities are their maturity, default risk, and marketability. Consistent with Chapter 12's discussion of risk and return, managers of marketable securities portfolios have an opportunity to increase expected returns in exchange for taking on higher risk. Marketable securities managers almost always resolve this trade-off in favour of low risk. Because this portfolio is a liquidity reserve, preservation of capital is generally the primary goal.

MATURITY Maturity refers to the time period over which interest and principal payments are made. From Chapter 7, we know that for a given change in the level of interest rates, the prices of longer maturity securities change more than those of shorter maturity securities. As a consequence, firms that invest in long-term maturity securities are accepting greater risk than firms that invest in securities with short-term maturities.

We called this type of risk interest rate risk. Firms often limit their investments in marketable securities to those maturing in less than 90 days to avoid the risk of losses in value from changing interest rates. Of course, the expected return on securities with short-term maturities is usually (but not always) less than the expected return on securities with longer maturities.

For example, suppose you are the treasurer of a firm with $10 million needed to make a major capital investment after 90 days. You have decided to invest in obligations of the Government of Canada to eliminate all possible default risk. The newspaper (or your computer screen) provides you with the list of securities and rates in Figure 19.7. The safest investment is three-month Treasury bills yielding 3.08 percent. Because this matches the maturity of the

FIGURE 19.7

Money market quotations

YIELDS & RATES

Supplied by Reuters. Indicative late afternoon rates.

CANADIAN YIELDS

	Latest	Prev day	Week ago	4 wks ago
T-Bills				
1-month	4.09	4.09	4.07	3.97
3-month	4.14	4.17	4.15	4.09
6-month	4.18	4.22	4.18	4.14
1-year	4.28	4.32	4.23	4.23
Bonds				
2-year	4.16	4.19	4.07	4.15
5-year	4.25	4.31	4.17	4.32
7-year	4.33	4.39	4.24	4.40
10-year	4.39	4.45	4.29	4.47
30-year	4.44	4.50	4.35	4.50
Banker's acceptances *(ask price)*				
1-month	4.30	4.31	4.30	4.13
3-month	4.34	4.34	4.32	4.25
6-month	4.37	4.37	4.34	4.30
3-mth forward rate agreement				
3-month	4.39	4.39	4.30	4.30
6-month	4.44	4.45	4.33	4.38
9-month	4.47	4.48	4.35	4.44

U.S. YIELDS

	Latest	Prev day	Week ago	4 wks ago
T-Bills				
1-month	4.74	4.75	4.74	4.58
3-month	4.83	4.85	4.81	4.79
6-month	5.04	5.07	5.00	5.00
Bonds				
2-year	5.02	5.03	4.95	4.96
5-year	5.01	5.03	4.97	5.03
10-year	5.10	5.12	5.07	5.15
30-year	5.19	5.22	5.17	5.24
Commercial paper				
1-month	4.99	5.02	4.96	4.85
3-month	5.01	5.01	5.01	4.90
6-month	5.15	5.10	5.07	5.07
3-mth forward rate agreement				
3-month	5.40	5.41	5.34	5.31
6-month	5.43	5.44	5.36	5.38
9-month	5.38	5.40	5.30	5.35

INTERNATIONAL

Euro-deposit rates (bid)

		Latest	Prev day	Wk ago	4 wks ago
US$	1-month	5.07	5.05	5.03	5.02
	3-month	5.22	5.19	5.17	5.11
	6-month	5.33	5.27	5.27	5.17
C$	3-month	4.26	4.25	4.22	4.13
euro	3-month	2.91	2.89	2.86	2.82
¥	3-month	0.26	0.25	0.20	0.06
£	3-month	4.63	4.61	4.63	4.60

London interbank offer rate US$

	Latest	Prev day	Wk ago	4 wks ago
1-month	5.13	5.11	5.09	5.07
3-month	5.27	5.24	5.22	5.16
6-month	5.39	5.33	5.32	5.27

BANK RATES

Canada		U.S.	
Bank of Can.	4.50	Discount	6.00
O/N MM Fin Rate	4.13	Prime	8.00
Prime	6.00	Fed Funds	5.00
Call Loan Ave.	4.25		

Source: *The National Post, FP Investing,* June 2, 2006, p. FP14. Used with permission.

investment with the planned holding period, there is no interest rate risk. After three months, the Treasury bills mature for a certain future cash flow of $10 million.[7]

If you invest instead in a 10-year Canada bond, the expected return is higher, 4.39 percent, but so is the risk. Again drawing on Chapter 7, if interest rates rise over the next three months, the bond drops in price. The resulting capital loss reduces the yield, possibly below the 4.14 percent on Treasury bills.

www.dbrs.com
www.standardandpoors.com

DEFAULT RISK   Default risk refers to the probability that interest and principal will not be paid in the promised amounts on the due dates (or not paid at all). In Chapter 7, we observed that various financial reporting agencies, such as the Dominion Bond Rating Service (DBRS) and Standard and Poor's (S&P), compile and publish ratings of various corporate and public securities. These ratings are connected to default risk. Of course, some securities have negligible default risk, such as Canada Treasury bills. Given the purposes of investing idle corporate cash, firms typically avoid investing in marketable securities with significant default risk.

Small variations in default risk are reflected in the rates in Figure 19.7. For example, consider the rates on three alternative 90-day (three-month) investments. Since the maturities are the same, they differ only in default risk. In increasing order of default risk, the securities are Treasury bills (4.14 percent yield), banker's acceptances (4.34 percent yield), and commercial paper (5.01 percent yield June 1, 2006). Recall from Chapter 18 that all three are unsecured paper. Treasury bills (the least risky) are backed by the credit of the Government of Canada. Commercial paper (the highest risk) is backed by the credit of the issuing large corporation. Bankers acceptances are a slightly less risky variation on commercial paper, as they are guaranteed by a chartered bank as well as by the issuing corporation.

In Their Own Words . . .   Geoff Martin on Online Billing

ELECTRONIC BILL PAYMENT and collection is finally starting to become the "killer app" that pundits have long predicted it would be, and the Government of Canada is leading the charge.

It has placed first worldwide in online services for four years running, according to a yearly study by global technology services firm Accenture. And with the leadership of the federal Government On-Line (GOL) program (gol-ged.gc.ca), which aims to provide a majority of Canadian government services securely and efficiently, our lead over the two countries tied for second place, Singapore and the United States, continues to widen.

Since it deals with virtually every Canadian citizen and business, the Canada Revenue Agency (CRA) is leading the way with the GOL program. Last year, 10 million Canadians filed their taxes online, but CRA expects to significantly expand its services before the next tax deadline, to entice even greater numbers.

With their acquisition of webdoxs from BCE Emergis in July 2004, Canada Post's online payment service, called epost,

is also poised to become a global trail-blazer in e-billing. While epost currently offers services that allow its more than 400,000 registered users in major cities such as Calgary, Winnipeg, Toronto, and Ottawa to pay their municipal taxes and other bills online, the scheduled launch of merged services between epost and webdoxs in December will connect more than one million registered customers with the services of 97 companies. In Toronto, the service will enable electronic payment for 7 of the 10 monthly bills received by an average household.

With numbers ramping upwards so sharply right across the country, it doesn't take a crystal ball to determine that e-billing is very quickly taking over in Canada. While the paperless society we've long been promised still seems like a distant fairy tale, Canadian governments and businesses seem poised to achieve one of the world's first truly cashless societies in the very near future.

This discussion is excerpted from G. Martin, "No cash please,"
Summit Ottawa: Oct 2004. Vol. 7, Iss. 6, p. 11. Used with permission.

---

7 Treasury bills are sold on a discount basis so the future cash flow includes principal and interest.

MARKETABILITY   Marketability refers to how easy it is to convert an asset to cash; so marketability and liquidity mean much the same thing. Some money market instruments are much more marketable than others. At the top of the list are Treasury bills, which can be bought and sold very cheaply and very quickly in large amounts.

TAXES   Interest earned on money market securities is subject to federal and provincial corporate tax. Capital gains and dividends on common and preferred stock are taxed more lightly, but these long-term investments are subject to significant price fluctuations and most managers consider them too risky for the marketable securities portfolio. One exception is the strategy of **dividend capture.** Under this strategy portfolio managers purchase high-grade preferred stock or blue chip common stock just before a dividend payment. They hold the stock only long enough to receive the dividend. In this way, firms willing to tolerate price risk for a short period can benefit from the dividend exclusion that allows corporations to receive dividends tax free from other Canadian corporations.

dividend capture
A strategy in which an investor purchases securities to own them on the day of record and then quickly sells them; designed to attain dividends but avoid the risk of a lengthy hold.

Check out international short-term rates online at www.bloomberg.com

Some Different Types of Money Market Securities

The money market securities listed in Figure 19.7 are generally highly marketable and short-term. They usually have low risk of default. They are issued by the federal government (for example, Treasury bills), domestic and foreign banks (certificates of deposit), and business corporations (commercial paper). Of the many types, we illustrate only a few of the most common here.

Treasury bills are obligations of the federal government that mature in 1, 2, 3, 6, or 12 months. They are sold at weekly auctions and traded actively over the counter by banks and investment dealers.

Commercial paper refers to short-term securities issued by finance companies, banks, and corporations. Typically, commercial paper is unsecured.[8] Maturities range from a few weeks to 270 days. There is no active secondary market in commercial paper. As a consequence, the marketability is low; however, firms that issue commercial paper often repurchase it directly before maturity. The default risk of commercial paper depends on the financial strength of the issuer. DBRS and S&P publish quality ratings for commercial paper. These ratings are similar to the bond ratings we discussed in Chapter 7.

As explained earlier, bankers acceptances are a form of corporate paper stamped by a chartered bank that adds its guarantee of principal and interest.

Certificates of deposit (CDs) are short-term loans to chartered banks. Rates quoted are for CDs in excess of $100,000. There are active markets in CDs of 3-month, 6-month, 9-month, and 12-month maturities, particularly in the United States.

Our brief look at money markets illustrates the challenges and opportunities for treasurers today. Securitization has produced dramatic growth in bankers acceptances and commercial paper.

CONCEPT QUESTIONS

1. What are some reasons firms find themselves with idle cash?

2. What are some types of money market securities?

3. How does the design of money market securities reflect the trends of securitization, globalization, and financial engineering?

SUMMARY AND CONCLUSIONS

This chapter has described the computer-based cash management systems used by large corporations in Canada and worldwide. By moving cash efficiently and maximizing the amount available for short-term investment, the treasurer adds value to the firm. Our discussion made the following key points:

1. A firm holds cash to conduct transactions and to compensate banks for the various services they render.

---

8 Commercial paper and bankers acceptances are sources of short-term financing for their issuers. We discuss them in more detail in Chapter 18.

2. The optimal amount of cash for a firm to hold depends on the opportunity cost of holding cash and the uncertainty of future cash inflows and outflows.

3. The difference between a firm's available balance and its book balance is the firm's net float. The float reflects the fact that some cheques have not cleared and are thus uncollected.

4. The firm can use a variety of procedures to manage the collection and disbursement of cash in such a way as to speed the collection of cash and control payments. Large firms use computerized cash management systems that include over-the-counter collections and lockboxes, concentration banking, and electronic disbursements through zero-balance accounts.

5. Because of seasonal and cyclical activities, to help finance planned expenditures, or as a contingency reserve, firms temporarily find themselves with a cash surplus. The money market offers a variety of possible vehicles for parking this idle cash.

Key Terms

adjustment costs (page 581)
debit card (page 588)
dividend capture (page 595)
float (page 583)
lockboxes (page 588)
precautionary motive (page 580)

same day value (page 589)
smart card (page 587)
speculative motive (page 580)
target cash balance (page 581)
transaction motive (page 580)
zero-balance account (page 591)

Chapter Review Problem and Self-Test

19.1 Float Measurement On a typical business day, a firm writes and mails cheques totalling $1,000. These cheques clear in six days on average. Simultaneously, the firm receives $1,300. The cash is available in one day on average. Calculate the disbursement float, the collection float, and the net float. How do you interpret the answer?

Answer to Self-Test Problem

19.1 The disbursement float is 6 days × $1,000 = $6,000. The collection float is one day × –$1,300 = –$1,300. The net float is $6,000 + (–$1,300) = $4,700. In other words, at any given time, the firm typically has uncashed cheques outstanding of $6,000. At the same time, it has uncollected receipts of $1,300. Thus, the firm's book balance is typically $4,700 less than its available balance, a positive $4,700 net float.

Concepts Review and Critical Thinking Questions

1. Is it possible for a firm to have too much cash? Why would shareholders care if a firm accumulates large amounts of cash?

2. What options are available to a firm if it believes it has too much cash? How about too little?

3. Are shareholders and creditors likely to agree on how much cash a firm should keep on hand?

4. In the discussion at the beginning of this chapter, do you think the motivations for holding cash are reasonable?

5. What is the difference between cash management and liquidity management?

6. Why is a preferred stock with a dividend tied to short-term interest rates an attractive short-term investment for corporations with excess cash?

7. Which would a firm prefer: a net collection float or a net disbursement float? Why?

8. For each of the short-term marketable securities given here, provide an example of the potential disadvantages the investment has for meeting a corporation's cash management goals.
   a. Treasury bills
   b. Ordinary preferred stock
   c. Negotiable certificates of deposit (CDs)
   d. Commercial paper
   e. 10-year Canada bonds

9. It is sometimes argued that excess cash held by a firm can aggravate agency problems (discussed in Chapter 1) and, more generally, reduce incentives for shareholder wealth maximization. How would you frame the issue here?

10. One option a firm usually has with any excess cash is to pay its suppliers more quickly. What are the advantages and disadvantages of this use of excess cash?

11. Another option usually available is to reduce the firm's outstanding debt. What are the advantages and disadvantages of this use of excess cash?

Questions and Problems

Basic
(Questions 1–7)

1. Calculating Float   In a typical month, the Timmons Corporation receives 90 cheques totalling $85,000. These are delayed six days on average. What is the average daily float?

2. Calculating Net Float   Each business day, on average, a company writes cheques totalling $25,000 to pay its suppliers. The usual clearing time for the cheques is four days. Meanwhile, the company is receiving payments from its customers each day, in the form of cheques, totalling $40,000. The cash from the payments is available to the firm after two days.

   a. Calculate the company's disbursement float, collection float, and net float.

   b. How would your answer to part (*a*) change if the collected funds were available in one day instead of two?

3. Costs of Float   Purple Feet Wine, Inc., receives an average of $9,000 in cheques per day. The delay in clearing is typically four days. The current interest rate is .025 percent per day.

   a. What is the company's float?

   b. What is the most Purple Feet should be willing to pay today to eliminate its float entirely?

   c. What is the highest daily fee the company should be willing to pay to eliminate its float entirely?

4. Float and Weighted Average Delay   Your neighbour goes to the post office once a month and picks up two cheques, one for $16,000 and one for $3,000. The larger cheque takes four days to clear after it is deposited; the smaller one takes five days.

   a. What is the total float for the month?

   b. What is the average daily float?

   c. What are the average daily receipts and weighted average delay?

5. NPV and Collection Time   Your firm has an average receipt size of $80. A bank has approached you concerning a lockbox service that will decrease your total collection time by two days. You typically receive 12,000 cheques per day. The daily interest rate is .016 percent. If the bank charges a fee of $190 per day, should the lockbox project be accepted? What would the net annual savings be if the service were adopted?

6. Using Weighted Average Delay   A mail-order firm processes 5,000 cheques per month. Of these, 65 percent are for $50 and 35 percent are for $70. The $50 cheques are delayed two days on average; the $70 cheques are delayed three days on average.

   a. What is the average daily collection float? How do you interpret your answer?

   b. What is the weighted average delay? Use the result to calculate the average daily float.

   c. How much should the firm be willing to pay to eliminate the float?

   d. If the interest rate is 7 percent per year, calculate the daily cost of the float.

   e. How much should the firm be willing to pay to reduce the weighted average float by 1.5 days?

7. Value of Delay   No More Pencils, Inc., disburses cheques every two weeks that average $70,000 and take seven days to clear. How much interest can the company earn annually if it delays transfer of funds from an interest-bearing account that pays .02 percent per day for these seven days? Ignore the effects of compounding interest.

Intermediate
(Questions 8–11)

8. NPV and Reducing Float   No More Books Corporation has an agreement with Lollipop Bank whereby the bank handles $8 million in collections a day and requires a $500,000 compensating balance. No More Books is contemplating cancelling the agreement and dividing its eastern region so that two other banks will handle its business. Banks A and B will each handle $4 million of collections a day, and each requires a compensating balance of $300,000. No More Books's financial management expects that collections will be accelerated by one day if the eastern region is divided. Should the company proceed with the new system? What will be the annual net savings? Assume that the T-bill rate is 5 percent annually.

9. Lockboxes and Collection Time   Bird's Eye Treehouses, Inc., a Saskatoon company, has determined that a majority of its customers are located in the Manitoba area. It therefore is considering using a lockbox system offered by a Canadian bank located in Winnipeg. The bank has estimated that use of the system will reduce collection time by two days. Based on the following information, should the lockbox system be adopted?

Average number of payments per day	600
Average value of payment	$1,100
Variable lockbox fee (per transaction)	$0.35
Annual interest rate on money market securities	6.0%

How would your answer change if there were a fixed charge of $1,000 per year in addition to the variable charge?

Intermediate
(continued)

10. **Calculating Transactions Required** Cow Chips, Inc., a large fertilizer distributor based in Alberta, is planning to use a lockbox system to speed up collections from its customers located on the East Coast. A Montreal-area bank will provide this service for an annual fee of $25,000 plus 10 cents per transaction. The estimated reduction in collection and processing time is one day. If the average customer payment in this region is $5,500, how many customers each day, on average, are needed to make the system profitable for Cow Chips? Treasury bills are currently yielding 5 percent per year.

11. **Float** The Victor Company disburses cheques every two weeks that average $250,000 in total and take three days to clear. How much cash can the Victor Company save annually if it delays the transfer of funds from an interest-bearing account that pays 0.02 percent per day for these three days?

Challenge
(Question
12)

12. **Concentration Banking** Mojo Corporation currently employs a lockbox system with collection centres in Vancouver, Calgary, Montreal, and Halifax. Each lockbox centre, on average, handles $130,000 in payments every day. Mojo's current policy is to invest these payments in short-term marketable securities daily at the collection centre banks. Every two weeks, the investment accounts are swept and the proceeds are wire-transferred to Mojo's headquarters in Winnipeg to meet the company's payroll. The investment accounts pay .015 percent per day, and wire transfers cost .15 percent of the amount transferred.

   a. What is Mojo's total net cash flow available from its lockbox system to meet the payroll?

   b. Suppose Late Nite Bank, located just outside Winnipeg, offers to set up a concentration bank system for Mojo. Late Nite will accept each of the lockbox centre's daily payments via automated clearinghouse, ACH, transfers (in lieu of wire transfers) and deposit the funds in the same marketable securities investments yielding .015 percent per day. ACH-transferred funds are not available for use for one day. If the ACH transfers cost $700 each, should Mojo proceed with the concentration bank plan?

   c. In part (b), at what cost of ACH transfers would Mojo be indifferent between the two systems?

Internet Application Questions

1. Cash management today involves integrating various functions such as invoicing and electronic deposits. For many mid-sized businesses, such tasks end up consuming valuable scarce resources if done in-house. SAP Canada (www3.sap.com/canada) provides consulting and implementation services in all cash and liquidity management. Search SAP's website and discuss what kinds of companies will find SAP Canada's services particularly useful.

2. ITG Canada (www.itginc.com/canada) provides equity trading research for institutions and brokers. Click on their website and explain what "soft dollar" arrangements are.

3. Digital Insight (www.digitalinsight.com) specializes in Internet-based solutions for cash management, Internet banking, and e-commerce, among other things. The following link describes their AXIS cash management program (www.digitalinsight.com/pdf/AXIS_Cash_Management_4.pdf). Describe the main features of their cash management product.

4. Chrysler Financial sells commercial paper in Canada and the U.S. to interested institutional investors. Go to the Chrysler Financial website at investor.chryslerfinancial.com and find out current information about the company's commercial paper. What is the credit rating for the paper in Canada and the U.S.? What firms provided the ratings? What is the minimum size Chrysler Financial will sell in Canada and the U.S.? For what duration?

5. What are the highest and lowest historical interest rates for commercial paper in Canada? Go to the Bank of Canada website at www.bankofcanada.ca and follow the link "Rates and Statistics," then "Canadian Interest Rates" and "Selected Historical Interest Rates." Find the highest and lowest interest rates for one-month and three-month prime corporate paper. What are they and when did they occur? What implications do these rates have for short-term financial planning and liquidity management?

Suggested Readings

We have benefitted from the following books on short-term finance:

Hill, N. C., and W. L. Sartoris. *Short-Term Financial Management,* 3rd ed. New York: Prentice Hall, 1994, chaps. 6–10.
Scherr, Frederick C. *Modern Working Capital Management.* Englewood Cliffs, NJ: Prentice-Hall, 1989.

To keep up with Canadian practices, a good source is various issues of *Canadian Treasurer,* Treasury Management Association of Canada at *www.tmac.ca.*

CASH MANAGEMENT MODELS

The BAT Model

The Baumol-Allais-Tobin (BAT) model is a classic means of analyzing the cash management problem. We illustrate how this model can be used to actually establish the target cash balance. It is a straightforward model and very useful for illustrating the factors in cash management and, more generally, current asset management.

To develop the BAT model, suppose the Golden Socks Corporation starts at Time 0 with a cash balance of C = $1.2 million. Each week, outflows exceed inflows by $600,000. As a result, the cash balance drops to zero at the end of Week 2. The average cash balance is the beginning balance ($1.2 million) plus the ending balance ($0) divided by 2, or ($1.2 million + $0)/2 = $600,000 over the two-week period. At the end of Week 2, Golden Socks replaces its cash by depositing another $1.2 million.

As we have described, the cash management strategy for Golden Socks is very simple and boils down to depositing $1.2 million every two weeks. This policy is shown in Figure 19A.1. Notice how the cash balance declines by $600,000 per week. Since we bring the account up to $1.2 million, the balance hits zero every two weeks. This results in the sawtooth pattern displayed in Figure 19A.1.

Implicitly, we assume the net cash outflow is the same every day and it is known with certainty. These two assumptions make the model easy to handle. We indicate what happens when they do not hold in the next section.

If C were set higher, say, at $2.4 million, cash would last four weeks before the firm would have to sell marketable securities, but the firm's average cash balance would increase to $1.2 million (from $600,000). If C were set at $600,000, cash would run out in one week and the firm would have to replenish cash more frequently, but its average cash balance would fall from $600,000 to $300,000.

Because transaction costs must be incurred whenever cash is replenished (for example, the brokerage costs of selling marketable securities), establishing large initial balances lowers the trading costs connected with cash management. However, the larger the average cash balance, the greater is the opportunity cost (the return that could have been earned on marketable securities).

To determine the optimal strategy, Golden Socks needs to know the following three things:

FIGURE 19A.1

Cash balances for the Golden Socks Corporation

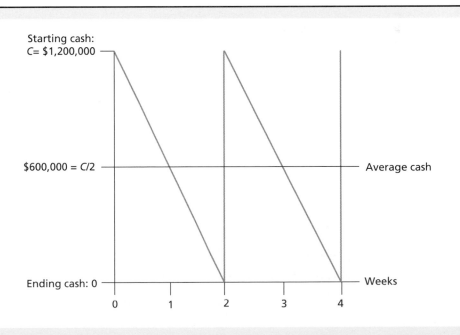

The Golden Socks Corporation starts at Time 0 with cash of $1,200,000. The balance drops to zero by the second week. The average cash balance is $C/2$ = $1,200,000/2 = $600,000 over the period.

F = The fixed cost of making a securities trade to replenish cash

T = The total amount of new cash needed for transaction purposes over the relevant planning period, say, one year

R = The opportunity cost of holding cash; the interest rate on marketable securities

With this information, Golden Socks can determine the total costs of any particular cash balance policy. It can then determine the optimal cash balance policy.

THE OPPORTUNITY COSTS   To determine the opportunity costs of holding cash, we have to find out how much interest is forgone. Golden Socks has, on average, $\$C/2$ in cash. This amount could be earning interest at rate R. So the total dollar opportunity costs of cash balances are equal to the average cash balance multiplied by the interest rate:

$$\text{Opportunity costs} = (C/2) \times R \qquad [19A.1]$$

For example, the opportunity costs of various alternatives are given here assuming that the interest rate is 10 percent:

Initial Cash Balance	Average Cash Balance	Opportunity Cost ($R = 0.10$)
C	$C/2$	$(C/2) \times R$
$4,800,000	$2,400,000	$240,000
2,400,000	1,200,000	120,000
1,200,000	600,000	60,000
600,000	300,000	30,000
300,000	150,000	15,000

In our original case where the initial cash balance is $1.2 million, the average balance is $600,000. The interest we could have earned on this (at 10 percent) is $60,000, so this is what we give up with this strategy. Notice that the opportunity cost increases as the initial (and average) cash balance rises.

THE TRADING COSTS   To determine the total trading costs for the year, we need to know how many times Golden Socks has to sell marketable securities during the year. First, the total amount of cash disbursed during the year is $600,000 per week or $T = \$600,000 \times 52$ weeks $= \$31.2$ million. If the initial cash balance is set at $C = 1.2$ million, Golden Socks would sell $1.2 million of marketable securities $T/C = \$31.2$ million/$1.2 million $= 26$ times per year. It costs F dollars each time, so trading costs are given by:

$$\$31.2 \text{ million}/\$1.2 \text{ million} \times F = 26 \times F$$

In general, the total trading costs are given by:

$$\text{Trading costs} = (T/C) \times F \qquad [19A.2]$$

In this example, if F were $1,000 (an unrealistically large amount) the trading costs would be $26,000. We can calculate the trading costs associated with some different strategies as follows:

Total Amount of Disbursements during Relevant Period	Initial Cash Balance	Trading Costs ($F = \$1,000$)
T	C	$(T/C) \times F$
$31,200,000	$4,800,000	$ 6,500
31,200,000	2,400,000	13,000
31,200,000	1,200,000	26,000
31,200,000	600,000	52,000
31,200,000	300,000	104,000

THE TOTAL COST   Now that we have the opportunity costs and the trading costs, we can calculate the total cost by adding them together:

$$\begin{aligned} \text{Total cost} &= \text{Opportunity costs} + \text{Trading costs} \\ &= (C/2) \times R + (T/C) \times F \end{aligned} \qquad [19A.3]$$

Using these numbers, we have:

Cash Balance	Opportunity Costs	+	Trading Costs	=	Total Cost
$4,800,000	$240,000		$ 6,500		$246,500
2,400,000	120,000		13,000		133,000
1,200,000	60,000		26,000		86,000
600,000	30,000		52,000		82,000
300,000	15,000		104,000		119,000

Notice how the total cost starts at almost $250,000 and declines to about $80,000 before starting to rise again.

THE SOLUTION   We can see from the preceding schedule that a $600,000 cash balance results in the lowest total cost of the possibilities presented: $82,000. But what about $700,000 or $500,000 or other possibilities? It appears that the optimum balance is somewhere between $300,000 and $1.2 million. With this in mind, we could easily proceed by trial and error to find the optimum balance. It is not difficult to find it directly, however, so we do this next.

Take a look back at Figure 19.1. As drawn, the optimal size of the cash balance, C^*, occurs where the two lines cross. At this point, the opportunity costs and the trading costs are exactly equal. So, at C^*, we must have that:

$$\text{Opportunity costs} = \text{Trading costs}$$
$$C^*/2 \times R = (T/C^*) \times F$$

With a little algebra, we can write:

$$C^{*2} = (2T \times F)/R$$

To solve for C^*, we take the square root of both sides to get:

$$C^* = \sqrt{(2T \times F)/R} \tag{19A.4}$$

This is the optimum initial cash balance.

For Golden Socks, we have $T = \$31.2$ million, $F = \$1,000$, and $R = 10\%$. We can now find the optimum cash balance as:

$$C^* = \sqrt{(2 \times \$31,200,000 \times \$1,000/.10)}$$
$$= \$\sqrt{(624 \text{ billion})}$$
$$= \$789,937$$

We can verify this answer by calculating the following costs at this balance as well as at a little more and a little less:

Cash Balance	Opportunity Costs	+	Trading Costs	+	Total Cost
$850,000	$42,500		$36,706		$79,206
800,000	40,000		39,000		79,000
789,937	39,497		39,497		78,994
750,000	37,500		41,600		79,100
700,000	35,000		44,571		79,571

The total cost at the optimum is $78,994, and it does appear to increase as we move in either direction.

It is worth noting that there is considerable room on either side of the optimum cash point, within which the total cost does not vary significantly. This means that the optimum cash point should be considered a guideline, rather than a firm requirement.

The Miller–Orr Model: A More General Approach

We now describe a cash management system designed to deal with cash inflows and outflows that fluctuate randomly from day to day. With this model, we again concentrate on the cash balance; in contrast to the BAT model, we assume this balance fluctuates up and down randomly and that the average change is zero.

EXAMPLE 19A.1: The BAT Model

The Vulcan Corporation has cash outflows of $100 per day, seven days a week. The interest rate is 5 percent, and the fixed cost of replenishing cash balances is $10 per transaction. What is the optimal initial cash balance? What is the total cost?

The total cash needed for the year is 365 days × $100 = $36,500. From the BAT model, the optimal initial balance is:

$$C^* = \sqrt{(2T \times F)/R}$$
$$= \sqrt{2 \times \$36,500 \times \$10/.05}$$
$$= \sqrt{\$14.6 \text{ million}}$$
$$= \$3,821$$

The average cash balance is $3,821/2 = $1,911, so the opportunity cost is $1,911 × .05 = $96. Since we need $100 per day, the $3,821 balance lasts $3,821/$100 = 38.21 days. We need to resupply the account 365/38.21 = 9.6 times, so the trading (order) cost is $96. The total cost is $192.

The BAT model is possibly the simplest and most stripped-down sensible model for determining the optimal cash position. Its chief weakness is that it assumes steady, certain cash outflows. We next discuss a more involved model designed to deal with these problems.

THE BASIC IDEA   Figure 19A.2 shows how the system works. It operates in terms of an upper limit to the amount of cash (U^*) and a lower limit (L), and a target cash balance (C^*). The firm allows its cash balance to wander around between the lower and upper limits. As long as the cash balance is somewhere between U^* and L, nothing happens.

When the cash balance reaches the upper limit (U^*), as it does at point X, the firm moves $U^* - C^*$ dollars out of the account and into marketable securities. This action moves the cash balance down to C^*. In the same way, if the cash balance falls to the lower limit (L), as it does at point Y, the firm sells $C^* - L$ worth of securities and deposits the cash in the account. This action takes the cash balance up to C^*.

USING THE MODEL   To get started, management sets the lower limit (L). This limit is essentially a safety stock; so where it is set depends on how much risk of a cash shortfall the firm is willing to tolerate.

Like the BAT model, the optimal cash balance depends on trading costs and opportunity costs. Once again, the cost per transaction of buying and selling marketable securities, F, is assumed to be fixed. Also, the opportunity cost of holding cash is R, the interest rate per period on marketable securities.

FIGURE 19A.2

The Miller–Orr model

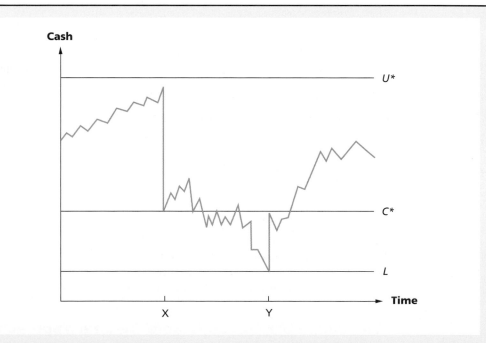

U^* is the upper control limit. L is the lower control limit. The target cash balance is C^*. As long as cash is between L and U^*, no transaction is made.

The only extra piece of information needed is σ^2, the variance of the cash flow per period. For our purposes, the period can be anything, a day or a week, for example, as long as the interest rate and the variance are based on the same length of time.

Given L, which is set by the firm, Miller and Orr show that the cash balance target, C^*, and the upper limit, U^*, that minimize the total costs of holding cash are:[9]

$$C^* = L + (3/4 \times F \times \sigma^2/R)^{1/3} \qquad\qquad\qquad \text{[19A.5]}$$

$$U^* = 3 \times C^* - 2 \times L \qquad\qquad\qquad\qquad \text{[19A.6]}$$

Also, the average cash balance in the Miller–Orr model is:

$$\text{Average cash balance} = (4 \times C^* - L)/3 \qquad\qquad \text{[19A.7]}$$

The derivation of these expressions is relatively complex, so we do not present it here. Fortunately, as we illustrate next, the results are not difficult to use.

For example, suppose $F = \$10$, the interest rate is 1 percent per month, and the standard deviation of the monthly net cash flows is $200. The variance of the monthly net cash flows is:

$$\sigma^2 = (\$200)^2 = \$40,000$$

We assume a minimum cash balance of $L = \$100$. We can calculate the cash balance target, C^*, as:

$$\begin{aligned}
C^* &= L + (3/4 \times F \times \sigma^2/R)^{1/3} \\
&= \$100 + (3/4 \times \$10 \times \$40,000/.01)^{1/3} \\
&= \$100 + (30,000,000)^{1/3} \\
&= \$100 + 311 = \$411
\end{aligned}$$

The upper limit, U^*, is thus:

$$\begin{aligned}
U^* &= 3 \times C^* - 2 \times L \\
&= 3 \times \$411 - 2 \times \$100 \\
&= \$1,033
\end{aligned}$$

Finally, the average cash balance is:

$$\begin{aligned}
\text{Average cash balance} &= (4 \times C^* - L)/3 \\
&= (4 \times \$411 - \$100)/3 \\
&= \$515
\end{aligned}$$

The advantage of the Miller–Orr model is that it improves our understanding of the problem of cash management by considering the effect of uncertainty as measured by the variation in net cash inflows.

The Miller–Orr model shows that the greater the uncertainty is (the higher σ^2 is), the greater is the difference between the target balance and the minimum balance. Similarly, the greater the uncertainty is, the higher is the upper limit and the higher is the average cash balance. These all make intuitive sense. For example, the greater the variability is, the greater is the chance of the balance dropping below the minimum. We thus keep a higher balance to guard against this happening.

CONCEPT QUESTIONS

1. What is the basic trade-off in the BAT model?

2. Describe how the Miller–Orr model works.

---

9 M. H. Miller and D. Orr, "A Model of the Demand for Money by Firms," *Quarterly Journal of Economics*, August 1966.

Appendix Review Problem and Self-Test

A.1 **The BAT Model** Given the following information, calculate the target cash balance using the BAT model:

Annual interest rate	12%
Fixed order cost	$100
Total cash needed	$240,000

What are the opportunity cost of holding cash, the trading cost, and the total cost? What would these be if $15,000 were held instead? If $25,000 were held?

Answers to Appendix Self-Test Problem

A.1 From the BAT model, we know that the target cash balance is:

$$C^* = \sqrt{(2T \times F)/R}$$
$$= \sqrt{2 \times \$240,000 \times 100)/.12}$$
$$= \sqrt{\$400,000,000}$$
$$= \$20,000$$

The average cash balance will be $C^*/2 = \$20,000/2 = \$10,000$. The opportunity cost of holding $10,000 when the going rate is 12 percent is $10,000 \times .12 = \$1,200$. There will be $240,000/20,000 = 12$ orders during the year, so the order cost, or trading cost, is also $12 \times \$100 = \$1,200$. The total cost is thus $2,400.

If $15,000 is held, then the average balance is $7,500. Verify that the opportunity, trading, and total costs in this case are $900, $1,600, and $2,500, respectively. If $25,000 is held, these numbers are $1,500, $960, and $2,460, respectively.

Appendix Questions and Problems

A1. **Changes in Target Cash Balances** Indicate the likely impact of each of the following on a company's target cash balance. Use the letter I to denote an increase and D to denote a decrease. Briefly explain your reasoning in each case.

a. Commissions charged by brokers decrease.

b. Interest rates paid on money market securities rise.

c. The compensating balance requirement of a bank is raised.

d. The firm's credit rating improves.

e. The cost of borrowing increases.

f. Direct fees for banking services are established.

A2. **Using the BAT Model** Given the following information, calculate the target cash balance using the BAT model:

Annual interest rate	7%
Fixed order cost	$10
Total cash needed	$5,000

How do you interpret your answer?

A3. **Opportunity versus Trading Costs** White Whale Corporation has an average daily cash balance of $400. Total cash needed for the year is $25,000. The interest rate is 5 percent, and replenishing the cash costs $6 each time. What are the opportunity cost of holding cash, the trading cost, and the total cost? What do you think of White Whale's strategy?

A4. **Costs and the BAT Model** Debit and Credit Bookkeepers needs a total of $4,000 in cash during the year for transactions and other purposes. Whenever cash runs low, it sells off $300 in securities and transfers the cash in. The interest rate is 6 percent per year, and selling off securities costs $25 per sale.

a. What is the opportunity cost under the current policy? The trading cost? With no additional calculations, would you say that Debit and Credit keeps too much or too little cash? Explain.

b. What is the target cash balance derived using the BAT model?

A5. **Determining Optimal Cash Balances** The Joe Elvis Company is currently holding $700,000 in cash. It projects that over the next year its cash outflows will exceed cash inflows by $360,000 per month. How much of the current cash holding should be retained and how much should be used to increase the company's holdings of marketable securities? Each time these securities are bought or sold through a broker, the company pays a fee of $500. The annual interest rate on money market securities is 6.5 percent. After the initial investment of excess cash, how many times during the next 12 months will securities be sold?

A6. **Interpreting Miller-Orr** Econoline Crush, Inc., uses a Miller-Orr cash management approach with a lower limit of $40,000, an upper limit of $125,000, and a target balance of $60,000. Explain what each of these points represents and then explain how the system will work.

A7. **Using Miller-Orr** Slap Shot Corporation has a fixed cost associated with buying and selling marketable securities of $100. The interest rate is currently .021 percent per day, and the firm has estimated that the standard deviation of its daily net cash flows is $75. Management has set a lower limit of $1,100 on cash holdings. Calculate the target cash balance and upper limit using the Miller-Orr model. Describe how the system will work.

A8. **Interpreting Miller-Orr** Based on the Miller-Orr model, describe what will happen to the lower limit, the upper limit, and the spread (the distance between the two) if the variation in net cash flow grows. Give an intuitive explanation for why this happens. What happens if the variance drops to zero?

A9. **Using Miller-Orr** The variance of the daily cash flows for the Pele Bicycle Shop is $960,000. The opportunity cost to the firm of holding cash is 7 percent per year. What should be the target cash level and the upper limit if the tolerable lower limit has been established as $150,000? The fixed cost of buying and selling securities is $500 per transaction.

A10. **Using BAT** All Night Corporation has determined that its target cash balance if it uses the BAT model is $2,200. The total cash needed for the year is $21,000, and the order cost is $10. What interest rate must All Night be using?

CHAPTER 20

Credit and Inventory Management

In October 2005, Staples Business Depot became one of the first Canadian retailers to test radio frequency identification technology (Gen2 RFID) in its logistics and store level operations. These high-tech tags are replacing bar codes because they can be read from a distance. Staples Business Depot followed Wal-Mart's lead in testing this relatively new technology.

In April 2004, retailing giant Wal-Mart began using these RFID tags on cases and pallets in a small group of stores in Dallas, Texas. Wal-Mart is expected to save billions each year when RFIDs are fully implemented across the company. Specifically, it will save $6.7 billion in labour costs by eliminating the need to scan each pallet individually, $600 million by reducing out-of-stock items, $575 million by reducing theft, $300 million with better tracking, and $180 million by reducing inventory. The total cost savings for Wal-Mart is estimated at $8.35 billion per year! As this example suggests, proper management of inventory can have a significant impact on the profitability of a company and the value investors place on it.

www.staples.ca

MOST FIRMS hold inventories to ensure that they have finished goods to meet sales demand and raw materials and work in process when they are needed in production. Deciding how much to hold is important to managers in production and marketing. Because inventories represent a significant investment with carrying costs, the financial manager is also involved in the decision. Our discussion of inventory looks at a traditional approach that focuses on the trade-off between carrying costs and shortage costs. We also present just-in-time inventory that offers an innovative solution.

This chapter also covers credit management. When a firm sells goods and services, it can demand cash on or before the delivery date, or it can extend credit to customers and allow some delay in payment. The next few sections provide an idea of what is involved in the firm's decision to grant credit to its customers. Granting credit is investing in a customer, an investment tied to the sale of a product or service.

Why do firms grant credit? Not all do, but the practice is extremely common. The obvious reason is that offering credit is a way of stimulating sales. The costs associated with granting credit are not trivial: First, there is the chance that the customer will not pay. Second, the firm has to bear the costs of carrying the receivables. The credit policy decision thus involves a trade-off between the benefits of increased sales and the costs of granting credit. We examine this trade-off in the next sections.

CREDIT AND RECEIVABLES

From an accounting perspective, when credit is granted, an account receivable is created. These receivables include credit to other firms, called *trade credit,* and credit granted consumers, called *consumer credit.* About 10 percent of all the assets of Canadian industrial firms are in the form of accounts receivable. For retail firms, the figure is much higher. So receivables obviously represent a major investment of financial resources by Canadian businesses.

Furthermore, trade credit is a very important source of financing for corporations. Looking back at Table 18.2 in Chapter 18, Canadian Tire financed about 49 percent of total assets through accounts payable, more than any other single source of short-term financing. However we look at it, receivables and receivables management are key aspects of a firm's short-term financial policy.

Components of Credit Policy

If a firm decides to grant credit to its customers, it must establish procedures for extending credit and collecting. In particular, the firm has to deal with the following components of credit policy:

terms of sale
Conditions on which a firm sells its goods and services for cash or credit.

1. **Terms of sale.** The terms of sale establish how the firm proposes to sell its goods and services. A basic distinction is whether the firm requires cash or extends credit. If the firm does grant credit to a customer, the terms of sale specify (perhaps implicitly) the credit period, the cash discount and discount period, and the type of credit instrument.

credit analysis
The process of determining the probability that customers will or will not pay.

2. **Credit analysis.** In granting credit, a firm determines how much effort to expend trying to distinguish between customers who pay and customers who do not pay. Firms use a number of devices and procedures to determine the probability that customers will not pay, and put together, these are called *credit analysis.*

collection policy
Procedures followed by a firm in collecting accounts receivable.

3. **Collection policy.** After credit has been granted, the firm has the potential problem of collecting the cash when it becomes due, for which it must establish a collection policy.

In the next several sections, we discuss these components of credit policy that collectively make up the decision to grant credit.

The Cash Flows from Granting Credit

In a previous chapter, we described the accounts receivable period as the time it takes to collect on a sale. Several events occur during that period. These are the cash flows associated with granting credit, and they can be illustrated with a cash flow diagram:

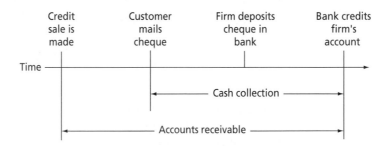

The cash flows of granting credit

As our time line indicates, the typical sequence of events when a firm grants credit is (1) the credit sale is made, (2) the customer sends a cheque to the firm, (3) the firm deposits the cheque, and (4) the firm's account is credited for the amount of the cheque.

Based on our discussion in the previous chapter, it is apparent that one of the factors influencing the receivables period is float. Thus, one way to reduce the receivables period is to speed up cheque mailing, processing, and clearing. Because we cover this subject elsewhere, we ignore float in our subsequent discussion and focus on what is likely to be the major determinant of the receivables period, credit policy. We come back to float at the end when we look at a computerized implementation of credit policy.

The Investment in Receivables

The investment in accounts receivable for any firm depends on the amount of credit sales and the average collection period. For example, if a firm's average collection period (ACP) is 30 days, at any given time there are 30 days' worth of sales outstanding. If sales run $1,000 per day, the firm's accounts receivable are equal to 30 days × $1,000 per day = $30,000.

As our example illustrates, a firm's receivables generally are equal to its average daily sales multiplied by its average collection period (ACP):

$$\text{Accounts receivable} = \text{Average daily sales} \times \text{ACP} \qquad [20.1]$$

Thus, a firm's investment in accounts receivable depends on factors that influence credit sales and collections.

We have seen the average collection period in various places, including Chapters 3 and 18. Recall that we use the terms *days' sales in receivables, receivables period,* and *average collection period* interchangeably to refer to the length of time it takes for the firm to collect on a sale.

CONCEPT QUESTIONS

1. What are the basic components of credit policy?

2. What are the basic components of the terms of sale if a firm chooses to sell on credit?

TERMS OF THE SALE

As we just described, the terms of a sale are made up of three distinct elements:

1. The period for which credit is granted (the credit period).
2. The cash discount and the discount period.
3. The type of credit instrument.

Within a given industry, the terms of sales are usually fairly standard, but across industries these terms vary quite a bit. In many cases, the terms of sale are remarkably archaic and literally date to previous centuries. Organized systems of trade credit that resemble current practice can be easily traced to the great fairs of medieval Europe, and they almost surely existed long before then.

Why Trade Credit Exists

Set aside the venerable history of trade credit for a moment and ask yourself why it should exist.[1] After all, it is quite easy to imagine that all sales could be for cash. From the firm's viewpoint, this would get rid of receivables carrying costs and collection costs. Bad debts would be zero (assuming the firm was careful to accept no counterfeit money).

Imagine this cash-only economy in the context of perfectly competitive product and financial markets. Competition would force companies to lower their prices to pass the savings from immediate collections on to customers. Any company that chose to grant credit to its customers would have to raise its prices accordingly to survive. A purchaser who needed financing over the operating cycle could borrow from a bank or the money market. In this perfect market environment, it would make no difference to the seller or the buyer whether credit were granted.

In practice, firms spend significant resources setting credit policy and managing its implementation. So deviations from perfect markets—market imperfections—must explain why trade credit exists. We look briefly at several imperfections and how trade credit helps to overcome them.

---

1 Our discussion draws on N. C. Hill and W. S. Sartoris, *Short-Term Financial Management,* 2d ed. (New York: Macmillan, 1992), chap. 14.

In practice, both the buyer and seller have imperfect information. Buyers lack perfect information on the quality of the product. For this reason, the buyer may prefer credit terms that give time to return the product if it is defective or unsuitable. When the seller offers credit, it signals potential customers that the product is of high quality and likely to provide satisfaction.[2]

In addition, in practice, any firm that grants credit or a loan lacks perfect information on the creditworthiness of the borrower. Although it is costly for a bank or other third-party lender to acquire this information, a seller that has been granting trade credit to a purchaser likely has it already. Further, the seller may have superior information on the resale value of the product serving as collateral. These information advantages may allow the seller to offer more attractive, more flexible credit terms and be more liberal in authorizing credit.

Finally, perfect markets have zero transaction costs but, in reality, it is costly to set up a bank borrowing facility or to borrow in money markets. We discussed some of the costs in Chapter 18. It may be cheaper to utilize credit from the seller.

These reasons go a long way toward explaining the popularity of trade credit. Whatever the reasons, setting credit policy involves major decisions for the firm.

The Basic Form

The easiest way to understand the terms of sale is to consider an example. For bulk candy, terms of 2/10, net 60 are common.[3] This means that customers have 60 days from the invoice date to pay the full amount. However, if payment is made within 10 days, a 2 percent cash discount can be taken.

Consider a buyer who places an order for $1,000, and assume that the terms of the sale are 2/10, net 60. The buyer has the option of paying $1,000 \times (1 - .02) = \$980$ in 10 days, or paying the full $1,000 in 60 days.

When the terms are stated as just net 30, then the customer has 30 days from the invoice date to pay the entire $1,000, and no discount is offered for early payment.

The Credit Period

credit period
The length of time that credit is granted.

The **credit period** is the basic length of time for which credit is granted. The credit period varies widely from industry to industry, but it is almost always between 30 and 120 days. When a cash discount is offered, the credit period has two components: the net credit period and the cash discount period. In most cases, the credit period and the cash discount conform to industry practice. Firms do not often deviate from the industry norm. For this reason, we focus on examples at the industry level.

The net credit period is the length of time the customer has to pay. The cash discount period, as the name suggests, is the time during which the discount is available. With 2/10, net 30, for example, the net credit period is 30 days and the cash discount period is 10 days.

invoice
Bill for goods or services provided by the seller to the purchaser.

THE INVOICE DATE The invoice date is the beginning of the credit period. An **invoice** is a written account of merchandise shipped to the buyer. For individual items, by convention, the invoice date is usually the shipping date or the billing date, *not* the date the buyer receives the goods or the bill.

Many other arrangements exist. For example, the terms of sale might be ROG, for "receipt of goods." In this case, the credit starts when the customer receives the order. This might be used when the customer is in a remote location.

End-of-month (EOM) terms are fairly common. With EOM dating, all sales made during a particular month are assumed to be made at the end of that month. This is useful when a buyer makes purchases throughout the month, but the seller bills only once a month.

---

2 This use of signalling is very similar to dividend signalling discussed in Chapter 17. There corporations signalled the quality of projected cash flows by maintaining dividends even when earnings were down.

3 The terms of sale cited from specific industries in this section and elsewhere are drawn from Theodore N. Beckman, *Credits and Collections: Management and Theory* (New York: McGraw-Hill, 1962).

For example, terms of 2/10th EOM tell the buyer to take a 2 percent discount if payment is made by the 10th of the month, otherwise the full amount is due after that. Confusingly, the end of the month is sometimes taken to be the 25th day of the month. MOM, for middle of month, is another variation.

Seasonal dating is sometimes used to encourage sales of seasonal products during the off-season. A product that is sold primarily in the spring, such as bicycles or sporting goods, can be shipped in January with credit terms of 2/10, net 30. However, the invoice might be dated May 1, so the credit period actually begins at that time. This practice encourages buyers to order early.

LENGTH OF THE CREDIT PERIOD   A number of factors influence the length of the credit period. One of the most important is the *buyer's* inventory period and operating cycle. All other things being equal, the shorter these are, the shorter the credit period normally is.

Based on our discussion in Chapter 18, the operating cycle has two components: the inventory period and the receivables period. The inventory period is the time it takes the buyer to acquire inventory (from us), process it, and sell it. The receivables period is the time it then takes the buyer to collect on the sale. Note that the credit period that we offer is effectively the buyer's payables period.

By extending credit, we finance a portion of our buyer's operating cycle and thereby shorten the cash cycle. When our credit period exceeds the buyer's inventory period, we are financing not only the buyer's inventory purchases but also part of the buyer's receivables.

Furthermore, if our credit period exceeds our buyer's operating cycle, we are effectively providing financing for aspects of our customer's business beyond the immediate purchase and sale of our merchandise. The reason is that the buyer has a loan from us even after the merchandise is resold, and the buyer can use that credit for other purposes. For this reason, the length of the buyer's operating cycle is often cited as an appropriate upper limit to the credit period.

A number of other factors influence the credit period. Many of these also influence our customers' operating cycles; so, once again, these are related subjects. Among the most important are:

1. *Perishability and collateral value.* Perishable items have relatively rapid turnover and relatively low collateral value. Credit periods are thus shorter for such goods. For example, a food wholesaler selling fresh fruit and produce might use net seven terms. Alternatively, jewellery might be sold for 5/30, net four months.

2. *Consumer demand.* Products that are well established generally have more rapid turnover. Newer or slow-moving products often have longer credit periods to entice buyers. Also, as we have seen, sellers may choose to extend much longer credit periods for off-season sales (when customer demand is low).

3. *Cost, profitability, and standardization.* Relatively inexpensive goods tend to have shorter credit periods. The same is true for relatively standardized goods and raw materials. These all tend to have lower markups and higher turnover rates, both of which lead to shorter credit periods. There are exceptions. Auto dealers, for example, generally pay for cars as they are received.

4. *Credit risk.* The greater the credit risk of the buyer, the shorter the credit period is likely to be (assuming that credit is granted at all).

5. *The size of the account.* If the account is small, the credit period is shorter. Small accounts are more costly to manage, and the customers are less important.

6. *Competition.* When the seller is in a highly competitive market, longer credit periods may be offered as a way of attracting customers.

7. *Customer type.* A single seller might offer different credit terms to different buyers. A food wholesaler, for example, might supply grocers, bakeries, and restaurants. Each group would probably have different credit terms. More generally, sellers often have both wholesale and retail customers, and they frequently quote different terms to each.

Cash Discounts

cash discount
A discount given for a cash purchase.

As we have seen, **cash discounts** are often part of the terms of sale. The practice of granting discounts for cash purposes goes back more than 100 years and is widespread today. One reason discounts are offered is to speed the collection of receivables. This reduces the amount of credit being offered, and the firm must trade this off against the cost of the discount.

Notice that when a cash discount is offered, the credit is essentially free during the discount period. The buyer only pays for the credit after the discount expires. With 2/10, net 30, a rational buyer either pays in 10 days to make the greatest possible use of the free credit or pays in 30 days to get the longest possible use of the money in exchange for giving up the discount. So, by giving up the discount, the buyer effectively gets $30 - 10 = 20$ days' credit.

Another reason for cash discounts is that they are a legal way of charging higher prices to customers that have had credit extended to them. In both Canada and the United States, the law prohibits discrimination in charging different prices to different buyers for the same product. In this sense, cash discounts are a convenient way of separately pricing the credit granted to customers.

ELECTRONIC CREDIT TERMS   In Chapter 19, we showed how electronic disbursements saved time and money. To induce buyers to pay electronically or to give discounts to large customers, some firms offer discounts of around 1 percent for electronic payment one day after the goods are delivered. If electronic disbursement is coupled with electronic data interchange, the buyer and seller negotiate the discount and the date for payment.

COST OF THE CREDIT   In our examples, it might seem that the discounts are rather small. With 2/10, net 30, for example, early payment gets the buyer only a 2 percent discount. Does this provide a significant incentive for early payment? The answer is yes because the implicit interest rate is extremely high.

To see why the discount is important, we will calculate the cost to the buyer of not paying early. To do this, we will find the interest rate the buyer is effectively paying for the trade credit. Suppose the order is for $1,000. The buyer can pay $980 in 10 days or wait another 20 days and pay $1,000. It's obvious that the buyer is effectively borrowing $980 for 20 days and that the buyer pays $20 in interest on the "loan." What's the interest rate?

This interest is ordinary discount interest, which we discussed in Chapter 5. With $20 in interest on $980 borrowed, the rate is $20/$980 = 2.0408\%$. This is relatively low, but remember that this is the rate per 20-day period. There are $365/20 = 18.25$ such periods in a year, so, by not taking the discount, the buyer is paying an effective annual rate (EAR) of:

$$EAR = (1.020408)^{18.25} - 1 = 44.6\%$$

From the buyer's point of view, this is an expensive source of financing!

Given that the interest rate is so high here, it is unlikely that the seller benefits from early payment. Ignoring the possibility of default by the buyer, the decision by a customer to forgo the discount almost surely works to the seller's advantage.

TRADE DISCOUNTS   In some circumstances, the discount is not really an incentive for early payment but is instead a *trade discount,* a discount routinely given to some type of buyer. For example, with our 2/10th, EOM terms, the buyer takes a 2 percent discount if the invoice is paid by the 10th, but the bill is considered due on the 10th, and overdue after that. Thus, the credit period and the discount period are effectively the same, and there is no reward for paying before the due date.

EXAMPLE 20.1: What's the Rate?

Ordinary tiles are often sold 3/30, net 60. What effective annual rate does a buyer pay by not taking the discount? What would the APR be if one were quoted?

Here we have 3 percent discount interest on $60 - 30 = 30$ days' credit. The rate per 30 days is $.03/.97 = 3.093\%$. There are $365/30 = 12.17$ such periods in a year, so the effective annual rate is:

$$EAR = (1.03093)^{12.17} - 1 = 44.9\%$$

The APR, as always, would be calculated by multiplying the rate per period by the number of periods:

$$APR = .03093 \times 12.17 = 37.6\%$$

An interest rate calculated like this APR is often quoted as the cost of the trade credit, and, as this example illustrates, can seriously understate the true cost.

THE CASH DISCOUNT AND THE ACP   To the extent that a cash discount encourages customers to pay early, it shortens the receivables period and, all other things being equal, reduces the firm's investment in receivables.

For example, suppose a firm currently has terms of net 30 and an ACP of 30 days. If it offers terms of 2/10, net 30, perhaps 50 percent of its customers (in terms of volume of purchases) would pay in 10 days. The remaining customers would still take an average of 30 days to pay. What would the new average collection period (ACP) be? If the firm's annual sales are $15 million (before discounts), what happens to the investment in receivables?

If half of the customers take 10 days to pay and half take 30, the new average collection period is:

$$\text{New ACP} = .50 \times 10 \text{ days} + .50 \times 30 \text{ days} = 20 \text{ days}$$

The ACP thus falls from 30 days to 20 days. Average daily sales are $15 million/365 = $41,096 per day. Receivables thus fall by $41,096 \times 10 = $410,960.

Credit Instruments

credit instrument
The evidence of indebtedness.

The **credit instrument** is the basic evidence of indebtedness. Most trade credit is offered on *open account*. This means the only formal instrument of credit is the invoice that is sent with the shipment of goods and that the customer signs as evidence the goods have been received. Afterward, the firm and its customers record the exchange on their books of account.

At times, the firm may require the customer to sign a *promissory note*. This is a basic IOU and might be used when the order is large, when there is no cash discount involved, and when the firm anticipates a problem in collections. Promissory notes are not common, but they can eliminate controversies later about the existence of debt.

One problem with promissory notes is that they are signed after delivery of the goods. To obtain a credit commitment from a customer before the goods are delivered, a firm arranges a *commercial draft*. Typically, the firm draws up a commercial draft calling for the customer to pay a specific amount by a specified date. The draft is then sent to the customer's bank with the shipping invoices.

When immediate payment on the draft is required, it is called a *sight draft*. If immediate payment is not required, the draft is a *time draft*. When the draft is presented and the buyer accepts it—meaning the buyer promises to pay it in the future—it is called a *trade acceptance* and is sent back to the selling firm. The seller can keep the acceptance, in effect providing trade credit financing to the buyer, or sell it to someone else. The third party buying the acceptance is a money market investor. This investor is now financing the buyer and the seller receives immediate payment less discount interest.

To make the trade acceptance more salable, a chartered bank may stamp it, meaning the bank is guaranteeing payment. Then the draft becomes a *bankers acceptance*. This arrangement is common in international trade and widely used domestically. Bankers acceptances are actively traded in the money market as we discussed in Chapter 19.

A firm can also use a conditional sales contract as a credit instrument. This is an arrangement where the firm retains legal ownership of the goods until the customer has completed payment. Conditional sales contracts usually are paid in installments and have an interest cost built into them.

CONCEPT QUESTIONS

1. What considerations enter into the determination of the terms of sale?

2. Explain what terms of "3/45, net 90" mean. What is the implicit interest rate?

20.3

ANALYZING CREDIT POLICY

In this section, we take a closer look at the factors that influence the decision to grant credit. Granting credit makes sense only if the NPV from doing so is positive. We thus need to look at the NPV of the decision to grant credit.

Credit Policy Effects

In evaluating credit policy, there are five basic factors to consider:

1. *Revenue effects.* When the firm grants credit, there is a delay in revenue collections as some customers take advantage of the credit offered and pay later. However, the firm may be able to charge a higher price if it grants credit and it may be able to increase the quantity sold. Total revenues may thus increase.

2. *Cost effects.* Although the firm may experience delayed revenues if it grants credit, it still incurs the costs of sales immediately. Whether or not the firm sells for cash or credit, it still has to acquire or produce the merchandise (and pay for it).

3. *The cost of debt.* When the firm grants credit, it must arrange to finance the resulting receivables. As a result, the firm's cost of short-term borrowing is a factor in the decision to grant credit.[4]

4. *The probability of nonpayment.* If the firm grants credit, some percentage of the credit buyers do not pay. This can't happen, of course, if the firm sells for cash.

5. *The cash discount.* When the firm offers a cash discount as part of its credit terms, some customers choose to pay early to take advantage of the discount.

Evaluating a Proposed Credit Policy

To illustrate how credit policy can be analyzed, we start with a relatively simple case. Locust Software has been in existence for two years; it is one of several successful firms that develop computer programs. Currently, Locust sells for cash only.

Locust is evaluating a request from some major customers to change its current policy to net 30 days. To analyze this proposal, we define the following:

P = Price per unit
v = Variable cost per unit
Q = Current quantity sold per month
Q' = Quantity sold under new policy
R = Monthly required return

For now, we ignore discounts and the possibility of default. Also, we ignore taxes because they don't affect our conclusions.

NPV OF SWITCHING POLICIES   To illustrate the NPV of switching credit policies, suppose we had the following for Locust:

P = $49
v = $20
Q = 100
Q' = 110

If the required return is 2 percent per month, should Locust make the switch?

Currently, Locust has monthly sales of $P \times Q$ = $4,900. Variable costs each month are $v \times Q$ = $2,000, so the monthly cash flow from this activity is:

$$\text{Cash flow (old policy)} = (P - v)Q \qquad\qquad [20.2]$$
$$= (\$49 - 20) \times 100$$
$$= \$2,900$$

---

4 The cost of short-term debt is not necessarily the required return on receivables, although it is commonly assumed to be. As always, the required return on an investment depends on the risk of the investment, not the source of the financing. The buyer's cost of short-term debt is closer in spirit to the correct rate. We maintain the implicit assumption that the seller and the buyer have the same short-term debt cost. In any case, the time periods in credit decisions are relatively short, so a relatively small error in the discount rate does not have a large effect on our estimated NPV.

This is not the total cash flow for Locust, of course, but it is all that we need to look at because fixed costs and other components of cash flow are the same whether or not the switch is made.

If Locust does switch to net 30 days on sales, the quantity sold rises to $Q' = 110$. Monthly revenues increase to $P \times Q'$, and costs are $v \times Q'$. The monthly cash flow under the new policy is thus:

$$
\begin{aligned}
\text{Cash flow (new policy)} &= (P - v)Q' \\
&= (\$49 - 20) \times 110 \\
&= \$3,190
\end{aligned}
\tag{20.3}
$$

Going back to Chapter 10, the relevant incremental cash flow is the difference between the new and old cash flows:

$$
\begin{aligned}
\text{Incremental cash inflow} &= (P - v)(Q' - Q) \\
&= (\$49 - 20) \times (110 - 100) \\
&= \$290
\end{aligned}
$$

This says the benefit each month of changing policies is equal to the gross profit per unit sold $(P - v) = \$29$, multiplied by the increase in sales $(Q' - Q) = 10$. The present value of the future incremental cash flows is thus:

$$
PV = [(P - v)(Q' - Q)]/R
\tag{20.4}
$$

For Locust, this present value works out to be:

$$
PV = (\$29 \times 10)/.02 = \$14,500
$$

Notice that we have treated the monthly cash flow as a perpetuity since the same benefit would be realized each month forever.

Now that we know the benefit of switching, what's the cost? There are two components to consider: First, since the quantity sold rises from Q to Q', Locust has to produce $Q' - Q$ more units today at a cost of $v(Q' - Q) = \$20 \times (110 - 100) = \$200$. Second, the sales that would have been collected this month under the current policy $(P \times Q = \$4,900)$ are not collected. This happens because the sales made this month won't be collected until 30 days later under the new policy. The cost of the switch is the sum of these two components:

$$
\text{Cost of switching} = PQ + v(Q' - Q)
\tag{20.5}
$$

For Locust, this cost would be $\$4,900 + 200 = \$5,100$.

Putting it all together, the NPV of the switch is:

$$
\text{NPV of switching} = -[PQ + v(Q' - Q)] + (P - v)(Q' - Q)/R
\tag{20.6}
$$

For Locust, the cost of switching is $\$5,100$. As we saw, the benefit is $\$290$ per month, forever. At 2 percent per month, the NPV is:

$$
\begin{aligned}
\text{NPV} &= -\$5,100 + \$290/.02 \\
&= -\$5,100 + 14,500 \\
&= \$9,400
\end{aligned}
$$

Therefore, the switch is very profitable.

A BREAK-EVEN APPLICATION   Based on our discussion thus far, the key variable for Locust is $Q' - Q$, the increase in unit sales. The projected increase of 10 units is only an estimate, so there is some forecasting risk. Under the circumstances, it's natural to wonder what increase in unit sales is necessary to break even.

Earlier, the NPV of the switch was defined as:

EXAMPLE 20.2: We'd Rather Fight than Switch

Suppose a company is considering a switch from all cash to net 30, but the quantity sold is not expected to change. What is the NPV of the switch? Explain.

In this case, $Q' - Q$ is zero, so the NPV is just $-P \times Q$. What this says is that the effect of the switch is simply to postpone one month's collections forever, with no benefit from doing so.

$$NPV = -[PQ + v(Q' - Q)] + (P - v)(Q' - Q)/R$$

We can calculate the break-even point explicitly by setting the NPV equal to zero and solving for $(Q' - Q)$:

$$NPV = 0 = -[PQ + v(Q' - Q)] + (P - v)(Q' - Q)/R \qquad [20.7]$$

$$Q' - Q = (PQ)/[(P - v)/R - v]$$

For Locust, the break-even sales increase is thus:

$$Q' - Q = \$4,900/[\$29/.02 - \$20]$$
$$= 3.43 \text{ units}$$

This tells us that the switch is a good idea as long as we are confident we can sell at least 3.43 more units.

CONCEPT QUESTIONS

1. What are the important effects to consider in a decision to offer credit?

2. Explain how to estimate the NPV of a credit policy switch.

OPTIMAL CREDIT POLICY

So far, we've discussed how to compute net present value for a switch in credit policy. We have not discussed the optimal amount of credit or the optimal credit policy. In principle, the optimal amount of credit is determined where the incremental cash flows from increased sales are exactly equal to the incremental costs of carrying the increased investment in accounts receivable.

The Total Credit Cost Curve

The trade-off between granting credit and not granting credit isn't hard to identify, but it is difficult to quantify precisely. As a result, we can only describe an optimal credit policy.

To begin, the carrying costs associated with granting credit come in three forms:

1. The required return on receivables.
2. The losses from bad debts.
3. The costs of managing credit and credit collections.

We have already discussed the first and second of these. Making up the third cost of managing credit are the expenses associated with running the credit department. Firms that don't grant credit have no such department and no such expense. These three costs all increase as credit policy is relaxed.

If a firm has a very restrictive credit policy, all the preceding costs are low. In this case, the firm has a shortage of credit, so there is an opportunity cost. This opportunity cost is the extra potential profit from credit sales that is lost because credit is refused. This forgone benefit comes from two sources, the increase in quantity sold, Q' versus Q, and, potentially, a higher price. These costs go down as credit policy is relaxed.

credit cost curve
Graphical representation of the sum of the carrying costs and the opportunity costs of a credit policy.

The sum of the carrying costs and the opportunity costs of a particular credit policy is called the total **credit cost curve.** We have drawn such a curve in Figure 20.1. As this figure illustrates, there is a point where the total credit cost is minimized. This point corresponds to the optimal amount of credit or, equivalently, the optimal investment in receivables.

If the firm extends more credit than this minimum, the additional net cash flow from new customers does not cover the carrying costs of the investment in receivables. If the level of receivables is less than this amount, the firm is forgoing valuable profit opportunities.

In general, the costs and benefits from extending credit depend on the characteristics of particular firms and industries. All other things being equal, for example, it is likely that firms with (1) excess capacity, (2) low variable operating costs, and (3) repeat customers extend credit more

FIGURE 20.1

The costs of granting credit

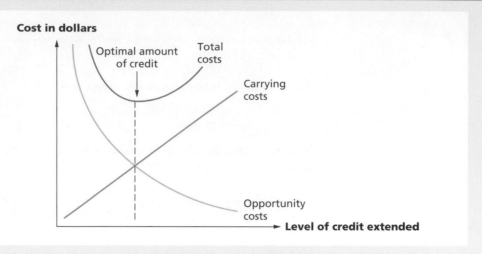

Carrying costs are the cash flows that must be incurred when credit is granted. They are positively related to the amount of credit extended.
Opportunity costs are the lost sales from refusing credit. These costs go down when credit is granted.

liberally than otherwise. See if you can explain why each of these contributes to a more liberal credit policy.

Organizing the Credit Function

As we stated earlier, firms selling only for cash save the expense of running a credit department. In practice, firms that do grant credit may achieve some of these savings by contracting out all or part of the credit function to a factor, an insurance company, or a **captive finance company.** Chapter 18 discussed factoring, an arrangement where the firm sells its receivables to a factor that takes on all responsibility for credit checking, authorization, and collection. The factor also guarantees payment, ruling out defaults. Factors often provide accounts receivable financing as well. Small firms may find factoring cheaper than an in-house credit department.

Firms that run internal credit operations are self-insured against default risk. An alternative is to buy credit insurance through an insurance company. The insurance company offers coverage up to a preset dollar limit for accounts. As you would expect, accounts with a higher credit rating merit higher insurance limits.

Exporters may qualify for credit insurance through Export Development Canada (EDC), a Crown corporation of the federal government. For example, in late 2004, EDC supported Q'Max Solutions of Calgary, Alberta, which won a contract with Mexican oil company Pemex for US $68.9 million.[5]

Large corporations commonly extend credit through a subsidiary called a captive finance company, instead of a credit department. General Motors Corporation, for example, finances its dealers and car buyers through General Motors Acceptance Corporation (GMAC). Consumer and dealer receivables are the assets of GMAC and they are financed largely through commercial paper. Setting up the credit function as a separate legal entity has potential advantages in facilitating borrowing against receivables. Since they are segregated on the balance sheet of a captive, the receivables may make better collateral. As a result, the captive may be able to carry more debt and save on borrowing costs.[6]

captive finance company
Wholly owned subsidiary that handles credit extension and receivables financing through commercial paper.

www.gmcanada.com

---

5 More information about EDC is at *www.edc.ca*

6 The trend toward securitization of receivables through wholly owned subsidiaries discussed in Chapter 18 is supporting evidence. This somewhat controversial view of finance captives comes from G. S. Roberts and J. A. Viscione, "Captive Finance Subsidiaries and the M-Form Hypothesis," *Bell Journal of Economics,* Spring 1981, pp. 285–95.

A related issue in credit administration, whether through a finance captive or in-house, is the importance of having a set of written credit policies.[7] The policy covers credit terms, the information needed for credit analysis, collection procedures and the monitoring of receivables. Having the policy clearly stated helps control possible conflicts between the credit department and sales. For example, during the economic slowdown of 2001–2002, some Canadian companies tightened their credit granting rules to offset the higher probability of customer bankruptcy. Other companies eased credit to promote sales and to provide flexibility for regular customers. The decision depends on the considerations we analyzed earlier. Either way, sales and credit have to work together.

CONCEPT QUESTIONS

1. What are the carrying costs of granting credit?

2. What are the opportunity costs of not granting credit?

3. Why do many large U.S. and Canadian corporations form captive finance subsidiaries?

www.qualcomm.com

20.5 | CREDIT ANALYSIS

Thus far, we have focused on establishing credit terms. Once a firm decides to grant credit to its customers, it must then establish guidelines for determining who is allowed to buy on credit as well as the credit limits to be set. Since the forces of competition often leave a firm little discretion in setting credit terms, credit managers focus on credit analysis, along with collection and receivables monitoring. Credit analysis refers to the process of deciding whether to extend credit to a particular customer. It usually involves two steps: gathering relevant information and determining creditworthiness.

Credit analysis is important simply because potential losses on receivables can be substantial. For example, in early 2001 Qualcomm was forced to evaluate the impact of an announcement from Globalstar that it had suspended further payments on its debt. Globalstar was attempting to build a worldwide satellite-telephone network, and was a significant customer for Qualcomm. The need to write off this debt cost Qualcomm some U.S. $595 million.

When Should Credit Be Granted?

Imagine that a firm is trying to decide whether to grant credit to a customer. This decision can get complicated. For example, the answer depends on what happens if credit is refused. Will the customer simply pay cash or will the customer not make the purchase? To avoid this and other difficulties, we use some special cases to illustrate the key points.

A ONETIME SALE We start by considering the simplest case. A new customer wishes to buy one unit on credit at a price of P' per unit. If credit is refused, the customer would not make a purchase.

Furthermore, we assume that, if credit is granted, in one month, the customer either pays up or defaults. The probability of the second of these events is π. In this case, the probability (π) can be interpreted as the percentage of new customers who do not pay. Our business does not have repeat customers, so this is strictly a one-time sale. Finally, the required return on receivables is R per month and the variable cost is v per unit.

The analysis here is straightforward. If the firm refuses credit, the incremental cash flow is zero. If it grants credit, it spends v (the variable cost) this month and expects to collect $(1 - \pi)P'$ next month. The NPV of granting credit is:

$$\text{NPV} = -v + (1 - \pi)P'/(1 + R) \qquad \textbf{[20.8]}$$

---

7 Our discussion draws on "A Written Credit Policy Can Overcome a Host of Potential Problems," Joint Venture Supplement, *The Financial Post*, June 20, 1991.

For example, for Locust Software, this NPV is:

$$NPV = -\$20 + (1 - \pi) \times \$50/(1.02)$$

With, say, a 20 percent rate of default, this works out to be:

$$NPV = -\$20 + .80 \times \$50/1.02 = \$19.22$$

Therefore, credit should be granted.

Our example illustrates an important point. In granting credit to a new customer, a firm risks its variable cost (v). It stands to gain the full price (P'). For a new customer, then, credit may be granted even if the default probability is high. For example, the break-even probability can be determined by setting the NPV equal to zero and solving for π:

$$NPV = 0 = -\$20 + (1 - \pi) \times \$50/(1.02)$$
$$(1 - \pi) = \$20/\$50 \times 1.02$$
$$\pi = 59.2\%$$

Locust should extend credit as long as there is at least a $1 - .592 = 40.8\%$ chance or better of collecting. This explains why firms with higher markups tend to have looser credit terms.

A common rule of thumb restates this information by asking, how many good accounts do we have to sell and collect to make up for the mistake of one write-off? Working with accounting numbers instead of NPVs, we can restate the break-even point as follows:

$$\text{Profit} = 0 = -\text{ variable cost} \times \text{probability of loss} + \text{profit margin}$$
$$\times \text{probability of payment}$$
$$0 = -v \times \pi + (P' - v)(1 - \pi)$$

In the Locust example, we have at the break-even point:

$$\text{Profit} = 0 = -\$20 \times \pi + (\$50 - \$20)(1 - \pi)$$

With a little algebra, we can solve for $\pi = 60$ percent the same as we had earlier except for rounding error due to ignoring the present value. Notice that the break-even probability of default is simply the profit margin $= \$30/\$50 = 60\%$. This makes sense since the seller breaks even if losses offset profits. Business people interpret this as saying that for every write-off we have to sell and collect around .6 good accounts.

Finally, notice that the break-even percentage of 60 percent is much higher than the break-even percentage of .04 percent we calculate in Appendix 20A, because that percentage is calculated assuming that $Q = Q'$, implying there are no new customers. The percentage calculated here applies to a potential new customer only.

The important difference is that, if we extend credit to an old customer, we risk the total sales price (P), since this is what we collect if we do not extend credit. If we extend credit to a new customer, we risk only our variable cost.

REPEAT BUSINESS   A second, very important factor to keep in mind is the possibility of repeat business. We can illustrate this by extending our onetime example. We make one important assumption: A new customer who does not default the first time remains a customer forever and never defaults. If the firm grants credit, it spends v this month. Next month, it either gets nothing if the customer defaults or it gets P if the customer pays. If the customer does pay, he or she buys another unit on credit and the firm spends v again. The net cash inflow for the month is thus $P - v$. In every subsequent month, this same $P - v$ occurs as the customer pays for the previous month's order and places a new one.

It follows from our discussion that, in one month, the firm has $0 with probability π. With probability $(1 - \pi)$, however, the firm has a new customer. The value of a new customer is equal to present value of $(P - v)$ every month forever:

$$PV = (P - v)/R$$

The NPV of extending credit is therefore:

$$NPV = -v + (1 - \pi)(P - v)/R \qquad \text{[20.9]}$$

For Locust, this is:

$$NPV = -\$20 + (1 - \pi) \times (\$49 - \$20)/.02$$
$$= -\$20 + (1 - \pi) \times \$1,450$$

Even if the probability of default is 90 percent, the NPV is:

$$NPV = -\$20 + .10 \times \$1,450 = \$125$$

Locust should extend credit unless default is a virtual certainty. The reason is that it costs only $20 to find out who is a good customer and who is not. A good customer is worth $1,450, however, so Locust can afford quite a few defaults.

Our repeat business example probably exaggerates the acceptable default probability, but it does illustrate that often the best way to do credit analysis is simply to extend credit to almost anyone. It also points out that the possibility of repeat business is a crucial consideration. In such cases, the important thing is to control the amount of credit initially offered so the possible loss is limited. The amount can be increased with time. Most often, the best predictor of whether customers will pay in the future is whether they have paid in the past.

Credit Information

If a firm does want credit information on customers, there are a number of sources. Information commonly used to assess creditworthiness includes the following:

1. *Financial statements.* A firm can ask a customer to supply financial statement information such as balance sheets and income statements. Minimum standards and rules of thumb based on financial ratios like the ones we discussed in Chapter 3 can be used as a basis for extending or refusing credit.

2. *Credit reports on a customer's payment history with other firms.* Quite a few organizations sell information on the credit strength and credit history of business firms. Dun & Bradstreet Canada provides subscribers with a credit reference book and credit reports on individual firms. Ratings and information are available for a huge number of firms, including very small ones. Creditel of Canada also provides credit reporting and has the capability to send reports electronically.

    Many firms have mechanized rules that allow for automatic approval of, say, all credit requests up to a preset dollar amount for firms with high ratings. Potential customers with ratings below some minimum are automatically rejected. All others are investigated further.

3. *Banks.* Banks may provide some assistance to their business customers in acquiring information on the creditworthiness of other firms.

4. *The customer's payment history with the firm.* The most obvious way to obtain information about the likelihood of a customer not paying is to examine whether the customer paid in the past and how much trouble collecting turned out to be.

Figure 20.2 illustrates just part of a Dun & Bradstreet credit report. As you can see, quite detailed information is available.

www.dunandbradstreet.com

spread
The gap between the interest rate a bank pays on deposits and the rate it charges on loans.

EXAMPLE 20.3: Good and Bad Accounts at a Financial Institution

Suppose a lending officer at a chartered bank or other financial institution lends $1,000 to a customer who defaults completely. When this happens the lender has to write off the full $1,000. How many good $1,000 loans, paid in full and on time, does the lender have to make to offset the loss and break even on the lending portfolio?

To answer the question, we need to know the profit margin on loans. In banking this is called the **spread** between the lending rate and the cost of funds to the bank. The spread varies over the interest rate cycle but is usually around 2 or 3 percent. Supposing the spread is 2.5 percent, the bank makes $25 on every $1,000 loan. This means the lender must make $1,000/$25 = 40 good loans for every write-off. Our example illustrates one reason banks are conservative lenders. Low spreads leave little room for loan losses.

Credit Evaluation and Scoring

five Cs of credit
The following five basic credit factors to be evaluated: character, capacity, capital, collateral, and conditions.

No magical formulas can assess the probability that a customer will not pay. In very general terms, the classic **five Cs of credit** are the basic factors to be evaluated:

1. *Character.* The customer's willingness to meet credit obligations.
2. *Capacity.* The customer's ability to meet credit obligations out of operating cash flows.
3. *Capital.* The customer's financial reserves.
4. *Collateral.* A pledged asset in the case of default.
5. *Conditions.* General economic conditions in the customer's line of business.

credit scoring
The process of quantifying the probability of default when granting consumer credit.

Credit scoring refers to the process of calculating a numerical rating for a customer based on information collected and then granting or refusing credit based on the result. For example, a firm might rate a customer on a scale of 1 (very poor) to 10 (very good) on each of the five Cs of credit using all the information available about the customer. A credit score could then be calculated based on the total. From experience, a firm might choose to grant credit only to customers with a score of more than, say, 30.

Firms such as credit card issuers have developed elaborate statistical models for credit scoring. This approach has the advantage of being objective as compared to scoring based on judgments on the five Cs. Usually, all the legally relevant and observable characteristics of a large pool of customers are studied to find their historic relation to default rates. Based on the results, it is possible to determine the variables that best predict whether or not a customer will pay and then calculate a credit score based on those variables.

multiple discriminant analysis (MDA)
Statistical technique for distinguishing between two samples on the basis of their observed characteristics.

Computerized scoring models employ a statistical technique called **multiple discriminant analysis (MDA)** to predict which customers will be good or bad accounts.[8] Similar to regression analysis, MDA chooses a set of variables that best discriminate between good and bad credits with hindsight in a sample for which the outcomes are known. The variables are then used to classify new applications that come in. For consumer credit, for example, these variables include length of time in current job, monthly income, whether the customer's home is owned or rented, other financial obligations, and so on. For business customers, ratios are the relevant variables.

To illustrate how MDA works without getting into the derivation, suppose only two ratios explain whether a business customer is creditworthy: sales/total assets and EBIT/total assets. What MDA does is draw a line to separate good (G) from bad (B) accounts as shown in Figure 20.3. The equation for the line is:

$$\text{Score} = Z = 0.4 \times [\text{Sales/Total assets}] + 3.0 \times \text{EBIT/Total assets} \qquad [20.10]$$

For example, suppose Locust Software has a credit application from Kiwi Computers. Kiwi's financial statements reveal sales/total assets of 1.8 and EBIT/total assets of .16. We can calculate Kiwi's score as:

$$Z = 0.4 \times 1.8 + 3.0 \times .16 = 1.2$$

The line in Figure 20.3 is drawn at a cutoff score of .90. Because Kiwi's score is higher, it lies above the line and the model predicts it will be a good account. The decision rule is to grant credit to all accounts with scores more than 0.9, that is to all accounts above the line.

To test the track record of scoring models, researchers have compared their predictions with actual outcomes. If the models were perfect, all good accounts would be above the line and all bad accounts below it. As you can see in Figure 20.3, the model does a reasonable job but there are some errors. For this reason, firms using scoring models assign scores near the line to a grey area for further investigation.

As you might expect, statistical scoring models work best when there is a large sample of similar credit applicants. Research on scoring models bears this out: the models are most useful in consumer credit.

Because credit-scoring models and procedures determine who is and is not creditworthy, it is not surprising that they have been the subject of government regulation. In particular, the kinds of background and demographic information that can be used in the credit decision are

---

8 Our discussion of scoring models draws on Hill and Sartoris, *Short-Term Financial Management,* chap. 14; and
L. Kryzanowski et al., *Business Solvency Risk Analysis* (Montreal: Institute of Canadian Bankers, 1990), chap. 6.

FIGURE 20.2

A Dun & Bradstreet
credit report

```
D&B Payment Analysis Report Sample

        COPYRIGHT 2001 DUN & BRADSTREET INC. - PROVIDED UNDER CONTRACT
              FOR THE EXCLUSIVE USE OF SUBSCRIBER XXX-XXXXXX.

                ATTN: sample
  BUSINESS SUMMARY               DATE PRINTED: January 18, 200-
  D-U-N-S: 80-473-5132           SIC 27 52 COMMERCIAL PRINTING
  GORMAN MANUFACTURING COMPANY, INC
                                 SALES: ($)          17,685,297
                                 HISTORY:            CLEAR
                                 CONTROL DATE:       1965
                                 YEAR STARTED:       MAY 21 1965
                                 EMPLOYS:            105
  492 KOLLER STREET              EMPLOYS HERE:       100
  SAN FRANCISCO, CA 94110
  TEL: 650 555-0000              LESLIE SMITH, PRES

  Evidence of open Suit(s), Lien(s) and Judgment(s) in the D&B database
  PAYDEX - Based on most recent 12 mos. trade   55 - 26 Days Beyond Terms
  PAYDEX - Based on most recent 90 Days trade   48 - 36 Days Beyond Terms
  Payments Within Terms (not dollar weighted)   47%
  ------------------------------------------------------------------------
  PAYMENT TRENDS
  PAYDEX scores below are based on dollar weighted trade in most recent 12 mos.
      PRIOR 4 QTRS                    CURRENT 12 MONTHS
      ''''''''98 ''''''''98 ''''''''98 ''''''''98   '''''''''99 '''''''00
      MAR JUN SEP DEC    FEB MAR APR MAY JUN JUL AUG SEP OCT NOV DEC JAN

  Firm     73  75  72  72   75  71  69  69  68  58  56  55  61  61  55  55
  Industry
  Quartiles
  Upper    79  80  80  79       79           79          80          79
  Median   75  75  76  75       75           75          75          75
  Lower    66  66  67  67       67           66          67          66

  Industry PAYDEX based on:             KEY TO PAYDEX SCORES:
  SIC: 2752                                80 -   Within terms
  1,286 Firms                              75 -    8 Days Beyond Terms
                                           55 -   26 Days Beyond Terms
  ------------------------------------------------------------------------
  PUBLIC FILINGS SUMMARY
  Currently, there is indication of open suit(s), lien(s), and/or judgment(s)
  in D&B's Public Records database:
         Suit(s) 2          Lien(s) 2          Judgment(s) 1
  The public record items contained in this report may have been paid,
  terminated, vacated or released prior to the date this report was printed.
  ------------------------------------------------------------------------
  SPECIAL EVENTS
  12/03/9-    On Mar 26, 199- the subject experienced a fire due to an earthquake.
              According to Leslie Smith, president, damages amounted to $35,000 which
              were fully covered by their insurance company. The business was closed
              for two days while employees settled personal matters.
  ------------------------------------------------------------------------
  SUMMARY OF PAYMENT HABITS
  DOLLAR RANGE COMPARISONS
  SUPPLIERS THAT         NUMBER OF         TOTAL           % OF DOLLAR AMOUNTS
  EXTEND CREDIT OF...    EXPERIENCES    DOLLAR AMOUNT      PAID WITHIN TERMS
                            #                $                    %
  OVER $100,000            18           4,900,000                52
  $50,000 - 99,999         15             955,000                78
  $15,000 - 49,999         30             750,000                86
  $ 5,000 - 14,999         46             330,000                77
  $ 1,000 -  4,999         31              59,500                75
  Under $1,000             14               5,600                48

  OTHER PAYMENT CATEGORIES:
  Cash Experiences      3      76,000    50,000
  Paying Record Unknown 14    326,500   200,000
  Unfavorable Comments  10    145,500   100,000
  Placed For Collection:
       with D&B         0           0
       other           52         N/A
  Highest Now Owing           $1,000,000  Based on all trade
  Highest Past Due             $500,000   Based on all trade
  Average High Credit           $46,913   Based on industry trade

                                              D&B
                                           Dun & Bradstreet
```

limited. For example, suppose a consumer applicant was formerly bankrupt but has discharged all obligations. After a waiting period that varies from province to province, this information cannot be used in the credit decision.

Credit scoring is used for business customers by Canadian chartered banks. Scoring for small business loans offers the advantages of objective analysis without taking more of the lending officer's time than could be justified for a small account.

FIGURE 20.3

Credit scoring with multiple discriminant analysis

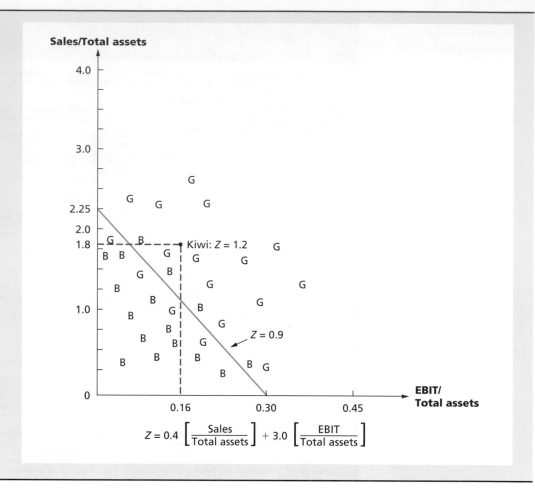

$$Z = 0.4 \left[\frac{\text{Sales}}{\text{Total assets}} \right] + 3.0 \left[\frac{\text{EBIT}}{\text{Total assets}} \right]$$

Many Canadian banks have online information and application forms for small businesses. For example, visit the website of TD Canada Trust (*www.tdcanadatrust.com/smallbusiness/index.jsp*) or Royal Bank of Canada (*www.royalbank.com/business/services/small_ bus_loan.html*).

CONCEPT QUESTIONS

1. What is credit analysis?

2. What are the five Cs of credit?

3. What are credit scoring models and how are they used?

20.6   COLLECTION POLICY

The collection policy is the final element management considers in establishing a credit policy. Collection policy involves monitoring receivables to spot trouble and obtaining payment on past-due accounts.

Monitoring Receivables

To keep track of payments by customers, most firms monitor outstanding accounts. First, a firm normally keeps track of its average collection period through time. If a firm is in a seasonal business, the ACP fluctuates during the year, but unexpected increases in the ACP are a cause for concern. Either customers in general are taking longer to pay, or some percentage of accounts receivable is seriously overdue.

aging schedule
A compilation of accounts receivable by the age of each account.

The **aging schedule** is a second basic tool for monitoring receivables. To prepare one, the credit department classifies accounts by age.[9] Suppose a firm has $100,000 in receivables. Some of these accounts are only a few days old, but others have been outstanding for quite some time. The following is an example of an aging schedule.

Aging Schedule

Age of Account	Amount	Percent of Total Value of Accounts Receivable
0–10 days	$ 50,000	50%
11–60 days	25,000	25
61–80 days	20,000	20
Over 80 days	5,000	5
	$100,000	100%

If this firm has a credit period of 60 days, 25 percent of its accounts are late. Whether or not this is serious depends on the nature of the firm's collection and customers. Often, accounts beyond a certain age are almost never collected. "The older the receivable, the less value it is to the business and the harder it is to collect."[10] Monitoring the age of accounts is very important in such cases.

Firms with seasonal sales find the percentages on the aging schedule changing during the year. For example, if sales in the current month are very high, total receivables also increase sharply. This means the older accounts, as a percentage of total receivables, become smaller and might appear less important. Some firms have refined the aging schedule so that they have an idea of how it should change with peaks and valleys in their sales.

Collection Effort

A firm's credit policy should include the procedures to follow for customers who are overdue. A sample set of procedures is given in Table 20.1 for an account due in 30 days. The time line is an important part of the table since experienced credit managers stress the need for prompt action.

The step at 90 days is severe: refusing to grant additional credit to the customer until arrearages are cleared up. This may antagonize a normally good customer, and it points to a potential conflict of interest between the collections department and the sales department.

After 120 days, the firm takes legal action only if the account is large. Legal action is expensive and, as we saw in Chapter 16, if the customer goes bankrupt as a result, there is usually little chance of recovering a significant portion of the credit extended. When this happens, the credit-granting firm is just another unsecured creditor. The firm can simply wait, or it can sell its

TABLE 20.1
Schedule of actions to follow up late payments (Stated terms: Net 30 days)

If Payment Is Not Made By:	Action
40 days	Telephone call to customer's payables department Send duplicate invoice if needed
50 days	Second telephone call to customer's payables department
60 days	Warning letter (mild)
75 days	Warning letter (strong)
90 days	Telephone call to management level Notify that future deliveries will be made only on a COD basis until payment is made
120 days	Stop further deliveries 1. Initiate appropriate legal action if the account is large 2. Turn over to a collection agency if the account is small

Source: Ned C. Hill and William C. Sartoris, *Short-Term Financial Management*, 2d ed. (New York: Macmillan, 1992), p. 392.

---

9 Aging schedules are used elsewhere in business. For example, aging schedules are often prepared for inventory items.

10 The quotation is from S. Horvitch, "Debt Collection: When to Drop the Hammer on Delinquent Customers," *The Financial Post*, March 15, 1991, p. 39.

receivable. For example, when FoxMeyer Health filed for bankruptcy in August 1996, it owed $20 million to Bristol-Myers Squibb for drug purchases. Once FoxMeyer filed for bankruptcy, Bristol-Myers tried to sell its receivable at a discount. The purchaser would then have been the creditor in the bankruptcy proceedings and would have gotten paid when the bankruptcy was settled. Similar trade claims against FoxMeyer initially traded as high as 49 cents on the dollar, but settled to about 20 cents less than a month later. Thus, if Bristol-Myers had cashed out at that price, it would have sold its $20 million claim for about $4 million, a hefty discount. Of course, Bristol-Myers would have gotten its money immediately rather than waiting for an uncertain future amount. Smaller accounts are turned over to a collection agency. Agency commissions range up to 50 percent of the amount collected.

Credit Management in Practice

CO-OP Atlantic is a groceries and fuel distributor located in Moncton, New Brunswick. Its credit manager, Gary Steeves, is responsible for monitoring and collecting over $450 million in receivables annually. CO-OP's customers include large grocery stores with balances of more than $1 million as well as several thousand small accounts with balances around $1,000. By installing a computerized system, CO-OP has reduced its average collection period by two days with a savings (NPV) of millions. The system improved monitoring of receivables and credit granting analysis. It also saved on labour costs in processing receivables documentation.

To make monitoring easy, treasury credit staff call up customer information from a central data base. For example, in the home fuel division, aging schedules are used to identify overdue accounts that require authorization by an analyst before further deliveries can be made. Under the old manual system, this information was not available. The system also provides collections staff with a daily list of accounts due for a telephone call together with a complete history of each.

Credit analysis centres around an early warning system that examines the solvency risk of existing and new commercial accounts. The software scores the accounts based on financial ratios. By mechanizing the analysis, CO-OP is now able to score all its large commercial accounts. Under the manual system, detailed financial analysis was done on an exception basis and often came too late.

CO-OP achieved these gains in monitoring and analysis without adding any staff in the credit department. The department has the same number of people as it did 10 years earlier when sales were half the present level. Gary Steeves estimates automation saved the company over $100,000 in additional wages.

CONCEPT QUESTIONS

1. What tools can a manager use to monitor receivables?
2. What is an aging schedule?
3. Describe collection procedures and the reasons for them.
4. Describe the key features of a computerized credit system.

20.7 INVENTORY MANAGEMENT

Like receivables, inventories represent a significant investment for many firms. For a typical Canadian manufacturing operation, inventories often exceed 20 percent of assets. For a retailer, inventories could represent more than 25 percent of assets. From our discussion in Chapter 18, we know that a firm's operating cycle is made up of its inventory period and its receivables period. This is one reason for discussing credit and inventory policy together. Beyond this, both credit policy and inventory policy are used to drive sales, and the two must be coordinated to ensure that the process of acquiring inventory, selling it, and collecting on the sale proceeds smoothly.

For example, changes in credit policy designed to stimulate sales must be simultaneously accompanied by planning for adequate inventory.

The Financial Manager and Inventory Policy

Despite the size of an average firm's investment in inventories, the financial manager typically does not have primary control over inventory management. Instead, other functional areas such as purchasing, production, and marketing normally share decision-making authority. Inventory management has become an increasingly important specialty in its own right; often financial management has only input into the decision. For this reason, we only survey some basics of inventory and inventory policy in the sections ahead.

Inventory Types

For a manufacturer, inventory is normally classified into one of three categories: The first category is *raw material*. This is whatever the firm uses as a starting point in its production process. Raw materials might be something as basic as iron ore for a steel manufacturer or something as sophisticated as disk drives for a computer manufacturer.

The second type of inventory is *work-in-progress,* which is just what the name suggests, namely, unfinished product. How large this portion of inventory is depends on the length and organization of the production process. The third and final type of inventory is *finished goods,* that is, products ready to ship or sell. Merchandise inventory being held by retail and wholesale firms for sale could also be categorized as finished goods.

There are three things to keep in mind concerning inventory types. First, the names for the different types can be a little misleading because one company's raw materials could be another's finished goods. For example, going back to our steel manufacturer, iron ore would be a raw material, and steel would be the final product. An auto body panel stamping operation has steel as its raw material and auto body panels as its finished goods, and an automobile assembler has body panels as raw materials and automobiles as finished products.

The second thing to keep in mind is that the different types of inventory can be quite different in their liquidity. Raw materials that are commodity-like or relatively standardized can be easy to convert to cash. Work-in-progress, on the other hand, can be quite illiquid and have little more than scrap value. As always, the liquidity of finished goods depends on the nature of the product.

Finally, a very important distinction between finished goods and other types of inventories is the demand for an inventory item that becomes a part of another item is usually termed *derived* or *dependent* demand because a company's demand for the input item depends on its need for finished items. In contrast, the firm's demand for finished goods is not derived from demand for other inventory items, so it is sometimes said to be *independent.*

Inventory Costs

As we discussed in Chapter 18, two basic types of costs are associated with current assets in general and with inventory in particular. The first of these are *carrying costs*. Here, carrying costs represent all the direct and opportunity costs of keeping inventory on hand.

These include:

1. Storage and tracking costs.
2. Insurance and taxes.
3. Losses due to obsolescence, deterioration, or theft.
4. The opportunity cost of capital on the invested amount.

The sum of these costs can be substantial, roughly ranging from 20 to 40 percent of inventory value per year.

The other type of costs associated with inventory are *shortage costs*. These are costs associated with having inadequate inventory on hand. The two components are restocking costs and costs related to safety reserves. Depending on the firm's business, restocking or order costs are either the costs of placing an order with suppliers or the cost of setting up a production run. The costs related to safety reserves are opportunity losses such as lost sales and loss of customer goodwill that result from having inadequate inventory.

A basic trade-off in inventory management exists because carrying costs increase with inventory levels while shortage or restocking costs decline with inventory levels. The goal of inventory management is thus to minimize the sum of these two costs. We consider approaches to this goal in the next section.

CONCEPT QUESTIONS

1. What are the different types of inventory?

2. What are three things to remember when examining inventory types?

3. What are the basic goals of inventory management?

INVENTORY MANAGEMENT TECHNIQUES

As we described earlier, the goal of inventory management is usually framed as cost minimization. Three techniques are discussed in this section, ranging from the relatively simple to the very complex.

The ABC Approach

The ABC is a simple approach to inventory management where the basic idea is to divide inventory into three (or more) groups. The underlying rationale is that a small portion of inventory in terms of quantity might represent a large portion in terms of inventory value. For example, this situation would exist for a manufacturer that uses some relatively expensive, high-tech components and some relatively inexpensive basic materials in producing its products.

Figure 20.4 illustrates an ABC comparison of items by their percentage of inventory value and the percentage of items represented. As Figure 20.4 shows, the A Group constitutes only 10 percent of inventory by item count, but it represents over half the value of inventory. The A Group items are thus monitored closely, and inventory levels are kept relatively low. At the other end, basic inventory items, such as nuts and bolts, also exist; because these are crucial and inexpensive, large quantities are ordered and kept on hand. These would be C Group items. The B Group is made up of in-between items.

The Economic Order Quantity (EOQ) Model

The economic order quantity (EOQ) model is the best-known approach to explicitly establishing an optimum inventory level. The basic idea is illustrated in Figure 20.5, which plots the various costs associated with holding inventory (on the vertical axis) against inventory levels (on the horizontal axis). As shown, inventory carrying costs rise as inventory levels increase, while, at the same time, restocking costs decrease. From our general discussion in Chapter 18 and our discussion of the total credit cost curve in this chapter, the general shape of the total inventory cost curve is familiar. With the EOQ model, we attempt to specifically locate the minimum total cost point, Q^*.

In our following discussion, keep in mind that the actual cost of the inventory itself is not included. The reason is that the *total* amount of inventory the firm needs in a given year is dictated by sales. What we are analyzing here is how much the firm should have on hand at any particular time. More precisely, we are trying to determine what size order the firm should place when it restocks its inventory.

INVENTORY DEPLETION   To develop the EOQ, we assume that the firm's inventory is sold at a steady rate until it hits zero. At that point, the firm restocks its inventory back to some

FIGURE 20.4

ABC inventory analysis

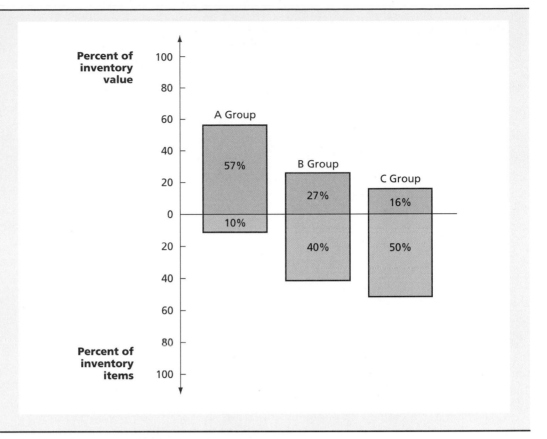

optimal level. For example, suppose the Trans Can Corporation starts out today with 3,600 units of a particular item in inventory. Annual sales of this item are 46,800 units, which is about 900 per week. If Trans Can sells 900 units in inventory each week, after four weeks, all the available inventory would be sold, and Trans Can would restock by ordering (or manufacturing) another 3,600 and start over. This selling and restocking process produces the sawtooth pattern for inventory holdings shown in Figure 20.6. As this figure illustrates, Trans Can always starts with 3,600 units in inventory and ends up at zero. On average, then, inventory is half of 3,600, or 1,800 units.

THE CARRYING COSTS   Going back to Figure 20.5, we see that carrying costs are normally assumed to be directly proportional to inventory levels. Suppose we let Q be the quantity of inventory that Trans Can orders each time (3,600 units); we call this the restocking quantity. Average inventory would then just be $Q/2$, or 1,800 units. If we let CC be the carrying cost per unit per year, Trans Can's total carrying costs are as follows:

$$\text{Total carrying costs} = \text{Average inventory} \times \text{Carrying costs per unit} \qquad [20.11]$$
$$= (Q/2) \times CC$$

In Trans Can's case, if carrying costs were \$0.75 per unit per year, total carrying costs would be the average inventory of 1,800 multiplied by \$0.75, or \$1,350 per year.

THE SHORTAGE COSTS   For now, we focus only on the restocking costs. In essence, we assume the firm never actually runs short on inventory, so that costs relating to safety reserves are not important. Later, we return to this issue.

Restocking costs are normally assumed to be fixed. In other words, every time we place an order, there are fixed costs associated with that order (remember the cost of the inventory itself is not considered here). Suppose we let T be the firm's total unit sales per year. If the firm orders Q units each time, it needs to place a total of T/Q orders. For Trans Can, annual sales were 46,800,

FIGURE 20.5

Costs of holding inventory

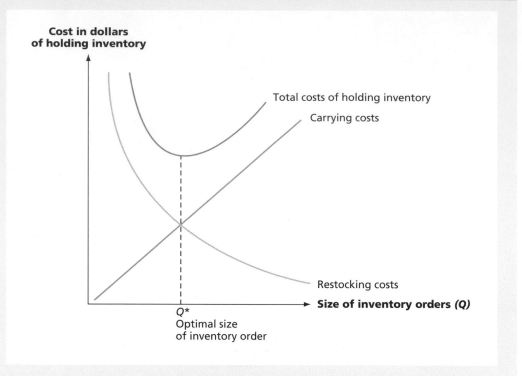

Restocking costs are increased when the firm holds a small quantity of inventory.
Carrying costs are increased when there is a large quantity of inventory on hand.
Total costs are the sum of the carrying and restocking costs.

FIGURE 20.6

Inventory holdings for the Trans Can Corporation

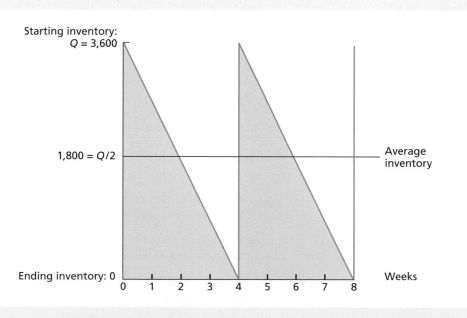

The Trans Can Corporation starts with inventory of 3,600 units. The quantity drops to zero by the fourth week.
The average inventory is $Q/2 = 3,600/2 = 1,800$ over the period.

and the order size was 3,600. Trans Can thus places a total of 46,800/3,600 = 13 orders per year. If the fixed cost per order is F, the total restocking cost for the year would be:

$$\text{Total restocking cost} = \text{Fixed cost per order} \times \text{Number of orders} \qquad [20.12]$$
$$= F \times (T/Q)$$

For Trans Can, order costs might be $50 per order, so the total restocking cost for 13 orders would be $50 × 13 = $650 per year.

THE TOTAL COSTS   The total costs associated with holding inventory are the sum of the carrying costs and the restocking costs:

$$\text{Total costs} = \text{Carrying costs} + \text{Restocking costs} \qquad [20.13]$$
$$= (Q/2) \times CC + F \times (T/Q)$$

Our goal is to find the value of Q, the restocking quantity that minimizes this cost. To see how we might go about this, we can calculate total costs for some different values of Q. For the Trans Can Corporation, we had carrying costs (CC) of $0.75 per unit per year, fixed costs per order (F) of $50 per order, and total unit sales (T) of 46,800 units. With these numbers, some possible total costs are (check some of these for practice):

Restocking Quantity (c)	Carrying Costs (Q/2 × CC)	+	Restocking Costs (F × T/Q)	=	Total Costs
500	$ 187.50		$4,680.00		$4,867.50
1,000	375.00		2,340.00		2,715.00
1,500	562.50		1,560.00		2,122.50
2,000	750.00		1,170.00		1,920.00
2,500	937.50		936.00		1,873.50
3,000	1,125.00		780.00		1,905.00
3,500	1,312.50		668.60		1,981.10

Inspecting the numbers, we see that total costs start at almost $5,000, and they decline to just under $1,900. The cost-minimizing quantity appears to be approximately 2,500.

To find the precise cost-minimizing quantity, we can look back at Figure 20.5. What we notice is that the minimum point occurs right where the two lines cross. At this point, carrying costs and restocking costs are the same. For the particular types of costs we have assumed here, this is always true; so we can find the minimum point just by setting these costs equal to each other and solving for Q^*:

$$\text{Carrying costs} = \text{Restocking costs} \qquad [20.14]$$
$$(Q^*/2) \times CC = F \times (T/Q^*)$$

With a little algebra, we get that

$$Q^{*2} = \frac{2T \times F}{CC} \qquad [20.15]$$

To solve for Q^*, we take the square root of both sides to find that

$$Q^* = \sqrt{\frac{2T \times F}{CC}} \qquad [20.16]$$

This reorder quantity, which minimizes the total inventory cost, is called the economic order quantity (EOQ). For the Trans Can Corporation, the EOQ is

$$Q^* = \sqrt{\frac{2T \times F}{CC}} \qquad [20.17]$$

$$= \sqrt{\frac{(2 \times 46,800) \times \$50}{\$.75}}$$

$$= \sqrt{6,240,000}$$

$$= 2,498 \text{ units}$$

Thus, for Trans Can, the economic order quantity is actually 2,498 units. At this level, check that the restocking costs and carrying costs are identical (they're both $926.75).[11]

Extensions to the EOQ Model

Thus far, we have assumed a company lets its inventory run down to zero and then reorders. In reality, a company reorders before its inventory goes to zero for two reasons: First, by always having at least some inventory on hand, the firm minimizes the risk of a stockout and the resulting losses of sales and customers. Second, when a firm does reorder, there is some time lag between placing the order and when the inventory arrives. Thus, to finish our discussion of the EOQ, we consider two extensions, safety stocks and reordering points.

SAFETY STOCKS A safety stock refers to the minimum level of inventory that a firm keeps on hand. Inventories are reordered whenever the level of inventory falls to the safety stock level. The top of Figure 20.7 illustrates how a safety stock can be incorporated into our EOQ model.

EXAMPLE 20.4: Carrying Costs

Thiewes Shoes begins each period with 100 pairs of hiking boots in stock. This stock is depleted each period and reordered. If the carrying cost per pair of boots per year is $3, what are the total carrying costs for the hiking boots?

Inventories always start at 100 items and end at zero, so average inventory is 50 items. At an annual cost of $3 per item, total carrying costs are $150.

EXAMPLE 20.5: Restocking Costs

In our previous example, suppose Thiewes sells a total of 600 pairs of boots in a year. How many times per year does Thiewes restock? Suppose the restocking cost is $20 per order. What are total restocking costs?

Thiewes orders 100 items each time. Total sales are 600 items per year, so Thiewes restocks six times per year, or about every two months. The restocking costs would be 6 orders × $20 per order = $120.

EXAMPLE 20.6: The EOQ

Based on our previous two examples, what size orders should Thiewes place? How often will Thiewes restock? What are the carrying and restocking costs? The total costs?

We know that the total number of pairs of boots ordered for the year (T) is 600. The restocking cost (F) is $20 per order, and the carrying cost (CC) is $3. We can calculate the EOQ for Thiewes as shown to the right.

Since Thiewes sells 600 pairs per year, it restocks 600/89.44 = 6.71 times.[12] The total restocking costs are $20 × 6.71 = $134.16. Average inventory is 89.44/2 = 44.72 pairs

of boots. The carrying costs will be $3 × 44.72 = $134.16, the same as the restocking costs. The total costs are thus $268.33.

$$EOQ^* = \sqrt{\frac{2T \times F}{CC}}$$

$$= \sqrt{\frac{(2 \times 600) \times \$20}{\$3}}$$

$$= \sqrt{8,000}$$

$$= 89.44 \text{ units}$$

---

11 In general, EOQ is the minimum point on the total cost curve in Figure 20.4 where the derivative of total cost with respect to quantity is zero. From Equation 20.13:

$$\frac{d \text{ (Total cost)}}{dQ} = \frac{CC}{2} - \frac{T \times F}{Q^2} = 0$$

To find the optimal value of Q, we solve this equation for Q:

$$\frac{CC}{2} = \frac{T \times F}{Q^2}$$

$$Q^2 = \frac{2T \times F}{CC}$$

$$Q = \sqrt{\frac{2T \times F}{CC}}$$

12 In practice, Thiewes would order 90 pairs of boots. It should also be pointed out that the EOQ model provides a guideline value, though there is some flexibility in the number chosen around this optimal point (without significantly increasing the total cost). For example, a convenient order size might be multiples of a dozen, so that 84 or 96 could be the number selected.

Notice that adding a safety stock simply means the firm does not run its inventory all the way down to zero. Other than this, the situation is identical to our earlier discussion of the EOQ.

REORDER POINTS   To allow for delivery time, a firm places orders before inventories reach a critical level. The reorder points are the times at which the firm actually places its inventory orders. These points are illustrated in the middle of Figure 20.7. As shown, the reorder points simply occur some fixed number of days (or weeks or months) before inventories are projected to reach zero.

One of the reasons a firm keeps a safety stock is to allow for uncertain delivery times. So we can combine our reorder point and safety stock discussions in the bottom part of Figure 20.7. The result is a generalized EOQ in which the firm orders in advance of anticipated needs and also keeps a safety stock of inventory to guard against unforeseen fluctuations in demand and delivery time.

Canadian Tire uses a modified EOQ approach to set target inventory levels for the thousands of items stocked in each store. Because the company markets its stores as providing one-stop shopping, it seeks a high service level with few stockouts. Safety stocks are set accordingly. An in-store computer, on-line with the cash registers, monitors sales and automatically sends an order to the warehouse computer when the stock level drops to the reorder point.

www.canadiantire.ca

Managing Derived-Demand Inventories

As we described previously, the demand for some inventory types is derived from, or dependent on, other inventory needs. A good example is an auto manufacturer where the demand for finished products depends on consumer demand, marketing programs, and other factors related to projected unit sales. The demand for inventory items such as tires, batteries, headlights, and other components is then completely determined by the number of autos planned.

Materials Requirements Planning (MRP)

Production and inventory specialists have developed computer-based systems for ordering and/or scheduling production of demand-dependent inventories. These systems fall under the general heading of *materials requirements planning* (MRP). The basic idea behind MRP is that, once finished goods inventory levels are set, it is possible to back out what levels of work-in-progress inventories must exist to meet the need for finished goods. From there, it is possible to back out what raw materials inventories must be on hand. This ability to schedule backward from finished goods inventories stems from the dependent nature of work-in-progress and raw materials inventories. MRP is particularly important for complicated products where a variety of components are needed to create the finished product.

just-in-time inventory (JIT)
Design for inventory in which parts, raw materials, and other work-in-process is delivered exactly as needed for production. Goal is to minimize inventory.

Just-In-Time Inventory

EOQ is a useful tool for many firms especially in the retail sector but the cutting edge of inventory management in manufacturing is a relatively new approach called **just-in-time inventory** or **just-in-time production**.[13] The basic idea is that raw materials, parts, and other work-in-

---

EXAMPLE 20.7: The Reorder Point for Hiking Boots

Suppose Thiewes Shoes wishes to hold a safety stock of hiking boots equal to six days' sales. If the store is open 300 days per year, what should be the safety stock? What is the reorder point for hiking boots?

The safety stock is $6/300 \times 600$ pairs = 12 pairs

The reorder point is when 12 pairs are on hand. If sales are evenly distributed, there will still be 6.71 orders per year.

---

13 Our discussion of just-in-time inventory draws on J. Loring, "Inventory: Taking Stock," *Canadian Business,* April 1991; E. Corcoran, "Milliken & Co., Managing the Quality of a Textile Revolution," *Scientific American,* April 1990; and Hill and Sartoris, *Short-Term Financial Management,* chaps. 17 and 20. A good source of just-in-time production is J. D. Blackburn, ed., *Time-Based Competition: The Next Battleground in American Manufacturing* (Homewood, IL: Business One Irwin, 1991).

FIGURE 20.7

Safety stocks and reorder points

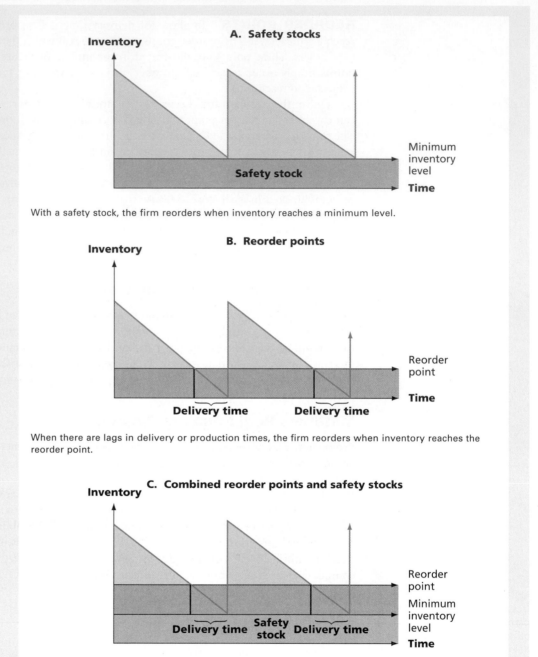

A. Safety stocks

With a safety stock, the firm reorders when inventory reaches a minimum level.

B. Reorder points

When there are lags in delivery or production times, the firm reorders when inventory reaches the reorder point.

C. Combined reorder points and safety stocks

By combining safety stocks and reorder points, the firm maintains a buffer against unforeseen events.

process should be delivered at the exact time they are needed on the factory floor. Raw materials and work-in-process are no longer seen as a necessary buffer to decouple stages of production. Instead, all stages of production are recoupled and the goal is to reduce inventories of raw materials and work-in-process to zero.

At the heart of just-in-time inventory is a different approach to ordering or setup costs. Under the traditional EOQ approach, these are considered fixed. As we saw, higher ordering costs translate into larger, less frequent orders. When producing for inventory, large setup costs in switching production from one product to another mean longer production runs. Either way, the firm carries a large work-in-process inventory as the next stage of production gradually draws

www.toyota.co.jp

down the stock of work-in-process. If a manufacturer produces many different products, the burden of different work-in-process for each becomes excessive.

This was the problem faced by Toyota in Japan after World War II. To be competitive, the company needed to make a mix of vehicles, so no one model had a long production run. The solution was to attack setup time and reduce it dramatically, by up to 75 percent. Thus, just-in-time inventory (production) was born.

Making just-in-time inventory work requires detailed materials requirements planning (MRP). As all stages of production are recoupled, careful coordination is needed. There are no longer inventory buffers to fall back on to cover planning errors or equipment downtime. This difference between the traditional approach and just-in-time inventory in resolving problems is captured in the following analogy drawn from a Japanese parable:

> The ship of enterprise floats on a lake of inventory. Problems can be thought of as rocks in the lake on which one is sailing a boat. The safety stock inventory approach is to raise the water level in the lake so that the rocks are not seen. The just-in-time approach is to chart carefully the location of the rocks and sail around them while keeping the water level at a minimum.[14]

When a manufacturer outsources parts and other work-in-process, planning must include suppliers. With the new approach, suppliers have to be capable of delivering smaller orders more often with precision timing. Suppliers need to receive high-quality information on the schedule of deliveries and to communicate continually with the buyer on the location of all shipments. So, in many ways, just-in-time inventory transfers the demands of inventory management from the manufacturer to its suppliers.

Manufacturers and suppliers use electronic data interchange (EDI) over integrated computer systems. The cash management system discussed in Chapter 19 is an example of EDI featuring communications between a firm and its bank. In implementing a just-in-time system, the firm and its supplier electronically exchange all information from the initial order to acknowledgment of the final payment.

Beyond information requirements, suppliers must meet very high quality standards. Manufacturers receive parts and use them at once so there is no room for defects. Quality control and preventive maintenance becomes very important.

JUST-IN-TIME INVENTORY AT GM OF CANADA   Since just-in-time methods were born in the automobile industry, it is not surprising that automakers in Canada are leading the way in applying them.[15] GM uses more than 900 suppliers at its plants in Canada, and most of them now ship daily or weekly. The reduction in inventory has been dramatic. Changes in the manufacturing process have also been employed to reduce inventory. For example, at a GM plant in Windsor, Ontario, a huge bay was once filled with a three-month supply of door panels. The inventory is completely gone, replaced by a unit that builds the panels just-in-time. The result is that inventory turns over once every 3.5 days, for a turnover ratio of 365/3.5 = 104. Under the old system, inventory turned over 24 times per year. GM saves around $1 million for each extra inventory turn.

There are potential problems, however, with just-in-time manufacturing methods. Consider the aftermath of the terrorist attacks in the U.S. on September 11, 2001. The U.S.–Canada border came to a virtual standstill, and many shipments of parts were delayed. Several auto plants were forced to close temporarily due to parts shortages. Another potential problem is that rapidly changing prices of raw materials such as steel can have negative impacts on automakers like General Motors. When using just-in-time methods, if prices rise significantly in a very short period, the cost of the raw materials will be much greater, since the company will be constantly buying.

---

14 Hill and Sartoris, *Short-Term Financial Management*, p. 457.

15 This section draws on J. Loring, "Inventory: Taking Stock," *Canadian Business,* April 1991, pp. 46–52.

In Their Own Words . . .

Just-in-Time Inventory on the Internet at the Boyd Group

CALGARY—The Boyd Group Inc. is hoping to put a dent in the e-commerce world when it comes to automotive parts and inventory systems.

And the Winnipeg-based firm plans to unroll an Internet-based initiative within a year to improve customer service and enhance the 60-shop chain's relationship with insurance companies.

Terry Smith, president and chief executive, said his company has hammered out an agreement with Automotive Refinish Technologies Inc. to testdrive *bodyshopmall.com*.

The e-commerce site, open only to commercial repair shops, is aimed at maximizing productivity and cutting costs through better management of parts.

"Bulk ordering and consolidation of shipping, which saves on transportation costs, means there is an immediate bottom line impact," said the 47-year-old executive. "We have a more sophisticated inventory management system with the future promise of something that is really leading edge."

The company, traded on the Toronto Stock Exchange, has already hooked up outlets in Winnipeg and Brandon, Man., to the website, and 11 of its Manitoba shops will be connected by July. Expansion to other locations on both sides of the border will be determined by results of the pilot program.

The firm has worked on the project for about a year with ART, a large player in the North American auto repair industry and a

subsidiary of BASF AG, an international conglomerate. ART is paying for the cost of designing and running the website.

Mr. Smith said *body shopmall.com* will evolve in the next couple of years, eventually becoming sophisticated enough to automatically order replacement parts. This would put his firm on a just-in-time inventory footing, similar to the one used so successfully by Wal-Mart, and improve earnings.

After doubling in size for each of the past three years, the new goal for Boyd is to grow to annual revenue of $500 million during the next five years from the expected total of about $100 million in 2000. Mr. Smith said e-commerce and upcoming Internet initiatives will help move his company towards the aggressive target.

This discussion is from F. Greenslade, "Terry Smith is using the Web to transform the Boyd Group," *National Post Online*, May 8, 2000. Used with permission.

CONCEPT QUESTIONS

1. Why do firms hold inventories?

2. Explain the basic idea behind the EOQ solution for inventory management.

3. What is just-in-time inventory? How does it differ from the more traditional EOQ approach?

20.9

SUMMARY AND CONCLUSIONS

This chapter covered the basics of credit policy and inventory management. The major topics we discussed include:

1. The components of credit policy. We discussed the terms of sale, credit analysis, and collection policy. Under the general subject of terms of sale, the credit period, the cash discount and discount period, and the credit instrument were described.

2. Credit policy analysis. We develop the cash flows from the decision to grant credit and show how the credit decision can be analyzed in an NPV setting. The NPV of granting credit depends on five factors: revenue effects, cost effects, the cost of debt, the probability of non-payment, and the cash discount.

3. Optimal credit policy. The optimal amount of credit the firm offers depends on the competitive conditions under which it operates. These conditions determine the carrying costs

associated with granting credit and the opportunity costs of the lost sales from refusing to offer credit. The optimal credit policy minimizes the sum of these two costs.

4. Credit analysis. We looked at the decision to grant credit to a particular customer. We saw that two considerations are very important: the cost relative to the selling price and the possibility of repeat business.

5. Collection policy. Collection policy is the method of monitoring the age of accounts receivable and dealing with past-due accounts. We describe how an aging schedule can be prepared and the procedures a firm might use to collect on past-due accounts.

6. Motives for holding inventory. Like cash, firms hold inventory for precautionary and speculative motives. The main reason for holding inventory is the transactions motive to have supplies for production and product to meet customer demand.

7. The economic order quantity (EOQ) model. This traditional approach to inventory sets the optimal order size and with it the average inventory, trading off ordering or setup costs against carrying costs. The optimal inventory minimizes the sum of these costs.

8. Just-in-time inventory. A new approach, JIT reduces inventory by scheduling production and deliveries of work-in-process to arrive just in time for the next stage of production. Implementation requires detailed planning with suppliers and advanced information and communications systems such as Electronic Data Interchange (EDI).

Key Terms

aging schedule (page 623)
captive finance company (page 616)
cash discount (page 610)
collection policy (page 607)
credit analysis (page 607)
credit cost curve (page 615)
credit instrument (page 612)
credit period (page 609)

credit scoring (page 620)
five Cs of credit (page 620)
invoice (page 609)
just-in-time inventory (JIT) (page 631)
multiple discriminant analysis (MDA) (page 620)
spread (page 619)
terms of sale (page 607)

Chapter Review Problems and Self-Test

20.1 Credit Policy The Cold Fusion Corporation (manufacturer of the Mr. Fusion home power plant) is considering a new credit policy. The current policy is cash only. The new policy would involve extending credit for one period. Based on the following information, determine if a switch is advisable. The interest rate is 2.0 percent per period.

	Current Policy	New Policy
Price per unit	$ 175	$ 175
Cost per unit	$ 130	$ 130
Sales per period in units	1,000	1,100

20.2 Discounts and Default Risk The ICU Binocular Corporation is considering a change in credit policy. The current policy is cash only, and sales per period are 5,000 units at a price of $95. If credit is offered, the new price would be $100 per unit and the credit would be extended for one period. Unit sales are not expected to change, and all customers would take the credit. ICU anticipates that 2 percent of its customers will default. If the required return is 3 percent per period, is the change a good idea? What if only half the customers take the offered credit?

20.3 Credit Where Credit Is Due You are trying to decide whether or not to extend credit to a particular customer. Your variable cost is $10 per unit; the selling price is $14. This customer wants to buy 100 units today and pay in 60 days. You think there is a 10 percent chance of default. The required return is 3 percent per 60 days. Should you extend credit? Assume this is a onetime sale and the customer will not buy if credit is not extended.

20.4 The EOQ Heusen Computer Manufacturing starts each period with 4,000 CPUs in stock. This stock is depleted each month and reordered. If the carrying cost per CPU is $1, and the fixed order cost is $10, is Heusen following an economically advisable strategy?

Answers to Self-Test Problems

20.1   If the switch is made, an extra 100 units per period would be sold at a gross profit of $175 − 130 = $45 each. The total benefit is thus $45 × 100 = $4,500 per period. At 2.0 percent per period forever, the PV is $4,500/.02 = $225,000.

      The cost of the switch is equal to this period's revenue of $175 × 1,000 units = $175,000 plus the cost of producing the extra 100 units, 100 × $130 = $13,000. The total cost is thus $188,000, and the NPV is $225,000 − 188,000 = $37,000. The switch should be made.

20.2   The costs per period are the same whether or not credit is offered; so we can ignore the production costs. The firm currently sells and collects $95 × 5,000 = $475,000 per period. If credit is offered, sales rise to $100 × 5,000 = $500,000.

      Defaults will be 2 percent of sales, so the cash inflow under the new policy is .98 × $500,000 = $490,000. This amounts to an extra $15,000 every period. At 3 percent per period, the PV is $15,000/.03 = $500,000. If the switch is made, ICU would give up this month's revenues of $475,000; so the NPV of the switch is $25,000. If only half switch, then the NPV is half as large: $12,500.

20.3   If the customer pays in 60 days, then you collect $14 × 100 = $1,400. There's only a 90 percent chance of collecting this; so you expect to get $1,400 × .90 = $1,260 in 60 days. The present value of this is $1,260/1.03 = $1,223.3. Your cost is $10 × 100 = $1,000; so the NPV is $223.3. Credit should be extended.

20.4   We can answer by first calculating Heusen's carrying and restocking costs. The average inventory is 2,000 CPUs, and, since the carrying costs are $1 per CPU, total carrying costs are $2,000. Heusen restocks every month at a fixed order cost of $10, so the total restocking costs are $120. What we see is that carrying costs are large relative to reorder costs, so Heusen is carrying too much inventory.

      To determine the optimal inventory policy, we can use the EOQ model. Because Heusen orders 4,000 CPUs 12 times per year, total needs (T) are 48,000 CPUs. The fixed order cost is $10, and the carrying cost per unit (CC) is $1. The EOQ is therefore:

$$\text{EOQ} = \sqrt{\frac{2T \times F}{CC}}$$
$$= \sqrt{\frac{(2 \times 48,000) \times \$10}{\$1}}$$
$$= \sqrt{960,000}$$
$$= 979.8 \text{ units}$$

We can check this by noting that the average inventory is about 490 CPUs, so the carrying cost is $490. Heusen would have to reorder 48,000/979.8 = 49 times. The fixed reorder cost is $10, so the total restocking cost is also $490.

Concepts Review and Critical Thinking Questions

1.   Describe each of the following:
   a. Sight draft
   b. Time draft
   c. Banker's acceptance
   d. Promissory note
   e. Trade acceptance

2.   In what form is trade credit most commonly offered? What is the credit instrument in this case?

3.   What are the costs associated with carrying receivables? What are the costs associated with not granting credit? What do we call the sum of the costs for different levels of receivables?

4.   What are the five Cs of credit? Explain why each is important.

5.   What are some of the factors that determine the length of the credit period? Why is the length of the buyer's operating cycle often considered an upper bound on the length of the credit period?

6.   In each of the following pairings, indicate which firm would probably have a longer credit period and explain your reasoning.
   a. Firm A sells a miracle cure for baldness; Firm B sells toupees.
   b. Firm A specializes in products for landlords; Firm B specializes in products for renters.
   c. Firm A sells to customers with an inventory turnover of 10 times; Firm B sells to customers with an inventory turnover of 20 times.
   d. Firm A sells fresh fruit; Firm B sells canned fruit.
   e. Firm A sells and installs carpeting; Firm B sells rugs.

7.   What are the different inventory types? How do the types differ? Why are some types said to have dependent demand whereas other types are said to have independent demand?

8.   If a company moves to a JIT inventory management system, what will happen to inventory turnover? What will happen to total asset turnover? What will happen to return on equity, ROE? (Hint: remember the Du Pont equation from Chapter 3.)

9.   If a company's inventory carrying costs are $5 million per year and its fixed order costs are $8 million per year, do you think the firm keeps too much inventory on hand or too little? Why?

10. Looking back at the Dell Computer example we used to open the chapter, why would you say it is to Dell's advantage to have such a short inventory period? If doing this is so valuable, why don't all other PC manufacturers simply switch to Dell's approach?

Questions and Problems

Basic
(Questions
1–12)

1. **Cash Discounts** You place an order for 200 units of inventory at a unit price of $95. The supplier offers terms of 2/10, net 30.

   a. How long do you have to pay before the account is overdue? If you take the full period, how much should you remit?

   b. What is the discount being offered? How quickly must you pay to get the discount? If you do take the discount, how much should you remit?

   c. If you don't take the discount, how much interest are you paying implicitly? How many days' credit are you receiving?

2. **Size of Accounts Receivable** The Graham Corporation has annual sales of $65 million. The average collection period is 48 days. What is Graham's average investment in accounts receivable as shown on the balance sheet?

3. **ACP and Accounts Receivable** Kyoto Joe, Inc., sells earnings forecasts for Japanese securities. Its credit terms are 2/10, net 30. Based on experience, 65 percent of all customers will take the discount.

   a. What is the average collection period for Kyoto Joe?

   b. If Kyoto Joe sells 1,200 forecasts every month at a price of $2,200 each, what is its average balance sheet amount in accounts receivable?

4. **Size of Accounts Receivable** Vitale, Baby!, Inc., has weekly credit sales of $18,000, and the average collection period is 29 days. The cost of production is 80 percent of the selling price. What is Vitale's average accounts receivable figure?

5. **Terms of Sale** A firm offers terms of 2/9, net 40. What effective annual interest rate does the firm earn when a customer does not take the discount? Without doing any calculations, explain what will happen to this effective rate if:

   a. The discount is changed to 3 percent.

   b. The credit period is increased to 60 days.

   c. The discount period is increased to 15 days.

6. **ACP and Receivables Turnover** Music City, Inc., has an average collection period of 52 days. Its average daily investment in receivables is $46,000. What are annual credit sales? What is the receivables turnover?

7. **Size of Accounts Receivable** Essence of Skunk Fragrances, Ltd., sells 4,000 units of its perfume collection each year at a price per unit of $400. All sales are on credit with terms of 2/15, net 40. The discount is taken by 60 percent of the customers. What is the amount of the company's accounts receivable? In reaction to sales by its main competitor, Sewage Spray, Essence of Skunk is considering a change in its credit policy to terms of 4/10, net 30 to preserve its market share. How will this change in policy affect accounts receivable?

8. **Size of Accounts Receivable** The Orbison Corporation sells on credit terms of net 25. Its accounts are, on average, 9 days past due. If annual credit sales are $8 million, what is the company's balance sheet amount in accounts receivable?

9. **Evaluating Credit Policy** Air Spares is a wholesaler that stocks engine components and test equipment for the commercial aircraft industry. A new customer has placed an order for 8 high-bypass turbine engines, which increase fuel economy. The variable cost is $1.5 million per unit, and the credit price is $1.8 million each. Credit is extended for one period, and based on historical experience, payment for about 1 out of every 200 such orders is never collected. The required return is 2.5 percent per period.

   a. Assuming that this is a one-time order, should it be filled? The customer will not buy if credit is not extended.

   b. What is the break-even probability of default in part (a)?

   c. Suppose that customers who don't default become repeat customers and place the same order every period forever. Further assume that repeat customers never default. Should the order be filled? What is the break-even probability of default?

   d. Describe in general terms why credit terms will be more liberal when repeat orders are a possibility.

10. **Credit Policy Evaluation** Champions, Inc., is considering a change in its cash-only sales policy. The new terms of sale would be net one month. Based on the following information, determine if Champions should proceed or not. Describe the buildup of receivables in this case. The required return is 1.5 percent per month.

	Current Policy	New Policy
Price per unit	$ 800	$ 800
Cost per unit	$ 475	$ 475
Unit sales per month	1,130	1,195

11. **EOQ** Redan Manufacturing uses 2,000 switch assemblies per week and then reorders another 2,000. If the relevant carrying cost per switch assembly is $20, and the fixed order cost is $2,600, is Redan's inventory policy optimal? Why or why not?

12. **EOQ** The Trektronics store begins each week with 180 phasers in stock. This stock is depleted each week and reordered. If the carrying cost per phaser is $51 per year and the fixed order cost is $150, what is the total carrying cost?

**Basic
(continued)**

What is the restocking cost? Should Trektronics increase or decrease its order size? Describe an optimal inventory policy for Trektronics in terms of order size and order frequency.

**Intermediate
(Questions
13–15)**

13. **EOQ Derivation** Prove that when carrying costs and restocking costs are as described in the chapter, the EOQ must occur at the point where the carrying costs and restocking costs are equal.

14. **Credit Policy Evaluation** The Jungle Corporation is considering a change in its cash-only policy. The new terms would be net one period. Based on the following information, determine if Jungle should proceed or not. The required return is 3 percent per period.

	Current Policy	New Policy
Price per unit	$ 75	$ 80
Cost per unit	$ 43	$ 43
Unit sales per month	3,200	3,500

15. **Credit Policy Evaluation** Happiness Systems currently has an all-cash credit policy. It is considering making a change in the credit policy by going to terms of net 30 days. Based on the following information, what do you recommend? The required return is 2 percent per month.

	Current Policy	New Policy
Price per unit	$ 340	$ 345
Cost per unit	$ 260	$ 265
Unit sales per month	1,800	1,850

**Challenge
(Questions
16–19)**

16. **Break-Even Quantity** In Problem 14, what is the break-even quantity for the new credit policy?

17. **Credit Markup** In Problem 14, what is the break-even price per unit that should be charged under the new credit policy? Assume that the sales figure under the new policy is 3,300 units and all other values remain the same.

18. **Credit Markup** In Problem 15, what is the break-even price per unit under the new credit policy? Assume all other values remain the same.

19. **Safety Stocks and Order Points** Saché, Inc., expects to sell 700 of its designer suits every week. The store is open seven days a week and expects to sell the same number of suits every day. The company has an EOQ of 500 suits and a safety stock of 100 suits. Once an order is placed, it takes three days for Saché to get the suits in. How many orders does the company place per year? Assume that it is Monday morning before the store opens, and a shipment of suits has just arrived. When will Saché place its next order?

MINI CASE

Piepkorn Manufacturing Working Capital Management

You have recently been hired by Piepkorn Manufacturing to work in the newly established treasury department. Piepkorn Manufacturing is a small company that produces cardboard boxes in a variety of sizes for different purchasers. Gary Piepkorn, the owner of the company, works primarily in the sales and production areas of the company. Currently, the company puts all receivables in one shoe box and all payables in another. Because of the disorganized system, the finance area needs work, and that's what you've been brought in to do.

The company currently has a cash balance of $164,000, and plans to purchase new box folding machinery in the fourth quarter at a cost of $240,000. The purchase of the machinery will be made with cash because of a discount offered. The company's policy is to maintain a minimum cash balance of $100,000. All sales and all purchases are made on credit.

Gary Piepkorn has projected the following gross sales for each of the next four quarters:

	Q1	Q2	Q3	Q4
Gross sales	$695,000	$708,000	$741,000	$757,000

Also, gross sales for the first quarter of next year are projected at $784,000. Piepkorn currently has an accounts receivable period of 57 days, and an accounts receivable balance of $426,000. Ten percent of the accounts receivable balance is from a company that has just entered bankruptcy, and it is likely this portion of the accounts receivable will never be collected.

Piepkorn typically orders 50 percent of next quarter's projected gross sales in the current quarter, and suppliers are typically paid in 53 days. Wages, taxes, and other costs run about 25 percent of gross sales. The company has a quarterly interest payment of $85,000 on its long-term debt.

The company uses a local bank for its short-term financial needs. It pays 1.5 percent per quarter in all short-term borrowing and maintains a money market account that pays 1 percent per quarter on all short-term deposits.

Gary has asked you to prepare a cash budget and short-term financial plan for the company under the current policies. He has also asked you to prepare additional plans based on changes in several inputs.

1. Use the numbers given to complete the cash budget and short-term financial plan.

2. Rework the cash budget and short-term financial plan assuming Piepkorn changes to a minimum balance of $80,000.

3. You have looked at the credit policy offered by your competitors and have determined that the industry standard credit policy is 1/10, net 45. The discount will begin to be offered on the first day of the first quarter. You want to examine how this credit policy would affect the cash budget and short-term financial plan. If this credit policy is implemented, you believe that 25 percent of all sales will take advantage of it, and the accounts receivable period will decline to 38 days. Rework the cash budget and short-term financial plan under the new credit policy and a minimum cash balance of $80,000. What interest rate are you effectively offering customers?

4. You have talked to the company's suppliers about the credit terms Piepkorn receives. Currently, the company receives terms of net 45. The suppliers have stated that they would offer new credit terms of 2/15, net 40. The discount would begin to be offered in the first day of the first quarter. What interest rate are the suppliers offering the company? Rework the cash budget and short-term financial plan assuming you take the credit terms on all orders and the minimum cash balance is $80,000.

PIEPKORN MANUFACTURING
Cash Budget

	Q1	Q2	Q3	Q4
Beginning cash balance				
Net cash inflow				
Ending cash balance				
Minimum cash balance				
Cumulative surplus (deficit)				

PIEPKORN MANUFACTURING
Short-Term Financial Plan

	Q1	Q2	Q3	Q4
Beginning cash balance				
Net cash inflow				
New short-term investments				
Income from short-term investments				
Short-term investments sold				
New short-term borrowing				
Interest on short-term borrowing				
Short-term borrowing repaid				
Ending cash balance				
Minimum cash balance				
Cumulative surplus (deficit)				
Beginning short-term investments				
Ending short-term investments				
Beginning short-term debt				
Ending short-term debt				

Internet Application Questions

1. Working capital financing is no longer an area limited to traditional banks. In fact, for some high-growth industries, specialized companies such as RFC Capital step in and provide both advice and working capital loans, sometimes leading a syndicate. Click on the RFC Capital link below and describe their most recent working capital financing arrangement.

   www.rfccapital.com/

2. Export Development Canada (EDC) (www.edc.ca) provides trade finance and risk management services to Canadian exporters and investors in up to 200 markets. Founded in 1944, EDC is a Crown corporation that operates as a commercial financial institution. One of their products is Equity Investments (www.edc.ca/english/finance_equity_investments.htm). This product allows a Canadian exporter to benefit from risk sharing of equity capital. Describe the advantage of this product *vis-à-vis* a more traditional line of credit (www.edc.ca/english/financing_lines_of_credit.htm).

3. How do you think banks make personal credit line decisions? As a student, you often face a banker who is trying to ascertain your "credit score." The following site takes some of the mystery out of the personal credit approval process.

   www.creditcarecenter.com

   Based on the credit-scoring model provided in the link above, what are three of the most important items banks look at when making the personal credit decision?

Suggested Readings

An excellent textbook on short-term financial decisions is:
   Hill, N. C., and W. L. Sartoris. *Short-Term Financial Management,* 3rd ed. New York: Prentice Hall, 1994.

Information on credit management in Canada is available from the Canadian Institute of Credit and Financial Management, Mississauga, Ontario and from Export Development Corporation's website: *www.edc.ca.*

For more on MRP, JIT, and related acronyms see Chase, Richard B., F. Robert Jacobs, and Nicholas J. Aquilano. *Operations Management for Competitive Advantage,* 11th ed. Burr Ridge, IL: McGraw-Hill/Irvin, 2005.

MORE ON CREDIT POLICY ANALYSIS

This Appendix takes a closer look at credit policy analysis by investigating some alternative approaches and by examining the effect of cash discounts and the possibility of non-payment.

Two Alternative Approaches

From our chapter discussion, we know how to analyze the NPV of a proposed credit policy switch. Now we discuss two alternative approaches: the "one-shot" approach and the accounts receivable approach. These are very common means of analysis; our goal is to show that these two and our NPV approach are all the same. Afterward, we use whichever of the three is most convenient.

THE ONE-SHOT APPROACH   If the switch is not made, Locust would have a net cash flow this month of $(P - v)Q = \$29 \times 100 = \$2,900$. If the switch is made, Locust would invest $vQ' = \$20 \times 110 = \$2,200$ this month and receive $PQ' = \$49 \times 110 = \$5,390$ next month. Suppose we ignore all other months and cash flows and view this as a one-shot investment. Is Locust better off with $2,900 in cash this month, or should Locust invest the $2,200 to get $5,390 next month?

   The present value of the $5,390 to be received next month is $5,390/1.02 = $5,284.31; the cost is $2,200, so the net benefit is $5,284.31 − 2,200 = $3,084.31. If we compare this to the net cash flow of $2,900 under the current policy, Locust should switch. The NPV is $3,084.31 − 2,900 = $184.31.

   In effect, Locust can repeat this one-shot investment every month and thereby generate an NPV of $184.31 every month (including the current one). The PV of this series of NPVs is:

   $$\text{Present value} = \$184.31 + \$184.31/.02 = \$9,400$$

This PV is the same as our previous answer.

THE ACCOUNTS RECEIVABLE APPROACH   Our second approach is the one that is most commonly discussed and is very useful. By extending credit, the firm increases its cash flow through increased gross profits. However, the firm must increase its investment in receivables and bear the carrying cost of doing so. The accounts receivable approach focuses on the expense of the incremental investment in receivables compared to the increased gross profit.

As we have seen, the monthly benefit from extending credit is given by the gross profit per unit $(P - v)$ multiplied by the increase in quantity sold $(Q' - Q)$. For Locust, this benefit was $(\$49 - 20) \times (110 - 100)$ = \$290 per month.

If Locust makes the switch, receivables rise from zero (since there are no credit sales) to PQ', so Locust must invest in receivables. The necessary investment has two components: The first part is what Locust would have collected under the old policy (PQ). Locust must carry this amount in receivables each month because collections are delayed by 30 days.

The second part is related to the increase in receivables that results from the increase in sales. Since unit sales increase from Q to Q', Locust must produce this quantity today even though it won't collect for 30 days. The actual cost to Locust of producing the extra quantity is equal to v per unit, so the investment necessary to provide the extra quantity sold is $v(Q' - Q)$.

In sum, if Locust switches, its investment in receivables is equal to the $P \times Q$ in revenues that are given up plus an additional $v(Q' - Q)$ in production costs:

Incremental investment in receivables $= PQ + v(Q' - Q)$

The required return on this investment (the carrying cost of the receivables) is R per month; so, for Locust, the accounts receivable carrying cost is:

$$\text{Carrying cost} = [PQ + v(Q' - Q)] \times R$$
$$= [\$4,900 + 200] \times .02$$
$$= \$102 \text{ per month}$$

Since the monthly benefit is \$290 and the cost per month is only \$102, the net benefit per month is \$290 - 102 = \$188 per month. Locust earns this \$188 every month, so the PV of the switch is:

$$\text{Present value} = \$188/.02$$
$$= \$9,400$$

Again, this is the same figure we previously calculated.

One of the advantages of looking at the accounts receivable approach is that it helps us interpret our earlier NPV calculation. As we have seen, the investment in receivables necessary to make the switch is $PQ + v(Q' - Q)$. If you look back at our original NPV calculation, this is precisely what we had as the cost to Locust of making the switch. Our earlier NPV calculation thus amounts to a comparison of the incremental investment in receivables to the PV of the increased future cash flows.

There is one final thing to notice. The increase in accounts receivable is PQ', and this amount corresponds to the amount of receivables shown on the balance sheet. However, the incremental investment in receivables is $PQ + v(Q' - Q)$. It is straightforward to verify that this second quantity is smaller by $(P - v)(Q' - Q)$. This difference is the gross profit on the new sales, which Locust does not actually have to put up to switch credit policies.

Put another way, whenever we extend credit to a new customer who would not otherwise pay cash, all we risk is our cost, not the full sales price. This is the same issue we discussed in Section 20.5.

EXAMPLE 20A.1: Extra Credit

Looking back at Locust Software, determine the NPV of the switch if the quantity sold is projected to increase by only 5 units instead of 10. What will be the investment in receivables? What is the carrying cost? What is the monthly net benefit from switching?

If the switch is made, Locust gives up $P \times Q = \$4,900$ today. An extra five units have to be produced at a cost of \$20 each, so the cost of switching is $\$4,900 + (5 \times \$20) = \$5,000$. The benefit of selling the extra five units each month is $5 \times$ $(\$49 - 20) = \$145$. The NPV of the switch is $-\$5,000 + \$145/.02 = \$2,250$, so it's still profitable.

The \$5,000 cost of switching can be interpreted as the investment in receivables. At 2 percent per month, the carrying cost is $.02 \times \$5,000 = \$100$. Since the benefit each month is \$145, the net benefit from switching is \$45 per month ($\$145 - \$100$). Notice that the PV of \$45 per month forever at 2 percent is $\$45/.02 = \$2,250$ as we calculated.

Discounts and Default Risk

We now look at cash discounts, default risk, and the relationship between the two. To get started, we define the following:

π = Percentage of credit sales that go uncollected
d = Percentage discount allowed for cash customers
P' = Credit price (the no-discount price)

The cash price (P) is equal to the credit price (P') multiplied by $(1 - d)$: $P = P'(1 - d)$ or, equivalently, $P' = P/(1 - d)$.

The situation at Locust is now a little bit more complicated. If a switch is made from the current policy of no credit, the benefit to the switch comes from both the higher price (P') and, potentially, the increased quantity sold (Q').

Furthermore, in our previous case, it was reasonable to assume that all customers took the credit since it was free. Now, not all customers take the credit because a discount is offered. In addition, of the customers who do take the credit offered, a certain percentage (π) do not pay.

To simplify the following discussion, we assume the quantity sold (Q) is not affected by the switch. This assumption isn't crucial, but it does cut down on the work. We also assume that all customers take the credit terms. This assumption also isn't crucial. It actually doesn't matter what percentage of our customers take the offered credit.[16]

NPV OF THE CREDIT DECISION   Currently Locust sells Q units at a price of $P = \$49$. Locust is considering a new policy that involves 30 days' credit and an increase in price to $P' = \$50$ on credit sales. The cash price remains at \$49, so Locust is effectively allowing a discount of $(\$50 - \$49)/\$50 = 2\%$ for cash.

What is the NPV to Locust of extending credit? To answer, note that Locust is already receiving $(P - v)Q$ every month. With the new, higher price, this rises to $(P' - v)Q$ assuming that everybody pays. However, since π percent of sales would not be collected, Locust collects only on $(1 - \pi) \times P'Q$; so net receipts are $[(1 - \pi)P' - v] \times Q$.

The net effect of the switch for Locust is thus the difference between the cash flows under the new policy and the old policy:

Net incremental cash flow = $[(1 - \pi)P' - v] \times Q - (P - v) \times Q$

Since $P = P' \times (1 - d)$, this simplifies to:[17]

Net incremental cash flow = $P'Q \times (d - \pi)$ [20A.1]

If Locust does make the switch, the cost of the investment in receivables is just $P \times Q$ since $Q = Q'$. The NPV of the switch is thus:

NPV = $-PQ + P'Q \times (d - \pi)/R$ [20A.2]

For example, suppose that, based on industry experience, the percentage of deadbeats (π) is 1 percent. What is the NPV of changing credit terms for Locust? We can plug in the relevant numbers as follows:

$$\begin{aligned} \text{NPV} &= -PQ + P'Q \times (d - \pi)/R \\ &= -\$49 \times 100 + \$50 \times 100 \times (.02 - .01)/.02 \\ &= -\$2,400 \end{aligned}$$

Since the NPV of the change is negative, Locust shouldn't switch.

---

16 The reason is that all customers are offered the same terms. If the NPV of offering credit is \$100, assuming that all customers switch, it is \$50 if only 50 percent of our customers switch. The hidden assumption is that the default rate is a constant percentage of credit sales.

17 To see this, note that the net incremental cash flow is:

Cash flow = $[(1 - \pi) \times P' - v] \times Q - (P - v) \times Q$
               = $[(1 - \pi) \times P' - P] \times Q$

Since $P = P' \times (1 - d)$, this can be written as:

Net incremental cash flow = $[(1 - \pi) \times P' - (1 - d) \times P'] \times Q$
                                          = $P' \times Q \times (d - \pi)$

In our expression for NPV, the key elements are the cash discount percentage (d) and the default rate (π). One thing we see immediately: If the percentage of sales that goes uncollected exceeds the discount percentage, $d - \pi$ is negative. Obviously, the NPV of the switch would be negative as well. More generally, our result tells us that the decision to grant credit here is a trade-off between getting a higher price, thereby increasing sales, and not collecting on some fraction of those sales.

With this in mind, $P'Q \times (d - \pi)$ is the increase in sales less the portion of the increase that won't be collected. This increase is the incremental cash inflow from the switch in credit policy. If d is 5 percent and π is 2 percent, for example, loosely speaking, revenues are increasing by 5 percent because of the higher price, but collections rise by only 3 percent since the default rate is 2 percent. Unless $d > \pi$, we actually have a decrease in cash inflows from the switch.

A BREAK-EVEN APPLICATION   Since the discount percentage (d) is controlled by the firm, the key unknown is the default rate (π). What is the break-even default rate for Locust Software?

We can answer by finding the default rate that makes the NPV equal to zero.

$$NPV = 0 = -PQ + P'Q \times (d - \pi)/R$$

Rearranging things a bit:

$$PR = P'(d - \pi)$$
$$\pi = d - R \times (1 - d)$$

For Locust, the break-even default rate works out to be:

$$\pi = .02 - .02 \times (.98)$$
$$= .0004$$
$$= .04\%$$

This is quite small because the implicit interest rate Locust is charging its credit customers (2 percent discount interest per month, or about $.02/.98 = 2.0408\%$) is only slightly greater than the required return of 2 percent per month. As a result, there's not much room for defaults if the switch is going to make sense.

CONCEPT QUESTIONS

1. What is the incremental investment that a firm must make in receivables if credit is extended?

2. Describe the trade-off between the default rate and the cash discount.

Appendix Review Problems and Self-Test

A.1   Credit Policy   Rework Chapter Review Problem and Self-Test 20.1 using the one-shot and accounts receivable approaches. As before, the required return is 2.0 percent per period, and there will be no defaults. The basic information is:

	Current Policy	New Policy
Price per unit	$175	$175
Cost per unit	$130	$130
Sales per period in units	1,000	1,100

A.2   Discounts and Default Risk   The De Long Corporation is considering a change in credit policy. The current policy is cash only, and sales per period are 2,000 units at a price of $110. If credit is offered, the new price will be $120 per unit and the credit will be extended for one period. Unit sales are not expected to change, and all customers are expected to take the credit. De Long anticipates that 4 percent of its customers will default. If the required return is 2 percent per period, is the change a good idea? What if only half the customers take the offered credit?

Answers to Appendix Self-Test Problems

A.1 As we saw earlier, if the switch is made, an extra 100 units per period will be sold at a gross profit of $175 – 130 = $45 each. The total benefit is thus $45 × 100 = $4,500 per period. At 2.0 percent per period forever, the PV is $4,500/.02 = $225,000.

The cost of the switch is equal to this period's revenue of $175 × 1,000 units = $175,000 plus the cost of producing the extra 100 units, 100 × $130 = $13,000. The total cost is thus $188,000, and the NPV is $225,000 – 188,000 = $37,000. The switch should be made.

For the accounts receivable approach, we interpret the $188,000 cost as the investment in receivables. At 2.0 percent per period, the carrying cost is $188,000 × .02 = $3,760 per period. The benefit per period we calculated as $4,500; so the net gain per period is $4,500 – 3,760 = $740. At 2.0 percent per period, the PV of this is $740/.02 = $37,000.

Finally, for the one-shot approach, if credit is not granted, the firm will generate ($175 – 130) – 1,000 = $45,000 this period. If credit is extended, the firm will invest $130 × 1,100 = $143,000 today and receive $175 × 1,100 = $192,500 in one period. The NPV of this second option is $192,500/1.02 – 143,000 = $45,725.49. The firm is $45,725.49 – 45,000 = $725.49 better off today and in each future period because of granting credit. The PV of this stream is $725.49 + 725.49/.02 = $37,000 (allowing for a rounding error).

A.2 The costs per period are the same whether or not credit is offered; so we can ignore the production costs. The firm currently has sales of, and collects, $110 × 2,000 = $220,000 per period. If credit is offered, sales will rise to $120 × 2,000 = $240,000.

Defaults will be 4 percent of sales, so the cash inflow under the new policy will be .96 × $240,000 = $230,400. This amounts to an extra $10,400 every period. At 2 percent per period, the PV is $10,400/.02 = $520,000. If the switch is made, De Long will give up this month's revenues of $220,000; so the NPV of the switch is $300,000. If only half of the customers take the credit, then the NPV is half as large: $150,000. So, regardless of what percentage of customers take the credit, the NPV is positive. Thus, the change is a good idea.

Appendix Questions and Problems

A1. **Evaluating Credit Policy**   Bismark Co. is in the process of considering a change in its terms of sale. The current policy is cash only; the new policy will involve one period's credit. Sales are 70,000 units per period at a price of $530 per unit. If credit is offered, the new price will be $552. Unit sales are not expected to change, and all customers are expected to take the credit. Bismark estimates that 2 percent of credit sales will be uncollectible. If the required return is 2 percent per period, is the change a good idea?

A2. **Credit Policy Evaluation**   The Johnson Company sells 3,000 pairs of running shoes per month at a cash price of $90 per pair. The firm is considering a new policy that involves 30 days' credit and an increase in price to $91.84 per pair on credit sales. The cash price will remain at $90, and the new policy is not expected to affect the quantity sold. The discount period will be 10 days. The required return is 1 percent per month.

   a. How would the new credit terms be quoted?

   b. What is the investment in receivables required under the new policy?

   c. Explain why the variable cost of manufacturing the shoes is not relevant here.

   d. If the default rate is anticipated to be 10 percent, should the switch be made? What is the break-even credit price? The break-even cash discount?

A3. **Credit Analysis**   Silicon Wafers, Inc. (SWI), is debating whether or not to extend credit to a particular customer. SWI's products, primarily used in the manufacture of semiconductors, currently sell for $1,850 per unit. The variable cost is $1,200 per unit. The order under consideration is for 12 units today; payment is promised in 30 days.

   a. If there is a 20 percent chance of default, should SWI fill the order? The required return is 2 percent per month. This is a one-time sale, and the customer will not buy if credit is not extended.

   b. What is the break-even probability in part (*a*)?

c. This part is a little harder. In general terms, how do you think your answer to part (*a*) will be affected if the customer will purchase the merchandise for cash if the credit is refused? The cash price is $1,700 per unit.

A4. **Credit Analysis** Consider the following information on two alternative credit strategies:

	Refuse Credit	Grant Credit
Price per unit	$ 51	$ 55
Cost per unit	$ 29	$ 31
Quantity sold per quarter	3,300	3,500
Probability of payment	1.0	.90

The higher cost per unit reflects the expense associated with credit orders, and the higher price per unit reflects the existence of a cash discount. The credit period will be 90 days, and the cost of debt is .75 percent per month.

a. Based on this information, should credit be granted?

b. In part (*a*), what does the credit price per unit have to be to break even?

c. In part (*a*), suppose we can obtain a credit report for $2 per customer. Assuming that each customer buys one unit and that the credit report correctly identifies all customers who will not pay, should credit be extended?

A5. **NPV of Credit Policy Switch** Suppose a corporation currently sells Q units per month for a cash-only price of P. Under a new credit policy that allows one month's credit, the quantity sold will be Q' and the price per unit will be P'. Defaults will be π percent of credit sales. The variable cost is v per unit and is not expected to change. The percentage of customers who will take the credit is α, and the required return is R per month. What is the NPV of the decision to switch? Interpret the various parts of your answer.

Topics in Corporate Finance

CHAPTER 21 *International Corporate Finance*

Chapter 21 discusses international financial management. It describes the special factors that affect firms with significant foreign operations. The most important new factor that foreign operations introduce is foreign exchange rates. This chapter discusses how to deal with foreign exchange rates in financial management.

CHAPTER 22 *Leasing*

Leasing is a way businesses finance plant, property, and equipment. Just about any long-term asset that can be purchased can be leased. Leasing an asset is much like borrowing the needed funds and simply buying the asset. When is leasing preferable to long-term borrowing? This is the question we answer in Chapter 22.

CHAPTER 23 *Mergers and Acquisitions*

Chapter 23 describes the corporate finance of mergers and acquisitions. It shows that the acquisition of one firm by another is essentially a capital budgeting decision, and the NPV framework still applies. This chapter discusses the tax, accounting, and legal aspects of mergers and acquisitions along with recent developments in areas such as takeover defences.

CHAPTER 21

International Corporate Finance

In early 2002, major currencies including the German mark, Italian lira, and French franc became footnotes in history, replaced by the euro (EUR). In an extraordinary turn of events, the 11 countries that originally made up the European Economic and Monetary Union (EMU) turned their sovereign currencies and much of the control of their monetary policies over to the new European Central Bank. Some of the major proponents of the new system were businesses in these 11 countries; many business leaders believed the union was necessary to enhance competitiveness with countries such as the United States. And the adoption of the euro continues to be popular. As of June 2006, there are 25 member states, 2 acceding countries, and 3 candidate countries on the verge of EU membership. As the euro spreads, it will become more widely used than the U.S. dollar (in June 2006, EUR 1 was equivalent to approximately US $1.2778) and will play an increasingly important role in the global economy. In this chapter, we explore the role played by currencies and exchange rates, along with a number of other key topics in international finance.

www.alcan.ca
www.mccain.ca

CORPORATIONS WITH significant foreign operations are often called *international corporations* or *multinationals*. Such corporations must consider many financial factors that do not directly affect purely domestic firms. These include foreign exchange rates, differing interest rates from country to country, complex accounting methods for foreign operations, foreign tax rates, and foreign government intervention.

Key topics of international financial management, foreign exchange rates, for example, are also of interest to many smaller Canadian businesses. Canada has an open economy linked very closely by a free-trade agreement to its largest trading partner, the United States. There are also very important economic and financial ties to Europe, the Pacific Rim, and other major economies worldwide. To illustrate, in the Atlantic Provinces, independent fish plants that supply the Boston market also wholesale lobster to Europe. These smaller corporations do not qualify as multinationals in the league of Alcan or McCain, but their financial managers must know how to manage foreign exchange risk.

The basic principles of corporate finance still apply to international corporations; like domestic companies, they seek to invest in projects that create more value for the shareholders than they cost and to arrange financing that raises cash at the lowest possible cost. In other words, the net present value principle holds for both foreign and domestic operations, but it is usually more complicated to apply the NPV rule to foreign investments.

One of the most significant complications of international finance is foreign exchange. The foreign exchange markets provide important information and opportunities for an international corporation when it undertakes capital budgeting and financing decisions. As we discuss, international exchange rates, interest rates, and inflation rates are closely related. We spend much of this chapter exploring the connection between these financial variables.

We won't have much to say here about the role of cultural and social differences in international business. Also, we do not discuss the implications of differing political and economic systems. These factors are of great importance to international businesses, but it would take another book to do them justice. Consequently, we focus only on some purely financial considerations in international finance and some key aspects of foreign exchange markets.

21.1

TERMINOLOGY

Chapter 1 had a lot to say about trends in world financial markets, including globalization. The first step in learning about international finance is to conquer the new vocabulary. As with any specialty, international finance is rich in jargon. Accordingly, we get started on the subject with a highly eclectic vocabulary exercise.

The terms that follow are presented alphabetically, and they are not of equal importance. We chose these particular ones because they appear frequently in the financial press or because they illustrate some of the colourful language of international finance.

cross-rate
The implicit exchange rate between two currencies (usually non-U.S.) quoted in some third currency (usually the U.S. dollar).

1. The **cross-rate** is the implicit exchange rate between two currencies when both are quoted in some third currency. Usually the third currency is the U.S. dollar.

Eurobond
International bonds issued in multiple countries but denominated in a single currency (usually the issuer's currency).

2. A **Eurobond** is a bond issued in multiple countries, but denominated in a single currency, usually the issuer's home currency. Such bonds have become an important way to raise capital for many international companies and governments. Eurobonds are issued outside the restrictions that apply to domestic offerings and are syndicated and traded mostly from London. Trading can and does occur anywhere there is a buyer and a seller.

Eurocurrency
Money deposited in a financial centre outside of the country whose currency is involved.

3. **Eurocurrency** is money deposited in a financial centre outside of the country whose currency is involved. For instance, Eurodollars—the most widely used Eurocurrency—are U.S. dollars deposited in banks outside the U.S. banking system. EuroCanadian are Canadian dollar bank deposits outside Canada.

Export Development Canada (EDC)
Federal Crown corporation that promotes Canadian exports by making loans to foreign purchasers.

4. **Export Development Canada (EDC)** is a federal Crown corporation with a mandate to promote Canadian exports. EDC provides financing for foreign companies that purchase Canadian exports. EDC also insures exporters' receivables and provides coverage against loss of assets due to political risks in foreign markets. Most of EDC's customers are small businesses.[1]

foreign bonds
International bonds issued in a single country, usually denominated in that country's currency.

5. **Foreign bonds,** unlike Eurobonds, are issued in a single country and are usually denominated in that country's currency. Often, the country in which these bonds are issued draws distinctions between them and bonds issued by domestic issuers, including different tax laws, restrictions on the amount issued, or tougher disclosure rules.

Foreign bonds often are nicknamed for the country where they are issued: Yankee bonds (United States), Samurai bonds (Japan), Rembrandt bonds (the Netherlands), and Bulldog bonds (Britain). Partly because of tougher regulations and disclosure requirements, the foreign-bond market hasn't grown in past years with the vigor of the Eurobond market. A substantial portion of all foreign bonds are issued in Switzerland.

1 More information about EDC is available at its website: *www.edc.ca*

gilts
British and Irish government securities, including issues of local British authorities and some overseas public-sector offerings.

London Interbank Offer Rate (LIBOR)
The rate most international banks charge one another for overnight Eurodollar loans.

swaps
Agreements to exchange two securities or currencies.

6. **Gilts,** technically, are British and Irish government securities, although the term also includes issues of local British authorities and some overseas public-sector offerings.

7. The **London Interbank Offer Rate (LIBOR)** is the rate that most international banks charge one another for loans of Eurodollars overnight in the London market. LIBOR is a cornerstone in the pricing of money market issues and other short-term debt issues by both government and corporate borrowers. Interest rates are frequently quoted as some spread over LIBOR, then they float with the LIBOR rate.

8. There are two basic kinds of **swaps:** interest rate and currency. An *interest rate swap* occurs when two parties exchange a floating-rate payment for a fixed-rate payment or vice versa. *Currency swaps* are agreements to deliver one currency in exchange for another. Often both types of swaps are used in the same transaction when debt denominated in different currencies is swapped. Chartered banks make an active market in arranging swaps, and swap volumes have grown rapidly.

CONCEPT QUESTIONS

1. What are the differences between a Eurobond and a foreign bond?

2. What are Eurodollars?

FOREIGN EXCHANGE MARKETS AND EXCHANGE RATES

foreign exchange market
The market where one country's currency is traded for another's.

The **foreign exchange market** is undoubtedly the world's largest financial market. It is the market where one country's currency is traded for another's. Most of the trading takes place in a few currencies: the U.S. dollar ($), the European Union Euro (EUR), the British pound sterling (£), the Japanese yen (¥), and the Swiss franc (SF). Table 21.1 lists some of the more common currencies and their symbols.

The foreign exchange market is an over-the-counter market, so there is no single location where traders get together. Instead, market participants are located in the major banks around the world. They communicate using computers, telephones, and other telecommunications

TABLE 21.1
International currency symbols (2006)

For current exchange rates visit www.xe.com

Country	Currency	Symbol
Australia	Dollar	A$
Austria	Euro	EUR
Belgium	Euro	EUR
Canada	Dollar	Can$
Denmark	Krone	DKr
Finland	Euro	EUR
France	Euro	EUR
Germany	Euro	EUR
Greece	Euro	EUR
India	Rupee	Rs
Iran	Rial	RI
Italy	Euro	EUR
Japan	Yen	¥
Kuwait	Dinar	KD
Mexico	Peso	Ps
Netherlands	Euro	EUR
Norway	Krone	NKr
Saudi Arabia	Riyal	SR
Singapore	Dollar	S$
South Africa	Rand	R
Spain	Euro	EUR
Sweden	Krona	SEK
Switzerland	Franc	SF
United Kingdom	Pound	£
United States	Dollar	$

devices. For example, one communications network for foreign transactions is the Society for Worldwide Interbank Financial Telecommunications (SWIFT), a Belgian not-for-profit co-operative. Using data transmission lines, a bank in Toronto, the centre of Canada's foreign exchange trading, can send messages to a bank in London via SWIFT regional processing centres.

The many different types of participants in the foreign exchange market include the following:

1. Importers who pay for goods involving foreign currencies by converting foreign exchange.
2. Exporters who receive foreign currency and may want to convert to the domestic currency.
3. Portfolio managers who buy or sell foreign stocks and bonds.
4. Foreign exchange brokers who match buy and sell orders.
5. Traders who "make a market" in foreign exchange.
6. Speculators who try to profit from changes in exchange rates.

Exchange Rates

exchange rate
The price of one country's currency expressed in another country's currency.

An **exchange rate** is simply the price of one country's currency expressed in another country's currency. In practice, almost all trading of currencies worldwide takes place in terms of the U.S. dollar.

EXCHANGE RATE QUOTATIONS   Figure 21.1 reproduces exchange rate quotations as they appear in *The National Post*. Notice that the rates were supplied to *The National Post* by Reuters. The top right of Figure 21.1 is the cross-rates of seven main currencies. Because of the heavy volume of transactions in U.S. dollars, U.S./Canada rates appear first in the next portion of Figure 21.1. The first row (labelled "Canada $") gives the number of Canadian dollars it takes to buy one unit of foreign currency. For example, the U.S./Canada spot rate is quoted at 1.1129, which means you can buy one U.S. dollar today with 1.1129 Canadian dollars.[2]

The final section (labelled "Per C$") shows the indirect exchange rate. This is the amount of U.S. currency per Canadian dollar. The U.S./Canada spot rate is quoted here at 0.8986 U.S. dollars for one Canadian dollar. Naturally this second exchange rate is just the reciprocal of the first one, 1/0.8986 = 1.1129.

The rest of Figure 21.1 shows the exchange rates for other foreign currencies. Notice that the most important currencies are listed first: British pounds, European euros, and Japanese yen. In this part of the figure, the table labelled "Per C$" gives the price of one unit of the foreign currency in Canadian dollars. For example, you can buy one British pound for $2.0642 Canadian. The table labelled "Per US$" repeats the price of one unit of foreign currency in U.S. dollars. You can buy the same one British pound for $1.8554 U.S.

CROSS-RATES AND TRIANGLE ARBITRAGE   Using the U.S. dollar or the euro as the common denominator in quoting exchange rates greatly reduces the number of possible cross-currency quotes. For example, with five major currencies, there would potentially be

---

EXAMPLE 21.1: A yen for Fast Cars

Suppose you have $1,000. Based on the rates in Figure 21.1, how many Japanese yen can you get? Alternatively, if a Porsche costs EUR 100,000, how many dollars will you need to buy it? (EUR is the abbreviation for euros.)

The exchange rate for yen is given in Canadian dollars per yen as 0.0098 (top right section under yen). Your $1,000 thus gets you:

$1,000/0.0098 dollars per yen = 102,041 yen

Since the exchange rate in dollars per euro is 1.5930, you need:

EUR 100,000 × 1.4231 $ per EUR = $142,310

---

2 The spot rate is for immediate trading. Forward rates are for future transactions and are discussed in detail later.

FIGURE 21.1

Exchange rate quotations

FOREIGN EXCHANGE

*Supplied by Reuters. Indicative late afternoon rates. * inverted*

MAJOR CURRENCIES

Per US$	Latest	Prev day	Week ago	4 wks ago	% chg on day	% chg in wk	% chg 4 wk
Canada $	1.1129	1.1127	1.1005	1.0993	0.02	1.13	1.24
euro*	1.2792	1.2833	1.2814	1.2797	-0.32	-0.17	-0.04
Japan yen	113.51	113.28	112.57	110.34	0.21	0.84	2.88
UK pound*	1.8554	1.8605	1.8704	1.8656	-0.28	-0.80	-0.55
Swiss franc	1.2214	1.2153	1.2187	1.2172	0.51	0.22	0.35
Australia $*	0.7407	0.7402	0.7520	0.7752	0.07	-1.50	-4.45
Mexico peso	11.3620	11.3090	11.3410	10.8545	0.47	0.19	4.68
Hong Kong	7.7619	7.7598	7.7583	7.7516	0.03	0.05	0.13
Singapore $	1.5863	1.5837	1.5788	1.5615	0.16	0.47	1.59
China renminbi	8.0160	8.0120	8.0215	8.0033	0.05	-0.07	0.16
India rupee	45.88	45.82	46.31	44.85	0.12	-0.93	2.29

Per C$	Latest	Prev day	Week ago	4 wks ago	% chg on day	% chg in wk	% chg 4 wk
US $	0.8986	0.8988	0.9087	0.9097	-0.02	-1.11	-1.23
euro*	1.4231	1.4274	1.4098	1.4059	-0.30	0.95	1.22
Japan yen	101.97	101.78	102.25	100.33	0.18	-0.28	1.63
UK pound*	2.0642	2.0696	2.0577	2.0498	-0.26	0.32	0.70
Swiss franc	1.0972	1.0919	1.1071	1.1068	0.48	-0.89	-0.86
Australia $*	0.8240	0.8233	0.8271	0.8515	0.09	-0.38	-3.24
Mexico peso	10.2030	10.1609	10.2989	9.8668	0.42	-0.93	3.41
Hong Kong	6.9730	6.9730	7.0482	7.0492	0.00	-1.07	-1.08
Singapore $	1.4244	1.4224	1.4340	1.4196	0.14	-0.67	0.34
China renminbi	7.2028	7.2008	7.2890	7.2807	0.03	-1.18	-1.07
India rupee	41.22	41.18	42.08	40.80	0.11	-2.04	1.04

CURRENCY CROSS RATES

	C$	US$	euro	Yen	£	Sw. fr.	A$
C$	---·-	1.1129	1.4231	0.0098	2.0642	0.9114	0.8246
US$	0.8986	---·-	1.2792	0.0088	1.8554	0.8187	0.7407
euro	0.7027	0.7818	---·-	0.6886	1.4501	0.6399	0.5788
¥	101.97	113.51	145.17	---·-	210.55	92.92	84.05
£	0.4845	0.5390	0.6893	0.4747	---·-	0.4412	0.3991
Sw. fr.	1.0972	1.2214	1.5620	1.0758	2.2656	---·-	0.9044
A$	1.2127	1.3502	1.7265	1.1891	2.5042	1.1051	---·-
Gold	696.91	626.10	489.41	71075	337.41	764.78	845.17

FORWARD EXCHANGE RATES

Per US$	Spot	1-mo	3-mo	6-mo	1-yr	2-yr	3-yr	4-yr	5-yr
Canada $	1.1129	1.1125	1.1117	1.1094	1.1040	1.0947	1.0872	1.0830	1.0835
euro*	1.2792	1.2797	1.2818	1.2860	1.2963	1.3165	1.3343	1.3500	1.3695
Japan yen	113.51	113.50	113.49	113.48	113.46	113.42	113.39	113.35	113.32
UK pound*	1.8554	1.8518	1.8455	1.8378	1.8263	1.8121	1.8040	1.7935	1.7906

Per C$	Spot	1-mo	3-mo	6-mo	1-yr	2-yr	3-yr	4-yr	5-yr
US $	0.8986	0.8989	0.8995	0.9014	0.9058	0.9135	0.9198	0.9234	0.9229
euro*	1.4231	1.4248	1.4280	1.4316	1.4376	1.4412	1.4506	1.4620	1.4839
Japan yen	101.97	101.76	101.34	100.73	99.42	96.47	93.57	90.58	87.52
UK pound*	2.0642	2.0601	2.0516	2.0390	2.0167	1.9847	1.9628	1.9441	1.9418

Source: *The National Post*, FP Investing, June 8, 2006, p. FP19. Used with permission.

10 exchange rates instead of just 4.[3] Also, the fact that the dollar is used throughout cuts down on inconsistencies in the exchange rate quotations.

Earlier, we defined the cross-rate as the exchange rate for a non-U.S. currency expressed in another non-U.S. currency. For example, suppose we observed the following:

¥ per $1US = 100.00
A$ per $1US = 1.50

Suppose the cross-rate is quoted as:

¥ per A$ = 50.00

What do you think?

The cross-rate here is inconsistent with the exchange rates. To see this, suppose you have $100US. If you convert this to Australian dollars, you receive:

$100US × A$1.5 per $1 = A$150

If you convert this to yen at the cross-rate, you have:

A$150 × ¥50 per A$1 = ¥7,500

However, if you just convert your U.S. dollars to yen without going through Australian dollars, you have:

$100US × ¥100 per $1 = ¥10,000

What we see is that the yen has two prices, ¥100 per $1US and ¥75 per $1US, depending on how we get them.

To make money, we want to buy low, sell high. The important thing to note is that yen are cheaper if you buy them with U.S. dollars because you get 100 yen instead of just 75. You should proceed as follows:

---

3 In discussing cross-rates, we follow Canadian practice of using the U.S. dollar. There are four exchange rates instead of five because one exchange rate would involve the exchange rate for a currency with itself. More generally, it might seem there should be 25 exchange rates with five currencies. There are 25 different combinations, but, of these, five involve the exchange rate of a currency for itself. Of the remaining 20, half of them are redundant because they are just the reciprocals of the exchange rate. Of the remaining 10, six can be eliminated by using a common denominator.

1. Buy 10,000 yen for $100US.
2. Use the 10,000 yen to buy Australian dollars at the cross-rate. Since it takes 50 yen to buy an Australian dollar, you receive ¥10,000/50 = A$200.
3. Use the A$200 to buy U.S. dollars. Since the exchange rate is A$1.5 per dollar, you receive A$200/1.5 = $133.33, for a round-trip profit of $33.33.
4. Repeat steps 1 through 3.

This particular activity is called *triangle arbitrage* because the arbitrage involves moving through three different exchange rates.

$$¥100/1\$$$

$$A\$1.5/1\$ = \$.67/A\$1 \quad \leftarrow \quad A\$.02/¥1 = ¥50/A\$1$$

To prevent such opportunities, it is not difficult to see that since a U.S. dollar buys you either 50 yen or 1.5 Australian dollars, the cross-rate must be:

$$(¥50/\$1US)/(A\$1.5/\$1US) = ¥33.33/A\$1$$

If it were anything else, there would be a triangle arbitrage opportunity.

Types of Transactions

spot trade
An agreement to trade currencies based on the exchange rate today for settlement in two days.

There are two basic types of trades in the foreign exchange market: spot trades and forward trades. A **spot trade** is an agreement to exchange currency on the spot; this actually means the transaction is completed or settled within two business days. The exchange rate on a spot trade is called the **spot exchange rate**. Implicitly, all of the exchange rates and transactions we have discussed so far have referred to the spot market.

spot exchange rate
The exchange rate on a spot trade.

FORWARD EXCHANGE RATES   A **forward trade** is an agreement to exchange currency at some time in the future. The exchange rate used is agreed on today and is called the **forward exchange rate**. A forward trade would normally be settled sometime in the next 12 months, but some forward rates are quoted for as far as 10 years into the future.

forward trade
Agreement to exchange currency at some time in the future.

Look back at Figure 21.1 to see forward exchange rates quoted for some of the major currencies. For example, the spot exchange rate for the U.S. dollar is $1.1129. The six month forward exchange rate is U.S. $1 = 1.1094. This means you can buy one U.S. dollar today for $1.1129, or you can agree to take delivery of a U.S. dollar in six months and pay $1.1094 at that time.

forward exchange rate
The agreed-on exchange rate to be used in a forward trade.

Notice that the U.S. dollar is less expensive in the forward market ($1.1094 versus $1.1129). Since the U.S. dollar is less expensive in the future than it is today, it is said to be selling at a discount relative to the Canadian dollar in the forward market. For the same reason, the Canadian dollar is said to be selling at a premium relative to the U.S. dollar. To see the discount, compare the spot and six-month forward rates in the "Per C$" section of Figure 21.1. The Canada/U.S. spot rate is 0.8986 and the six-month forward rate is 0.9014. The Canadian dollar is selling at a premium in the forward market since buyers with U.S. dollars will pay more for it six months from today.

EXAMPLE 21.2: Shedding Some Pounds

Suppose the exchange rates for the British pound and the euro are:

Pounds per $1US = 0.60
    EUR per $1US = 0.90

The cross-rate is 1.6 euros per pound. Is this consistent? Explain how to go about making some money.

The cross-rate should be EUR 0.90/£ .60 = EUR 1.5 per pound. You can buy a pound for EUR 1.5 in one market, and

you can sell a pound for EUR 1.6 in another. So we want to first get some pounds, then use the pounds to buy some euros, and then sell the euros. Assuming you have $100US, you could:

1. Exchange U.S. dollars for pounds: $100US × 0.6 = £60.
2. Exchange pounds for euros: £60 × 1.6 = EUR 96.
3. Exchange euros for U.S. dollars: EUR 96/.90 = $106.67.

This would result in a $6.67 U.S. round-trip profit.

Why does the forward market exist? One answer is that it allows businesses and individuals to lock in a future exchange rate today, thereby eliminating any risk from unfavourable shifts in the exchange rate.

EXAMPLE 21.3

In Figure 21.1, the spot exchange rate and the six-month forward rate in dollars per pound are $2.0642 = 1 pound and $2.0390 = 1 pound, respectively. If you expect 1 million pounds in six months, you will get 1 million pounds × $2.0390 per pound = $2.0390 million. Since it is less expensive to buy a pound in the forward market than in the spot market ($2.0390 versus $2.0642), the pound is selling at a discount relative to the dollar.

EXAMPLE 21.4

From Figure 21.1, the spot and 12-month forward rates in yen per dollars are 101.97 yen = $1 and $99.42, respectively. You plan to convert ¥10 million in 12 months so you need to know the forward exchange rate in dollar per yen.

$1 = 99.42 yen
1 yen = 1/99.42 = $0.0100583

So your ¥10 million converts to $100,583. The spot exchange rate in dollars per yen is 1/101.97 = $0.0098068.

Either way you look at it, the yen is selling at a forward discount. It would take less dollars to buy one yen. And if you converted your funds today, instead of waiting 12 months, you would get less yen.

CONCEPT QUESTIONS

1. What is triangle arbitrage?
2. What do we mean by the six-month forward exchange rate?

21.3 PURCHASING POWER PARITY

Now that we have discussed what exchange rate quotations mean, we can address an obvious question: What determines the level of the spot exchange rate? In addition, we know that exchange rates change through time. A related question is: What determines the rate of change in exchange rates? At least part of the answer in both cases goes by the name of **purchasing power parity (PPP)**, the idea that the exchange rate adjusts to keep purchasing power constant among currencies. As we discuss next, there are two forms of PPP, absolute and relative.

purchasing power parity (PPP)
The idea that the exchange rate adjusts to keep purchasing power constant among currencies.

Absolute Purchasing Power Parity

The basic idea behind *absolute purchasing power parity* is that a commodity costs the same regardless of what currency is used to purchase it or where it is selling. This is a very straightforward concept. If a beer costs £2 in London, and the exchange rate is £.60 per dollar, then a beer costs £2/.60 = $3.33 in Montreal. In other words, absolute PPP says $5 will buy you the same number of, say, cheeseburgers anywhere in the world.

More formally, let S_0 be the spot exchange rate between the British pound and the Canadian dollar today (Time 0). Here we are quoting exchange rates as the amount of foreign currency per dollar. Let P_{CDN} and P_{UK} be the current Canadian and British prices, respectively, on a particular commodity, say, apples. Absolute PPP simply says that:

$$P_{UK} = S_0 \times P_{CDN}$$

This tells us that the British price for something is equal to the Canadian price for that same something, multiplied by the exchange rate.

The rationale behind PPP is similar to that behind triangle arbitrage. If PPP did not hold, arbitrage would be possible (in principle) by moving apples from one country to another. For example, suppose apples in Halifax are selling for $4 per bushel, while in London the price is £2.40 per bushel. Absolute PPP implies that:

$$P_{UK} = S_0 \times P_{CDN}$$
$$£2.40 = S_0 \times \$4$$
$$S_0 = £2.40/\$4 = £.60$$

That is, the implied spot exchange rate is £.60 per dollar. Equivalently, a pound is worth $1/£.60 = $1.67.

Suppose, instead, the actual exchange rate is £.50. Starting with $4, a trader could buy a bushel of apples in Halifax, ship it to London, and sell it there for £2.40. Our trader then converts the £2.40 into dollars at the prevailing exchange rate, S_0 = £.50, yielding a total of £2.40/.50 = $4.80. The round-trip gain is 80 cents.

Because of this profit potential, forces are set in motion to change the exchange rate and/or the price of apples. In our example, apples would begin moving from Halifax to London. The reduced supply of apples in Halifax would raise the price of apples there, and the increased supply in Britain would lower the price of apples in London.

In addition to moving apples around, apple traders would be busily converting pounds back into dollars to buy more apples. This activity increases the supply of pounds and simultaneously increases the demand for dollars. We would expect the value of a pound to fall. This means the dollar is getting more valuable, so it will take more pounds to buy one dollar. Since the exchange rate is quoted as pounds per dollar, we would expect the exchange rate to rise from £.50.

For absolute PPP to hold, several things must be true:

1. The transactions cost of trading apples—shipping, insurance, wastage, and so on—must be zero.

2. There are no barriers to trading apples, such as tariffs, taxes, or other political barriers such as voluntary restraint agreements.

3. Finally, an apple in Halifax must be identical to an apple in London. It won't do for you to send red apples to London if the English eat only green apples.

Given the fact that the transaction costs are not zero and that the other conditions are rarely exactly met, it is not surprising that absolute PPP is really applicable only to traded goods, and then only to very uniform ones.

For this reason, absolute PPP does not imply that a Mercedes costs the same as a Ford or that a nuclear power plant in France costs the same as one in Ontario. In the case of the cars, they are not identical. In the case of the power plants, even if they were identical, they are expensive and very difficult to ship. Still, we can observe major violations of PPP. For example, on a European trip in the summer of 2003, one of the authors noticed that a 500 ml bottle of Dutch beer cost 2 pounds (around $4.50 Canadian) in London but only 1.5 euros (around $2.40 Canadian) in Lisbon. This difference led thousands of students to plan vacations in Portugal instead of England. Despite the resulting increased demand for euros, the exchange rate has not adjusted to reflect PPP.

One interesting application of the theory behind purchasing power parity is the Big Mac Index updated and published regularly by *The Economist*.[4] The index calculates the exchange rate to the U.S. dollar that would result in McDonald's Big Mac burgers costing the same around the world (using the U.S. cost as a base). This calculated value is compared with the actual current exchange rate to determine if a currency is overvalued or undervalued. At the time of writing, the index supported the widespread belief that China was keeping its currency undervalued to promote its exports. In August 2006, the Big Mac index showed that the Chinese renminbi was 58 percent undervalued against the U.S. dollar. A Big Mac in China cost 10.5 RMB while its average cost in the U.S. was US$3.10. To make the two prices equal would have required an exchange rate of RMB 3.39 to the U.S. dollar, compared with the actual rate of RMB 8.03.

---

4 This discussion is largely based on "McCurrencies," *The Economist*, April 24, 2003. For the latest on the index visit the website *www.economist.com/markets/Bigmac/index.cfm*.

Relative Purchasing Power Parity

As a practical matter, a relative version of purchasing power parity has evolved. *Relative purchasing power parity* does not tell us what determines the absolute level of the exchange rate. Instead, it tells what determines the change in the exchange rate over time.

THE BASIC IDEA   Suppose again that the British pound/Canadian dollar exchange rate is currently $S_0 = £.50$. Further suppose that the inflation rate in Britain is predicted to be 10 percent over the coming year and (for the moment) the inflation rate in Canada is predicted to be zero. What do you think the exchange rate will be in a year?

If you think about it, a dollar currently costs .50 pounds in Britain. With 10 percent inflation, we expect prices in Britain to generally rise by 10 percent. So we expect that the price of a dollar will go up by 10 percent and the exchange rate should rise to $£.50 \times 1.1 = £.55$.

If the inflation rate in Canada is not zero, we need to worry about the relative inflation rates in the two countries. For example, suppose the Canadian inflation rate is predicted to be 4 percent. Relative to prices in Canada, prices in Britain are rising at a rate of $10\% - 4\% = 6\%$ per year. So we expect the price of the dollar to rise by 6 percent, and the predicted exchange rate is $£.50 \times 1.06 = £.53$.

THE RESULT   In general, relative PPP says that the change in the exchange rate is determined by the difference in the inflation rates between the two countries. To be more specific, we use the following notation:

S_0 = Current (Time 0) spot exchange rate (foreign currency per dollar)
$E[S_t]$ = Expected exchange rate in t periods
h_{CDN} = Inflation rate in Canada
h_{FC} = Foreign country inflation rate

Based on our discussion, relative PPP says the expected percentage change in the exchange rate over the next year, $(E[S_1] - S_0)/S_0$, is:

$$(E[S_1] - S_0)/S_0 = h_{FC} - h_{CDN} \qquad [21.1]$$

In words, relative PPP simply says that the expected percentage change in the exchange rate is equal to the difference in inflation rates. If we rearrange this slightly, we get:

$$E[S_1] = S_0 \times [1 + (h_{FC} - h_{CDN})] \qquad [21.2]$$

This result makes a certain amount of sense, but care must be used in quoting the exchange rate.

In our example involving Britain and Canada, relative PPP tells us the exchange rate rises by $h_{FC} - h_{CDN} = 10\% - 4\% = 6\%$ per year. Assuming the difference in inflation rates doesn't change, the expected exchange rate in two years, $E[S_2]$, is therefore:

$$\begin{aligned} E[S_2] &= E[S_1] \times (1 + .06) \\ &= .53 \times 1.06 \\ &= .562 \end{aligned}$$

Notice that we could have written this as:

$$\begin{aligned} E[S_2] &= .53 \times 1.06 \\ &= (.50 \times 1.06) \times 1.06 \\ &= .50 \times 1.06^2 \end{aligned}$$

In general, relative PPP, says the expected exchange rate at sometime in the future, $E[S_t]$, is:

$$E[S_t] = S_0 \times [1 + (h_{FC} - h_{CDN})]^t \qquad [21.3]$$

As we shall see, this is a very useful relationship.

Because we don't really expect absolute PPP to hold for most goods, we focus on relative PPP, or RPPP, in the following discussion.

Currency Appreciation and Depreciation

We frequently hear these statements: The dollar strengthened (or weakened) in financial markets today or the dollar is expected to appreciate (or depreciate) relative to the pound. When we say the dollar strengthens or appreciates, we mean the value of a dollar rises, so it takes more foreign currency to buy a Canadian dollar.

What happens to the exchange rates as currencies fluctuate in value depends on how exchange rates are quoted. Since we are quoting them as units of foreign currency per dollar, the exchange rate moves in the same direction as the value of the dollar: It rises as the dollar strengthens, and it falls as the dollar weakens.

Relative PPP tells us the exchange rate rises if the Canadian inflation rate is lower than the foreign country's. This happens because the foreign currency depreciates in value and therefore weakens relative to the dollar.

CONCEPT QUESTIONS

1. What does absolute PPP say? Why might it not hold for many goods?

2. According to relative PPP, what determines the change in exchange rates?

EXAMPLE 21.5: It's All Relative

Suppose the Japanese exchange rate is currently 130 yen per dollar. The inflation rate in Japan over the next three years will run, say, 2 percent per year while the Canadian inflation rate will be 6 percent. Based on relative PPP, what would the exchange rate be in three years?

Since the Canadian inflation rate is higher, we expect a dollar to become less valuable. The exchange rate change would be 2% − 6% = −4% per year. Over three years, the exchange rate falls to:

$$E[S_3] = S_0 \times [1 + (h_{FC} - h_{CDN})]^3$$
$$= 130 \times [1 + (-.04)]^3$$
$$= 115.02$$

INTEREST RATE PARITY, UNBIASED FORWARD RATES, AND THE INTERNATIONAL FISHER EFFECT

The next issue we need to address is the relationship between the spot exchange rates, forward exchange rates, and interest rates. To get started, we need some additional notation:

$$F_t = \text{Forward exchange rate for settlement at time } t$$
$$R_{CDN} = \text{Canadian nominal risk-free interest rate}$$
$$R_{FC} = \text{Foreign country nominal risk-free interest rate}$$

As before, use S_0 to stand for the spot exchange rate. You can take the Canadian nominal risk-free rate, R_{CDN}, to be the T-bill rate.

Covered Interest Arbitrage

Suppose we observe the following information about Canada and the European Union (E.U.):

$$S_0 = \text{EUR } 0.65 \qquad R_{CDN} = 10\%$$
$$F_1 = \text{EUR } 0.60 \qquad R_G = 5\%$$

where R_G is the nominal risk-free rate in the E.U. The period is one year, so F_1 is the one-year forward rate.

Do you see an arbitrage opportunity here? There is one. Suppose you have $1 to invest, and you want a riskless investment. One option you have is to invest the $1 in a riskless Canadian investment such as a one-year T-bill. If you do this, in one period your $1 will be worth:

$$\text{\$ value in 1 period} = \$1 \times (1 + R_{CDN})$$
$$= \$1.10$$

Alternatively, you can invest in the European risk-free investment. To do this, you need to convert your $1 to euros and simultaneously exercise a forward trade to convert euros back to dollars in one year. The necessary steps would be as follows:

1. Convert your $1 to $1 \times S_0 = EUR 0.65.
2. At the same time, enter into a forward agreement to convert euros back to dollars in one year. Since the forward rate is EUR 0.60, you get $1 for every EUR 0.60 that you have in one year.
3. Invest your EUR 0.65 in Europe at R_G. In one year, you have:

$$\text{EUR value in 1 year} = EUR\ 0.65 \times (1 + R_G)$$
$$= EUR\ 0.65 \times 1.05$$
$$= EUR\ 0.6825$$

4. Convert your EUR 0.6825 back to dollars at the agreed-on rate of EUR 0.60 = $1. You end up with:

$$\text{\$ value in 1 year} = EUR\ 0.6825/0.60$$
$$= \$1.1375$$

Notice that the value in one year from this strategy can be written as:

$$\text{\$ value in 1 year} = \$1 \times S_0 \times (1 + R_G)/F_1$$
$$= \$1 \times 0.65 \times (1.05)/0.60$$
$$= \$1.1375$$

The return on this investment is apparently 13.75 percent. This is higher than the 10 percent we get from investing in Canada. Since both investments are risk-free, there is an arbitrage opportunity.

To exploit the difference in interest rates, you need to borrow, say, $5 million at the lower Canadian rate and invest it at the higher European rate. What is the round-trip profit from doing this? To find out, we can work through the preceding steps:

1. Convert the $5 million at EUR 0.65 = $1 to get EUR 3.25 million.
2. Agree to exchange euros for dollars in one year at EUR 0.60 to the dollar.
3. Invest the EUR 3.25 million for one year at $R_G = 5\%$. You end up with EUR 3.4125 million.
4. Convert the EUR 3.4125 million back to dollars to fulfill the forward contract. You receive EUR 3.4125 million/0.60 = $5.6875 million.
5. Repay the loan with interest. You owe $5 million plus 10 percent interest, for a total of $5.5 million. You have $5,687,500, so your round-trip profit is a risk-free $187,500.

The activity that we have illustrated here goes by the name of *covered interest arbitrage*. The term *covered* refers to the fact that we are covered in the event of a change in the exchange rate because we lock in the forward exchange rate today.

Interest Rate Parity (IRP)

If we assume that significant covered interest arbitrage opportunities do not exist, there must be some relationship between spot exchange rates, forward exchange rates, and relative interest rates. To see what this relationship is, note that, in general, strategy 1—investing in a riskless Canadian investment—gives us $(1 + R_{CDN})$ for every dollar we invest. Strategy 2—investing in a foreign risk-free investment—gives us $S_0 \times (1 + R_{FC})/F_1$ for every dollar we invest. Since these have to be equal to prevent arbitrage, it must be the case that:

$$(1 + R_{CDN}) = S_0 \times (1 + R_{FC})/F_1$$

interest rate parity (IRP)
The condition stating that the interest rate differential between two countries is equal to the difference between the forward exchange rate and the spot exchange rate.

Rearranging this a bit gets us the famous **interest rate parity (IRP)** condition:

$$F_1/S_0 = (1 + R_{FC})/(1 + R_{CDN}) \qquad [21.4]$$

A very useful approximation for IRP illustrates very clearly what is going on and is not difficult to remember. If we define the percentage forward premium or discount as $(F_1 - S_0)/S_0$, IRP says this percent premium or discount is approximately equal to the difference in interest rates:

$$(F_1 - S_0)/S_0 = R_{FC} - R_{CDN} \qquad [21.5]$$

Very loosely, what IRP says is that any difference in interest rates between two countries for some period is just offset by the change in the relative value of the currencies, thereby eliminating any arbitrage possibilities. Notice that we could also write:

$$F_1 = S_0 \times [1 + (R_{FC} - R_{CDN})] \qquad [21.6]$$

In general, if we have t periods instead of just one, the IRP approximation would be written as:

$$F_t = S_0 \times [1 + (R_{FC} - R_{CDN})]^t \qquad [21.7]$$

Forward Rates and Future Spot Rates

unbiased forward rates (UFR)
The condition stating that the current forward rate is an unbiased predictor of the future exchange rate.

In addition to PPP and IRP, there is one more basic relationship we need to discuss. What is the connection between the forward rate and the expected future spot rate? The **unbiased forward rates (UFR)** condition says the forward rate, F_1, is equal to the expected future spot rate, $E[S_1]$:

$$F_1 = E[S_1]$$

With t periods, UFR would be written as:

$$F_t = E[S_t]$$

Loosely, the UFR condition says that, on average, the forward exchange rate is equal to the future spot exchange rate.

If we ignore risk, the UFR condition should hold. Suppose the forward rate for the Japanese yen is consistently lower than the future spot rate by, say, 10 yen. This means that anyone who wanted to convert dollars to yen in the future would consistently get more yen by not agreeing to a forward exchange. The forward rate would have to rise to get anyone interested.

Similarly, if the forward rate were consistently higher than the future spot rate, anyone who wanted to convert yen to dollars would get more dollars per yen by not agreeing to a forward trade. The forward exchange rate would have to fall to attract such traders.

For these reasons, the forward and actual future spot rates should be equal to each other on average. What the future spot rate will actually be is uncertain, of course. The UFR condition may not hold if traders are willing to pay a premium to avoid this uncertainty. If the condition does

EXAMPLE 21.6: Parity Check

Suppose the exchange rate for Japanese yen, S_0, is currently ¥120 = \$1. If the interest rate in Canada is R_{CDN} = 10% and the interest rate in Japan is R_J = 5%, what must the forward rate be to prevent covered interest arbitrage?

From IRP, we have:

$$F_1 = S_0 \times [1 + (R_J - R_{CDN})]$$
$$= ¥120 \times [1 + (.05 - .10)]$$
$$= ¥120 \times .95$$
$$= ¥114$$

Notice that the yen sells at a premium relative to the dollar (why?).

hold, the six-month forward rate that we see today should be an unbiased predictor of what the exchange rate will actually be in six months.

Putting It All Together

We have developed three relationships, PPP, IRP, and UFR, that describe the relationships between key financial variables such as interest rates, exchange rates, and inflation rates. We now explore the implications of these relationships as a group.

UNCOVERED INTEREST PARITY   To start, it is useful to collect our international financial market relationships in one place:

$$\text{RPPP: } E[S_1] = S_0 \times [1 + (h_{FC} - h_{CDN})]$$
$$\text{IRP: } F_1 = S_0 \times [1 + (R_{FC} - R_{CDN})]$$
$$\text{UFR: } F_1 = E[S_1]$$

We begin by combining UFR and IRP. Since $F_1 = E[S_1]$ from the UFR condition, we can substitute $E[S_1]$ for F_1 in IRP. The result is:

$$E[S_1] = S_0 \times [1 + (R_{FC} - R_{CDN})] \tag{21.8}$$

uncovered interest parity (UIP)
The condition stating that the expected percentage change in the exchange rate is equal to the difference in interest rates.

This important relationship is called **uncovered interest parity (UIP)**, and it plays a key role in our international capital budgeting discussion that follows. With t periods, UIP becomes:

$$E[S_t] = S_0 \times [1 + (R_{FC} - R_{CDN})]^t \tag{21.9}$$

THE INTERNATIONAL FISHER EFFECT   Next, we compare RPPP and UIP. Both of them have $E[S_1]$ on the left side, so their right sides must be equal. We thus have that:

$$S_0 \times [1 + (h_{FC} - h_{CDN})] = S_0 \times [1 + (R_{FC} - R_{CDN})]$$
$$h_{FC} - h_{CDN} = R_{FC} - R_{CDN}$$

international Fisher effect (IFE)
The theory that real interest rates are equal across countries.

This tells us that the difference in risk-free returns between Canada and a foreign country is just equal to the difference in inflation rates. Rearranging this slightly gives us the **international Fisher effect (IFE)**:

$$R_{CDN} - h_{CDN} = R_{FC} - h_{FC} \tag{21.10}$$

The IFE says that real rates are equal across countries.[5]

The conclusion that real returns are equal across countries is really basic economics. If real returns were higher in, say, the United States than in Canada, money would flow out of Canadian financial markets and into U.S. markets. Asset prices in the United States would rise and their returns would fall. At the same time, asset prices in Canada would fall and their returns would rise. This process acts to equalize real returns.

Having said all this, we need to note several things: First, we really haven't explicitly dealt with risk in our discussion. We might reach a different conclusion about real returns once we do, particularly if people in different countries have different tastes and attitudes toward risk. Second, there are many barriers to the movement of money and capital around the world. Real returns might be different between two countries for long periods of time if money can't move freely between them.

Despite these problems, we expect capital markets to become increasingly internationalized. As this occurs, any differences in real rates that do exist will probably diminish. The laws of economics have very little respect for national boundaries.

CONCEPT QUESTIONS

1. What is covered interest arbitrage?

2. What is the international Fisher effect?

---

5 Notice that our result here is the approximate real rate, $R - h$ (see Chapter 7), because we used approximations for PPP and IRP. For the exact result, see the Mini Case at the end of the chapter.

EXAMPLE 21.7: Taking a High Toll

Suppose a municipal authority is constructing a tunnel connecting two parts of a major Canadian city separated by a river. The tunnel will cost $100 million to build. Work will be complete in one year at which time the authority will pay off the present construction loan and replace it with long-term financing from capital markets. The loan will be paid off over 10 years with tolls collected from tunnel users.

In the meantime, it is time to renew the construction loan for one year. A group of Canadian banks has offered to lend $100 million for one year at 11 percent. A Japanese bank has offered a yen loan at 7 percent. Should the authority borrow in yen for one year to save 4 percent in interest— $4 million?

While you are considering, you come across the following information on exchange rates: the spot exchange rate is ¥110 per Canadian dollar ($0.009091 per ¥). The 12-month forward rate is ¥106 per dollar ($.0094340 per yen).

According to the UFR condition, the forward rate shows that the yen is expected to rise in value. It follows that the authority is naive if it expects to save $4 million by borrowing in Japan. The UIP condition tells us the yen should rise by just enough so that exchange losses on paying back the loan in more expensive yen exactly offset the lower interest rate. To prove this, we compare the balloon payments at the end of one year for borrowing in Canadian dollars and in yen. If the authority borrows in Canadian dollars at 11 percent, the principal and interest at the end of one year would be $111 million.

If the borrowing is in yen, the treasurer of the authority executes the following steps:

1. Borrow the equivalent of $100 million in yen. Converting at today's spot rate, this is $100 million × 110 = ¥11 billion.

2. At the end of 12 months, the authority owes ¥11 billion × (1.07) = ¥11.77 billion.

3. After 12 months, the authority purchases ¥11.77 billion in the spot market to repay the loan. The cost depends on the unknown future spot rate for the yen. By borrowing in Japan, the authority is gambling that the yen will not appreciate in value by enough to cancel the gains of the lower interest rate. In other words, the authority is betting that the future cost of buying ¥11.77 billion will not exceed $111 million. This gives us a break-even future spot rate:

$$\text{¥}11.77 \text{ billion} = \$111 \text{ million} \times F_1$$
$$F_1 = 11.77 \text{ billion}/111 \text{ million}$$
$$F_1 = 106.036$$

If the authority gambles, it could break even if the future spot rate is around 106 yen per dollar. This translates to 1/106 = $.009434 per yen. If the yen appreciates more, the authority loses. Suppose the yen goes up to $.01 or 100 yen to the dollar. Then the authority has to repay ¥11.77 billion × .01 = $118 million. This is equivalent to borrowing at 18 percent!

Our advice in this case is to borrow in Canada to eliminate foreign exchange risk. Or, if there is a good reason to borrow abroad, say better access to funds, the authority should hedge in the forward market.[6] Under this approach, steps 1 and 2 are the same. With a forward contract taken out when the borrowing is initiated, the future exchange rate is locked in at ¥106 to the dollar. Due to the IRP condition, it is no coincidence that this is the break-even rate.

 21.5

INTERNATIONAL CAPITAL BUDGETING

Kihlstrom Equipment, a Canadian-based international company, is evaluating an overseas investment. Kihlstrom's exports of high-tech communications equipment have increased to such a degree that it is considering building a plant in France. The project would cost EUR 2.5 million to launch. The cash flows are expected to be EUR 1.1 million a year for the next three years.[7]

The current spot exchange rate for euros is EUR 0.65. Recall that this is euros per dollar, so a euro is worth $1/0.65 = $1.54. The risk-free rate in Canada is 5 percent, and the risk-free rate in France is 7 percent. Notice that the exchange rate and the two interest rates are observed in financial markets, not estimated.[8] Kihlstrom's required return on dollar investments of this sort is 10 percent.

Should Kihlstrom take this investment? As always, the answer depends on the NPV, but how do we calculate the net present value of this project in Canadian dollars? There are two basic ways to do this:

1. *The home currency approach.* Convert all the euro cash flows into dollars, and then discount at 10 percent to find the NPV in dollars. Notice that for this approach, we have to come up with the future exchange rates to convert the future projected euro cash flows into dollars.

---

6 Currency futures or swaps offer another possible hedging vehicle. Chapter 24 discusses futures in more detail.

7 In our discussion of Kihlstrom, all cash flows and interest rates are nominal unless we state otherwise.

8 For example, the interest rates might be the short-term Eurodollar and euro deposit rates offered by large money centre banks.

In Their Own Words . . .   Richard M. Levich on Forward Exchange Rates

THAT IS THE RELATIONSHIP between today's three-month forward exchange rate, which can be observed in the market, and the spot exchange rate of three months from today, which cannot be observed until the future? One popular answer is that there is no relationship. As every bank trader knows, the possibility of covered interest arbitrage between domestic and foreign securities establishes a close link between the forward premium and the interest rate differential. At any moment, a trader can check his screen and observe that the forward premium and the interest rate differentials are nearly identical, especially when Eurocurrency interest rates are used. Thus, the trader might say, "The forward rate reflects today's interest differential. It has nothing to do with expectations."

To check the second popular belief, that the forward rate reflects exchange rate expectations, takes a bit more work. Take today's three-month forward rate as of January 15 and compare it to the spot exchange rate that actually exists three months later on April 15. This produces one observation on the forward rate as a forecaster—not enough to accept or reject a theory. The idea that the forward rate might be an unbiased predictor of the future spot rate suggests that, on average and looking at many observations, the prediction error is small. So collect more data using the forward rate of April 15 and match it with the spot rate of July 15, and then the forward rate of July 15 matched to the spot rate of October 15, and so on. Look at the data for 8 to 10 years to have a large sample of observations.

The data suggest [for full citation see Suggested Readings] that in the early 1980s when the U.S. dollar was very strong, the forward rate significantly underestimated the strength of the dollar, and the forward rate was a biased predictor. But from 1985 to 1987 when the dollar depreciated sharply, the forward rate tended to overestimate the strength of the dollar, and the forward rate was again a biased predictor, but with the opposite sign as the earlier period. Looking at all of the 1980s—you guessed it—the forward rate was on average very close to the future spot exchange rate.

There are two messages here. First, even if there were "no relationship" between the forward rate and the future spot rate, the treasurer of General Motors would want to know exactly what that "nonrelationship" was. Because if the forward rate were consistently 3 percent higher than, or consistently 5 percent lower than, the future spot rate, the treasurer would be facing a tantalizing profit opportunity. A watch that is three minutes fast or five minutes slow is a very useful watch, as long as the bias is known and consistent. And finally, the data from the 1980s have revalidated Michael Mussa's [for full citation see Suggested Readings] interpretation of the 1970s. Mussa observed that "the forward rate is an unbiased predictor of the future spot rate, [it] is close to the best available predictor . . . but [it] is probably not a very good predictor."

Richard M. Levich is professor of finance and international business at New York University. He has written extensively on exchange rates and other issues in international economics and finance.

---

2. *The foreign currency approach.* Determine the required return on euro investments, and discount the euro cash flows to find the NPV in euros. Then convert this euro NPV to a dollar NPV. This approach requires us to somehow convert the 10 percent dollar required return to the equivalent euro required return.

The difference between these two approaches is primarily a matter of when we convert from euros to dollars. In the first case, we convert before estimating the NPV. In the second case, we convert after estimating NPV.

It might appear that the second approach is superior because we only have to come up with one number, the euro discount rate. Furthermore, since the first approach requires us to forecast future exchange rates, it probably seems that there is greater room for error. As we illustrate next, however, based on our results the two approaches are really the same.

Method 1: The Home Currency Approach

To convert the project future cash flows into dollars, we invoke the uncovered interest parity (UIP) relation to come up with the project exchange rates. Based on our discussion, the expected exchange rate at time t, $E[S_t]$ is:

$$E[S_t] = S_0 \times [1 + (R_E - R_{CDN})]^t$$

where R_E stands for the nominal risk-free rate in France. Since R_E is 7 percent, R_{CDN} is 5 percent, and the current exchange rate (S_0) is EUR 0.65:

$$E[S_t] = 0.65 \times [1 + (.07 - .05)]^t$$
$$= 0.65 \times 1.02^t$$

The projected exchange rates for the communications equipment project are thus:

Year	Expected Exchange Rate
1	EUR 0.65×1.02^1 = EUR 0.663
2	EUR 0.65×1.02^2 = EUR 0.676
3	EUR 0.65×1.02^3 = EUR 0.690

Using these exchange rates, along with the current exchange rate, we can convert all of the euro cash flows to dollars:

Year	(1) Cash Flow in EUR	(2) Expected Exchange Rate	(3) Cash Flow in \$ (1)/(2)
0	–EUR 2.5	EUR 0.650	–\$3.85
1	1.1	0.663	1.66
2	1.1	0.676	1.63
3	1.1	0.690	1.59

To finish, we calculate the NPV in the ordinary way:

$$NPV = -\$3.85 + \$1.66/1.10 + \$1.63/1.10^2 + \$1.59/1.10^3$$
$$= \$.2 \text{ million}$$

So the project appears to be profitable.

Method 2: The Foreign Currency Approach

Kihlstrom requires a nominal return of 10 percent on the dollar-denominated cash flows. We need to convert this to a rate suitable for euro-denominated cash flows.

Based on the international Fisher effect, we know that the difference in the nominal rates is:

$$R_E - R_{CDN} = h_E - h_{CDN}$$
$$= 7\% - 5\% = 2\%$$

The appropriate discount rate for estimating the euro cash flows from the project is approximately equal to 10 percent plus an extra 2 percent to compensate for the greater euro inflation rate.

If we calculate the NPV of the euro cash flows at this rate, we get:

$$NPV_E = -EUR\ 2.5 + EUR\ 1.1/1.12 + EUR\ 1.1/1.12^2 + EUR\ 1.1/1.12^3$$
$$= EUR\ 0.142 \text{ million}$$

The NPV of this project is EUR 0.142 million. Taking this project makes us EUR 0.142 million richer today. What is this in dollars? Since the exchange rate today is EUR 0.65, the dollar NPV of the project is:

$$NPV_\$ = NPV_E/S_0 = EUR\ 0.142/0.65 = \$.2 \text{ million}$$

This is the same dollar NPV as we previously calculated.

The important thing to recognize from our example is that the two capital budgeting procedures are actually the same and always give the same answer.[9] In this second approach, the fact

---

9 Actually, there will be a slight difference because we are using the approximate relationships. If we calculate the required return as $(1.10) \times (1 + .02) - 1 = 12.2\%$, we get exactly the same NPV. See the Mini Case at the end of the chapter for more detail.

that we are implicitly forecasting exchange rates is simply hidden. Even so, the foreign currency approach is computationally a little easier.

Unremitted Cash Flows

The previous example assumed that all aftertax cash flows from the foreign investment could be remitted to (paid out to) the parent firm. Actually, substantial differences can exist between the cash flows generated by a foreign project and the amount that can actually be remitted or repatriated to the parent firm.

A foreign subsidiary can remit funds to a parent in many ways, including the following:

1. Dividends.
2. Management fees for central services.
3. Royalties on the use of a trade name and patents.

However cash flows are repatriated, international firms must pay special attention to remittance because there may be current and future controls on remittances. Many governments are sensitive to the charge of being exploited by foreign national firms. In such cases, governments are tempted to limit the ability of international firms to remit cash flows. Funds that cannot currently be remitted are sometimes said to be blocked.

CONCEPT QUESTIONS

1. What financial complications arise in international capital budgeting? Describe two procedures for estimating NPV in this case.

2. What are blocked funds?

21.6   FINANCING INTERNATIONAL PROJECTS

The Cost of Capital for International Firms

An important question for firms with international investments is whether the required return for international projects should be different from that of similar domestic projects. The answer to this question depends on:

1. Segmentation of the international financial market.
2. Foreign political risk of expropriation, foreign exchange controls, and taxes.

We save political risk for later discussion and focus here on the first point.

Suppose barriers prevented shareholders in Canada from holding foreign securities. If this were the case, the financial markets of different countries would be segmented. Further suppose that firms in Canada did not face the same barriers. In such a case, a firm engaging in international investing could provide indirect diversification for Canadian shareholders that they could not achieve by investing within Canada. This could lead to lowering of the risk premium on international projects.

On the other hand, if there were no barriers to international investing for shareholders, investors could get the benefit of international diversification for themselves by buying foreign securities. Then, the project cost of capital for Canadian firms would not depend on where the project was located.

To resolve this issue, researchers have compared the variance of purely domestic stock portfolios with international portfolios. The result is that international portfolios have lower variance. Because investors are not fully diversified internationally, firms can benefit from a lower cost of capital for international projects that provide diversification services for the firms' shareholders.[10]

---

[10] B. H. Solnik, "Why Not Diversify Internationally Rather than Domestically?" *Financial Analysts Journal,* July–August 1974.

International Diversification and Investors

As we just saw, there is evidence that international diversification by firms presently provides a service that investors cannot obtain themselves at reasonable cost. Holding foreign securities may subject investors to increased tax, trading, and information costs. Financial engineering is aiding investors in avoiding some of these costs. As a result, as investors diversify globally, the cost of capital advantage to firms is likely to decline.

An *Index Participation* (IP) is a current example of a financially engineered vehicle for international diversification.[11] An IP on the Standard & Poor's 500 Stock Average, for example, gives an investor an asset that tracks this well-known U.S. market index. IPs are highly liquid, thus reducing trading costs. Information costs are also reduced since the holder need not research each of the 500 individual stocks that make up the index.

International diversification for Canadian investors is being made easier by the lowering of an important barrier. Effective 2001, the maximum allowable foreign holding for pension funds and Registered Retirement Savings Plans (RRSPs) increased to 30 percent. Increased demand is fueling the development of new products to exploit this opportunity.

These and other financial engineering developments have helped to integrate the international financial market. Still, recent research suggests that local market effects influence prices of shares of firms with subsidiaries listed in different markets. For example, Royal Dutch Petroleum and Shell Transport are "twin" companies that merged in 1907. Each retains its own shares, Royal Dutch trading primarily in New York and Shell mainly trading in London. When the New York market goes up relative to London, researchers found that Royal Dutch shares rise relative to Shell even though there is no change in the companies' cash flows. All this means that, despite globalization of markets, some segmentation remains making international diversification worthwhile.[12]

Sources of Short- and Intermediate-Term Financing

In raising short-term and medium-term cash, Canadian international firms have a choice between borrowing from a chartered bank at the Canadian rate or borrowing EuroCanadian (or other Eurocurrency) from a bank outside Canada through the Eurocurrency market.

The Eurocurrency markets are the **Eurobanks** that make loans and accept deposits in foreign currencies. Most Eurocurrency trading involves the borrowing and lending of time deposits at Eurobanks. For example, suppose the Bank of Nova Scotia (BNS) receives a 30-day Eurodollar deposit from McCain in London. The BNS then makes a U.S. dollar-denominated loan to the Bank of Tokyo. Ultimately, the Bank of Tokyo makes a loan to a Japanese importer with invoices to pay in the United States. As our example shows, the Eurocurrency market is not a retail market. The customers are large corporations, banks, and governments.

One important characteristic of the Eurocurrency market is that loans are made on a floating rate basis. The interest rates are set at a fixed margin above the London Interbank Offered Rate (LIBOR) for the given period and currency involved. For example, if LIBOR is 8 percent and the margin is 0.5 percent for Eurodollar loans in a certain risk class, called a *tier,* the Eurodollar borrower pays an interest rate of 8.5 percent. Eurodollar loans have maturities ranging up to 10 years.

Securitization and globalization have produced alternatives to borrowing from a Eurobank. Under a **Note Issuance Facility (NIF),** a large borrower issues short-term notes with maturities usually three to six months but ranging to one year.[13] Banks may underwrite NIFs or sell them to investors. In the latter case, where banks simply act as an agent, the Euronotes issued are called *Euro-*

Eurobanks
Banks that make loans and accept deposits in foreign currencies.

Note Issuance Facility (NIF)
Large borrowers issue notes up to one year in maturity in the Euromarket. Banks underwrite or sell notes.

---

11 G. Axford and Y. Lin, "Surprise! Currency Risk Improves International Investment," *Canadian Treasury Management Review,* Royal Bank of Canada, March–April 1990.

12 Our discussion is based on K.A. Froot and E.M.Dabora, "How are stock prices affected by the location of trade?" *Journal of Financial Economics* 53, August 1999, pp. 189–216. For more information on the effects of globalization on market correlation, see Dwarka Lakhan, "Increasing correlation reduces benefits of global diversification," *Canadian Treasurer,* August/September 2003 and G. Andrew Karolyi, "International stock market correlations," *Canadian Investment Review,* Summer 2001.

13 Our discussion of NIFs draws on A. L. Melnik and S. E. Plaut, *The Short-Term Eurocredit Market* (New York: New York University Salomon Center, 1991), chap. 4.

commercial paper (ECP). ECP is similar to domestic commercial paper but, because the Eurocredit market is not regulated, offers greater flexibility in available maturities and tax avoidance.

The drive to escape regulation (part of the regulatory dialectic introduced in Chapter 1) explains the attraction and growth of the Euromarkets. Eurocurrency markets developed to allow borrowers and banks to operate without regulation and taxes mainly in the United States. They offer borrowers an opportunity to tap large amounts of short-term funds quickly and at competitive rates. As banking regulations—for example capital rules—become tighter, alternatives to bank borrowing, such as NIFs, are growing and sharing the Euromarket with banks.

THE EUROBOND MARKET   Eurobonds are denominated in a particular currency and are issued simultaneously in the bond markets of several countries. The prefix *Euro* means the bonds are issued outside the countries in whose currencies they are denominated. For example, a French automobile firm issues 50,000 bonds with a face value of $1,000 (U.S.) each. When the bonds are issued, they are managed by London merchant bankers and listed on the London Stock Exchange.

Most Eurobonds are bearer bonds. The ownership of the bonds is established by possession of the bond. In contrast, foreign bonds (issued by foreign borrowers in a domestic capital market) are registered. This makes Eurobonds more attractive to Belgian dentists, investors who have a disdain for tax authorities.

Most issues of Eurobonds are arranged by underwriting. However, some Eurobonds are privately placed. Eurobonds appear as straight bonds, floating-rate notes, convertible bonds, zero coupon bonds, mortgage-backed bonds, and dual-currency bonds.

CONCEPT QUESTIONS

1. Can firms reduce their risk and with it their costs of capital through diversifying with international projects?

2. What are the main sources of short and intermediate financing in Euro-markets?

3. Describe a Eurobond and its advantages over a foreign bond.

exchange rate risk
The risk related to having international operations in a world where relative currency values vary.

EXCHANGE RATE RISK

Exchange rate risk is the natural consequence of international operations in a world where relative currency values move up and down. Managing exchange rate risk is an important part of international finance. As we discuss next, there are three different types of exchange rate risk or exposure: short-run exposure, long-run exposure, and translation exposure.

Transaction Exposure

Transaction exposure is the day-to-day fluctuations in exchange rates that create short-run risks for international firms. Transaction exposure is also called short-run exposure. Most such firms have contractual agreements to buy and sell goods in the near future at set prices. When different currencies are involved, such transactions have an extra element of risk.

For example, imagine you are importing imitation pasta from Italy and reselling it in Canada under the Impasta brand name. Your largest customer has ordered 10,000 cases of Impasta. You place the order with your supplier today, but you won't pay until the goods arrive in 60 days. Your selling price is $6 per case. Your cost is 3.5 euros per case, and the exchange rate is currently EUR 0.65, so it takes 0.65 euros to buy $1.

At the current exchange rate, your cost in dollars from filling the order is EUR 3.5/0.65 = $5.38 per case, so your pretax profit on the order is 10,000 × ($6 − $5.38) = $6,200. However, the exchange rate in 60 days will probably be different, so your profit depends on what the future exchange rate turns out to be.

For example, if the rate goes to EUR 0.70, your cost is EUR 3.5/0.70 = $5 per case. Your profit goes to $10,000. If the exchange rate goes to, say, EUR 0.58, then your cost is EUR 3.5/0.58 = $6, and your profit is zero.

The short-run exposure in our example can be reduced or eliminated in several ways. The most obvious means of hedging is to enter into a forward exchange agreement to lock in an exchange rate. For example, suppose the 60-day forward rate is EUR 0.67. What is your profit if you hedge? What profit should you expect if you don't?

If you hedge, you lock in an exchange rate of EUR 0.67. Your cost in dollars is thus EUR 3.5/0.67 = $5.22 per case, so your profit is 10,000 × ($6 − $5.22) = $7,800. If you don't hedge, assuming that the forward rate is an unbiased predictor (in other words, assuming the UFR condition holds), you should expect the exchange rate to actually be EUR 0.67 in 60 days. You should expect to make $7,800.

Alternatively, if this is not feasible, you could simply borrow the dollars today, convert them into euros, and invest the euros for 60 days to earn some interest. From IRP, this amounts to entering into a forward contract.

Should the treasurer hedge or speculate? There are usually two reasons the treasurer should hedge:

1. In an efficient foreign exchange rate market, speculation is a zero NPV activity. Unless the treasurer has special information, nothing is gained from foreign exchange speculation.

2. The costs of hedging are not large. The treasurer can use forward contracts to hedge, and if the forward rate is equal to the expected spot, the costs of hedging are negligible.

MORE ADVANCED SHORT-TERM HEDGES Of course, there are ways to hedge foreign exchange risk other than with forward contracts. Currency swaps, currency options, and other financially engineered products are taking considerable business away from the forward exchange market.[14] A currency swap is an arrangement between a borrower, a second borrower, called a **counterparty,** and a bank. The borrower and the counterparty each raise funds in a different currency and then swap liabilities. The bank guarantees the borrower's and counterparty's credit as in a bankers acceptance. The result is that the borrower obtains funds in the desired currency at a lower rate than for direct borrowing.

For example, in 1986 the federal government of Canada made an 80 billion yen bond issue and swapped part of it into U.S. dollars. The interest rate was six-month LIBOR and the ending liability was in U.S. dollars, not yen. The interest cost turned out to be 54 basis points below the cost of direct borrowing in the United States.

Currency options are similar to options on stock (discussed in Chapter 25) except the exercise price is an exchange rate.[15] They are exchange traded in the United States with exercise prices in various currencies including the Canadian dollar. Currency options can be exercised at any time before maturity. In the jargon of options, they are **American options.** A call option on the Canadian dollar gives the holder the right, but not the obligation, to buy C$ at a fixed exercise price in U.S.$. It increases in value as the C$ exchange rate in U.S.$ rises. A put option allows the holder to sell C$ at the exercise price. A put becomes more valuable when the C$ declines against the U.S.$.

The basic idea behind hedging with options is to take an options position opposite to the cash position. For this reason, hedge analysis starts by looking at the unhedged position of the business. For example, suppose an exporter expects to collect receivables totalling $1 million (U.S.) in 30 days. Suppose the present C$ exchange rate is $.74 (U.S.). If the rate remains at 74 cents, the exporter receives $1 million U.S./.74= $1,351,351 (Can) after 30 days. The exporter is at risk if the exchange rate rises so that the $1 million (U.S.) buys fewer Canadian dollars. For example, if the exchange rate rises to .77, the exporter receives only $1 million U.S./.77 = $1,298,701 (Can). The loss of $52,650 comes out of profits.

Since the exporter loses if the exchange rate rises, buying call options is an appropriate hedge. Calls on the C$ increase in value if the exchange rate rises. The profit on the calls helps

counterparty
Second borrower in currency swap. Counterparty borrows funds in currency desired by principal.

American options
A call or put option that can be exercised on or before its expiration date.

---

14 Our discussion of currency swaps in practice draws on B. Critchley, "Explosion of New Products Cuts Foreign Currency Risk," *The Financial Post*, September 14, 1987. Further discussion of swaps is found in Chapter 24.

15 See Chapter 25 for a thorough introduction to options. Our discussion of currency options simplifies the description by discussing options on currency. In practice, options are written against currency futures contracts.

offset the loss on exchange. To implement this strategy, the exporter likely seeks expert advice on how many calls to buy and, more generally, the relative cost of hedging with options rather than with forwards.

Canadian sports teams like the Toronto Blue Jays and the Edmonton Oilers also face exchange rate risk. These organizations import talent, paying salaries in U.S. dollars while realizing most of their revenues from Canadian game attendance and television in Canadian dollars. The Jays estimate that a fluctuation of one cent in the Canadian dollar changes the profit for the franchise by about $700,000 over a year. The losses due to exchange rate differences are significant. Unlike the auto manufacturers in our prior example, there is little a sports team can do to avoid this long-run exposure. In this case, hedging is likely the best policy.

Economic Exposure

Economic exposure is another term for long-run exposure. In the long run, the value of a foreign operation can fluctuate because of unanticipated changes in relative economic conditions. For example, imagine that we own a labour-intensive assembly operation located in another country to take advantage of lower wages. Through time, unexpected changes in economic conditions can raise the foreign wage levels to the point where the cost advantage is eliminated or even becomes negative.

Hedging long-run exposure is more difficult than hedging short-term risks. For one thing, organized forward markets don't exist for such long-term needs. Instead, the primary option that firms have is to try to match up foreign currency inflows and outflows. The same thing goes for matching foreign currency-denominated assets and liabilities. For example, a firm that sells in a foreign country might try to concentrate its raw material purchases and labour expense in that country. That way, the dollar values of its revenues and costs will move up and down together. Probably the best examples of this type of hedging are the so-called transplant auto manufacturers such as BMW, Honda, Mercedes, and Toyota, which now build locally a substantial portion of the cars they sell in the United States and Canada, thereby obtaining some degree of immunization against exchange rate movements. There can still be problems with this strategy. For example, many cars are built in Canada and exported to the United States. With the falling U.S. dollar in 2003, the Canadian dollar production costs are taking up a larger portion of revenue.

Similarly, a firm can reduce its long-run exchange rate risk by borrowing in the foreign country. Fluctuations in the value of the foreign subsidiary's assets will then be at least partially offset by changes in the value of the liabilities.

For example, the turmoil in the Asian currency markets in 1997 caught many companies napping, but not Avon. The U.S. cosmetics manufacturer had a significant exposure in Asia, with sales there comprising about 20 percent of the company's worldwide volume. To protect itself against currency fluctuations, Avon produced nearly all of its products in the country where they were sold, and purchased nearly all related raw materials in the same country as well. That way, their production costs and revenues were in the same currency. In addition, operating loans were denominated in the currency of the country where production was located to tie interest rates and payments to the local currency. All of this protects profits in the foreign market, but Avon still had the exposure related to translating profits back into dollars. To reduce that exposure, the company began having its foreign operating units remit earnings weekly rather than monthly to minimize "translation" risk, the subject of our next section.

Translation Exposure

When a Canadian company calculates its accounting net income and EPS for some period, it must translate everything into dollars. This can create some problems for the accounts when there are significant foreign operations. In particular, two issues arise:

1. What is the appropriate exchange rate to use for translating each balance sheet account?
2. How should balance sheet accounting gains and losses from foreign currency translation be handled?

www.edmontonoilers.com
www.bluejays.com

www.bmw.com
www.world.honda.com
www.mercedes-benz.com
www.toyota.co.jp

To illustrate the accounting problem, suppose we started a small foreign subsidiary in Lilliputia a year ago. The local currency is the gulliver, abbreviated GL. At the beginning of the year, the exchange rate was GL 2 = Cdn. $1, and the balance sheet in gullivers looked like this:

Assets	GL 1,000	Liabilities	GL 500
		Equity	500

At 2 gullivers to the dollar, the beginning balance sheet in dollars was:

Assets	$500	Liabilities	$250
		Equity	250

Lilliputia is a quiet place, and nothing at all actually happened during the year. As a result, net income was zero (before consideration of exchange rate changes). However, the exchange rate did change to 4 gullivers = $1 purely because the Lilliputian inflation rate is much higher than the Canadian inflation rate.

Since nothing happened, the accounting ending balance sheet in gullivers is the same as the beginning one. However, if we convert it to dollars at the new exchange rate, we get:

Assets	$250	Liabilities	$125
		Equity	125

Notice that the value of the equity has gone down by $125, even though net income was zero. Despite the fact that absolutely nothing really happened, there is a $125 accounting loss. How to handle this $125 loss has been a controversial accounting question.

One obvious and consistent way to handle this loss is simply to report the loss on the parent's income statement. During periods of volatile exchange rates, this kind of treatment can dramatically impact an international company's reported EPS. This is purely an accounting phenomenon; even so, such fluctuations are disliked by financial managers.

The current compromise approach to translation gains and losses is based on rules set out in Canadian Institute of Chartered Accountants (CICA) S. 1650. The rules divide a firm's foreign subsidiaries into two categories: integrated and self-sustaining. For the most part, the rules require that all assets and liabilities must be translated from the subsidiary's currency into the parent's currency using the exchange rate that currently prevails.[16] Because Canadian accountants consolidate the financial statements of subsidiaries more than 50 percent owned by the parent firm, translation gains and losses are reflected on the income statement of the parent company.

For a self-sustaining subsidiary, any translation gains and losses that occur are accumulated in a special account within the shareholders' equity section of the parent company's balance sheet. This account might be labelled something like "unrealized foreign exchange gains (losses)." These gains and losses are not reported on the income statement. As a result, the impact of translation gains and losses is not recognized explicitly in net income until the underlying assets and liabilities are sold or otherwise liquidated.

www.cica.ca

Managing Exchange Rate Risk

For a large multinational firm, the management of exchange rate risk is complicated by the fact that many different currencies may be involved in many different subsidiaries. It is very likely that a change in some exchange rate benefits some subsidiaries and hurts others. The net effect on the overall firm depends on its net exposure.

For example, suppose a firm has two divisions: Division A buys goods in Canada for dollars and sells them in Britain for pounds. Division B buys goods in Britain for pounds and sells them in Canada for dollars. If these two divisions are of roughly equal size in their inflows and outflows, the overall firm obviously has little exchange rate risk.

---

16 The rules also define the current exchange rate differently for the types of subsidiaries. An integrated subsidiary uses the exchange rate observed on the last day of its fiscal year. For a self-sustaining subsidiary, the exchange rate prescribed is the average rate over the year. For detailed discussion of CICA 1650, see A. Davis and G. Pinches, *Canadian Financial Management*, 4th ed. (Toronto, Ontario: Prentice-Hall, 2000).

In our example, the firm's net position in pounds (the amount coming in less the amount going out) is small, so the exchange rate risk is small. However, if one division, acting on its own, were to start hedging its exchange rate risk, the overall firm's exchange risk would go up. The moral of the story is that multinational firms have to be conscious of the overall position that the firm has in a foreign currency. For this reason, exchange risk management is probably best handled on a centralized basis.

> ### CONCEPT QUESTIONS
>
> **1.** What are the different types of exchange rate risk?
>
> **2.** How can a firm hedge short-run exchange rate risk? Long-run exchange rate risk?

political risk
Risk related to changes in value that arise because of political actions.

POLITICAL RISK

One final element of risk in international investing concerns **political risk.** Political risk refers to changes in value that arise as a consequence of political actions. This is not purely a problem faced by international firms. For example, changes in Canadian or provincial tax laws and regulations may benefit some Canadian firms and hurt others, so political risk exists nationally as well as internationally. For example, the possibility of Quebec separation is seen by many as a political risk affecting firms located in the province. When firms announce plans to relocate to Toronto, stock market reaction is usually positive.[17]

Some countries do have more political risk than others, however. In such cases, the extra political risk may lead firms to require higher returns on overseas investments to compensate for the risk that funds will be blocked, critical operations interrupted, and contracts abrogated. For example, the rate of return required for an overseas investment made in "A" rated Chile would be less than the rate of return required for a foreign investment made in "C" rated Argentina. In the most extreme case, the possibility of outright confiscation may be a concern in countries with relatively unstable political environments.

Political risk also depends on the nature of the business; some businesses are less likely to be confiscated because they are not particularly valuable in the hands of a different owner. An assembly operation supplying subcomponents that only the parent company uses would not be an attractive takeover target, for example. Similarly, a manufacturing operation that requires the use of specialized components from the parent is of little value without the parent company's cooperation.

Natural resource developments, such as copper mining or oil drilling, are just the opposite. Once the operation is in place, much of the value is in the commodity. The political risk for such investments is much higher for this reason. Also, the issue of exploitation is more pronounced with such investments, again increasing the political risk.

Political risk can be hedged in several ways, particularly when confiscation or nationalization is a concern. As we stated earlier, insurance against political risk is available from Export Development Canada. Further, the use of local financing, perhaps from the government of the foreign country in question, reduces the possible loss because the company can refuse to pay on the debt in the event of unfavourable political activities. Based on our previous discussion, structuring the operation so that it requires significant parent company involvement to function is another way some firms try to reduce political risk.

At the other extreme, some companies avoid the implicit threats in the methods just discussed while trying to be good corporate citizens in the host country. This approach is an international application of the view of the corporation as responsible to shareholders and stakeholders that we presented in Chapter 1.

---

17 Our source here is: H. Bhabra, U. Lel, and D. Tirtirolu, "Stock Market's Reaction to Business Relocations: Canadian Evidence," *Canadian Journal of Administrative Sciences*, December 2002, vol. 19, number 4, pp. 346–358.

CONCEPT QUESTIONS

1. What is political risk?

2. What are some ways of hedging political risks?

 **21.9**

SUMMARY AND CONCLUSIONS

The international firm has a more complicated life than the purely domestic firm. Management must understand the connection between interest rates, foreign currency exchange rates, and inflation. It must also become aware of a large number of different financial market regulations and tax systems. This chapter is intended to be a concise introduction to some of the financial issues that come up in international investing.

Our coverage was necessarily brief. The main topics we discussed include:

1. Some basic vocabulary. We briefly defined some exotic terms such as *LIBOR* and *Eurodollar.*

2. The basic mechanics of exchange rate quotations. We discussed the spot and forward markets and how exchange rates are interpreted.

3. The fundamental relationships between international financial variables:

   a. Absolute and relative purchasing power parity (PPP).

   b. Interest rate parity (IRP).

   c. Unbiased forward rates (UFR).

   Absolute purchasing power parity states that $1 should have the same purchasing power in each country. This means that an orange costs the same whether you buy it in Montreal or in Tokyo.

   Relative purchasing power parity means the expected percentage change in exchange rates between the currencies of two countries is equal to the difference in their inflation rates.

   Interest rate parity implies that the percentage difference between the forward exchange rate and the spot exchange rate is equal to the interest rate differential. We showed how covered interest arbitrage forces this relationship to hold.

   The unbiased forward rates condition indicates that the current forward rate is a good predictor of the future spot exchange rate.

4. International capital budgeting. We showed that the basic foreign exchange relationships imply two other conditions:

   a. Uncovered interest parity.

   b. International Fisher effect.

   By invoking these two conditions, we learned how to estimate NPVs in foreign currencies and how to convert foreign currencies into dollars to estimate NPV in the usual way.

5. Exchange rate and political risk. We described the various types of exchange rate risk and discussed some commonly used approaches to managing the effect of fluctuating exchange rates on the cash flows and value of the international firm. We also discussed political risk and some ways of managing exposure to it.

Key Terms

American options (page 667)
counterparty (page 667)
cross-rate (page 649)
Eurobanks (page 665)
Eurobond (page 649)
Eurocurrency (page 649)
exchange rate (page 651)
exchange rate risk (page 666)
Export Development Canada (EDC) (page 649)
foreign bonds (page 649)
foreign exchange market (page 650)
forward exchange rate (page 653)
forward trade (page 653)

gilts (page 650)
interest rate parity (IRP) (page 659)
international Fisher effect (IFE) (page 660)
London Interbank Offer Rate (LIBOR) (page 650)
Note Issuance Facility (NIF) (page 665)
political risk (page 670)
purchasing power parity (PPP) (page 654)
spot exchange rate (page 653)
spot trade (page 653)
swaps (page 650)
unbiased forward rates (UFR) (page 659)
uncovered interest parity (UIP) (page 660)

Chapter Review Problems and Self-Test

21.1 **Relative Purchasing Power Parity**   The inflation rate in Canada is projected at 6 percent per year for the next several years. The German inflation rate is projected to be 2 percent during that time. The exchange rate is currently EUR 0.6. Based on relative PPP, what is the expected exchange rate in two years?

21.2 **Covered Interest Arbitrage**   The spot and 12-month forward rates on the Swiss franc are SF 1.8 and SF 1.7, respectively. The risk-free interest rate in Canada is 8 percent, and the risk-free rate in Switzerland is 5 percent. Is there an arbitrage opportunity here? How would you exploit it?

Answers to Self-Test Problems

21.1 From relative PPP, the expected exchange rate in two years, $E[S_2]$ is:

$$E[S_2] = S_0 \times [1 + (h_G - h_{CDN})]^2$$

where h_G is the European inflation rate. The current exchange rate is EUR 0.6, so the expected exchange rate is:

$$
\begin{aligned}
E[S_2] &= EUR\ 0.6 \times [1 + (.02 - .06)]^2 \\
&= EUR\ 0.6 \times .96^2 \\
&= EUR\ 0.55
\end{aligned}
$$

21.2 From interest rate parity, the forward rate should be (approximately):

$$
\begin{aligned}
F_1 &= S_0 \times [1 + (R_{FC} - R_{CDN})] \\
&= 1.8 \times [1 + .05 - .08] \\
&= 1.75
\end{aligned}
$$

Since the forward rate is actually SF 1.7, there is an arbitrage opportunity.

To exploit the arbitrage, we first note that dollars are selling for SF 1.7 each in the forward market. From IRP, this is too cheap because they should be selling for SF 1.75. So we want to arrange to buy dollars with Swiss francs in the forward market. To do this, we can:

1. Today: Borrow, say, $10 million for 12 months. Convert it to SF 18 million in the spot market, and forward contract at SF 1.7 to convert it back to dollars in one year. Invest the SF 18 million at 5 percent.

2. In one year: Your investment has grown to SF 18 × 1.05 = SF 18.9 million. Convert this to dollars at the rate of SF 1.7 = $1. You have SF 18.9 million/1.7 = $11,117,647. Pay off your loan with 8 percent interest at a cost of $10 million × 1.08 = $10,800,000 and pocket the difference of $317,647.

Concepts Review and Critical Thinking Questions

1. Suppose the exchange rate for the Swiss franc is quoted as SF 1.50 in the spot market and SF 1.53 in the 90-day forward market.
   a. Is the dollar selling at a premium or a discount relative to the franc?
   b. Does the financial market expect the franc to strengthen relative to the dollar? Explain.
   c. What do you suspect is true about relative economic conditions in Canada and Switzerland?

2. Suppose the rate of inflation in the European Union will run about 3 percent higher than the Canadian

inflation rate over the next several years. All other things being the same, what will happen to the euro versus dollar exchange rate? What relationship are you relying on in answering?

3. The exchange rate for the Australian dollar is currently A$1.15. This exchange rate is expected to rise by 10 percent over the next year.
   a. Is the Australian dollar expected to get stronger or weaker?
   b. What do you think about the relative inflation rates in Canada and Australia?
   c. What do you think about the relative nominal interest rates in Canada and Australia? Relative real rates?

4. Which of the following most accurately describes a Yankee bond?
   a. A bond issued by General Motors in Japan with the interest payable in U.S. dollars.
   b. A bond issued by General Motors in Japan with the interest payable in yen.
   c. A bond issued by Toyota in the United States with the interest payable in yen.
   d. A bond issued by Toyota in the United States with the interest payable in dollars.
   e. A bond issued by Toyota worldwide with the interest payable in dollars.

5. Are exchange rate changes necessarily good or bad for a particular company?

6. Duracell International confirmed in October 1995 that it was planning to open battery-manufacturing plants in China and India. Manufacturing in these countries allows Duracell to avoid import duties of between 30 and 35 percent that have made alkaline batteries prohibitively expensive for some consumers. What additional advantages might Duracell see in this proposal? What are some of the risks to Duracell?

7. Given that many multinationals based in many countries have much greater sales outside their domestic markets than within them, what is the particular relevance of their domestic currency?

8. Are the following statements true or false? Explain why.
   a. If the general price index in Great Britain rises faster than that in Canada, we would expect the pound to appreciate relative to the dollar.

   b. Suppose you are a European machine tool exporter and you invoice all of your sales in foreign currency. Further suppose that the European Union monetary authorities begin to undertake an expansionary monetary policy. If it is certain that the easy money policy will result in higher inflation rates in the European Union relative to those in other countries, then you should use the forward markets to protect yourself against future losses resulting from the deterioration in the value of the euro.
   c. If you could accurately estimate differences in the relative inflation rates of two countries over a long period of time, while other market participants were unable to do so, you could successfully speculate in spot currency markets.

9. Some countries encourage movements in their exchange rate relative to those of some other country as a short-term means of addressing foreign trade imbalances. For each of the following scenarios, evaluate the impact the announcement would have on a Canadian importer and a Canadian exporter doing business with the foreign country.
   a. Officials in Ottawa announce that they are comfortable with a rising deutsche mark relative to the dollar.
   b. British monetary authorities announce that they feel the pound has been driven too high by currency speculators relative to the U.S. dollar.
   c. The Argentinian government announces that it will devalue the peso in an effort to improve its economy.
   d. The Brazilian government announces that it will print billions of new cruzeiros and inject them into the economy, in an effort to reduce the country's 40 percent unemployment rate.

10. We discussed five international capital market relationships: relative PPP, IRP, UFR, UIP, and the international Fisher effect. Which of these would you expect to hold most closely? Which do you think would be most likely to be violated?

Questions and Problems

Basic
(Questions 1–13)

1. **Using Exchange Rates**   Take a look back at Figure 21.1 to answer the following questions:
   a. If you have $100, how many euros can you get?
   b. How much is one euro worth?
   c. If you have five million euros, how many dollars do you have?
   d. Which is worth more, an Indian Rupee or a Hong Kong dollar?
   e. Which is worth more, a Mexican peso or a Japanese yen?
   f. How many Swiss francs can you get for a euro? What do you call this rate?
   g. Per unit, what is the most valuable currency of those listed? The least valuable?

2. **Using the Cross-Rate**   Use the information in Figure 21.1 to answer the following questions:
   a. Which would you rather have, $100 or £100? Why?
   b. Which would you rather have, EUR 100 or £100? Why?

Basic
(continued)

c. What is the cross-rate for euros in terms of British pounds? For British pounds in terms of euros?

3. **Forward Exchange Rates**   Use the information in Figure 21.1 to answer the following questions:

    a. What is the six-month forward rate for the Japanese yen in yen per Canadian dollar? Is the yen selling at a premium or a discount? Explain.

    b. What is the three-month forward rate for euros in Canadian dollars per euro? Is the dollar selling at a premium or a discount? Explain.

    c. What do you think will happen to the value of the dollar relative to the yen and the euro, based on the information in the figure? Explain.

4. **Using Spot and Forward Exchange Rates**   Suppose the spot exchange rate for the U.S. dollar is $0.85 and the six-month forward rate is $0.82.

    a. Which is worth more, a U.S. dollar or a Canadian dollar?

    b. Assuming absolute PPP holds, what is the cost in the United States of an Elkhead beer if the price in Canada is Can$2.19? Why might the beer actually sell at a different price in the United States?

    c. Is the Canadian dollar selling at a premium or a discount relative to the U.S. dollar?

    d. Which currency is expected to appreciate in value?

    e. Which country do you think has higher interest rates—the United States or Canada? Explain.

5. **Cross-Rates and Arbitrage**   Suppose the Japanese yen exchange rate is ¥107 = $1, and the British pound exchange rate is £1 =$2.29.

    a. What is the cross-rate in terms of yen per pound?

    b. Suppose the cross-rate is ¥250 = £1. Is there an arbitrage opportunity here? If there is, explain how to take advantage of the mispricing.

6. **Interest Rate Parity**   Use Figure 21.1 to answer the following questions. Suppose interest rate parity holds, and the current six-month risk-free rate in Canada is 4 percent. What must the six-month risk-free rate be in the European Union? In Japan? In Britain?

7. **Interest Rates and Arbitrage**   The treasurer of a major Canadian firm has $30 million to invest for three months. The annual interest rate in Canada is .45 percent per month. The interest rate in Great Britain is .60 percent per month. The spot exchange rate is £.56, and the three-month forward rate is £0.59. Ignoring transactions costs, in which country would the treasurer want to invest the company's funds? Why?

8. **Inflation and Exchange Rates**   Suppose the current exchange rate for the euro is EUR 0.70. The expected exchange rate in three years is EUR 0.73. What is the difference in the annual inflation rates for Canada and Europe over this period? Assume that the anticipated rate is constant for both countries. What relationship are you relying on in answering?

9. **Exchange Rate Risk**   Suppose your company imports high-tech computer motherboards from Japan. The exchange rate is given in Figure 21.1. You have just placed an order for 30,000 motherboards at a cost to you of 113,000 Japanese yen each. You will pay for the shipment when it arrives in 90 days. You can sell the motherboards for $1500 each. Calculate your profit if the exchange rate goes up or down by 10 percent over the next 90 days. What is the break-even exchange rate? What percentage rise or fall does this represent in terms of the Japanese yen versus the Canadian dollar?

10. **Exchange Rates and Arbitrage**   Suppose the spot and six-month forward rates on the Norwegian Krone are Kr 5.50 and Kr 5.57, respectively. The annual risk-free rate in Canada is 5 percent, and the annual risk-free rate in Norway is 4 percent.

    a. Is there an arbitrage opportunity here? If so, how would you exploit it?

    b. What must the six-month forward rate be to prevent arbitrage?

11. **The International Fisher Effect**   You observe that the inflation rate in the United States is 3.5 percent per year and that T-bills currently yield 4.1 percent annually. What do you estimate the inflation rate to be in:

    a. The Netherlands, if short-term Dutch government securities yield 5 percent per year?

    b. Canada, if short-term Canadian government securities yield 7 percent per year?

    c. France, if short-term French government securities yield 10 percent per year?

12. **Spot versus Forward Rates**   Suppose the spot and three-month forward rates for the yen are ¥89 and ¥85, respectively.

    a. Is the yen expected to get stronger or weaker?

    b. What would you estimate is the difference between the inflation rates of Canada and Japan?

13. **Expected Spot Rates**   Suppose the spot exchange rate for the Hungarian forint is HUF 215. Interest rates in Canada are 3.6 percent per year. They are triple that in Hungary. What do you predict the exchange rate will be in one year? In two years? In five years? What relationship are you using?

Intermediate (Questions 14–15)

14. **Capital Budgeting** You are evaluating a proposed expansion of an existing subsidiary located in Switzerland. The cost of the expansion would be SF 27.0 million. The cash flows from the project would be SF 7.5 million per year for the next five years. The dollar required return is 13 percent per year, and the current exchange rate is SF 1.15. The going rate on Eurodollars is 8.5 percent per year. It is 7.2 percent per year on Euroswiss.

 a. What do you project will happen to exchange rates over the next four years?

 b. Based on your answer in (a), convert the projected franc flows into dollar flows and calculate the NPV.

 c. What is the required return on franc flows? Based on your answer, calculate the NPV in francs and then convert to dollars.

15. **Big Mac Index** Suppose that a Big Mac in the United Kingdom costs 3.50 British pounds. The same Big Mac in the United States costs US$3.50. Using Figure 21.1, is the British pound overvalued or undervalued? By how much? What exchange would be required to make the two prices equal?

Advanced (Question 16)

16. **Interest Rate Parity** A U.S. corporation, Magic Potion, Inc., intends to import $1,000,000 worth of cosmetic products from France and will make the payment in euros three months from now. The foreign exchange spot rate of the euro to the U.S. dollar is EUR 0.98/$. Annual interest rates for the U.S. dollar and the euro are 4 percent and 7 percent respectively.

 a. What is the three-month forward rate for the euro if interest rate parity holds?

 b. How can Magic Potion use currency trading to hedge against the foreign exchange risk associated with the purchase?

MINI CASE

From our discussion of the Fisher effect in Chapter 7, we know that the actual relationship between a nominal rate, R, a real rate, r, and an inflation rate, h, can be written as:

$$1 + r = (1 + R)/(1 + h)$$

 This is the *domestic* Fisher effect.

 a) What is the nonapproximate form of the international Fisher effect?

 b) Based on your answer in (a), what is the exact form for UIP? (Hint: Recall the exact form of IRP and use UFR.)

 c) What is the exact form for relative PPP? (Hint: Combine your previous two answers.)

 d) Recalculate the NPV for the Kihlstrom drill bit project (discussed in Section 21.5) using the exact forms for UIP and the international Fisher effect. Verify that you get precisely the same answer either way.

 e) Conduct a sensitivity analysis on your answer in part (d). Consider a 8.7 percent variation in the major variables (risk-free rates in each country, initial project cost, cash flows, required project return rate).

 f) Discuss how you would attempt to reduce the risk of variation associated with each variable in part (e).

Internet Application Questions

The following web-links are related to equities that trade on foreign exchanges in the form of depository receipts. Trading on foreign exchanges allows the issuing firm to raise capital internationally, and benefit from increased scrutiny by foreign analysts.

1. What are American Depository Receipts (ADRs)? How are ADRs created? Go to the following website operated by JP Morgan, the company that pioneered the use of ADRs in 1927. Look under Overview at www.adr.com/. What are the advantages of investing in ADRs vis-à-vis the underlying foreign stock?

2. The Bank of New York is an important player in sponsoring ADRs. Go to its website at www.adrbny.com and search for Hitachi (CUSIP: 433578507) ADR. What is the price of Hitachi ADR on the NYSE? Explain the meaning of RATIO on the ADR listings page. If 1USD = ¥100, what do you think is the price of Hitachi's shares on the Tokyo Stock Exchange (in ¥)? You can find Hitachi's share prices on the TSE's website at www.tse.or.jp/english/index.shtml.

3. Go to the following website operated by Citibank, another big player in the ADR creation market: wwss.citissb.com/adr/www/adr_info/index.htm. Explain how the dividend payment process works for ADRs. As a Canadian investor, do you face more foreign currency risk when you buy Hitachi's ADRs on the NYSE, or Hitachi's shares on the Tokyo Stock Exchange?

4. As mentioned earlier in the chapter, one of the more famous examples of a violation of absolute purchasing power parity is the Big Mac index calculated by *The Economist*. This index calculates the dollar price of a McDonald's Big Mac in different countries. You can find the Big Mac index at www.economist.com/markets/bigmac/index.cfm. Using the most recent index,

which currency is most overvalued compared to the U.S. dollar? Which currency is most undervalued compared to the U.S. dollar? Is the Canadian dollar over or undervalued? Why is the price of a Big Mac not the same in every country?

5. Go to www.marketvector.com and find the exchange rates section. Is the Canadian dollar expected to appreciate or depreciate compared to the U.S. dollar over the next six months? What is the difference in the annual inflation rates for the United States and Canada over this period? Assume that the anticipated rate is constant for both countries. What relationship are you relying on in your answers?

6. Go to the *Financial Times* site at www.ft.com, and find the currency section under the "Markets" link. Find the current exchange rate between the U.S. dollar and the euro. You can also locate interest rate information at this site. Find the Canadian dollar and euro interest rates. What must the one year forward rate be to prevent arbitrage? What principle are you relying on in your answer?

7. Nestle has American Depository Receipts listed on the Nasdaq. Many ADRs listed on U.S. exchanges are for fractional shares. In the case of Nestle, four ADRs are equal to one registered share. Find the information for Nestle by logging on to the S&P Market Insights website and using the ticker symbol "3NSRGY."

   a. Click on the "Mthly. Adj. Prices" link and find Nestle's closing price for May 2003. Assume the exchange rate on that day was $/SFr 0.75 and Nestle shares traded for SFr 285. Is there an arbitrage opportunity available? If so, how would you take advantage of it?

   b. What exchange rate is necessary to eliminate the arbitrage opportunity available in part (*a*)?

Suggested Readings

The following is a good book on the modern theory of international markets:

Shapiro, A. C. *Multinational Financial Management*. 8th ed. New York: John Wiley & Sons, Inc., 2006.

These two articles describe budgeting for international projects:

Lessard, D. R. "Evaluating Foreign Projects: An Adjusted Present Value Approach." In *International Financial Management*, ed. D. R. Lessard. New York: Warren, Gorham & Lamont, 1979.
Shapiro, A. S. "Capital Budgeting for the Multinational Corporation." *Financial Management* 7 (Spring 1978).

For more information on the relationship between the forward rate and the spot rate, see:

Levich, Richard M. "Is the Foreign Exchange Market Efficient?" *Oxford Review of Economic Policy* 5, no. 3 (1989).

A good discussion of the risks facing Canadian exporters is at the Export Development Canada's website: *www.edc.ca.*

CHAPTER 22

Leasing

Computers and communications equipment are the most popular kinds of equipment for leasing in Canada. Next come aircraft leases—big ticket items ranging up to $200 million for a Boeing 787 Dream Liner. As we will see in this chapter, leasing is just another form of financing for businesses and, for reasons we will discuss, the computer industry is particularly suited to leasing rather than buying.

Leasing is a way businesses finance plant, property, and equipment. Just about any asset that can be purchased can be leased, and there are many good reasons for leasing. For example, when we take vacations or business trips, renting a car for a few days is a convenient thing to do. After all, buying a car and selling it a week later would be a great nuisance. According to the Canadian Finance & Leasing Association, the industry had over $103 billion of financing in place in 2006. We discuss additional reasons for leasing in the sections that follow.

www.aircanada.ca
www.cfla-acfl.ca

ALTHOUGH CORPORATIONS do both short-term leasing and long-term leasing, this chapter is primarily concerned with long-term leasing, where long-term typically means more than five years. As we discuss in greater detail shortly, leasing an asset on a long-term basis is much like borrowing the needed funds and simply buying the asset. Thus, long-term leasing is a form of financing much like long-term debt. When is leasing preferable to long-term borrowing? This is the question we seek to answer in this chapter.[1]

22.1

lessee
The user of an asset in a leasing agreement. Lessee makes payments to lessor.

lessor
The owner of an asset in a leasing agreement. Lessor receives payments from the lessee.

LEASES AND LEASE TYPES

A lease is a contractual agreement between two parties: the lessee and the lessor. The **lessee** is the user of the equipment; the **lessor** is the owner. Typically, a company first decides on the asset that it needs. Then it must decide how to finance the asset. If the firm decides to lease, it then negotiates a lease contract with a lessor for use of that asset. The lease agreement establishes that the lessee has the right to use the asset and, in return, must make periodic payments to the lessor, the owner of the asset. The lessor is usually either the asset's manufacturer or an independent leasing company. If the lessor is an independent leasing company, it must buy the asset from a manufacturer. The lessor then delivers the asset to the lessee, and the lease goes into effect. Some

---

1 Our discussion of lease valuation is drawn, in part, from Chapter 21 of S.A. Ross, R.W. Westerfield, J.F. Jaffe, and G.S. Roberts, *Corporate Finance*, 4th Canadian ed. (Whitby, Ontario: McGraw-Hill Ryerson, 2005), which contains a more comprehensive treatment and discusses some subtle, but important, issues not covered here.

lessors play both roles. G.E. Capital, for example, leases GE's own products and also leases aircraft to Air Canada.

Leasing versus Buying

As far as the lessee is concerned, it is the use of the asset that is important, not necessarily who has title to it. One way to obtain the use of an asset is to lease it. Another way is obtain outside financing and buy it. Thus, the decision to lease or buy amounts to a comparison of alternative financing arrangements for the use of an asset.

You may think of leasing analysis as an extension of the capital budgeting decision. The lessee has already done capital budgeting analysis and found that buying the asset has a positive NPV. Leasing analysis investigates whether acquiring the use of the asset through leasing is better still.

Figure 22.1 compares leasing and buying. The lessee, Canadian Enterprises, might be a hospital, a law firm, or any other firm that uses computers. The lessor is an independent leasing company that purchased the computer from a manufacturer such as Hewlett-Packard Company (HP). Leases of this type, where the leasing company purchases the asset from the manufacturer, are called *direct leases*. Of course, HP might choose to lease its own computers, and many companies have set up wholly owned subsidiaries called *captive finance companies* to lease out their products.[2]

As shown in Figure 22.1, Canadian Enterprises ends up using the asset either way. The key difference is that in the case of buying, Canadian Enterprises arranges the financing, purchases the asset, and holds title to the asset. In the case of leasing, the leasing company arranges the financing, purchases the asset, and holds title to it.

FIGURE 22.1

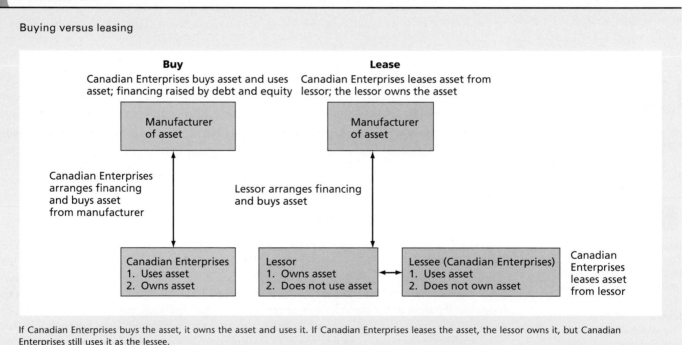

Buying versus leasing

If Canadian Enterprises buys the asset, it owns the asset and uses it. If Canadian Enterprises leases the asset, the lessor owns it, but Canadian Enterprises still uses it as the lessee.

---

2 Captive finance companies (or subsidiaries) may do a number of other things, such as purchase the parent company's accounts receivable. General Motors Acceptance Corporation (GMAC) and GE Capital are examples of captive finance companies. We discuss captive finance companies in Chapter 20.

Operating Leases

operating lease
Usually a shorter-term lease where the lessor is responsible for insurance, taxes, and upkeep. Often cancellable on short notice.

Years ago, a lease where the lessee received an equipment operator along with the equipment was called an **operating lease.** Today, an operating lease (or service lease) is difficult to define precisely, but this form of leasing has several important characteristics.

First, with an operating lease, the payments received by the lessor are usually not enough to fully recover the cost of the asset. A primary reason is that operating leases are often relatively short-term. In such cases, the life of the lease can be much less than the economic life of the asset. For example, if you lease a car for two years, the car has a substantial residual value at the end of the lease, and the lease payments you make would pay off only a fraction of the original cost of the car.

A second characteristic is that an operating lease frequently requires that the lessor maintain the asset. The lessor is also responsible for any taxes or insurance. Of course, these costs would be passed on, at least in part to the lessee in the form of higher lease payments.

The third, and perhaps most interesting, feature of an operating lease is the cancellation option. This option gives the lessee the right to cancel the lease contract before the expiration date. If the option to cancel is exercised, the lessee returns the equipment to the lessor and ceases to make payments. The value of a cancellation clause depends on whether technological and/or economic conditions are likely to make the value of the asset to the lessee less than the value of the future lease payments under the lease.

To leasing practitioners, these three characteristics constitute an operating lease. However, as we see shortly, accountants use the term in a somewhat different way.

Financial Leases

financial lease
Typically, a longer-term, fully amortized lease under which the lessee is responsible for upkeep. Usually not cancellable without penalty.

Financial leases are the other major type of lease. In contrast to an operating lease, the payments made under a financial lease are usually sufficient to cover fully the lessor's cost of purchasing the asset and pay the lessor a return on the investment. For this reason, a financial lease is sometimes said to be a fully amortized or full-payout lease whereas an operating lease is said to be partially amortized.

For both operating and financial leases, formal legal ownership of the leased asset resides with the lessor. However, in terms of economic function, we see that the lessee enjoys the risk/reward of ownership in a financial lease. Operating leases, on the other hand, are more like a rental agreement.

With a financial lease, the lessee (not the lessor) is usually responsible for insurance, maintenance, and taxes. Importantly, a financial lease generally cannot be cancelled, at least not without a significant penalty. In other words, the lessee must make the lease payments or face possible legal action.

The characteristics of a financial lease, particularly the fact it is fully amortized, make it very similar to debt financing, so the name is a sensible one. Three special types of financial leases are of particular interest, *tax-oriented leases, sale and leaseback* agreements and *leveraged leases*. We consider these next.

tax-oriented lease
A financial lease in which the lessor is the owner for tax purposes. Also called a true lease or a tax lease.

TAX-ORIENTED LEASES   A lease in which the lessor is the owner of the leased asset for tax purposes is called a **tax-oriented lease.** Such leases are also called tax leases or true leases. In contrast, a *conditional sales agreement lease* is not a true lease. Here, the "lessee" is the owner for tax purposes. Conditional sales agreement leases are really just secured loans. The financial leases we discuss in this chapter are all tax leases.

Tax-oriented leases make the most sense when the lessee is not in a position to use tax credits or depreciation deductions that come with owning the asset. By arranging for someone else to hold title, a tax lease passes these benefits on. The lessee can benefit because the lessor may return a portion of the tax benefits to the lessee in the form of lower lease costs.

SALE AND LEASEBACK AGREEMENTS   A sale and leaseback occurs when a company sells an asset it owns to another firm and immediately leases it back. In a sale and leaseback, two things happen:

1. The lessee receives cash from the sale of the asset.

2. The lessee continues to use the asset.

sale and leaseback
A financial lease in which the lessee sells an asset to the lessor and then leases it back.

An example of a **sale and leaseback** occurred in January 1989 when Air Canada arranged a sale and leaseback of four Boeing 767-200ER aircraft. The purchaser was a Canadian financial institution and the transaction proceeds were $260 million. Further examples include Canadian universities and hospitals that set up sale-leaseback deals for library books and medical equipment. With a sale and leaseback, the lessee may have the option of repurchasing the leased assets at the end of the lease. Tax changes have restricted sale-leasebacks in recent years.

leveraged lease
A financial lease where the lessor borrows a substantial fraction of the cost of the leased asset.

LEVERAGED LEASES   A **leveraged lease** is a tax-oriented lease involving three parties: a lessee, a lessor, and a lender. A typical arrangement might go as follows:

1. The lessee selects the asset, gets the value of using the asset, and makes the periodic lease payments.

2. The lessor usually puts up no more than 40 to 50 percent of the financing, is entitled to the lease payments, has title to the asset, and pays interest to the lenders.

3. The lenders supply the remaining financing and receive interest payments. Thus, the arrangement on the right side of Figure 22.1 would be a leveraged lease if the bulk of the financing were supplied by creditors.

The lenders in a leveraged lease typically use a non-recourse loan. This means the lender cannot turn to the lessor in case of a default. However, the lender is protected in two ways:

1. The lender has a first lien on the asset.

2. The lender may actually receive the lease payments from the lessee. The lender deducts the principal and interest due, and forwards whatever is left to the lessor.

CONCEPT QUESTIONS

1. What are the specific differences between an operating lease and a financial lease?

2. What is a tax-oriented lease?

3. What is a sale and leaseback agreement?

22.2   ACCOUNTING AND LEASING

www.cica.ca

Before 1979, leasing was frequently called *off balance sheet financing*. As the name implies, a firm could arrange to use an asset through a lease and not disclose the existence of the lease contract on the balance sheet. Lessees only had to report information on leasing activity in the footnotes of their financial statements.

Of course, this meant firms could acquire the use of a substantial number of assets and incur a substantial long-term financial commitment through financial leases while not disclosing the impact of these arrangements in their financial statements. Operating leases, being cancellable at little or no penalty, do not involve a firm financial commitment. So operating leases did not generate much concern about complete disclosure. As a result, the accounting profession wanted to distinguish clearly between operating and financial leases to ensure that the impact of financial leases was included in the financial statements.

In 1979, the Canadian Institute of Chartered Accountants implemented new rules for lease accounting (CICA 3065). The basic idea is that all financial leases (called *capital leases* in CICA 3065) must be capitalized. This requirement means that the present value of the lease payments must be calculated and reported along with debt and other liabilities on the right side of the lessee's balance sheet.[3] The same amount must be shown as an asset on the left side of the

---

3 The income statement is also affected. The asset created is amortized over the lease life and reported income is adjusted downward.

balance sheet. Operating leases are not disclosed on the balance sheet. We discuss exactly what constitutes a financial or operating lease for accounting purposes next.

The accounting implications of CICA 3065 are illustrated in Table 22.1. Imagine a firm that has $100,000 in assets and no debt, implying that the equity is also $100,000. The firm needs a truck that costs $100,000 (it's a big truck), that it can lease or buy. The top of the table shows the balance sheet assuming that the firm borrows the money and buys the truck.

If the firm leases the truck, one of two things happen: If the lease is an operating lease, the balance sheet looks like the one in the center of the table. In this case, neither the asset (the truck) nor the liability (the lease payments) appear. If the lease is a capital (financial) lease, the balance sheet would look like the one at the bottom of the table, where the truck is shown as an asset and the present value of the lease payments is shown as a liability.

As we discussed earlier, it is difficult, if not impossible, to give a precise definition of what constitutes a financial or operating lease. For accounting purposes, a lease is declared to be a financial lease, and must therefore be disclosed, if at least one of the following criteria is met:

1. The lease transfers ownership of the property to the lessee by the end of the term of the lease.
2. The lessee has an option to purchase the asset at a price below fair market value (bargain purchase price option) when the lease expires.
3. The lease term is 75 percent or more of the estimated economic life of the asset.
4. The present value of the lease payments is at least 90 percent of the fair market value of the asset at the start of the lease.

If one or more of the four criteria is met, the lease is a capital lease; otherwise, it is an operating lease for accounting purposes.

A firm might be tempted to try and cook the books by taking advantage of the somewhat arbitrary distinction between operating leases and capital leases. Suppose a trucking firm wants to lease the $100,000 truck in our example in Table 22.1. The truck is expected to last for 15 years. A (perhaps unethical) financial manager could try to negotiate a lease contract for 10 years with lease payments having a present value of $89,000. These terms would get around criteria 3 and 4. If criteria 1 and 2 are similarly circumvented, the arrangement would be an operating lease and would not show up on the balance sheet.

There are several alleged benefits to hiding financial leases. One of the advantages to keeping leases off the balance sheet has to do with fooling financial analysts, creditors, and investors. The idea is that if leases are not on the balance sheet, they would not be noticed.

Financial managers who devote substantial effort to keeping leases off the balance sheet are probably wasting time. Of course, if leases are not on the balance sheet, traditional measures of

TABLE 22.1

Leasing and the balance sheet

1. **Initial balance sheet (the company buys a $100,000 truck with debt)**

Truck	$100,000	Debt	$100,000
Other assets	100,000	Equity	100,000
Total assets	$200,000	Total debt plus equity	$200,000

2. **Operating lease (the company has an operating lease for the truck)**

Truck	$ 0	Debt	$ 0
Other assets	100,000	Equity	100,000
Total assets	$100,000	Total debt plus equity	$100,000

3. **Capital (financial) lease (the company has a capital lease for the truck)**

Assets under capital lease	$100,000	Obligations under capital lease	$100,000
Other assets	100,000	Equity	100,000
Total assets	$200,000	Total debt plus equity	$200,000

In the first case, a $100,000 truck is purchased with debt. In the second case, an operating lease is used; no balance sheet entries are created. In the third case, a capital (financial) lease is used; the lease payments are capitalized as a liability, and the leased truck appears as an asset.

financial leverage, such as the ratio of total debt to total assets, understate the true degree of financial leverage. As a consequence, the balance sheet appears stronger than it really is, but it seems unlikely that this type of manipulation could mislead many people.

Nonetheless, firms do try to hide leases. For example, a controversial type of lease, known as a synthetic lease, has come to be widely used. The details are a little complex; in essence, a company arranges for a separate entity to purchase an asset (often a building) and then lease that asset back to the company. If the deal is properly structured, the company is considered the owner of the property for tax purposes, but for accounting purposes, the transaction is classified as an operating lease. Faced with investor criticism of this practice, some firms, such as Krispy Kreme Doughnuts, have announced that they will no longer engage in synthetic leasing.

Having said all of this, there are some reasons why a firm might reasonably try to come in under the radar of the accounting lease test. For example, if a firm's managers are told that capital spending is frozen, an operating lease may still be an option. Alternatively, a firm might face a restriction on additional borrowing (a loan covenant, perhaps). A financial lease counts as debt, but an operating lease does not.

CONCEPT QUESTIONS

1. For accounting purposes, what constitutes a capital lease?

2. How are capital leases reported?

www.cra-arc.gc.ca

TAXES, CANADA REVENUE AGENCY (CRA), AND LEASES

The lessee can deduct lease payments for income tax purposes if the lease is qualified by Canada Revenue Agency (CRA). The tax shields associated with lease payments are critical to the economic viability of a lease, so CRA guidelines are an important consideration. Tax rules on leasing have changed considerably in the last few years and further changes may occur. The discussion that follows gives you a good idea of rules in force at the time of writing.

Essentially, CRA requires that a lease be primarily for business purposes and not merely for tax avoidance. In particular, CRA is on the lookout for leases that are really conditional sales agreements in disguise. The reason is that, in a lease, the lessee gets a tax deduction on the full lease payment. In a conditional sales agreement, only the interest portion of the payment is deductible. When CRA detects one or more of the following, it disallows the lease:

1. The lessee automatically acquires title to the property after payment of a specified amount in the form of rentals.

2. The lessee is required to buy the property from the lessor during or at the termination of the lease.

3. The lessee has the right during or at the expiration of the lease to acquire the property at a price less than fair market value.

These rules also apply to sale-leaseback agreements. CRA auditors rule that a sale-leaseback is really a secured loan if they find one of the three terms in the sale-leaseback agreement.

Once leases are qualified for tax purposes, lessors still must be aware of further tax regulations limiting their use of CCA tax shields on leased assets. Current regulations allow lessors to deduct CCA from leasing income only. Any unused CCA tax shields cannot be passed along to other companies owned by the same parent holding company.

CONCEPT QUESTIONS

1. Why is CRA concerned about leasing?

2. What are some of the standards CRA uses in evaluating a lease?

THE CASH FLOWS FROM LEASING

To begin our analysis of the leasing decision, we need to identify the relevant cash flows. The first part of this section illustrates how this is done. A key point, and one to watch for, is that taxes are a very important consideration in a lease analysis.

The Incremental Cash Flows

Consider the business decision facing TransCanada Distributors, a distribution firm that runs a fleet of company cars for its sales staff. Business has been expanding and the firm needs 50 additional cars to provide basic transportation in support of sales. The type of car required can be purchased wholesale for $10,000. TransCanada has determined that each car can be expected to generate an additional $6,000 per year in added sales for the next five years.

TransCanada has a corporate tax rate (combined federal and provincial) of 40 percent. The cars would qualify for a CCA rate of 40 percent (as rental cars) and, due to the hard-driving habits of TransCanada's sales staff, the cars would have no residual value after five years. Using all this information, a TransCanada financial analyst determines that acquiring the 50 cars is a capital budgeting decision with a positive NPV. At this point, TransCanada receives an offer from Financial Leasing company to lease the cars to TransCanada for lease payments of $2,500 per year for each car over the five-year period. Lease payments are made at the beginning of the year. With the lease, TransCanada would remain responsible for maintenance, insurance, and operating expenses.

Susan Smart has been asked to compare the direct incremental cash flows from leasing the cars to the cash flows associated with buying them. The first thing she realizes is that, because TransCanada has the cars either way, the $6,000 saving is realized whether the cars are leased or purchased. Thus, this cost saving, and any other operating costs or revenues, can be ignored in the analysis because they are not incremental.

On reflection, Smart concludes that there are only three important cash flow differences between leasing and buying:[4]

1. If the cars are leased, TransCanada must make a lease payment of $2,500 each year. However, lease payments are fully tax deductible, so there is a tax shield of $1,000 on each lease payment. The aftertax lease payment is $2,500 − $1,000 = $1,500. This is a cost of leasing instead of buying.[5]

2. If the cars are leased, TransCanada does not own them and cannot depreciate them for tax purposes.

Table 22.2 shows the CCA and UCC schedule for one car.[6] Notice that CCRA's half-year rule means that the eligible UCC is only $5,000 when the car is put in use in Year 0. Table 22.2 also shows the tax shield on CCA for each year. For example, in Year 0, the tax shield is $2,000 × .40 = $800. The tax shields for years 1–4 are calculated in the same way. In Year 5, the car is scrapped for a zero salvage value. We assume that the asset pool is closed at this time, so there is a tax shield on the terminal loss of $1,037 × .40 = $415.[7] All these tax shields are lost to TransCanada if it leases so they are a cost of leasing.

3. If the cars are leased, TransCanada does not have to spend $10,000 apiece today to buy them. This is a benefit to leasing.

---

4 There is a fourth consequence that we do not discuss here. If the car has a non-trivial salvage value and we lease, we give up that salvage value. This is another cost of leasing instead of buying.

5 Lease payments are made at the beginning of the year as shown in Table 22.3. Firms pay taxes later but our analysis ignores this difference for simplicity.

6 To keep the lease and purchase alternatives comparable, we assume here that TransCanada buys the cars at the beginning of period 0.

7 If the pool were continued, the remaining UCC of $1,037 would be depreciated to infinity as explained in Chapter 2.

TABLE 22.2

Tax shield on CCA for car

Year	UCC	CCA	Tax Shields
0	$5,000	$2,000	$ 800
1	8,000	3,200	1,280
2	4,800	1,920	768
3	2,880	1,152	461
4	1,728	691	276
5	1,037		415

TABLE 22.3

Incremental cash flows for TransCanada from leasing one car instead of buying

	Year					
	0	1	2	3	4	5
Investment	$10,000					
Lease payment	–2,500	–$ 2,500	–$2,500	–$2,500	$2,500	
Payment shield	1,000	1,000	1,000	1,000	1,000	
Forgone tax shield	–800	–1,280	–768	–461	–276	–$415
Total cash flow	$ 7,700	–$ 2,780	–$2,268	–$1,961	–$1,776	–$415

The cash flows from leasing instead of buying are summarized in Table 22.3. Notice that the cost of the car shows up with a positive sign in Year 0. This is a reflection of the fact that TransCanada saves $10,000 by leasing instead of buying.

A NOTE ON TAXES   Susan Smart has assumed that TransCanada can use the tax benefits of the CCA allowances and the lease payments. This may not always be the case. If TransCanada were losing money, it would not pay taxes and the tax shelters would be worthless (unless they could be shifted to someone else). As we mentioned, this is one circumstance under which leasing may make a great deal of sense. If this were the case, the relevant lines in Table 22.3 would have to be changed to reflect a zero tax rate. We return to this point later.

> **CONCEPT QUESTIONS**
>
> **1.** What are the cash flow consequences of leasing instead of buying?
>
> **2.** Explain why the $10,000 in Table 22.3 is a positive number.

LEASE OR BUY?

From our discussion thus far, Smart's analysis comes down to this: If TransCanada Distributors leases instead of buying, it saves $10,000 today because it avoids having to pay for the car, but it must give up the cash outflows detailed in Table 22.3 in exchange. We now must decide whether getting $10,000 today and then paying back these cash flows is a good idea.

A Preliminary Analysis

Suppose TransCanada were to borrow $10,000 today and promise to make aftertax payments of the cash flows shown in Table 22.3 over the next five years. This is essentially what the firm does when it leases instead of buying. What interest rate would TransCanada be paying on this "loan"? Going back to Chapter 9, we need to find the unknown rate that solves the following equation:

$$0 = 7,700 - \frac{2,780}{1+i} - \frac{2,268}{(1+i)^2} - \frac{1,961}{(1+i)^3} - \frac{1,776}{(1+i)^4} - \frac{415}{(1+i)^5}$$

The equation may be solved by trial and error using Excel 4.0 or any compatible spreadsheet to show that the discount rate is 7.8 percent aftertax.

The cash flows of our hypothetical loan are identical to the cash flows from leasing instead of borrowing, and what we have illustrated is that when TransCanada leases the car, it effectively arranges financing at an aftertax rate of 7.8 percent. Whether this is a good deal or not depends on what rate TransCanada would pay if it simply borrowed the money. For example, suppose the firm can arrange a five-year loan with its bank at a rate of 11 percent. Should TransCanada sign the lease or should it go with the bank?

Because TransCanada is in a 40 percent tax bracket, the aftertax interest rate would be 11 × (1 − .40) = 6.6 percent. This is less than the 7.8 percent implicit aftertax rate on the lease. In this particular case, TransCanada is better off borrowing the money because it gets a better rate.

We have seen that TransCanada should buy instead of lease. The steps in our analysis can be summarized as follows:

1. Calculate the incremental aftertax cash flows from leasing instead of borrowing.
2. Use these cash flows to calculate the implicit aftertax interest rate on the lease.
3. Compare this rate to the company's aftertax borrowing cost and choose the cheaper source of financing.

The most important thing about our discussion thus far is that in evaluating a lease, the relevant rate for the comparison is the company's aftertax borrowing rate. The fundamental reason is that the alternative to leasing is long-term borrowing, so the aftertax borrowing rate on such borrowing is the relevant benchmark.

THREE POTENTIAL PITFALLS There are three potential problems with the implicit rate on the lease that we calculated: First, this rate can be interpreted as the internal rate of return (IRR) on the decision to lease instead of buy, but doing so can be confusing. To see why, notice that the IRR from leasing is 7.8 percent, which is greater than TransCanada's aftertax borrowing cost of 6.6 percent. Normally, the higher the IRR the better, but we decided that leasing was a bad idea here. The reason is that the cash flows are not conventional; the first cash flow is positive and the rest are negative, which is just the opposite of the conventional case (see Chapter 9 for a discussion). With this cash flow pattern, the IRR represents the rate we pay, not the rate we earn, so the lower the IRR the better.

A second, and related, potential pitfall is that we calculated the advantage of leasing instead of borrowing. We could have done just the opposite and come up with the advantage to borrowing instead of leasing. If we did this, the cash flows would be the same, but the signs would be reversed. The IRR would be the same. Now, however, the cash flows are conventional, so we interpret the 7.8 percent IRR as saying that borrowing is better.

The third potential problem is that our implicit rate is based on the net cash flows of leasing instead of borrowing. There is another rate that is sometimes calculated that is just based on the lease payments. If we wanted to, we could note that the lease provides $10,000 in financing and requires five payments of $2,500 each. It is tempting to determine an implicit rate based on these numbers, but the resulting rate is not meaningful for making lease versus buy decisions because it ignores the CCA tax shields. It should not be confused with the implicit return on leasing instead of borrowing and buying.

Perhaps because of these potential confusions, the IRR approach we have outlined thus far is not as widely used as an NPV-based approach that we describe next.

NPV Analysis

Now that we know the relevant rate for evaluating a lease versus buy decision is the firm's aftertax borrowing cost, an NPV analysis is straightforward. We simply discount the cash flows in Table 22.3 back to the present at TransCanada's borrowing rate of 6.6 percent as follows:

$$NPV = 7,700 - \frac{2,780}{(1.066)} - \frac{2,268}{(1.066)^2} - \frac{1,961}{(1.066)^3} - \frac{1,776}{(1.066)^4} - \frac{415}{(1.066)^5} = -\$199$$

net advantage to leasing (NAL)
The NPV of the decision to lease an asset instead of buying it.

The NPV from leasing instead of buying is −$199, verifying our earlier conclusion that leasing is a bad idea. Once again, notice the signs of the cash flows; the first is positive, the rest are negative. The NPV that we have computed here is often called the **net advantage to leasing** and abbreviated NAL. Surveys indicate that the NAL approach is the most popular means of lease analysis in the business world.

A Misconception

In our lease versus buy analysis, it looks as if we ignored the fact that if TransCanada borrows $10,000 to buy the car, it has to repay the money with interest. In fact, we reasoned that if TransCanada leased the car, it would be better off by $10,000 today because it wouldn't have to pay for the car. It is tempting to argue that if TransCanada borrowed the money, it wouldn't have to come up with the $10,000. Instead, the firm would make a series of principal and interest payments over the next five years. This observation is true, but not particularly relevant. The reason is that if TransCanada borrows $10,000 at an aftertax cost of 6.6 percent, the present value of the aftertax loan payments is simply $10,000, no matter what the repayment schedule is (assuming that the loan is fully amortized). Thus, we could write down the aftertax loan repayments and work with these, but it would just be extra work for no gain. (See Problem 10 at the end of the chapter for an example.)

EXAMPLE 22.1: Lease Evaluation

In our TransCanada example, suppose the firm is able to negotiate a lease payment of $2,000 per year. What would be the NPV of the lease in this case?

Table 22.4 shows the new cash flows. You can verify that the NPV of the lease (net advantage to leasing) at 6.6 percent is now a substantial $1,126.

EXAMPLE 22.2: Lease Evaluation with a Continuing Asset Pool

In our original TransCanada example, the firm wrote off the entire book value of the cars in Year 5 as it closed the asset pool. Suppose, more generally, that TransCanada has other assets in the same class so that the unused UCC is depreciated to zero to infinity. In this case, we use the CCA tax shield formula introduced in Chapter 10 and recast our analysis in the following formula:

$$NPV_{lease} = NAL = \text{Investment} - PV \text{ (aftertax lease payments)} - PVCCATS$$

$$NAL = I - \sum_{t=0}^{4} \frac{L(1-T)}{(1+i)^t} - \frac{[T\,d\,I]}{i+d} \times \frac{[1+0.5i]}{1+i}$$

$$NAL = 10,000 - \sum_{t=0}^{4} \frac{\$2,500(1-.40)}{(1+0.066)^t} -$$

$$\frac{0.40 \times 0.40 \times \$10,000}{0.066 + 0.40} \times \frac{1.033}{1.066}$$

$$NAL = \$10,000 - \$6,627 - \$3,327$$
$$NAL = \$46$$

With the full tax shield on CCA available instead of just the write-off in Year 5, the NAL increases from the original value of –$199 to +$46.

TABLE 22.4
Revised NAL spreadsheet

		Year				
	0	1	2	3	4	5
Investment	$10,000					
Lease payment	–2,000	–$ 2,000	–$2,000	–$2,000	$2,000	
Payment shield	800	800	800	800	800	
Forgone tax shield	–800	–1,280	–768	–461	–276	–$415
Total cash flow	$ 8,000	–$ 2,480	–$1,968	–$1,661	–$1,476	–$415
NAL	$ 1,126					

CONCEPT QUESTIONS

1. What is the relevant discount rate for evaluating whether or not to lease an asset? Why?

2. Explain how to go about a lease versus buy analysis.

22.6   A LEASING PARADOX

We previously looked at the lease versus buy decision from the perspective of the potential lessee, TransCanada Distributors. We now turn things around and look at the lease from the perspective of the lessor, Financial Leasing Company. The cash flows associated with the lease from the lessor's perspective are shown in Table 22.5. First, the lessor must buy each car for $10,000, so there is a $10,000 outflow today. Next, Financial Leasing depreciates the car at a CCA rate of 40 percent to obtain the CCA tax shields shown. Finally, the lessor receives a lease payment of $2,500 each year on which it pays taxes at a 40 percent tax rate. The aftertax lease payment received is $1,500.

What we see is that the cash flows to Financial Leasing (the lessor) are exactly the opposite of the cash flows to TransCanada Distributers (the lessee). This makes perfect sense because Financial Leasing and TransCanada are the only parties to the transaction, and the lease is a zero-sum game. In other words, if the lease has a positive NPV to one party, it must have a negative NPV to the other. Financial Leasing hopes that TransCanada will do the deal because the NPV would be +$199, just what TransCanada would lose.

We seem to have a paradox. In any leasing arrangement, one party must inevitably lose (or both parties exactly break even). Why would leasing occur? We know that leasing is very important in the business world, so the next section describes some factors that we have omitted thus far from our analysis. These factors can make a lease attractive to both parties.

EXAMPLE 22.3: It's the Lease We Can Do

In our TransCanada example, a lease payment of $2,500 makes the lease unattractive to TransCanada and a lease payment of $2,000 makes the lease very attractive. What payment would leave TransCanada indifferent to leasing or not leasing?

TransCanada is indifferent when the NPV from leasing is zero. For this to happen, the present value of the cash flows from leasing instead of buying would have to be –$10,000. From our previous efforts, we know the answer is to set the payments somewhere between $2,500 and $2,000. To find the exact payment, we use our spreadsheet as shown in Table 22.6. It turns out that the NPV of leasing is zero for a payment of $2,425.

TABLE 22.5
Cash flows to the lessor

	Year					
	0	**1**	**2**	**3**	**4**	**5**
Investment	$10,000					
Lease payment	2,500	$ 2,500	$2,500	$2,500	$2,500	
Payment shield	–1,000	–1,000	–1,000	–1,000	–1,000	
Forgone tax shield	800	1,280	768	461	276	$415
Total cash flow	–$ 7,700	$ 2,780	$2,268	$1,961	$1,776	$415
NAL	$ 199					

TABLE 22.6
Indifference lease payments

	Year					
	0	**1**	**2**	**3**	**4**	**5**
Investment	$10,000					
Lease payment	–2,425	–$ 2,425	–$2,425	–$2,425	–$2,425	
Payment shield	970	970	970	970	970	
Forgone tax shield	–800	–1,280	–768	–461	–276	–$415
Total cash flow	$ 7,745	–$ 2,735	–$2,223	–$1,916	–$1,731	–$415
NAL	$ 0					

CONCEPT QUESTIONS

1. Why do we say that leasing is a zero-sum game?

2. What paradox does the first question create?

Resolving the Paradox

A lease contract is not a zero-sum game between the lessee and lessor when their effective tax rates differ. In this case, the lease can be structured so that both sides benefit. Any tax benefits from leasing can be split between the two firms by setting the lease payments at the appropriate level, and the shareholders of both firms benefit from this tax transfer arrangement. The loser is Canada Revenue Agency.

This works because a lease contract swaps two sets of tax shields. The lessor obtains the CCA tax shields due to ownership. The lessee receives the tax shield on lease payments made. In a full-payout lease, the total dollar amounts of the two sets of tax shields may be roughly the same, but the critical difference is the timing. CCA tax shields are accelerated deductions reducing the tax burden in early years. Lease payments, on the other hand, reduce taxes by the same amount in every year. As a result, the ownership tax shields often have a greater present value provided the firm is fully taxed.

The basic logic behind structuring a leasing deal makes a firm in a high tax bracket want to act as the lessor. Low tax (or untaxed) firms are lessees because they are not able to use the tax advantages of ownership, such as CCA and debt financing. These ownership tax shields are worth less to the lessee because the lessee faces a lower tax rate or may not have enough taxable income to absorb the accelerated tax shields in the early years.

Overall, less tax is paid by the lessee and lessor combined and this tax savings occurs sooner rather than later. The lessor gains on the tax side; the lessee may lose but the amount of any loss is less than the lessor gains. To make the lease attractive, the lessor must pass on some of the tax savings in the form of lower lease payments. In the end, the lessor gains by keeping part of the tax savings, the lessee gains through a lower lease payment, and CRA pays for both gains through a reduction in tax revenue.

To see how this would work in practice, recall the example of Section 22.3 and the situation of Financial Leasing. The value of the lease it proposed to TransCanada was $199. The value of the lease to TransCanada was exactly the opposite −$199. Since the lessor's gains came at the expense of the lessee, no deal could be arranged. However, if TransCanada pays no taxes and the lease payments are reduced to $2,437 from $2,500, both Financial Leasing and TransCanada find there is positive NPV in leasing.

To see this, we can rework Table 22.3 with a zero tax rate. This would be the case when TransCanada has enough alternate tax shields to reduce taxable income to zero for the foresee-able future.[8] In this case, notice that the cash flows from leasing are simply the lease payments of $2,437 because no CCA tax shield is lost and the lease payment is not tax deductible. The cash flows from leasing are thus:

	Year					
	0	1	2	3	4	5
Cost of car	$10,000					
Lease payment	−2,437	−$2,437	−$2,437	−$2,437	−$2,437	0
Cash flow	$ 7,563	−$2,437	−$2,437	−$2,437	−$2,437	0

The value of the lease for TransCanada is

$$NAL = \$7,563 - \$2,437 \times (1 - 1/1.11^4)/.11$$
$$= \$2.34$$

which is positive. Notice that the discount rate here is 11 percent because TransCanada pays no taxes; in other words, this is both the pretax and the aftertax rate.

From Table 22.7, the value of the lease to Financial Leasing can be worked out as +$32.

As a consequence of different tax rates, the lessee (TransCanada) gains $2.34, and the lessor (Financial Leasing) gains $32 CRA loses. What this example shows is that the lessor and the

---

8 Strictly speaking, the UCC of the cars would be carried on the books until the firm is able to claim CCA. However, the present value of the CCA tax shield would be low; so for the sake of simplicity, we ignore it here.

TABLE 22.7
Revised cash flows to lessor

	Year					
	0	1	2	3	4	5
Investment	−$10,000					
Lease payment	2,437	$ 2,437	$2,437	$2,437	$2,437	
Payment shield	−974	−974	−974	−974	−974	
CCA tax shield	800	1,280	768	461	276	$415
Total cash flow	−$ 7,738	$ 2,742	$2,230	$1,923	$1,739	$415
NPV lessor	$ 32					

lessee can gain if their tax rates are different. The lease contract allows the lessor to take advantage of the CCA and interest tax shields that cannot be used by the lessee. CRA experiences a net loss of tax revenue, and some of the tax gains to the lessor are passed on to the lessee in the form of lower lease payments.

Leasing and Capital Budgeting

Recall that we began the TransCanada car leasing example by saying that the firm had already made a capital budgeting decision to acquire the 50 cars. Our analysis focused on whether to buy the cars or to lease them. For this reason we ignored the added sales generated by the car acquisition because they would be realized whether the cars were purchased or leased. We focused on what was incremental in developing the formula for the NPV of the decision to lease instead of buy. We called this the net advantage to leasing or NAL.

In our initial analysis, both TransCanada and the lessor, Financial Leasing, had the same tax rate and, as a result, NAL was −$199. This meant that if TransCanada leased the cars, the NPV of the capital budgeting decision would be $199 lower than if the firm bought the cars.

We then modified the example to recognize that, in practice, leasing deals are often designed to take benefit from a situation in which the lessor faces a higher tax rate than the lessee. In particular, we showed that when TransCanada pays no tax and Financial Leasing faces the same 40 percent tax rate as earlier, the NALs are positive to both parties. This occurs because the loser is CRA.

From a capital budgeting perspective, in this realistic case, the NAL to TransCanada of $2.34 tells us that the NPV of acquiring one car increases by this amount by using lease financing.

REASONS FOR LEASING

Proponents of leasing make many claims about why firms should lease assets rather than buy them. Some of the reasons given to support leasing are good, while some are not. We discuss here the reasons for leasing we think are good and some that we think are not so good.

Good Reasons for Leasing

If leasing is a good choice, it is probably because one or more of the following is true:

1. Taxes may be reduced by leasing.
2. The lease contract may reduce certain types of uncertainty that might otherwise decrease the value of the firm.
3. Transaction costs can be lower for a lease contract than for buying the asset.

TAX ADVANTAGES As we have hinted in various places, by far the most important reason for long-term leasing is tax avoidance. If the corporate income tax were repealed, long-term leasing would become much less important. The tax advantages of leasing exist because firms are in different tax brackets. A potential tax shield that cannot be used by one firm can be transferred to another by leasing. We saw this in our earlier discussion on resolving the paradox.

A REDUCTION OF UNCERTAINTY We have noted that the lessee does not own the property when the lease expires. The value of the property at this time is called the *residual value* (or salvage value). At the time the lease contract is signed, there may be substantial uncertainty as to what the residual value of the asset is. A lease contract is a method that transfers this uncertainty from the lessee to the lessor.

Transferring the uncertainty about the residual value of an asset to the lessor makes sense when the lessor is better able to bear the risk. For example, if the lessor is the manufacturer, the lessor may be better able to assess and manage the risk associated with the residual value. The transfer of uncertainty to the lessor amounts to a form of insurance for the lessee. A lease, therefore, provides something besides long-term financing. Of course, the lessee pays for this insurance implicitly, but the lessee may view the insurance as a relative bargain.

LOWER TRANSACTION COSTS The costs of changing ownership of an asset many times over its useful life are frequently greater than the costs of writing a lease agreement. Consider the choice that confronts a person who lives in Vancouver but must do business in Halifax for two days. It seems obvious that it will be cheaper to rent a hotel room for two nights than it would be to buy a condominium for two days and then to sell it. Thus, transactions costs may be the major reason for short-term leases (operating leases). However, they are probably not the major reason for long-term leases.

FEWER RESTRICTIONS AND SECURITY REQUIREMENTS As we discussed in Chapter 7, with a secured loan, the borrower will generally agree to a set of restrictive covenants, spelled out in the indenture, or loan agreement. Such restrictions are not generally found in lease agreements. Also, with a secured loan, the borrower may have to pledge other assets as security. With a lease, only the leased asset is so encumbered.

Bad Reasons for Leasing

LEASING AND ACCOUNTING INCOME Leasing can have a significant effect on the appearance of the firm's financial statements. If a firm is successful at keeping its leases off the books, the balance sheet and income statement can be made to look better. As a consequence, accounting-based performance measures such as return on assets (ROA) can appear to be higher.

For example, off-the-books leases (that is, operating leases) result in an expense, namely, the lease payment. However, in the early years of the lease, the expense is usually lower in accounting terms than if the asset were purchased. If an asset is purchased with debt financing, capital cost allowance and interest expenses are subtracted from revenues to determine accounting net income. With accelerated depreciation under the CCA rules, the total of the depreciation deduction and the interest expense almost always exceeds the lease payments. Thus, accounting net income is greater with leasing.

In addition, because an operating lease does not appear on the balance sheet, total assets (and total liabilities) are lower than they would be if the firm borrowed the money and bought the asset. From Chapter 3, ROA is computed as net income divided by total assets. With an operating lease, the net income is bigger and total assets are smaller, so ROA is larger.

As we have discussed, however, the impact that leasing has on a firm's accounting statements is not likely to fool anyone. As always, what matters are the cash flow consequences. Whether or not a lease has a positive NPV has little to do with its effect on a firm's financial statements.

100 PERCENT FINANCING It is often claimed that an advantage to leasing is that it provides 100 percent financing, whereas secured equipment loans require an initial down payment. Of course, a firm can simply borrow the down payment from another source that provides unsecured credit. Moreover, leases do usually involve a down payment in the form of an advance lease payment (or security deposit). Even when they do not, leases may implicitly be secured by assets of the firm other than those being leased (leasing may give the appearance of 100 percent financing, but not the substance).

Having said this, we should add that it may be the case that a firm (particularly a small one) simply cannot obtain debt financing because, for example, additional debt would violate a loan agreement. Operating leases frequently do not count as debt, so they may be the only source of financing available. In such cases, it is not lease or buy—it is lease or die!

OTHER REASONS FOR LEASING   There are, of course, many special reasons for some companies to find advantages in leasing. For example, leasing may be used to circumvent capital expenditure control systems set up by bureaucratic firms. Government cutbacks have made leasing increasingly popular with municipalities, universities, school boards, and hospitals (the MUSH sector).

Leasing Decisions in Practice

The reduction-of-uncertainty motive for leasing is the one that is most often cited by corporations. For example, computers have a way of becoming technologically outdated very quickly, and computers are very commonly leased instead of purchased. In a recent U.S. survey, 82 percent of the responding firms cited the risk of obsolescence as an important reason for leasing, whereas only 57 percent cited the potential for cheaper financing.

Yet, cheaper financing based on shifting tax shields is an important motive for leasing. One piece of evidence is Canadian lessors' strong reaction to 1989 changes in tax laws restricting sale and lease-backs. Further evidence comes from a study analyzing decisions taken by Canadian railroads to lease rolling stock. The study examined 20 lease contracts and found that, in 17 cases, leasing provided cheaper financing than debt.[9] A third study confirmed the importance of taxes in leasing decisions. Looking at financial information for Canadian firms between 1985 and 1995, the research showed that firms with lower marginal tax rates tend to use more lease financing.

CONCEPT QUESTIONS

1. Explain why differential tax rates may be a good reason for leasing.

2. If leasing is tax-motivated, who has the higher tax bracket, the lessee or lessor?

SUMMARY AND CONCLUSIONS

A large fraction of Canada's equipment is leased rather than purchased. This chapter describes different lease types, accounting and tax implications of leasing, and how to evaluate financial leases.

1. Leases can be separated into two types, financial and operating. Financial leases are generally longer-term, fully amortized, and not cancellable. In effect, the lessor obtains economic but not legal ownership. Operating leases are usually shorter-term, partially amortized, and cancellable; they can be likened to a rental agreement.

2. The distinction between financial and operating leases is important in financial accounting. Financial leases must be reported on a firm's balance sheet; operating leases are not. We discussed the specific accounting criteria for classifying leases as financial or operating.

3. Taxes are an important consideration in leasing, and the Canada Revenue Agency has some specific rules about what constitutes a valid lease for tax purposes.

4. A long-term financial lease is a source of financing much like long-term borrowing. We showed how to go about an NPV analysis of the leasing decision to decide whether leasing is cheaper than borrowing. A key insight was that the appropriate discount rate is the firm's aftertax borrowing rate.

5. We saw that differential tax rates can make leasing an attractive proposition to all parties. We also mentioned that a lease decreases the uncertainty surrounding the residual value of the leased asset. This is a primary reason cited by corporations for leasing.

---

9 T. K. Mukherjee, "A Survey of Corporate Leasing Analysis," *Financial Management* 20 (Autumn 1991), pp. 96–107; C. R. Dipchand, A. C. Gudikunst, and G. S. Roberts, "An Empirical Analysis of Canadian Railroad Leases," *Journal of Financial Research* 3 (Spring 1980), pp. 57–67; L. Shanker, "Tax Effects and the Leasing Decisions of Canadian Corporations," *Canadian Journal of Administrative Sciences* 14, June 1997, pp. 195–205.

Key Terms

Chapter Review Problems and Self-Test

22.1 Your company wants to purchase a new network file server for its wide-area computer network. The server costs $24,000. It will be obsolete in three years. Your options are to borrow the money at 10 percent or lease the machine. If you lease it, the payments will be $9,000 per year, payable at the beginning of each year. If you buy the server, you can apply a CCA rate of 30 percent per year. The tax rate is 40 percent. Assuming the asset pool remains open, should you lease or buy?

22.2 In the previous question again assuming the asset pool remains open, what is the NPV of the lease to the lessor? At what lease payment do the lessee and the lessor both break even?

Answers to Self-Test Problems

22.1 Because the asset pool remains open after the useful life of the network file server, we can answer this question by using the net advantage to leasing (NAL) formula shown in Example 22.2 of the text. This formula is:

$$\text{NAL} = I - \sum_{t=0}^{2} \frac{L(1-T)}{(1+i)t} - \frac{[TdI]}{i+d} \times \frac{[1+0.5i]}{1+i}$$

We are given all the information necessary to solve for NAL:

I = the investment necessary to purchase the asset
  = $24,000

t = the number of years, beginning at zero, that the new asset would be used
  = 3 (Year 0, Year 1, and Year 2)

L = the amount of money required to lease the asset for one year
  = $9,000

T = the applicable tax rate
  = 40%

i = the applicable aftertax interest rate
  = 10%$(1 - T)$
  = 10%$(.6)$
  = 6%

d = the applicable CCA rate
  = 30%

We then plug all of these numbers into the formula:

NAL = $24,000

$$- \sum_{t=0}^{2} \frac{\$9,000(1-.40)}{(1+0.06)_t} - \frac{0.40 \times 0.30 \times \$24,000}{0.06 + 0.30} \times \frac{1.03}{1.06}$$

NAL = $24,000 − $15,299 − $7,774

NAL = $927

Because the NAL formula gives a positive value of $927, there is a net advantage to lease the file server.

22.2 The answer to the first part of the question is that the lessor has a NPV of −$927. The lessor has lost what the lessee has gained. To solve the second question posed in 22.2 we can again refer to the NAL formula:

$$\text{NAL} = I - \sum_{t=0}^{2} \frac{L(1-T)}{(1+i)^t} - \frac{[TdI]}{i+d} \times \frac{[1+0.5i]}{1+i}$$

We also use much of the information used to solve Problem 22.1. However, instead of using the value of $9,000 for L, we make NAL = 0 and solve for L. We merely have to plug in the values for the information we know and rearrange the formula so that we may solve for L:

$$0 = 24,000 - \sum_{t=0}^{2} \frac{L(1-.40)}{(1+0.06)^t} - \frac{0.40 \times 0.30 \times \$24,000}{0.06 + 0.30} \times \frac{1.03}{1.06}$$

$$0 = \$24,000 - \sum_{t=0}^{2} \frac{L(0.6)}{(1.06)^t} - \$7,774$$

$$\$16,226 = \sum_{t=0}^{2} \frac{L(0.6)}{(1.06)^t}$$

$$\$16,226 = \frac{L(0.6)}{(1.06)^0} + \frac{L(0.6)}{(1.06)^1} + \frac{L(0.6)}{(1.06)^2}$$

$$\$16,226 = .600L + .566L + .534L$$

$$\$16,266 = 1.7L$$

$$L = \$9,545$$

As we can now see, some of the tax advantages of the lessee have been transferred to the lessor and they are now in a break-even situation.

Concepts Review and Critical Thinking Questions

1. What are the key differences between leasing and borrowing? Are they perfect substitutes?

2. Taxes are an important consideration in the leasing decision. Who is more likely to lease, a profitable corporation in a high tax bracket or a less profitable one in a low tax bracket? Why?

3. What are some of the potential problems with looking at IRRs in evaluating a leasing decision?

4. Comment on the following remarks:
   a. Leasing reduces risk and can reduce a firm's cost of capital.
   b. Leasing provides 100 percent financing.
   c. If the tax advantages of leasing were eliminated, leasing would disappear.

5. Discuss the accounting criteria for determining whether or not a lease must be reported on the balance sheet. In each case, give a rationale for the criterion.

6. Discuss CCRA's criteria for determining whether or not a lease is valid. In each case, give a rationale for the criterion.

7. What is meant by the term *off-balance sheet financing?* When do leases provide such financing, and what are the accounting and economic consequences of such activity?

8. Why might a firm choose to engage in a sale and lease-back transaction? Give two reasons.

9. Explain why the aftertax borrowing rate is the appropriate discount rate to use in lease evaluation.

   Questions 10 and 11 refer to the Air Canada leasing example we used to open the chapter.

10. Why would a leasing company be willing to buy planes from Boeing and then lease them to Air Canada? How is this different from just loaning money to Air Canada to buy the planes?

11. What do you suppose happens to the leased planes at the end of the 10-year lease period?

Questions and Problems

Basic
(Question 1)

1. **Lease or Buy**   Assuming the asset pool was closed when the network file server became obsolete, re-do Self-Test Problem 22.1.

Intermediate
(Questions 2–10)

Using the following information, work the next six problems: You work for a nuclear research laboratory that is contemplating leasing a diagnostic scanner (leasing is a very common practice with expensive, high-tech equipment). The scanner costs $2.5 million and it qualifies for a 30 percent CCA rate. Because of radiation contamination, it is valueless in four years. You can lease it for $800,000 per year for four years.

2. **Lease or Buy**   Assume the tax rate is 37 percent. You can borrow at 7.5 percent pretax. Should you lease or buy?

3. **Lessor View of Leasing**   What are the cash flows from the lease from the lessor's point of view? Assume a 37 percent tax bracket.

4. **Break-even Lease**   What would the lease payment have to be for both lessor and lessee to be indifferent to the lease?

5. **Tax Effects on Leasing**   Assume that your company does not contemplate paying taxes for the next several years. What are the cash flows from leasing?

6. **Leasing Profits**   In the previous equation, over what range of lease payments will the lease be profitable for both parties?

7. **Lease or Buy**   Rework Problem 2 assuming the scanner qualifies for a special CCA rate of 50 percent per year.

Use the following information to work Problems 8 through 10

The Wildcat Oil Company is trying to decide whether to lease or buy a new computer-assisted drilling system for its oil exploration business. Management has already determined that acquisition of the system has a positive NPV. The system costs $6 million and qualifies for a 25 percent CCA rate. The equipment will have a $650,000 salvage value in 5 years. Wildcat's tax rate is 36 percent, and the firm can borrow at 8.5 percent. Southtown Leasing Company has offered to lease the drilling equipment to Wildcat for payments of $1,350,000 per year. Southtown's policy is to require its lessees to make payments at the start of the year.

Intermediate
(continued)

8. **Lease or Buy**   What is the NAL for Wildcat? What is the maximum lease payment that would be acceptable to the company?

9. **Leasing and Salvage Value**   Suppose it is estimated that the equipment will have no salvage value at the end of the lease. What is the maximum lease payment acceptable to Wildcat now?

10. **Deposits in Leasing**   Many lessors require a security deposit in the form of a cash payment or other pledged collateral. Suppose Southtown requires Wildcat to pay a $400,000 security deposit at the inception of the lease. If the lease payment is still $1,350,000 a year, is it advantageous for Wildcat to lease the equipment now?

Challenge
(Questions
11–13)

11. **Lease versus Borrow**   Return to the case of the diagnostic scanner used in Problems 2 through 7. Suppose the entire $2.5 million purchase price of the scanner is borrowed. The rate on the loan is 7.5 percent, and the loan will be repaid in equal installments. Create a lease versus buy analysis that explicitly incorporates the loan payments. Show that the NPV of leasing instead of buying is not changed from what it was in Problem 2. Why is this so?

12. **Lease or Buy**   In the Self-Test Problem 21.1, suppose the server had a projected value of $900. How would you conduct the lease versus buy analysis?

13. **Break-even Lease**   An asset costs $367.48. The CCA rate for this asset is 25 percent. The asset's useful life is two years. It will have no salvage value. The corporate tax rate on ordinary income is 35 percent. The interest rate on risk-free cash flows is 10 percent.

    a. What set of lease payments will make the lessee and the lessor equally well off?

    b. Show the general condition that will make the value of a lease to the lessor the negative of the value to the lessee.

    c. Assume that the lessee pays no taxes and the lessor is in the 35 percent tax bracket. For what range of lease payments does the lease have a positive NPV for both parties?

MINI CASE

Lease or Buy Tollufson Corporation has decided to purchase a new machine that costs $15,000. The machine will be worthless after three years. CCA for this type of machine is 40 percent. Tollufson is in the 34 percent combined tax bracket. The Royal Canadian Bank has offered Tollufson a three-year loan for $15,000. The repayment schedule is three yearly principal repayments of $5,000 and an interest charge of 9 percent on the outstanding balance of the loan at the beginning of each year. Nine percent is the marketwide rate of interest. Both principal repayments and interest are due at the end of each year.

York Leasing Corporation offers to lease the same machine to Tollufson. Lease payments of $5,700 per year are due at the end of each of the three years of the lease.

a)   Should Tollufson lease the machine or buy it with bank financing?

b)   What is the annual lease payment that will make Tollufson indifferent to whether it leases or purchases the machine?

c)   What interest rate on the loan (and in the marketplace) will make Tollufson indifferent to whether it leases the machine or not?

d)   Considering the current economic conditions, how likely is it that the interest rate on the loan will change to the rate determined in part (c)? Explain.

e)   How does the analysis change if the machine has a salvage value of $400 at the end of the three years?

f)   Who is responsible for the repair of leased equipment? Do you think the lessor will always be responsive to the needs of the lessee on a timely basis? What other concerns might there be in leases?

Internet Application Questions

1. There are some very sensible reasons for leasing assets, and some that make you think deeper. The following site argues mostly in favour of leasing. One of its arguments is that since leasing payments are typically lower than loan payments on a purchase, the "savings" can be invested in higher yield instruments such as equity funds, and you therefore come out ahead at the end of the term. Is this a reasonable criticism of the borrow-and-buy alternative to leasing?

    www.leaseguide.com/lease03.htm

2. OK, are you ready for a test drive? CARS4U.COM provides a unique Internet-based car buying and leasing service where they will deliver the car of your choice to your doorstep (well, driveway). Look at the information for the VW Jetta below and decide whether the lease is preferable to financing and purchasing. To get the interest rate, add 1 percent to the current prime rate from Royal Bank (www.royalbank.com/rates/prime.html). Leasing and financing assumptions are provided below and in the link.

Term:	36 months
Cash down payment:	$2,500
Trade-in allowance:	$0
Interest rate:	Current market rate
Lease only:	50% Residual Value/Buyback

2006 Volkswagen Jetta 2.0T

MSRP:	$24,795
Est. Lease:	$360
Cars4U.com Price:	$24,654
Est. Financing:	$808
Rebate:	TBA
Vehicle Type:	Sedan
Engine:	2.0 litres, turbo charged 4 cylinder engine, 200 horsepower and 4 valves per cylinder
Fuel Economy:	City: 10 L/100 km Highway: 7 L/100 km

Suggested Readings

A classic article on lease valuation is:

Myers, S., D. A. Dill, and A. J. Bautista. "Valuation of Financial Lease Contracts." *Journal of Finance,* June 1976.

A good review and discussion of leasing is contained in:

Smith, C. W., Jr., and L. M. Wakeman. "Determinations of Corporate Leasing Policy." *Journal of Finance,* July 1985.

Current information on leasing in Canada is provided by the Canadian Finance and Leasing Association at their website: *www.canadianleasing.ca.*

CHAPTER 23

Mergers and Acquisitions

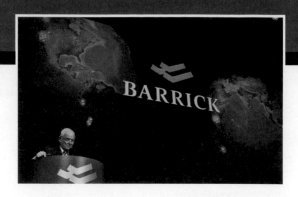

The year 2005 was a standout one for mergers in Canada. In 2005, the total value of announced deals was $166 billion, a 47 percent increase from 2004. Thirty-four mega-deals (transactions over $1 billion) occurred in 2005, with a total value of $103 billion. Merger activity in 2005 included Barrick Gold Corporation's takeover of Placer Dome Inc. for US $10.4 billion, creating the world's largest gold producer, and Bain Capital Partners, LLC's sale of a directory business to Yellow Pages Income Fund for $2.6 billion. Activity has picked up dramatically since 2002, when the total value of merger transactions was $91 billion. All this activity raises two basic questions: Why does a firm choose to merge with or acquire another, and how does it happen? This chapter explores these two issues.

www.barrickgold.com
www.baincapital.com

THERE IS NO MORE dramatic or controversial activity in corporate finance than the acquisition of one firm by another or the merger of two firms. It is the stuff of headlines in the financial press, and occasionally it is an embarrassing source of scandal.

The acquisition of one firm by another is, of course, an investment made under uncertainty, and the basic principles of valuation apply. Another firm should be acquired only if doing so generates a positive net present value to the shareholders of the acquiring firm. However, because the NPV of an acquisition candidate can be difficult to determine, mergers and acquisitions are interesting topics in their own right.

Some of the special problems that come up in this area of finance include:

1. The benefits from acquisitions can depend on such things as strategic fits. Strategic fits are difficult to define precisely, and it is not easy to estimate the value of strategic fits using discounted cash flow techniques.

2. There can be complex accounting, tax, and legal effects that must be considered when one firm is acquired by another.

3. Acquisitions are an important control device for shareholders. Some acquisitions are a consequence of an underlying conflict between the interests of existing managers and shareholders. Agreeing to be acquired by another firm is one way that shareholders can remove existing managers.

4. Mergers and acquisitions sometimes involve "unfriendly" transactions. In such cases, when one firm attempts to acquire another, it does not always involve quiet negotiations. The sought-after firm often resists takeover and may resort to defensive tactics with exotic names such as poison pills or greenmail.

We discuss these and other issues associated with mergers in the next section. We begin by introducing the basic legal, accounting, and tax aspects of acquisitions.

 **23.1**

THE LEGAL FORMS OF ACQUISITIONS

There are three basic legal procedures that one firm can use to acquire another firm:

1. Merger or consolidation.
2. Acquisition of stock.
3. Acquisition of assets.

Although these forms are different from a legal standpoint, the financial press frequently does not distinguish between them. To make the terminology more confusing, both the Canadian and Ontario Business Corporation Acts refer to combinations of firms as **amalgamations**. In our discussion, we use the term *merger* regardless of the actual form of the acquisition.

In our discussion, we frequently refer to the acquiring firm as the *bidder*. This is the company that makes an offer to distribute cash or securities to obtain the stock or assets of another company. The firm that is sought (and perhaps acquired) is often called the *target firm*. The cash or securities offered to the target firm are the *consideration* in the acquisition.

amalgamations
Combinations of firms that have been joined by merger, consolidation, or acquisition.

Merger or Consolidation

A **merger** refers to the complete absorption of one firm by another. The acquiring firm retains its name and its identity, and it acquires all the assets and liabilities of the acquired firm. After a merger, the acquired firm ceases to exist as a separate business entity.

A **consolidation** is the same as a merger except that a new firm is created. In a consolidation, both the acquiring firm and the acquired firm terminate their previous legal existence and become part of a new firm. For this reason, the distinction between the acquiring and the acquired firm is not as important in a consolidation as it is in a merger.

The rules for mergers and consolidations are basically the same. Acquisition by merger or consolidation results in a combination of the assets and liabilities of acquired and acquiring firms; the only difference is whether or not a new firm is created. We henceforth use the term *merger* to refer generically to both mergers and consolidations.

There are some advantages and some disadvantages to using a merger to acquire a firm:

1. A primary advantage is that a merger is legally simple and does not cost as much as other forms of acquisition. The reason is that the firms simply agree to combine their entire operations. Thus, for example, there is no need to transfer title to individual assets of the acquired firm to the acquiring firm.
2. A primary disadvantage is that a merger must be approved by a vote of the shareholders of each firm.[1] Typically, two-thirds (or even more) of the share votes are required for approval. Obtaining the necessary votes can be time consuming and difficult. Furthermore, as we later discuss in greater detail, the cooperation of the target firm's existing management is almost a necessity for a merger. This cooperation may not be easily or cheaply obtained.

merger
The complete absorption of one company by another, where the acquiring firm retains its identity and the acquired firm ceases to exist as a separate entity.

consolidation
A merger in which a new firm is created and both the acquired and acquiring firm cease to exist.

Acquisition of Stock

A second way to acquire another firm is to simply purchase the firm's voting stock in exchange for cash, shares of stock, or other securities. This process often starts as a private offer from the management of one firm to another. Regardless of how it starts, at some point the offer is taken directly to the target firm's shareholders. This can be accomplished by a **tender offer.** A tender offer is a public offer to buy shares. It is made by one firm directly to the shareholders of another firm.

If the shareholders choose to accept the offer, they tender their shares by exchanging them for cash or securities (or both), depending on the offer. A tender offer is frequently contingent on the bidder's obtaining some percentage of the total voting shares. If not enough shares are tendered, the offer might be withdrawn or reformulated.

tender offer
A public offer by one firm to directly buy the shares from another firm.

---

1 As we discuss later, obtaining majority assent is less of a problem in Canada than in the United States because fewer Canadian corporations are widely held.

circular bid
Corporate takeover bid communicated to the shareholders by direct mail.

stock exchange bid
Corporate takeover bid communicated to the shareholders through a stock exchange.

The takeover bid is communicated to the target firm's shareholders by public announcements such as newspaper advertisements. Takeover bids may be either by **circular bid** mailed directly to the target's stockholders or by **stock exchange bid** (through the facilities of the TSX or other exchange). In either case, Ontario securities law requires that the bidder mail a notice of the proposed share purchase to shareholders. Furthermore, the management of the target firm must also respond to the bid, including their recommendation to accept or to reject the bid. For a circular bid, the response must be mailed to shareholders. If the bid is made through a stock exchange, the response is through a press release.

The following factors are involved in choosing between an acquisition by stock and a merger:

1. In an acquisition by stock, no shareholder meetings have to be held and no vote is required. If the shareholders of the target firm don't like the offer, they are not required to accept it and need not tender their shares.
2. In an acquisition by stock, the bidding firm can deal directly with the shareholders of the target firm by using a tender offer. The target firm's management and board of directors can be bypassed.
3. Acquisition by stock is occasionally unfriendly. In such cases, a stock acquisition is used in an effort to circumvent the target firm's management, which is usually actively resisting acquisition. Resistance by the target firm's management often makes the cost of acquisition by stock higher than the cost of a merger.
4. Frequently, a significant minority of shareholders holds out in a tender offer. The target firm cannot be completely absorbed when this happens, and this may delay realization of the merger benefits or otherwise be costly.
5. Complete absorption of one firm by another requires a merger. Many acquisitions by stock end up with a formal merger later.

Acquisition of Assets

A firm can effectively acquire another firm by buying most or all of its assets. This accomplishes the same thing as buying the company. In this case, however, the target firm does not necessarily cease to exist, it just has its assets sold. The shell still exists unless its shareholders choose to dissolve it.

This type of acquisition requires a formal vote of the shareholders of the selling firm. One advantage to this approach is that there is no problem with minority shareholders holding out. However, acquisition of assets may involve transferring titles to individual assets. The legal process of transferring assets can be costly.

Acquisition Classifications

Financial analysts typically classify acquisitions into three types:

1. *Horizontal acquisition.* This is acquisition of a firm in the same industry as the bidder. The firms compete with each other in their product markets. A good example is the acquisition of Canada Life Financial by Great-West Lifeco in 2003.
2. *Vertical acquisition.* A vertical acquisition involves firms at different steps of the production process. The acquisition by an airline company of a travel agency would be a vertical acquisition. For example, America Online's (AOL's) purchase of Netscape for $4.21 billion in 1998 was essentially a vertical merger. AOL is a huge online service provider, while Netscape provides Internet and electronic commerce software.
3. *Conglomerate acquisition.* When the bidder and the target firm are not related to each other, the merger is called a conglomerate acquisition. The acquisition of Federated Department Stores by Campeau Corporation, a real estate company, was considered a conglomerate acquisition.

www.greatwestlife.com
www.aol.com

A Note on Takeovers

Takeover is a general and imprecise term referring to the transfer of control of a firm from one group of shareholders to another. A takeover thus occurs whenever one group takes control from another.[2] This can occur in three ways: acquisitions, proxy contests, and going-private transactions. Thus, takeovers encompass a broader set of activities than just acquisitions. These activities can be depicted as follows:

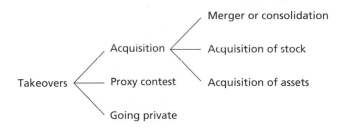

As we have mentioned, a takeover achieved by acquisition occurs by merger, tender offer, or purchase of assets. In mergers and tender offers, the bidder buys the voting common stock of the target firm.

Takeovers can also occur with **proxy contests.** Proxy contests occur when a group attempts to gain controlling seats on the board of directors by voting in new directors. A proxy is the right to cast someone else's votes. In a proxy contest, proxies are solicited by an unhappy group of shareholders from the rest of the shareholders.

In **going-private transactions,** all the equity shares of a public firm are purchased by a small group of investors. Usually, the group includes members of incumbent management and some outside investors. Such transactions have come to be known generically as **leveraged buyouts (LBOs)** because a large percentage of the money needed to buy the stock is usually borrowed. Such transactions are also termed *MBOs* (management buyouts) when existing management is heavily involved.[3] The shares of the firm are delisted from stock exchanges and no longer can be purchased in the open market. An example of an MBO was management's purchase of Sun Media Corp., publisher of *The Financial Post* and *Toronto Sun,* from Rogers Communications. CIBC Wood Gundy also purchased some of the shares.

LBOs were common in the late 1980s, and some recent ones have been quite large. The 1989 LBO of RJR Nabisco, the U.S. tobacco and food products giant, was one of the largest private transactions of any kind ever. The acquisition price in that buyout was an astonishing U.S. $30.6 billion. In that LBO, as with most large ones, much of the financing came from junk bond sales (see Chapter 7 for a discussion of junk bonds). In 1999, the $2.55 (Cdn) billion LBO of Shoppers Drug Mart by KKR, the Ontario Teachers' Pension Plan Board, and CIBC World Markets provides a good example of a large Canadian buyout.

There have been a large number of mergers and acquisitions in recent years many of them involving very familiar companies. Table 23.1 lists some of the largest mergers in Canada in recent years.

Alternatives to Merger

Firms don't have to merge to combine their efforts. At a minimum, two (or more) firms can simply agree to work together. They can sell each other's products, perhaps under different brand names, or jointly develop a new product or technology. Firms will frequently establish a **strategic alliance,** which is usually a formal agreement to cooperate in pursuit of a joint goal. An even more formal arrangement is a **joint venture,** which commonly involves two firms putting up the money to establish a new firm. For example, Saskatoon-based Shore Gold Inc. became an equal partner with dominant De Beers Group in a joint venture to look for diamonds in a region just east of Prince Albert, Saskatchewan.

proxy contests
Attempts to gain control of a firm by soliciting a sufficient number of shareholder votes to replace existing management.

going-private transactions
All publicly owned stock in a firm is replaced with complete equity ownership by a private group.

leveraged buyouts (LBOs)
Going-private transactions in which a large percentage of the money used to buy the stock is borrowed. Often, incumbent management is involved.

strategic alliance
Agreement between firms to cooperate in pursuit of a joint goal.

joint venture
Typically an agreement between firms to create a separate, co-owned entity established to pursue a joint goal.

---

2 A takeover bid has a narrowed meaning as we explained earlier. *Control* may be defined as having a majority vote on the board of directors.

3 LBOs and MBOs can involve proxy contests for control of the company. Recall that proxy contests, like the one at Diamond Fields, were discussed in greater detail in Chapter 8.

TABLE 23.1   25 large mergers and acquisitions involving Canadian companies

Rank	(in Cdn $ millions)	Acquisition	Target Company	Acquiring Company
1	51.0	Nov '00	Seagram Co. Ltd.	Vivendi
2	15.1	May '98	Polygram NV	Seagram Co. Ltd.
3	15.0	Sep '03	John Hancock Financial Services	Manulife Financial
4	12.2	Apr '95	E.I. du Pont de Nemours	Seagram Co. Ltd.
5	12.1	Dec '05	Placer Dome	Barrick Gold
6	11.0	Jan '98	*Nova Corp.	TransCanada Pipelines
7	10.7	Feb '00	Newbridge Networks Corp.	Alcatel
8	9.8	May '98	Bay Networks Inc.	Northern Telecom Ltd.
9	9.2	Jan '02	*PanCanadian Energy Corp.	Alberta Energy Co.
10	8.0	Jan '00	Canada Trust	TD Bank
11	7.8	Apr '95	MCA Inc.	Seagram Co. Ltd.
12	7.3	Dec '01	Clarica Life	Sun Life Financial
13	7.1	Feb '00	Donohue Inc.	Abitibi-Consolidated
14	7.0	Mar '99	*AT&T Canada Corp.	Metronet Communications
15	6.9	Aug '05	Terasen Inc.	Kinder Morgan Inc.
16	5.7	Oct '97	*HSN Inc.	Seagram Co. Ltd.
17	5.5	Mar '05	Telesystem International Wireless	Vodafone Group
18	5.2	Apr '97	Dome Petroleum Ltd.	Amoco Corp.
19	4.9	Jan '89	Texaco Canada Inc.	Imperial Oil Ltd.
20	4.9	Jul '98	Tropicana Products Ltd.	Pepsi Co. Inc.
21	4.6	Aug '00	Clearnet Communications	Telus Corp.
22	4.5	Sep '05	Acclaim Energy Trust*	Starpoint Energy Trust
23	4.5	Jul '04	Adolph Coors Co.	Molson Inc.
24	4.4	Aug '90	STC PLC	Northern Telecom Ltd.
25	4.2	Jun '00	Gold Fields	Franco-Nevada

*No defined target or acquirer

Source: *Mergers & Acquisitions in Canada*—various issues and *www.canoe.ca/MergerMania/home.html*

> **CONCEPT QUESTIONS**
>
> **1.** What is a merger? How does a merger differ from other acquisition forms?
>
> **2.** What is a takeover?

TAXES AND ACQUISITIONS

If one firm buys another firm, the transaction may be taxable or tax free. In a *taxable acquisition*, the shareholders of the target firm are considered to have sold their shares, and they have capital gains or losses that are taxed. In a *tax-free acquisition*, since the acquisition is considered an exchange instead of a sale, no capital gain or loss occurs at that time.

Determinants of Tax Status

The general requirements for tax-free status are that the acquisition involves two Canadian corporations subject to corporate income tax and that there be a continuity of equity interest. In other words, the shareholders in the target firm must retain an equity interest in the bidder.

The specific requirements for a tax-free acquisition depend on the legal form of the acquisition; in general, if the buying firm offers the selling firm cash for its equity, it is a taxable acquisition. If shares of stock are offered, it is a tax-free acquisition.

In a tax-free acquisition, the selling shareholders are considered to have exchanged their old shares for new ones of equal value, and no capital gains or losses are experienced.

Taxable versus Tax-Free Acquisitions

There are two factors to consider when comparing a tax-free acquisition and a taxable acquisition: the capital gains effect and the write-up effect. The *capital gains effect* refers to the fact that the target firm's shareholders may have to pay capital gains taxes in a taxable acquisition. They may demand a higher price as compensation, thereby increasing the cost of the merger. This is a cost of taxable acquisition.

The tax status of an acquisition also affects the appraised value of the assets of the selling firm. In a taxable acquisition, the assets of the selling firm are revalued or "written up" from their historic book value to their estimated current market value. This is the *write-up effect*, and it is important because the depreciation expense on the acquired firm's assets can be increased in taxable acquisitions. Remember that an increase in depreciation is a non-cash expense, but it has the desirable effect of reducing taxes.

CONCEPT QUESTIONS

1. What factors influence the choice between a taxable and a tax-free acquisition?

2. What is the write-up effect in a taxable acquisition?

ACCOUNTING FOR ACQUISITIONS

Firms keep two distinct sets of books: the shareholders' books and the tax books. In this section, we are considering the shareholders' books. When one firm buys another firm, the acquisition will be treated as a purchase on the shareholders' books.

The purchase accounting method of reporting acquisitions requires that the assets of the target firm be reported at their fair market value on the books of the bidder. This allows the bidder to establish a new cost basis for the acquired assets. With this method, an asset called *goodwill* is created for accounting purposes. Goodwill is the difference between the purchase price and the estimated fair value of the assets acquired.

To illustrate, suppose Firm A acquires Firm B, thereby creating a new firm, AB. The balance sheets for the two firms on the date of the acquisition are shown in Table 23.2. Suppose Firm A pays $18 million in cash for Firm B. The money is raised by borrowing the full amount. The fixed assets in Firm B are appraised at $14 million fair market value. Since the working capital is $2 million, the balance sheet assets are worth $16 million. Firm A thus pays $2 million in excess of the estimated market value of these assets. This amount is the goodwill.[4]

The last balance sheet in Table 23.2 shows what the new firm looks like under purchase accounting. Notice that:

1. The total assets of Firm AB increase to $38 million. The fixed assets increase to $30 million. This is the sum of the fixed assets of Firm A and the revalued fixed assets of Firm B ($16 million + 14 million = $30 million). Note that the tax effect of the write-up is ignored in this example.

TABLE 23.2
Accounting for acquisitions: Purchase (in $ millions)

Firm A				Firm B			
Working capital	$ 4	Equity	$20	Working capital	$ 2	Equity	$10
Fixed assets	16			Fixed assets	8		
Total	$20		$20	Total	$10		$10

Firm AB			
Working capital	$ 6	Debt	$18
Fixed assets	30	Equity	20
Goodwill	2		
Total	$38		$38

The market value of the fixed assets of Firm B is $14 million. Firm A pays $18 million for Firm B by issuing debt.

---

4 Remember, there are assets such as employee talents, good customers, growth opportunities, and other intangibles that don't show up on the balance sheet. The $2 million excess pays for these.

2. The $2 million excess of the purchase price over the fair market value is reported as goodwill on the balance sheet.[5]

CONCEPT QUESTION

1. What is the role of goodwill in purchase accounting for mergers?

GAINS FROM ACQUISITION

To determine the gains from an acquisition, we need to first identify the relevant incremental cash flows, or, more generally, the source of value. In the broadest sense, acquiring another firm makes sense only if there is some concrete reason to believe that the target firm will somehow be worth more in our hands than it is worth now. As we will see, there are a number of reasons why this might be so.

Synergy

Suppose Firm A is contemplating acquiring Firm B. The acquisition will be beneficial if the combined firm will have value that is greater than the sum of the values of the separate firms. If we let V_{AB} stand for the value of the merged firm, then the merger makes sense only if:

$$V_{AB} > V_A + V_B$$

where V_A and V_B are the separate values. A successful merger thus requires that the value of the whole exceed the sum of the parts.

The difference between the value of the combined firm and the sum of the values of the firms as separate entities is the incremental net gain from the acquisition, ΔV:

$$\Delta V = V_{AB} - (V_A + V_B)$$

synergy
The positive incremental net gain associated with the combination of two firms through a merger or acquisition.

www.disney.com

When ΔV is positive, the acquisition is said to generate **synergy.** For example, when Walt Disney bought Capital Cities/ABC for $4 billion in 1995, Disney chairman Michael Eisner predicted the combined companies would find synergies "under every rock," adding that in this case, "1 and 1 will add up to 4." That's a lot of synergy!

If Firm A buys Firm B, it gets a company worth V_B plus the incremental gain, ΔV. The value of Firm B to Firm A (V_B^*) is thus:

$$\text{Value of Firm B to Firm A} = V^*_B = \Delta V + V_B$$

We place an * on V_B^* to emphasize that we are referring to the value of Firm B to Firm A, not the value of Firm B as a separate entity.

V_B^* can be determined in two steps: (1) estimating V_B and (2) estimating ΔV. If B is a public company, then its market value as an independent firm under existing management (V_B) can be observed directly. If Firm B is not publicly owned, then its value will have to be estimated based on similar companies that are. Either way, the problem of determining a value for V_B^* requires determining a value for ΔV.

To determine the incremental value of an acquisition, we need to know the incremental cash flows. These are the cash flows for the combined firm less what A and B could generate separately. In other words, the incremental cash flow for evaluating a merger is the difference between the cash flow of the combined company and the sum of the cash flows for the two companies considered separately. We will label this incremental cash flow as ΔCF.

From our discussions in earlier chapters, we know that the incremental cash flow, ΔCF, can be broken down into four parts:

$$\Delta CF = \Delta EBIT + \Delta \text{Depreciation} - \Delta \text{Tax} - \Delta \text{Capital requirements}$$
$$= \Delta \text{Revenue} - \Delta \text{Cost} - \Delta \text{Tax} - \Delta \text{Capital requirements}$$

---

5 You might wonder what would happen if the purchase price were less than the estimated fair market value. Amusingly, to be consistent, it seems that the accountants would need to create a liability called ill will! Instead, the fair market value is revised downward to equal the purchase price.

EXAMPLE 23.1: Synergy

Firms A and B are competitors with very similar assets and business risks. Both are all-equity firms with aftertax cash flows of $10 per year forever, and both have an overall cost of capital of 10 percent. Firm A is thinking of buying Firm B. The aftertax cash flow from the merged firm would be $21 per year. Does the merger generate synergy? What is V_B^*? What is ΔV?

The merger does generate synergy because the cash flow from the merged firm is $\Delta CF = \$1$ greater than the sum of the individual cash flows ($21 versus $20). Assuming that the risks stay the same, the value of the merged firm is $21/.10 = $210. Firms A and B are each worth $10/.10 = $100, for a total of $200. The incremental gain from the merger, ΔV, is thus $210 − 200 = $10. The total value of Firm B to Firm A, V_B^* is $100 (the value of B as a separate company) plus $10 (the incremental gain), or $110.

where ΔRevenue is the difference in revenues, ΔCost is the difference in costs, ΔTax is the difference in taxes, and ΔCapital requirements is the change in new fixed assets and net working capital.

Based on this breakdown, the merger will make sense only if one or more of these cash flow components are beneficially affected by the merger. The possible cash flow benefits of mergers and acquisitions thus fall into four basic categories: revenue enhancement, cost reductions, lower taxes, and reductions in capital needs.

Revenue Enhancement

One important reason for an acquisition is that the combined firm may generate greater revenues than two separate firms. Increases in revenue may come from marketing gains, strategic benefits, and increases in market power.

MARKETING GAINS   It is frequently claimed that mergers and acquisitions can produce greater operating revenues from improved marketing. For example, improvements might be made in the following areas:

1. Previously ineffective media programming and advertising efforts.
2. A weak existing distribution network.
3. An unbalanced product mix.

STRATEGIC BENEFITS   Some acquisitions promise a strategic advantage. This is an opportunity to take advantage of the competitive environment if certain things occur or, more generally, to enhance management flexibility with regard to the company's future operations. In this regard, a strategic benefit is more like an option than it is a standard investment opportunity.

For example, suppose a sewing machine firm can use its technology to enter other businesses. The small-motor technology from the original business can provide opportunities to begin manufacturing small appliances and electric typewriters. Similarly, electronics expertise gained in producing typewriters can be used to manufacture electronic printers.

The word *beachhead* describes the process of entering a new industry to exploit perceived opportunities. The beachhead is to spawn new opportunities based on intangible relationships. One example is Procter & Gamble's initial acquisition of the Charmin Paper Company as a beachhead that allowed Procter & Gamble to develop a highly interrelated cluster of paper products—disposable diapers, paper towels, feminine hygiene products, and bathroom tissue.[6]

MARKET POWER   One firm may acquire another to increase its market share and market power. In such mergers, profits can be enhanced through higher prices and reduced competition for customers. In theory, such mergers are controlled by law. In practice, however, horizontal mergers are far more common in Canada than the United States due to weaker legal restrictions against combinations of competitors that might limit market competition.[7]

www.pg.com

---

6 This example comes from Michael Porter's *Competitive Advantage* (New York: Free Press, 1985).

7 From the mid-1950s to the mid-1980s, only one merger in Canada was blocked under the *Combines Investigation Act*. In the same period, U.S. antitrust laws "prevented several hundred horizontal mergers" according to B. E. Eckbo, "Mergers and the Market for Corporate Control: the Canadian Evidence," *Canadian Journal of Economics*, May 1986, pp. 236–60.

Cost Reductions

One of the most basic reasons to merge is that a combined firm may operate more efficiently than two separate firms. A firm can obtain greater operating efficiency in several different ways through a merger or an acquisition.

ECONOMIES OF SCALE   Economies of scale relate to the average cost per unit of producing goods and services. As Figure 23.1 shows, when the per-unit cost of production falls as the level of production increases, an economy of scale exists.

Frequently, the phrase *spreading overhead* is used in connection with economies of scale. This expression refers to the sharing of central facilities such as corporate headquarters, top management, and computer services.

ECONOMIES OF VERTICAL INTEGRATION   Operating economies can be gained from vertical combinations as well as from horizontal combinations. The main purpose of vertical acquisitions is to make coordinating closely related operating activities easier. Benefits from vertical integration are probably the reason most forest product firms that cut timber also own sawmills and hauling equipment. Such economies may explain why some airline companies have purchased hotels and car rental companies.

Technology transfers are another reason for vertical integration. Consider the merger of General Motors Corporation and Hughes Aircraft in 1985. It seems natural that an automobile manufacturer might acquire an advanced electronics firm if the special technology of the electronics firm can be used to improve the quality of the automobile.

COMPLEMENTARY RESOURCES   Some firms acquire others to make better use of existing resources or to provide the missing ingredient for success. Think of a ski equipment store that could merge with a tennis equipment store to produce more even sales over both the winter and summer seasons, and thereby better use store capacity.

EVIDENCE ON REVENUE ENHANCEMENT AND COST REDUCTION   Most of the evidence on merger gains is measured in returns to shareholders. We discuss this later to see who gains in mergers. To attribute any gains from mergers to specific advantages like market share requires an industrial organization approach. A study of Canadian mergers in the 1970s finds that gains occurred in market share, productivity, or profitability. This suggests that revenue enhancement and cost reduction are valid reasons at least for some mergers. Inefficiencies in real goods markets explain why it is sometimes cheaper to acquire resources and strategic

www.gm.com

FIGURE 23.1

Economies of scale

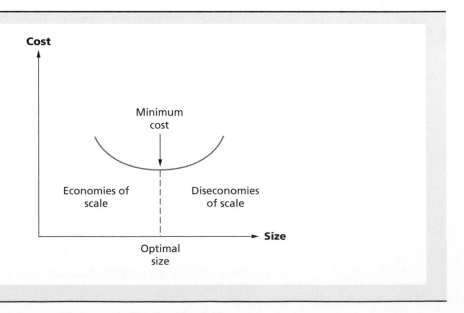

www.telus.com

links through mergers. This was the main motive for widespread mergers in the Canadian oil and mining industries in recent years.

Scale economies and increasing market share are also important in current mergers. For example, when Roger Wireless acquired Fido for $1.4 billion in cash in 2004, one of the main motives was to expand its wireless GSM network in Quebec. Figure 23.2 shows features of the two firms.

Tax Gains

Tax gains often are a powerful incentive for some acquisitions. The possible tax gains from an acquisition include the following:

1. The use of tax losses.
2. The use of unused debt capacity.
3. The use of surplus funds.
4. The ability to write up the value of depreciable assets.

NET OPERATING LOSSES   Firms that lose money on a pretax basis do not pay taxes. Such firms can end up with tax losses that they cannot use. These tax losses are referred to as NOL (an acronym for net operating losses).

A firm with net operating losses may be an attractive merger partner for a firm with significant tax liabilities. Absent any other effects, the combined firm would have a lower tax bill than the two firms considered separately. This is a good example of how a firm can be more valuable merged than standing alone. For example, tax savings made possible by Dome Petroleum's large losses were an important attraction to Amoco when it bought Dome in 1988.

There is an important qualification to our NOL discussion. Canadian tax laws permit firms that experience periods of profit and loss to even things out through loss carry-back and carry-

---

FIGURE 23.2

Features of Rogers Wireless and Fido

WIRELESS HOOKUP

In 2004, Rogers Wireless made a takeover bid for Microcell Communications, providers of the Fido cell phone service in Canada. Rogers Wireless planned to finance the $1.4 billion bid with cash on hand and a loan from its parent company, Rogers Communications. The two companies will have a combined customer base of 5.1 million, making the merged company the leader in the Canadian wireless market.

Rogers Wireless

Rogers Wireless is one of Canada's biggest wireless companies, competing with other wireless giants Bell Mobility and Telus for market share. Rogers Wireless offers a wide range of wireless services – personal plans, business plans, pay-as-you-go, and wireless data plans. Rogers Wireless joined the Rogers telecommunications family in 1985.

Headquarters: Toronto, Ontario
CEO: Nadir Mohamed
Employees: 2,380

Fido

Fido is a Canadian wireless communications company that uses the popular global system for mobile (GSM) standard. Rogers uses the same mobile system, which makes Fido an attractive takeover target for Rogers. Fido was launched by Microcell in 1996, offering customers personal communications services and wireless data services. With just over 1.3 million customers, Fido is Canada's smallest major cell phone provider, but it is also Canada's most competitive.

Headquarters: Montreal, Quebec
CEO: André Tremblay
Employees: 2,229*

Source: www.sedar.com, www.rogers.com, and *Computing Canada*. Willowdale: Oct 8, 2004. vol. 30, Iss. 14; pg. 12.

forward provisions. A firm that has been profitable in the past but has a loss in the current year can get refunds of income taxes paid in the three previous years. After that, losses can be carried forward for up to seven years. Thus, a merger to exploit unused tax shields must offer tax savings over and above what can be accomplished by firms via carry-overs.

UNUSED DEBT CAPACITY   Some firms do not use as much debt as they are able. This makes them potential acquisition candidates. Adding debt can provide important tax savings, and many acquisitions are financed with debt. The acquiring company can deduct interest payments on the newly created debt and reduce taxes.[8]

SURPLUS FUNDS   Another quirk in the tax laws involves surplus funds. Consider a firm that has a free cash flow available after all taxes have been paid and after all positive net present value projects have been financed.

In this situation, aside from purchasing fixed income securities, the firm has several ways to spend the free cash flow, including:

1. Pay dividends.
2. Buy back its own shares.
3. Acquire shares in another firm.

We discussed the first two options in Chapter 17. We saw that an extra dividend increases the income tax paid by some investors. And, under Canada Customs and Revenue Agency regulations, share repurchase does not always reduce the taxes paid by shareholders when compared to paying dividends.

To avoid these problems, the firm can buy another firm. By doing this, the tax problem associated with paying a dividend is avoided.

ASSET WRITE-UPS   We have previously observed that, in a taxable acquisition, the assets of the acquired firm can be revalued. If the value of the assets is increased, tax deductions for depreciation are a gain.

Changing Capital Requirements

All firms must make investments in working capital and fixed assets to sustain an efficient level of operating activity. A merger may reduce the combined investments needed by the two firms. For example, Firm A may need to expand its manufacturing facilities while Firm B has significant excess capacity. It may be much cheaper for Firm A to buy Firm B than to build from scratch.

In addition, acquiring firms may see ways of more effectively managing existing assets. This can occur with a reduction in working capital by more efficient handling of cash, accounts receivable, and inventory. Finally, the acquiring firm may also sell certain assets that are not needed in the combined firm.

Avoiding Mistakes

Evaluating the benefit of a potential acquisition is more difficult than a standard capital budgeting analysis because so much of the value can come from intangible, or otherwise difficult to quantify, benefits. Consequently, there is a great deal of room for error. Here are some general rules to remember:

1. *Do not ignore market values.* There is no point and little gain to estimating the value of a publicly traded firm when that value can be directly observed. The current market value represents the consensus of investors concerning the firm's value (under existing management). Use this value as a starting point. If the firm is not publicly held, the place to start is with similar firms that are publicly held.

---

8 While unused debt capacity can be a valid reason for a merger, hindsight shows that many mergers in the 1980s overused debt financing. We discuss this in more detail later.

2. *Estimate only incremental cash flows.* It is important to estimate the cash flows that are incremental to the acquisition. Only incremental cash flows from an acquisition add value to the acquiring firm. Acquisition analysis should thus focus only on the newly created, incremental cash flows from the proposed acquisition.

3. *Use the correct discount rate.* The discount rate should be the required rate of return for the incremental cash flows associated with the acquisition. It should reflect the risk associated with the use of funds, not the source. In particular, if Firm A is acquiring Firm B, Firm A's cost of capital is not particularly relevant. Firm B's cost of capital is a much more appropriate discount rate because it reflects the risk of Firm B's cash flows.

4. *Be aware of transaction costs.* An acquisition may involve substantial (and sometimes astounding) transaction costs. These include fees to investment bankers, legal fees, and disclosure requirements. Fees generated by leveraged buyouts during the 1980s amounted to U.S. $4.7 billion![9]

A Note on Inefficient Management

There are firms whose value could be increased with a change in management. These firms are poorly run or otherwise do not efficiently use their assets to create shareholder value. Mergers are a means of replacing management in such cases.[10]

Furthermore, the fact that a firm might benefit from a change in management does not necessarily mean that existing management is dishonest, incompetent, or negligent. Instead, just as some athletes are better than others, so might some management teams be better at running a business. This can be particularly true during times of technological change or other periods when innovations in business practice are occurring. In any case, to the extent that they can identify poorly run firms or firms that otherwise would benefit from a change in management, corporate raiders provide a valuable service to target firm shareholders and society in general.

The consumption of perks by top management is another inefficiency that may be eliminated by acquisition. For example, Ross Johnson (former CEO of RJR Nabisco) is described as "a relentlessly cheerful rogue who reveled in all the apartments, country-club memberships, jets, Jaguars, and scotch his corporate treasuries could afford."[11]

The Negative Side of Takeovers

While most financial analysts would likely agree that corporate raiders can deliver benefits to society, there is concern over whether the cost is too high. Critics of takeovers (and especially LBOs) are concerned that social costs are not counted when the post-takeover search for efficiency gains leads to plant closures and layoffs. When plants close or move, workers and equipment can be turned to other uses only at some cost to society. For example, taxpayers may need to subsidize retraining and relocation programs for workers or tax incentives for investment. For example, in the late 1990s larger companies bought two major financial institutions headquartered in London, Ontario: Canada Trust and London Life. In both cases, the head offices moved elsewhere, raising fears of lost jobs and economic dislocation.

Critics of takeovers argue that they reduce trust between management and labour thus reducing efficiency and increasing costs. They point to Japan, Germany, and Korea, where there are few takeovers, as examples of more efficient economics. They argue that, as an alternative to takeovers a strong board of outside directors could maximize management's efficiency.[12]

---

9 P. J. Regan, "Junk Bonds—Opportunity Knocks?" *Financial Analysts Journal,* May–June 1990, p. 13.

10 Another alternative is for a firm to spin off or divest negative NPV divisions. See Chapter 11 for more discussion of the abandonment option.

11 B. Burroughs, "Barbarians in Retreat," *Vanity Fair,* March 1993, p. 226.

12 This section draws on C. Robinson's points in "C. Robinson versus W. Block, Are Corporate Takeovers Good or Bad? A Debate," *Canadian Investment Review,* Fall 1991, pp. 53–60; and on a piece by the late W. S. Allen, "Relegating Corporate Takeovers to the 'Campeaust' Heap: A Proposal," *Canadian Investment Review,* Spring 1990, pp. 71–76.

23.5

SOME FINANCIAL SIDE EFFECTS OF ACQUISITIONS

In addition to the various possibilities we discussed, mergers can have some purely financial side effects; that is, things that occur regardless of whether the merger makes economic sense or not. Two such effects are particularly worth mentioning: EPS growth and diversification.

EPS Growth

earnings per share (EPS)
Net income minus any cash dividends on preferred stock, divided by the number of shares of common stock outstanding.

An acquisition can create the appearance of growth in **earnings per share (EPS).** This may fool investors into thinking the firm is doing better than it really is. What happens is easiest to see with an example.

Suppose Global Resources, Ltd., acquires Regional Enterprises. The financial positions of Global and Regional before the acquisition are shown in Table 23.3. Because the merger creates no additional value, the combined firm (Global Resources after acquiring Regional) has a value that is equal to the sum of the values of the two firms before the merger.

Both Global and Regional have 100 shares outstanding before the merger. However, Global sells for $25 per share versus $10 per share for Regional. Global therefore acquires Regional by exchanging 1 of its shares for every 2.5 Regional shares. Since there are 100 shares in Regional, it takes 100/2.5 = 40 shares in all.

After the merger, Global has 140 shares outstanding, and several things happen (see Column 3 of Table 23.3):

1. The market value of the combined firm is $3,500. This is equal to the sum of the values of the separate firms before the merger. If the market is smart, it realizes the combined firm is worth the sum of the values of the separate firms.

2. The earnings per share of the merged firm are $1.43. The acquisition enables Global to increase its earnings per share from $1 to $1.43, an increase of 43 percent.

3. Because the stock price of Global after the merger is the same as before the merger, the price/earnings ratio must fall. This is true as long as the market is smart and recognizes that the total market value has not been altered by the merger.

If the market is fooled, it might mistake the 43 percent increase in earnings per share for true growth. In this case, the price/earnings ratio of Global may not fall after the merger. Suppose the price/earnings ratio of Global remains equal to 25. Since the combined firm has earnings of $200, the total value of the combined firm increases to $5,000 (25 × $200). The per share value of Global increases to $35.71 ($5,000/140).

This is earnings growth magic. Like all good magic, it is just illusion. For it to work, the shareholders of Global and Regional must receive something for nothing. This, of course, is unlikely with so simple a trick.

Diversification

diversification
Investment in more than one asset; returns do not move proportionally in the same direction at the same time, thus reducing risk.

Diversification is commonly mentioned as a benefit to a merger. For example, U.S. Steel Corporation included diversification as a benefit in its acquisition of Marathon Oil Company, a merger that ranked in size just behind Campeau's purchase of Federated Department Stores. The problem is that diversification per se probably does not create value.

Going back to Chapter 13, diversification reduces unsystematic risk. We also saw that the value of an asset depends on its systematic risk and that diversification does not directly affect

TABLE 23.3
Financial positions of
Global Resources and
Regional Enterprises

	Global Resources before Merger	Regional Enterprises before Merger	Global Resources after Merger	
			The Market Is Smart	The Market Is Fooled
Earnings per share	$ 1.00	$ 1.00	$ 1.43	$ 1.43
Price per share	$ 25.00	$ 10.00	$ 25.00	$ 35.71
Price/earnings ratio	25	10	17.5	25
Number of shares	100	100	140	140
Total earnings	$ 100	$ 100	$ 200	$ 200
Total value	$2,500	$1,000	$3,500	$5,000

Exchange ratio: 1 share in Global for 2.5 shares in Regional.

systematic risk. Since the unsystematic risk is not especially important, there is no particular benefit to reducing it.

An easy way to see why diversification isn't an important benefit to mergers is to consider someone who owned stock in U.S. Steel and Marathon Oil. Such a shareholder is already diversified between these two investments. The merger doesn't do anything that the shareholders can't do for themselves.

More generally, shareholders can get all the diversification they want by buying stock in different companies. As a result, they won't pay a premium for a merged company just for the benefit of diversification.

By the way, we are not saying that U.S. Steel (now USX Corporation) made a mistake. At the time of the merger, U.S. Steel was a cash-rich company (more than 20 percent of its assets were in the form of cash and marketable securities). It is not uncommon to see firms with surplus cash articulating a "need" for diversification.

CONCEPT QUESTIONS

1. Why can a merger create the appearance of earnings growth?

2. Why is diversification by itself not a good reason for a merger?

23.6 THE COST OF AN ACQUISITION

We've discussed some of the benefits of acquisition. We now need to discuss the cost of a merger.[13] We learned earlier that the net incremental gain to a merger is:

$$\Delta V = V_{AB} - (V_A + V_B)$$

Also, the total value of Firm B to Firm A, V^*_B, is:

$$V^*_B = V_B + \Delta V$$

The NPV of the merger is therefore:

$$\text{NPV} = V^*_B - \text{Cost to Firm A of the acquisition} \qquad [23.1]$$

To illustrate, suppose we have the following premerger information for Firm A and Firm B:

	Firm A	Firm B
Price per share	$ 20	$ 10
Number of shares	25	10
Total market value	$500	$100

---

13 For a more complete discussion of the costs of a merger and the NPV approach, see S. C. Myers, "A Framework for Evaluating Mergers," in *Modern Developments in Financial Management*, ed. S. C. Myers (New York: Praeger Publishers, 1976).

Both of these firms are 100 percent equity. You estimate that the incremental value of the acquisition, ΔV, is $100.

The board of Firm B has indicated that it agrees to a sale if the price is $150, payable in cash or stock. This price for Firm B has two parts. Firm B is worth $100 as a stand-alone, so this is the minimum value that we could assign to Firm B. The second part, $50, is called the *merger premium,* and it represents the amount paid more than the stand-alone value.

Should Firm A acquire Firm B? Should it pay in cash or stock? To answer, we need to determine the NPV of the acquisition under both alternatives. We can start by noting that the value of Firm B to Firm A is:

$$V^*_B = \Delta V + V_B$$
$$= \$100 + 100 = \$200$$

The total value received by A from buying Firm B is thus $200. The question then is, how much does Firm A have to give up? The answer depends on whether cash or stock is used as the means of payment.

Case I: Cash Acquisition

The cost of an acquisition when cash is used is just the cash itself. So, if Firm A pays $150 in cash to purchase all the shares of Firm B, the cost of acquiring Firm B is $150. The NPV of a cash acquisition is:

$$NPV = V^*_B - \text{Cost}$$
$$= \$200 - 150 = \$50$$

The acquisition is, therefore, profitable.

After the merger, Firm AB still has 25 shares outstanding. The value of Firm A after the merger is:

$$V_{AB} = V_A + (V^*_B - \text{Cost})$$
$$= \$500 + 200 - 150$$
$$= \$550$$

This is just the premerger value of $500 plus the $50 NPV. The price per share after the merger is $550/25 = $22, a gain of $2 per share.

Case II: Stock Acquisition

Things are somewhat more complicated when stock is the means of payment. In a cash merger, the shareholders in B receive cash for their stock, and, as in the previous U.S. Steel/Marathon Oil example, they no longer participate in the company. Thus, as we have seen, the cost of the acquisition is the amount of cash needed to pay off B's stockholders.

In a stock merger, no cash actually changes hands. Instead, the shareholders in B come in as new shareholders in the merged firm. The value of the merged firm is equal to the premerger values of Firms A and B plus the incremental gain from the merger, ΔV:

$$V_{AB} = V_A + V_B + \Delta V$$
$$= \$500 + 100 + 100$$
$$= \$700$$

To give $150 worth of stock for Firm B, Firm A has to give up $150/$20 = 7.5 shares. After the merger, there are thus 25 + 7.5 = 32.5 shares outstanding and the per share value is $700/32.5 = $21.54.

Notice that the per-share price after the merger is lower under the stock purchase option. The reason has to do with the fact that B's shareholders own stock in the new firm.

It appears that Firm A paid $150 for Firm B. However, it actually paid more than that. When all is said and done, B's stockholders own 7.5 shares of stock in the merged firm. After the merger, each of these shares is worth $21.54. The total value of the consideration received by B's shareholders is thus 7.5 × $21.54 = $161.55.

This $161.55 is the true cost of the acquisition because it is what the sellers actually end up receiving. The NPV of the merger to Firm A is:

$$\text{NPV} = V^*_B - \text{Cost}$$
$$= \$200 - 161.55 = \$38.45$$

We can check this by noting that A started with 25 shares worth $20 each. The gain to A of $38.45 works out to be $38.45/25 = $1.54 per share. The value of the stock increases to $21.54 as we calculated.

When we compare the cash acquisition to the stock acquisition, we see that the cash acquisition is better in this case, because Firm A gets to keep all the NPV if it pays in cash. If it pays in stock, Firm B's stockholders share in the NPV by becoming new shareholders in A.

Cash versus Common Stock

The distinction between cash and common stock financing in a merger is an important one. If cash is used, the cost of an acquisition is not dependent on the acquisition gains. All other things being the same, if common stock is used, the cost is higher because Firm A's shareholders must share the acquisition gains with the shareholders of Firm B. However, if the NPV of the acquisition is negative, the loss is shared between the two firms.

Whether to finance an acquisition by cash or by shares of stock depends on several factors, including:[14]

1. *Sharing gains.* If cash is used to finance an acquisition, the selling firm's shareholders do not participate in the potential gains of the merger. Of course, if the acquisition is not a success, the losses are not shared, and shareholders of the acquiring firm are worse off than if stock were used.

2. *Taxes.* Acquisition by cash usually results in a taxable transaction. Acquisition by exchanging stock is generally tax free.

3. *Control.* Acquisition by cash does not affect the control of the acquiring firm. Acquisition with voting shares may have implications for control of the merged firm.

In 1999 and early 2000, high stock prices in the technology sector resulted in a number of acquisitions financed with shares as companies like JDS Uniphase and Nortel Networks expanded through acquisitions.

CONCEPT QUESTIONS

1. Why does the true cost of a stock acquisition depend on the gain from the merger?

2. What are some important factors in deciding whether to use stock or cash in an acquisition?

 23.7

DEFENSIVE TACTICS

Target firm managers frequently resist takeover attempts. Resistance usually starts with press releases and mailings to shareholders presenting management's viewpoint. It can eventually lead to legal action and solicitation of competing bids. Managerial action to defeat a takeover attempt may make target shareholders better off if it elicits a higher offer premium from the bidding firm or another firm.

Of course, management resistance may simply reflect pursuit of self-interest at the expense of shareholders. This is a controversial subject. At times, management resistance has greatly increased the amount ultimately received by shareholders. At other times, management resistance appears to have defeated all takeover attempts to the detriment of shareholders.

---

14 In Canada, cash transactions ranged from 41 percent to 50 percent of annual transaction value between 1997 and 2001 according to *Mergers & Acquisitions in Canada: 2001 Annual Directory* (Toronto: Crosbie & Company, 2002), p. 5.

In this section, we describe various defensive tactics that have been used by target firms' managements to resist unfriendly attempts. The law surrounding these defences is not settled, and some of these manoeuvres may ultimately be deemed illegal or otherwise unsuitable. Our discussion of defensive tactics that may serve to entrench management at the expense of shareholders takes us into **corporate governance.** In addition to describing management's actions, we comment on how large pension funds and other institutional investors strive to reform the corporate governance practices of companies in which they invest.

corporate governance
Rules and practices relating to how corporations are governed by management, directors, and shareholders.

The Control Block and the Corporate Charter

control block
An interest controlling 50 percent of outstanding votes plus one; thereby it may decide the fate of the firm.

If one individual or group owns 51 percent of a company's stock, this **control block** makes a hostile takeover virtually impossible. In the extreme, one interest may own all the stock. Examples are privately owned companies such as Olympia and York Developments Ltd. and Crown corporations such as Ontario Hydro. Many Canadian companies are subsidiaries of foreign corporations that own control blocks. Many domestically owned companies have controlling shareholders.[15]

As a result, control blocks are typical in Canada although they are the exception in the United States. Table 23.4 shows that only 15 of the top 100 corporations in Canada as widely held versus 73 for the United States.[16] This situation has changed somewhat in recent years, with approximately one-third of the top 100 corporations in Canada widely held as of 2003. One important implication is that minority shareholders need protection in Canada. One key group of minority shareholders are pension funds and other institutional investors. They are becoming increasingly vocal in opposing defensive tactics that are seen to be entrenching management at the expense of stockholders. We discuss several examples next.

For widely held companies, their corporate charters establish the conditions that allow for takeovers. The *corporate charter* refers to the articles of incorporation and corporate by-laws that establish the governance rules of the firm. Firms can amend their corporate charters to make acquisitions more difficult. For example, usually two-thirds of the shareholders of record must approve a merger. Firms can make it more difficult to be acquired by changing this to 80 percent or so. This is called a *supermajority amendment.*

Another device is to stagger the election of the board members. This makes it more difficult to elect a new board of directors quickly. We discuss staggered elections in Chapter 8.

Repurchase/Standstill Agreements

Managers of target firms may attempt to negotiate standstill agreements. Standstill agreements are contracts where the bidding firm agrees to limit its holdings in the target firm. These agreements usually lead to the end of takeover attempts.

In the U.S., standstill agreements often occur at the same time that a targeted repurchase is arranged. In a targeted repurchase, a firm buys a certain amount of its own stock from an individual investor, usually at a substantial premium. These premiums can be thought of as payments to potential bidders to eliminate unfriendly takeover attempts. Critics of such payments view

TABLE 23.4
Ownership makeup of the top 100 corporations

	Canada	United States
Widely held	15	73
Control block	50	25
Privately owned	28	2
Government owned	7	0

Source: D.H. Thain and D.S.R. Leighton, "Ownership Structure and the Board," *Canadian Investment Review,* Fall 1991, pp. 61–66.

15 Important exceptions are chartered banks. As we showed in Chapter 1, at the time of writing, the *Bank Act* prohibited any one interest from owning more than 10 percent of the shares.

16 The top 100 corporations in Canada are from *The Financial Post 500.* The U.S. corporations come from Fortune 500. The table is from D. H. Thain and D. S. R. Leighton, "Ownership Structure and the Board," *Canadian Investment Review,* Fall 1991, pp. 61–66.

greenmail
A targeted stock repurchase where payments are made to potential bidders to eliminate unfriendly takeover attempts.

them as bribes and label them **greenmail.** Paying greenmail may harm minority shareholders if it heads off a takeover that would raise the stock price.

Standstill agreements also occur in takeover attempts in Canada but without greenmail, which is ruled out by securities laws. For example, in March 2006, Wendy's International Inc. entered into a standstill agreement with the Nelson Peltz-led investor group that has a 5.5 percent stake in the fast-food empire. The investor group agreed to not acquire more than a 10 percent stake in Wendy's International before June 30, 2007. Also included in the agreement was that the investor group would not submit any shareholder proposals or solicit proxies during the 15-month standstill agreement period. In exchange for entering into the agreement, Wendy's promised to expand its board of directors from 12 to 15 members and nominate three candidates representing the Nelson Peltz-led investor group. Even so, critics of standstill agreements argue that in cases like this, such agreements often cause losses for minority shareholders by averting takeovers at a premium price.

Exclusionary Offers and Non-Voting Stock

www.magna.com
www.canadiantire.ca

An exclusionary offer is the opposite of a targeted repurchase. Here the firm or an outside group makes an offer for a given amount of stock while excluding targeted shareholders, often holders of non-voting shares. This kind of an offer is made easier in Canada since non-voting shares are more prevalent than in the United States. As of 2003, 52 out of 220 companies that made up the S&P/TSX Composite had dual class share structures, with some 39 of them controlled by a single shareholder or family. For example, the Stronach family owned only 0.8 percent of the equity in the firm but controlled 66.2 percent of the votes at Magna International (the highest voting power to equity ownership ratio for a composite company). Magna, in turn, held voting control at Decoma and Tesma International (both also part of the S&P/TSX Composite) through use of dual class share structures.[17]

A well-known example occurred in 1986 when the Canadian Tire Dealers Association offered to buy 49 percent of Canadian Tire's voting shares from the founding Billes family. The dealers' bid was at $169 per share for voting shares trading at $40 before the bid. The non-voting shares were priced at $14. Further, since the dealers were the principal buyers of Canadian Tire products, control of the company would have allowed them to adjust prices to benefit themselves over the non-voting shareholders.[18] At the time of writing in 2003, the Billes family still retained control of 61.4 percent of the votes at Canadian Tire though only 3.8 percent of the shares (the second highest voting power to equity ratio for a composite company).[19]

The offer was voided by the Ontario Securities Commission and it appears that any future exclusionary offers are likely to be viewed as an illegal form of discrimination against one group of shareholders.

Share Rights Plans

poison pill
A financial device designed to make unfriendly takeover attempts unappealing, if not impossible.

shareholder rights plan
Provisions allowing existing shareholders to purchase stock at some fixed price should an outside takeover bid take place, discouraging hostile takeover attempts.

A **poison pill** is a tactic designed to repel would-be suitors. The term comes from the world of espionage. Agents are supposed to bite a pill of cyanide rather than permit capture. Presumably, this prevents enemy interrogators from learning important secrets.

In the equally colourful world of corporate finance, a poison pill is a financial device designed to make it impossible for a firm to be acquired without management's consent—unless the buyer is willing to commit financial suicide.

In recent years, many of the largest firms in the United States and Canada have adopted poison pill provisions of one form or another, often calling them **shareholder rights plans** (SRPs) or something similar. Inco introduced the first poison pill in Canada in 1988.

---

17 This discussion is drawn from S. Maich, "Stronach has most votes, least shares," *National Post,* June 11, 2003, IN1.

18 Chapter 8 discusses restricted voting stock and Canadian Tire in detail.

19 S. Maich, "Stronach has most votes, least shares," *National Post,* June 11, 2003, IN1.

SRPs differ quite a bit in detail from company to company; we describe a kind of generic approach here. In general, when a company adopts an SRP, it distributes share rights to its existing shareholders.[20] These rights allow shareholders to buy shares of stock (or preferred stock) at some fixed price.

The rights issued with an SRP have a number of unusual features. First, the exercise or subscription price on the right is usually set high enough so the rights are well out of the money, meaning the purchase price is much higher than the current stock price. The rights are often good for 10 years, and the purchase or exercise price is usually a reasonable estimate of what the stock will be worth at that time.

Second, unlike ordinary stock rights, these rights can't be exercised immediately, and they can't be bought and sold separately from the stock. Also, they can essentially be cancelled by management at any time; often, they can be redeemed (bought back) for a penny apiece, or some similarly trivial amount.

Things get interesting when, under certain circumstances, the rights are triggered. This means the rights become exercisable, they can be bought and sold separately from the stock, and they are not easily cancelled or redeemed. Typically, the rights are triggered when someone acquires 20 percent of the common stock or otherwise announces a tender offer.

When the rights are triggered, they can be exercised. Since they are out of the money, this fact is not especially important. Certain other features come into play, however. The most important is the flip-over provision.

The flip-over provision is the poison in the pill. In the event of a merger, the holder of a right can pay the exercise price and receive common stock in the merged firm worth twice the exercise price. In other words, holders of the right can buy stock in the merged firm at half price.[21]

The rights issued in connection with an SRP are poison pills because anyone trying to force a merger would trigger the rights. When this happens, all the target firm's shareholders can effectively buy stock in the merged firm at half price. This greatly increases the cost of the merger to the bidder because the target firm's shareholders end up with a much larger percentage of the merged firm.

Notice that the flip-over provision doesn't prevent someone from acquiring control of a firm by purchasing a majority interest. It just acts to prevent a complete merger of the two firms. Even so, this inability to combine can have serious tax and other implications for the buyer.

The intention of a poison pill is to force a bidder to negotiate with management. This can be bad news for shareholders of the target firm if it discourages takeovers and entrenches inefficient management. On the other hand, poison pills could be positive for the target's shareholders if they allow management time to find competing offers that maximize the selling price.

In Canada, several arrangements exist that make poison pills more beneficial to target shareholders than in the U.S. First, the Ontario Securities Commission and its counterparts in other provinces, intervene in takeover bids to rule on the acceptability of poison pills. In many cases, the result has been to extend the waiting period and increase shareholder value.[22] Still, most large Canadian institutional investors like the Caisse de depot or Ontario Teachers' Pension Plan consider the introduction of poison pills to be a bad corporate governance practice.

www.lacaisse.com
www.otpp.com

Going Private and Leveraged Buyouts

As we have previously discussed, going private refers to what happens when the publicly owned stock in a firm is replaced with complete equity ownership by a private group, which may include elements of existing management. As a consequence, the firm's stock is taken off the market (if it is an exchange-traded stock, it is delisted) and is no longer traded.

---

20 We discuss ordinary share rights in Chapter 15.

21 Some plans also contain flip-in provisions. These allow the holder to buy stock in the target company at half price when the target company is the surviving company in a merger. Simultaneously, the rights owned by the raider (the acquirer) are voided. A merger where the target is the surviving company is called a *reverse merger*.

22 For a detailed discussion of poison pills in Canada, see P. Halpern, "Poison Pills: The Next Decade," *Canadian Investment Review* 11, Winter 1998, pp. 69–70.

One result of going private is that takeovers via tender offer can no longer occur since there are no publicly held shares. In this sense, an LBO (or, more specifically, a management buyout or MBO) can be a takeover defence. However, it's only a defence for management. From the stockholder's point of view, an LBO is a takeover because they are bought out.

In an LBO, the selling shareholders are invariably paid a premium more than the market price, just as they are in a merger.[23] As with a merger, the acquirer profits only if the synergy created is greater than the premium. Synergy is quite plausible in a merger of two firms, and we delineated a number of types of synergy earlier in the chapter. However, it is much more difficult to explain synergy in an LBO, because only one firm is involved.

There are generally two reasons given for the ability of an LBO to create value: First, the extra debt provides a tax deduction, which, as earlier chapters suggest, leads to an increase in firm value. Most LBOs are on firms with stable earnings and with low to moderate debt.[24] The LBO may simply increase the firm's debt to its optimum level.

Second, the LBO usually turns the previous managers into owners, thereby increasing their incentive to work hard. The increase in debt is a further incentive because the managers must earn more than the debt service to obtain any profit for themselves.

LBOs to Date: The Record

Since the mid-1980s, ongoing experience with LBOs has revealed some weaknesses both in the concept and the financing vehicle—junk bonds.

Problems facing LBOs in the early 1990s are exemplified in the trials of Robert Campeau whose real estate company took over Allied Stores in 1986 and then Federated Department Stores in 1988.

Campeau was correct; Federated Department Stores assets were undervalued at the pre-takeover share price of $33 but hindsight shows that the $73.50 per share takeover price was too high. Further, the deal was overleveraged with 97 percent debt financing. With either a lower purchase price, or lower leverage, the deal might have survived.[25]

Despite an injection of $300 million from Olympia & York Developments Ltd. (then owned by the Reichmann family of Toronto), Campeau Corporation had to default on its bank loans. As a result, the National Bank of Canada took over 35 percent of Campeau's voting stock in January 1990. Shortly after, Allied and Federated filed for bankruptcy protection in the United States. Over the next year, Campeau sold just under $2 billion in Canadian real estate to try to reduce its debt to manageable levels in order to survive.[26] In January 1991, Campeau Corporation's name was changed to Candev with a 65 percent control block in the hands of Olympia & York. Robert Campeau lost his seat on the board and all but 2 percent of the company's stock. LBO problems reflected on the high-yield or junk bonds used heavily to finance them. For example, when Allied and Federated sought bankruptcy protection in 1990, Campeau junk bonds that had a face value of $1,000 sold for $110.[27] In a more positive example, Kohlberg Kravis Roberts and Ontario Teachers' Pension Plan bought Yellow Pages from Bell Canada in a $3-billion LBO in 2002. In July 2003, they sold part of their holding for $1 billion in an income trust IPO.[28]

---

23 H. DeAngelo, L. DeAngelo and E. M. Rice, "Going Private: Minority Freezeouts and Shareholder Wealth," *Journal of Law and Economics* 27 (1984). They show that the premiums paid to existing shareholders in U.S. LBOs and other going-private transactions are about the same as interfirm acquisitions.

24 T. Melman, "Leveraged Buyouts: How Everyone Can Win," *Canadian Investment Review,* Spring 1990, pp. 67–70, discusses LBOs from a management perspective.

25 S. N. Kaplan, "Campeau's Acquisition of Federated, Value Destroyed or Value Added?" *Journal of Financial Economics,* December 1989, pp. 189–212.

26 S. Horvitch, "Campeau 'Selling Itself' to Survive," *The Financial Post,* July 1, 1991, p. 22.

27 See Edward Altman in Chapter 7 for more on problems with junk bonds in the United States.

28 Our discussion draws on Laura Santini, "Deals & Dealmakers: Ontario Teachers' Makes Grade With Private-Equity Plays," *Wall Street Journal,* August 15, 2005, p. C1.

In Their Own Words . . .

Andrew Willis on the Leverage Buyout Experience at Shoppers Drug Mart

CANADA has been very, very good to Kohlberg Kravis Roberts.

The world's best-known leveraged buyout firm took a few more chips off the table yesterday by leading a syndicate of owners that sold up to 20 million shares in Shoppers Drug Mart for $460 million.

KKR, made famous for its *Barbarians at the Gate* takeover of RJR Nabisco, bought Canada's biggest drugstore chain from conglomerate Imasco just four years ago. The management-led buyout saw KKR and backers that included the Ontario Teachers Pension Plan Board and CIBC World Markets put up $5 a share to buy Shoppers equity, and borrow the rest of the $2.55-billion purchase price.

Today, Shoppers is a $5-billion company, with a stock that was halted for the share sale after changing hands at $23.55 on the Toronto Stock Exchange. In the Street's term, KKR and friends have a four-bagger. Their original investment has increased fourfold in as many years. (It's worth noting that Shoppers management did not opt to sell any of their shares.)

After this share sale, the KKR-led group will hold roughly 60 percent of Shoppers, down from 70 percent of the chain.

"We are pleased to have this opportunity to expand our shareholder base with additional long-term investors, while at the same time increasing the size and liquidity of the company's public float," Glenn Murphy, Shoppers chairman and CEO, said in a press release late yesterday.

Shoppers' controlling shareholders commissioned CIBC World Markets and Merrill Lynch to do what's known as an overnight marketed deal. The dealers announced they were selling shares late yesterday. During the evening and early morning, they called potential investors. A price for the new shares will be set before trading begins this morning. Given the communications reach of modern technology—cell-phones and BlackBerrys—such a campaign allows for a major sales effort.

This is the second time that KKR and its partners at Shoppers have cashed in part of their winnings. Last June, the financiers moved $644-million worth of stock, selling at $23 a share.

Over 26 years, KKR has purchased $110-billion (U.S.) worth of companies, averaging 3.5 buyouts a year.

Shoppers is the firm's second major win in this country. In the 1990s, KKR had another four-bagger when it bought, then quickly resold, Canadian General Insurance.

Andrew Willis writes for *The Globe and Mail*. His comments are reproduced with permission from the May 7, 2003 edition. Photo: Darryl James/*The Globe and Mail*.

Other Defensive Devices

As corporate takeovers become more common, other colourful terms have become popular.

- *Golden parachutes.* Some target firms provide compensation to top-level management if a takeover occurs. This can be viewed as a payment to management to make it less concerned for its own welfare and more interested in shareholders when considering a takeover bid. Alternatively, the payment can be seen as an attempt to enrich management at the shareholders' expense.

- *Crown jewels.* Firms often sell major assets—crown jewels—when faced with a takeover threat. This is sometimes referred to as the *scorched earth strategy.*

- *White knight.* Target firms sometimes seek a competing bid from a friendly bidder—a white knight—who promises to maintain the jobs of existing management and to refrain from selling the target's assets.

Chapters, one of Canada's largest bookstore chains, was taken over for $121 million in February of 2001 by Trilogy Retail Enterprises, a firm headed by Indigo founder Heather Reisman and spouse Gerald Schwartz, of Onex Corp. The takeover was launched with the intention of merging Indigo and Chapters to create a Canadian bookstore super-chain.

Before giving in to Trilogy Retail Enterprises' final takeover bid of $121 million, Chapters' board of directors and management explored takeover defenses. Chapters had a poison pill in place to prevent a hostile takeover. When Trilogy made a partial bid which, if successful, would have given Trilogy 53 percent of Chapters, Chapters shareholders (other than the hostile bidder) had a right to purchase additional Chapters' shares at half the market price. As well, 51 days after Trilogy's initial bid, Chapters announced an offer from a white knight, Future Shop, which the Chapters' board recommended to the shareholders. Chapters entered into a support agreement with Future Shop which provided that the poison pill would only be waived for competing bids upon the take-up of Chapters' shares by Future Shop, and would remain in place to give Future Shop time to prepare and mail their offer. The poison pill was eventually removed because the OSC found that Future Shop had already had substantial time to prepare its bid. In the end, Future Shop's role as a white knight forced Trilogy to raise its bid to $121 million, finally resulting in the takeover after months of media-publicized drama.

CONCEPT QUESTIONS

1. What can a firm do to make takeover less likely?

2. What is a share rights plan? Explain how the rights work.

3. What are the main problems faced by LBOs in the early 1990s?

23.8 SOME EVIDENCE ON ACQUISITIONS

One of the most controversial issues surrounding our subject is whether mergers and acquisitions benefit shareholders. Quite a few studies have attempted to estimate the effect of mergers and takeovers on stock prices of the bidding and target firms. These are called *event studies* because they estimate abnormal stock-price changes on and around the offer-announcement date—the event. Abnormal returns are usually defined as the difference between actual stock returns and a market index, to take account of the influence of marketwide effects on the returns of individual securities.

Table 23.5 summarizes the results of numerous studies that look at the effects of merger and tender offers on stock prices in the United States. Table 23.6 shows the highpoints of three studies on mergers in Canada. Both tables are relevant because firms from one country often purchase companies in the other.

The tables show that the shareholders of target companies in successful takeovers gain substantially. Starting with U.S. takeovers in Table 23.5, when the takeover is accomplished by merger, the gains are 20 percent; when the takeover is via tender offer, the gains are 30 percent.

The Canadian studies did not distinguish among tender offers, mergers, and proxy contests in looking at target returns. The first two studies listed in Table 23.6 found gains of 9–10 percent, more modest than for the United States. The other studies found that target firm shareholders in going-private transactions enjoyed an abnormal return of 23 to 25 percent, a figure consistent with U.S. results in Table 23.5.

The Canadian study of going-private transactions also looked at whether minority shareholders suffer. You can see from Table 23.6 that the answer is no. Returns to minority shareholders hardly differ from returns that occurred when firms went private with no majority shareholder.[29]

TABLE 23.5

Stock price changes in successful U.S. corporate takeovers

Takeover Technique	Target	Bidders
Tender offer	30%	4%
Merger	20	0
Proxy contest	8	NA*

*NA = Not applicable.
Modified from Michael C. Jensen and Richard S. Ruback, "The Market for Corporate Control: The Scientific Evidence," *Journal of Financial Economics* 11 (April 1983), pp. 7, 8. © Elsevier Science Publishers B.V. (North-Holland).

---

29 In contrast, in a later study of takeovers and dual class shares in Canada, Smith and Amoako-Adu find that shareholders with superior voting shares enjoy higher returns: B.F. Smith and B. Amoako-Adu, "A Comparative Analysis of Takeovers of Single and Dual Class Firms," *Financial Review* 29 (February 1994).

TABLE 23.6

Abnormal returns in successful Canadian mergers

	Target	Bidder
1,271 aquired, 242 targets, 1994–2000**	10%	1%
1,930 mergers, 1964–1983*	9	3
119 mergers, 1963–1982†	23	11
173 going-private transactions, 1977–1989‡	25	NA
Minority buyouts	27	
Non-controlling bidder	24	

*From B. Espen Eckbo, "Mergers and the Market for Corporate Control: The Canadian Evidence," *Canadian Journal of Economics,* May 1986, pp. 236–60. The test for bidders excluded firms involved in multiple mergers.

†From A. L. Calvet and J. Lefoll, "Information Asymmetry and Wealth Effect of Canadian Corporate Acquisitions," *Financial Review,* November 1987, pp. 415–31.

‡Modified from B. Amoako-Adu and B. Smith, "How Do Shareholders Fare in Minority Buyouts?" *Canadian Investment Review,* Fall 1991, pp. 79–88.

** From A. Yuce and A. Ng, "Effects of Private and Public Canadian Mergers," *Canadian Journal of Administrative Sciences,* June 2005, pp. 111–124.

For both countries, these gains are a reflection of the merger premium that is typically paid by the acquiring firm. These gains are excess returns, that is, the returns over and above what the shareholders would normally have earned.

The shareholders of bidding firms do not fare as well. According to the U.S. studies summarized in Table 23.5, bidders experience gains of 4 percent in tender offers, but this gain is about zero in mergers.[30] Canadian research places bidders' gains in a range from 1 to 11 percent. It also suggests that bidding firms do poorly over a longer, three-year, period after the merger.[31]

What conclusions can be drawn from Tables 23.5 and 23.6? First, the evidence strongly suggests that the shareholders of successful target firms achieve substantial gains as a result of takeovers. The gains appear to be larger in tender offers than in mergers. This may reflect the fact that takeovers sometimes start with a friendly merger proposal from the bidder to the management of the target firm. If management rejects the offer, the bidding firm may take the offer directly to the shareholders with a tender offer. As a consequence, tender offers are frequently unfriendly.

Also, the target firm's management may actively oppose the offer with defensive tactics. This often has the result of raising the tender offer from the bidding firm; on average, friendly mergers may be arranged at lower premiums than unfriendly tender offers.

The second conclusion we can draw is that the shareholders of bidding firms earn significantly less from takeovers. The balance is more even for Canadian mergers. This may be because there is less competition among bidders in Canada. Two reasons for this are that the Canadian capital market is smaller and that federal government agencies review foreign investments.[32]

In fact, studies have found that the acquiring firms actually lose value in many mergers. These findings are a puzzle, and there are a variety of explanations:

1. Anticipated merger gains may not have been completely achieved, and shareholders thus experienced losses. This can happen if managers of bidding firms tend to overestimate the gains from acquisition, as we saw happened to Campeau Corporation.

2. The bidding firms are often much larger than the target firms. Thus, even though the dollar gains to the bidder may be similar to the dollar gains earned by shareholders of the target firm, the percentage gains are much lower.[33]

3. Another possible explanation for the low returns to the shareholders of bidding firms in takeovers is simply that management may not be acting in the interest of shareholders

---

30 Loughran and Vijh find that bidders experience below-average returns for five years after acquisitions: T. Loughran and A. Vijh, "Do Long-Term Shareholders Benefit from Corporate Acquisitions," *Journal of Finance* (December 1997).

31 P. André, M. Kooli and J-F L'Her, "The Long-Run Performance of Mergers and Acquisitions: Evidence from the Canadian Stock Market," *Financial Management,* Winter 2004, pp. 27–43.

32 P. Halpern, "Poison Pills," p. 66; and A. L. Calvet and J. Lefoll, "Information Asymmetry," p. 432.

33 This factor cannot explain the imbalance in returns in the first Canadian study in Table 23.6. In this sample, bidder and target firms were about the same size.

when it attempts to acquire other firms. Perhaps, it is attempting to increase the size of the firm, even if this reduces its value per share.

4. The market for takeovers may be sufficiently competitive that the NPV of acquiring is zero because the prices paid in acquisitions fully reflect the value of the acquired firms. In other words, the sellers capture all the gain.

5. Finally, the announcement of a takeover may not convey much new information to the market about the bidding firm. This can occur because firms frequently announce intentions to engage in merger programs long before they announce specific acquisitions. In this case, the stock price in the bidding firm may already reflect anticipated gains from mergers.

CONCEPT QUESTIONS

1. What does the evidence say about the benefits of mergers and acquisitions to target company shareholders?

2. What does the evidence say about the benefits of mergers and acquisitions to acquiring company shareholders?

3. What is the evidence on whether minority shareholders are shortchanged in mergers?

divestiture
The sale of assets, operations, divisions, and/or segments of a business to a third party.

equity carve-out
The sale of stock in a wholly owned subsidiary via an IPO.

spin-off
The distribution of shares in a subsidiary to existing parent company shareholders.

split-up
The splitting up of a company into two or more companies.

DIVESTITURES AND RESTRUCTURINGS

In contrast to a merger or acquisition, a **divestiture** occurs when a firm sells assets, operations, divisions, and/or segments to a third party. Note that divestitures are an important part of M&A activity. After all, one company's acquisition is usually another's divestiture. Also, following a merger, it is very common for certain assets or divisions to be sold. Such sales may be required by antitrust regulations; they may be needed to raise cash to help pay for a deal; or the divested units may simply be unwanted by the acquirer.

Divestitures also occur when a company decides to sell off a part of itself for reasons unrelated to mergers and acquisitions. This can happen when a particular unit is unprofitable or not a good strategic fit. Or, a firm may decide to cash out of a very profitable operation. Finally, a cash-strapped firm may have to sell assets just to raise capital (this commonly occurs in bankruptcy).

A divestiture usually occurs like any other sale. A company lets it be known that it has assets for sale and seeks offers. If a suitable offer is forthcoming, a sale occurs.

In some cases, particularly when the desired divestiture is a relatively large operating unit, companies will elect to do an **equity carve-out**. To do a carve-out, a parent company first creates a completely separate company of which the parent is the sole shareholder. Next, the parent company arranges an initial public offering (IPO) in which a fraction, perhaps 20 percent or so, of the parent's stock is sold to the public, thus creating a publicly held company. An example of an equity carve-out is Wendy's International selling a small portion of wholly-owned Tim Hortons via IPO in March 2006.

Instead of a carve-out, a company can elect to do a **spin-off**. In a spin-off, the company simply distributes shares in the subsidiary to its existing shareholders on a pro rata basis. Shareholders can keep the shares or sell them as they see fit. Very commonly, a company will first do an equity carve-out to create an active market for the shares and then subsequently do a spin-off of the remaining shares at a later date. Many well-known companies were created by this route. For example, insurance giant Allstate was spun off by Sears; Palm Computing was a 3Com spin-off; and Energizer was a spin-off of Ralston Purina, a company that produced pet food and batteries.

In a less common, but more drastic move, a company can elect to do (or be forced to do) a **split-up**. A split-up is just what the name suggests: A company splits itself into two or more new companies. Shareholders have their shares in the old company swapped for shares in the new companies. Probably the most famous split-up occurred in the United States in the 1980s. As a result of an antitrust suit brought by the Justice Department, AT&T was forced to split up through the creation of seven regional phone companies (the so-called Baby Bells). Today, the Baby Bells survive as companies such as BellSouth, SBC Communications, and Verizon.

CONCEPT QUESTIONS

1. What is an equity carve-out? Why might a firm wish to do one?

2. What is a split-up? Why might a firm choose to do one?

23.10

SUMMARY AND CONCLUSIONS

This chapter introduced you to the extensive literature on mergers and acquisitions. We touched on a number of issues, including:

1. Form of merger. One firm can acquire another in several different ways. The three legal forms of acquisition are merger and consolidation, acquisition of stock, and acquisition of assets.

2. Tax issues. Mergers and acquisitions can be taxable or tax-free transactions. The primary issue is whether the target firm's shareholders sell or exchange their shares. Generally, a cash purchase is a taxable merger, while a stock exchange is not taxable. In a taxable merger, there are capital gains effects and asset write-up effects to consider. In a stock exchange, the target firm's shareholders become shareholders in the merged firm.

3. Merger valuation. If Firm A is acquiring Firm B, the benefits (ΔV) from an acquisition are defined as the value of the combined firm (V_{AB}) less the value of the firms as separate entities (V_A and V_B), or:

$$\Delta V = V_{AB} - (V_A + V_B)$$

The gain to Firm A from acquiring Firm B is the increased value of the acquired firm (ΔV) plus the value of B as a separate firm. The total value of Firm B to Firm A, V^*_B, is thus:

$$V^*_B = \Delta V + V_B$$

An acquisition benefits the shareholders of the acquiring firm if this value is greater than the cost of the acquisition. The cost of an acquisition can be defined in general terms as the price paid to the shareholders of the acquired firm. The cost frequently includes a merger premium paid to the shareholders of the acquired firm. Moreover, the cost depends on the form of payment, that is, the choice between cash or common stock.

4. The possible benefits of an acquisition come from several possible sources, including the following:

   a. Revenue enhancement.
   b. Cost reduction.
   c. Lower taxes.
   d. Changing capital requirements.

5. Some of the most colourful language of finance comes from defensive tactics in acquisition battles. *Poison pills, golden parachutes,* and *greenmail* are terms that describe various antitakeover tactics.

6. Mergers and acquisitions have been extensively studied. The basic conclusions are that, on average, the shareholders of target firms do very well, while the shareholders of bidding firms do not appear to gain anywhere near as much.

In Their Own Words . . . Claude Lamoureux on Corporate Governance

GOVERNANCE MATTERS to a company's performance. The point is well made in a study by Paul Gompers and Joy Ishii published in Harvard's Quarterly Journal of Economics entitled "Corporate Governance and Equity Prices." That study constructed an index of 24 governance rules and applied it to the performance of 1,500 firms during the 1990s. It found that companies with best governance practices had a higher stock return during this decade.

Yes, good governance matters. And more companies are paying attention. For instance, the Canadian banks are notable for their responsiveness to shareholder concerns. They and many of our large corporations are listening and have made changes to executive compensation and in some cases have even ended stock options for directors. But these are still the exceptions, not the rule.

Judging by the attitude of many companies during this year's proxy season and shareholder meetings, it is as if the recent spate of governance, accounting, and disclosure scandals never happened. There is no groundswell in the boardrooms of North America. Many directors and executives still do not accept that shareholders own the firms they govern and manage, and deserve to be treated as owners.

Ontario Teachers' has been advocating governance changes for more than a decade. It is clear to us that entrenched corporate reactionaries won't change unless change is forced upon them. First, by legislation. Second, through a strong and national securities regulator. Third, by informed and determined shareholders banding together to make things happen.

Let's look at how these forces might shape a better governance world. Do we really need more rules and regulations? I would like to say no, but unfortunately the answer is yes. Voluntary compliance by publicly traded companies does not work well enough to protect shareholder interests. The Toronto Stock Exchange has had voluntary guidelines since 1995. The majority of listed companies do not bother to report in their annual report or proxy circular whether or not they comply with the guidelines. Most who do state that they do not comply. Why should they? The TSX has no enforcement role. The TSX is the wrong body to impose governance compliance. Enforcement should be expressed in legislation and carried out by securities regulators.

Not surprisingly, the opinion in Canada's boardrooms is that we do not need more legislation and regulations. We heard that in the Canadian reaction to the Sarbanes-Oxley Act. We should not delude ourselves that there are deep differences between our corporate culture and capital markets compared with the U.S. The argument is often put forward that Canada is different from the U.S. because we have a greater number of small companies. We also have many firms that are family owned or controlled by a single shareholder. They often assert control through multiple

voting shares that are grossly out of proportion to their economic exposure as shareholders. Surely, if a company sells shares to the public it should be held to the same governance standards as any other public company—irrespective of size or controlling ownership.

This brings me to the second force that is needed to effectively shape corporate governance—a national securities regulator with the powers to act. Unlike other nations with sophisticated capital markets, Canada does not have a national securities regulator. We rank sixth in the world in terms of market capitalization. That is less than two percent of global market capitalization, and about five percent of North American market capitalization. Yet regulating this tiny market from the global perspective is carved up among thirteen jurisdictions. This balkanization is a disservice to Canadian investors, a burden on corporate issuers, and a discouragement to foreign investors.

Clear and enforceable legislation and an empowered national securities regulator would do a lot to move governance standards forward. But in our view the most vital force for change must be shareholders asserting their ownership rights. That means making management accountable to directors as the stewards for the shareholders.

Clearly the soft stuff is important. Good governance is about more than laws and regulations. It has to do with human nature and how individuals interact with each other.

Recently a group of institutional investors incorporated the Canadian Coalition for Good Governance as a non-profit corporation. In case you missed it, let me remind you of its mission. It is to represent institutional shareholders—as well as small shareholders—through the promotion of best corporate governance practices and align the interests of boards and management with those of shareholders. So how can we improve the situation? First, we should change the way directors are elected. The practice of voting for a slate of directors should be abolished. Second, more candidates should be nominated than there are board seats so that shareholders have choice. A third suggestion is a mandatory annual meeting of directors with major shareholders. Specifically, with shareholders who have owned shares for at least one year. Long-term shareholders are informed shareholders. They want the company to do well over the long term.

Speech entitled "In Their Own Words... Claude Lamoureux on Corporate Governance," excerpted with permission from a speech delivered in May 2003. For more information on corporate governance, see *www-otpp.com*.

Key Terms

amalgamations (page 697)
circular bid (page 698)
consolidation (page 697)
control block (page 712)
corporate governance (page 712)
diversification (page 708)
divestiture (719)
earnings per share (EPS) (page 708)
equity carve-out (719)
going-private transactions (page 699)
greenmail (page 713)
joint venture (699)

leveraged buyouts (LBOs) (page 699)
merger (page 697)
poison pill (page 713)
proxy contests (page 699)
shareholder rights plan (page 713)
spin-off (719)
split-up (719)
stock exchange bid (page 698)
strategic alliance (699)
synergy (page 702)
tender offer (page 697)

Chapter Review Problems and Self-Test

23.1 Merger Value and Cost Consider the following information for two all-equity firms, A and B:

	Firm A	Firm B
Shares outstanding	100	50
Price per share	$50	$30

Firm A estimates that the value of the synergistic benefit from acquiring Firm B is $200. Firm B has indicated it would accept a cash purchase offer of $35 per share. Should Firm A proceed?

23.2 Stock Mergers and EPS Consider the following information for two all-equity firms, A and B:

	Firm A	Firm B
Total earnings	$1,000	$400
Shares outstanding	100	80
Price per share	$ 50	$ 30

Firm A is acquiring Firm B by exchanging 25 of its shares for all the shares in B. What is the cost of the merger if the merged firm is worth $11,000? What will happen to Firm A's EPS? Its P/E ratio?

Answers to Self-Test Problems

23.1 The total value of Firm B to Firm A is the premerger value of B plus the $200 gain from the merger. The premerger value of B is $30 × 50 = $1,500, so the total value is $1,700. At $35 per share, A is paying $35 × 50 = $1,750; the merger therefore has a negative NPV of –$50. At $35 per share, B is not an attractive merger partner.

23.2 After the merger, the firm would have 125 shares outstanding. Since the total value is $11,000, the price per share is $11,000/125 = $88, up from $80. Since Firm B's stockholders end up with 25 shares in the merged firm, the cost of the merger is 25 × $88 = $2,200, not 25 × 80 = $2,000. Also, the combined firm has $1,000 + 400 = $1,400 in earnings, so EPS will be $1,400/125 = $11.20, up from $1,000/100 = $10. The old P/E ratio was $80/$10 = 8. The new one is $88/11.20 = 7.86.

Concepts Review and Critical Thinking Questions

1. Define each of the following terms:
   a. Greenmail
   b. White knight
   c. Golden parachute
   d. Crown jewels
   e. Shark repellent
   f. Corporate raider
   g. Poison pill
   h. Tender offer
   i. Leveraged buyout, or LBO
2. Explain why diversification *per se* is probably not a good reason for merger.
3. In January 1996, Dun and Bradstreet Corp. announced plans to split into three entities: an information services core to include Moody's credit-rating agencies, a company that would include the Nielsen media-rating

business, and a third entity that would focus on tracking consumer packaged-goods purchases. D&B was not alone, because many companies voluntarily split up in the 1990s. Why might a firm do this? Is there a possibility of reverse synergy?

4. Are poison pills good or bad for stockholders? How do you think acquiring firms are able to get around poison pills?
5. Describe the advantages and disadvantages of a taxable merger as opposed to a tax-free exchange. What is the basic determinant of tax status in a merger? Would an LBO be taxable or nontaxable? Explain.
6. What does it mean to say that a proposed merger will take advantage of available economies of scale? Suppose Eastern Power Co. and Western Power Co. are located in different time zones. Both of them operate

at 60 percent of capacity except for peak periods, when they operate at 100 percent of capacity. The peak periods begin at 9:00 a.m. and 5:00 p.m. local time and last about 45 minutes. Explain why a merger between Eastern and Western might make sense.

7. What types of actions might the management of a firm take to fight a hostile acquisition bid from an unwanted suitor? How do the target-firm shareholders benefit from the defensive tactics of their management team? How are the target-firm shareholders harmed by such actions? Explain.

8. Suppose a company in which you own stock has attracted two takeover offers. Would it ever make sense for your company's management to favour the lower offer? Does the form of payment affect your answer at all?

9. Acquiring-firm stockholders seem to benefit very little from takeovers. Why is this finding a puzzle? What are some of the reasons offered for it?

10. What is the difference between an equity carve-out and a spin-off? Why would a corporation choose to do one over the other? Describe a situation where an equity carve-out would be more advantageous than a spin-off. Describe a situation where a spin-off would be more advantageous than an equity carve-out.

Questions and Problems

**Basic
(Questions
1–8)**

1. **Calculating Synergy**   Pearl Inc. has offered $740 million cash for all the common stock in Jam Corporation. Based on recent market information, Jam is worth $650 million as an independent operation. If the merger makes economic sense for Pearl, what is the minimum estimated value of the synergistic benefits from the merger?

2. **Balance Sheets for Mergers**   Consider the following premerger information about Firm X and Firm Y:

	Firm X	Firm Y
Total earnings	$40,000	$15,000
Shares outstanding	20,000	20,000
Per-share values:		
Market	$ 49	$ 18
Book	$ 20	$ 7

Assume that Firm X acquires Firm Y by paying cash for all the shares outstanding at a merger premium of $5 per share. Assuming that neither firm has any debt before or after the merger, construct the postmerger balance sheet for Firm X, using the purchase accounting method.

3. **Balance Sheets for Mergers**   Assume that the following balance sheets are stated at book value. Construct a postmerger balance sheet assuming that Meat Co. purchases Loaf, Inc. and the pooling of interests method of accounting is used.

MEAT CO.

Current assets	$ 10,000	Current liabilities	$ 3,100
Net fixed assets	14,000	Long-term debt	1,900
		Equity	19,000
Total	$24,000	Total	$24,000

LOAF, INC.

Current assets	$3,400	Current liabilities	$1,600
Net fixed assets	5,400	Long-term debt	900
		Equity	6,500
Total	$9,000	Total	$9,000

4. **Incorporating Goodwill**   In the previous problem, suppose the fair market value of Loaf's fixed assets is $12,000 versus the $3,400 book value shown. Meat pays $17,000 for Loaf and raises the needed funds through an issue of long-term debt. Construct the postmerger balance sheet now, assuming that the purchase method of accounting is used.

5. **Balance Sheets for Mergers**   Silver Enterprises has acquired All Gold Mining in a merger transaction. Construct the balance sheet for the new corporation if the merger is treated as a purchase for accounting purposes. The market value of All Gold Mining's fixed assets is $2,800; the market values for current and other assets are the same as the book values. Assume that Silver Enterprises issues $8,400 in new long-term debt to finance the acquisition. The following balance sheets represent the premerger book values for both firms.

SILVER ENTERPRISES

Current assets	$2,600	Current liabilities	$1,800
Other assets	800	Long-term debt	900
Net fixed assets	3,900	Equity	4,600
Total	$7,300	Total	$7,300

ALL GOLD MINING			
Current assets	$1,100	Current liabilities	$900
Other assets	350	Long-term debt	0
Net fixed assets	2,800	Equity	3,350
Total	$4,250	Total	$4,250

6. **Cash versus Stock Payment**   Penn Corp. is analyzing the possible acquisition of Teller Company. Both firms have no debt. Penn believes the acquisition will increase its total aftertax annual cash flows by $3.1 million indefinitely. The current market value of Teller is $78 million, and that of Penn is $135 million. The appropriate discount rate for the incremental cash flows is 12 percent. Penn is trying to decide whether it should offer 40 percent of its stock or $94 million in cash to Teller's shareholders.

   a. What is the cost of each alternative?

   b. What is the NPV of each alternative?

   c. Which alternative should Penn choose?

7. **EPS, PE, and Mergers**   The shareholders of Jolie Company have voted in favour of a buyout offer from Pitt Corporation. Information about each firm is given here:

	Jolie	Pitt
Price-earning ratio	5.25	21
Shares outstanding	60,000	180,000
Earnings	$300,000	$675,000

   Jolie's shareholders will receive one share of Pitt stock for every three shares they hold in Jolie.

   a. What will the EPS of Pitt be after the merger? What will the PE ratio be if the NPV of the acquisition is zero?

   b. What must Pitt feel is the value of the synergy between these two firms? Explain how your answer can be reconciled with the decision to go ahead with the takeover.

8. **Cash versus Stock as Payment**   Consider the following premerger information about a bidding firm (Firm B) and a target firm (Firm T). Assume that both firms have no debt outstanding.

	Firm B	Firm T
Shares outstanding	1,500	900
Price per share	$34	$24

   Firm B has estimated that the value of the synergistic benefits from acquiring Firm T is $3,000.

   a. If Firm T is willing to be acquired for $27 per share in cash, what is the NPV of the merger?

   b. What will the price per share of the merged firm be assuming the conditions in (a)?

   c. In part (a), what is the merger premium?

   d. Suppose Firm T is agreeable to a merger by an exchange of stock. If B offers three of its shares for every five of T's shares, what will the price per share of the merged firm be?

   e. What is the NPV of the merger assuming the conditions in (d)?

9. **Cash versus Stock as Payment**   In Problem 9, are the shareholders of Firm T better off with the cash offer or the stock offer? At what exchange ratio of B shares to T shares would the shareholders in T be indifferent between the two offers?

10. **Effects of a Stock Exchange**   Consider the following premerger information about Firm A and Firm B:

	Firm A	Firm B
Total earnings	$900	$600
Shares outstanding	550	220
Price per share	$ 40	$ 15

   Assume that Firm A acquires Firm B via an exchange of stock at a price of $20 for each share of B's stock. Both A and B have no debt outstanding.

   a. What will the earnings per share, EPS, of Firm A be after the merger?

   b. What will Firm A's price per share be after the merger if the market incorrectly analyzes this reported earnings growth (that is, the price-earnings ratio does not change)?

   c. What will the price-earnings ratio of the postmerger firm be if the market correctly analyzes the transaction?

   d. If there are no synergy gains, what will the share price of A be after the merger? What will the price-earnings ratio be? What does your answer for the share price tell you about the amount A bid for B? Was it too high? Too low? Explain.

Intermediate 11. Merger NPV Show that the NPV of a merger can be expressed as the value of the synergistic benefits, ΔV, less the
(continued) merger premium.

Challenge 12. Calculating NPV Foxy News, Inc., is considering making an offer to purchase Pulitzer Publications. The vice presi-
(Question 12) dent of finance has collected the following information:

	Foxy	Pulitzer
Price-earning ratio	12.5	9
Shares outstanding	1,000,000	550,000
Earnings	$2,000,000	$580,000
Dividends	600,000	290,000

Foxy also knows that securities analysts expect the earnings and dividends of Pulitzer to grow at a constant rate of
5 percent each year. Foxy management believes that the acquisition of Pulitzer will provide the firm with some
economies of scale that will increase this growth rate to 7 percent per year.

a. What is the value of Pulitzer to Foxy?

b. What would Foxy's gain be from this acquisition?

c. If Foxy were to offer $18 in cash for each share of Pulitzer, what would the NPV of the acquisition be?

d. What's the most Foxy should be willing to pay in cash per share for the stock of Pulitzer?

e. If Foxy were to offer 100,000 of its shares in exchange for the outstanding stock of Pulitzer, what would the
NPV be?

f. Should the acquisition be attempted, and, if so, should it be as in (*c*) or as in (*e*)?

g. Foxy's outside financial consultants think that the 7 percent growth rate is too optimistic and a 6 percent rate is
more realistic. How does this change your previous answers?

Internet Application Questions

1. The Competition Bureau (www.competition.ic.gc.ca) in Canada reviews all mergers for approval. Its main concern is whether
a proposed merger is likely to reduce competition. In this regard, it has set guidelines that allow investors and firms to determine whether a proposed merger passes the Competition Bureau's test. These guidelines are explained in the link below.

www.competitionbureau.gc.ca/internet/index.cfm?itemid=1245&1g=e

Use the guidelines described above to make your own evaluation of the efficacy of the following mergers:

a. A vertical merger involving a timber mill and a pulp producer, and a conglomerate merger involving a liquor company and
a film studio.

b. Great-West Lifeco's (www.greatwestlife.com) bid to acquire Canada Life (www.canadalife.ca).

c. What is the Efficiency Exception principle in evaluating mergers?

2. Former investment bankers provide tools and information to analyze mergers and acquisitions on the website
www.dealmaven.com/home.aspx. The "Ask the Maven" section of the site provides free tips and advice. Browse the section to
find a quick method for determining whether or not a deal will be dilutive or accretive to earnings per share. Apply this analysis to a recently announced merger or acquisition.

Suggested Readings

Current institutional investors' policies on corporate governance are on the following websites:
Ontario Teachers' Pension Plan: *www.otpp.com*
Caisse de depot et placement du Quebec: *www.lacaisse.com*

Four fascinating paperbacks on LBOs are:
C. Bruck. *The Predators Ball, The Inside Story of Drexel Burnham, and the Rise of the Junk Bond Raiders,* New York: Penguin
Books, 1989; B. Burroughs and J. Helyar. *Barbarians at the Gate, The Fall of RJR Nabisco,* New York: Harper Perennial, 1991;
J. Rothchild. *Going for Broke—How Robert Campeau Bankrupted the Retail Industry, Jolted the Junk Bond Market, and
Brought the Booming Eighties to a Crashing Halt,* Toronto: Simon & Schuster, 1991; A. Risberg. *Mergers and Acquisitions,*
New York: Routledge, 2006.

CHAPTER 24

Risk Management: An Introduction to Financial Engineering

Export Development Canada (EDC) is a Canadian Crown corporation that assists Canadian exporters to compete in global markets by providing them with a variety of risk management and financial services. In its 2005 Annual Report, EDC reported that it used currency and interest rate swaps to reduce its funding costs, to minimize market risk, and for asset liability manage-ment purposes. The Crown corporation issued bonds with a fixed coupon rate in a foreign currency. It then engaged in two swaps. A currency swap converted the debt obligation from the foreign currency to U.S. dollars. An interest rate swap exchanged the fixed coupon for a floating rate. As we will see in this chapter, swaps are just one of the tools used by firms to manage risk.

www.edc.ca

SINCE THE EARLY 1970S, prices for all types of goods and services have become increasingly volatile. This is a cause for concern because sudden and unexpected shifts in prices can create expensive disruptions in operating activities for even very well run firms. As a result, firms are increasingly taking steps to shield themselves from price volatility through the use of new and innovative financial arrangements.

The purpose of this chapter is to introduce you to some of the basics of financial risk management. The activities we discuss here are on the frontier of modern, real-world financial management. By describing one of the rapidly developing areas in corporate finance, we hope to leave you with a sense of how the art and practice of financial management evolve in response to changes in the financial environment.

24.1

hedging
Reducing a firm's exposure to price or rate fluctuations. Also, immunization.

derivative security
A financial asset that represents a claim to another financial asset.

HEDGING AND PRICE VOLATILITY

In broad terms, reducing a firm's exposure to price or rate fluctuations is called **hedging.** The term *immunization* is sometimes used as well. As we will discuss, there are many different types of hedging and many different techniques. Frequently, when a firm desires to hedge a particular risk, there will be no direct way of doing so. The financial manager's job in such cases is to create a way by using available financial instruments to create new ones. This process has come to be called *financial engineering*.

Corporate risk management often involves the buying and selling of **derivative securities.** A derivative security is a financial asset that represents a claim to another financial asset. For example, a stock option gives the owner the right to buy or sell stock, a financial asset, so stock options are derivative securities.

Financial engineering frequently involves creating new derivative securities, or else combining existing derivatives to accomplish specific hedging goals. In a world where prices were very stable and changed only slowly, there would be very little demand for financial engineering. As this is being written, however, financial engineering is very much a growth industry. As we illustrate next, the reason is that the financial world has become more risky.[1]

Price Volatility: A Historical Perspective

In trying to understand why we claim that the financial world has become more risky, you will find it useful to look back at the history of prices. Figure 24.1 provides a very long-term view of price levels for England. The price-level series shown begins in 1666 and runs through the mid-1980s. The remarkable fact revealed by this series is that for the first 250 years, prices changed very little (except in wartime). In contrast, in the last 30 or 40 years, prices have increased dramatically. Figure 24.2 illustrates the same point with a somewhat shorter series for Canada.

As we saw in Chapter 12, the rate of change in prices has slowed in recent years. The important lesson, however, is that even though the inflation rate is now relatively low in Canada and the United States, the uncertainty about the future rate of inflation remains. Beyond the unexpected changes in overall price levels, there are three specific areas of particular importance to businesses in which volatility has also increased dramatically: interest rates, exchange rates, and commodity prices.

Interest Rate Volatility

We know that debt is a vital source of financing for corporations, and interest rates are a key component of a firm's cost of capital. Up until 1979, interest rates in the United States were relatively stable because the Federal Reserve actively managed rates to keep them that way. This goal has since been abandoned, and interest rate volatility has increased sharply.

FIGURE 24.1

Price levels in England
(1850 = 100)

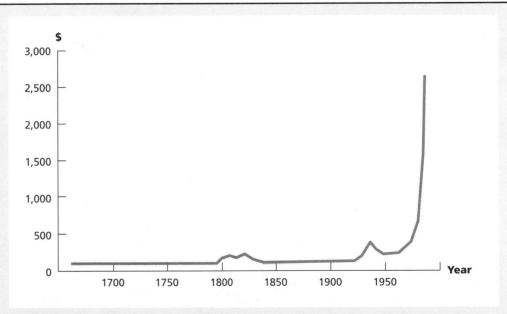

Source: Charles W. Smithson and Clifford W. Smith with D. Sykes Wilford, *Managing Financial Risk: A Guide to Derivative Products, Financial Engineering, and Value Maximization,* 3rd ed. (Burr Ridge, Ill.: Irwin Professional Publishing, 1998).

---

1 This discussion is based on Charles W. Smithson and Clifford W. Smith with D. Sykes Wilford, *Managing Financial Risk: A Guide to Derivative Products, Financial Engineering, and Value Maximization,* 3rd ed. (Burr Ridge, Ill.: Irwin Professional Publishing, 1998).

FIGURE 24.2

Price levels in Canada
(1992 = 100)

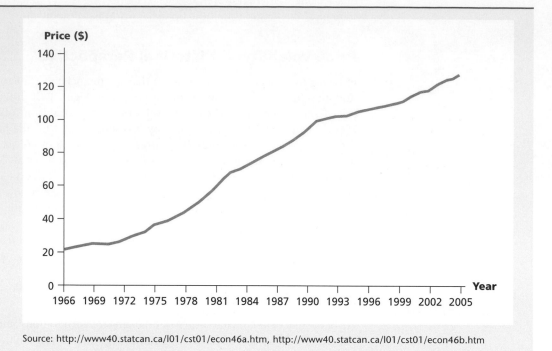

Source: http://www40.statcan.ca/l01/cst01/econ46a.htm, http://www40.statcan.ca/l01/cst01/econ46b.htm

www.bankofcanada.ca

Similarly, in March 1980, the Bank of Canada dropped its discretionary interest rate policy in favour of a system which allows for floating interest rates. Figure 24.3 illustrates the volatility of three- to five-year Government of Canada bond rates in recent years.

FIGURE 24.3

Three- to five-year Government of Canada bond rates: 1999–2006

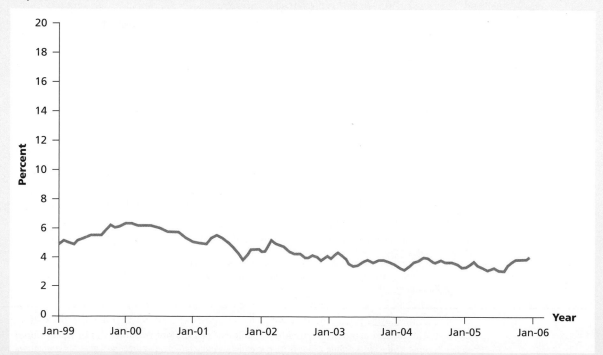

Source: www.bankofcanada.ca

In Their Own Words . . .

Abolhassan Jalilvand on Derivatives Use in Canada

OUR RESEARCH TEAM sent a detailed questionnaire to the 548 largest Canadian nonfinancial corporations (by dollar value of sales) selected from the Montreal Exchange databases. We received 154 useable responses, which provided a reasonable response rate. A total of 116 firms (75 percent) are users of derivatives products.

We can draw on prior studies for Europe and the U.S. to put our findings into perspective. The widespread use of derivatives in Canada is similar to findings for Europe. However, the use of derivatives varies considerably (from 35 to 85 percent) among U.S. firms depending on which survey we look at.

Looking more closely at Canadian derivatives users, we find that managing currency risk is the top objective followed by interest rate and commodity price risks. This ranking is similar to what other researchers report for U.S. and European companies. Of our 154 Canadian firms sampled, 97 operated globally and 57 are national. The majority is exchange listed. The firms represent 19 different industries with the top three categories being consumer products, industrial products, and merchandising. Roughly a third of the firms were in regulated industries.

The majority of users stated that the most important objectives for using derivatives were to manage the volatility of cash flows and earnings and to reduce the cost of funds. This is

consistent with the Wharton-Chase survey for the U.S. Nonusers emphasized two reasons for not using derivatives: their limited exposure to different types of risk and lack of information on derivative products. Multinational companies are far more likely (88 percent) to use derivatives than national firms (56 percent). Non-regulated companies are more likely to use derivatives (83 percent) versus regulated companies (62 percent). All the gold and silver, paper and forest, pipelines, and agricultural companies that responded use derivatives. These companies have high exposure to commodity price risk. The lowest percentage of derivative users is in technology, health care, and distribution.

Abolhassan Jalilvand is Dean, School of Business Administration, Loyola University, Chicago. His comments here are excerpted with permission from the Canadian Journal of Administrative Sciences 16, September 1999.

Before 1980, Canadian firms were able to plan for and predict their future borrowing costs with some confidence. In today's financial world, because of the increased uncertainty surrounding interest rates, this is no longer the case.

Exchange Rate Volatility

As we discussed in Chapter 21, international operations have become increasingly important to Canadian businesses. Consequently, exchange rates and exchange rate volatility have also become increasingly important. Figure 24.4 plots the U.S. dollar–Canadian dollar exchange rate and illustrates that exchange rate volatility has increased enormously since the early 1970s.

The reason for the increase in exchange rate volatility was the breakdown of the so-called Bretton Woods accord. Under the Bretton Woods system, exchange rates were fixed for the most part and significant changes occurred only rarely. As a result, importers and exporters could predict with relative certainty what exchange rates were likely to be in the future. In today's post-Bretton Woods era, exchange rates are set by market forces, and future exchange rates are very difficult to predict with precision.

Commodity Price Volatility

Commodity prices (the prices for basic goods and materials) are the third major area in which volatility has risen. Oil is one of the most important commodities, and, as Figure 24.5 shows, oil prices have become increasingly uncertain since the early 1970s.

The behaviour of oil prices is not unique; many other key commodities have experienced increased volatility over the past two decades.

FIGURE 24.4

Canadian dollar–U.S. dollar exchange rate: 1971–2006

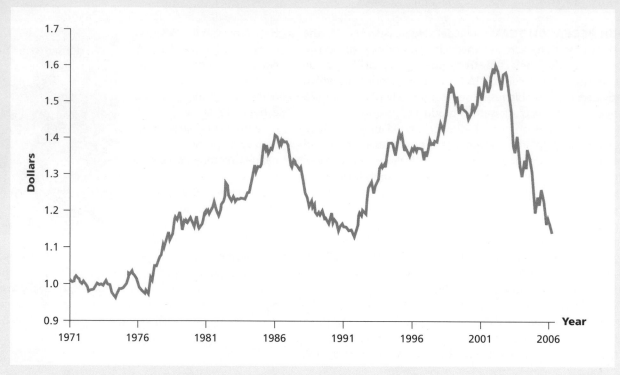

Source: www.bankofcanada.ca, www.federalreserve.gov/releases

FIGURE 24.5

Percentage changes in oil price: 1995–2006

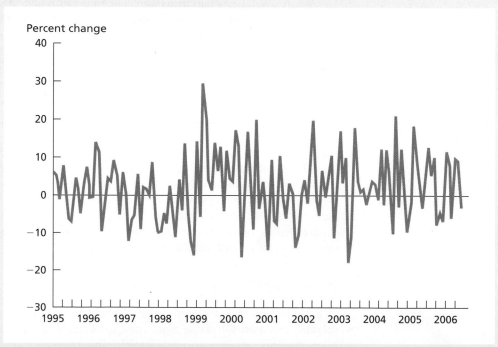

Source: http://tonto.eia.doe.gov/dnav/pet/hist/wtotworldw.htm

The Impact of Financial Risk: The U.S. Savings and Loan Industry

The best-known example of the effect of financial risk is the collapse of the once-thriving U.S. savings and loan, or S&L, industry. At one time, the S&L industry was relatively simple. S&Ls accepted short-term deposits, and they made long-term, fixed-rate home mortgage loans. Before the increases in interest rate volatility came about, short-term interest rates were almost always lower than long-term rates, so the S&Ls simply profited from the spread.

When short-term interest rates became highly volatile, they exceeded long-term rates on various occasions, sometimes by substantial amounts. Suddenly, the S&L business got very complicated. Depositors removed their funds because higher rates were available elsewhere, but homeowners held on to their low-interest rate mortgages. S&Ls were forced into borrowing over the short term at very high rates. They began taking greater risks in lending in an attempt to earn higher returns, but this frequently resulted in much higher default rates, another problem with which the S&Ls were unfamiliar.

There were other economic and political factors that contributed to the astounding size of the S&L disaster, but the root cause was the increase in interest rate volatility. Today, surviving S&Ls and other financial institutions take specific steps to insulate themselves from interest rate volatility.

CONCEPT QUESTIONS

1. What is hedging?

2. Why do firms place greater emphasis on hedging now than they did in the past?

MANAGING FINANCIAL RISK

We've seen that price and rate volatility have increased in recent decades. Whether or not this is a cause for concern for a particular firm depends on the nature of the firm's operations and its financing. For example, an all-equity firm would not be as concerned about interest rate fluctuations as a highly leveraged one. Similarly, a firm with little or no international activity would not be overly concerned about exchange rate fluctuations.

To effectively manage financial risk, financial managers need to identify the types of price fluctuations that have the greatest impact on the value of the firm. Sometimes these will be obvious, but sometimes they will not be. For example, consider a forest products company. If interest rates increase, then its borrowing costs will clearly rise. Beyond this, however, the demand for housing typically declines as interest rates rise. As housing demand falls, so does demand for lumber. An increase in interest rates thus leads to increased financing costs and, at the same time, decreased revenues.

The Risk Profile

risk profile
A plot showing how the value of the firm is affected by changes in prices or rates.

The basic tool for identifying and measuring a firm's exposure to financial risk is the **risk profile.** The risk profile is a plot showing the relationship between changes in the price of some good, service, or rate and changes in the value of the firm. Constructing a risk profile is conceptually very similar to performing a sensitivity analysis (described in Chapter 11).

To illustrate, consider an agricultural products company that has a large-scale wheat-farming operation. Because wheat prices can be very volatile, we might wish to investigate the firm's exposure to wheat price fluctuations, that is, its risk profile with regard to wheat prices. To do this, we plot changes in the value of the firm (ΔV) versus unexpected changes in wheat prices (ΔP_{wheat}). Figure 24.6 shows the result.

The risk profile in Figure 24.6 tells us two things. First, because the line slopes up, increases in wheat prices will increase the value of the firm. Because wheat is an output, this comes as no surprise. Second, because the line has a fairly steep slope, this firm has a significant exposure to wheat price fluctuations, and it may wish to take steps to reduce that exposure.

FIGURE 24.6

Risk profile for a wheat grower

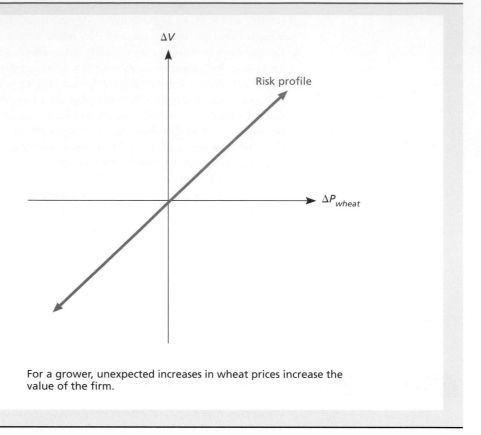

For a grower, unexpected increases in wheat prices increase the value of the firm.

Reducing Risk Exposure

Fluctuations in the price of any particular good or service can have very different effects on different types of firms. Going back to wheat prices, we now consider the case of a food processing operation. The food processor buys large quantities of wheat and has a risk profile like that illustrated in Figure 24.7. As with the agricultural products firm, the value of this firm is sensitive to wheat prices, but, because wheat is an input, increases in wheat prices lead to decreases in firm value.

Both the agricultural products firm and the food processor are exposed to wheat price fluctuations, but any fluctuations have opposite effects for the two firms. If these two firms get together, then much of the risk can be eliminated. The grower and the processor can simply agree that, at set dates in the future, the grower will deliver a certain quantity of wheat, and the processor will pay a set price. Once the agreement is signed, both firms will have locked in the price of wheat for as long as the contract is in effect, and both of their risk profiles with regard to wheat prices will be completely flat during that time.

We should note that, in reality, a firm that hedges financial risk usually won't be able to create a completely flat risk profile. For example, our wheat grower doesn't actually know what the size of the crop will be ahead of time. If the crop is larger than expected, then some portion of the crop will be unhedged. If the crop is small, then the grower will have to buy more to fulfill the contract and will thereby be exposed to the risk of price changes. Either way, there is some exposure to wheat price fluctuations, but, by hedging, that exposure is sharply reduced.

There are a number of other reasons why perfect hedging is usually impossible, but this is not really a problem. With most financial risk management, the goal is to reduce the risk to more bearable levels and thereby flatten out the risk profile, not necessarily to eliminate the risk altogether.

In thinking about financial risk, there is an important distinction to be made. Price fluctuations have two components. Short-run, essentially temporary changes are the first component.

FIGURE 24.7

Risk profile for a wheat buyer

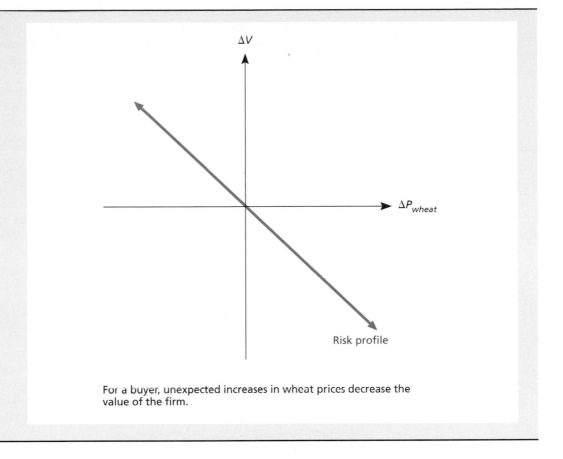

For a buyer, unexpected increases in wheat prices decrease the value of the firm.

The second component has to do with more long-run, essentially permanent changes. As we discuss next, these two types of changes have very different implications for the firm.

Hedging Short-Run Exposure

Short-run, temporary changes in prices result from unforeseen events or shocks. Some examples are sudden increases in orange juice prices because of a late Florida freeze, increases in oil prices because of political turmoil, and increases in lumber prices because available supplies are low following a hurricane. Price fluctuations of this sort are often called *transitory* changes.

Short-run price changes can drive a business into financial distress even though, in the long run, the business is fundamentally sound. This happens when a firm finds itself with sudden cost increases that it cannot pass on to its customers immediately. A negative cash flow position is created, and the firm may be unable to meet its financial obligations.

For example, wheat crops might be much larger than expected in a particular year because of unusually good growing conditions. At harvest time, wheat prices will be unexpectedly low. By that time, a wheat farmer will have already incurred most of the costs of production. If prices drop too low, revenues from the crop will be insufficient to cover the costs, and financial distress may result.

transactions exposure
Short-run financial risk arising from the need to buy or sell at uncertain prices or rates in the near future.

Short-run financial risk is often called **transactions exposure.** This name stems from the fact that short-term financial exposure typically arises because a firm must make transactions in the near future at uncertain prices or rates. With our wheat farmer, for example, the crop must be sold at the end of the harvest, but the wheat price is uncertain. Alternatively, a firm may have a bond issue that will mature next year that it will need to replace, but the interest rate that the firm will have to pay is not known.

As we will see, short-run financial risk can be managed in a variety of ways. The opportunities for short-term hedging have grown tremendously in recent years, and firms in Canada and the United States are increasingly hedging away transitory price changes.

Cash Flow Hedging: A Cautionary Note

One thing to notice is that, in our discussion thus far, we have talked conceptually about hedging the value of the firm. In our example concerning wheat prices, however, what is really hedged is the firm's near-term cash flow. In fact, at the risk of ignoring some subtleties, we will say that hedging short-term financial exposure, hedging transactions exposure, and hedging near-term cash flows amount to much the same thing.

It will usually be the case that directly hedging the value of the firm is not really feasible, and, instead, the firm will try to reduce the uncertainty of its near-term cash flows. If the firm is thereby able to avoid expensive disruptions, then cash flow hedging will act to hedge the value of the firm, but the linkage is indirect. In such cases, care must be taken to ensure that the cash flow hedging does have the desired effect.

For example, imagine a vertically integrated firm with an oil-producing division and a gasoline-retailing division. Both divisions are affected by fluctuations in oil prices. However, it may well be that the firm as a whole has very little transactions exposure because any transitory shifts in oil prices simply benefit one division and cost the other. The overall firm's risk profile with regard to oil prices is essentially flat. Put another way, the firm's *net* exposure is small. If one division, acting on its own, were to begin hedging its cash flows, then the firm as a whole would suddenly be exposed to financial risk. The point is that cash flow hedging should not be done in isolation. Instead, a firm needs to worry about its net exposure. As a result, any hedging activities should probably be done on a centralized, or at least cooperative, basis.

Hedging Long-Term Exposure

Price fluctuations can also be longer-run, more permanent changes. These result from fundamental shifts in the underlying economics of a business. If improvements in agricultural technology come about, for example, then wheat prices will permanently decline (in the absence of agricultural price subsidies!). If a firm is unable to adapt to the new technology, then it will not be economically viable over the long run.

economic exposure
Long-term financial risk arising from permanent changes in prices or other economic fundamentals.

A firm's exposure to long-run financial risks is often called its **economic exposure.** Because long-term exposure is rooted in fundamental economic forces, it is much more difficult, if not impossible, to hedge on a permanent basis. For example, is it possible that a wheat farmer and a food processor could permanently eliminate exposure to wheat price fluctuations by agreeing on a fixed price forever?

The answer is no, and, in fact, the effect of such an agreement might even be the opposite of the one desired. The reason is that if, over the long run, wheat prices were to change on a permanent basis, one party to this agreement would ultimately be unable to honour it. Either the buyer would be paying too much, or the seller would be receiving too little. In either case, the loser would become uncompetitive and be forced to take political and legal action to reopen the contract. This happened in Canada with the long-term agreement by the province of Newfoundland to sell power from Churchill Falls to Hydro Quebec. When prices rose in the 1990s, the contract was renegotiated.

Conclusion

In the long run, a business is either economically viable or it will fail. No amount of hedging can change this simple fact. Nonetheless, by hedging over the near term, a firm gives itself time to adjust its operations and thereby adapt to new conditions without expensive disruptions. So, drawing our discussion in this section together, we can say that, by managing financial risks, the firm can accomplish two important things. The first is that the firm insulates itself from otherwise troublesome transitory price fluctuations. The second is that the firm gives itself a little breathing room to adapt to fundamental changes in market conditions.

CONCEPT QUESTIONS

1. What is a risk profile? Describe the risk profiles with regard to oil prices for an oil producer and a gasoline retailer.

2. What can a firm accomplish by hedging financial risk?

HEDGING WITH FORWARD CONTRACTS

Forward contracts are among the oldest and most basic tools for managing financial risk. Our goal in this section is to describe forward contracts and discuss how they are used to hedge financial risk.

Forward Contracts: The Basics

forward contract
A legally binding agreement between two parties calling for the sale of an asset or product in the future at a price agreed upon today.

A **forward contract** is a legally binding agreement between two parties calling for the sale of an asset or product in the future at a price agreed upon today. The terms of the contract call for one party to deliver the goods to the other on a certain date in the future, called the *settlement date*. The other party pays the previously agreed-upon *forward price* and takes the goods. Looking back, note that the agreement we discussed between the wheat grower and the food processor was, in fact, a forward contract.

Forward contracts can be bought and sold. The *buyer* of a forward contract has the obligation to take delivery and pay for the goods; the *seller* has the obligation to make delivery and accept payment. The buyer of a forward contract benefits if prices increase because the buyer will have locked in a lower price. Similarly, the seller wins if prices fall because a higher selling price has been locked in. Note that one party to a forward contract can win only at the expense of the other, so a forward contract is a zero-sum game.

The Payoff Profile

payoff profile
A plot showing the gains and losses that will occur on a contract as the result of unexpected price changes.

The **payoff profile** is the key to understanding how forward contracts and other contracts that we discuss later are used to hedge financial risks. In general, a payoff profile is a plot showing the gains and losses on a contract that result from unexpected price changes. For example, suppose we were examining a forward contract on oil. Based on our discussion, the buyer of the forward contract is obligated to accept delivery of a specified quantity of oil at a future date and pay a set price. Part A of Figure 24.8 shows the resulting payoff profile on the forward contract from the buyer's perspective.

Figure 24.8 shows that, as oil prices increase, the buyer of the forward contract benefits by having locked in a lower-than-market price. If oil prices decrease, then the buyer loses because that buyer ends up paying a higher-than-market price. For the seller of the forward contract, things are simply reversed. The payoff profile of the seller is illustrated in Part B of Figure 24.8.

FIGURE 24.8

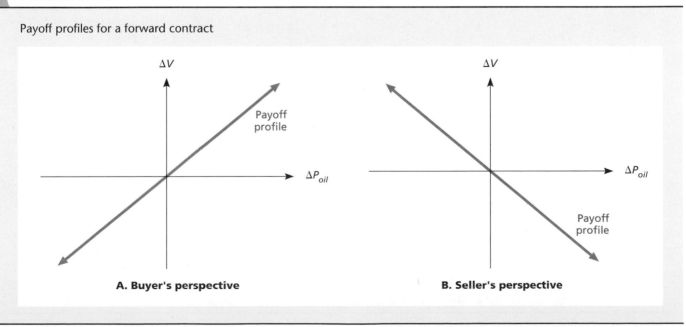

Payoff profiles for a forward contract

A. Buyer's perspective

B. Seller's perspective

Hedging with Forwards

To illustrate how forward contracts can be used to hedge, we consider the case of a utility that uses oil to generate power. The prices that our utility can charge are regulated and cannot be changed rapidly. As a result, sudden increases in oil prices are a source of financial risk. The utility's risk profile is illustrated in Figure 24.9.

If we compare the risk profile in Figure 24.9 to the buyer's payoff profile on a forward contract shown in Figure 24.8, we see what the utility needs to do. The payoff profile for the buyer of a forward contract on oil is exactly the opposite of the utility's risk profile with respect to oil. If the utility buys a forward contract, its exposure to unexpected changes in oil prices will be eliminated. This result is shown in Figure 24.10.

Our utility example illustrates the fundamental approach to managing financial risk. We first identify the firm's exposure to financial risk using a risk profile. We then try to find a financial arrangement, such as a forward contract, that has an offsetting payoff profile.

www.mitsubishi.com

A CAVEAT   Figure 24.10 shows that the utility's net exposure to oil price fluctuations is zero. If oil prices rise, then the gains on the forward contract will offset the damage from increased costs. However, if oil prices decline, the benefit from lower costs will be offset by losses on the forward contract.

For example, in September 1995, Japanese carmaker Mitsubishi Motors revealed the results of its hedging program against the U.S. dollar. Earlier in the year, when the dollar was trading at less than 90 yen, Mitsubishi had used currency contracts to lock in an exchange rate of about 90 yen to the dollar through the end of March 1996. Unfortunately for the auto manufacturer, by September, the dollar had climbed to 98.35 yen. In this case, Mitsubishi lost out by hedging.

This example illustrates an important thing to remember about hedging with forward contracts. Price fluctuations can be good or bad, depending on which way they go. If we hedge with forward contracts, we do eliminate the risk associated with an adverse price change. However, we also eliminate the potential gain from a favourable move. You might wonder if we couldn't somehow just hedge against unfavourable moves. We can, and we describe how in a subsequent section.

CREDIT RISK   Another important thing to remember is that with a forward contract, no money changes hands when the contract is initiated. The contract is simply an agreement to transact in the future, so there is no up-front cost to the contract. However, because a forward contract

FIGURE 24.9

Risk profile for an oil buyer

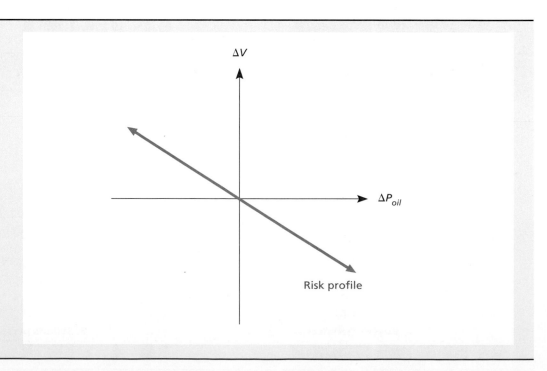

FIGURE 24.10

Hedging with forward contracts

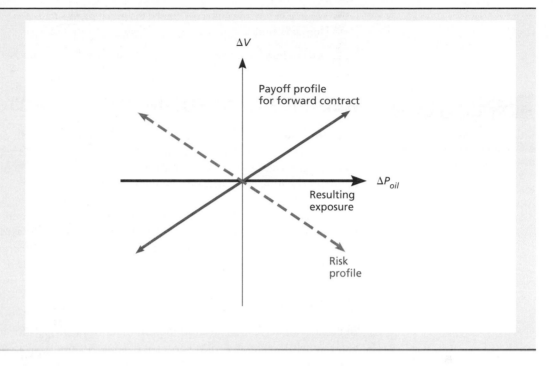

is a financial obligation, there is credit risk. When the settlement date arrives, the party on the losing end of the contract has a significant incentive to default on the agreement. As we discuss in the next section, a variation on the forward contract exists that greatly diminishes this risk.

www.jaguar.com
www.ford.com

FORWARD CONTRACTS IN PRACTICE   Where are forward contracts commonly used to hedge? Because exchange rate fluctuations can have disastrous consequences for firms that have significant import or export operations, forward contracts are routinely used by such firms to hedge exchange rate risk. For example, Jaguar, the U.K. auto manufacturer (and subsidiary of Ford Motor Co.), historically hedged the U.S. dollar–British pound exchange rate for six months into the future. (The subject of exchange rate hedging with forward contracts is discussed in greater detail in Chapter 21.)

Another good example of hedging with forward contracts is the Forward Sales Program that Barrick Gold Corporation used to use. When the program was in full use, Barrick would commit to sell a fixed number of ounces of gold at a future date established by the company over a period of between 10 and 15 years. The contract provided for a premium above the current spot rates based on the difference between the market LIBOR rates and the gold lease rates.[2] Between 1991 and 2002, Barrick claims to have secured additional revenue of $2.2 billion using the program. If gold prices rose above the contract price, Barrick would choose to sell into the spot market to maximize revenue. The long contract term and the flexibility in choosing a delivery date reduce the risks associated with forward contracts. Two problems can occur, however, that would negatively impact the returns associated with hedging. First, a situation of "backwardation" in which the gold lease rates are higher than short-term interest rates can occur. In this situation, forward prices under the program would be lower than spot prices, resulting in a negative premium. Second, gold prices could rise to the point where the contract expires and the gold must be delivered at a rate less than market prices. When this occurred in 2004 and 2005, pressure on management from shareholders led to a reduction in the use of the Forward Sales Program, and Barrick Gold pledged to eventually reduce the hedge book to zero.

---

2 The gold lease rate is the fee charged by a central bank to a gold bullion dealer that borrows gold from the central bank.

futures contract
A forward contract with the feature that gains and losses are realized each day rather than only on the settlement date.

HEDGING WITH FUTURES CONTRACTS

A **futures contract** is exactly the same as a forward contract with one exception. With a forward contract, the buyer and seller realize gains or losses only on the settlement date. With a futures contract, gains and losses are realized on a daily basis. If we buy a futures contract on oil, then, if oil prices rise today, we have a profit and the seller of the contract has a loss. The seller pays up, and we start again tomorrow with neither party owing the other.

The daily resettlement feature found in futures contracts is called *marking-to-market*. As we mentioned earlier, there is a significant risk of default with forward contracts. With daily marking-to-market, this risk is greatly reduced. This is probably why organized trading is much more common in futures contracts than in forward contracts (outside of international trade).

Trading in Futures

In Canada and elsewhere around the world, futures contracts for a remarkable variety of items are routinely bought and sold. The types of contracts available are traditionally divided into two groups, commodity futures and financial futures. With a financial future, the underlying goods are financial assets such as stocks, bonds, or currencies. With a commodity future, the underlying goods can be just about anything other than a financial asset.

There are commodity futures contracts on a wide variety of agricultural products such as corn, orange juice, and, yes, pork bellies. There is even a contract on fertilizer. There are commodity contracts on precious metals such as gold and silver, and there are contracts on basic goods such as copper and lumber. There are contracts on various petroleum products such as crude oil, heating oil, and gasoline.

Wherever there is price volatility, there may be a demand for a futures contract, and new futures contracts are introduced on a fairly regular basis. For example, by some estimates, the potential value of wholesale trade in electricity in the United States is more than $100 billion a year, dwarfing the market for many other commodities such as gold, copper, wheat, and corn. Electricity producers, who own generating capacity, are "long" large quantities of the commodity. As the market develops, new futures contracts will allow energy producers and (large) consumers to hedge their transactions in electricity. Whether such contracts will be successful remains to be seen. Many new contracts don't pan out because there is not enough volume; such contracts are simply discontinued.

It is even possible to have derivatives that are not linked to prices. The Chicago Mercantile Exchange has introduced weather futures for which the underlying is the number of snow days in a winter. Bombardier, the Canadian multinational manufacturer of Ski-Doo® snowmobiles, is using such snow derivatives to hedge its cash back promise to customers if there is no snow.[3]

www.cme.com
www.bombardier.com

Futures Exchanges

There are a number of futures exchanges in the United States and elsewhere, and more are being established. The Chicago Board of Trade (CBT) is among the largest. Other notable exchanges include the Chicago Mercantile Exchange (CME), the International Money Market (IMM), the New York Futures Exchange (NYFE), a part of the NYSE, the Winnipeg Commodity Exchange (WPG), and the Montreal Exchange (ME).

---

3 C. Smith, "Weather derivatives: An enormous potential," *Financial Times*, Derivatives Survey, June 28, 2000, p. vi.

Figure 24.11 gives a sample of *The National Post* listing for selected futures contracts. Taking a look at the canola contracts in the lower left portion of the table, note that the contracts trade on WPG, one contract calls for the delivery of 20 metric tons of canola, and prices are quoted in Canadian dollars per metric ton. The months in which the contracts mature are given in the third column.

For the canola contract with a June 2006 maturity, the first number in the row is the high price for the lifetime of the contract ($341 per metric ton), and the following number is the lifetime low price ($251.50). The number after the maturity month is the opening price ($278.70) followed by the highest price ($279) and the lowest price ($276.20) for the day. The *settlement price* is the next number ($277.30), and it is the closing price for the day. For purposes of marking-to-market, this is the figure used. The change (−0.40) listed next is the movement in the settlement price since the previous trading session. Finally, the previous *open interest* (79,182), the number of contracts outstanding at the end of the previous trading session, is shown. At the end of the section, the volume of trading in all maturities is shown for the previous trading session (10,124), along with the previous day's total open interest for all maturities.

To see how large futures trading can be, we take a look at the International Money Market (IMM) British Pounds contracts (under the currency heading). One contract is for 62,500 pounds. The previous day's total open interest for all months is 128,560 contracts. The total value outstanding is therefore 8.0 billion British pounds for this one type of contract!

Hedging with Futures

Hedging with futures contracts is conceptually identical to hedging with forward contracts, and the payoff profile on a futures contract is drawn just like the profile for a forward contract. The only difference in hedging with futures is that the firm will have to maintain an account with an investment dealer so that gains and losses can be credited or debited each day as a part of the marking-to-market process.

Even though there is a large variety of futures contracts, it is unlikely that a particular firm will be able to find the precise hedging instrument it needs. For example, we might produce a particular grade or variety of oil, and find that no contract exists for exactly that grade. However, all oil prices tend to move together, so we could hedge our output using futures contracts on other grades of oil. Using a contract on a related, but not identical, asset as a means of hedging is called **cross-hedging**.

cross-hedging
Hedging an asset with contracts written on a closely related, but not identical, asset.

When a firm does cross-hedge, it does not actually want to buy or sell the underlying asset. This presents no problem because the firm can reverse its futures position at some point before maturity. This simply means that if the firm sells a futures contract to hedge something, it will buy the same contract at a later date, thereby eliminating its futures position. In fact, futures contracts are very rarely held to maturity by anyone (despite horror stories of individuals waking up to find mountains of soybeans in their front yards), and, as a result, actual physical delivery very rarely takes place.

A related issue has to do with contract maturity. A firm might wish to hedge over a relatively long period of time, but the available contracts might have shorter maturities. A firm could therefore decide to roll over short-term contracts, but this entails some risks. For example, in stark contrast to Barrick's relative success with its Forward Sales Program, Ashanti Goldfields experienced considerable trouble in 1999 with its hedging program. In Ashanti's case, the company elected to hedge future gold production with futures contracts. The firm took a chance that gold prices would decline. Instead, gold prices actually rose dramatically and Ashanti had to mark-to-market its futures contracts. In late 1999, Ashanti was forced to announce a $570 million loss on hedging. Almost half of the loss was owed to creditors immediately. The result was a liquidity crisis, and a significant drop in the share price of Ashanti. The primary problem was hedging a long-term production plan with contracts that were marked-to-market daily.

CONCEPT QUESTIONS

1. What is a futures contract? How does it differ from a forward contract?

2. What is cross-hedging? Why is it important?

FIGURE 24.11

Sample: *The National Post* futures price quotations

Futures Prices

Friday June 16, 2006

CURRENCY

Australian Dollar (CME)
A$100,000, US$ per A$; 0.0001 = $10 per contract

LIFETIME High	LIFETIME Low	Month	DAILY Open	DAILY High	DAILY Low	DAILY Settle	DAILY Change	Previous open interest
0.7789	0.7006	Jun-06	0.7415	0.7446	0.7374	0.7383	–0.0024	44,780
0.7775	0.7001	Sep-06	0.7409	0.7438	0.7363	0.7375	–0.0024	34,887

Est. vol. 29,367 Prev. vol. 28,420 Prev. open int. 80,011

British Pound (CME)
62,500 pounds, US$ per pound; 0.0002 = $12.50 per contract

High	Low	Month	Open	High	Low	Settle	Change	Previous open interest
1.9035	1.7076	Jun-06	1.8528	1.8558	1.8472	1.8515	0.0037	52,059
1.906	1.7282	Sep-06	1.8568	1.8597	1.8505	1.8551	0.0037	76,332

Est. vol. 50,248 Prev. vol. 70,016 Prev. open int. 128,560

Canadian Dollar (CME)
C$100,000, US$ per C$; 0.0001 = $10 per contract

High	Low	Month	Open	High	Low	Settle	Change	Previous open interest
0.9152	0.795	Jun-06	0.8962	0.9001	0.8889	0.8905	–0.0065	44,974
0.9175	0.797	Sep-06	0.8989	0.9026	0.8912	0.8929	–0.0066	84,363
0.9184	0.8425	Dec-06	0.8945	0.905	0.8936	0.8953	–0.0066	1,841
0.9196	0.859	Mar-07	...	0.8991	0.8977	0.8977	–0.0066	160

Est. vol. 47,590 Prev. vol. 51,837 Prev. open int. 131,455

European Currency (CME)
125,000 ECUs, US$ per unit; 0.0001 = $12.50 per contract

High	Low	Month	Open	High	Low	Settle	Change	Previous open interest
1.3795	1.1798	Jun-06	1.2654	1.2672	1.2618	1.2648	0.0034	85,338
1.3074	1.1864	Sep-06	1.2732	1.2751	1.2693	1.2726	0.0034	118,374

Est. vol. 149,119 Prev. vol. 216,170 Prev. open int. 204,637

Japanese Yen (CME)
12.5 million yen, US$ per yen (scaled .00); 0.0001 = $12.50 per contract

High	Low	Month	Open	High	Low	Settle	Change	Previous open interest
0.9949	0.8455	Jun-06	0.87	0.873	0.8679	0.8688	–0.0011	82,588
0.9435	0.8572	Sep-06	0.8811	0.8843	0.8791	0.88	–0.0012	137,368
0.96	0.8644	Dec-06	0.8915	0.8954	0.8908	0.8911	–0.0012	20,035

Est. vol. 65,869 Prev. vol. 90,362 Prev. open int. 240,019

Mexican Peso (CME)
500,000 new pesos, US$ per peso; 0.000025 = $12.50 per contract

High	Low	Month	Open	High	Low	Settle	Change	Previous open interest
0.095	0.0845	Jun-06	0.0877	0.088	0.0874	0.0874	–0.0004	45,355
0.0944	0.0825	Sep-06	0.0874	0.0875	0.0868	0.0869	–0.0004	42,394
0.0936	0.0834	Dec-06	...	....	0.0867	0.0864	–0.0004	23,207
0.0926	0.0851	Mar-07	...	....	...	0.0858	–0.0004	1,489

Est. vol. 14,409 Prev. vol. 23,921 Prev. open int. 112,658

Swiss Franc (CME)
125,000 francs, US$ per franc; 0.0001 = $12.50 per contract

High	Low	Month	Open	High	Low	Settle	Change	Previous open interest
0.8635	0.7633	Jun-06	0.8132	0.8152	0.8101	0.8131	0.0016	72,118
0.8497	0.7712	Sep-06	0.8211	0.8234	0.8179	0.8212	0.0016	48,504

Est. vol. 44,792 Prev. vol. 33,594 Prev. open int. 120,687
Est. vol. 0 Prev. vol. 0 Prev. open int. 52

U.S. Dollar Index (FINEX)
1000 x index points and US cents; 0.01 = $10 per contract

High	Low	Month	Open	High	Low	Settle	Change	Previous open interest
91.65	83.41	Jun-06	85.82	86.05	85.7	85.94	–0.12	15,653
91.35	83.03	Sep-06	85.47	85.69	85.26	85.52	–0.12	22,045
89.74	82.7	Dec-06	85.05	85.24	85.05	85.17	–0.12	2,153

Prev. vol. 2,468 Prev. open int. 39,856

FOOD AND FIBRE

Canola (WPG)
20 metric tons, C$ per metric ton; 10 cents = $2 per contract

LIFETIME High	LIFETIME Low	Month	DAILY Open	DAILY High	DAILY Low	DAILY Settle	DAILY Change	Previous open interest
341	251.5	Jun-06	278.7	279	276.2	277.3	–0.4	13,594
355.5	265.5	Nov-06	297.6	298	295	296.7	0.1	53,049
317.5	275	Jan-07	305.3	305.6	304.5	304.7	–0.6	5,119
323	288	May-07	...	...	...	318	–4.8	1,016
332.6	298.8	Jul-07	...	...	...	322.6	–2.4	2,409
340	298.1	Nov-07	322.2	327	322.2	324.6	–1.4	3,438

Prev. vol. 10,124 Prev. open int. 79,182
Prev. vol. 0 Prev. open int. 35

Cattle - Live (CME)
40,000 lbs., US cents per lb.; 2.5 cents per cwt = $10 per contract

High	Low	Month	Open	High	Low	Settle	Change	Previous open interest
88	72.75	Jun-06	80.95	81.8	80.4	81.65	0.7	13,229
86.75	74.5	Aug-06	82.7	83.5	82.3	83.45	0.85	124,478
89.5	78.35	Oct-06	85.95	86.4	85.5	86.05	0.1	48,751
90.5	80.425	Dec-06	87.15	88	86.8	87.85	0.75	30,050
91.4	82.6	Feb-07	89.5	90.2	89.25	90.1	0.6	10,062
89.25	81.5	Apr-07	87	87.3	86.9	87.275	0.025	2,161
82.6	77.8	Jun-07	82.1	82.6	82.1	82.3	0.05	1,040

Est. vol. 27,581 Prev. vol. 55,682 Prev. open int. 229,771

Cocoa (CSCE)
10 metric tons, US$ per metric ton; $1 = $10 per contract

High	Low	Month	Open	High	Low	Settle	Change	Previous open interest
1895	1390	Jul-06	1540	1545	1500	1525	–2	9,595
1912	1410	Sep-06	1553	1555	1516	1539	2	66,694
1832	1438	Dec-06	1580	1585	1548	1569	...	21,236
1713	1465	Mar-07	1612	1613	1583	1599	–1	15,569
1690	1495	May-07	1628	...	...	1619	–1	6,076
1740	1505	Jul-07	...	...	...	1639	–1	2,987
1726	1590	Sep-07	...	...	...	1658	–1	8,664
1720	1607	Dec-07	...	...	...	1677	–2	6,617

Prev. vol. 19,766 Prev. open int. 137,448
Prev. vol. 0 Prev. open int. 40

Coffee (CSCE)
37,500 lbs., US cents per lb.; 0.01 cent = $3.75 per contract

High	Low	Month	Open	High	Low	Settle	Change	Previous open interest
148.5	89	Jul-06	96.75	97.2	94.5	95.25	–1.3	25,677
148.5	96.8	Sep-06	99.2	99.6	96.9	97.7	–1.25	72,546
200	99.85	Dec-06	103.3	103.5	101	101.6	–1.3	14,865
143.6	103.4	Mar-07	107	107.2	104.7	105.4	–1.3	5,469
136.25	106	May-07	109.7	109.7	107	107.75	–1.3	1,468
137.25	110	Sep-07	...	...	...	112.15	–1.2	1,077
139.5	115.6	Dec-07	117	117	115.9	115.45	–1.1	1,041

Prev. vol. 24,747 Prev. open int. 123,115

INTEREST RATE

Canadian 3 Month Banker's Acceptance (ME)
$1,000,000, points of 100%; 0.01 = $25 per contract

LIFETIME High	LIFETIME Low	Month	DAILY Open	DAILY High	DAILY Low	DAILY Settle	DAILY Change	Previous open interest
97.09	95.33	Jun-06	95.57	95.58	95.56	95.56	–0.015	80,692
97	95.19	Sep-06	95.48	95.49	95.46	95.47	...	149,754
96.88	95.37	Dec-06	95.41	95.43	95.4	95.41	0.01	176,194
96.78	95.02	Mar-07	95.41	95.44	95.4	95.41	0.01	58,326
96.38	95.38	Jun-07	95.43	95.43	95.42	95.42	0.01	14,138
96.27	95.4	Sep-07	95.43	95.43	95.43	95.43	0.01	8,798
95.98	95.35	Dec-07	95.45	95.45	95.45	95.45	0.01	4,747

Vol. 30,323 Prev. vol. 69,420 Prev. open int. 493,079

Canadian Govt. Bonds 2 Year (ME)
$100,000, points of 100%; 0.01 = $10 per contract

High	Low	Month	Open	High	Low	Settle	Change	Previous open interest
103.1	102.815	Sep-06	102.88	102.88	102.88	102.84	0.02	2,255

Vol. 1 Prev. vol. 33 Prev. open int. 2,265

Canadian Govt. Bonds 10 Year (ME)
$100,000, points of 100%; 0.01 = $10 per contract

High	Low	Month	Open	High	Low	Settle	Change	Previous open interest
113.04	109.72	Jun-06	111.2	111.2	111.2	111.17	0.15	24,783
112.64	110.87	Sep-06	111.9	112.05	111.8	111.85	0.15	300,190

Vol. 15,636 Prev. vol. 28,361 Prev. open int. 324,973

METAL

Gold (COMEX)
100 troy ozs., US$ per troy oz.; 10 cents = $10 per contract

LIFETIME High	LIFETIME Low	Month	DAILY Open	DAILY High	DAILY Low	DAILY Settle	DAILY Change	Previous open interest
739.2	435.5	Aug-06	579	589	570.5	581.7	11.4	193.887
742	436.5	Oct-06	588.5	594.4	580	587.7	11.5	10,532
753	338	Dec-06	591.2	601.1	582.3	593.5	11.5	29,178
755	469	Feb-07	602.6	604.3	595.5	599.3	11.6	14,195
765	490	Apr-07	600.5	600.5	598	605	11.6	2,012
771	367	Jun-07	610	615	603	610.7	11.7	12,813
707	550	Oct-07	...	...	...	622.2	11.7	2,280
800	368	Dec-07	636.3	636.3	621	627.9	11.7	14,680
730	617.5	Feb-08	...	...	...	633.6	11.7	1,215
761	411	Jun-08	...	...	...	645.1	11.9	1,031
808	437	Dec-08	...	...	...	662.5	12	5,406
849	476	Jun-09	678	678	678	679.9	12.1	2,950

Prev. vol. 59,960 Prev. open int. 291,254

PETROLEUM

Crude Oil (NYME)
1,000 US barrels, US$ per barrel; 0.01 = $10 per contract

LIFETIME High	LIFETIME Low	Month	DAILY Open	DAILY High	DAILY Low	DAILY Settle	DAILY Change	Previous open interest
76.95	30.05	Jul-06	70.14	70.45	68.8	69.88	0.38	97,647
77.08	32.65	Aug-06	70.48	70.85	69.05	70.2	0.27	227,967
77.52	29.75	Sep-06	71.13	71.44	69.8	70.89	0.33	92,991
77.8	35.81	Oct-06	70.85	71.87	70.35	71.42	0.36	41,629
77.95	35.64	Nov-06	71.94	72.21	70.8	71.87	0.38	25,077
78	19.1	Dec-06	72.3	72.67	71.05	72.23	0.4	110,485
77.85	39.54	Jan-07	72.95	72.95	72.4	72.51	0.42	35,475
77.59	38.15	Feb-07	...	...	...	72.69	0.43	14,005
77.62	37.8	Mar-07	...	...	...	72.81	0.45	15,096
76.5	49.8	Apr-07	...	...	...	72.85	0.46	9,812
75.25	42	May-07	72.15	72.15	72.15	72.84	0.47	8,903
77.3	31.15	Jun-07	72.87	72.87	72.1	72.8	0.48	34,769
76.25	64.53	Jul-07	71.9	71.9	71.9	72.69	0.49	10,231
75.8	45.8	Aug-07	71.9	71.9	71.9	72.55	0.5	5,804
74.25	46	Sep-07	...	...	...	72.41	0.51	8,130
74.1	57	Oct-07	...	...	...	72.27	0.52	4,333
74.12	50.25	Nov-07	...	...	...	72.1	0.53	6,283
76.2	19.5	Dec-07	71	71.05	70.9	71.92	0.54	87,644
74.71	60.5	Jan-08	...	...	...	71.7	0.53	3,218
61.3	60.4	Feb-08	...	...	...	71.48	0.52	4,181
74.55	60.3	Mar-08	...	...	...	71.26	0.52	3,319
62.35	62.35	Apr-08	...	...	...	71.04	0.54	1,390
68.3	68.3	May-08	...	...	...	70.82	0.56	1,155
73.65	55.4	Jun-08	69.7	69.7	69.7	70.61	0.58	19,645
...	...	Jul-08	...	...	...	70.4	0.59	2,415
...	...	Sep-08	...	...	...	70.04	0.61	3,125
...	...	Nov-08	...	...	...	69.7	0.63	1,075
74.4	19.75	Dec-08	68.5	68.7	68.5	69.52	0.64	39,043
...	...	Jan-09	...	...	...	69.37	0.65	2,418
...	...	Feb-09	...	...	...	69.23	0.66	1,703
72	67.6	Jun-09	67.6	67.6	67.6	68.67	0.67	4,430
...	...	Nov-09	...	...	...	67.97	0.72	1,004
73	22.5	Dec-09	...	67.5	67.5	67.82	0.72	25,213
65.8	65.8	Jun-10	...	...	...	67.04	0.72	1,070
72.65	27.15	Dec-10	66	66	65.3	66.32	0.72	41,120
70.7	36.1	Dec-11	...	64.75	64.75	65.14	0.77	15,513
70.4	52.75	Decc-12	63.4	63.4	63.4	64.24	0.82	8,946

Prev. vol. 289,569 Prev. open int. 1,020,466

Source: *The National Post,* June 16, 2006. Used with permission. A pdf version of this figure is on the OLC.

swap contract
An agreement by two parties to exchange, or swap, specified cash flows at specified intervals in the future.

www.ibm.com
www.worldbank.com

HEDGING WITH SWAP CONTRACTS

As the name suggests, a **swap contract** is an agreement by two parties to exchange, or swap, specified cash flows at specified intervals. Swaps are a recent innovation; they were first introduced to the public in 1981 when IBM and the World Bank entered into a swap agreement. The market for swaps has grown tremendously since that time.

A swap contract is really just a portfolio, or series, of forward contracts. Recall that with a forward contract, one party promises to exchange an asset (e.g., bushels of wheat) for another asset (cash) on a specific future date. With a swap, the only difference is that there are multiple exchanges instead of just one. In principle, a swap contract could be tailored to exchange just about anything. In practice, most swap contracts fall into one of three basic categories: currency swaps, interest rate swaps, and commodity swaps. Other types will surely develop, but we will concentrate on just these three.

Currency Swaps

With a *currency swap,* two companies agree to exchange a specific amount of one currency for a specific amount of another at specific dates in the future. For example, suppose a Canadian firm has a German subsidiary and wishes to obtain debt financing for an expansion of the subsidiary's operations. Because most of the subsidiary's cash flows are in euros, the company would like the subsidiary to borrow and make payments in euros, thereby hedging against changes in the euros–dollar exchange rate. Unfortunately, the company has good access to Canadian debt markets, but not to German debt markets.

At the same time, a German firm would like to obtain Canadian dollar financing. It can borrow cheaply in euros, but not in dollars. Both firms face a similar problem. They can borrow at favourable rates, but not in the desired currency. A currency swap is a solution. These two firms simply agree to exchange dollars for euros at a fixed rate at specific future dates (the payment dates on the loans). Each firm thus obtains the best possible rate and then arranges to eliminate exposure to exchange rate changes by agreeing to exchange currencies, a neat solution. A further benefit is that the two firms can lower their transaction costs by working together in a swap.

Interest Rate Swaps

Imagine a firm that wishes to obtain a fixed-rate loan, but can only get a good deal on a floating-rate loan, that is, a loan for which the payments are adjusted periodically to reflect changes in interest rates. Another firm can obtain a fixed-rate loan, but wishes to obtain the lowest possible interest rate and is therefore willing to take a floating-rate loan. (Rates on floating-rate loans are generally lower than rates on fixed-rate loans; why?) Both firms could accomplish their objectives by agreeing to exchange loan payments; in other words, the two firms would make each other's loan payments. This is an example of an *interest rate swap;* what is really being exchanged is a floating interest rate for a fixed one.

Interest rate swaps and currency swaps are often combined. One firm obtains floating-rate financing in a particular currency and swaps it for fixed-rate financing in another currency. Also, note that payments on floating-rate loans are always based on some index, such as the one-year Treasury rate. An interest rate swap might involve exchanging one floating-rate loan for another as a way of changing the underlying index.

Commodity Swaps

As the name suggests, a *commodity swap* is an agreement to exchange a fixed quantity of a commodity at fixed times in the future. Commodity swaps are the newest type of swap, and the market for them is small relative to that for other types. The potential for growth is enormous, however.

Swap contracts for oil have been engineered. For example, say that an oil user has a need for 20,000 barrels every quarter. The oil user could enter into a swap contract with an oil producer to supply the needed oil. What price would they agree on? As we mentioned previously, they can't fix a price forever. Instead, they could agree that the price would be equal to the *average* daily oil price from the previous 90 days. As a result of their using an average price, the impact of the relatively large daily price fluctuations in the oil market would be reduced, and both firms would benefit from a reduction in transactions exposure.

The Swap Dealer

Unlike futures contracts, swap contracts are not traded on organized exchanges. The main reason is that they are not sufficiently standardized. Instead, the *swap dealer* plays a key role in the swaps market. In the absence of a swap dealer, a firm that wished to enter into a swap would have to track down another firm that wanted the opposite end of the deal. This search would probably be expensive and time-consuming.

Instead, a firm wishing to enter into a swap agreement contacts a swap dealer, and the swap dealer takes the other side of the agreement. The swap dealer will then try to find an offsetting transaction with some other party or parties (perhaps another firm or another dealer). Failing this, a swap dealer will hedge its exposure using futures contracts.

Banks are the dominant swap dealers in Canada and the United States. As a large swap dealer, a bank would be involved in a variety of contracts. It would be swapping fixed-rate loans for floating-rate loans with some parties and doing just the opposite with other participants. The total collection of contracts in which a dealer is involved is called the *swap book*. The dealer will try to keep a balanced book to limit its net exposure. A balanced book is often called a *matched book*.

Interest Rate Swaps: An Example

To get a better understanding of swap contracts and the role of the swap dealer, we consider a floating-for-fixed interest rate swap. Suppose Company A can borrow at a floating rate equal to prime plus 1 percent or at a fixed rate of 10 percent. Company B can borrow at a floating rate of prime plus 2 percent or at a fixed rate of 9.5 percent. Company A desires a fixed-rate loan, whereas Company B desires a floating-rate loan. Clearly, a swap is in order.

Company A contacts a swap dealer, and a deal is struck. Company A borrows the money at a rate of prime plus 1 percent. The swap dealer agrees to cover the loan payments, and, in exchange, the company agrees to make fixed-rate payments to the swap dealer at a rate of, say, 9.75 percent. Notice that the swap dealer is making floating-rate payments and receiving fixed-rate payments. The company is making fixed-rate payments, so it has swapped a floating payment for a fixed one.

Company B also contacts a swap dealer. The deal here calls for Company B to borrow the money at a fixed rate of 9.5 percent. The swap dealer agrees to cover the fixed loan payments, and the company agrees to make floating-rate payments to the swap dealer at a rate of prime plus, say, 1.5 percent. In this second arrangement, the swap dealer is making fixed-rate payments and receiving floating-rate payments.

What's the net effect of these machinations? First, Company A gets a fixed-rate loan at a rate of 9.75 percent, which is cheaper than the 10 percent rate it can obtain on its own. Second, Company B gets a floating-rate loan at prime plus 1.5 instead of prime plus 2. The swap benefits both companies.

The swap dealer also wins. When all the dust settles, the swap dealer receives (from Company A) fixed-rate payments at a rate of 9.75 percent and makes fixed-rate payments (for Company B) at a rate of 9.5 percent. At the same time, it makes floating-rate payments (for Company A) at a rate of prime plus 1 percent and receives floating-rate payments at a rate of prime plus 1.5 percent (from Company B). Notice that the swap dealer's book is perfectly balanced, in terms of risk, and it has no exposure to interest rate volatility.

Figure 24.12 illustrates the transactions in our interest rate swap. Notice that the essence of the swap transactions is that one company swaps a fixed payment for a floating payment, while the other exchanges a floating payment for a fixed one. The swap dealer acts as an intermediary and profits from the spread between the rates it charges and the rates it receives.

FIGURE 24.12

Illustration of an interest rate swap

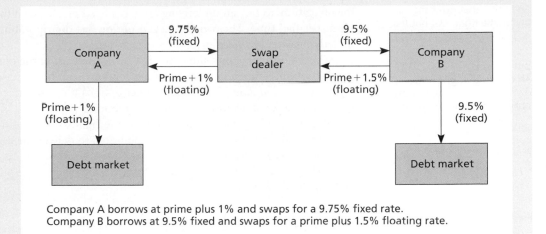

Company A borrows at prime plus 1% and swaps for a 9.75% fixed rate.
Company B borrows at 9.5% fixed and swaps for a prime plus 1.5% floating rate.

Credit Default Swaps (CDS)

credit default swap
A contract that pays off when a credit event occurs, default by a particular company termed the reference entity, giving the buyer the right to sell corporate bonds issued by the reference entity at their face value.

Credit default swaps, along with other credit derivatives, make up one of the fastest growing markets in the financial world. A credit default swap (CDS) is a contract that pays off when a credit event occurs—default by a particular company, termed the reference entity. In this case, the buyer of the CDS has the right to sell corporate bonds issued by the reference entity to the CDS seller at their face value. Since bonds in default trade at a deep discount, the right to sell bonds at their face value becomes quite valuable when a default occurs.

Credit default swaps are an important risk management tool for financial institutions. By buying a CDS on a borrower, a bank sets up a payment in the event the borrower defaults on its loan. In effect, CDS is a form of insurance against credit losses.[4]

CONCEPT QUESTIONS

1. What is a swap contract? Describe three types.

2. Describe the role of the swap dealer.

3. Explain the cash flows in Figure 24.12.

HEDGING WITH OPTION CONTRACTS

The contracts we have discussed thus far—forwards, futures, and swaps—are conceptually similar. In each case, two parties agree to transact on a future date or dates. The key is that both parties are obligated to complete the transaction.

option contract
An agreement that gives the owner the right, but not the obligation, to buy or sell a specific asset at a specific price for a set period of time.

In contrast, an **option contract** is an agreement that gives the owner the right, but not the obligation, to buy or sell (depending on the option type) some asset at a specified price for a specified time. Here we will quickly discuss some option basics and then focus on using options to hedge volatility in commodity prices, interest rates, and exchange rates. In doing so, we will sidestep a wealth of detail concerning option terminology, option trading strategies, and option valuation.

---

4 For more on credit default swaps, see J.C. Hull, *Fundamentals of Futures and Options Markets*, Fifth Edition, Pearson Prentice Hall, NJ, 2005, Chapter 21.

Option Terminology

call option
An option that gives the owner the right, but not the obligation, to buy an asset.

put option
An option that gives the owner the right, but not the obligation, to sell an asset.

Options come in two flavours, puts and calls. The owner of a **call option** has the right, but not the obligation, to buy an underlying asset at a fixed price, called the *strike price* or *exercise price*, for a specified time. The owner of a **put option** has the right, but not the obligation, to sell an underlying asset at a fixed price for a specified time.

The act of buying or selling the underlying asset using the option contract is called *exercising* the option. Some options ("American" options) can be exercised anytime up to and including the *expiration date* (the last day); other options ("European" options) can only be exercised on the expiration date. Most options are American.

Because the buyer of a call option has the right to buy the underlying asset by paying the strike price, the seller of a call option is obligated to deliver the asset and accept the strike price if the option is exercised. Similarly, the buyer of the put option has the right to sell the underlying asset and receive the strike price. In this case, the seller of the put option must accept the asset and pay the strike price.

Options versus Forwards

There are two key differences between an option contract and a forward contract. The first is obvious. With a forward contract, both parties are obligated to transact; one party delivers the asset, and the other party pays for it. With an option, the transaction occurs only if the owner of the option chooses to exercise it.

The second difference between an option and a forward contract is that, whereas no money changes hands when a forward contract is created, the buyer of an option contract gains a valuable right and must pay the seller for that right. The price of the option is frequently called the *option premium.*

Option Payoff Profiles

Figure 24.13 shows the general payoff profile for a call option from the owner's viewpoint. The horizontal axis shows the difference between the asset's value and the strike price on the option. As illustrated, if the price of the underlying asset rises above the strike price, then the owner of the option will exercise the option and enjoy a profit. If the value of the asset falls below the strike price, the owner of the option will not exercise it. Notice that this payoff profile does not consider the premium that the buyer paid for the option.

The payoff profile that results from buying a call is repeated in Part A of Figure 24.14. Part B shows the payoff profile on a call option from the seller's side. A call option is a zero-sum game, so the seller's payoff profile is exactly the opposite of the buyer's.

Part C of Figure 24.14 shows the payoff profile for the buyer of a put option. In this case, if the asset's value falls below the strike price, then the buyer profits because the seller of the put must pay the strike price. Part D shows that the seller of the put option loses out when the price falls below the strike price.

Option Hedging

Suppose a firm has a risk profile that looks like the one in Part A of Figure 24.15. If the firm wishes to hedge against adverse price movements using options, what should it do? Examining the different payoff profiles in Figure 24.14, we see that the one that has the desirable shape is C, buying a put. If the firm buys a put, then its net exposure is as illustrated in Part B of Figure 24.15.

In this case, by buying a put option, the firm has eliminated the downside risk, that is, the risk of an adverse price movement. However, the firm has retained the upside potential. In other words, the put option acts as a kind of insurance policy. Remember that this desirable insurance is not free; the firm pays for it when it buys the put option.

FIGURE 24.13

Call option payoff profile for an option buyer

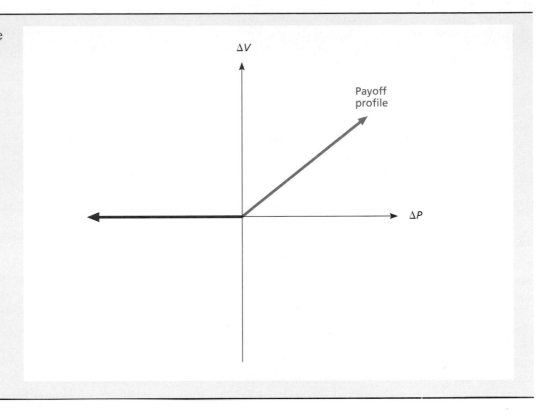

Hedging Commodity Price Risk with Options

We saw earlier that there are futures contracts available for a variety of basic commodities. In addition, there are an increasing number of options available on these same commodities. In fact, the options that are typically traded on commodities are actually options on futures contracts, and, for this reason, they are called *futures options*.

The way these work is as follows: When a futures call option on, for example, wheat is exercised, the owner of the option receives two things. The first is a futures contract on wheat at the current futures price. This contract can be immediately closed at no cost. The second thing the owner of the option receives is the difference between the strike price on the option and the current futures price. The difference is simply paid in cash.

Figure 24.16 gives a few futures options quotations from *The National Post*. Briefly, looking at the canola options, note that the first column of numbers tells us the different striking prices that are available. The next three columns are call option prices (or premiums) for three different months of expiration. The final three columns are put option prices for the same three months.

Suppose you buy the 290 futures call option. You will pay $19 per metric ton for the option (they're actually sold in multiples of 20 but we'll ignore this). If you exercise your option, you will receive a futures contract on canola and the difference between the current futures price and the strike price of $290 in cash.

Hedging Exchange Rate Risk with Options

Figure 24.16 shows that there are futures options available on *foreign currencies* as well as on commodities. These work in exactly the same way as commodities futures options. In addition, there are other traded options with which the underlying asset is just currency rather than a

www.nationalpost.com

FIGURE 24.14

Option payoff profiles

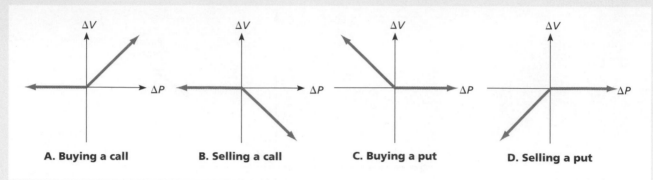

A. Buying a call   B. Selling a call   C. Buying a put   D. Selling a put

futures contract on a currency. Firms with significant exposure to exchange rate risk will frequently purchase put options to protect against adverse exchange rate changes.

Hedging Interest Rate Risk with Options

The use of options to hedge against interest rate risk is a very common practice, and there are a variety of options available to serve this purpose. Some are futures options like the ones we have been discussing, and these trade on organized exchanges. For example, we mentioned the Treasury bond contract in our discussion of futures. There are options available on this contract and a number of other financial futures as well. Beyond this, there is a thriving over-the-counter market in interest rate options. We will describe some of these options in this section.

FIGURE 24.15

Hedging with options

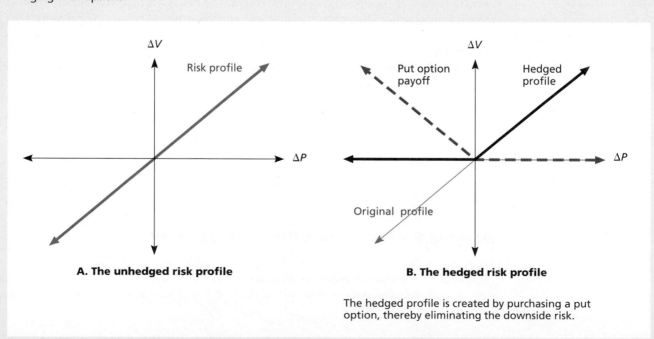

A. The unhedged risk profile   B. The hedged risk profile

The hedged profile is created by purchasing a put option, thereby eliminating the downside risk.

FIGURE 24.16

Sample: *The National Post* futures option price quotations

Futures Options Prices
Friday June 16, 2006

CURRENCY
British Pound (CME)
62,500 pounds, US cents per pound

Strike	Calls-Settle			Puts-Settle		
Strike	July	Aug	Sept	July	Aug	Sept
1750	r	s	10.64	0.02	s	0.21
1780	7.54	s	8.06	0.05	s	0.62
1810	4.71	s	s	0.21	r	1.23
1820	3.87	4.45	4.99	0.37	0.96	1.52
1830	3.1	s	4.33	0.6	s	1.85
1840	2.36	3.06	3.72	0.85	1.56	2.23
1850	1.69	s	3.17	1.18	s	2.66
1860	1.13	2.06	2.66	1.62	2.55	3.15
1870	0.74	1.67	2.19	2.23	s	3.66
1880	0.46	s	1.76	2.94	s	4.22
1900	0.17	0.83	1.1	s	s	s
1920	0.08	0.5	0.8	s	s	s
1950	0.03	s	0.48	s	s	s

Est. call vol. 75   Est. put vol. 403
Prev. open int. 6,191   Prev. open int. 3,351

FOOD AND FIBRE
Canola (WPG)
20 metric tons, C$ per metric ton

Strike	Calls-Settle			Puts-Settle		
Strike	July	Nov	Jan	July	Nov	Jan
240	37.3	57.4	65.3	0.1	0.7	0.6
250	27.3	48.1	56	0.1	1.4	1.3
260	17.4	30.5	47.1	0.1	2.0	2.4
270	8.3	31.6	39	1	4.9	4.3
280	2.4	24.8	31.7	5.1	8.1	7
290	0.4	19	25.3	13.1	12.3	10.6

Prev. open int. 2,288   Prev. open int. 9,172

OATS (CBOT)
5,000 bushels, US cents per bushel

Strike	Calls-Settle			Puts-Settle		
Strike	July	Sept	Dec	July	Sept	Dec
150	s	s	s	s	0.25	0.75
170	26.625	s	29.25	0.25	2.25	3.75
180	16.875	18.875	22.75	0.375	4.875	7.25
190	7.5	13	17.5	1.125	9.125	s
200	1.75	8.75	13.5	5.25	s	s
210	0.25	5.75	10.25	s	s	s

Prev. open int. 2,356   Prev. open int. 1,389

METAL
Copper (COMEX)
25,000 lbs., US cents per lb.

Strike	Calls-Settle			Puts-Settle		
Strike	July	Aug	Sept	July	Aug	Sept
16000	169.15	166.15	162.75	0.05	0.15	1.35
24000	89.2	91.65	94.6	0.1	5.85	13.05
27500	55.6	62.1	66.05	1.5	11.2	19.25
28000	51.15	58.1	62.15	2.05	12.15	20.35
28500	46.8	54.1	58.3	2.7	13.15	21.45
30000	33.65	42.65	47.1	4.55	16.65	25.15
32500	16.35	28.7	33.1	12.2	27.55	35.9
35000	6.6	19.35	23.1	27.4	43.1	50.7
37000	4.25	15.55	16.25	45.05	59.2	63.75
37500	3.9	14.8	14.8	49.7	63.45	67.2
40000	2.75	10.6	8.8	73.5	84.1	86.05
60000	0.05	s	0.9	270.85	s	277.9
62000	0.05	s	s	290.85	s	s

Prev. open int. 3,872   Prev. open int. 4,689

PETROLEUM
Crude Oil (NYME)
1,000 US barrels, US$ per barrel

Strike	Calls-Settle			Puts-Settle		
Strike	July	Aug	Sept	July	Aug	Sept
30	r	40.2	s	s	0.01	0.01
40	r	30.2	30.89	r	0.01	0.01
44.5	s	25.7	s	s	0.01	s
45	r	s	s	r	0.01	0.01
48	s	s	s	r	0.01	0.01
49.5	s	s	s	r	0.01	0.01
50	r	s	20.89	r	0.01	0.01
50.5	s	s	s	r	0.01	0.01
52	s	s	s	r	0.01	0.02
52.5	r	s	s	r	0.01	0.02
53	s	s	s	r	0.01	0.03
54	r	r	s	r	0.01	0.04
55	r	15.2	15.9	r	0.01	0.06
56	r	14.2	s	r	0.01	0.08
57	r	13.2	s	r	0.01	0.11
57.5	r	12.7	13.46	r	0.02	0.13
58	r	12.2	12.98	r	0.02	0.16
58.5	s	s	12.51	r	0.03	0.18
59	r	11.22	12.04	r	0.04	0.21
59.5	r	10.73	11.57	r	0.05	0.24
60	r	10.24	11.11	r	0.06	0.28
60.5	r	9.75	10.65	r	0.08	0.32
61	r	9.27	10.2	r	0.1	0.37
61.5	r	8.8	9.76	r	0.12	0.42
62	r	8.33	9.32	r	0.15	0.48
62.5	r	7.86	8.89	r	0.19	0.55
63	r	7.4	8.46	r	0.23	0.62
63.5	r	6.95	8.04	r	0.27	0.7
64	r	6.51	7.63	r	0.33	0.79
64.5	r	6.08	7.23	r	0.4	0.89
65	r	5.66	6.84	r	0.47	0.99
65.5	r	5.24	6.46	r	0.56	1.11
66	r	4.85	6.09	r	0.66	1.24
66.5	r	4.46	5.73	r	0.78	1.37
67	r	4.1	5.38	r	0.91	1.52
67.5	r	3.75	5.04	r	1.06	1.68
68	r	3.44	4.73	r	1.25	1.86
68.5	r	3.11	4.42	r	1.42	2.05
69	r	2.8	4.13	r	1.6	2.26
69.5	r	2.54	3.86	r	1.85	2.48
70	r	2.29	3.59	r	2.09	2.71
70.5	r	2.05	3.34	r	2.35	2.95
71	r	1.83	3.1	r	2.62	3.2
71.5	r	1.62	2.87	r	2.92	3.47
72	r	1.43	2.65	r	3.23	3.75
72.5	r	1.26	2.45	r	3.56	4.05
73	r	1.11	2.26	r	3.9	4.35
73.5	r	0.98	2.07	r	4.27	4.67
74	r	0.86	1.91	r	4.64	5
74.5	r	0.75	1.75	r	5.03	5.34
75	r	0.65	1.61	r	5.44	5.69
75.5	r	0.57	1.47	r	5.85	6.05
76	r	0.49	1.35	s	6.27	6.42
76.5	r	0.42	1.23	s	6.7	6.8
77	r	0.36	1.12	r	7.14	7.19
77.5	r	0.31	1.02	r	s	7.59
78	r	0.27	0.94	r	8.04	8
78.5	r	0.23	0.86	s	8.5	s
79	r	0.2	0.79	r	s	8.85
79.5	r	0.17	0.73	s	s	s
80	r	0.15	0.67	r	9.92	9.72
80.5	r	0.13	0.61	s	s	s
81	r	0.12	0.56	r	s	s
82	r	0.09	0.47	r	s	s
82.5	r	0.08	0.43	r	12.35	11.98
83	r	0.07	0.4	r	s	12.44
83.5	r	0.06	0.36	s	s	s
84	r	0.05	0.33	s	s	s
84.5	r	0.05	0.31	r	s	s
85	r	0.04	0.28	r	14.81	14.32
86	r	0.03	0.24	s	s	s
87	r	0.02	0.2	s	s	s
88	r	0.02	0.17	s	s	17.2
89	r	0.01	0.14	s	s	s
90	r	0.01	0.12	s	s	s
91	r	0.01	0.1	s	s	s
92	r	0.01	0.09	s	s	s
93	r	0.01	0.07	s	s	s
94	s	0.01	0.06	s	s	s
95	r	0.01	0.05	s	s	s
96	r	0.01	0.05	s	s	s
100	r	0.01	0.03	s	s	s
104	r	0.01	0.01	s	s	s
108	r	0.01	0.01	s	s	s
110	r	0.01	0.01	s	s	s

Prev. open int. 623,165   Prev. open int. 866,434
Source: The National Post, June 16, 2006. Used with permission.

Source: *The National Post*, June 16, 2006. Used with permission.

A PRELIMINARY NOTE Some interest rate options are actually options on interest-bearing assets such as bonds (or on futures contracts for bonds). Most of the options that are traded on exchanges fall into this category. As we will discuss in a moment, some others are actually options on interest rates. The distinction is important if we are thinking about using one type or the other to hedge. To illustrate, suppose we want to protect ourselves against an increase in interest rates using options; what should we do?

We need to buy an option that increases in value as interest rates go up. One thing we can do is buy a *put* option on a bond. Why a put? Remember that when interest rates go up, bond values go down, so one way to hedge against interest rate increases is to buy put options on bonds. The other way to hedge is to buy a *call* option on interest rates. We discuss this alternative in more detail in the next section.

We actually saw interest rate options in Chapter 7 when we discussed the call feature on a bond. Remember that the call provision gives the issuer the right to buy back the bond at a set price, known as the *call price*. What happens is that if interest rates fall, the bond's price will rise. If it rises above the call price, the buyer will exercise its option and acquire the bond at a bargain price. The call provision can thus be viewed as either a call option on a bond or a put option on interest rates.

INTEREST RATE CAPS An *interest rate cap* is a call option on an interest rate. Suppose a firm has a floating-rate loan. It is concerned that interest rates will rise sharply and the firm will experience financial distress because of the increased loan payment. To guard against this, the firm can purchase an interest rate cap from a bank. What will happen is that if the loan payment ever rises above an agreed-upon limit (the "ceiling"), the bank will pay the difference between the actual payment and the ceiling to the firm in cash.

A *floor* is a put option on an interest rate. If a firm buys a cap and sells a floor, the result is a *collar*. By selling the put and buying the call, the firm protects itself against increases in interest rates beyond the ceiling by the cap. However, if interest rates drop below the floor, the put will be exercised against the firm. The result is that the rate the firm pays will not drop below the floor rate. In other words, the rate the firm pays will always be between the floor and the ceiling.

OTHER INTEREST RATE OPTIONS We will close out our chapter by briefly mentioning two relatively new types of interest rate options. Suppose a firm has a floating-rate loan. The firm is comfortable with its floating-rate loan, but it would like to have the right to convert it to a fixed-rate loan in the future.

What can the firm do? What it wants is the right, but not the obligation, to swap its floating-rate loan for a fixed-rate loan. In other words, the firm needs to buy an option on a swap. Swap options exist, and they have the charming name *swaptions*.

We've seen that there are options on futures contracts and options on swap contracts, but what about options on options? Such options are called *compound* options. As we have just discussed, a cap is a call option on interest rates. Suppose a firm thinks that, depending on interest rates, it might like to buy a cap in the future. As you can probably guess, in this case, what the firm might want to do today is buy an option on a cap. Inevitably, it seems, an option on a cap is called a *caption,* and there is a growing market for these instruments.

CONCEPT QUESTIONS

1. Suppose that the unhedged risk profile in Figure 24.15 sloped down instead of up. What option-based hedging strategy would be suitable in this case?

2. What is a futures option?

3. What is a caption? Who might want to buy one?

24.7

SUMMARY AND CONCLUSIONS

This chapter has introduced some of the basic principles of financial risk management and financial engineering. The motivation for risk management and financial engineering stems from the fact that a firm will frequently have an undesirable exposure to some type of risk. This is particularly true today because of the increased volatility in key financial variables such as interest rates, exchange rates, and commodity prices.

We describe a firm's exposure to a particular risk with a risk profile. The goal of financial risk management is to alter the firm's risk profile through the buying and selling of derivative assets such as futures contracts, swap contracts, and options contracts. By finding instruments with appropriate payoff profiles, a firm can reduce or even eliminate its exposure to many types of risk.

Hedging cannot change the fundamental economic reality of a business. What it can do is allow a firm to avoid expensive and troublesome disruptions that might otherwise result from short-run, temporary price fluctuations. Hedging also gives a firm time to react and adapt to changing market conditions. Because of the price volatility and rapid economic change that characterize modern business, intelligently dealing with volatility has become an increasingly important task for financial managers.

There are many other option types available in addition to those we have discussed, and more are created every day. One very important aspect of financial risk management that we have not discussed is that options, forwards, futures, and swaps can be combined in a wide variety of ways to create new instruments. These basic contract types are really just the building blocks used by financial engineers to create new and innovative products for corporate risk management.

Key Terms

call option (page 746)
credit default swap (page 745)
cross-hedging (page 741)
derivative security (page 728)
economic exposure (page 736)
forward contract (page 737)
futures contract (page 740)

hedging (page 728)
option contract (page 745)
payoff profile (page 737)
put option (page 746)
risk profile (page 733)
swap contract (page 743)
transactions exposure (page 735)

Chapter Review Problems and Self-Test

24.1 **Futures Contracts** Suppose Golden Grain Farms (GGF) expects to harvest 50,000 bushels of wheat in September. GGF is concerned about the possibility of price fluctuations between now and September. The futures price for September wheat is $2 per bushel, and the relevant contract calls for 5,000 bushels. What action should GGF take to lock in the $2 price? Suppose the price of wheat actually turns out to be $3.

Evaluate GGF's gains and losses. Do the same for a price of $1. Ignore marking-to-market.

24.2 **Options Contracts** In the previous question, suppose that September futures put options with a strike price of $2 per bushel cost $.15 per bushel. Assuming that GGF hedges using put options, evaluate its gains and losses for wheat prices of $1, $2, and $3.

Answers to Self-Test Problems

24.1 GGF wants to deliver wheat and receive a fixed price, so it needs to *sell* futures contracts. Each contract calls for delivery of 5,000 bushels, so GGF needs to sell 10 contracts. No money changes hands today.

If wheat prices actually turn out to be $3, then GGF will receive $150,000 for its crop, but it will have a loss of $50,000 on its futures position when it closes that position because the contracts require it to sell 50,000 bushels of wheat at $2, when the going price is $3. GGF thus nets $100,000 overall.

If wheat prices turn out to be $1 per bushel, then the crop will be worth only $50,000. However, GGF will have a profit of $50,000 on its futures position, so GGF again nets $100,000.

24.2 If GGF wants to insure against a price decline only, it can buy 10 put contracts. Each contract is for 5,000 bushels, so the cost per contract is 5,000 × $.15 = $750. For 10 contracts, the cost will be $7,500.

If wheat prices turn out to be $3, then GGF will not exercise the put options (why not?). Its crop is worth $150,000, but it is out the $7,500 cost of the options, so it nets $142,500.

If wheat prices fall to $1, the crop is worth $50,000. GGF will exercise its puts (why?) and thereby force the seller of the puts to pay $2 per bushel. GGF receives a total of $100,000. If we subtract the cost of the puts, we see that GGF's net is $92,500. In fact, verify that its net at any price of $2 or lower is $92,500.

Concepts Review and Critical Thinking Questions

1. If a firm is selling futures contracts on lumber as a hedging strategy, what must be true about the firm's exposure to lumber prices?

2. If a firm is buying call options on pork belly futures as a hedging strategy, what must be true about the firm's exposure to pork belly prices?

3. What is the difference between a forward contract and a futures contract? Why do you think that futures contracts are much more common? Are there any circumstances under which you might prefer to use forwards instead of futures? Explain.

4. Bubbling Crude Corporation, a large Alberta oil producer, would like to hedge against adverse movements in the price of oil, since this is the firm's primary source of revenue. What should the firm do? Provide at least two reasons why it probably will not be possible to achieve a completely flat risk profile with respect to oil prices.

5. A company produces an energy intensive product and uses natural gas as the energy source. The competition primarily uses oil. Explain why this company is exposed to fluctuations in both oil and natural gas prices.

6. If a textile manufacturer wanted to hedge against adverse movements in cotton prices, it could buy cotton futures contracts or buy call options on cotton futures contracts. What would be the pros and cons of the two approaches?

7. Explain why a put option on a bond is conceptually the same as a call option on interest rates.

8. A company has a large bond issue maturing in one year. When it matures, the company will float a new issue. Current interest rates are attractive, and the company is concerned that rates next year will be higher. What are some hedging strategies that the company might use in this case?

9. Explain why a swap is effectively a series of forward contracts. Suppose a firm enters into a swap agreement with a swap dealer. Describe the nature of the default risk faced by both parties.

10. Suppose a firm enters into a fixed-for-floating interest rate swap with a swap dealer. Describe the cash flows that will occur as a result of the swap.

11. What is the difference between transactions and economic exposure? Which can be hedged more easily? Why?

12. Refer to Figure 24.11 in the text to answer this question. If a Canadian company exports its goods to Japan, how would it use a futures contract on Japanese yen to hedge its exchange rate risk? Would it buy or sell yen futures? In answering, pay attention to how the exchange rate is quoted in the futures contract.

13. For the following scenarios, describe a hedging strategy using futures contracts that might be considered. If you think that a cross-hedge would be appropriate, discuss the reasons for your choice of contract.
    a. A public utility is concerned about rising costs.
    b. A candy manufacturer is concerned about rising costs.
    c. A corn farmer fears that this year's harvest will be at record high levels across the country.
    d. A manufacturer of photographic film is concerned about rising costs.
    e. A natural gas producer believes there will be excess supply in the market this year.
    f. A bank derives all its income from long-term, fixed-rate residential mortgages.
    g. A stock mutual fund invests in large, blue-chip stocks and is concerned about a decline in the stock market.
    h. A Canadian importer of Swiss army knives will pay for its order in six months in Swiss francs.
    i. A Canadian exporter of construction equipment has agreed to sell some cranes to a German construction firm. The Canadian firm will be paid in euros in three months.

14. Looking back at the Export Development Corporation (EDC) example we used to open the chapter, why would you say EDC used a swap agreement? In other words, why didn't EDC just go ahead and issue fixed-rate bonds since the net effect of issuing variable-rate bonds and then doing a swap is to create a fixed-rate bond?

Questions and Problems

Basic
(Questions 1–4)

1. **Futures Quotes** Refer to Figure 24.11 in the text to answer this question. Suppose you purchase a September 2006 cocoa futures contract on June 16, 2006. What will your profit or loss be if the cocoa prices turn out to be $1,550 per metric ton at expiration?

2. **Futures Quotes** Refer to Figure 24.11 in the text to answer this question. Supposed you sell December 2006 gold futures on June 16, 2006. What will your profit or loss be if gold prices turn out to be $490 per ounce at expiration? What if gold prices are $650 per ounce at expiration?

3. **Futures Options Quotes** Refer to Figure 24.16 in the text to answer this question. Suppose you purchase a September 2006 call option on crude oil futures with a strike price of $55. How much does your option cost per barrel of oil? What is the total cost? Suppose the price of oil futures is $57 per barrel at expiration of the options contract. What is your net profit or loss from this position? What if oil futures prices are $40 per barrel at expiration?

Basic
(continued)

4. **Put and Call Payoffs**   Suppose a financial manager buys call options on 50,000 barrels of oil with an exercise price of $35 per barrel. She simultaneously sells a put option on 50,000 barrels of oil with the same exercise price of $35 per barrel. Consider her gains and losses of oil prices are $30, $32, $35, $38, and $40. What if oil futures prices are $43.24 per barrel at expiration?

Intermediate
(Questions
5–6)

5. **Hedging with Futures**   Refer to Figure 24.11 in the text to answer this question. Suppose today is June 16, 2006, and your firm is a jewellery manufacturer that needs 1,000 ounces of gold in October for the fall production run. You would like to lock in your costs today, because you're concerned that gold prices might go up between now and October.

   a. How could you use gold futures contracts to hedge your risk exposure? What price would you be effectively locking in?

   b. Suppose gold prices are $580 per ounce in October. What is the profit or loss on your futures position? Explain how your futures position has eliminated your exposure to price risk in the gold market.

6. **Interest Rate Swaps**   ABC Company and XYZ Company need to raise funds to pay for capital improvements at their manufacturing plants. ABC Company is a well-established firm with an excellent credit rating in the debt market; it can borrow funds either at 10 percent fixed rate or at LIBOR + 1 percent floating rate. XYZ Company is a fledgling start-up firm without a strong credit history. It can borrow funds either at 9 percent fixed rate or at LIBOR + 3 percent floating rate.

   a. Is there an opportunity here for ABC and XYZ to benefit by means of an interest rate swap?

   b. Suppose you've just been hired at a bank that acts as a dealer in the swaps market, and your boss has shown you the borrowing rate information for your clients ABC and XYZ. Describe how you could bring these two companies together in an interest rate swap that would make both firms better off, while netting your bank a 2.0 percent profit.

Challenge
(Questions
7–8)

7. **Financial Engineering**   Suppose there were call options and forward contracts available on coal, but no put options. Show how a financial engineer could synthesize a put option using the available contracts. What does your answer tell you about the general relationship between puts, calls, and forwards?

8. **Hedging**   You are assigned to the risk management department of Squeaky Wheels Inc., a U.S. chain of auto service shops with outlets in North America and internationally. Your office is located in Albany, New York, U.S.A. and the earnings of Squeaky are stated in U.S. dollars. Your responsibility is to manage the foreign exchange risk arising from operations in the European Community.

   The current exchange rate is $1.33 U.S. per euro. Currently Squeaky earns net profits from EC operations of 1 million euros per month, which are repatriated to the U.S. head office. The firm also has pension obligations to retired employees in the EC of 1.5 million euros per month. Pension funds for the entire company are managed in the U.S. head office and invested in U.S. assets. While the pension obligations are quite stable, monthly profits are subject to fluctuation with economic conditions and seasonality.

   The CFO has identified one month as the appropriate planning horizon and foreign exchange forward contracts with a major bank, currency futures and currency futures options (puts and calls) as possible hedging vehicles. To complete your engagement, do the following:

   a. Assess Squeaky's exchange rate exposure.

   b. Explain how Squeaky could hedge with each of the possible vehicles. For each, state the appropriate position (buy or sell) and state your reasons briefly.

   c. Suppose the CFO is committed to hedging all the foreign exchange risk from European operations. How would these considerations affect your recommendation on the best choice of hedging vehicle?

Internet Application Questions

1. Value at Risk is a powerful tool to analyze the risk of a portfolio. VaR attempts to estimate the dollar loss on a portfolio based on small probabilities. The following link explains all about VaR.

   www.gloriamundi.org/introduction.asp

   Assuming that returns on a portfolio are normally distributed, reconcile the VaR measure to more traditional measures of risk such as the standard deviation of returns.

2. The Winnipeg Commodities Exchange (www.wce.ca) provides several education tools to help understand the world of futures trading. The following link explains the mechanics of futures trading and common futures jargon, and provides examples of hedging.

   www.wce.ca/ – search for "hedging" in their search box

   Explain how a wheat farmer in Saskatchewan as well as a baker in Quebec can benefit from using futures.

3. Information on derivative instruments and markets can be found at www.numa.com. Among the resources you can access is an "Options Strategy Guide." What technique(s) does the guide suggest if you are moderately bullish on the market? What about if you are neutral, expecting short-term weakness, and a longer term rally?

4. The Montreal Stock Exchange is the main market for derivative products in Canada. The exchange provides an options calculator on its website at www.m-x.org/accueil_en.php. Locate an option in the newspaper or on the exchange's website, and calculate its value using the online calculator.

Suggested Readings

A highly readable discussion of derivatives use in Canada is:

Jalilvand, A., "Why Firms Use Derivatives: Evidence from Canada." *Canadian Journal of Administrative Sciences* 16, September 1999, pp. 213–228.

A more detailed discussion of derivatives can be found in:

Hull, J. *Options, Futures and Other Derivative Securities*. 6th ed., Upper Saddle River, N.J.: Prentice-Hall, 2006.

CHAPTER 25

Options and Corporate Securities

Noranda Inc., an international mining and metals company based in Canada, sold 10 year debentures in 1997 maturing on April 29, 2007. The bonds carry a low coupon rate of 5 percent. Why? Because the holders of these bonds can, at their option, exchange their bonds for 3.63 shares of Noranda common stock. Such bonds are called convertible bonds, for obvious reasons, and they are just one example of the use of options in corporate finance. We examine these and other options in this chapter.

www.noranda.com

option
A contract that gives its owner the right to buy or sell some asset at a fixed price on or before a given date.

OUR PREVIOUS CHAPTER briefly examined options and their use in risk management. Options are a much broader topic, however, and there is much more to them than we have discussed so far. In fact, options are a part of everyday life. "Keep your options open" is sound business advice, and "We're out of options" is a sure sign of trouble. Options are obviously valuable, but actually putting a dollar value on one is not easy. How to value options is an important topic of research, and option pricing is one of the great success stories of modern finance.

In finance, an **option** is an arrangement that gives its owner the right to buy or sell an asset at a fixed price anytime on or before a given date. The most familiar options are stock options. These are options to buy and sell shares of common stock, and we discuss them in some detail. Almost all corporate securities have implicit or explicit option features. Furthermore, the use of such features is expanding with the growth of financial engineering. As a result, understanding securities that involve option features requires a general knowledge of the factors that determine an option's value.

This chapter starts with a description of different types of options. We identify and discuss the general factors that determine option values and show how ordinary debt and equity have option-like characteristics. We then illustrate how option features are incorporated into corporate securities by discussing warrants, convertible bonds, and other option-like securities.

25.1 OPTIONS: THE BASICS

An option is a contract that gives its owner the right to buy or sell some asset at a fixed price on or before a given date. For example, an option on a building might give the holder of the option the right to buy the building for $1 million anytime on or before the Saturday before the third Wednesday in January 2010.

Options are a unique type of financial contract because they give the buyer the right, but not the obligation, to do something. The buyer uses the option only if it is profitable to do so; otherwise the option can be thrown away.

There is a special vocabulary associated with options. Here are some important definitions:

exercising the option
The act of buying or selling the underlying asset via the option contract.

striking price
The fixed price in the option contract at which the holder can buy or sell the underlying asset. Also the exercise price or strike price.

expiration date
The last day on which an option can be exercised.

American option
An option that can be exercised at any time until its expiration date.

European option
An option that can be exercised only on the expiration date.

call option
The right to buy an asset at a fixed price during a particular period of time.

put option
The right to sell an asset at a fixed price during a particular period of time. The opposite of a call option.

www.cboe.com

1. **Exercising the option.** The act of buying or selling the underlying asset via the option contract is called exercising the option.
2. **Striking price or exercise price.** The fixed price specified in the option contract at which the holder can buy or sell the underlying asset is called the striking price or exercise price. The striking price is often just called the *strike price.*
3. **Expiration date.** An option usually has a limited life. The option is said to expire at the end of its life. The last day on which the option can be exercised is called the expiration date.
4. **American and European options.** An American option may be exercised anytime up to the expiration date. A European option can be exercised only on the expiration date.

Puts and Calls

As we discussed in our previous chapter, options come in two basic types: puts and calls. Call options are the more common of the two and our discussion focuses mostly on calls. A **call option** gives the owner the right to buy an asset at a fixed price during a particular time period. It may help you to remember that a call option gives you the right to "call in" an asset.

A **put option** is essentially the opposite of a call option. Instead of giving the holder the right to buy some asset, it gives the holder the right to sell that asset for a fixed exercise price. If you buy a put option, you can force the seller to buy the asset from you for a fixed price and thereby "put it to him."

What about an investor who sells a call option? The seller receives money up front and has the obligation to sell the asset at the exercise price if the option holder wants it. Similarly, an investor who sells a put option receives cash up front and is then obligated to buy the asset at the exercise price if the option holder demands it.[1]

The asset involved in an option could be anything. The options that are most widely bought and sold, however, are stock options. These are options to buy and sell shares of stock. Because these are the best-known options, we study them first. As we discuss stock options, keep in mind that the general principles apply to options involving any asset, not just shares of stock.

Stock Option Quotations

In the 1970s and 1980s, organized trading in options grew from literally zero into some of the world's largest markets. The tremendous growth in interest in derivative securities resulted from the greatly increased volatility in financial markets, which we discussed in Chapter 1.[2] Exchange trading in options began in 1973 on the Chicago Board Options Exchange (CBOE). The CBOE is still the largest organized options market; options are traded in a number of other places today, including London, Paris, Tokyo, and Hong Kong.

Option trading in Canada began in 1975 on the Montreal Exchange. Today options are traded on the Montreal Exchange and are cleared through the Canadian Derivatives Clearing Corp. (CDCC). The CDCC stands between option buyers and option sellers, called writers. Put and call options involving stock in some of the best-known corporations in Canada are traded daily. Almost all such options are American (as opposed to European). Trading in Canadian options and other derivative securities has grown rapidly in the last 10 years as banks, pension funds, and other financial institutions gain experience with hedging techniques using derivative securities.

---

1 An investor who sells an option is often said to have "written" the option.

2 Our discussion of the history of options trading draws on L. Gagnon, "Exchange-Traded Financial Derivatives in Canada: Finally Off the Launching Pad," *Canadian Investment Review,* Fall 1990, pp. 63–70, and J. Ilkiw, "From Suspicion to Optimism: The Story of Derivative Use by Pension Funds in Canada," *Canadian Investment Review,* Summer 1994, pp. 19–22.

To get started with option specifics, we look at a simplified *National Post* quotation for a CDCC option:

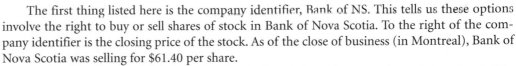

Stk	Exp	P/C	Bid	Ask
Bank of NS (BNS)				**45.10**
44	July	C	1.30	1.40
46	July	C	0.30	0.40

www.scotiabank.com

The first thing listed here is the company identifier, Bank of NS. This tells us these options involve the right to buy or sell shares of stock in Bank of Nova Scotia. To the right of the company identifier is the closing price of the stock. As of the close of business (in Montreal), Bank of Nova Scotia was selling for $61.40 per share.

On the next line is the expiration date for the first option. July means the option expires in July 2006. All CDCC options expire after the close of trading on the third Friday of the expiration month.

To the left of the expiration date is the striking (or exercise) price. The first Bank of Nova Scotia option listed here has an exercise price of $44. The second option also has an exercise price of $46. Both are call options (marked by the "C").

The first option listed would be described as the "Bank of NS $44 call." The asking price for this option is $1.40. If you pay the $1.40, you have the right, between now and the third Friday in July, to buy one share of Bank of Nova Scotia stock for $44. Actually, trading occurs in round lots (multiples of 100 shares), so one option contract costs $1.40 × 100 = $140.

www.me.org

Figure 25.1 contains a more detailed quote reproduced from *The National Post*. (You can also get option quotes online at the Montreal Exchange's website.) From our previous discussion, we know that these are Bank of Nova Scotia options and the Bank of Nova Scotia closed at $45.10 per share on the Montreal Exchange. Notice that multiple striking prices ranging from $42 to $48 are available. Expiration dates range from July 2006 to January 2007.

To check your understanding of option quotes, suppose you wanted the right to buy 100 shares of ATI Technologies for $17 any time between now and the third Friday in January 2007. What should you order and how much will it cost you?

Since you want the right to buy the stock for $17, you need to buy a call option with a $17 exercise price. Place an order for one ATI Jan $17 call. Since the Jan $17 call is quoted at $2.35 asking price, you have to pay $2.35 per share, or $235 in all (plus commission).

Option Payoffs

Looking at Figure 25.1, suppose you were to buy 50 Bank of NS July $46 call contracts. The option is quoted at a $0.40 asking price, so the contracts cost $40 each. You would spend a total of 50 × $40 = $2,000. You wait a while and the expiration date rolls around. Now what? You have the right to buy Bank of Nova Scotia stock for $46 per share. If Bank of Nova Scotia is selling for less than $46 a share, this option isn't worth anything, and you throw it away. In this case, we say the option has finished "out of the money" since the stock price exceeds the exercise price. Suppose Bank of Nova Scotia rises to, say, $53 per share. Since you have the right to buy Bank of Nova Scotia at $46, you make a profit of $7 on each share on exercise. Each contract involves 100 shares, so you make $7 per share × 100 shares per contract = $700 per contract. Finally, you own 50 contracts, so the value of your options is a handsome $35,000. Notice that since you invested $2,000, your net profit is $32,000.

Ending Stock Price	Option Value (50 Contracts)	Net Profit (Loss)	Stock Value (44 shares)	Net Profit (Loss)
$40	$ —	$ (2,000)	$1,760	$(240)
45	$ —	$ (2,000)	$1,980	$ (20)
50	$20,000	$18,000	$2,200	$ 200
55	$45,000	$43,000	$2,420	$ 420
60	$70,000	$68,000	$2,640	$ 640
65	$95,000	$93,000	$2,860	$ 860

As our example indicates, the gains and losses from buying call options can be quite large. To illustrate further, suppose you had simply purchased the stock with $2,000 instead of buying

FIGURE 25.1

Options quotations

Stock Options — 10 Most active options

Company	Volume	Interest
Alcan	3,135	39,786
RogersComBNV	2,940	17,384
iShares i60	2,747	38,656
Nortel Networks	2,439	93,101
EnCana	2,393	55,562
Sun Life Finl	2,244	10,412
Cdn Nat Res	2,188	33,486
Cdn Natl Rail	1,995	14,055
Goldcorp	1,880	21,058
Talisman Enrg	1,859	34,837

CDCC Trades

Total	57,739	1,283,042

StkExp	P/C	Vol	Bid	Ask	Opint
ACE Aviation RV (ACE)					30.94
32 July	C	450	0.6	0.8	178
Total option vol. 450			Total open int. 3,355		
ATI Technlgys (ATY)					16.59
15 July	P	55	0.45	0.55	118
16 July	P	78	0.75	0.9	354
17 July	C	56	0.95	1.05	240
18 July	C	150	0.55	0.7	409
16 Oct	P	10	1.4	1.5	83
17 Oct	C	20	1.7	1.85	658
15 Jan	C	10	3.25	3.4	90
17 Jan	C	10	2.2	2.35	99
Total option vol. 576			Total open int. 9,149		
Aber Diamond (ABZ)					35.24
34 July	P	10	1.05	1.25	40
36 July	C	40	1.05	1.2	11
36 July	P	10	2.05	2.25	2
32 Oct	P	2	1.65	1.85	0
Total option vol. 62			Total open int. 722		
Agnico-Eagle (AEM)					30.38
28 July	C	25	3.3	3.5	12
28 July	P	4	0.95	1.1	10
34 July	C	35	0.75	0.9	79
28 Sept	P	3	1.9	2.1	93
28 Dec	C	10	5.6	5.85	0
34 Dec	C	22	3.1	3.35	20
Total option vol. 119			Total open int. 4,527		
Alcan (AL)					47.24
44 July	C	67	4.75	4.85	203
44 July	P	70	1.35	1.45	308
46 July	C	20	3.5	3.6	335
46 July	P	168	2.05	2.15	319
48 July	C	156	2.45	2.6	369
48 July	P	513	3.05	3.15	295
50 July	C	88	1.7	1.8	501
50 July	P	191	4.25	4.4	516
46 Aug	P	76	2.75	2.9	0
50 Aug	C	20	2.4	2.5	0
50 Aug	P	29	4.9	5.05	0
44 Oct	P	97	2.7	2.85	322
46 Oct	P	60	3.5	3.7	48
48 Oct	C	10	4.2	4.35	57
48 Oct	P	20	4.5	4.65	186
50 Oct	C	23	3.3	3.45	174
50 Oct	P	21	5.6	5.75	138
46 Jan	C	10	6.3	6.5	194
46 Jan	P	1	4.3	4.5	326
48 Jan	C	11	5.3	5.5	341
Total option vol. 3,034			Total open int. 32,459		

StkExp	P/C	Vol	Bid	Ask	Opint
BCE (BCE)					26.69
24 July	C	50	2.75	2.85	345
26 July	C	131	0.95	1.05	260
26 July	P	25	0.15	0.3	165
27 July	C	948			0
28 July	C	32	0.1	0.15	517
28 July	P	10	1.3	1.4	232
24 Aug	C	20	2.85	3	226
26 Aug	C	30	1.15	1.3	663
28 Aug	C	17	0.2	0.3	2,386
28 Aug	P	26	1.35	1.45	1,711
24 Nov	C	50	3.1	3.25	232
26 Nov	P	218	0.75	0.9	873
28 Nov	C	110	0.6	0.7	498
24 Jan	C	50	3.2	3.35	651
Total option vol. 1,785			Total open int. 32,193		
BCE LEAPS 2008 (LBC)					26.69
24 Jan	C	0	3.9	4.1	172
24 Jan	P	0	1.3	1.45	240
26 Jan	C	0	2.7	2.9	400
26 Jan	P	17	2.05	2.2	383
28 Jan	C	10	1.8	2	446
28 Jan	P	0	3.05	3.25	442
30 Jan	C	0	1.15	1.3	425
30 Jan	P	0	4.35	4.55	1,082
Total option vol. 49			Total open int. 6,566		
Ballard Power (BLD)					6.53
6 July	C	1	0.9	1	220
8 July	C	47	0.2	0.25	288
7 Oct	P	5	1.3	1.45	96
8 Jan	C	1	0.85	1	31
Total option vol. 94			Total open int. 8,873		
Bank of Mtl (BMO)					59.38
58 July	P	57	0.55	0.7	65
60 July	C	137	0.9	1.05	506
61 July	C	312			0
58 Aug	P	5	1.1	1.25	0
60 Aug	C	110	1.25	1.4	0
60 Aug	P	10	2.05	2.2	0
56 Oct	C	10	4.55	4.75	31
58 Oct	P	5	1.75	1.85	224
56 Jan	C	10	5.35	5.55	125
58 Jan	C	5	4.1	4.25	206
Total option vol. 1,251			Total open int. 31,052		
Bank of Mtl LEAPS 2008 (LBM)					59.38
56 Jan	C	0	7.6	7.85	53
56 Jan	P	6	4.1	4.3	170
58 Jan	C	0	6.45	6.75	65
58 Jan	P	0	4.85	5.1	78
60 Jan	C	0	5.45	5.7	251
60 Jan	P	17	5.8	6.05	110
62 Jan	C	0	4.55	4.8	85
62 Jan	P	0	6.8	7.1	221
Total option vol. 43			Total open int. 6,427		
Bank of NS (BNS)					45.1
42 July	P	110	0.1	0.2	2,385
44 July	C	50	1.3	1.4	1,135
44 July	P	94	0.45	0.55	1,553
46 July	C	75	0.3	0.4	2,957
46 July	P	2	1.5	1.65	673
48 July	P	80	3.25	3.35	529
42 Aug	P	60	0.25	0.35	0

StkExp	P/C	Vol	Bid	Ask	Opint
42 Oct	P	300	0.6	0.75	991
44 Oct	C	40	2.2	2.35	979
46 Oct	C	142	1.15	1.25	652
46 Oct	P	60	2.15	2.35	829
48 Oct	C	4	0.55	0.65	874
42 Jan	C	2	4.15	4.3	739
46 Jan	C	10	1.8	1.9	970
48 Jan	C	3	1.05	1.15	763
Total option vol. 1,112			Total open int. 45,454		
Bank of NS LEAPS 2008 (LBQ)					45.1
42 Jan	C	0	6.15	6.4	704
42 Jan	P	0	2.65	2.85	327
44 Jan	C	0	5.05	5.25	485
44 Jan	P	0	3.4	3.6	226
46 Jan	C	50	4	4.2	562
46 Jan	P	3	4.3	4.5	731
48 Jan	C	53	3.15	3.3	880
48 Jan	P	0	5.4	5.6	193
Total option vol. 136			Total open int. 8,617		
Barrick (ABX)					30.5
30 July	C	14	1.45	1.55	1,225
30 July	P	150	0.8	0.9	1,326
32 July	C	122	0.6	0.65	790
32 July	P	26	1.9	1.95	1,035
32 Aug	C	10	1.05	1.15	0
28 Oct	P	10	1	1.15	566
30 Oct	C	55	2.7	2.85	206
30 Oct	P	3	1.8	1.9	460
32 Oct	C	10	1.8	1.95	327
32 Oct	P	43	2.85	3	511
32.5 Jan	C	22	2.4	2.45	366
32.5 Jan	P	10	3.65	3.8	567
Total option vol. 658			Total open int. 40,886		

Source: *The National Post*, June 20, 2006. http://www.canada.com/nationalpost/financialpost/fpmarketdata/options_stock.html. Used with permission.

call options. You would have about $2,000/45.10 = 44.35 shares. We can now compare what you have when the options expire for different stock prices.

The option position clearly magnifies the gains and losses on the stock by a substantial amount. The reason is that payoff on your 50 option contracts is based on $50 \times 100 = 5,000$ shares of stock instead of just 44.

In our example, if the stock price changes by only a small amount, you lose all $2,000, with the option. With the stock, you still have about what you started with. Also notice that the option can never be worth less than zero because you can always just throw it away. As a result, you can never lose more than your original investment ($2,000 in our example).

Recognize that stock options are a zero-sum game. By this we mean that whatever the buyer of a stock option makes, the seller loses and vice versa. To illustrate, suppose that in our example you had sold 50 option contracts. You would receive $2,000 upfront, and you would be obligated to sell the stock for $46 if the buyer of the option wished to exercise it. In this situation, if the stock price ends up at or less than $46, you would be $2,000 ahead. If the stock price ends up more than $46, you have to sell something for less than it is worth, so you lose the difference. For example, if the stock price were $51, you would have to sell $50 \times 100 = 5,000$ shares at $46 per share, so you would be out $51 - 46 = $5 per share, or $25,000. Because you received $2,000 up front, your net loss is $23,000. We can summarize some other possibilities as follows:

Ending Stock Price	Net Profit to Option Seller
$40	$2,000
45	2,000
50	(18,000)
55	(43,000)
60	(68,000)
65	(93,000)

Notice that the net profits to the option buyer (just calculated) are the opposites of these amounts.

Put Payoffs

Looking at Figure 25.1, suppose you buy 10 Ballard October 7 put contracts. How much does this cost (ignoring commissions)? Just before the option expires, Ballard is selling for $5 per share. Is this good news or bad news? What is your net profit?

The option is quoted at 1.45, so one contract costs $100 \times 1.45 = 145. Your 10 contracts total $1,450. You now have the right to sell 1,000 shares of Ballard for $7 per share—this is most definitely good news. You can buy 1,000 shares at $5 and sell them for $7. Your puts are thus worth $2 \times 1,000 = $2,000$. Since you paid $1,450, your net profit is $2,000 - 1,450 = 550.

Long-Term Equity Anticipation Securities (LEAPS)

Figure 25.1 also shows listings for Long-Term Equity Anticipation Securities or LEAPS for short. LEAPS are long-term calls and puts that expire in January for terms of at least one year up to 2⅔ years. For example, Figure 25.1 lists call LEAPS for Bank of Montreal expiring in January 2008—about 1½ years from the time of the price quotes.

CONCEPT QUESTIONS

1. What is a call option? A put option?

2. If you thought a stock was going to drop sharply in value, how might you use stock options to profit from the decline?

FUNDAMENTALS OF OPTION VALUATION

Now that we understand the basics of puts and calls, we can discuss what determines their values. We focus on call options in the following discussion, but the same type of analysis can be applied to put options.

Value of a Call Option at Expiration

We have already described the payoffs from call options for different stock prices. To continue this discussion, the following notation is useful:

S_1 = Stock price at expiration (in one period)
S_0 = Stock price today
C_1 = Value of the call option on the expiration date (in one period)
C_0 = Value of the call option today
E = Exercise price on the option

From our previous discussion, remember that if the stock price (S_1) is not more than the exercise price (E) on the expiration date, the call option (C_1) is worth zero. In other words:

$$C_1 = 0 \text{ if } S_1 \leq E$$

Or, equivalently:

$$C_1 = 0 \text{ if } (S_1 - E) \leq 0 \qquad [25.1]$$

This is the case where the option is out of the money when it expires.

If the option finishes in the money, $S_1 > E$, the value of the option at expiration is equal to the difference:

$$C_1 = S_1 - E \text{ if } S_1 > E$$

Or, equivalently:

$$C_1 = S_1 - E \text{ if } (S_1 - E) > 0 \qquad [25.2]$$

For example, suppose we have a call option with an exercise price of $10. The option is about to expire. If the stock is selling for $8, we have the right to pay $10 for something worth only $8. Our option is thus worth exactly zero because the stock price is less than the exercise price on the option ($S_1 \leq E$). If the stock is selling for $12, the option has value. Since we can buy the stock for $10, it is worth ($S_1 - E$) = $12 - $10 = $2.

Figure 25.2 plots the value of a call option at expiration against the stock price. The result looks something like a hockey stick. Notice that for every stock price less than E, the value of the option is zero. For every stock price greater than E, the value of the call option is ($S_1 - E$). Also, once the stock price exceeds the exercise price, the option's value goes up dollar for dollar with the stock price.

The Upper and Lower Bounds on a Call Option's Value

Now that we know how to determine C_1, the value of the call at expiration, we turn to a somewhat more challenging question: How can we determine C_0, the value sometime before expiration? We discuss this in the next several sections. For now, we establish the upper and lower bounds for the value of a call option.

THE UPPER BOUND   What is the most a call option could sell for? If you think about it, the answer is obvious. A call option gives you the right to buy a share of stock, so it can never be worth more than the stock itself. This tells us the upper bound on a call's value: A call option always sells for less than the underlying asset. So, in our notation, the upper bound is:

$$C_0 \leq S_0 \qquad [25.3]$$

FIGURE 25.2

Value of a call option at expiration for different stock prices

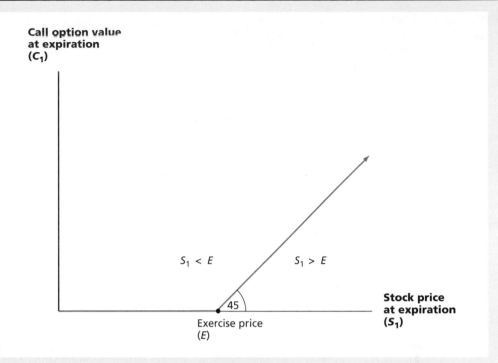

As shown, the value of a call option at expiration is equal to zero if the stock price is less than or equal to the exercise price. The value of the call is equal to the stock price minus the exercise price ($S_1 - E$) if the stock price exceeds the exercise price. The resulting "hockey stick" shape is highlighted.

THE LOWER BOUND   What is the least a call option could sell for? The answer here is a little less obvious. First, the call can't sell for less than zero, so $C_0 \geq 0$. Furthermore, if the stock price is greater than the exercise price, the call option is worth at least $S_0 - E$.

To see why, suppose we had a call option selling for $4. The stock price is $10, and the exercise price is $5. Is there a profit opportunity here? The answer is yes because you could buy the call for $4 and immediately exercise it by spending an additional $5. Your total cost of acquiring the stock is $4 + 5 = $9. If you turn around and immediately sell the stock for $10, you pocket a $1 certain profit.

Opportunities for riskless profits such as this one are called *arbitrages* or arbitrage opportunities. One who arbitrages is called an arbitrageur. The root for the term *arbitrage* is the same as the root for the word *arbitrate*, and an arbitrageur essentially arbitrates prices. In a well-organized market, significant arbitrages are, of course, rare.

In the case of a call option, to prevent arbitrage, the value of the call today must be greater than the stock price less the exercise price:

$$C_0 \geq S_0 - E$$

If we put our two conditions together, we have:

$$\begin{aligned} &C_0 \geq 0 \text{ if } S_0 - E < 0 \\ &C_0 \geq S_0 - E \text{ if } S_0 - E \geq 0 \end{aligned} \qquad [25.4]$$

These conditions simply say that the lower bound on the call's value is either zero or $S_0 - E$, whichever is bigger.

Our lower bound is called the **intrinsic value** of the option, and it is simply what the option would be worth if it were about to expire. With this definition, our discussion thus far can be restated as follows: At expiration, an option is worth its intrinsic value; it is generally worth more than that any time before expiration.

intrinsic value
The lower bound of an option's value, or what the option would be worth if it were about to expire.

FIGURE 25.3

Value of a call option before expiration for different stock prices

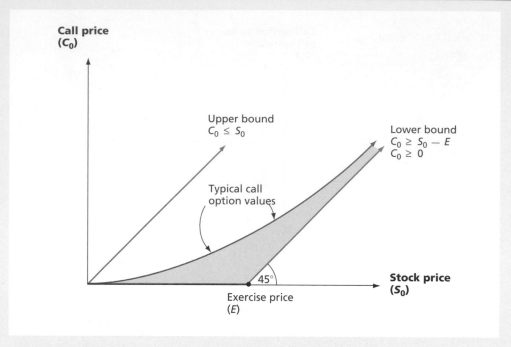

As shown, the upper bound on a call's value is given by the value of the stock ($C_0 \leq S_0$). The lower bound is either $S_0 - E$ or 0, whichever is larger. The highlighted curve illustrates the value of a call option prior to maturity for different stock prices.

Figure 25.3 displays the upper and lower bounds on the value of a call option. Also plotted is a curve representing typical call option values for different stock prices before maturity. The exact shape and location of this curve depends on a number of factors. We begin our discussion of these factors in the next section.

EXAMPLE 25.1: Upper and Lower Bounds for ATI Technologies Calls

Look back at the options listed for ATI in Figure 25.1. Calculate the upper and lower limits for the Jan 15 call. Does the actual price in the newspaper fall between these limits?

ATI stock closed at $16.59 and this is the upper bound. For this call, the stock price (S_0) is greater than the exercise price (E). In the jargon of options, this call is in the money. The lower bound call value is $1.59:

$S_0 - E = \$16.59 - \$15.00 = \$1.59$

The actual price of this call is $3.40 (asking), which lies between the upper and lower bounds.

www.ati.com

A Simple Model: Part I

Option pricing can be a complex subject. Fortunately, as is often the case, many of the key insights can be illustrated with a simple example. Suppose we are looking at a call option with one year to expiration and an exercise price of $105. The stock currently sells for $100, and the risk-free rate, R_f, is 20 percent.

The value of the stock in one year is uncertain, of course. To keep things simple, suppose we know the stock price will either be $110 or $130. Importantly, we don't know the odds associated with these two prices. In other words, we know the possible values for the stock, but not the probabilities associated with those values.

Since the exercise price on the option is $105, we know the option will be worth either $110 − 105 = $5 or $130 − 105 = $25, but, once again, we don't know which. We do know one thing, however: Our call option is certain to finish in the money.

THE BASIC APPROACH   Here is the crucial observation: It is possible to duplicate exactly the payoffs on the stock using a combination of the option and the risk-free asset. How? Do the following: Buy one call option and invest $87.50 in a risk-free asset (such as a T-bill).

What will you have in a year? Your risk-free asset earns 20 percent, so it is worth $87.50 × 1.20 = $105. Your option is worth $5 or $25, so the total value is either $110 or $130, just like the stock:

Stock Value		Risk-Free Asset Value	+	Call Value	=	Total Value
$110	versus	$105	+	$ 5	=	$110
130	versus	105	+	25	=	130

As illustrated, these two strategies—buy a share of stock versus buy a call and invest in the risk-free asset—have exactly the same payoffs in the future.

Because these two strategies have the same future payoffs, they must have the same value today or else there would be an arbitrage opportunity. The stock sells for $100 today, so the value of the call option today, C_0, is:

$$\$100 = \$87.50 + C_0$$
$$C_0 = \$12.50$$

Where did we get the $87.50? This is just the present value of the exercise price on the option, calculated at the risk-free rate:

$$E/(1 + R_f) = \$105/1.20 = \$87.50$$

Thus, our example shows that the value of a call option in this simple case is given by:

$$S_0 = C_0 + E/(1 + R_f)$$
$$C_0 = S_0 - E/(1 + R_f)$$

[25.5]

In words, the value of the call option is equal to the stock price minus the present value of the exercise price.

A MORE COMPLICATED CASE   Obviously, our assumption that the stock price would be either $110 or $130 is a vast oversimplification. We can now develop a more realistic model by assuming the stock price can be anything greater than or equal to the exercise price. Once again, we don't know how likely the different possibilities are, but we are certain the option will finish somewhere in the money.

We again let S_1 stand for the stock price in one year. Now consider our strategy of investing $87.50 in a riskless asset and buying one call option. The riskless asset is again worth $105 in one year, and the option is worth $S_1 − \$105$, depending on what the stock price is.

When we investigate the combined value of the option and the riskless asset, we observe something very interesting:

$$\text{Combined value} = \text{Riskless asset value} + \text{Option value}$$
$$= \$105 + (S_1 - \$105)$$
$$= S_1$$

Just as we had before, buying a share of stock has exactly the same payoff as buying a call option and investing the present value of the exercise price in the riskless asset.

Once again, to prevent arbitrage, these two strategies must have the same cost, so the value of the call option is equal to the stock price less the present value of the exercise price:

$$C_0 = S_0 - E/(1 + R_f)$$

Our conclusion from this discussion is that determining the value of a call option is not diffi-cult as long as we are certain the option will finish somewhere in the money.[3]

Four Factors Determining Option Values

If we continue to suppose that our option is certain to finish in the money, we can readily iden-tify four factors that determine an option's value. There is a fifth factor that comes into play if the option can finish out of the money. We discuss this last factor in the next section.

For now, if we assume that the option expires in t periods, the present value of the exercise price is $E/(1 + R_f)^t$, and the value of the call is:

$$\text{Call option value} = \text{Stock value} - \text{Present value of the exercise price} \qquad [25.6]$$
$$C_0 = S_0 - E/(1 + R_f)^t$$

If we look at this expression, the value of the call obviously depends on four things:

1. *The stock price.* The higher the stock price (S_0) is, the more the call is worth. This comes as no surprise because the option gives us the right to buy the stock at a fixed price.

2. *The exercise price.* The higher the exercise price (E) is, the less the call is worth. This is also not a surprise since the exercise price is what we have to pay to get the stock.

3. *The time to expiration.* The longer the time to expiration is (the bigger t is), the more the option is worth. Once again, this is obvious. Since the option gives us the right to buy for a fixed length of time, its value goes up as that length of time increases.

4. *The risk-free rate.* The higher the risk-free rate (R_f) is, the more the call is worth. This result is a little less obvious. Normally, we think of asset values going down as rates rise. In this case, the exercise price is a cash outflow, a liability. The current value of that liabil-ity goes down as the discount rate goes up.

CONCEPT QUESTIONS

1. What is the value of a call option at expiration?

2. What are the upper and lower bounds on the value of a call option any time before expiration?

3. Assuming the stock price is certain to be greater than the exercise price on a call option, what is the value of the call? Why?

VALUING A CALL OPTION

We now investigate the value of a call option when there is the possibility that the option will finish out of the money. We again examine the simple case of two possible future stock prices. This case lets us identify the remaining factor that determines an option's value.

A Simple Model: Part II

From our previous example, we have a stock that currently sells for $100. It will be worth either $110 or $130 in a year, and we don't know which. The risk-free rate is 20 percent. We are now looking at a different call option, however. This one has an exercise price of $120 instead of $105. What is the value of this call option?

This case is a little harder. If the stock ends up at $110, the option is out of the money and worth nothing. If the stock ends up at $130, the option is worth $130 – 120 = $10.

---

3 You're probably wondering what would happen if the stock price were less than the present value of the exercise price, resulting in a negative value for the call option. This can't happen because we are certain the stock price will be at least E in one year since we know the stock will finish in the money. If the current price of the stock is less than $E/(1 + R_f)$, the return on the stock is certain to be greater than the risk-free rate, thereby creating an arbitrage opportunity. For example, if the stock were currently selling for $80, the minimum return would be ($105 – $80)/$80 = 31.25%. Since we can borrow at 20 percent, we can earn a certain minimum return of 11.25 percent per dollar borrowed. This, of course, is an arbitrage.

Our basic approach to determining the value of the call option is the same. We show once again that it is possible to combine the call option and a risk-free investment in a way that exactly duplicates the payoff from holding the stock. The only complication is that it's a little harder to determine how to do it.

For example, suppose we bought one call and invested the present value of the exercise price in a riskless asset as we did before. In one year, we would have $120 from the riskless investment plus an option worth either zero or $10. The total value is either $120 or $130. This is not the same as the value of the stock ($110 or $130), so the two strategies are not comparable.

Instead, consider investing the present value of $110 (the lower stock price) in a riskless asset. This guarantees us a $110 payoff. If the stock price is $110, any call options we own are worthless, and we have exactly $110 as desired.

When the stock is worth $130, the call option is worth $10. Our risk-free investment is worth $110, so we are $130 − 110 = $20 short. Since each call option is worth $10, we need to buy two of them to replicate the stock.

Thus, in this case, investing the present value of the lower stock price in a riskless asset and buying two call options exactly duplicates owning the stock. When the stock is worth $110, we have $110 from our risk-free investment. When the stock is worth $130, we have $110 from the risk-free investment plus two call options worth $10 each.

Because these two strategies have exactly the same value in the future, they must have the same value today or else arbitrage would be possible:

$$S_0 = \$100 = 2 \times C_0 + \$110/(1 + R_f)$$
$$2 \times C_0 = \$100 - \$110/1.20$$
$$C_0 = \$4.17$$

Each call option is thus worth $4.17.

The Fifth Factor

We now illustrate the fifth (and last) factor that determines an option's value. Suppose that everything in our previous example is the same except the stock price can be $105 or $135 instead of $110 or $130. Notice that this change makes the stock's future price more volatile than before.

We investigate the same strategy that we used before: Invest the present value of the lower stock price ($105) in the risk-free asset and buy two call options. If the stock price is $105, as before, the call options have no value and we have $105 in all.

If the stock price is $135, each option is worth $S_1 - E = \$135 - 120 = \$15$. We have two calls, so our portfolio is worth $\$105 + 2 \times \$15 = \$135$. Once again, we have exactly replicated the value of the stock.

EXAMPLE 25.2: Don't Call Us, We'll Call You

We are looking at two call options on the same stock, one with an exercise price of $20 and one with an exercise price of $30. The stock currently sells for $35. Its future price will either be $25 or $50. If the risk-free rate is 10 percent, what are the values of these call options?

The first case (the $20 exercise price) is not difficult since the option is sure to finish in the money. We know that the value is equal to the stock price less the present value of the exercise price:

$$C_0 = S_0 - E/(1 + R_f)$$
$$= \$35 - \$20/1.1$$
$$= \$16.82$$

In the second case, the exercise price is $30, so the option can finish out of the money. At expiration, the option is worth $0 if the stock is worth $25. The option is worth $50 − 30 = $20 if it finishes in the money.

As before, we start by investing the present value of the lower stock price in the risk-free asset. This costs $25/1.1 = $22.73. At expiration, we have $25 from this investment.

If the stock price is $50, we need an additional $25 to duplicate the stock payoff. Since each option is worth $20, we need $25/$20 = 1.25 options. So, to prevent arbitrage, investing the present value of $25 in a risk-free asset and buying 1.25 call options has the same value as the stock:

$$S_0 = 1.25 \times C_0 + \$25/(1 + R_f)$$
$$\$35 = 1.25 \times C_0 + \$25/(1 + .10)$$
$$C_0 = \$9.82$$

Notice that this second option had to be worth less because it has the higher exercise price.

What has happened to the option's value? More to the point, the variance of the return on the stock has increased. Does the option's value go up or down? To find out, we need to solve for the value of the call just as we did before:

$$S_0 = \$100 = 2 \times C_0 + \$105/(1 + R_f)$$
$$2 \times C_0 = \$100 - \$105/1.20$$
$$C_0 = \$6.25$$

The value of the call option has gone up from $4.17 to $6.25.

Based on our example, the fifth and final factor that determines an option's value is the variance of the return on the underlying asset. Furthermore, the greater that variance is, the more the option is worth. This result appears a little odd at first, and it may be somewhat surprising to learn that increasing the risk (as measured by return variance) on the underlying asset increases the value of the option.

The reason that increasing the variance on the underlying asset increases the value of the option isn't hard to see in our example. Changing the lower stock price to $105 from $110 doesn't hurt a bit because the option is worth zero in either case. However, moving the upper possible price to $135 from $130 makes the option worth more when it is in the money.

More generally, increasing the variance of the possible future prices on the underlying asset doesn't affect the option's value when the option finishes out of the money. The value is always zero in this case. On the other hand, increasing that variance when the option is in the money only increases the possible payoffs, so the net effect is to increase the option's value. Put another way, since the downside risk is always limited, the only effect is to increase the upside potential.

In later discussion, we use the usual symbol, σ^2, to stand for the variance of the return on the underlying asset.

A Closer Look

Before moving on, it is useful to consider one last example. Suppose the stock price is $100 and it will either move up or down by 20 percent. The risk-free rate is 5 percent. What is the value of a call option with a $90 exercise price?

The stock price will either be $80 or $120. The option is worth zero when the stock is worth $80, and it's worth $120 - 90 = \$30$ when the stock is worth $120. We therefore invest the present value of $80 in the risk-free asset and buy some call options.

When the stock finishes at $120, our risk-free asset pays $80, leaving us $40 short. Each option is worth $30 in this case, so we need $40/\$30 = 4/3$ options to match the payoff on the stock. The option's value must thus be given by:

$$S_0 = 4/3 \times C_0 + \$80/1.05$$
$$C_0 = (3/4) \times (\$100 - \$76.19)$$
$$= \$17.86$$

option delta
The change in the stock price divided by the change in the call price.

To make our result a little bit more general, notice that the number of options you need to buy to replicate the stock is always equal to the change in stock price divided by the change in call price, where the change in stock price is the difference in the possible stock prices and the change in call price is the difference in the possible option values. The change in the stock price divided by the change in the call price is termed the **option delta**. In our current case, for example, the change in the stock price would be $120 - 80 = \$40$ and the change in the call price would be $30 - 0 = \$30$, so the change in the stock price divided by the change in the call price is $40/\$30 = 4/3$, as we calculated.

Notice also that when the stock is certain to finish in the money, the change in the stock price divided by the change in the call price is always exactly equal to one, so one call option is always needed. Otherwise, the change in the stock price divided by the change in the call price is greater than one, so more than one call option is needed.

This concludes our discussion of option valuation. The most important thing to remember is that the value of an option depends on five factors. Table 25.1 summarizes these factors and the direction of the influence for both puts and calls. In Table 25.1, the sign in parentheses indicates

Factor	Calls	Puts
Current value of the underlying asset	(+)	(−)
Exercise price on the option	(−)	(+)
Time to expiration on the option	(+)	(+)
Risk-free rate	(+)	(−)
Variance of return on underlying asset	(+)	(+)

TABLE 25.1
Five factors that determine option values

the direction of the influence.[4] In other words, the sign tells us whether the value of the option goes up or down when the value of a factor increases. For example, notice that increasing the exercise price reduces the value of a call option. Increasing any of the other four factors increases the value of the call. Notice also that the time to expiration and the variance act the same for puts and calls. The other three factors have opposite signs.

We have not considered how to value a call option when the option can finish out of the money and the stock price can take on more than two values. A very famous result, the Black–Scholes option pricing model, is needed in this case. For developing this model, Myron Scholes and Robert Merton shared the 1997 Nobel Prize for economics. We cover this subject in the chapter appendix.

EXAMPLE 25.3: Option Prices and Time to Expiration and Variance

According to Table 25.1, when other things are held equal, increasing either time to expiration or stock price variance raises the prices of puts and calls. Is this theory consistent with the actual option prices in Figure 25.1?

We can look at time to expiration and pricing for BCE options. Starting with calls, all the other four factors are constant if we compare calls with the same

exercise price but different expiration dates. There are three BCE calls with a $30 exercise price:

Call	Bid Price
July	0.1
Aug	0.2
Nov	0.6

CONCEPT QUESTIONS

1. What are the five factors that determine an option's value?

2. What is the effect of an increase in each of the five factors on the value of a call option? Give an intuitive explanation for your answer.

3. What is the effect of an increase in each of the five factors on the value of a put option? Give an intuitive explanation for your answer.

25.4

EMPLOYEE STOCK OPTIONS

employee stock option (ESO)
An option granted to an employee by a company giving the employee the right to buy shares of stock in the company at a fixed price for a fixed time.

Options are important in corporate finance in a lot of different ways. In this section, we begin to examine some of these by taking a look at **employee stock options,** or ESOs. An ESO is, in essence, a call option that a firm gives to employees giving them the right to buy shares of stock in the company. The practice of granting options to employees has become widespread. It is almost universal for upper management (see Figure 25.4), but some companies, like The Gap and Starbucks, grant options to almost every employee. At the end of 1994, 90 percent of firms listed on the Toronto Stock Exchange had a bonus plan and used stock options.[5] Thus, an understanding of ESOs is important. Why? Because you may very soon be an ESO holder!

---

4 The signs in Table 25.1 are for American options. For a European put option, the effect of increasing the time to expiration is ambiguous, and the direction of the influence can be positive or negative.

5 X. Zhou, "CEO Pay, Firm Size, and Corporate Performance: Evidence from Canada," University of Sydney, Australia, October 2000.

FIGURE 25.4

Executive stock options in Canada

Who holds the most stock options?

Value of in-the-money stock options held by executives at the company's fiscal 2005 year-end. It indicates the potential profit that could have been reaped if the options had been exercised at the year-end, based on the company's closing share price.

Vested options are those that were available for the CEO to exercise at year-end.
Unvested options are those that were not available for the CEO to exercise at year-end.
Total is the total of vested and unvested options.

CEO	Company	Vested Options	Unvested Options	Total
Michael Lazaridis	Research in Motion Ltd.	$87,721,322	$29,777,956	$117,499,278
James Balsillie	Research in Motion Ltd.	87,721,322	29,777,956	117,499,278
Dominic D'Alessandro	Manulife Financial Corp.	70,293,295	15,098,556	85,391,851
Hunter Harrison	Canadian National Railway Co.	61,737,385	15,732,187	77,469,572
Richard George	Suncor Energy Inc.	57,194,504	15,113,760	72,308,264
André Desmarais	Power Corp. of Canada	68,412,112	1,416,380	69,828,492
Paul Desmarais Jr.	Power Corp. of Canada	64,470,300	1,416,380	65,886,680
Raymond McFeetors	Great-West Lifeco Inc.	52,627,414	10,354,747	62,982,161
James Buckee	Talisman Energy Inc.	28,501,908	30,254,500	58,756,408
Bruce Flatt	Brookfield Asset Management Inc.	51,945,308	5,340,191	57,285,499
Charles Fischer	Nexen Inc.	44,538,700	8,329,250	52,867,950

Source: http://www.theglobeandmail.com/v5/content/topCEOs/

See www.esopassociation.org for a site devoted to employee stock options.

ESO Features

Since ESOs are basically call options, we have already covered most of the important aspects. However, ESOs have a few features that make them different from regular stock options. The details differ from company to company, but a typical ESO has a 10-year life, which is much longer than most ordinary options. Unlike traded options, ESOs cannot be sold. They also have what is known as a "vesting" period. Often, for up to three years or so, an ESO cannot be exercised and also must be forfeited if an employee leaves the company. After this period, the options "vest," which means they can be exercised. Sometimes, employees who resign with vested options are given a limited time to exercise their options.

Why are ESOs granted? There are basically two reasons. First, going back to Chapter 1, the owners of a corporation (the shareholders) face the basic problem of aligning shareholder and management interests and also of providing incentives for employees to focus on corporate goals. ESOs are a powerful motivator because, as we have seen, the payoffs on options can be very large. High-level executives in particular stand to gain enormous wealth if they are successful in creating value for stockholders. Research studies in the U.S., Canada, and other countries find that, over the 1990s, the use of executive stock options served its goal of helping to tie executive compensation to company performance.[6] The decline of stock prices from 2001 to 2003, especially in the tech sector, had made options granted earlier almost worthless in motivating employees. For example, 750,000 options granted in 2000 to John Roth, then Nortel CEO, had an exercise price of $118.68. By 2005, Nortel was trading at around $4 (after trading as low as $0.69 in late 2002)!

The second reason some companies rely heavily on ESOs is that an ESO has no immediate, upfront, out-of-pocket cost to the corporation. In smaller, possibly cash-strapped, companies, ESOs are simply a substitute for ordinary wages. Employees are willing to accept them instead of

---

6 The most current study for Canada is by X. Zhou, referenced in footnote 5.

cash, hoping for big payoffs in the future. In fact, ESOs are a major recruiting tool, allowing businesses to attract talent that they otherwise could not afford.

New Canadian GAAP changes are making businesses think twice about how to use ESOs.[7] In January 2002, the Accounting Standards Board (AcSB) introduced new regulations regarding the accounting treatment of stock options and stock option–related compensation. The new regulations required many corporations using executive stock options as a form of compensation to recognize these options as a compensation expense against company earnings. This can have a tremendous impact on the bottom line of many companies. For example, Cott Corp.'s net income before option compensation was $6.13 million in 2002. Under the new guidelines, the impact of option compensation decreased the company's net income to a loss of $2.36 million. Nortel Networks was also negatively impacted by the new guidelines. The impact of option compensation increased Nortel's net losses from $5.631 billion to $7.13 billion in 2002.

In 2003, Microsoft halted its stock options plan entirely, instead granting restricted Microsoft shares to a wide range of employees.[8] According to Microsoft CEO Steve Ballmer, the move towards granting restricted stock instead of ESOs would increase morale and retention. Another advantage that restricted stock offers is actual ownership of part of the company that links the personal objectives of the employee to the corporate objectives. Intel has since decided to scrap its own ESO plan in favour of restricted stock. This trend does not mean the end of ESOs. It only indicates that companies are becoming more conservative with their ESO plans and are looking to find the alternatives that best suit the company's corporate structure.

ESO Repricing

ESOs are almost always "at the money" when they are issued, meaning that the stock price is equal to the strike price. Notice that, in this case, the intrinsic value is zero, so there is no value from immediate exercise. Of course, even though the intrinsic value is zero, an ESO is still quite valuable because of, among other things, its very long life.

If the stock falls significantly after an ESO is granted, then the option is said to be "underwater." On occasion, a company will decide to lower the strike price on underwater options. Such options are said to be "restruck" or "repriced."

The practice of repricing ESOs is very controversial. Companies that do it argue that once an ESO becomes deeply out of the money, it loses its incentive value because employees recognize there is only a small chance that the option will finish in the money. In fact, employees may leave and join other companies where they receive a fresh options grant.

Critics of repricing point out that a lowered strike price is, in essence, a reward for failing. They also point out that if employees know that options will be repriced, then much of the incentive effect is lost. Today, many companies award options on a regular basis, perhaps annually or even quarterly. That way, an employee will always have at least some options that are near the money even if others are underwater. Also, regular grants ensure that employees always have unvested options, which gives them an added incentive to stay with their current employer rather than forfeit the potentially valuable options.

For more information on ESOs, try the National Center for Employee Ownership at www.nceo.org.

CONCEPT QUESTIONS

1. What are the key differences between a traded stock option and an ESO?

2. What is ESO repricing? Why is it controversial?

25.5

EQUITY AS A CALL OPTION ON THE FIRM'S ASSETS

Now that we understand the basic determinants of an option's value, we turn to examining some of the many ways that options appear in corporate finance. One of the most important insights we gain from studying options is that the common stock in a leveraged firm (one that

---

7 Prem M. Lobo. "Weighing the Options," *CA Magazine*. Toronto: Sept 2005. Vol. 138, Iss. 7; pp. 47–49.

8 J. Nicholas Hoover. "The Options Mess," *InformationWeek*. Manhasset: July 10, 2006. Iss. 1097; p. 21.

has issued debt) is effectively a call option on the assets of the firm. This is a remarkable observation, and we explore it next.

An example is the easiest way to get started. Suppose a firm has a single debt issue outstanding. The face value is $1,000, and the debt is coming due in a year. There are no coupon payments between now and then, so the debt is effectively a pure discount bond. In addition, the current market value of the firm's assets is $950, and the risk-free rate is 12.5 percent.

In a year, the stockholders will have a choice. They can pay off the debt for $1,000 and thereby acquire the assets of the firm free and clear, or they can default on the debt. If they default, the bondholders will own the assets of the firm.

In this situation, the shareholders essentially have a call option on the assets of the firm with an exercise price of $1,000. They can exercise the option by paying the $1,000, or they cannot exercise the option by defaulting. Whether they choose to exercise obviously depends on the value of the firm's assets when the debt becomes due.

If the value of the firm's assets exceeds $1,000, the option is in the money, and the stockholders would exercise by paying off the debt. If the value of the firm's assets is less than $1,000, the option is out of the money, and the stockholders would optimally choose to default. What we now illustrate is that we can determine the values of the debt and equity using our option pricing results.

Case I: The Debt Is Risk-Free

Suppose that in one year the firm's assets will either be worth $1,100 or $1,200. What is the value today of the equity in the firm? The value of the debt? What is the interest rate on the debt?

To answer these questions, we recognize that the option (the equity in the firm) is certain to finish in the money because the value of the firm's assets ($1,100 or $1,200) always exceeds the

---

In Their Own Words . . .   Boyd Erman on Options Timing

SOME OF CANADA'S biggest companies may be manipulating the timing of stock-option grants to give executives bigger bonuses, signalling the options-rigging scandal may not be confined to the United States.

Prompted by probes of U.S. companies such as Home Depot Inc. and Apple Computer Inc., Toronto-based Veritas Investment Research analyzed option grants by 60 of Canada's biggest, most heavily traded companies, and found signs that some may be timing grants for periods when stock prices are depressed. That benefits executives by supercharging any gains in the value of the options.

The review "suggests that options timing is alive and well in Canada, as evidenced by a statistical drop in prices towards the date of the options grant and an upswing in prices immediately after," study authors Sam La Bell and Chris Sylvestre concluded.

Companies can rig the game by backdating options grants to a day when the stock was low or timing grants to follow bad news or precede good news.

The Veritas report did not single out specific companies, citing the "circumstantial nature of the evidence." The review looked at the members of the Standard & Poor's/TSX 60 index, which includes the big banks, insurers, and other familiar names.

Options are designed to give executives an incentive to drive up share prices. Options give holders the right to buy stock at a pre-set exercise price at some point in the future. Options become profitable when the market price of the stock rises above the exercise price.

Timing options to create built-in gains undermines the whole point of the bonuses, from a shareholder perspective. Doing so also contravenes Toronto Stock Exchange regulations.

The Veritas study showed that stock prices for the 60 companies were on average half a percentage point higher 10 days before the grant date and more than a percentage point higher 15 days afterward. Grant dates chosen at random should show no such pattern, according to Veritas.

"You do see a pattern, so that makes you wonder," Mr. La Bell said in an interview.

"But to actually prove one company or another is doing anything wrong is very difficult," he added. "Coincidence is a pretty powerful defence."

Source: Boyd Erman, "Options timing alive and well in Canada." *National Post,* September 12, 2006, canada.com. Used with permission.

face value of the debt. From our discussion in previous sections, we know that the option value is simply the difference between the value of the underlying asset and the present value of the exercise price (calculated at the risk-free rate). The present value of $1,000 in one year at 12.5 percent is $888.89. The current value of the firm is $950, so the option (the firm's equity) is worth $950 − 888.89 = $61.11.

What we see is that the equity, which is effectively an option to purchase the firm's assets, must be worth $61.11. The debt must therefore actually be worth $888.89. In fact, we really didn't need to know about options to handle this example, because the debt is risk free. The reason is that the bondholders are certain to receive $1,000. Since the debt is risk free, the appropriate discount rate (and the interest rate on the debt) is the risk-free rate. Therefore, we know immediately that the current value of the debt is $1,000/1.125 = $888.89. The equity is thus worth $950 − 888.89 = $61.11 as we calculated.

Case II: The Debt Is Risky

Suppose now that the value of the firm's assets in one year will be either $800 or $1,200. This case is a little more difficult because the debt is no longer risk free. If the value of the assets turns out to be $800, the shareholders will not exercise their option and thereby default. The stock is worth nothing in this case. If the assets are worth $1,200, the stockholders will exercise their option to pay off the debt and enjoy a profit of $1,200 − 1,000 = $200.

What we see is that the option (the equity in the firm) is worth either zero or $200. The assets are worth either $1,200 or $800. Based on our discussion in previous sections, a portfolio that has

---

In Their Own Words . . .

Robert C. Merton on Applications of Options Analysis

ORGANIZED MARKETS for trading options on stocks, fixed-income securities, currencies, financial futures, and a variety of commodities are among the most successful financial innovations of the past two decades.

Commercial success is not, however, the reason that option pricing analysis has become one of the cornerstones of finance theory. Instead, its central role derives from the fact that option-like structures permeate virtually every part of the field.

From the first observation more than 30 years ago that leveraged equity has the same payoff structure as a call option, option pricing theory has provided an integrated approach to the pricing of corporate liabilities, including all types of debt, preferred stocks, warrants, and rights. The same methodology has been applied to the pricing of pension fund insurance, deposit insurance, and other government loan guarantees. It has also been used to evaluate various labour contract provisions such as wage floors and guaranteed employment including tenure.

A significant and recent extension of options analysis has been to the evaluation of operating or "real" options in capital budgeting decisions. For example, a facility that can use various inputs to produce various outputs provides the firm with operating options not available from a specialized facility that uses a fixed set of inputs to produce a single type of

output. Similarly, choosing among technologies with different proportions of fixed and variable costs can be viewed as evaluating alternative options to change production levels, including abandonment of the project. Research and development projects are essentially options to either establish new markets, expand market share, or reduce production costs. As these examples suggest, options analysis is especially well suited to the task of evaluating the "flexibility" components of projects. These are precisely the components whose values are especially difficult to estimate by using traditional capital budgeting techniques.

Robert C. Merton is the John and Natty McArthur University Professor at Harvard University. He previously held the J. C. Penney Professor of Management, A.P. Sloan School of Management at MIT. He shared the 1997 Nobel Prize for economics for major contributions to financial theory and practice through his work on pricing options and other contingent claims.

the present value of $800 invested in a risk-free asset and ($1,200 − $800)/($200 − $0) = 2 call options exactly replicates the assets of the firm.

The present value of $800 at the risk-free rate of 12.5 percent is $800/1.125 = $711.11. This amount, plus the value of the two call options, is equal to $990, the current value of the firm:

$$\$990 = 2 \times C_0 + \$711.11$$
$$C_0 = \$139.45$$

Because the call option is actually the firm's equity, the value of the equity is $139.45. The value of the debt is thus $990 − 139.45 = $850.55.

Finally, since the debt has a $1,000 face value and a current value of $850.55, the interest rate is $1,000/$850.55 − 1 = 17.6%. This exceeds the risk-free rate, of course, since the debt is now risky.

EXAMPLE 25.4: Equity as a Call Option

Swenson Software has a pure discount debt issue with a face value of $100. The issue is due in a year. At that time, the assets in the firm will be worth either $55 or $160, depending on the sales success of Swenson's latest product. The assets of the firm are currently worth $110. If the risk-free rate is 10 percent, what is the value of the equity in Swenson? The value of the debt? The interest rate on the debt?

To replicate the assets of the firm, we need to invest the present value of $55 in the risk-free asset. This costs $55/1.10 = $50. If the assets turn out to be worth $160, the option is

worth $160 − 100 = $60. Our risk-free asset would be worth $55, so we need ($160 − $55)/$60 = 1.75 call options. Since the firm is currently worth $110, we have:

$$\$110 = 1.75 \times C_0 + \$50$$
$$C_0 = \$34.29$$

The equity is thus worth $34.29; the debt is worth $110 − 34.29 = $75.71. The interest rate on the debt is about $100/$75.71 − 1 = 32.1%.

CONCEPT QUESTIONS

1. Why do we say that the equity in a leveraged firm is effectively a call option on the firm's assets?

2. All other things being the same, would the stockholders of a firm prefer to increase or decrease the volatility of the firm's return on assets? Why? What about the bondholders? Give an intuitive explanation.

25.6

warrant
A security that gives the holder the right to purchase shares of stock at a fixed price over a given period of time.

sweeteners or equity kickers
A feature included in the terms of a new issue of debt or preferred shares to make the issue more attractive to initial investors.

www.domtar.com

WARRANTS

A **warrant** is a corporate security that looks a lot like a call option. It gives the holder the right, but not the obligation, to buy shares of common stock directly from a company at a fixed price for a given time period. Each warrant specifies the number of shares of stock that the holder can buy, the exercise price, and the expiration date.[9]

The differences in contractual features between the call options that are traded on the Montreal Exchange and warrants are relatively minor. Warrants usually have much longer maturity periods, however. In fact, some warrants are actually perpetual and have no fixed expiration date.

Warrants are often called **sweeteners** or **equity kickers** because they are usually issued in combination with privately placed loans, bonds, or common or preferred shares. Throwing in some warrants is a way of making the deal a little more attractive to the lender, and it is very common. In fact, the use of warrants is becoming more popular judging by the increasing number listed on the TSX.

In most cases, warrants are attached to the bonds when issued. The loan agreement states whether the warrants are detachable from the bond. Usually, the warrant can be detached immediately and sold by the holder as a separate security.

---

9 Rights are another closely related corporate security. Their purpose, however, is to allow current shareholders to maintain proportionate ownership of the company when new shares are issued. The number of shares that can be purchased with each right will be calculated to maintain the proportionate ownership. We discuss rights in Chapter 15.

For example, Domtar Inc. is one of the world's largest producers of lumber, paper, and other wood products. On December 18, 2002, the company filed final documents with regulatory authorities to allow the sale in Canada and the United States of 18,170,249 units at a price of $16.50 each. Each unit consisted of one common share of Domtar stock and one warrant to purchase a common share of Domtar stock for $17.55 for up to one year from the closing of the offering. These shares were held by the Société Générale de Financement du Québec, a Québec-based economic development agency, which had received them in return for providing business development capital. The following year, after the common shares and the warrants were sold, the share price never exceeded $16.0525, making it very unlikely that many would have used their warrants. Those that did use them would have been disappointed, as the stock has never risen above $18 since December 2002 and the stock price has since dropped to $6.60 per share, as of June 19, 2006.

As soon as the units were issued, the common shares and warrants were detachable. This meant that the warrants could be traded immediately on the TSX under the symbol "DTC.WT." The warrants opened trading in December at a value slightly over $1.55, with the common shares trading at $16.35 per share.

Just as we saw with call options, the lower limit on the value of a warrant is zero if Domtar's stock price is less than $17.55 per share. If the price of Domtar's common stock rises to more than $17.55 per share, the lower limit is the stock price minus $17.55. The upper limit is the price of Domtar's common stock. A warrant to buy one share of common stock cannot sell at a price more than the price of the underlying common stock.

If, on the warrant expiration date, Domtar stock traded for less than $17.55, the warrants would expire worthless.

With the growth of financial engineering, warrant issuers are creating new varieties. Some warrant issues give investors the right to buy the issuers' bonds instead of their stock. In addition, warrants are issued on their own instead of as sweeteners in a bond issue. In 1991, the Toronto-Dominion Bank combined these features in a $2.7 million stand-alone issue. The TD warrants gave the right to purchase debentures to be issued in the future.[10]

Echo Bay Mines Ltd. of Edmonton designed an innovative financing package including gold purchase warrants with a preferred share issue. The warrants gave the holder the right to buy gold at an exercise price of $595 (U.S.) per ounce. When the warrants were issued in 1981, gold was trading at $500 (U.S.) per ounce. A further condition restricted exercise of the warrants to cases where Echo Bay met certain production levels. As a result, how much these warrants were worth depended both on how well the company was doing and on gold prices.[11]

The Difference between Warrants and Call Options

As we have explained, from the holder's point of view, warrants are very similar to call options on common stock. A warrant, like a call option, gives its holder the right to buy common stock at a specified price. From the firm's point of view, however, a warrant is very different from a call option sold on the company's common stock.

The most important difference between call options and warrants is that call options are issued by individuals and warrants are issued by firms. When a call option is exercised, one investor buys stock from another investor. The company is not involved. When a warrant is exercised, the firm must issue new shares of stock. Each time a warrant is exercised, the firm receives some cash and the number of shares outstanding increases.

To illustrate, suppose the Endrun Company issues a warrant giving holders the right to buy one share of common stock at $25. Further suppose the warrant is exercised. Endrun must print one new stock certificate. In exchange for the stock certificate, it receives $25 from the holder.

In contrast, when a call option is exercised, there is no change in the number of shares outstanding. Suppose Bethany Enger purchases a call option on the common stock of the Endrun

www.td.com
www.kinross.com

---

10 B. Critchley, "The Top 10 Financings, Innovative Fund-Raising in Corporate Canada for '91," *Financial Post*, December 16, 1991, p. 15.

11 P. P. Boyle and E. F. Kirzner, "Pricing Complex Options: Echo-Bay Ltd. Gold Purchase Warrants," *Canadian Journal of Administrative Sciences* 2, no. 12 (December 1985), pp. 294–306.

Company from Thomas Swift. The call option gives Enger the right to buy one share of common stock of the Endrun Company for $25.

If Enger chooses to exercise the call option, Swift is obligated to give her one share of Endrun's common stock in exchange for $25. If Swift does not already own a share, he must go into the stock market and buy one.

The call option amounts to a side bet between Enger and Swift on the value of the Endrun Company's common stock. When a call option is exercised, one investor gains and the other loses. The total number of outstanding Endrun shares remains constant, and no new funds are made available to the company.

Warrants and the Value of the Firm

Because the company is not involved in buying or selling options, puts and calls have no effect on the value of the firm. However, the firm is the original seller when warrants are involved, and warrants do affect the value of the firm. We compare the effect of call options and warrants in this section.

Imagine that Spencer Gould and Jennifer Rockefeller are two investors who together purchase six ounces of platinum at $500 per ounce. The total investment is $6 \times \$500 = \$3,000$, and each of the investors puts up half. They incorporate, print two stock certificates, and name the firm the GR Company. Each certificate represents a one-half claim to the platinum, and Gould and Rockefeller each own one certificate. The net effect of all of this is that Gould and Rockefeller have formed a company with platinum as its only asset.

THE EFFECT OF A CALL OPTION   Suppose Gould later decides to sell a call option to Franchesca Fiske. The call option gives Fiske the right to buy Gould's share for $1,800 in one year.

At the end of the year, platinum is selling for $700 per ounce, so the value of the GR Company is $6 \times \$700 = \$4,200$. Each share is worth $\$4,200/2 = \$2,100$. Fiske exercises her option, and Gould must turn over his stock certificate and receive $1,800.

How would the firm be affected by the exercise? The number of shares won't be affected. There are still two of them, now owned by Rockefeller and Fiske. The shares are still worth $2,100. The only thing that happens is that, when Fiske exercises her option, she profits by $2,100 − 1,800 = \$300$. Gould loses by the same amount.

THE EFFECT OF A WARRANT   This story changes if a warrant is issued. Suppose Gould does not sell a call option to Fiske. Instead, Spencer Gould and Jennifer Rockefeller get together and decide to issue a warrant and sell it to Fiske. This means that, in effect, the GR Company decides to issue a warrant.

The warrant gives Fiske the right to receive a share of stock in the company at an exercise price of $1,800. If Fiske decides to exercise the warrant, the firm issues another stock certificate and gives it to Fiske in exchange for $1,800.

Suppose again that platinum rises to $700 an ounce. The firm is worth $4,200. Further suppose that Fiske exercises her warrant. Two things would occur:

1. Fiske would pay $1,800 to the firm.
2. The firm would print one stock certificate and give it to Fiske. The stock certificate represents a one-third claim on the platinum of the firm.

Fiske's one-third share seems to be worth only $\$4,200/3 = \$1,400$. This is not correct, because we have to add the $1,800 contributed to the firm by Fiske. The value of the firm increases by this amount, so:

$$\text{New value of firm} = \text{Value of platinum} + \text{Fiske's contribution to the firm}$$
$$= \$4,200 + 1,800$$
$$= \$6,000$$

Because Fiske has a one-third claim on the firm's value, her share is worth $\$6,000/3 = \$2,000$. By exercising the warrant, Fiske gains $\$2,000 − 1,800 = \$200$. This is illustrated in Table 25.2.

When the warrant is exercised, the exercise money goes to the firm. Since Fiske ends up owning one-third of the firm, she effectively gets back one-third of what she pays in. Because she really gives up only two-thirds of $1,800 to buy the stock, the effective exercise price is $2/3 \times$ $1,800 = $1,200.

Fiske effectively pays out $1,200 to obtain a one-third interest in the assets of the firm (the platinum). This is worth $4,200/3 = $1,400. Fiske's gain, from this perspective, is $1,400 - 1,200 = $200 (exactly what we calculated earlier).

WARRANT VALUE AND STOCK VALUE   What is the value of the common stock of a firm that has issued warrants? Let's look at the market value of the GR Company just before and just after the exercise of Fiske's warrant. Just after exercise, the balance sheet looks like this:

Cash	$1,800	Stock	$6,000
Platinum	4,200	(3 shares)	
Total	$6,000	Total	$6,000

As we saw, each share of stock is worth $6,000/3 = $2,000.

Whoever holds the warrant profits by $200 when the warrant is exercised; thus, the warrant is worth $200 just before expiration. The balance sheet for the GR Company just before expiration is thus:

Platinum	$4,200	Warrant	$200
		Stock	4,000
		(2 shares)	
Total	$4,200	Total	$4,200

We calculate the value of the stock as the value of the assets ($4,200) less the value of the warrant ($200).

Notice that the value of each share just before expiration is $4,000/2 = $2,000 just as it is after expiration. The value of each share of stock is thus not changed by the exercise of the warrant. There is no dilution of share value from the exercise.

EARNINGS DILUTION   Warrants and convertible bonds frequently cause the number of shares to increase. This happens (1) when the warrants are exercised and (2) when the bonds are converted. As we have seen, this increase does not lower the per share value of the stock. However, it does cause the firm's net income to be spread over a larger number of shares; thus, earnings per share decrease.

TABLE 25.2
Effect of a call option versus a warrant on the GR Company

	Value of Firm Based on Price of Platinum per Ounce	
	$700	**$600**
No Warrant or Call Option		
Gould's share	$2,100	$1,800
Rockefeller's share	2,100	1,800
Firm value	$4,200	$3,600
Call Option		
Gould's claim	$ 0	$1,800
Rockefeller's claim	2,100	1,800
Fiske's claim	2,100	0
Firm value	$4,200	$3,600
Warrant*		
Gould's share	$2,000	$1,800
Rockefeller's share	2,000	1,800
Fiske's share	2,000	0
Firm value	$6,000	$3,600

*If the price of platinum is $700, the value of the firm is equal to the value of six ounces of platinum plus the excess dollars paid into the firm by Fiske. This amount is $4,200 + 1,800 = $6,000.

Firms with significant amounts of warrants and convertible issues outstanding generally calculate and report earnings per share on a *fully diluted basis*. This means the calculation is based on the number of shares that would be outstanding if all the warrants were exercised and all the convertibles were converted. Since this increases the number of shares, the fully diluted EPS is lower than an EPS calculated only on the basis of shares actually outstanding.

CONCEPT QUESTIONS

1. What is a warrant?

2. Why are warrants different from call options?

CONVERTIBLE BONDS

convertible bond
A bond that can be exchanged for a fixed number of shares of stock for a specified amount of time.

A **convertible bond** is similar to a bond with warrants. The most important difference is that a bond with warrants can be separated into distinct securities (a bond and some warrants), but a convertible bond cannot be. A convertible bond gives the holder the right to exchange the bond for a fixed number of shares of stock anytime up to and including the maturity date of the bond.

Preferred shares can frequently be converted into common shares. A convertible preferred share is the same as a convertible bond except that it has an infinite maturity date.[12]

Features of a Convertible Bond

The basic features of a convertible bond can be illustrated by examining a particular issue. The example we used to start this chapter features Noranda, a large international mining and metals producer. In 1997, Noranda issued convertible subordinated debentures maturing in 10 years in 2007. The particular feature that makes the Noranda bonds interesting is that they are convertible into the common stock of Noranda anytime before maturity at a **conversion price** of $27.55 per share. Since each bond has a face value of $100, this means the holder of a Noranda convertible bond can exchange that bond for $100/27.55 = 3.63 shares of Noranda common stock. The number of shares received for each debenture, 3.63 in this example, is called the **conversion ratio.**

conversion price
The dollar amount of a bond's par value that is exchangeable for one share of stock.

On March 1, 2006, Placer Dome's common stock was trading at $22.60 per share on the New York Stock Exchange. The conversion price of $20.925 is thus ($20.925-$22.60)/$22.60 = -7.4 percent or 7.4 percent lower than the actual common stock price. This 7.4 percent is called the **conversion premium**. It reflects that the conversion option in Placer Dome convertible bonds is out of the money.

conversion ratio
The number of shares per $1,000 bond received for conversion into stock.

conversion premium
Difference between the conversion price and the current stock price divided by the current stock price.

Value of a Convertible Bond

Even though the conversion feature of the convertible bond cannot be detached like a warrant, the value of the bond can still be decomposed into its bond value and the value of the conversion feature. We discuss how this is done next.

straight bond value
The value of a convertible bond if it could not be converted into common stock.

STRAIGHT BOND VALUE   The **straight bond value** is what the convertible bond would sell for if it could not be converted into common stock. This value depends on the general level of interest rates on debentures and on the default risk of the issuer.

Suppose that straight debentures issued by Noranda are priced to yield 8 percent. The straight bond value of Noranda convertible bonds can be determined by discounting the $5 annual coupon payment and maturity value at 8 percent, just as we did in Chapter 7:[13]

$$\text{Straight bond value} = \$5 \times (1 - 1/1.08^4)/.08 + \$100/1.08^4$$
$$= \$16.56 + 73.50$$
$$= \$90.06$$

---

12 The dividends paid are, of course, not tax deductible for the corporation. Interest paid on a convertible bond is tax deductible.

13 For simplicity, we assume that the Noranda convertible had four years to maturity in June 2003.

The straight bond value of a convertible bond is a minimum value in the sense that the bond is always worth at least this amount. As we discuss, it is usually worth more.

conversion value
The value of a convertible bond if it was immediately converted into common stock.

CONVERSION VALUE   The **conversion value** of a convertible bond is what the bond would be worth if it were immediately converted into common stock. This value is computed by multiplying the current price of the stock by the number of shares received when the bond is converted.

For example, each Noranda convertible bond could be converted into 3.63 shares of common stock. Noranda common was selling for $13.28 at the time of writing in June 2003. Thus, the conversion value is 3.63 × $13.28 = $48.21.

A convertible cannot sell for less than its conversion value or an arbitrage exists. If Noranda's convertible sold for less than $48.21, investors would buy the bonds and convert them into common stock and sell the stock. The arbitrage profit would be the difference between the value of the stock and the bond's conversion value.

FLOOR VALUE   As we have seen, convertible bonds have two floor values: the straight bond value and the conversion value. The minimum value of a convertible bond is given by the greater of these two values. For the Noranda issue, the conversion value is $48.21, while the straight bond value is $84.38. At a minimum, this bond is thus worth $84.38.

Figure 25.5 plots the minimum value of a convertible bond against the value of the stock. The conversion value is determined by the value of the firm's underlying common stock. As the value of common stock rises and falls, the conversion value rises and falls with it. For example, if the value of Noranda's common stock increases by $1, the conversion value of its convertible bonds increases by $3.63.

In Figure 25.5, we have implicitly assumed that the convertible bond is default-free. In this case, the straight bond value does not depend on the stock price, so it is plotted as a horizontal line. Given the straight bond value, the minimum value of the convertible depends on the value of the stock. When this is low, the minimum value of a convertible is most significantly influ-

---

FIGURE 25.5

Minimum value of a convertible bond versus the value of the stock for a given interest rate

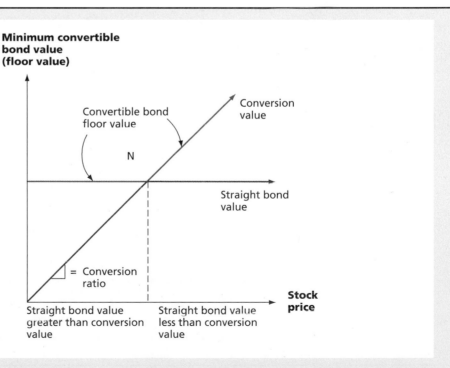

As shown, the minimum or "floor" value of a convertible bond is either its straight bond value or its conversion value, whichever is greater.

enced by the underlying value as straight debt. This is the case for the Noranda convertible as the straight bond value, $90.06, far exceeds the conversion value of $48.21. However, when the value of the firm is very high, the value of a convertible bond is mostly determined by the underlying conversion value. This is also illustrated in Figure 25.5.

OPTION VALUE   The value of a convertible bond always exceeds the straight bond value and the conversion value unless the firm is in default or the bondholders are forced to convert. The reason is that holders of convertibles do not have to convert immediately. Instead, by waiting, they can take advantage of whichever is greater in the future, the straight bond value or the conversion value.

This option to wait has value, and it raises the value of the convertible bond over its floor value. The total value of the convertible is thus equal to the sum of the floor value and the option value. This is illustrated in Figure 25.6. Notice the similarity between this picture and the representation of the value of a call option in Figure 25.3.

Figure 25.6 shows the Noranda convertible. Because the stock price, $13.28, at the time, was well below the conversion price of $27.55, the bond was trading based mainly on its straight bond value of $90.06. However, due to the option value, the actual price was slightly higher.

CONCEPT QUESTIONS

1. What is the conversion ratio, the conversion price, and the conversion premium?

2. What three elements make up the value of a convertible bond?

FIGURE 25.6

Value of a convertible bond versus value of the stock for a given interest rate

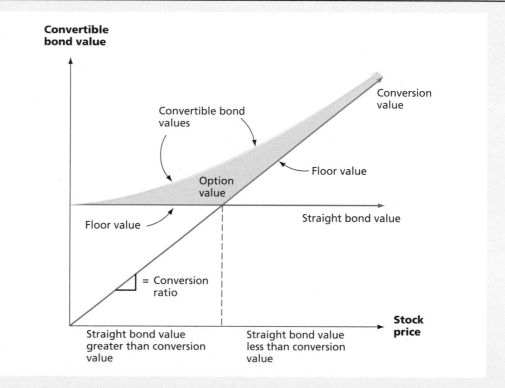

As shown, the value of a convertible bond is the sum of its floor value and its option value (highlighted region).

REASONS FOR ISSUING WARRANTS AND CONVERTIBLES

Until recently, bonds with warrants and convertible bonds were not well understood. Surveys of financial executives have provided the most popular textbook reasons for warrants and convertibles. Here are two of them:

1. They allow companies to issue cheap bonds by attaching sweeteners to the bonds. Sweeteners allow the coupon rate on convertibles and bonds with warrants to be set at less than the market rates on straight bonds.
2. They give companies the chance to issue common stock at a premium more than current prices in the future. In this way, convertibles and bonds with warrants represent deferred sales of common stock at relatively high prices.

These justifications for convertibles and bonds with warrants are frequently mixed into free lunch explanations.

The Free Lunch Story

Suppose the RWJR Company can issue straight (non-convertible) subordinated debentures at 10 percent. It can also issue convertible bonds at 6 percent with a conversion value of $800. The conversion value means the holders can convert a convertible bond into 40 shares of common stock, which currently trades at $20.

A company treasurer who believes in free lunches might argue that convertible bonds should be issued because they represent a cheaper source of financing than either straight subordinated bonds or common stock. The treasurer points out that, if the company does poorly and the stock price does not rise to more than $20, the convertible bondholders do not convert the bonds into common stock. In this case, the company has obtained debt financing at below-market rates by attaching worthless equity kickers.

On the other hand, if the firm does well, the bondholders would convert. The company issues 40 shares. Because the company receives a bond with a face value of $1,000 in exchange for issuing 40 shares of common stock, the conversion price is $25.

Effectively, if the bondholders convert, the company has issued common stock at $25 per share. This is 20 percent more than the current common stock price of $20, so the company gets more money per share of stock. Thus, the treasurer happily points out, regardless of whether the company does well or poorly, convertible bonds are the cheapest form of financing. RWJR can't lose.

The problem with this story is that we can turn it around and create an argument showing that issuing warrants and convertibles is always a disaster. We call this the expensive lunch story.

The Expensive Lunch Story

Suppose we take a closer look at the RWJR Company and its proposal to sell convertible bonds. If the company performs badly and the stock price falls, bondholders do not exercise their conversion option. This suggests the RWJR Company should have issued common stock when prices were high. By issuing convertible bonds, the company lost a valuable opportunity.

On the other hand, if the company does well and the stock price rises, bondholders convert. Suppose the stock price rises to $40. The bondholders convert and the company is forced to sell stock worth $40 for an effective price of only $25. The new shareholders benefit. Put another way, if the company prospers, it would have been better to have issued straight debt so that the gains would not have to be shared.

Whether the convertible bonds are converted or not, the company has done worse than with straight bonds or new common stock. Issuing convertible bonds is a terrible idea.

Which is correct—the free lunch story or the expensive lunch story?

TABLE 25.3
The case for and
against convertibles

	If Firm Does Poorly	If Firm Prospers
Convertible bonds	Low stock price and no conversion	High stock price and conversion
versus:		
Straight bonds	Cheap financing because coupon rate is lower (good outcome)	Expensive financing because bonds are converted, which dilutes existing equity (bad outcome)
Common stock	Expensive financing because the firm could have issued common stock at high prices (bad outcome)	Cheap financing because firm issues stock at high prices when bonds are converted (good outcome)

A Reconciliation

Reconciling our two stories requires only that we remember our central goal: Increase the wealth of the existing shareholders. Thus, with 20-20 hindsight, issuing convertible bonds turns out to be worse than issuing straight bonds and better than issuing common stock if the company prospers. The reason is that the prosperity has to be shared with bondholders after they convert.

In contrast, if a company does poorly, issuing convertible bonds turns out to be better than issuing straight bonds and worse than issuing common stock. The reason is that the firm benefited from the lower coupon payments on the convertible bond.

Both of our stories thus have a grain of truth; we just need to combine them. This is done in Table 25.3. Exactly the same arguments would be used in a comparison of a straight debt issue versus a bond/warrant package.

> **CONCEPT QUESTIONS**
>
> 1. What is wrong with the view that it is cheaper to issue a bond with a warrant or a convertible feature because the required coupon is lower?
>
> 2. What is wrong with the theory that says a convertible can be a good security to issue because it can be a way to sell stock at a price that is higher than the current stock price?

 **25.9**

OTHER OPTIONS

We've discussed two of the more common option-like securities, warrants and convertibles. Options appear in many other places. We briefly describe a few such cases in this section.

The Call Provision on a Bond

As we discussed in Chapter 7, most corporate bonds are callable. A call provision allows a corporation to buy the bonds at a fixed price for a fixed time period. In other words, the corporation has a call option on the bonds. The cost of the call feature to the corporation is the cost of the option.

Convertible bonds are almost always callable. This means a convertible bond is really a package of three securities: a straight bond, a call option held by the bondholder (the conversion feature), and a call option held by the corporation (the call provision).

Put Bonds

The owner of a put bond has the right to force the issuer to repurchase the bond at a fixed price for a fixed period of time. Such a bond is a combination of a straight bond and a put option, hence the name.

For example, Canada Savings Bonds are put bonds since the holder can force the Government of Canada to repurchase them (through a financial institution acting as its agent) at 100 percent of the purchase price. The put option is exercisable at any time after the first two months of the bond's life. A more exotic, financially engineered example comes from Chapter 7 where we briefly discussed a LYON, a liquid yield option note. This is a callable, putable, convertible, pure discount bond. It is thus a package of a pure discount bond, two call options, and a put option. In 1991, Rogers Communication issued the first LYON in Canada.

The Overallotment Option

In Chapter 15, we mentioned that underwriters are frequently given the right to purchase additional shares of stock from a firm in an initial public offering (IPO). We called this the overallotment option. We now recognize that this provision is simply a call option (or, more accurately, a warrant) granted to the underwriter. The value of the option is an indirect form of compensation paid to the underwriter.

Insurance and Loan Guarantees

Insurance of one kind or another is a financial feature of everyday life. Most of the time, having insurance is like having a put option. For example, suppose you have $1 million in fire insurance on an office building. One night, your building burns down, reducing its value to nothing. In this case, you would effectively exercise your put option and force the insurer to pay you $1 million for something worth very little.

Loan guarantees are a form of insurance. If you lend money to a borrower who defaults, with a guaranteed loan you can collect from someone else, often the government. For example, when you lend money to a financial institution (by making a deposit), your loan is guaranteed (up to $60,000) by the federal government provided your institution is a member of the Canada Deposit Insurance Corporation (CDIC).

The federal government, with a loan guarantee, has provided a put option to the holders of risky debt. The value of the put option is the cost of the loan guarantee. Loan guarantees are not cost-free. This point was made absolutely clear to the CDIC when two banks collapsed in western Canada in 1985.

Because the put option allows a risky firm to borrow at subsidized rates, it is an asset to the stockholders. The riskier the firm, the greater the value of the guarantee and the more it is worth to the shareholders. Researchers modified the Black–Scholes model presented in this chapter's appendix to value the put option in CDIC deposit insurance for one of the Canadian banks that failed. They found that financial markets provided early warning of bank failures as the value of the put option increased significantly before the bank failed.[14]

U.S. taxpayers learned the same lesson about loan guarantees at far greater cost in the savings and loan collapse. The cost to U.S. taxpayers of making good on the guaranteed deposits in these institutions is a staggering amount.

One result of all this is that accountants in Canada, urged on by the auditor general, are forcing government agencies to report guarantees and other contingent liabilities in their financial statements. This may induce greater caution in extending guarantees in the first place.

Managerial Options

real option
An option with payoffs in real goods.

We introduced managerial options in our discussion of capital budgeting in Chapter 11. These options represent opportunities that managers can exploit if certain things happen in the future. Returning to such options, we now see that they represent **real options**—options with payoffs in real goods as opposed to asset prices. One example of a real option is production flexibility as we explain next.

---

14 R. Giammarino, E. Schwartz, and J. Zechner, "Market Valuation of Bank Assets and Deposit Insurance in Canada," *Canadian Journal of Economics*, February 1989, pp. 109–27.

The value of flexibility in production has long been recognized, but at what price? All other things being equal, a company would rather have production facilities that can quickly and cheaply adapt to changing circumstances than a plant that is limited in what and how much it can produce. Changing demand for products often necessitates changes in products and the changing costs of raw materials and other inputs can mean that the production process now in use may no longer be the cost-minimizing one.

However, a flexible production facility costs more than building one that is suited to one line of products or one pattern of inputs. In addition, a plant that is designed to be used with one product line and one pattern of inputs is usually optimized for those conditions. It is more efficient for that purpose than a flexible plant producing the same line of products and using the same inputs. A company building a production facility must trade off the advantages of flexibility against the additional costs.

world.honda.com

AUTOMOBILE PRODUCTION   The market for automobiles is notoriously fickle. The hottest seller can be sports cars in one year and sport utility vehicles in the next. When you consider that it usually takes more than two years to design and bring a new model into production, the risks of the business become apparent.

In an effort to cope with this ever-changing environment, Honda built a production facility in Canada which may be the ultimate in flexible production. According to popular accounts, this plant has the capacity to switch production from one car model to another in a matter of days! By contrast, it can take other manufacturers six months or longer to switch production from one model to another. In addition, a new model can require an entirely new set of assembly lines.

That is the good news. The bad news is that a flexible plant costs about $1.4 billion versus $1 billion for a typical automobile plant. The real question in building such a plant is whether the flexibility is worth the additional $400 million investment.

To find an answer to this question, we have to examine the value of having a flexible plant. Perhaps the most important variable determining which cars to produce is the changing demands and tastes for car models. For simplicity, let us assume that the flexible plant can produce either minivans or four door sedans. Suppose, too, that it has a capacity of 300,000 vehicles a year and that it can produce either one type or the other, but not both at the same time. To illustrate our point, we will assume that the plant can be switched only once, three years from now, and that the lifetime of the plant is 10 years.

Currently there is a high demand for minivans, and the company forecasts that it will need to produce minivans at full capacity, 300,000 vehicles per year, for the next three years. Three years from now, though, there is a 50-percent chance that the public will prefer sedans rather than minivans and that only 50,000 minivans per year could be produced and sold. Both the fixed plant and the flexible plant have a capacity of 300,000 vehicles per year. The profit for the flexible plant is $1,000 per vehicle on minivans and $1,100 per vehicle on sedans. A fixed plant dedicated to minivan production can only produce minivans, but it does so more efficiently. The cash flow from having the fixed plant produce minivans is $1,200 per minivan, rather than the $1,000 per minivan for the flexible plant.

The profits from a plant that is committed to producing minivans for the next 10 years will be $360 million per year for the first three years ($300,000 \times $1,200$) and then will either continue at this rate for the next seven years or will drop to $60 million per year if demand switches to sedans ($50,000 \times $1,200$). On the other hand, if demand switches to sedans, a flexible plant will be able to switch its production. Therefore, the profit from a flexible plant will stay at $300 million per year for the first three years ($300,000 \times $1,000$) and then will either rise to $330 million if sedans come into favour ($300,000 \times $1,100$) or stay at $300 million per year if it sticks to minivans. This demonstrates the smoothing of cash flows from having a flexible plant.

The company faces a seemingly simple choice now. It can either invest $1 billion in a committed plant to produce minivans for the next 10 years or it can invest $1.4 billion to give itself the option of switching from minivans to sedans in three years.

The possible results are illustrated in Figure 25.7.

Using a 15-percent discount rate, the present value of the cash flows generated by building a fixed plant dedicated to minivans is

$$\text{PV (Fixed Plant)} = \$360/1.15 + \$360/1.15^2 + \ldots + \$360/1.15^{10}$$
$$= \$1.807 \text{ billion}$$

FIGURE 25.7

Yearly profits from a fixed plant and a flexible plant

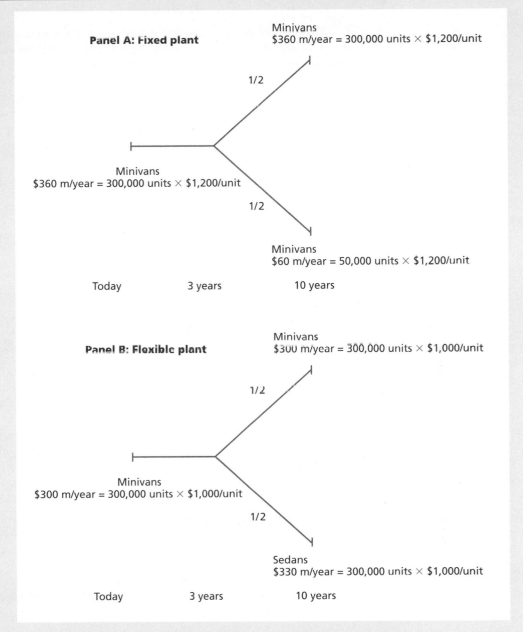

Panel A: Fixed plant

Minivans
$360 m/year = 300,000 units × $1,200/unit

1/2

Minivans
$360 m/year = 300,000 units × $1,200/unit

1/2

Minivans
$60 m/year = 50,000 units × $1,200/unit

Today   3 years   10 years

Panel B: Flexible plant

Minivans
$300 m/year = 300,000 units × $1,000/unit

1/2

Minivans
$300 m/year = 300,000 units × $1,000/unit

1/2

Sedans
$330 m/year = 300,000 units × $1,000/unit

Today   3 years   10 years

This graph shows the annual profits from a fixed plant and a flexible plant. A fixed plant can only produce minivans. Thus, if demand turns to sedans, the fixed plant will only sell 50,000 minivans. By contrast, the flexible plant can produce sedans if demand turns to that item. However, profit per unit is less in a flexible plant.

if minivan production stays in demand. However, the present value will drop to

$$\text{PV (Fixed Plant)} = \$360/1.15 + \$360/1.15^2 + \$360/1.15^3 + \$60/1.15^4 + \ldots + \$60/1.15^{10}$$
$$= \$.986 \text{ billion}$$

if sedans come into favour.

If minivans stay in demand, the present value of the cash flows from a flexible plant will be

$$\text{PV (Flexible Plant)} = \$300/1.15 + \$300/1.15^2 + \ldots + \$300/1.15^{10}$$
$$= \$1.506 \text{ billion}$$

If sedans displace minivans in customers' affections, then

$$\text{PV (Flexible Plant)} = \$300/1.15 + \$300/1.15^2 + \$300/1.15^3 + \$330/1.15^4 + \ldots +$$
$$\$330/1.15^{10}$$
$$= \$1.588 \text{ billion}$$

There is a 50-percent chance that minivans will stay in fashion and a 50-percent chance that they will not. If we assume that the firm is risk-neutral between these two possibilities, the expected present value is the average of the two. Of course, this may not be the case. It may be that a switch in tastes to sedans is correlated with changes in GNP or broad market movements, in which case we would have to do a beta adjustment to compute the present value correctly. For now we will assume that this risk adjustment is already incorporated in the 15-percent discount rate and take the expected present value. While we will develop a more accurate technique to solve such problems later in this chapter, our current assumption is quite reasonable as a practical matter. Thus,

$$\text{Expected PV (Fixed Plant)} = (1/2)\$1.807 \text{ billion} + (1/2)\$.986 \text{ billion}$$
$$= \$1.396 \text{ billion}$$

and

$$\text{Expected PV (Flexible Plant)} = (1/2)\$1.506 \text{ billion} + (1/2)\$1.588 \text{ billion}$$
$$= \$1.547 \text{ billion}$$

Comparing these calculations, we can see that the additional expected present value of having the flexibility to switch production is

$$\text{Expected PV (Flexible Plant)} - \text{Expected PV (Fixed Plant)}$$
$$= \$1.547 \text{ billion} - \$1.396 \text{ billion}$$
$$= \$151 \text{ million}$$

In other words, flexibility in this case is worth $151 million. Since the flexible plant costs $400 million more to build, the NPV of the flexible plant is less than that of the fixed plant. The price of flexibility is too high.

A recent study showed that the decision to open or close gold mining operations could also be explained by the real options model.[15] The study found that mine closures are strongly influenced by factors like price and volatility of gold, the firm's operating costs, closing costs, and the size of gold reserves at the mine.

CONCEPT QUESTIONS

1. Explain how car insurance acts like a put option.
2. Explain why government loan guarantees are not free.
3. Explain how managerial options can change capital budgeting decisions.

 **SUMMARY AND CONCLUSIONS**

This chapter described the basics of option valuation and discussed option-like corporate securities. In it, we saw that:

1. Options are contracts giving the right, but not the obligation, to buy and sell underlying assets at a fixed price during a specified time period.

   The most familiar options are puts and calls involving shares of stock. These options give the holder right, but not the obligation, to sell (the put option) or buy (the call option) shares of common stock at a given price.

   As we discussed, the value of any option depends only on five factors:
   a. The price of the underlying asset.

---

15 A. Moel and P. Tufano, "When Are Real Options Exercised? An Empirical Study of Mine Closings," *The Review of Financial Studies*, Spring 2002.

b. The exercise price.

c. The expiration date.

d. The interest rate on risk-free bonds.

e. The volatility of the underlying asset's value.

2. A warrant gives the holder the right to buy shares of common stock directly from the company at a fixed exercise price for a given period of time. Typically, warrants are issued in a package with privately placed bonds. Often, they can be detached afterward and traded separately.

3. A convertible bond is a combination of a straight bond and a call option. The holder can give up the bond in exchange for a fixed number of shares of stock. The minimum value of a convertible bond is given by its straight bond value or its conversion value, whichever is greater.

4. Convertible bonds, warrants, and call options are similar, but important differences do exist:

a. Warrants and convertible securities are issued by corporations. Call options are issued by and traded between individual investors.

b. Warrants are usually issued privately and combined with a bond. In most cases, the warrants can be detached immediately after the issue. In some cases, warrants are issued with preferred stock, with common stock, or in publicly traded bond issues.

c. Warrants and call options are exercised for cash. The holder of a warrant gives the company cash and receives new shares of the company's stock. The holder of a call option gives another individual cash in exchange for common stock. Convertible bonds are exercised by exchange; the individual gives the company back the bond in exchange for stock.

5. Many other corporate securities have option features. Bonds with call provisions, bonds with put provisions, and debt backed by a loan guarantee are just a few examples.

Key Terms

American and European options (page 756)
call option (page 756)
conversion premium (page 776)
conversion price (page 776)
conversion ratio (page 776)
conversion value (page 777)
convertible bond (page 776)
employee stock option (ESO) (page 767)
exercising the option (page 756)
expiration date (page 756)

intrinsic value (page 761)
option (page 755)
option delta (page 766)
put option (page 756)
real option (page 781)
straight bond value (page 776)
striking price or exercise price (page 756)
sweeteners or equity kickers (page 772)
warrant (page 772)

Chapter Review Problems and Self-Test

25.1 Value of a Call Option Stock in the Barsoom Corporation is currently selling for $20 per share. In one year, the price would either be $20 or $30. T-bills with one year to maturity are paying 10 percent. What is the value of a call option with a $20 exercise price? A $24 exercise price?

25.2 Convertible Bonds The Kau Corporation, publisher of Gourmand magazine, has a convertible bond issue currently selling in the market for $900. Each bond can be exchanged for 100 shares of stock at the holder's option.

The bond has a 6 percent coupon, payable annually, and it matures in 12 years. Kau's debt is BBB-rated. Debt with this rating is priced to yield 12 percent. Stock in Kau is trading at $6 per share.

What is the conversion ratio on this bond? The conversion price? The conversion premium? What is the floor value of the bond? What is its option value?

Answers to Self-Test Problems

25.1   With a $20 exercise price, the option can't finish out of the money (it can finish "at the money" if the stock price is $20). We can replicate the stock by investing the present value of $20 in T-bills and buying one call option. Buying the T-bill would cost $20/1.1 = $18.18.

   If the stock ends up at $20, the call option is worth zero and the T-bill pays $20. If the stock ends up at $30, the T-bill again pays $20, and the option is worth $30 − 20 = $10, so the package is worth $30. Since the T-bill/call option combination exactly duplicates the payoff on the stock, it has to be worth $20 or arbitrage is possible. Using the notation from the chapter, we can calculate the value of the call option:

$$S_0 = C_0 + E/(1 + R_f)$$
$$\$20 = C_0 + \$18.18$$
$$C_0 = \$1.82$$

   With the $24 exercise price, we start by investing the present value of the lower stock price in T-bills. This guarantees us $20 when the stock price is $20. If the stock price is $30, the option is worth $30 − 24 = $6. We have $20 from our T-bill, so we need $10 from the options to match the stock. Since each option is worth $6, we need to buy $10/$6 = 1.67 call options. Notice that the difference in the possible stock prices is $10 ($\Delta S$) and the difference in the possible option prices is $6 ($\Delta C$), so $\Delta S/\Delta C = 1.67$.

   To complete the calculation, the present value of the $20 plus 1.67 call options has to be worth $20 to prevent arbitrage, so:

$$\$20 = 1.67 \times C_0 + \$20/1.1$$
$$C_0 = \$1.82/1.67$$
$$= \$1.09$$

25.2   Since each bond can be exchanged for 100 shares, the conversion ratio is 100. The conversion price is the face value of the bond ($1,000) divided by the conversion ratio, $1,000/100 = $10. The conversion premium is the percentage difference between the current price and the conversion price, ($10 − $6)/$6 = 67%.

   The floor value of the bond is the greater of its straight bond value and its conversion value. Its conversion value is what the bond is worth if it is immediately converted: $100 \times \$6 = \$600$. The straight bond value is what the bond would be worth if it were not convertible. The annual coupon is $60, and the bond matures in 12 years. At a 12 percent required return, the straight bond value is:

$$\text{Straight bond value} = \$60 \times (1 - 1/1.12^{12})/.12 + \$1,000/1.12^{12}$$
$$= \$371.66 + 256.68$$
$$= \$628.34$$

   This exceeds the conversion value, so the floor value of the bond is $628.34. Finally, the option value is the value of the convertible in excess of its floor value. Since the bond is selling for $900, the option value is:

$$\text{Option value} = \$900 - 628.34$$
$$= \$271.66$$

Concepts Review and Critical Thinking Questions

1.   What is a call option? A put option? Under what circumstances might you want to buy each? Which one has greater *potential* profit? Why?

2.   Complete the following sentence for each of these investors:
   a. A buyer of call options
   b. A buyer of put options
   c. A seller (writer) of call options
   d. A seller (writer) of put options
   "The (buyer/seller) of a (put/call) option (pays/receives) money for the (right/obligation) to (buy/sell) a specified asset at a fixed price for a fixed length of time."

3.   What is the intrinsic value of a call option? How do we interpret this value?

4.   What is the value of a put option at maturity? Based on your answer, what is the intrinsic value of a put option?

5.   You notice that shares of stock in the Patel Corporation are going for $50 per share. Call options with an exercise price of $35 per share are selling for $10. What's wrong here? Describe how you can take advantage of this mispricing if the option expires today.

6.   If the risk of a stock increases, what is likely to happen to the price of call options on the stock? To the price of put options? Why?

7.   True or false: The unsystematic risk of a share of stock is irrelevant in valuing the stock because it can be diversified away; therefore, it is also irrelevant for valuing a call option on the stock. Explain.

8.   Suppose a certain stock currently sells for $30 per share. If a put option and a call option are available with $30 exercise prices, which do you think will sell for more, the put or the call? Explain.

9.   Suppose the interest rate on T-bills suddenly and unexpectedly rises. All other things being the same, what is the impact on call option values? On put option values?

10. When you take out an ordinary student loan, it is usually the case that whoever holds that loan is given a guarantee by the federal government, meaning that the government will make up any payments you skip. This is just one example of the many loan guarantees made by the federal government. Such guarantees don't show up in calculations of government spending or in official deficit figures. Why not? Should they show up?

Questions and Problems

Basic
(Questions
1–13)

1.   **Calculating Option Values**   T-bills currently yield 5.5 percent. Stock in Nina Manufacturing is currently selling for $55 per share. There is no possibility that the stock will be worth less than $50 per share in one year.

   a.   What is the value of a call option with a $45 exercise price? What is the intrinsic value?

   b.   What is the value of a call option with a $35 exercise price? What is the intrinsic value?

   c.   What is the value of a put option with a $45 exercise price? What is the intrinsic value?

2.   **Understanding Option Quotes**   Use the option quote information shown here to answer the questions that follow. The stock is currently selling for $83.

Option and NY Close	Expiration	Strike Price	Calls		Puts	
			Vol.	Last	Vol.	Last
RWJ						
	Mar	80	230	2.80	160	0.80
	Apr	80	170	6	127	1.40
	Jul	80	139	8.05	43	3.90
	Oct	80	60	10.20	11	3.65

   a.   Are the call options in the money? What is the intrinsic value of an RWJ Corp. call option?

   b.   Are the put options in the money? What is the intrinsic value of an RWJ Corp. put option?

   c.   Two of the options are clearly mispriced. Which ones? At a minimum, what should the mispriced options sell for? Explain how you could profit from the mispricing in each case.

3.   **Calculating Payoffs**   Use the option quote information shown here to answer the questions that follow. The stock is currently selling for $114.

Option and NY Close	Expiration	Strike Price	Calls		Puts	
			Vol.	Last	Vol.	Last
Macrosoft						
	Feb	110	85	7.60	40	.60
	Mar	110	61	8.80	22	1.55
	May	110	22	10.25	11	2.85
	Aug	110	3	13.05	3	4.70

   a.   Suppose you buy 10 contracts of the February 110 call option. How much will you pay, ignoring commissions?

   b.   In part (a), suppose that Macrosoft stock is selling for $140 per share on the expiration date. How much is your options investment worth? What if the terminal stock price is $125? Explain.

   c.   Suppose you buy 10 contracts of the August 110 put option. What is your maximum gain? On the expiration date, Macrosoft is selling for $104 per share. How much is your options investment worth? What is your net gain?

   d.   In part (c), suppose you *sell* 10 of the August 110 put contracts. What is your net gain or loss if Macrosoft is selling for $103 at expiration? For $132? What is the break-even price, that is, the terminal stock price that results in a zero profit?

4.   **Calculating Option Values**   The price of Ervin Corp. stock will be either $75 or $95 at the end of the year. Call options are available with one year to expiration. T-bills currently yield 6 percent.

   a.   Suppose the current price of Ervin stock is $80. What is the value of the call option if the exercise price is $70 per share?

   b.   Suppose the exercise price is $90 in part (a). What is the value of the call option now?

Basic   5. **Calculating Option Values**   The price of Tara, Inc., stock will be either $60 or $80 at the end of the year. Call options
(continued)   are available with one year to expiration. T-bills currently yield 5 percent.

   a. Suppose the current price of Tara stock is $70. What is the value of the call option if the exercise price is $45 per
         share?

   b. Suppose the exercise price is $70 in part (*a*). What is the value of the call option now?

6. **Using the Pricing Equation**   A one-year call option *contract* on Cheesy Poofs Co. stock sells for $1,200. In one year,
    the stock will be worth $45 or $65 per share. The exercise price on the call option is $60. What is the current value of
    the stock if the risk-free rate is 5 percent?

7. **Equity as an Option**   Rackin Pinion Corporation's assets are currently worth $1,050. In one year, they will be worth
    either $1,000 or $1,400. The risk-free interest rate is 5 percent. Suppose Rackin Pinion has an outstanding debt issue
    with a face value of $1,000.

   a. What is the value of the equity?

   b. What is the value of the debt? The interest rate on the debt?

   c. Would the value of the equity go up or down if the risk-free rate were 20 percent? Why? What does your answer
         illustrate?

8. **Equity as an Option**   Buckeye Industries has a bond issue with a face value of $1,000 that is coming due in one year.
    The value of Buckeye's assets is currently $1,200. Jim Tressell, the CEO, believes that the assets in the firm will be worth
    either $800 or $1,400 in a year. The going rate on one-year T-bills is 4 percent.

   a. What is the value of Buckeye's equity? The value of the debt?

   b. Suppose Buckeye can reconfigure its existing assets in such a way that the value in a year will be $500 or $1,700.
         If the current value of the assets is unchanged, will the stockholders favour such a move? Why or why not?

9. **Calculating Conversion Value**   A $1,000 par convertible debenture has a conversion price for common stock of
    $80 per share. With the common stock selling at $90, what is the conversion value of the bond?

10. **Convertible Bonds**   The following facts apply to a convertible bond making semiannual payments:

Conversion price	$40/share
Coupon rate	7.5%
Par value	$1,000
Yield on nonconvertible debentures of same quality	9%
Maturity	20 years
Market price of stock	$38/share

   a. What is the minimum price at which the convertible should sell?

   b. What accounts for the premium of the market price of a convertible bond over the total market value of the
         common stock into which it can be converted?

11. **Calculating Values for Convertibles**   You have been hired to value a new 30-year callable, convertible bond. The bond
     has a 7 percent coupon, payable annually, and its face value is $1,000. The conversion price is $65 and the stock cur-
     rently sells for $50.

   a. What is the minimum value of the bond? Comparable nonconvertible bonds are priced to yield 9 percent.

   b. What is the conversion premium for this bond?

12. **Calculating Warrant Values**   A bond with 25 detachable warrants has just been offered for sale at $1,000. The bond
     matures in 15 years and has an annual coupon of $105. Each warrant gives the owner the right to purchase two shares
     of stock in the company at $15 per share. Ordinary bonds (with no warrants) of similar quality are priced to yield
     12 percent. What is the value of one warrant?

13. **Option to Wait**   Your company is deciding whether to invest in a new machine. The new machine will increase cash
     flow by $280,000 per year. You believe the technology used in the machine has a 10-year life; in other words, no matter
     when you purchase the machine, it will be obsolete 10 years from today. The machine is currently priced at $1,500,000.
     The cost of the machine will decline by $125,000 per year until it reaches $1,000,000, where it will remain. If your
     required return is 12 percent, should you purchase the machine? If so, when should you purchase it?

Intermediate 14. **Abandonment Value**   We are examining a new project. We expect to sell 7,000 units per year at $60 net cash flow
(Questions   apiece for the next 10 years. In other words, the annual operating cash flow is projected to be $60 × 7,000 = $420,000.
14–19)   The relevant discount rate is 16 percent, and the initial investment required is $1,800,000.

   a. What is the base-case NPV?

   b. After the first year, the project can be dismantled and sold for $1,400,000. If expected sales are revised based on the
         first year's performance, when would it make sense to abandon the investment? In other words, at what level of
         expected sales would it make sense to abandon the project?

   c. Explain how the $1,400,000 abandonment value can be viewed as the opportunity cost of keeping the project in one year.

Intermediate
(continued)

15. **Abandonment** In the previous problem, suppose you think it is likely that expected sales will be revised upwards to 9,000 units if the first year is a success and revised downwards to 4,000 units if the first year is not a success.

    a. If success and failure are equally likely, what is the NPV of the project? Consider the possibility of abandonment in answering.

    b. What is the value of the option to abandon?

16. **Abandonment and Expansion** In the previous problem, suppose the scale of the project can be doubled in one year in the sense that twice as many units can be produced and sold. Naturally, expansion would only be desirable if the project is a success. This implies that if the project is a success, projected sales after expansion will be 18,000. Again assuming that success and failure are equally likely, what is the NPV of the project? Note that abandonment is still an option if the project is a failure. What is the value of the option to expand?

17. **Intuition and Option Value** Suppose a share of stock sells for $65. The risk-free rate is 5 percent, and the stock price in one year will be either $75 or $85.

    a. What is the value of a call option with a $75 exercise price?

    b. What's wrong here? What would you do?

18. **Intuition and Convertibles** Which of the following two sets of relationships, at time of issuance of convertible bonds, is more typical? Why?

	A	B
Offering price of bond	$ 800	$1,000
Bond value (straight debt)	800	950
Conversion value	1,000	900

19. **Convertible Calculations** Alicia, Inc., has a $1,000 face value convertible bond issue that is currently selling in the market for $950. Each bond is exchangeable at any time for 20 shares of the company's stock. The convertible bond has an 8 percent coupon, payable semiannually. Similar nonconvertible bonds are priced to yield 10 percent. The bond matures in 10 years. Stock in Alicia sells for $46 per share.

    a. What are the conversion ratio, conversion price, and conversion premium?

    b. What is the straight bond value? The conversion value?

    c. In part (b), what would the stock price have to be for the conversion value and the straight bond value to be equal?

    d. What is the option value of the bond?

Challenge
(Questions
20–21)

20. **Pricing Convertibles** You have been hired to value a new 25-year callable, convertible bond. The bond has a 6.80 percent coupon, payable annually. The conversion price is $150, and the stock currently sells for $44.75. The stock price is expected to grow at 12 percent per year. The bond is callable at $1,200, but, based on prior experience, it won't be called unless the conversion value is $1,300. The required return on this bond is 10 percent. What value would you assign?

21. **Abandonment Decisions** For some projects, it may be advantageous to terminate the project early. For example, if a project is losing money, you might be able to reduce your losses by scrapping out the assets and terminating the project, rather than continuing to lose money all the way through to the project's completion. Consider the following project of Hand Clapper, Inc. The company is considering a four-year project to manufacture clap-command garage door openers. This project requires an initial investment of $8 million that will be depreciated straight-line to zero over the project's life. An initial investment in net working capital of $2 million is required to support spare parts inventory; this cost is fully recoverable whenever the project ends. The company believes it can generate $7 million in pretax revenues with $3 million in total pretax operating costs. The tax rate is 38 percent and the discount rate is 16 percent. The market value of the equipment over the life of the project is as follows:

Year	Market Value (millions)
1	$6.50
2	6.00
3	3.00
4	0.00

    a. Assuming Hand Clapper operates this project for four years, what is the NPV?

    b. Now compute the project NPV assuming the project is abandoned after only one year, after two years, and after three years. What economic life for this project maximizes its value to the firm? What does this problem tell you about not considering abandonment possibilities when evaluating projects?

Internet Application Questions

1. The 1997 Nobel prize for economics (www.nobel.se/economics/laureates/1997/index.html) was awarded to Robert C. Merton and Myron S. Scholes for their early pioneering work in options pricing. The following site contains the transcript of an interview conducted by the Public Broadcasting Service (www.pbs.org) of the U.S. and the two professors. The interview explains the principles behind options pricing, and the excitement the news of the Nobel prize generated for the recipients. In two short sentences, can you paraphrase Scholes' and Merton's explanation of the intuition behind their options pricing formula?

   www.pbs.org/newshour/bb/business/july-dec97/nobel_10-14.html

2. The Chicago Board of Options Exchange (CBOE) (www.cboe.com) is the premier venue for trading options in the United States. The CBOE provides one of the best educational links to understand both the valuation of options, and the institutional details such as trading practices. Click on the CBOE link below to take a self-paced tutorial in options pricing and trading.

   www.cboe.com/LearnCenter/cboeducation/default.aspx

   When you are done with the tutorial, go back to the CBOE site and find and describe securities called LEAPS (www.cboe.com/OptProd/LEAPS.asp). Note that the Canadian derivatives exchange, the counterpart of the CBOE, is the Montreal Exchange (www.me.org).

3. Visit the website of the Montreal Exchange (www.me.org). What are the three most active options on this trading day? What is the company, series, strike price, and volume of the three highest volume calls? Find the same information for puts?

4. The Montreal Exchange (www.me.org) also provides information on expiration dates. Using the "Trading Calendar" tool, on what day do equity options expire in the current month? On what day do they expire next month?

Suggested Readings

For a detailed discussion of options read:
   Hull, J. *Options, Futures, and Other Derivative Securities.* Englewood Cliffs, NJ: Prentice-Hall, 6th ed., 2006.

THE BLACK–SCHOLES OPTION PRICING MODEL

In our discussion of call options in this chapter, we did not discuss the general case where the stock can take on any value and the option can finish out of the money. The general approach to valuing a call option falls under the heading of the *Black–Scholes Option Pricing Model (OPM),* a very famous result in finance. In addition to its theoretical importance, the OPM has great practical value. Many option traders carry hand-held calculators programmed with the Black–Scholes formula.

This appendix briefly discusses the Black–Scholes model. Because the underlying development is relatively complex, we present only the result and then focus on how to use it.

From our earlier discussion, when a t-period call option is certain to finish somewhere in the money, its value today, C_0, is equal to the value of the stock today, S_0, less the present value of the exercise price, $E/(1 + R_f)^t$:

$$C_0 = S_0 - E/(1 + R_f)^t$$

If the option can finish out of the money, this result needs modifying. Black and Scholes show that the value of a call option in this case is given by:

$$C_0 = S_0 \times N(d_1) - E/(1 + R_f)^t \times N(d_2) \qquad [25A.1]$$

where $N(d_1)$ and $N(d_2)$ are probabilities that must be calculated. This is the Black–Scholes OPM.[16]

In the Black–Scholes model, $N(d_1)$ is the probability that a standardized, normally distributed random variable (widely known as a z variable) is less than or equal to d_1, and $N(d_2)$ is the probability of a value that is less than or equal to d_2. Determining these probabilities requires a table such as Table 25A.1.

To illustrate, suppose we were given the following information:

There's a Black-Scholes calculator (and a lot more) at www.cboe.com

---

16 Strictly speaking, the risk-free rate in the Black–Scholes model is the continuously compounded risk-free rate. Continuous compounding is discussed in Chapter 6.

TABLE 25A.1 Cumulative normal distribution

d	N(d)	d	N(d)	d	N(d)	d	N(d)	d	N(d)	d	N(d)
−3.00	.0013	−1.58	.0571	−0.76	.2236	0.06	.5239	0.86	.8051	1.66	.9515
−2.95	.0016	−1.56	.0594	−0.74	.2297	0.08	.5319	0.88	.8106	1.68	.9535
−2.90	.0019	−1.54	.0618	−0.72	.2358	0.10	.5398	0.90	.8159	1.70	.9554
−2.85	.0022	−1.52	.0643	−0.70	.2420	0.12	.5478	0.92	.8212	1.72	.9573
−2.80	.0026	−1.50	.0668	−0.68	.2483	0.14	.5557	0.94	.8264	1.74	.9591
−2.75	.0030	−1.48	.0694	−0.66	.2546	0.16	.5636	0.96	.8315	1.76	.9608
−2.70	.0035	−1.46	.0721	−0.64	.2611	0.18	.5714	0.98	.8365	1.78	.9625
−2.65	.0040	−1.44	.0749	−0.62	.2676	0.20	.5793	1.00	.8414	1.80	.9641
−2.60	.0047	−1.42	.0778	−0.60	.2743	0.22	.5871	1.02	.8461	1.82	.9656
−2.55	.0054	−1.40	.0808	−0.58	.2810	0.24	.5948	1.04	.8508	1.84	.9671
−2.50	.0062	−1.38	.0838	−0.56	.2877	0.26	.6026	1.06	.8554	1.86	.9686
−2.45	.0071	−1.36	.0869	−0.54	.2946	0.28	.6103	1.08	.8599	1.88	.9699
−2.40	.0082	−1.34	.0901	−0.52	.3015	0.30	.6179	1.10	.8643	1.90	.9713
−2.35	.0094	−1.32	.0934	−0.50	.3085	0.32	.6255	1.12	.8686	1.92	.9726
−2.30	.0107	−1.30	.0968	−0.48	.3156	0.34	.6331	1.14	.8729	1.94	.9738
−2.25	.0122	−1.28	.1003	−0.46	.3228	0.36	.6406	1.16	.8770	1.96	.9750
−2.20	.0139	−1.26	.1038	−0.44	.3300	0.38	.6480	1.18	.8810	1.98	.9761
−2.15	.0158	−1.24	.1075	−0.42	.3373	0.40	.6554	1.20	.8849	2.00	.9772
−2.10	.0179	−1.22	.1112	−0.40	.3446	0.42	.6628	1.22	.8888	2.05	.9798
−2.05	.0202	−1.20	.1151	−0.38	.3520	0.44	.6700	1.24	.8925	2.10	.9821
−2.00	.0228	−1.18	.1190	−0.36	.3594	0.46	.6773	1.26	.8962	2.15	.9842
−1.98	.0239	−1.16	.1230	−0.34	.3669	0.48	.6844	1.28	.8997	2.20	.9861
−1.96	.0250	−1.14	.1271	−0.32	.3745	0.50	.6915	1.30	.9032	2.25	.9878
−1.94	.0262	−1.12	.1314	−0.30	.3821	0.52	.6985	1.32	.9066	2.30	.9893
−1.92	.0274	−1.10	.1357	−0.28	.3897	0.54	.7054	1.34	.9099	2.35	.9906
−1.90	.0287	−1.08	.1401	−0.26	.3974	0.56	.7123	1.36	.9131	2.40	.9918
−1.88	.0301	−1.06	.1446	**−0.24**	**.4052**	0.58	.7191	1.38	.9162	2.45	.9929
−1.86	.0314	−1.04	.1492	−0.22	.4129	0.60	.7258	1.40	.9192	2.50	.9938
−1.84	.0329	−1.02	.1539	−0.20	.4207	0.62	.7324	1.42	.9222	2.55	.9946
−1.82	.0344	−1.00	.1587	−0.18	.4286	0.64	.7389	1.44	.9251	2.60	.9953
−1.80	.0359	−0.98	.1635	−0.16	.4365	0.66	.7454	1.46	.9279	2.65	.9960
−1.78	.0375	−0.96	.1685	−0.14	.4443	0.68	.7518	1.48	.9306	2.70	.9965
−1.76	.0392	−0.94	.1736	−0.12	.4523	0.70	.7580	1.50	.9332	2.75	.9970
−1.74	.0409	−0.92	.1788	−0.10	.4602	0.72	.7642	1.52	.9357	2.80	.9974
−1.72	.0427	−0.90	.1841	−0.08	.4681	0.74	.7704	1.54	.9382	2.85	.9978
−1.70	.0446	−0.88	.1894	−0.06	.4761	0.76	.7764	1.56	.9406	2.90	.9981
−1.68	.0465	−0.86	.1949	−0.04	.4841	0.78	.7823	1.58	.9429	2.95	.9984
−1.66	.0485	−0.84	.2005	−0.02	.4920	0.80	.7882	1.60	.9452	3.00	.9986
−1.64	.0505	−0.82	.2061	0.00	.5000	0.82	.7939	1.62	.9474	3.05	.9989
−1.62	.0526	−0.80	.2119	0.02	.5080	0.84	.7996	1.64	.9495		
−1.60	.0548	−0.78	.2177	0.04	.5160						

This table shows the probability ($N(d)$) of observing a value less than or equal to d. For example, as illustrated, if d is −.24, then $N(d)$ is .4052.

$$S_0 = \$100$$
$$E = \$80$$
$$R_f = 1\% \text{ per month}$$
$$d_1 = 1.20$$
$$d_2 = .90$$
$$t = 9 \text{ months}$$

Based on this information, what is the value of the call option, C_0?

To answer, we need to determine $N(d_1)$ and $N(d_2)$. In Table 25A.1, we first find the row corresponding to a d of 1.20. The corresponding probability, $N(d)$, is .8849, so this is $N(d_1)$. For d_2, the associated probability $N(d_2)$ is .8159. Using the Black–Scholes OPM, the value of the call option is thus:

$$C_0 = S_0 \times N(d_1) - E/(1 + R_f)^t \times N(d_2)$$
$$= \$100 \times .8849 - \$80/1.01^9 \times .8159$$
$$= \$88.49 - 59.68$$
$$= \$28.81$$

As this example illustrates, if we are given values for d_1 and d_2 (and the table), using the Black–Scholes model is not difficult. In general, however, we are not given the values of d_1 and d_2, and we must calculate them instead. This requires a little extra effort. The values for d_1 and d_2 for the Black–Scholes OPM are given by:

$$d_1 = [\ln(S_0/E) + (R_f + 1/2 \times \sigma^2) \times t]/[\sigma \times \sqrt{t}]$$
$$d_2 = d_1 - \sigma \times \sqrt{t}$$

[25A.2]

In these expressions, σ is the standard deviation of the rate of return on the underlying asset. Also, $\ln(S_0/E)$ is the natural logarithm of the current stock price divided by the exercise price (most calculators have a key labelled *ln* to perform this calculation).

The formula for d_1 looks intimidating, but using it is mostly a matter of "plug and chug" with a calculator. To illustrate, suppose we have the following:

$S_0 = \$70$
$E = \$80$
$R_f = 1\%$ per month
$\sigma = 2\%$ per month
$t = 9$ months

With these numbers, d_1 is:

$$
\begin{aligned}
d_1 &= [\ln(S_0/E) + (R_f + 1/2 \times \sigma^2) \times t]/[\sigma \times \sqrt{t}] \\
&= [\ln(.875) + (.01 + 1/2 \times .02^2) \times 9]/[.02 \times 3] \\
&= [-.1335 + .0918]/.06 \\
&\approx -.70
\end{aligned}
$$

Given this result, d_2 is:

$$
\begin{aligned}
d_2 &= d_1 - \sigma \times \sqrt{t} \\
&= -.70 - .02 \times 3 \\
&= -.76
\end{aligned}
$$

Referring to Table 25A.1, the values for $N(d_1)$ and $N(d_2)$ are .2420 and .2236, respectively. The value of the option is thus:

$$
\begin{aligned}
C_0 &= S_0 \times N(d_1) - E/(1 + R_f)^t \times N(d_2) \\
&= \$70 \times .2420 - \$80/1.01^9 \times .2236 \\
&= \$.58
\end{aligned}
$$

This may seem a little small, but the stock price would have to rise by \$10 before the option would even be in the money.

Notice that we quoted the risk-free rate, the standard deviation, and the time to maturity in months in this example. We could have used days, weeks, or years as long as we are consistent in quoting all three of these using the same time units.

A question that sometimes comes up concerns the probabilities $N(d_1)$ and $N(d_2)$. Just what are they the probabilities of? In other words, how do we interpret them? The answer is that they don't really correspond to anything in the real world. We mention this because there is a common misconception about $N(d_2)$ in particular. It is frequently thought to be the probability that the stock price will exceed the strike price on the expiration day, which is also the probability that a call option will finish in the money. Unfortunately, that's not correct, at least not unless the expected return on the stock is equal to the risk-free rate.

Tables such as Table 25A.1 are the traditional means of looking up "*z*" values, but they have been mostly replaced by computers. They are not as accurate because of rounding, and they also have only a limited number of values. The following *Spreadsheet Strategies* box shows how to calculate Black–Scholes call option prices using a spreadsheet.

SPREADSHEET STRATEGIES

	A	B	C	D	E	F	G	H	I	J	K
1											
2			Using a spreadsheet to calculate Black-Scholes option prices								
3											
4	XYZ stock has a price of $65 and an annual return standard deviation of 50%. The riskless										
5	interest rate is 5%. Calculate call and put option prices with a strike of $60 and a 3-month										
6	time to expiration.										
7											
8	Stock =	65		d1 =	0.4952		N(d1) =	0.6898			
9	Strike =	60									
10	Sigma =	0.5		d2 =	0.2452		N(d2) =	0.5968			
11	Time =	0.25									
12	Rate =	0.05									
13											
14		Call = Stock x N(d1) – Strike x exp(– Rate x Time) x N(d2) =									$9.47
15											
16		Put = Strike x exp(– Rate x Time) + Call – Stock							=		$3.72
17											
18	Formula entered in E8 is =(LN(B8/B9)+(B12+0.5*B10^2)*B11)/(B10*SQRT(B11))										
19	Formula entered in E10 is =E8–B10*SQRT(B11)										
20	Formula entered in H8 is =NORMSDIST(E8)										
21	Formula entered in K10 is =NORMSDIST(E10)										
22	Formula entered in K14 is =B8*H8–B9*EXP(–B12*B11)*H10										
23	Formula entered in K16 is =B9*EXP(–B12*B11)+K14–B8										

Appendix Review Problems and Self-Test

A.1 **Black–Scholes OPM: Part I** Calculate the Black–Scholes price for a six-month option given the following:

$S_0 = \$80$
$E = \$70$
$R_f = 10\%$ per year
$d_1 = .82$
$d_2 = .74$

A.2 **Black–Scholes OPM: Part II** Calculate the Black–Scholes price for a nine-month option given the following:

$S_0 = \$80$

$E = \$70$

$\sigma = .30$ per year

$R_f = 10\%$ per year

Answers to Appendix Self-Test Problems

A.1 $C_0 = 80 \times N(.82) - 70/(1.10)^{.5} \times N(.74)$

From Table 25A.1, the values for $N(.82)$ and $N(.74)$ are .7939 and .7704, respectively. The value of the option is about $12.09. Notice that since the interest rate (and standard deviation) is quoted on an annual basis, we used a t value of .50, representing a half year, in calculating the present value of the exercise price.

A.2 We first calculate d_1 and d_2:

$d_1 = [\ln(S_0/E) + (R_f + 1/2 \times \sigma^2) \times t]/(\sigma \times \sqrt{t}]$
$= [\ln(80/70) + (.10 + 1/2 \times .30^2) \times (.75)]/[.30 \times \sqrt{75}]$
$= .9325$

$$d_2 = d_1 - \sigma \times \sqrt{t}$$
$$= .9325 - .30 \times \sqrt{75}$$
$$= .6727$$

From Table 25A.1, $N(d_1)$ appears to be roughly .825, and $N(d_2)$ is about .75. Plugging these in, we determine that the option's value is $17.12. Notice again that we used an annual t value of $9/12 = .75$ in this case.

Appendix Questions and Problems

For Problems A.1 through A.3, round computed values for d_1 and d_2 to the nearest values in Table 25A.1 for determining $N(d_1)$ and $N(d_2)$, respectively.

Basic
(Questions
A.1 and A.2)

A.1 Using the OPM   Calculate the Black–Scholes option price in each of the cases that follow. The risk-free rate and standard deviation are quoted in annual terms. The last three cases may require some thought.

Stock Price	Exercise Price	Risk-Free Rate	Maturity	Standard Deviation	Call Price
$31	$37.50	07%	3 months	0.21	
40	29	03%	6 months	.15	
89	63	12%	9 months	0.24	
97	99	08%	12 months	.30	
0	35	05%	12 months	0.44	
125	17	04%	Forever	.35	
129	0	03%	6 months	0.21	
121	113	06%	6 months	.00	
50	74	13%	12 months	∞	

A.2 Equity as an Option and the OPM   Childs Manufacturing has a discount bank loan that matures in one year and requires the firm to pay $2,950. The current market value of the firm's assets is $3,400. The annual *variance* for the firm's return on assets is 0.29, and the annual risk-free interest rate is 4.5 percent. Based on the Black–Scholes model, what is the market value of the firm's debt and equity?

Intermediate
(Question
A.3)

A.3 Changes in Variance and Equity Value   Suppose that, in the previous problem, Childs is considering two mutually exclusive investments. Project A has an NPV of $135, and Project B has an NPV of $215. As a result of taking Project A, the variance of the firm's return on assets will increase to .39. If Project B is taken, the variance will fall to .22.

a. What is the value of the firm's debt and equity if Project A is undertaken? If Project B is undertaken?

b. Which project would the stockholders prefer? Can you reconcile your answer with the NPV rule?

c. Suppose the stockholders and bondholders are in fact the same group of investors. Would this affect the answer to part *(b)*?

d. What does this problem suggest to you about stockholder incentives?

Glossary

Accounting Break-Even The sales level that results in zero project net income. (page 317)

Accounts Payable Period The time between receipt of inventory and payment for it. (page 549)

Accounts Receivable Financing A secured short-term loan that involves either the assignment or factoring of receivables. (page 566)

Accounts Receivable Period The time between sale of inventory and collection of the receivable. (page 549)

Adjusted Present Value (APV) Base case net present value of a project's operating cash flows plus present value of any financing benefits. (page 439)

Adjustment Costs The costs associated with holding too little cash. Also shortage costs. (page 581)

Agency Problem The possibility of conflicts of interest between the shareholders and management of a firm. (page 11)

Aggregation Process by which smaller investment proposals of each of a firm's operational units are added up and treated as one big project. (page 88)

Aging Schedule A compilation of accounts receivable by the age of each account. (page 623)

Amalgamations Combinations of firms that have been joined by merger, consolidation, or acquisition. (page 697)

American Option An option that can be exercised at any time until its expiration date. (page 756)

American Options A call or put option that can be exercised on or before its expiration date. (page 667)

Annual Percentage Rate (APR) The interest rate charged per period multiplied by the number of periods per year. (page 160)

Annuity A level stream of cash flows for a fixed period of time. (page 147)

Annuity Due An annuity for which the cash flows occur at the beginning of the period. (page 153)

Arbitrage Pricing Theory (APT) An equilibrium asset pricing theory that is derived from a factor model by using diversification and arbitrage. It shows that the expected return on any risky asset is a linear combination of various factors. (page 399)

Arithmetic Average Return The return earned in an average year over a multiyear period. (page 354)

Average Accounting Return (AAR) An investment's average net income divided by its average book value. (page 248)

Average Tax Rate Total taxes paid divided by total taxable income. (page 40)

Balance Sheet Financial statement showing a firm's accounting value on a particular date. (page 27)

Bankruptcy A legal proceeding for liquidating or reorganizing a business. Also, the transfer of some or all of a firm's assets to its creditors. (page 503)

Bearer Form Bond issued without record of the owner's name; payment is made to whoever holds the bond. (page 187)

Benefit/Cost Ratio The profitability index of an investment project. (page 258)

Best Efforts Underwriting Underwriter sells as much of the issue as possible, but can return any unsold shares to the issuer without financial responsibility. (page 454)

Beta Coefficient Amount of systematic risk present in a particular risky asset relative to an average risky asset. (page 388)

Bond Refunding The process of replacing all or part of an issue of outstanding bonds. (page 209)

Bought Deal One underwriter buys securities from an issuing firm and sells them directly to a small number of investors. (page 454)

Business Risk The equity risk that comes from the nature of the firm's operating activities. (page 490)

Call Option An option that gives the owner the right, but not the obligation, to buy an asset. (page 746)

Call Option The right to buy an asset at a fixed price during a particular period of time. (page 756)

Call Premium Amount by which the call price exceeds the par value of the bond. (page 188)

Call Protected Bond during period in which it cannot be redeemed by the issuer. (page 188)

Call Provision Agreement giving the corporation the option to repurchase the bond at a specified price before maturity. (page 188)

Canada Plus Call Call provision which compensates bond investors for interest differential, making call unattractive for issuer. (page 188)

Canada Yield Curve A plot of the yields on Government of Canada notes and bonds relative to maturity. (page 199)

Capital Asset Pricing Model (CAPM) Equation of the SML showing relationship between expected return and beta. (page 397)

Capital Budgeting The process of planning and managing a firm's investment in long-term assets. (page 3)

Capital Cost Allowance (CCA) Depreciation for tax purposes, not necessarily the same as depreciation under GAAP. (page 43)

Capital Cost Allowance (CCA) Depreciation method under Canadian tax law allowing for the accelerated write-off of property under various classifications. (page 272)

Capital Gains The increase in value of an investment over its purchase price. (page 40)

Capital Gains Yield The dividend growth rate or the rate at which the value of an investment grows. (page 222)

Capital Intensity Ratio A firm's total assets divided by its sales, or the amount of assets needed to generate $1 in sales. (page 94)

Capital Markets Financial markets where long-term debt and equity securities are bought and sold. (page 19)

Capital Rationing The situation that exists if a firm has positive NPV projects but cannot find the necessary financing. (page 330)

Capital Structure The mix of debt and equity maintained by a firm. (page 4)

Captive Finance Company Wholly owned subsidiary that handles credit extension and receivables financing through commercial paper. (page 616)

Carrying Costs Costs that rise with increases in the level of investment in current assets. (page 554)

Cash Break-Even The sales level where operating cash flow is equal to zero. (page 322)

Cash Budget A forecast of cash receipts and disbursements for the next planning period. (page 560)

Cash Cycle The time between cash disbursement and cash collection. (page 549)

Cash Discount A discount given for a cash purchase. (page 610)

Cash Flow from Assets The total of cash flow to bondholders and cash flow to shareholders, consisting of the following: operating cash flow, capital spending, and additions to net working capital. (page 34)

Cash Flow Time Line Graphical representation of the operating cycle and the cash cycle. (page 549)

Cash Flow to Creditors A firm's interest payments to creditors less net new borrowings. (page 36)

Cash Flow to Shareholders Dividends paid out by a firm less net new equity raised. (page 36)

CCA Tax Shield Tax saving that results from the CCA deduction, calculated as depreciation multiplied by the corporate tax rate. (page 282)

Circular Bid Corporate takeover bid communicated to the stockholders by direct mail. (page 698)

Clean Price The price of a bond net of accrued interest; this is the price that is typically quoted. (page 196)

Clientele Effect Stocks attract particular groups based on dividend yield and the resulting tax effects. (page 527)

Collection Policy Procedures followed by a firm in collecting accounts receivable. (page 607)

Common-Base-Year Statement A standardized financial statement presenting all items relative to a certain base year amount. (page 61)

Common-Size Statement A standardized financial statement presenting all items in percentage terms. Balance sheets are shown as a percentage of assets and income statements as a percentage of sales. (page 60)

Common Stock Equity without priority for dividends or in bankruptcy. (page 224)

Compounding The process of accumulating interest in an investment over time to earn more interest. (page 121)

Compound Interest Interest earned on both the initial principal and the interest reinvested from prior periods. (page 121)

Consol A type of perpetuity. (page 154)

Consolidation A merger in which an entirely new firm is created and both the acquired and acquiring firm cease to exist. (page 697)

Contingency Planning Taking into account the managerial options that are implicit in a project. (page 327)

Control Block An interest controlling 50 percent of outstanding votes plus one; thereby it may decide the fate of the firm. (page 712)

Conversion Premium Difference between the conversion price and the current stock price divided by the current stock price. (page 776)

Conversion Price The dollar amount of a bond's par value that is exchangeable for one share of stock. (page 776)

Conversion Ratio The number of shares per $1,000 bond received for conversion into stock. (page 776)

Conversion Value The value of a convertible bond if it was immediately converted into common stock. (page 777)

Convertible Bond A bond that can be exchanged for a fixed number of shares of stock for a specified amount of time. (page 776)

Corporate Governance Rules for corporate organization and conduct. (page 13)

Corporate Governance Rules and practices relating to how corporations are governed by management, directors, and shareholders. (page 712)

Corporation A business created as a distinct legal entity owned by one or more individuals or entities. (page 6)

Cost of Debt The return that lenders require on the firm's debt. (page 418)

Cost of Equity The return that equity investors require on their investment in the firm. (page 414)

Counterparty Second borrower in currency swap. Counterparty borrows funds in currency desired by principal. (page 667)

Coupon Rate The annual coupon divided by the face value of a bond. (page 178)

Coupons The stated interest payments made on a bond. (page 177)

Covenants A promise by the firm, included in the debt contract, to perform certain acts. A restrictive covenant imposes constraints on the firm to protect the interests of the debtholder. (page 566)

Credit Analysis The process of determining the probability that customers will or will not pay. (page 607)

Credit Cost Curve Graphical representation of the sum of the carrying costs and the opportunity costs of a credit policy. (page 615)

Credit Default Swap A contract that pays off when a credit event occurs, default by a particular company termed the reference entity, giving the buyer the right to sell corporate bonds issued by the reference entity at their face value. (page 745)

Credit Instrument The evidence of indebtedness. (page 612)

Credit Period The length of time that credit is granted. (page 609)

Credit Scoring The process of quantifying the probability of default when granting consumer credit. (page 620)

Cross-Hedging Hedging an asset with contracts written on a closely related, but not identical, asset. (page 741)

Cross-Rate The implicit exchange rate between two currencies (usually non-U.S.) quoted in some third currency (usually the U.S. dollar). (page 649)

Cumulative Voting Procedure where a shareholder may cast all votes for one member of the board of directors. (page 237)

Date of Payment Date on the dividend cheques. (page 518)

Date of Record Date on which holders of record are designated to receive a dividend. (page 517)

Debenture Unsecured debt, usually with a maturity of 10 years or more. (page 187)

Debit Card An automated teller machine card used at the point of purchase to avoid the use of cash. As this is not a credit card, money must be available in the user's bank account. (page 588)

Debt Capacity The ability to borrow to increase firm value. (page 100)

Declaration Date Date on which the board of directors passes a resolution to pay a dividend. (page 517)

Default Risk Premium The portion of a nominal interest rate or bond yield that represents compensation for the possibility of default. (page 200)

Deferred Call Call provision prohibiting the company from redeeming the bond before a certain date. (page 188)

Degree of Operating Leverage The percentage change in operating cash flow relative to the percentage change in quantity sold. (page 324)

Depreciation (CCA) Tax Shield Tax saving that results from the CCA deduction, calculated as depreciation multiplied by the corporate tax rate. Also CCA Tax Shield. (page 282)

Derivative Securities Options, futures, and other securities whose value derives from the price of another, underlying, asset. (page 22)

Derivative Security A financial asset that represents a claim to another financial asset. (page 728)

Dilution Loss in existing shareholders' value, in terms of either ownership, market value, book value, or EPS. (page 471)

Direct Bankruptcy Costs The costs that are directly associated with bankruptcy, such as legal and administrative expenses. (page 495)

Dirty Price The price of a bond including accrued interest, also known as the *full* or *invoice price*. This is the price the buyer actually pays. (page 196)

Discount Calculate the present value of some future amount. (page 128)

Discounted Cash Flow (DCF) Valuation The process of valuing an investment by discounting its future cash flows. (page 242)

Discounted Payback Period The length of time required for an investment's discounted cash flows to equal its initial cost. (page 247)

Discount Rate The rate used to calculate the present value of future cash flows. (page 129)

Distribution Payment made by a firm to its owners from sources other than current or accumulated earnings. (page 516)

Diversification Investment in more than one asset; returns do not move proportionally in the same direction at the same time, thus reducing risk. (page 708)

Divestiture The sale of assets, operations, divisions, and/or segments of a business to a third party. (page 719)

Dividend Payment made out of a firm's earnings to its owners, either in the form of cash or stock. (page 516)

Dividend Capture A strategy in which an investor purchases securities to own them on the day of record and then quickly sells them; designed to attain dividends but avoid the risk of a lengthy hold. (page 595)

Dividend Growth Model Model that determines the current price of a stock at its dividend next period, divided by the discount rate less the dividend growth rate. (page 219)

Dividend Payout Ratio Amount of cash paid out to shareholders divided by net income. (page 93)

Dividend Tax Credit Tax formula that reduces the effective tax rate on dividends. (page 40)

Dividend Yield A stock's cash dividend divided by its current price. (page 222)

Dividends Return on capital of corporation paid by company to shareholders in either cash or stock. (page 225)

Du Pont Identity Popular expression breaking ROE into three parts: profit margin, total asset turnover, and financial leverage. (page 73)

Dutch Auction Underwriting The type of underwriting in which the offer price is set based on competitive bidding by investors. Also known as a *uniform price auction*. (page 454)

Earnings Per Share (EPS) Net income minus any cash dividends on preferred stock, divided by the number of shares of common stock outstanding. (page 708)

Economic Exposure Long-term financial risk arising from permanent changes in prices or other economic fundamentals. (page 736)

Economic Value Added (EVA) Performance measure based on WACC. (page 423)

Effective Annual Rate (EAR) The interest rate expressed as if it were compounded once per year. (page 158)

Efficient Capital Market Market in which security prices reflect available information. (page 357)

Efficient Markets Hypothesis (EMH) The hypothesis is that actual capital markets, such as the TSX, are efficient. (page 357)

Employee Stock Option (ESO) An option granted to an employee by a company giving the employee the right to buy shares of stock in the company at a fixed price for a fixed time. (page 767)

Equity Carve-Out The sale of stock in a wholly owned subsidiary via an IPO. (page 719)

Equivalent Annual Cost (EAC) The present value of a project's costs calculated on an annual basis. (page 291)

Erosion The portion of cash flows of a new project that come at the expense of a firm's existing operations. (page 270)

Eurobanks Banks that make loans and accept deposits in foreign currencies. (page 665)

Eurobond International bonds issued in multiple countries but denominated in a single currency (usually the issuer's currency). (page 649)

Eurocurrency Money deposited in a financial centre outside of the country whose currency is involved. (page 649)

European Option An option that can be exercised only on the expiration date. (page 756)

Exchange Rate The price of one country's currency expressed in another country's currency. (page 651)

Exchange Rate Risk The risk related to having international operations in a world where relative currency values vary. (page 666)

Ex-Dividend Date Date two business days before the date of record, establishing those individuals entitled to a dividend. (page 517)

Exercise Price The fixed price in the option contract at which the holder can buy or sell the underlying asset. Also called the striking price or strike price. (page 756)

Exercising the Option The act of buying or selling the underlying asset via the option contract. (page 756)

Expected Return Return on a risky asset expected in the future. (page 370)

Expiration Date The last day on which an option can be exercised. (page 756)

Export Development Canada (EDC) Federal Crown corporation that promotes Canadian exports by making loans to foreign purchasers. (page 649)

Ex Rights Period when stock is selling without a recently declared right, normally beginning four business days before the holder-of-record date. (page 468)

External Financing Needed (EFN) The amount of financing required to balance both sides of the balance sheet. (page 94)

Face Value The principal amount of a bond that is repaid at the end of the term. Also par value. (page 177)

Financial Break-Even The sales level that results in a zero NPV. (page 322)

Financial Distress Costs The direct and indirect costs associated with going bankrupt or experiencing financial distress. (page 495)

Financial Engineering Creation of new securities or financial processes. (page 22)

Financial Lease Typically, a longer-term, fully amortized lease under which the lessee is responsible for upkeep. Usually not cancellable without penalty. (page 679)

Financial Ratios Relationships determined from a firm's financial information and used for comparison purposes. (page 62)

Financial Risk The equity risk that comes from the financial policy (i.e., capital structure) of the firm. (page 490)

Firm Commitment Underwriting Underwriter buys the entire issue, assuming full financial responsibility for any unsold shares. (page 454)

Fisher Effect The relationship between nominal returns, real returns, and inflation. (page 197)

Five Cs of Credit The following five basic credit factors to be evaluated: character, capacity, capital, collateral, and conditions. (page 620)

Fixed Costs Costs that do not change when the quantity of output changes during a particular time period. (page 315)

Float The difference between book cash and bank cash, representing the net effect of cheques in the process of clearing. (page 583)

Forecasting Risk The possibility that errors in projected cash flows lead to incorrect decisions. (page 309)

Foreign Bonds International bonds issued in a single country, usually denominated in that country's currency. (page 649)

Foreign Exchange Market The market where one country's currency is traded for another's. (page 650)

Forward Contract A legally binding agreement between two parties calling for the sale of an asset or product in the future at a price agreed upon today. (page 737)

Forward Exchange Rate The agreed-on exchange rate to be used in a forward trade. (page 653)

Forward Trade Agreement to exchange currency at some time in the future. (page 653)

Free Cash Flow Another name for cash flow from assets. (page 35)

Futures Contract A forward contract with the feature that gains and losses are realized each day rather than only on the settlement date. (page 740)

Future Value (FV) The amount an investment is worth after one or more periods. Also compound value. (page 121)

General Cash Offer An issue of securities offered for sale to the general public on a cash basis. (page 452)

Generally Accepted Accounting Principles (GAAP) The common set of standards and procedures by which audited financial statements are prepared. (page 30)

Geometric Average Return The average compound return earned per year over a multiyear period. (page 354)

Gilts British and Irish government securities, including issues of local British authorities and some overseas public-sector offerings. (page 650)

Going-Private Transactions All publicly owned stock in a firm is replaced with complete equity ownership by a private group. (page 699)

Greenmail A targeted stock repurchase where payments are made to potential bidders to eliminate unfriendly takeover attempts. (page 713)

Growing Annuity A finite number of growing annual cash flows. (page 156)

Growing Perpetuity A constant stream of cash flows without end that is expected to rise indefinitely. (page 154)

Half-year Rule CRA's requirement to figure CCA on only one-half of an asset's installed cost for its first year of use. (page 44)

Hard Rationing The situation that occurs when a business cannot raise financing for a project under any circumstances. (page 330)

Hedging Reducing a firm's exposure to price or rate fluctuations. Also, immunization. (page 728)

Holder-of-Record Date The date on which existing shareholders on company records are designated as the recipients of stock rights. Also the date of record. (page 468)

Homemade Dividends Idea that individual investors can undo corporate dividend policy by reinvesting dividends or selling shares of stock. (page 520)

Homemade Leverage The use of personal borrowing to change the overall amount of financial leverage to which the individual is exposed. (page 485)

Income Statement Financial statement summarizing a firm's performance over a period of time. (page 32)

Incremental Cash Flows The difference between a firm's future cash flows with a project and without the project. (page 269)

Indenture Written agreement between the corporation and the lender detailing the terms of the debt issue. (page 186)

Indirect Bankruptcy Costs The difficulties of running a business that is experiencing financial distress. (page 495)

Inflation Premium The portion of a nominal interest rate that represents compensation for expected future inflation. (page 199)

Information Content Effect The market's reaction to a change in corporate dividend payout. (page 527)

Initial Public Offering (IPO) A company's first equity issue made available to the public. Also an unseasoned new issue. (page 452)

Interest on Interest Interest earned on the reinvestment of previous interest payments. (page 121)

Interest Rate Parity (IRP) The condition stating that the interest rate differential between two countries is equal to the difference between the forward exchange rate and the spot exchange rate. (page 659)

Interest Rate Risk Premium The compensation investors demand for bearing interest rate risk. (page 199)

Interest Tax Shield The tax saving attained by a firm from interest expense. (page 491)

Internal Growth Rate The growth rate a firm can maintain with only internal financing. (page 99)

Internal Rate of Return (IRR) The discount rate that makes the NPV of an investment zero. (page 250)

International Fisher Effect (IFE) The theory that real interest rates are equal across countries. (page 660)

Intrinsic Value The lower bound of an option's value, or what the option would be worth if it were about to expire. (page 761)

Inventory Loan A secured short-term loan to purchase inventory. (page 568)

Inventory Period The time it takes to acquire and sell inventory. (page 549)

Invoice Bill for goods or services provided by the seller to the purchaser. (page 609)

Joint Venture Typically an agreement between firms to create a separate, co-owned entity established to pursue a joint goal. (page 699)

Just-in-Time Inventory (JIT) Design for inventory in which parts, raw materials, and other work-in-process is delivered exactly as needed for production. Goal is to minimize inventory. (page 631)

Lessee The user of an asset in a leasing agreement. Lessee makes payments to lessor. (page 677)

Lessor The owner of an asset in a leasing agreement. Lessor receives payments from the lessee. (page 677)

Letter of Credit A written statement by a bank that money will be paid, provided conditions specified in the letter are met. (page 566)

Leveraged Buyouts (LBOs) Going-private transactions in which a large percentage of the money used to buy the stock is borrowed. Often, incumbent management is involved. (page 699)

Leveraged Lease A financial lease where the lessor borrows a substantial fraction of the cost of the leased asset. (page 680)

Liquidation Termination of the firm as a going concern. (page 503)

Liquidity Premium The portion of a nominal interest rate or bond yield that represents compensation for lack of liquidity. (page 201)

Lockboxes Special post office boxes set up to intercept and speed up accounts receivable payments. (page 588)

Lockup Agreement The part of the underwriting contract that specifies how long insiders must wait after an IPO before they can sell stock. (page 455)

London Interbank Offer Rate (LIBOR) The rate most international banks charge one another for overnight Eurodollar loans. (page 650)

Loss Carry-forward, Carry-back Using a year's capital losses to offset capital gains in past or future years. (page 42)

Managerial Options Opportunities that managers can exploit if certain things happen in the future. (page 327)

M&M Proposition I The value of the firm is independent of its capital structure. (page 486)

M&M Proposition II A firm's cost of equity capital is a positive linear function of its capital structure. (page 487)

Marginal or Incremental Cost The change in costs that occurs when there is a small change in output. (page 316)

Marginal Tax Rate Amount of tax payable on the next dollar earned. (page 40)

Market Risk Premium Slope of the SML, the difference between the expected return on a market portfolio and the risk-free rate. (page 397)

Maturity Date Specified date at which the principal amount of a bond is paid. (page 178)

Maturity Factoring Short-term financing in which the factor purchases all of a firm's receivables and forwards the proceeds to the seller as soon as they are collected. (page 567)

Merger The complete absorption of one company by another, where the acquiring firm retains its identity and the acquired firm ceases to exist as a separate entity. (page 697)

Money Markets Financial markets where short-term debt securities are bought and sold. (page 19)

Multiple Discriminant Analysis (MDA) Statistical technique for distinguishing between two samples on the basis of their observed characteristics. (page 620)

Multiple Rates of Return One potential problem in using the IRR method if more than one discount rate makes the NPV of an investment zero. (page 254)

Mutually Exclusive Investment Decisions One potential problem in using the IRR method if the acceptance of one project excludes that of another. (page 255)

Net Acquisitions Total installed cost of capital acquisitions minus adjusted cost of any disposals within an asset pool. (page 45)

Net Advantage to Leasing (NAL) The NPV of the decision to lease an asset instead of buying it. (page 685)

Net Present Value (NPV) The difference between an investment's market value and its cost. (page 241)

Net Present Value Profile A graphical representation of the relationship between an investment's NPVs and various discount rates. (page 251)

Nominal Rates Interest rates or rates of return that have not been adjusted for inflation. (page 196)

Non-cash Items Expenses charged against revenues that do not directly affect cash flow, such as depreciation. (page 33)

Normal Distribution A symmetric, bell-shaped frequency distribution that can be defined by its mean and standard deviation. (page 351)

Note Unsecured debt, usually with a maturity under 10 years. (page 187)

Note Issuance Facility (NIF) Large borrowers issue notes up to one year in maturity in the Euromarket. Banks underwrite or sell notes. (page 665)

Operating Cash Flow Cash generated from a firm's normal business activities. (page 34)

Operating Cycle The time period between the acquisition of inventory and when cash is collected from receivables. (page 549)

Operating Lease Usually a shorter-term lease where the lessor is responsible for insurance, taxes, and upkeep. Often cancellable on short notice. (page 679)

Operating Leverage The degree to which a firm or project relies on fixed costs. (page 323)

Operating Loan Loan negotiated with banks for day-to-day operations. (page 564)

Opportunity Cost The most valuable alternative that is given up if a particular investment is undertaken. (page 270)

Option A contract that gives its owner the right to buy or sell some asset at a fixed price on or before a given date. (page 755)

Option Contract An agreement that gives the owner the right, but not the obligation, to buy or sell a specific asset at a specific price for a set period of time. (page 745)

Option Delta The change in the stock price divided by the change in the call price. (page 766)

Oversubscription Privilege Allows shareholders to purchase unsubscribed shares in a rights offering at the subscription price. (page 469)

Partnership A business formed by two or more co-owners. (page 5)

Payback Period The amount of time required for an investment to generate cash flows to recover its initial cost. (page 245)

Payoff Profile A plot showing the gains and losses that will occur on a contract as the result of unexpected price changes. (page 737)

Percentage of Sales Approach Financial planning method in which accounts are projected depending on a firm's predicted sales level. (page 92)

Perpetuity An annuity in which the cash flows continue forever. (page 154)

Planning Horizon The long-range time period the financial planning process focuses on, usually the next two to five years. (page 88)

Plowback Ratio Retained earnings divided by net income. Also called the retention ratio. (pages 93, 416)

Poison Pill A financial device designed to make unfriendly takeover attempts unappealing, if not impossible. (page 713)

Political Risk Risk related to changes in value that arise because of political actions. (page 670)

Portfolio Group of assets such as stocks and bonds held by an investor. (page 373)

Portfolio Weight Percentage of a portfolio's total value in a particular asset. (page 373)

Precautionary Motive The need to hold cash as a safety margin to act as a financial reserve. (page 580)

Preferred Stock Stock with dividend priority over common stock, normally with a fixed dividend rate, often without voting rights. (page 226)

Present Value (PV) The current value of future cash flows discounted at the appropriate discount rate. (page 127)

Principle of Diversification Principle stating that spreading an investment across a number of assets eliminates some, but not all, of the risk. (page 386)

Private Placements Loans, usually long term in nature, provided directly by a limited number of investors. (page 473)

Profitability Index (PI) The present value of an investment's future cash flows divided by its initial cost. Also benefit/cost ratio. (page 258)

Pro Forma Financial Statements Financial statements projecting future years' operations. (page 272)

Prospectus Legal document describing details of the issuing corporation and the proposed offering to potential investors. (page 451)

Protective Covenant Part of the indenture limiting certain transactions that can be taken during the term of the loan, usually to protect the lender's interest. (page 188)

Proxy Grant of authority by shareholder allowing for another individual to vote his or her shares. (page 237)

Proxy Contests Attempts to gain control of a firm by soliciting a sufficient number of shareholder votes to replace existing management. (page 699)

Public Issue Creation and sale of securities on public markets. (page 450)

Purchasing Power Parity (PPP) The idea that the exchange rate adjusts to keep purchasing power constant among currencies. (page 654)

Pure Play Approach Use of a WACC that is unique to a particular project. (page 426)

Put Option An option that gives the owner the right, but not the obligation, to sell an asset. (page 746)

Put Option The right to sell an asset at a fixed price during a particular period of time. The opposite of a call option. (page 756)

Real Rates Interest rates or rates of return that have been adjusted for inflation. (page 196)

Real Option An option with payoffs in real goods. (page 781)

Realized Capital Gains The increase in value of an investment, when converted to cash. (page 41)

Recaptured Depreciation The taxable difference between adjusted cost of disposal and UCC when UCC is smaller. (page 45)

Red Herring Preliminary prospectus distributed to prospective investors in a new issue of securities. (page 451)

Registered Form Registrar of company records ownership of each bond; payment is made directly to the owner of record. (page 187)

Regular Cash Dividend Cash payment made by a firm to its owners in the normal course of business, usually made four times a year. (page 516)

Regular Underwriting The purchase of securities from the issuing company by an investment banker for resale to the public. (page 454)

Regulatory Dialectic The pressures financial institutions and regulatory bodies exert on each other. (page 23)

Reorganization Financial restructuring of a failing firm to attempt to continue operations as a going concern. (page 503)

Repurchase Another method used to pay out a firm's earnings to its owners, which provides more preferable tax treatment than dividends. (page 534)

Residual Dividend Approach Policy where a firm pays dividends only after meeting its investment needs while maintaining a desired debt-to-equity ratio. (page 529)

Retention Ratio Retained earnings divided by net income. Also called the plowback ratio. (pages 93, 416)

Retractable Bond Bond that may be sold back (put) to the issuer at a prespecified price before maturity. (page 193)

Return on Equity (ROE) Net income after interest and taxes divided by average common shareholders' equity. (page 416)

Reverse Split Procedure where a firm's number of shares outstanding is reduced. (page 538)

Rights Offer A public issue of securities in which securities are first offered to existing shareholders. Also called a rights offering. (page 452)

Risk Premium The excess return required from an investment in a risky asset over a risk-free investment. (page 347)

Risk Profile A plot showing how the value of the firm is affected by changes in prices or rates. (page 733)

Sale and Leaseback A financial lease in which the lessee sells an asset to the lessor and then leases it back. (page 680)

Same Day Value Bank makes proceeds of cheques deposited available the same day before cheques clear. (page 589)

Scenario Analysis The determination of what happens to NPV estimates when we ask what-if questions. (page 311)

Seasoned Equity Offering (SEO) A new equity issue of securities by a company that has previously issued securities to the public. (page 452)

Seasoned New Issue A new issue of securities by a firm that has already issued securities in the past. (page 452)

Security Market Line (SML) Positively sloped straight line displaying the relationship between expected return and beta. (page 396)

Sensitivity Analysis Investigation of what happens to NPV when only one variable is changed. (page 312)

Shareholder Rights Plan Provisions allowing existing shareholders to purchase stock at some fixed price should an outside takeover bid take place, discouraging hostile takeover attempts. (page 713)

Shortage Costs Costs that fall with increases in the level of investment in current assets. (page 554)

Simple Interest Interest earned only on the original principal amount invested. (page 121)

Simulation Analysis A combination of scenario and sensitivity analyses. (page 313)

Sinking Fund Account managed by the bond trustee for early bond redemption. (page 188)

Smart Card Much like an automated teller machine card; one use is within corporations to control access to information by employees. (page 587)

Soft Rationing The situation that occurs when units in a business are allocated a certain amount of financing for capital budgeting. (page 330)

Sole Proprietorship A business owned by a single individual. (page 5)

Sources of Cash A firm's activities that generate cash. (page 57)

Speculative Motive The need to hold cash to take advantage of additional investment opportunities, such as bargain purchases. (page 580)

Spin-Off The distribution of shares in a subsidiary to existing parent company shareholders. (page 719)

Split-Up The splitting up of a company into two or more companies. (page 719)

Spot Exchange Rate The exchange rate on a spot trade. (page 653)

Spot Trade An agreement to trade currencies based on the exchange rate today for settlement in two days. (page 653)

Spread Compensation to the underwriter, determined by the difference between the underwriter's buying price and offering price. (page 453)

Spread The gap between the interest rate a bank pays on deposits and the rate it charges on loans. (page 619)

Stakeholder Anyone who potentially has a claim on a firm. (page 13)

Stand-Alone Principle Evaluation of a project based on the project's incremental cash flows. (page 269)

Standard Deviation The positive square root of the variance. (page 348)

Standby Fee Amount paid to underwriter participating in standby underwriting agreement. (page 469)

Standby Underwriting Agreement where the underwriter agrees to purchase the unsubscribed portion of the issue. (page 469)

Stated or Quoted Interest Rate The interest rate expressed in terms of the interest payment made each period. Also, quoted interest rate. (page 158)

Statement of Cash Flows A firm's financial statement that summarizes its sources and uses of cash over a specified period. (page 58)

Static Theory of Capital Structure Theory that a firm borrows up to the point where the tax benefit from an extra dollar in debt is exactly equal to the cost that comes from the increased probability of financial distress. (page 496)

Stock Dividend Payment made by a firm to its owners in the form of stock, diluting the value of each share outstanding. (page 536)

Stock Exchange Bid Corporate takeover bid communicated to the shareholders through a stock exchange. (page 698)

Stock Split An increase in a firm's shares outstanding without any change in owner's equity. (page 536)

Straight Bond Value The value of a convertible bond if it could not be converted into common stock. (page 776)

Straight Voting Procedure where a shareholder may cast all votes for each member of the board of directors. (page 237)

Strategic Alliance Agreement between firms to co-operate in pursuit of a joint goal. (page 699)

Strategic Options Options for future, related business products or strategies. (page 329)

Striking Price The fixed price in the option contract at which the holder can buy or sell the underlying asset. Also the exercise price or strike price. (page 756)

Stripped Bond/Zero-Coupon Bond A bond that makes no coupon payments, thus initially priced at a deep discount. (page 192)

Stripped Common Shares Common stock on which dividends and capital gains are repackaged and sold separately. (page 520)

Sunk Cost A cost that has already been incurred and cannot be removed and therefore should not be considered in an investment decision. (page 269)

Sustainable Growth Rate The growth rate a firm can maintain given its debt capacity, ROE, and retention ratio. (page 100)

Swap Contract An agreement by two parties to exchange, or swap, specified cash flows at specified intervals in the future. (page 743)

Swaps Agreements to exchange two securities or currencies. (page 650)

Sweeteners or Equity Kickers A feature included in the terms of a new issue of debt or preferred shares to make the issue more attractive to initial investors. (page 772)

Syndicate A group of underwriters formed to reduce the risk and help to sell an issue. (page 453)

Syndicated Loans Loans made by a group of banks or other institutions. (page 473)

Synergy The positive incremental net gain associated with the combination of two firms through a merger or acquisition. (page 702)

Systematic Risk A risk that influences a large number of assets. Also called market risk. (page 383)

Systematic Risk Principle Principle stating that the expected return on a risky asset depends only on that asset's systematic risk. (page 388)

Target Cash Balance A firm's desired cash level as determined by the trade-off between carrying costs and shortage costs. (page 581)

Target Payout Ratio A firm's long-term desired dividend-to-earnings ratio. (page 533)

Tax-Oriented Lease A financial lease in which the lessor is the owner for tax purposes. Also called a true lease or a tax lease. (page 679)

Tender Offer A public offer by one firm to directly buy the shares from another firm. (page 697)

Term Loans Direct business loans of, typically, one to five years. (page 473)

Term Structure of Interest Rates The relationship between nominal interest rates on default-free, pure discount securities and time to maturity; that is, the pure time value of money. (page 198)

Terminal Loss The difference between UCC and adjusted cost of disposal when the UCC is greater. (page 45)

Terms of Sale Conditions on which a firm sells its goods and services for cash or credit. (page 607)

Trading Range Price range between highest and lowest prices at which a stock is traded. (page 537)

Transactions Exposure Short-run financial risk arising from the need to buy or sell at uncertain prices or rates in the near future. (page 735)

Transaction Motive The need to hold cash to satisfy normal disbursement and collection activities associated with a firm's ongoing operations. (page 580)

Trust Receipt An instrument acknowledging that the borrower holds certain goods in trust for the lender. (page 568)

Unbiased Forward Rates (UFR) The condition stating that the current forward rate is an unbiased predictor of the future exchange rate. (page 659)

Uncovered Interest Parity (UIP) The condition stating that the expected percentage change in the exchange rate is equal to the difference in interest rates. (page 660)

Unlevered Cost of Capital The cost of capital of a firm that has no debt. (page 491)

Unsystematic Risk A risk that affects at most a small number of assets. Also called unique or asset-specific risks. (page 383)

Uses of Cash A firm's activities in which cash is spent. Also applications of cash. (page 57)

Value at Risk (VaR) Statistical measure of maximum loss used by banks and other financial institutions to manage risk exposures. (page 353)

Variable Costs Costs that change when the quantity of output changes. (page 315)

Variance The average squared deviation between the actual return and the average return. (page 348)

Venture Capital Financing for new, often high-risk ventures. (page 449)

Warrant A security that gives the holder the right to purchase shares of stock at a fixed price over a given period of time. (page 772)

Weighted Average Cost of Capital (WACC) The weighted average of the costs of debt and equity. (page 420)

Working Capital Management Planning and managing the firm's current assets and liabilities. (page 5)

Yield to Maturity (YTM) The market interest rate that equates a bond's present value of interest payments and principal repayment with its price. (page 178)

Zero-Balance Account A chequing account in which a zero balance is maintained by transfers of funds from a master account in an amount only large enough to cover cheques presented. (page 591)

Zero Coupon Bond A bond that makes no coupon payments, thus initially priced at a deep discount. Also Stripped Bond. (page 192)

Appendix A Mathematical Tables

Table A.1: Future value of $1 at the end of t periods = $1(1 + r)^t$

INTEREST RATE

Period	1%	2%	3%	4%	5%	6%	7%	8%	9%
1	1.0100	1.0200	1.0300	1.0400	1.0500	1.0600	1.0700	1.0800	1.0900
2	1.0201	1.0404	1.0609	1.0816	1.1025	1.1236	1.1449	1.1664	1.1881
3	1.0303	1.0612	1.0927	1.1249	1.1576	1.1910	1.2250	1.2597	1.2950
4	1.0406	1.0824	1.1255	1.1699	1.2155	1.2625	1.3108	1.3605	1.4116
5	1.0510	1.1041	1.1593	1.2167	1.2763	1.3382	1.4026	1.4693	1.5386
6	1.0615	1.1262	1.1941	1.2653	1.3401	1.4185	1.5007	1.5869	1.6771
7	1.0721	1.1487	1.2299	1.3159	1.4071	1.5036	1.6058	1.7138	1.8280
8	1.0829	1.1717	1.2668	1.3686	1.4775	1.5938	1.7182	1.8509	1.9926
9	1.0937	1.1951	1.3048	1.4233	1.5513	1.6895	1.8385	1.9990	2.1719
10	1.1046	1.2190	1.3439	1.4802	1.6289	1.7908	1.9672	2.1589	2.3674
11	1.1157	1.2434	1.3842	1.5395	1.7103	1.8983	2.1049	2.3316	2.5804
12	1.1268	1.2682	1.4258	1.6010	1.7959	2.0122	2.2522	2.5182	2.8127
13	1.1381	1.2936	1.4685	1.6651	1.8856	2.1329	2.4098	2.7196	3.0658
14	1.1495	1.3195	1.5126	1.7317	1.9799	2.2609	2.5785	2.9372	3.3417
15	1.1610	1.3459	1.5580	1.8009	2.0789	2.3966	2.7590	3.1722	3.6425
16	1.1726	1.3728	1.6047	1.8730	2.1829	2.5404	2.9522	3.4259	3.9703
17	1.1843	1.4002	1.6528	1.9479	2.2920	2.6928	3.1588	3.7000	4.3276
18	1.1961	1.4282	1.7024	2.0258	2.4066	2.8543	3.3799	3.9960	4.7171
19	1.2081	1.4568	1.7535	2.1068	2.5270	3.0256	3.6165	4.3157	5.1417
20	1.2202	1.4859	1.8061	2.1911	2.6533	3.2071	3.8697	4.6610	5.6044
21	1.2324	1.5157	1.8603	2.2788	2.7860	3.3996	4.1406	5.0338	6.1088
22	1.2447	1.5460	1.9161	2.3699	2.9253	3.6035	4.4304	5.4365	6.6586
23	1.2572	1.5769	1.9736	2.4647	3.0715	3.8197	4.7405	5.8715	7.2579
24	1.2697	1.6084	2.0328	2.5633	3.2251	4.0489	5.0724	6.3412	7.9111
25	1.2824	1.6406	2.0938	2.6658	3.3864	4.2919	5.4274	6.8485	8.6231
30	1.3478	1.8114	2.4273	3.2434	4.3219	5.7435	7.6123	10.063	13.268
40	1.4889	2.2080	3.2620	4.8010	7.0400	10.286	14.974	21.725	31.409
50	1.6446	2.6916	4.3839	7.1067	11.467	18.420	29.457	46.902	74.358
60	1.8167	3.2810	5.8916	10.520	18.679	32.988	57.946	101.26	176.03

Continued on next page

10%	12%	14%	15%	16%	18%	20%	24%	28%	32%	36%
1.1000	1.1200	1.1400	1.1500	1.1600	1.1800	1.2000	1.2400	1.2800	1.3200	1.3600
1.2100	1.2544	1.2996	1.3225	1.3456	1.3924	1.4400	1.5376	1.6384	1.7424	1.8496
1.3310	1.4049	1.4815	1.5209	1.5609	1.6430	1.7280	1.9066	2.0972	2.3000	2.5155
1.4641	1.5735	1.6890	1.7490	1.8106	1.9388	2.0736	2.3642	2.6844	3.0360	3.4210
1.6105	1.7623	1.9254	2.0114	2.1003	2.2878	2.4883	2.9316	3.4360	4.0075	4.6526
1.7716	1.9738	2.1950	2.3131	2.4364	2.6996	2.9860	3.6352	4.3980	5.2899	6.3275
1.9487	2.2107	2.5023	2.6600	2.8262	3.1855	3.5832	4.5077	5.6295	6.9826	8.6054
2.1436	2.4760	2.8526	3.0590	3.2784	3.7589	4.2998	5.5895	7.2058	9.2170	11.703
2.3579	2.7731	3.2519	3.5179	3.8030	4.4355	5.1598	6.9310	9.2234	12.166	15.917
2.5937	3.1058	3.7072	4.0456	4.4114	5.2338	6.1917	8.5944	11.806	16.060	21.647
2.8531	3.4785	4.2262	4.6524	5.1173	6.1759	7.4301	10.657	15.112	21.199	29.439
3.1384	3.8960	4.8179	5.3503	5.9360	7.2876	8.9161	13.215	19.343	27.983	40.037
3.4523	4.3635	5.4924	6.1528	6.8858	8.5994	10.699	16.386	24.759	36.937	54.451
3.7975	4.8871	6.2613	7.0757	7.9875	10.147	12.839	20.319	31.691	48.757	74.053
4.1772	5.4736	7.1379	8.1371	9.2655	11.974	15.407	25.196	40.565	64.359	100.71
4.5950	6.1304	8.1372	9.3576	10.748	14.129	18.488	31.243	51.923	84.954	136.97
5.0545	6.8660	9.2765	10.761	12.468	16.672	22.186	38.741	66.461	112.14	186.28
5.5599	7.6900	10.575	12.375	14.463	19.673	26.623	48.039	85.071	148.02	253.34
6.1159	8.6128	12.056	14.232	16.777	23.214	31.948	59.568	108.89	195.39	344.54
6.7275	9.6463	13.743	16.367	19.461	27.393	38.338	73.864	139.38	257.92	468.57
7.4002	10.804	15.668	18.822	22.574	32.324	46.005	91.592	178.41	340.45	637.26
8.1403	12.100	17.861	21.645	26.186	38.142	55.206	113.57	228.36	449.39	866.67
8.9543	13.552	20.362	24.891	30.376	45.008	66.247	140.83	292.30	593.20	1178.7
9.8497	15.179	23.212	28.625	35.236	53.109	79.497	174.63	374.14	783.02	1603.0
10.835	17.000	26.462	32.919	40.874	62.669	95.396	216.54	478.90	1033.6	2180.1
17.449	29.960	50.950	66.212	85.850	143.37	237.38	634.82	1645.5	4142.1	10143.
45.259	93.051	188.88	267.86	378.72	750.38	1469.8	5455.9	19427.	66521.	*
117.39	289.00	700.23	1083.7	1670.7	3927.4	9100.4	46890.	*	*	*
304.48	897.60	2595.9	4384.0	7370.2	20555.	56348.	*	*	*	*

*The factor is greater than 99,999.

Table A.2: Present value of $1 to be received after t periods = $1/(1 + r)^t$

INTEREST RATE

Period	1%	2%	3%	4%	5%	6%	7%	8%	9%
1	0.9901	0.9804	0.9709	0.9615	0.9524	0.9434	0.9346	0.9259	0.9174
2	0.9803	0.9612	0.9426	0.9246	0.9070	0.8900	0.8734	0.8573	0.8417
3	0.9706	0.9423	0.9151	0.8890	0.8638	0.8396	0.8163	0.7938	0.7722
4	0.9610	0.9238	0.8885	0.8548	0.8227	0.7921	0.7629	0.7350	0.7084
5	0.9515	0.9057	0.8626	0.8219	0.7835	0.7473	0.7130	0.6806	0.6499
6	0.9420	0.8880	0.8375	0.7903	0.7462	0.7050	0.6663	0.6302	0.5963
7	0.9327	0.8706	0.8131	0.7599	0.7107	0.6651	0.6227	0.5835	0.5470
8	0.9235	0.8535	0.7894	0.7307	0.6768	0.6274	0.5820	0.5403	0.5019
9	0.9143	0.8368	0.7664	0.7026	0.6446	0.5919	0.5439	0.5002	0.4604
10	0.9053	0.8203	0.7441	0.6756	0.6139	0.5584	0.5083	0.4632	0.4224
11	0.8963	0.8043	0.7224	0.6496	0.5847	0.5268	0.4751	0.4289	0.3875
12	0.8874	0.7885	0.7014	0.6246	0.5568	0.4970	0.4440	0.3971	0.3555
13	0.8787	0.7730	0.6810	0.6006	0.5303	0.4688	0.4150	0.3677	0.3262
14	0.8700	0.7579	0.6611	0.5775	0.5051	0.4423	0.3878	0.3405	0.2992
15	0.8613	0.7430	0.6419	0.5553	0.4810	0.4173	0.3624	0.3152	0.2745
16	0.8528	0.7284	0.6232	0.5339	0.4581	0.3936	0.3387	0.2919	0.2519
17	0.8444	0.7142	0.6050	0.5134	0.4363	0.3714	0.3166	0.2703	0.2311
18	0.8360	0.7002	0.5874	0.4936	0.4155	0.3503	0.2959	0.2502	0.2120
19	0.8277	0.6864	0.5703	0.4746	0.3957	0.3305	0.2765	0.2317	0.1945
20	0.8195	0.6730	0.5537	0.4564	0.3769	0.3118	0.2584	0.2145	0.1784
21	0.8114	0.6598	0.5375	0.4388	0.3589	0.2942	0.2415	0.1987	0.1637
22	0.8034	0.6468	0.5219	0.4220	0.3418	0.2775	0.2257	0.1839	0.1502
23	0.7954	0.6342	0.5067	0.4057	0.3256	0.2618	0.2109	0.1703	0.1378
24	0.7876	0.6217	0.4919	0.3901	0.3101	0.2470	0.1971	0.1577	0.1264
25	0.7798	0.6095	0.4776	0.3751	0.2953	0.2330	0.1842	0.1460	0.1160
30	0.7419	0.5521	0.4120	0.3083	0.2314	0.1741	0.1314	0.0994	0.0754
40	0.6717	0.4529	0.3066	0.2083	0.1420	0.0972	0.0668	0.0460	0.0318
50	0.6080	0.3715	0.2281	0.1407	0.0872	0.0543	0.0339	0.0213	0.0134

Continued on next page

10%	12%	14%	15%	16%	18%	20%	24%	28%	32%	36%
0.9091	0.8929	0.8772	0.8696	0.8621	0.8475	0.8333	0.8065	0.7813	0.7576	0.7353
0.8264	0.7972	0.7695	0.7561	0.7432	0.7182	0.6944	0.6504	0.6104	0.5739	0.5407
0.7513	0.7118	0.6750	0.6575	0.6407	0.6086	0.5787	0.5245	0.4768	0.4348	0.3975
0.6830	0.6355	0.5921	0.5718	0.5523	0.5158	0.4823	0.4230	0.3725	0.3294	0.2923
0.6209	0.5674	0.5194	0.4972	0.4761	0.4371	0.4019	0.3411	0.2910	0.2495	0.2149
0.5645	0.5066	0.4556	0.4323	0.4104	0.3704	0.3349	0.2751	0.2274	0.1890	0.1580
0.5132	0.4523	0.3996	0.3759	0.3538	0.3139	0.2791	0.2218	0.1776	0.1432	0.1162
0.4665	0.4039	0.3506	0.3269	0.3050	0.2660	0.2326	0.1789	0.1388	0.1085	0.0854
0.4241	0.3606	0.3075	0.2843	0.2630	0.2255	0.1938	0.1443	0.1084	0.0822	0.0628
0.3855	0.3220	0.2697	0.2472	0.2267	0.1911	0.1615	0.1164	0.0847	0.0623	0.0462
0.3505	0.2875	0.2366	0.2149	0.1954	0.1619	0.1346	0.0938	0.0662	0.0472	0.0340
0.3186	0.2567	0.2076	0.1869	0.1685	0.1372	0.1122	0.0757	0.0517	0.0357	0.0250
0.2897	0.2292	0.1821	0.1625	0.1452	0.1163	0.0935	0.0610	0.0404	0.0271	0.0184
0.2633	0.2046	0.1597	0.1413	0.1252	0.0985	0.0779	0.0492	0.0316	0.0205	0.0135
0.2394	0.1827	0.1401	0.1229	0.1079	0.0835	0.0649	0.0397	0.0247	0.0155	0.0099
0.2176	0.1631	0.1229	0.1069	0.0930	0.0708	0.0541	0.0320	0.0193	0.0118	0.0073
0.1978	0.1456	0.1078	0.0929	0.0802	0.0600	0.0451	0.0258	0.0150	0.0089	0.0054
0.1799	0.1300	0.0946	0.0808	0.0691	0.0508	0.0376	0.0208	0.0118	0.0068	0.0039
0.1635	0.1161	0.0829	0.0703	0.0596	0.0431	0.0313	0.0168	0.0092	0.0051	0.0029
0.1486	0.1037	0.0728	0.0611	0.0514	0.0365	0.0261	0.0135	0.0072	0.0039	0.0021
0.1351	0.0926	0.0638	0.0531	0.0443	0.0309	0.0217	0.0109	0.0056	0.0029	0.0016
0.1228	0.0826	0.0560	0.0462	0.0382	0.0262	0.0181	0.0088	0.0044	0.0022	0.0012
0.1117	0.0738	0.0491	0.0402	0.0329	0.0222	0.0151	0.0071	0.0034	0.0017	0.0008
0.1015	0.0659	0.0431	0.0349	0.0284	0.0188	0.0126	0.0057	0.0027	0.0013	0.0006
0.0923	0.0588	0.0378	0.0304	0.0245	0.0160	0.0105	0.0046	0.0021	0.0010	0.0005
0.0573	0.0334	0.0196	0.0151	0.0116	0.0070	0.0042	0.0016	0.0006	0.0002	0.0001
0.0221	0.0107	0.0053	0.0037	0.0026	0.0013	0.0007	0.0002	0.0001	*	*
0.0085	0.0035	0.0014	0.0009	0.0006	0.0003	0.0001	*	*	*	*

*The factor is zero to four decimal places.

Table A.3: Present value of an annuity of $1 per period for t periods = $[1 - 1/(1 + r)^t]/r$

INTEREST RATE

Number of Periods	1%	2%	3%	4%	5%	6%	7%	8%	9%
1	0.9901	0.9804	0.9709	0.9615	0.9524	0.9434	0.9346	0.9259	0.9174
2	1.9704	1.9416	1.9135	1.8861	1.8594	1.8334	1.8080	1.7833	1.7591
3	2.9410	2.8839	2.8286	2.7751	2.7232	2.6730	2.6243	2.5771	2.5313
4	3.9020	3.8077	3.7171	3.6299	3.5460	3.4651	3.3872	3.3121	3.2397
5	4.8534	4.7135	4.5797	4.4518	4.3295	4.2124	4.1002	3.9927	3.8897
6	5.7955	5.6014	5.4172	5.2421	5.0757	4.9173	4.7665	4.6229	4.4859
7	6.7282	6.4720	6.2303	6.0021	5.7864	5.5824	5.3893	5.2064	5.0330
8	7.6517	7.3255	7.0197	6.7327	6.4632	6.2098	5.9713	5.7466	5.5348
9	8.5660	8.1622	7.7861	7.4353	7.1078	6.8017	6.5152	6.2469	5.9952
10	9.4713	8.9826	8.5302	8.1109	7.7217	7.3601	7.0236	6.7101	6.4177
11	10.3676	9.7868	9.2526	8.7605	8.3064	7.8869	7.4987	7.1390	6.8052
12	11.2551	10.5753	9.9540	9.3851	8.8633	8.3838	7.9427	7.5361	7.1607
13	12.1337	11.3484	10.6350	9.9856	9.3936	8.8527	8.3577	7.9038	7.4869
14	13.0037	12.1062	11.2961	10.5631	9.8986	9.2950	8.7455	8.2442	7.7862
15	13.8651	12.8493	11.9379	11.1184	10.3797	9.7122	9.1079	8.5595	8.0607
16	14.7179	13.5777	12.5611	11.6523	10.8378	10.1059	9.4466	8.8514	8.3126
17	15.5623	14.2919	13.1661	12.1657	11.2741	10.4773	9.7632	9.1216	8.5436
18	16.3983	14.9920	13.7535	12.6593	11.6896	10.8276	10.0591	9.3719	8.7556
19	17.2260	15.6785	14.3238	13.1339	12.0853	11.1581	10.3356	9.6036	8.9501
20	18.0456	16.3514	14.8775	13.5903	12.4622	11.4699	10.5940	9.8181	9.1285
21	18.8570	17.0112	15.4150	14.0292	12.8212	11.7641	10.8355	10.0168	9.2922
22	19.6604	17.6580	15.9369	14.4511	13.1630	12.0416	11.0612	10.2007	9.4424
23	20.4558	18.2922	16.4436	14.8568	13.4886	12.3034	11.2722	10.3741	9.5802
24	21.2434	18.9139	16.9355	15.2470	13.7986	12.5504	11.4693	10.5288	9.7066
25	22.0232	19.5235	17.4131	15.6221	14.0939	12.7834	11.6536	10.6748	9.8226
30	25.8077	22.3965	19.6004	17.2920	15.3725	13.7648	12.4090	11.2578	10.2737
40	32.8347	27.3555	23.1148	19.7928	17.1591	15.0463	13.3317	11.9246	10.7574
50	39.1961	31.4236	25.7298	21.4822	18.2559	15.7619	13.8007	12.2335	10.9617

Continued on next page

10%	12%	14%	15%	16%	18%	20%	24%	28%	32%	36%
0.9091	0.8929	0.8772	0.8696	0.8621	0.8475	0.8333	0.8065	0.7813	0.7576	0.7353
1.7355	1.6901	1.6467	1.6257	1.6052	1.5656	1.5278	1.4568	1.3916	1.3315	1.2760
2.4869	2.4018	2.3216	2.2832	2.2459	2.1743	2.1065	1.9813	1.8684	1.7663	1.6735
3.1699	3.0373	2.9137	2.8550	2.7982	2.6901	2.5887	2.4043	2.2410	2.0957	1.9658
3.7908	3.6048	3.4331	3.3522	3.2743	3.1272	2.9906	2.7454	2.5320	2.3452	2.1807
4.3553	4.1114	3.8887	3.7845	3.6847	3.4976	3.3255	3.0205	2.7594	2.5342	2.3388
4.8684	4.5638	4.2883	4.1604	4.0386	3.8115	3.6046	3.2423	2.9370	2.6775	2.4550
5.3349	4.9676	4.6389	4.4873	4.3436	4.0776	3.8372	3.4212	3.0758	2.7860	2.5404
5.7590	5.3282	4.9464	4.7716	4.6065	4.3030	4.0310	3.5655	3.1842	2.8681	2.6033
6.1446	5.6502	5.2161	5.0188	4.8332	4.4941	4.1925	3.6819	3.2689	2.9304	2.6495
6.4951	5.9377	5.4527	5.2337	5.0286	4.6560	4.3271	3.7757	3.3351	2.9776	2.6834
6.8137	6.1944	5.6603	5.4206	5.1971	4.7932	4.4392	3.8514	3.3868	3.0133	2.7084
7.1034	6.4235	5.8424	5.5831	5.3423	4.9095	4.5327	3.9124	3.4272	3.0404	2.7268
7.3667	6.6282	6.0021	5.7245	5.4675	5.0081	4.6106	3.9616	3.4587	3.0609	2.7403
7.6061	6.8109	6.1422	5.8474	5.5755	5.0916	4.6755	4.0013	3.4834	3.0764	2.7502
7.8237	6.9740	6.2651	5.9542	5.6685	5.1624	4.7296	4.0333	3.5026	3.0882	2.7575
8.0216	7.1196	6.3729	6.0472	5.7487	5.2223	4.7746	4.0591	3.5177	3.0971	2.7629
8.2014	7.2497	6.4674	6.1280	5.8178	5.2732	4.8122	4.0799	3.5294	3.1039	2.7668
8.3649	7.3658	6.5504	6.1982	5.8775	5.3162	4.8435	4.0967	3.5386	3.1090	2.7697
8.5136	7.4694	6.6231	6.2593	5.9288	5.3527	4.8696	4.1103	3.5458	3.1129	2.7718
8.6487	7.5620	6.6870	6.3125	5.9731	5.3837	4.8913	4.1212	3.5514	3.1158	2.7734
8.7715	7.6446	6.7429	6.3587	6.0113	5.4099	4.9094	4.1300	3.5558	3.1180	2.7746
8.8832	7.7184	6.7921	6.3988	6.0442	5.4321	4.9245	4.1371	3.5592	3.1197	2.7754
8.9847	7.7843	6.8351	6.4338	6.0726	5.4509	4.9371	4.1428	3.5619	3.1210	2.7760
9.0770	7.8431	6.8729	6.4641	6.0971	5.4669	4.9476	4.1474	3.5640	3.1220	2.7765
9.4269	8.0552	7.0027	6.5660	6.1772	5.5168	4.9789	4.1601	3.5693	3.1242	2.7775
9.7791	8.2438	7.1050	6.6418	6.2335	5.5482	4.9966	4.1659	3.5712	3.1250	2.7778
9.9148	8.3045	7.1327	6.6605	6.2463	5.5541	4.9995	4.1666	3.5714	3.1250	2.7778

Table A.4: Future value of an annuity of $1 per period for t periods $= [(1 + r)^t - 1]/r$

INTEREST RATE

Number of Periods	1%	2%	3%	4%	5%	6%	7%	8%	9%
1	1.0000	1.0000	1.0000	1.0000	1.0000	1.0000	1.0000	1.0000	1.0000
2	2.0100	2.0200	2.0300	2.0400	2.0500	2.0600	2.0700	2.0800	2.0900
3	3.0301	3.0604	3.0909	3.1216	3.1525	3.1836	3.2149	3.2464	3.2781
4	4.0604	4.1216	4.1836	4.2465	4.3101	4.3746	4.4399	4.5061	4.5731
5	5.1010	5.2040	5.3091	5.4163	5.5256	5.6371	5.7507	5.8666	5.9847
6	6.1520	6.3081	6.4684	6.6330	6.8019	6.9753	7.1533	7.3359	7.5233
7	7.2135	7.4343	7.6625	7.8983	8.1420	8.3938	8.6540	8.9228	9.2004
8	8.2857	8.5830	8.8932	9.2142	9.5491	9.8975	10.260	10.637	11.028
9	9.3685	9.7546	10.159	10.583	11.027	11.491	11.978	12.488	13.021
10	10.462	10.950	11.464	12.006	12.578	13.181	13.816	14.487	15.193
11	11.567	12.169	12.808	13.486	14.207	14.972	15.784	16.645	17.560
12	12.683	13.412	14.192	15.026	15.917	16.870	17.888	18.977	20.141
13	13.809	14.680	15.618	16.627	17.713	18.882	20.141	21.495	22.953
14	14.947	15.974	17.086	18.292	19.599	21.015	22.550	24.215	26.019
15	16.097	17.293	18.599	20.024	21.579	23.276	25.129	27.152	29.361
16	17.258	18.639	20.157	21.825	23.657	25.673	27.888	30.324	33.003
17	18.430	20.012	21.762	23.698	25.840	28.213	30.840	33.750	36.974
18	19.615	21.412	23.414	25.645	28.132	30.906	33.999	37.450	41.301
19	20.811	22.841	25.117	27.671	30.539	33.760	37.379	41.446	46.018
20	22.019	24.297	26.870	29.778	33.066	36.786	40.995	45.762	51.160
21	23.239	25.783	28.676	31.969	35.719	39.993	44.865	50.423	56.765
22	24.472	27.299	30.537	34.248	38.505	43.392	49.006	55.457	62.873
23	25.716	28.845	32.453	36.618	41.430	46.996	53.436	60.893	69.532
24	26.973	30.422	34.426	39.083	44.502	50.816	58.177	66.765	76.790
25	28.243	32.030	36.459	41.646	47.727	54.865	63.249	73.106	84.701
30	34.785	40.568	47.575	56.085	66.439	79.058	94.461	113.28	136.31
40	48.886	60.402	75.401	95.026	120.80	154.76	199.64	259.06	337.88
50	64.463	84.579	112.80	152.67	209.35	290.34	406.53	573.77	815.08
60	81.670	114.05	163.05	237.99	353.58	533.13	813.52	1253.2	1944.8

Continued on next page

10%	12%	14%	15%	16%	18%	20%	24%	28%	32%	36%
1.0000	1.0000	1.0000	1.0000	1.0000	1.0000	1.0000	1.0000	1.0000	1.0000	1.0000
2.1000	2.1200	2.1400	2.1500	2.1600	2.1800	2.2000	2.2400	2.2800	2.3200	2.3600
3.3100	3.3744	3.4396	3.4725	3.5056	3.5724	3.6400	3.7776	3.9184	4.0624	4.2096
4.6410	4.7793	4.9211	4.9934	5.0665	5.2154	5.3680	5.6842	6.0156	6.3624	6.7251
6.1051	6.3528	6.6101	6.7424	6.8771	7.1542	7.4416	8.0484	8.6999	9.3983	10.146
7.7156	8.1152	8.5355	8.7537	8.9775	9.4420	9.9299	10.980	12.136	13.406	14.799
9.4872	10.089	10.730	11.067	11.414	12.142	12.916	14.615	16.534	18.696	21.126
11.436	12.300	13.233	13.727	14.240	15.327	16.499	19.123	22.163	25.678	29.732
13.579	14.776	16.085	16.786	17.519	19.086	20.799	24.712	29.369	34.895	41.435
15.937	17.549	19.337	20.304	21.321	23.521	25.959	31.643	38.593	47.062	57.352
18.531	20.655	23.045	24.349	25.733	28.755	32.150	40.238	50.398	63.122	78.998
21.384	24.133	27.271	29.002	30.850	34.931	39.581	50.895	65.510	84.320	108.44
24.523	28.029	32.089	34.352	36.786	42.219	48.497	64.110	84.853	112.30	148.47
27.975	32.393	37.581	40.505	43.672	50.818	59.196	80.496	109.61	149.24	202.93
31.772	37.280	43.842	47.580	51.660	60.965	72.035	100.82	141.30	198.00	276.98
35.950	42.753	50.980	55.717	60.925	72.939	87.442	126.01	181.87	262.36	377.69
40.545	48.884	59.118	65.075	71.673	87.068	105.93	157.25	233.79	347.31	514.66
45.599	55.750	68.394	75.836	84.141	103.74	128.12	195.99	300.25	459.45	700.94
51.159	63.440	78.969	88.212	98.603	123.41	154.74	244.03	385.32	607.47	954.28
57.275	72.052	91.025	102.44	115.38	146.63	186.69	303.60	494.21	802.86	1298.8
64.002	81.699	104.77	118.81	134.84	174.02	225.03	377.46	633.59	1060.8	1767.4
71.403	92.503	120.44	137.63	157.41	206.34	271.03	469.06	812.00	1401.2	2404.7
79.543	104.60	138.30	159.28	183.60	244.49	326.24	582.63	1040.4	1850.6	3271.3
88.497	118.16	158.66	184.17	213.98	289.49	392.48	723.46	1332.7	2443.8	4450.0
98.347	133.33	181.87	212.79	249.21	342.60	471.98	898.09	1706.8	3226.8	6053.0
164.49	241.33	356.79	434.75	530.31	790.95	1181.9	2640.9	5873.2	12941.	28172.3
442.59	767.09	1342.0	1779.1	2360.8	4163.2	7343.9	22729.	69377.	*	*
1163.9	2400.0	4994.5	7217.7	10436.	21813.	45497.	*	*	*	*
3034.8	7471.6	18535.	29220.	46058.	*	*	*	*	*	*

*The factor is greater than 99,999.

Appendix B   Answers to Selected End-of-Chapter Problems

CHAPTER 2

2. Net Income = $126,100
4. EPS = $4.20
   DPS = $1.60
6. Total Taxes Payable = $50,778
8. Net Capital Spending = $1.425 million
10. Cash Flow to Creditors = $0.04 million
12. OCF = $400,000
14. Depreciation expense = $6,092
16. a. Shareholders' Equity = $800
    b. Shareholders' Equity = $(300)
18. a. NI = $(115,000)
    b. OCF = $100,000
20. a. NI = $30
    b. OCF = $2,380
    c. CF from assets = −$470
    d. CFC = $450
22. Amount distributed to income trust unitholders = $500,000
    Net after-tax receipt by investors = $280,000
26. Cash flow from assets = $206
    Cash flow to creditors = −$867
    Cash flow to stockholders = $1,073
28. Based on Ontario's dividend tax credit rate from text:
    After tax rate of return on dividends = 11.19%
    After tax rate of return on interest = 4.07%
    After tax rate of return on capital gains = 5.37%
30. Year 1: Beginning UCC = $50,000; CCA = $10,000;
    Ending UCC = $40,000
    Year 2: Beginning UCC = $90,000; CCA = $18,000;
    Ending UCC = $72,000
    Year 3: Beginning UCC = $72,000; CCA = $14,400;
    Ending UCC = $57,600
    Year 4: Beginning UCC = $57,600; CCA = $11,520;
    Ending UCC = $46,080
    Year 5: Beginning UCC = $46,080; CCA = $9,216;
    Ending UCC = $36,864
32. CCA for 2005 = $520,000
    CCA for 2006 = $951,000
34. a. $1,738.50
    b. Based on Ontario's dividend tax credit rate from text: $5,246.88
    c. $6,037.50
36. a. $20,245.23
    b. There are no tax consequences.

CHAPTER 3

2. Net income = $2.61 million; ROA = 7.05%; ROE = 10.88%
4. Inventory turnover = 6.55 times; Days' sales in inventory = 55.71 days;
   Average inventory period = 55.71 days
6. EPS = $2.61; DPS = $0.89; BVPS = $36.11; Market-to-book ratio = 2.16 times; PE ratio = 29.87 times
8. Debt-equity ratio = 0.24
10. 82.19 days
12. Equity multiplier = 2.40; ROE = 20.88%; Net income = $108,576
18. $94.80
20. Net fixed assets = $6,178.06
22. ROE Firm A = ROE Firm B = 50%
24. $2,142,000

28. 160 days
30. PE = 21.36 times; DPS = $1.60; Market-to-book ratio = 8.29 times

CHAPTER 4

2. EFN = −$1,035
4. EFN = $16,865.52
6. Internal growth rate = 5.23%
8. Maximum increase in sales = $7,469.27
12. Sustainable growth rate = 8.70%
14. Sustainable growth rate = 14.28%; ROE = 25.89%
16. Maximum sales growth = 17.65%
18. Maximum growth = 42.86%
20. Profit margin = 13.76%
22. TAT = 1.47 times
24. Sustainable growth rate = 22.50%; New borrowing = $19,125;
    Internal growth rate = 7.20%
26. 14.16%; 14.16%; 12.40%
28. EFN = −$62,161
30. EFN @ 20% = $10,639; EFN @ 15% = −$7,943; EFN @ 25% = $29,221;
    EFN @ 17.14% = 0
32. Maximum sustainable growth rate = 5.49%

CHAPTER 5

2. $13,760.80; $25,319.70; $169,151.87; $315,795.75
4. 7.63%; 10.66%; 9.97%; 8.12%
6. 9.75%
8. 5.94%
10. $130,258,959.12
12. $7,249.01
14. $0.10
16. a. 6.35%
    b. 19.90%
    c. 5.68%
18. $145,780.97; $56,204.87
20. 28.07 years

CHAPTER 6

2. @ 5%: PV(X) = $28,431.29; PV(Y) = $25,976.86
   @ 22%: PV(X) = $15,145.14; PV(Y) = $17,181.84
4. 15 years: PV = $27,381.89
   40 years: PV = $35,204.58
   75 years: PV = $35,971.70
   Forever: PV $36,000
6. PV = $456,262.25
8. $3,327.58
10. PV = $187,500
12. 11.46%; 7.23%; 9.42%; 18.53%
14. Royal Canadian Bank = 12.91%; First United Bank = 12.78%
16. $6,077.42
18. $12,405.67
20. Payment = $1,158.16; EAR = 8.52%
22. EAR = 313,916,515.7%; APR = 1,733.33%
24. FV = $129,845.71
26. PV = $18,407.91
28. PV = $10,015.75

30. 7.70% semiannual; 3.78% quarterly; 1.24% monthly

32. $19,546.19

34. $158.13; $442.38; $1,316.88

36. Case 1: PV = $137,969.76; Case 2: PV = $138,477.32

38. G: 11.20%; H: 12.06%

40. 102.10 payments

42. $335,411.32

44. $18,758,930.79

46. Profit = $7,700.77; Break-even rate = 16.89%

48. PV = $110,240.46

50. Value = $29,700.29

52. PV(5) = $27,194.83; PV(3) = $21,417.72; PV(0) = $14,969.38

54. Payment = $1,361.82

56. Third year: $1,800; Life of loan: $9,000

58. $26,216.03

60. EAR = 13.64%

62. Refundable fee: APR = 7.58%; EAR = 7.85%
Nonrefundable fee: APR = 7.50%; EAR = 7.76%

64. Without fee: @ 19.2% = 101.39 months; @ 9.2% = 63.30 months
With fee: @ 9.2% = 64.94 months

66. Balloon payment = $229,278.34

68. 6.25%

72. a. APR = 520%; EAR = 14,104.29%
b. APR = 577.78%; EAR = 23,854.63%
c. APR = 1,309.92%; EAR = 11,851,501.94%

CHAPTER 7

4. 11.09%

6. $1,055.83

8. 9.16%

10. 6.60%

12. 8.52%

16. If the YTM suddenly rises to 12 percent:
$\Delta P_{Sam}\% = -3.47\%$
$\Delta P_{Dave}\% = -13.76\%$
If the YTM suddenly falls to 8 percent:
$\Delta P_{Sam}\% = +3.63\%$
$\Delta P_{Dave}\% = +17.29\%$

18. YTM = 7.77%
Effective annual yield = 7.92%

20. Clean price = $1,134

22. 20 years

26. a. Number of coupon bonds to sell = 15,000; Number of zero coupon bonds to sell = 114,181
b. Coupon bonds: repayment = $15,000,000; Zeroes: repayment = $114,181,000

28. P: Capital gains yield = −1.26%; D: Capital gains yield = +1.48%

30. P_M = $13,474.20
P_N = $2,840.91

CHAPTER 8

2. R = 11.46%

4. P_0 = $42.35

6. D_0 = $4.20 / 1.06 = $3.96

8. R = 7.30%

10. P_0 = $38.04

12. P_0 = $31.18

14. D_1 = $2.75

16. D_0 = $2.78

18. NI = $133,928,571

20. a. P_0 = $39.75

b. P_0 = $41.78

22. R = 9.85%

24. a. P_0 = $2.79
b. NPVGO = $206,579
c. P_0 = $3.82

CHAPTER 9

2. Initial cost = $3,000: Payback = 3.57 years
Initial cost = $5,000: Payback = 5.95 years
Initial cost = $7,000: No payback

4. Initial cost = $8,000: Discounted payback = 1.32 years
Initial cost = $13,000: Discounted payback = 2.20 years
Initial cost = $18,000: Discounted payback = 3.14 years

6. AAR = 19.44%

8. Required return = 11%: NPV = $7,423.84
Required return = 30%: NPV = − $1,324.53

10. IRR = 26.83%

12. a. IRR Project A = 16.60%
IRR Project B = 15.72%
b. NPV Project A = $3,491.88
NPV Project B = $4,298.06
c. Crossover rate = 13.75%

14. a. NPV = $13,570,247.93
b. IRR = 72.75%; −83.46%

16. a. PI_I = 1.243
PI_{II} = 1.393
b. NPV_I = $7,302.78
NPV_{II} = $1,963.19

18. At a zero discount rate: NPV = $125,516
At an infinite discount rate: NPV = − $568,240
IRR = 10.71%

22. IRR = 25%; 33.33%; 42.86%; and 66.67%

CHAPTER 10

2. Annual sales = $366,500,000

4. OCF = $256,308; Tax shield = $45,900

8. NPV = $463,960

12. Net cash flow = $44,995

14. NPV = $805,551

16. NPV − $3,773,067

20. Annual cash flow = $564,750,000

22. IRR = 20.80%

24. $82,696 per system

26. Incorporating the half-year rule: OCF = $69,800

28. Method 1: EAC = −$2,063.96; Method 2: EAC = −$2,451.48

30. Techron I: EAC = −$90,457; Techron II: EAC − −$87,746

32. EAC = −$64,062

34. NPV = −$93,546

36. NPV = −$279,885

38. Underground: EAC = −$1,017,496; Above ground: EAC = −$783,926

40. Price per share = $17.52

42. System A: EAC = −$214,243; System B: EAC = −$183,216

44. Using replacement chains: Sal 5000: NPV = −$311,171;
DET 1000: NPV = −$341,700

46. a. NPV = $652,820
b. Abandon in 1 year: NPV = $159,292; Abandon in 2 years: NPV = $637,484; Abandon in 3 years: NPV = $508,366

48. a. $69,901.70
b. $64,547.46

50. NPV = $6,220,041; IRR = 38.09%

52. a. NPV = −$137,677
b. New computer: EAC = −$50,941; Old computer: EAC = −$29,545

CHAPTER 11

2. Total costs = $5,997,500; Marginal cost = $34.65; Average cost = $39.98; Minimum revenue = $346,500

6. Best-case NPV = $3,109,608; Worst-case NPV = –$1,848,883

8. D = $612,200; P = $88.22; VC = $56.62

10. Financial break-even quantity = 22,162

12. OCF = $68,750; DOL = 3.182

14. FC = $28,000; At 11,000 units: OCF = $20,400; At 9,000 units: OCF = $11,600

18. At 110,000 units: DOL = 1.3371; At the accounting breakeven level: DOL = 2.8095

20. a. NPV = $482,999.60
    b. Abandon if Q < 3,997 units

22. NPV = $2,474,000.81; Value of option to expand = $2,222,791

24. Best-case NPV = $34,527,281; Worst-case NPV = –$13,433,120

28. a. OCF Years 1-5: $1,196,750; $1,251,350; $1,226,780; $1,207,124; $1,191,399
        NPV = $2,492,871.53
    b. NPV = –$103,020.07

30. For Year 1 quantities: Accounting break-even = 9,545.45; Cash break-even = 4,329.36; Financial break-even = 18,356.73

CHAPTER 12

2. Dividend yield = 2.73%; Capital gains yield = 12.50%

4. 12.024%; 8.904%

6. a. $120
   b. 11.43%
   c. 7.14%

8. From 1957–2005: 4.67%

10. a. 4.11%; 5.62%
    b. 18.65%; 1.82%
    c. –1.51%; 19.83%

12. a. 8.60%
    b. 8.20%

16. 38.00%; Standard deviation = 22.15%

18. 11.13%; 10.62%

20. 0.01; < 0.0001

22. 24.88%

CHAPTER 13

2. Expected return = 14.06%

4. X: $6,400; Y: $3,600

6. Expected return = 12.50%

8. Expected return = 14.50%

10. a. Expected return = 13.29%
    b. Variance = 0.03171; Standard deviation = 17.81%

12. Correlation = 0.6: Variance = 0.0198, Standard deviation = 0.1407
    Correlation = 0.5: Variance = 0.0187, Standard deviation = 0.1369
    Correlation = 1.0: Variance = 0.0241, Standard deviation = 0.1551

14. Beta = 1.10

16. Beta = 1.67

18. Risk-free rate = 4.33%

20. Slope = 0.0846

22. Risk-free rate = 3.07%

26. Investment in C = $343,333; Investment in the risk-free asset = $206,667; Beta of the risk-free asset = 0

28. Beta (I) = 3.07, Standard deviation (I) = 12.15%;
    Beta (II) = 0.65, Standard deviation (II) = 20.39%

CHAPTER 14

2. 14.25%

4. 15.14%; 14.86%

6. Pretax cost = 7.37%; Aftertax cost = 4.79%

8. Book value = $100 million; Market value = $68 million; Aftertax cost = 5.48%

10. 13.69%

12. a. E/V = 0.2603; D/V = 0.7397
    b. E/V = 0.7978; D/V = 0.2022

14. a. 7.50%
    b. 13.78%

16. a. D/V = 0.2431; P/V = 0.0904; E/V = 0.6665
    b. 13.58%

18. b. 7.2%
    c. $16,156,463

20. Break-even cost = $42,385,321

22. $2,860,617

CHAPTER 15

2. a. maximum = $40; minimum > 0
   b. 1,428,571; 3.64
   c. $38.92; $1.08

4. $5,000; –$500

6. 804,348

8. No change; declines by $0.83; declines by $3.33

10. BVPS = $200.63; MVPS = $64.11; EPS = $35.06; NPV = –$748,107

12. $41.60

14. $12,711.13

CHAPTER 16

2. a. EPS = $1.46; $3.64; $4.73
   b. EPS = $1.13; $4.77; $6.59

4. a. I: EPS = $1.33; II: EPS = $0.83
   b. I: EPS = $4.67; II: EPS = $9.17

6. a. EPS = $7.59; $8.06; 7.14
   b. EBIT = $7,700
   c. EBIT = $7,700
   d. EBIT = $7,700

8. a. $800
   b. $960
   c. Sell 40 shares

10. $4.55 million

12. a. 12%
    b. 12.87%
    c. 14.60%
    d. 10.95%; 9.90%

14. $280,682; $301,682

16. V = $187,000

CHAPTER 17

2. a. New shares issued = 1,000
   b. New shares issued = 2,500

4. a. $39.00
   b. $56.52
   c. $45.61
   d. $113.75
   e. 250,000; 172,500; 213,750; 85,714

6. Shares outstanding = 4,885; Price = $35.00

8. Shares outstanding = 392,000; Capital surplus = $2,448,000
10. New borrowings = $576; Capital outlays = $1,296
12. a. $720,000
  b. No dividend paid
14. Current share price = $30.85; D = $18.98
16. a. Price = $15; $40
  b. EPS = $0.95, $2.53; PE = $15.79; 15.79

CHAPTER 18

2. Cash = $6,450; Current assets = $10,150
4. a. I, I; **b.** I, N; **c.** D, D; **d.** D, D; **e.** D, N; **f.** I, I
6. Operating cycle = 92.75 days; Cash cycle = 42.48 days
8. a. The payables period = 0

	Q1	Q2	Q3	Q4
Payment of accounts	$157.50	$195.00	$150.00	$155.25

b.

	Q1	Q2	Q3	Q4
Payment of accounts	$135.00	$157.50	$195.00	$150.00

c.

	Q1	Q2	Q3	Q4
Payment of accounts	$142.50	$170.00	$180.00	$151.75

10. a. $106,666.67
  b. $117,141.86
  c. $136,928.57; $160,021.43; $183,200.00
12. a. 7.90%
  b. $580,667
14. a. EAR = 7.86%; EAR = 6.95%
  b. Interest saved = $99,589.86; Total interest paid = $754,160.63
18. a. 5.523%
  b. 5.538%

CHAPTER 19

2. a. $100,000; −$80,000; $20,000
  b. $100,000; −$40,000; $60,000
4. a. $79,000
  b. $2,633.33
  c. $633.33; 4.16 days
6. a. $23,083
  b. 2.43 days
  c. $23,083
  d. $4.28
  e. $14,250
8. NPV = $7.9 million; Net savings = $395,000
10. 105 customers per day
12. a. $7,276,172
  b. $7,246,777
  c. $175.53

CHAPTER 20

2. $8,547,945
4. $74,571
6. Annual credit sales = $322,885; Accounts receivable turnover = 7.02 times
8. $745,205
10. NPV = $473,458
12. Carrying cost = $4,590; Order cost = $7,800; EOQ = 235; Orders = 40 per year
14. NPV = $650,433
16. 2,954
18. $349.69

CHAPTER 21

2. c. 1.4501 euros/pound; 0.6893 pounds/euro
4. b. $1.86 US
6. European risk-free rate = 3.38%; Japanese risk-free rate = 2.74%; British risk-free rate = 5.29%
8. The European annual inflation rate is 1.409% higher than the Canadian rate
10. b. Kr 5.4724
12. b. The inflation rate in Canada is 4.49% higher than it is in Japan
14. b. NPV = $306,704
  c. Required return = 11.531%; NPV = SFr 352,913.35 = $306,881.17
16. a. Three-month forward rate = 1.0709 euros/dollar

CHAPTER 22

2. NAL = −$164,728.53
4. Break-even payment before tax = $764,531.75
6. If payments are between $694,343.04 and $699,697.19 the lease will be profitable to both
8. NAL = $23,845.54; Maximum acceptable lease payment before tax = $1,358,261.33
10. NAL = −$69,228.94
12. NAL = $423.23

CHAPTER 23

6. a. Cash cost = $94 million; Equity cost = $95.5 million
  b. NPV all cash = $9.83 million; NPV all stock = $8.30 million
8. a. $300
  b. $34.20
  c. $2,700
  d. $37.06
  e. $4,588.24
10. a. $2.27
  b. $55.56
  c. 17.60 times
  d. Price = $38.33; PE = 16.87 times
12. a. $8,094,783
  b. $2,874,783
  c. −$1,805,217
  d. $14.72
  e. $5,086,166
  g. NPV all cash = −$3,540,000; NPV all stock = $3,509,091

CHAPTER 24

2. Gain $103.5 per ounce transacted; Lose $56.5 per ounce transacted
4. −$5; −$3; $0; $3; $5

CHAPTER 25

4. a. $13.96
  b. $2.31
6. $90.86
8. a. Equity = $287.18; Debt = $912.82
  b. Equity = $419.55. Stockholders will favour the move.
10. $950
12. $4.09
14. a. NPV = $229,955.54
  b. Abandon if sales < 5,065 units
16. NPV = $1,309,942.84; Value of option to expand = $1,072,212.80
20. $859.80

Subject Index

Name Index

Equation Index